The Oxford Handbook of Cognitive Neuroscience

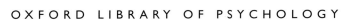

Editor in Chief PETER E. NATHAN

The Oxford Handbook of Cognitive Neuroscience

Volume 2: The Cutting Edges

Edited by

Kevin N. Ochsner

Stephen M. Kosslyn

OXFORD

UNIVERSITY PRESS

OXFORD
UNIVERSITY PRESS

Oxford University Press is a department of the University of Oxford.
It furthers the University's objective of excellence in research, scholarship,
and education by publishing worldwide.

Oxford   New York
Auckland   Cape Town   Dar es Salaam   Hong Kong   Karachi
Kuala Lumpur   Madrid   Melbourne   Mexico City   Nairobi
New Delhi   Shanghai   Taipei   Toronto

With offices in
Argentina   Austria   Brazil   Chile   Czech Republic   France   Greece
Guatemala   Hungary   Italy   Japan   Poland   Portugal   Singapore
South Korea   Switzerland   Thailand   Turkey   Ukraine   Vietnam

Oxford is a registered trademark of Oxford University Press
in the UK and certain other countries.

Published in the United States of America by
Oxford University Press
198 Madison Avenue, New York, NY 10016

Library of Congress Cataloging-in-Publication Data

The Oxford handbook of cognitive neuroscience / edited by Kevin Ochsner, Stephen M. Kosslyn.
    volumes cm.—(Oxford library of psychology)
ISBN 978–0–19–998870–9
1. Cognitive neuroscience—Handbooks, manuals, etc.   2. Neuropsychology—Handbooks, manuals, etc.
I. Ochsner, Kevin N. (Kevin Nicholas)   II. Kosslyn, Stephen Michael, 1948–   III. Title: Handbook of cognitive neuroscience.
QP360.5.O94 2013
612.8′233—dc23
2013026213

9 8 7 6 5 4 3 2 1
Printed in China
on acid-free paper

SHORT CONTENTS

OXFORD LIBRARY OF PSYCHOLOGY

The *Oxford Library of Psychology*, a landmark series of handbooks, is published by Oxford University Press, one of the world's oldest and most highly respected publishers, with a tradition of publishing significant books in psychology. The ambitious goal of the *Oxford Library of Psychology* is nothing less than to span a vibrant, wide-ranging field and, in so doing, to fill a clear market need.

Encompassing a comprehensive set of handbooks, organized hierarchically, the *Library* incorporates volumes at different levels, each designed to meet a distinct need. At one level are a set of handbooks designed broadly to survey the major subfields of psychology; at another are numerous handbooks that cover important current focal research and scholarly areas of psychology in depth and detail. Planned as a reflection of the dynamism of psychology, the *Library* will grow and expand as psychology itself develops, thereby highlighting significant new research that will have an impact on the field. Adding to its accessibility and ease of use, the *Library* will be published in print and, later on, electronically.

The *Library* surveys psychology's principal subfields with a set of handbooks that capture the current status and future prospects of those major subdisciplines. This initial set includes handbooks of social and personality psychology, clinical psychology, counseling psychology, school psychology, educational psychology, industrial and organizational psychology, cognitive psychology, cognitive neuroscience, methods and measurements, history, neuropsychology, personality assessment, developmental psychology, and more. Each handbook undertakes to review one of psychology's major subdisciplines with breadth, comprehensiveness, and exemplary scholarship. In addition to these broadly conceived volumes, the *Library* also includes a large number of handbooks designed to explore in depth more specialized areas of scholarship and research, such as stress, health and coping, anxiety and related disorders, cognitive development, or child and adolescent assessment. In contrast to the broad coverage of the subfield handbooks, each of these latter volumes focuses on an especially productive, more highly focused line of scholarship and research. Whether at the broadest or most specific level, however, all of the *Library* handbooks offer synthetic coverage that reviews and evaluates the relevant past and present research and anticipates research in the future. Each handbook in the *Library* includes introductory and concluding chapters written by its editor to provide a roadmap to the handbook's table of contents and to offer informed anticipation of significant future developments in that field.

An undertaking of this scope calls for handbook editors and chapter authors who are established scholars in the areas about which they write. Many of the nation's and world's most productive and best-respected psychologists have agreed to edit *Library* handbooks or write authoritative chapters in their areas of expertise.

For whom has the *Oxford Library of Psychology* been written? Because of its breadth, depth, and accessibility, the *Library* serves a diverse audience, including graduate students in psychology and their faculty mentors, scholars, researchers, and practitioners in psychology and related fields. Each will find in the *Library* the information they seek on the subfield or focal area of psychology in which they work or are interested.

Befitting its commitment to accessibility, each handbook includes a comprehensive index, as well as extensive references to help guide research. And because the *Library* was designed from its inception as an online as well as a print resource, its structure and contents will be readily and rationally searchable online. Further, once the *Library* is released online, the handbooks will be regularly and thoroughly updated.

In summary, the *Oxford Library of Psychology* will grow organically to provide a thoroughly informed perspective on the field of psychology, one that reflects both psychology's dynamism and its increasing interdisciplinarity. Once published electronically, the *Library* is also destined to become a uniquely valuable interactive tool, with extended search and browsing capabilities. As you begin to consult this handbook, we sincerely hope you will share our enthusiasm for the more than 500-year tradition of Oxford University Press for excellence, innovation, and quality, as exemplified by the *Oxford Library of Psychology*.

Peter E. Nathan
Editor-in-Chief
Oxford Library of Psychology

ABOUT THE EDITORS

Kevin N. Ochsner

Kevin N. Ochsner is Associate Professor of Psychology at Columbia University. He graduated *summa cum laude* from the University of Illinois where he received his B.A. in Psychology. Ochsner then received a M.A. and Ph.D. in psychology from Harvard University working in the laboratory of Dr. Daniel Schacter, where he studied emotion and memory. Also at Harvard, he began his postdoctoral training in the lab or Dr. Daniel Gilbert, where he first began integrating social cognitive and neuroscience approaches to emotion-cognition interactions, and along with Matthew Lieberman published the first articles on the emerging field of social cognitive neuroscience. Ochsner later completed his postdoctoral training at Stanford University in the lab of Dr. John Gabrieli, where he conducted some of the first in functional neuroimaging studies examining the brain systems supporting cognitive forms of regulation. He is now director the Social Cognitive Neuroscience Laboratory at Columbia University, where current studies examine the psychological and neural bases of emotion, emotion regulation, empathy and person perception in both healthy and clinical populations. Ochsner has received various awards for his research and teaching, including the American Psychological Association's Division 3 New Investigator Award, the Cognitive Neuroscience Society's Young Investigator Award, and Columbia University's Lenfest Distinguished Faculty Award.

Stephen M. Kosslyn

Stephen M. Kosslyn is the Founding Dean of the university at the Minerva Project, based in San Francisco. Before that, he served as Director of the Center for Advanced Study in the Behavioral Sciences and Professor of Psychology at Stanford University, and was previously chair of the Department of Psychology, Dean of Social Science, and the John Lindsley Professor of Psychology in Memory of William James at Harvard University. He received a B.A. from UCLA and a Ph.D. from Stanford University, both in psychology. His original graduate training was in cognitive science, which focused on the intersection of cognitive psychology and artificial intelligence; faced with limitations in those approaches, he eventually turned to study the brain. Kosslyn's research has focused primarily on the nature of visual cognition, visual communication, and individual differences; he has authored or coauthored 14 books and over 300 papers on these topics. Kosslyn has received the American Psychological Association's Boyd R. McCandless Young Scientist Award, the National Academy of Sciences Initiatives in Research Award, a Cattell Award, a Guggenheim Fellowship, the J-L. Signoret

Prize (France), an honorary Doctorate from the University of Caen, an honorary Doctorate from the University of Paris Descartes, an honorary Doctorate from Bern University, and election to Academia Rodinensis pro Remediatione (Switzerland), the Society of Experimental Psychologists, and the American Academy of Arts and Sciences.

CONTRIBUTORS

Adam K. Anderson
Department of Psychology
University of Toronto
Rotman Research Institute
Baycrest Centre
Toronto, Ontario, Canada

Daniel Ansari
Numerical Cognition Laboratory
Department of Psychology
University of Western Ontario
London, Ontario, Canada

Lauren Y. Atlas
Department of Psychology
New York University
New York, NY

David Badre
Department of Cognitive, Linguistic, and
    Psychological Sciences
Brown University
Providence, RI

Lisa Feldman Barrett
Psychiatric Neuroimaging Research
    Program
Harvard Medical School, Martinos Center
    for Biomedical Imaging
Massachusetts General Hospital
Department of Psychology
Northeastern University
Boston, MA

Karina S. Blair
Department of Health and Human Services
National Institute of Mental Health
National Institutes of Health
Bethesda, MD

R. J. R. Blair
Department of Health and Human Services
National Institute of Mental Health
National Institutes of Health
Bethesda, MD

J. Douglas Bremner
Departments of Psychiatry and Behavioral
    Sciences and Radiology
Emory University School of Medicine
Atlanta, GA
Atlanta VA Medical Center
Decatur, GA

Jason T. Buhle
New York State Psychiatric Institute
Columbia University
New York, NY

Samuel R. Chamberlain
Department of Psychiatry
University of Cambridge
Addenbrooke's Hospital
Cambridge, UK

Kalina Christoff
Department of Psychology
University of British Columbia
Vancouver, British Columbia, Canada

Eveline A. Crone
Developmental and Educational
    Psychology
Institute of Psychology
Leiden University
Leiden, The Netherlands

Jean Decety
Department of Psychology
University of Chicago
Chicago, IL

Naomi I. Eisenberger
Department of Psychology
University of California, Los Angeles
Los Angeles, CA

Naomi A. Fineberg
National OCDs Treatment Service
Hertfordshire Partnership NHS
    Foundation Trust
Welwyn Garden City, UK
University of Hertfordshire
Hatfield, UK

Jennifer M. B. Fugate
  Department of Psychology
  Boston College
  Department of Psychology
  Northeastern University
  Boston, MA

Vittorio Gallese
  Department of Neuroscience
  University of Parma, Italy
  Brain Center for Social and Motor
    Cognition
  Italian Institute of Technology
  Parma, Italy

Isabel Gauthier
  Department of Psychology
  Vanderbilt University
  Nashville, TN

Tobias Grossmann
  Max Planck Institute for Human Cognitive
    and Brain Sciences
  Leipzig, Germany

Berna Güroğlu
  Developmental and Educational
    Psychology
  Institute of Psychology
  Leiden University
  Leiden, The Netherlands

Todd F. Heatherton
  Department of Psychological and Brain
    Sciences
  Dartmouth College
  Hanover, NH

Mark H. Johnson
  Centre for Brain and Cognitive
    Development
  School of Psychology
  Birkbeck College
  University of London
  London, UK

William M. Kelley
  Department of Psychological and Brain
    Sciences
  Dartmouth College
  Hanover, NH

Stephen M. Kosslyn
  Center for Advanced Study in the
    Behavioral Sciences
  Stanford University
  Stanford, CA

Kristen A. Lindquist
  Mind/Brain/Behavior Initiative
  Harvard University
  Department of Neurology
  Harvard Medical School
  Martinos Center for Biomedical Imaging
  Massachusetts General Hospital
  Cambridge, MA

Bradley C. Love
  Cognitive, Perceptual, and Brain Sciences
  University College London
  London, UK

Fred W. Mast
  Department of Psychology
  University of Bern
  Bern, Switzerland

Samuel M. McClure
  Department of Psychology
  Stanford University
  Stanford, CA

Rankin W. McGugin
  Department of Psychology
  Vanderbilt University
  Nashville, TN

Peter Mende-Siedlecki
  Department of Psychology
  Princeton University
  Princeton, NJ

Andreas Meyer-Lindenberg
  Central Institute of Mental Health
  Mannheim, Germany

Joseph M. Moran
  Department of Psychology
  Harvard University
  Cambridge, MA

Keely A. Muscatell
  Department of Psychology
  University of California, Los Angeles
  Los Angeles, CA

Kevin N. Ochsner
  Department of Psychology
  Columbia University
  New York, NY

Luiz Pessoa
  Department of Psychology
  University of Maryland
  College Park, MD

Lukas Pezawas
Division of Biological Psychiatry
Medical University of Vienna
Vienna, Austria

Aina Puce
Department of Psychological and Brain
Sciences
Indiana University
Bloomington, IN

T. W. Robbins
Department of Psychology and
Behavioral and Clinical Neuroscience
Institute
University of Cambridge
Cambridge, UK

Andreia Santos
Central Institute of Mental Health
Mannheim, Germany

Rebecca Saxe
Department of Brain and Cognitive
Sciences
Massachusetts Institute of Technology
Cambridge, MA

Maya U. Shankar
Stanford University
Stanford, CA

Jennifer A. Silvers
Department of Psychology
Columbia University
New York, NY

Rebecca M. Todd
Department of Psychology
University of Toronto
Rotman Research Institute
Baycrest Centre
Toronto, Ontario, Canada

Alexander Todorov
Department of Psychology
Princeton University
Princeton, NJ

Chandan J. Vaidya
Department of Psychology
Georgetown University
Children's Research Institute
Children's National Medical Center
Washington, DC

Stephan E. Vogel
Department of Psychology
Georg-August-University of Göttingen
Göttingen, Germany

Tor D. Wager
Department of Psychology & Neuroscience
University of Colorado at Boulder
Boulder, CO

Nick Yeung
Department of Experimental Psychology
University of Oxford
Oxford, UK

Liane Lee Young
Psychology Department
Boston College
Boston, MA

CONTENTS

Introduction to *The Oxford Handbook of Cognitive Neuroscience*: Cognitive Neuroscience: Where Are We Now?

Kevin N. Ochsner *and* Stephen M. Kosslyn

Abstract

This book consists of two volumes that review the current state of the art in cognitive neuroscience. Volume 2 has four sections. The first section explores emotion and its link to perception and attention, how emotion affects cognition, and genetic and developmental approaches to emotion. The second section deals with self and social cognition. It includes chapters that examine topics such as the perception of nonverbal cues and perception–action links, face recognition, empathy and social interaction, impression formation, and drawing of inferences about others' mental states. The third section is about higher cognitive functions and covers topics ranging from conflict monitoring and cognitive control, the hierarchical control of action, decision-making, categorization, thinking, expectancies, and numerical cognition. Finally, the fourth section contains four chapters that illustrate how disruptions of the mechanisms of cognition and emotion produce abnormal functioning in individuals. This section covers topics such as attention deficit–hyperactivity disorder, anxiety, obsessive-compulsive disorder, and post-traumatic stress disorder.

Key Words: cognitive neuroscience, emotion, self, social cognition, cognitive functions, anxiety, attention, face recognition, empathy, categorization

On a night in the late 1970s, something important happened in a New York City taxicab: A new scientific field was named. En route to a dinner at the famed Algonquin Hotel, the neuroscientist Michael Gazzaniga and the cognitive psychologist George Miller coined the term "cognitive neuroscience." This field would go on to change the way we think about the relationship between behavior, mind, and brain.

This is not to say that the field was *born* on that day. Indeed, as Hermann Ebbinghaus (1910) noted, "Psychology has a long past, but a short history," and cognitive neuroscience clearly has a rich and complex set of ancestors. Although it is difficult to say exactly when a new scientific discipline came into being, the groundwork for this field had begun to be laid decades before the term was coined. As has been chronicled in detail elsewhere (Gardner, 1985; Posner & DiGirolamo, 2000), as behaviorism gave way to the cognitive revolution, and as computational

and neuroscientific approaches to understanding the mind became increasingly popular, a Zeitgeist emerged—researchers in numerous allied fields came to believe that understanding the relationships between behavior and the mind required understanding their relationship to the brain.

This two-volume set reviews the current state of the art in cognitive neuroscience, some 35 years after the field was named. In these intervening years the field has grown tremendously—so much so, in fact, that cognitive neuroscience is now much less a bounded discipline focused on specific topics and more an approach that permeates psychological and neuroscientific inquiry. As such, no collection of chapters could possibly encompass its entire breath and depth. That said, this two-volume set attempts systematically to survey eight core areas of cognitive neuroscientific inquiry, four per volume, in a total of 55 chapters.

As an appetizer to this scientific feast, this introductory chapter offers a quick sketch of some central elements of the cognitive neuroscience approach and a brief overview of the eight main sections of the handbook's two volumes.

The Cognitive Neuroscience Approach

Among the many factors that gave rise to cognitive neuroscience, we highlight three signal events. In part, we explicitly highlight these events because they lay bare elements of the cognitive neuroscience approach that have become so commonplace that their importance may be forgotten even as they implicitly influence the ways research is conducted.

Multiple Levels of Analysis

The first crucial influence on cognitive neuroscience was a book by the late British vision scientist David Marr. Published in 1982, the book *Vision* made the case that we can only understand visual perception if we integrate descriptions cast at three distinct, but fundamentally interrelated (Kosslyn & Maljkovic 1990), levels of analysis. At the topmost *computational* level one describes the problem at hand, such as how one can see edges, derive three-dimensional structure of shapes, and so on; this level characterizes "what" the system does. At the middle *algorithm* level one describes how a specific computational problem is solved by a system that includes specific processes that operate on specific representations; this level characterizes "how" the system operates. And at the lowest *implementation* level one describes how these representations and processes that comprise the algorithm are instantiated in the brain. All three levels are crucial, and characteristics of the description at each level affect the way we must describe characteristics at the other levels.

This approach proved enormously influential in vision research, and researchers in other domains quickly realized that it could be applied more broadly. This multilevel approach is now the foundation for cognitive neuroscience inquiry more generally, although we often use different terminology to refer to these levels of analysis. For instance, many researchers now talk about the levels of behavior and experience, psychological processes (or information-processing mechanisms), and neural systems (Mitchell, 2006; Ochsner, 2007; Ochsner & Lieberman, 2001). But the core idea is still the same as that articulated by Marr: A complete understanding of the ways in which vision, memory, emotion, or any other cognitive or emotional faculty operates necessarily involves connecting descriptions of phenomena across levels of analysis.

The resulting multilevel descriptions have many advantages over the one- or two-level accounts typical of traditional approaches in allied disciplines such as cognitive psychology. These advantages include the ability to use both behavioral and brain data in combination—rather than just one or the other taken alone—to draw inferences about psychological processes. In so doing, one constructs theories that are constrained by, must connect to, and must make sense in the context of, more types of data than theories couched solely at the behavioral or the behavioral and psychological levels. We return to some of these advantages later.

The Use of Multiple Methods

If we are to study human abilities and capacities at multiple levels of analysis, we must necessarily use multiple types of methods to do so. In fact, many methods exist to measure phenomena at each of the levels of analysis, and new measures are continually being invented (Churchland & Sejnowski, 1988).

Today, this observation is taken as a given by many graduate students who study cognitive neuroscience. Of course, we should use studies of patient populations, electrophysiological methods, functional imaging methods, transcranial magnetic stimulation (TMS, which uses magnetic fields to temporarily impair neural functioning in a specific brain area), and other new techniques as they are developed. But this view wasn't always the norm. This fact is illustrated nicely by a debate that took place in the early 1990s about whether and how neuroscience data should inform psychological models of cognitive processes. On one side was the view from *cognitive neuropsychology*, which argued that studies of patient populations may be sufficient to understand the structure of cognitive processing (Caramazza, 1992). By studying the ways in which behavior changed as a result of the unhappy accidents of nature (e.g., strokes, traumatic brain injuries) that caused lesions of language areas, memory areas, and so on, we could discover the processing modules that comprise the mind. The assumption here was that researchers could identify direct relationships between behavioral deficits and specific areas of the brain that were damaged. On the other side of the debate was the view from *cognitive neuroscience* that the more methods we used, the better (Kosslyn & Intriligator, 1992). Because every method has its limitations, the argument went, the more methods we could bring to bear, the more likely we were to have a correct picture of how behavior was related to neural functioning. In the case of patient populations, for example, in some cases the deficits in behavior might not simply reflect the normal functions of the damaged regions; rather, they could reflect reorganization of function after brain damage or diffuse damage to multiple regions that affects multiple separate functions. If so, then observing patterns of dissociations and associations of abilities following brain damage would not necessarily allow researchers to delineate the structure of cognitive processing. Other methods would be required (such as neuroimaging) to complement studies of brain-damaged patients.

The field quickly adopted the second perspective, drawing on multiple methods when constructing and testing theories of cognitive processing. Researchers realized that they could use multiple methods together in complementary ways: They could use functional imaging methods to describe the network of processes active in the healthy brain when engaging in a particular behavior; they could use lesion methods or TMS to assess the causal relationships between activity in specific brain areas and particular forms of information processing (which in turn give rise to particular types of behavior); they could use electrophysiological methods to study the temporal dynamics of cortical systems as they interactively relate to the behavior of interest; and so on. The cognitive neuroscience approach adopted the idea that no single technique provides all the answers.

That said, there is no denying the fact that some techniques have proved more powerful and generative than others during the past 35 years. In particular, it is difficult to overstate the impact of functional imaging of the healthy intact human brain, first ushered in by positron emission tomography (PET) studies in the late 1980s (Petersen, Fox, Posner, Mintun, & Raichle, 1988) and given a tremendous boost by the advent and subsequent boom of functional magnetic resonance imaging (fMRI) in the early 1990s (Belliveau et al., 1992). Functional imaging is in many ways the single most important contributor to the rise of cognitive neuroscience. Without the ability to study cortical and subcortical brain systems in action in healthy adults, it is not clear whether cognitive neuroscience would have become the central paradigm it is today.

However, we must offer a cautionary note: As noted earlier, functional imaging is by no means the be-all and end-all of cognitive neuroscience techniques. Like any other method, it has its own strengths and weaknesses (which have been described in detail elsewhere, e.g., Poldrack, 2006, 2008, 2011; Van Horn & Poldrack, 2009; Yarkoni, Poldrack, VanEssen, & Wager, 2010). Researchers trained in cognitive neuroscience understand many if not all of these limitations, but unfortunately, many outside the field do not. This can cause two problems. The first is that newcomers to the field may improperly use functional imaging in the service of overly simplistic "brain mapping" (for example, seeking to identify "love spots" in the brain; Fisher, Aron, Mashek, Li, & Brown, 2002) and may commit other inferential errors (Poldrack, 2006). The second, less appreciated problem is that when nonspecialists read about studies of such overly simplistic hypotheses, they may assume that all cognitive neuroscientists traffic in this kind of experimentation and theorizing. As the contributions to the chapters in these volumes make clear, most cognitive neuroscientists appreciate the strengths and limits of the various techniques they use, and they understand that functional imaging is simply one of a number of techniques that allow neuroscience data to *constrain* theories of psychological processes. In the next subsection we turn to exactly this point.

Constraints and Convergence

One implication of using multiple methods to study phenomena at multiple levels of analysis is that we have numerous types of data. These data provide converging evidence for, and constrain the nature of, theories of human cognition, emotion, and behavior. That is, the data must fit together, painting different facets of the same picture (this is what we mean by *convergence*), even though each of them alone does not dictate a particular interpretation but rather only narrows the range of possible interpretations (this is what we mean by *constraining* the nature of theories). Researchers in cognitive neuroscience acknowledge that data always can be interpreted in various ways, but they also rely on the fact that data limit the range of viable interpretations—and the more types of data, the more strongly they will narrow down the range of possible theories. In this sense, constraints and convergence are the very core of the cognitive neuroscience approach (Ochsner & Kosslyn, 1999).

We note that the principled use of constraining and converging evidence does not privilege evidence couched at any one level of analysis. Brain data are not more important, more real, or more intrinsically valuable than behavioral data, and vice versa. Rather, both kinds of data constrain the range of possible theories of psychological processes, and, as such, both are valuable.

In addition, both behavioral and brain data can spark changes in theories of psychological processes. This claim stands in contrast to claims made by those who have argued that brain data can never change, or in any way constrain, a psychological theory. According to this view, brain data are ambiguous without a psychological theory through which to interpret them (Kihlstrom, 2010). Such arguments fail to appreciate the fact that the goal of cognitive neuroscience is to construct theories couched at all three levels of analysis. Moreover, behavioral and brain data are dependent variables collected in the same experiments. This is not arbitrary; we have ample evidence that behavior and brain function are intimately related: When the brain is damaged in a particular location, specific behaviors are disrupted—and when a person engages in specific behaviors, specific brain areas are activated. Dependent measures are always what science uses to constrain theorizing, and thus it follows that *both* behavioral and brain data *must* constrain our theories of the intervening psychological processes.

This point is so important that we want to illustrate it with a two examples. The first begins with classic studies of the amnesic patient known for decades only by his initials, H.M. (Corkin, 2002). After he passed away, his brain was famously donated to science and dissected live on the Internet in 2009 (see http://thebrainobservatory.ucsd.edu/hm_live.php). We now know that his name was Henry. In the 1960s, Henry suffered from treatment-intractable epilepsy that arose because of abnormal neural tissue in his temporal lobes. At the time, he suffered horribly from seizures, and the last remaining course of potential treatment was a neurosurgical operation that removed the tips of Henry's temporal lobes (and with them the neural origins of his epileptic seizures).

When Henry awakened after his operation the epilepsy was gone, but so was his ability to form new memories of events he experienced. Henry was stuck in the eternal present, forevermore awakening each day with his sense of time frozen at the age at which he had the operation. The time horizon for his experience was about two minutes, or the amount of time information could be retained in short-term memory before it required transfer to a longer-term episodic memory store.

To say that the behavioral sequelae of H.M.'s operation were surprising to the scientific community at that time is an understatement. Psychologists and neuroscientists spent the better part of the next 20 to 30 years reconfiguring their theories of memory in order to accommodate these and subsequent findings. It wasn't until the early 1990s that the long-reaching theoretical implications of Henry's amnesia finally became clear (Schacter & Tulving, 1994), when a combination of behavioral, functional imaging, and patient lesion data converged to implicate a multiple-systems account of human memory.

This understanding of H.M.'s deficits was hard-won and emerged only after an extended "memory systems debate" in psychology and neuroscience (Schacter & Tulving, 1994). This debate was between, on the one hand, behavioral and psychological theorists who argued that we have a single memory system (which has multiple processes) and, on the other hand, neuroscience-inspired theorists who argued that we have multiple memory systems (each of which instantiates a particular kind of process or processes). The initial observation of H.M.'s amnesia, combined with decades of subsequent careful experimentation using multiple behavioral and neuroscience techniques, decisively came down on the side of the multiple–memory systems theorists. Cognitive processing relies on multiple types of memory, and each uses a distinct set of representations and processes. This was a clear victory for the cognitive neuroscience approach over purely behavioral approaches.

A second example of the utility of combining neuroscientific and behavioral evidence comes from the "imagery debate" (Kosslyn, Thompson, & Ganis, 2006). On the one hand, psychologists and philosophers argued that the experience of visual mental imagery is just an experience, with no functional consequences. In this view, the pictorial characteristics of visual mental images that are evident to experience are epiphenomenal, like heat produced by a light bulb when someone is reading—something that could be experienced but plays no role in accomplishing the function. On the other hand, cognitive neuroscientists argued that visual mental images are analogous to visual percepts in that they use space in a representation to specify space in the world.

This debate went back and forth for many years without resolution, and at one point a mathematical proof was offered that behavioral data alone could never resolve it (Anderson, 1978). The advent of neuroimaging helped bring this debate to a close (Kosslyn et al., 2006). The brain areas that comprise early visual cortex each are topographically mapped, such that adjacent locations in the visual world are represented in adjacent locations in visual cortex. When it was shown in the early 1990s that increasing size of a visual mental image corresponded to increasingly larger swaths of activation in topographically mapped visual cortex, there was clear evidence that visual mental images were, indeed, analogous to visual percepts.

We have written as if both debates—about memory systems and mental imagery representation—are now definitely closed. But this is a simplification; not everyone is convinced of one or another view. Our crucial point here is that the advent of neuroscientific data has shifted the terms of the debate. When only behavioral data were available, in both cases the two alternative positions seemed equally plausible. But after the relevant neuroscientific data were introduced, the burden of proof shifted dramatically to one side, and a clear consensus emerged in the field.

In the years since these debates, evidence from cognitive neuroscience has constrained theories of a wide range of phenomena. Many such examples are chronicled in this handbook.

Overview of the Handbook

Cognitive neuroscience in the new millennium is a the broad and diverse field, defined by a multileveled integrative approach. To provide a systematic overview of this field, we have divided this handbook into two volumes.

Volume 1

The first volume surveys classic areas of interest in cognitive neuroscience: perception, attention, memory, and language. Twenty years ago, when Kevin Ochsner was a graduate student and Stephen Kosslyn was one of his professors, research on these topics formed the backbone of cognitive neuroscience research. And this is still true today, for two reasons.

First, when cognitive neuroscience took off, these were the areas of research within psychology that had the most highly developed behavioral, psychological, and neuropsychological (i.e., patient-based) models in place. And in the case of research on perception, attention, and memory, these were topics for which fairly detailed models of the underlying neural circuitry already had been developed on the basis of rodent and nonhuman primate studies. As such, these areas were poised to benefit from the use of brain-based techniques in humans.

Second, research on the representations and processes used in perception, attention, memory, and language in many ways forms a foundation for studying other kinds of complex behaviors, which are the focus of the second volume. This is true in terms of both the findings themselves and the evidence such findings provided that the cognitive neuroscience approach could be successful.

With this in mind, each of the four sections in Volume 1 includes a selection of chapters that covers core processes and the ways in which they develop across the lifespan and may break down in special populations.

The first section, on perception, comprises chapters on the core abilities to represent and recognize objects and spatial relations. In addition, this section contains chapters on the use of top-down cognitive processes in visual perception and on the ways in which such processes enable us to construct and use mental images. We also include chapters on perceptual abilities that have seen tremendous research growth in the last 5 to 10 years, such as the study of olfaction, audition, and music perception. Finally, there is chapter on disorders of perception.

The second section, on attention, comprises chapters on the core abilities to attend to auditory and spatial information as well as on the relationships between attention, action, and visual motor control. These chapters are followed by chapters on the development of attention and its breakdown in various disorders.

The third section, on memory, includes chapters on the core abilities to maintain information in working memory as well as semantic memory, episodic memory, and the consolidation process that governs the transfer of information from working to semantic and episodic memory. There is also a chapter on the ability to acquire skills, which depends on different systems than those used in other forms of memory, and a chapter on changes in memory function with older age and the ways in which memorial processes break down in various disorders.

Finally, the fourth section, on language, comprises chapters on core abilities such as speech perception and production, the distinction between linguistic competence and performance, semantics, the capacity for written language, and multimodal and developmental aspects of speech perception.

Volume 2

Whereas Volume 1 addresses the classics of cognitive neuroscience, Volume 2 is the "new wave" of research that has developed primarily in the last

10 years. As noted earlier, in many ways the success of these relatively newer research directions builds on the successes of research in the classic domains. Indeed, our knowledge of the systems implicated in perception, attention, memory, and language literally—and in this handbook—provided the foundation for the work described in Volume 2.

The first section, on emotion, begins with core processes involved in interactions between emotion, perception, and attention, as well as the generation and regulation of emotion. This is followed by chapters that provide models for understanding broadly how emotion affects cognition as well as the contribution that bodily sensation and control makes to affective and other processes. This section concludes with chapters on genetic and developmental approaches to emotion.

The second section, on self and social cognition, begins with a chapter on the processes that give rise to the fundamental ability to know and understand oneself. This is followed by chapters on increasingly complex abilities involved in perceiving others, starting with the perception of nonverbal cues and perception–action links. From there the chapters go on to address face recognition, impression formation, drawing of inferences about others' mental states, empathy, and social interaction. This section concludes with a chapter on the development of social cognitive abilities.

The third section, on higher cognitive functions, surveys abilities that depend, in large part, on processes in the frontal lobes of the brain, which interact with the kinds of core perceptual, attentional, and memorial processes described in Volume 1. Here we include chapters on conflict monitoring and cognitive control, the hierarchical control of action, thinking, decision-making, categorization, expectancies, numerical cognition, as well as a chapter on neuromodulatory influences on higher cognitive abilities.

Finally, in the fourth section, four chapters illustrate how disruptions of the mechanisms of cognition and emotion produce abnormal functioning in clinical populations. This section begins with a chapter on attention deficit–hyperactivity disorder and from there moves to chapters on anxiety, post-traumatic stress disorder, and obsessive-compulsive disorder.

Summary

Before moving from the appetizer to the main course, we offer two last thoughts.

First, we edited this handbook with the goal of providing a comprehensive compendium of research on cognitive neuroscience that will be widely accessible to a broad audience. Toward this end, the chapters comprising this handbook are available online to be downloaded individually. This is the first time chapters of a handbook of this sort have been made available in this way, and we hope this facilitates access to and dissemination of some of cognitive neuroscience's greatest hits.

Second, we hope that, whoever you are—a student, an advanced researcher, an interested layperson—this handbook whets your appetite for learning more about this exciting and growing field. Although reading survey chapters of the sort provided here is an excellent way to become oriented in the field and to start building your knowledge of the topics that interest you most, we encourage you to take your interests to the next level: Delve into the primary research articles cited in these chapters—and perhaps even get involved in doing this sort of research!

References

Anderson, J. R. (1978). Arguments concerning representations for mental imagery. *Psychological Review, 85,* 249–277.

Belliveau, J. W., Kwong, K. K., Kennedy, D. N., Baker, J. R., Stern, C.E., et al. (1992). Magnetic resonance imaging mapping of brain function. Human visual cortex. *Investigative Radiology, 27* (Suppl 2), S59–S65.

Caramazza, A. (1992). Is cognitive neuropsychology possible? *Journal of Cognitive Neuroscience, 4,* 80–95.

Churchland, P. S., & Sejnowski, T. J. (1988). Perspectives on cognitive neuroscience. *Science, 242,* 741–745.

Corkin, S. (2002). What's new with the amnesic patient H.M.? *Nature Reviews. Neuroscience, 3,* 153–160.

Fisher, H. E., Aron, A., Mashek, D., Li, H., & Brown, L. L. (2002). Defining the brain systems of lust, romantic attraction, and attachment. *Archives of Sex Behavior, 31,* 413–419.

Gardner, H. (1985). *The mind's new science: A history of the cognitive revolution.* New York: Basic Books.

Kihlstrom, J. F. (2010). Social neuroscience: The footprints of Phineas Gage. Social Cognition, 28, 757–782.

Kosslyn, S. M., & Intriligator, J. I. (1992). Is cognitive neuropsychology plausible? The perils of sitting on a one-legged stool. Journal of Cognitive Neuroscience, 4, 96–105.

Kosslyn, S. M., & Koenig, O. (1992). *Wetmind: The new cognitive neuroscience.* New York: Free Press.

Kosslyn, S. M., & Maljkovic, V. M. (1990). Marr's metatheory revisited. *Concepts in Neuroscience, 1,* 239–251.

Kosslyn, S. M., Thompson, W. L., & Ganis, G. (2006). *The case for mental imagery.* New York: Oxford University Press.

Marr, D. (1982). *Vision: A computational investigation into the human representation and processing of visual information.* San Francisco: W.H. Freeman.

Mitchell, J. P. (2006). Mentalizing and Marr: An information processing approach to the study of social cognition. *Brain Research, 1079,* 66–75.

Ochsner, K. (2007). Social cognitive neuroscience: Historical development, core principles, and future promise. In A. Kruglanksi & E. T. Higgins (Eds.), *Social psychology: A handbook of basic principles* (pp. 39–66). New York: Guilford Press.

Ochsner, K. N., & Kosslyn, S. M. (1999). The cognitive neuroscience approach. In B. M. Bly & D. E. Rumelhart (Eds.), *Cognitive science* (pp. 319–365). San Diego: Academic Press.

Ochsner, K. N., & Lieberman, M. D. (2001). The emergence of social cognitive neuroscience. *American Psychologist, 56,* 717–734.

Petersen, S. E., Fox, P. T., Posner, M. I., Mintun, M., & Raichle, M. E. (1988). Positron emission tomographic studies of the cortical anatomy of single-word processing. *Nature, 331,* 585–589.

Poldrack, R. A. (2006). Can cognitive processes be inferred from neuroimaging data? *Trends in Cognitive Sciences, 10,* 59–63.

Poldrack, R. A. (2008). The role of fMRI in cognitive neuroscience: Where do we stand? *Current Opinion in Neurobiology, 18,* 223–227.

Poldrack, R. A. (2011). Inferring mental states from neuroimaging data: From reverse inference to large-scale decoding. *Neuron, 72,* 692–697.

Posner, M. I., & DiGirolamo, G. J. (2000). Cognitive neuroscience: Origins and promise. *Psychological Bulletin, 126,* 873–889.

Schacter, D. L., & Tulving, E. (1994). (Eds.) *Memory systems 1994.* Cambridge, MA: MIT Press. viii, 407 pp.

Van Horn, J. D., & Poldrack, R. A. (2009). Functional MRI at the crossroads. *International Journal of Psychophysiology, 73,* 3–9.

Yarkoni, T., Poldrack, R. A., Van Essen, D. C., & Wager, T. D. (2010). Cognitive neuroscience 2.0: Building a cumulative science of human brain function. *Trends in Cognitive Sciences, 14,* 489–496.

PART 1

Emotion

Salience, State, and Expression: The Influence of Specific Aspects of Emotion on Attention and Perception

Rebecca M. Todd *and* Adam K. Anderson

Abstract

This chapter focuses on the influence of emotion on cognitive processes, and underlying neural mechanisms. The influence of three aspects of emotional processing on perception and attention is discussed. First, literature on enhanced attention to emotionally arousing stimuli is reviewed. Addressed are the ongoing controversies about the relative automaticity of this "motivated attention" as well as those about its neural substrates, individual differences, and developmental changes. Next, evidence is presented that production of some facial expressions serves to enhance, and others to reduce, incoming sensory information. The chapter also reviews studies that investigate how sustained emotional states influence the nature and scope of selective attention. In particular, the role of positive affect in broadening attention by "unbiasing" competition for perceptual processing is addressed. Finally, findings are presented in relation to a view of the amygdala as a key hub linking cognitive and emotional process via allocation of bodily and cognitive resources.

Key Words: amygdala, attention, emotion, motivated attention, attention–emotion interactions, visual processing, facial expression

Introduction

Countless song lyrics attest to the enhanced vividness of experience conveyed by emotion. Emotional events seem to be lived with a special vividness, at least from the perspective of later recall, and emotionally compelling objects in the environment—a familiar face, a potentially threatening figure on a dark street, an accident, a delicious dessert in a bakery window—capture the eye as we navigate through the world, influencing selective attentional processes. It is, of course, well established that far more information falls on the retina than can enter awareness. We continuously filter "the wheat from the chaff" of incoming sensory information, selectively allocating attention to what is important to us and suppressing distracting or irrelevant information. This chapter will focus on the role of emotion in tuning attentional processes involved in gating sensory information, and on neural mechanisms underlying this influence.

Talking about "the influence of emotion on cognition" is more a convenient shorthand than an accurate description of how things work, however. Emotion is not a monolithic entity, and there is ongoing disagreement within emotion theory over the parsing of "cognitive" vs. "emotional" aspects of emotional experience. Appraisal theories of emotion parse emotional processes into cognition-emotion amalgams comprised of "cognitive" appraisals, which range from relatively pre-attentive to explicit and elaborated processes and include attention, perception, and evaluation as well as reflection, memory, and planning. These are thought to influence more "emotional" processes such as arousal, action tendency, emotional expression, and feeling tone (Arnold, 1969; Frijda & Zeeleberg, 2001; Lazarus, 1991; Roseman, Spindel, & Jose, 1990; Scherer, 2000). According to these theories, appraisals of an event's emotional significance for one's own well-being determine physiological responses associated with emotion along with the subjective experience of emotional arousal. Although over the course of more than a century, debate has periodically raged over whether appraisal is required for, and whether it necessarily precedes, emotional response—that is, whether "emotion" requires "cognition" (Cannon, 1927; James, 1884; Lazarus, 1982; Zajonc, 1980, 1984)—these arguments ultimately founder on difficulties in defining where appraisal ends and emotion begins. Moreover, from the perspective of cognitive neuroscience, convergent evidence suggests that it is not possible to neatly separate "emotional" from "cognitive" brain regions or neural processes (Lewis, 2005; Pessoa, 2008).

Emotion theories also often parse emotional processes according to the time scale at which they occur. For example, a discrete emotional episode may be distinguished from a mood state. An emotional episode typically involves an event that triggers a constellation of appraisal/arousal/action tendency/emotional expression/feeling tone associated with a specific emotion, and unfolds over seconds to minutes; in contrast, a mood does not necessarily have a specific trigger or object and can last for hours or weeks (Ekman, 1994). At a third time-scale, over the course of a lifespan, habitual patterns of emotional response to a given type of events are thought to form the basis for important individual differences in personality (Ekman, 1994; Lewis, 2005). Dynamic theories of emotion hold that emotional and cognitive processes mutually interact at a number of time scales, from the scale of milliseconds (rapid emotional events) to that of years (personality) (Lewis, 2005). Here, emotional arousal influences perception and attention, which in turn filter the world to select information that further influences emotional state.

Although a definitive taxonomy of emotional processes has proved elusive, investigating ways in which somatic and neural responses associated with emotional episodes, or sustained states of heightened arousal associated with moods, interact with specific attentional and perceptual processes has greatly deepened our understanding of how emotion and cognition are intertwined. In this chapter, we will review the influence of three aspects of emotional processing on attention and perception: The first aspect focuses on the influence of emotionally arousing stimuli, the second on the production of emotional facial expressions, and the third on sustained positive and negative emotional states.

The first domain encompasses the attentional prioritization of emotionally salient objects and events related to appraisal of aspects of the external world that have consequences for our well-being. Here we will review studies contributing to evidence that emotionally salient events burn longer and brighter in the mind's eye—that they grab visual attention, enhance visual cortex activation, and are more likely to enter awareness than relatively neutral objects when attentional resources are limited. We will discuss ongoing controversies about the relative automaticity of this "motivated attention" as well as about its neural substrates. Finally, we will review evidence that typical patterns of motivated attention change over development and discuss ways in which individual differences in habitual biases in motivated attention, at an extreme end of the spectrum, can be associated with psychopathology.

The second line of research is embedded in a tradition in emotion research that has focused more on emotional expression than appraisal. This line of research has its roots in Darwin's proposal that producing emotional facial expressions serves a basic, evolutionarily conserved function of gating perceptual information. Here we will discuss evidence that production of some facial expressions serves to enhance, and others to reduce, incoming sensory information.

Finally, the third research stream focuses on how sustained emotional "mood" states influence the nature and scope of selective attention. Here, human imaging studies have begun building on behavioral evidence that sustained emotional state tonically tunes perceptual filters. In particular, we will focus on the role of positive affect in broadening attention in an "unbiasing" of competition for perceptual processing.

Models of Attentional Capture

Attentional filtering is generally discussed in terms of "top-down" and "bottom-up" processes that, according to the influential *biased competition* model (Desimone & Duncan, 1995), allow selection among competing objects within the visual field (Desimone & Duncan, 1995; Kastner & Ungerleider, 2001). *Bottom-up processing* refers to the relatively automatic capture of attention by physical features of stimuli such as contrast, the sudden onset of motion, or color—all aspects of "visual saliency" that allow one feature of a visual scene to stand out from its surround (Itti & Koch, 2000, 2001). A visually salient object or feature, such as a bright light in a dull landscape, or a person who suddenly starts running down a sidewalk of slow pedestrians, tends to grab attention regardless of relevance to current goals. In contrast, *top-down processes* have been defined as those that involve a prioritizing of visual information that is shaped by expectations, effortful attentional processes, and explicit goals that must be maintained in working memory. These executive top-down processes allow us to apply rules to develop "control sets" (Folk, Remington, & Johnston, 1992) that tune one's attentional filters depending on what is presently demanded. In the context of a laboratory experiment, establishing a control set might involve attending to one type of stimulus while ignoring another. In daily life, control sets allow us attend to traffic while driving, ignoring an otherwise interesting conversation or beautiful scenery. It is now well-established that attention to an object enhances visual cortex response to it, and top-down influences on visual processing are mediated by a network—or several networks—of frontal and parietal regions implemented in deliberate attention allocation and goal-directed behavior (Corbetta, Kincade, & Shulman, 2002; Dosenbach, Fair, Cohen, Schlaggar, & Petersen, 2008).

But where does emotion fit into this view of selective attention, which emphasizes perceptual salience and explicit goals? How, for example, might emotionally arousing images of decapitated bodies or erotic images of couples (images frequently rated as highly arousing) influence competition for attentional and visual resources? Over a lifetime, can one develop emotional control settings, or is emotional processing more bottom-up? Like bottom-up visual salience, emotional salience is generally linked to aspects of the stimulus itself rather than to explicit goals and can capture attention even when it detracts from task-related goals. Yet emotionally salient images are not salient because of their physical features but because of emotional associations—related to our motivational goals—with the content of images, although there may be basic trigger features, such as eye whites or low-spatial frequency information, which we discuss below. Moreover, emotional influences on visual processing involve feedback to visual cortex from other brain regions involved in tagging motivational relevance in a top-down fashion (Bar et al., 2006). For this reason, along with other researchers (Barrett & Bar, 2009; Seeley et al., 2007), we propose that distinct emotional-salience networks, including the amygdala and orbitofrontal cortices, mediate an alternate form of top-down selection bias involved in the evaluation of the motivational relevance of an object or event. In this chapter we refer to "emotional salience" vs. "executive" top-down networks to refer to these distinct but mutually interacting top-down networks.

Although nodes of emotional-salience and executive networks share few direct connections with each other (Ghashghaei, Hilgetag, & Barbas, 2007; Seeley et al., 2007), emotional and executive top-down process typically interact with each other as well as with bottom-up processes. Both visually and emotionally salient stimuli can capture attentional resources at the expense of explicit executive goals, yet explicit goals modulate the capture of attention by both (Corbetta & Shulman, 2002). Evidence suggests that processing even the most basic qualities of a stimulus (orientation, color, motion) is reduced during inattention (Joseph, Chun, & Nakayama, 1997; Mack & Rock, 1998; O'Connor, Fukui, Pinsk, & Kastner, 2002), and that motivationally salient stimuli require some degree of attention for processing (Pessoa, Kastner, & Ungerleider, 2002), although the issue of attentional demands for emotional processing is still under debate.

Biasing Competition: Motivated Attention to Salient Stimuli
Enhanced Visual Processing of Emotionally Arousing Images

A body of research on motivated attention has established evidence that emotionally salient stimuli enjoy privileged perceptual processing—that emotionally arousing images are processed more rapidly and more vividly than neutral images and require less executive attention to reach awareness. This body of research has consistently demonstrated that emotionally salient images elicit higher levels of activation in the visual cortices than neutral stimuli. Functional magnetic resonance imaging (fMRI) and positron emission tomography (PET) studies have found that, in primary visual cortex (Padmala & Pessoa, 2008) as well as downstream regions involved in categorical object processing, positive and negative emotionally arousing images elicit greater activation than neutral ones (Anderson & Phelps, 2001; Bradley et al., 2003; Lane, Chua, & Dolan, 1999; Lang et al., 1998). Event-related potential studies suggest that the effect of motivational salience on visual processing is also rapid, occurring within 170 ms—and possibly as early as 50–80 ms—of stimulus onset for faces (Blau, Maurer, Tottenham, & McCandliss, 2007; Pizzagalli, Regard, & Lehmann, 1999), and as early as 200 ms for complex scenes (Schupp, Junghofer, Weike, & Hamm, 2003; Schupp et al.,

2008; Smith, Cacioppo, Larsen, & Chartrand, 2003). As brain regions activated in these imaging studies have also been shown to be responsive to manipulations of executive attention (Lane et al., 1999; Pessoa et al., 2002), further questions have centered on investigating interactions between prioritized emotional-salience responses and executive attentional demands.

The Advantage of Emotional Stimuli under Conditions of Limited Attention
ATTENTIONAL BLINK

A series of studies investigated the hypothesis that emotionally significant events enjoy a privileged attentional status during perceptual processing, requiring fewer executive resources than those needed for neutral stimuli to reach awareness. The studies employed emotional variants of an attentional blink (AB) paradigm in which two target words are embedded in a stream of rapidly presented distractor items (Figure 2.1) (Anderson, 2005). The blink effect occurs when the second target (T2) is presented within 500 ms of the first target (T1). During this brief time window, awareness

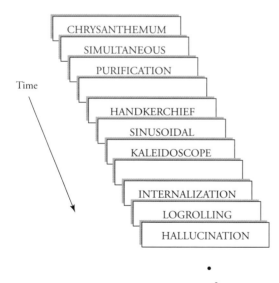

Figure 2.1 Diagram of a dual-target rapid, serial, visual presentation (RSVP) task used to measure the attentional blink. Fifteen words were briefly presented. Participants were instructed to ignore words appearing in black and to report the identity of the target words appearing in green. The time lag between the first (T1) and second (T2) target was varied. When T2 is presented within 600 ms of T1, the attentional blink typically occurs.

Reprinted by permission from Macmillan Publishers Ltd: [Nature] Anderson, A. K., & Phelps, E. A. Lesions of the human amygdala impair enhanced perception of emotionally salient events. *Nature, 411*(6835), 305–309, copyright (2001).

of T2 is impaired, a phenomenon thought to occur because perceptual encoding of a stimulus requires short-term consolidation processes that are limited in capacity. During short-term consolidation, attention can be seen as the glue that binds featural aspects of a stimulus so that an object is processed as a whole. This featural binding is required in turn for an item to enter working memory. The attentional blink is generally interpreted in terms of temporally limited processing resources, where the processing of T1 takes up most of the attentional resources required for the consolidation of the stimulus in working memory. These attentional resources are then unavailable for processing T2 until consolidation processes are complete. In other words, the blink is thought to reflect attentional limitations, during perceptual encoding, that gate the experience of seeing.

In order to probe the effects of stimulus salience on awareness, a series of AB experiments were conducted (Anderson, 2005). The first study compared the blink effect for negatively valenced high-arousal words (e.g., "rape"), negative low-arousal words (e.g., "hurt"), and neutral words (e.g., "rule"). Results showed that there was the smallest blink effect, or the greatest AB sparing, for negative high-arousal words over negative low-arousal words, which in turn were spared over neutral words. In other words, the word was more likely to be perceived, and thus the typically found attentional blink "spared," if the word was high in arousal. The second study showed that the same pattern held for positive words and suggested that the blink is modulated by emotional arousal elicited by the stimulus rather than by valence. Subsequent studies have demonstrated an emotional advantage for emotional faces as well as words (De Martino, Kalisch, Rees, & Dolan, 2009; Vermeulen, Godefroid, & Mermillod, 2009).

The next series of experiments was designed to rule out the possibility that the AB sparing was driven by other distinctive features of the arousing words. One study controlled for potential confounds due to idiosyncratic physical features of the emotional stimuli by using neutral words created from arousing words by transposing one letter (e.g., "rape" became "rope," "cancer" became "dancer"). The typical AB sparing was present for the emotionally arousing words but not for the orthographically similar T2 words, suggesting that observers did not reveal a response bias toward reporting negatively arousing words under conditions of uncertainty (e.g., rape vs. rope) and that low-level features common to arousing words were not responsible for AB sparing. In the next experiment, to ensure that the special status of arousing words did not reflect that novelty or distinctiveness related to neutral words, unusual neutral words as "Ballyhoo" and "Crump" were used. Again, AB sparing was observed for the emotionally arousing words relative to the unusual neutral words. To ensure that it was not the relative rarity or unexpectedness of arousing words driving the AB sparing, the task was next reversed so that neutral targets were surrounded by arousing distractors. Here neutral targets were reported less accurately when surrounded by arousing distractors than by neutral distractors. Thus, there was *less* AB sparing, or more of an attentional blink, when neutral targets were rare than when they were common, confirming that AB sparing was not the result of encountering unexpected words.

Over all of the experiments, the arousal content of T2 words effected a significant change in the magnitude and time course of the attentional blink. The change was not related to the physical features or the novelty of the arousing words, suggesting that arousing T2 words enjoy a privileged attentional status that allows them to more easily reach awareness. In fact, the studies demonstrated that AB sparing was not a property of the stimuli themselves but the observer's subjective emotional response to them, as AB sparing for arousing stimuli was predicted by the degree of experienced emotional arousal. Moreover, these results indicated that, when attentional resources were limited, emotional events required less attention to initially enter awareness.

Such findings are supported by data from lesion studies providing further evidence that emotionally salient stimuli enjoy privileged access to limited attentional resources. A study of patients with "spatial neglect," who were unaware of images presented in one hemifield when presented with images in both hemifields simultaneously, suggested that patients were less likely to be "blind" to emotional faces than to neutral faces that were presented in the neglected hemifield (Vuilleumier & Schwartz, 2001). Thus, convergent AB and lesion study evidence is consistent with the idea that emotionally arousing events enjoy a degree of attentional independence during encoding. Perceptual representations of arousing events may burn brighter and longer relative to competing neutral distractor events. This greedy capture of precious resources may maintain the focus of consciousness on emotionally provocative events. However, for the brain to prioritize attention to emotionally salient stimulus events, increased attention should logically be preceded by accelerated perceptual processing during initial encoding.

Further studies investigated neural mechanisms that might allow such a salience-related privileging of emotionally arousing stimuli to be partially independent of limitations in executive processing. Specifically, it was proposed that the amygdala, which sends projections to numerous regions of visual cortex (Amaral, Behniea, & Kelly, 2003), may work by "diminishing the burden" of top-down processing resources when stimuli are emotionally important. Evidence for this proposal came from a study using the AB paradigm in patients with amygdala lesions (Anderson & Phelps, 2001). This lesion study was designed to investigate the hypothesis that, in addition to its more established role in enhancing long term memory consolidation, the amygdala plays a critical role during initial encoding, modulating perceptual consolidation to enhance both detection of and memory for motivationally salient stimuli.

In this study, AB performance was measured in SP, a patient with bilateral amygdala lesions, and a group of healthy controls. SP showed a normal AB effect for neutral targets, but unlike the controls she did not show the pattern of AB sparing for negatively arousing words. To rule out a more global deficit in perceptual encoding, the authors manipulated the visual similarity of targets and distractors. SP showed AB sparing for more perceptually discriminable words but no AB sparing for emotional words. This finding suggested that the affective modulation of perceptual awareness is dissociable from modulation by low-level perceptual features, and only the former is mediated by the amygdala. The authors concluded that the amygdala modulates perceptual awareness with respect to emotional but not perceptual salience.

The next question addressed whether the lack of AB sparing for negative words was linked to lack of overall comprehension of the emotional value of words. SP and patients with left amygdala lesions were asked to rate the valence and arousal levels of target words. All participants rated the negative stimuli as more negative and more arousing than neutral words, indicating that impaired influence of emotional content on perceptual awareness was not related to overall differences in comprehension of the emotional value of words. Further studies with SP and other lesion patients indicated that amygdala activation is causally related to the perception but not the generation of emotional expressions (Anderson & Phelps, 2000) and that amygdala damage does not result in altered magnitude or frequency of emotional states (Anderson & Phelps, 2002). Thus, amygdala lesions do not necessarily decrease the experienced aspect of one's own emotion nor understanding of the overall significance of arousing stimuli. Here it was concluded that the amygdala is not necessary for the experience of an emotional state, which in humans may be more tied to internal emotional representations than to direct perceptual experience. Rather, these studies suggest that amygdala lesions impair the enhanced perceptual processing of emotionally arousing stimuli, as well as the prominence of emotionally salient events in memory.

Taken together, these findings suggest that amygdala lesions result in an inability to modulate the *efficiency* of perceptual processing mediated by other brain regions. Signals from the amygdala may enhance sensitivity in perceptual cortices as the amygdala trains the visual system to respond at lower activation thresholds. Less attention is then required for salient stimuli to activate the visual cortices. An fMRI study by Lim and colleagues (Lim, Padmala, & Pessoa, 2009) set out to directly investigate such a link between amygdala activation, enhanced visual processing, and the behavioral AB advantage for emotionally salient stimuli. In this study, fMRI data were collected during an AB task that was combined with aversive conditioning, which allows researchers to measure responses to affectively significant stimuli without confounds that are based on low-level differences in the image related to bottom-up visual salience. Here, T1 was a face and T2 was either a scene (a house or a building) or a non-scene. Participants had to report the identity of the face and whether T2 was a house or building, or a non-scene. In the learning phase of the study, for each participant, either the house or the building was paired with shock on 50% of trials (CS+) vs. no shock in any trials (CS–).

As predicted, there was an AB advantage for CS+ trials, with greater accuracy for CS+ than for CS– trials. fMRI results showed greater activation in the parahippocampal place area (PPA), a region of the visual cortex that responds preferentially to scenes, and in the amygdala for CS+ trials than for CS– trials. Trial by trial, PPA and amygdala activation predicted accuracy in identifying T2 more strongly for CS+ than for CS– trials, suggesting that emotional learning strengthens the neural representation of a scene, rendering it more likely to reach awareness. The trial-by-trial analysis indicated that improved performance for salient items in an AB task relies on representations in sensory cortex. Further mediation analysis revealed that, trial-by-trial, for CS+ trials, the relation between amygdala activation and behavioral accuracy was mediated by activation in the PPA. Finally, as amygdala activation increased, the link between visual cortex activation and behavior became stronger. The authors concluded that emotional salience provides an AB advantage via enhanced visual processing that is modulated by the amygdala.

Building on previous research, this study demonstrated that a key function of the amygdala is to segregate neural representations of the "significant from the mundane," playing a role in appraisal by shaping perceptual experience directly. Here, the amygdala may work by diminishing the burden of central (executive) processing resources when stimuli are emotionally important. At the end of the chapter, we will discuss convergent evidence suggesting that it plays an important node in a top-down salience network, working in tandem with prefrontal regions implicated in evaluative processing and selective attention to establish control settings that bias attention in visual cortices to emotionally salient events.

Further research has focused on the role of norepinephrine in the capture of attentional resources by salient stimuli. Norepinephrine plays a role in the regulation of blood pressure as well as on amygdala modulation of emotional memory (Roozendaal, McEwen, & Chattarji, 2009). A study by De Martino and colleagues (De Martino, Strange, & Dolan, 2008) combined a pharmacological manipulation with an AB task to see if increasing levels of norepinephrine in the brain enhance the advantage for emotional stimuli in capturing attentional resources. In one variation of this study, one group of participants was given a placebo and another was given reboxetine, a selective norepinephrine reuptake inhibitor, before performing a version of the emotional AB task. Although all participants showed greater accuracy for emotionally arousing words, the participants who received reboxetine showed more accuracy for arousing, but not neutral, trials than those given the placebo. These results suggest that the increased levels of adrenaline are selectively associated with privileged access to awareness for emotionally salient stimuli. They contribute to a picture in which the emotional advantage mediated by the amygdala, as a key hub of emotional-salience networks, is associated with allocation of somatic resources influencing heart rate, blood pressure, corticosteroid release, and respiration (Davis & Whalen, 2001).

Based on the accumulated evidence, we suggest that the amygdala is a hub of an evolutionarily conserved system for top-down processing that is more tightly linked to the allocation of bodily resources than are executive systems. The behavioral, lesion, fMRI, and pharmacological studies reviewed above demonstrated that (1) emotionally salient stimuli gain privileged access to awareness when attentional resources are limited; (2) this emotional advantage is dependent on an intact amygdala; (3) it is enhanced by the presence of norepinephrine in the brain; and (4) the influence of amygdala activation on salient stimulus recognition is mediated by increased activation in visual cortex. Future studies can investigate the developmental time course of the AB emotional advantage to test the hypothesis that it may emerge earlier in life, and deteriorate later, than attentional processes dominated by frontoparietal networks.

THE GREAT AUTOMATICITY DEBATE

The data reviewed above suggest that emotionally arousing events are "special" in that they have privileged access to attentional resources, and this privileging of such events is crucially linked to amygdala facilitation of perceptual processing. Thus, understanding the role of the amygdala is key to understanding selective attention to salient stimuli. Our knowledge of amygdala function continues to evolve, however. For some time the amygdala was conceived as a primitive threat-detector—the neural embodiment of an ancient animal id that functions automatically before more reasoned processes can kick in. That image has been challenged on a number of fronts.

One of these fronts involves the automaticity of amygdala function. Bringing earlier debates about whether emotion requires cognition into the realm of cognitive neuroscience, one debate has centered on whether visual processing of emotionally potent images, along with the amygdala activation that such images elicit, requires awareness. At the end of the 1990s, the answer seemed to be an easy "no." A body of behavioral data suggested preferential behavioral responses to subliminally presented threat cues (Mathews & MacLeod, 1986) and that skin conductance responses are modulated by masked fear-conditioned faces, even when subjects are unable to report seeing the face (Ohman & Soares, 1998; Soares & Ohman, 1993). Building on such evidence, two high-profile imaging studies were published showing evidence of selective amygdala responses to masked, threatening faces, flashed for ~30 ms, even when subjects reported no awareness of the faces (Morris, Ohman, & Dolan, 1998; Whalen et al., 1998). These were followed by studies demonstrating amygdala activation to briefly presented masked eye whites (Whalen et al., 2004); studies indicated that amygdala response to rapid, masked fearful faces was linked to trait anxiety (Etkin et al., 2004). On the basis of this evidence, some researchers concluded that emotional processing was evolutionarily hard-wired, automatic, and independent of awareness (Ohman, 2002). Such automaticity was thought to serve the adaptive function of facilitating rapid responses to threatening events when actions need to be quicker than the speed of thought. After all, if a tiger is about to pounce, she who contemplates the implications of running vs. freezing is unlikely to pass on her genes.

Yet these data generated a conundrum: If amygdala response to arousing images increases activation in the visual cortex, and yet the visual cortex needs to send categorical information about the identity of an object to the amygdala in order for the amygdala to tag its salience, how can either the amygdala or visual cortex discriminate emotional salience before there has been time for the visual cortex to extract categorical information? One proposed explanation came from the dual-route model of emotional processing, which was based on Ledoux's (1996) work with fear conditioning in rats. An adaptation of this model proposed that in humans there may be two routes by which the amygdala receives information about the visual world. (1) A subcortical, thalamo-amygdala "low road" is thought to send visual information directly to the amygdala, bypassing the neocortex, using low spatial-frequency information. Information sent through this route is thought to be crude but to contain enough information about emotional salience to influence amygdala activation—which in turn can enhance processing in the perceptual cortices. (2) A slower cortical "high road" is thought to send more detailed information to the amygdala after a feedforward volley of information through the perceptual cortices.

Another line of research further investigated attentional modulation of amygdala specificity, suggesting an alternate-route model of emotional-salience processing, if not a specifically subcortical one. In an initial study, Vuilleumier and Schwartz (2001) collected fMRI data while manipulating how much attention was devoted to target stimuli, which were either houses or faces with fearful or neutral expressions. This study found that while activity in face sensitive fusiform regions and house-sensitive parahippocampal regions was modulated by high vs. low levels of attention, amygdala activation discriminated fearful from neutral faces regardless of the level of attention devoted to the faces.

In a further fMRI study probing graded levels of amygdala sensitivity under conditions of greater vs. less attention (Anderson, Christoff, Panitz, De Rosa, & Gabrieli, 2003), images of fearful, neutral, and disgusted faces were directly superimposed on images of buildings (Figure 2.2). Participants were asked to judge either the gender of the faces (attended condition) or whether they were viewing the inside or the outside of a building (unattended condition). Again, results showed a direct effect of attention on visual cortex activation. As in the Vuilleumier and Schwartz (2001) study, the fusiform face area showed greater activation in the attended condition, when participants attended to faces, whereas the PPA showed relatively greater activation in the unattended condition, when participants attended to places. Thus, activation in visual cortex was directly related to the degree of attention paid to the stimulus, regardless of emotional content of the images.

In contrast, for the amygdala, there was an interaction between the degree of attention paid to

a stimulus and the response to emotional expression. When participants were attending to faces, the amygdala showed greater activation for fear faces than either disgusted or neutral faces. But when participants were not attending the faces, the amygdala responded equally to fear and disgust. Further, the amygdala again responded equally to fear faces during attended and unattended conditions, results suggesting that partial attentional distraction did not diminish the response to fearful faces. The authors concluded that, in conditions of impoverished attention, the amygdala responds to emotional salience, just more globally or crudely, and that increased attention enhances the specificity of the amygdala response.

With expressions of disgust there was an inverse relationship between cortical and amygdala processing that varied with attention: Cortical processing of disgust faces (in the insula) in attended conditions increased as amygdala processing decreased. This pattern was reversed in unattended conditions, during which amygdala processing increased and cortical processing decreased. Thus, when attention was impoverished, there was more crude amygdala processing relative to fine-grained categorization and processing of detail mediated by the cortex. These data suggest that, whereas the amygdala tags motivational relevance, or salience, the cortex mediates refined categorical processing, and attention enhances the latter relative to the former.

These results indicate that, although the magnitude of amygdala response may be mediated by an alternate route, which is partially independent of slower feedforward processing, the specificity of its response depends on extrastriate input. The evidence is consistent with models proposing a faster route that allows for rapid, relatively inattentive processing of crude visual features related to stimulus salience; slower routes allow more detailed but slower and more attentionally gated processing. Amygdala response may thus be influenced by inputs that are less attention-dependent as well as by inputs that require more attention. More recent evidence suggests that visual processing of emotional salience can indeed occur very rapidly, possibly in under 100 ms (West, Anderson, Ferber, & Pratt, 2011). There is also growing evidence that rapid emotional-salience detection may be mediated by a number of alternate routes, some cortical and some not necessarily implicating the amygdala (Bar et al., 2006; Barrett & Bar, 2009; Pessoa & Adolphs, 2010). Yet, although emotional-salience processes may be partially independent of executive

Figure 2.2 Example stimulus from face–place object selection task. Before each trial, participants saw a prompt indicating whether they should attend to the gender of the face (attended condition) or to whether they were viewing the interior or exterior of a building (unattended condition).

Reprinted with permission from *The Journal of Neuroscience*. Anderson, A. K., Christoff, K., Stappen, I., Panitz, D., Ghahremani, D. G., Glover, G., et al. (2003).

resources, and although there may be fast or sub-cortical routes to salience processing, it does not follow that salience processes are necessarily fully automatic.

Challenges to the View of the Amygdala as Automatic Threat Detector

A challenge to a view of amygdala function as purely automatic came from Pessoa and colleagues (Pessoa et al., 2002), who were guided by the following question: Given evidence that even low-level featural processing in early visual cortex is gated by attention, why should amygdala processing of emotional salience be any different? The studies reviewed above manipulated levels of attention devoted to faces in such a way that faces remained above the threshold of awareness in all conditions. Focusing more on the threshold of awareness, Pessoa et al. (2002) hypothesized that the amygdala would no longer respond to facial emotion if the attentional load was high enough to prevent any attentional resources being allocated to faces at all. To test this hypothesis, they first looked at amygdala responses to facial emotion in a highly attentionally demanding distractor task (discriminate the orientation of bars that are very similarly oriented) and an easy task that focused attention on the face (determine the gender). Not only was amygdala activation greater in the attended than unattended condition, but there was greater left amygdala activation for happy and fearful faces than for neutral faces in the low-attention task. In the high-attention task, there was no discrimination of stimulus valence, suggesting that amygdala activation does in fact require attentional resources. Face-selective regions of fusiform gyrus also showed an effect of facial emotion only in the attended condition, suggesting that category-specific processing of emotional expression in the visual cortex also requires attention. However, while this study indicates that a degree of attention is required for amygdala responses to stimulus salience, it is important to bear in mind that one cannot make definitive conclusions based on null fMRI results. Moreover, the task used in this study had a design that differed from those of the studies whose conclusions it challenged, and the results were therefore not *directly* comparable.

Further studies challenged the manner in which awareness was measured in masking studies finding "unconscious" threat processing. When signal detection methods were used as a more sensitive measure of fearful face identification, it was found that many participants could actually identify facial emotion when masked stimuli were presented for 33 ms, the presentation window typically used in subliminal masking studies (Pessoa, Japee, & Ungerleider, 2005)—and in some cases at 17 ms (Szczepanowski & Pessoa, 2007). An fMRI masking study found that when fearful faces were presented for 33 ms and participants were unaware of the fearful face, there was no differential amygdala activation. Yet when they were presented for 67 ms and participants correctly identified them, both the amygdala and the fusiform gyrus showed reliable preferential responses for fearful faces. Moreover, not only did the amygdala show stronger activation for trials in which fearful faces were correctly identified than when they were not identified, it showed stronger activation for trials in which fear faces were correctly identified than for trials in which they were present but not reported. These studies provided further evidence of the importance of executive attention for emotional-salience processing.

Lesion studies have also challenged the view of the amygdala as being involved in rapid, automatic emotional evaluation. One study of a patient with bilateral amygdala lesions found that, although she could not explicitly identify fearful facial expressions, she showed a normal capacity to correctly identify threatening stimuli when presented rapidly or at the threshold of awareness (Todd & Anderson, 2009; Tsuchiya, Moradi, Felsen, Yamazaki, & Adolphs, 2009). In this case, the typical bias for faster identification of fearful faces, thought to be linked to the amygdala role in automatic fear processing, was present, but the capacity for more explicit evaluation of facial emotion was missing. Thus, although the amygdala may be sensitive to rapid tagging of threatening stimuli, it may not be necessary for it—at least for fearful faces.

At present, the controversy over whether and how much the emotional advantage depends on awareness remains unresolved, with data on both sides. We suggest that, while there is evidence that amygdala sensitivity to emotional salience is influenced by attention, emotional stimuli may gain privileged access to attentional resources when attention is limited, and the degree of privileging may very depending on context and attentional load (Bishop, Jenkins, & Lawrence, 2007).

It is worth noting that many of the studies cited in both sides of the debate have used expressions of facial fear as stimuli; another set of issues arises around the special nature of fear faces as elicitors of emotional responses. The standard assumption about fearful faces is that they signal danger to conspecifics, we are biologically predisposed to respond to them, and they are thus indicators of threat in the environment (Ohman, 2002). But fearful faces are rated low in arousal, fail to elicit the same autonomic responses as strongly salient scenes (Anderson, Yamaguchi, Grabski, & Lacka, 2006), and are characterized by unique high spatial-frequency signatures (Schyns, Petro, & Smith, 2009). They are also quite bizarre looking and outside of the daily experience of those of us who do not watch a lot of horror movies. Thus, fear faces may be somewhat unique and problematic as exemplar emotionally salient stimuli. Results of studies relying on fearful faces are more conclusive in cases where they are replicated using emotional scenes and/or aversive conditioning that allow them to be generalized to the experience of fear or emotional processing in general.

Other challenges to the standard view of the amygdala have focused on the prevalent notion that the amygdala is primarily sensitive to threat. Historically, the view of the amygdala as a threat detector emerged in part because nonhuman animal research had mapped fear circuitry in great detail. Moreover, in human research, effects of arousal and valence were frequently conflated because many negative or fear-relevant stimuli (such as a decapitated body) elicit higher levels of arousal than commonly used positive stimuli (such as a bunny). A challenge to the view of the amygdala as a threat detector came from research suggesting that the amygdala responds to the arousal level of a stimulus rather than its valence.

In order to address this confound, an fMRI study by Anderson, Christoff, Stappen, and colleagues (2003) used olfactory stimuli to dissociate arousal and valence. Here fMRI data were collected while participants were presented with high and low concentrations of citral, which has a pleasant, lemony odor, and valeric, which is generally perceived to be unpleasant. Results showed that the amygdala responded to the intensity of the odor for pleasant and unpleasant odors alike. In contrast, the orbitofrontal cortex (OFC) was sensitive to valence rather than intensity, with the lateral OFC responding more to unpleasant odors and the medial OFC to pleasant odors. Moreover, activation patterns in the amygdala correlated with participants' ratings of the intensity but not the valence of the odors and responded to all odors more than to clean air. Thus, there were differences in amygdala activation when valence was held constant and intensity manipulated but not when intensity was held constant and valence manipulated. These data suggest that

amygdala activation is related directly to the experience of intensity, notwithstanding whether the stimulus is experienced as pleasant or unpleasant. One interpretation is that the amygdala is primarily responsive to crude stimulus properties rather than to more differentiated valence-dependent properties, which may depend on further processing mediated by the orbitofrontal cortices.

The finding that the amygdala responds more to how arousing a stimulus is, rather than to how good or bad it is, is supported by a body of accumulating evidence that the amygdala responds as—if not more—strongly to positive than negative stimuli if positive stimuli are matched to negative in arousal (Sergerie, Chochol, & Armony, 2008). Other studies have found the amygdala to be responsive to ambiguity (Whalen, 2007), to the regulation of social distance (Kennedy, Glascher, Tyszka, & Adolphs, 2009), and to extended as well as rapid processing of stimulus salience (Tsuchiya et al., 2009; Todd & Anderson, 2009).

What is tagged as salient may also change from moment to moment according to the demands of a task. Studies have shown evidence suggesting that amygdala responses to specific classes of stimuli are modulated by a change in social and motivational context (Cunningham, Van Bavel, & Johnsen, 2008; Van Bavel, Packer, & Cunningham, 2008). For example, in a study where participants were asked to evaluate famous people, Cunningham and colleagues (2008) found that the amygdala responded preferentially to names of celebrities that participants felt positive about when they were asked to evaluate positivity, and to names of celebrities they felt negative about when asked to rate negativity. Thus, the amygdala's response pattern shifted as the motivational relevance of stimuli changed according to momentary task demands. Such convergent findings have inspired some researchers to reconceive of the role of the amygdala: from threat detector to "biological relevance detector" that influences processes at a range of time scales, and from rapid stimulus consolidation to extended regulation of social and mnemonic processes (Adolphs, 2008; Cunningham et al., 2008; Davis & Whalen, 2001; Sander, Grafman, & Zalla, 2003).

Individual Differences and Developmental Changes in Motivated Attention

In addition to normative findings that emotionally arousing images elicit greater visual cortex activation and enjoy privileged access to awareness, there is also evidence of individual and developmental differences in attentional biases toward positive vs. negative stimuli. With regard to individual differences, a large body of behavioral and event-related brain potential (ERP) evidence indicates that temperamental anxiety is associated with selective processing of threatening stimuli and that this processing bias is rapid and relatively automatic (Armony & Dolan, 2002; Bishop et al., 2007; Holmes, Nielsen, & Green, 2008). Such biases are associated with lower thresholds for amygdala activation to threat (Bishop et al., 2007; McClure et al., 2007) Moreover, there is evidence that attentional biases are linked to trauma (Beck, Freeman, Shipherd, Hamblen, & Lackner, 2001; Buckley, Blanchard, & Neill, 2000; Vythilingam et al., 2007) and can be learned through conditioning (Armony & Dolan, 2002; Lim, Padmala, & Pessoa, 2008; Padmala & Pessoa, 2008). In an extreme example of processing bias, people suffering from post-traumatic stress disorder (PTSD) show heightened amygdala and perceptual sensitivity to stimuli associated with the trauma (Gilboa et al., 2004; Hendler et al., 2003). Although the majority of research to date has focused on biases to threat, there is increasing evidence of individual and developmental differences in biases for positive stimuli (Brosch, Sander, Pourtois, & Scherer, 2008; Mather et al., 2004). Thus, consistent with the amygdala's role in learning emotional associations, experience and temperament may both play a role in individual differences in what stimuli are tagged as salient.

Individual differences in motivated attention processes unfold on time scales ranging from the milliseconds required for heightened perception of a salient event, to the scale of minutes-to-hours implicated in sustained mood states, to a developmental scale of years as emotional habits are developed in childhood and honed throughout the lifespan (Lewis, 2005; Lewis & Todd, 2007). Recent research has also found evidence of normative developmental changes in the valence or category of images that preferentially activate the amygdala. In a developmental study (Todd, Evans, Morris, Lewis, & Taylor, 2011) young children (aged 4–8 years) and young adults (18–33 years) viewed images of personally familiar (mother's) and unfamiliar faces with angry and happy expressions. Adults showed a tendency toward greater amygdala activation for angry faces. In contrast, children showed preferential amygdala activation for happy vs. angry faces. This study adds to behavioral evidence suggesting that, like older adults, young children have a bias toward positively valenced stimuli (Mather et al., 2004;

Qu & Zelazo, 2007; van Duijvenvoorde, Zanolie, Rombouts, Raijmakers, & Crone, 2008). These data suggest that, although by the time children enter school amygdala cortical circuits supporting privileged visual encoding of salient stimuli appear to be in place, the salience of positive vs. negative stimuli may shift with developmental context.

Moreover, individual differences may become increasingly pronounced over development as amygdala-mediated associative learning—the development of emotional control sets—tunes the visual system toward specific categories of stimuli (Lewis & Todd, 2007). For example, research by Fox and colleagues suggests that children with at least one short serotonin transporter allele (5HTTLPR), a genetic profile associated with both temperamental fearfulness and increased amygdala reactivity, are more likely to experience a family environment that highlights threat. This repeated experience with caregivers in turn reinforces an attention bias to threatening stimuli (Fox, Hane, & Pine, 2007; Fox et al., 2005). Nonetheless, such developmental reinforcement of threat bias is not inevitable. Children high in negative affect who are also high in the trait capacity for effortful control, which includes the ability to volitionally focus and shift attention, do not show the attention bias to threat that is characteristic of children with high negative affect and low effortful control (Lonigan & Vasey, 2009). Thus, the amygdala response to emotional relevance would appear to be modulated by executive processes on a developmental as well as a momentary time scale. Future research can investigate the development of co-activation patterns between the amygdala and visual cortices that are correlated with the emergence of individual differences in both *what* and *how* salient stimuli are preferentially processed.

Modulating Attention Perception by Emotional Expression Production

The investigation of normative and individual preferential responses to salient stimuli focuses on only one of many facets of emotional response traditionally discussed in terms of appraisal. Another tradition in emotion research, linking perception and action, has focused motor responses involved in producing emotional expressions (Ekman, Sorenson, & Friesen, 1969; Tracy & Matsumoto, 2008). It was Darwin who first suggested that facial expressions of emotion serve to modify preparedness for perception and action in the face of an important event (Darwin, 1872/1988). He proposed that the role of facial expressions in social signaling may be built upon a more basic function in restricting or increasing access to sensory information. One line of research has investigated the effect of producing facial expressions on enhancing or reducing sensory processing.

Inspired by Darwin's proposal, Susskind and colleagues (2008) asked the following: Is the role of facial expressions in social communication built upon muscular patterns that serve the more basic pattern of expanding or reducing sensory intake? A series of studies set out to examine two Darwinian principals of expressive behavior: the principal of *function* and the principal of *form* (Darwin, 1872/1988). According to the principle of function, facial expressions arise from muscle actions that serve an adaptive function for the producer of the expression. According to the principle of form, expressions that serve opposite functions, such as increasing or reducing sensory intake, are opposite to each other in muscle action pattern.

To test the principal of form, a computer graphics model of facial expression was used to test statistically whether facial expressions of fear and disgust were opposite in form (Susskind et al., 2008). By manipulating prototypical models of facial expressions, the researchers created a prototype expression for fear and then manipulated shape- and surface-reflectance features to create an "anti-fear" face. Not only were anti-fear faces most similar to disgust faces based on featural characteristics but, in an expression recognition task, participants also rated anti-fear faces as disgust more than as any other emotion. The same process was repeated with disgust. Again, "anti-disgust" faces were most structurally similar to, and most likely to be rated as, fear faces. The next step was to model the muscular-action patterns underlying the oppositions in fear and disgust expressions (Figure 2.3). In comparison with disgust, the fear expression was characterized by an expanding, elongating longitudinal action around the mouth, nose, and eyes, suggesting muscular actions involved in sensory vigilance. Disgust invoked the opposite, a longitudinal compression suggesting muscular actions involved in sensory rejection.

The next study set out to test whether fear and disgust are opposite in *function*, allowing expanded vs. reduced perception. Using the computer model to further test predictions regarding specific measures of sensory regulation, it was found that fear was characterized by eye-lid opening and brow raising, and disgust in eyelid lowering and eye closing,

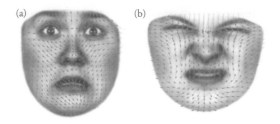

Figure 2.3 Opposition in facial actions between fear and disgust expressions. Arrows show patterns of facial muscle actions from anti-fear to fear (**a**) and anti-disgust to disgust (**b**), which indicate expansion vs. compression longitudinally from the bridge of the nose. This longitudinal movement results in raised vs. lowered brows, opened vs. closed eyes, and the elongation vs. compression of the nose that accompanies raised and lowered lips.

Reprinted by permission from Macmillan Publishers Ltd: [Nature Neuroscience]. Susskind, J. M., Lee, D. H., Cusi, A., Feiman, R., Grabski, W., & Anderson, A. K. Expressing fear enhances sensory acquisition. *Nature Neuroscience, 11*(7), 843–850, copyright (2008).

altering visual input. A further study tested the effects of facial expression on the visual field in human participants. In initial perimetry tests, participants stood in front of a grid and judged visual field size while posing fear and disgust expressions relative to neutral expressions. Production of fear expressions was found to increase the perceived visual field, specifically the upper half, consistent with raised brows and lids. Production of disgust expressions was found to decrease the size of the perceived visual field, consistent with brow lowering and the cheek raising that results from a wrinkled nose. Moreover, eye actions filmed during the production of facial expressions predicted subjective impressions of visual field size. The facial expression that was produced also predicted participants' objectively measured ability to detect simple sensory onsets in the upper level of the visual field, again with fear enhancing and disgust reducing stimulus detection. Overall, these studies demonstrated that producing facial expressions of fear and disgust regulates the size of the visual field, and thus the amount of visual information coming in from the world.

A final study examined whether the expansion of the eyes in fear faces might serve to prepare action patterns for increased scanning of the visual environment. In the next study, eye movements were measured as participants performed saccades between two horizontal targets while posing fear, disgust, and neutral expressions. Eye movements were fastest for fear and slowest for disgust, demonstrating that fear faces also increase the speed of foveation of objects in the visual field.

This series of studies provides evidence that, prior to their function in social communication, fear and disgust expressions may serve a basic physical function that allows us to take in more of the visual world when faced with threat, and less when faced with contamination. In the case of fear, visual capacity is increased in the face of a novel or unexpected stimulus, enabling subsequent activation of a repertoire of defensive and protective actions. We propose that, in this case, the amygdala again may serve as a key link between one's physical and emotional state and attentional modulation of visual processing via processes associated with emotional expression in addition to those traditionally associated with appraisal. Through its downstream connections, the amygdala can also relay signals to the body to modulate perception by priming muscular action. The effect of emotion on stimulus processing is not restricted to the central nervous system but begins through configuring one's face to maximize or minimize exposure of the sensory organs.

Emotional State and the Scope and Speed of Visual Processing

Production of a fleeting facial expression has a brief muscular influence on the scope of perception. In contrast, in a sustained emotional state, neurotransmitters can tonically influence cortical processes, thus producing changes in the style of processing, modulating attention or action readiness by globally modulating neuronal excitability and signal-to-noise ratio (Gu, 2002; Lewis, 2005; Panksepp, 1998). A whole other body of research has focused on the effects of emotional state on cognition and perception. Whereas our discussion of motivated attention to salient stimuli has focused on the effects of emotional arousal, regardless of valence, many studies of emotional state on cognitive processing have focused on the valence of the emotion, positing opposing effects of positive and negative affect. Whereas negative emotional states have been associated with a narrowed "weapon focus" on relevant details of a stimulus (Easterbrook, 1959), positive emotional states are commonly associated with a more flexible, exploratory attentional style, with a focus on gist rather than detail (Fredrickson, 2002; Fredrickson & Joiner, 2002; Gasper & Clore, 2002; Isen, Daubman, & Nowicki, 1987; Rowe, Hirsh, & Anderson, 2007). Although there are competing theories about the effects of valence on attention and perception, which we discuss further below, one hypothesis is that whereas a negative state narrows perceptual processing, positive emotion broadens the attentional lens, unbiasing competition to allow more distracting or task-irrelevant information to enter perception. Several imaging studies support this view.

One study examined whether mood *literally* contracts or expands the area (rather than the amplitude) of processing in the visual cortex (Schmitz, De Rosa, & Anderson, 2009). Specifically, this study probed the effect of mood on responses in extrastriate visual cortex to specific categories of objects. The authors hypothesized that negative mood would decrease the processing of task-irrelevant visual distractions. Conversely, positive mood should decrease the ability to filter irrelevant information. In this fMRI study, positive and negative affect were induced by showing series of positive, neutral, or negatively valenced (threatening) pictures before participants performed a visuospatial attention task. After a block of these mood induction images, participants viewed small, foveal pictures of faces that were surrounded by larger images of houses and were asked to report the gender of the face. Thus, the task required participants to attend to a central image and ignore information from a peripheral one. Cortical activation was then measured in the PPA, which responds more to houses than to faces. Results showed that negative affect was associated with less PPA activation than that with positive or neutral states, indicating that negative mood was associated with less cortical processing of irrelevant peripheral visual information. Repetition suppression, which is a reduction in brain activation that occurs when the same image is repeated one or more times, was then employed to investigate differences in the *degree* of peripheral information-processing associated with mood. Here, positive mood evoked the greatest amount of repetition suppression in the PPA, suggesting greater initial processing of peripheral information in a positive emotional state. Moreover, participant reports of greater positive affect predicted increased perceptual encoding of unattended peripheral stimuli, whereas reports of greater negative valence predicted less peripheral place processing. Finally, investigation of patterns of co-activation between the PPA and primary visual cortex suggested an increase in coupling between these regions with positive affect, and a decrease in coupling with negative affect. This finding suggests that a positive mood state facilitates the flow of sensory information between early visual-processing regions and extrastriate regions specialized for higher-level processing. In contrast, negative states are associated with a more circumscribed processing of sensory inputs.

This study demonstrated that emotional state can influence visual cortical processing regardless of the salience of the stimuli. Moreover, positive and negative states created opposite effects, with positive affect increasing task-irrelevant peripheral processing and negative affect reducing it. Thus, emotional states fundamentally bias the attentional lens through which perceptual experience is filtered. The analysis of functional connectivity further suggests that this biasing effect has an impact on initial stages of visual processing—that emotional state tunes the perceptual cortices to differentially process incoming perceptual information, and that this may be more nonselective with positive affect, which unbiases attention to let more task-irrelevant information in.

Another study probed the effects of mood state on the speed, rather than the scope, of cortical processing (Kuhbandner et al., 2009). In a between-subject design, participants were shown humorous, sad, or neutral film clips for mood induction, and electroencephalographic (EEG) data were collected while they tried to identify masked words shown at presentation times that ranged from 17 to 67 ms. To assess the effects of mood on perceptual gating, alpha power was measured over occipitoparietal sites prior to stimulus onset. Behavioral results showed that the threshold for word detection was lowest in the negative-mood condition and highest in the positive-mood condition, suggesting that sadness increased the speed of visual processing and that positive affect slowed it. Alpha power, which decreases with executive task demand, is thought to be negatively correlated with frontally mediated inhibitory processes implicated in selective attentional filters (Ergenoglu et al., 2004; Hanslmayr et al., 2005) and thus positively correlated with decreased filtering. Here, relative alpha power prior to stimulus onset was highest in the positive mood condition and lowest in the negative, suggesting a decrease in perceptual inhibition processes that was consistent with increased activity in perceptual cortices, or an *unbiasing* of attention with positive mood.

The two studies described above provide suggestive initial evidence that positive affect expands, and negative affect contracts, both the scope and the speed of visual perception, a finding consistent with the influence of mood on the biasing and unbiasing of visual attention. However, research on the effect of mood on the mechanisms of perceptual gating is just getting under way, and future studies are required to further test the hypothesis that positive affect unbiases neural competition in the visual cortices. Other studies are beginning explore neural systems implicated in the effects of positive mood state on higher-order tasks that tap creativity and insight decision-making (Kounios et al., 2006; Subramaniam, Kounios, Parrish, & Jung-Beeman, 2009). One hypothesis is that low-arousal positive affect facilitates exploratory behavior, mediated by frontopolar and dorsal cingulate regions, rather than exploitative behavior linked to frontostriatal dopaminergic reward circuits (Daw, O'Doherty, Dayan, Seymour, & Dolan, 2006; Schmitz et al., 2009). Whereas exploitation involves relying on strategies that reliably maximize currently available rewards, exploration entails gathering information about alternative courses of action, which may be more risky but potentially more profitable (Cohen, McClure, & Yu, 2007).

Individual differences in the tendency toward exploratory vs. exploitative behavior have been linked to differences in prefrontal dopamine metabolism. A uniquely human val158met polymorphism in the gene regulating catechol-*O*-methyltransferase (COMT), an enzyme involved in degradation of dopamine in the prefrontal cortex, has been associated with an exploratory style of cognition. Individuals with two copies of the met allele (met/met) have 25 to 75% less COMT enzyme activity, resulting in higher levels of extracellular dopamine in the prefrontal cortex, than those with two copies of the val allele (val/val) (Chen et al., 2004). According to the tonic-phasic hypothesis, the met/met variant is characterized by high levels of tonic dopaminergic activity that render its carriers more focused but more rigid (Bilder, Volavka, Lachman, & Grace, 2004; de Frias et al., 2010). In contrast, the val/val variant is characterized by higher levels of subcortical phasic activity that render val/val carriers more distractible but also more exploratory and flexible (Krugel et al., 2009). Thus, the val/val allele has been associated with exploratory behavior specifically and may more facilitate enhanced trait and state effects of positive emotions on perception and attention. An investigation of links between genetic influences on dopaminergic systems, neural systems underlying exploratory behavior, and positive affect is an important area for future research.

While the studies described in detail here have explored the influence of relatively low-arousal positive-state attentional processes, other models of positive affect propose that such valence effects may depend on the level of approach and avoidance elicited in the task. This, in turn, may be related to the degree of arousal of the stimuli or activation of exploitative rather than to exploratory systems. Studies by Harmon-Jones and colleagues have provided evidence that stimuli that are high in approach motivation, such as images of cake shown to hungry young women, *narrow* the scope of attentional focus (Gable & Harmon-Jones, 2008). They found that relative left-hemisphere frontal alpha power, thought to be a measure of approach motivation, was linked to attentional narrowing (Harmon-Jones & Gable, 2009) and was greater for participants who were hungrier and liked dessert better when they viewed dessert pictures. However, as these studies used discrete, arousing positive stimuli, it can be argued that they tapped stimulus-specific processes related to motivated attention rather than evoking a sustained emotional state.

There are also several competing models that make alternate predictions about the effects of positive affect on perception. One is that positive emotion leads to reliance on whatever attentional set is dominant at the moment, which may or may not entail a broadening of attention (Gasper & Clore, 2002). In contrast with models that predict greater cognitive flexibility with positive affect (Dreisbach & Goschke, 2004; Subramaniam et al., 2009), this model predicts decreased capacity to switch tasks or sets. Areas for future research include probing the possible effects of positive and negative emotional states on establishment of emotional control sets that gate attentional selection according to task demands, as well as the influence of individual personality differences on the effect of emotional state on attentional gating.

Beyond the Influence of Emotion on Attention and Perception

Another area that remains to be investigated concerns the effects of specific negative emotional states. Some of the studies described here used induced sadness and others, anxiety. Yet sadness and anxiety are associated with different levels of arousal and elicit different action tendencies, and thus they might have very different effects on attentional speed and scope. It will be important for future studies to discriminate between the effects of specific positive and negative emotional states.

Other important areas of cognitive neuroscience research into cognition–emotion interactions are beyond the scope of this chapter. These include a growing body of research on the influence of emotion and motivation on executive processes (Pessoa, 2009) and memory (LaBar & Cabeza, 2006); how these vary between individuals and in development; and their role in psychopathology (Bishop, 2009; Koenigs & Grafman, 2009). Another line of research focuses on the role of cognitive control processes on emotional responses, including the study of the effect of specific emotion-regulation strategies (Goldin, McRae, Ramel, & Gross, 2008; Ochsner et al., 2004) and mindfulness practices and cognitive behavioral therapies on emotional reactivity.

Conclusion

We conclude by returning to discussion of emotional-salience networks that tune perceptual processing according to stimulus salience or emotional state. Here we focus on the role of the amygdala as a central hub of networks mediating all three types of emotional processing reviewed here: (1) motivated attention linked to aspects of what has been traditionally thought of as appraisal, (2) effects of motor responses involved in facial expression production, and (3) tuning of perceptual filters by sustained affective state. We argue that the amygdala is optimally positioned to allocate somatic and attentional resources associated with aspects of emotion traditionally associated with both "cognitive" and "emotional" processes in order to tag and respond to what is important in the world.

Convergent evidence suggests that the amygdala is positioned to integrate information from numerous cortical and subcortical regions, facilitating prioritization and allocation of central and peripheral resources in service of one's goals. Geographically, the amygdala is optimally located to integrate information from the body and the world and, in turn, influence both cortical and subcortical and peripheral responses. Research suggests that it is anatomically linked to all but eight cortical structures (Young, Scannell, Burns, & Blakemore, 1994) and is literally central to the connectional topography of the central nervous system. In addition to sending direct projections to all levels of the visual cortex in the ventral visual stream (Amaral et al., 2003), it is also linked to frontal and parietal regions that mediate top-down attention (Young et al., 1994). Functional studies of resting-state connectivity also point to the central position of the amygdala in a "salience" network implicated in emotional processing (Seeley et al., 2007). Thus, we argue that it is optimally positioned to allocate resources in all three aspects of emotional processing.

1. Amygdala role in motivated attention. The amygdala has numerous connections with sensory regions that mediate distinct aspects of visual processing (Amaral et al., 2003). Research reviewed in this chapter further suggests a functional influence of the amygdala on regions of visual cortex, contributing to a view of amygdala function that emphasizes its appraisal-related role in tagging salient objects for further perceptual processing and facilitating an advantage for emotionally salient stimuli in reaching awareness. The amygdala also has dense reciprocal connections with prefrontal cortical regions such as the orbitofrontal cortex (OFC), implicated in evaluating motivational importance of an event in light of past experience (Ghashghaei et al., 2007). Strong connections between the amygdala and the OFC suggest a role for the amygdala in focusing attention on emotionally salient stimuli; connections from the OFC to the amygdala (Barbas, 2007) suggest rapid OFC prediction of stimulus identity or salience that influences amygdala as well as visual-cortex processing (Bar et al., 2006; Barrett & Bar, 2009). Taken together, these data emphasize the importance of amygdala–OFC–visual cortex connections that bias attention to salient events. Animal research suggests that the amygdala is also functionally associated with the thalamic pulvinar nucleus and the superior colliculus, subcortical structures important for attention and eye movements. Amygdala activation also increases thalamic sensitivity to information from the retina (Cain, Kapp, & Puryear, 2002), although such functional connections have yet to be established in primates.

2. Production of facial expressions. Research on the production of facial expressions further implicates the importance of motor responses to emotional events in gating perceptual processing. We argue that the amygdala should also play an important role in prioritizing such motor responses. Via connections to the hypothalamus and brainstem (Saha, 2005; Saha, Drinkhill, Moore, & Batten, 2005; Veening, Swanson, & Sawchenko, 1984), the amygdala can evoke basic action repertoires (such as freezing and startle responses and facial actions linked to emotional expression) and trigger changes in heart rate, blood pressure, galvanic skin response, corticosteroid release, pupil dilation, and respiration (Davis & Whalen, 2001). Thus, connections from the amygdala to lower structures facilitate activation of physiological responses associated with "emotion" at the same time as connections from the amygdala up to the cortex allow the amygdala to harness such "cognitive" processes as perception, attention, memory, and planned action.

3. Effects of emotional state on perceptual tuning. The effects of sustained emotional state on the scope and speed of cortical processing reviewed in this chapter may reflect an influence of subcortical processes that tonically influence visual processing. Schmitz et al. (2009) found amygdala activation to be associated with negative affective states that narrowed the scope of visual processing. One possible route for sustained amygdala influence on visual processing is via neurotransmitters that tonically influence visual processing. Stimulation of the amygdala increases overall cortical arousal and plays a role in attentional vigilance (Davis & Whalen, 2001; Hurlemann et al., 2007). In addition to upward connections with cortical systems, the amygdala has numerous downward projections to brainstem and basal forebrain regions that release neurotransmitters with global effects on cortical function (e.g., Krettek & Price, 1978). Such neurotransmitters as noradrenaline, acetylcholine, dopamine, and serotonin all in turn influence cortical and subcortical regions—including the amygdala—implicated in state-related tuning of visual processes (Beane & Marrocco, 2004; Botly & De Rosa, 2009; Sarter et al., 1996; Vitay & Hamker, 2008).

In conclusion, convergent research suggests that the amygdala may be crucially involved in influences of emotion on perception and attention on a number of time scales and via several cortical circuits. As a central hub that receives somatic and cortical information and influences the extent of both bodily and perceptual responses, the amygdala can guide allocation of both physical and attentional resources in a range of circumstances and at different times. Because the amygdala is implicated in emotional learning, its activation patterns are informed by past experiences, and it harnesses our central and peripheral responses accordingly.

We propose that all of these amygdala-mediated processes contribute to emotional-salience systems. Such systems enable us establish "emotional control sets" that change with moment-to-moment context but are tuned over a lifetime. One role of this ongoing processing bias is to maintain a moment-to-moment modulation of perception, based on experience, so that as we go about our day-to-day business, we see the things that count in the current context. From a phylogenetic brain systems perspective, evolutionarily older systems may serve to harness more sophisticated and elaborated "executive" systems, in parallel modulating the allocation of limited resources in the body and the brain. The amygdala may represent a central hub that adaptively harnesses these mental and bodily resources in responding to threats and challenges. When life is good, reduced amygdala vigilance to arousing events may be associated with attentional broadening that allows us to take in less immediately relevant information, and such distractibility is linked to creativity. Yet amygdala plasticity can also contribute to maladaptive salience, as in PTSD, which is characterized by a rigid biasing of perception and memory to trauma-related aspects of the environment. In this case, the adaptive emotional prioritizing of perception and attention can go awry, and the attentional lens loses its flexibility, becoming fixed on external stimuli and internal cognitions more associated with life's threat than with its rewards.

Future Directions

Additional research is needed in order to address the following areas:

1. Research on resting-state networks and effective connectivity that integrate subcortical regions that may be implicated in emotional-salience networks.

2. Investigation of the developmental time course of the attentional blink emotional advantage can test the hypothesis that it may emerge earlier in life, and deteriorate later, than attentional processes dominated by frontoparietal networks.

3. Investigation of development of co-activation patterns between the amygdala and visual cortices that are correlated with the emergence of individual differences in both *what* and *how* salient stimuli are preferentially processed.

4. An investigation of links between genetic influences on dopaminergic systems, neural systems underlying exploratory behavior, and positive affect.

5. Probing the possible effect of emotional state on control sets that gate attentional selection according to task demands, as well as individual personality differences in influence of emotional state on attentional gating.

Further Reading

Anderson, A. K., & Phelps, E. A. (2001). Lesions of the human amygdala impair enhanced perception of emotionally salient events. *Nature, 411*(6835), 305–309.

Anderson, A. K., Christoff, K., Stappen, I., Panitz, D., Gahremani, G., et al. (2003b). Dissociated neural representations of intensity and valence in human olfaction. *Nature Neuroscience, 6*(2), 196–202.

Darwin, C. (1872/1988). *The expression of the emotions in man and animals*. New York: Oxford University Press.

Lewis, M. D. (2005). Bridging emotion theory and neurobiology through dynamic systems modeling. *Behavioral and Brain Sciences, 28*(2), 169–194.

Pessoa, L. (2008). On the relationship between emotion and cognition. *Nature Reviews Neuroscience, 9*(2), 148–158.

Power, M. & Dagliesh, T. (2007). *Cognition and emotion: From order to disorder*, 2nd edition (2007). Hove, East Sussex, UK: Psychology Press.

Schmitz, T. W., De Rosa, E., & Anderson, A. K. (2009). Opposing influences of affective state valence on visual cortical encoding. *Journal of Neuroscience, 29*(22), 7199–7207.

Susskind, J. M., Lee, D. H., Cusi, A., Feiman, R., Grabski, W., & Anderson, A. K. (2008). Expressing fear enhances sensory acquisition. *Nature Neuroscience, 11*(7), 843–850.

References

Adolphs, R. (2008). Fear, faces, and the human amygdala. *Current Opinion Neurobiology, 18*(2), 166–172.

Amaral, D. G., Behniea, H., & Kelly, J. L. (2003). Topographic organization of projections from the amygdala to the visual cortex in the macaque monkey. *Neuroscience, 118*(4), 1099–1120.

Anderson, A. K. (2005). Affective influences on the attentional dynamics supporting awareness. *Journal of Experimental Psychology: General, 134*(2), 258–281.

Anderson, A. K., Christoff, K., Panitz, D., De Rosa, E., & Gabrieli, J. D. (2003). Neural correlates of the automatic processing of threat facial signals. *Journal of Neuroscience, 23*(13), 5627–5633.

Anderson, A. K., Christoff, K., Stappen, I., Panitz, D., Gahremani, G., et al. (2003). Dissociated neural representations of intensity and valence in human olfaction. *Nature Neuroscience, 6*(2), 196–202.

Anderson, A. K., & Phelps, E. A. (2000). Expression without recognition: Contributions of the human amygdala to emotional communication. *Psychological Science, 11*(2), 106–111.

Anderson, A. K., & Phelps, E. A. (2001). Lesions of the human amygdala impair enhanced perception of emotionally salient events. *Nature, 411*(6835), 305–309.

Anderson, A. K., & Phelps, E. A. (2002). Is the human amygdala critical for the subjective experience of emotion? Evidence of intact dispositional affect in patients with amygdala lesions. *Journal of Cognitive Neuroscience, 14*(5), 709–720.

Anderson, A. K., Yamaguchi, Y., Grabski, W., & Lacka, D. (2006). Emotional memories are not all created equal: Evidence for selective memory enhancement. *Learning and Memory, 13*(6), 711–718.

Armony, J. L., & Dolan, R. J. (2002). Modulation of spatial attention by fear-conditioned stimuli: An event-related fMRI study. *Neuropsychologia, 40*(7), 817–826.

Arnold, M. B. (1969). Human emotion and action. In T. Mischel (Ed.), *Human action: Conceptual and empirical issues* (pp. 167–197). New York: Academic Press.

Bar, M., Kassam, K. S., Ghuman, A. S., Boshyan, J., Schmid, A. M., Dale, A. M., et al. (2006). Top-down facilitation of visual recognition. *Proceedings of the National Academy of Sciences U S A*, *103*(2), 449–454.

Barbas, H. (2007). Specialized elements of orbitofrontal cortex in primates. *Annals of the New York Academy of Sciences*, *1121*, 10–32.

Barrett, L. F., & Bar, M. (2009). See it with feeling: Affective predictions during object perception. *Philosophical Transactions of the Royal Society: B Biological Sciences*, *364*(1521), 1325–1334.

Beane, M., & Marrocco, R. T. (2004). Norepinephrine and acetylcholine mediation of the components of reflexive attention: Implications for attention deficit disorders. *Progress in Neurobiology*, *74*(3), 167–181.

Beck, J. G., Freeman, J. B., Shipherd, J. C., Hamblen, J. L., & Lackner, J. M. (2001). Specificity of Stroop interference in patients with pain and PTSD. *Journal of Abnormal Psychology*, *110*(4), 536–543.

Bilder, R. M., Volavka, J., Lachman, H. M., & Grace, A. A. (2004). The catechol-*O*-methyltransferase polymorphism: Relations to the tonic-phasic dopamine hypothesis and neuropsychiatric phenotypes. *Neuropsychopharmacology*, *29*(11), 1943–1961.

Bishop, S. J. (2009). Trait anxiety and impoverished prefrontal control of attention. *Nature Neuroscience*, *12*(1), 92–98.

Bishop, S. J., Jenkins, R., & Lawrence, A. D. (2007). Neural processing of fearful faces: Effects of anxiety are gated by perceptual capacity limitations. *Cerebral Cortex*, *17*(7), 1595–1603.

Blau, V. C., Maurer, U., Tottenham, N., & McCandliss, B. D. (2007). The face-specific N170 component is modulated by emotional facial expression. *Behavioral and Brain Functions*, *3*, 7.

Botly, L. C., & De Rosa, E. (2009). The nucleus basalis magnocellularis contributes to feature binding in the rat. *Physiology & Behavior*, *97*(3-4), 313–320.

Bradley, M. M., Sabatinelli, D., Lang, P. J., Fitzsimmons, J. R., King, W., & Desai, P. (2003). Activation of the visual cortex in motivated attention. *Behavioral Neuroscience*, *117*(2), 369–380.

Brosch, T., Sander, D., Pourtois, G., & Scherer, K. R. (2008). Beyond fear: Rapid spatial orienting toward positive emotional stimuli. *Psychological Science*, *19*(4), 362–370.

Buckley, T. C., Blanchard, E. B., & Neill, W. T. (2000). Information processing and PTSD: A review of the empirical literature. *Clinical Psychology Review*, *20*(8), 1041–1065.

Cain, M. E., Kapp, B. S., & Puryear, C. B. (2002). The contribution of the amygdala to conditioned thalamic arousal. *Journal of Neuroscience*, *22*(24), 11026–11034.

Cannon, W. (1927). The James-Lange theory of emotions: A critical examination. *American Journal of Psychology*, *39*, 106–124.

Chen, J., Lipska, B. K., Halim, N., Ma, Q. D., Matsumoto, M., Melhem, S., et al. (2004). Functional analysis of genetic variation in catechol-O-methyltransferase (COMT): effects on mRNA, protein, and enzyme activity in postmortem human brain. *American Journal of Human Genetics*, *75*(5), 807–821.

Cohen, J. D., McClure, S. M., & Yu, A. J. (2007). Should I stay or should I go? How the human brain manages the trade-off between exploitation and exploration. *Philosophical Transactions of the Royal Society: B Biological Sciences*, *362*(1481), 933–942.

Corbetta, M., Kincade, J. M., & Shulman, G. L. (2002). Neural systems for visual orienting and their relationships to spatial working memory. *Journal of Cognitive Neuroscience*, *14*(3), 508–523.

Corbetta, M., & Shulman, G. L. (2002). Control of goal-directed and stimulus-driven attention in the brain. *Nature Reviews Neuroscience*, *3*(3), 201–215.

Cunningham, W. A., Van Bavel, J. J., & Johnsen, I. R. (2008). Affective flexibility: Evaluative processing goals shape amygdala activity. *Psychological Science*, *19*(2), 152–160.

Darwin, C. (1872/1988). *The expression of the emotions in man and animals*. New York: Oxford University Press.

Davis, M., & Whalen, P. J. (2001). The amygdala: Vigilance and emotion. *Molecular Psychiatry*, *6*(1), 13–34.

Daw, N. D., O'Doherty, J. P., Dayan, P., Seymour, B., & Dolan, R. J. (2006). Cortical substrates for exploratory decisions in humans. *Nature*, *441*(7095), 876–879.

de Frias, C. M., Marklund, P., Eriksson, E., Larsson, A., Öman, L., Annerbrink, K., et al. (2010). Influence of *COMT* gene polymorphism on fMRI-assessed sustained and transient activity during a working memory task. *Journal of Cognitive Neuroscience*, *22*(7), 1614–1622

De Martino, B., Kalisch, R., Rees, G., & Dolan, R. J. (2009). Enhanced processing of threat stimuli under limited attentional resources. *Cerebral Cortex*, *19*(1), 127–133.

De Martino, B., Strange, B. A., & Dolan, R. J. (2008). Noradrenergic neuromodulation of human attention for emotional and neutral stimuli. *Psychopharmacology (Berlin)*, *197*(1), 127–136.

Desimone, R., & Duncan, J. (1995). Neural mechanisms of selective visual attention. *Annual Review of Neuroscience*, *18*, 193–222.

Dosenbach, N. U., Fair, D. A., Cohen, A. L., Schlaggar, B. L., & Petersen, S. E. (2008). A dual-networks architecture of top-down control. *Trends in Cognitive Sciences*, *12*(3), 99–105.

Dreisbach, G., & Goschke, T. (2004). How positive affect modulates cognitive control: Reduced perseveration at the cost of increased distractibility. *Journal of Experimental Psychology: Learning Memory and Cognition*, *30*(2), 343–353.

Easterbrook, J. A. (1959). The effect of emotion on cue utilization and the organization of behavior. *Psychological Review*, *66*(3), 183–201.

Ekman, P. (1994). Moods, emotions, and traits. In P. Ekman & R. J. Davidson (Eds.), *The nature of emotion: Fundamental questions*. New York: Oxford University Press, 56-58.

Ekman, P., Sorenson, E. R., & Friesen, W. V. (1969). Pancultural elements in facial displays of emotion. *Science*, *164*(875), 86–88.

Ergenoglu, T., Demiralp, T., Bayraktaroglu, Z., Ergen, M., Beydagi, H., & Uresin, Y. (2004). Alpha rhythm of the EEG modulates visual detection performance in humans. *Brain Research: Cognitive Brain Research*, *20*(3), 376–383.

Etkin, A., Klemenhagen, K. C., Dudman, J. T., Rogan, M. T., Hen, R., Kandel, E. R., et al. (2004). Individual differences in trait anxiety predict the response of the basolateral amygdala to unconsciously processed fearful faces. *Neuron*, *44*(6), 1043–1055.

Folk, C. L., Remington, R. W., & Johnston, J. C. (1992). Involuntary covert orienting is contingent on attentional control settings. *Journal of Experimental Psychology: Human Perception and Performance, 18*(4), 1030–1044.

Fox, N. A., Hane, A. A., & Pine, D. S. (2007). Plasticity for affective neurocircuitry: How the environment affects gene expression. *Current Directions in Psychological Science, 16*(1), 1–5.

Fox, N. A., Nichols, K. E., Henderson, H. A., Rubin, K., Schmidt, L., Hamer, D., et al. (2005). Evidence for a gene–environment interaction in predicting behavioral inhibition in middle childhood. *Psychological Science, 16*(12), 921–926.

Fredrickson, B. L. (2002). The broaden-and-build theory of positive emotions. *Philosophical Transactions of the Royal Society of London, 52*, 1122–1131.

Fredrickson, B. L., & Joiner, T. (2002). Positive emotions trigger upward spirals toward emotional well-being. *Psychological Science, 13*(2), 172–175.

Frijda, N., & Zeelenberg, M. (2001). Appraisal: What is the dependent? In A. S. K. R. Scherer, & T. Johnstone (Ed.), *Appraisal processes in emotion: Theory, methods, research* (pp. 141–155). Oxford, UK: Oxford University Press.

Gable, P. A., & Harmon-Jones, E. (2008). Approach-motivated positive affect reduces breadth of attention. *Psychological Science, 19*(5), 476–482.

Gasper, K., & Clore, G. L. (2002). Attending to the big picture: Mood and global versus local processing of visual information. *Psychological Science, 13*(1), 34–40.

Ghashghaei, H. T., Hilgetag, C. C., & Barbas, H. (2007). Sequence of information processing for emotions based on the anatomic dialogue between prefrontal cortex and amygdala. *Neuroimage, 4*(3), 905–923.

Gilboa, A., Shalev, A. Y., Laor, L., Lester, H., Louzoun, Y., Chisin, R., et al. (2004). Functional connectivity of the prefrontal cortex and the amygdala in posttraumatic stress disorder. *Biological Psychiatry, 5*(3), 263–272.

Goldin, P. R., McRae, K., Ramel, W., & Gross, J. J. (2008). The neural bases of emotion regulation: Reappraisal and suppression of negative emotion. *Biological Psychiatry, 3*(6), 577–586.

Gu, Q. (2002). Neuromodulatory transmitter systems in the cortex and their role in cortical plasticity. *Neuroscience, 1*(4), 815–835.

Hanslmayr, S., Klimesch, W., Sauseng, P., Gruber, W., Doppelmayr, M., Freunberger, R., et al. (2005). Visual discrimination performance is related to decreased alpha amplitude but increased phase locking. *Neuroscience Letters, 5*(1), 64–68.

Harmon-Jones, E., & Gable, P. A. (2009). Neural activity underlying the effect of approach-motivated positive affect on narrowed attention. *Psychological Science, 20*(4), 406–409 .

Hendler, T., Rotshtein, P., Yeshurun, Y., Weizmann, T., Kahn, I., Ben-Bashat, D., et al. (2003). Sensing the invisible: differential sensitivity of visual cortex and amygdala to traumatic context. *Neuroimage, 9*(3), 587–600.

Holmes, A., Nielsen, M. K., & Green, S. (2008). Effects of anxiety on the processing of fearful and happy faces: An event-related potential study. *Biological Psychology, 7*(2), 159–173.

Hurlemann, R., Matusch, A., Hawellek, B., Klingmuller, D., Kolsch, H., Maier, W., et al. (2007). Emotion-induced retrograde amnesia varies as a function of noradrenergic-glucocorticoid activity. *Psychopharmacology (Berlin), 4*(2), 261–269.

Isen, A. M., Daubman, K. A., & Nowicki, G. P. (1987). Positive affect facilitates creative problem solving. *Journal of Personality and Social Psychology, 2*(6), 1122–1131.

Itti, L., & Koch, C. (2000). A saliency-based search mechanism for overt and covert shifts of visual attention. *Vision Research, 0*(10-12), 1489–1506.

Itti, L., & Koch, C. (2001). Computational modelling of visual attention. *Nature Reviews Neuroscience, 2*(3), 194–203.

James, W. (1884). What is an emotion? *Mind, 9*, 188–205.

Joseph, J. S., Chun, M. M., & Nakayama, K. (1997). Attentional requirements in a "preattentive" feature search task. *Nature, 7*(6635), 805–807.

Kastner, S., & Ungerleider, L. G. (2001). The neural basis of biased competition in human visual cortex. *Neuropsychologia, 9*(12), 1263–1276.

Kennedy, D. P., Glascher, J., Tyszka, J. M., & Adolphs, R. (2009). Personal space regulation by the human amygdala. *Nature Neuroscience, 2*(10), 1226–1227.

Koenigs, M., & Grafman, J. (2009). Posttraumatic stress disorder: The role of medial prefrontal cortex and amygdala. *Neuroscientist, 5*(5), 540–548.

Kounios, J., Frymiare, J. L., Bowden, E. M., Fleck, J. I., Subramaniam, K., Parrish, T. B., et al. (2006). The prepared mind: neural activity prior to problem presentation predicts subsequent solution by sudden insight. *Psychological Science, 7*(10), 882–890.

Krettek, J. E., & Price, J. L. (1978). Amygdaloid projections to subcortical structures within the basal forebrain and brainstem in the rat and cat. [Research Support, U.S. Gov't, P.H.S.]. *Journal of Comparative Neurology, 178*(2), 225–254.

Krugel, L. K., Biele, G., Mohr, P. N., Li, S. C., & Heekeren, H. R. (2009). Genetic variation in dopaminergic neuromodulation influences the ability to rapidly and flexibly adapt decisions. *Proceedings of the National Academy of Sciences USA, 106*(42), 17951–17956.

Kuhbandner, C., Hanslmayr, S., Maier, M. A., Pekrun, R., Spitzer, B., Pastotter, B., et al. (2009). Effects of mood on the speed of conscious perception: Behavioural and electrophysiological evidence. *Social, Cognitive & Affective Neuroscience, 4*(3), 286–293.

LaBar, K. S., & Cabeza, R. (2006). Cognitive neuroscience of emotional memory. *Nature Reviews Neuroscience, 7*(1), 54–64.

Lane, R. D., Chua, P. M., & Dolan, R. J. (1999). Common effects of emotional valence, arousal and attention on neural activation during visual processing of pictures. *Neuropsychologia, 7*(9), 989–997.

Lang, P. J., Bradley, M. M., Fitzsimmons, J. R., Cuthbert, B. N., Scott, J. D., Moulder, B., et al. (1998). Emotional arousal and activation of the visual cortex: An fMRI analysis. *Psychophysiology, 5*(2), 199–210.

Lazarus, R. S. (1982). Thoughts on the relations between emotion and cognition. *American Psychologist, 37*, 1019–1024.

Lazarus, R. S. (1991). Progress on a cognitive-motivational-relational theory of emotion. *American Psychologist, 6*(8), 819–834.

Ledoux, J. E. (1996). *The emotional brain: The mysterious underpinnings of emotional life.* New York: Simon & Schuster.

Lewis, M. D. (2005). Bridging emotion theory and neurobiology through dynamic systems modeling. *Behavioral and Brain Sciences, 8*(2), 169–194.

Lewis, M. D., & Todd, R. M. (2007). The self-regulating brain: Cortical-subcortical feedback and the development of intelligent action. *Cognitive Development, 2(*4), 406–430.

Lim, S. L., Padmala, S., & Pessoa, L. (2008). Affective learning modulates spatial competition during low-load attentional conditions. *Neuropsychologia, 6(*5), 1267–1278.

Lim, S. L., Padmala, S., & Pessoa, L. (2009). Segregating the significant from the mundane on a moment-to-moment basis via direct and indirect amygdala contributions. *Proceedings of the National Academy of Sciences U S A, 6(*39), 16841–16846.

Lonigan, C. J., & Vasey, M. W. (2009). Negative affectivity, effortful control, and attention to threat-relevant stimuli. *Journal of Abnormal Child Psychology, 37(*3), 387–399.

Mack, A., & Rock, I. (1998). *Inattentional blindness.* Cambridge, MA: MIT Press.

Mather, M., Canli, T., English, T., Whitfield, S., Wais, P., Ochsner, K., et al. (2004). Amygdala responses to emotionally valenced stimuli in older and younger adults. *Psychological Science, 5(*4), 259–263.

Mathews, A., & MacLeod, C. (1986). Discrimination of threat cues without awareness in anxiety states. *Journal of Abnormal Psychology, 5(*2), 131–138.

McClure, E. B., Monk, C. S., Nelson, E. E., Parrish, J. M., Adler, A., Blair, R. J., et al. (2007). Abnormal attention modulation of fear circuit function in pediatric generalized anxiety disorder. *Archives of General Psychiatry, 4(*1), 97–106.

Morris, J. S., Ohman, A., & Dolan, R. J. (1998). Conscious and unconscious emotional learning in the human amygdala. *Nature, 3(*6684), 467–470.

Ochsner, K. N., Ray, R. D., Cooper, J. C., Robertson, E. R., Chopra, S., Gabrieli, J. D., et al. (2004). For better or for worse: Neural systems supporting the cognitive down- and up-regulation of negative emotion. *Neuroimage, 3(*2), 483–499.

O'Connor, D. H., Fukui, M. M., Pinsk, M. A., & Kastner, S. (2002). Attention modulates responses in the human lateral geniculate nucleus. *Nature Neuroscience, 5(*11), 1203–1209.

Ohman, A. (2002). Automaticity and the amygdala: Nonconscious responses to emotional faces. *Current Directions in Psychological Science, 1(*2), 62–66.

Ohman, A., & Soares, J. J. (1998). Emotional conditioning to masked stimuli: Expectancies for aversive outcomes following nonrecognized fear-relevant stimuli. *Journal of Experimental Psychology.: General, 7(*1), 69–82.

Padmala, S., & Pessoa, L. (2008). Affective learning enhances visual detection and responses in primary visual cortex. *Journal of Neuroscience, 8(*24), 6202–6210.

Panksepp, J. (1998). *Affective neuroscience: The foundations of human and animal emotions.* New York: Oxford University Press.

Pessoa, L. (2008). On the relationship between emotion and cognition. *Nature Reviews Neuroscience, 9(*2), 148–158.

Pessoa, L. (2009). How do emotion and motivation direct executive control? *Trends in Cognitive Sciences, 3(*4), 160–166.

Pessoa, L., & Adolphs, R. (2010). Emotion processing and the amygdala: from a "low road" to "many roads" of evaluating biological significance. *Nature Reviews Neuroscience, 1(*11), 773–783.

Pessoa, L., Japee, S., & Ungerleider, L. G. (2005). Visual awareness and the detection of fearful faces. *Emotion, 5(*2), 243–247.

Pessoa, L., Kastner, S., & Ungerleider, L. G. (2002). Attentional control of the processing of neural and emotional stimuli. *Brain Research: Cognitive Brain Research, 5(*1), 31–45.

Pizzagalli, D., Regard, M., & Lehmann, D. (1999). Rapid emotional face processing in the human right and left brain hemispheres: An ERP study. *Neuroreport, 0(*13), 2691–2698.

Qu, L., & Zelazo, P. D. (2007). The facilitative effect of positive stimuli on children's flexible rule use. *Cognitive Development, 22,* 456–473.

Roozendaal, B., McEwen, B. S., & Chattarji, S. (2009). Stress, memory and the amygdala. *Nature Reviews Neuroscience, 0(*6), 423–433.

Roseman, I. J., Spindel, M. S., & Jose, P. E. (1990). Appraisals of emotion-eliciting events: Testing a theory of discrete emotions. *Journal of Personality and Social Psychology, 9(*5), 899–915.

Rowe, G., Hirsh, J. B., & Anderson, A. K. (2007). Positive affect increases the breadth of attentional selection. *Proceedings of the National Academy of Sciences U S A, 4(*1), 383–388.

Saha, S. (2005). Role of the central nucleus of the amygdala in the control of blood pressure: Descending pathways to medullary cardiovascular nuclei. *Clinical and Experimental Pharmacology and Physiology, 2(*5-6), 450–456.

Saha, S., Drinkhill, M. J., Moore, J. P., & Batten, T. F. (2005). Central nucleus of amygdala projections to rostral ventrolateral medulla neurones activated by decreased blood pressure. *European Journal of Neuroscience, 1(*7), 1921–1930.

Sander, D., Grafman, J., & Zalla, T. (2003). The human amygdala: An evolved system for relevance detection. *Reviews in the Neurosciences, 4(*4), 303–316.

Sarter, M., Bruno, J. P., Givens, B., Moore, H., McGaughy, J., & McMahon, K. (1996). Neuronal mechanisms mediating drug-induced cognition enhancement: Cognitive activity as a necessary intervening variable. *Brain Research: Cognitive Brain Research, 3(*3-4), 329–343.

Scherer, K. R. (2000). Emotions as episodes of subsystem synchronization driven by nonlinear appraisal processes. In M. D. L. I. Granic (Ed.), *Emotion, development, and self-organization: Dynamic systems approaches to emotional development* (pp. 70–99). Cambridge, UK: Cambridge University Press.

Schmitz, T. W., De Rosa, E., & Anderson, A. K. (2009). Opposing influences of affective state valence on visual cortical encoding. *Journal of Neuroscience, 9(*22), 7199–7207.

Schupp, H. T., Junghofer, M., Weike, A. I., & Hamm, A. O. (2003). Emotional facilitation of sensory processing in the visual cortex. *Psychological Science, 14(*1), 7–13.

Schupp, H. T., Stockburger, J., Schmalzle, R., Bublatzky, F., Weike, A. I., & Hamm, A. O. (2008). Visual noise effects on emotion perception: Brain potentials and stimulus identification. *Neuroreport, 9(*2), 167–171.

Schyns, P. G., Petro, L. S., & Smith, M. L. (2009). Transmission of facial expressions of emotion co-evolved with their efficient decoding in the brain: Behavioral and brain evidence. *PLoS One, 4(*5), e5625.

Seeley, W. W., Menon, V., Schatzberg, A. F., Keller, J., Glover, G. H., Kenna, H., et al. (2007). Dissociable intrinsic connectivity networks for salience processing and executive control. *Journal of Neuroscience, 7(*9), 2349–2356.

Sergerie, K., Chochol, C., & Armony, J. L. (2008). The role of the amygdala in emotional processing: A quantitative meta-analysis of functional neuroimaging studies. *Neuroscience and Biobehavioral Reviews, 2(*4), 811–830.

Smith, N. K., Cacioppo, J. T., Larsen, J. T., & Chartrand, T. L. (2003). May I have your attention, please: Electrocortical responses to positive and negative stimuli. *Neuropsychologia, 1(*2), 171–183.

Soares, J. J., & Ohman, A. (1993). Backward masking and skin conductance responses after conditioning to nonfeared but fear-relevant stimuli in fearful subjects. *Psychophysiology*, *0*(5), 460–466.

Subramaniam, K., Kounios, J., Parrish, T. B., & Jung-Beeman, M. (2009). A brain mechanism for facilitation of insight by positive affect. *Journal of Cognitive Neuroscience*, *1*(3), 415–432.

Susskind, J. M., Lee, D. H., Cusi, A., Feiman, R., Grabski, W., & Anderson, A. K. (2008). Expressing fear enhances sensory acquisition. *Nature Neuroscience*, *11*(7), 843–850.

Szczepanowski, R., & Pessoa, L. (2007). Fear perception: Can objective and subjective awareness measures be dissociated? *Journal of Vision*, *7*(4), 10.

Todd, R. M. & Anderson, A. K. (2009). Six degrees of separation: The amygdala regulates social behavior and perception. *Nature Neuroscience*, *2*(10), 1–3.

Todd, R. M., Evans, J. W., Morris, D., Lewis, M. D., & Taylor, M. J. (2011). The changing face of emotion: Age-related patterns of amygdala activation to salient faces. *Social, Cognitive & Affective Neuroscience*, *6*(1), 12–23.

Tracy, J. L., & Matsumoto, D. (2008). The spontaneous expression of pride and shame: evidence for biologically innate nonverbal displays. *Proceedings of the National Academy of Science U S A*, *5*(33), 11655–11660.

Tsuchiya, N., Moradi, F., Felsen, C., Yamazaki, M., & Adolphs, R. (2009). Intact rapid detection of fearful faces in the absence of the amygdala. *Nature Neuroscience*, *2*(10), 1224–1225.

Van Bavel, J. J., Packer, D. J., & Cunningham, W. A. (2008). The neural substrates of in-group bias: a functional magnetic resonance imaging investigation. *Psychological Science*, *19*(11), 1131–1139.

van Duijvenvoorde, A. C., Zanolie, K., Rombouts, S. A., Raijmakers, M. E., & Crone, E. A. (2008). Evaluating the negative or valuing the positive? Neural mechanisms supporting feedback based learning across development. *Journal of Neuroscience*, *8*(38), 9495–9503.

Veening, J. G., Swanson, L. W., & Sawchenko, P. E. (1984). The organization of projections from the central nucleus of the amygdala to brainstem sites involved in central autonomic regulation: A combined retrograde transport–immunohistochemical study. *Brain Research*, *3*(2), 337–357.

Vermeulen, N., Godefroid, J., & Mermillod, M. (2009). Emotional modulation of attention: Fear increases but disgust reduces the attentional blink. *PLoS One*, *4*(11), e7924.

Vitay, J., & Hamker, F. H. (2008). Sustained activities and retrieval in a computational model of the perirhinal cortex. *Journal of Cognitive Neuroscience*, *0*(11), 1993–2005.

Vuilleumier, P., & Schwartz, S. (2001). Beware and be aware: capture of spatial attention by fear-related stimuli in neglect. *Neuroreport*, *2*(6), 1119–1122.

Vythilingam, M., Blair, K. S., McCaffrey, D., Scaramozza, M., Jones, M., Nakic, M., et al. (2007). Biased emotional attention in post-traumatic stress disorder: A help as well as a hindrance? *Psychological Medicine*, *7*(10), 1445–1455.

West, G. L., Anderson, A. K., Ferber, S., & Pratt, J. (2011). Electrophysiological evidence for biased competition in V1 for fear expressions. *Journal of Cognitive Neuroscience*, *23*(11), 3410–3418.

Whalen, P. J. (2007). The uncertainty of it all. *Trends in Cognitive Sciences*, *11*(12), 499–500.

Whalen, P. J., Kagan, J., Cook, R. G., Davis, F. C., Kim, H., Polis, S., et al. (2004). Human amygdala responsivity to masked fearful eye whites. *Science*, *6*(5704), 2061.

Whalen, P. J., Rauch, S. L., Etcoff, N. L., McInerney, S. C., Lee, M. B., & Jenike, M. A. (1998). Masked presentations of emotional facial expressions modulate amygdala activity without explicit knowledge. *Journal of Neuroscience*, *8*(1), 411–418.

Young, M. P., Scannell, J. W., Burns, G. A., & Blakemore, C. (1994). Analysis of connectivity: Neural systems in the cerebral cortex. *Annual Review of Neuroscience*, *5*(3), 227–250.

Zajonc, R. (1980). Feeling and thinking: Preferences need no inferences. *American Psychologist*, *35*, 151–175.

Zajonc, R. (1984). On the primacy of affect. *American Psychologist*, *39*, 117–123.

Emotion: Generation or Construction?

Jennifer M. B. Fugate, Kristen A. Lindquist, *and* Lisa Feldman Barrett

Abstract

In *The Expression of the Emotions in Man and Animals* (1872), Charles Darwin argued that emotions (as states of mind) cause stereotypic expressions in the face and body. Instead of offering a theoretical model of emotion, however, Darwin wrote about emotion in a teleological fashion to support his argument that humans have a common ancestry with other mammals. This chapter examines the concept of "emotion generation" and whether it is supported by cognitive neuroscience evidence as it exists within the natural kind model of emotion. It reviews several recent meta-analyses of the neuroimaging literature on emotion that investigated the link between brain regions and discrete emotion categories. It also discusses the concept of "emotion construction" and how it is supported by the cognitive neuroscience evidence as it exists within a psychological construction approach to emotion. Moreover, it presents meta-analytic evidence showing that emotions can be decomposed into more basic neural networks corresponding to a set of hypothesized psychological ingredients. The chapter concludes by considering what a psychological construction approach can offer to the cognitive neuroscience study of emotion.

Key Words: Charles Darwin, emotion, cognitive neuroscience, emotion generation, neuroimaging, brain regions, emotion construction, neural networks, psychological construction approach

For almost a century, scientists have assumed that emotion is a faculty of the mind—a distinctive mental state that is generated in reaction to some stimulus. Many assume that this mental state is triggered in an obligatory way (called the "basic emotion" approach) or that some kind of meaning analysis must first take place (called the "appraisal" approach). Some scientists assume that a unique subjective experience is associated with mental states that belong to different categories (such as anger, sadness, fear), whereas others characterize emotional states in purely behavioral terms (for a review, see Barrett, Mesquita, Ochsner, & Gross, 2007). Like all faculty models of psychology, these models of emotion assume that there are objective indicators of a person's mental (in this case emotional) state. By measuring facial muscle activity, vocal acoustics,

autonomic physiology, or brain activation, it should be possible to know what state a mind is really in. Any variability in measurable responses is assumed to result from regulation of these more stereotyped responses (for a discussion, see Barrett, 2009b). The guiding hypothesis in these models, collectively referred to as the "natural kind model"[1] (Barrett, 2006a) or the "modal model" (Barrett, Ochsner, & Gross, 2007), is that different emotion categories correspond to inherited, architecturally distinct circuits in the brain. These modules have been discussed as particular gross anatomical locations (e.g., Calder, 2003, Ekman, 1999) or networks (e.g., Izard, 2011; Panksepp, 1998). Still others propose that emotions are triggered by inherited, central mechanisms like "affect programs" that are metaphorical in nature and do not necessarily correspond to a particular brain locale (e.g., Ekman & Cordaro, 2011). The general idea is that emotion categories are respected by the brain (as well as by autonomic patterns and physiology more generally; see Ekman & Cordaro, 2011).

From the natural kind point of view, it makes sense to ask about the neural correlates of emotion generation, but emotion generation is not a meaningful scientific concept in all models of emotion (Gross & Barrett, 2011). Another approach—one that avoids the pitfalls of faculty psychology—hypothesizes that emotions, like all mental states, arise from a set of more basic psychological ingredients that are not themselves specific to any discrete emotion category or to the category emotion itself. This is called the "psychological construction" approach. In this view, emotions are not "generated" as discrete states with a beginning and an end; instead they emerge when people perceive the varieties of arrangements of bodily states, behaviors, and subjective feelings. These perceptions emerge or "pop out" from the stream of mental activity as momentary "gestalts." They could be called "perceptual acts" because these perceptions are thought to emerge just as visual and auditory percepts do (i.e., as sensory input that is made meaningful by prior experience). We refer to them as "conceptual acts," however, because the category knowledge that is used to make sensory input meaningful is organized by humans to solve human problems (getting along vs. getting ahead) and is communicated and learned through culture. This conceptual knowledge is assumed to have multimodal sensory aspects (Barrett, 2006b; Niedenthal, Barsalou, Winkielman, Krauth-Gruber, & Ric, 2005; Wilson-Mendenhall, Barrett, Simmons, & Barsalou, 2011), however, dissolving the boundary between perception and conception.

In a psychological construction approach, emotions are hypothesized to be perceptions of the body in relation to the world and, like all perceptions, live in the head of the perceiver (Barrett, 2006a, 2006b, 2009a; Russell, 2003). This is not to say that emotions exist *only* in the head of the perceiver. Rather, it is more correct to say that they cannot exist without a perceiver. You experience yourself as angry or you see another person's face as angry or you experience a dog's behavior as angry, but anger does not exist independently of someone's perception of it. Psychological construction models treat each discrete emotion category as an ontologically subjective category that corresponds to a range of mental events that don't necessarily share any core features in common. That is, discrete emotions are

not psychic entities. The topography of the brain is not expected to respect these categories or even the broader categories of emotion and cognition. Instead, the hypothesis is that the brain can be understood in terms of a set of distributed networks (with both cortical and subcortical contributions) that correspond to a more basic set of psychological ingredients (e.g., affect, working memory, categorization). A further hypothesis is that each instance of emotion corresponds to a brain state constituted from broad-scale distributed networks that implement these ingredients, and so questions about the brain basis of emotion are really questions about the brain basis of the mind (i.e., identifying and understanding the interplay of these ingredients).

In this chapter, we briefly review the concept of emotion generation, after which we examine whether there is any cognitive neuroscience evidence to support this concept as it exists within the natural kind model of emotion. To do so, we review several recent meta-analyses of the neuroimaging literature on emotion assessing whether brain regions consistently and specifically correspond to discrete emotion categories. Next, we discuss the concept of emotion construction and examine how the cognitive neuroscience evidence supports this concept as it exists within a psychological construction approach to emotion. Here we again turn to meta-analytic evidence demonstrating that emotions can be decomposed into more basic neural networks that correspond to a set of hypothesized psychological ingredients (that are not themselves specific to emotions). Finally, we consider what a psychological construction approach can offer to the cognitive neuroscience study of emotion.

The Concept of Emotion Generation
Hypotheses

With his publication of *The Expression of the Emotions in Man and Animals* in 1872 (1965), Charles Darwin wrote that emotions (as states of mind) cause stereotypic expressions in the face and body. Many psychologists take this idea as the starting point of the natural kind approach to emotion. In point of fact, however, Darwin did not offer a theoretical model of emotion as much as he tried to show that his ideas about natural selection were plausible (c.f. Fridlund, 1992; Russell, 1994). He wrote about emotion in a teleological fashion to bolster his argument that humans have a common ancestry with other mammals. Many of the central natural kind assumptions about emotion attributed to Darwin were actually introduced by later theorists as they attempted to reconcile Darwin's writings with those of William James.

In 1884, James (simultaneously with Carl Lange, in 1885[1922]) challenged Darwin's ordering of events by suggesting that emotion results from the normal sensory processing of somatic, visceral, and motor (James) or vascular and motor (Lange) cues from the body, rather than the other way around.[2] As James famously wrote, "The bodily changes follow directly the perception of the exciting fact, and our feeling of these same changes as they occur is the emotion" (p. 189). James, like Darwin, defined emotion as a state of mind. Both appeared to rely on the idea that bodily responses are reflexively triggered in an instinctual or habitual fashion. In Darwin's view, emotional states of mind were triggered by the world and caused bodily expressions. In James' view, bodily responses were triggered by the world and were experienced as emotion. Both assumed that the bodily responses in question (and, therefore, the experience of emotion in James' case, and the expression of emotion in Darwin's case) derive from the structure of the nervous system.

Contemporaries of James and Lange took it upon themselves to reconcile those views with Darwin's by distinguishing between the "state" of emotion and the "feeling" of emotion. In so doing, they created a set of assumptions that still anchor the scientific study of emotion today. These theorists performed an *ontological reduction of emotion by redefinition*, such that the generation of emotion was separated from the generation of emotional experience. Emotion was redefined as a physical or functional state of the body (e.g., the state of being angry), and the experience of emotion was reduced to nothing more than the perception of that biological state (e.g., a feeling of anger). John Dewey (1895), for example, wrote that objects in the world triggered "action tendencies," and that these propensities to act in a particular way were, in essence, the emotional state. Feedback from this state constituted the experience of emotion (also see Bull, 1945). In a similar view (McDougall, 1908/1921), emotions were said to be stereotyped behavioral states generated by instincts, and feedback from these states, especially from the face, was thought to produce the experience of emotion (Allport, 1924). These ideas were resurrected four decades later by Tomkins (1962, 1963) when he introduced the concept of "affect programs" as emotion generation machinery. Tomkins' facial feedback hypothesis, in which feedback from the face results in the experience of emotion, served as the basis for the modern basic

emotion approach. Many basic emotion models still assume that discrete emotional states belonging to a single category (e.g., fear) are generated in an inherited brain location or circuit that is consistent with and distinct from those that generate other discrete emotional states (e.g., Calder, 2003; Damasio et al., 2000; Ekman, 1999; Panksepp, 1998).

The concept of emotion generation retained its meaning in the earliest appraisal models even when David Irons (1894) criticized both Darwin and James for insisting that "instincts" were the main causes of emotion. Irons suggested that a meaning analysis (a "psychical disturbance" or "feeling attitude") within the person caused emotion by intervening between the object and the resulting physical changes. Irons observed that the physical changes for a given category of emotion (e.g., anger) are highly variable from instance to instance, yet people experience the same kind of emotion each time despite such variation. The experience of a particular category of emotion, despite such variation, is similar because there is a common "psychical" element—the meaning analysis of the object. Essentially, Irons argued that people assess an object's meaning in relation to the self, such that the same object can generate two different emotions or no emotion at all. This idea was resurrected by Magda Arnold (1960a, 1960b) and is echoed in several modern appraisal models of emotion. In these models, appraisals are considered to be the literal mechanisms that trigger biologically basic emotional responses characterized either by stereotyped outputs (e.g., Lazarus, 1966, 1991, 2001; Roseman, 1984, 1991, 2001) or as loosely coordinated response tendencies that are configured in a contextually sensitive fashion (Frijda, 1986; Scherer, 1984, 2001).[3] To date, appraisal models have not really concerned themselves with the brain basis for emotion generation, focusing instead on psychological models or the brain basis of emotion regulation (for an exception using neural networks, see Sander, Grandjean, & Scherer, 2005; Scherer, 2009).

Cognitive Neuroscience Evidence

Cognitive neuroscience investigations of emotion generation have generally based their experiments on the natural kind approach and have been preoccupied with identifying the brain locations of discrete emotion categories (as specific locales but more recently as specific networks).[4] Meta-analyses of the neuroimaging literature are useful for evaluating the success of this enterprise, for at least three reasons. First, a meta-analysis summarizes hundreds of empirical studies by statistical means; this is particularly beneficial given the high rate of false positives and largely variable experimental and statistical methods used across individual studies (see Wager, Lindquist, & Kaplan, 2007). Second, not only are meta-analytic results more reliable than the findings from any given study, but they also make it possible to statistically model the influence of between-study methodological and statistical differences. Third, most individual experiments contrast only one emotion with another or with a "neutral" state, suggesting that activity is only different from, but not necessarily specific to, the emotion. Meta-analytic studies can help overcome this limitation by directly comparing the activation patterns of different discrete emotions to each other in order to assess the hypothesis that different emotions correspond to distinct locales (or networks) of activation.

There are several existing meta-analyses examining the hypothesis that different emotion categories are generated in distinct brain locales (Murphy, Nimmo-Smith, & Lawrence, 2003; Phan, Wager, Taylor, & Liberzon, 2002; Vytal & Hamann, 2010). All of these studies assess the neural correlates of anger, disgust, fear, happiness, and sadness by collapsing across studies of the experience and perception of emotion (and thus do not address the question of emotion generation specifically). The results of these meta-analyses are summarized in Table 3.1. For a brain region to be the locus of generation for a certain emotion category, the neural activation within this area must be consistent; for example, every instance of a particular emotion category, such as fear, should correspond to increased activation in a particular brain region (or network of regions), regardless of the sample or the induction method. The neural activation must also be specific; for example, the increased neural activation associated with the instances of a particular emotion category should occur only for that emotion category and not for any other (see Barrett & Wager, 2006). As can be seen from Table 3.1, neither criterion, at a gross anatomical level, was satisfied for four of the five discrete emotion categories across the meta-analyses.[5]

The meta-analyses did not find that instances of the category sadness were consistently associated with increased activation in any brain region or set of regions. Phan et al. (2002) reported that sadness was associated with increased activation in the ventral anterior cingulate cortex (ACC). Murphy et al. (2003) reported that sadness was associated with increased activation in the dorsal ACC. Vytal and Hamann (2010) reported that sadness was associated with increased activation in a host of brain regions (including, but not limited to, dorsomedial prefrontal cortex, lateral prefrontal cortex, and aspects of the basal ganglia).

The meta-analyses also did not find consistent increases in activation for instances of the category anger at the gross anatomical level. Murphy et al. and Vytal and Hamann reported that anger was consistently associated with increased activation in the orbitofrontal cortex (OFC), but Phan et al. found that anger was not consistently associated with increased activation in any region more than another. Furthermore, increased OFC activation was not specific to anger; Vytal and Hamann also found evidence for overlapping OFC activation for disgust, fear, and sadness.

There was also limited consistency for the category happiness at the gross anatomical level. Phan et al. reported that happiness was consistently associated with increased activation in the basal ganglia, whereas Murphy et al. found that happiness was consistently associated with increased activation in the dorsal ACC. Vytal and Hamann found that happiness was consistently associated with increased activation in the (ventral) ACC and basal ganglia, along with such regions including (but not limited to) the insula and thalamus.

Instances of the category disgust were also not consistently associated with increased activation in any brain region across the various meta-analyses. Phan et al. reported that the basal ganglia was associated with increased activation in disgust, whereas Murphy et al. found that the insula/operculum and globus pallidus showed consistent increases in activation. Lastly, Vytal and Hamann reported that a host of brain regions were consistently associated with increased activation in disgust, including (but not limited to) the OFC, amygdala, ACC, insula, and medial prefrontal cortex.

Only instances of the category fear showed some consistency across meta-analyses at the gross anatomical level. All meta-analyses found evidence that instances of fear were routinely associated with increased activity in the amygdala. Increases in amygdala activation were not specific to the category fear, however. Murphy et al. and Phan et al. found that fear activated the amygdala, but Vytal and Hamann reported that anger and disgust were also associated with increased activation in overlapping areas of the amygdala. Furthermore, none of these meta-analyses ruled out the alternative hypothesis

Table 3.1 Previous Meta-Analytic Findings at the Gross Anatomical Level*

Emotion	Brain Region	Meta-Analysis (Number of Studies)		
		Phan et al., 2002 (55)	Murphy et al., 2003 (28)	Vytal & Hamann, 2010 (81)
Anger	Amygdala		*	*
	Insula			
	OFC		*	*
	Basal ganglia			
Sad	Amygdala			
	Insula			*
	OFC			*
	ACC	* (Subcollosal)	* (Supracollosal)	
	Basal ganglia			* (Parts)
Fear	Amygdala	*	*	*
	Insula			*
	OFC			*
	ACC			* (Dorsal)
	Basal ganglia			
Disgust	Amygdala			*
	Insula		*	*
	OFC			*
	ACC			* (Dorsal)
	Basal ganglia	*		
Happiness	Amygdala			
	Insula			*
	OFC			
	ACC		*	* (Ventral)
	Basal ganglia	*		* (Putamen)

* Phan et al. (2002) and Murphy et al. (2003) counted peak activations in a given anatomically defined area. In theses meta-analyses, consistency was determined by the percentage of study contrasts for a given emotion category that reported activation in a given area (e.g., 60% of contrasts assessing fear reported increased activation within the amygdala). By contrast, Vytal and Hamann (2010) used the activation likelihood method (ALE), which places a Gaussian distribution around reported peaks and then sums the peaks and their distributions for each condition to make a statistical map of activations. In this method, consistency is a larger concentration of peaks in a given area for one emotion contrast than expected in the null distribution (e.g., a greater concentration of peaks in the amygdala for fear than would be expected in the null distribution of peaks).
Abbreviations: ACC = anterior cingulate cortex; OFC = orbitofrontal cortex.

that the amygdala codes for something more basic, such as stimulus salience or uncertainty (including novelty) (see Barrett & Bliss-Moreau, 2009; Bliss-Moreau, Owren, & Barrett, 2010; Duncan & Barrett, 2007; Whalen, 1998, 2007). Additional imaging findings support the idea that the amygdala shows increased activation in response to novel stimuli (e.g., Blackford, Avery, Cowan, Shelton, &

Zald, 2011; Blackford, Buckholz, Avery, & Zald, 2010; Moriguchi et al., 2011; Weierich, Wright, Negreira, Dickerson, & Barrett, 2010; Wright et al., 2003, 2008; Wright, Wedig, Williams, Rauch, & Albert, 2006). The majority of studies included in the imaging meta-analyses did not control for the possibility that fearful faces (the most widely used stimulus to elicit increased amygdala response) are relatively novel (Whalen et al.,,2001).

Furthermore, it is not clear that increased amygdala response is even necessary for fear. For example, the amygdala does not show an increase in activation to fearful faces with averted eye gazes (even though they signal more imminent danger) (e.g., Adams, Gordon, Baird, Ambady, & Kleck, 2003; Ewbank, Fox, & Calder, 2010; Straube, Dietrich, Motes-Lasch, Mentzel, & Miltner, 2010) or fearful faces that are masked with visual noise, rather than a neutral face (Kim et al., 2010). And, even when viewing fearful faces with forward-gazing eyes, amygdala activation habituates quickly (e.g., Fischer et al., 2003). Moreover, even individuals with amygdala lesions can recognize fearful faces (Adolphs et al., 2005; Tsuchiya, Moradi, Felsen, Yamazaki, & Adolphs, 2009) and bodies (Atkinson, Heberlein, & Adolphs, 2007).

The lack of consistency and specificity across meta-analyses was mirrored within each meta-analysis, again failing to support a key natural kind assumption of emotion generation. For instance, although all three meta-analyses found evidence for a fear–amygdala link, consistency in this activation within a given meta-analysis was modest at best. Phan and colleagues (2002) found that 60% of the studies involving fear showed an increase in amygdala activation, but Murphy and colleagues reported that less than 40% of fear studies preferentially activated the amygdala (see Barrett & Wager, 2006, for the Phan et al. (2002) and Murphy et al. (2003) findings). The clearest lack of specificity can be seen in the analysis by Vytal and Hamann (2010), where on average, the same brain region was activated in three of the five emotion categories tested (e.g., the amygdala in anger, fear, and disgust) (see Table 3.1). Although it could be argued that different groups of neurons within a brain region might be specific to different emotion categories, a detailed look at the clusters of increased activation within the amygdala do not support this argument. No significant clusters of activation in the left amygdala remained significant when the categories of anger and fear were directly compared, suggesting overlap in the loci of activation.

In addition to their inconsistent findings, these published meta-analyses suffer from several methodological weaknesses in their statistical approach. First, the previous meta-analyses did not separately examine studies of emotion experience and emotion perception. Our own meta-analytic research suggests that the neural correlates of these two mental states are sufficiently different from one another and that they should be considered distinct psychological phenomena (Wager et al., 2008). Moreover, separating experience from perception allows us to more specifically address the question of whether there are distinct emotion generators in the brain. Second, the previous meta-analyses ignored the nested structure of neuroimaging data. Each published experiment reports a number of locations of peak activation for each emotion contrast (e.g., anger vs. neutral). All three meta-analyses treated each and every peak as an independent data point when, in fact, peaks from the same study are not independent of one another. Because individual imaging studies vary in the number of peak activations that they report for each contrast (in part based on the processing and thresholding decisions made during data analysis and the number of subjects in the study), some studies will contribute more to the final meta-analytic summary than will others, biasing the results. Third, the three published meta-analyses did not control for other methodological variables that influence the generalizability of the findings (e.g., fixed vs. random effects, differences in sample size).

In collaboration with Tor Wager's laboratory, our lab (Lindquist, Wager, Kober, Bliss-Moreau, & Barrett, 2012) used a meta-analytic approach that overcomes some of the past statistical problems to specifically test the idea that discrete emotion categories (anger, sadness, fear, disgust, and happiness) are consistently and specifically generated in different brain locales or networks. The result is the most comprehensive meta-analysis of neuroimaging studies on discrete emotions to date (containing 91 studies of discrete emotion categories published between 1993 and 2007). Our method (the multilevel kernel density analysis, or MKDA; see Wager et al., 2007, for a description) respects the multilevel structure of neuroimaging data and institutes measures of quality control (i.e., it weighs data from random effects analyses more heavily and weighs the contributions of contrasts by their sample size). We also distinguished between emotion experience and emotion perception in our analyses. For the purposes of this chapter, we only discuss the results of our meta-analysis of emotion experience. Table 3.2 lists those brain regions with consistent increases in activity at greater than chance levels for the discrete emotion experiences of anger, sadness, fear, happiness, and disgust (computed as a χ^2 analysis).

In general, we found few areas of consistent activity for each emotion category. For instance, the experience of anger was consistently associated with increased activity in a single voxel within the left anterior insula. The experience of happiness was not consistently associated with increased activity in any brain region at greater than chance levels. Perhaps the best evidence of consistency was found for the experiences of sadness, fear, and disgust, although the activations were not specific to any of these emotion categories. For instance, the experience of sadness was associated with increased

activation in a total of 19 voxels across the entorhinal cortex (Brodmann's area [BA] 34) (also activated during the perception of fear), basal ganglia (putamen), visual cortex (BA 21), midbrain (periacquiductal gray [PAG]), and dorsomedial prefrontal cortex (dmPFC; BA 9) (also activated in any study using recall or films) (Lindquist et al., 2012). The experience of fear was consistently associated with increased activation of 209 voxels across the visual cortex (BAs 18, 21, 37) (also showing increased activation in a range of perceptions and experiences, including in the perception of disgust, the experience of happiness, in studies using visual stimuli [films and pictures], and in studies of unpleasant affect more generally). The experience of disgust was consistently associated with increased activation in a total of 281 voxels

Table 3.2 Absolute Differences in Brain Activation from Lindquist et al. (2012)

Emotion	x	y	z	Voxels	Brain Region	BA
Anger	−44	20	−2	1	L. anterior insula	
Sad	52	−10	−16	2	R. middle temporal gyrus	21
	−24	2	−12	10	L. med temp	34
	0	-38	−10	1	Midbrain (PAG)	
	26	4	−4	1	R. putamen	
	28	8	−2	3	R. putamen	
	22	4	−2	1	R. putamen	
	2	50	38	1	R. dmPFC	9
Fear	48	−72	2	127	R. occipitotemporal	37
	8	−96	4	10	R. parastriate	18
	−52	−70	8	72	L. m. temporal	21
Disgust	−20	−6	−24	50	L. basal lateral amygdala	
	26	2	−20	59	R. basal lateral amygdala	
	−30	36	−18	167	L. lateral OFC	11
	−26	−6	−20	1	entorhinal	34
	−32	−2	−20	2	L. basal lateral amygdala	
	−46	−58	−14	1	L. occipitotemporal	37
	−42	−58	−10	1	L. occipitotemporal	37
Happiness	None					

Abbreviations: BA = Broca's area; dmPFC = dorsomedial prefrontal cortex; L. = left; m. = medial; OFC = orbitofrontal cortex; R. = right PAG = periacquiductal gray.

across the bilateral amygdala (also consistently activated in the perception of fear and in studies of high arousal affect more generally), entorhinal cortex, lateral OFC (BA 11), and visual cortex (BA 37). Taken together, these meta-analytic results do not support the idea that the experience of discrete emotions are generated by distinct brain locales or networks. What little consistency that existed across studies was not specific to any single emotion category, as would be predicted by a natural kind view of emotion.

This lack of consistency and specificity is mirrored in meta-analyses focusing on correspondence between brain activity and other psychological categories. For example, several different brain regions are commonly activated across task domains such as working memory, long-term memory, inhibition, and task switching (Van Snellenberg & Wager, 2009; Wager & Smith, 2003). A host of brain regions, including ventromedial prefrontal cortex (vmPFC) and dmPFC are active during emotion, person perception, object perception, and long-term memory (see Buckner, Andrews-Hanna, & Schacter, 2008, for a review). The amygdala consistently activated during studies of emotion, learning, and social cognition (Costafreda, Brammer, David, & Fu, 2008). Even the anterior insula (involved in representing visceral cues in subjective awareness; Craig, 2002, 2009) is a brain region that shows increased activation across a range of tasks, including working memory, task switching, emotion, language, and sensory processing (Nelson et al., 2010).

Studies using electrical brain stimulation also do not support the idea of distinct brain generators for different emotion categories (for a discussion, see Barrett, Lindquist, & Gendron, 2007). In 1973, after reviewing decades of empirical evidence, neuroscientist Elliot Valenstein (1973) wrote,

> The impression exists that if electrodes are placed in a specific part of the brain, a particular behavior can inevitably be evoked. Those who have participated in this research know that this is definitely not the case. In a large percentage of cases, animals do not display any specific behavior in response to stimulation, even though great care may have been exerted to position the brain electrodes with as much precision as possible. Even in rats, where the behavior is more stereotyped than in monkeys and man, brain stimulation produces very variable results. (p. 88)

For example, a well-controlled electrical stimulation study of the temporal lobe (including the amygdala) in humans produced absolutely no evidence of distinct brain generators of emotion (Halgren, Walter, Cherlow, & Crandall, 1978). Of the 3,495 stimulations that were performed on 36 patients, only 267 elicited a mental response of any sort (35 reports of emotional experience reported as anger, fear, tension, or nervousness were observed across 8 patients). Mental responses were highly variable within participants across time, and across participants. Stimulation of a given anatomical site produced different experiences in different patients, and stimulation at different sites produced the same mental content.

Newer brain stimulation evidence is consistent with Valenstein's conclusion. For example, Blomstedt, Tisch, and Hariz (2008) reported that stimulation of the subthalamic nucleus (STN) in a single individual elicits crying and bouts of acute depression, suggesting that the STN might be the brain generator for depression. Yet, STN stimulation is widely used to increase mobility in Parkinson's disease (e.g., Bejjani et al., 2000; Limousin et al., 1995), and only a few published studies cite evidence of depression-like behavior upon STN stimulation. Even within these reports, only 5 to 10% of patients reported depression or showed depression-like behavior upon stimulation (see Bejjani et al., 1999; Doshi, Chhaya, & Bhatt, 2002). Moreover, other studies (e.g., Romito et al., 2002) have found evidence for mania upon stimulation of the STN in patients with Parkinson's disease, drawing into question whether the STN is even linked to unpleasant affect more generally.

The lack of consistency and specificity in the brain data related to emotion is reflected in behavioral and psychophysiological findings. These findings are important because some natural kind models still hypothesize that different profiles of response are diagnostic for each emotion category, even when distinctive neural circuitry cannot be specified (e.g., Ekman & Cordaro, 2011). The bulk of evidence shows that behaviors are associated with the situational demands of the immediate context, rather than with an emotion category per se. For example, in rats, freezing, vigilance, flight, and defensive aggression are all behavioral adaptations associated with the category fear (for a discussion, see Barrett 2006a, 2009b; Suvak & Barrett, 2011). Although animal research has carefully worked out the neural circuits associated with many such behavioral adaptations (e.g., Fanselow & Poulos, 2005), not all of these adaptations involve the amygdala (e.g., Kopchia, Altman, & Commissaris, 1992; Reynolds & Berridge, 2008; Vazdarjanova & McGaugh, 1998). Context is also important in determining whether or not stereotyped increases in heart rate or blood pressure occur with freezing behavior (Iwata & LeDoux, 1988). Even basic pleasure-related behaviors are context dependent. For example, sweet-tasting foods result in more lip licking and tongue protrusions in both rats and human infants when they are hungry compared to when they are full (Berridge, 1991; Berridge, Flynn, Schulkin, & Grill, 1984; Berridge & Schulkin, 1989). Under normal conditions, extremely salty liquids (above the concentration of sea water) result in mouth gapes. When a rat is extremely salt deprived, however, these same liquids induce lip licking. Thus, even highly stereotyped responses appear to be mediated by the context (in these examples, the physical state of the animal).

Likewise, changes in the peripheral nervous system do not unambiguously differentiate between discrete emotion categories. Although individual studies find distinctive patterns for different emotion categories, these patterns are not consistent across studies (Barrett, 2006a; Cacioppo, Berntson, Larsen, Poehlmann, & Ito, 2000) and instead appear to correspond to threat and challenge (Quigley, Barrett, & Weinstein, 2002; Tomaka, Blascovich, Kelsey, & Leitten, 1993; Tomaka, Blascovich, Kibler, & Ernst, 1997), positive vs. negative affect (Cacioppo et al., 2000), or valence and arousal (Lang, Greenwald, Bradley, & Hamm, 1993). The same is true for facial actions measured with facial electromyography (EMG). Facial EMG activity corresponds to differences in hedonic valence (Cacioppo et al., 2000) or intensity (Messinger, 2002) (but also see Niedenthal, Winkielman, Mondillon, & Vermeulen, 2009). A similar point can be made about acoustic cues as well (for a review see Bachorowski & Owren, 2008; Russell, 2003). The fact that certain physiological studies support the natural kind view, even as the larger body of work disconfirms it, is an important source of evidence that should be considered alongside the brain data.

The Concept of Psychological Construction
Hypotheses

In the psychological construction approach to emotion, emotions are not hypothesized to be unique in form, function, and cause when compared to other mental states such as cognition and perception. Instead, the hypothesis is that emotion words like *anger*, *sadness*, and *fear* name folk categories that divide up the continuous and contextually sensitive range of mental events consisting of highly variable measurable outcomes (e.g., facial muscle movements, peripheral physiology, behavior). From this perspective, emotions are not "caused" by dedicated brain mechanisms and therefore are not "generated" in the traditional sense of the word. Instead, the psychological construction approach assumes that all mental states, including emotion, emerge from an ongoing, continually modifiable constructive process that involves more basic ingredients that are not themselves specific to emotion. The general idea of a psychological construction approach is that, every waking moment, the brain is continually generating configurations of bodily states and behaviors that are yoked to the specific context. As a result, an instance of emotion (say, an instance of anger) corresponds to a brain state, not activity within a single location or circuit. In a descriptive sense, the brain can be said to be constructing the present by performing a meaning analysis of all incoming sensory input, both from the body and from the world. Depending on the proclivities of the perceiver, and the focus of attention, sensory input can be categorized as a body symptom, an emotion, a perception of the world, a memory, a belief, and so on. A common theme among psychological construction models is that cognition, emotion, and perception are not reified as separate processes (Barrett, 2009a; Duncan & Barrett, 2007; for a similar view, see Pessoa, 2008).

Across the history of psychological construction views (see Gendron & Barrett, 2009), all models have hypothesized that one primary psychological ingredient of the mind is some form of information from the body. William James (1884) emphasized the importance of raw sensory processing of somatic, visceral, vascular, and motor cues from the body as the basic building block of the mind, as did Duffy (1957), Schachter and Singer (1962), and Mandler (1975), who referred to this ingredient as "arousal." Wundt (1878/1897) focused on the mental counterpart of those internal cues, which he called "affect." Wundt's conception of affect is similar to what Russell (2003) and Barrett (2006a, 2006b; Barrett & Bliss-Moreau, 2009) refer to as "core affect." Other models that do not take an explicit psychological construction approach hypothesize motivational states to approach or avoid objects in the world. These tendencies can also be considered a basic psychological ingredient of the mind (and, therefore, of emotion) (e.g., Davidson, 1992; Lang, Bradley, & Cuthbert, 1997).

Most psychological construction models include a second psychological ingredient, which is some process by which internal sensory cues or affect are made meaningful. For example, this meaning analysis is seen as produced by ideas (Wundt, 1878/1897), social referencing (Schachter & Singer, 1962), attribution (Russell, 2003), or categorization (Barrett, 2006b, 2009a). Most models assume that the process of making meaning of sensory cues (be they experienced as sensory or as affect) is not deliberate, intentional, or effortful; instead, the meaning analysis is assumed to proceed automatically with little sense of agency or effort.

Of course, there is variety within the psychological construction approach. *Elemental* psychological construction models ontologically reduce mental categories to their more basic psychological ingredients, so that categories like fear, memory, and perception have no scientific value (e.g., Duffy, 1957; James, 1884; Russell, 2003). *Emergent* models view such categories as having meaning, not as explanatory mechanisms, but at other levels of analysis (e.g., as ontologically subjective categories they have functional distinctions for human perceivers in making mental-state inferences that allow communicating about and predicting human action; e.g., Clore & Ortony, 2008; Coan, 2010; for a discussion see Barrett, 2009b). Wundt (1878/1897), for example, wrote that emotions are emergent, and considered emotions (and all mental states) to be like hydrogen and oxygen atoms that combine to form a water molecule. Hydrogen is still hydrogen even when it is in a water molecule; oxygen is still oxygen. But when they come together to form a water molecule, they have features that neither one has alone. In some models, psychological ingredients combine in stages (e.g., Russell, 2003; Schachter & Singer, 1962; Wundt, 1878/1897). In other models, they are combined in parallel in an ongoing fashion according to constraint satisfaction logic, where each is influencing the other in real time (Barrett, Mesquita et al. 2007). In this constraint satisfaction approach, executive attention is implicated as a third psychological ingredient to manage construction smoothly and efficiently (usually accomplished without conscious awareness) (Barrett, 2009a; Barrett, Tugade, & Engle, 2004).

The psychological construction approach crafted in our lab is an emergent model that includes several additional features (see Barrett, 2006b, 2009a). First, emotion words constitute a fourth psychological ingredient (see Barrett, Lindquist et al., 2007, for a review of the empirical evidence supporting this view). This is because the psychological events that belong to a single category such as anger or fear have few statistical regularities to ground the categories. With such heterogeneity across instances within a single category, something other than perceptual similarity is needed for the human brain to learn the category. We hypothesize that emotion words (e.g., *anger* and *angry*) introduce a kind of statistical regularity to an otherwise heterogeneous set of instances, allowing various instances of anger to be grouped together into a single category. In our view, emotion categories are ontologically subjective (Searle, 1995), or observer dependent (Barrett, 2009a), and emotion words play a role in the construction of each and every mental state that is experienced as emotional.

Furthermore, our model outlines a specific set of cognitive neuroscience hypotheses for the brain basis of the psychological category emotion, as well as for discrete emotion categories such as anger, sadness, fear, disgust, and happiness. With the exception of William James (who wrote that emotions were not associated with special brain locations but were instead realized in the same sensory and motor areas responsible for other kinds of mental states), psychological construction models of emotion have not included specific hypotheses about how emotions would be represented in the brain. We hypothesize that, as a collection of instances, psychological categories correspond to a "neural reference space." According to Gerald Edelman (1987), a neural reference space composes the variety of brain states corresponding to a class of mental events.

Taking inspiration from connectionist and network approaches to the brain (e.g., Fuster, 2006; Mesulam, 1998; O'Reilly & Munakata, 2000; Poldrack, Halchenko, & Hanson, 2009; Raichle & Snyder, 2007; Seeley et al., 2007; Smith et al., 2009), we further hypothesize that basic psychological ingredients correspond to large-scale distributed networks within the brain that constitute the fundamental building blocks of mental states. An instance of emotion is a brain state that is constituted within this workspace by a combination (or recipe) of these ingredients. Because our model is relatively new, we cannot definitively claim to know the most basic or primitive psychological descriptions of brain networks. Our proposals for basic psychological ingredients thus far are really more like basic domains of psychological functions (e.g., core affect, conceptualization, attention, and language) that are a first approximation in the trajectory of a longer research program; they will very likely be refined as the research proceeds. Our psychological ingredients, as they currently stand, probably reflect a class of processes that are associated with assemblies of neurons within a distributed network, rather than a one-to-one mapping of ingredient to network. Ideally, with more research, it will be possible to identify distributed brain networks that are associated with psychological primitives (or the most basic psychological descriptions that cannot be further reduced to anything else psychological).

Cognitive Neuroscience Evidence

As part of our larger meta-analytic emotion project, we performed a multidimensional scaling on our meta-analytic database, revealing that the neural reference space for emotion consists of six general functional groupings of brain regions (see Figure 3.1; Kober et al., 2008). We did not find

that that these groupings were specific to any discrete emotion. Instead, they appear to correspond to some of the basic psychological ingredients proposed in psychological construction models. Furthermore, these functional groupings resemble networks that exist within the intrinsic connectivity of the human brain.[6] Intrinsic connectivity reveals many topographically distinct networks that appear to have distinct mechanistic functions, some of which appear similar to the basic ingredients in our psychological construction model (Corbetta, Patel, & Shulman, 2008; Corbetta & Shulman, 2002; Dosenbach et al., 2007; Seeley et al., 2007; Smith et al., 2009; Sridharan, Levitin, & Menon, 2008; Yeo et al., 2011).

The psychological ingredient of *core affect* is reflected by two functional groups in the brain

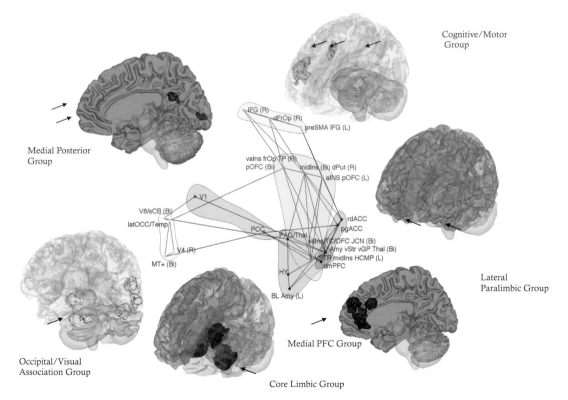

Figure 3.1 Functional networks in the neural reference space from Kober et al. (2008). Colors correspond to six functional networks. Points closer together on the graph tend to have stronger positive co-activation, and connected lines represent significant Tau-b (τ) association values between pairs of regions. The connectivity map has been "pruned" such that the relationships depicted are direct, meaning that they were not completely mediated by any other single intervening region. Direct relationships were assessed by mediation analyses considering each possible mediating region in turn, with 1,000 bootstrap samples per analysis (see Kober et al., 2008, for further details). Abbreviations: a, anterior; d, dorsal; fr, frontal; L, left; lat/l, lateral; med/m medial; p, posterior; pg, pregenual; r, rostral; R, right; s superior; v, ventral; ACC, anterior cingulate cortex; Amy, amygdala; Bi, ; BL, ; CB, cerebellum; frOP, frontal operculum; GP, globus pallidus; HCMP, hippocampus; HY, hypothalamus; IFG, inferior frontal gyrus; INS, insula; JCN, ; MT, ; OCC, occipital cortex; OFC, orbitofrontal cortex; PAG, periaqueductal gray; PCC, posterior cingulate cortex; PFC, prefrontal cortex; preSMA, pre-supplementary motor area; Put, ; STR, Str, striatum (Cau/Put); TC, temporal cortex; Temp, ; Thal, thalamus; V1–8, visual cortices 1–8.

Figure adapted from Kober et al. (2008), reprinted with permission from Elsevier.

identified in the neural reference space for emotion (Kober et al., 2008). One functional group includes core limbic structures such as the PAG, hypothalamus, thalamus, and amygdala. The PAG is thought to play a role in the regulation of autonomic responses and serve as an integrative center receiving direct cortical inputs and projecting to the lower brainstem and hypothalamus (e.g., Bandler, Keary, Floyd, & Price, 2000; Bandler & Shipley, 1991; Mantyh, 1983; Muthusamy, 2007; Sillery et al., 2005), whereas the amygdala plays a role in representing salience and motivational relevance (Weireich et al., 2010; Whalen, 1998). The other functional group includes paralimbic structures and the insula, temporal pole, OFC, and basal ganglia (including the ventral striatum and putamen). The insula is implicated in interoceptive awareness of the body (Craig, 2002, 2009). The temporal pole is implicated in language but is also implicated in studies of emotion (perhaps because it helps represent abstract social concepts; e.g., Zahn et al., 2007, 2009). The lateral OFC is a multimodal area involved in the context-based representation of value, which it accomplishes via the integration of exteroceptive information (from the world) and interoceptive information (from the body) (see Kringelbach & Rolls, 2004; Öngür, Ferry, & Price, 2003), whereas the medial OFC is involved in cortical control of autonomic and hormonal responses (Öngür et al., 2003). The basal ganglia consist of a set of nuclei involved in motivation and motor control. The ventral striatum, in particular, supports effortful behavior, including that involved in motivation, reward, and punishment (Delgado, Nystrom, Fissell, Noll, & Fiez, 2000; O'Doherty, Kringelbach, Rolls, Hornack, & Andrews, 2001). In addition, the ventral striatum is involved in gating attention to novel, salient, and unexpected stimuli (Berridge & Robinson, 1988; Horvitz, 2000, 2002; Salamone, Correa, Mingote, & Weber, 2005) (described in Barrett, Lindquist et al., 2007). Taken together, these brain regions create a representation of core affect. Core affect is like a homeostatic barometer—it is the body's way of telling you what is valuable and motivationally relevant in a given context at a particular point in time (Barrett & Bliss-Moreau, 2009; Barrett & Russell, 1999; Russell, 2003). Core affect is often (but need not be) experienced as a hedonic state with some degree of arousal.

Our second psychological ingredient, *categorization*, is reflected by two functional groups identified within the neural reference space for emotion (Kober et al., 2008). Together, these groups have been referred to as the "default" network (Raichle et al., 2001), the "context" network (Bar, 2007), and simply the "core" network (Andrews-Hanna, Reidler, Sepulcre, & Buckner, 2010). The brain regions within this network include dmPFC, portions of the medial temporal lobe (including the hippocampus and entorhinal and parahippocampal cortices), and the posterior cingulate/retrosplenial area. This network has been implicated in remembering the past and envisioning the future, theory-of-mind tasks, default mental activity (spontaneous, highly associative mental activity), first impressions, fictitious imaginings, emotion regulation, context framing, and moral decision-making (c.f. Buckner & Carroll, 2007; for reviews see Adolphs, 2001; Bar, 2007; Blakemore, Winston, & Frith, 2004; Lane & McRae, 2004; Ochsner et al., 2004; Spreng, Mar, & Kim, 2008). This network is also disrupted in diseases marked with emotional dysfunction, including schizophrenia, autism, and Alzheimer's disease (see Buckner et al., 2008, for a review). There is a lot of debate as to the precise function of this network, but one approach is to ask what all of these psychological tasks have in common. We think they require some reactivation of prior experience to make the present moment meaningful in a way that involves episodic projection or simulation. Thus, this network is critical to the phenomena that psychologists refer to as categorization, memory, and conceptual knowledge. Said another way, categorization gives meaning to the present state of affect and surrounding context (Barrett, 2006a, 2006b), forming what Edelman (1989) has referred to as "the remembered present."

A third psychological ingredient, *attention*, is reflected mainly by one functional group identified within the neural reference space for emotion (Kober et al., 2008). This group includes the motor/sensory regions, as well as parts of the inferior frontal gyrus (IFG) and frontal operculum (frOP). The pre–sensory motor cortex has been linked to the representation of intentional actions (Lau, Rogers, Haggard, & Passingham, 2004) or the preparation of responses (Stuss & Alexander, 2007), whereas the IFG and frOP are involved in tasks requiring cognitive control, such as switching, working memory, and response inhibition (e.g., Aron, Fletcher, Bullmore, Sahakian, & Robbins, 2003; Aron et al., 2004; Badre, Poldrack, Pare-Blagoev, Insler, & Wagner, 2005; Gabrieli, Poldrack, & Desmond, 1998; Martin & Chao, 2001; Poldrack et al., 1999; Wager, Jonides, Smith, & Nichols, 2005; Wager,

Maril, Bjork, & Schacter, 2001). We hypothesize that controlled attention (although not necessarily deliberate) helps negotiate which conceptual elements are activated and which are suppressed during categorization (see Barrett et al., 2004, for a discussion).

Lastly, the fourth psychological ingredient, *language*, is reflected by two functional groups identified by Kober et al. (2008) as part of the neural reference space for emotion. These groups include the anterior temporal lobe and the left vlPFC. The anterior temporal lobe has been implicated in language comprehension and the representation of semantic knowledge. More recent findings linked the anterior temporal lobe to the representation of abstract social categories (e.g., Ross & Olson, 2010; Zahn et al., 2007, 2009). The vlPFC has been implicated in the retrieval, maintenance, and manipulation of conceptual knowledge stored elsewhere in the brain (Gabrieli et al., 1998; Martin & Chao, 2001; Poldrack et al., 1999; Wagner et al., 2001).

Kober et al. (2008) identified two additional functional groups within the neural reference space for emotion. Both groups are thought to play a role in visual processing and attention, including the processing of emotional stimuli. One intriguing possibility is that the limbic system enhances activation in the ventral stream when viewing emotional content (Amaral, Behniea, & Kelly, 2003; for a discussion, see Duncan & Barrett, 2007). To this end, functional groups for exteroceptive sensory processing (e.g., vision, olfaction, audition) might be important additional ingredients in the neural reference space for emotion and would be consistent with the older view that perceptions of the world are part of what it means to be in an emotional state (vs. causes of that state) (e.g., Dewey, 1895; Lambie & Marcel, 2002).

Consistent with a psychological construction view, then, our meta-analytic findings suggest that emotions are constituted as a combination of a more general set of psychological ingredients within the human brain. In our most recent thinking, we have hypothesized that future research might attempt to identify the networks that correspond to the most basic psychological ingredients that are "psychologically primitive" (Barrett, 2009a), in the sense that they cannot be decomposed into more meaningful units at a psychological level.

Future Directions

The findings we have reviewed here demonstrate that natural kind assumptions about emotion

generation, however intuitive as they may seem, are not well supported by the existing cognitive neuroscience literature. Emotion generators seem not to exist in the brain, at least as they were originally conceived. Instead, the meta-analytic evidence is more consistent with the idea that emotions can be decomposed into more basic psychological processes that correspond to large-scale networks in the brain. Taken together, these networks form a neural reference space for emotion. Emotions emerge within this reference space when core affect, categorization, executive function, and language constrain one another to produce the experience of a discrete emotion.

Although we hypothesize that these four psychological ingredients are important components in our model, future research will refine these into more basic psychological primitives. For example, our meta-analysis revealed that regions in left lateral prefrontal cortex showed consistent increases in activation during the experience of anger, a state characterized by approach-related motivation (Carver & Harmon-Jones, 2009). These findings, along with a rich electroencephalography (EEG) literature (e.g., Fox, 1991; Sutton & Davidson, 1997), suggest that this group of brain regions might comprise a network that supports approach-related motivation within the distributed network for core affect (Lindquist et al., 2012). We might also add an ingredient for exteroceptive sensory sensation to our theoretical framework, since visual cortex was one of the most frequently activated brain regions in our meta-analysis (Lindquist et al., 2012).

Another avenue for future research is neuroimaging studies of emotion that allow for richer, contextualized constructions of emotion. In a recent study, participants were asked to construct a multimodal representation of social and physical situations, including changes in core affect that could be conceptualized as fear or anger (e.g., taking a jog at night without knowing the route and becoming lost) (Wilson-Mendenhall et al., 2011). In that study, we found strong evidence for neural correlates of social vs. physical situations, but regardless of whether participants were asked to construct a situated conceptualization of fear or anger, the pattern of brain imaging data was largely overlapping and engaged the networks identified in our meta-analysis.

A richer empirical approach also means moving beyond the presentation of faces or pictures or constructions of prototypical emotional experiences and providing more authentic contexts for experiencing emotion in the scanner. For example, one recent neuroimaging study used a social stress-induction technique in which participants were told they would have to perform a difficult mental math task in front of researchers (Wager et al., 2009). This sort of social stress induction better mimics the motivated performance tasks that individuals perform in the real world. Such designs will not only provide more realistic emotional instances to be modeled empirically but will also help us better explore how conceptual and associative systems are brought online to create the variety of contextually rich emotional experiences.

Developing a clearer understanding of how ingredients join and shape one another in real time is also an important avenue of future work. There are at least three types of neuroimaging experiments that could directly test our psychological construction hypothesis. First, researchers could construct emotion by directly manipulating ingredients to produce emergent emotions (e.g., manipulate categorization in the presence of affective states; for an example in the behavioral literature, see Lindquist & Barrett, 2008). Second, researchers could deconstruct emotion by impairing one or more constituent ingredients (e.g., temporarily impairing access to linguistic concepts via semantic satiation; e.g., Gendron, Lindquist, Barsalou, & Barrett, 2012; Lindquist, Barrett, Bliss-Moreau, & Russell, 2006); or by disrupting activity in brain regions in the networks for psychological ingredients via transcranial magnetic stimulation). Finally, researchers could carefully titrate the involvement of various ingredients and test the outcome (e.g., manipulating the extent to which participants engage the categorization vs. the core affect network to alter whether participants experience an emotion, a thought, or a memory). Recently, such an approach has been used by Spreng and colleagues to understand how the frontoparietal control network can modulate both autobiographical planning and visual–spatial planning (previously thought to be independent of one another, representing internally vs. externally focused cognition, respectively) (Spreng, Stevens, Chamberlain, Gilmore, & Schacter, 2010). A similar approach could be used to understand the dynamic interplay between networks representing psychological primitives important to emotion and other mental, constructed states.

In future directions, we will also continue to build upon and expand our psychological constructionist model to better understand the neural basis of the mind. First, it will be important to use multivariate reduction techniques (e.g., Kober et al., 2008) on databases of studies assessing other psychological domains (e.g., memory, perception, empathy, theory of mind) to test whether our proposed ingredients are the basic psychological operations that cut across all mental states. Second, it would be important to see whether these ingredients map to intrinsic networks in the brain (as are observed in resting-state analyses) or whether they are task-related functional networks (that join together specifically for the purposes of a given psychological operation). Finally, it would be interesting to see whether there are modal combinations of these networks that occur in individual mental categories (e.g., superordinate categories like emotion and memory, or subordinate categories like anger and fear). This could be achieved via pattern classification analyses assessing which combination of ingredients tends to characterize specific mental states. Such pattern classification techniques could then allow us to predict which emotional experiences individual subjects are likely to be experiencing in a given instance.

Implications

The implications of a psychological construction view of emotion for cognitive neuroscience are twofold. First, there are not "emotional" and "cognitive" regions of the brain, so it cannot be said that emotions influence cognition, or vice versa. Furthermore, brain areas should be thought of as functionally *selective* for a specific emotion in a given instance, rather than functionally *specific*. As a consequence, the function of a brain region would be described in terms of its more general role in instantiating a psychological ingredient (e.g., core affect, categorization, language, controlled attention) rather than as the emergent mental state it helps to produce (e.g., anger, fear).

Second, a neuroscientific approach based on population coding or network modeling is needed to understand the construction of emotion (and the construction of all mental states). Although construction views have a long history in the science of psychology (e.g., James, 1884; Wundt, 1878/1897), ours is the first to outline clear hypotheses regarding how functional neural networks underlie the more basic psychological ingredients of the mind. With neuroimaging, we can directly examine the ingredients underlying mental states ranging from emotions to memories to cognitions. A psychological construction account would suggest that these mental states differ in degree rather than kind, and suggests a very different model of the mind.

Acknowledgments

The preparation of this chapter was supported by a National Research Service Award (F32MH083455) from the National Institute of Mental Health to Jennifer Fugate, as well as by the National Institutes of Health Director's Pioneer Award (DP1OD003312), a grant from the National Science Foundation (BCS 0721260) and from the National Institute on Aging (AG030311), and a contract with the U.S. Army Research Institute for the Behavioral and Social Sciences (W91WAW-08-C-0018) to Lisa Feldman Barrett. The views, opinions, and/or findings contained in this article are solely those of the author(s) and should not be construed as an official Department of the Army or Department of Defense position, policy, or decision, unless so designated by other documentation. The content also does not necessarily represent the official views of the National Institutes of Health.

Notes

1. The assumptions of essence (a common cause) and homeostatic causal mechanisms (also called a "definable set of observable properties") are at the heart of what is called a "natural kind" category (see Barrett, 2006a). To assume that emotions are a natural kind is to assume that there are measurable markers in the world of what does, and what does not, belong to each category (see Barrett, 2006a). Psychology has viewed many mental phenomena as natural-kinds. For example, memory, personality, and intelligence have all been considered entities at some point in psychology; more recently, however, they are viewed as emergent features of the mind.

2. James' opinion on the ordering of the emotional sequence was anticipated by philosophers such as Descartes (1649/1989; see Irons, 1895), Spinoza (1677/1982), and Malebranche (1674–1675/1997; see Titchener, 1910), and a similar view was proposed by Wundt (1878/1897). Because of the similarity in their views, James and Lange have often been concatenated into a single perspective, and Lange's basic emotion leanings are misattributed to James. Whereas James stressed that variability in emotional responding is the norm, Lange argued that emotions can be scientifically studied because there is an objective physiological signature for each emotion kind (i.e., he assumed discrete emotions were biologically primitive). In reference to Lange's model of emotion, James wrote, "Dr. Lange simplifies and universalizes the phenomena a little too much" (p. 446).

3. Other appraisal models, where appraisals are descriptions of experience (of meaning or mental content), remain agnostic as to the causes (or generators) of emotion (e.g., Clore, Ortony, & Collins, 1998; Smith & Ellsworth, 1985) and are consistent with a psychological construction approach to emotion (e.g., Clore & Ortony, 2008).

4. Although the focus of the natural kind approach has been in the spatial domain ("where" in the brain), some researchers have looked for specificity in the temporal domain (using event-related potential). There is little evidence thus far to support claims about the temporal specificity of discrete emotion categories (see Schienle & Schäfer, 2009, for a review).

5. Phan and colleagues did not directly test the specificity of each emotion category, nor did they provide coordinates of mean activation within a brain region that could be used to test whether activation at a more precise level was specific across studies. Murphy and colleagues did provide mean activation coordinates for emotion categories, but their statistical aggregation methods were less precise than those used by Vytal and Hamann, making it difficult to compare the activation at anything more than a gross anatomical level. It is possible that there might be specificity at a more precise level (e.g., cluster of voxels, individual voxels, or even individual neurons), but this is unlikely due to important context effects in the brain (for a review, see Barrett et al., 2010). For example, even neurons in V1 (one of the most highly specialized areas of cortex in humans with well-defined receptive fields) respond to more than one type of sensory cue (e.g., Stolarova, Keil, & Moratti, 2006). Recent research has shown that even individual neurons in the nucleus accumbens can sometimes code for reward and sometimes for threat, depending on the context (Reynolds & Berridge, 2008).

6. Intrinsic connectivity networks are identified by examining correlations in low-frequency signals in fMRI data recorded when there is no external stimulus or task (hence the misnomer "resting state" or "default" activity) (Beckmann, DeLuca, Devlin, & Smith, 2005; Biswal, Yetkin, Haughton, & Hyde, 1995; Buckner & Vincent, 2007; Fox et al., 2005; Greicius, Krasnow, Reiss, & Menon, 2003). The temporal dynamics of these low-frequency signals reveal networks of regions that increase and decrease in their activity together in a correlated fashion.

References

Adams, R. B., Gordon, H. L., Baird, A. A., Ambady, N., & Kleck, R. E. (2003). Effects of gaze on amygdala sensitivity to anger and fear faces. *Science*, *300*(5625), 1536.

Adolphs, R. (2001). The neurobiology of social cognition. *Current Opinion in Neurobiology*, *11*, 231–223.

Adolphs, R., Gosselin, F., Buchanan, T. W., Tranel, D., Schyns, P., & Damasio, A. R. (2005). A mechanism for impaired fear recognition after amygdale damage. *Nature*, *433*(7021), 22–23.

Allport, F. (1924). *Social psychology.* New York: Houghton Mifflin.

Amaral, D. G., Behniea, H., & Kelly, J. L. (2003). Topographical organization of projections from the amygdala to the visual cortex in the Macaque monkey. *Neuroscience*, *118*, 1099–1120.

Andrews-Hanna, J. R., Reidler, J. S., Sepulcre, J., & Buckner, R. L. (2010). Functional-anatomical fractionation of the brain's default network. *Neuron*, *65*, 550–562.

Aron, A. R., Fletcher, P. C., Bullmore, E. T., Sahakian, B. J., & Robbins, T. W. (2003). Stop-signal inhibition disrupted by damage to right inferior frontal gyrus in humans. *Nature Neuroscience*, *6*, 115–116.

Aron, A. R., Shohamy, D., Clark, J., Myers, C., Gluck, M. A., & Poldrack, R. A. (2004). Human midbrain sensitivity to cognitive feedback and uncertainty during classification learning. *Journal of Neurophysiology*, *92*, 1144–1152.

Arnold, M. B. (1960a). *Emotion and personality: Vol. 1. Psychological aspects.* New York: Columbia University Press.

Arnold, M. B. (1960b). *Emotion and personality: Vol. 2. Physiological aspects.* New York: Columbia University Press.

Atkinson, A., Heberlein A. S., Adolphs, R. (2007). Spared ability to recognise fear from static and moving whole-body cues following bilateral amygdala damage. *Neuropsychologia, 45,* 2772–2782.

Bachorowski, J. A., & Owren, M. J. (2008). Vocal expressions of emotion. In Lewis, M., Haviland-Jones, J. M., & Barrett, L. F. (Eds.), *The handbook of emotion, 3rd edition* (pp. 196–210). New York: Guilford Press.

Badre, D., Poldrack, R. A., Pare-Blagoev, E. J., Insler, R. Z., & Wagner, A. D. (2005). Dissociable controlled retrieval and generalized selection mechanisms in ventrolateral prefrontal cortex. *Neuron, 47,* 907–918.

Bandler, R., Keary, K. A., Floyd, N., & Price, J. (2000). Central circuits mediating patterned autonomic activity during active vs. passive emotional coping. *Brain Research Bulletin, 53,* 95–104.

Bandler, R., & M. Shipley, M. (1991). Columnar organization in midbrain periaqueductal gray: Modules for emotional expression? *Trends in Neuroscience, 17,* 379–389.

Bar, M. (2007). The Proactive Brain: Using analogies and associations to generate predictions. *Trends in Cognitive Sciences, 11,* 280–289.

Barrett, L. F. (2006a). Are emotions natural kinds? *Perspectives on Psychological Science, 1,* 28–58.

Barrett, L. F. (2006b). Solving the emotion paradox: Categorization and the experience of emotion. *Personality and Social Psychology Review, 10,* 20–46.

Barrett, L. F. (2009a). The future of psychology: Connecting mind to brain. *Perspectives in Psychological Science, 4,* 326–339.

Barrett, L. F. (2009b). Variety is the spice of life: A psychologist constructionist approach to understanding variability in emotion. *Cognition and Emotion, 23,* 1284–1306.

Barrett, L. F., & Bliss-Moreau, E. (2009). Affect as a psychological primitive. *Advances in Experimental Social Psychology, 41,* 167–218.

Barrett, L. F., Lindquist, K. A., & Gendron, M. (2007). Language as context for the perception of emotion. *Trends in Cognitive Sciences, 11,* 327–332.

Barrett, L. F., Mesquita, B., Ochsner, K. N., & Gross, J. J. (2007). The experience of emotion. *Annual Review of Psychology, 58,* 373–403.

Barrett, L. F., Ochsner, K., & Gross, J. (2007). The automaticity of emotion. In J. Bargh (Ed.), *Social psychology and the unconscious: The automaticity of higher mental processes* (pp. 249–271). New York: Psychology Press.

Barrett, L. F., & Russell, J. A. (1999). Structure of current affect. *Current Directions in Psychological Science, 8,* 10–14.

Barrett, L. F., Tugade, M. M., & Engle, R. W. (2004). Individual differences in working memory capacity and dual-process theories of the mind. *Psychological Bulletin, 130,* 553–573.

Barrett, L. F., & Wager, T. D. (2006). The structure of emotion: Evidence from neuroimaging studies. *Current Directions in Psychological Science, 15,* 79–83.

Beckmann, C. F., DeLuca, M., Devlin, J. T., & Smith, S. M. (2005). Investigations into resting-state connectivity using independent component analysis. *Philosophical Transactions of the Royal Society of London B: Biological Sciences, 360,* 1001–1013.

Bejjani, B. P., Damier, P., Arnulf, I., Thivard, L., Bonnet, A. M., Dormont, D., et al. (1999). Transient acute depression induced by high-frequency deep-brain stimulation. *New England Journal of Medicine, 340,* 1476–1480.

Bejjani, B., Dormont, D., Pidoux, B., Yelnik, J., Damier, P., Arnulf, I., et al. (2000). Bilateral subthalamic stimulation for Parkinson's disease by using three-dimensional stereotactic magnetic resonance imaging and electro physiological guidance. *Journal of Neurosurgery, 92,* 615–625.

Berridge, K. C. (1991). Modulation of taste affect by hunger, caloric satiety, and sensory-specific satiety in the rat. *Appetite, 16,* 103–120.

Berridge, K. C., Flynn, F. W., Schulkin, J., & Grill, H. J. (1984). Sodium depletion enhances salt palatability in rats. *Behavioral Neuroscience, 98,* 652–660.

Berridge, K. C., & Robinson, T. E. (1988). What is the role of dopamine in reward: Hedonic impact, reward learning, or incentive salience? *Brain Research Reviews, 28*(3), 309–369.

Berridge, K. C., & Schulkin, J. (1989). Palatability shift of a salt-associated incentive during sodium depletion. *Quarterly Journal of Experimental Psychology, 41,* 121–138.

Biswal, B., Yetkin, F. Z., Haughton, V. M., & Hyde, J. S. (1995). Functional connectivity in the motor cortex of resting human brain using echo-planar MRI. *Magnetic Resonance in Medicine, 34,* 537–541.

Blackford, J. U., Avery, S. N., Cowan, R. L., Shelton, R. C., & Zald, D. H. (2011). Sustained amygdala response to both novel and newly familiar faces characterizes inhibited temperament. *Social, Cognitive, & Affective Neuroscience, 8,* 143–150.

Blackford, J. U., Buckholz, J. W., Avery, S. N., & Zald, D. H. (2010). A unique role for the human amygdala in novelty detection. *Neuroimage, 50,* 1188–1193.

Blakemore, S.-J., Winston, J., & Frith, U. (2004). Social cognitive neuroscience: Where are we heading? *Trends in Cognitive Sciences, 8,* 216–222.

Bliss-Moreau, E., Owren, M., & Barrett, L. F. (2010). I like the sound of your voice: Affective learning about the human voice. *Journal of Experimental Social Psychology, 46,* 557–563.

Blomstedt, P., Hariz, I., Lees, A., Silberstein, P., Limousin, P., Yelnik, J., et al. (2008). Acute severe depression induced by intraoperative stimulation of the substantia nigra: A case report. *Parkinsonism Related Disorders, 14,* 253–256.

Blomstedt, P., Tisch, S., & Hariz, M. I. (2008). Pallidal deep brain stimulation in the treatment of Meige syndrome. *Acta Neurologica Scandinavica, 118,* 198–202.

Buckner, R. L., Andrews-Hanna, J. R., & Schacter, D. L. (2008). The brain's default network: Anatomy, function, and relevance to disease. *Annals of the New York Academy of Sciences, 1124,* 1–38.

Buckner, R. L., & Carroll, D. C. (2007). Self-projection and the brain. *Trends in Cognitive Sciences, 11,* 49–57.

Buckner, R. L., & Vincent, J. L. (2007). Unrest at rest: Default activity and spontaneous network correlations. *Neuroimage, 37,* 1091–1096.

Bull, N. (1945). Towards a clarification of the concept of emotion. *Psychosomatic Medicine, 7,* 210.

Cacioppo, J., Berntson, C., Larsen, J., Poehlmann, K., & Ito, T. (2000). The psychophysiology of emotion. In M. Lewis, J. M. Haviland-Jones (Eds.), *Handbook of emotions* (2nd ed., pp. 173–191). New York: Guilford.

Calder, A. J. (2003). Disgust discussed. *Annals of Neurology, 53,* 427–428.

Carver, C. S., & Harmon-Jones, E. (2009). Anger is an approach-related affect: Evidence and implications. *Psychological Bulletin, 135,* 183–204.

Clore, G. L., & Ortony, A. (2008). Appraisal theories: How cognition shapes affect into emotion. In M. Lewis, J. M. Haviland-Jones, & L. F. Barrett (Eds.), *Handbook of emotions* (3rd ed., pp. 628–642). New York: Guilford Press.

Clore, G. L., Ortony, A., & Collins, A. (1998). *The cognitive structure of emotions.* New York: Cambridge University Press.

Coan, J. A. (2010). Emergent ghosts of the emotion machine. *Emotion Review, 2,* 274–285.

Corbetta, M., Patel, G. H., & Shulman, G. L. (2008). The reorienting system of the human brain: From environment to theory of mind. *Neuron, 58,* 306–324.

Corbetta, M., & Shulman, G. L. (2002). Control of goal-directed and stimulus-driven attention in the brain. *Nature Reviews Neuroscience, 3,* 215–229.

Costafreda, S. G., Brammer, M. J., David, A. S., & Fu, C. H. Y. (2008). Predictors of amygdala activation during the processing of emotional stimuli: A meta-analysis of 385 PET and fMRI studies. *Brain Research Reviews, 58,* 57–50.

Craig, A. D. (2002). How do you feel? Interoception: The sense of the physiological condition of the body. *Nature Reviews. Neuroscience, 3,* 655–666.

Craig, A. D. (2009). How do you feel—now? The anterior insula and human awareness. *Nature Reviews Neuroscience, 10,* 59–70.

Damasio, A. R., Grabowski, T. J., Bechara, A., Damasio, H., Ponto, L. L., Parvizi, J., et al. (2000). Subcortical and cortical brain activity during the feeling of self-generated emotions. *Nature Neuroscience, 3,* 1049–1056.

Darwin, C. (1872/1965). *The expression of emotions in man and animals.* Chicago: University of Chicago Press. (Original work published 1872).

Davidson, R. J. (1992). Anterior cerebral asymmetry and the nature of emotion. *Brain and Cognition, 20,* 125–151.

Delgado, M. R., Nystrom, L. E., Fissell, C., Noll, D. C., & Fiez, J. A. (2000). Tracking the hemodynamic responses to reward and punishment in the striatum. *Journal of Neurophysiology, 84,* 3072–3077.

Descartes, R. (1649/1989). *The passions of the soul* (S. Voss, Trans.). Indianapolis, IN: Hackett Publishing. (Original work published 1649).

Dewey, J. (1895). The theory of emotion. II. The significance of emotions. *Psychological Review, 2,* 13–32.

Dosenbach, N. U., Fair, D. A., Miezin, F. M., Cohen, A. L., Wenger, K. K., Dosenbach, R. A. T., et al. (2007). Distinct brain networks for adaptive and stable task control in humans. *Proceedings of the National Academy of Sciences U S A, 104,* 11073–11078.

Doshi, P. K., Chhaya, N., & Bhatt, M. H. (2002). Depression leading to attempted suicide after bilateral subthalamic nucleus stimulation for Parkinson's disease. *Movement Disorders, 17,* 1084–1085.

Duffy, E. (1957). The psychological significance of the concept of "arousal" or "activation." *Psychological Review, 64,* 265–275.

Duncan, S., & Barrett, L. F. (2007). Affect as a form of cognition: A neurobiological analysis. *Cognition and Emotion, 21,* 1184–1211.

Edelman, G. M. (1987). *Neural Darwinism: The theory of neuronal group selection.* New York: Basic Books.

Edelman, G. M. (1989). *The remembered present: A biological theory of consciousness.* New York: Basic Books.

Ekman, P. (1999). Basic emotions. In: Dalgleish & Power (Eds.), *Handbook of cognition and emotion* (pp.46–60). New York: Wiley.

Ekman, P., & Cordaro, D. (2011). What is meant by calling emotion basic. *Emotion Review, 3,* 364–370.

Ewbank, M. P., Fox, E., & Calder, A. J. (2010). The interaction between gaze and facial expression in the amygdala and extended amygdala is modulated by anxiety. *Frontiers in Human Neuroscience, 4,* 1–11.

Fanselow, M. S., & Poulos, A. M. (2005). The neuroscience of mammalian associative learning. *Annual Review of Psychology, 56,* 207–234.

Fischer, H., Wright, C. I., Whalen, P. J., McInerney, S. C., Shin, L. M., & Rauch, S. L. (2003). Brain habituation during repeated exposure to fearful and neutral faces: A functional MRI study. *Brain Research Bulletin, 59,* 387–392.

Fridlund, A. J. (1992). The behavioral ecology and sociality of human face. In M. S. Clark (Ed.), *Emotion: Review of personality and social psychology,* Vol. 13 (pp. 90–121). Newbury Park, CA: Sage.

Frijda, N. H. (1986). *The emotions.* New York: Cambridge University Press.

Fox, M. D., Snyder, A. Z., Vincent, J. L., Corbetta, M., Van Essen, D. C., & Raichle, M. E. (2005). The human brain is intrinsically organized into dynamic, anticorrelated functional networks. *Proceedings of the National Academy of Science U S A, 102,* 9673–9678.

Fox, N. A. (1991). If it's not left, it's right. *American Psychologist, 46,* 863–872.

Fuster, J. M. (2006). The cognit: A network model of cortical representation. *International Journal of Psychophysiology: Official Journal of the International Organization of Psychophysiology, 60,* 125–132.

Gabrieli, J. D. E., Poldrack, R. A., & Desmond, J. E. (1998). The role of left prefrontal cortex in language and memory. *Proceedings of the National Academy of Sciences U S A, 95,* 906–913.

Gendron, M., & Barrett, L. F. (2009). Reconstructing the past: A century of ideas about emotion in psychology. *Emotion Review, 1,* 1–24.

Gendron, M., Lindquist, K. A., Barsalou, L., & Barrett, L. F. (2012). Emotion words shape emotion percepts. *Emotion, 12,* 314–325.

Greicius, M. D., Krasnow, B., Reiss, A. L., & Menon, V. (2003). Functional connectivity in the resting brain: A network analysis of the default mode hypothesis. *Proceedings of the National Academy of Sciences U S A, 100,* 253–258.

Gross, J. J., & Barrett, L. F. (2011). Emotion generation and emotion regulation: One or two depends on your point of view. *Emotion Review, 3,* 8–16.

Halgren, E., Walter, R., Cherlow, D., & Crandall, P. (1978). Mental phenomena evoked by electrical stimulation of the human hippocampal formation and amygdala. *Brain, 101,* 83–117.

Horvitz, J. C. (2000). Mesolimbocortical and nigrostriatal dopamine responses to salient non-reward events. *Neuroscience, 96,* 651–656.

Horvitz, J. C. (2002). Dopamine gating of glutamatergic sensorimotor and incentive motivational input signals to the striatum. *Behavioural Brain Research, 137,* 65–74.

Irons, D. (1894). Prof. James' theory of emotion. *Mind, 3,* 77–97.

Irons, D. (1895). Descartes and modern theories of emotion. *Philosophical Review, 4,* 291–302.

Iwata J., & LeDoux J. E. (1988). Dissociation of associative and nonassociative concomitants of classical fear conditioning in the freely behaving rat. *Behavioral Neuroscience, 102,* 66–76.

Izard, C. (2011). Forms and function of emotions: matters of emotion–cognition interactions. *Emotion Review, 3,* 371–378.

James, W. (1884). What is an emotion? *Mind,* 188–205.

Kim, M. J., Loucks, R. A., Neta, M., Davis, F. C., Oler, J. A., Mazzulla, E. C., et al. (2010). Behind the mask: The influence of mask-type on amygdala responses to fearful faces. *Social, Cognitive & Affective Neuroscience, 5*(4): 363–368.

Kober, H., Barrett, L. F., Joseph, J., Bliss-Moreau, E., Lindquist, K., & Wager, T. D. (2008). Functional grouping and cortical-subcortical interactions in emotion: A meta-analysis of neuroimaging studies. *Neuroimage, 42,* 998–1031.

Kopchia, K. L., Altman, H. J., & Commissaris, R. L. (1992). Effects of lesions of the central nucleus of the amygdala on anxiety-like behaviors in the rat. *Pharmacology, Biochemistry, and Behavior, 43,* 453–461.

Kringelbach, M. L., & Rolls, E. T. (2004). The functional neuroanatomy of the human orbitofrontal cortex: Evidence from neuroimaging and neuropsychology. *Progress in Neurobiology, 72,* 341–372.

Lambie, J. A., & Marcel, A. J. (2002). Consciousness and the varieties of emotion experience: A theoretical framework. *Psychological Review, 109,* 219–259.

Lane, R. D., & McRae, K. (2004). Neural substrates of conscious emotional experience: A cognitive-neuroscientific perspective. In B. M. Amsterdam and J. Benjamins (Eds.), *Consciousness, emotional self-regulation and the brain* (pp. 87–122). Amsterdam: John Benjamins.

Lang, P. J., Bradley, M. M., & Cuthbert, B. N. (1997). Motivated attention: Affect, activation, and action. In P. J. Lang, R. F. Simons, & M. T. Balaban (Eds.), *Attention and orienting: Sensory and motivational processes* (pp. 97–135). Mahwah, NJ: Erlbaum.

Lang, P.J., Greenwald, M., Bradley, M. M., & Hamm, A. O. (1993). Looking at pictures: Evaluative, facial, visceral, and behavioral responses. *Psychophysiology, 30,* 261–273.

Lange, C. G. (1885/1922). The emotions: A psychophysiological study (I. A. Haupt, Trans.) In K. Dunlap (Ed.), *The emotions* (pp. 33–90). Baltimore: Williams & Wilkins (original work published 1885).

Lau, H. C., Rogers, R. D., Haggard, P., & Passingham, R. E. (2004). Attention to intention. *Science, 303* (5661), 1208–1210.

Lazarus, R. S. (1966). *Psychological stress and the coping process.* New York: McGraw-Hill.

Lazarus, R. S. (1991). *Emotion and adaptation.* New York: Oxford University Press.

Lazarus, R. S. (2001). Relational meaning and discrete emotions. In K. R. Scherer, A. Schorr, & T. Johnstone (Eds.), *Appraisal processes in emotion* (pp. 37–67). New York: Oxford University Press.

Limousin, P., Pollak, P., Benazzouz, A., Hoffmann, D., Le Bas, J. F., Broussolle, E., et al. (1995). Effect of parkinsonian signs and symptoms of bilateral sub-thalamic nucleus stimulation. *Lancet, 14,* 345, 91–95.

Lindquist, K., & Barrett, L. F. (2008). Constructing emotion: The experience of fear as a conceptual act. *Psychological Science, 19,* 898–903.

Lindquist, K., Barrett, L. F., Bliss-Moreau, E., & Russell, J. A. (2006). Language and the perception of emotion. *Emotion, 6,* 125–138.

Lindquist, K. A., Wager, T. D., Kober, H., Bliss-Moreau, E., & Barrett, L. F. (2012). The brain basis of emotion: A meta-analytic review. *Behavioral and Brain Sciences, 35,* 121–143.

Malebranche, N. (1674–1675/1997). *Search after truth* (T. M. Lennon, & P. J. Olscamp, Trans.). Cambridge: Cambridge University Press (original work published in French 1674–1675).

Mandler, G. (1975). *Mind and emotion.* New York: Wiley.

Mantyh, P. W. W. (1983). Connections of midbrain periaqueductal gray in the monkey. I. Ascending efferent projections. *Journal of Neurophysiology, 49,* 567–581.

Martin, A., & Chao, L. L. (2001). Semantic memory and the brain: Structure and processes. *Current Opinion in Neurobiology, 11,* 194–201.

McDougall, W. (1908/1921). *An introduction to social psychology.* Boston: John W. Luce (original work published 1908).

Messinger, D. S. (2002). Positive and negative: Infant facial expressions and emotions. *Current Directions in Psychological Science, 11,* 1–6.

Mesulam, M. M. (1998). From sensation to cognition. *Brain: A Journal of Neurology, 121* (Pt 6), 1013–1052.

Moriguchi, Y., Negreira, A., Weierich, M., Dautoff, R., Dickerson, B. C., Wright, C. I., et al. (2011). Differential hemodynamic response in affective circuitry with aging: An fMRI study of novelty, valence, and arousal. *Journal of Cognitive Neuroscience, 23,* 1027–1041.

Murphy, F. C., Nimmo-Smith, I., & Lawrence, A. D. (2003). Functional neuroanatomy of emotions: A meta-analysis. *Cognitive, Affective & Behavioral Neuroscience, 3,* 207–233.

Muthusamy, K. A. (2007). Connectivity of the human pedunculopontine nucleus region and diffusion. *Journal of Neurosurgery, 107,* 814–820.

Nelson, S. M., Dosenbach, N. U. F., Cohen, A. L., Wheeler, M. E., Schlagger, B. L., & Petersen, S. E. (2010). Role of the anterior insula in task-level control and focal attention. *Brain Structure Function, 214,* 669–680.

Niedenthal, P. M., Barsalou, L. W., Winkielman, P., Krauth-Gruber, S., & Ric, F. (2005). Embodiment in attitudes, social perception, and emotion. *Personality and Social Psychology Review, 9,* 184–211.

Niedenthal, P. M., Winkielman, P., Mondillon, L., & Vermeulen, N. (2009). Embodiment of emotional concepts: Evidence from EMG measures. *Journal of Personality and Social Psychology, 96,* 1120–1136.

Ochsner, K. N., Ray, R. D., Cooper, J. C., Robertson, E. R., Chopra, S., Gabrieli, J. D. E., et al. (2004). For better or for worse: Neural systems supporting the cognitive down- and up-regulation of negative emotion. *Neuroimage, 23,* 483–499.

O'Doherty, J., Kringelbach, M. L., Rolls, E. T., Hornack, J., & Andrews, C. (2001). Abstract reward and punishment representations in the human orbitofrontal cortex. *Nature Neuroscience, 4,* 95–102.

Öngür, D., Ferry, A. T., & Price, J. L. (2003) Architectonic analysis of the human orbital and medial prefrontal cortex. *Journal of Comparative Neurology, 460,* 425–449.

O'Reilly, R. C., & Munakata, Y. (2000). *Computational explorations in cognitive neuroscience.* Cambridge, MA: MIT Press.

Panksepp, J. (1998). *Affective neuroscience: The foundations of human and animal emotions.* New York: Oxford University Press.

Pessoa, L. (2008). On the relationship between emotion and cognition. *Nature Reviews Neuroscience, 2,* 148–158.

Phan, K. L., Wager, T., Taylor, S. F., & Liberzon, I. (2002). Functional neuroanatomy of emotion: A meta-analysis of emotion activation studies in PET and fMRI. *Neuroimage, 16* (2), 331–348.

Poldrack, R. A., Halchenko, Y., & Hanson, S. J. (2009). Decoding the large-scale structure of brain function by classifying mental states across individuals. *Psychological Science, 20,* 1364–1372.

Poldrack, R. A., Wagner, A. D., Prull, M., Desmond, J. E., Glover, G. H., & Gabrieli, J. D. E. (1999). Functional specialization for semantic and phonological processing in the left inferior prefrontal cortex. *Neuroimage, 10,* 15–35.

Quigley, K. S., Barrett, L. F., & Weinstein, S. (2002). Cardiovascular patterns associated with threat and challenge appraisals: Individual responses across time. *Psychophysiology, 39,* 1–11.

Raichle, M. E., MacLeod, A. M., Snyder, A. Z., Powers, W. J., Gusnard, D. A., & Shulman, G. L. (2001). A default mode of brain function. *Proceedings of the National Academy of Sciences U S A, 98,* 676–682.

Raichle, M. E., & Snyder, A. Z. (2007). A default mode of brain function: A brief history of an evolving idea. *Neuroimage, 37,* 1083–1090.

Reynolds, S. M., & Berridge, K. C. (2008). Emotional environments retune the valence of appetitive versus fearful functions in nucleus accumbens. *Nature Neuroscience, 11,* 423–425.

Romito, L. M., Scerrati, M., Contarino, M. F., Bentivoglio, A. R., Tonali, P., & Albanese, A. (2002). Long-term follow up of subthalamic nucleus stimulation in Parkinson's disease. *Neurology, 58,* 1546–1550.

Roseman, I. J. (1984). Cognitive determinants of emotion: A structural theory. *Review of Personality and Social Psychology, 5,* 11–36.

Roseman, I. J. (1991). Appraisal determinants of discrete emotions. *Cognition and Emotion, 5,* 161–200.

Roseman, I. J. (2001). A model of appraisal in the emotion system: Integrating theory, research, and applications. In K. R. Scherer, A. Schorr, & T. Johnstone (Eds.), *Appraisal processes in emotion: Theory, methods, research* (pp. 68–91). New York: Oxford University Press.

Ross, L. A., & Olson, I. R. (2010). Social cognition and the anterior temporal lobes. *Neuroimage, 49,* 3452–3462.

Russell, J. A. (1994). Is there universal recognition of emotion from facial expression? A review of the cross-cultural studies. *Psychological Bulletin, 115,* 102–141.

Russell, J. A. (2003). Core affect and the psychological construction of emotion. *Psychological Review, 110,* 145–172.

Salamone, J. D., Correa, M., Mingote, S. M., & Weber, S. M. (2005). Beyond the reward hypothesis: Alternative functions of nucleus accumbens dopamine. *Current Opinion in Pharmacology, 5,* 34–41.

Sander, D., Grandjean, D., & Scherer, K. R. (2005). A systems approach to appraisal mechanisms in emotion. *Neural Networks, 18,* 317–352.

Schachter, S., & Singer, J. (1962). Cognitive, social, and physiological determinants of an emotional state. *Psychological Review, 69,* 379–399.

Scherer, K. R. (1984). Emotion as a multicomponent process: A model and some cross-cultural data. In P. Shaver (Ed.), *Review of personality and social psychology* (Vol. 5) (pp. 37–63). Beverly Hills, CA: Sage.

Scherer, K. R. (2001). Appraisal considered as a process of multilevel sequential checking. In K. R. Scherer, A. Schorr, & T. Johnstone (Eds.), *Appraisal processes in emotion: Theory, methods, research* (pp. 92–120). New York: Oxford University Press.

Scherer, K. R. (2009). The dynamic architecture of emotion: Evidence for the component process model. *Cognition & Emotion, 23,* 1307–1351.

Schienle, A., & Schäfer, A. (2009). In search of specificity: functional MRI in the study of emotional experience. *International Journal of Psychophysiology, 73,* 22–26.

Searle, J. R. (1995). *The construction of social reality.* New York: Free Press.

Seeley, W. W., Menon, V., Schatzberg, A. F., Keller, J., Glover, G. H., Kenna, H., et al. (2007). Dissociable intrinsic connectivity networks for salience processing and executive control. *Journal of Neuroscience, 27,* 2349.

Sillery, E., Bittar, R. G., Robson, M. D., Behrens, T. E., Stein, J., Aziz, T. Z., et al. (2005). Connectivity of the human periventricular-periaqueductal gray region. *Journal of Neurosurgery, 103,* 1030–1040.

Smith, C. A., & Ellsworth, P. C. (1985). Patterns of cognitive appraisal in emotion. *Journal of Personality and Social Psychology, 48,* 813–838.

Smith, S. M., Fox, P. T., Miller, K. L., Glahen, D. C., Fox, M., Flippini, N., et al. (2009). Correspondence of the brain's functional architecture during activation and rest. *Proceedings of the National Academy of Sciences U S A, 106,* 13040–13045.

Spinoza, B. (1677/1982). *Ethics* (S. Shirley, Trans.). Indianapolis: Hackett (original work published 1677).

Spreng, R. N., Mar, R. A., & Kim, A. S. (2008). The common neural basis of autobiographical memory, prospection, navigation, theory of mind, and the default mode: A quantitative meta-analysis. *Journal of Cognitive Neuroscience 21,* 489–510.

Spreng, R. N., Stevens, W. D., Chamberlain, J. P., Gilmore, A. W., & Schacter, D. L. (2010). Default network activity, coupled with frontoparietal control network, supports goal-directed cognition. *Neuroimage, 53,* 303–317.

Sridharan, D., Levitin, D. J., & Menon, V. A. (2008). Critical role for the right fronto-insular cortex in switching between central-executive and default-mode networks. *Proceedings of the National Academy of Sciences U S A, 105,* 12569–12574.

Stolarova, M., Keil, A., & Moratti, S. (2006). Modulation of the C1 visual event-related component by conditioned stimuli: Evidence for sensory plasticity in early affective perception. *Cerebral Cortex, 16,* 876–887.

Straube, T., Dietrich, C., Motes-Lasch, M., Mentzel, H.-J., & Miltner, W. H. (2010). The volatility of the amygdala response to masked fearful eyes. *Human Brain Mapping, 31,* 1601–1608.

Stuss, D. T., & Alexander, M. P. (2007). Is there a dysexecutive syndrome? *Philosophical Transactions of the Royal Society, Series B. Biological Sciences, 362,* 901–915.

Sutton, S. K., & Davidson, R. J. (1997). Prefrontal brain asymmetry: A biological substrate of the behavioral approach and inhibition systems. *Psychological Science, 8,* 204–210.

Suvak, M. K., & Barrett, L. F. (2011). The brain basis of PTSD: A psychological construction analysis. *Journal of Traumatic Stress, 24,* 3–24.

Titchener, E. B. (1910). *A text-book of psychology.* New York: Macmillan.

Tomaka, J., Blascovich, J., Kelsey, R. M., & Leitten, C. (1993). Subjective, physiological, and behavioral effects of threat and challenge appraisal. *Journal of Personality and Social Psychology*, *65*, 248–260.

Tomaka, J., Blascovich, J., Kibler, J., & Ernst, J. (1997) Cognitive and physiological antecedents of threat and challenge appraisals. *Journal of Personality and Social Psychology*, *73*, 63–72.

Tomkins, S. S. (1962). *Affect, imagery, and consciousness: Vol. 1. The positive affects.* New York: Springer.

Tomkins, S. S. (1963). *Affect, imagery, and consciousness: Vol. 2. The negative affects.* New York: Springer.

Tsuchiya, N., Moradi, F., Felsen, C., Yamazaki, M., & Adolphs, R. (2009). Intact rapid detection of fearful faces in the absence of the amygdala. *Nature Neuroscience*, *12*, 1224–1225.

Valenstein, E. S. (1973). *Brain control.* New York: Wiley.

Van Snellenberg, J. X., & Wager, T. D. (2009). Cognitive and motivational functions of the human prefrontal cortex. In A.-L. Christensen, D. Bougakov, & E. Goldberg (Eds.), *Luria's legacy in the 21st century* (pp. 30–61). New York: Oxford University Press.

Vazdarjanova, A., & McGaugh, J. L. (1998). Basolateral amygdala is not critical for cognitive memory of contextual fear conditioning. *Proceedings of the National Academy of Sciences U S A*, *95*, 15003–15007.

Vytal, K., & Hamann, S. (2010). Neuroimaging support for discrete neural correlates of basic emotions: A voxel-based meta-analysis. *Journal of Cognitive Neuroscience*, *22*, 2864–2885.

Wager, T., Barrett, L. F., Bliss-Moreau, E., Lindquist, K. A., et al (2008). The neuroimaging of emotion. In M. Lewis, J. M. Haviland-Jones, & L. F. Barrett (Eds.), *Handbook of emotions* (3rd ed., pp. 249–271). New York: Guilford.

Wager, T. D., Jonides, J., Smith, E. E., & Nichols, T. E. (2005). Towards a taxonomy of attention-shifting: Individual differences in fMRI during multiple shift types. *Cognitive, Affective, and Behavioral Neuroscience*, *5*, 127–134.

Wager, T. D., Lindquist, M., & Kaplan, L. (2007). Meta-analysis of functional neuroimaging data: Current and future directions. *Social, Cognitive & Affective Neuroscience*, *2*, 150–158.

Wager, T. D., & Smith, E. E. (2003). Neuroimaging studies of working memory: A meta-analysis. *Cognitive, Affective & Behavioral Neuroscience*, *3*, 255–274.

Wager, T. D., Waugh, C. E., Lindquist, M., Noll, D. C., Fredrickson, B. L., & Taylor, S. F. (2009). Brain mediators of cardiovascular responses to social threat, Part I: Reciprocal dorsal and ventral sub-regions of the medial prefrontal cortex and heart-rate reactivity. *Neuroimage*, *47*, 821–835.

Wagner, A. D., Maril, A., Bjork, R. A., & Schacter, D. L. (2001). Prefrontal contributions to executive control: fMRI evidence for functional distinctions within lateral prefrontal cortex. *Neuroimage*, *14*, 1337–1347.

Weireich, M. R., Wright, C. I., Negreira, A., Dickerson, B. C., & Barrett, L. F. (2010). Novelty as a dimension in the affective brain. *Neuroimage*, *49*, 2871–2878.

Whalen, P. J. (1998). Fear, vigilance, and ambiguity: Initial neuroimaging studies of the human amygdala. *Current Directions in Psychological Science*, *7*, 177–188.

Whalen, P. J. (2007). The uncertainty of it all. *Trends in Cognitive Sciences*, *11*, 499–500.

Whalen, P. J., Shin, L. M., McInerney, S. C., Fischer, H., Wright, C. I., & Rauch, S. L. (2001). A functional MRI study of human amygdala responses to facial expressions of fear vs. anger. *Emotion*, *1*, 70–83.

Wilson-Mendenhall, C. D., Barrett, L. F., Simmons, W. K., & Barsalou, L. W. (2011). Grounding emotion in situated conceptualization. *Neuropsychologia*, *49*, 1105–1127.

Wright, C. I., Martis, B., Schwartz, C. E., Shin, L. M., Fischer H, H., McMullin, K., et al. (2003). Novelty responses and differential effects of order in the amygdala, substantia innominata, and inferior temporal cortex. *Neuroimage*, *18*, 660–669.

Wright, C. I., Negreira, A., Gold, A. L., Britton, J. C., Williams, D., & Barrett, L. F. (2008). Neural correlates of novelty in young and elderly adults. *Neuroimage*, *42*, 956–968.

Wright, C. I., Wedig, M. M., Williams, D., Rauch, S. L., & Albert, M. S. (2006). Novel fearful faces activate the amygdala in healthy young and elderly adults. *Aging*, *27*, 361–374.

Wundt, W. (1878/1897). *Outlines of psychology* (C. H. Judd, Trans.). Oxford, England: Engelman.

Yeo, B. T. T., Krienen, F. M., Sepulcre, J., Sabuncu, M. R., Lashkari, D., Hollinshead, M., et al. (2011). The organization of the human cerebral cortex estimated by functional connectivity. *Journal of Neurophysiology*, *106*, 1125–1165.

Zahn, R., Moll., J., Krueger, F., Heuy, E. D., Garrido, G., & Grafman, J. (2007). Social concepts are represented in the superior anterior temporal cortex. *Proceedings of the National Academy of Sciences U S A*, *104*, 6430–6435.

Zahn, R., Moll, J., Paiva, M., Garrido, G., Krueger, F., Huey, E. D., et al. (2009). The neural basis of human social values: evidence from functional MRI. *Cerebral Cortex*, *19*, 276–283.

The Neuroscience of Emotion Regulation: Basic Mechanisms and Their Role in Development, Aging, and Psychopathology

Jennifer A. Silvers, Jason T. Buhle, *and* Kevin N. Ochsner

Abstract

When life's gentle breezes turn into threatening gales, we humans have a remarkable ability to adapt accordingly. This adaptability grants us a degree of control over not just our circumstances but also our emotional responses to them. We can keep our cool under stress, resist harmful temptations, and emerge resilient from all manner of trials and tribulations. We do so using a diversity of emotion regulation strategies that allow us to alter the nature, magnitude, and duration of our emotional responses in a variety of circumstances. The ability to regulate one's emotions is one of the keys to leading a healthy and productive life and the failure to do so is a hallmark of many types of psychopathology, as well as a normal part of development for children and adolescents. A major motivator of the emerging science of emotion regulation is the need to better understand why and how these failures occur and lay the foundation for efforts to improve emotion regulation skills. With this in mind, the goals of this chapter are twofold. In the first section, a model of the cognitive control of emotion in healthy adults is outlined. In the second section, this model is used as a vantage point from which to survey recent efforts to examine emotion regulation in the contexts of development, aging, and psychopathology.

Key Words: emotion, emotion regulation, cognitive control, amygdala, prefrontal cortex

I can't change the direction of the wind, but I can adjust my sails.
—*James Dean*

Cognitive Control of Emotion

In this initial section of the chapter we outline a model that broadly describes the psychological and neural processes by which cognitive strategies can be used to control our emotions (Figure 4.1). First, we will outline a psychological process model of emotion generation and regulation. Next, we will consider the neural sources of regulation—the regions that generate and implement the regulatory processes that comprise a given strategy. Finally, we will consider the neural targets of regulation—the regions that are affected by regulatory processes.

Process Model of Emotion Generation and Regulation

EMOTION GENERATION

The time line at the bottom of Figure 4.1A depicts four basic steps involved in the generation of an emotional response (Barrett, Mesquita, Ochsner, & Gross, 2007). In the first step, a stimulus is perceived in its current situational context. The stimulus could be internal in origin, such as a thought, feeling, or sensation, or external, such as a facial expression, gesture, action, or event. At the second stage, one attends to some of these stimuli or their

(a) Process Model of Emotion Regulation

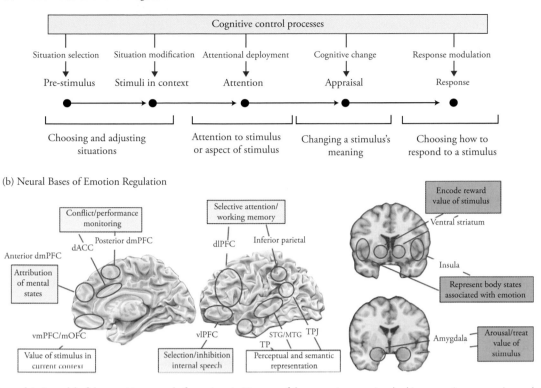

(b) Neural Bases of Emotion Regulation

Figure 4.1 A model of the cognitive control of emotion. **A**. Diagram of the processing steps involved in generating an emotion and the ways in which cognitive control processes (blue box) might be used to regulate them. As described in the text, the effects of different emotion regulation strategies (the red arrows descednding from the cognitive control processes box) can be understood in terms of the stages of of the emotion generation sequence that they impact. **B**. Neural systems involved in using cognitive strategies, such as reappraisal, to regulate emotion (left, blue boxes) and systems involved in generating those responses (left, pink boxes). dACC, dorsal anterior cingulate cortex; dlPFC, dorsolateral prefrontal cortex; dmPFC, dorsomedial prefrontal cortex; mOFC, medial orbitofrontal cortex; MTG, middle temporal gyrus; STG, superior temporal gyrus; TP, temporal polar region; TPJ, temporoparietal junction; vmPFC, ventromedial prefrontal cortex.

attributes. The focus of attention determines what information feeds forward to subsequent emotion generation stages. Ignored or unattended stimuli may be either excluded from these subsequent stages or receive reduced processing. The third stage involves appraising the significance of stimuli in terms of their relevance to one's current goals, wants, or needs. According to appraisal theories of emotion, this is the stage at which an emotion takes on both its valence (whether it is positive or negative) and its more specific characterization (e.g., anger, fear, sadness) (Scherer, Schorr, & Johnstone, 2001). Finally, in the fourth stage these appraisals coalesce into an emotional response, consisting of some combination of emotional experience, emotion-expressive behavior, and autonomic activity. Although these three indicators of emotional response do not always correlate with one another, for reasons that are not perfectly understood (Mauss, Levenson,

McCarter, Wilhelm, & Gross, 2005), emotion regulation strategies can effect changes in some or all of them, depending on the strategy.

EMOTION REGULATION

Emotion regulation involves the modification of emotional responses through the engagement of top-down control processes. Building on previous work, our model of emotion regulation distinguishes among five classes of strategies whose effects on emotion can be understood in terms of the stage of the emotion generation sequence that they impact (Gross, 1998b). In the present chapter, we focus on conscious, goal-driven regulatory strategies rather than implicit or non-conscious ones because they have been studied far more frequently.

As illustrated by the top portion of Figure 4.1A, the first two strategies involve changing the nature of the stimulus inputs to the emotion generation cycle. In *situation selection*, one keeps oneself away from stimuli that elicit unwanted emotions and puts oneself in the presence of stimuli that elicit desired emotions. For example, a recovering alcoholic may choose to skip a happy hour with coworkers, or a dieter may stay away from the sections of the grocery store that offer desserts. *Situation modification* is when one is in the presence of a stimulus that elicits an unwanted emotion and one changes something about the situation to alter its impact (Davis, Gross, & Ochsner, 2011). For the recovering alcoholic, this may mean leaving a party when friends begin to become intoxicated.

Given that we cannot always avoid or alter our external circumstances, at times we must regulate our emotions by changing our internal responses. A third strategy, *attentional deployment*, describes the allocation of attention among stimuli or components of a particular stimulus. This strategy can be further broken down into two subtypes (Ochsner & Gross, 2005). *Selective attention* involves moving the focus of attention toward or away from stimuli or their attributes (e.g., Anderson, Christoff, Panitz, De Rosa, & Gabrieli, 2003; Etkin, Egner, Peraza, Kandel, & Hirsch, 2006). For example, the recovering alcoholic may attempt to avert his gaze from an ad on the subway promoting the latest flavored vodka. *Distraction* involves limiting attentional resources by introducing a competing working-memory demand (e.g., Buhle, Stevens, Friedman, & Wager, 2012; Buhle & Wager, 2009; Kanske, Heissler, Schonfelder, Bongers, & Wessa, 2011; McRae et al., 2010). For example, the alcoholic may throw himself into a difficult problem at work when the urge to drink arises.

Cognitive change involves altering the way one thinks about an emotional stimulus so as to alter one's emotional response to it. This change may occur when generating an initial emotional response, as when expectations, beliefs, or mindsets influence one's appraisal of a stimulus, or subsequently, as when one changes the way one thinks about the stimulus (Atlas & Wager, 2012; Buhle & Wager, 2010; Meissner et al., 2011). The most commonly studied exemplar of cognitive change is *reappraisal*, which involves reinterpreting the meaning of a stimulus, or mentally modifying the emotional relevance of it, in order to change subsequent emotional responses. Reappraisal is one of the most cognitively complex strategies, drawing on language and memory to reference semantic knowledge about the stimulus, working memory to maintain and manipulate appraisals, response

selection to pick goal-congruent appraisals, and self-monitoring to ensure that one is reappraising successfully (Ochsner, Bunge, Gross, & Gabrieli, 2002; Ochsner & Gross, 2005).

Reappraisals themselves can be accomplished in a number of ways. Two of the most common subtypes are reinterpretation and distancing. *Reinterpretation* involves changing how one understands or "interprets" the emotion-eliciting situation or stimulus (e.g., Ochsner et al., 2002). In the case of the alcoholic, he might think about how a beer contains many calories, and that turning down a drink will help him achieve his weight loss goals. *Distancing* involves changing one's personal connection to, or psychological distance from, the emotion-eliciting stimulus (e.g., Ochsner et al., 2004). For example, the alcoholic facing a surging desire to drink may reduce the intensity of his emotional response by imagining himself as an objective friend viewing the situation from the outside.

Finally, *response modulation* strategies target the systems for emotion-expressive behavior. The most commonly studied exemplar is *expressive suppression* (e.g., Goldin, McRae, Ramel, & Gross, 2008; Gross, 1998a; Hayes et al., 2010), which entails keeping the face still so that an observer cannot detect that one is experiencing an emotion. Because expressive suppression only targets the final stage of the emotion generation process, it influences emotional experience subtly, if at all (Davis, Senghas, & Ochsner, 2009; Goldin et al., 2008). However, the effort expended during expressive suppression may increase physiological arousal (Gross, 1998a). Other forms of response modulation, such as expressive enhancement (Bonanno, Papa, Lalande, Westphal, & Coifman, 2004; Jackson, Malmstadt, Larson, & Davidson, 2000) and expressive change, also exist, but they have received little attention in the neuroimaging literature thus far.

The differences among these strategies may lead to differences in long-term efficacy and real-world use. For example, reappraisal, but not distraction, has been shown to have long-lasting effects on one's tendency to have an emotional response to a stimulus (Kross & Ayduk, 2008), presumably because only reappraisal involves an active change in how one represents the affective meaning of that stimulus. However, the active change induced by reappraisal requires engagement with the emotional content, which may be difficult or unappealing. One recent study showed that participants, when allowed to choose which emotion regulation strategy to implement, typically used reappraisal in low-intensity negative situations but preferred the disengagement-based strategy of distraction in high-intensity negative situations (Sheppes, Scheibe, Suri, & Gross, 2011).

Neural Bases of Emotion Regulation

Over the last decade, functional imaging research in healthy human adults has provided tremendous insight into the nature of the source regions that implement regulatory strategies as well as the target systems that are acted upon during reappraisal. This section discusses core conclusions that can be drawn from reappraisal research and a general model of emotion regulation that can be derived from it.

REAPPRAISAL AS A PARADIGM CASE

Reappraisal is an appropriate starting point for developing a model of the cognitive control of emotion, for five reasons. First, because reappraisal is among the most cognitively complex strategies, a model of emotion regulation derived from reappraisal work may be generally applicable to relatively simpler strategies and phenomena. Second, the majority of neuroimaging studies to date have focused on reappraisal. Third, reappraisal is deeply engrained in our culture, as evidenced by countless well-known aphorisms reminding us that "life is what you make of it," "April showers bring forth may flowers," and "it's all grist to the mill." Fourth,

in contrast to other areas of emotion regulation research (see Extending the Model to Other Forms of Emotion Regulation, below) reappraisal studies tend to be more methodologically and conceptually similar to one another and thus provide a stronger base for mechanistic inferences. Finally, reappraisal is an important component of many therapeutic techniques, including cognitive behavioral therapy (Beck, 2005) and dialectical behavioral therapy (Lynch, Trost, Salsman, & Linehan, 2007). With these considerations in mind, we now review the neural systems that have been most consistently observed in studies of reappraisal (Ochsner & Gross, 2008).

IMPLEMENTAITON OF REAPPRAISAL

Figure 4.1B schematically illustrates the brain systems shown by current research to be involved in the cognitive control of emotion via reappraisal, and Figure 4.2 plots peak activation foci for 43 studies (see Table 4.1) of reappraisal in healthy individuals. As these plots demonstrate, a great deal of evidence now supports the hypothesis that the cognitive regulation of emotion is implemented largely by the same frontoparietal control regions that regulate memory, attention, and other thought processes (Ochsner et al., 2002). In this section we consider the possible roles in reappraisal of some of the most commonly observed regions, including dorsolateral prefrontal

A   Sources of reappraisal

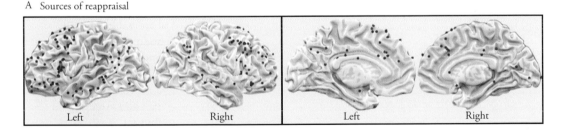

B   Targets of reappraisal

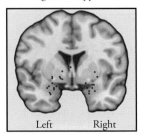

Figure 4.2 Plots of activation foci from the reappraisal studies described in the text and Table 4.1. Contrasts in which the goal was to increase emotion are excluded from these plots, as such contrasts combine both source and target activity. **A.** Plots of foci for contrasts identifying sources of reappraisal (e.g., reappraise > look). **B.** Plots of foci for contrasts identifying targets of reappraisal (e.g., look > reappraise). A mask was used to limit foci to the amygdala and striatum.

Table 4.1 Studies of Brain Systems Involved in Cognitive Control of Emotion via Reappraisal*

Study	Participants	Goal	Valence	Tactic	Amygdala?
		Design			
Beauregard et al., 2001	HYA	Dec	Pos	Dist	No
Domes et al., 2010	HYA	Both	Neg	Both	Yes
Eippert et al., 2007	HYA	Both	Neg	Both	Yes
Erk et al., 2010	HC	Dec	Neg	Dist	Yes
Goldin et al., 2008	HYA	Dec	Neg	Reint	Yes
Harenski & Hamann, 2006	HYA	Dec	Neg	Both	Yes
Hayes et al., 2010	HYA	Dec	Neg	Reint	Yes
Herwig et al., 2007	HYA	Dec	Both	Reint	Yes
Hollmann et al., 2012	HYA	Dec	Pos (food)	Reint	No
Ichikawa et al., 2011	HYA	Both	Neg (errors)	Reint	No
Kanske et al., 2011	HYA	Dec	Both	Both	Yes
Kim & Hamann, 2007	HYA	Dec	Both	Reint	Inc pos only
Kober et al., 2010	HYA smokers & nonsmokers	Dec	Pos (food/cigarettes)	Reint	Yes
Koenigsburg et al., 2010	HYA	Dec	Neg	Dist	Yes
Krendl et al., 2012	HYA	Dec	Neg	Unclear	Yes
Kross et al., 2009	HYA	Dec	Neg	Reint	No
Lang et al., 2011	HC	Both	Neg	Dist	Inc only
Levesque et al., 2003	HYA	Dec	Neg	Dist	No
Mak et al., 2009	HYA	Dec	Both	Unclear	No
McRae et al., 2008	HYA	Dec	Neg	Reint	Yes
McRae et al., 2010	HYA	Dec	Neg	Reint	Yes
McRae, Gross, et al., 2012	Healthy aged 10-22	Dec	Neg	Reint	No
McRae, Misra, et al., 2012	HYA	Dec	Neg	Reint	Yes
Modinos et al., 2010	HYA	Dec	Neg	Reint	Yes
New et al., 2009	HC	Both	Neg	Reint	Yes
Ochsner et al., 2002	HYA	Dec	Neg	Reint	Yes
Ochsner et al., 2004	HYA	Both	Neg	Both	Yes
Ochnser et al., 2009	HYA	Inc	Neg	Both	Yes
Ohira et al., 2006	HYA	Dec	Both	Unclear	Yes

Table 4.1 (Continued)

Study	Participants	Goal	Valence	Tactic	Amygdala?
			Design		
Opitz et al., 2012	HYA & HOA	Both	Neg	Reint	No
Phan et al., 2005	HYA	Dec	Neg	Reint	Yes
Pitskel et al., 2011	Healthy aged 7–17	Both	Neg	Reint	Yes
Schardt et al., 2010	HYA	Dec	Neg	Dist	Yes
Schulze et al., 2010	HC	Both	Neg	Both	No
Staudinger et al., 2009	HYA	Dec	Pos	Dist	No
Staudinger et al., 2011	HYA	Dec	Pos	Dist	No
Urry et al., 2006	HOA	Both	Neg	Reint	Inc only
Urry et al., 2009	HOA	Both	Neg	Reint	Yes
van Reekum et al., 2007	HOA	Both	Neg	Reint	Dec only
Vrticka et al., 2011	HYA	Dec	Both	Reint	Yes
Wager et al., 2008	HYA	Dec	Neg	Reint	Yes
Walter et al., 2009	HYA	Dec	Neg	Dist	Yes
Winecoff et al., 2010	HYA & HOA	Dec	Both	Dist	Yes

*Studies are ordered first by alphabetical order and second by year and are listed in the References section. Only studies that reported contrasts (i.e., not only functional connectivity or correlational analyses) for psychologically healthy individuals are included here. If a study included a patient sample but still reported results for its healthy adult controls separately, it was included. All studies used event-related designs except the nine studies designated by * in the "Timing of reapp cue" column, which indicates that they used a block design. Also, for the stimulus type column, photo stimuli were drawn from the international affective picture system unless otherwise specified.

Abbreviations, by column: **Participants:** HYA = healthy young adult participants typically 18–30 years old, HOA = healthy older adults participants typically aged 60 years or older, HC = healthy adult control participants matched to patients. **Goal:** goal pursued by participants to increase or decrease emotional responses, Dec = decrease, Inc = increase, Both = both increase and decrease conditions were used. **Valence:** positive- or negative-valenced emotional stimuli, Neg = negative, Pos = positive, Both = both positive and negative stimuli were used. **Tactic:** type of reappraisal used—distancing or reinterpreting, Both = both distancing and reinterpreting were used (this only applies to Ochsner et al., 2004) or participants were given choice of distancing or reappraising, Dist = become more or less psychologically distant, Reint = cognitively reinterpret; Unclear = unclear as to what tactic was instructed. Stim Type = stimulus type, Timing of reapp cue = timing of instruction cue to reappraise relative to onset of stimulus, where early is just prior to stimulus onset and late is a few seconds after stimulus onset. **Amygdala?:** whether modulation of amygdala was reported.

cortex (dlPFC), inferior parietal cortex (iPC), dorsal anterior cingulate (dACC) and adjacent posterior medial prefrontal cortex (dmPFC), ventrolateral prefrontal cortex (vlPFC), and anterior dmPFC.

It is important to note that neuroimaging studies of reappraisal have varied along a number of experimentally significant dimensions, including tactics (reinterpretation or distancing), valence of stimuli and emotions elicited (positive or negative), and modulatory direction (decrease or increase), and a number of studies have even directly examined how altering these dimensions impacts neural responses during reappraisal. In keeping with the scope of

this chapter, the present discussion will largely consider reappraisal as a whole, looking at general patterns that are consistent across these variations. We encourage the interested reader to see another review for a more thorough assessment of how paradigm differences meaningfully influence patterns of neural recruitment (Ochsner, Silvers, & Buhle, 2012).

Dorsolateral Prefrontal Cortex and Inferior Parietal Cortex

Together, the dlPFC and iPC are believed to constitute a dorsal frontoparietal network for the endogenous control of attention and working memory (Corbetta & Shulman, 2002). While attention and working memory are supported by complex interactions between dlPFC and iPC, the precise roles they play in these processes are somewhat distinct. On the one hand, dlPFC appears to play more of an executive role in working memory and attentional processes by maintaining goals (Ptak, 2011) and monitoring the contents of working memory (Champod & Petrides, 2010). On the other hand, iPC appears to initiate shifts in attention to goal-relevant stimuli (Ptak, 2012) and to manipulate components in working memory in accordance with goal states represented in dlPFC (Champod & Petrides, 2010). In the context of reappraisal, this network may be used to direct attention to reappraisal-relevant stimulus features, to hold in mind reappraisal goals, and to manipulate information during the construction of new appraisals.

Dorsal Anterior Cingulate and Posterior Dorsomedial Prefrontal Cortex

Neuroimaging and lesion research has broadly associated the dACC and posterior dmPFC with the initiation and maintenance of controlled processing (Bush, Luu, & Posner, 2000; Ochsner et al., 2001; Paus, 2001). In the most well-known models, dACC and posterior dmPFC detect conflict, errors, or other performance signals, and may then call upon dlPFC to implement needed control (Botvinick, Braver, Barch, Carter, & Cohen, 2001; Botvinick, Cohen, & Carter, 2004; Gehring & Knight, 2000; MacDonald, Cohen, Stenger, & Carter, 2000; Miller, 2000; Miller & Cohen, 2001). In other models, dACC and posterior dmPFC do not play a role in monitoring but are directly responsible for activating and sustaining task representations and goals (Stuss & Alexander, 2007). In the context of reappraisal, these regions might track the extent to which one's current reappraisals are changing emotional responses in the intended way and recruit dlPFC to improve or modify reappraisal processes as necessary (Denny, Silvers, & Ochsner, 2009; Ochsner & Barrett, 2001; Ochsner & Gross, 2004), or dACC and posterior dmPFC may serve to directly activate and sustain the task representations and goals needed to implement reappraisals.

An alternative view of the dACC and posterior dmPFC is that these regions help coordinate appropriate autonomic responses during emotion generation and regulation. When stimulated, the dACC is one of the few cortical areas that can cause changes in heart rate, respiration, and gastric motility (Burns &

Wyss, 1985; Hurley-Gius & Neafsey, 1986; Kaada, Pribram, & Epstein, 1949; Pool & Ransohoff, 1949). In both animals and humans, dACC and posterior dmPFC lesions have been shown to alter cardiac and skin conductance responses to stimuli with learned affective and physiological significance as well as to increasingly demanding cognitive tasks (Buchanan & Powell, 1982a,b; Naccache et al., 2005; Neafsey, 1990; Zahn, Grafman, & Tranel, 1999). Neuroimaging studies also suggest that dACC and posterior dmPFC mediate skin conductance responses to conditioned stimuli and are specifically involved in the acquisition of conditioned aversive responses (Etkin, Egner, & Kalisch, 2011; Schiller & Delgado, 2010). Taken together, these data suggest that the dACC is important for controlling learned physiological responses and may therefore also be critical for modifying physiological responses in the context of reappraisal (e.g., reducing skin conductance responses to an aversive stimulus that is being reappraised).

Ventrolateral Prefrontal Cortex

Left vlPFC has been implicated in the selection of goal-appropriate responses and information from semantic memory (Badre & Wagner, 2007; Thompson-Schill, Bedny, & Goldberg, 2005) and in the production of speech (Bookheimer, 2002; Huang, Carr, & Cao, 2002), including internal speech (Hinke et al., 1993; Huang et al., 2002). In the context of reappraisal, left vlPFC may be used to deliberately select semantic elements needed to construct a new stimulus-appropriate, verbally mediated reappraisal. We would expect this type of semantic selection to be especially important during *reinterpretation*, a reappraisal tactic that involves changing one's interpretation of the elements of the situation or stimulus that elicits emotion. Conversely, we would expect less of a need for semantic selection during *distancing*, a reappraisal tactic that involves changing one's personal connection to, or psychological distance from, the stimulus that elicits emotion. In line with this psychological prediction, reinterpretation more frequently evokes activity in left vlPFC than does distancing (Ochsner et al., 2012).

Right vlPFC has been implicated in the inhibition of prepotent, goal-inappropriate responses (Aron, Robbins, & Poldrack, 2004; Konishi et al., 1999; Lieberman et al., 2007; Ochsner, 2005). In the context of reappraisal, right vlPFC may serve to inhibit one's initial appraisal in favor of a goal-congruent reappraisal. Consideration of the type of reappraisal implemented can provide a useful test of this hypothesized function. While decreasing an emotional response would typically require the inhibition of an initial appraisal and its replacement with a less negative alternative, increasing a response would typically only involve amplifying one's initial response, and so inhibitory demands should be lower. In keeping with this psychological interpretation, several studies that compared decreasing and increasing found greater right vlPFC activation for the decreasing condition (Kim & Hamann, 2007; Ochsner et al., 2004; Urry, 2009), and this pattern seems to hold across the larger set of studies that have examined decreasing or increasing conditions separately (Ochsner et al., 2012).

Anterior Dorsomedial Prefrontal Cortex

Anterior dmPFC has been implicated in the reflection on and making judgments about the mental states of oneself and others (Amodio & Frith, 2006; Denny, Kober, Wager, & Ochsner, 2012; Mitchell, 2009; Olsson & Ochsner, 2008) (see Chapter 2 in this book). In the context of reappraisal, one possibility is that anterior dmPFC might be important for both assessing the effect of one's initial appraisal on one's mental state and assessing one's new mental state following reappraisal. Alternatively, or perhaps additionally, anterior dmPFC might support attention to and elaboration of emotional states, intentions, and outcomes of the individuals depicted in the photographic stimuli typically used in these studies. This second possibility is consistent with the predominance of anterior dmPFC in reappraisal tasks in which the goal is to increase emotion (Ochsner et al., 2012). Of the 12 studies that directly compared increasing emotion to a control condition where participants responded naturally, 6 showed increases in anterior dmPFC (Domes et al., 2010; Ichikawa et al., 2011; Lang et al., 2011; Ochsner et al., 2004, 2009). Of the six that did not, most showed activation in neighboring areas (such as anterior cingulate and paracingulate cortex) (Eippert et al., 2007; New, Fan, et al., 2009; Pitskel, Bolling, Kaiser, Crowley, & Pelphrey, 2011; Schulze et al., 2010; Urry, 2009; van Reekum et al., 2007).

TARGETS OF REAPPRAISAL

In the previous section, we reviewed the regions believed to be responsible for the implementation of reappraisal. These regions can be thought of as the sources of emotional control. But what are the targets of this control? Given that reappraisal effectively modulates self-reported emotional experience

as well as other behavioral and physiological correlates of emotion, we would also expect to see modulation in regions involved in generating emotions. In this section, we review the putative target regions that have garnered the most attention in the reappraisal literature thus far, including the amygdala, ventral striatum, and insula.

As described earlier, neuroimaging studies of reappraisal have varied along a number of dimensions, including tactics, stimulus and emotional valence, and regulatory goals. Again, we will largely consider reappraisal as a whole, looking at patterns that cut across together these different task dimensions. However, we will pay special attention to task differences that occur as a function of valence, as differently valenced emotions can be expected to involve considerably different appraisal systems. For a more detailed discussion of the variability seen in different types of reappraisal tasks, we direct the interested reader to a recent review by Ochsner et al. (2012).

Amygdala

The amygdala is believed to support the detection and appraisal of stimuli relevant to one's current or chronic affective goals (Cunningham, Arbuckle, Jahn, Mowrer, & Abduljalil, 2011; Cunningham, Van Bavel, & Johnsen, 2008). While the amygdala most consistently has been shown to respond to aversive stimuli such as punishments, fearful facial expressions, and negatively valenced films or images (Neta & Whalen, 2011; Vuilleumier & Pourtois, 2007; Whalen et al., 2004), it has also been shown to respond to positive stimuli, such as rewards, as well as other forms of salient, nonaffective stimuli (Anderson, Christoff, Stappen, et al., 2003; Davis & Whalen, 2001; Hariri & Whalen, 2011; Phelps, 2006).

As can be seen in Figure 4.2B, many studies have reported changes in the amygdala as a consequence of reappraisal. These studies have most typically involved the reduction of negative affect, with only a few studies examining, and showing, increases in amygdala when the goal was to increase an emotion or the valence was positive (see Table 4.1). Notably, the few cases in which the modulation of positively valenced emotions resulted in amygdala modulation were left-lateralized (Herwig et al., 2007; Ohira et al., 2006; Vrticka, Sander, & Vuilleumier, 2011; Winecoff, Labar, Madden, Cabeza, & Huettel, 2010). While this is consistent with some older hypotheses about valence lateralization (Davidson & Sutton, 1995), the imaging literature in general has not borne this out (Sergerie, Chochol, &

Armony, 2008; Wager, Phan, Liberzon, & Taylor, 2003), and the reliability and reasons for lateralization effects in reappraisal await further work.

Ventral Striatum

The ventral striatum is believed to be involved in learning the relationships between cues (ranging from social signals, such as smiling faces, to actions to abstract objects) and rewarding or reinforcing outcomes (Knutson & Cooper, 2005; O'Doherty, 2004; Schultz, 2007).

As can be seen in Figure 4.2B, a number of studies have reported changes in the ventral striatum as a consequence of reappraisal. As with the amygdala, reappraisal of both positive and negative emotions has been shown to modulate the striatum. However, in contrast to the amygdala, changes in ventral striatum have been seen less frequently for negative emotions and more frequently for positive emotions (Ochsner et al., 2012). That said, because only a relatively small number of studies have examined positively valenced emotions, it is difficult to draw firm conclusions. As noted above, an important future direction for reappraisal studies is to more thoroughly examine how valence influences regulatory targets.

Insula

The insular cortex has been theorized to represent a viscerotopic map of ascending inputs from the body (Mufson & Mesulam, 1982) that some believe is essential to negative affective experience in general (Craig, 2009; Wager & Feldman Barrett, 2004). Within the insula, more posterior regions are associated with the representation of sensations from the body, while more anterior regions have been linked with motivational and affective states, such as disgust, that have a strong visceral component (Augustine, 1996; Calder, Lawrence, & Young, 2001; Craig, 2009; Critchley, Wiens, Rotshtein, Ohman, & Dolan, 2004; Nitschke, Sarinopoulos, Mackiewicz, Schaefer, & Davidson, 2006; Wager & Feldman Barrett, 2004).

While several studies have reported target-related activity in the posterior insula, only a few studies have reported modulation in anterior insula. One possible explanation for this surprising dearth of findings in the anterior insula may stem from the proximity of this region to vlPFC regions involved in the implementation of reappraisal. Target regions are typically detected using the reverse contrast used to detect source regions. For example, a contrast between reappraisal and a passive-viewing,

naturalistic response condition may be used to detect source regions that support the implementation of reappraisal, while the reverse contrast may be used to detect target regions modulated by reappraisal. As described above and depicted in Figure 4.2A, vlPFC regions are often activated in the implementation of reappraisal. This increase in activity may overwhelm any decrease that would otherwise be observed in adjacent portions of anterior insula.

OTHER AREAS INVOLVED IN REAPPRAISAL

Several other areas that appear to be involved in reappraisal do not fit neatly into the source–target dichotomy. One such area is the ventromedial prefrontal cortex (vmPFC), which has been proposed as both a source and target of reappraisal. We will review evidence in support of the hypothesis that modulation of these emotion-processing regions results from earlier modulation of semantic and perceptual representations in temporal and occipital regions known to support perceptual and semantic representations (see Figure 4.1B).

Ventromedial Prefrontal Cortex

The vmPFC is hypothesized to integrate memorial and semantic information stored in the medial temporal lobes, affective appraisals of specific stimuli formed by subcortical structures such as the amygdala and ventral striatum, and inputs from other regions that provide information about current behavioral and motivational goals such as the brainstem and prefrontal cortex (Cunningham, Johnsen, & Waggoner, 2011; Davachi, 2006; Fellows, 2011; Murray, O'Doherty, & Schoenbaum, 2007; Ochsner et al., 2002; Ongur, Ferry, & Price, 2003; Price, 1999; Rudebeck & Murray, 2011; Schoenbaum, Takahashi, Liu, & McDannald, 2011). As such, vmPFC activity may scale with the affective value one attributes to a stimulus in a situational and goal-dependent manner (Oya et al., 2005; Roy, Shohamy, & Wager, 2012; Schoenbaum, Saddoris, & Stalnaker, 2007; Schoenbaum et al., 2011). Examples of this include affective learning, including fear extinction and reversal learning, the finding that vmPFC responses to an image of a healthy food are modulated by whether one has the goal to eat healthily (Hare, Camerer, & Rangel, 2009), and the finding that vmPFC lesions lead to context-inappropriate affective responses in both humans and animals (Beer, Heerey, Keltner, Scabini, & Knight, 2003; Damasio, 1994; Murray et al., 2007).

At present, the vmPFC's role in reappraisal remains somewhat ambiguous. While some have suggested that it may be used to implement reappraisal (Diekhof, Geier, Falkai, & Gruber, 2011; Schiller & Delgado, 2010), in simple main-effect contrast analyses, vmPFC was not found to be more strongly recruiting during reappraisal than when responding naturally. However, in such contrasts a handful of studies have found vmPFC activity to be *diminished* when down-regulating emotion in comparison to when responding naturally or when up-regulating emotion, particularly for positive stimuli (Kanske et al., 2011; Kim & Hamann, 2007; Kober et al., 2010; Schardt et al., 2010; Winecoff et al., 2010). This finding suggests that vmPFC may actually be a target of reappraisal.

Several studies have also found that individuals showing more robust modulation of the amygdala or insula during reappraisal tend to show stronger inverse connectivity between vmPFC and these appraisal structures (Pitskel et al., 2011; Urry et al., 2006). Additionally, it appears that such connectivity differs between individuals according to psychiatric status (Erk, Mikschl, et al., 2010; Johnstone, van Reekum, Urry, Kalin, & Davidson, 2007), genotyping (Schardt et al., 2010), or reappraisal success (Wager, Davidson, Hughes, Lindquist, & Ochsner, 2008). Taken together, these findings suggest that vmPFC may relate to between-individual differences in regulation, although more work is needed to further clarify why this may be the case.

Perceptual and Semantic Representations

Related to how we conceptualize the role of the vmPFC is the question of how reappraisal may modulate not only affective appraisal systems but also systems that process and represent perceptual and semantic properties of affective stimuli. As shown in Figure 4.2, reappraisal often involves activation of middle and superior temporal cortex, regions known to represent high-level visual stimuli, including facial features and biological motion (Allison, Puce, & McCarthy, 2000; Brefczynski-Lewis, Berrebi, McNeely, Prostko, & Puce, 2011; Wheaton, Thompson, Syngeniotis, Abbott, & Puce, 2004); temporal polar regions thought to be involved semantic knowledge about emotion and the binding of emotional and perceptual representations (Olson, Plotzker, & Ezzyat, 2007); and the temporal–parietal junction, a region involved in perspective taking that may be critical when one generates and compares alternative appraisals of a stimulus (Saxe, 2006; Young, Camprodon, Hauser, Pascual-Leone, & Saxe, 2010).

In order to understand the functional role that these temporal regions play in reappraisal, at least three issues need to be addressed. First, there is the issue of how consistently these regions are recruited across different types of emotion regulation. It makes theoretical sense that such regions would be important for reappraisal given that reappraisal involves changing the meaning of a stimulus. However, it is less clear whether other regulatory strategies that do not involve changing the meaning of a stimulus might rely on such areas. The fact that direct comparisons between reappraisal and distraction have shown that the two strategies differentially recruit posterior temporal cortex (reappraisal relies on these regions more) supports the notion that activity in this region may differ across regulatory strategies (Kanske et al., 2011; McRae et al., 2010).

Second, there is the question as to what cognitive process or processes are driving activation of these temporal regions. Greater activity might reflect increased attention to perceptual and semantic aspects of stimuli. Alternatively, greater activity may reflect increased retrieval of alternative interpretations of reappraised stimuli, or the process of actively restructuring one's mental image of the stimulus. Future work should attempt to distinguish among these possibilities.

Third is the question of how these temporal regions fit into the neural model of emotion regulation described earlier and depicted in Figure 4.1B. One possibility is that they play an intermediary role between prefrontal control systems and affective appraisal systems (Ochsner et al., 2002, 2012). According to this view, PFC and parietal regions could change one's mental representation of a stimulus's meaning from the top down, directly altering perceptual and semantic processing in these temporal regions. This reappraised representation in turn feeds forward to the amygdala and other structures that trigger affective responses. Because the amygdala now "sees" the reappraised stimulus, its response changes. While consistent with the existing data, these hypotheses have yet to be directly tested.

Extending the Model to Other Forms of Emotion Regulation

The majority of functional imaging studies of emotion regulation have focused on reappraisal. That said, the other four main classes of emotion regulation strategies diagrammed in Figure 4.1A have been targeted by imaging studies to varying degrees. Given the robustness of the neurocognitive model depicted in Figure 4.1B in accounting for reappraisal, the question naturally arises as to whether this model can be generalized to account for other types of emotion regulation strategies. Here, we briefly discuss each of the four other classes of regulation, using the model derived from reappraisal as a starting point for analysis.

SITUATION SELECTION AND MODIFICATION

While situation-focused strategies are effective in certain situations (Davis et al., 2011), they are difficult to study in a neuroimaging context, so little is known about the neural processes involved in humans. In the rodent literature, a typical avoidance conditioning paradigm consists of a rat learning to perform an action that allows it to avoid or remove the presentation of an aversive stimulus (Everitt et al., 1999; LeDoux & Gorman, 2001). In a handful of studies examining avoidance conditioning in humans, it has been shown that avoidance conditioning relies on vlPFC and dlPFC control systems and modulates the amygdala (Delgado, Jou, Ledoux, & Phelps, 2009; Prevost, McCabe, Jessup, Bossaerts, & O'Doherty, 2011; Schlund & Cataldo, 2010; Schlund et al., 2010). These findings provide preliminary evidence for the notion that situation selection may depend on systems relevant for maintaining regulatory goals and selecting context-appropriate avoidance responses.

ATTENTIONAL DEPLOYMENT

In comparison to situation selection and modification, there have been numerous human neuroimaging studies of attentional deployment, second in number only to studies of reappraisal. As described above, such research can be broken down into two types of studies. The first type involves the use of selective attention to shift visual–spatial attention away from an affectively valenced stimulus or stimulus attribute and toward a neutral one. The second type focuses on the use of distraction to shift the focus of attention away from an affective stimulus and onto some internally maintained mental representation (e.g., a relevant working memory load, self-generated stimulus-irrelevant thoughts, a pleasant mental image). As has been suggested elsewhere (Buhle, Wager, & Smith, 2010; Ochsner & Gross, 2005), interpretation of results found in both types of studies is challenged by three issues. First, the vast majority of selective attention studies, and many studies of distraction, use stimuli that do not elicit strong emotional responses, such as facial expressions of emotion. As such, these studies

are concerned with the regulation of evaluative judgment or perception rather than with affective responding per se. Second, among the studies that have used highly arousing and affect-inducing stimuli, the stimulus of choice has almost always been physical pain. While the experience of pain has a strong negatively valenced affective component, this component may itself have a distinct neural signature that depends in part on dedicated pain-specific neural pathways (Apkarian, Bushnell, Treede, & Zubieta, 2005; Tracey & Mantyh, 2007). Whether or not regulation of pain is similar to or different from the regulation of negative affective responses more generally remains an empirical question in need of testing. Third, attentional deployment studies tend to be highly heterogeneous, often employing very different methods of controlling the focus and level of attention, often without a clear or consistently defined dependent variable for how well attention was controlled. Despite these limitations, it is worth noting that the results of attentional deployment studies are generally consistent with the model depicted in Figure 4.1B in so far as activation of prefrontal systems and modulation of affect systems (like the amygdala) are often (but not always) reported.

RESPONSE MODULATION

Only two imaging studies have examined response modulation (Goldin et al., 2008; Hayes et al., 2010). Both focused on expressive suppression, the ability to hide behavioral manifestations of emotion (Gross, 1998a), asking participants to suppress facial expressions of disgust elicited by a film clip (Goldin et al., 2008; Hayes et al., 2010). Both studies found that expressive suppression activated dorsolateral and ventrolateral PFC regions associated with maintaining goals, response selection, and inhibition (Aron et al., 2004; Badre & Wagner, 2007; Thompson-Schill et al., 2005), and it activated the insula, which is involved in the formation of affective responses. Amygdala findings were more mixed, however, with one study reporting increases (Goldin et al., 2008) and one reporting decreases (Hayes et al., 2010) in activity during suppression. Increases in insula and amygdala fit with psychophysiological studies demonstrating that expressive suppression enhances autonomic measures of emotional responding (Gross, 1998a).

In total, the available literature on emotion regulation strategies other than reappraisal is in some cases limited and in other cases somewhat confusing, but in general it supports the idea that all emotion regulation strategies depend on interactions between cognitive control and affect-generative regions.

Emotion Regulation in Development, Aging, and Psychopathology

The first goal of this chapter was to review and synthesize current functional imaging research on emotion regulation in healthy adults. Another important direction for emotion regulation research is the translation of basic findings to special populations. Two domains in which this will prove particularly significant is understanding (1) how our emotional lives evolve as we grow from childhood through adolescence into adulthood and old age, and (2) how emotional reactivity and regulation are impacted in psychopathology.

Development of Emotion Regulation

There is growing evidence that childhood and adolescence are critical times for development of the emotion regulatory abilities needed to adaptively balance affective impulses and the deleterious health behaviors they can promote. Demands for self-regulation are high in adolescence in particular as individuals experience increased independence, hormonal changes, and a changing social environment (Blakemore, 2008; Casey, Getz, & Galvan, 2008; Somerville, Jones, & Casey, 2010). Most individuals successfully navigate the challenges of adolescence by developing regulatory skills that will help them to cope with stressors for the rest of their lives. However, for some individuals adolescence marks the beginning of a lifelong struggle with emotion regulation and mental and physical health. Not only does the peak age of onset for mental illness occur during adolescence (Kessler et al., 2005), but lifelong problems with alcohol and substance abuse, obesity, and eating disorders (Aldao, Nolen-Hoeksema, & Schweizer, 2010; Baumeister & Heatherton, 1996; Chandler, Fletcher, & Volkow, 2009; Gupta,

Zachary Rosenthal, Mancini, Cheavens, & Lynch, 2008; Herman, Polivy, Lank, & Heatherton, 1987; Houben & Wiers, 2009; Volkow et al., 2010) often also have their origins in adolescence. Thus a critical question is how emotion regulatory mechanisms develop during adolescence when individuals are at greatest risk for developing maladaptive patterns of emotional regulation and unhealthy behaviors.

While a considerable number of behavioral studies have suggested that, on average, adolescents experience more extreme affect (both positive and negative) and more variable mood states in their everyday lives than do adults (Larson, Csikszentmihalyi, & Graef, 1980; Larson, Moneta, Richards, & Wilson, 2002; Larson & Richards, 1994), this work has been somewhat contradictory regarding the reasons for these data. For example, this work does not make clear whether emotional responsivity decreases linearly from childhood to adolescence to adulthood (Carthy, Horesh, Apter, Edge, & Gross, 2010; Murphy, Eisenberg, Fabes, Shepard, & Guthrie, 1999); whether it changes in a quadratic fashion, with emotionality being highest in adolescents (Casey et al., 2008, 2010); or whether it is both linear and quadratic in nature (Larson et al., 2002; Thomas, De Bellis, Graham, & LaBar, 2007) (see Figure 4.3).

To address this issue, studies would need to disentangle the developmental trajectories of emotional reactivity and regulation. To date, however, few studies have done so (for notable exceptions, see Murphy et al., 1999; Silk, Steinberg, & Morris, 2003), which makes it difficult to determine whether age-related differences in emotional responsivity are due to differences in bottom-up emotional reactivity or top-down emotion regulation. That said, reappraisal has been examined in limited age groups (Carthy et al., 2010; Levesque et al., 2004; Moore, Mischel, & Zeiss, 1976; Pitskel et al., 2011), with two studies comparing emotional

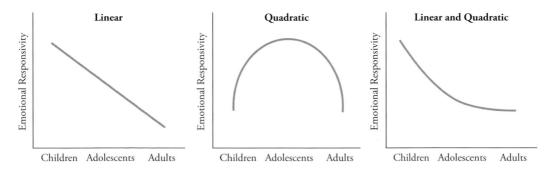

Figure 4.3 Three theoretical trajectories for emotional responsivity in development.

reactivity (baseline responsiveness to affective stimuli) and regulation success (the ability to use regulatory strategies to modulate emotional responses) in individuals at the beginning, middle, and end of adolescence (McRae, Gross, et al., 2012; Silvers et al., 2012). Both of these studies found that emotional reactivity remains relatively constant across adolescence while regulation success improves.

Imaging studies have just begun to address the reactivity-vs.-regulation issue using a combination of structural and functional methods. In general, this work has been motivated by two kinds of findings, the first from studies of emotional reactivity and the second from studies of the development of control systems.

First, volumetric MRI studies indicate that the amygdala increases in size during puberty, with some studies concluding that these changes occur rapidly at the beginning of adolescence before tapering off (Ostby et al., 2009), and others reporting steady linear increases over the course of adolescence (Giedd et al., 1996; Schumann et al., 2004). These structural findings may help to explain why in functional imaging studies adolescents are particularly sensitive to the motivational properties of affective stimuli (Casey et al., 2010), showing enhanced striatal and amygdala responsivity to the receipt of rewards (Ernst et al., 2005; Galvan et al., 2006; Geier, Terwilliger, Teslovich, Velanova, & Luna, 2009; van Leijenhorst, Crone, & Bunge, 2006; van Leijenhorst et al., 2010) and perception of fear faces (Hare et al., 2008; Killgore & Yurgelun-Todd, 2001, 2007; Monk et al., 2003; Thomas et al., 2001), respectively. Second, there is evidence of structure–function–behavior relationships in "cold" forms of cognitive control (such as working memory and response inhibition) during adolescent development. Here studies have shown that prefrontal control systems mature later than subcortical systems, with PFC white matter increasing linearly throughout adolescence (Barnea-Goraly et al., 2005; Giedd et al., 1999; Pfefferbaum et al., 1994) and pruning of PFC gray matter starting around puberty and continuing into one's 20s (Gogtay et al., 2004). Strikingly, these structural changes are paralleled by improved performance on control tasks, with performance improvements correlating with decreased activation of task-irrelevant regions and increasingly focal activations in task-relevant regions (Casey, Tottenham, Liston, & Durston, 2005; Durston & Casey, 2006; Durston et al., 2006; Luna, Padmanabhan, & O'Hearn, 2010).

Building on these findings, current studies have aimed to examine emotion-regulatory processes in adolescence in two ways. First, studies of selective attention have shown that children and adolescents are more susceptible to the influence of affective stimuli than adults, showing age-related inverted-U response patterns in the striatum and amygdala to happy and fear faces, respectively, that peak during adolescence (Hare et al., 2008; Somerville, Hare, & Casey, 2011), coupled with age-related declines in vlPFC activation (Somerville et al., 2011). While face stimuli do not generally elicit strong affective responses, these data are generally consistent with adolescent hyperesponsivity to affective stimuli coupled with immature control circuitry (Somerville et al., 2010). Second, a handful of imaging studies have begun to assess reappraisal in developmental samples (Levesque et al., 2004; McRae, Gross, et al., 2012; Perlman et al., 2012; Pitskel et al., 2011). While limited age ranges and small sample sizes have constrained the interpretability of some studies, there is evidence to suggest that age is associated with both linear and quadratic (inverted U-shaped) increases in activity in dorsal and lateral prefrontal regions known to support reappraisal in adults (McRae, Gross, et al., 2012). What's more, a recent study comparing adolescents with major depressive disorder (MDD) to healthy controls found that healthy controls recruited vlPFC to a greater extent than did adolescents with MDD (Perlman et al., 2012).

While developmental cognitive neuroscience research on emotion regulation remains a relatively "young" area, two conclusions can be gleaned from extant data. The first is that the ability to control one's emotions appears to follow a developmental trajectory similar to what has been observed in studies of "cold" cognitive tasks, although perhaps more protracted. The second is that this shift toward greater emotional control is supported by structural and functional maturation in prefrontal control regions known to support reappraisal in healthy adults.

Emotion Regulation in Aging

Over the next 20 years, the age distribution in the United States will shift such that older adults (65 years of age or older) will comprise ~20% of the population (Vincent & Velkoff, 2010). As such, understanding the psychological and neural mechanisms supporting emotional health in older adults is of importance at both the individual and societal levels. When considering emotion regulation in aging, we are faced with something of a paradox (Mather, 2012). On the one hand, much behavioral research has suggested that with old age comes a more positive outlook, or "rosy glow," that brings with it more stable and satisfying emotional well-being (Carstensen & Mikels, 2005; Carstensen et al., 2011; Scheibe & Carstensen, 2010). On the other hand, age-related cortical thinning is seen in lateral and dorsal PFC regions known to support reappraisal (Fjell et al., 2009), along with declines in performance on "cold" cognitive control tasks (e.g., response inhibition) that depend on these regions (Park & Reuter-Lorenz, 2009). How might we reconcile these two observations?

In comparison to younger adults, older adults report less negative affect and show reduced autonomic and amygdala responses to aversive stimuli (Levenson, Carstensen, & Gottman, 1994; St. Jacques, Bessette-Symons, & Cabeza, 2009; Tsai, Levenson, & Carstensen, 2000). Given that the amygdala remains structurally intact during aging and that age-related decreases in amygdala activity are often accompanied by enhanced prefrontal activity (Nashiro, Sakaki, & Mather, 2012), some investigators have suggested that age-related decreases in negative affect may be driven by the use of top-down regulation strategies. Supporting this notion is the fact that age-related bias toward reporting more positive and less negative emotion in response to stimuli is strongest for low-arousal stimuli for which top-down appraisal processes may play a greater role in generating and regulating emotions (Streubel & Kunzmann, 2011). While this evidence is suggestive, only two studies have directly examined whether there are age-related changes in reappraisal-related modulation of the amygdala. One found that older adults could successfully decrease amygdala responses to both positive and negative photos (Winecoff et al., 2010). The other reported no baseline amygdala responses in old or young adults (Opitz, Rauch, Terry, & Urry, 2012), so regulatory effects could not be examined.

While older adults report that they regularly use reappraisal (Gross et al., 1997), several experimental studies have suggested that they are actually less able to decrease negative emotion (Opitz et al., 2012; Shiota & Levenson, 2009; Tucker, Feuerstein, Mende-Siedlecki, Ochsner, & Stern, 2012; Winecoff et al., 2010). However, this reduced ability may be a function of the reappraisal tactic used. While older adults show deficits in reappraising when using a neutralizing tactic, in which one attempts to think about stimuli in unemotional terms, they are just as good as young adults when using a positivizing tactic (Shiota & Levenson, 2009), through which one seeks positive ways to reframe a stimulus's meaning (McRae, Ciesielski, & Gross, 2012). Interestingly, another study found that while older adults were unable to effectively use reappraisal to *decrease* their negative affect, they were able to use reappraisal to *increase* negative affect (Opitz et al., 2012). Given that anterior dmPFC has been implicated in up-regulation of emotion in prior work (Ochsner et al., 2004), this suggests that older adults may be better at reappraising when the reappraisal goals rely on dmPFC-supported processes, in comparison to when reappraisal goals rely on processes supported by dorsal and lateral PFC. Indeed, both older and younger adults recruit dmPFC to a similar degree in several tasks known to involve this area, including making self-referential (Gutchess, Kensinger, & Schacter, 2007) or semantic (Ritchey, Bessette-Symons, Hayes, & Cabeza, 2011) judgments about valenced stimuli, and more generally when viewing positive stimuli (Kensinger & Schacter, 2008; Leclerc & Kensinger, 2008, 2011). Consistent with these hypotheses, two neuroimaging studies of reappraisal in older adults have shown weaker vlPFC activity accompanied by impaired ability to decrease negative emotion (Opitz et al., 2012; Winecoff et al., 2010). Furthermore, one of these studies found that activity in a dACC region adjacent to anterior dmPFC in older adults was associated with greater success at increasing negative emotion (Opitz et al., 2012).

Taken together, this work suggests that older adults have preserved reappraisal abilities when reappraising using a positivizing tactic or when the reappraisal goal is to increase emotion. However, it may also be the case that older adults struggle to reappraise when asked to use tactics and follow goals that are not consistent with their chronic regulatory tendencies or to draw upon cognitive processes that decline with age, such as working memory and response selection processes involved in neutralizing negative emotion that are supported in lateral PFC.

Emotion Regulation in Psychopathology

A second important goal for translational research will be to understand how potential dysfunction in the mechanisms of emotion generation and regulation may underlie various forms of psychopathology. This translational direction is being pursued in studies of reappraisal across various disorders, ranging from borderline personality disorder (Koenigsberg et al., 2010; Lang et al., 2011; Schulze et al., 2010), to depression (Erk, Mikschl, et al., 2010; Heller et al., 2009; Johnstone et al., 2007) to anxiety disorders (Goldin, Manber, Hakimi, Canli, & Gross, 2009; Goldin, Manber-Ball, Werner, Heimberg, & Gross, 2009), including phobia (Hermann et al., 2009) and post-traumatic stress disorder (Lang et al., 2011; New, Fan, et al., 2009). In the next section of this chapter, we will highlight the research findings to date on the neural bases of emotion regulation in each of these disorders.

BORDERLINE PERSONALITY DISORDER

Emotional instability, particularly in the context of interpersonal relationships, is one of the hallmarks of borderline personality disorder (BPD) (Gunderson, 2007; Gunderson & Lyons-Ruth, 2008). Not only is this instability a trademark feature of BPD, it is also one of the most destructive aspects of this disorder in that it is associated with suicidality, extreme anger, and feelings of emptiness (Koenigsberg et al., 2001; Linehan, 1993). Structural MRI research has linked this tendency to experience heightened emotional reactivity to decreased amygdala and insula volumes, regions associated with emotional responding, as well as reduced ACC volumes, a region associated with emotion regulation (Nunes et al., 2009; Rusch et al., 2003; Schmahl, Vermetten, Elzinga, & Douglas Bremner, 2003; Soloff et al., 2012; Tebartz van Elst et al., 2003). Building on these findings, fMRI studies have found that individuals with BPD show exaggerated amygdala responses during passive viewing of emotional stimuli (Donegan et al., 2003; Herpertz et al., 2001; Koenigsberg, Siever, et al., 2009; Minzenberg, Fan, New, Tang, & Siever, 2007; Schnell, Dietrich, Schnitker, Daumann, & Herpertz, 2007) and atypical prefrontal recruitment during cognitive control tasks (New, Hazlett, et al., 2009; Silbersweig et al., 2007; Völlm et al., 2004; Wingenfeld et al., 2009).

At present, three studies have assessed the neural correlates of reappraisal in individuals with BPD. While these studies differed in terms of stimulus type (pictures vs. emotional scripts), reappraisal goal (increase vs. decrease), and reappraisal tactic (reinterpretation vs. distancing), taken together they suggest two basic patterns of results. First, individuals with BPD did not differ from healthy controls on behavioral measures of baseline emotional reactivity or reappraisal success (Koenigsberg, Fan, et al., 2009; Lang et al., 2011). The second, somewhat contradictory pattern, is that in comparison to healthy controls, during reappraisal individuals

with BPD showed both heightened amygdala responses and diminished recruitment of cortical regions involved in cognitive control, including dlPFC, vlPFC, and, most consistently, dACC and anterior dmPFC (Koenigsberg, Fan, et al., 2009; Lang et al., 2011; Schulze et al., 2010). Prior work has suggested that high alexithymic traits, the tendency to have difficulty in recognizing and expressing emotions, exist in BPD (Berenbaum, 1996; Domes, Grabe, Czieschnek, Heinrichs, & Herpertz, 2011) and that high alexithymic traits are also associated with diminished activity in dACC and anterior and posterior dmPFC during mentalizing and emotional interference tasks (McRae, Reiman, Fort, Chen, & Lane, 2008; Moriguchi et al., 2006, 2007). Taken together, these behavioral and imaging findings suggest that individuals with BPD are less adept than healthy controls at self-monitoring and making online evaluations of reappraisal success and, perhaps, their own emotions more generally.

MAJOR DEPRESSIVE DISORDER

Major depressive disorder (MDD) is characterized by prolonged dysphoric mood as well as disrupted motivation, thought, and behavior (Drevets & Todd, 1997). To date, a central focus of neuroimaging research on MDD has been evaluating whether MDD symptomology is caused by a bottom-up enhancement of responses to negative stimuli, diminished responses to positive stimuli, impaired top-down regulatory ability, or some combination of these three. In keeping with these ideas, fMRI work has suggested that individuals with MDD exhibit (1) atypical resting-state activity in anterior dmPFC and ventral striatum (Kuhn & Gallinat, 2013), as well as (2) enhanced amygdala and (3) diminished striatal responses to emotional stimuli (Delvecchio et al., 2012; Hamilton et al., 2012). Structural studies also are generally consistent, with two recent meta-analyses showing that individuals with MDD show diminished hippocampal, prefrontal, and orbitofrontal volumes in comparison to healthy controls (Arnone, McIntosh, Ebmeier, Munafo, & Anderson, 2012; Kempton et al., 2011). Somewhat confusing, however, is a separate meta-analysis focusing specifically on the amygdala, which found that amygdala volumes were enlarged for individuals with MDD on medication relative to healthy controls but diminished for unmedicated individuals with MDD relative to healthy controls (Hamilton, Siemer, & Gotlib, 2008). These data raise questions about the relationships between structural volumes and functional responsivity that have yet to be resolved.

With this somewhat cloudy picture as a backdrop, five studies have examined the neural mechanisms of reappraisal in depression. While these studies examined different reappraisal tactics (reinterpretation vs. distancing), goals (increase vs. decrease emotion), and emotional valence (positive vs. negative), three general trends have emerged. First, individuals with MDD do not differ from healthy controls on behavioral measures of reappraisal success (Beauregard, Paquette, & Levesque, 2006; Erk, Mikschl, et al., 2010), although in one study individuals with MDD reported that it was more difficult to reappraise than did healthy controls (Beauregard et al., 2006). Second, regulation of subcortical responses to affective stimuli is impacted by MDD, with one study finding that individuals with MDD fail to sustain ventral striatal responses during up-regulation of positive emotion (Heller et al., 2009), another finding that they show enhanced amygdala responses during down-regulation of negative affect (Beauregard et al., 2006), and yet another finding that individuals with MDD do not show enduring reappraisal-related modulation of the amygdala (Erk, Mikschl, et al., 2010). Third, in three out of the four studies that compared neural responses in a reappraise "respond naturally" contrast in individuals with MDD relative to healthy controls, depressed individuals recruited larger swaths of PFC during reappraisal than did healthy controls. This suggests less efficiency during emotion regulation in individuals with MDD (Beauregard et al., 2006; Johnstone et al., 2007; Light et al., 2012). Fourth, all studies that examined prefrontal-subcortical dynamics found that functional connectivity between the PFC and the amygdala (Erk, Mikschl, et al., 2010; Johnstone et al., 2007) or ventral striatum (Heller et al., 2009) in individuals with MDD was either diminished or showed an opposite pattern of what was observed in healthy controls.

PHOBIAS, ANXIETY DISORDERS, AND PTSD

State anxiety may be defined as a feeling of agitation or arousal caused by the perception of a real or imagined threat (Amstadter, 2008). In anxiety disorders (AD), specific (e.g., social anxiety disorder [SAD], phobias, and post-traumatic stress disorder [PTSD]) or varied (e.g., generalized anxiety disorder [GAD]) triggers chronically activate this anxious state (American Psychiatric Association, 1995). Within the context of our model of emotion regulation, AD may represent an inability to accurately appraise what is threatening, an inability to reappraise threat, or both.

In support of the appraisal possibility, relatively greater activation of the insula and amygdala has been shown in response to negative or threatening social stimuli across different types of AD (Etkin & Wager, 2007). These relative hyperactivations have been observed in response to negative emotional facial expressions (Blair et al., 2008; Evans et al., 2008; Goldin, Manber, et al., 2009; Klumpp, Angstadt, & Phan, 2012; Labuschagne et al., 2010), during a speech preparation task in individuals with SAD (Lorberbaum et al., 2004), to trauma-themed pictures and scripts for individuals with PTSD (Simmons & Matthews, 2012), and to phobogenic stimuli for individuals with spider phobia (Alpers et al., 2009; Caseras et al., 2010; Dilger et al., 2003; Goossens, Schruers, Peeters, Griez, & Sunaert, 2007; Larson et al., 2006; Lipka, Miltner, & Straube, 2011; Schienle, Schafer, Walter, Stark, & Vaitl, 2005; Schweckendick et al., 2011; Straube, Mentzel, & Miltner, 2006; Wendt, Lotze, Weike, Hosten, & Hamm, 2008). It should be noted, however, that appraisal-related activity is somewhat different for PTSD than for other ADs in that most ADs are associated with hyperactivation of the insula whereas PTSD is not, nor is PTSD associated with hyperactivation of the entire amygdala, but rather only more ventral portions (Etkin & Wager, 2007).

GAD is unusual in its lack of specificity for what produces anxious feelings, and it is perhaps for this reason that some neuroimaging studies have found anticipation or viewing of fear-related stimuli to elicit greater amygdala responses in GAD (Etkin & Schatzberg, 2011; McClure et al., 2007; Nitschke et al., 2009), while others have found no differences in amygdala responses between individuals with GAD and healthy controls (Palm, Elliott, McKie, Deakin, & Anderson, 2011). Still others have observed hypoactive amygdala responses in GAD (Blair et al., 2008).

In summary, inappropriate threat appraisals in AD appear to be linked to abnormal activity in structures involved in perceiving, responding to, and remembering fear-inducing stimuli, such as the amygdala and insula (Etkin & Wager, 2007).

In addition to the hyperactivations observed in targets of emotion regulation described above, a number of abnormalities associated with AD have been noted in prefrontal control regions. However, the specific pattern of atypical brain recruitment appears to vary across disorders. While most fMRI studies in AD samples report typical or enhanced recruitment of prefrontal regions, particularly dorsal ACC and anterior dmPFC, most fMRI studies of PTSD report diminished recruitment of both dorsal and ventral mPFC (Damsa, Kosel, & Moussally, 2009; Etkin & Wager, 2007).

In healthy adults, use of strategies like "reality checking," which involves using a type of emotional distancing (i.e., thinking about participating in an fMRI experiment on emotion from a more objective perspective), or attentional deployment strategies such as self-distraction to regulate state anxiety elicits activity in anterior and posterior dmPFC and dlPFC and reduces activity in the amygdala and insula (Herwig et al., 2007; Kalisch et al., 2005). Two fMRI studies have examined reappraisal in individuals with SAD (Goldin, Manber, et al., 2009; Goldin, Manber-Ball, et al., 2009), one study has examined reappraisal in spider phobia (Hermann et al., 2009), and one study has examined reappraisal in PTSD (New, Fan, et al., 2009). Across these studies of different subtypes of AD, three patterns have emerged. First, none of these studies observed behavioral differences between individuals with AD and healthy controls. Second, none of these studies found group differences with regard to amygdala modulation during reappraisal, although other types of effects have been reported. For example, one study found that spider phobics were less effective at down-regulating insula activity to phobogenic stimuli than to generally aversive stimuli (Hermann et al., 2009), and another study found less functional connectivity between prefrontal control regions and the amygdala during down-regulation for individuals with SAD than that in healthy controls (Goldin, Manber-Ball, et al., 2009). Third, although the precise set of prefrontal regions associated with reappraisal varied from study to study, all four studies found evidence to suggest that individuals with AD recruit anterior and posterior dmPFC, dlPFC, and vlPFC to a lesser degree than healthy controls (Goldin, Manber, et al., 2009; Goldin, Manber-Ball, et al., 2009; New, Fan, et al., 2009), or they recruit these regions to a lesser degree when regulating responses to phobogenic stimuli than to other types of emotional stimuli (Hermann et al., 2009).

SUMMARY OF TRANLSATIONAL FINDINGS

Taken together, the translational work to date emphasizes the need to examine emotion regulation in development, aging, and psychopathology using converging evidence from the behavioral and fMRI literatures. In doing so, we have already made great strides toward identifying how emotional reactivity and regulation abilities interact to predict emotional stability, yet much more work must still be done. While it is clear that breakdowns in prefrontal control systems and subcortical affective appraisal systems contribute to regulatory failures in the young, the elderly, and the mentally ill, there is still a need to carefully and precisely characterize the nature of these breakdowns on a population-by-population basis. Additionally, when looking between those populations that *are* well-characterized, there is a need to understand why they differ. For example, why does more prefrontal recruitment result in diminished regulatory success in some cases (e.g., MDD) while less recruitment results in diminished regulatory success in other cases (e.g., BPD)? This is just one of many questions that have yet to be fully addressed by translational emotion regulation work.

Summary and Future Directions

The overarching goal of this chapter has been to review and synthesize current functional imaging research on emotion regulation and to apply it to development, aging and psychopathology. In the first part of this chapter, we outlined a basic model of the processes and neural systems that support emotion generation and regulation. At its core, this model specifies how prefrontal, cingulate, and parietal control systems modulate activity in affective appraisal regions as well as occipitotemporal regions involved in semantic and perceptual representations. Such dynamics may differ across regulatory contexts as a function of one's goal, tactic, and the nature of the stimuli and emotions being regulated (Ochsner et al., 2012).

With this model in place, the second part of this chapter sought to translate the model to constrain and interpret findings on emotion regulation in developmental, aging, and clinical populations. This approach is critical both for understanding the mechanisms underlying normal variability and for testing the boundaries of our basic model of emotion regulation.

While this chapter sought to clarify and synthesize our existing knowledge about basic and applied aspects of emotion regulation, it is important to note the limitations of our current knowledge. On the basic side, four questions stand out. First, more direct comparisons between paradigms that differ in terms of goals, tactics, and stimulus types are needed to clarify the basic mechanisms underlying reappraisal. Second, additional work is needed to determine what roles the brain systems supporting reappraisal play in related phenomena such as attentional deployment and situational selection and modification. Third, it will be essential to not only refine our understanding of the distinctions between different regulatory processes but also to address new questions about how emotion regulation operates. For example, while it is critical that regulation strategies have immediate effects on emotional responses, it is equally important, if not more so, to determine what their long-term effects are. Fourth, assessing whether regulatory effects are enduring is significant for both everyday and clinical contexts where one might repeatedly re-encounter an emotionally evocative stimulus (e.g., having daily interactions with a difficult co-worker). At present, this issue has only been addressed in three studies. In one study, reappraisal diminished arousal-related event-related potential (ERP) activity for up to 30 minutes (Macnamara, Ochsner, & Hajcak, 2011). In a second study, reappraisal diminished amygdala responses for up to 40 minutes in healthy adults, but not those with major depression (Erk, Mikschl, et al., 2010). In a third study, reappraisal differentially impacted amygdala responses as a function of successful recall 1 year later (Erk, von Kalckreuth, & Walter, 2010). However, reappraisal did not affect whether or not stimuli were remembered. Taken together, these studies suggest that reappraisal may result in long-term changes in the neural response to emotional stimuli, but more work is clearly needed to characterize the extent of this duration and the mediating psychological processes.

On the translational side, as discussed in this chapter, two major goals will prove important for guiding future research. The first is to understand from a neural and cognitive perspective how and why emotional behavior changes as we transition from childhood to adolescence, from adolescence to adulthood, and from adulthood to old age. Evaluation of the neural bases of emotional development has the potential to enhance mental health and well-being in at least two ways. First, neuroimaging data may enable us to better parse emotional reactivity and regulation than self-report data alone. For example, when questionnaire or diary studies compare self-reports of emotion across individuals at different ages, it can be difficult to determine whether bottom-up or top-down processes drive age effects. By using converging evidence from both fMRI and behavioral data, however, we may elucidate what drives

emotional changes across development (i.e., is activity in sources or targets of reappraisal more strongly linked to affective ratings?). This will be critical for achieving a second goal for this line of work: developing appropriate interventions for individuals at different points in the lifespan. For example, if vlPFC develops relatively late in adolescence and deteriorates relatively early in old age, then the young and the old ought to be better at using reappraisal subtypes that rely less strongly on vlPFC, such as distancing, than those that rely more strongly on vlPFC, such as reinterpretation. If this is the case, it may be more effective to teach these populations distancing strategies in interventions than reinterpretation strategies.

A second important goal for translational research is to clarify how potential dysfunction in the mechanisms of emotion generation and regulation may underlie psychopathology. While this review discussed this solely in the context of depression (Erk, Mikschl, et al., 2010; Heller et al., 2009; Johnstone et al., 2007), BPD (Koenigsberg et al., 2010; Lang et al., 2011; Schulze et al., 2010), and ADs (Goldin, Manber, et al., 2009), including phobia (Hermann et al., 2009) and PTSD (Lang et al., 2011; New, Fan, et al., 2009), this line of work may also extend to other clinical populations as well as to addicted populations (Kober et al., 2010; Volkow et al., 2010). Examining the neural bases of emotion generation and regulation in psychopathology has at least two potential benefits. First, doing so may elucidate disorder-specific patterns of altered function in emotion generation and regulation systems. Second, neuroimaging of emotion regulation processes may be used before and after treatment regimes as a biomarker to predict and assess treatment response. While such studies are only beginning to emerge, they hold great promise for understanding why some individuals improve and others do not, as well as whether different treatments (e.g., pharmacological vs. cognitive behavioral therapy) have different mechanisms of action.

By integrating basic and translational perspectives on emotion regulation, we may be better suited to identify which individuals are at greatest risk for maladaptive health behaviors and emotional outcomes, at what ages this risk is greatest, and which regulatory mechanisms could be targeted in future interventions during particular points in the life course. While this remains a far-off goal, establishing basic and applied models of emotion regulation is a necessary stepping stone for ultimately achieving it.

Acknowledgments

Preparation of this article was supported by NIH grants AG039279, MH076137, and DA022541 awarded to Kevin N. Ochsner as well as fellowship MH094056 awarded to Jennifer A. Silvers. Preparation was also supported by NIH grant HD069178. This grant is supported by the Common Fund, which is managed by the OD/Office of Strategic Coordination (OSC).

References

Aldao, A., Nolen-Hoeksema, S., & Schweizer, S. (2010). Emotion-regulation strategies across psychopathology: A meta-analytic review. *Clinical Psychology Review*, *30*(2), 217–237.

Allison, T., Puce, A., & McCarthy, G. (2000). Social perception from visual cues: Role of the STS region. *Trends in Cognitive Sciences*, *4*(7), 267–278.

Alpers, G. W., Gerdes, A. B., Lagarie, B., Tabbert, K., Vaitl, D., & Stark, R. (2009). Attention and amygdala activity: An fMRI study with spider pictures in spider phobia. *Journal of Neural Transmission*, *116*(6), 747–757.

American Psychiatric Association. (1995). *Diagnostic and statistical manual of mental disorders, fourth edition, primary care version*. Washington, DC: Author.

Amodio, D. M., & Frith, C. D. (2006). Meeting of minds: the medial frontal cortex and social cognition. *Nature Reviews Neuroscience*, *7*(4), 268–277.

Amstadter, A. (2008). Emotion regulation and anxiety disorders. *Journal of Anxiety Disorders*, *22*(2), 211–221.

Anderson, A. K., Christoff, K., Panitz, D., De Rosa, E., & Gabrieli, J. D. (2003). Neural correlates of the automatic processing of threat facial signals. *Journal of Neuroscience*, *23*(13), 5627–5633.

Anderson, A. K., Christoff, K., Stappen, I., Panitz, D., Ghahremani, D. G., Glover, G., et al. (2003). Dissociated neural representations of intensity and valence in human olfaction. *Nature Neuroscience*, *6*(2), 196–202.

Apkarian, A. V., Bushnell, M. C., Treede, R. D., & Zubieta, J. K. (2005). Human brain mechanisms of pain perception and regulation in health and disease. *European Journal of Pain*, *9*(4), 463–484.

Arnone, D., McIntosh, A. M., Ebmeier, K. P., Munafo, M. R., & Anderson, I. M. (2012). Magnetic resonance imaging studies in unipolar depression: systematic review and meta-regression analyses. *European Neuropsychopharmacology*, *22*(1), 1–16.

Aron, A. R., Robbins, T. W., & Poldrack, R. A. (2004). Inhibition and the right inferior frontal cortex. *Trends in Cognitive Sciences*, *8*(4), 170–177.

Atlas, L. Y., & Wager, T. D. (2012). How expectations shape pain. *Neuroscience Letters*.

Augustine, J. R. (1996). Circuitry and functional aspects of the insular lobe in primates including humans. *Brain Research Brain Research Review*, *22*(3), 229–244.

Badre, D., & Wagner, A. D. (2007). Left ventrolateral prefrontal cortex and the cognitive control of memory. *Neuropsychologia*, *45*(13), 2883–2901.

Barnea-Goraly, N., Menon, V., Eckert, M., Tamm, L., Bammer, R., Karchemskiy, A., et al. (2005). White matter development during childhood and adolescence: A cross-sectional diffusion tensor imaging study. *Cerebral Cortex*, *15*(12), 1848–1854.

Barrett, L. F., Mesquita, B., Ochsner, K. N., & Gross, J. J. (2007). The experience of emotion. *Annual Review of Psychology*, *58*, 373–403.

Baumeister, R. F., & Heatherton, T. F. (1996). Self-regulation failure: An overview. *Psychological Inquiry*, *7*, 1–15.

Beauregard, M., Levesque, J., & Bourgouin, P. (2001). Neural correlates of conscious self-regulation of emotion. *Journal of Neuroscience*, *21*(18), RC165.

Beauregard, M., Paquette, V., & Levesque, J. (2006). Dysfunction in the neural circuitry of emotional self-regulation in major depressive disorder. *Neuroreport*, *17*(8), 843–846.

Beck, A. T. (2005). The current state of cognitive therapy: A 40-year retrospective. *Archives of General Psychiatry*, *62*(9), 953–959.

Beer, J. S., Heerey, E. A., Keltner, D., Scabini, D., & Knight, R. T. (2003). The regulatory function of self-conscious emotion: insights from patients with orbitofrontal damage. *Journal of Personality and Social Psychology*, *85*(4), 594–604.

Berenbaum, H. (1996). Childhood abuse, alexithymia and personality disorder. *Journal of Psychosomatic Research*, *41*(6), 585–595.

Blair, K., Shaywitz, J., Smith, B. W., Rhodes, R., Geraci, M., Jones, M., et al. (2008). Response to emotional expressions in generalized social phobia and generalized anxiety disorder: Evidence for separate disorders. *American Journal of Psychiatry*, *165*(9), 1193–1202.

Blakemore, S. J. (2008). The social brain in adolescence. *Nature Reviews Neuroscience*, *9*(4), 267–277.

Bonanno, G. A., Papa, A., Lalande, K., Westphal, M., & Coifman, K. (2004). The importance of being flexible: The ability to both enhance and suppress emotional expression predicts long-term adjustment. *Psychological Science*, *15*(7), 482–487.

Bookheimer, S. (2002). Functional MRI of language: New approaches to understanding the cortical organization of semantic processing. *Annual Review of Neuroscience*, *25*, 151–188.

Botvinick, M. M., Braver, T. S., Barch, D. M., Carter, C. S., & Cohen, J. D. (2001). Conflict monitoring and cognitive control. *Psychological Review*, *108*(3), 624–652.

Botvinick, M. M., Cohen, J. D., & Carter, C. S. (2004). Conflict monitoring and anterior cingulate cortex: An update. *Trends in Cognitive Sciences*, *8*(12), 539–546.

Brefczynski-Lewis, J. A., Berrebi, M. E., McNeely, M. E., Prostko, A. L., & Puce, A. (2011). In the blink of an eye: Neural responses elicited to viewing the eye blinks of another individual. *Frontiers in Human Neuroscience*, *5*, 68.

Buchanan, S. L., & Powell, D. A. (1982a). Cingulate cortex: Its role in Pavlovian conditioning. *Journal of Comparative and Physiological Psychology*, *96*(5), 755–774.

Buchanan, S. L., & Powell, D. A. (1982b). Cingulate damage attenuates conditioned bradycardia. *Neuroscience Letters*, *29*(3), 261–268.

Buhle, J. T., Stevens, B. L., Friedman, J. J., & Wager, T. D. (2012). Distraction and placebo: Two separate routes to pain control. *Psychological Science*, *23*(3), 246–253.

Buhle, J. T., & Wager, T. D. (2009). Performance-dependent inhibition of pain by an executive working memory task. *Pain*, *149*(1), 19–26. .

Buhle, J. T., & Wager, T. D. (2010). Does meditation training lead to enduring changes in the anticipation and experience of pain? *Pain*, *150*(3), 382–383.

Buhle, J. T., Wager, T. D., & Smith, E. E. (2010). Using the Stroop task to study emotion regulation. In R. Hassin, K. N.

Ochsner, & Y. Trope (Eds.), *Self control in society, mind, and brain* (pp. 93–113). New York: Oxford University Press.

Burns, S. M., & Wyss, J. M. (1985). The involvement of the anterior cingulate cortex in blood pressure control. *Brain Research, 340*(1), 71–77.

Bush, G., Luu, P., & Posner, M. I. (2000). Cognitive and emotional influences in anterior cingulate cortex. *Trends in Cognitive Sciences, 4*(6), 215–222.

Calder, A. J., Lawrence, A. D., & Young, A. W. (2001). Neuropsychology of fear and loathing. *Nature Reviews Neuroscience, 2*(5), 352–363.

Carstensen, L. L., & Mikels, J. A. (2005). At the intersection of emotion and cognition: Aging and the positivity effect. *Current Directions in Psychological Science, 14*(3), 117–121.

Carstensen, L. L., Turan, B., Scheibe, S., Ram, N., Ersner-Hershfield, H., Samanez-Larkin, G. R., et al. (2011). Emotional experience improves with age: Evidence based on over 10 years of experience sampling. *Psychology and Aging, 26*(1), 21–33.

Carthy, T., Horesh, N., Apter, A., Edge, M. D., & Gross, J. J. (2010). Emotional reactivity and cognitive regulation in anxious children. *Behaviour Research and Therapy, 48*(5), 384–393.

Caseras, X., Mataix-Cols, D., Trasovares, M. V., Lopez-Sola, M., Ortriz, H., Pujol, J., et al. (2010). Dynamics of brain responses to phobic-related stimulation in specific phobia subtypes. *European Journal of Neuroscience, 32*(8), 1414–1422.

Casey, B. J., Getz, S., & Galvan, A. (2008). The adolescent brain. *Developmental Review, 28*(1), 62–77.

Casey, B. J., Jones, R. M., Levita, L., Libby, V., Pattwell, S. S., Ruberry, E. J., et al. (2010). The storm and stress of adolescence: Insights from human imaging and mouse genetics. *Developmental Psychobiology, 52*(3), 225–235.

Casey, B. J., Tottenham, N., Liston, C., & Durston, S. (2005). Imaging the developing brain: What have we learned about cognitive development? *Trends in Cognitive Sciences, 9*(3), 104–110.

Champod, A. S., & Petrides, M. (2010). Dissociation within the frontoparietal network in verbal working memory: A parametric functional magnetic resonance imaging study. *Journal of Neuroscience, 30*(10), 3849–3856.

Chandler, R. K., Fletcher, B. W., & Volkow, N. D. (2009). Treating drug abuse and addiction in the criminal justice system: Improving public health and safety. *JAMA: Journal of the American Medical Association, 301*(2), 183–190.

Corbetta, M., & Shulman, G. L. (2002). Control of goal-directed and stimulus-driven attention in the brain. *Nature Reviews Neuroscience, 3*(3), 201–215

Craig, A. D. (2009). How do you feel—now? The anterior insula and human awareness. *Nature Reviews Neuroscience, 10*(1), 59–70.

Critchley, H. D., Wiens, S., Rotshtein, P., Ohman, A., & Dolan, R. J. (2004). Neural systems supporting interoceptive awareness. *Nature Neuroscience, 7*(2), 189–195.

Cunningham, W. A., Arbuckle, N. L., Jahn, A., Mowrer, S. M., & Abduljalil, A. M. (2011). Aspects of neuroticism and the amygdala: Chronic tuning from motivational styles. *Neuropsychologia, 48*(12), 3399–3404.

Cunningham, W. A., Johnsen, I. R., & Waggoner, A. S. (2011). Orbitofrontal cortex provides cross-modal valuation of self-generated stimuli. *Social Cognitive and Affective Neuroscience, 6*(3), 286–293.

Cunningham, W. A., Van Bavel, J. J., & Johnsen, I. R. (2008). Affective flexibility: Evaluative processing goals shape amygdala activity. *Psychological Science, 19*(2), 152–160.

Damasio, A. (1994). *Descartes' error: Emotion, reason, and the human brain*. New York: G.P. Putnam.

Damsa, C., Kosel, M., & Moussally, J. (2009). Current status of brain imaging in anxiety disorders. *Current Opinion in Psychiatry, 22*(1), 96–110.

Davachi, L. (2006). Item, context and relational episodic encoding in humans. *Current Opinion in Neurobiology, 16*(6), 693–700.

Davidson, R. J., & Sutton, S. K. (1995). Affective neuroscience: The emergence of a discipline. *Current Opinion in Neurobiology, 5*(2), 217–224.

Davis, J. I., Gross, J. J., & Ochsner, K. N. (2011). Psychological distance and emotional experience: What you see is what you get. *Emotion, 11*(2), 438–444.

Davis, J. I., Senghas, A., & Ochsner, K. N. (2009). How does facial feedback modulate emotional experience? *Journal of Research in Personality, 43*(5), 822–829.

Davis, M., & Whalen, P. J. (2001). The amygdala: Vigilance and emotion. *Molecular Psychiatry, 6*(1), 13–34.

Delgado, M. R., Jou, R. L., Ledoux, J. E., & Phelps, E. A. (2009). Avoiding negative outcomes: Tracking the mechanisms of avoidance learning in humans during fear conditioning. *Frontiers in Behavioral Neuroscience, 3*, 33.

Delvecchio, G., Fossati, P., Boyer, P., Brambilla, P., Falkai, P., Gruber, O., et al. (2012). Common and distinct neural correlates of emotional processing in bipolar disorder and major depressive disorder: A voxel-based meta-analysis of functional magnetic resonance imaging studies. *European Neuropsychopharmacology, 22*(2), 100–113.

Denny, B. T., Kober, H., Wager, T. D., & Ochsner, K. N. (2012). A meta-analysis of functional neuroimaging studies of self- and other judgments reveals a spatial gradient for mentalizing in medial prefrontal cortex. *Journal of Cognitive Neuroscience, 24*(8), 1742–1752.

Denny, B. T., Silvers, J. A., & Ochsner, K. N. (2009). How we heal what we don't want to feel: The functional neural architecture of emotion regulation. In A. M. Kring & D. M. Sloan (Eds.), *Emotion regulation and psychopathology: A transdiagnostic approach to etiology and treatment* (pp. 59–87). New York: Guilford Press.

Diekhof, E. K., Geier, K., Falkai, P., & Gruber, O. (2011). Fear is only as deep as the mind allows: A coordinate-based meta-analysis of neuroimaging studies on the regulation of negative affect. *Neuroimage, 58*(1), 275–285.

Dilger, S., Straube, T., Mentzel, H. J., Fitzek, C., Reichenbach, J. R., Hecht, H., et al. (2003). Brain activation to phobia-related pictures in spider phobic humans: An event-related functional magnetic resonance imaging study. *Neuroscience Letters, 348*(1), 29–32.

Domes, G., Grabe, H. J., Czieschnek, D., Heinrichs, M., & Herpertz, S. C. (2011). Alexithymic traits and facial emotion recognition in borderline personality disorder. *Psychotherapy and Psychosomatics, 80*(6), 383–385.

Domes, G., Schulze, L., Bottger, M., Grossmann, A., Hauenstein, K., Wirtz, P. H., et al. (2010). The neural correlates of sex differences in emotional reactivity and emotion regulation. *Human Brain Mapping, 31*(5), 758–769.

Donegan, N. H., Sanislow, C. A., Blumberg, H. P., Fulbright, R. K., Lacadie, C., Skudlarski, P., et al. (2003). Amygdala hyperreactivity in borderline personality disorder: Implications for emotional dysregulation. *Biological Psychiatry*, *54*(11), 1284–1293.

Drevets, W. C., & Todd, R. D. (1997). Depression, mania and other related disorders. In S. B. Guze (Ed.), *Adult psychiatry*. St. Louis, MO: Mosby.

Durston, S., & Casey, B. J. (2006). What have we learned about cognitive development from neuroimaging? *Neuropsychologia*, *44*(11), 2149–2157.

Durston, S., Davidson, M. C., Tottenham, N., Galvan, A., Spicer, J., Fossella, J. A., et al. (2006). A shift from diffuse to focal cortical activity with development. *Developmental Science*, *9*(1), 1–8.

Eippert, F., Veit, R., Weiskopf, N., Erb, M., Birbaumer, N., & Anders, S. (2007). Regulation of emotional responses elicited by threat-related stimuli. *Human Brain Mapping*, *28*(5), 409–423.

Erk, S., Mikschl, A., Stier, S., Ciaramidaro, A., Gapp, V., Weber, B., et al. (2010). Acute and sustained effects of cognitive emotion regulation in major depression. *Journal of Neuroscience*, *30*(47), 15726–15734.

Erk, S., von Kalckreuth, A., & Walter, H. (2010). Neural long-term effects of emotion regulation on episodic memory processes. *Neuropsychologia*, *48*(4), 989–996.

Ernst, M., Nelson, E. E., Jazbec, S., McClure, E. B., Monk, C. S., Leibenluft, E., et al. (2005). Amygdala and nucleus accumbens in responses to receipt and omission of gains in adults and adolescents. *Neuroimage*, *25*(4), 1279–1291.

Etkin, A., Egner, T., & Kalisch, R. (2011). Emotional processing in anterior cingulate and medial prefrontal cortex. *Trends in Cognitive Sciences*, *15*(2), 85–93.

Etkin, A., Egner, T., Peraza, D. M., Kandel, E. R., & Hirsch, J. (2006). Resolving emotional conflict: A role for the rostral anterior cingulate cortex in modulating activity in the amygdala. *Neuron*, *51*(6), 871–882.

Etkin, A., & Schatzberg, A. F. (2011). Common abnormalities and disorder-specific compensation during implicit regulation of emotional processing in generalized anxiety and major depressive disorders. *Am Journal of Psychiatry*, *168*(9), 968–978.

Etkin, A., & Wager, T. D. (2007). Functional neuroimaging of anxiety: A meta-analysis of emotional processing in PTSD, social anxiety disorder, and specific phobia. *American Journal of Psychiatry*, *164*(10), 1476–1488.

Evans, K. C., Wright, C. I., Wedig, M. M., Gold, A. L., Pollack, M. H., & Rauch, S. L. (2008). A functional MRI study of amygdala responses to angry schematic faces in social anxiety disorder. *Depression and Anxiety*, *25*(6), 496–505.

Everitt, B. J., Parkinson, J. A., Olmstead, M. C., Arroyo, M., Robledo, P., & Robbins, T. W. (1999). Associative processes in addiction and reward. The role of amygdala-ventral striatal subsystems. *Annals of New York Academy of Science*, *877*, 412–438.

Fellows, L. K. (2011). Orbitofrontal contributions to value-based decision making: Evidence from humans with frontal lobe damage. *Annals of New York Academy of Science*, *1239*, 51–58.

Fjell, A. M., Westlye, L. T., Amlien, I., Espeseth, T., Reinvang, I., Raz, N., et al. (2009). High consistency of regional cortical thinning in aging across multiple samples. *Cerebral Cortex*, *19*(9), 2001–2012.

Galvan, A., Hare, T. A., Parra, C. E., Penn, J., Voss, H., Glover, G., et al. (2006). Earlier development of the accumbens relative to orbitofrontal cortex might underlie risk-taking behavior in adolescents. *Journal of Neuroscience*, *26*(25), 6885–6892.

Gehring, W. J., & Knight, R. T. (2000). Prefrontal-cingulate interactions in action monitoring. *Nature Neuroscience*, *3*(5), 516–520.

Geier, C. F., Terwilliger, R., Teslovich, T., Velanova, K., & Luna, B. (2009). Immaturities in reward processing and its influence on inhibitory control in adolescence. *Cerebral Cortex*, *20*(7), 1623–1629.

Giedd, J. N., Blumenthal, J., Jeffries, N. O., Castellanos, F. X., Liu, H., Zijdenbos, A., et al. (1999). Brain development during childhood and adolescence: A longitudinal MRI study. *Nature Neuroscience*, *2*(10), 861–863.

Giedd, J. N., Vaituzis, A. C., Hamburger, S. D., Lange, N., Rajapakse, J. C., Kaysen, D., et al. (1996). Quantitative MRI of the temporal lobe, amygdala, and hippocampus in normal human development: Ages 4-18 years. *Journal of Comparative Neurology*, *366*(2), 223–230.

Gogtay, N., Giedd, J. N., Lusk, L., Hayashi, K. M., Greenstein, D., Vaituzis, A. C., et al. (2004). Dynamic mapping of human cortical development during childhood through early adulthood. *Proceedings of the National Academy of Sciences U S A*, *101*(21), 8174–8179.

Goldin, P. R., Manber, T., Hakimi, S., Canli, T., & Gross, J. J. (2009). Neural bases of social anxiety disorder: Emotional reactivity and cognitive regulation during social and physical threat. *Archives of General Psychiatry*, *66*(2), 170–180.

Goldin, P. R., Manber-Ball, T., Werner, K., Heimberg, R., & Gross, J. J. (2009). Neural mechanisms of cognitive reappraisal of negative self-beliefs in social anxiety disorder. *Biological Psychiatry*, *66*(12), 1091–1099

Goldin, P. R., McRae, K., Ramel, W., & Gross, J. J. (2008). The neural bases of emotion regulation: Reappraisal and suppression of negative emotion. *Biological Psychiatry*, *63*(6), 577–586.

Goossens, L., Schruers, K., Peeters, R., Griez, E., & Sunaert, S. (2007). Visual presentation of phobic stimuli: Amygdala activation via an extrageniculostriate pathway? *Psychiatry Research*, *155*(2), 113–120.

Gross, J. J. (1998a). Antecedent- and response-focused emotion regulation: Divergent consequences for experience, expression, and physiology. *Journal of Personality and Social Psychology*, *74*(1), 224–237.

Gross, J. J. (1998b). The emerging field of emotion regulation: An integrative review. *Review of General Psychological*, *2*, 271–299.

Gross, J. J., Carstensen, L. L., Pasupathi, M., Tsai, J., Skorpen, C. G., & Hsu, A. Y. (1997). Emotion and aging: Experience, expression, and control. *Psychological Aging*, *12*(4), 590–599.

Gross, J. J., & Thompson, R. A. (2007). *Handbook of emotion regulation*. New York: Guilford Press.

Gunderson, J. G. (2007). Disturbed relationships as a phenotype for borderline personality disorder. *American Journal of Psychiatry*, *164*(11), 1637–1640.

Gunderson, J. G., & Lyons-Ruth, K. (2008). BPD's interpersonal hypersensitivity phenotype: A gene-environment-developmental model. *Journal of Personal Disorders*, *22*(1), 22–41.

Gupta, S., Zachary Rosenthal, M., Mancini, A. D., Cheavens, J. S., & Lynch, T. R. (2008). Emotion regulation skills mediate the effects of shame on eating disorder symptoms in women. *Eating Disorders*, *16*(5), 405–417.

Gutchess, A. H., Kensinger, E. A., & Schacter, D. L. (2007). Aging, self-referencing, and medial prefrontal cortex. *Social Neuroscience*, 2(2), 117–133.

Hamilton, J., Siemer, M., & Gotlib, I. (2008). Amygdala volume in major depressive disorder: A meta-analysis of magnetic resonance imaging studies. *Molecular Psychiatry*, 13, 993–1000.

Hamilton, J. P., Etkin, A., Furman, D. J., Lemus, M. G., Johnson, R. F., & Gotlib, I. H. (2012). Functional neuroimaging of major depressive disorder: A meta-analysis and new integration of baseline activation and neural response data. *American Journal of Psychiatry*, 169(7), 693–703.

Hare, T. A., Camerer, C. F., & Rangel, A. (2009). Self-control in decision-making involves modulation of the vmPFC valuation system. *Science*, 324(5927), 646–648.

Hare, T. A., Tottenham, N., Galvan, A., Voss, H. U., Glover, G. H., & Casey, B. J. (2008). Biological substrates of emotional reactivity and regulation in adolescence during an emotional go–no-go task. *Biological Psychiatry*, 63(10), 927–934.

Harenski, C. L., & Hamann, S. (2006). Neural correlates of regulating negative emotions related to moral violations. *Neuroimage*, 30(1), 313–324.

Hariri, A. R., & Whalen, P. J. (2011). The amygdala: Inside and out. *F1000 Biology Reports*, 3, 2.

Hayes, J. P., Morey, R. A., Petty, C. M., Seth, S., Smoski, M. J., McCarthy, G., et al. (2010). Staying cool when things get hot: Emotion regulation modulates neural mechanisms of memory encoding. *Frontiers in Human Neuroscience*, 4, 230.

Heller, A. S., Johnstone, T., Shackman, A. J., Light, S. N., Peterson, M. J., Kolden, G. G., et al. (2009). Reduced capacity to sustain positive emotion in major depression reflects diminished maintenance of fronto-striatal brain activation. *Proceedings of the National Academy of Sciences U S A*, 106(52), 22445–22450.

Herman, C. P., Polivy, J., Lank, C. N., & Heatherton, T. F. (1987). Anxiety, hunger, and eating behavior. *Journal of Abnormal Psychology*, 96, 264–269.

Hermann, A., Schafer, A., Walter, B., Stark, R., Vaitl, D., & Schienle, A. (2009). Emotion regulation in spider phobia: Role of the medial prefrontal cortex. *Social Cognitive Affective Neuroscience*, 4(3), 257–267.

Herpertz, S. C., Dietrich, T. M., Wenning, B., Krings, T., Erberich, S. G., Willmes, K., et al. (2001). Evidence of abnormal amygdala functioning in borderline personality disorder: A functional MRI study. *Biological Psychiatry*, 50(4), 292–298.

Herwig, U., Baumgartner, T., Kaffenberger, T., Bruhl, A., Kottlow, M., Schreiter Gasser, U., et al. (2007). Modulation of anticipatory emotion and perception processing by cognitive control. *Neuroimage*, 37(2), 652–662.

Hinke, R. M., Hu, X., Stillman, A. E., Kim, S. G., Merkle, H., Salmi, R., et al. (1993). Functional magnetic resonance imaging of Broca's area during internal speech. *Neuroreport*, 4(6), 675–678.

Hollmann, M., Hellrung, L., Pleger, B., Schlogl, H., Kabisch, S., Stumvoll, M., et al. (2012). Neural correlates of the volitional regulation of the desire for food. *International Journal of Obesity* (London), 36(5), 648–655.

Houben, K., & Wiers, R. W. (2009). Response inhibition moderates the relationship between implicit associations and drinking behavior. *Alcohol Clinical Experimental Research*, 33(4), 626–633.

Huang, J., Carr, T. H., & Cao, Y. (2002). Comparing cortical activations for silent and overt speech using event-related fMRI. *Human Brain Mapping*, 15(1), 39–53.

Hurley-Gius, K. M., & Neafsey, E. J. (1986). The medial frontal cortex and gastric motility: Microstimulation results and their possible significance for the overall pattern of organization of rat frontal and parietal cortex. *Brain Research*, 365(2), 241–248.

Ichikawa, N., Siegle, G. J., Jones, N. P., Kamishima, K., Thompson, W. K., Gross, J. J., et al. (2011). Feeling bad about screwing up: Emotion regulation and action monitoring in the anterior cingulate cortex. *Cognitive, Affective, and Behavioral Neuroscience*, 11(3), 354–371.

Jackson, D. C., Malmstadt, J. R., Larson, C. L., & Davidson, R. J. (2000). Suppression and enhancement of emotional responses to unpleasant pictures. *Psychophysiology*, 37(4), 515–522.

Johnstone, T., van Reekum, C. M., Urry, H. L., Kalin, N. H., & Davidson, R. J. (2007). Failure to regulate: Counterproductive recruitment of top-down prefrontal-subcortical circuitry in major depression. *Journal of Neuroscience*, 27(33), 8877–8884.

Kaada, B. R., Pribram, K. H., & Epstein, J. A. (1949). Respiratory and vascular responses in monkeys from temporal pole, insula, orbital surface and cingulate gyrus; a preliminary report. *Journal of Neurophysiology*, 12(5), 347–356.

Kalisch, R., Wiech, K., Critchley, H. D., Seymour, B., O'Doherty, J. P., Oakley, D. A., et al. (2005). Anxiety reduction through detachment: Subjective, physiological, and neural effects. *Journal of Cognitive Neuroscience*, 17(6), 874–883.

Kanske, P., Heissler, J., Schonfelder, S., Bongers, A., & Wessa, M. (2011). How to regulate emotion? Neural networks for reappraisal and distraction. *Cerebral Cortex*, 21(6), 1379–1388.

Kempton, M. J., Salvador, Z., Munafo, M. R., Geddes, J. R., Simmons, A., Frangou, S., et al. (2011). Structural neuroimaging studies in major depressive disorder. Meta-analysis and comparison with bipolar disorder. *Archives of General Psychiatry*, 68(7), 675–690.

Kensinger, E. A., & Schacter, D. L. (2008). Neural processes supporting young and older adults' emotional memories. *Journal of Cognitive Neuroscience*, 20(7), 1161–1173.

Kessler, R. C., Berglund, P., Demler, O., Jin, R., Merikangas, K. R., & Walters, E. E. (2005). Lifetime prevalence and age-of-onset distributions of DSM-IV disorders in the National Comorbidity Survey Replication. *Archives of General Psychiatry*, 62(6), 593–602.

Killgore, W. D., & Yurgelun-Todd, D. A. (2001). Sex differences in amygdala activation during the perception of facial affect. *Neuroreport*, 12(11), 2543–2547.

Killgore, W. D., & Yurgelun-Todd, D. A. (2007). Unconscious processing of facial affect in children and adolescents. *Social Neuroscience*, 2(1), 28–47.

Kim, S. H., & Hamann, S. (2007). Neural correlates of positive and negative emotion regulation. *Journal of Cognitive Neuroscience*, 19(5), 1–23.

Klumpp, H., Angstadt, M., & Phan, K. L. (2012). Insula reactivity and connectivity to anterior cingulate cortex when processing threat in generalized social anxiety disorder. *Biological Psychology*, 89(1), 273–276.

Knutson, B., & Cooper, J. C. (2005). Functional magnetic resonance imaging of reward prediction. *Current Opinion in Neurology*, 18(4), 411–417.

Kober, H., Mende-Siedlecki, P., Kross, E. F., Weber, J., Mischel, W., Hart, C. L., et al. (2010). Prefrontal-striatal pathway underlies cognitive regulation of craving. *Proceeding of the National Academy of Sciences U S A, 107*(33), 14811–14816.

Koenigsberg, H. W., Fan, J., Ochsner, K. N., Liu, X., Guise, K. G., Pizzarello, S., et al. (2009). Neural correlates of the use of psychological distancing to regulate responses to negative social cues: A study of patients with borderline personality disorder. *Biological Psychiatry, 66*(9), 854–863.

Koenigsberg, H. W., Fan, J., Ochsner, K. N., Liu, X., Guise, K. G., Pizzarello, S., et al. (2010). Neural correlates of using distancing to regulate emotional responses to social cues. *Neuropsychologia, 48*(6), 1813–1822.

Koenigsberg, H. W., Harvey, P. D., Mitropoulou, V., New, A. S., Goodman, M., Silverman, J., et al. (2001). Are the interpersonal and identity disturbances in the borderline personality disorder criteria linked to the traits of affective instability and impulsivity? *Journal of Personality Disorders, 15*(4), 358–370.

Koenigsberg, H. W., Siever, L. J., Lee, H., Pizzarello, S., New, A. S., Goodman, M., et al. (2009). Neural correlates of emotion processing in borderline personality disorder. *Psychiatry Research, 172*(3), 192–199.

Konishi, S., Nakajima, K., Uchida, I., Kikyo, H., Kameyama, M., & Miyashita, Y. (1999). Common inhibitory mechanism in human inferior prefrontal cortex revealed by event-related functional MRI. *Brain, 122*(Pt 5), 981–991.

Krendl, A. C., Kensinger, E. A., & Ambady, N. (2012). How does the brain regulate negative bias to stigma? *Social, Cognitive, and Affective Neuroscience, 7*(6), 715–726.

Kross, E., & Ayduk, O. (2008). Facilitating adaptive emotional analysis: Distinguishing distanced-analysis of depressive experiences from immersed-analysis and distraction. *Personality and Social Psychology Bulletin, 34*(7), 924–938.

Kross, E., Davidson, M., Weber, J., & Ochsner, K. (2009). Coping with emotions past: The neural bases of regulating affect associated with negative autobiographical memories. *Biological Psychiatry, 65*(5), 361–366.

Kuhn, S., & Gallinat, J. (2013). Resting-state brain activity in schizophrenia and major depression: A quantitative meta-analysis. *Schizophrenia Bulletin, 39*(2), 358–365.

Labuschagne, I., Phan, K. L., Wood, A., Angstadt, M., Chua, P., Heinrichs, M., et al. (2010). Oxytocin attenuates amygdala reactivity to fear in generalized social anxiety disorder. *Neuropsychopharmacology, 35*(12), 2403–2413.

Lang, P. J., Greenwald, M. K., Bradley, M. M., & Hamm, A. O. (1993). Looking at pictures: Affective, facial, visceral, and behavioral reactions. *Psychophysiology, 30*(3), 261–273.

Lang, S., Kotchoubey, B., Frick, C., Spitzer, C., Grabe, H. J., & Barnow, S. (2011). Cognitive reappraisal in trauma-exposed women with borderline personality disorder. *Neuroimage, 59*(2), 1727–1734.

Larson, C. L., Schaefer, H. S., Siegle, G. J., Jackson, C. A., Anderle, M. J., & Davidson, R. J. (2006). Fear is fast in phobic individuals: amygdala activation in response to fear-relevant stimuli. *Biological Psychiatry, 60*(4), 410–417.

Larson, R. W., Moneta, G., Richards, M. H., & Wilson, S. (2002). Continuity, stability, and change in daily emotional experience across adolescence. *Child Development, 73*(4), 1151–1165.

Leclerc, C. M., & Kensinger, E. A. (2008). Age-related differences in medial prefrontal activation in response to emotional images. *Cognitive, Affective, and Behavioral Neuroscience, 8*(2), 153–164.

Leclerc, C. M., & Kensinger, E. A. (2011). Neural processing of emotional pictures and words: A comparison of young and older adults. *Developmental Neuropsychology, 36*(4), 519–538.

LeDoux, J. E., & Gorman, J. M. (2001). A call to action: Overcoming anxiety through active coping. *American Journal of Psychiatry, 158*(12), 1953–1955.

Levenson, R. W., Carstensen, L. L., & Gottman, J. M. (1994). The influence of age and gender on affect, physiology, and their interrelations: A study of long-term marriages. *Journal of of Personality and Social Psychology, 67*(1), 56–68.

Levesque, J., Eugene, F., Joanette, Y., Paquette, V., Mensour, B., Beaudoin, G., et al. (2003). Neural circuitry underlying voluntary suppression of sadness. *Biological Psychiatry, 53*(6), 502–510.

Levesque, J., Joanette, Y., Mensour, B., Beaudoin, G., Leroux, J. M., Bourgouin, P., et al. (2004). Neural basis of emotional self-regulation in childhood. *Neuroscience, 129*(2), 361–369.

Lieberman, M. D., Eisenberger, N. I., Crockett, M. J., Tom, S. M., Pfeifer, J. H., & Way, B. M. (2007). Putting feelings into words: Affect labeling disrupts amygdala activity in response to affective stimuli. *Psychological Science, 18*(5), 421–428.

Light, S. N., Heller, A. S., Johnstone, T., Kolden, G. G., Peterson, M. J., Kalin, N. H., et al. (2012). Reduced right ventrolateral prefrontal cortex activity while inhibiting positive affect is associated with improvement in hedonic capacity after 8 weeks of antidepressant treatment in major depressive disorder. *Biological Psychiatry, 70*(10), 962–968.

Linehan, M. M. (1993). *Cognitive-behavioral treatment of borderline personality disorder.* New York: Guilford Press.

Lipka, J., Miltner, W. H., & Straube, T. (2011). Vigilance for threat interacts with amygdala responses to subliminal threat cues in specific phobia. *Biological Psychiatry, 70*(5), 472–478.

Lorberbaum, J. P., Kose, S., Johnson, M. R., Arana, G. W., Sullivan, L. K., Hamner, M. B., et al. (2004). Neural correlates of speech anticipatory anxiety in generalized social phobia. *Neuroreport, 15*(18), 2701–2705.

Luna, B., Padmanabhan, A., & O'Hearn, K. (2010). What has fMRI told us about the development of cognitive control through adolescence? *Brain and Cognition, 72*(1), 101–113.

Lynch, T. R., Trost, W. T., Salsman, N., & Linehan, M. M. (2007). Dialectical behavior therapy for borderline personality disorder. *Annual Review of Clinical Psychology, 3*, 181–205.

MacDonald, A. W., Cohen, J. D., Stenger, V. A., & Carter, C. S. (2000). Dissociating the role of the dorsolateral prefrontal and anterior cingulate cortex in cognitive control. *Science, 288*(5472), 1835–1838.

Macnamara, A., Ochsner, K. N., & Hajcak, G. (2011). Previously reappraised: The lasting effect of description type on picture-elicited electrocortical activity. *Social, Cognitive & Affective Neuroscience, 6*(3), 348–358.

Mak, A. K., Hu, Z. G., Zhang, J. X., Xiao, Z. W., & Lee, T. M. (2009). Neural correlates of regulation of positive and negative emotions: An fMRI study. *Neuroscience Letters, 457*(2), 101–106.

Mather, M. (2012). The emotion paradox in the aging brain. *Annals of the New York Academy of Sciences, 1251*, 33–49.

Mauss, I. B., Levenson, R. W., McCarter, L., Wilhelm, F. H., & Gross, J. J. (2005). The tie that binds? Coherence among emotion experience, behavior, and physiology. *Emotion*, 5(2), 175–190.

McClure, E. B., Monk, C. S., Nelson, E. E., Parrish, J. M., Adler, A., Blair, R. J. R., et al. (2007). Abnormal attention modulation of fear circuit function in pediatric generalized anxiety disorder. *Archives of General Psychiatry*, 64(1), 97–106.

McRae, K., Ciesielski, B., & Gross, J. J. (2012). Unpacking cognitive reappraisal: Goals, tactics, and outcomes. *Emotion*, 12(2), 250–255.

McRae, K., Gross, J. J., Weber, J., Robertson, E. R., Sokol-Hessner, P., Ray, R. D., et al. (2012). The development of emotion regulation: An fMRI study of cognitive reappraisal in children, adolescents and young adults. *Social, Cognitive & Affective Neuroscience*, 7(1), 11–22.

McRae, K., Hughes, B., Chopra, S., Gabrieli, J. D., Gross, J. J., & Ochsner, K. N. (2010). The neural bases of distraction and reappraisal. *Journal of Cognitive Neuroscience*, 22(2), 248–262.

McRae, K., Misra, S., Prasad, A. K., Pereira, S. C., & Gross, J. J. (2012). Bottom-up and top-down emotion generation: Implications for emotion regulation. *Social, Cognitive & Affective Neuroscience*, 7(3), 253–262.

McRae, K., Reiman, E. M., Fort, C. L., Chen, K., & Lane, R. D. (2008). Association between trait emotional awareness and dorsal anterior cingulate activity during emotion is arousal-dependent. *Neuroimage*, 41(2), 648–655.

Meissner, K., Bingel, U., Colloca, L., Wager, T. D., Watson, A., & Flaten, M. A. (2011). The placebo effect: Advances from different methodological approaches. *Journal of Neuroscience*, 31(45), 16117–16124.

Miller, E. K. (2000). The prefrontal cortex and cognitive control. *Nature Reviews Neuroscience*, 1(1), 59–65.

Miller, E. K., & Cohen, J. D. (2001). An integrative theory of prefrontal cortex function. *Annual Review of Neuroscience*, 24, 167–202.

Minzenberg, M. J., Fan, J., New, A. S., Tang, C. Y., & Siever, L. J. (2007). Fronto-limbic dysfunction in response to facial emotion in borderline personality disorder: An event-related fMRI study. *Psychiatry Research*, 155(3), 231–243.

Mitchell, J. P. (2009). Inferences about mental states. *Philosophy Transactions of the Royal Society of London. Series B Biological Sciences*, 364(1521), 1309–1316.

Modinos, G., Ormel, J., & Aleman, A. (2010). Individual differences in dispositional mindfulness and brain activity involved in reappraisal of emotion. *Social, Cognitive & Affective Neuroscience*, 5(4), 369–377.

Monk, C. S., Grillon, C., Baas, J. M., McClure, E. B., Nelson, E. E., Zarahn, E., et al. (2003). A neuroimaging method for the study of threat in adolescents. *Developmental Psychobiology*, 43(4), 359–366.

Moore, B., Mischel, W., & Zeiss, A. (1976). Comparative effects of the reward stimulus and its cognitive representation in voluntary delay. *Journal of Personality and Social Psychology*, 34(3), 419–424.

Moriguchi, Y., Decety, J., Ohnishi, T., Maeda, M., Mori, T., Nemoto, K., et al. (2007). Empathy and judging other's pain: An fMRI study of alexithymia. *Cerebral Cortex*, 17(9), 2223–2234.

Moriguchi, Y., Ohnishi, T., Lane, R. D., Maeda, M., Mori, T., Nemoto, K., et al. (2006). Impaired self-awareness and theory of mind: An fMRI study of mentalizing in alexithymia. *Neuroimage*, 32(3), 1472–1482.

Mufson, E. J., & Mesulam, M. M. (1982). Insula of the old world monkey. II: Afferent cortical input and comments on the claustrum. *Journal of Comparative Neurology*, 212(1), 23–37.

Murphy, B. C., Eisenberg, N., Fabes, R. A., Shepard, S., & Guthrie, I. K. (1999). Consistency and change in children's emotionality and regulation: A longitudinal study. *Merrill-Palmer Quarterly Journal of Developmental Psychology*, 45(3), 413–444.

Murray, E. A., O'Doherty, J. P., & Schoenbaum, G. (2007). What we know and do not know about the functions of the orbitofrontal cortex after 20 years of cross-species studies. *Journal of Neuroscience*, 27(31), 8166–8169.

Naccache, L., Dehaene, S., Cohen, L., Habert, M. O., Guichart-Gomez, E., Galanaud, D., et al. (2005). Effortless control: Executive attention and conscious feeling of mental effort are dissociable. *Neuropsychologia*, 43(9), 1318–1328.

Nashiro, K., Sakaki, M., & Mather, M. (2012). Age differences in brain activity during emotion processing: Reflections of age-related decline or increased emotion regulation? *Gerontology*, 58(2), 156–163.

Neafsey, E. J. (1990). Prefrontal cortical control of the autonomic nervous system: Anatomical and physiological observations. *Progress in Brain Research*, 85, 147–165; discussion 165–146.

Neta, M., & Whalen, P. J. (2011). The primacy of negative interpretations when resolving the valence of ambiguous facial expressions. *Psychological Science*, 21(7), 901–907.

New, A. S., Fan, J., Murrough, J. W., Liu, X., Liebman, R. E., Guise, K. G., et al. (2009). A functional magnetic resonance imaging study of deliberate emotion regulation in resilience and posttraumatic stress disorder. *Biological Psychiatry*, 66(7), 656–664.

New, A. S., Hazlett, E. A., Newmark, R. E., Zhang, J., Triebwasser, J., Meyerson, D., et al. (2009). Laboratory induced aggression: A positron emission tomography study of aggressive individuals with borderline personality disorder. *Biological Psychiatry*, 66(12), 1107–1114.

Nitschke, J. B., Sarinopoulos, I., Mackiewicz, K. L., Schaefer, H. S., & Davidson, R. J. (2006). Functional neuroanatomy of aversion and its anticipation. *Neuroimage*, 29(1), 106–116.

Nitschke, J. B., Sarinopoulos, I., Oathes, D. J., Johnstone, T., Whalen, P. J., Davidson, R. J., et al. (2009). Anticipatory activation in the amygdala and anterior cingulate in generalized anxiety disorder and prediction of treatment response. *American Journal of Psychiatry*, 166(3), 302–310.

Nunes, P. M., Wenzel, A., Borges, K. T., Porto, C. R., Caminha, R. M., & de Oliveira, I. R. (2009). Volumes of the hippocampus and amygdala in patients with borderline personality disorder: A meta-analysis. *Journal of Personality Disorders*, 23(4), 333–345.

Ochsner, K. N. (2005). Characterizing the functional architecture of affect regulation: Emerging answers and outstanding questions. In J. T. Cacioppo (Ed.), *Social neuroscience: People thinking about people* (pp. 245–268). Cambridge, MA: MIT Press.

Ochsner, K. N., & Barrett, L. F. (2001). A multiprocess perspective on the neuroscience of emotion. In T. J. Mayne & G. A. Bonanno (Eds.), *Emotions: Current issues and future directions* (pp. 38–81). New York, NY: The Guilford Press.

Ochsner, K. N., Bunge, S. A., Gross, J. J., & Gabrieli, J. D. (2002). Rethinking feelings: An FMRI study of the cognitive regulation of emotion. *Journal of Cognitive Neuroscience*, 14(8), 1215–1229.

Ochsner, K. N., & Gross, J. J. (2004). Thinking makes it so: A social cognitive neuroscience approach to emotion regulation. In R. F. Baumeister & K. D. Vohs (Eds.), *Handbook of self-regulation: Research, theory, and applications* (pp. 229–255).

Ochsner, K. N., & Gross, J. J. (2005). The cognitive control of emotion. *Trends in Cognitive Sciences, 9*(5), 242–249.

Ochsner, K. N., & Gross, J. J. (2008). Cognitive emotion regulation: Insights from social cognitive and affective neuroscience. *Currents Directions in Psychological Science, 17*(1), 153–158.

Ochsner, K. N., Kosslyn, S. M., Cosgrove, G. R., Cassem, E. H., Price, B. H., Nierenberg, A. A., et al. (2001). Deficits in visual cognition and attention following bilateral anterior cingulotomy. *Neuropsychologia, 39*(3), 219–230.

Ochsner, K. N., Ray, R. D., Cooper, J. C., Robertson, E. R., Chopra, S., Gabrieli, J. D. E., et al. (2004). For better or for worse: Neural systems supporting the cognitive down- and up-regulation of negative emotion. *Neuroimage, 23*(2), 483–499.

Ochsner, K. N., Ray, R. R., Hughes, B., McRae, K., Cooper, J. C., Weber, J., et al. (2009). Bottom-up and top-down processes in emotion generation: Common and distinct neural mechanisms. *Psychological Science, 20*(11), 1322–1331.

Ochsner, K. N., Silvers, J. A., & Buhle, J. T. (2012). Functional imaging studies of emotion regulation: A synthetic review and evolving model of the cognitive control of emotion. *Annals of the New York Academy of Sciences, 1251*, E1–E24.

O'Doherty, J. P. (2004). Reward representations and reward-related learning in the human brain: Insights from neuroimaging. *Current Opinion in Neurobiology, 14*(6), 769–776.

Ohira, H., Nomura, M., Ichikawa, N., Isowa, T., Iidaka, T., Sato, A., et al. (2006). Association of neural and physiological responses during voluntary emotion suppression. *Neuroimage, 29*(3), 721–733.

Olson, I. R., Plotzker, A., & Ezzyat, Y. (2007). The enigmatic temporal pole: A review of findings on social and emotional processing. *Brain, 130*(Pt 7), 1718–1731.

Olsson, A., & Ochsner, K. N. (2008). The role of social cognition in emotion. *Trends in Cognitive Sciences, 12*(2), 65–71.

Ongur, D., Ferry, A. T., & Price, J. L. (2003). Architectonic subdivision of the human orbital and medial prefrontal cortex. *Journal of Comparative Neurology, 460*(3), 425–449.

Opitz, P. C., Rauch, L. C., Terry, D. P., & Urry, H. L. (2012). Prefrontal mediation of age differences in cognitive reappraisal. *Neurobiology of Aging, 33*(4), 645–655.

Ostby, Y., Tamnes, C. K., Fjell, A. M., Westlye, L. T., Due-Tonnessen, P., & Walhovd, K. B. (2009). Heterogeneity in subcortical brain development: A structural magnetic resonance imaging study of brain maturation from 8 to 30 years. *Journal of Neuroscience, 29*(38), 11772–11782.

Oya, H., Adolphs, R., Kawasaki, H., Bechara, A., Damasio, A., & Howard, M. A., 3rd. (2005). Electrophysiological correlates of reward prediction error recorded in the human prefrontal cortex. *Proceedings of the National Academy of Science U S A, 102*(23), 8351–8356.

Palm, M. E., Elliott, R., McKie, S., Deakin, J. F., & Anderson, I. M. (2011). Attenuated responses to emotional expressions in women with generalized anxiety disorder. *Psychological Medicine, 41*(5), 1009–1018.

Park, D. C., & Reuter-Lorenz, P. (2009). The adaptive brain: aging and neurocognitive scaffolding. *Annual Review of Psychology, 60*, 173–196.

Paus, T. (2001). Primate anterior cingulate cortex: where motor control, drive and cognition interface. *Nature Reviews Neuroscience, 2*(6), 417–424.

Perlman, G., Simmons, A. N., Wu, J., Hahn, K. S., Tapert, S. F., Max, J. E., et al. (2012). Amygdala response and functional connectivity during emotion regulation: A study of 14 depressed adolescents. *Journal of Affective Disorders, 139*(1), 75–84.

Pfefferbaum, A., Mathalon, D. H., Sullivan, E. V., Rawles, J. M., Zipursky, R. B., & Lim, K. O. (1994). A quantitative magnetic resonance imaging study of changes in brain morphology from infancy to late adulthood. *Archives of Neurology, 51*(9), 874–887.

Phan, K. L., Fitzgerald, D. A., Nathan, P. J., Moore, G. J., Uhde, T. W., & Tancer, M. E. (2005). Neural substrates for voluntary suppression of negative affect: A functional magnetic resonance imaging study. *Biological Psychiatry, 57*(3), 210–219.

Phelps, E. A. (2006). Emotion and cognition: Insights from studies of the human amygdala. *Annual Review of Psychology, 57*, 27–53.

Pitskel, N. B., Bolling, D. Z., Kaiser, M. D., Crowley, M. J., & Pelphrey, K. A. (2011). How grossed out are you? The neural bases of emotion regulation from childhood to adolescence. *Developmental Cognitive Neuroscience, 1*(3), 324–337.

Pool, J. L., & Ransohoff, J. (1949). Autonomic effects on stimulating rostral portion of cingulate gyri in man. *Journal of Neurophysiology, 12*(6), 385–392.

Prevost, C., McCabe, J. A., Jessup, R. K., Bossaerts, P., & O'Doherty, J. P. (2011). Differentiable contributions of human amygdalar subregions in the computations underlying reward and avoidance learning. *European Journal of Neuroscience, 34*(1), 134–145.

Price, J. L. (1999). Prefrontal cortical networks related to visceral function and mood. *Annals of the New York Academy Science, 877*, 383–396.

Ptak, R. (2012). The frontoparietal attention network of the human brain: Action, saliency, and a priority map of the environment. *Neuroscientist, 18*(5), 501–515

Ritchey, M., Bessette-Symons, B., Hayes, S. M., & Cabeza, R. (2011). Emotion processing in the aging brain is modulated by semantic elaboration. *Neuropsychologia, 49*(4), 640–650.

Roy, M., Shohamy, D., & Wager, T. D. (2012). Ventromedial prefrontal-subcortical systems and the generation of affective meaning. *Trends in Cognitive Sciences, 16*(3), 147–156.

Rudebeck, P. H., & Murray, E. A. (2011). Balkanizing the primate orbitofrontal cortex: Distinct subregions for comparing and contrasting values. *Annals of the New York Academy of Sciences, 1239*, 1–13.

Rusch, N., van Elst, L. T., Ludaescher, P., Wilke, M., Huppertz, H. J., Thiel, T., et al. (2003). A voxel-based morphometric MRI study in female patients with borderline personality disorder. *Neuroimage, 20*(1), 385–392.

Saxe, R. (2006). Uniquely human social cognition. *Current Opinion in Neurobiology, 16*(2), 235–239.

Schardt, D. M., Erk, S., Nusser, C., Nothen, M. M., Cichon, S., Rietschel, M., et al. (2010). Volition diminishes genetically mediated amygdala hyperreactivity. *Neuroimage, 53*(3), 943–951.

Scheibe, S., & Carstensen, L. L. (2010). Emotional aging: recent findings and future trends. *The Journals of Gerontology. Series B: Psychological Science and Social Science, 65B*(2), 135–144.

Scherer, K. R., Schorr, A., & Johnstone, T. (Eds.). (2001). *Appraisal processes in emotion: Theory, methods, research*. New York: Oxford University Press.

Schienle, A., Schafer, A., Walter, B., Stark, R., & Vaitl, D. (2005). Brain activation of spider phobics towards disorder-relevant, generally disgust- and fear-inducing pictures. *Neuroscience Letters, 388*(1), 1–6.

Schiller, D., & Delgado, M. R. (2010). Overlapping neural systems mediating extinction, reversal and regulation of fear. *Trends in Cognitive Sciences, 14*(6), 268–276.

Schlund, M. W., & Cataldo, M. F. (2010). Amygdala involvement in human avoidance, escape and approach behavior. *Neuroimage, 53*(2), 769–776.

Schlund, M. W., Siegle, G. J., Ladouceur, C. D., Silk, J. S., Cataldo, M. F., Forbes, E. E., et al. (2010). Nothing to fear? Neural systems supporting avoidance behavior in healthy youths. *Neuroimage, 52*(2), 710–719.

Schmahl, C. G., Vermetten, E., Elzinga, B. M., & Douglas Bremner, J. (2003). Magnetic resonance imaging of hippocampal and amygdala volume in women with childhood abuse and borderline personality disorder. *Psychiatry Research, 122*(3), 193–198.

Schnell, K., Dietrich, T., Schnitker, R., Daumann, J., & Herpertz, S. C. (2007). Processing of autobiographical memory retrieval cues in borderline personality disorder. *Journal of Affective Disorders, 97*, 253–259.

Schoenbaum, G., Saddoris, M. P., & Stalnaker, T. A. (2007). Reconciling the roles of orbitofrontal cortex in reversal learning and the encoding of outcome expectancies. *Annals of the New York Academy of Science, 1121*, 320–335.

Schoenbaum, G., Takahashi, Y., Liu, T. L., & McDannald, M. A. (2011). Does the orbitofrontal cortex signal value? *Annals of the New York Academy of Science, 1239*, 87–99.

Schultz, W. (2007). Multiple dopamine functions at different time courses. *Annual Review of Neuroscience, 30*, 259–288.

Schulze, L., Domes, G., Kruger, A., Berger, C., Fleischer, M., Prehn, K., et al. (2010). Neuronal correlates of cognitive reappraisal in borderline patients with affective instability. *Biological Psychiatry, 69*(6), 564–573.

Schumann, C. M., Hamstra, J., Goodlin-Jones, B. L., Lotspeich, L. J., Kwon, H., Buonocore, M. H., et al. (2004). The amygdala is enlarged in children but not adolescents with autism; the hippocampus is enlarged at all ages. *Journal of Neuroscience, 24*(28), 6392–6401.

Schweckendiek, J., Klucken, T., Merz, C. J., Tabbert, K., Walter, B., Ambach, W., et al. (2011). Weaving the (neuronal) web: Fear learning in spider phobia. *Neuroimage, 54*(1), 681–688.

Sergerie, K., Chochol, C., & Armony, J. L. (2008). The role of the amygdala in emotional processing: A quantitative meta-analysis of functional neuroimaging studies. *Neuroscience and Biobehavioral Review, 32*(4), 811–830.

Sheppes, G., Scheibe, S., Suri, G., & Gross, J. J. (2011). Emotion-regulation choice. *Psychological Science, 22*(11), 1391–1396.

Shiota, M. N., & Levenson, R. W. (2009). Effects of aging on experimentally instructed detached reappraisal, positive reappraisal, and emotional behavior suppression. *Psychology and Aging, 24*(4), pp.

Silbersweig, D., Clarkin, J. F., Goldstein, M., Kernberg, O. F., Tuescher, O., Levy, K. N., et al. (2007). Failure of frontolimbic inhibitory function in the context of negative emotion in borderline personality disorder. *American Journal of Psychiatry, 164*(12), 1832–1841.

Silvers, J. A., McRae, K., Gabrieli, J. D. E., Gross, J. J., Remy, K. A., & Ochsner, K. N. (2012). Age-related differences in emotional reactivity, regulation and rejection sensitivity in adolescence. *Emotion, 12*(6), 1235–1247.

Simmons, A. N., & Matthews, S. C. (2012). Neural circuitry of PTSD with or without mild traumatic brain injury: A meta-analysis. *Neuropharmacology, 62*(2), 598–606.

Soloff, P. H., Pruitt, P., Sharma, M., Radwan, J., White, R., & Diwadkar, V. A. (2012). Structural brain abnormalities and suicidal behavior in borderline personality disorder. *Journal of Psychiatric Research, 46*(4), 516–525.

Somerville, L. H., Hare, T., & Casey, B. J. (2011). Frontostriatal maturation predicts cognitive control failure to appetitive cues in adolescents. *Journal of Cognitive Neuroscience, 23*(9), 2123–2134.

Somerville, L. H., Jones, R. M., & Casey, B. J. (2010). A time of change: Behavioral and neural correlates of adolescent sensitivity to appetitive and aversive environmental cues. *Brain and Cognition, 72*(1), 124–133.

Staudinger, M. R., Erk, S., Abler, B., & Walter, H. (2009). Cognitive reappraisal modulates expected value and prediction error encoding in the ventral striatum. *Neuroimage, 47*(2), 713–721.

Staudinger, M. R., Erk, S., & Walter, H. (2011). Dorsolateral prefrontal cortex modulates striatal reward encoding during reappraisal of reward anticipation. *Cerebral Cortex, 21*(11), 2578–2588.

St. Jacques, P. L., Bessette Symons, B., & Cabeza, R. (2009). Functional neuroimaging studies of aging and emotion: Fronto-amygdalar differences during emotional perception and episodic memory. *Journal of the International Neuropsychological Society, 15*(6), 819–825.

Straube, T., Mentzel, H. J., & Miltner, W. H. (2006). Neural mechanisms of automatic and direct processing of phobogenic stimuli in specific phobia. *Biological Psychiatry, 59*(2), 162–170.

Streubel, B., & Kunzmann, U. (2011). Age differences in emotional reactions: Arousal and age-relevance count. *Psychology and Aging, 26*(4), 966–978.

Stuss, D. T., & Alexander, M. P. (2007). Is there a dysexecutive syndrome? *Philosophical Transactions of the Royal Society of London. Series B: Biological Sciences, 362*(1481), 901–915.

Tebartz van Elst, L., Hesslinger, B., Thiel, T., Geiger, E., Haegele, K., Lemieux, L., et al. (2003). Frontolimbic brain abnormalities in patients with borderline personality disorder: A volumetric magnetic resonance imaging study. *Biological Psychiatry, 54*(2), 163–171.

Thomas, K. M., Drevets, W. C., Dahl, R. E., Ryan, N. D., Birmaher, B., Eccard, C. H., et al. (2001). Amygdala response to fearful faces in anxious and depressed children. *Archives of General Psychiatry, 58*(11), 1057–1063.

Thomas, L. A., De Bellis, M. D., Graham, R., & LaBar, K. S. (2007). Development of emotional facial recognition in late childhood and adolescence. *Developmental Science, 10*(5), 547–558.

Thompson-Schill, S. L., Bedny, M., & Goldberg, R. F. (2005). The frontal lobes and the regulation of mental activity. *Current Opinion in Neurobiology, 15*(2), 219–224.

Tracey, I., & Mantyh, P. W. (2007). The cerebral signature for pain perception and its modulation. *Neuron, 55*(3), 377–391.

Tsai, J. L., Levenson, R. W., & Carstensen, L. L. (2000). Autonomic, subjective, and expressive responses to emotional films in older and younger Chinese Americans and European Americans. *Psychology and Aging, 15*(4), 684–693.

Tucker, A. M., Feuerstein, R., Mende-Siedlecki, P., Ochsner, K. N., & Stern, Y. (2012). Double dissociation: Circadian off-peak times increase emotional reactivity; aging impairs emotion regulation via reappraisal. *Emotion, 12*(5), 869–874.

Urry, H. L. (2009). Using reappraisal to regulate unpleasant emotional episodes: Goals and timing matter. *Emotion, 9*(6), 782–797.

Urry, H. L., van Reekum, C. M., Johnstone, T., & Davidson, R. J. (2009). Individual differences in some (but not all) medial prefrontal regions reflect cognitive demand while regulating unpleasant emotion. *Neuropsychologia, 47*(3), 852–863.

Urry, H. L., van Reekum, C. M., Johnstone, T., Kalin, N. H., Thurow, M. E., Schaefer, H. S., et al. (2006). Amygdala and ventromedial prefrontal cortex are inversely coupled during regulation of negative affect and predict the diurnal pattern of cortisol secretion among older adults. *Journal of Neuroscience, 26*(16), 4415–4425.

van Leijenhorst, L., Crone, E. A., & Bunge, S. A. (2006). Neural correlates of developmental differences in risk estimation and feedback processing. *Neuropsychologia, 44*(11), 2158–2170.

van Leijenhorst, L., Zanolie, K., Van Meel, C. S., Westenberg, P. M., Rombouts, S. A., & Crone, E. A. (2010). What motivates the adolescent? Brain regions mediating reward sensitivity across adolescence. *Cerebral Cortex, 20*(1), 61–69.

van Reekum, C. M., Johnstone, T., Urry, H. L., Thurow, M. E., Schaefer, H. S., Alexander, A. L., et al. (2007). Gaze fixations predict brain activation during the voluntary regulation of picture-induced negative affect. *Neuroimage, 36*(3), 1041–1055.

Vincent, G. A., & Velkoff, V. A. (2010). *The next four decades: The older population in the United States 2010 to 2050.* Retrieved from http://www.census.gov/prod/2010pubs/p25-1138.pdf.

Volkow, N. D., Fowler, J. S., Wang, G. J., Telang, F., Logan, J., Jayne, M., et al. (2010). Cognitive control of drug craving inhibits brain reward regions in cocaine abusers. *Neuroimage, 49*(3), 2536–2543.

Völlm, B., Richardson, P., Stirling, J., Elliott, R., Dolan, M., Chaudhry, I., et al. (2004). Neurobiological substrates of antisocial and borderline personality disorder: Preliminary results of a functional fMRI study. *Criminal Behaviour and Mental Health, 14*(1), 39–54.

Vrticka, P., Sander, D., & Vuilleumier, P. (2011). Effects of emotion regulation strategy on brain responses to the valence and social content of visual scenes. *Neuropsychologia, 49*(5), 1067–1082.

Vuilleumier, P., & Pourtois, G. (2007). Distributed and interactive brain mechanisms during emotion face perception: Evidence from functional neuroimaging. *Neuropsychologia, 45*(1), 174–194.

Wager, T. D., Davidson, M. L., Hughes, B. L., Lindquist, M. A., & Ochsner, K. N. (2008). Prefrontal-subcortical pathways mediating successful emotion regulation. *Neuron, 59*(6), 1037–1050.

Wager, T. D., & Feldman Barrett, L. (2004). From affect to control: Functional specialization of the insula in motivation and regulation. *PsycExtra.* Retrieved from http://psych-www.colorado.edu/~tor/Papers/Wager_Feldman_Barrett_2004_Insula_meta-analysis.pdf.

Wager, T. D., Phan, K. L., Liberzon, I., & Taylor, S. F. (2003). Valence, gender, and lateralization of functional brain anatomy in emotion: a meta-analysis of findings from neuroimaging. *Neuroimage, 19*(3), 513–531.

Walter, H., von Kalckreuth, A., Schardt, D., Stephan, A., Goschke, T., & Erk, S. (2009). The temporal dynamics of voluntary emotion regulation. *PLoS One, 4*(8), e6726.

Wendt, J., Lotze, M., Weike, A. I., Hosten, N., & Hamm, A. O. (2008). Brain activation and defensive response mobilization during sustained exposure to phobia-related and other affective pictures in spider phobia. *Psychophysiology, 45*(2), 205–215.

Whalen, P. J., Kagan, J., Cook, R. G., Davis, F. C., Kim, H., Polis, S., et al. (2004). Human amygdala responsivity to masked fearful eye whites. *Science, 306*(5704), 2061.

Wheaton, K. J., Thompson, J. C., Syngeniotis, A., Abbott, D. F., & Puce, A. (2004). Viewing the motion of human body parts activates different regions of premotor, temporal, and parietal cortex. *Neuroimage, 22*(1), 277–288.

Winecoff, A., Labar, K. S., Madden, D. J., Cabeza, R., & Huettel, S. A. (2010). Cognitive and neural contributors to emotion regulation in aging. *Social, Cognitive & Affective Neuroscience, 6*(2), 165–176.

Wingenfeld, K., Rullkoetter, N., Mensebach, C., Beblo, T., Mertens, M., Kreisel, S., et al. (2009). Neural correlates of the individual emotional Stroop in borderline personality disorder. *Psychoneuroendocrinology, 34*(4), 571–586.

Young, L., Camprodon, J. A., Hauser, M., Pascual-Leone, A., & Saxe, R. (2010). Disruption of the right temporoparietal junction with transcranial magnetic stimulation reduces the role of beliefs in moral judgments. *Proceedings of the National Academy of Science U S A, 107*(15), 6753–6758.

Zahn, T. P., Grafman, J., & Tranel, D. (1999). Frontal lobe lesions and electrodermal activity: Effects of significance. *Neuropsychologia, 37*(11), 1227–1241.

CHAPTER 5

The Impact of Emotion on Cognition

Luiz Pessoa

Abstract

This chapter summarizes ways in which emotion affects cognition. First, some of the interactions between emotion and cognition are reviewed, with an emphasis on interactions between emotion and (1) perception and attention and (2) executive functions (behavioral inhibition and working memory). The overall focus is on brain systems, and less on psychological processes, as obtained by behavioral data. Second, the dual competition framework is presented, which was developed to explain how affective significance influences information processing in the brain. The framework describes influences of emotion at both the perceptual and the executive (i.e., "central") levels.

Key Words: emotion, cognition, amygdala, threat, executive functions, control, affective significance, perception

Introduction

This chapter discusses interactions between emotion and cognition, with an emphasis on the effects of emotion on cognition; see Chapter 2 in this Handbook for a discussion of the effects of cognition on emotion. In addressing this topic, it would be natural to attempt to define what is meant by "emotion" and by "cognition" (see Oatley, Keltner, & Jenkins, 2006). However, we will not do so here with any degree of precision, because it may be disadvantageous to dichotomize processes into emotional and cognitive categories. It is often argued that, in science, definitions are all-important for understanding. On the contrary, paraphrasing Oatley et al. (2006), it may be the case that, in the context of this chapter, understanding may have to precede proper definition.

Cognition typically refers to processes such as memory, attention, language, problem solving, and planning—given the difficulty of a precise definition, one often resorts to enumerating distinct "cognitive dimensions." Many cognitive processes are thought to involve sophisticated functions that may

be uniquely human. They often involve so-called controlled processes, such as when the pursuit of a goal (e.g., maintaining information in mind) needs to be protected from interference (e.g., a distracting stimulus). A prototypical example of a neural correlate of a cognitive process is the sustained firing of cells in dorsolateral prefrontal cortex as a monkey maintains information "in mind" for brief periods of time (Fuster, 2008). With the advent of functional magnetic resonance imaging (fMRI), a growing body of literature has documented (and continues to document) how a variety of cognitive processes are linked to specific parts of the brain. According to this literature, in the vast majority of cases, cognitive processes appear to engage cortical regions.

Whereas there is relative agreement on the constituent processes of cognition, the same cannot be said about emotion. Accordingly, some investigators use definitions that incorporate the concepts of drive and motivation: "emotions are states elicited by rewards and punishers" (Rolls, 2005). Others favor the view that emotions are involved in the conscious (or unconscious) evaluation of events (Arnold, 1960) (i.e., appraisals). Some approaches focus on basic emotions (Ekman, 1992) (e.g., fear, anger), while others focus on an extended set of emotions, including moral ones (Haidt, 2003; Moll, Zahn, de Oliveira-Souza, Krueger, & Grafman, 2005) (e.g., pride, envy). Strong evidence also links emotions to the body (Damasio, 1994). Brain structures linked to emotion are often subcortical, such as the amygdala, ventral striatum, and hypothalamus. These structures are often considered evolutionarily conserved, or "primitive." They are also believed to operate fast and in an "automatic fashion," such that certain trigger features (e.g., the white of the eyes in a fearful expression [Whalen et al., 2004]) are relatively unfiltered when evoking responses that may be important for survival. Accordingly, an individual may not be necessarily conscious of a stimulus that may have triggered brain responses in an affective brain region, especially the amygdala. For discussion of this approach, see the studies by Ohman (2002) and Pessoa (2005).

The first objective of this chapter will be to illustrate some of the interactions between emotion and cognition. Given the enormous scope of this topic, by necessity, the examples will be relatively focused and will emphasize the brain systems involved in the interactions between emotion and (1) perception and attention and (2) executive functions (behavioral inhibition and working memory). The emphasis will be on brain systems, and less on psychological processes, as obtained by behavioral data. Other valuable sources for this discussion include works by Damasio (1994, 1999), Dolan (2003) LeDoux (1996), Phelps (2006), and Rolls (2005).

Before proceeding, however, a brief historical note is in order. The emotion–cognition debate came into sharp focus with the report of the mere-exposure effect (Kunst-Wilson & Zajonc, 1980), which led to a strong belief that affect was primary to and independent of cognition. It can be said that the mere-exposure effect and other behavioral findings shifted ongoing debates toward viewing affect as being related to unconscious processing and subcortical activity, with cognition being related to conscious processing and cortical involvement. Interestingly, behavioral findings were interpreted in the context of the "low route" suggested by LeDoux (1996), which was purported to carry affective information subcortically (but see Pessoa & Adolphs, 2010, in preparation). These early behavioral studies provided a strong impetus to the wave of neuroscience research in the late 1990s (and

beyond) that investigated related phenomena. For some of the early theoretical arguments, see those by Lazarus (1984) and Zajonc (1984).

Following the initial general review, I will present my own proposal that describes how the processing of affectively significant items influences information processing in the brain. In doing so, influences of emotion at both the perceptual and the executive levels will be discussed.

Interactions Between Emotion and Cognition
Perception and Attention

Viewing of emotion-laden visual stimuli is linked to heightened and more extensive visual-system activation (Pessoa, Kastner, & Ungerleider, 2002; Vuilleumier, 2005). For instance, viewing faces with emotional expressions evokes greater responses throughout ventral occipitotemporal visual cortex than when viewing neutral faces (Figure 5.1). Visual responses are also stronger when subjects view emotional scenes (e.g., a war scene) than when they view neutral scenes (e.g., a lake scene). Increased visual activation is observed in both "late" visual areas, such as the fusiform gyrus and superior temporal sulcus, and early visual cortex in occipital cortex. Studies have shown that, in humans, even retinotopically organized visual cortex, including visual areas V1 and V2 along the calcarine fissure, is modulated by the affective significance of a stimulus (Padmala & Pessoa, 2008).

Enhanced visual activation when viewing emotional stimuli is consistent with observed improvements in behavioral performance in several visual tasks. For instance, there is some evidence that angry and happy faces are detected faster in visual search tasks (Eastwood, Smilek, & Merikle, 2001). Other emotional stimuli, such as a snake or spider, may also be detected faster (Ohman, Flykt, & Esteves, 2001). Stronger evidence comes from studies of the *attentional blink* paradigm, in which subjects are asked to report the occurrence of two targets (T1 and T2) among a rapid stream of visual stimuli. When T2 follows T1 after a brief delay, participants are more likely to miss it, as if they had blinked (hence the name). The attentional blink is believed to reflect a capacity-limited processing stage, possibly linked to a process of identification and consolidation of the first target for subsequent conscious report. Interestingly, the attentional blink has been shown to be modulated by emotional stimuli, as subjects are significantly better at detecting T2 when it is an emotion-laden word (e.g., "rape") than when it is a neutral word (Anderson, 2005). Lim and colleagues

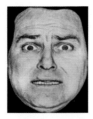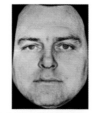

Fearful > Neutral

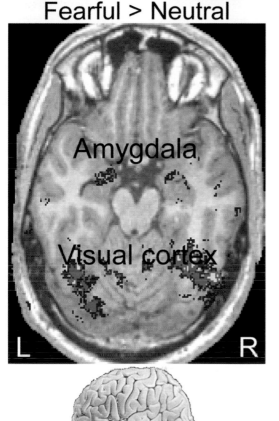

Figure 5.1 Emotional modulation of visual processing. Large portions of occipitotemporal cortex were more strongly driven by fearful faces than by neutral ones. The strongest differential responses were observed in visual regions that included the fusiform gyrus, a ventral temporal area known to be strongly driven by face stimuli.

Original data from Pessoa, McKenna, Gutierrez, and Ungerleider. (2002).

have shown an advantage for affectively significant items in the attentional blink that is based on only the learning history of specific items (e.g., house or building stimuli previously paired with mild shock) (Lim, Padmala, & Pessoa, 2009).

Converging evidence for a link between perception, attention, and emotion comes from additional studies. For example, patients who present with unilateral inattention due to spatial hemineglect (often as a result of right-hemisphere parietal lesions) are better at detecting happy or angry faces than at detecting neutral ones (Vuilleumier & Schwartz, 2001). These findings are consistent with the notion that emotional faces may direct the allocation of attention. For instance, in one study, emotional faces were flashed at spatial locations that subsequently displayed low-contrast visual stimuli (Phelps, Ling, & Carrasco, 2006). Subjects exhibited improved performance for detecting targets shown at those locations, which suggests that attention was deployed to them, thereby facilitating visual detection.

How is the increase in perceptual processing and attentional capture that is observed during the perception of affective stimuli instantiated in the brain? In a study of the attentional blink, Lim et al. (2009) observed that trial-by-trial fluctuations of responses in the amygdala were predictive of behavioral performance in the task—the greater the evoked response, the higher the likelihood that the subject would correctly detect an emotional T2 stimulus. Thus, it appears that the amygdala may underlie a form of *emotional modulation* of information that in many ways parallels attentional effects observed with nonemotional information (Pessoa, Kastner, et al., 2002; Vuilleumier, 2005). There are several ways in which emotional modulation may be accomplished, as further elaborated later in the section Dual Competition Model. Here, we will focus our discussion on the mechanism most often highlighted in the literature, namely that direct projections from the amygdala to visual cortex enhance visual processing. The amygdala sends projections across nearly all levels of the visual system, including anterior regions in temporal cortex and posterior regions in occipital cortex (including V1 and V2) (Amaral, Price, Pitkanen, & Carmichael, 1992). Thus, the amygdala is well situated to modulate sensory processing according to the affective significance of a visual object—exactly as observed in our study (Lim et al., 2009).

An important issue when considering interactions between emotion, and perception and attention is whether the perception of emotion-laden stimuli is "automatic," that is, independent of attention and awareness. This question has received considerable attention because specific answers to this question ("no" or "yes") suggest potentially different relationships between emotion and cognition (more or less independence between the two, respectively). Interestingly, evidence both for and against automaticity has been presented. For instance, emotional faces evoke responses in the amygdala when attention is diverted to other stimuli (Anderson, Christoff, Panitz, De Rosa, & Gabrieli, 2003; Vuilleumier, Armony, Driver, & Dolan, 2001). Perhaps even more strikingly, amygdala responses are sometimes reported for emotional faces that subjects are not conscious of (Etkin et al., 2004; Morris, Ohman, & Dolan, 1998; Whalen et al., 1998, 2004). Furthermore, cases of so-called affective blindsight have been reported (de Gelder, Vroomen, Pourtois, & Weiskrantz, 1999). These and other related findings suggest that at least some types of emotional perception occur outside of "cognitive" processing and, so the argument goes, may rely on direct subcortical pathways conveying visual information to the amygdala (LeDoux, 1996) (but see Dual Competition Model, below). At the same time, some findings have suggested that the perception of emotion-laden items requires attention, as revealed by attentional manipulations designed to more effectively consume processing resources, leaving relatively few for the processing of unattended emotional items (Bishop, Duncan, & Lawrence, 2004; Bishop, Jenkins, & Lawrence, 2007; Hsu & Pessoa, 2007; Lim, Padmala, & Pessoa, 2008; Pessoa, Padmala, & Morland, 2005; Pessoa, McKenna, Gutierrez, & Ungerleider, 2002). Furthermore, it also appears that amygdala responses evoked by "unaware" stimuli depend somewhat on the manner by which awareness is operationally defined (Merikle, Smilek, & Eastwood, 2001), such that no unaware responses are observed when awareness is defined, for instance, via signal detection theory methods (Pessoa, Japee, Sturman, & Ungerleider, 2006; but see Whalen, et al., 2004). Overall, the automaticity debate remains unresolved and controversial (Bishop, 2007; Pessoa, 2005; Vuilleumier, 2005; Wiens, 2006).

Executive Functions

The impact of emotion on cognition is rich and varied and has been documented in a range of different tasks. In this section, I will briefly illustrate these interactions in two cognitive domains involving executive functions. The first examples come from an important dimension of executive function that involves inhibiting and controlling behavior. *Response inhibition*, namely the processes required to cancel an intended action, is believed to involve control regions in prefrontal cortex (e.g., dorsolateral prefrontal cortex, anterior cingulate cortex,

and inferior frontal cortex) (Aron, Robbins, & Poldrack, 2004; Rubia, Smith, Brammer, & Taylor, 2003). Response inhibition is often investigated by using so-called go/no-go tasks in which subjects are asked to execute a motor response when shown the "go" stimulus (e.g., press a key as fast as possible when you see a letter stimulus) but to withhold the response when shown the "no-go" stimulus (e.g., do not respond when you see the letter *Y*). Typically, the go and no-go stimuli are shown as part of a rapid stream of stimuli (e.g., a sequence of letters). One study investigated the interaction between the processing of emotional words and response inhibition (Goldstein et al., 2007). Response inhibition following negative words (e.g., "worthless") engaged the dorsolateral prefrontal cortex. Interestingly, this region was not recruited by negative valence or inhibitory task demands per se; instead, the dorsolateral cortex was sensitive to the explicit interaction between behavioral inhibition and the processing of negatively valenced words.

Working memory, another important cognitive operation, involves the maintenance and updating of information in mind when the information is no longer available to sensory systems (e.g., when keeping a phone number in mind for a few seconds before dialing the number). Evidence for cognitive–emotional interaction comes from working memory studies as well. For instance, when participants were asked to keep in mind neutral or emotional pictures, maintenance-related activity in dorsolateral prefrontal cortex was modulated by the valence of the picture, with pleasant pictures enhancing activity and unpleasant pictures decreasing activity relative to neutral ones (Perlstein, Elbert, & Stenger, 2002). Interestingly, emotional pictures did not affect dorsolateral responses during a second experimental condition in which participants were *not* required to keep information in mind. This indicates that the modulation of sustained activity by emotional valence was particular to the experimental context requiring active maintenance. In another study, participants watched short videos intended to induce emotional states (e.g., clips from uplifting or sad movies), after which they performed challenging working memory tasks (Gray, Braver, & Raichle, 2002). Lateral prefrontal cortex activity on both hemispheres reflected equally the emotional and working memory task components. In other words, prefrontal activity did not stem from the working memory task alone or from the mood that ensued from viewing the video but instead resulted from an interaction between emotion and cognition.

In summary, the examples presented in this section highlight the notion that many of the effects of emotion on cognition are best viewed as interactions between the two; the resulting processes and signals are neither purely cognitive nor emotional. Instead, the "cognitive" or "emotional" nature of the processes is blurred in a way that highlights the integration of these entities in the brain.

Dual Competition Model

As reviewed in the first part of this chapter, the impact of affective significance on behavioral performance and the brain is well documented. In general, however, the mechanisms by which this impact is manifested remain poorly understood. And whereas some progress has been made concerning the interactions between emotion and specific cognitive processes (Pessoa, 2008; Phelps, 2006), important gaps in our knowledge about them still remain. Here, I will summarize a conceptual framework that attempts to describe how affective significance impacts the flow of information processing in the brain. Originally, the framework was proposed to explain how both emotion and motivation interact with executive control to determine behavioral outcome (Pessoa, 2009). It was suggested that both emotion and motivation (e.g., as manipulated via reward) signals are integrated with executive functions so as to effectively incorporate *value* into the unfolding of behavior. I called the proposed framework the "dual competition model" to reflect the suggestion that affective significance influences competition at both the perceptual and executive levels—and because the impact is due to both emotion and motivation. The framework draws upon several ideas in the literature, including biased competition (Desimone & Duncan, 1995) and resource theory (Kahneman, 1973; Lavie, Hirst, de Fockert, & Viding, 2004; Norman & Bobrow, 1975; Park, Kim, & Chun, 2007); see also work by Braver, Gray, and Burgess (2007) and Robbins (2007) for complementary proposals. Some of the main elements of the model as it relates to emotional processing are described below. For further developments of the motivational side of the model, please see the study by Pessoa and Engelmann (2010).

Objects compete for limited perceptual processing capacity and control of behavior (Desimone & Duncan, 1995; Pashler, 1998). Because processing capacity is limited, selective attention to one part of the visual field comes at the cost of neglecting other parts. Thus, a popular notion is that there is *competition* for neural resources (Bundesen, 1990;

Desimone, 1998; Desimone & Duncan, 1995; Duncan, 1996, 1998; Grossberg, 1980; Harter & Aine, 1984). According to a well-known proposal, the *biased competition model* (Desimone & Duncan, 1995), the competition among stimuli for neural representation, which occurs within the visual cortex itself, can be biased in several ways. One way is by bottom-up sensory-driven mechanisms, such as stimulus salience. For example, stimuli that are colorful or of high contrast will be at a competitive advantage. But another way is by attentional top-down feedback, which is thought to be generated in areas outside the visual cortex, such as frontoparietal areas. For example, directed attention to a particular location in space facilitates processing of stimuli presented at that location. In this way, even objects that are not physically salient may win the competition and influence ongoing behavior. The stimulus that wins the competition for neural representation will gain further access to multiple systems and, thereby, the ability to guide subsequent actions.

By combining both bottom-up and top-down factors, *biased competition* provides a good starting point for the understanding of an object's impact on behavior. However, in order to understand the flow of information processing more generally, it is necessary to go beyond the role of perceptual competition and explicitly incorporate the impact of executive control functions on item processing; more is needed to determine the fate of objects than a simple biasing mechanism. This is because, as described below, *executive control and competition* are critically important in determining how an object will influence ongoing behaviors.

Executive control involves a host of selection and adjustment processes, including perceptual selection, detection and resolution of conflict, monitoring of performance levels, prioritization and switching between tasks, and maintenance of contextual information. Behavioral research supports the notion that executive control is not unitary and that different mechanisms may have their own limited processing capacities, or resources (Kahneman, 1973; Norman & Bobrow, 1975). Neuropsychological research also supports the dissociation of executive functions, as well as the fractionation of the central executive (Baddeley, 2003; Norman & Shallice, 1986; Stuss & Knight, 2002). While the exact fractionation of executive functions is subject to debate, it likely involves at least three major functions (Miyake et al., 2000; Smith & Jonides, 1999): inhibition, shifting, and updating. However, ample evidence also suggests some *unity* of executive functions, consistent with the notion that mechanisms are shared across them (Duncan, Emslie, Williams, Johnson, & Freer, 1996; Miyake et al., 2000). This capacity sharing has important implications for the understanding of human information processing because it leads to *executive competition*: subcomponents of executive control are mutually interacting, such that resources devoted to one component will detract from those available to other functions. For instance, if resources required to carry out response inhibition are partly shared with those needed during shifting, an individual needing to withhold responding in a trial may exhibit an increased switching cost if asked in close temporal succession to switch between tasks (e.g., Verbruggen, Liefooghe, & Vandierendonck, 2004).

Perceptual Competition and Related Mechanisms

With these basic notions outlined, we are now in a position to address our main question of interest: How does the affective significance of an item alter information processing in the brain? To understand this, we need to work out the impact of affective significance on both perceptual competition and executive control and competition (Figure 5.2). Let us start with perceptual competition. Perceptual competition, which takes place in visual cortex, is

affected because emotional content enhances sensory representations of emotion-laden items (arrow 2). As discussed earlier in this chapter, the amygdala is well positioned to mediate this enhancement given that its rich set of efferents reach multiple levels of the visual cortex, including the primary visual cortex (Amaral et al., 1992). Although the direct role of the amygdala in the modulation of visual processing is often emphasized (Figure 5.3), several other mechanisms are also likely involved (see discussion below).

How does visual input reach the amygdala (arrow 1 in Figure 5.2) in the first place? A popular notion is that a subcortical pathway involving the superior colliculus and the pulvinar nucleus of the thalamus conveys visual information to the amygdala. The subcortical nature of the pathway would allow signals to engage the amygdala rapidly and in a manner that would be independent of attention, an idea inspired by work on auditory processing in rodents, by LeDoux and colleagues (LeDoux, 1996). Based on both physiological and anatomical information, we have challenged this notion of a subcortical "low road" pathway that is capable of conveying affective information in a rapid and automatic fashion, at least in humans (Pessoa & Adolphs, 2010, in preparation). We propose instead that inputs reach the amygdala via several parallel cortical routes. Subsequently, feedback signals from the amygdala would modulate responses in visual cortex according to the affective significance of the visual item.

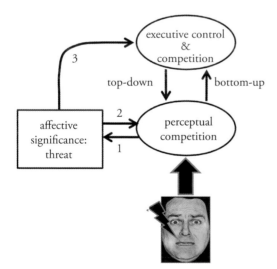

Figure 5.2 Dual competition model. The affective significance of a visual item (e.g., due to its facial expression and/or pairing with mild shock) influences information processing in the brain via effects at both the perceptual and executive-control levels. The evaluation of affective significance is suggested to rely on several brain structures, including the amygdala, orbitofrontal cortex, anterior insula, and anterior cingulate cortex.

Adapted from Pessoa (2009) with permission.

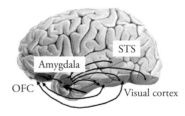

Figure 5.3 Emotional modulation of visual processing. The amygdala (red), which receives inputs from anterior portions of visual cortex (green), projects back to multiple levels, including very early visual cortex (areas V1/V2). Emotional modulation also likely depends on reciprocal connections with the orbitofrontal cortex (OFC, blue). In this case, only more anterior regions of visual cortex are affected. Other portions of the visual system, including the superior temporal sulcus (STS, orange), are also modulated as a function of emotional content. Note that the amygdala is drawn on the lateral surface for illustration only, as this subcortical structure lies near the brain medial surface.

Reproduced from Pessoa, Kaster, and Ungerleider (2002) with permission.

An additional modulatory mechanism relies on the orbitofrontal cortex (OFC), a structure that has important roles in the evaluation of incoming stimuli (Barrett & Bar, 2009). The OFC is reciprocally interconnected with visual cortex, especially more anterior portions (areas TEO and TE, for example) (Barbas, 1995; Cavada, Company, Tejedor, Cruz-Rizzolo, & Reinoso-Suarez, 2000). Indeed, it has been suggested by Bar and colleagues that the OFC may be responsible for a first, coarse processing of the stimulus, narrowing the set of alternative perceptual interpretations (Bar, 2003; Barrett & Bar, 2009). Although Bar et al.'s proposal initially focused on nonemotional stimuli, in all likelihood the OFC plays an important role in the modulation of affective items as well (Barrett & Bar, 2009).

Another class of modulatory mechanisms relies on frontoparietal "attentional control sites," such as those in lateral PFC, frontal eye field, and intraparietal sulcus, which are in a position to modulate visual processing according to an item's behavioral relevance. These sites are believed to be "control sites" that provide the source of "top-down" attentional signals (Corbetta & Shulman, 2002; Kastner & Ungerleider, 2000). Here I would suggest that they are co-opted by evaluative sites including the amygdala, OFC, anterior insula, and the anterior cingulate cortex (ACC), based on the affective significance of the stimulus. The direct connectivity between the "evaluative" and the "control" sites is generally believed to be weak (Ghashghaei, Hilgetag, & Barbas, 2007), and indirect routes involving one or two intermediate steps are probably involved. For instance, in monkeys the distribution and density of axonal terminals from the amygdala in lateral prefrontal cortices was reported as "light" (compared to "moderate" and "heavy"), although present (Ghashghaei et al., 2007). In a case like this, connections from the amygdala to lateral PFC via parts of more dorsal ACC that are richly innervated by the amygdala (Ghashghaei et al., 2007) may generate stronger effects. It is noteworthy that the existence of additional steps probably only delays the impact of affective significance on evoked responses by ~10 ms per stage (Nowak & Bullier, 1997), which clearly still allows for fast effects to take place. The modulation discussed here involves sites heavily implicated in the context of executive control and competition (discussed below), a property that further highlights the tight link between "bottom-up" and "top-down" processes illustrated in Figure 5.2 ("perceptual competition" and "executive control & competition," respectively). In other words, the distinction between bottom-up and top-down is schematic only, given that, in reality, the mechanisms are inherently interdependent.

A third important mechanism may involve the pulvinar complex of the thalamus. Based on anatomical and physiological considerations, we have recently proposed that the importance of the pulvinar for affective processing is not due to its putative role as part of a subcortical pathway, as is often assumed in the literature, but instead due to its connectivity with other cortical regions (Pessoa & Adolphs, 2010, in preparation). Briefly, the medial nucleus of the pulvinar, which projects to the amygdala, is part of several thalamocortical loops that include the OFC, cingulate cortex, and insula (in addition to frontal and parietal sites). Given this broad connectivity pattern, we have suggested that the medial nucleus may be involved in two general functions that directly impact emotional processing: determining behavioral relevance and value. Accordingly, our suggestion extends the role of the pulvinar in attentional processes (Shipp, 2004) to the more general case of affective significance. And consistent with the notion that the "driving input" (as opposed to modulatory input) to the pulvinar is from the cortex (as opposed to from the superior colliculus; Guillery, 1995; Sherman & Guillery, 1996), we suggest that cortical signals from evaluative sites

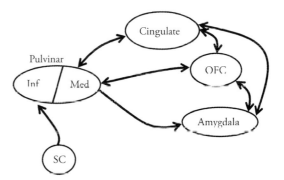

Figure 5.4 A role for the pulvinar nucleus of the thalamus in affective processing. Contrary to current suggestions in the literature that the importance of the pulvinar to emotion resides in its critical location as part of a colliculo-pulvino-amygdalar subcortical pathway, it is proposed here that the pulvinar coordinates and integrates a range of cortical signals involving stimulus valuation and that such signals can then be further integrated in the amygdala. As indicated in the diagram, the contribution of the pulvinar needs to be understood in terms of the network interactions that it participates in. Note too that visual input from the superior colliculus (SC) is sent to the inferior pulvinar (Inf), which is not directly interconnected with the amygdala. Abbreviations: Inf, inferior; Med, medial; OFC: orbitofrontal cortex; SC, superior colliculus.

are integrated in the medial pulvinar as they are conveyed to the amygdala (Figure 5.4).

Executive Control and Competition

Let us now turn to the effects of emotional content on executive control and competition (see arrow 3 in Figure 5.2), which, as stated previously, are critical in determining the impact of an affective item on behavior. The magnitude of the effect of emotional content on behavior is expected to depend on whether the item is low or high in threat. When threat content is relatively low, processing is biased in favor of the emotional item (Figure 5.5A). In particular, the spatial locus of the emotional item is privileged, possibly because items that are low in threat are somewhat ambiguous and so may attract further attention as part of additional information gathering (Whalen, 1998). In general, in the low-threat case, although emotional items are prioritized, the impact on behavior is modest (but positive), and in this sense it can be said that a "soft prioritization" of processing occurs. Importantly, emotional content enhances task-relevant processing with relatively minor effects on irrelevant stimuli and other executive functions that may be concurrently needed. In other words, *common-pool resources*—i.e., processing resources that are strongly shared by several executive functions (see also Bishop, 2007; Eysenck, Derakshan, Santos, & Calvo, 2007; Mathews & Mackinstosh, 1998)—are not significantly consumed by the emotional item because the threat is low. Furthermore, because the effect on performance is relatively weak, behavioral findings may be difficult to replicate and may be observed only in highly anxious individuals (e.g., Fox, Russo, Bowles, & Dutton, 2001). Finally, whereas low-threat emotional stimuli may comprise a privileged stimulus category, their processing is highly dynamic and depends on the interplay of a host of factors that sculpt the associated neural responses, including attention, task context, awareness, and perceptual interpretation (Pessoa, 2005).

A more dramatic effect of emotional content on behavior is expected when emotional content is high in threat. In the laboratory, these are situations involving stimuli that have been paired with shock or, possibly, high-arousal pictures (e.g., mutilation pictures). In this situation, resources are diverted toward the processing of the item at hand, and because the mobilization of the resources is more extreme, the effects on behavior are considerably more dramatic (Lang, Davis, & Ohman, 2000; Panksepp, 1998). In the present context, the main

impact on behavior comes from the recruitment of attentional/effortful control that is required to prioritize the processing of high-threat information (Figure 5.5B). It can be said then that a "hard prioritization" occurs. Attentional/effortful control involves processing resources strongly shared by several executive functions. Because high threat is expected to recruit such common-pool resources, it will impair other executive functions that are reliant on them, including inhibition, shifting, and updating. For instance, in a recent study, performance

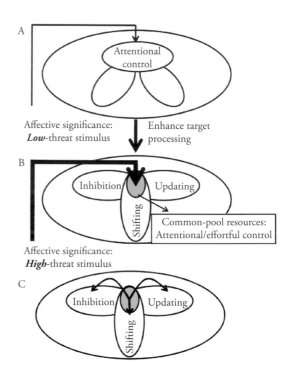

Figure 5.5 Executive control and competition are viewed as involving multiple mechanisms, or resources. Larger unfilled ellipses represent executive control; smaller shapes represent processing resources. **A.** When the threat level is low, affective significance enhances processing of the item. Other executive functions are not strongly affected (smaller ellipses). **B, C.** Processes are hypothesized to share resources, here called "common-pool resources" (see intersections indicated in gray), such that the engagement of one will detract from the processing of the other. Common-pool resources are proposed to be necessary for general functions of attentional/effortful control. **B.** High-threat, emotion-laden stimuli will typically recruit common-pool resources that allow their processing to be prioritized, which will detract from other mechanisms sharing those resources. **C.** High threat will also trigger specific executive functions to handle the challenges to the organism, as indicated by the arrows. For instance, "updating" might be needed to refresh the contents of working memory, "shifting" might be recruited to switch the current task set, and "inhibition" could be called for to cancel previously planned actions.

Adapted from Pessoa (2009) with permission.

during response inhibition was compromised when participants viewed high- vs. low-arousing pictures (Verbruggen & De Houwer, 2007). Specifically, emotional scenes preceding both *go* and *stop* stimuli increased the stop-signal reaction time, a measure of the temporal evolution of inhibitory processes (for another example see Blair et al., 2007). The processing of threat typically will require further actions and, in addition to the consumption of common resources, may involve the triggering of multiple mechanisms that are specific to the task at hand (Figure 5.5C). These will likely depend on several frontoparietal sites that are important for effortful behaviors, including sites in lateral PFC and in parietal cortex (e.g., intraparietal sulcus).

The notion of resources has been employed repeatedly to account for the limits of human information processing. Naturally, in many contexts it is challenging to perform multiple functions at once, so the notion of resource availability is a natural one. Despite its popularity, the concept has at times rightly been criticized as vague (Navon, 1984). Although no great breakthroughs can be claimed in this area, some inroads have been made in terms of operationalizing the concept and clarifying the mechanisms involved. For example, Lavie and colleagues (2004) have shown that loading on more "central resources," such as those needed for working memory or dual-task coordination tasks, results in the use of mechanisms needed to reduce distractor processing (which are needed to guarantee focus on the task at hand). Chun and collaborators have further refined these findings and shown that the impact of a task that requires central resources on "other" processing, such as distractor processing, depends on the extent to which target-distractor processing shares the same resource pool (Park et al., 2007).

A potential approach to understanding resource consumption by threat is to probe the correspondence of brain sites sensitive to specific experimental conditions. It is particularly instructive, for instance, to determine the overlap between manipulations of threat level and those involving attention—given the assumption that attentional manipulations are sensitive to changes in the distribution of processing resources. The "attentional network" has been extensively researched and is believed to involve frontoparietal regions, including the middle frontal gyrus (MFG), ACC, inferior frontal gyrus (IFG), and anterior insula (Corbetta & Shulman, 2002; Kastner & Ungerleider, 2000). In order to assess brain regions sensitive to high levels

of threat, the activation sites for the contrast of CS+ vs. CS– of 34 aversive-conditioning studies were reviewed. Although great emphasis has been placed on involvement of the amygdala in the processing of threat, this summary revealed that several frontal activation sites were consistently reported, including MFG, ACC, IFG, and anterior insula (Figure 5.6). This informal exercise appears to indicate that high-threat processing engages key nodes of the attentional network, consistent with the notion that it is linked to resource consumption.

This link is interesting but admittedly weak, as it simply used "attentional network" as a proxy for "resource consumption." Although activation of the

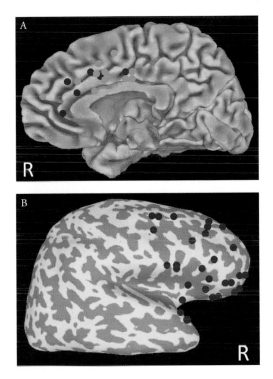

Figure 5.6 Threat processing and prefrontal cortex. Summary of results from 34 positron emission tomography (PET) and fMRI studies of conditioning, from 1995 to 2008, illustrating the coordinates provided for the contrast of threat (CS+) versus safety (CS–). **A.** Activation peaks observed in the medial prefrontal cortex (including the anterior cingulate cortex) are shown in green for right hemisphere results and red for left hemisphere results (all coordinates were projected onto a midline view for display purposes). **B.** Results for the right lateral surface are shown on an inflated surface to reveal multiple prefrontal cortical sites (sites that were not on the lateral surface per se are shown at the corresponding lateral site), which include the middle frontal gyrus and inferior frontal gyrus. In addition, multiple sites were observed in the anterior insula. Note that the surface inflation pushed away some of the activation sites relative to their standard anatomical positions.

Reproduced from Pessoa (2009) with permission.

attentional network likely indicates that effortful conditions have been encountered, a more rigorous link is desirable. We reasoned that it would be possible to further operationalize resource consumption by linking observed evoked fMRI responses and behavioral performance. For instance, in one experiment (Lim et al., 2008), subjects performed a search task under low and high attentional demands (Figure 5.7A, B), which were then contrasted to determine brain sites sensitive to the availability of processing resources. Differential responses (high vs. low) were observed in several frontoparietal regions commonly associated with the attentional network, including those listed above. In the same study, subjects were also shown task-irrelevant threat and safe faces (Figure 5.7A, B). Interestingly, increased responses to threat vs. safe stimuli were observed in several of the same frontoparietal regions. To further test the idea that additional processing resources were recruited during the viewing of threatening stimuli (relative to safe), we correlated evoked fMRI responses by threat and safe stimuli in the regions that were also modulated by attentional load with behavioral accuracy during the task. As illustrated in Figure 5.7C, the higher the ACC recruitment during the threat condition, the worse the behavioral performance (relative to the safe condition). A similar pattern of results was observed in multiple regions, including MFG, IFG, and anterior insula, in addition to superior parietal lobule (although the exact spatial overlap between attentional load and threat effects varied slightly for these regions). Consistent with the increased processing of shock-paired stimuli, threat stimuli exhibited increased behavioral priming and fMRI repetition effects relative to unpaired faces during a subsequent implicit-memory task (Lim et al., 2008). These findings suggest that consumption of processing resources engaged by task-irrelevant threat faces, as indexed via ACC responses, impaired performance on the main task—in this case, likely because the threat faces were task irrelevant (see below).

What are the neural substrates of the interactions between emotion and cognition outlined above? When items are high in threat, robust interactions between affective processing and executive functions are proposed to take place via at least three types of neural mechanisms (Figure 5.8). First, it is hypothesized that threat processing engages attentional/effortful control mechanisms in several frontoparietal sites, including lateral PFC, ACC, and intraparietal sulcus. Some of these sites are illustrated in Figure 5.8. Here I would

emphasize that the ACC engagement will include the *dorsal* site discussed above in the context of resource consumption (see Figure 5.7C, inset). Thus, the present proposal sharply contrasts with the idea that the ACC is subdivided into two sectors: a more anterior and "emotional" one, and a more posterior and "cognitive" one (Bush, Luu, & Posner, 2000). As argued elsewhere (Pessoa, 2008), in most settings, it is artificial to segregate brain regions into these two dichotomous labels (see also Etkin, Egner, & Kalisch, 2011; Shackman et al.,

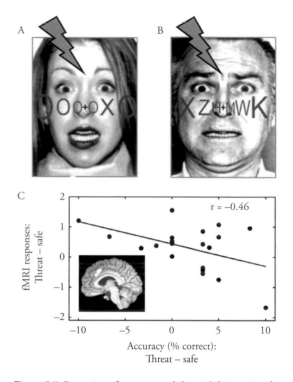

Figure 5.7 Processing of resources and threat. Subjects viewed an array of letters superimposed on task-irrelevant faces and were asked to report whether or not the target letter *X* was present. During the threat condition, faces were previously paired with mild electrical shock (as indicated here), whereas safe stimuli were never paired with shock (threat/safe was crossed the low/high attentional load). **A.** During the low attentional load condition, the target appeared among a uniform array of distractors (pop-out condition). **B.** During the high attentional load condition, a nonuniform array of letters was employed (search condition). **C.** Differential responses to task-irrelevant threat and safe stimuli were inversely correlated with behavioral performance, suggesting that the processing of threat captured processing resources needed for task execution as a function of threat-related responses. Results are shown for a region of interest in the anterior cingulate cortex (inset) that was defined in terms of a separate contrast of high vs. low attentional load (shown in white).

Data reanalyzed from Lim et al. (2008). Adapted from Pessoa (2009) with permission.

2011). Of the frontoparietal sites listed above, the ACC may be particularly important because of its role in integrating inputs from multiple sources, including affective and motivational inputs (Devinsky, Morrell, & Vogt, 1995; Rushworth, Buckley, Behrens, Walton, & Bannerman, 2007), and in this respect works in close cooperation with the anterior insula and OFC (Barbas, 1995). The ACC has also been suggested as being involved in conflict detection, error-likelihood processing, and error monitoring, and it helps determine the benefits and costs of acting. I would suggest further that ACC engagement during threat will impair executive function because common-pool resources that are required to prioritize threat processing are taken up. In other words, the ACC sites engaged by high threat are at the intersection of the resources needed for several executive functions, as indicated by the gray region in Figure 5.5B.

As noted earlier, a second effect of threat is to trigger specific executive functions to handle the ongoing challenges to the organism (Figure 5.8, thick arrows; see also Figure 5.5C). For instance, "updating" might be needed to refresh the contents of working memory, "shifting" might be recruited to switch the current task set, and "inhibition" could be called for to cancel previously planned actions. Again, this recruitment is suggested to depend, at least in part, on the ACC, whose signals are known to influence activity in other brain regions and to modulate cognitive, motor, and visceral responses (Devinsky et al., 1995). For instance, the ACC may engage lateral PFC, which is important in the

manipulation of information, among other important functions. In this manner, additional *specific* processing resources are diverted to the processing of threat information (Figure 5.8). This type of organization is aligned with the proposal that the ACC monitors and detects response conflict at first and subsequently engages lateral PFC territories that further assist in resolution of the conflict (Botvinick, Braver, Barch, Carter, & Cohen, 2001). It is also possible that affective information represented in regions such as the amygdala, OFC, and anterior insula is conveyed (possibly indirectly) to lateral PFC and parietal sites without having to first engage the ACC. In this scenario, the ACC would not function as a central "distributing hub" (as suggested in Figure 5.8) but simply as one of the several players that are engaged during these cognitive–emotional interactions. The merits of these two viewpoints need to be clarified by future research. In concluding our discussion of the involvement of frontoparietal regions in interactions between emotion and executive function, it is important to note that these are some of the same regions initially implicated in having an important effect on perceptual competition—perceptual and executive processes are closely interdependent—in other words, no sharp distinction exists between bottom-up and top-down processes.

A third effect of threat on executive functions involves *state* changes that are implemented via ascending systems (Heimer & Van Hoesen, 2006; Sarter & Bruno, 2000) (Figure 5.8). For instance, the basal forebrain system is known to modulate cortical activity and is not only involved in more general functions such as arousal but also more specific attentional mechanisms (Sarter & Bruno, 2000). More generally, the overall anatomical arrangement of the basal forebrain might involve multiple functional–anatomical macrosystems (Alheid & Heimer, 1988; Zahm, 2006), with wide-ranging effects on brain computations and important clinical implications (Alheid & Heimer, 1988; Pessoa, 2008; Sarter & Bruno, 1999).

Conclusion

The goals of this chapter were twofold. The first was to summarize some important interactions between emotion and cognition, including those that have been documented in detail in the past two decades. Such interactions illustrate contributions of emotion to perception and attention, and to more general executive functions such as response inhibition and working memory. The second goal of the

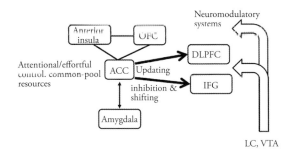

LC, VTA

Figure 5.8 Effects of threat on executive function. Shown here are key brain regions mediating the interactions between emotion and executive control function. A central player in these interactions is the anterior cingulate cortex. Abbreviations: ACC, anterior cingulate cortex; DLPFC, dorsolateral prefrontal cortex; IFG, inferior frontal gyrus; LC, locus coeruleus; OFC, orbitofrontal cortex; VTA, ventral tegmental area.

Adapted from Pessoa (2009) with permission.

chapter was to describe a general framework developed to describe how emotion directs information processing in the brain. In this framework, the dual competition model, interactions between emotion and cognition are illustrated at both the perceptual and executive levels.

Historically, emotion and cognition have been viewed as largely separate entities. And one way in which emotion was often contrasted to cognition was by linking the former with "irrational" or "suboptimal" processes (Oatley et al., 2006) that were more "basic," namely more linked to survival, than cognitive ones. Although much thinking on the relation between emotion and cognition has changed in the past two decades, versions of this viewpoint still are quite frequent in the literature (even if at times implicitly). Research in the past two decades suggests, however, that such view is likely deficient and that in order to understand how complex behaviors are carried out in the brain, an understanding of the interactions between the two may be indispensable. Interestingly, neuroimaging in humans may have been one factor contributing to this changing viewpoint, and if there is some truth to this statement, neuroimaging may eventually be redeemed from the often-stated criticism of the technique amounting to "neo-phrenology." Because neuroimaging techniques afford whole-brain investigations, it has become increasingly evident that large portions of both cortex and subcortex are engaged during emotional manipulations (Kober et al., 2008).

A more radical notion can also be entertained: it may be important to go beyond understanding interactions between emotion and cognition, some of which are suggested to be mutually antagonistic (Drevets & Raichle, 1998), to understanding how cognition and emotion are effectively *integrated* in the brain. As stated recently, "at some point of processing functional specialization is lost, and emotion and cognition conjointly and equally contribute to the control of thought and behavior" (Gray et al., 2002). A key implication from this viewpoint is that, in general, it may be simply counterproductive to attempt to separate emotion and cognition. Instead, their interdependence challenges a simple division of labor into separate "cognitive" and "emotional" domains (Duncan & Barrett, 2007). And, in the context of brain organization, it may be contended that all dichotomizations in terms of emotional and cognitive areas break down when a more in-depth evaluation of the associated functions is carried out.

Future Directions

Following are questions that future research on the interaction between emotion and cognition needs to address:

1. How do interactions between emotion and perception, described here for the case of visual perception, depend on the specific sensory modality considered?

2. Can positive stimuli ever lead to a "hard prioritization" of processing that is comparable to that of threat?

3. Is the impact of higher levels of threat the same across distinct executive functions? For instance, does an affectively potent item impair conflict processing and behavioral inhibition to a similar extent?

4. Should executive functions be viewed as being tied to specific regions, or are they better conceptualized as engaging specific networks of brain regions?

5. In a related fashion, affective significance is often described in terms of responses in the amygdala and possibly a few other key regions (e.g., orbitofrontal cortex, anterior insula). Is affective significance better conceptualized as a "network property," for instance, one that *simultaneously* involves contributions from the these regions?

Acknowledgments

The author wishes to acknowledge support from the National Institute of Mental Health (R01 MH071589) and Phil Spechler for assistance with the chapter's figures and references.

Further Reading

Damasio, A. R. (1994). *Descartes' error: Emotion, reason, and the human brain.* New York: G.P. Putnam.

Duncan, S., & Barrett, L. F. (2007). Affect is a form of cognition: A neurobiological analysis. *Cognition and Emotion, 21,* 1184–1211.

LeDoux, J. E. (1996). *The emotional brain.* New York: Simon & Schuster.

Pessoa, L. (2008). On the relationship between emotion and cognition. *Nature Reviews Neuroscience, 9,* 148–158.

Phelps, E. A. (2006). Emotion and cognition: insights from studies of the human amygdala. *Annual Review of Psychology, 57,* 27–53.

Rolls, E. T. (2005). *Emotion explained.* Oxford: Oxford University Press.

References

Alheid, G. F., & Heimer, L. (1988). New perspectives in basal forebrain organization of special relevance for neuropsychiatric disorders: The striatopallidal, amygdaloid, and corticopetal components of substantia innominata. *Neuroscience, 27*(1), 1–39.

Amaral, D. G., Price, J. L., Pitkanen, A., & Carmichael, S. T. (1992). Anatomical organization of the primate amygdaloid complex. In J. Aggleton (Ed.), *The amygdala: Neurobiological aspects of emotion, memory, and mental dysfunction* (pp. 1–66). New York: Wiley-Liss.

Anderson, A. K. (2005). Affective influences on the attentional dynamics supporting awareness. *Journal of Experimental Psychology: General, 134*(2), 258–281.

Anderson, A. K., Christoff, K., Panitz, D., De Rosa E., & Gabrieli, J. D. (2003). Neural correlates of the automatic processing of threat facial signals. *Journal of Neuroscience, 23*(13), 5627–5633.

Arnold, M. B. (1960). *Emotion and personality.* New York: Columbia University Press.

Aron, A. R., Robbins, T. W., & Poldrack, R. A. (2004). Inhibition and the right inferior frontal cortex. *Trends in Cognitive Sciences, 8*(4), 170–177.

Baddeley, A. (2003). Working memory: Looking back and looking forward. *Nature Reviews Neuroscience, 4*(10), 829–839.

Bar, M. (2003). A cortical mechanism for triggering top-down facilitation in visual object recognition. *Journal of Cognitive Neuroscience, 15*(4), 600–609.

Barbas, H. (1995). Anatomic basis of cognitive-emotional interactions in the primate prefrontal cortex. *Neuroscience and Biobehavioral Reviews, 19*(3), 449–510.

Barrett, L. F., & Bar, M. (2009). See it with feeling: Affective predictions during object perception. *Philosophical Transactions of the Royal Society of London B: Biological Sciences, 364*(1521), 1325–1334.

Bishop, S. J. (2007). Neurocognitive mechanisms of anxiety: An integrative account. *Trends in Cognitive Sciences, 11*(7), 307–316.

Bishop, S. J., Duncan, J., & Lawrence, A. D. (2004). State anxiety modulation of the amygdala response to unattended threat-related stimuli. *Journal of Neuroscience, 24*(46), 10364–10368.

Bishop, S. J., Jenkins, R., & Lawrence, A. D. (2007). Neural processing of fearful faces: Affects of anxiety are gated by perceptual capacity limitations. *Cerebral Cortex, 17*(7), 1595–1603.

Blair, K. S., Smith, B. W., Mitchell, D. G., Morton, J., Vythilingam, M., Pessoa, L., et al. (2007). Modulation of emotion by cognition and cognition by emotion. *Neuroimage, 35*(1), 430–440.

Botvinick, M. M., Braver, T. S., Barch, D. M., Carter, C. S., & Cohen, J. D. (2001). Conflict monitoring and cognitive control. *Psychological Review, 108*(3), 624–652.

Braver, T. S., Gray, J. R., & Burgess, G. C. (2007). Explaining the many varieties of working memory variation: Dual mechanisms of cognitive control. In A. R. A. Conway, C. Jarrold, M. J. Kane, A. Miyake, & J. N. Towse (Eds.), *Variation in working memory* (pp. 76–106). Oxford, UK: Oxford University Press.

Bundesen, C. (1990). A theory of visual attention. *Psychological Review, 97*, 523–547.

Bush, G., Luu, P., & Posner, M. I. (2000). Cognitive and emotional influences in anterior cingulate cortex. *Trends in Cognitive Sciences, 4*(6), 215–222.

Cavada, C., Company, T., Tejedor, J., Cruz-Rizzolo, R. J., & Reinoso-Suarez, F. (2000). The anatomical connections of the macaque monkey orbitofrontal cortex. A review. *Cerebral Cortex, 10*(3), 220–242.

Corbetta, M., & Shulman, G. L. (2002). Control of goal-directed and stimulus-driven attention in the brain. *Nature Reviews Neuroscience, 3*(3), 201–215.

Damasio, A. R. (1994). *Descartes' error: Emotion, reason, and the human brain.* New York: Putnam.

Damasio, A. R. (1999). *The feeling of what happens: Body and emotion in the making of consciousness.* New York: Harcourt Brace.

de Gelder, B., Vroomen, J., Pourtois, G., & Weiskrantz, L. (1999). Non-conscious recognition of affect in the absence of striate cortex. *Neuroreport, 10*(18), 3759–3763.

Desimone, R. (1998). Visual attention mediated by biased competition in extrastriate visual cortex. *Philosophical Transactions of the Royal Society of London B: Biological Sciences, 353* , 1245–1255.

Desimone, R., & Duncan, J. (1995). Neural mechanisms of selective attention. *Annual Review of Neuroscience, 18* , 193–222.

Devinsky, O., Morrell, M. J., & Vogt, B. A. (1995). Contributions of anterior cingulate cortex to behaviour. *Brain, 118* (Pt 1), 279–306.

Dolan, R. (2003). Emotion, cognition, and behavior. *Science, 298*(5596), 1191–1194.

Drevets, W. C., & Raichle, M. E. (1998). Reciprocal suppression of regional cerebral blood flow during emotional versus higher cognitive processes: Implications for interactions between emotion and cognition. *Cognition & Emotion, 12*(3), 353–385.

Duncan, J. (1996). Cooperating brain systems in selective perception and action. In T. Inui & J. L. McClelland (Eds.), *Attention and performance XVI* (pp. 549–578). Cambridge, MA: MIT Press.

Duncan, J. (1998). Converging levels of analysis in the cognitive neuroscience of visual attention. *Philosophical Transactions of the Royal Society of London B: Biological Sciences, 353* , 1307–1317.

Duncan, J., Emslie, H., Williams, P., Johnson, R., & Freer, C. (1996). Intelligence and the frontal lobe: The organization of goal-directed behavior. *Cognitive Psychology, 30*(3), 257–303.

Duncan, S., & Barrett, L. F. (2007). Affect is a form of cognition: A neurobiological analysis. *Cognition & Emotion, 21*(6), 1184–1211.

Eastwood, J. D., Smilek, D., & Merikle, P. M. (2001). Differential attentional guidance by unattended faces expressing positive and negative emotion. *Perception & Psychophysics, 63*(6), 1004–1013.

Ekman, P. (1992). An argument for basic emotions. *Cognition & Emotion, 6* , 169–200.

Etkin, A., Egner, T., & Kalisch, R. (2011). Emotional processing in anterior cingulate and medial prefrontal cortex. *Trends in Cognitive Sciences, 15*(2), 85–93.

Etkin, A., Klemenhagen, K. C., Dudman, J. T., Rogan, M. T., Hen, R., Kandel, E. R., & Hirsch, J. (2004). Individual differences in trait anxiety predict the response of the basolateral amygdala to unconsciously processed fearful faces. *Neuron, 44*(6), 1043–1055.

Eysenck, M. W., Derakshan, N., Santos, R., & Calvo, M. G. (2007). Anxiety and cognitive performance: Attentional control theory. *Emotion, 7*(2), 336–353.

Fox, E., Russo, R., Bowles, R., & Dutton, K. (2001). Do threatening stimuli draw or hold visual attention in subclinical anxiety? *Journal of Experimental Psychology: General, 130*(4), 681–700.

Fuster, J. M. (2008). *The prefrontal cortex.* San Diego, CA: Academic Press.

Ghashghaei, H. T., Hilgetag, C. C., & Barbas, H. (2007). Sequence of information processing for emotions based on the anatomic dialogue between prefrontal cortex and amygdala. *Neuroimage, 34*(3), 905–923.

Goldstein, M., Brendel, G., Tuescher, O., Pan, H., Epstein, J., Beutel, M., et al. (2007). Neural substrates of the interaction of emotional stimulus processing and motor inhibitory control: An emotional linguistic go/no-go fMRI study. *Neuroimage, 36*(3), 1026–1040.

Gray, J. R., Braver, T. S., & Raichle, M. E. (2002). Integration of emotion and cognition in the lateral prefrontal cortex. *Proceedings of the National Academy of Sciences U S A, 99*(6), 4115–4120.

Grossberg, S. (1980). How does a brain build a cognitive code? *Psychological Review, 87*(1), 1–51.

Guillery, R. W. (1995). Anatomical evidence concerning the role of the thalamus in corticocortical communication: A brief review. *Journal of Anatomy, 187* (Pt 3), 583–592.

Haidt, J. (2003). The moral emotions. In R. J. Davidson, K. R. Scherer, & H. H. Goldsmith (Eds.), *Handbook of affective sciences* (pp. 852–870). Oxford: Oxford University Press.

Harter, M. R., & Aine, C. J. (1984). Brain mechanisms of visual selective attention. In R. Parasuraman & D. R. Davies (Eds.), *Varieties of attention* (pp. 293–321). Orlando, FL: Academic.

Heimer, L., & Van Hoesen, G. W. (2006). The limbic lobe and its output channels: Implications for emotional functions and adaptive behavior. *Neuroscience and Biobehavioral Reviews, 30*(2), 126–147.

Hsu, S. M., & Pessoa, L. (2007). Dissociable effects of bottom-up and top-down factors on the processing of unattended fearful faces. *Neuropsychologia, 45*(13), 3075–3086.

Kahneman, D. (1973). *Attention and effort.* Englewood Cliffs, NJ: Prentice-Hall.

Kastner, S., & Ungerleider, L. G. (2000). Mechanisms of visual attention in the human cortex. *Annual Review of Neuroscience, 23* , 315–341.

Kober, H., Barrett, L. F., Joseph, J., Bliss-Moreau, E., Lindquist, K., & Wager, T. D. (2008). Functional grouping and cortical-subcortical interactions in emotion: A meta-analysis of neuroimaging studies. *Neuroimage, 42*(2), 998–1031.

Kunst-Wilson, W. R., & Zajonc, R. B. (1980). Affective discrimination of stimuli that cannot be recognized. *Science, 207*(4430), 557–558.

Lang, P. J., Davis, M., & Ohman, A. (2000). Fear and anxiety: Animal models and human cognitive psychophysiology. *Journal of Affective Disorders, 61*(3), 137–159.

Lavie, N., Hirst, A., de Fockert, J. W., & Viding, E. (2004). Load theory of selective attention and cognitive control. *Journal of Experimental Psychology: General, 133*(3), 339–354.

Lazarus, R. S. (1984). On the primacy of cognition. *American Psychologist, 39*(2), 124–129.

LeDoux, J. E. (1996). *The emotional brain.* New York: Simon & Schuster.

Lim, S. L., Padmala, S., & Pessoa, L. (2008). Affective learning modulates spatial competition during low-load attentional conditions. *Neuropsychologia, 46*(5), 1267–1278.

Lim, S. L., Padmala, S., & Pessoa, L. (2009). Segregating the significant from the mundane on a moment-to-moment basis

via direct and indirect amygdala contributions. *Proceedings of the National Academy of Sciences U S A, 106*(39), 16841–16846.

Mathews, A., & Mackinstosh, B. (1998). A cognitive model of selective processing in anxiety. *Cognitive Therapy and Research, 22*(6), 539–560.

Merikle, P. M., Smilek, D., & Eastwood, J. D. (2001). Perception without awareness: Perspectives from cognitive psychology. *Cognition, 79*(1-2), 115–134.

Miyake, A., Friedman, N. P., Emerson, M. J., Witzki, A. H., Howerter, A., & Wager, T. D. (2000). The unity and diversity of executive functions and their contributions to complex "frontal lobe" tasks: A latent variable analysis. *Cognitive Psychology, 41*(1), 49–100.

Moll, J., Zahn, R., de Oliveira-Souza, R., Krueger, F., & Grafman, J. (2005). The neural basis of human moral cognition. *Nature Reviews Neuroscience, 6*(10), 799–809.

Morris, J. S., Ohman, A., & Dolan, R. J. (1998). Conscious and unconscious emotional learning in the human amygdala. *Nature, 393*(6684), 467–470.

Navon, D. (1984). Resources—a theoretical soup stone? *Psychological Review, 91*(2), 216–234.

Norman, D. A., & Bobrow, D. G. (1975). On data-limited and resource-limited processes. *Cognitive Psychology, 7* , 44–64.

Norman, D. A., & Shallice, T. (1986). Attention to action: Willed and automatic control of behavior. In R.J. Davidson, G.E. Schwartz, & D. Shapiro (Eds.), *Consciousness and self-regulation.* New York: Plenum.

Nowak, L. G., & Bullier, J. (1997). The timing of information transfer in the visual system. In K. Rockland, J. Kass, & A. Peters (Eds.), *Cerebral cortex: Extrastriate cortex in primate* (Vol. 21, pp. 205–241). New York: Plenum.

Oatley, K., Keltner, D., & Jenkins, J. M. (2006). *Understanding emotions.* Malden, MA: Blackwell Publishing.

Ohman, A. (2002). Automaticity and the amygdala: Nonconscious responses to emotional faces. *Current Directions in Psychological Science, 11* , 62–66.

Ohman, A., Flykt, A., & Esteves, F. (2001). Emotion drives attention: Detecting the snake in the grass. *Journal of Experimental Psychology: General, 130*(3), 466–478.

Padmala, S., & Pessoa, L. (2008). Affective learning enhances visual detection and responses in primary visual cortex. *Journal of Neuroscience, 28*(24), 6202–6210.

Panksepp, J. (1998). *Affective neuroscience: The foundations of human and animal emotions.* New York: Oxford University Press.

Park, S., Kim, M. S., & Chun, M. M. (2007). Concurrent working memory load can facilitate selective attention: Evidence for specialized load. *Journal of Experimental Psychology: Human Perception and Performance, 33*(5), 1062–1075.

Pashler, H. (1998). *The psychology of attention.* Cambridge, MA: MIT Press.

Perlstein, W. M., Elbert, T., & Stenger, V. A. (2002). Dissociation in human prefrontal cortex of affective influences on working memory-related activity. *Proceedings of the National Academy of Sciences U S A, 99*(3), 1736–1741.

Pessoa, L. (2005). To what extent are emotional visual stimuli processed without attention and awareness? *Current Opinion in Neurobiology, 15*(2), 188–196.

Pessoa, L. (2008). On the relationship between emotion and cognition. *Nature Reviews Neuroscience, 9*(2), 148–158.

Pessoa, L. (2009). How do emotion and motivation direct executive function? *Trends in Cognitive Sciences, 13*(4), 160–166.

Pessoa, L., & Adolphs, R. (2010). Emotion processing and the amygdala: From a "low road" to "many roads" of evaluating biological significance. *Nature Reviews Neuroscience, 11*(11), 773–783. doi: 10.1038/nrn2920

Pessoa, L., & Adolphs, R. (in preparation). Subcortical affective processing: A critical analysis and re-evaluation.

Pessoa, L., & Engelmann, J. B. (2010). How does motivation affect perception and attentional control? *Frontiers in Neuroscience.*

Pessoa, L, Japee, S., Sturman, D., & Ungerleider, L. G. (2006). Target visibility and visual awareness modulate amygdala responses to fearful faces. *Cerebral Cortex, 16*(3), 366–375.

Pessoa, L., Kastner, S., & Ungerleider, L. G. (2002). Attentional control of the processing of neutral and emotional stimuli. *Cognitive Brain Research, 15*(1), 31–45.

Pessoa, L., McKenna, M., Gutierrez, E., & Ungerleider, L.G. (2002). Neural processing of emotional faces requires attention. *Proceedings of the National Academy of Sciences U S A, 99*(17), 11458–11463.

Pessoa, L, Padmala, S., & Morland, T. (2005). Fate of unattended fearful faces in the amygdala is determined by both attentional resources and cognitive modulation. *Neuroimage, 28*(1), 249–255.

Phelps, E. A. (2006). Emotion and cognition: Insights from studies of the human amygdala. *Annual Review of Psychology, 57*, 27–53.

Phelps, E. A., Ling, S., & Carrasco, M. (2006). Emotion facilitates perception and potentiates the perceptual benefits of attention. *Psychological Science, 17*(4), 292–299.

Robbins, T. W. (2007). Shifting and stopping: Fronto-striatal substrates, neurochemical modulation and clinical implications. *Philosophical Transactions of the Royal Society of London B: Biological Sciences, 362*(1481), 917–932.

Rolls, E. T. (2005). *Emotion explained.* Oxford: Oxford University Press.

Rubia, K, Smith, A. B., Brammer, M. J., & Taylor, E. (2003). Right inferior prefrontal cortex mediates response inhibition while mesial prefrontal cortex is responsible for error detection. *Neuroimage, 20*(1), 351–358.

Rushworth, M. F., Buckley, M. J., Behrens, T. E., Walton, M. E., & Bannerman, D. M. (2007). Functional organization of the medial frontal cortex. *Current Opinion in Neurobiology, 17*(2), 220–227.

Sarter, M., & Bruno, J. P. (1999). Abnormal regulation of corticopetal cholinergic neurons and impaired information processing in neuropsychiatric disorders. *Trends in Neuroscience, 22*(2), 67–74.

Sarter, M., & Bruno, J. P. (2000). Cortical cholinergic inputs mediating arousal, attentional processing and dreaming: Differential afferent regulation of the basal forebrain by telencephalic and brainstem afferents. *Neuroscience, 95*(4), 933–952.

Shackman, A. J., Salomons, T. V., Slagter, H. A., Fox, A. S., Winter, J. J., & Davidson, R. J. (2011). The integration of negative affect, pain and cognitive control in the cingulate cortex. *Nature Reviews Neuroscience, 12*(3), 154–167.

Sherman, S. M., & Guillery, R. W. (1996). Functional organization of thalamocortical relays. *Journal of Neurophysiology, 76*(3), 1367–1395.

Shipp, S. (2004). The brain circuitry of attention. *Trends in Cognitive Sciences, 8*(5), 223–230.

Smith, E. E., & Jonides, J. (1999). Storage and executive processes in the frontal lobes. *Science, 283*(5408), 1657–1661.

Stuss, D., & Knight, R. T. (Eds.). (2002). *Principles of frontal lobe function.* Oxford: Oxford University Press.

Verbruggen, F., & De Houwer, J. (2007). Do emotional stimuli interfere with response inhibition? Evidence from the stop signal paradigm. *Cognition & Emotion, 21*(2), 391–403.

Verbruggen, F., Liefooghe, B., & Vandierendonck, A. (2004). The interaction between stop signal inhibition and distractor interference in the flanker and Stroop task. *Acta Psychologica (Amsterdam), 116*(1), 21–37.

Vuilleumier, P. (2005). How brains beware: Neural mechanisms of emotional attention. *Trends in Cognitive Sciences, 9*(12), 585–594.

Vuilleumier, P., Armony, J. L., Driver, J., & Dolan, R. J. (2001). Effects of attention and emotion on face processing in the human brain: An event-related fMRI study. *Neuron, 30*(3), 829–841.

Vuilleumier, P., & Schwartz, S. (2001). Emotional facial expressions capture attention. *Neurology, 56*(2), 153–158.

Whalen, P. J. (1998). Fear, vigilance, and ambiguity: Initial neuroimaging studies of the human amygdala. *Current Directions in Psychological Science, 7*(6), 177–188.

Whalen, P. J., Kagan, J., Cook, R. G., Davis, F. C., Kim, H., Polis, S., et al. (2004). Human amygdala responsivity to masked fearful eye whites. *Science, 306*(5704), 2061.

Whalen, P. J., Rauch, S. L., Etcoff, N. L., McInerney, S. C., Lee, M. B., & Jenike, M. A. (1998). Masked presentations of emotional facial expressions modulate amygdala activity without explicit knowledge. *Journal of Neuroscience, 18*(1), 411–418.

Wiens, S. (2006). Subliminal emotion perception in brain imaging: Findings, issues, and recommendations. *Progress in Brain Research, 156*, 105–121.

Zahm, D. S. (2006). The evolving theory of basal forebrain functional-anatomical "macrosystems." *Neuroscience and Biobehavioral Reviews, 30*(2), 148–172.

Zajonc, R. B. (1984). On the primacy of affect. *American Psychologist, 39*(2), 117–123.

Genetics and Emotion

Andreia Santos, Lukas Pezawas, *and* Andreas Meyer-Lindenberg

Abstract

That genes influence how we feel and behave is without question. Yet despite decades of research, the mechanisms through which this occurs are only recently coming into focus. This chapter reviews studies that have contributed toward narrowing the gap in knowledge regarding genes and emotional behavior. First, the discussion focuses on Williams syndrome, a genetic "lesional" model, which offers an exceptional framework for understanding the relationship between genes, brain circuits, and atypical socioemotional behavior. The chapter then reviews recent findings for the more common case of mood disorders, for which as for most psychiatry conditions the genetics are complex. The concepts of intermediate phenotypes and imaging genetics will be introduced here as tools to address this question. Finally, evidence at the neurochemical level is presented which suggests that prosocial neuropeptides play a crucial role in the neurobiological chain linking genes and emotion.

Key Words: Williams syndrome, microdeletion syndrome, amygdala, fusiform face area, serotonin, 5-HTTLPR, brain-derived neurotrophic factor (BDNF), monoamine oxidase a (MAO-A)

Introduction

Several lines of thought lead to the topic of genetics of emotion: social-emotional behavior is critical for survival in primates, who live in complex societies, and aspects of social interaction style and temperament are heritable in humans. In addition, abnormal social-emotional behavior is a key component of a wide range of neurodevelopmental and neuropsychiatric diseases. As well as being debilitating, these disorders impose enormous medical and economic burdens, making understanding of the mechanisms underlying them crucial. However, the genetic architecture of psychiatric risk and social-emotional behavior is complex and is dominated by multiple interacting contributing factors. Identifying the genes and understanding the neural mechanisms linking genes to behavior is thus one of the greater challenges for modern biomedical research, albeit a promising one (Meyer-Lindenberg & Weinberger,

2006). Within this framework, disorders with a known major genetic "lesion" affecting social-emotional behavior, such as Williams syndrome (WS), offer an exceptional framework for understanding the relationship between genes, brain circuits, cognition, and social-emotional behavior. The first section of this chapter will provide a description of WS and review studies on social-emotional processing in the disorder. This section will also highlight the role of the amygdala on socioemotional processing and its involvement in WS.

Things get more complex, however, when we consider the genetic contributions to common psychiatric conditions and normal socioemotional behaviors. Because genes do not encode for psychopathology, it is reasonable to expect that the association or penetrance of gene effects will be greater at the level of relatively simpler and biologically based phenotypes. The intermediate-phenotype concept represents a strategy for characterizing the neural systems affected by risk gene variants to elucidate quantitative, mechanistic aspects of brain function implicated in psychiatric disease. This concept will be briefly recapitulated in this chapter. As an important example of this strategy, we will review the development of imaging genetics, a method for mapping neural structure and activity as a function of genotype in living humans. The introduction of imaging genetics as a research tool (Hariri & Weinberger, 2003) has encouraged a conceptual transformation by showing that the greater power of intermediate phenotypes lies in using genetic risk variants as tools for the discovery of the mediating neural mechanisms that bridge the gap from DNA sequence to pathological behavior. We will focus here on mood disorders as our example of highly heritable disorders that have been linked to abnormal neural and behavioral emotion processing. It is important to note that most of the arguments apply equally to other complex psychiatric disorders, such as schizophrenia (Meyer-Lindenberg & Weinberger, 2006), attention-deficit hyperactivity disorder (Waldman & Gizer, 2006), addictions (Goldman, Oroszi, & Ducci, 2005), and autism (Belmonte et al., 2004).

Finally, this chapter will briefly review findings on other quantitative parameters from neurochemistry, such as neuropeptide levels, that can be powerful tools for indexing intermediate neurobiological processes influenced by genetic variation.

Williams Syndrome: A Unique "Experiment of Nature"

In order to understand the neurobiological basis of social-emotional behavior, we need to understand the relationships between functionally relevant brain areas, its genetic underpinnings, and neurochemical pathways (Meyer-Lindenberg, 2008). This is a challenging task requiring a multidisciplinary approach, preferably within the same homogeneous populations and including a sufficient number of participants. Contrary to behaviorally defined disorders, such as autism spectrum disorders (ASD), which are as a rule genetically highly complex and encompass a spectrum of clinical subgroups, genetic neurodevelopmental disorders are etiologically homogeneous and allow researchers to link known genetic alterations to a specific phenotype (for a review see Walter, Mazaika, & Reiss, 2009). Indeed, in the last decades, research on "experiments of nature" (Reiss et al., 2004) such as WS has provided insights into the impact of a major alteration in the expression of

only a few genes on atypical brain development and function. Such research has also revealed neural systems that have been implicated in socioemotional cognition and behavior in general (for a review see Meyer-Lindenberg, Mervis, & Berman, 2006). In the next sections, the main features characterizing WS are presented, with a focus on recent studies on socioemotional processing in the disorder.

A Unique Combination of Behavioral, Cognitive, Neuroanatomical, and Genetic Features

WS is a rare genetic syndrome caused by a microdeletion of ~26 contiguous genes on chromosome band 7q11.23 in one of the two chromosomes 7 (Donnai & Karmiloff-Smith, 2000; Korenberg et al., 2000; Peoples et al., 2000). This leads to a gene dosage effect that includes the gene for elastin (*ELN*) in over 96% of individuals with WS (Lowery et al., 1995). The microdeletion is due to a hemizygous deletion during meiosis (Urbán et al., 1996) of repetitive sequences flanking the region (Korenberg et al., 2000). It is characterized by a unique combination of behavioral, cognitive, neuroanatomical, and genetic features (see further details below). Its estimated incidence ranges from 1 in 20,000 (Morris, Demsey, Leonard, Dilts, & Blackburn, 1988) to 1 in 7,500 (Strømme, Bjørnstad, & Ramstad, 2002) live births. Because the genes involved in WS are known and the dosage of at least some of these genes is clearly abnormal, the study of neurobiological mechanisms associated with the deviant behavior (e.g., hypersociability) in WS affords a good means of investigating the genetic influences on complex brain socioemotional cognitive functions in a "bottom-up" way (Meyer-Lindenberg, Mervis, et al., 2006).

The hallmark of WS behavior is undoubtedly the high sociability, the so-called hypersociability (Jones et al., 2000), that is uniquely found in this condition. Individuals with WS show a worrisome tendency to approach strangers and have a lack of social inhibition. From the earliest stages of development, they are observed clinically as overfriendly and socially fearless. They show an eager drive toward social engagement, even with people they objectively consider to be not approachable (Frigerio et al., 2006). They are also highly empathetic (Klein-Tasman & Mervis, 2003). At the same time, they experience increased nonsocial anxiety and substantial problems in social adjustment, and have poor social judgment and poor peer relationships (e.g., Gosch & Pankau, 1997), all of which suggest that "more [sociability] is not always better" (Santos, 2008).

Along with these striking behavioral abnormalities, individuals with WS have an uneven cognitive profile, with some abilities being only mildly affected (e.g., verbal abilities; for a review see Mervis & Becerra, 2007) while others are severely impaired (e.g., visuoconstructive abilities; Rondan, Santos, Mancini, Livet, & Deruelle, 2008). The IQ scores of individuals with WS also suggest that it is not a unitary condition characterized by homogeneous slowness of cognitive development but by a variety of conditions in which some cognitive functions may be more disrupted than others (for a review see Santos, Milne, Rosset, & Deruelle, 2007). Regarding socioemotional cognitive abilities, individuals with WS have a *peak* and *valley* (deviant) profile, with social-emotional relevance significantly boosting performance of WS groups. In our studies such groups showed dissociated abilities to process emotion in human vs. nonhuman faces (Santos et al., 2007; Santos, Rossett, Deruelle, 2009), emotional vs. nonemotional contextual cues (Santos, Rondan, Milne, Démonet, & Deruelle, 2008), and verbal vs. visual theory of mind (Santos & Deruelle, 2009). They also exhibited diminished threat detection (Santos, Silva, Rosset, & Deruelle, 2010), in accordance with evidence for abnormalities in brain areas for social threat processing (e.g., amygdala) in WS.

At the neural level, there is evidence for atypical brain structure (e.g., decreased depth of the intraparietal sulcus and abnormal size of amygdala and orbitofrontal cortex; Meyer-Lindenberg et al., 2004; Reiss et al., 2004; Thompson et al., 2005), function (e.g., decreased amygdala reactivity to threatening faces; Meyer-Lindenberg, Hariri, et al., 2005), and connectivity (e.g., decreased interactions between the fusiform face area and the amygdala; Sarpal et al., 2008). These findings suggest that brains of individuals with WS develop differently from the outset. Such brain development probably has subtle but widespread repercussions at the cognitive and behavioral levels.

In the following sections, we review some of our findings on social-emotional processing in WS and relate them to amygdala abnormalities found at the neural level in the disorder.

Socioemotional Processing in Williams Syndrome

I. FACIAL-EMOTIONAL PROCESSING

Facial-emotion processing functions are thought to be important evolutionary skills that have helped drive the development of our social behavior. Human faces are a special site for conveying social and emotional information; they are a means by which intentions and desires from others can be inferred and are a crucial reference for social communication. It has been argued that the remarkable ease with which people can instantly recognize a face depends on perceptual processes, as evident, for instance, in our superior ability to recognize faces in an upright rather than inverted orientation (e.g., Farah, Tanaka, & Drain, 1995). There is little doubt that normally developing individuals use configural strategies to process faces (e.g., Bukach, Gauthier, & Tarr, 2006). Moreover, it has been shown that this mechanism breaks down when faces are presented in an inverted orientation, as inversion disrupts a face's usual configuration (e.g., Rhodes, Brake, & Atkinson, 1993). Interestingly, early studies on face processing in WS failed to show this inversion effect in individuals with WS, as their overall scores were similar to those of normal controls (Deruelle, Mancini, Livet, Cassé-Perrot, & de Schonen, 1999; Karmiloff-Smith, 1997). This evidence launched the debate of whether face-processing skills in WS relied (or not) on the use of atypical (local rather than configural) perceptual strategies (Rondan et al., 2008). One of the reasons that this issue has been debated is that previous studies had focused mainly on the perceptual mechanisms underlying face processing and often neglected the possibility that more social mechanisms could also interfere with face-processing skills in WS (Santos et al., 2007). Given the unusual and striking social profile characterizing WS, these latter mechanisms should certainly be considered. On the basis of this reasoning, we investigated whether the ability to process faces in WS relates to increased interest in social stimuli or, alternatively, whether it depends on more general mechanisms, not exclusively social in origin, such as visual perceptual strategies (Santos et al., 2009). A facial-expression task (Rosset, Rondan, Da Fonseca, Santos, Assouline, & Deruelle, 2008) was used, because one of the biggest reasons for faces being considered as a special social stimulus is that they can express a wide range of emotional states. A special feature of this task was that it included not only photographs of real faces (as was the case for previous studies in the literature) but also human and nonhuman cartoon faces. Importantly, this allowed for a control for the effect of social relevance (real faces are more socially relevant than cartoon faces) on face-processing performance patterns. In addition, these three types of faces were presented either upright or inverted, allowing a control for the use of typical configural face-processing perceptual strategies. This study included 29 individuals with WS who were individually matched to 29 chronological age (CA)- and 29 mental age (MA)-matched, normally developing controls (in order to control for the effects of life experience and overall intellectual functioning, respectively). Results showed that a face's social relevance has an increased impact in WS individuals relative to typically developing controls, which cannot be explained by a reliance on atypical perceptual abilities. More precisely, it was found that individuals with WS process facial expressions of emotion at the level expected of their MA and even of their CA controls, but only when the expressions were displayed in human faces (photographs of real faces and human cartoon faces). This was not the case for nonhuman faces. The contribution of these findings toward understanding how deletion of a set of genes can affect social-emotional processing and behavior is presented later in this chapter.

II. PROCESSING OF EMOTIONAL VS. NONEMOTIONAL CONTEXTUAL CUES

Contextual cues are important for discriminating simple emotions and complex mental states from facial expressions (Ellis & Young, 1989). The ability to process contextual cues is a relevant aspect of social cognition, as it may influence (or be influenced by) one's experience with social contexts. As mentioned earlier, individuals with WS show increased interest in social stimuli and drive toward social interaction. Given this aspect of hypersociability in WS, we have hypothesized that individuals' ability to extract emotional information from contextual cues would be boosted compared to that of extracting nonemotional information from the same cues.

To test this hypothesis, we used two tasks including similar visual scenes but in which either a facial expression of emotion (emotionally relevant task) or an object (nonemotionally relevant task) was missing (see Figure 6.1; Santos et al., 2008). This study included 16 individuals with WS individually matched to 16 CA- and 16 MA-matched typically developing controls. Their ability to use contextual cues to recognize the missing emotional vs. nonemotional information was compared. Although both tasks were closely matched, individuals with WS showed a different pattern of performance as a function of the task. Individuals with WS performed at similar levels to MA- and even CA-matched controls on the facial-expression but not on the object-recognition task, which suggests that their ability

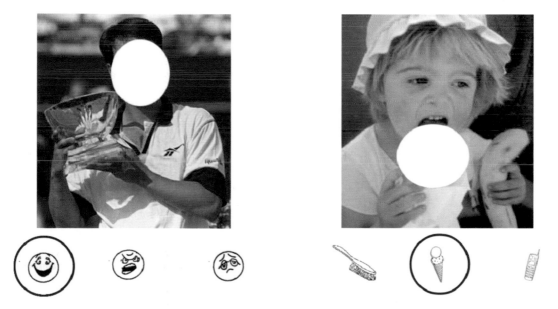

Figure 6.1 Example of stimuli used to investigate processing of emotional vs. nonemotional contextual cues in Williams syndrome (Santos et al., 2008; Da Fonseca, Santos, et al., 2009). **Left**: Example of a stimulus used in the facial expression recognition task. The top picture corresponds to a visual scene in which a character's facial expression was masked. The bottom three pictures are response options: picture 1 is the correct response (happy), and picture 2 (angry) and picture 3 (sad) are distracters. **Right**: Example of stimulus used in the object recognition task. The top picture corresponds to a visual scene in which an object was masked. The bottom three pictures are response options: picture 2 is the correct response (ice cream), and picture 1 (hair brush) and picture 3 (cell phone) are distracters.

to use contextual cues depends on the emotional relevance of the task. In other words, the findings indicated that emotional relevance boosts context processing in WS to the point of overcoming MA- and reaching CA-expected levels of performance (Santos et al., 2008).

III. PROCESSING OF THREATENING FACIAL EXPRESSIONS

Detection of social threat has clear adaptive value (Darwin, 1872/1965), and social-emotional skills are critical for survival. There is a clear evolutionary advantage for humans who can efficiently recognize and detect social threat in their environment, as this ability enables them to anticipate danger, prepare defensive behavior, and escape potentially dangerous situations (e.g., Öhman, Lundqvist, & Esteves, 2001; Öhman & Mineka, 2001, 2003). From early in life and throughout development, we learn to use facial expressions as powerful sources of social information that is crucial for guiding behavior toward or away from interaction. While facial expressions of emotion in general provide a wealth of information, angry faces in particular provide specific information on potential social threat. Indeed, these are universally read as critical cues for interpersonal threat and potent warning signals. Angry faces seem thus to hold a special status for normally developing individuals, and some would argue that humans are biologically prepared, or "hard-wired," for the recognition of anger or threat specifically (Öhman, 1993).

In agreement with this, there is a great deal of evidence supporting the idea that angry faces capture attention and are processed promptly and efficiently (Vuilleumier & Schwartz, 2001). The empirical basis for specific mechanisms with regard to anger comes mostly from studies using visual search paradigms, such as the "face-in-the-crowd" task. In this task, participants are instructed to detect the presence or absence of a target emotional face among a crowd of distracter faces. In a pioneering study using this task, Hansen and Hansen (1988) showed an *anger superiority* effect, with angry faces being detected more quickly and accurately than happy faces, independent of the number of distracters—they "pop out" when happy faces do not. Interestingly, this anger superiority effect holds even for neurodevelopmental disorders, such as autism and Asperger syndrome (Ashwin, Wheelwright, & Baron-Cohen, 2006; Krysko & Rutherford, 2009), and for anxiety disorders (for a review see Bar-Haim, Lamy, Pergamin, Bakermans,-Kranenburg, Van IJzendoorn, 2007).

To examine whether the anger superiority effect could be found in WS, we conducted a study comparing 21 children with WS to 21 MA-matched controls (Santos et al., 2010). This study included two visual search tasks examining detection of angry or happy target faces and controlling for attentional aspects related to the size of crowd surrounding the faces (see Figure 6.2). Participants were asked to respond "yes" or "no" (two–forced choice paradigm) if there was one angry face ("Angry Task") or one happy face ("Happy Task") in the crowd. The target face was surrounded by either two, five, or eight distracters (happy or angry faces depending on the target face).

The results showed no group differences for viewing happy faces; however, for angry faces, the WS group, but not the control group, showed a significant performance decrease for the eight-distracters condition, indicating absence of an anger superiority effect. Findings of this study were in agreement with the WS social-behavior profile. Together with high sociability and an unusual interest toward social

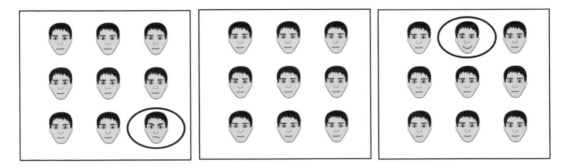

Figure 6.2 Example of stimuli used to investigate threat detection in Williams syndrome (Santos et al., 2010). Illustration of trials including nine faces, with either one target surrounded by eight distracters (target-present trials) or nine distracters (target-absent trials). **Left:** Target-present trial of the Angry Task. **Center:** No-target trial of both Angry and Happy Tasks. **Right:** Target-present trial of the Happy Task.

information, WS individuals show an enhanced drive to interact with others, including strangers. Putatively, this absence of fear of strangers is related to atypical perception of social threat and decreased detection of threatening social stimuli. However, the detection of social threat is a crucial ability for one to respond to social demands in an adaptive and protective manner (Öhman et al., 2001; Öhman & Mineka, 2001, 2003). Findings of this study suggest a link between reduced ability to detect social threat and genetically determined reduced social fear in WS.

Insights Gained from Studies on Socioemotional Processing in WS

These studies have shown that individuals with the genetic microdeletion WS process crucial social-emotional information, such as faces, contextual cues, and threatening stimuli, in a deviant fashion relative to typically developing individuals.

Based on the theoretical framework of adult neuropsychology, evidence for double dissociations within a syndrome and within domains could be interpreted in terms of impaired vs. intact cognitive modules, or as being the result of a dissociation between independently functioning modules of cognition—one being responsible for the processing of emotionally relevant features, such as human facial traits and emotional cues (spared), and another being responsible for the processing of nonemotional stimuli, such as nonhuman facial features and objects (impaired). Within this framework, WS was seen for a long time as a promising model to bolster innate modularity claims (for a critical review see Karmiloff-Smith, Brown, Grice, & Paterson, 2003), that is, to demonstrate the existence of genetically determined, innate, and independently functioning modules, some of which are intact (e.g., language and face processing) and others impaired (e.g., visuospatial cognition). However, findings of the studies reported above challenge the notion of clear-cut intactness by showing atypical patterns of social-emotional processing in WS, which can hardly be interpreted on the basis of a modular view of cognition. Importantly, WS patterns of performance were found to be deviant, not delayed, spared, or impaired, relative to that of controls across the studies. Because in individuals with WS the neurocomputational constraints are altered since the time of conception, the atypical patterns found at the cognitive level are probably the result of *atypical* development rather than being solely a reflection of intact and impaired modules since the

initial state (for a review, see Karmiloff-Smith & Thomas, 2003). Findings of these studies provide a contribution to the debate of modular vs. neuro-constructivist approaches of social-cognitive development, lending strong support to the latter.

Importantly, these studies also provide intriguing clues to a link between social-emotional cognition and behavior. Studies on a contrasting model of social behavior, autism, using the same tasks as those used with WS, have highlighted this issue. Individuals with autism show profound impairments in social functioning (e.g., difficulties interacting with other and attending to people) and emotional reciprocity, whereas WS individuals have a quite the opposite profile. Such contrast in social behavior—*hypo*sociable vs. *hyper*sociable—is at the origin of the idea that the two syndromes are mirror images of one another and that what is spared in WS might be impaired in autism (Tager-Flusberg, Plesa Skewerer, & Joseph, 2006).

Rosset and colleagues (2008) examined face processing in 20 individuals with autism relative to CA-matched controls using the same methodology as that used with WS (see above; Santos et al., 2009). Contrary to what was found in the WS study, the performance of individuals with autism was found to be dependent on perceptual (orientation of the faces) but not on socially relevant mechanisms (human status of faces). More precisely, unlike WS individuals, those with autism achieved levels of performance similar to those of controls across all face types, yet used atypical perceptual strategies when processing human faces (Rosset et al., 2008). A further study examined the ability to extract emotional vs. nonemotional information from contextual cues in a group of 19 individuals with autism relative to 19 CA-matched normally developing individuals (Da Fonseca, Santos, et al., 2009). This study used the same task as that used by Santos et al. (2008) in studying WS. Again, contrasting results were found for autism, with significantly poorer performance on the emotionally relevant task but not on the nonemotionally relevant task than that of controls (Da Fonseca, Santos, et al., 2009; see also Da Fonseca, Séguier, Santos, Poinso, & Deruelle, 2009, for similar findings in children with attention-deficit hyperactivity disorder).

Taken together, these studies support the idea that comparison of WS and autism offers a unique perspective on the deviances that may occur in socio-emotional processing during atypical development, as they indicate that the cognitive mechanisms typically underlying emotional processing can be differently affected in these neurogenetic syndromes. At the neurobiological level, fundamental neurocognitive mechanisms underlying social function also appear to be abnormal in autism and WS, as studies have suggested amygdalar dysfunctions in both disorders (autism: Critchley et al., 2000; WS: Meyer-Lindenberg, Hariri, et al., 2005; see further details below). In the next section, we discuss the role of the amygdala in emotion processing, with a special focus on evidence for amygdala abnormalities in WS.

The Amygdala: A Key Region for Emotion Processing

The amygdalar cortex serves as a complex neural hub critically involved in both normal behavior and mental illness (LeDoux, 2007). Its almond-shaped body encompasses several nuclei receiving inputs originating from the hippocampus, sensory thalamus, sensory and association cortices, sensory brainstem, olfactory regions, and medial prefrontal cortex. Two nuclei—the central and the basal nucleus—act as effector organs and project to a multiplicity of neural targets, thus managing fear-related actions via projections to the ventral striatum (running to safety) and brainstem (freezing) (LeDoux, 2007). In behavioral studies the amygdala has been predominantly associated with fear conditioning and reaction; however, it likely plays a role in functions other than fear-related ones, such as signaling of face salience (Santos, Mier, Kirsch & Meyer-Lindenberg, 2011), reward processing, and generation of emotional states associated with

aggressive, maternal, sexual, and ingestive behaviors (Costafreda, Brammer, David, & Fu, 2008; LeDoux, 2007; Sergerie, Chochol, Armony, 2008). Although most of these concepts have evolved from animal studies, human imaging experiments support their validity in humans (Stein et al., 2007).

Because of its prominent role in emotion processing, the amygdala has been implicated in neurogenetic disorders affecting the social-emotional sphere, such as WS. Meyer-Lindenberg, Hariri, and colleagues (2005) were the first to conduct a functional magnetic resonance imaging (fMRI) study investigating amygdala functioning and regulation in individuals with WS relative to controls. This study included two tasks requiring processing of threatening stimuli, either faces or scenes, known to engage the amygdala (Hariri, Tessitore, et al., 2002). Interestingly, these two tasks elicited significant group differences in amygdala activation. Relative to controls, individuals with WS showed reduced amygdala activation for threatening faces but increased amygdala activation for threatening scenes (see Figure 6.3). Both results were found to be in agreement with the WS atypical social profile: diminished amygdala reactivity to threatening faces was associated with absence of fear from strangers and consequent social disinhibition, and abnormally increased reactivity to threatening scenes may be a potential mechanism for excessive nonsocial anxiety (e.g., specific phobias) in WS. Similar reactivity differences as a function of the task were also found in the prefrontal cortex, where controls differentially activated orbitofrontal and dorsolateral and medial prefrontal cortex for

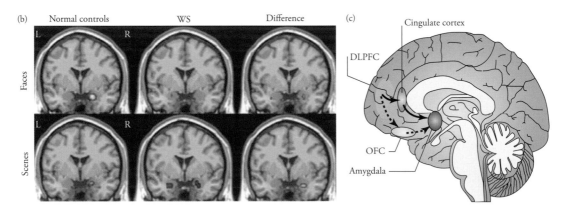

Figure 6.3 Left: Amygdala activation ($p < 0.05$, corrected for multiple comparisons) for face and scene stimuli. First column, normal controls (NC); second column, high-functioning participants with Williams syndrome (WS); third column, significant differences between groups (blue, NC > WS; red, WS > NC) in the amygdala. **Right:** Schema depicting key regions for social cognition and emotional regulation affected in WS: amygdala, orbitofrontal cortex (OFC), dorsolateral prefrontal cortex (DLPFC), and cingulate cortex.

Left panel reproduced, with permission, from Meyer-Lindenberg, Hariri, et al. (2005). Right panel adapted, with permission, from Martin (1996) Appleton & Lange.

threatening faces, whereas WS individuals showed a task-invariant pattern of activation. Given that both medial prefrontal cortex and orbitofrontal cortex are densely interconnected with the amygdala and that dorsolateral prefrontal cortex and ?? have been implicated in regulation of the amygdala, these findings provide evidence for a dysregulation of amygdala–prefrontal systems (involved in social and nonsocial fear signaling; e.g., Schultz, 2005) in WS, which may account for the gregarious behavioral profile, the lack of socially related fear, and the presence of nonsocial anxieties commonly reported in this condition (Meyer-Lindenberg, Hariri, et al., 2005).

A study by Sarpal et al. (2008) further showed significant reductions in functional connectivity between the fusiform face area (FFA) and the amygdala and prefrontal cortex (see Figure 6.4), areas possibly involved in the hypersocial symptoms of WS. This finding suggests that the afferent flow of face-emotion-related information into the amygdala is impaired in WS. Reduced amygdala activation to fearful social visual stimuli was also found in a group of subjects with WS and mental retardation (Haas et al., 2009). This study showed increased activation to positive stimuli (happy faces), adding a new facet to the neural mechanisms underlying prosocial behavior in WS. Dysregulation of the amygdala by prefrontal cortex may lead to changed activation profiles not only between socially relevant and less relevant stimuli but also across a range of stimulus valence.

Unraveling the Genetic Mechanisms of Neuropsychiatric Disorders

To narrow the gaps in the causal chain between genes and behavior, the identification and definition of intermediate phenotypes is of special relevance (Gottesman & Gould, 2003; Siebner, Callicott, Sommer, & Mattay, 2009). *Intermediate phenotypes* are biomarkers closer to the biology of the illness, with higher penetrance of genetic than the multifaceted phenomenon of behavior (e.g., Viding & Blakemore, 2007). This approach is an alternative method for measuring phenotypic variation that may facilitate identification of susceptibility genes for complexly inherited traits and aid in our understanding of these disorders by elucidating the neural mechanisms influenced by risk gene variants. The aim of the approach is to reduce complex clinical phenomena and enhance disease diagnosis through more tractable mapping of underlying genes. Because genetic effects on behavior are neurally mediated, the functional impact of genetic variation can only be understood if it is considered in terms of its effects on shaping brain development, structure, and functions (Meyer-Lindenberg & Weinberger, 2006). In this context, the rapidly emerging field of *imaging genetics* is relevant. In the imaging genetics approach, the power of neuroimaging to characterize various aspects of brain structure and function related to behavioral traits, cognition, and emotional regulation is combined with genetic data to link interindividual variation in imaging parameters to genetic variants that these individuals carry (e.g., Meyer-Lindenberg & Zink, 2007). This approach is a special instance of an intermediate phenotype: it benefits from the fact that genes are likely to have a bigger effect on biological processing than on emergent behavioral phenomena—that is, the penetrance is likely to be higher on the neural systems level. Imaging genetics leverages the genetic information

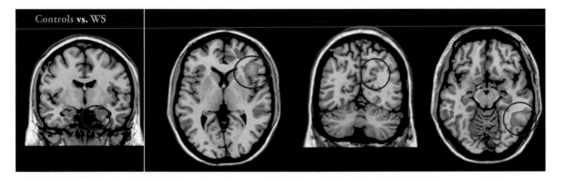

Figure 6.4 Results from between-group comparisons in right amygdala, right inferior frontal gyrus, right intraparietal sulcus, and right middle temporal gyrus (from left to right, respectively). Greater fusiform face area (FFA) connectivity was observed in control than in WS participants in bilateral amygdala and right inferior frontal gyrus. The bilateral intraparietal sulcus exhibited significantly greater parahippocampal place area connectivity in controls than in participants with WS. Participants with WS showed significantly more parahippocampal place area connectivity than controls with posterior regions, including middle temporal gyrus.

Reproduced, with permission, from Sarpal et al. (2008).

usually obtained in large-scale association studies to investigate the effects of common genetic variants on neural structure and function with high penetrance (Meyer-Lindenberg & Weinberger, 2006) in the normal population, while controlling for false positives (Meyer-Lindenberg et al., 2008).

Contribution of Imaging Genetics: Lessons from Mood Disorder Research

The birth of imaging genetics (Hariri & Weinberger, 2003) as a strategy for mapping neural phenotypes as a function of genotype has fostered new enthusiasm in mood disorders research,

because this approach enables assessment of the neural impact of candidate genes *in vivo* and thus provides a new level of evidence (Scharinger, Rabl, Sitte, & Pezawas, 2010). Questions explored thus far include the neural effects of single genes, and gene–gene (epistasis) and gene–environment interactions on systems neurobiology.

Given the genetic sophistication of mood disorders, imaging genetics studies corroborate the assumption that the effects of risk genes converge at brain systems of emotion processing (Canli, Ferri, & Duman, 2009). These regions are involved in the identification of stimulus-related emotional

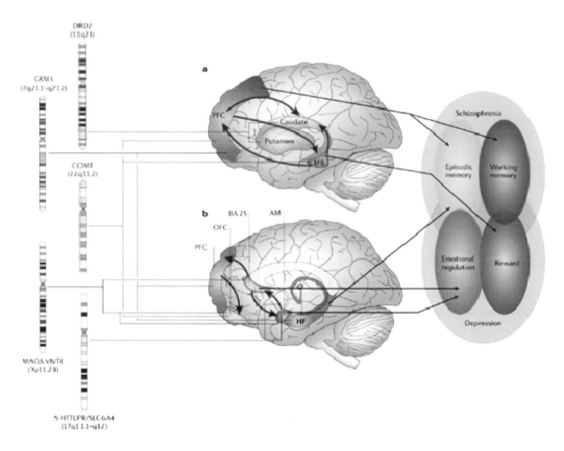

Figure 6.5 Through interaction with each other and the environment, multiple genetic risk variants affect multiple neural systems linked to several neuropsychological and behavioral domains that are impaired, in differing proportions, in psychiatric diseases. No one-to-one mapping exists between genes and neural-system mechanisms or between mechanisms and behavior. As examples, the following genetic variants are depicted (chromosomal variation in parentheses): GRM3 single nucleotide polymorphism 4 (Egan et al., 2004; 7q21.1–q21.2), dopamine receptor D2 (DRD2) Taq 1a (Cohen, Young, Baek, Kessler, & Ranganath, 2005; 11q23;), catechol-*O*-methyltransferase (COMT) Val66Met (Egan et al., 2001; Meyer-Lindenberg, Kohn, et al., 2005; 22q11.2), serotonin transporter length polymorphism (5-HTTLPR/SLC6A4; Hariri, Mattay, et al., 2002; Pezawas et al., 2005; 17q11.1–q12), and monoamine oxidase A variable number tandem repeat (MAOA VNTR) (Meyer-Lindenberg, Buckholtz, et al., 2006; Xp11.23). These are shown to affect a circuit linking the prefrontal cortex (PFC) with the midbrain (MB) and striatum (caudate and putamen) (**a**), which is relevant for schizophrenia, and a circuit that connects the amygdala (AM) with regulatory cortical and limbic areas (**b**), which is implicated in depression and anxiety. These circuits, in turn, mediate risk for schizophrenia and depression as well as various neuropsychological functions. The connections shown correspond to published work and indicate that a given gene will influence a variety of neural circuits, which in turn influence several behavioral and clinical parameters. BA 25, Brodmann's area 25; HF, hippocampal formation; OFC, orbitofrontal cortex.

Reproduced with permission from Meyer-Lindenberg & Weinberger (2006).

significance as well as the initiation and regulation of affective states, emotional response, and subsequent emotion-related behavior (Phillips, Drevets, Rauch, & Lane, 2003a,b).

The mounting evidence of gene effects on brain systems of emotion processing is accompanied by a more in-depth understanding of the anatomical interrelationship between regions of emotion processing (Price & Drevets, 2010), highlighting the crucial role of the orbital and medial prefrontal cortex (OMPFC) for mood disorders (see Figure 6.5). The OMPFC comprises two major networks (Price & Drevets, 2010): (1) the sensory-related orbital network, which acts as a system for integrating multimodal stimuli as well as a system for assessing the value of those stimuli; and (2) the output-related medial prefrontal network, which can modulate visceral function in relation to emotion and is interconnected to important structures such as the amygdala, cingulate cortex, and hippocampus.

Here we will focus on the amygdala, given its crucial role in emotion processing and its involvement in pathological states such as major depressive disorder (MDD) (Phillips et al., 2003b) and anxiety disorders (Domschke & Dannlowski, 2010). Positron emission tomography (PET) and fMRI studies have frequently shown increased amygdala activation in patients with acute MDD (Savitz & Drevets, 2009). Since MDD is predominantly treated with drugs selectively inhibiting serotonin (5-HT) uptake (selective serotonin re-uptake inhibitors [SSRIs]), genetic variation of the serotonin transporter (5-HTT) and its coding gene (*SLC6A4*) has become a major target of study within the neuroscientific community. Genetic variation, such as a variable number of tandem repeats (VNTR) polymorphism in the promoter region (5-HTTLPR) of *SLC6A4*, has been related to neuroticism (Lesch et al., 1996) and is thought to be a risk factor for MDD (Schinka, Busch, & Robichaux-Keene, 2004; Sen, Burmeister, & Ghosh, 2004) in the context of environmental adversity (Barr et al., 2004; Caspi et al., 2003). Recently, however, these findings have been questioned by meta-analyses (Flint & Munafo, 2008; Munafo, Durrant, Lewis, & Flint, 2009; Munafo, Freimer, et al., 2009; Risch et al., 2009). This highlights the difficulties in unravelling genetically complex disorders that have been attributed to clinical, neurobiological, and genetic heterogeneity as well as the problems regarding the sample size necessary to detect such effects (Flint & Munafo, 2008). Specifically, variable penetrance, epistasis, imprinting, epigenetics, pleiotropy (Murphy &

Lesch, 2008), and further functional genetic variability in *SLC6A4*, such as a single nucleotide polymorphism (A-G substitution, rs25531) within the L allele (Hu et al., 2006) and a VNTR in the second intron (Hranilovic et al., 2004), are probable other factors contributing to this inconsistency.

Despite these problems inherent to genetic association studies, imaging genetics studies investigating the impact of 5-HTTLPR on amygdala reactivity in normal subjects offer a much more homogeneous picture (Brown and Hariri, 2006; Munafo, Brown, & Hariri, 2008). With the exception of one study (Surguladze et al., 2008), all such studies have suggested that S allele carriers of European ancestry show exaggerated amygdala activation in the presence of fearful or negatively valenced stimuli compared to subjects with the L/L genotype (Bertolino et al., 2005; Brown & Hariri, 2006; Canli, Omura, et al., 2005; Dannlowski et al., 2008, 2010; Friedel et al., 2009; Hariri, Mattay, et al., 2002; Hariri et al., 2005; Heinz et al., 2005; Perlis et al., 2008; Pezawas et al., 2005; Smolka et al., 2007; Williams, Gatt, Schofield, et al., 2010), a finding that does not necessarily apply to other ethnicities (Lee & Ham, 2008b). Interestingly, this difference might also exist during resting state (Canli et al., 2006; Rao et al., 2007), hence baseline periods may have an impact on those results (Canli, Omura, et al., 2005; Heinz et al., 2007). Such findings are in accordance with animal studies demonstrating that high levels of 5-HT are accompanied by blood level oxygen–dependent (BOLD) signal increases (Preece et al., 2009), which is thought to apply to adult S allele carriers.

Currently, only a limited number of studies have investigated the effects of 5-HTTLPR on brain development in humans, although 5-HT is one of the best-studied brain developmental factors available (Gaspar, Cases, & Maroteaux, 2003). Three voxel-based morphometry (VBM) studies in large samples of healthy subjects indicate that S allele carrier status implies a smaller relative amygdala volume (Frodl et al., 2008; Pezawas et al., 2005, 2008), whereas two studies investigating smaller samples either reported the opposite (Scherk et al., 2009) or did not detect any genetic impact on amygdala volume (Canli, Omura, et al., 2005). Regarding studies of 5-HTTLPR effects on amygdala function or development in acute MDD, results are sparse, and further replications are needed. Studies have reported S allele–associated activation increases of the amygdala (Dannlowski et al., 2007, 2008; Friedel et al., 2009) as well as, counterintuitively, increases in amygdala volume, in a small-scale study of bipolar patients (Scherk et al., 2009).

Massive evidence provided by imaging genetics studies suggests a specific role of *SLC6A4* in amygdala regulation and development in healthy subjects. Therefore, it is not surprising that other genes involved in clearing 5-HT from the synaptic cleft have been identified as significant factors. One example is the X chromosome–linked monoamine oxidase A gene (*MAOA*). *MAOA* is expressed in the outer mitochondrial membrane of monoaminergic neurons and is a key enzyme in the degradation of 5-HT. A functional VNTR polymorphism in the promoter region of the *MAOA* gene has been found to impact gene expression by genetic variability of its highly active MAOA-H and less active MAOA-L allele (Sabol, Hu, & Hamer, 1998). Like 5-HTTLPR, *MAOA* is also believed to interact with environmental factors in the formation of complex behaviors, such as antisocial behavior, which is less likely to occur in maltreated children with MAOA-H allele status (Caspi et al., 2002). *MAOA* has frequently been related to aggressive and impulsive behavior; however, studies have also reported an association with MDD (Schulze et al., 2000; Yu et al., 2005). With regard to amygdala regulation, one study revealed increased amygdala reactivity and decreased amygdala volume in healthy Caucasian MAOA-L carriers (Meyer-Lindenberg, Buckholtz, et al., 2006), a finding that was replicated in an Asian sample (Lee & Ham, 2008a). Furthermore, it has been suggested that the *MAOB* gene is related to amygdala volume (Good et al., 2003), a conclusion based on studies of X-monosomal Turner syndrome patients exhibiting functional (Skuse, Morris, & Dolan, 2005) and volumetric (Cutter et al., 2006; Good et al., 2003; Kesler et al., 2004) amygdala alterations. These can also be found in Turner patients with partial X-chromosome deletions only lacking the genetic locus Xp11.3 containing *MAOB* (Good et al., 2003). Complementary findings indicating X-chromosomal effects on amygdala volume also exist for Klinefelter syndrome (Patwardhan et al., 2002; Shen et al., 2004).

While *SLC6A4* and *MAOA* are critically involved in the elimination of 5-HT, the tryptophan hydroxylase 2 gene (*TPH2*) is critical for the synthesis of 5-HT. Several functional variants with an impact on *TPH2* expression are known (Haghighi et al., 2008). The T allele of G(-703)T TPH2 (rs4570625) has been associated with increased amygdala reactivity in two studies of healthy subjects (Brown et al., 2005; Canli, Congdon, et al., 2005), whereas the opposite was reported in an Asian sample, once more suggesting the significance of ethnic background (Lee & Ham, 2008b).

The power of the serotonergic system in the context of amygdala activation is further featured by imaging genetics studies, highlighting an important role of 5-HT receptor genes, such as the 5-HT$_{1A}$ autoreceptor gene (*HTR1A*) crucially involved in the regulation of 5-HT signaling (Lemonde et al., 2003). G allele carriers of C(-1019)G HTR1A (rs6295), a functional single nucleotide polymorphism (SNP) in the promoter region of *HTR1A*, have been associated with decreased transcriptional repression, leading to increased 5-HT$_{1A}$ density and diminished amygdala activation in healthy subjects (Fakra et al., 2009), a finding that has not been replicated in a non-Caucasian sample (Lee & Ham, 2008b). Supportive evidence stems from a PET study reporting an inverse relationship between 5-HT$_{1A}$ autoreceptor binding in the dorsal raphe nuclei and amygdala reactivity (Fisher et al., 2006). In MDD patients, increased amygdala reactivity has been found in G allele carriers (Dannlowski et al., 2007).

Additionally, other monoamines such as dopamine (DA) have been implicated in depression, as anhedonia is a prominent clinical symptom of depression and euphoria can be induced by dopaminergic drugs. Since DA transporters are lacking in the cortex, the monoamine-degrading enzyme catechol-*O*-methyltransferase (COMT) is of specific importance for DA catabolism and has been linked to a variety of psychiatric disorders, including MDD (Craddock, Owen, & O'Donovan, 2006). The Met allele of Val158Met COMT (rs4680) has been associated with significantly lower enzymatic activity than that with the Val allele (Chen et al., 2004), putatively affecting tonic and phasic dopamine levels (Bilder, Volavka, Lachman, & Grace, 2004). In imaging genetics studies, Met allele-associated volume increase (Cerasa et al., 2008; Ehrlich et al., 2010; Taylor et al., 2007) and amygdala hyperreactivity (Smolka et al., 2005, 2007; Williams, Gatt, Grieve, et al., 2010) have been reported. A minority of studies found contrary (Kempton et al., 2009) or even lacking effects (Drabant et al., 2006), likely due to sexual dimorphism (Harrison & Tunbridge, 2008).

The complex relationship between genotypes is highlighted by the fact that 5-HT affects *BDNF* expression via induction of the cyclic adenosine monophosphate response element-binding protein gene (*CREB1*), which alone has been related to altered amygdala activation in a single study (Perlis et al., 2008). This relationship between monoamines and neurotrophins has converged in the controversially discussed (Groves, 2007) neuroplasticity hypothesis of depression (Castren, 2005), which placed brain-derived neurotrophic factor (BDNF) in the spotlight of mood disorder research (Berton et al., 2006; Krishnan et al., 2007). Neurons transfected with Met BDNF of Val66Met BDNF (rs6265), which has been related to anxious behavior in animal models and antidepressant drug resistance (Chen et al., 2006), showed reduced depolarization-induced secretion and failed to localize BDNF to secretory granules and dendritic processes (Egan et al., 2003). Hence, the Met allele has been related to a smaller amygdala volume (Montag, Weber, Fliessbach, Elger, & Reuter, 2009), likely dependent of aging effects (Sublette et al., 2008). However, the majority of these studies have been unable to detect effects on amygdala volume (Frodl et al., 2007; Matsuo et al., 2009; Nemoto et al., 2006; Pezawas et al., 2004; Schofield et al., 2009). On a behavioral level the Val allele has predominantly been associated with increased trait anxiety (Lang et al., 2005; Sen et al., 2003; Willis-Owen et al., 2005). Like morphological studies, activation studies are inconclusive, with one study reporting increased amygdala reactivity associated with the Val allele (Gasic et al., 2009), while the bulk of studies has been unable to provide such evidence (Egan et al., 2003; Hariri et al., 2003; Hashimoto et al., 2008; Montag Reuter, Newport, Elger, & Weber, 2008; Schofield et al., 2009).

Currently, most imaging genetics studies are conducted within the framework of "classical" depression concepts, such as the monoamine and neuroplasticity hypothesis. However, many more gene candidates have been proposed as being important in MDD and for amygdala regulation (Kato, 2007). One example is C(-385)A FAAH (rs324420) of the fatty acid amid hydrolase gene (FAAH), which plays a role in the catabolism of endogenous ligands of the cannabinoid receptor and has been demonstrated to alter amygdala reactivity in healthy subjects (Hariri et al., 2009). Similarly, a study investigated the cannabinoid receptor 1 gene (CNR1) in MDD (Domschke et al., 2008). Furthermore, presence of rs333229 of the choline transporter gene 1 (SLC5A7) indicates increased amygdala reactivity and has been associated with depression and autonomic variability in heart rate (Neumann et al., 2006). A microsatellite 312 bp variant (RS1) near the promoter region of the arginine vasopressin receptor 1A gene (AVPR1A) was found to be related to decreased harm avoidance and increased amygdala reactivity in healthy subjects (Meyer-Lindenberg et al., 2009). Another stress-related neuropeptide, neuropeptide Y (NPY), showed robust amygdala activation and increased trait anxiety via lower haplotype-driven NPY expression in healthy subjects (Cotton, Flint, & Campbell, 2009; Zhou et al., 2008). Also, regulator of G protein signaling 2 (RGS2) gene—linked to anxious behavior in rodents—has been associated with introversion and increased amygdala activation (Smoller et al., 2008). A(10398)G mitochondrial DNA (mtDNA), which is important for calcium regulation in neurons and probably mental illness, has been related to volumetric alterations within the amygdala (Yamasue et al., 2008). And finally, variation in two loci of D-amino acid oxidase activator G72 (DAOA), a gene associated with schizophrenia and bipolar disorder as well as MDD and neuroticism (Rietschel et al., 2008), has been associated with alterations in amygdala gray matter density in patients with bipolar disorder (Zuliani et al., 2009).

Progress in genetics highlights the importance of gene gene and gene environment interactions for understanding the complex depression phenotype, and imaging genetics studies applying such models have been launched. Gene gene interactions, epistasis, in particular, reflect this sort of complex relationship, and animals genetically engineered to be hypomorphic at BDNF and SLC6A4 have shown such effects (Murphy et al., 2003). This finding is supported by a genetically humanized mouse model demonstrating that anxious behavior in animals carrying Met BDNF alleles are unresponsive to SSRI treatment, which can be seen as pharmacological analogue of 5-HTTLPR S alleles (Krishnan et al., 2007). These findings are supported by a recent imaging genetics study investigating epistasis between 5-HTTLPR and Val66Met BDNF in healthy subjects that demonstrated for the amygdala a Met allele-dependent volumetric reduction of the known S allele effect (Pezawas et al., 2008). Furthermore, additive amygdalar effects of the Met allele of Val158Met COMT and S/L_G alleles of 5-HTTLPR and rs25531 (Smolka et al., 2007) as well as the T allele of G(-703)T TPH2 and the S allele of 5-HTTLPR (Canli, Congdon, Todd Constable, & Lesch, 2008) were identified in healthy subjects, whereas additive effects of C(-1019) G HTR1A, 5-HTTLPR and rs25531 have been found in MDD patients (Dannlowski et al., 2007). Finally, gene–environment interactions impacting amygdala activity have been demonstrated between 5-HTTLPR (Canli et al., 2006) and Val66Met BDNF (Gatt et al., 2009) and life stress.

Contribution of Imaging Genetics Studies to Understanding Mood Disorders

Using mood disorders as a reference, this section has presented recent insights gained from a translational approach to investigate and define neural mechanisms of psychiatric illness based on genetic risk. Although methodological problems in this fast-moving area of research exist and must be tackled in the interest of reliable and replicable results, we believe that this methodology of using genetic variation as a tool for the discovery of brain mechanisms will become a widely applied and fruitful research field in psychiatry and related disciplines. Besides neural mechanisms, other quantitative parameters, such as those from neurochemistry, may be powerful tools to index intermediate neurobiological processes influenced by genetic variation. The next section will discuss how neuropeptides critically involved in social-emotional regulation may constitute an additional pathway linking genes and behavior.

Genes, Neuropeptides, and Social-Emotional Mechanisms

Convergent work over the last two decades has established the neuropeptides oxytocin (OT) and vasopressin (VP) as central players in the regulation of social-emotional behavior (see Donaldson & Young, 2008, for a review) in mammalian species. OT and VP differ by structure in just two of nine amino acids (nonapeptides). OT is synthesized in the hypothalamus. The neural architecture of the oxytocinergic system is evolutionarily conserved and targets, among others, brain areas critical for emotion regulation (e.g., amygdala, lateral septum, and brainstem). In contrast, the regional expression of oxytocin receptors is highly variable. It is therefore a neuropeptide likely to be directly related to social behavior and an excellent candidate biomarker for the coordination of emotional states and feelings with physiological processes (e.g., Carter, 1998).

Findings from animal and human studies point unequivocally to the involvement of OT in social behavior (for reviews see Bartz & Hollander, 2006; Heinrichs & Domes, 2008; Lim & Young, 2006). For instance, administration of OT has been found to increase the amount of social interactions in rats (Witt, Winslow, & Insel, 1992), prairie voles (Cho, DeVries, Williams, & Carter, 1999), and

Mongolian gerbils (Razzoli, Cushing, Carter, & Valsecchi, 2003). Moreover, in the prairie vole (a monogamous species), OT administration has been found to facilitate partner preference formation (Cho et al., 1999), whereas an OT antagonist appears to reduce this behavior (Insel & Young, 2001). In addition, several studies have shown that in humans, intranasal administration of OT increases trust behavior (Kosfeld, Heinrichs, Zak, Fischbacher, & Fehr, 2005), modulates emotion processing (Di Simplicio, Massey-Chase, Cowen, & Harmer, 2009), and improves social cognition skills (Andari et al., 2010; Domes, Heinrichs, Michel, et al., 2007). Recently, OT administration has also been found to increase the duration of positive relative to negative behavior during couple conflict interaction (Ditzen et al., 2009), gaze toward the eye region of human faces (Guastella, Mitchell, & Dadds, 2008), and trustworthiness and attractiveness (Theodoridou, Rowe, Penton-Voak, & Rogers, 2009).

Neuroimaging findings of our own group have shown that the mechanism whereby OT induces trust may be through suppression of social fear signaling in the amygdala and linked structures (Kirsch et al., 2005). In line with this, intranasally administered OT was fund to affect trust behavior via a specific reduction in activation in the neural circuitry of trust, including the amygdala (Baumgartner, Heinrichs, Vonlanthen, Fischbacher, & Fehr, 2008). In addition, OT has been found to attenuate amygdala responses to facial expressions irrespective of their valence (Domes, Heinrichs, Gläscher, et al., 2007).

In autism spectrum disorder (ASD), a neurodevelopmental disorder characterized by marked impairments in the social-emotional sphere, there is evidence that variations in the brain receptor for OT, encoded by OXTR, and in the brain receptor for VP, encoded by AVPR1A, are associated with disease risk. Furthermore, we have shown that these same variants have an impact on amygdala reactivity in healthy carriers (Meyer-Lindenberg et al., 2009). Although there is contradictory evidence for lower (Andari et al., 2010; Modahl et al., 1998) and higher (Jansen et al., 2006) OT plasma levels in individuals with ASD relative to typically developing controls, it has been shown that OT administration improves social cognition skills in individuals with ASD. Thus OT may have therapeutic benefits for the treatment of social deficits. In addition, Carter (2007) proposed the intriguing theory that the male vulnerability to ASD (4:1 male to female ration in ASD) may be due to disruptions in the VP system and possibly to an excess of VP during development, because VP is androgen dependent and VP plays a key role in male behavior. While no such evidence exists for WS, the combination of increased hypersociability and trust with reduced amygdala activation to socially fear-inducing stimuli is strongly reminiscent of the discussed imaging and behavioral findings regarding OT, and it would be of great interest to examine the hypothesis that OT is involved in the striking hypersocial phenotype of WS.

Conclusion

Although there is clear evidence that many complex behaviors and neuropsychiatric disorders have a high heritable component (Sullivan, Neale, & Kendler, 2000), identifying these genes and understanding the neural mechanisms linking genes to behavior will be one of the greater challenges for research in the next years (Meyer-Lindenberg, & Weinberger, 2006). These studies should contribute to the development of combined medical, social, and educative procedures for individuals with debilitating social-emotional difficulties (e.g., autism and schizophrenia). Of relevance is the therapeutic potential of this work that is most tantalizing to the clinician: prosocial cognition and neuropeptides, for instance, may provide an alternative pathway for treating social-emotional dysfunctions. To further develop these innovative therapies, an understanding of the neural mechanisms through which genes affect cognition and behavior and of how neuropeptides act in human brain is fundamental.

References

Andari, E., Duhamel, J., Zalla, T., Herbrecht, E., Leboyer, M., & Sirigu, A. (2010). Promoting social behavior with oxytocin in high-functioning autism spectrum disorders *Proceedings of the National Academy of Sciences U S A*, *107*(9), 4389–4394.

Ashwin, C., Wheelwright, S., & Baron-Cohen, S. (2006). Finding a face in the crowd: Testing the anger superiority effect in Asperger syndrome. *Brain and Cognition*, *61*(1), 78–95.

Bar-Haim, Y., Lamy, D., Pergamin, L., Bakermans-Kranenburg, M. J., & Van IJzendoorn, M. H. (2007). Threat-related attentional bias in anxious and non-anxious individuals: A meta-analytic study. *Psychological Bulletin*, *133*(1), 1–24.

Barr, C. S., Newman, T. K., Schwandt, M., Shannon, C., Dvoskin, R. L., Lindell, S. G., et al. (2004). Sexual dichotomy of an interaction between early adversity and the serotonin transporter gene promoter variant in rhesus macaques. *Proceedings of the National Academy of Sciences U S A*, *101*, 12358–12363.

Bartz, J. A., & Hollander, E. (2006). The neuroscience of affiliation: Forging links between basic and clinical research on neuropeptides and social behavior. *Hormones and Behaviour*, *50*(4), 518–528.

Baumgartner, T., Heinrichs, M., Vonlanthen, A., Fischbacher, U., & Fehr, E. (2008). Oxytocin shapes the neural circuitry of trust and trust adaptation in humans. *Neuron*, *58*(4), 639–650.

Belmonte, M. K., Allen, G., Beckel-Mitchener, A., Boulanger, L. M., Carper, R. A., & Webb, S. J. (2004). Autism and abnormal development of brain connectivity. *Journal of Neuroscience*, *24*(42), 9228–9231.

Bertolino, A., Arciero, G., Rubino, V., Latorre, V., De Candia, M., Mazzola, V., et al. (2005). Variation of human amygdala response during threatening stimuli as a function of 5HTTLPR genotype and personality style. *Biological Psychiatry*, *57*, 1517–1525.

Berton, O., McClung, C. A., Dileone, R. J., Krishnan, V., Renthal, W., Russo, S. J., et al. (2006). Essential role of BDNF in the mesolimbic dopamine pathway in social defeat stress. *Science*, *311*, 864–868.

Bilder, R. M., Volavka, J., Lachman, H. M., & Grace, A. A. (2004). The catechol-O-methyltransferase polymorphism: Relations to the tonic-phasic dopamine hypothesis and neuropsychiatric phenotypes. *Neuropsychopharmacology*, *29*, 1943–1961.

Brown, S. M., & Hariri, A. R. (2006). Neuroimaging studies of serotonin gene polymorphisms: Exploring the interplay of genes, brain, and behavior. *Cognitive, Affective & Behavioral Neuroscience*, *6*, 44–52.

Brown, S. M., Peet, E., Manuck, S. B., Williamson, D. E., Dahl, R. E., Ferrell, R. E., & Hariri, A.R. (2005). A regulatory variant of the human tryptophan hydroxylase-2 gene biases amygdala reactivity. *Molecular Psychiatry*, *10*, 884–888, 805.

Bukach, C. M., Gauthier, I., & Tarr, M. J. (2006). Beyond faces and modularity: The power of an expertise framework. *Trends in Cognitive Sciences*, *10*(4), 159–166.

Canli, T., Congdon, E., Gutknecht, L., Constable, R. T., & Lesch, K. P. (2005). Amygdala responsiveness is modulated by tryptophan hydroxylase-2 gene variation. *Journal of Neural Transmission*, *112*, 1479–1485.

Canli, T., Congdon, E., Todd Constable, R., & Lesch, K. P. (2008). Additive effects of serotonin transporter and tryptophan hydroxylase-2 gene variation on neural correlates of affective processing. *Biological Psychology*, *79*, 118–125.

Canli, T., Ferri, J., & Duman, E. A. (2009). Genetics of emotion regulation. *Neuroscience*, *164*, 43–54.

Canli, T., Omura, K., Haas, B. W., Fallgatter, A., Constable, R. T., & Lesch, K. P. (2005). Beyond affect: A role for genetic variation of the serotonin transporter in neural activation during a cognitive attention task. *Proceedings of the National Academy of Sciences U S A*, *102*, 12224–12229.

Canli, T., Qiu, M., Omura, K., Congdon, E., Haas, B. W., Amin, Z., et al. (2006). Neural correlates of epigenesis. *Proceedings of the National Academy of Sciences U S A*, *103*, 16033–16038.

Carter, C. S. (1998). Neuroendocrine perspectives on social attachment and love. *Psychoneuroendocrinology*, *23*(8), 779–818.

Carter, C. S. (2007). Sex differences in oxytocin and vasopressin: Implications for autism spectrum disorders? *Behavioral Brain Research*, *176*(1), 170–186.

Caspi, A., McClay, J., Moffitt, T. E., Mill, J., Martin, J., Craig, I. W., et al. (2002). Role of genotype in the cycle of violence in maltreated children. *Science*, *297*, 851–854.

Caspi, A., Sugden, K., Moffitt, T. E., Taylor, A., Craig, I. W., Harrington, H., et al. (2003). Influence of life stress on depression: Moderation by a polymorphism in the 5-HTT gene. *Science, 301*, 386–389.

Castren, E. (2005). Is mood chemistry? *Nature Reviews Neuroscience, 6*, 241–246.

Cerasa, A., Gioia, M. C., Labate, A., Liguori, M., Lanza, P., & Quattrone, A. (2008b). Impact of catechol-*O*-methyltransferase Val(108/158) Met genotype on hippocampal and prefrontal gray matter volume. *Neuroreport, 19*, 405–408.

Chen, J., Lipska, B. K., Halim, N., Ma, Q.D., Matsumoto, M., Melhem, S., et al. (2004). Functional analysis of genetic variation in catechol-*O*-methyltransferase (COMT): Effects on mRNA, protein, and enzyme activity in postmortem human brain. *American Journal of Human Genetics, 75*, 807–821.

Chen, Z. Y., Jing, D., Bath, K. G., Ieraci, A., Khan, T., Siao, C.J., et al. (2006). Genetic variant BDNF (Val66Met) polymorphism alters anxiety-related behavior. *Science, 314*, 140–143.

Cho, M. M., DeVries, A. C., Williams, J. R., & Carter, C. S. (1999). The effects of oxytocin and vasopressin on partner preferences in male and female prairie voles (*Microtus ochrogaster*). *Behavioral Neuroscience, 113*(5), 1071–1079.

Cohen, M.X., Young, J., Baek, J.M., Kessler, C., & Ranganath, C. (2005). Individual differences in extraversion and dopamine genetics reflect reactivity of neural reward circuitry. *Cognitive Brain Research, 25*, 851–861.

Costafreda, S. G., Brammer, M. J., David, A. S., & Fu, C. H. (2008). Predictors of amygdala activation during the processing of emotional stimuli: A meta-analysis of 385 PET and fMRI studies. *Brain Research Reviews, 58*, 57–70.

Cotton, C. H., Flint, J., & Campbell, T. G. (2009). Is there an association between NPY and neuroticism? *Nature, 458*, E6; discussion E7.

Craddock, N., Owen, M. J., & O'Donovan, M. C. (2006). The catechol-*O*-methyl transferase (COMT) gene as a candidate for psychiatric phenotypes: Evidence and lessons. *Molecular Psychiatry, 11*, 446–458.

Critchley, H. D., Daly, E. M., Bullmore, E. T., Williams, S. C., Van Amelsvoort, T., et al. (2000). The functional neuroanatomy of social behaviour: Changes in cerebral blood flow when people with autistic disorder process facial expressions. *Brain, 123* (Pt 11), 2203–2212.

Cutter, W. J., Daly, E. M., Robertson, D. M., Chitnis, X. A., van Amelsvoort, T. A., Simmons, A., et al. (2006). Influence of X chromosome and hormones on human brain development: A magnetic resonance imaging and proton magnetic resonance spectroscopy study of Turner syndrome. *Biological Psychiatry, 59*, 273–283.

Da Fonseca, D., Santos, A., Rosset, D. B., Rondan, C., Poinso, F., & Deruelle, C. (2009). Can children with autism spectrum disorders extract emotions out of contextual cues? *Research in Autism Spectrum Disorders, 3*(1), 50–56.

Da Fonseca, D., Séguier, V., Santos, A., Poinso, F., & Deruelle, C. (2009). Emotion understanding in children with ADHD. *Child Psychiatry and Human Development, 40*(1), 111–121.

Dannlowski, U., Konrad, C., Kugel, H., Zwitserlood, P., Domschke, K., Schöning, S., et al. (2010). Emotion specific modulation of automatic amygdala responses by 5-HTTLPR genotype. *Neuroimage, 53*(3), 893–898.

Dannlowski, U., Ohrmann, P., Bauer, J., Deckert, J., Hohoff, C., Kugel, H., et al. (2008). 5-HTTLPR biases amygdala activity in response to masked facial expressions in major depression. *Neuropsychopharmacology, 33*, 418–424.

Dannlowski, U., Ohrmann, P., Bauer, J., Kugel, H., Baune, B. T., Hohoff, C., et al. (2007). Serotonergic genes modulate amygdala activity in major depression. *Genes, Brain and Behavior, 6*, 672–676.

Darwin, C. (1872/1965). *The expression of emotions in man and animals*. Chicago: University of Chicago Press.

Deruelle, C., Mancini, J., Livet, M. O., Cassé-Perrot, C. & de Schonen, S. (1999). Configural and local processing of faces in children with Williams syndrome. *Brain and Cognition, 41*, 276–298.

Di Simplicio, M., Massey-Chase, R., Cowen, P., & Harmer, C. (2009). Oxytocin enhances processing of positive versus negative emotional information in healthy male volunteers. *Journal of Psychopharmacology, 23*(3), 241–248.

Ditzen, B., Schaer, M., Gabriel, B., Bodenmann, G., Ehlert, U., & Heinrichs, M. (2009). Intranasal oxytocin increases positive communication and reduces cortisol levels during couple conflict. *Biological Psychiatry, 65*(9), 728–731.

Domes, G., Heinrichs, M., Gläscher, J., Büchel, C., Braus, D. F., & Herpertz, S. C. (2007). Oxytocin attenuates amygdala responses to emotional faces regardless of valence. *Biological Psychiatry, 62*(10), 1187–1190.

Domes, G., Heinrichs, M., Michel, A., Berger, C., & Herpertz, S. C. (2007). Oxytocin improves "mind-reading" in humans. *Biological Psychiatry, 61*(6), 731–733.

Domschke, K., & Dannlowski, U. (2010). Imaging genetics of anxiety disorders. *Neuroimage, 53*(3), 822–831.

Domschke, K., Dannlowski, U., Ohrmann, P., Lawford, B., Bauer, J., Kugel, H., et al. (2008). Cannabinoid receptor 1 (CNR1) gene: Impact on antidepressant treatment response and emotion processing in major depression. *European Neuropsychopharmacology, 18*, 751–759.

Donaldson, Z. R., & Young, L. J. (2008). Oxytocin, vasopressin, and the neurogenetics of sociality. *Science, 322*(5903), 900–904.

Donnai, D., & Karmiloff-Smith, A. (2000) Williams syndrome: From genotype through to the cognitive phenotype. *American Journal of Medical Genetics: Seminars in Medical Genetics, 97*(2), 164–171.

Drabant, E. M., Hariri, A. R., Meyer-Lindenberg, A., Munoz, K. E., Mattay, V. S., Kolachana, B. S., et al. (2006). Catechol *O*-methyltransferase val158met genotype and neural mechanisms related to affective arousal and regulation. *Archives of General Psychiatry, 63*, 1396–1406.

Egan, M. F., Goldberg, T. E., Kolachana, B. S., Callicott, J. H., Mazzanti, C. M., Straub R. E., et al. (2001) Effect of COMT Val108/158 Met genotype on frontal lobe function and risk for schizophrenia. *Proceeding of the National Academy of Science U S A, 98*, 6917–6922.

Egan, M. F., Kojima, M., Callicott, J. H., Goldberg, T. E., Kolachana, B. S., Bertolino, A., et al. (2003). The BDNF val66met polymorphism affects activity-dependent secretion of BDNF and human memory and hippocampal function. *Cell, 112*, 257–269.

Egan, M. F., Straub, R. E., Goldberg, T. E., Yakub, I., Callicott, J. H., Hariri, A. R., et al. (2004). Variation in GRM3 affects cognition, prefrontal glutamate, and risk for schizophrenia. *Proceeding of the National Academy of Science U S A, 101*, 12604–12609.

Ehrlich, S., Morrow, E. M., Roffman, J. L., Wallace, S. R., Naylor, M., Bockholt, J., et al. (2010). The COMT Val108/158Met polymorphism and medial temporal lobe volumetry in patients with schizophrenia and healthy adults. *Neuroimage, 53*(3), 922–1000.

Ellis, H. D., & Young, A. W. (1989) Are faces special? In A. W. Young & H. D. Ellis (Eds.), *Handbook of research on face processing* (pp. 1–26). Amsterdam: Elsevier.

Fakra, E., Hyde, L. W., Gorka, A., Fisher, P. M., Munoz, K. E., Kimak, M., et al. (2009). Effects of HTR1A C(-1019)G on amygdala reactivity and trait anxiety. *Archives of General Psychiatry, 66*, 33–40.

Farah, M. J., Tanaka J. W., & Drain, H. M. (1995). What causes the face inversion effect? *Journal of Experimental Psychology: Human Perception and Performance, 21*, 628–634.

Fisher, P. M., Meltzer, C. C., Ziolko, S. K., Price, J. C., Moses-Kolko, E. L., Berga, S. L., & Hariri, A. R. (2006). Capacity for 5-HT1A-mediated autoregulation predicts amygdala reactivity. *Nature Neuroscience, 9*, 1362–1363.

Flint, J., & Munafo, M. R. (2008). Forum: Interactions between gene and environment. *Current Opinion in Psychiatry, 21*, 315–317.

Friedel, E., Schlagenhauf, F., Sterzer, P., Park, S. Q., Bermpohl, F., Strohle, A., et al. (2009). 5-HTT genotype effect on prefrontal-amygdala coupling differs between major depression and controls. *Psychopharmacology (Berlin), 205*, 261–271.

Frigerio, E., Burt, D. M., Gagliardi, C., Cioffi, G., Martelli, S., et al. (2006). Is everybody always my friend? Perception of approachability in Williams syndrome. *Neuropsychologia, 44*, 254–259.

Frodl, T., Koutsouleris, N., Bottlender, R., Born, C., Jager, M., Morgenthaler, M., et al. (2008). Reduced gray matter brain volumes are associated with variants of the serotonin transporter gene in major depression. *Molecular Psychiatry, 13*, 1093–1101.

Frodl, T., Schule, C., Schmitt, G., Born, C., Baghai, T., Zill, P., et al. (2007). Association of the brain-derived neurotrophic factor Val66Met polymorphism with reduced hippocampal volumes in major depression. *Archives of General Psychiatry, 64*, 410–416.

Gaspar, P., Cases, O., & Maroteaux, L. (2003). The developmental role of serotonin. News from mouse molecular genetics. *Nature Reviews Neuroscience, 4*, 1002–1012.

Gasic, G. P., Smoller, J. W., Perlis, R. H., Sun, M., Lee, S., Kim, B. W., et al. (2009). BDNF, relative preference, and reward circuitry responses to emotional communication. *American Journal of Medical Genetics Part B: Neuropsychiatric Genetics, 150B* (6), 762–781.

Gatt, J. M., Nemeroff, C. B., Dobson-Stone, C., Paul, R. H., Bryant, R. A., Schofield, P. R., et al. (2009). Interactions between BDNF Val66Met polymorphism and early life stress predict brain and arousal pathways to syndromal depression and anxiety. *Molecular Psychiatry, 14*, 681–695.

Goldman, D., Oroszi, G., & Ducci, F. (2005). The genetics of addictions: Uncovering the genes. *Nature Reviews Genetics, 6*(7), 521–532.

Good, C. D., Lawrence, K., Thomas, N. S., Price, C. J., Ashburner, J., Friston, K. J., et al. (2003). Dosage-sensitive X-linked locus influences the development of amygdala and orbitofrontal cortex, and fear recognition in humans. *Brain, 126*, 2431–2446.

Gosch, A., & Pankau, R. (1994). Social-emotional and behavioral adjustment in children with Williams-Beuren syndrome. *American Journal of Medical Genetics, 52*, 291–296.

Gottesman, I. I., & Gould, T. D. (2003). The endophenotype concept in psychiatry: Etymology and strategic intentions. *American Journal of Psychiatry, 160*, 636–645.

Groves, J. O. (2007). Is it time to reassess the BDNF hypothesis of depression? *Molecular Psychiatry, 12*, 1079–1088.

Guastella, A. J., Mitchell, P. B., & Dadds, M. R. (2008). Oxytocin increases gaze to the eye region of human faces. *Biological Psychiatry, 63*(1), 3–5.

Haas, B. W., Mills, D., Yam, A., Hoeft, F., Bellugi, U., & Reiss, A. (2009). Genetic influences on sociability: Heightened amygdale reactivity and event-related responses to positive social stimuli in Williams syndrome. *Journal of Neuroscience, 29*(4), 1132–11349.

Haghighi, F., Bach-Mizrachi, H., Huang, Y. Y., Arango, V., Shi, S., Dwork, A. J., et al. (2008). Genetic architecture of the human tryptophan hydroxylase 2 gene: Existence of neural isoforms and relevance for major depression. *Molecular Psychiatry, 13*, 813–820.

Hansen, C. H., & Hansen, R. D. (1988). Finding the face in the crowd: An anger superiority effect. *Journal of Personality and Social Psychology, 54*(6), 917–924.

Hariri, A. R., Drabant, E. M., Munoz, K. E., Kolachana, B. S., Mattay, V. S., Egan, M. F., & Weinberger, D. R. (2005). A susceptibility gene for affective disorders and the response of the human amygdala. *Archives of General Psychiatry, 62*, 146–152.

Hariri, A. R., Goldberg, T. E., Mattay, V. S., Kolachana, B. S., Callicott, J. H., Egan, M. F., & Weinberger, D. R. (2003). Brain-derived neurotrophic factor val66met polymorphism affects human memory-related hippocampal activity and predicts memory performance. *Journal of Neuroscience, 23*, 6690–6694.

Hariri, A. R., Gorka, A., Hyde, L. W., Kimak, M., Halder, I., Ducci, F., et al. (2009). Divergent effects of genetic variation in endocannabinoid signaling on human threat- and reward-related brain function. *Biological Psychiatry, 66*, 9–16.

Hariri, A. R., Mattay, V. S., Tessitore, A., Kolachana, B., Fera, F., Goldman, D., et al., (2002). Serotonin transporter genetic variation and the response of the human amygdala. *Science, 297*(5580), 400–403.

Hariri, A. R., Tessitore, A., Mattay, V. S., Fera, F., Weinberger, D. R. (2002). The amygdala response to emotional stimuli: A comparison of faces and scenes. *Neuroimage, 17*(1), 317–323.

Hariri, A. R., & Weinberger, D. R. (2003). Imaging genomics. *British Medical Bulletin, 65*, 259–270.

Harrison, P. J., & Tunbridge, E. M. (2008). Catechol-*O*-methyltransferase (COMT): A gene contributing to sex differences in brain function, and to sexual dimorphism in the predisposition to psychiatric disorders. *Neuropsychopharmacology, 33*, 3037–3045.

Hashimoto, R., Moriguchi, Y., Yamashita, F., Mori, T., Nemoto, K., Okada, T., et al. (2008). Dose-dependent effect of the Val66Met polymorphism of the brain-derived neurotrophic factor gene on memory-related hippocampal activity. *Neuroscience Research, 61*, 360–367.

Heinrichs, M., & Domes, G. (2008). Neuropeptides and social behaviour: Effects of oxytocin and vasopressin in humans. *Progress in Brain Research, 170*, 337–350.

Heinz, A., Braus, D. F., Smolka, M. N., Wrase, J., Puls, I., Hermann, D., et al. (2005). Amygdala-prefrontal coupling depends on a genetic variation of the serotonin transporter. *Nature Neuroscience, 8*, 20–21.

Heinz, A., Smolka, M. N., Braus, D. F., Wrase, J., Beck, A., Flor, H., et al. (2007). Serotonin transporter genotype

(5-HTTLPR): Effects of neutral and undefined conditions on amygdala activation. *Biological Psychiatry, 61*, 1011–1014.

Hranilovic, D., Stefulj, J., Schwab, S., Borrmann-Hassenbach, M., Albus, M., Jernej, B., & Wildenauer, D. (2004). Serotonin transporter promoter and intron 2 polymorphisms: Relationship between allelic variants and gene expression. *Biological Psychiatry, 55*, 1090–1094.

Hu, X. Z., Lipsky, R. H., Zhu, G., Akhtar, L. A., Taubman, J., Greenberg, B. D., et al. (2006). Serotonin transporter promoter gain-of-function genotypes are linked to obsessive-compulsive disorder. *American Journal of Human Genetics, 78*, 815–826.

Insel, T. R., & Young, L. J. (2001). The neurobiology of attachment. *Nature Reviews Neuroscience, 2*(2), 129–136.

Jansen, L. M., Gispen-de Wied, C. C., Wiegant, V. M., Westenberg, H. G., Lahuis, B. E., van Engeland, H. (2006). Autonomic and neuroendocrine responses to a psychosocial stressor in adults with autistic spectrum disorder. *Journal of Autism and Developmental Disorders, 36*(7), 891–899.

Jones, W., Bellugi, U., Lai, Z., Chiles, M., Reilly, J., Lincoln, A., & Adolphs, R. (2000). Hypersociability in Williams syndrome. *Journal of Cognitive Neuroscience, 12*(Suppl 1), 30–46.

Karmiloff-Smith, A. (1997). Crucial differences between developmental cognitive neuroscience and adult neuropsychology. *Developmental Neuropsychology, 13*, 513–524.

Karmiloff-Smith, A, Brown, J. H., Grice, S., & Paterson, S. (2003). Dethroning the myth: Cognitive dissociations and innate modularity in Williams syndrome. *Developmental Neuropsychology, 23*, 227–242.

Karmiloff-Smith, A., & Thomas, M. (2003). What can developmental disorders tell us about the neurocomputational constraints that shape development? The case of Williams syndrome. *Development and Psychopathogy, 15*, 969–990.

Kato, T. (2007). Molecular genetics of bipolar disorder and depression. *Psychiatry and Clinical Neurosciences, 61*, 3–19.

Kempton, M. J., Haldane, M., Jogia, J., Christodoulou, T., Powell, J., Collier, D., et al. (2009). The effects of gender and COMT Val158Met polymorphism on fearful facial affect recognition: A fMRI study. *International Journal of Neuropsychopharmacology, 12*, 371–381.

Kesler, S. R., Garrett, A., Bender, B., Yankowitz, J., Zeng, S. M., & Reiss, A. L. (2004). Amygdala and hippocampal volumes in Turner syndrome: A high-resolution MRI study of X-monosomy. *Neuropsychologia, 42*, 1971–1978.

Kirsch, P., Esslinger, C., Chen, Q., Mier, D., Lis, S., Siddhanti, S. et al. (2005). Oxytocin modulates neural circuitry for social cognition and fear in humans. *Journal of Neuroscience, 25*(49), 11489–11493.

Klein-Tasman, B. P., & Mervis, C. B. (2003). Distinctive personality characteristics of 8-, 9-, and 10-year-olds with Williams syndrome. *Developmental Neuropsychology, 23*, 269–290.

Krishnan, V., Han, M. -H., Graham, D. L., Berton, O., Renthal, W., Russo, S. J., et al. (2007). Molecular adaptations underlying susceptibility and resistance to social defeat in brain reward regions. *Cell, 131*, 391–404.

Korenberg, J. R., Chen, X. N., Hirota, H., Lai, Z., Bellugi, U., et al. (2000). IV. Genome structure and cognitive map of Williams syndrome. *Journal of Cognitive Neuroscience, 12* (Suppl 1), 89–107.

Kosfeld, M., Heinrichs, M., Zak, P. J., Fischbacher, U., & Fehr, E. (2005). Oxytocin increases trust in humans. *Nature, 435*(7042), 673–676.

Krysko, K. M., & Rutherford, M. D. (2009). A threat-detection advantage in those with autism spectrum disorders. *Brain and Cognition, 69*(3), 472–480.

Lang, U. E., Hellweg, R., Kalus, P., Bajbouj, M., Lenzen, K. P., Sander, T., et al. (2005). Association of a functional BDNF polymorphism and anxiety-related personality traits. *Psychopharmacology (Berlin), 180*, 95–99.

LeDoux, J. (2007). The amygdala. *Current Biology, 17*, R868–R874.

Lee, B. T., & Ham, B. J. (2008a). Monoamine oxidase A-uVNTR genotype affects limbic brain activity in response to affective facial stimuli. *Neuroreport, 19*, 515–519.

Lee, B. T. & Ham, B. J. (2008b). Serotonergic genes and amygdala activity in response to negative affective facial stimuli in Korean women. *Genes, Brain and Behavior, 7*, 899–905.

Lemonde, S., Turecki, G., Bakish, D., Du, L., Hrdina, P. D., Bown, C. D., et al. (2003). Impaired repression at a 5-hydroxytryptamine 1A receptor gene polymorphism associated with major depression and suicide. *Journal of Neuroscience, 23*, 8788–8799.

Lesch, (1996).

Lim, M. M., & Young, L. J. (2006). Neuropeptidergic regulation of affiliative behavior and social bonding in animals. *Hormones and Behaviour, 50*(4), 506–517.

Lowery, M. C., Morris, C. A., Ewart, A., Brothman, L. J., Zhu, X. L., et al. (1995). Strong correlation of elastin deletions, detected by FISH, with Williams syndrome. *American Journal of Human Genetics, 57*, 49–53.

Martin, (1996).

Matsuo, K., Walss-Bass, C., Nery, F. G., Nicoletti, M. A., Hatch, J. P., Frey, B. N., et al. (2009). Neuronal correlates of brain-derived neurotrophic factor Val66Met polymorphism and morphometric abnormalities in bipolar disorder. *Neuropsychopharmacology, 34*, 1904–1913.

Mervis, C. B., & Becerra, A. M. (2007). Language and communicative development in Williams syndrome. *Mental Retardation and Developmental Disabilities Research Reviews, 13*(1), 3–15.

Meyer-Lindenberg, A. (2008). Impact of prosocial neuropeptides on human brain function. *Progress in Brain Research, 170*, 463–470.

Meyer-Lindenberg, A., Buckholtz, J., Kolachana, B. S., Pezawas, L., Blasi, G., Wabnitz, A., et al. (2006). Neural mechanisms of genetic risk for impulsivity and violence in humans. *Proceedings of the National Academy of Sciences USA, 103*(16), 6269–6274.

Meyer-Lindenberg, A., Hariri, A. R., Munoz, K. E., Morris, C. A., Mervis, C., et al. (2005). Neural correlates of genetically abnormal social cognition in Williams syndrome. *Nature Neuroscience, 8*(8), 991–993.

Meyer-Lindenberg, A., Kohn, P. D., Kolachana, B., Kippenhan, S., McInerney-Leo, A., Nussbaum, R., et al. (2005). Midbrain dopamine and prefrontal function in humans: Interaction and modulation by COMT genotype. *Nature Neuroscience, 8*(5), 594–596.

Meyer-Lindenberg, A., Kohn, P., Mervis, C. B., Kippenhan, J., S., Olsen, R. K., et al. (2004). Neural basis of genetically determined visuospatial construction deficit in Williams syndrome. *Neuron, 43*(5), 623–631.

Meyer-Lindenberg, A., Kolachana, B., Gold, B., Olsh, A., Nicodemus, K. K., Mattay, V., et al. (2009). Genetic variants in AVPR1A linked to autism predict amygdala activation and personality traits in healthy humans. *Molecular Psychiatry, 14*(10), 968–975.

Meyer-Lindenberg, A., Mervis, C. B., & Berman, K. F. (2006). Neural mechanisms in Williams syndrome: A unique window to genetic influences on cognition and behaviour. *Nature Neuroscience, 8*, 991–993.

Meyer-Lindenberg, A., Nicodemus, K. K., Egan, M. F., Callicott, J. H., Mattay, V., & Weinberger, D. R. (2008). False positives in imaging genetics. *Neuroimage, 40*(2), 655–661.

Meyer-Lindenberg, A., & Weinberger, D. R. (2006). Intermediate phenotypes and genetic mechanisms of psychiatric disorders. *Nature Reviews Neuroscience, 7*, 818–827.

Meyer-Lindenberg, A., & Zink, C. F. (2007). Imaging genetics for neuropsychiatric disorders. *Child and Adolescent Psychiatric Clinics of North America, 16*(3), 581–597.

Modahl, C., Green, L., Fein, D., Morris, M., Waterhouse, L., Feinstein, C., & Levin, H. (1998). Plasma oxytocin levels in autistic children. *Biological Psychiatry, 43*(4), 270–277.

Montag, C., Reuter, M., Newport, B., Elger, C., & Weber, B. (2008). The BDNF Val66Met polymorphism affects amygdala activity in response to emotional stimuli: Evidence from a genetic imaging study. *Neuroimage, 42*, 1554–1559.

Montag, C., Weber, B., Fliessbach, K., Elger, C., & Reuter, M. (2009). The BDNF Val66Met polymorphism impacts parahippocampal and amygdala volume in healthy humans: Incremental support for a genetic risk factor for depression. *Psychological Medicine, 39*, 1831–1839.

Morris, C. A., Demsey, S. A., Leonard, C. O., Dilts, C., & Blackburn, B. L. (1988). Natural history of Williams syndrome: Physical characteristics. *Journal of Pediatrics, 113*, 318–326.

Munafo, M. R., Brown, S. M., & Hariri, A. R. (2008). Serotonin transporter (5-HTTLPR) genotype and amygdala activation: a meta-analysis. *Biological Psychiatry, 63*, 852–857.

Munafo, M. R., Durrant, C., Lewis, G., & Flint, J. (2009). Gene X environment interactions at the serotonin transporter locus. *Biological Psychiatry, 65*, 211–219.

Munafo, M. R., Freimer, N. B., Ng, W., Ophoff, R., Veijola, J., Miettunen, J., et al. (2009). 5-HTTLPR genotype and anxiety-related personality traits: A meta-analysis and new data. *American Journal of Medical Genetics Part B: Neuropsychiatric Genetics, 150B*, 271–281.

Murphy, D. L., & Lesch, K. P. (2008). Targeting the murine serotonin transporter: Insights into human neurobiology. *Nature Reviews Neuroscience, 9*, 85–96.

Murphy, D. L., Uhl, G. R., Holmes, A., Ren Patterson, R., Hall, F.S., Sora, I., et al. (2003). Experimental gene interaction studies with SERT mutant mice as models for human polygenic and epistatic traits and disorders. *Genes, Brain and Behavior, 2*, 350–364.

Nemoto, K., Ohnishi, T., Mori, T., Moriguchi, Y., Hashimoto, R., Asada, T., & Kunugi, H. (2006). The Val66Met polymorphism of the brain-derived neurotrophic factor gene affects age-related brain morphology. *Neuroscience Letters, 397*, 25–29.

Neumann, S. A., Brown, S. M., Ferrell, R. E., Flory, J. D., Manuck, S. B., & Hariri, A. R. (2006). Human choline transporter gene variation is associated with corticolimbic reactivity and autonomic-cholinergic function. *Biological Psychiatry, 60*, 1155–1162.

Öhman, A. (1993). Fear and anxiety as emotional phenomena: Clinical phenomenology, evolutionary perspectives, and information processing mechanisms. In M. Lewis & J. M. Haviland (Eds.), *Handbook of emotions* (pp. 511–536). New York: Guilford Press.

Öhman, A., Lundqvist, D., & Esteves, F., (2001). The face in the crowd revisited: A threat advantage with schematic stimuli. *Journal of Personality and Social Psychology, 80*(3), 381–396.

Öhman, A., & Mineka, S. (2001). Fears, phobias, and preparedness: Toward an evolved module of fear and fear learning. *Psychological Review, 108*(3), 483–522.

Öhman, A., & Mineka, S. (2003). The malicious serpent: Snakes as a prototypical stimulus for an evolved module of fear. *Current Directions in Psychological Science, 12*(1), 5–9.

Patwardhan, A. J., Brown, W. E., Bender, B. G., Linden, M. G., Eliez, S., & Reiss, A. L. (2002). Reduced size of the amygdala in individuals with 47,XXY and 47,XXX karyotypes. *American Journal of Medical Genetics, 114*, 93–98.

Peoples, R., Franke, Y., Wang, Y. K., Pérez-Jurado, L., Paperna, T., Cisco, M., & Francke, U. (2000). A physical map, including a BAC/PAC clone contig, of the Williams-Beuren syndrome—deletion region at 7q11.23. *American Journal of Human Genetics, 66*(1), 47–68.

Perlis, R. H., Holt, D. J., Smoller, J. W., Blood, A. J., Lee, S., Kim, B. W., et al. (2008). Association of a polymorphism near CREB1 with differential aversion processing in the insula of healthy participants. *Archives of General Psychiatry, 65*, 882–892.

Pezawas, L., Meyer-Lindenberg, A., Drabant, E. M., Verchinski, B. A., Munoz, K. E., Kolachana, B. S., et al. (2005). 5-HTTLPR polymorphism impact anatomy and function of affective neural circuitry: A genetic mechanism for susceptibility to depression and anxiety disorders. *Nature Neuroscience, 8*, 828–834.

Pezawas, L., Meyer-Lindenberg, A., Goldman, A. L., Verchinski, B. A., Chen, G., Kolachana, B. S., et al. (2008). Evidence of biologic epistasis between BDNF and SLC6A4 and implications for depression. *Molecular Psychiatry, 13*, 709–716.

Pezawas, L., Verchinski, B. A., Mattay, V. S., Callicott, J. H., Kolachana, B. S., Straub, R. E., et al. (2004). The brain-derived neurotrophic factor val66met polymorphism and variation in human cortical morphology. *Journal of Neuroscience, 24*, 10099–10102.

Phillips, M. L., Drevets, W. C., Rauch, S. L., & Lane, R. (2003a). Neurobiology of emotion perception I: The neural basis of normal emotion perception. *Biological Psychiatry, 54*, 504–514.

Phillips, M. L., Drevets, W. C., Rauch, S. L., & Lane, R. (2003b). Neurobiology of emotion perception II: Implications for major psychiatric disorders. *Biological Psychiatry, 54*, 515–528.

Preece, M. A., Taylor, M. J., Raley, J., Blamire, A., Sharp, T., & Sibson, N. R. (2009). Evidence that increased 5-HT release evokes region-specific effects on blood-oxygenation level-dependent functional magnetic resonance imaging responses in the rat brain. *Neuroscience, 159*, 751–759.

Price, J. L., & Drevets, W. C. (2010). Neurocircuitry of mood disorders. *Neuropsychopharmacology, 35*, 192–216.

Rao, H., Gillihan, S. J., Wang, J., Korczykowski, M., Sankoorikal, G. M., Kaercher, K. A., et al. (2007). Genetic variation in serotonin transporter alters resting brain function in healthy individuals. *Biological Psychiatry, 62*, 600–606.

Razzoli, M., Cushing, B. S., Carter, C. S., & Valsecchi, P. (2003). Hormonal regulation of agonistic and affiliative behavior in female mongolian gerbils (*Meriones unguiculatus*). *Hormones and Behaviour, 43*(5), 549–553.

Reiss, A. L., Eckert, M. A., Rose, F. E., Karchemskiy, A., Kesler, S., Chang, M. et al. (2004). An experiment of nature: Brain anatomy parallels cognition and behaviour in Williams Syndrome. *Journal of Neuroscience, 24*(21), 5009–5015.

Rhodes, G., Brake, S., & Atkinson, A. (1993). What's lost in inverted faces? *Cognition, 47*, 25–27.

Rietschel, M., Beckmann, L., Strohmaier, J., Georgi, A., Karpushova, A., Schirmbeck, F., et al. (2008). G72 and its association with major depression and neuroticism in large population-based groups from Germany. *American Journal of Psychiatry, 165*, 753–762.

Risch, N., Herrell, R., Lehner, T., Liang, K. Y., Eaves, L., Hoh, J., et al. (2009). Interaction between the serotonin transporter gene (5-HTTLPR), stressful life events, and risk of depression: a meta-analysis. *Journal of the American Medical Association, 301*, 2462–2471.

Rondan, C., Santos, A., Mancini, J., Livet, M. O., & Deruelle, C. (2008). Global and local processing in Williams syndrome: Drawing versus perceiving. *Child Neuropsychology, 14*(3), 237–248.

Rosset, D., Rondan, C., Da Fonseca, D., Santos, A., Assouline, B., & Deruelle, C. (2008). Typical emotion processing for cartoon but not for real faces in children with autistic spectrum disorders. *Journal of Autism and Developmental Disorders, 38*(5), 919–925.

Sabol, S. Z., Hu, S., & Hamer, D. (1998). A functional polymorphism in the monoamine oxidase A gene promoter. *Human Genetics, 103*, 273–279.

Santos, A. (2008). *More is not always better: Atypical social cognition in (hypersociable) individuals with Williams syndrome.* PhD dissertation, Université Paul Sabatier, Toulouse III, France.

Santos, A., & Deruelle, C. (2009). Verbal peaks and visual valleys in theory of mind ability in Williams syndrome. *Journal of Autism and Developmental Disorders, 39*(4), 651–659

Santos, A., Mier, D., Kirsch, P., & Meyer-Lindenberg, A. (2011). Evidence for a general face salience signal in human amygdala. *Neuroimage, 54*(4), 3111–3116.

Santos, A., Milne, D., Rosset, D., & Deruelle, C. (2007). Challenging symmetry on mental retardation: Evidence from Williams syndrome. In E. B. Heinz (Ed.), *Mental retardation research advances* (pp. 147–174). New York: Nova Science Publishers.

Santos, A., Rondan, R., Milne, D., Démonet, J-F., & Deruelle, C. (2008). Social relevance boosts context processing in Williams syndrome. *Developmental Neuropsychology, 33*(4), 1–12.

Santos, A., Rosset, D., & Deruelle, C. (2009). Human versus non-human face processing: Evidence from Williams syndrome. *Journal of Autism and Developmental Disorders, 39*(11), 1552–1559.

Santos, A., Silva, C., Rosset, D., & Deruelle (2010). Just another face in the crowd: Evidence for decreased detection of angry faces in children with Williams syndrome. *Neuropsychologia, 48*(4), 1071–1078.

Sarpal, D., Buchsbaum, B. R., Kohn, P. D., Kippenhan, J. S., Mervis, C. B., et al. (2008). A genetic model for understanding higher order visual processing: Functional interactions of the ventral visual stream in Williams syndrome. *Cerebral Cortex, 18*(10), 2402–2409.

Savitz, J. B., & Drevets, W. C. (2009). Imaging phenotypes of major depressive disorder: Genetic correlates. *Neuroscience, 164*, 300–330.

Scharinger, C., Rabl, U., Sitte, H. H., & Pezawas, L. (2010). Imaging genetics of mood disorders. *Neuroimage, 53*(3), 810–821.

Scherk, H., Gruber, O., Menzel, P., Schneider-Axmann, T., Kemmer, C., Usher, J., et al. (2009). 5-HTTLPR genotype influences amygdala volume. *European Archives of Psychiatry and Clinical Neurosciences, 259*, 212–217.

Schinka, J. A., Busch, R. M., & Robichaux-Keene, N. (2004). A meta-analysis of the association between the serotonin transporter gene polymorphism (5-HTTLPR) and trait anxiety. *Molecular Psychiatry, 9*, 197–202.

Schofield, P. R., Williams, L. M., Paul, R. H., Gatt, J. M., Brown, K., Luty, A., et al. (2009). Disturbances in selective information processing associated with the BDNF Val66Met polymorphism: Evidence from cognition, the P300 and fronto-hippocampal systems. *Biological Psychology, 80*, 176–188.

Schultz, R. T. (2005). Developmental deficits in social perception in autism: The role of the amygdala and fusiform face are. *International Journal of Developmental Neuroscience, 23*(2-3), 125–141.

Schulze, T. G., Muller, D. J., Krauss, H., Scherk, H., Ohlraun, S., Syagailo, Y. V., et al. (2000). Association between a functional polymorphism in the monoamine oxidase A gene promoter and major depressive disorder. *American Journal of Medical Genetics, 96*, 801–803.

Sen, S., Burmeister, M., & Ghosh, D. (2004). Meta-analysis of the association between a serotonin transporter promoter polymorphism (5-HTTLPR) and anxiety-related personality traits. *American Journal of Medical Genetics Part B: Neuropsychiatric Genetics, 127B*, 85–89.

Sen, S., Nesse, R. M., Stoltenberg, S. F., Li, S., Gleiberman, L., Chakravarti, A., (2003). A BDNF coding variant is associated with the NEO personality inventory domain neuroticism, a risk factor for depression. *Neuropsychopharmacology, 28*, 397–401.

Sergerie, K., Chochol, C., & Armony, J. L. (2008). The role of the amygdala in emotional processing: A quantitative meta-analysis of functional neuroimaging studies. *Neuroscience & Biobehavioral Reviews, 32*, 811–830.

Shen, D., Liu, D., Liu, H., Clasen, L., Giedd, J., & Davatzikos, C. (2004). Automated morphometric study of brain variation in XXY males. *Neuroimage, 23*, 648–653.

Siebner, H. R., Callicott, J. H., Sommer, T., & Mattay, V. S. (2009). From the genome to the phenome and back: Linking genes with human brain function and structure using genetically informed neuroimaging. *Neuroscience, 164*(1), 1–6.

Skuse, D.H., Morris, J.S., & Dolan, R.J. 2005. Functional dissociation of amygdala-modulated arousal and cognitive appraisal, in Turner syndrome. *Brain 128*, 2084–2096.

Smolka, M. N., Buhler, M., Schumann, G., Klein, S., Hu, X.Z., Moayer, M., et al. (2007). Gene–gene effects on central processing of aversive stimuli. *Molecular Psychiatry, 12*, 307–317.

Smolka, M. N., Schumann, G., Wrase, J., Grusser, S. M., Flor, H., Mann, K., et al. (2005). Catechol-O-methyltransferase val158met genotype affects processing of emotional stimuli in the amygdala and prefrontal cortex. *Journal of Neuroscience, 25*, 836–842.

Smoller, J. W., Paulus, M. P., Fagerness, J. A., Purcell, S., Yamaki, L. H., Hirshfeld-Becker, D., et al. (2008). Influence of RGS2 on anxiety-related temperament, personality, and brain function. *Archives of General Psychiatry, 65*, 298–308.

Stein, J. L., Wiedholz, L. M., Bassett, D. S., Weinberger, D. R., Zink, C. F., Mattay, V. S., & Meyer-Lindenberg, A. (2007). A validated network of effective amygdala connectivity. *Neuroimage, 36*, 736–745.

Strømme, P., Bjørnstad, P. G., & Ramstad, K. (2002). Prevalence estimation of Williams syndrome. *Journal of Child Neurology, 17*, 269–271.

Sublette, M. E., Baca-Garcia, E., Parsey, R. V., Oquendo, M. A., Rodrigues, S. M., Galfalvy, H., et al. (2008). Effect of BDNF val66met polymorphism on age-related amygdala volume changes in healthy subjects. *Progress in Neuropsychopharmacology and Biological Psychiatry, 32*, 1652–1655.

Sullivan, P. F., Neale, M. C., & Kendler, K. S. (2000). The genetic epidemiology of major depression: Review and meta-analysis. *American Journal of Psychiatry, 157*(10), 1552–1562.

Surguladze, S. A., Elkin, A., Ecker, C., Kalidindi, S., Corsico, A., Giampietro, V., et al. (2008). Genetic variation in the serotonin transporter modulates neural system-wide response to fearful faces. *Genes, Brain and Behavior, 7*, 543–551.

Tager-Flusberg, H., Plesa Skewerer, D., & Joseph, R. M. (2006). Model syndromes for investigating social cognitive and affective neuroscience: A comparison of autism and Williams syndrome. *Social, Cognitive & Affective Neuroscience, 1*(3), 175–182.

Taylor, W. D., Zuchner, S., Payne, M. E., Messer, D. F., Doty, T. J., MacFall, J. R. (2007). The COMT Val158Met polymorphism and temporal lobe morphometry in healthy adults. *Psychiatry Research, 155*, 173–177.

Theodoridou, A., Rowe, A. C., Penton-Voak, I. S., & Rogers, P. J. (2009). Oxytocin and social perception: Oxytocin increases perceived facial trustworthiness and attractiveness. *Hormones and Behavior, 56*(1), 128–132.

Thompson, P. M., Lee, A. D., Dutton, R. A., Geaga, J. A., Hayashi, K. M., et al., (2005). Abnormal cortical complexity and thickness profiles mapped in Williams syndrome. *Journal of Neuroscience, 25*(16), 4146–4158.

Urbán, Z., Helms, C., Fekete, G., Csiszár, K., Bonnet, D., Munnich, A. et al. (1996). 7q11.23 deletions in Williams syndrome arise as a consequence of unequal meiotic crossover. *American Journal of Human Genetics, 59*(4), 958–962.

VIding, E., & Blakemore, S-J. (2007). Endophenotype approach to the study of developmental disorders: Implications for autism research. *Behavior Genetics, 37*, 51–60.

Vuilleumier, P., & Schwartz, S. (2001). Emotional facial expressions capture attention. *Neurology, 56*(2), 153–158.

Waldman, I. D., & Gizer, I. R. (2006). The genetics of attention deficit hyperactivity disorder. *Clinical Psychology Reviews, 26*(4), 396–432.

Walter, E., Mazaika, P. K., & Reiss, A. L. (2009). Insights into brain development from neurogenetic syndromes: Evidence from fragile X syndrome, Williams syndrome, Turner syndrome and velocardiofacial syndrome. *Neuroscience, 164*(1), 257–271.

Williams, L. M., Gatt, J. M., Grieve, S., Dobson-Stone, C., Paul, R. H., Gordon, E., & Schofield, P. R. (2010a). COMT Val108/158Met polymorphism effects on emotional brain function are modulated by level of awareness and associated with negativity biases. *Neuroimage, 53*(3), 918–925.

Williams, L. M., Gatt, J. M., Schofield, P. R., Olivieri, G., Peduto, A., & Gordon, E. (2010b). Negativity bias' in risk for depression and anxiety: Brain-body fear circuitry correlates, 5-HTTLPR and early life stress. *Neuroimage, 47*, 804–814.

Willis-Owen, S. A., Fullerton, J., Surtees, P. G., Wainwright, N. W., Miller, S., & Flint, J. (2005). The Val66Met coding variant of the brain-derived neurotrophic factor (BDNF) gene does not contribute toward variation in the personality trait neuroticism. *Biological Psychiatry, 58*, 738–742.

Witt, D. M., Winslow, J. T., & Insel, T. R. (1992). Enhanced social interactions in rats following chronic, centrally infused oxytocin. *Pharmacology Biochemistry and Behavior, 43*(3), 855–861.

Yamasue, H., Kakiuchi, C., Tochigi, M., Inoue, H., Suga, M., Abe, O., et al. (2008). Association between mitochondrial DNA 10398A>G polymorphism and the volume of amygdala. *Genes, Brain and Behavior, 7*, 698–704.

Yu, Y. W., Tsai, S. J., Hong, C. J., Chen, T. J., Chen, M. C., & Yang, C. W. (2005). Association study of a monoamine oxidase a gene promoter polymorphism with major depressive disorder and antidepressant response. *Neuropsychopharmacology, 30*, 1719–1723.

Zhou, Z., Zhu, G., Hariri, A. R., Enoch, M. A., Scott, D., Sinha, R., et al. (2008). Genetic variation in human NPY expression affects stress response and emotion. *Nature, 452*, 997–1001.

Zuliani, R., Moorhead, T.W., Job, D., McKirdy, J., Sussmann, J.E., Johnstone, E.C., Lawrie, S.M., Brambilla, P., Hall, J., McIntosh, A.M., 2009. Genetic variation in the G72 (DAOA) gene affects temporal lobe and amygdala structure in subjects affected by bipolar disorder. *Bipolar Disorder, 11*, 621–627.

Visceromotor Sensation and Control

Fred W. Mast

Abstract

Bodily afferent information has been known for over a century, but only quite recently has this area of research, called visceroception, received more attention. The representation of visceroceptive information will be presented with particular emphasis on recent neuroimaging research. Visceroception involves a wide network of cortical and subcortical brain areas, among which particular emphasis will be dedicated to the insula and its putative role in self-awareness. In essence, the findings are consistent with the James-Lange theory of emotions and with Damasio's "somatic-marker" hypothesis. Visceroception is much more than just the gut, and many more questions will need to be addressed in future research, for example, its relation to seemingly unrelated topics such as balance.

Key Words: balance, consciousness, emotion, insula, interoception, self-awareness, visceroception

Some years ago I took a cab in New York City and struck up a lively conversation with the driver. At that time I used to live in Boston and the driver explained to me that life in New England is much more provincial compared to life in New York City. At some point he made a remark and I still remember it today: "Do you know what's special about New York City?" the driver asked me loudly, through a thick New York accent. Before I had a chance to contemplate an answer, he continued by saying, "There is something visceral here, and you will not find that kind of feeling anywhere else in the world." Impressed by his eloquence, I knew immediately what he meant.

The term *visceral* refers to the internal organs of the body (the viscera), and common sense uses it rather for the description of instinctive behavior and gut reactions. *Visceroception* includes regulatory functions such as cardiac activity and digestive tract motility and acts, to some extent, in the background; it does not continuously reach the level of conscious awareness (e.g., movements of the intestines). Given

the limits of our attentional resources, this is probably to our advantage. Nevertheless, visceromotor sensations such as stomach and bladder filling or the urge to defecate, along with other viscerosensory experiences such as thirst or hunger, are not rare occurrences. Moreover, heartbeat is commonly felt, along with breathlessness, during physical exertion or in the case of irregularities (palpitations). While these can be considered warning signs (e.g., reaching the limits of distension of the walls of the stomach, bladder, or rectum), there are also pleasant viscerosensory sensations, such as satiety (visceral afferences from stomach volume and hormonal changes during digestion) or an orgasm (contraction of the pelvic organs).

Visceroception—From the Gut to the Brain

Visceroception works in conjunction with exteroception (e.g., smell or vision) and proprioception (e.g., stretch receptors in the muscles) and provides the brain with information about the physiological condition of the body. Unlike in the domains of proprioception and exteroception, visceral receptors are hidden well inside the body, centered around many vital organs, and are thus not easily accessible to experimental manipulation. Visceroceptive input includes mechanoreceptors (e.g., stretch of visceral walls), chemoreceptors (e.g., detecting changes in blood oxygen level), thermoreceptors (e.g., regulation of body skin temperature), and osmoreceptors (e.g., the release of vasopression to regulate water retention via the kidneys). Input to these receptors gives rise to different autonomic responses (e.g., changes in blood pressure). Furthermore, there is evidence to suggest a small number of visceral pain fibers, despite ongoing debate concerning an adequate stimulus for visceral pain (specificity vs. intensity of stretch, tension, or chemical signals; McMahon, 1997).

The spinoreticular pathway conveys inputs from visceral and somatic afferents to the reticular formation and the caudal raphe nuclei of the brainstem. Information is also processed via the spinomesencephalic tract, which is mostly involved in nociception (the encoding and processing of noxious stimuli). There is considerable convergence of visceral and somatic afferents in the spinal cord and brainstem. Vagal ascending afferents carry cardiovascular, pulmonary, respiratory, and gastrointestinal information and terminate in the nucleus of the solitary tract (NTS, nucleus tractus solitarius). NTS neurons project to various brain areas including the hypothalamus, nucleus accumbens, amygdala, thalamus, and the dorsal motor nucleus of the vagus (Travagli, Hermann, Browning, & Rogers, 2006). The NTS also plays an important role in visceral–somatic integration, which may also contribute to the phenomenon of referred pain (e.g., when heart problems are mislocalized and felt in the arm). It is noteworthy, however, that there is more convergence of visceral and somatic input in other brain areas, such as the medial frontal cortex (Cechetto & Saper, 1990).

An alternative route for viscerosensory information is via the spinothalamic tract, which originates in the dorsal horn and ascends to various thalamic nuclei. The spinothalamic tract has two divisions. The lateral part terminates in the ventral and ventroposterior thalamic areas, conveying pain information and possibly other visceral inputs. The medial pathway projects to the medial and intralaminar thalamic nuclei, and it is involved in visceral pain from the heart and gastrointestinal tract. According to Cechetto (1987), there are core thalamic regions that receive separate somatotopic,

gustatory, cardiopulmonary, and spinal input. These areas then project to the insular cortex, which we will address in more detail below. However, beyond the brainstem, it is difficult to track whether visceral input conveys afferent or efferent information, given that most connections are reciprocal.

The hypothalamus is an integrator of exteroceptive and visceroceptive information, and it also receives input from other brain areas, such as the hippocampus and the amygdala. The latter receives direct input from the NTS and is therefore a projection area of afferent visceroceptive input. The amygdala also shares connections with the insula, yet another pathway to relay reciprocal, visceroceptive information. The amygdala is involved in various types of processing of emotional information (e.g., evaluation of emotional stimuli, recognition of emotions in faces, and emotional reactions) and thus acts like a potential visceral–emotional converter. This is a rather simplified generalization, but we will see below that Damasio's "somatic-marker" hypothesis (Damasio et al., 2000) attributes an important role to the internal visceral information of the body in understanding emotional experience. In any case, it is clear that the processing of visceroceptive information does not end at the amygdala. Its higher cortical projections are elaborated in more detail in the next section.

Cortical Body State Representation

The insula has been proposed as the cortical substrate providing awareness of the physiological condition of the body (Craig, 2002, 2003, 2009). It is situated in the lateral sulcus and covered by the frontal, parietal, and temporal opercular lobes. The central sulcus of the insula divides into the anterior and the smaller posterior part. The ventral anterior parts are involved in the processing of emotion and empathy (Adolphs 2002; Dolan 2002; Frith and Singer 2008; Lamm and Singer 2010; Phillips, Drevets, Rauch, & Lane, 2003) and in the processing of olfactory information (Poellinger et al., 2001) and how olfaction interacts with gustatory information (Shipley & Geinisman, 1984), including the subjective evaluation of these stimuli. The processing of emotional information is in accordance with the anatomy of the insular cortex in monkeys, which has dense connections between the ventral anterior parts and limbic areas (Stefanacci & Amaral, 2002).

Another important finding, which is interesting in this context, is the knowledge that mirror neurons (observed, imagined, and executed actions show similar activations; see, e.g., Gerardin et al., 2000; Rizzolatti & Craighero, 2004) have been extended to the realm of emotions (Jabbi, Bastiaansen, & Keysers, 2008). More important is the fact that the ventral anterior insula and the adjacent frontal operculum have been proposed as a potential neural basis for this mirror neuron system. Jabbi et al. (2008) found that activation in these areas was independent of whether participants tasted bitter liquids, viewed someone else tasting the disgusting liquid, or when they imagined tasting the liquid. However, functional connectivity analyses between the frontal operculum and other brain areas differed depending on the condition used to induce disgust (Jabbi et al., 2008).

Neuroimaging studies have shown the activity of the dorsal anterior insula in response to many categories of stimuli that activate the insula, with the only exception being somatosensory information (Kurth, Zilles, Fox, Laird, & Eickhoff, 2010). The insula has dense connections to various frontal areas and has been suggested to be part of an inferior frontoparietal network involved in working memory and attention tasks (Mayer et al., 2007). Some evidence also implicates the insula in language processing (Riecker, Ackermann, Wildgruber, Dogil, & Grodd, 2000). Finally, the mid-posterior insula responds to visceral, sensorimotor, and painful stimulation. Penfield and Faulk (1955) in earlier investigations reported changes in gastric motility during deep brain stimulation of the mid-posterior insula, and it elicited visceroceptive and somatic sensations and influenced cardiovascular and respiratory functions.

There is strong evidence to suggest that parts of the insula are functionally differentiated. Alternatively, evidence from tracing studies in nonhuman primates (Augustine, 1996) shows that different insular areas are heavily interconnected. Moreover, the increased integration of interoceptive information along the posterior–anterior axis illustrates the insula's interconnectivity. For example, cool temperatures are represented linearly in the contralateral dorsal part of the posterior insula, whereas the subjective evaluation of these stimuli is associated with contralateral mid-insular and more strongly with right anterior regions (Craig, Chen, Bandy, & Reiman, 2000). The fact that temperature sensation is processed in the insula may appear surprising, and it suggests a less emphasized aspect in addition to its known role in exteroception. According to Craig et al. (2000), thermoregulatory behavior is nested with interoceptive functions, in particular with pain perception.

The involvement of the latter is obvious because the location of the thermosensory cortex corresponds to the brain area damaged in certain patients with post-stroke central pain (Schmahmann & Leifer, 1992).

In recent research, the insula has increasingly become the focus of attention for its role in body representation (Chaminade, Meltzoff, & Decety, 2005; Nunn, Frampton, Gordon, & Lask, 2008; Sachdev, Mondraty, Wen, & Guillford, 2008) and subjective emotional experience (Critchley, Wiens, Rotshtein, Ohman, & Dolan, 2004; Lane, Fink, Chau, & Dolan, 1997). In particular, Antonio Damasio (1999) has proposed that this region plays a key role in mapping visceral states associated with emotional experience, giving rise to conscious feelings. This is in essence a neurobiological formulation of the ideas of William James, who first proposed that subjective emotional experience (i.e., feelings) arise from the brain's interpretation of bodily states elicited by emotional events. In fact, the insula is activated in over 70% of the studies on disgust but in fewer than 40% of the studies focusing on other emotions (Murphy, Nimmo-Smith, & Lawrence, 2003).

Finally, the insula has connections with the anterior cingulate cortex, amygdala, hypothalamus, orbitofrontal cortex, temporal, parietal, and lateral frontal areas and is thus part of a highly interconnected and reciprocal neural network. Moreover, efferent insular connections to the somatosensory cortices SI and SII are somatotopically organized and constitute yet another visceral–somatic convergence. Its main function is to provide information about the localization and intensity of the stimulus.

Visceroception and Decision Making

Damasio (1999) developed the concept of somatic markers, which are involved in and support human decision making. When faced with different options it is sometimes difficult to come to a decision. It is challenging to anticipate the consequences associated with different options. In particular, when different alternatives have a high degree of uncertainty, decision making may overtax reasoning capabilities. This is when somatic markers may come into play. Marker signals represent the bodily state experienced previously in similar life situations. Thus, when we are faced with a particular situation, we not only recall from memory factual knowledge about this situation but at the same time reactivate the emotional experience, including its bodily states.

The somatic markers can help to constrain the range of different conceivable options, thus allowing for rapid decision making by endorsing or rejecting one or more options. Visceroceptive information is but one of several sources underpinning somatic markers. A core idea of the somatic-marker hypothesis is that emotions and feelings do not only arise after we decided among options, but they can be used before a certain decision is made. Indeed, viscerosensory information can be recalled from memory to aid the decision-making processes. Insula activation has been shown when participants recalled disgusting events (Fitzgerald et al., 2004). Moreover, the insula is activated in 60% of studies on emotional recall (Phan, Wagner, Taylor, & Liberzon, 2002) but not in emotional-film viewing, which does not activate the insula (Reiman et al, 1997).

Somatic markers can act at an overt or covert level (i.e., the somatic markers can act in the background). For a case in point, anticipatory skin conductance responses have been studied, and it has been shown that they may aid the participant in decision-making processes during gambling tasks (Bechara, Damasio, Tranel, & Damasio, 1997). Even though there is some debate concerning the role of anticipatory skin conductance (Tomb, Hauser, Deldin, & Caramazza, 2002), there still is strong empirical evidence supporting the reciprocal influence of visceroception and emotions in the decision-making process, which is the hallmark of the somatic-marker hypothesis (Damasio et al., 2000).

The processing of viscerosensory information can act on a subconscious level, in the background, but how is it that it can still exert strong influence on decision making, as proposed by Damasio's somatic-marker hypothesis? First, as outlined above, there are several pathways enabling afferent information to be conveyed from the inner organs to the brain, and this information need not be conscious in order to efficiently guide and influence decisions. Second, there is empirical evidence to suggest that some individuals do in fact experience sensory visceral awareness, such as an accurate perception of their own heartbeat (see, e.g., the review by Jones, 1994, on cardiac awareness and heart beat perception). However, many questions remain unresolved as to the underlying mechanism involved in cardiac awareness, such as the type of receptors involved and the precise visceral pathways taken (Khalsa, Rudrauf, Feinstein, & Tranel, 2009).

Visceroceptive cues can provide useful and helpful information to aid decision making, but what is the precise origin of the visceral sensations? Do these sensations necessarily start in the inner organs of the body? Or is it possible to bypass the periphery and trigger visceral sensations via other sensory cues?

Visceroception and the Perception of Disgust

Some readers may recall, from many years back when they were in college, the vivid and truly unpleasant experience of opening the refrigerator in their dormitory after having been away for spring break. The mere visual exposure to rotten food can trigger immediate and strong visceral reactions. It is the underlying neuronal mechanism of such a response that is of interest in the context of this chapter. It shows that visceral sensations can be triggered in the absence of adequate peripheral somatic stimulation (e.g., occurring after having eaten addled food). Alternative inputs, in this case visual, can trigger the same or at least similar responses (e.g., disgusting food: Calder et al., 2007; mutilation and contamination: Wright, He, Shapira, Goodman, & Liu, 2004). Thus we can conclude that visceroceptive sensations can arise from various sources of input and are not bound to visceral afferences from the peripheral nervous system.

In fact, Wicker et al. (2003) showed that the anterior insula is activated not only by the perception of disgusting odorants but also when study participants view video clips of other humans expressing disgust. The anterior insular cortex is modulated when we see disgusted faces, but activation is also dependent on the degree of disgust expressed in the face. In epileptic patients, deep brain electrodes have recorded activation in the anterior, but not the posterior, insula when the patients view disgusted facial expressions. This finding is in line with the insula's increased integration along the posterior–anterior axis. Calder et al. (2000) reported a patient with, among others, a left insula lesion. This patient had an impaired ability to recognize disgust expressed in faces while maintaining the ability to identify other facial emotions. Interestingly, the perception of auditory stimuli associated with disgust (e.g., retching) was also impaired in this patient, whereas the recognition other emotional sounds were preserved. The patient also experienced reduced feelings of disgust. It appears, therefore, that the insula can be implicated in one's own experience of disgust and the ability to recognize disgust in other faces.

A similar mechanism has been reported by Singer et al. (2004), who showed that the anterior insular cortex, along with the anterior cingulum, mediates empathy for pain. Considering that both anterior insular and anterior cingulate cortex are crucially involved in pain perception and pain-related visceromotor reactions, it is likely that empathy for pain is mediated by a mechanism similar to that postulated here for disgust.

The mirror neurons communicate with the limbic structures via the insula. This provides strong anatomical evidence for a mirror neuron network in the insula, mirroring actual sensations of disgust or pain empathy to those evoked from a visual and emotional input. Electrical stimulation of the insula, producing visceromotor reactions, provides further evidence for this motor-visceral interface and potential mirror system (Penfield and Faulk, 1955). In addition, stimulation of the anterior insula resulted in patients feeling nauseous and sick. More recently, Krolak-Salmon et al. (2003), using weaker stimulation parameters, were able to evoke unpleasant sensations in the throat and mouth. These findings support the link between the insula and the experience of disgust and related aversive visceral sensations, and visceromotor reactions.

In addition to processing the perception of disgust, the insula also responds in a more general way to aversive or threat-related stimuli (Schienle et al., 2002). Some studies have found insula activation to happy (Jabbi et al., 2008) or to emotional faces in general (Damasio et al., 2000). Phan et al. (2002) reviewed neuroimaging studies on the processing of emotions, and the meta-analysis did not confirm a specificity of the insula for disgust. Chen et al. (2009) studied the temporal dynamics of insula activation, and their results showed that early activation in the right insula is not specific to the valence of the emotion. Later, however, at about 350 ms after stimulus onset, the right insula showed stronger activation to disgust than to happy faces. Taking into account the temporal dynamics of the neural processes may help us better understand how different emotions are processed in the insula. Remember the example of the taxi driver in the introduction to this chapter. He equated living in New York City with a strongly engaging and positive bodily state. It is now known that positive visceral states can tap into the same mechanisms outlined above (Critchley et al., 2004; Jabby et al., 2008).

Visceroception and the Bodily Self

Ever since the great American philosopher and psychologist William James categorized at the end of the nineteenth century different aspects of the self, these aspects have been continuously refined and expanded to include many different sensory, emotional, and cognitive layers. This expansion has led to an excess of definitions in the absence of a widely accepted model of the self that is based on empirical neurobiological data. Recent approaches (e.g., Gallagher, 2005) converge on the relevance of the bodily self, that is, the processing of low-level multisensory body-related information, as one promising approach for the development of a comprehensive neurobiological model of the self and self-consciousness. Craig (2003, 2009, 2010) suggests a structural model of insula functioning during visceroception, in that the information progresses from an image of the homeostatic state of the body in the mid-insula to a more integrated processing stage in the anterior insula, which culminates in its role in awareness. Craig (2009) points out the existence of large spindle-typed neurons (called von Economo neurons, after the early neuroscientist), which are unique to the anterior insula and the anterior cingulate cortex. These types of neurons are present in humanoid primates and in a few other animals like elephants and whales. According to Craig, it is possible that these particular neurons constitute fast interconnections between the anterior insular cortex and the anterior cingulate cortex. Degenerative loss of these neurons leads to self-conscious emotion deficits (Sturm, Rosen, Allison, Miller, & Levenson, 2006).

Recently, Khalsa et al. (2009) identified the potential of a sensorimotor pathway for the perception of heartbeat. They documented a patient with bilateral insular lesions who had intact heartbeat awareness via the skin. Thus, somatosensory afferents from skin receptors constitute yet another pathway that contributes to the awareness of the cardiovascular state of the body, alongside and in addition to the network involving the insula and the anterior cingulum.

The insula, in combination with the right frontal cortex, is also involved in visual self-recognition in the context of other faces of highly familiar persons. The anterior part of the insula receives input from the anterior portion of the ventral bank of the superior temporal sulcus where the neurons are selective to the sight of faces (Perrett, Rolls, & Caan, 1982). Moreover, the right anterior insula, along with the right anterior cingulum, seems to play a role in the integration of information about oneself independent of the stimulus domain (Craig, 2009). In fact, the anterior insular cortex is involved in many different tasks, including attention, visual and auditory perception, expectations, time perception, subjective evaluation of others, self-reported orgasm ratings, and the experience of romantic love (for a review, see Craig, 2009).

Another finding provided by Moseley et al. (2008) illustrates the relationship between representation of the bodily self and visceroception, in particular the regulation of body skin temperature. The authors used the well-established rubber-hand paradigm, in which an artificial hand positioned on a table in front of the participant is, to some extent, experienced as one's own hand when the seen tactile stimulation on the rubber hand is synchronized with tactile stimulation applied to the real, but hidden, hand. Interestingly, when the rubber hand takes over body ownership, the skin temperature in the real hand diminishes as a result of disembodiment. This is compelling evidence that an altered state of the bodily self can affect the regulation of basic physiological processes in the periphery. Future research will need to explore the implications of this finding. For example, knowing that a full body version of the rubber-hand illusion leads to similar illusions of mislocalization (Lenggenhager, Tadi, Metzinger, & Blanke, 2007), it would be interesting to measure possible changes in body skin temperature and to see whether Moseley et al.'s finding extends to the entire body.

Visceroception and the Sense of Balance

Interestingly, information from the vestibular end organ also projects to the posterior end of the insula. The vestibular projection area has been called the parieto-insular vestibular cortex (PIVC; see, for example, Grüsser, Pause, & Schreiter, 1990). The PIVC extends about 6 to 8 mm in the anterior–posterior direction from the posterior part of the insula into the retroinsular region (stereotaxic coordinates: anterior 4–12 mm, lateral 16–19 mm, and vertical 3–6 mm). The vestibular organ is the primary sensory source of information for the detection of acceleration caused by translations or rotations of the head in space.

However, several studies suggest that we not only rely on vestibular information but also use extravestibular gravity-receptors situated in the body's trunk. For example, it has been demonstrated that the subjective visual vertical is affected by changes in visceroceptive input. Trousselard and colleagues (Trousselard, Barraud, Nougier, Raphel, & Cian, 2004) varied gastric fullness and induced an overload stomach stimulation by having participants consume 500 g of pasta right before the experiment began. The participants were placed in a tilt-chair and rolled sideways from 0 degrees to 90 degrees (horizontal body position). They were asked to adjust a luminous line to the vertical position under empty vs. full stomach load conditions. The investigators found better performance (i.e., less deviation from the physical vertical) in the full-stomach condition. The fact that the vestibular system would produce exactly the same gravity response in both conditions speaks for the existence of extralabyrinthine gravity-receptors in the trunk. The stomach load may act through the inertial forces exerted against gravity by the mechanoreceptors in the fundus. Interestingly, the subjective sense of fullness is associated with activation peaks in the bilateral posterior insula, and in the left mid-insula, anterior insula, and anterior cingulate cortex (Stephan et al., 2003).

Other experiments have helped to further isolate the location of visceral receptors involved in the detection of gravity. Evidence from studies with nephrectomized and paraplegic persons suggests involvement of the kidneys and the vascular system (Jarchow, Wirz, Haslwanter, Dietz, & Straumann, 2003; Mittelstaedt, 1992, 1996). It is at least conceivable that the cortical convergence of visceral (e.g., gastric) and vestibular information is also the source of the "gastric" feelings experienced during rapid vertical accelerations in an elevator or during roller coaster rides. Knowing more about the interoceptive input to human spatial orientation is also of applied interest. Such knowledge could help guide the rehabilitation process of patients suffering from vestibular lesions or be used to detect the possible impairment of balance functions in paraplegic patients, depending on the height of their spinal cord section.

Conclusion

Emotions would not be the same in the absence of afferent viscerosensory input from the body. Craig (2003) suggests that the "material me" is shaped by the representation of the visceral state of the body. This view emphasizes the basic experience of one's own existence, which precedes the perception of the environment and the objects within it. This is surprising because exteroception (e.g., vision, audition) has been more thoroughly investigated in humans than has visceroception, for which there is still a paucity of clear-cut research findings. Exteroception provides awareness of the continuity of the physical world that surrounds us, but visceroception ultimately provides the awareness of the physical self across time.

Future Directions

Despite the obvious importance of visceroceptive processes and mechanisms in not only basic bodily equilibrium but also higher order cognition, research in this area is scarce, and many questions remain unanswered. For instance, what is the proportion of visceral afferences that ascends to higher brain areas? Under what conditions do visceral afferents reach conscious awareness?

How close is the relationship between interoception and emotions? There is plenty of evidence showing that interoceptive processes are key to understanding emotions, but knowledge about the specificity of the somatic-visceral input is still lacking.

What is the role of visceroception in constituting the bodily self? In particular, the link between visceroception and body ownership is a cutting-edge topic for future investigations. Given the empirical evidence ascertained thus far, visceroception will play a pivotal role in future understanding of awareness.

Acknowledgments

The research for this chapter was supported by grants from the Swiss National Science Foundation. I thank Caroline Falconer and Nora Preuss for their help with this manuscript.

Further Reading

Damasio, A. (2000). *The feeling of what happens: Body and emotion in the making of consciousness*. New York: Hartcourt.

Cameron, O. G., (2002). *Visceral sensors neuroscience: Interoception*. New York: Oxford University Press.

Craig, A. D. (2009). How do you feel—now? The anterior insula and human awareness. *Nature Reviews, 10*, 59–70.

Gigerenzer, G. (2007). *Gut feelings: The intelligence of the unconscious*. London: Penguin Books.

References

Adolphs, R. (2002). Neural systems for recognizing emotion. *Current Opinion in Neurobiology, 12*(2), 169–177.

Augustine, J. R. (1996). Circuitry and functional aspects of the insular lobe in primates including humans. *Brain Research Reviews, 22*(3), 229–244.

Bechara, A., Damasio, H., Tranel, D., & Damasio, A. R. (1997). Deciding advantageously before knowing the advantageous strategy. *Science, 275*(5304), 1293–1295.

Calder, A. J., Keane, J., Manes, F., Antoun, N., & Young, A. W. (2000). Impaired recognition and experience of disgust following brain injury. *Nature Neuroscience, 3*(11), 1077–1078.

Calder, A. J., Beaver, J. D., Davis, M. H., Ditzhuijzen, J., Keane, J., & Lawrence, A. D. (2007). Disgust sensitivity predicts the insula and pallidal response to pictures of disgusting foods. *European Journal of Neuroscience, 25*, 3422–3428.

Cechetto, D. F. (1987). Central representation of visceral function. *Federation Proceedings, 46*(1), 17–23.

Cechetto, D. F., & Saper, C. B. (1990). Role of the cerebral cortex in autonomic function. In A. D. Loewy & K. M. Spyer (Eds.). *Central regulation of autonomic function*. New York: Oxford University Press, pp. 208–223.

Chaminade, T., Meltzoff, A. N., & Decety, J. (2005). An fMRI study of imitation: Action representation and body schema. *Neuropsychologia, 43*(1), 115–127.

Chen, Y. H., Dammers, J., Boers, F., Leiberg, S., Edgar, J. C., Roberts, T. P., & Mathiak, K. (2009). The temporal dynamics of insula activity to disgust and happy facial expressions: a magnetoencephalography study. *Neuroimage, 47*(4), 1921–1928.

Craig, A. D. (2002). How do you feel? Interoception: The sense of physiological sensation of the body. *Nature Reviews Neuroscience, 2002*(3), 655–666.

Craig, A. D. (2003). Interoception: The sense of the physiological condition of the body. *Current Opinion in Neurobiology, 13*(4), 500–505.

Craig, A. D. (2009). How do you feel—now? The anterior insula and human awareness. *Nature Reviews, 10*, 59–70.

Craig, A. D. (2010). The sentient self. *Brain Structure and Function, 214*(5–6), 563–577.

Craig, A. D., Chen, K., Bandy, D., & Reiman, E. M. (2000). Thermosensory activation of insular cortex. *Nature Neuroscience, 3*, 184–190.

Critchley, H. D., Wiens, S., Rotshtein, P., Ohman, A., & Dolan, R. J. (2004). Neural systems supporting interoceptive awareness. *Nature Neuroscience, 7*(2), 189–195.

Damasio, A. (1999). *The feeling of what happens: Body and emotion in the making of consciousness*. New York: Hartcourt.

Damasio, A. R., Grabowski, T. J., Bechara, A., Damasio, H., Ponto, L. L. B., Parvizi, J., & Hichwa, R. D. (2000). Subcortical and cortical brain activity during the feeling of self-generated emotions, *Nature Neuroscience, 3*, 1049–1056.

Dolan, R. J. (2002). The neurobiology of emotion and mood. *Memory and Emotion, 12*, 73–84.

Fitzgerald, D. M., Posse, S., Moore, G. J., Tanner, M. E., Nathan, P. J., & Phan, K. L. (2004). Neural correlates of internally generated disgust via autobiographical recall: A functional magnetic resonance imaging investigation. *Neuroscience Letters, 370*, 91–96.

Frith, C. D., & Singer, T. (2008). The role of social cognition in decision making. *Philosophical Transactions of the Royal Society, Series B. Biological Sciences, 363*(1511), 3875–3886.

Gallagher, S. (2005). *How the body shapes the mind*. Oxford: Oxford University Press.

Gerardin, E., Sirigu, A., Lehericy, S., Poline, J. B., Gaymard, B., et al. (2000). Partially overlapping neural networks for real and imagined hand movements. *Cerebral Cortex, 10*, 1093–1104.

Grüsser, O. J., Pause, M., & Schreiter, U. (1990). Localization and responses of neurones in the parieto-insular vestibular cortex of awake monkeys (*Macaca fascicularis*). *Journal of Physiology, 430*, 537–557.

Jabbi, M., Bastiaansen, J., & Keysers, C. (2008). A common anterior insula representation of disgust observation, experience and imagination shows divergent functional connectivity pathways. *Plos One, 3*(8), e2939.

Jarchow T., Wirz M., Haslwanter, T., Dietz, V., & Straumann, D. (2003). Perceived horizontal body position in healthy and paraplegic subjects: Effect of centrifugation. *Journal of Neurophysiology, 90*(5), 2973–2977.

Jones, G. E. (1994). Perception of visceral sensations: A review of recent findings, methodologies, and future directions. In J. R. Jennings, P. K. Ackles, & M. G. H. Coles (Eds.) *Advances in psychophysiology, Vol. 5*. London: Jessica Kingsley Publishers, pp. 155–192.

Khalsa, S. S., Rudrauf, D., Feinstein, J. S., & Tranel, D. (2009). The pathway of interoceptive awareness. *Nature Neuroscience, 12*, 1494–1496

Krolak-Salmon, P., Henaff, M. A., Isnard, J., Tallon-Baudry, C., Guenot, M., Vighetto, A., et al. (2003). An attention modulated response to disgust in human ventral anterior insula. *Annals of Neurology, 53*(4), 446–453.

Kurth, F., Zilles, K., Fox, P. T., Laird, A. R., & Eickhoff, S. B. (2010). A link between the systems: Functional differentiation and integration with in the human insula revealed by meta-analysis. *Brain Structure and Function, 214*, 519–534.

Lamm, C., & Singer, T. (2010). The role of anterior insular cortex in social emotions. *Brain Structure & Function, 214*(5-6), 579–591.

Lane, R. D., Fink, G. R., Chau, P. M. L., & Dolan, R. J. (1997). Neural activation during selective attention to subjective emotional responses. *Neuroreport, 8*(18), 3969–3972.

Lenggenhager, B., Tadi, T., Metzinger, T., & Blanke, O. (2007). Video ergo sum: Manipulating bodily self-consciousness. *Science, 317*(5841), 1096–1099.

Mayer, J.S., Bittner, R.A., Nikolic, D., Bledowski, C., Goebel, R., & Linden, D. E. (2007). Common neural substrates for visual working memory and attention. *Neuroimage, 36*, 441–453.

McMahon, S. B. (1997). Are there fundamental differences in the peripheral mechanisms of visceral and somatic pain? *Behavioral Brain Science, 20*, 381–391.

Mittelstaedt, H. (1992). Somatic versus vestibular gravity reception in man. *Sensing and Controlling Motion, 656*, 124–139.

Mittelstaedt, H. (1996). Somatic graviception. *Biological Psychology, 42*(1-2), 53–74.

Moseley, G. L., Olthof, N., Venema, A., Don, S., Wijers, M., Gallace, A., et al. (2008). Psychologically induced cooling of a specific body part caused by the illusory ownership of an artificial counterpart. *Proceedings of the National Academy of Sciences U S A, 105*(35), 13169–13173.

Murphy, F. C., Nimmo-Smith, I., & Lawrence, A. D. (2003). Functional neuroanatomy of emotions: A meta-analysis. *Cognitive, Affective & Behavioral Neuroscience, 3*(3), 207–233.

Nunn, K., Frampton, I., Gordon, I., & Lask, B. (2008). The fault is not in her parents but in her insula—a neurobiological hypothesis of anorexia nervosa. *European Eating Disorders Review, 16*(5), 355–360.

Penfield, W., & Faulk, M. E. (1955). The insula—further observations on its function. *Brain, 78*(4), 445–470.

Perrett, D. I., Rolls, E. T., & Caan, W. (1982) Visual neurones responsive to faces in the monkey temporal cortex. *Experimental Brain Research, 47*, 329–342.

Phan, K. L., Wagner, T., Taylor, S. F., & Liberzon, I. (2002). Functional neuroanatomy of emotion: A meta-analysis of emotion activation studies in PET and fMRI. *Neuroimage, 16*, 331–348.

Phillips, M. L., Drevets, W. C., Rauch, S. L., & Lane, R. (2003). Neurobiology of emotion perception I: The neural basis of normal emotion perception. *Biological Psychiatry, 54*(5), 504–514.

Poellinger, A., Thomas, R., Lio, P., Lee, A., Makris, N., Rosen, B. R., & Kwong, K. K. (2001). Activation and habituation in olfaction—an fMRI study. *Neuroimage, 13*, 547–560.

Reiman, E. M., Lane, R. D., Ahern, G. L., et al. (1997). Neuroanatomical correlates of externally and internally generated emotion. *American Journal of Psychiatry, 154*, 918–925.

Riecker, A., Ackermann, H., Wildgruber, D., Dogil, G., & Grodd, W. (2000) Opposite hemispheric lateralization effects during speaking and singing at motor cortex, insula and cerebellum. *Neuroreport, 11*, 1997–2000.

Rizzolatti, G., & Craighero, L. (2004). The mirror-neuron system. *Annual Review of Neuroscience, 27*, 169–192.

Sachdev, P., Mondraty, N., Wen, W., & Gulliford, K. (2008). Brains of anorexia nervosa patients process self-images differently from non-self-images: An fMRI study. *Neuropsychologia, 46*(8), 2161–2168.

Schienle, A., Stark, R., Walter, B., et al. (2002). The insula is not specifically involved in disgust processing: An fMRI study. *Neuroreport, 13*, 2023–2026.

Schmahmann, J. D., & Leifer, D. (1992). Parietal pseudothalamic pain syndrome: Clinical features and anatomic correlates. *Archives of Neurology, 49*, 1032–1037.

Shipley, M. T., & Geinisman, Y. (1984). Anatomical evidence for convergence of olfactory, gustatory, and visceral afferent pathways in mouse cerebral-cortex. *Brain Research Bulletin, 12*(3), 221–226.

Singer, T., Seymour, B., O'Doherty, J., Kaube, H., Dolan, R. J., & Frith, C. D. (2004). Empathy for pain involves the affective but not sensory components of pain. *Science, 303*(5661), 1157–1162.

Stefanacci, L., & Amaral, D. G. (2002) Some observations on cortical inputs to the macaque monkey amygdala: An anterograde tracing study. *Journal of Comparative Neurology, 451*, 301–323.

Stephan, E., Pardo, J. V., Faris, P. L., Hartman, B. K., Kim, S. W., Ivanov, E. H., et al.. (2003). Functional neuroimaging of gastric distention. *Journal of Gastrointestinal Surgery, 7*, 740–749.

Sturm, V. E., Rosen, H. J., Allison, S., Miller, B. L., & Levenson, R. W. (2006). Self-conscious emotion deficits in frontotemporal lobar degeneration. *Brain, 129*, 2508–2516.

Tomb, I., Hauser, M., Deldin, P., & Caramazza, A. (2002). Do somatic markers mediate decisions on the gambling task? *Nature Neuroscience, 5*(11), 1103–1104.

Travagli, R. A., Hermann, G. E., Browning, K. N., & Rogers, R. C. (2006). Brainstem circuits regulating gastric function. *Annual Review of Physiology, 68*, 279–305.

Trousselard, M., Barraud, P. A., Nougier, V., Raphel, C., & Cian, C. (2004). Contribution of tactile and interoceptive cues to the perception of the direction of gravity. *Cognitive Brain Research, 20*(3), 355–362.

Wicker, B., Keysers, C., Plailly, J., Royet, J. P., Gallese, V., & Rizzolatti, G. (2003). Both of us disgusted in my insula: The common neural basis of seeing and feeling disgust. *Neuron, 40*(3), 655–664.

Wright, P., He, G., Shapira, N.A., Goodman, W. K., Liu, Y. (2004). Disgust and the insula: fMRI responses to pictures of mutilation and contamination. *Neuroreport, 15*, 2347–2351.

Development of Emotion and Social Reasoning in Adolescence

Eveline A. Crone *and* Berna Güroğlu

Abstract

Adolescence can be seen as a period of pronounced cognitive advancements accompanied by significant changes in emotional and social behavior. Adolescents become more self-conscious and more focused on their social behavior and emotions. Recent studies have explored these changes in terms of brain maturation, brain function, and cognitive, emotional, and social development. This chapter examines the development of emotion and social reasoning in adolescence and how it is mediated by functionally different brain networks. It looks at brain maturation vis-à-vis developmental changes in reward processing, risk-taking, and social reasoning and proposes a working hypothesis that integrates neuroimaging data with behavioral studies. It also discusses use of the Ultimatum Game to probe social decision-making processes, along with the role of the insula, temporaparietal junction, and dorsolateral prefrontal cortex in the development of emotion processing and social reasoning in adolescents.

Key Words: emotion, social reasoning, adolescence, brain maturation, reward processing, risk-taking, Ultimatum Game, insula, temporaparietal junction, dorsolateral prefrontal cortex

Introduction

George had always been a happy, easygoing boy who liked to play sports and was pleasant to his friends and family. In the last few years he had lost interest in playing sports and spent more time on his computer chatting with friends. His parents complained that he talked less to them than he used to. On some days he was easy to talk to, whereas on other days it seemed like they did everything wrong. At the last family gathering, George was constantly listening to his iPod, and together with his cousins he had some beers in the back yard, even though his parents told him not to. Interestingly, George himself did not understand why he engaged in these risky activities, and he felt uneasy about his looks and the way he acted. Even though it may seem like George was going through a major transformation, these changes are more easily captured under

the interesting, unavoidable, and intriguing stage in development: adolescence.

Adolescence is a highly important transition phase between childhood and adulthood, marked by significant physical, social, cognitive, and emotional changes (Dahl & Gunner, 2009; Steinberg, 2008). The onset of adolescence is characterized by the start of pubertal maturation around the age of 10 years, during which children undergo rapid physical growth and experience the onset of sexual maturation (Shirtcliff, Dahl, & Pollack, 2009). One of the more salient achievements in adolescence is a steady increase in self-regulation. During adolescence, children increasingly master the ability to control their behavior for the benefit of future goals (Best, Miller, & Jones, 2009; Crone, Bunge, van der Molen, & Ridderinkhof, 2006; Cragg & Nation, 2008; Huizinga, Dolan, & van der Molen,

2006). Developmental studies have converged on the conclusion that increased capacity for self-regulation may be associated with maturation of the prefrontal cortex (PFC) and its connections to other brain areas (Gogtay et al., 2004). Prior studies showed that the regions important for mental flexibility and performance adaptation, including the PFC, parietal cortex, and anterior cingulate cortex (ACC), become increasingly engaged across childhood and adolescence (Crone, Zanolie, van Leijenhorst, Westenberg, & Rombouts, 2008; van Duijvenvoorde, Zanolie, Rombouts, Raijmakers, & Crone, 2008). These studies are consistent with results from a wider range of cognitive control paradigms, which have reported that developmental changes in cognitive control functions are associated with more focal and increased magnitude of activation in brain regions important for cognitive control in adults, including the lateral PFC, parietal cortex, and ACC (for a review, see Chapter 4 in this book). Self-regulation is thought to be central to human cognition, and therefore adolescence can be seen as a period of significant cognitive advancements.

These advances in self-regulation abilities in adolescence, however, are accompanied by pronounced changes in emotional and social behavior. The main developmental task during adolescence is the formation of self-identity with a particular focus on social relationships. Adolescents are increasingly self-conscious and become more focused on their social behavior and emotions, which is accompanied by more complex peer relationships. Scientists have began to examine and understand these changes in terms of brain maturation, brain function, and cognitive, emotional, and social development, which has led to biological models that provide a framework for understanding changes in development that are specific for adolescence.

This chapter will highlight these new insights with a focus on brain maturation vis-à-vis developmental changes in reward processing, risk-taking, and social reasoning. We will propose a working hypothesis that integrates brain imaging data with behavioral studies and that may provide a unifying approach toward understanding this erratic period in life.

Emotion, Reward Processing, and Risk-Taking

The emerging self-regulatory abilities in adolescence work in concert or in competition with emotions that become more intense and erratic in adolescence and that affect emotional functioning and social reasoning. Since Stanley Hall defined *adolescence* as the period of storm and stress in development in the early 1900s, many scientists have been puzzled by adolescent-specific changes in emotion and social reasoning, as these are often unpredictable and subject to individual differences (Arnett, 1992).

Affective behaviour in adolescence has been widely studied using risk-taking paradigms, which is typically measured as choice behavior that can result in short-term gain but long-term loss. Learning to make good decisions and avoid excessive risks is one of the most important abilities to be acquired during development. In order to make good decisions, we have to be able to control our impulses, judge the probability that we will be successful, and weigh the risk involved against the potential benefit. Adolescents perform well on risk-taking tasks that require the simple evaluation of probabilities (van Leijenhorst, Westenberg, & Crone, 2008). Developmental studies have demonstrated that adolescents become better at delaying gratification (Scheres et al., 2006), and the ability to weigh short-term against long-term benefits has been shown to improve throughout adolescence (Crone & van der Molen, 2004; Hooper, Luciana, Conklin, & Yarger, 2004).

It has been suggested that the heightened sensitivity to rewards is associated with increased sensitivity and vulnerability of subcortical brain regions in adolescence, which is most likely the result of biological changes that affect brain functioning (Casey, Getz, & Galvan, 2008). Specifically, gonadal hormones associated with the onset of puberty may have a modulating effect on subcortical brain regions, resulting in increased approach and/or avoidance behavior, whereas cortical development and function follows a developmental pattern independent of hormonal changes (Steinberg et al., 2008). There is compelling evidence from animal models that gonadal hormone changes in puberty induce a (second) organizational period that serves to guide the remodeling of the adolescent brain in sex-appropriate ways (Sisk & Zehr, 2005; Spear, 2009). Results derived from rodent studies indicate a remodeling of the dopaminergic system within the affective subcortical brain network which involves an initial postnatal rise starting in preadolescence and a subsequent reduction of dopamine receptor density in the striatum and prefrontal cortex. As a result, dopaminergic activity increases significantly in early adolescence and is higher during this period than before and after it (Sisk & Zehr, 2005; Spear,

2009). Given the important role of dopamine in the brain's reward circuitry, this redistribution of dopamine receptors may increase reward-seeking behavior in puberty and thus affect executive and self-regulatory functions.

This model has received initial support from empirical studies in which functional brain activation in children, adolescents, and adults was compared using risk or reward-seeking paradigms. Consistent with the assumption that risk-taking is associated with increased self-regulation and control, a set of studies by Ernst and colleagues demonstrated protracted development of brain regions important for self-regulation and cognitive control in risk-taking studies across adolescence (Ernst & Fudge, 2009; Ernst, Pine & Hardin, 2006; Eshel, Nelson, Blair, Pine, & Ernst, 2007). Eshel et al. (2007) examined behavioral and neural responses in a Wheel-of-Fortune task, in which participants chose between high-probability and low-probability gambles. A risky choice was defined as a choice from a low-probability option that could result in high reward, whereas a non-risky choice was defined as a choice from a high-probability option that would result in a smaller reward. The behavioral results demonstrated that adolescents were more willing to choose the risky option than the adults. When taking risks, increased activation in lateral PFC and ACC was observed, but this activation was more pronounced for adults than for adolescents. Thus, it may be that adolescents recruit prefrontal control areas to a lesser extent than adults when they take risks.

In a different set of studies, risky-choice evaluation was found to be associated with not only protracted development of PFC but also heightened sensitivity of brain regions important for reward processing. The heightened reward sensitivity was demonstrated in an fMRI experiment by Galvan et al. (2006) in which participants ranging in age from 7 to 29 years performed a task in which they could win small, medium-size, or large rewards. Using a pirates cartoon task, Galvan et al. asked participants to press the button at the location where a pirate appeared, which was then followed by a monetary reward (finding the treasure). Three different pirates resulted in three different reward magnitudes (small, medium, large). In response to receiving rewards, individuals in mid-adolescence (13–17 years) showed enhanced responses in the nucleus accumbens, which is part of the neural reward circuitry, relative to children (7–11 years) and adults (23–29 years). This region had previously been shown to play an important

role in processing rewards and motivating behavior in adults (Knutson, Adams, Fong, & Hommer, 2001; McClure, Berns, & Montague, 2003). In addition, Galvan et al. correlated real-life risk-taking indices, such as the Cognitive Appraisal of Risk Activities Scale and Connor's Impulsivity Scale, to neural activation in the pirates task described above. They demonstrated that those individuals who are likely to engage in risky activities in real-life show enhanced neural responses to reward in the nucleus accumbens (Galvan, Hare, Voss, Glover, & Casey, 2008). The authors interpreted this effect as indicating that those individuals who are prone to risky behavior are at further risk in adolescence when neural systems underlying risky behavior go through developmental changes (see also Ernst et al., 2005).

It should be noted that the opposite results have also been reported. Bjork et al. (2004) reported that adolescents show underactivation in the nucleus accumbens when faced with potential rewards, and no age differences were observed when study participants were receiving reward. According to these authors, adolescents need more stimulation to get the same rewarding experience as that of adults. We performed two studies in our laboratory which aimed to further investigate this apparent inconsistency. Our hypothesis was that it matters what the task demands are, given that the Galvan et al. study required simple reward prediction and outcome processing, whereas the Bjork et al. study required more complex reward prediction. In a first study, we took out all behavioral demands and asked participants to perform a passive slot machine game. Here we found that when faced with slot machine rewards, mid-adolescents show heightened activation in the nucleus accumbens to rewards, more so than early adolescents and adults. We concluded that the elevated reward sensitivity in adolescence is a relatively basic sensitivity and that this neural response occurs independently of whether participants need to perform accurately to receive the reward (van Leijenhorst et al., 2010a).

Subsequently, we examined whether and how adolescents were sensitive to outcomes after taking a risk. First, we were interested in examining whether the elevated reward sensitivity reported in two passive gambling tasks (Galvan et al., 2006; van Leijenhorst et al., 2010a) would also be found when adolescents were actively judging probabilities and taking risks, followed by outcomes. We were also interested in understanding the specificity of this elevated sensitivity, as adolescence has often been broadly defined, whereas there are pronounced

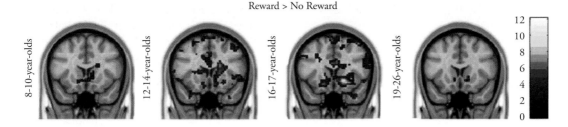

Figure 8.1 Enhanced neural activation in the striatum following reward in the cake gambling task. Between–age group contrasts show elevated activation in the caudate nucleus in adolescents aged 12–14 and 16–17 relative to that in children aged 8–10 and adults aged 19–26 (age–reward interaction). Images are displayed for each age group at *p* < .005 uncorrected (van Leijenhorst et al., 2010).

differences between phases of development (Giedd et al., 2006). For this reason, participants from four age groups (8–10, 12–14, 16–17, 19–26 years) were asked to play a risk-taking task (referred to as the cake gambling task) while functional MRI data were collected. The behavioral data demonstrated that all participants were sensitive to rewards, and increased risk-taking was observed when more rewards were at stake. The neuroimaging data demonstrated that, in individuals of mid- and late adolescence (12–14 and 16–17 years), there was increased neural response in the striatum to rewards that followed risky gambles (see Figure 8.1; van Leijenhorst et al., 2010b). The elevated neural response in the striatum was reported in several studies and was found specifically for mid- and late adolescence. Future studies should examine how these changes are related to task performance, for example, by predicting performance on the basis of observed neural activation.

Intriguingly, the same pattern of subcortical hypersensitivity in adolescence has been observed for negatively valenced stimuli. Using an emotional go/no-go task, Hare and colleagues (2008) asked 7- to 12-year-old children, 13- to 18-year-old adolescents, and 19- to 32-year-old adults to respond or inhibit their responses, based on the valence of a presented face. These faces could have fearful, calm, or happy expressions. All participants showed activation in the amygdala following the presentation of fearful faces, but this neural activation was increased in adolescents relative to that in children and adults. Greater amygdala activation was associated with lower trait anxiety scores, confirming that the amygdala response was associated with level of anxiety. These findings extended earlier results by Monk et al. (2003), who demonstrated that adolescents ages 9 to 17 have greater activation in the amygdala, relative to that in adults ages 25 to 36, to fearful than to neutral faces. In addition, a study by Guyer et al. (2008) also found that 9- to 17-year-old

adolescents have an elevated amygdala response to fearful faces, and that adults have increased amygdala–hippocampus connectivity when viewing fearful faces. The latter effect was interpreted in the context of a strengthening with age of memory storage and retrieval for emotionally salient stimuli.

Taking these findings together, it is clear that the slowly maturing PFC hypothesis cannot explain all changes in affective behavior; developmental changes in adolescence are associated with competition between at least two brain networks. The first, evolutionary older system builds on subcortical structures that have been linked to the processing of emotion, such as the amygdala and the nucleus accumbens; whereas a second, evolutionary younger system builds on cortical brain areas, including the PFC and the parietal cortex (Adolphs, 2003). Developmental changes in risk-taking are most likely associated with different developmental trajectories of these systems (Casey et al., 2008; Rivers, Reyna, & Mills, 2008; Steinberg, 2008). The slow development of brain regions important for cognitive control and self-regulation, together with the faster development of brain regions subserving reward sensitivity, may result in a fragile balance between emotional impulses and cognitive control.

Social Reasoning

Although the fragile-balance hypothesis provides a starting point for understanding erratic behaviour in adolescence, it is clear that emotional impulses toward rewards, risks, and aversive stimuli are not the only factor in explaining adolescent behavior. One of the more evident changes in adolescence is that adolescents form and interact in an increasingly complex social environment. During adolescence, friendships change and peers become increasingly important. Not only do adolescents spend more time in the presence of peers, but the opinions of peers also become more important (Harris, 1995).

Indeed, in an experimental study on the influence of peers on risk-taking, adolescents showed high sensitivity to the presence of peers by making a disproportionately greater number of risky decisions when they were with their peers (Gardner & Steinberg, 2005).

The increased sensitivity to rewards in the presence of peers led us to hypothesize that basic approach and avoidance sensitivities in adolescence may also account for sensitivity to social context. For example, it has been demonstrated that brain regions responding to feelings of envy and schadenfreude are also those that respond to physical pain and reward/pleasure, respectively (Takahashi et al., 2009). We hypothesized that increased capacity for making inferences about mental states of others influences choice behavior in adolescents, which may be associated with additional brain systems that come online during adolescence (Blakemore, 2008). We propose that heightened sensitivity in adolescence to social evaluation and reasoning results from heightened sensitivity in subcortical limbic regions, together with slow maturation of brain regions important for intention understanding.

Recently, brain models used to explain the emotion–cognitive balance in the developing brain have been extended by taking into account brain networks that facilitate our understanding of others and mentalizing about intentions. One of these models is the Social Information Processing Network (SIPN) model, which focuses specifically on developmental changes across adolescence (see Figure 8.2; Nelson, Leibenluft, McClure, & Pine, 2005). The SIPN model incorporates physiological and hormonal changes at puberty with developmental changes in brain circuits to explain normal and pathological social behavior across adolescence. The model is based on three basic nodes: the detection node, the affective node, and the cognitive node. The detection node is composed of brain areas such as the inferior occipital and temporal cortex (including the fusiform face area and the intraparietal gyrus), related to the perception and categorization of a stimulus based on its "social" properties. The function of this node is to determine the extent to which one can socially interact with the stimulus, depending on what the stimulus is doing or intending to do. Once a stimulus has been detected and categorized as being, for example, animate and

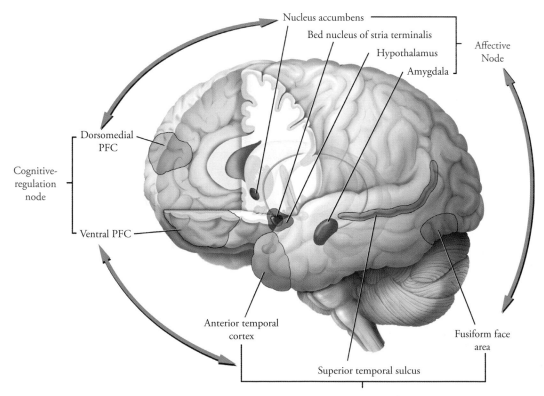

Figure 8.2 The social information processing network (Nelson et al., 2005). Reprinted with permission from Cambridge University Press.

social, the affective node, composed of the reward–punishment related brain areas such as the striatum, amygdala, hypothalamus, and the orbitofrontal cortex, is activated in order to determine the emotional valence of the stimulus. The emotional significance attached to the stimulus is crucial for the subsequent response, which is regulated by the third, cognitive, node. This cognitive node, composed of the PFC as well as the paracingulate and the temporal cortex, is more complex in terms of its broader regulatory function. It plays a role in perceiving the thoughts, goals, and feelings of others (i.e., the theory of mind [TOM]; see Chapter 13 in this book), executing control over prepotent responses, and planning and executing goal-directed behavior.

Nelson and colleagues (2005) have proposed that the hormonal and neural changes within the SIPN model are intermittently related to the socioemotional and behavioral changes across adolescence. Whereas the detection node matures quite early in life, the affective node experiences major changes with the onset of puberty. As in previously named models (e.g., Casey et al., 2008; Ernst et al., 2006), the hormonal changes during puberty alter regulation of the neurotransmitter systems involving oxytocin, vasopressin, serotonin, and dopamine, resulting in changes in social and emotional responsiveness. The changes in the affective node are reflected in social behavior in adolescence, particularly in terms of emotional responses to social stimuli such as increased reward sensitivity (Steinberg, 2007, 2008). Finally, the cognitive node is characterized by a prolonged trajectory of maturation that extends into late adolescence. The ventral and medial prefrontal regions and the superior temporal cortex, which underlie TOM-related functioning, mature across adolescence (Choudhury, Blakemore, & Charman, 2006). The late development of the prefrontal and temporal brain regions might explain the increase in executive functioning and perspective-taking skills into late adolescence and early adulthood (Blakemore & Choudhury, 2006; Blakemore, den Ouden, Choudhury, & Frith, 2007).

In a set of experiments, we tested this hypothesis, with a special focus on perspective-taking and regions previously implicated in mentalizing about one's own and others' intentions. Studies with healthy participants confirmed the role of mentalizing brain regions, such as the medial prefrontal cortex (MPFC) and the posterior superior temporal sulcus (pSTS)/temporaparietal junction (TPJ), during social emotion processing (Burnett, Bird, Moll, Frith, & Blakemore, 2009). The increasing perspective-taking skills that enable incorporation of intentionality understanding are of great importance in social decision-making processes across adolescence. We tested these social emotions, which accompany decision-making processes in social interactions, by studying the development of interpersonal concepts such as fairness, trust, and reciprocity. Economic game paradigms, including the Ultimatum Game (UG) and the Trust Game (TG), prove efficient in this investigation because of their feasibility in simple two-person interactions that can also be simulated in neuroimaging studies.

Ultimatum Game and the Role of Insula, TPJ, and DLPFC

In the UG, a proposer has the opportunity to divide a certain stake (e.g., 10 dollars) between him- or herself and another player. After the proposer has made an offer, the responder has two possibilities: accept the offer, in which case the stake will be divided as proposed by the first player, or reject the offer made by the proposer, which results in both players going empty handed. Thus, the UG provides the opportunity to examine the role of self-interest relative to fairness. That is, according to economic principles, the responder should never reject, because then both players would not receive anything. However, unfair splits are often rejected, indicating that choices are based not only on self-interest only but also on feelings of fairness and the aversion of inequity (De Dreu, Lualhati, & McCusker, 1994; van Dijk & Vermunt, 2000).

We were interested in understanding how adolescents are sensitive to fairness and the increasing role of perspective-taking abilities in judging fairness, as well as the neural underpinnings. In order to better incorporate intentionality understanding and perspective-taking skills, we used an alternative version of the UG, referred to as the mini-UG (Falk, Fehr, & Fischbacher, 2003). In this setup, proposers had to choose between two predetermined distributions of the stake (10 coins) and select one of the two offers; the responders, in turn, were informed about the available options for the proposers and could decide whether to accept or reject that offer (Güroğlu, van den Bos, & Crone, 2009). We manipulated intentionality by using four conditions against which an unfair distribution of the stake (i.e., 8/2 distribution, with 8 coins for self versus 2 coins for the responder) was pitted: (1) hyperunfair alternative (i.e., 10/0 distribution), (2) no alternative (i.e., 8/2 distribution), (3) fair alternative (i.e.,

A **Behavioral study**

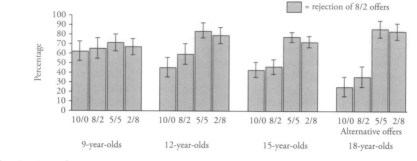

B **Neuroimaging study**

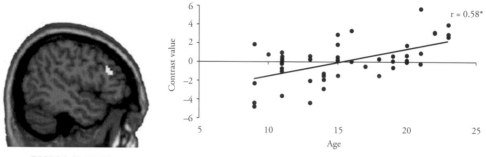

DLPFC (–48, 27, 27)

Figure 8.3 A. In the mini-Ultimate Game, there is a steady age-related increase in the ability to understand intentionality (Güroğlu et al., 2009). **B**. In the no-alternative condition (8/2 vs. 8/2 offer), an age-related difference emerges in recruitment of dorslolateral prefrontal cortex (DLPFC) such that the older adolescents and the adults show increased activation for reject > accept (Güroğlu et al., 2011).

5/5 distribution), and (4) hyperfair alternative (i.e., 2/8 distribution). Intention understanding was studied by examining the proportion trials on which responders rejected an unfair 8/2 division when this offer was pitted against one of the four alternatives. The behavioral findings showed that 9-year-olds did not make any differentiation between intentionality conditions: rejection rates of unfair 8/2 offers were independent of the alternative distribution available to the proposer (see Figure 8.3A). Intentionality considerations were already incorporated into decision-making by age 12 such that rejection of unfair offers was lower in the hyperunfair- and no-alternative conditions than in the fair- and hyper-fair-alternative conditions. However, there was a linear age-related increase in acceptance of unfair 8/2 offers when the proposer did not have a better alternative (8/2 vs. 8/2). In other words, changes in fairness considerations in social interactions were related to the development of intentionality understanding and perspective-taking skills across adolescence (Güroğlu et al., 2009).

In an fMRI study including adults, we demonstrated that the mentalizing brain regions, such as the medial PFC and TPJ, as well as subcortical brain areas, such as the insula and ventral striatum, were differentially sensitive to the social-context manipulations (Güroğlu, van den Bos, Rombouts, & Crone, 2010). The results replicated prior reports showing high insula activation during UG performance, especially when participants made choices that were against the norm (acceptance of unfair 8/2 offers when the proposer has a fair alternative, and rejection of unfair 8/2 offers when the proposer has no alternative). Of most interest was the role of the TPJ in intention understanding, which was most evident in the no-alternative condition. That is, rejecting an unfair 8/2 offer when the proposer had no alternative was associated with elevated activation in the TPJ, a region thought to be related to mentalizing and the shifting of attention from self to other (Decety & Lamm, 2007; Mitchell, 2008). Thus, the UG manipulations were successful in identifying brain regions sensitive to violation of personal norms and to intention understanding and perspective-taking.

Next, these data were complemented with fMRI data from children (mean age = 10), early-adolescent individuals (mean age = 13), and mid-adolescent individuals (mean age = 15) relative to young adults (mean age = 20) (Güroğlu, van den Bos, van Dijk, Rombouts, & Crone, 2011). Similar to what was found in the adult data, the insula was involved in UG performance, such that the insula was sensitive to the violation of personal norms, in children and adolescents. Again, the no-alternative condition, which is though to rely most on perspective-taking skills, yielded an interesting age–response interaction. This time, the most striking age differences were observed in dorsolateral prefrontal cortex (DLPFC), a brain region thought to be important for response selection and impulse control (Miller & Cohen, 2001) and which has previously shown to be highly sensitive to developmental change (Bunge & Wright, 2007), as well as in the TPJ. In the current paradigm, mid-adolescent individuals and young adults demonstrated higher DLFPC and TPJ activity during rejection of unfair 8/2 offers than when accepting these offers (see Figure 8.3B; Güroğlu et al., 2011). We interpreted these findings as showing that adolescent development is associated with increased cognitive control (as indicated by increased DLPFC activation) and increasing intentionality understanding (as indicated by increased TPJ activation).

Trust Game and the Role of MPFC, TPJ, and DLPFC

One brain region that has been implicated in mentalizing about self and other is the MPFC, although the role of the MPFC in development is not yet well understood. In a study where participants were asked to identify irony in cartoon drawings, children engaged the mPFC more than adults, whereas there was a shift toward activation in posterior regions in adults (Wang, Lee, Sigman, & Dapretto, 2006). Others have also reported increased MPFC activation in adolescents relative to that in adults (Blakemore, 2008; Pfeifer, Lieberman, & Dapretto, 2007). The heightened activation in MPFC in adolescence has been interpreted as increased self-referential processing in adolescence, based on prior literature showing that MPFC is mainly sensitive to self-oriented thoughts (Amodio & Frith, 2006).

We tested this hypothesis using a social decision-making paradigm in which self-referential thoughts and actions are most evident. This set of studies made use of the Trust Game (TG), in which one player (the trustor) is given a sum of money that he or she can divide between him- or herself and a second player, or the first player can decide to trust the money to the second player. In the latter case, the money is tripled and the second player has the possibility of reciprocating the trust by splitting the money between him- or herself and the trustor, or to keep all the money. If a second player does not reciprocate, this decision might be interpreted as self-serving. We tested the role of MPFC when trust was not reciprocated in the participants aged 12–14 years, 15–17 years, and 18–25 years while they played the TG as the second player (i.e., as trustee). As anticipated, abandonment of trust resulted in elevated activation in anterior MPFC (aMPFC) in adults and older adolescents. In contrast, in young adolescents (12–14 years), the aMPFC was increased for both the trust-abandoned and trust-reciprocated trials, which could be interpreted as broader self-referential processing (van den Bos, van Dijk, Westenberg, Rombouts, & Crone, 2009, 2010). These findings were accompanied by elevated activation in TPJ and DLPFC for older adolescents and adults relative to that in younger adolescents when receiving trust.

Similar results were found in another study that examined the neural correlates of perspective-taking and intentionality understanding. In this study, the posing of questions regarding intentional causality of situations compared to physical causality resulted in higher MPFC activity in adolescents than adults (Blakemore et al., 2007). These findings present converging evidence suggesting that the brain networks supporting understanding of intentionality and higher order perspective-taking develop across adolescence and shift from anterior (aMPFC) to posterior brain regions (pSTS/TPJ).

Conclusion

In this chapter, we discussed the development of emotion and social reasoning in adolescence and their mediation by functionally different brain networks. Current models of adolescent brain development suggest slow development of prefrontal and parietal cortex regions, which are important for impulse control and intention understanding, together with elevated sensitivity of subcortical brain regions (Blakemore, 2008; Casey et al., 2008; Nelson et al., 2005). This claim is supported by longitudinal studies demonstrating protracted development of cortical brain regions in terms of gray matter volume (Gogtay et al., 2004), by animal research suggesting that gonadal hormones induce increases in dopaminergic activity that influence affective subcortical brain systems (Quevedo, Benning, Gunnar, & Dahl, 2009; Sisk & Zehr,

2005; Spear, 2009), and by recent functional MRI studies providing initial evidence for this fragile balance between reward processing and social reasoning (Galvan et al., 2006; Güroğlu et al., 2009; van Leijenhorst et al., 2009).

In this chapter, we have demonstrated that adolescence is a time period of significant improvement in self-regulation, but it is also marked by vulnerabilities to affective input or social context. Although steady improvements are observed between childhood and adulthood in the ability to perform cognitive tasks, the developmental changes in emotion regulation and social competence have been found to follow complicated nonlinear age patterns. In particular, functional neuroimaging studies have shown that adolescent development is typically characterized by immature PFC activity (important for cognitive control and intelligent behavior) and enhanced responses in subcortical affective systems (important for emotional responses). Such activity suggests an intensification of emotional experience and an immature capacity of affective regulation and self-control in adolescence (Galvan et al., 2006; Hare et al., 2008). In future studies, it will be important to also examine within-subject changes and to identify early on those adolescents who are at risk for vulnerability to real-life risks (Galvan et al., 2008) or psychiatric disorders (Paus, Keshvan, & Giedd, 2008).

We suggest that the development of emotional functioning in adolescence and the underlying neural architecture that subserves these changes can also be applied to the domain of social reasoning. Previous studies examining changes in social functioning have used complex tasks that are difficult to disentangle and that leave open the question the means by which functional maturation of brain regions subserves the development of social reasoning. In this chapter, we illustrated how an experimental approach in which relatively simple social interaction games are presented in different conditions allows us to draw conclusions about specific changes in development. We also demonstrated the involvement of distinguishable brain networks which make differential contributions to the development of social reasoning. Thus, models of emotion development can be articulated further by taking into account the role of social factors in development. The task for future research is to gain converging evidence from behavioral, hormonal, neuroimaging, and connectivity analyses, which may provide a working model for the functionally segregated and emerging connectivity between brain regions that may account for adolescent development, as well as developmental changes in various aspects of emotional and social processing.

Most studies examining social decision-making processes focus on simulations of social interactions with anonymous others. Findings from economic-game paradigms such as the Ultimatum Game and the Trust Game rely on single-shot exchanges with interaction partners, neglecting the relationship aspect of real-life social interactions. Repetition of such interactions builds relationships over time that are closely related to many aspects of socioemotional well-being (Baumeister & Leary, 1995). Patterns of brain activity related to social interactions with familiar partners might be related to specific relationship characteristics that develop over time. This interplay between relationships and neural activity has been neglected because of the difficulties related to simulating real-life social interactions within the scanner. One example of such an attempt is a study implementing a social-interaction simulation task to examine the neural correlates of friendships (Güroğlu et al., 2008). In this study, emotion processing as well as empathy-related brain networks were particularly activated during social interactions with friends. Future studies need to focus on examining the mechanisms related to relationship patterns in order to better understand the neural basis of social behavior.

One of the challenges for future research is to further understand why, when, and how behavior is more erratic in adolescence than during other stages in life. Future studies should focus on the interplay between developmental, cognitive, emotional, and social neuroscience studies in order to examine how brain development contributes to the emergence of the many complex skills we use in daily life. In addition, future studies should identify not only the risks but also the opportunities of this highly potential developmental period in life.

Acknowledgments

Research conducted by the Eveline A. Crone was sponsored by an NWO-VIDI grant and an Innovative Ideas Grant of the European Research Council, and research conducted by Berna Güroğlu was sponsored by an NWO-VENI grant.

References

Adolphs, R. (2003). Cognitive neuroscience of human social behaviour. *Nature Reviews Neuroscience, 4*(3), 165–178.

Amodio, D. M., & Frith, C. D. (2006). Meeting of minds: The medial frontal cortex and social cognition. *Nature Reviews Neuroscience, 7*, 268–277.

Arnett, J. (1992). Reckless behavior in adolescence: A developmental perspective. *Developmental Reviews, 12*, 391–409.

Baumeister, R. F., & Leary, M. R. (1995). The need to belong: Desire for interpersonal attachments as a fundamental human motivation. *Psychological Bulletin, 117*(3), 497.

Best, J. R., Miller, P. H., & Jones, L. L. (2009). Executive function development after age 5: Changes and correlates. *Developmental Review, 29*, 180–200.

Bjork, J. M., Knutson, B., Fong, G. W., Caggiano, D. M., Bennett, S. M., & Hommer, D. W. (2004). Incentive-elicited brain activation in adolescents: Similarities and differences from young adults. *Journal of Neuroscience, 24*, 1793–1802.

Blakemore, S. J. (2008). The social brain in adolescence. *Nature Reviews Neuroscience, 9*, 267–277.

Blakemore, S.-J., & Choudhury, S. (2006). Development of the adolescent brain: implications for executive function and social cognition. *Journal of Child Psychology & Psychiatry, 47*(3/4), 296.

Blakemore, S.-J., den Ouden, H., Choudhury, S., & Frith, C. (2007). Adolescent development of the neural circuitry for thinking about intentions. *Social, Cognitive & Affective Neuroscience, 2*, 130–139.

Bunge, S. A., & Wright, S. B. (2007). Neurodevelopmental changes in working memory and cognitive control. *Current Opinion in Neurobiology, 17*(2);243–250.

Burnett, S., Bird, G., Moll, J., Frith, C., & Blakemore, S.-J. (2009). Development during adolescence of the neural processing of social emotion. *Journal of Cognitive Neuroscience, 21*(9), 1736–1750.

Casey, B. J., Getz, S., & Galvan, A. (2008). The adolescent brain. *Developmental Review, 28*, 62–77.

Choudhury, S., Blakemore, S.-J., & Charman, T. (2006). Social cognitive development during adolescence. *Social, Cognitive & Affective Neuroscience, 1*(3), 165–174.

Cragg, L., & Nation, K. (2008). Go or no-go? Developmental improvements in the efficiency of response inhibition in mid-childhood. *Developmental Science, 11*(6), 819–827.

Crone, E. A., Zanolie, K., van Leijenhorst, L., Westenberg, P. M., & Rombouts, S. A. (2008). Neural mechanisms supporting flexible performance adjustment during development. *Cognitive, Affective & Behavioral Neuroscience, 8*(2), 165–177.

Crone, E. A., & van der Molen, M. W. (2004). Developmental changes in real life decision making: Performance on a gambling task previously shown to depend on the ventromedial prefrontal cortex. *Developmental Neuropsychology, 35*(3), 251–279.

Crone, E. A., Bunge, S. A., van der Molen, M. W., & Ridderinkhof, K. R. (2006). Switching between tasks and responses: A developmental study. *Developmental Science, 9*(3), 278–287.

Dahl, R. E., & Gunner, M. R. (2009). Heightened stress responsiveness and emotional reactivity during pubertal maturation: Implications for psychopathology. *Development and Psychopathology, 21*, 1–6.

Decety, J., & Lamm, C. (2007). The role of the right temporoparietal junction in social interaction: How low-level computational processes contribute to meta-cognition. *Neuroscientist, 13*(6), 580–593.

De Dreu, C. K. W., Lualhati, J. C., & McCusker, C. M. (1994). Effects of gain-loss frames on satisfaction with self-other outcome differences. *European Journal of Social Psychology, 24*, 497–510.

Ernst, M., Nelson, E. E., Jazbec, S., McClure, E. B., Monk, C. S., Leibenluft, E., et al. (2005). Amygdala and nucleus accumbens in responses to receipt and omission of gains in adults and adolescents. *Neuroimage, 25*(4), 1279–1291.

Ernst, M., Pine, D. S., & Hardin, M. (2006). Triadic model of the neurobiology of motivated behavior in adolescence. *Psychological Medicine, 36*, 299–312.

Ernst, M., & Fudge, J. L. (2009). A developmental neurobiological model of motivated behavior: Anatomy, connectivity, and ontogeny of the triadic nodes. *Neuroscience and Biobehavioral Reviews, 33*(3), 367–382.

Eshel, N., Nelson, E. E., Blair, J. R., Pine, D. S., & Ernst, M. (2007). Neural substrates of choice selection in adults and adolescents: Development of the ventrolateral prefrontal and anterior cingulate cortices. *Neuropsychologia, 45*, 1270–1279.

Falk, A., Fehr, E., & Fischbacher, U. (2003). On the nature of fair behavior. *Economic Inquiry, (41)*, 20–26.

Galvan, A., Hare, T. A., Parra, C. E., Penn, J., Voss, H., Glover, G., & Casey, B. J. (2006). Earlier development of the accumbens relative to orbitofrontal cortex might underlie risk-taking behavior in adolescents. *Journal of Neuroscience, 26*, 6885–6892.

Galvan, A., Hare, T., Voss, H., Glover, G., & Casey, B. J. (2008). Risk-taking and the adolescent brain: Who is at risk? *Developmental Science, 10*(2), F8–F14.

Gardner, M., & Steinberg, L. (2005). Peer influence on risk taking, risk preference, and risky decision making in adolescence and adulthood: An experimental study. *Developmental Psychology, 4*, 625–635.

Giedd, J. N., Clasen, L. S., Lenroot, R., Greenstein, D., Wallace, G. L., Ordaz, S., et al. (2006). Puberty-related influences on brain development. *Molecular and Cellular Endocrinology, 254–255*, 154–162.

Gogtay, N., Giedd, J. N., Lusk, L., Hayashi, K. M., Greenstein, D., Vaituzis, A. C., et al. (2004). Dynamic mapping of human cortical development during childhood through early adulthood. *Proceedings of the National Academy of Science U S A 101*(21), 8174–8179.

Güroğlu, B., Haselager, G. J. T., van Lieshout, C. F. M., Takashima, A., Rijpkema, M., & Fernández, G. (2008). Why are friends special? Implementing a social interaction simulation task to probe the neural correlates of friendship. *Neuroimage, 39*(2), 903.

Güroğlu, B., van den Bos, W., & Crone, E. A. (2009). Fairness considerations: Increasing understanding of intentionality in adolescence. *Journal of Experimental Child Psychology, 104*, 398–409.

Güroğlu, B., van den Bos, W., Rombouts, S. A. R. B., & Crone, E. A. (2010). Unfair? It depends: Neural correlates of fairness in social context. *Social, Cognitive & Affective Neuroscience, 5*(4), 414–423.

Güroğlu, B., van den Bos, W., van Dijk, E. Rombouts, S. A. R. B., & Crone, E. A. (2011). Dissociable brain regions involved in development of fairness considerations. *Neuroimage, 57*(2), 634–641.

Guyer, A. E., Monk, C. S. McClure-Tone, E. B., Nelson, E. E., Roberson-Nay, R., Adler, A. D., et al. (2008). A developmental examination of amygdala response to facial expressions. *Journal of Cognitive Neuroscience, 20*(9), 1565–1582.

Hare, T. A., Tottenham, N., Galvan, A., Voss, H. U., Glover, G. H., & Casey, B. J. (2008). Biological substrates of emotional reactivity and regulation in adolescence during an emotional go–no-go task. *Biological Psychiatry*, 63, 927–934.

Harris, J. R. (1995). Where is the child's environment? A groups socialization theory of development. *Psychological Review*, 102(3), 458–489.

Hooper, C. J., Luciana, M., Conklin, H. M., & Yarger, R. S. (2004). Adolescents' performance on the Iowa Gambling Task: Implications for the development of decision making and ventromedial prefrontal cortex. *Developmental Psychology*, 40(6), 1148–1158.

Huizinga, M., Dolan, C. V., & van der Molen, M. W. (2006). Age-related change in executive function: developmental trends and a latent variable analysis. *Neuropsychologia*, 44(11), 2017–2036.

Knutson, B., Adams, C. M., Fong, G. W., & Hommer, D. (2001). Anticipation of increasing monetary reward selectively recruits nucleus accumbens. *Journal of Neuroscience*, 21, 1–5.

McClure, S. M., Berns, G. S., & Montague, P. R. (2003). Temporal prediction errors in a passive learning task activate human striatum. *Neuron*, 38, 339–346.

Miller, E. K., & Cohen, J. D. (2001). An integrative theory of prefrontal cortex function. *Annual Review of Neuroscience 24*, 167–202.

Mitchell, J. P. (2008). Activity in right temporo-parietal junction is not selective for theory-of-mind. *Cerebral Cortex*, 18(2), 262–271.

Monk, C. S., McClure, E. B., Nelson, E. E., Zrahn, E., Bilder, R., Leibenluft, E., et al. (2003). Adolescent immaturity in attention-related brain engagements to emotional facial expressions. *Neuroimage*, 20, 420–428.

Nelson, E. E., Leibenluft, E., McClure, E. B., & Pine, D. S. (2005). The social re-orientation of adolescence: A neuroscience perspective on the process and its relation to psychopathology. *Psychological Medicine*, 35(02), 163–174.

Paus, T., Keshvan, M., & Giedd, J. N. (2008). Why do many psychiatric disorders emerge during adolescence? *Nature Reviews*, 9, 947–957.

Pfeifer, J. H., Lieberman, M. D., & Dapretto, M. (2007). "I know you are but what am I?!" Neural basis of self and social knowledge retrieval in children and adults. *Journal of Cognitive Neuroscience*, 19, 1323–1337.

Quevedo, K. M., Benning, S. D., Gunnar, M. R., & Dahl, R. E. (2009). The onset of puberty: Effects on the psychophysiology of defensive and appetitive motivation. *Development and Psychopathology*, 21, 27–45.

Rivers, S. E., Reyna, V. F., & Mills, B. (2008). Risk taking under the influence: A fuzzy-trace theory of emotion in adolescence. *Developmental Review*, 28, 107–144.

Scheres, A., Dijkstra, M., Ainslie, E., Balkan, J., Reynolds, B., Sonuga-Barke, E., et al. (2006). Temporal and probabilistic discounting of rewards in children and adolescents: Effects of age and ADHD symptoms. *Neuropsychologia*, 44, 2092–2103.

Shirtcliff, E. A., Dahl. R. E., & Pollak, S. D. (2009). Pubertal development: Correspondence between hormonal and physical development. *Child Development*, 80, 327–337.

Sisk, C. L., & Zehr, J. L. (2005). Pubertal hormones organize the adolescent brain and behavior. *Annals of the New York Academy of Sciences*, 1007, 189–198.

Spear, L. P. (2009). Heightened stress responsivity and emotional reactivity during pubertal maturation: Implications for psychopathology. *Development and Psychopathology*, 21, 87–97.

Steinberg, L. (2007). Risk taking in adolescence: New perspectives from brain and behavioral science. *Current Directions in Psychological Science*, 16(2), 55–59.

Steinberg, L. (2008). A social neuroscience perspective on adolescent risk-taking. *Developmental Review*, 28(1), 78.

Steinberg, L., Albert, D., Cauffman, E., Banich, M, Graham, S., & Woolard, J. (2008). Age differences in sensation seeking and impulsivity as indexed by behavior and self-report: Evidence for a dual systems model. *Developmental Psychology*, 44, 1764–1778.

Takahashi, H., Kato, M., Matsuura, M., Mobbs, D., Suhara, T., & Okubo, Y. (2009). When your gain is my pain and your pain is my gain: neural correlates of envy and schadenfreude. *Science*, 323, 937–939

van den Bos, W., van Dijk, E., Westenberg, M., Rombouts, S. A. R. B., & Crone, E. A. (2009). What motivates repayment? Neural correlates of reciprocity in the Trust Game. *Social, Cognitive & Affective Neuroscience*, 4, 294–304.

van den Bos, W., van Dijk, E., Westenberg, M., Rombouts, S. A. R. B., & Crone, E. A. (2010). Changing brains, changing perspectives: The neurocognitive development of reciprocity. *Psychological Science*, 22(1), 60–70.

van Dijk, E., & Vermunt, R. (2000). Strategy and fairness in social decision making: Sometimes it pays to be powerless. *Journal of Experimental Social Psychology*, 36, 1–25.

van Duijvenvoorde, A. C., Zanolie, K., Rombouts, S. A., Raijmakers, M. E., & Crone, E. A. (2008). Evaluating the negative or valuing the positive? Neural mechanisms supporting feedback-based learning across development. *Journal of Neuroscience*, 28(38), 9495–9503.

van Leijenhorst, L., Gunther Moor, B., Zdeňa A., Op de Macks, Rombouts, S. A. R. B., Westenberg, P. M., & Crone, E. A. (2010b) Adolescent risky decision-making: Neurocognitive development of affective and control regions. *Neuroimage*, 51(1), 345–355.

van Leijenhorst, L., Westenberg, P. M., & Crone, E. A. (2008) A developmental study of risky decisions on the cake gambling task; age and gender analyses of probability estimation and reward evaluation. *Developmental Neuropsychology*, 33, 179–196.

van Leijenhorst, L., Zanolie, K., Van Meel, C. S., Westenberg, P. M., Rombouts, S. A. R. B., & Crone, E. A. (2010a). What motivates the adolescent? Brain regions mediating reward sensitivity in adolescence. *Cerebral Cortex*, 20(1), 61–69.

Wang, A. T., Lee, S. S., Sigman, M., & Dapretto, M. (2006). Developmental changes in the neural basis of interpreting communicative intent. *Social, Cognitive & Affective Neuroscience*, 1(2), 107–121.

PART 2

Self and Social Cognition

CHAPTER

9

Self-Knowledge

Joseph M. Moran, William M. Kelley, *and* Todd F. Heatherton

Abstract

Having an understanding of ourselves has been a fundamental topic for psychologists, philosophers, and laypeople alike since the beginnings of consciousness. Whether one's own sense of self has any special neurocognitive status has been hotly debated. This chapter reviews neuropsychological and neuroimaging evidence that argues for the special status of self-knowledge in memory. The contributing roles to self-knowledge of central nodes in the brain's default mode network of regions are also discussed. This review argues that these nodes may be functionally dissociated along multiple lines, with an important dissociation concerning the representation of psychological characteristics and the representation of physical characteristics. It is also argued that the medial prefrontal cortex, a critical node in the default mode network, enjoys anatomical and functional connectivity that together suggest a role for it in delineating the world into "me" and "not me." The chapter concludes with suggested lines of future inquiry that might provide more direct evidence of this role.

Key Words: self, memory, social cognition, social neuroscience, functional magnetic resonance imaging, cortical midline structures, medial prefrontal cortex, posterior cingulate cortex

"Who am I?" is a fundamental question in our inner mental lives. This question has most likely surfaced in some form or another in each individual since humans were first able to ask it, and it has been posed more formally by philosophers for millennia. As a central topic of investigation in the study of mind, the self has resisted definition, inquiry, and even existence at various points during its long history. Possession of a conscious sense of self has been held up as the defining characteristic of humanity. Whereas nonhuman animals have not been traditionally viewed as capable of acquiring the sort of conscious self reserved for humans, they do possess implicit, or nonconscious, aspects of the self (LeDoux, 2002). For instance, Damasio (1999) has distinguished between "core" and "extended" selves. The core self consists of a collection of processes making up the ongoing functions that differentiate self from other. The extended self, putatively limited

to humans, involves a more narrative structure, embodied in the here and now, but also is in possession of a future and a past as well as mental access to both through processes of memory and autonoetic consciousness (Tulving, 1985). Partitioning the self along similar lines, LeDoux (2002) has described differences between "implicit" and "explicit" selves: explicit self contains those processes that are present in consciousness, such as ongoing self-awareness, and implicit self refers to aspects of the self that are not accessible to conscious awareness, such as ongoing processes of memory consolidation.

Traditional studies of the self in the introspectionist school of psychology focused squarely on conscious aspects of the self. These aspects of the self are obviously more amenable to behavioral inquiry than their implicit counterparts, since implicit aspects of self are unavailable for conscious reflection. Fortunately, experimental psychology ultimately developed methods to go beyond the simple here and now and probe concepts such as self-knowledge more deeply. Unfortunately for this field, however, the rise of the behaviorist school of psychology set back for decades research into such ineffable concepts as "self." Indeed, for a significant period of time, the prevailing view was that even explicit aspects of the self were inaccessible by scientific methods and should therefore be ignored (methodological behaviorism) or disavowed entirely (radical behaviorism). Rejecting the strict adherence to the stimulus–response psychology of behaviorism, the architects of the cognitive revolution in the middle part of the last century allowed for the return of processes between the input and output stages of behavior. They reasoned that the workings of the mind resembled those of the computers that were beginning to exhibit complex behaviors and hence began to emphasize the *processes* occurring in cognition, a focus that continues in present-day cognitive psychology, cognitive neuroscience, and social cognition research.

Social psychology and cognitive science have been responsible for an explosion in interest in the processes that engender the explicit self; an Internet search in April 2012 for the word *self* in the title of research articles in the social sciences resulted in more than 400,000 papers through which to wade, should one desire a complete knowledge of the current literature of research about the self. Although this output is staggering, more questions than answers remain, one of the more troubling being how one might define the self. William James (1890) provides us with a prescient and valuable definition:

> In its widest possible sense ... a man's Self is the sum total of all that he CAN call his, not only his body and his psychic powers, but his clothes and his house, his wife and children, his ancestors and friends, his reputation and works, his land and horses, and yacht and bank-account ... if they wax and prosper, he feels triumphant; if they dwindle and die away, he feels cast down—not necessarily in the same degree for each thing, but in much the same way for all. (pp. 291–292)

This definition highlights the inclusive nature of the self-concept and the interplay between cognition and emotion that lies at the heart of the self. Indeed, James differentiates the self into three parts: "its constituents, the feelings and emotions they arouse, and the actions to which they prompt" (James, 1890, p. 292). Research in cognitive science

and in the field of personality and social psychology (see Baumeister, 1998) has made much headway in characterizing the nature of the self concept ("its constituents": cognition), the "feelings and emotions they arouse" (emotion) and "the actions to which they prompt" (motivation), but it has failed thus far to provide an integrative synthesis of these disparate aspects of self with their neural implementation.

Descartes notwithstanding, the brain is generally considered to be the seat of the mind, with the conscious self being the preeminent aspect of mind. Thus, any theory of the self that is successful must be capable of explaining the interaction between the mechanisms of mind that give rise to both conscious explicit and nonconscious implicit aspects of self and the physical machinery in which those mechanisms are instantiated. Thus far, cognitive science and the field of social cognition have achieved some early success in delineating the processes that underlie the cognitive self, such as self-referential processing, self-schemas, self-awareness, and memory encoding. Personality psychology has had much to say on the multifactorial structure of the self and personality and has given rise to important concepts in understanding individual differences in self, such as self-esteem. Neuroscientific research has begun to piece together the processes that underlie emotion and motivation.

To date, however, research in these fields has occurred customarily along parallel lines, with little cross-talk among disciplines and little use of findings from one field to inform investigations in another. The advent of cognitive neuroscience and, most recently, social neuroscience, however, has begun to change this prevailing pattern. The introduction of functional neuroimaging techniques over the past two decades has given researchers the capacity to study the working brain in action, thus providing a new window for examining previously intractable mental states, including the phenomenological experience of self (Heatherton, Macrae, & Kelley, 2004; Kelley et al., 2002; Macrae, Kelley, & Heatherton, 2004). One of the grander hopes of neuroimaging has been that it may allow us in part to go beyond the reported experiences of the participant and adjudicate among competing theoretical explanations for particular psychological phenomena.

Given the broad nature of such inquiry, it is perhaps surprising that there is a well-identified neural system that is engaged when people decide who they are by judging to what extent trait adjectives (e.g., kind, bold, clever) describe their characters.

The basic goal of this chapter is to demonstrate how studying the brain can inform research on various aspects of the self. We aim to (1) show how neuropsychology and brain imaging have been able to resolve competing positions in the behavioral literature regarding the "specialness" of self, (2) discuss how brain imaging can inform our understanding of the nature of self and self-reflection more specifically, and (3) suggest interesting future research avenues into the multifaceted and elusive sense of self. We begin first by focusing on the brain regions associated with self and their anatomical connections. We then present evidence for the specialness of self at the neural level and finally move on to provide a theoretical perspective that aims to make sense of the disparate research findings in the cognitive neuroscience of self.

Cognitive Neuroscience and the Self

Cognitive neuroscience is uncovering the existence of dissociable aspects of self at the neural level and has consistently implicated several cortical structures in aspects of the self. These structures include, but are not limited to, regions of the medial prefrontal cortex ([mPFC] both dorsal and ventral aspects of the anteromedial part of the medial frontal gyrus) and more posterior regions of cortex, such as the retrosplenial, posterior cingulate, and precuneal cortices [pCC]. These structures have been collectively referred to as the "cortical midline structures" (CMS) by Northoff and Bermpohl (2004), who advanced a theoretical position that mPFC may be responsible for evaluating information as to its self-relevance (dorsal mPFC) and for representing information that is self-relevant (ventral mPFC), and that pCC may be responsible for integrating information with respect to the self. Although this theoretical stance is certainly quite plausible, the empirical support for these putative different roles for these regions has been slow in coming. Indeed, while cognitive neuroscience has been successful in uncovering a broad-stroke network involved in self-reflection, there have been scant empirical studies conducted to determine the relative contributions of these regions in the domain of self-knowledge and what sorts of component processes and knowledge structures make up self-knowledge. We will thus review below the current literature to determine whether there is any reasonable basis for a dissociation between anterior and posterior cortical midline structures and what such a dissociation would mean for the component processes engaged when experimental participants are asked to reflect upon themselves.

Based on the available cognitive neuroscience evidence, three main conclusions can be drawn. First, we argue that an important function of mPFC is to facilitate access to the mental store of information regarding the self-concept. Second, ventral and dorsal aspects of mPFC may be dissociable with regard to their relative contributions to thinking about individuals who are similar or dissimilar to oneself, respectively (Denny, Kober, Waer, & Ochsner, 2012; Murray, Schaer, & Debbané, 2012). Third, the anterior and posterior CMS may be dissociable according to the relative task demands placed on accessing different aspects of self-knowledge. This dissociation may be associated with differential reliance on semantic and episodic memory, or on abstract and concrete aspects of self.

There are both neuroanatomical and neuroimaging data that may be brought to bear in support of these conclusions. With regard to neuroanatomy, medial PFC, more specifically the medial aspect of Brodmann's area (BA) 10, enjoys several features that distinguish it from other cortical regions. First, it is larger than any other prefrontal region in humans (Ongur, Ferry, & Price, 2003). Second, by proportion, it covers more of the cortex in humans than in other animals (Semendeferi, Armstrong, Schleicher, Zilles, & Van Hoesen, 2001). Third, on average, it has a greater density of dendritic spines and smaller density of cell bodies than that of other cortical regions (Jacobs et al., 2001). Fourth, mPFC is almost exclusively interconnected with other heteromodal processing regions in the prefrontal cortex (Barbas & Pandya, 1989; Petrides & Pandya, 1999), anterior temporal cortex (Amaral & Price, 1984; Moran, Mufson, & Mesulam, 1987), and cingulate gyrus (Arikuni, Sako, & Murata, 1994; Morecraft & Van Hoesen, 1993). Most of these connections are reciprocal in nature (Passingham, Stephen, & Kotter, 2002). These features leave mPFC well placed as a region involved in the integration of many disparate aspects of information processing and in the processing of abstract supramodal information. It is also a critical node in the "social brain" (Adolphs, 2001).

As mentioned earlier, pCC shares many reciprocal connections with mPFC. In addition, the subregions of pCC are strongly reciprocally connected with one another in a bilateral manner (Cavanna & Trimble, 2006). Along with mPFC, pCC is disproportionately larger in humans than in nonhuman primates (Goldman-Rakic, 1987). pCC shares many connections with subcortical and cortical regions and serves as "association cortex," enabling the brain to "integrate both external and self-generated information and to produce much of the mental activity that characterizes *Homo sapiens*" (Cavanna & Trimble, 2006, p. 568).

In noteworthy reviews of the functional neuroimaging literature, Northoff and colleagues (Northoff & Bermpohl, 2004; Northoff et al., 2006) explored the role of these "cortical midline structures" (Northoff & Bermpohl, 2004) in many tasks broadly classifiable as self-referential in nature. Northoff and colleagues (2006) argue that these regions form a functional anatomic "unit," suggesting that their coactivation may be necessary for successful self-reflection. While these conclusions are certainly valid in the climate of current neuroscientific research on the self, they are somewhat vague.

The present conjecture is that an important function of mPFC is to facilitate access to the self-schemata, a set of semantic memory structures that detail abstracted information about what the self is like and the wealth of information that is included in the self concept (Markus, 1977). This distinction of general and self-related semantic memory is supported by at least two major lines of research in neuropsychology and in neuroimaging. The role of mPFC in retrieving and manipulating information from the self-schemata is one that may be automatic and obligatory under circumstances where the individual's mind is unconstrained (e.g., Raichle et al., 2001), and it is attenuated in situations where an individual is required to perform some sort of goal-directed task (Gusnard, Akbudak, Shulman, & Raichle, 2001). One major prediction of this approach, therefore, is that the degree to which a given task either encourages or allows for this sort of nondirectional mental activity (e.g., Singer & Antrobus, 1972) will be reflected in the degree of mPFC activation elicited during performance of that task. This is not to say that activation is related to the given task, but that a byproduct of setting any goal-oriented task will be attenuation of the inherent tendency to self-reflect (i.e., mindwander, Singer & Antrobus, 1972) to a predictable degree: the more difficult a task is, the less resources one has available for engaging in task-independent thought. Indeed, the meta-analysis of Shulman and colleagues (1997) most obviously leads to this sort of argument, as that study showed that goal-directed tasks across many differing domains produced identical attenuation in activation in these structures.

Conversely, if a task is so simple as to be accomplished automatically (such as changing gears while driving), then it will produce no effect on activity

in the system that is designed to foster introspective self-reflections. Several neuroimaging studies have already shown this to be the case (d'Argembeau et al., 2005; McKiernan, D'Angelo, Kaufman, & Binder,, 2003, McKiernan, Kaufman, Kucera-Thompson, & Binder, 2006; Wicker, Ruby, Royet, & Fonlupt, 2003). Mason and colleagues (2007) argue strongly for just such a theoretical position, demonstrating that practiced tasks engage these regions much more than novel tasks (of the same ilk) and that this engagement tracks linearly with subjects' self-reported tendency to engage in stimulus-independent thoughts. Providing further evidence for the convergence of self-reflection during both active tasks and rest, Whitfield-Gabrieli and colleagues (2011) demonstrated significant overlap in involvement of mPFC when participants were asked about their own characters and when they were free to quietly rest, in comparison to a control semantic task.

In the ensuing sections, we will discuss evidence for a distinction between general and self-related semantic memory systems. We will then go on to develop a theoretical perspective to bring explanatory power to the discussion of mPFC activation by what appears to be a large variety of disparate experimental paradigms. This section focuses on the contribution of mPFC to self-reflection and self memory; in later sections we will discuss how mPFC and pCC might be differentiable with respect to self-reflection.

Self in Memory Is Special

Early work in cognitive psychology demonstrated that when participants are asked to encode a list of items with reference to themselves (e.g., "How 'confident' are you?"), later memory for those items is improved relative to other orientation conditions (e.g., "Is *confident* a positive or negative word?") (Rogers, Kuiper, & Kirker, 1977). Further, items deemed to be self-relevant (e.g., deciding that *confident* does describe the self) are remembered better than items deemed not self-relevant (Rogers et al., 1977). This effect is among the more robust in all of cognitive psychology (Symons & Johnson, 1997), and theorists have argued vociferously over its meaning. One camp (Maki & McCaul, 1985; Rogers et al., 1977) has suggested that the self serves as a special memory system, superordinate to the typical memory encoding system, while other theorists have argued that the self is simply a powerful but ordinary semantic structure, producing its memorial advantage through greater depth of encoding (Greenwald & Banaji, 1989). Once a hot topic of debate in the literature, it appears that the self's "specialness" in this domain is now well supported by the evidence.

Evidence from Neuropsychology

Two lines of research appear to support the position that self in memory is special. Evidence for a distinction between self and other at the level of semantic memory comes from a series of elegant studies by Klein and colleagues (Klein, Chan, & Loftus, 1999; Klein, Cosmides, Costabile, & Mei, 2002). Over the course of a number of investigations into the intact and compromised memory systems of several patient groups, they have demonstrated that episodic and semantic memory are dissociable with respect to the self. In a comprehensive review of their findings, Klein, Rozendal, and Cosmides (2002) detailed several disparate cases of individuals who show strikingly dissociable patterns of deficit. The first case concerned a woman (WJ) who had suffered a traumatic brain injury (TBI) in college (Klein, Loftus, & Kihlstrom, 1996). Because of her TBI, WJ was unable to recall any recent episodic autobiographical memories when cued with familiar nouns. Over a period of 4 weeks following the injury, her amnesia remitted, and she made a full recovery of her episodic memory faculties. Interestingly, the authors also had WJ rate herself on a series of trait adjectives immediately following the accident and again after the amnesia had remitted. Her ratings of herself did not differ between her amnestic and recovered periods. Since she was unable to produce any episodic memories of her traits during her period of amnesia, she must have been relying on a semantic memory system to assess accurately her traits.

While WJ's amnesia was only related to recent memories, and thus she may have been able to use older episodic memories to judge her personality, a more complete case of episodic amnesia argued against this explanation. Klein, Rozendal, and Cosmides (2002) described patient DB, who was "unable to consciously recollect a single thing he had ever done or experience from any period of his life," and who suffered profound anterograde amnesia. When tested on separate occasions about his self-trait knowledge, DB showed remarkable test–retest reliability and remarkable interrater reliability, compared with that of his daughter. Correlations between his own tests, and between his test and his daughter's were not different from those of age-matched controls and were both significantly

greater than zero (both r's > 0.63). Thus, the ability to self-reflect accurately is not dependent upon episodic memory, at least in the case of absent episodic recall due to adult-onset brain damage.

More striking, Klein and colleagues reported two patients who both had suffered developmental impairments in episodic memory, and both of whom evidenced intact and accurate self-reflective capabilities (patients KC, first described by Tulving, 1993, and RJ, first described by Klein et al., 1999). Thus, it appears that the ability to depict oneself accurately is entirely independent of episodic memory, and further that the acquisition of self-knowledge does not require episodic memory. In turn, then, we can assume that the system by which we gather and express trait self-knowledge appears to be dependent solely upon semantic memory processes.

Further differentiating self from other, Klein, Rozendal, and Cosmides (2002) summarized evidence of several cases demonstrating dissociations within the domain of semantic memory. From their work and that of others, it appears that self and other forms of general semantic memory are dissociable in certain patient groups, and that individuals can retain their ability to know what they are like in the presence of severely compromised general semantic knowledge. The evidence from neuropsychology indicates that within the broad domain of self, the ability to self-reflect upon one's own traits and the ability to perform this task accurately are skills dissociable from other forms of memory and are not dependent upon episodic retrieval processes.

Evidence from Neuroimaging

The second line of research supporting the general conclusion that self is special comes from neuroimaging. This work shows that self-referential processing is performed by different brain structures than those used for similar sorts of processing about general semantic information or familiar other individuals (e.g., Heatherton et al., 2006; Johnson et al., 2002; Kelley et al., 2002; Kjaer, Nowak, & Lou, 2002; Lou et al., 2004; Moran, Lee, & Gabrieli, 2011; Pfeifer, Lieberman, & Dapretto, 2007). More specifically, regions of mPFC became more active when relating trait adjectives to the self than when relating them to former President George W. Bush (Kelley et al., 2002), when reflecting on the traits of the self, rather than those of the Danish Queen (Kjaer et al., 2002), and when self-reflecting rather than answering questions about general semantic sentences (Johnson et al., 2002). Moreover, further evidence suggests that this region of mPFC predicts the memorial fate of words encoded in reference to the self (Macrae, Moran, Heatherton, Banfield, & Kelley, 2004) and is more active when successfully retrieving information encoded with reference to the self rather than when encoded in a general semantic manner (Fossati et al., 2004). This trio of findings provides compelling evidence that self-referential processing enjoys a distinct functional anatomical architecture that differs from that used for other forms of more general semantic processing.

Some data suggest, however, that the distinction between self and other at the level of the brain might be less clear-cut (Ochsner et al., 2005; Schmitz, Kawahara-Baccus, & Johnson, 2004; Seger, Stone, & Keenan, 2004). Each of these studies used blocked-design fMRI, and each reported similar neural activation patterns for self- and intimate-other judgments. Seger and colleagues (2004) imaged subjects while subjects made self-judgments about food preferences, friend-judgments about food preferences, and superficial judgments about food names (i.e., whether the food name contained two vowels). Medial PFC activity did not differ when self-judgments of food preference were contrasted directly with comparable judgments about an intimate-other's food preferences. Similarly, Ochsner and colleagues (2005) imaged subjects while they were making self-judgments of personality traits (similar to Craik et al., 1999; Johnson et al., 2002; Kelley et al., 2002), close other-judgments of personality traits, social-desirability judgments of personality traits, and syllable judgments of personality traits (i.e., whether the descriptor contained two syllables). Again, mPFC activity did not differ when self- and other-judgments were directly contrasted. Although Ochsner et al. (2005) and Seger et al. (2004) failed to observe differences in mPFC (i.e., BA 10) activity between self- and close-other judgments, it is difficult to interpret these findings as evidence for a shared neural representation because neither study replicated previously reported differences between self- and non-referential task conditions (e.g., Johnson et al., 2002; Kelley et al., 2002; Ochsner et al., 2005). Put simply, while mPFC activity did not differ between self and close-other conditions, it also did not differ between the self and the superficial control conditions (vowel and syllable counting) in each study. Thus it is difficult to know whether the reported null effects in mPFC for self- vs. close-other judgments reflect a common functional architecture or an inability to detect differences in mPFC activity.

A more compelling case for functional homogeneity in making self- and close-other judgments can be made on the basis of Schmitz and colleagues' (2004) finding that self-judgments and friend-judgments of trait adjectives both produced mPFC activation relative to a nonreferential control condition; however, mPFC activation did not differ between self- and friend-judgments. Two later studies also suggest that ventral mPFC activation for other people may be related to how similar the other people are to oneself, whereas dorsal mPFC activation may be insensitive to similarity of another person (Jenkins, Macrae, & Mitchell, 2008; Mitchell, Macrae, & Banaji, 2006). Cross-cultural research on self-reflection using participants from more interdependent cultures argues further for the notion that we may process similar others like ourselves (Zhang et al., 2006, see Kitayama and Park, 2010, for an excellent review). Zhang et al. (2006) showed across two experiments that when Chinese participants reflected on themselves relative to another, mPFC was more engaged for self when the other was not close, but equally engaged for self and mother. Similarly, Ying et al. (2002) showed equivalent memory performance and autonoetic awareness when participants thought about themselves and their mothers. A significant body of work by Han and colleagues has also investigated self-reflection in interdependent cultures. One intriguing investigation in particular (Han et al., 2010) revealed a reduction in activation in mPFC in Chinese Buddhists, a group trained in the doctrine of no-self. While this may indicate a lack of consensus regarding specialness of self, we would suggest that the experimental methods used (i.e., event-related vs. blocked designs) and the differences across experimental paradigms, participants, and cultures in the degree of "closeness" of the other people (Aron, Aron, Tudor, & Nelson, 1991) go some way toward resolving this discrepancy. To the degree that the other person is included in the self, we may see more activation in mPFC when considering traits of the other person and hence similar behavioral consequences for information processed about those other people (e.g., Symons & Johnson, 1997).

More recent work by Moran and colleagues (2011) provides direct evidence for the idea that activation in mPFC is driven by the closeness of the other person. The authors included self, mother, and former President George W. Bush as targets and showed that a region of ventral mPFC was more active when participants thought about the psychological traits of themselves and their mothers than when they thought about those of President Bush. Importantly, when thinking about the physical characteristics of the targets, ventral mPFC was only active for self. In a follow-up behavioral experiment, the authors showed that participants were more likely to consider their mother's psychological traits as important to their own conceptions of themselves, not their mother's physical characteristics. This finding fits nicely with Aron et al.'s (1991) theoretical perspective that we include the traits of close others in the self. It also extends the literature to show that while mPFC activation may overlap for some close others, it does so only to the degree that that information is in some way self relevant. Converging with this, Krienen, Tu, and Buckner (2010) demonstrated that mPFC was more active for close others regardless of their similarity to the self. That is, simple consideration of whether a person is a member of "my clan" might be enough to deem a person as more self-relevant than someone outside of the clan and hence drive greater activation in mPFC.

The preceding discussion supports the notion that the CMS are engaged when we think about ourselves and, perhaps in some circumstances, about other people. What it has not shown thus far is how we might think cogently about the component processes engaged during self-reflection and what specific roles these regions might play during self-reflection. We now turn to evidence that focuses on the specific roles of the regions in question and that suggests principled ways in which they might be dissociated in self-reflection.

Extending the neuroimaging literature, a study by Moran and colleagues (2006) showed that these effects occur in ventral mPFC and pCC regardless of hedonic valence. That is, the CMS were more responsive when participants viewed self-relevant words than when they viewed non-self-relevant words; this effect occurred regardless of whether the information was positive or negative in nature.

Earlier work by Phan et al. (2004) in the pictorial domain suggested this distinction in mPFC in the processing of International Affective Picture System (IAPS) pictures that differed in their self-relevance. Further, Moran, Heatherton, and Kelley (2009) demonstrated that these regions are engaged by canonically self-relevant information, even when current processing goals divert attention away from judging self-relevance. Following this work, Rameson and colleagues (2010) showed that these regions become more active when participants encounter information that is consistent with their self-schemata (e.g., images pertaining to athletics for athletes) during an orthogonal processing task (indicating whether people appear in the images).

These two studies in concert suggest that self-reflection may be obligatory or automatic in some senses and point to the idea that the resting state may be characterized by ongoing self-reflection (d'Argembeau & Salmon, 2012; d'Argembeau et al., 2005; Whitfield-Gabrieli et al., 2011). Their findings demonstrate that these regions of the brain are responsive when performing a task that requires participants to reflect on the self-relatedness of incoming stimuli, further differentiate items on the basis of the outcome of that self-reflective process, and respond to self-relevant information regardless of what processing demands are encouraged by ongoing tasks. If these regions serve to "tag" perceptual information as self-relevant, this set of functional properties suggests a dissociation between self and not-self in consciousness. If we have a set of regions that label incoming information in this way, then we might argue that one of their functions is to differentiate self from not-self. This would make sound evolutionary sense given that in the Jamesian concept of self, "self" includes many things that are not part of the body or person proper, extending to include people and things that are important (and helpful) to us.

Cortical Midline Structures Mediate Differentiable Aspects of Self-Knowledge

The previous discussion gives us lots of clues to suggest that the CMS might be specialized for self-reflection. Thus far we have discussed paradigms in which these two regions seem invariably to coactivate. One way in which we might learn more about self-reflection at the level of cognition and its brain representation is to investigate paradigms that reliably dissociate the contribution of anterior (mPFC) and posterior (pCC) nodes of the cortical midline. Several studies have focused on differentiating mPFC from pCC in self and have revealed tantalizingly plausible explanations for their dissociation. The first one comes from Marcia Johnson and colleagues (Johnson et al., 2006; Mitchell et al., 2009), who varied whether participants reflected with a promotion or prevention focus. Participants who thought about hopes and dreams (promotion focus, experiment 1) activated mPFC more than participants who thought about duties and obligations (prevention focus, experiment 2). The reverse pattern of activation was true in pCC. Strikingly, this result was replicated in a second within-subjects experiment (Johnson et al., 2006) and in a different cohort of young adults (Mitchell et al., 2009). These results demonstrate a nice dissociation along the lines of different aspects of self-knowledge. One way we might think about these different aspects of self-knowledge is along the lines of abstract and concrete thought. Thinking about our hopes and dreams may involve greater reliance on abstract thinking than thinking about duties and obligations, which typically are more concrete in nature. The anatomical connections of these regions leave them well-placed for such operations. The pCC obviously is well connected to regions involved in mental imagery and episodic retrieval, whereas mPFC is connected to regions involved in semantic memory, such as the lateral temporal lobes.

Further functional imaging evidence for a dissociation between mPFC and pCC along the lines of abstract and concrete processing comes from the previously mentioned study by Moran and colleagues (2011). In this study, a region of pCC was more responsive when participants thought about their own appearance than when they thought about their own character. Conversely, a region of dorsal mPFC was more active when participants thought about their own and others' character than when thinking about their own and others' appearance. Thus, across two lines of inquiry, anterior and posterior cortical midline structures were differentiable in their relative contribution to self-reflection. Since most prior work had used trait adjectives as stimuli, it is possible that coactivation of these structures reflects the fact that knowledge of one's own traits might be associated with retrieval of both concrete and abstract aspects of self-knowledge (or episodic and semantic aspects of self-knowledge).

The work just summarized takes a more nuanced approach and shows that having subjects focus on more concrete aspects of themselves (appearance, Moran et al., 2011; duties and obligations, Johnson et al., 2006) leads to preferential activation of the pCC. Conversely, having subjects focus on more abstract aspects of themselves (character traits, Moran et al., 2011; hopes and dreams, Johnson et al., 2006) leads to *preferential* activation of the mPFC. Since there is evidence that episodic knowledge and semantic self-knowledge are indeed distinct cognitive processes (Klein et al., 1999), it follows that there should be brain systems that are preferentially engaged by aspects of the self that are more reliant on concrete, episodic experiences (e.g., knowledge of one's appearance) and systems that are preferentially engaged by aspects of the self that are more about abstracted, semantic memory structures (e.g., knowledge of one's traits). One prediction of this theory is that traits that vary in the degree to which participants can recall specific episodes about them should vary in the degree to which they activate pCC (more for more trait-relevant episodes) and mPFC (less for less trait-relevant episodes).

A Role for mPFC in Abstracted, Semantic Representations

Consistent with the idea that mPFC might be more specifically associated with abstracted, semantic representations, many recent studies have demonstrated activation in this region by use of multiply different experimental paradigms and task domains, in addition to those encouraging self-referential processing. In agreement with this theoretical position, Mitchell (2009) has argued for a role for mPFC in "fuzzy" aspects of social cognition. Support for this assertion comes from work by Jenkins and Mitchell (2010), who demonstrated that mPFC is activated more when participants mentalize about people's ambiguous than about their unambiguous mental states. Mitchell's position helps clarify some of the disparate experimental contrasts that have been linked with increased activity in mPFC, detailed below:

• Evaluative vs. semantic judgments (Zysset, Huber, Samson, Ferstl, & von Cramon, 2003)
• Episodic vs. semantic judgments (Zysset, ahuber, Ferstl, & von Cramon, 2002)
• Listening to one's own voice (McGuire, Paulesu, Frackowiak, & Frith, 1996)
• Prediction error signal after someone lies to you (Behrens, Hunt, Woolrich, & Rushworth, 2008)
• Hearing one's own name and making eye contact (Kampe, Frith, & Frith, 2003)
• Remembering perceived vs. imagined items (Simons, Davis, Gilbert, Frith, & Burgess, 2006)
• Remembering internally generated vs. provided words (Vinogradov et al., 2006)
• Answering autobiographical vs. nonautobiographical questions (Nunez, Casey, Egner, Hare, & Hirsch, 2005)
• Positive correlation during simple tasks with mind wandering (Mason et al., 2007)
• Attending to internal vs. external aspects of the environment (Lane, Fink, Chau, & Dolan, 1997)
• Internal vs. external subjective decisions (Johnson et al., 2005)

- Watching others suffer the effects of one's retaliation (Lotze, Veit, Anders, & Birbaumer, 2007)
- Reading stories about intentional violation of social norms (Berthoz, Armony, Blair, & Dolan, 2002)
- Focused vs. random episodic recall (Andreasen, O'Leary, Cizadlo, Arndt, & Rezai, 1995)
- Retrieving affectively laden autobiographical memories (Fink et al., 1996)
- Motivated emotion regulation (Westen, Blagov, Harenski, Kilts, & Hamann, 2006)
- Self-as-object of a third party's attention (Schilbach et al., 2006)
- Taking a first- vs. third-person perspective (Vogeley et al., 2004)
- Viewing real-time interactions between third parties (Saxe, Xiao, Kovacs, Perrett, & Kanwisher, 2004)
- Reading false belief stories vs. false physical descriptions (Saxe & Kanwisher, 2003)
- Empathic processing (for a review, see Seitz, Nickel, & Azari, 2006)
- Playing economic games (McCabe, Houser, Ryan, Smith, & Trouard, 2001; Rilling, Sanfey, Aronson, Nystrom, & Cohen, 2004)
- Following the recognition heuristic (Volz et al., 2006)
- Deciding whether to buy items on the basis of price (Knutson, Rick, Wimmer, Prelec, & Loewenstein, 2007)
- Viewing culturally familiar vs. unfamiliar car brands (Schaefer, Berens, Heinze, & Rotte, 2006)
- Allowing beliefs to bias logical processing (Goel & Dolan, 2003)
- "Hot" vs. "cold" emotional reasoning (Goel & Dolan, 2004)
- Moral vs. semantic decision-making (Heekeren, Wartenburger, Schmidt, Schwintowski, & Villringer, 2003)
- Moral vs. basic emotion-processing (Moll et al., 2002)
- Resolving personal vs. impersonal moral dilemmas (Greene, Sommerville, Nystrom, Darley, & Cohen, 2001)
- Intending to deceive (Grezes, Frith, & Passingham, 2004; Walter et al., 2004)
- Judging stimulus beauty vs. judging stimulus symmetry (Jacobsen, Schubotz, Hofel, & von Cramon, 2006)
- Representing ongoing levels of reward for self and others (Zaki & Mitchell, 2011)

As can be seen from this list, the sources of activation for mPFC are manifold. One characteristic common to all of these contrasts, however, is the involvement of self in the condition eliciting mPFC activation, paired with a lack of (or decrease in) self-involvement in the condition being contrasted against.

"Self-involvement" is a vague concept at best and requires some definition. We regard self-involvement as the cognitive activity that is involved in accessing aspects of the self-concept (semantic memory schemata) in the service of whatever task one is currently engaged in. This function could involve reflection upon one's own traits ("am I indecisive?"), looking up answers to personal semantic facts (e.g., "my hometown is Boston"), updating the self-concept ("since trying Ethiopian food, I have become more worldly"), or retrieving autobiographical episodic memories that prime the retrieval of associated semantic memories. When thinking about others, we may often use a process of simulation, whereby we think about others in relation to our own selves (e.g., Mitchell, 2005). While the account that simulating others' minds through accessing our own does not hold true for all situations in which we think about others (e.g., Saxe, 2005), the data do suggest that (a) we engage in simulation when we think about others who are similar to ourselves, and (b) this is associated with mPFC activation (Mitchell et al., 2006). Thus, much of the source of activation for paradigms in which participants are thinking primarily about others could be a reliance on simulating the others' beliefs, desires, and so on by accessing their own beliefs and desires. Indeed, whether we are playing economic games (McCabe et al., 2001), watching others suffer the effects of one's retaliation (Lotze et al., 2007), engaging in moral or basic emotional reasoning (Moll et al., 2002), or representing another's false beliefs (Saxe & Kanwisher, 2003), the key commonality is that we must access our own understanding of the current state of the world in order to respond successfully in each situation.

Conclusions

The sum of the research presented here on self and other suggests several conclusions:

1. The mPFC and pCC seem to form a functional unit that is engaged when we think about ourselves.

2. This network is engaged particularly by information that holds relevance for the self.

3. These structures respond more when we think about ourselves than about other people, unless the characteristics of others we are considering are part of our own self-concept.

4. The involvement of mPFC and pCC in self-reflection is dissociable along the lines of thinking about abstract and concrete aspects of ourselves.

5. mPFC may serve as a central node in a special, superordinate, semantic network of self that is activated in service of many tasks that include some reflection on the self as a task component.

Future research should aim to compare multiple different kinds of tasks that encourage activation of the semantic network of self and of semantic networks of other individuals, to provide evidence that there may indeed be separable neural processing components that differentiate between ourselves and the external social and physical worlds.

References

Adolphs, R. (2001). The neurobiology of social cognition. *Current Opinion in Neurobiology, 11*(2), 231–239.

Amaral, D. G., & Price, J. L (1984). Amygdalo-cortical projections in the monkey (*Macaca fascicularis*). *Journal of Comparative Neurology, 230*(4), 465–496.

Andreasen, N. C., O'Leary, D. S., Cizadlo, T., Arndt, S., & Rezai, K. (1995). Remembering the past: Two facets of episodic memory explored with positron emission tomography. *American Journal of Psychiatry, 152*, 1576–1585.

Arikuni, T., Sako, H., & Murata, A. (1994). Ipsilateral connections of the anterior cingulate cortex with the frontal and medial temporal cortices in the macaque monkey. *Neuroscience Research, 21*(1), 19–39.

Aron, A., Aron, E. N., Tudor, M., & Nelson, G. (1991). Close relationships as including other in the self. *Journal of Personality and Social Psychology, 60*(2), 241–253.

Barbas, H., & Pandya, D. N. (1989). Architecture and intrinsic connections of the prefrontal cortex in the rhesus-monkey. *Journal of Comparative Neurology, 286*(3), 353–375.

Baumeister, R. F. (1998). The self. In D. T. Gilbert, S. T. Fiske, & G. Lindzey (Eds.), *Handbook of social psychology* (4th ed., pp. 680–740). New York: McGraw-Hill.

Behrens, T. E. J., Hunt, L. T., Woolrich, M. W., & Rushworth, M. F. S. (2008). Associative learning of social value. *Nature, 456*(7219), 245–249.

Berthoz, S., Armony, J. L., Blair, R. J. R., & Dolan, R. J. (2002). An fMRI study of intentional and unintentional (embarrassing) violation of social norms. *Brain, 125*, 1696–1708.

Cavanna, A. E., & Trimble, M. R. (2006). The precuneus: A review of its functional anatomy and behavioural correlates. *Brain, 129*, 564–583.

Craik, F. I. M., Moroz, T., Moscovitch, M., Stuss, D., Winocur, G., Tulving, E., & Kapur, S. (1999). In search of the self: A positron emission tomography study. *Psychological Science, 10*, 26–34.

Damasio A. (1999). *The feeling of what happens: Body and emotion in the making of consciousness*. New York: Harcourt Brace.

d'Argembeau, A., Collette, F., Van der Linden, M., Laureys, S., Del Fiore, G., Degueldre, C., Luxen, A., & Salmon, E. (2005). Self-referential reflective activity and its relationship with rest: A PET study. *Neuroimage, 25*, 616–624.

d'Argembeau, A., & Salmon, E. (2012). The neural basis of semantic and episodic forms of self-knowledge: Insights from functional neuroimaging. *Advances in Experimental Medicine and Biology, 239*, 276–290.

Denny, B. T., Kober H., Wager, T. D., & Ochsner, K. N. (2012). A meta-analysis of functional neuroimaging studies of self- and other judgments reveals a spatial gradient for mentalizing in medial prefrontal cortex. *Journal of Cognitive Neuroscience, 24*(8), 1742–1752.

Fink, G. R., Markowitsch, H. J., Reinkemeier, M., Bruckbauer, T., Kessler, J., & Heiss, W. D. (1996). Cerebral representation of one's own past: Neural networks involved in autobiographical memory. *Journal of Neuroscience, 16*, 4275–4282.

Fossati, P., Hevenor, S. J., Lepage, M., Graham, S. J., Grady, C., Keightley, M. L., et al. (2004). Distributed self in episodic memory: Neural correlates of successful retrieval of self-encoded positive and negative personality traits. *Neuroimage, 22*, 1596–1604.

Goel, V., & Dolan, R. J. (2003). Differential involvement of left prefrontal cortex in inductive and deductive reasoning. *Cognition, 93*(3), B109–B121.

Goel, V., & Dolan, R. J. (2004). Reciprocal neural response within lateral and ventral medial prefrontal cortex during hot and cold reasoning. *Neuroimage, 20*(4), 2314–2321.

Goldman-Rakic, P. S. (1987). Circuitry of the primate prefrontal cortex and the regulation of behavior by representational memory. In F. Plum & V. Mountcastle (Eds.), *Handbook of physiology: The nervous system, Vol. V.* (pp. 373–417). Bethesda, MD: American Physiological Society.

Greene, J. D., Sommerville, R. B., Nystrom, L. E., Darley, J. M., & Cohen, J. D. (2001). An fMRI investigation of emotional engagement in moral judgment. *Science, 293*(5537), 2105–2108.

Greenwald, A. G., & Banaji, M. R. (1989). The self as a memory system: Powerful, but ordinary. *Journal of Personality and Social Psychology, 57*, 41–54.

Grezes, J., Frith, C., & Passingham, R. E. (2004). Brain mechanisms for inferring deceit in the actions of others. *Journal of Neuroscience, 24*, 5500–5505.

Gusnard, D. A., Akbudak, E., Shulman, G. L., & Raichle, M. E. (2001). Medial prefrontal cortex and self-referential mental activity: Relation to a default mode of brain function. *Proceedings of the National Academy of Sciences U S A, 98*, 4259–4264.

Han, S., Gu, X., Mao, L., Ge, J., Wang, G., & Ma, Y. (2010). Neural substrates of self-referential processing in Chinese Buddhists. *Social, Cognitive & Affective Neuroscience, 5*, 332–339.

Heatherton, T. F., Macrae, C. N., & Kelley, W. M. (2004). A social brain sciences approach to studying the self. *Current Directions in Psychological Science, 13*, 190–193.

Heatherton, T. F., Wyland, C. L., Macrae, C. N., Demos, K. E., Denny, B. T., & Kelley, W. M. (2006). Medial prefrontal activity differentiates self from close others. *Social, Cognitive & Affective Neuroscience, 1*, 18.

Heekeren, H. R., Wartenburger, I., Schmidt, H., Schwintowski, H. P., & Villringer, A. (2003). An fMRI study of simple ethical decision-making. *Neuroreport 14*(9), 1215–1219.

Jacobs, B., Schall, M. Prather, M., Kapler, E., Driscoll, L., Baca, S., et al. (2001). Dendritic spine variation in human cerebral cortex: A quantitative Golgi study. *Cerebral Cortex, 11*(6), 558–571.

Jacobsen, T., Schubotz, R. I., Hofel, L., & von Cramon, D. Y. (2006). Brain correlates of aesthetic judgment of beauty. *Neuroimage 29*(1), 276–285.

James, W. (1890). *Principles of psychology* (Vol. 1). New York: Henry-Holt and Co.

Jenkins, A. C., Macrae, C. N., & Mitchell, J. P. (2008). Repetition suppression of ventromedial prefrontal activity during judgments of self and others. *Proceedings of the National Academy of Sciences U S A, 105*(11), 4507–4512.

Jenkins, A. C., & Mitchell, J. P. (2010). Mentalizing under uncertainty: Dissociated neural responses to ambiguous and unambiguous mental state inferences. *Cerebral Cortex, 20*(2), 404–410.

Johnson, M. K., Raye, C. L., Mitchell, K. J., Touryan, S. R., Greene, E. J., & Nolen-Hoeksema, S. (2006). Dissociating medial frontal and posterior cingulate activity during self-reflection. *Social, Cognitive & Affective Neuroscience, 1*, 56.

Johnson, S. C., Baxter, L. C., Wilder, L. S., Pipe, J. G., Heiserman, J. E., & Prigatano, G. P. (2002). Neural correlates of self reflection. *Brain, 125*, 1808–1814.

Johnson, S. C., Schmitz, T. W., Kawahara-Baccus, T. N., Rowley, H. A., Alexander A. L., Lee J. H., & Davidson R. J. (2005). The cerebral response during subjective choice with and without self-reference. *Journal of Cognitive Neuroscience, 17*, 1897–1906.

Kampe, K. K. W., Frith, C. D., & Frith, U. (2003). "Hey John": Signals conveying communicative intention toward the self activate brain regions associated with "mentalizing," regardless of modality. *Journal of Neuroscience, 23*(12), 5258–5263.

Kelley, W. M., Macrae, C. N., Wyland, C. L., Caglar, S., Inati, S., & Heatherton, T. F. (2002). Finding the self? An event-related fMRI study. *Journal of Cognitive Neuroscience, 14*, 785–794.

Kitayama, S., & Park, J. (2010). Cultural neuroscience of the self: Understanding the social grounding of the brain. *Social, Cognitive & Affective Neuroscience, 5*, 111–129.

Kjaer, T. W., Nowak, M., & Lou, H. C. (2002). Reflective self-awareness and conscious states: PET evidence for a common midline parietofrontal core. *Neuroimage, 17*(2), 1080–1086.

Klein, S. B., Chan, R. L., & Loftus, J. (1999). Independence of episodic and semantic self-knowledge: The case from autism. *Social Cognition, 17*, 413–436.

Klein, S. B., Cosmides, L., Costabile, K. A., & Mei, L. (2002). Is there something special about the self? A neuropsychological case study. *Journal of Research in Personality, 36*, 490–506.

Klein, S. B., Loftus, J., & Kihlstrom, J. F. (1996). Self-knowledge of an amnesic patient: Toward a neuropsychology of personality and social psychology. *Journal of Experimental Psychology. General, 125*(3), 250–260.

Klein, S. B., Rozendal, K., & Cosmides, L. (2002). A social-cognitive neuroscience analysis of the self. *Social Cognition, 20*(2), 105–135.

Knutson, B., Rick, S., Wimmer, G. E., Prelec, D., & Loewenstein, G. (2007). Neural predictors of purchases. *Neuron, 53*(1), 147–156.

Krienen, F., Tu, P.-C., & Buckner, R. L. (2010). Clan mentality: Evidence that the medial prefrontal cortex responds to close others. *Journal of Neuroscience, 30*(41), 13906–13915.

Lane, R. D., Fink, G. R., Chau, P. M., & Dolan, R. J. (1997). Neural activation during selective attention to subjective emotional responses. *Neuroreport, 8*, 3969–3972.

LeDoux, J., (2002). *Synaptic self: How our brain become who we are.* New York: Viking.

Lotze, M., Veit, R., Anders, S., & Birbaumer, N. (2007). Evidence for a different role of the ventral and dorsal medial prefrontal cortex for social reactive aggression: An interactive fMRI study. *Neuroimage, 34*(1), 470–478.

Lou, H. C., Luber, B., Crupain, M., Keenan, J. P., Nowka, M., Kjaer, T. W., Sackeim, H., & Lisanby, S. H. (2004). Parietal cortex and representation of the mental self. *Proceedings of the National Academy of Sciences U S A, 101*(17), 6827–6832.

Macrae, C. N., Kelley, W. M., & Heatherton, T. F. (2004). A self less ordinary: The medial prefrontal cortex and you. In M. S. Gazzaniga (Ed.), *Cognitive neurosciences III* (pp. 1067–1076). Cambridge, MA: MIT Press.

Macrae, C. N., Moran, J. M., Heatherton, T. F., Banfield, J. F., & Kelley, W. M. (2004). Medial prefrontal activity predicts memory for self. *Cerebral Cortex, 14*, 647–654.

Maki, R. H., & McCaul, K. D. (1985). The effects of self-reference versus other reference on the recall of traits and nouns. *Bulletin of the Psychonomic Society, 23*, 169–172.

Markus, H. (1977). Self-schemata and processing information about the self. *Journal of Personality and Social Psychology, 35*, 63–78.

Mason, M. F., Norton, M. I., Van Horn, J. D., Wegner, D. M., Grafton, S. T., & Macrae, C. N. (2007). Wandering minds: The default network and stimulus-independent thought. *Science, 315*, 393–395.

McCabe, K., Houser, D., Ryan, L., Smith, V., & Trouard, T. (2001). A functional imaging study of cooperation in two-person reciprocal exchange. *Proceedings of the National Academy of Sciences U S A, 98*, 11832–11835.

McGuire, P. K., Paulesu, E., Frackowiak, R. S., & Frith, C. D. (1996). Brain activity during stimulus independent thought. *Neuroreport, 7*, 2095–2099.

McKiernan, K. A., D'Angelo, B. R., Kaufman, J. N., & Binder, J. R. (2006). Interrupting the "stream of consciousness": An fMRI investigation. *Neuroimage, 29*, 1185–1191.

McKiernan, K. A., Kaufman, J. N., Kucera-Thompson, J., & Binder, J. R. (2003). A parametric manipulation of factors affecting task-induced deactivation in functional neuroimaging. *Journal of Cognitive Neuroscience, 15*, 394–408.

Mitchell, J. P. (2005). The false dichotomy between simulation and theory-theory: The argument's error. *Trends in Cognitive Sciences, 9*(8), 363–364.

Mitchell, J. P. (2009). Social psychology as a natural kind. *Trends in Cognitive Sciences, 13*(6), 246–251.

Mitchell, J. P., Macrae, C. N., & Banaji, M. R. (2006). Dissociable medial prefrontal contributions to judgments of similar and dissimilar others. *Neuron, 50*(4) 655–663.

Mitchell, K. J., Raye, C. L., Ebner, N. C., Tubridy, S. M., Frankel, H., & Johnson, M. K. (2009). Age-group differences in medial cortex activity associated with thinking about self-relevant agendas. *Psychological Aging, 24*(2), 438–449.

Moll, J., de Olveira-Souza, R., Eslinger, P. J., Bramati, I. E., Mourao-Miranda, J., Adnreiuolo, P. A., & Pessoa, L. (2002). The neural correlates of moral sensitivity: A functional magnetic resonance imaging investigation of basic and moral emotions. *Journal of Neuroscience, 22*(7), 2730–2736.

Moran, J. M., Heatherton, T. F., & Kelley, W. M. (2009). Modulation of cortical midline structures by implicit and explicit self-relevance evaluation. *Social Neuroscience, 4*(3), 197–211.

Moran, J. M., Lee, S. M., & Gabrieli, J. D. E. (2011). Dissociable neural systems supporting knowledge about human character and appearance in ourselves and others. *Journal of Cognitive Neuroscience, 23,* 2222–2230.

Moran, J. M., Macrae, C. N., Heatherton, T. F., Wyland, C. L., & Kelley, W. M. (2006). Neuroanatomical evidence for distinct cognitive and affective components of self. *Journal of Cognitive Neuroscience, 18,* 1586–1594.

Moran, M. A., Mufson, E. J., & Mesulam, M. M. (1987). Neural inputs into the temporopolar cortex of the rhesus monkey. *Journal of Comparative Neurology, 256*(1), 88–103.

Morecraft, R. J., & Van Hoesen, G. W. (1993). Frontal granular cortex input to the cingulate (M3), supplementary (M2) and primary (M1) motor cortices in the rhesus monkey. *Journal of Comparative Neurology, 337*(4), 669–689.

Murray, R. J., Schaer, M., & Debbané, M. (2012). Degrees of separation: A quantitative neuroimaging meta-analysis investigating self-specificity and shared neural activation between self- and other-reflection. *Neuroscience and Biobehavioral Reviews, 36*(3), 1043–1059.

Northoff, G., & Bermpohl, F. (2004). Cortical midline structures and the self. *Trends in Cognitive Sciences, 8,* 102–107.

Northoff, G., Heinzel, A., de Greck, M., Bermpohl, F., Dobrowolny, H., & Panksepp, J. (2006). Self-referential processing in our brain. *Neuroimage, 31*(1), 440–457.

Nunez, J. M., Casey, B. J., Egner, T., Hare, T., & Hirsch, J. (2005). Intentional false responding shares neural substrates with response conflict and cognitive control. *Neuroimage, 25*(1), 267–277.

Ochsner, K. N., Beer, J. S., Robertson, E. R., Cooper, J. C., Gabrieli, J. D. E., Kihlstrom, J. F., & D'Esposito, M. (2005). The neural correlates of direct and reflected self-knowledge. *Neuroimage, 28,* 797–814.

Ongur, D., Ferry, A. T., & Price, J. L. (2003). Architectonic subdivision of the human orbital and medial prefrontal cortex. *Journal of Comparative Neurology, 460*(3), 425–449.

Passingham, R. E., Stephan, K. E., & Kotter, R. (2002). The anatomical basis of functional localization in the cortex. *Nature Reviews Neuroscience, 3*(8), 606–616.

Petrides, M., & Pandya, D. N. (1999). Dorsolateral prefrontal cortex: Comparative cytoarchitectonic analysis in the human and the macaque brain and corticocortical connection patterns. *European Journal of Neuroscience, 11*(3), 1011–1036.

Pfeifer, J. H., Lieberman, M. D., & Dapretto, M. (2007). "I know you are but what am I?!": Neural bases of self- and social knowledge retrieval in children and adults. *Journal of Cognitive Neuroscience, 19,* 1323–1337.

Phan, K. L., Taylor, S. F., Welsh, R. C., Ho, S. H., Britton, J. C., & Liberzon, I. (2004). Neural correlates of individual ratings of emotional salience: A trial-related fMRI study. *Neuroimage, 21,* 768–780.

Raichle, M. E., MacLeod, A. M., Snyder, A. Z., Powers, W. J., Gusnard, D. A., & Shulman, G. L. (2001). A default mode of brain function. *Proceedings of the National Academy of Sciences U S A, 98,* 676–682.

Rameson, L. T., Satpute, A. B., & Lieberman, M. D. (2010). The neural correlates of implicit and explicit self-relevant processing. *NeuroImage, 50,* 701–708.

Rilling, J. K., Sanfey, A. G., Aronson, J. A., Nystrom, L. E., & Cohen, J. D. (2004). The neural correlates of theory of mind within interpersonal interactions. *Neuroimage, 22,* 1694–1703.

Rogers, T. B., Kuiper, N. A., & Kirker, W. S. (1977). Self-reference and the encoding of personal information. *Journal of Personality and Social Psychology, 35*(9), 677.

Saxe, R. (2005). Against simulation: The argument from error. *Trends in Cognitive Sciences, 9*(4), 174–179.

Saxe, R., & Kanwisher, N. (2003). People thinking about thinking people—the role of the right temporo-parietal junction in theory of mind. *Neuroimage, 19*(4), 1835–1842.

Saxe, R., Xiao, D. K., Kovacs, G., Perrett, D. I., & Kanwisher N. (2004). A region of right posterior superior temporal sulcus responds to observed intentional actions. *Neuropsychologia, 42*(11), 1435–1446.

Schaefer, M., Berens, H., Heinze, H. J., & Rotte, M. (2006). Neural correlates of culturally familiar brands of car manufacturers, *Neuroimage, 31,* 861–865.

Schilbach, L., Wohschlaeger, A. M., Kraemer, N. C., Newen, A., Shah, N. J., Fink, G. R., & Vogeley, K. (2006). Being with virtual others: Neural correlates of social interaction. *Neuropsychologia, 44,* 718–730.

Schmitz, T. W., Kawahara-Baccus, T. N., & Johnson, S. C. (2004). Metacognitive evaluation, self-relevance, and the right prefrontal cortex. *Neuroimage, 22*(2), 941–947.

Seger, C. A., Stone, M., & Keenan, J. P. (2004). Cortical activations during judgments about the self and another person. *Neuropsychologia, 42*(9), 1168–1177.

Seitz, R. J., Nickel, J., & Azari, N. P. (2006). Functional modularity of the medial prefrontal cortex: Involvement in human empathy. *Neuropsychology, 20*(6), 743–751.

Semendeferi, K., Armstrong, E., Schleicher, A., Zilles, K., & Van Hoesen G. W. (2001). Prefrontal cortex in humans and apes: A comparative study of area 10. *American Journal of Physical Anthroplogy, 114*(3), 224–241.

Shulman, G. L., Fiez, J. A., Corbetta, M., Buckner, R. L., Miezin, F. M., Raichle, M. E., & Petersen, S.E. (1997). Common blood flow changes across visual tasks: II. Decreases in cerebral cortex. *Journal of Cognitive Neuroscience, 9,* 648–663.

Simons, J. S., Davis, S. W., Gilbert, S. J., Frith, C. D., & Burgess, P. W. (2006). Discriminating imagined from perceived information engages brain areas implicated in schizophrenia. *Neuroimage, 32*(2), 696–703.

Singer, J. L., & Antrobus, J. S. (1972). Daydreaming, imaginal processes, and personality: A normative study. In P. W. Sheehan (Ed.), *The nature and function of imagery* (pp. 175–202). New York: Academic Press.

Symons, C. S., & Johnson, B. T. (1997). The self-reference effect in memory: A mcta-analysis. *Psychology Bulletin, 121,* 371–394.

Tulving, E. (1985). Memory and consciousness. *Canadian Psychology, 26,* 1–12.

Tulving, E. (1993). Self-knowledge of an amnesic individual is represented abstractly. In T. K. Srull & R. S. Wyer, Jr. (Eds.), *The mental representation of trait and autobiographical knowledge about the self* (pp. 147–156). Hillsdale, NJ: Erlbaum.

Vinogradov, S., Luks, T. L., Simpson, G. V., Schulman, B. J., Glenn, S., & Wong, A. E. (2006). Brain activation patterns during memory of cognitive agency. *Neuroimage, 31*(2), 896–905.

Vogeley, K., May, M., Ritzl, A., Falkai, P., Zilles, K., & Fink G. R. (2004). Neural correlates of first-person perspective as one constituent of human self-consciousness. *Journal of Cognitive Neuroscience, 16*(5), 817–827.

Volz, K. G., Schooler, L. J., Schubotz, R. I., Raab, M., Gigerenzer, G., & von Cramon, D. Y. (2006). Why you think Milan is larger than Modena: Neural correlates of the recognition heuristic. *Journal of Cognitive Neuroscience, 18*(11), 1924–1936.

Walter, H., Adenzato, M., Ciaramidaro, A., Enrici, I., Pia, L., & Bara, B. G. (2004). Understanding intentions in social interaction: the role of the anterior paracingulate cortex. *Journal of Cognitive Neuroscience, 16*, 1854–1863.

Westen, D., Blagov, P. S., Harenski, K., Kilts, C., & Hamann, S. (2006). Neural bases of motivated reasoning: An fMRI study of emotional constraints on partisan political judgment in the 2004 US Presidential election. *Journal of Cognitive Neuroscience, 18*(11), 1947–1958.

Whitfield-Gabrieli, S., Moran, J. M., Nieto-Castanon, A., Triantafyllou, C., Saxe, R., & Gabrieli, J. D. E. (2011). Associations and dissociations between default and self-reference networks in the human brain. *Neuroimage, 55*, 225–232.

Wicker, B., Ruby, P., Royet, J. P., & Fonlupt, P. (2003). A relation between rest and self in the brain. *Brain Research Review 43*, 224–230.

Ying, Z., & Li, Z. (2002). An experimental study on the self-reference effect. *Science in China Series C: Life Sciences 45*, 120–128.

Zaki, J., & Mitchell, J. P. (2011). Equitable decision making is associated with neural markers of intrinsic value. *Proceedings of the National Academy of Sciences U S A, 108*, 19761–19766.

Zhang, L., Zhou, T., Zhang, J., Liu, Z., Fan, J., & Zhu, Y. (2006). In search of the Chinese self: An fMRI study. *Science in China Series C: Life Sciences, 49* (1), 89–96.

Zysset, S., Huber, O., Ferstl, E. C., & von Cramon, D. Y. (2002). The anterior frontomedian cortex and evaluative judgment: An fMRI study. *Neuroimage, 15*, 983–991.

Zysset, S., Huber, O., Samson, A., Ferstl, E. C., & von Cramon, D. Y. (2003). Functional specialization within the anterior medial prefrontal cortex: A functional magnetic resonance imaging study with human subjects. *Neuroscience Letters 335*, 183–186.

Perception of Nonverbal Cues

Aina Puce

Abstract

Nonverbal cues are read signals from changes in another's behavior that do *not* involve speech or verbalization. We evaluate visual nonverbal cues, such as facial, head, hand, or body movements, as well as auditory, tactile, or olfactory cues. Nonverbal cues can be evaluated consciously or unconsciously, with chemosensory signals perhaps playing an important role in this process and not available to conscious awareness. Brain regions selectively responsive to nonverbal cues in others can be activated when we ourselves have similar affective or social experiences—this may include autonomic nervous system responses and electromyographic activity in facial muscles appropriate to the emotion being viewed. Nonverbal cues or signals can be intentional or unintentional on the part of the sender, and an intentional cue can be sent to deceive another. Ambiguities in received input might be caused by conflicting information sent across nonverbal and verbal dimensions. Similarly, anomalous or socially inappropriate cues might be received from individuals who have disorders of social cognition who may themselves be unable to evaluate social cues from others. This chapter discusses these various aspects of nonverbal cue perception and, at the end of the chapter, addresses some of the many unanswered questions in this exciting new area in social neuroscience.

Key Words: nonverbal cues, gaze, facial motion, hand actions, body motion, vocalizations, chemosensory signaling, pupil size, unconscious awareness

Introduction

How many times have we not heard someone complain that they are not a "mind reader" during a misunderstanding with another individual? Most of the time it is probably better to not know what is really on someone else's mind. However, being the curious human primates that we are, we continually try to infer what another individual might be thinking and feeling in everyday life. We do so from the inadvertent or deliberate nonverbal and verbal cues that we receive from others. In this context, *nonverbal cues* are incoming signals of changes in another's behavior that do *not* involve speech or verbalization.

We often evaluate visual nonverbal cues, such as facial, head, hand, or body movements—for example, a bowed head or a clenched fist. As visual primates, we notice these cues; however, the power of auditory, tactile, or olfactory cues should not be underestimated. Figure 10.1 illustrates how nonverbal cues from *multiple senses* might be sampled and interpreted over the course of a pleasant social interaction in which two individuals meet each other for the very first time. Visual, auditory, tactile, and olfactory cues may be evaluated consciously or unconsciously, and chemosensory signals might play an important role and not be available to conscious awareness. Nonverbal cues or signals can be intentional or unintentional on the part of the sender. An intentional cue might be sent to deceive another. Deception might be involved in some interactions, or the social messages being sent might be aberrant and awkward.

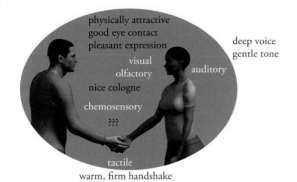

physically attractive
good eye contact
pleasant expression

deep voice
gentle tone

visual
olfactory

auditory

nice cologne

chemosensory

???

tactile

warm, firm handshake

Figure 10.1 Some nonverbal sensory cues that might influence an initial social interaction. Visual, auditory, olfactory, and tactile inputs (white print) might be evaluated consciously by a female protagonist (right) to form the impressions listed in the figure (in black print). Chemosensory signals (incoming via the olfactory system) as well as cues from other modalities might also be evaluated unconsciously.

A number of important issues underpin the study of nonverbal cues. This chapter is organized along the lines of some of the general themes, each of which straddles a number of subareas. First, the more elementary aspects of nonverbal cues are dealt with, such as interpreting visual face and body motion and vocalizations of others. Nonverbal cues from other sensory modalities are also addressed. Next, unconscious nonverbal cue perception is examined, an important source of information that can greatly affect our behavior. This perception may also come in the form of chemosensory signaling. Unintentional and intentional nonverbal cue production is discussed next, including the sending of a cue to deceive another. Additionally, ambiguities in nonverbal cue perception and interpretation are discussed. Both normal and aberrant cue perception are considered. Observer and observed synchrony is discussed in terms of how it affects a social interaction. Finally, some unanswered questions regarding nonverbal cue perception are posed at the end of the chapter, in the hope of encouraging further work in this exiting new discipline of social neuroscience.

Basic Underpinnings of Perception and Interpretation of Nonverbal Cues

Our ability to watch or play sports or appreciate many of the performing arts relies on the ability to effortlessly decode visual nonverbal cues sent by the athlete's or performer's body, irrespective of whether we ourselves have expertise in that particular type of activity or not (see, e.g., Pilgramm et al., 2010). The success of the motion picture industry originally relied on our visual-cue reading ability. Silent movie–era audiences were riveted by the (exaggerated) on-screen movements and antics of stars such as Charlie Chaplin and Buster Keaton, the latter being famous for keeping a completely expressionless face that was at odds with the situation in which his body found itself.

Our ability to understand the movements of others has fascinated visual scientists for many years. One very effective way of studying this question is to distill the very essence of human movement. In an ingenious experiment in the 1970s, Johansson dressed actors in black and placed them against a black background (Johansson, 1973). He attached white dots at the intersections formed by the joints on the body and filmed the actors as they moved. The point-light or "biological motion" movies he produced showed moving white dots that were unmistakably identified as (three-dimensional) human motion. This manipulation has formed the basis of many elegant contemporary psychophysical studies and has been used commonly in cognitive neuroscience in the explicit study of the neural mechanisms of biological motion (Beauchamp, Lee, Haxby, & Martin, 2003; Bonda, Petrides, Ostry, & Evans, 1996; Grossman & Blake, 2002; Petrini et al., 2011).

Human motion is complex, but the constraints imposed by human anatomy, the articulation of the joints, and the earth's gravitational force impart a certain predictability of the repertoire of motion that humans can produce (Cerveri et al., 2007; Smeesters, Hayes, & McMahon, 2007). Neuropsychological studies indicate that lesions of the occipitotemporal cortex can impair the ability to decode these visual nonverbal cues (Vaina & Gross, 2004), and a large number of neuroimaging studies have described focal brain activation in these same regions that is in response to viewing biological motion stimuli. Indeed, the posterior aspect of the superior temporal sulcus (pSTS) is consistently activated to these stimuli (for a good summary, see Deen & McCarthy, 2010). Interestingly, it has long been known that infants 4 to 6 months of age respond with preferential looking to biological motion stimuli (Fox & McDaniel, 1982). More recent evidence suggests that 8-month-old infants show differentiation in event-related potentials (ERPs) elicited in response to upright vs. inverted biological motion stimuli (Reid, Hoehl, & Striano, 2006).

Biological motion stimuli, which effectively capture the most essential and basic elements of human motion, however, lack important visual-form cues that can potentially enable us to interpret the subtleties of the actions of others. Stimuli depicting animations of avatar-based or real human movement to address these questions, while difficult to construct, have shown that the pSTS integrates visual form and motion (Puce et al., 2003) and can be active in response to human facial, hand, or body motion (Puce, Allison, Bentin, Gore, & McCarthy, 1998; Wheaton, Thompson, Syngeniotis, Abbott, & Puce, 2004), as is the premotor and inferior parietal cortex (Buccino et al., 2001; Wheaton et al., 2004). Body motion, or implied body motion from still images, has been shown to activate an inferior temporal extrastriate region of cortex in the vicinity of the posterior inferior temporal sulcus (ITS) that has come to be known as the extrastriate body area (EBA) (Astafiev, Stanley, Shulman, & Corbetta, 2004; Michels, Lappe, & Vaina, 2005; Schwarzlose, Baker, & Kanwisher, 2005).

While studies examining the EBA have argued that the activation reflects specialized processing for the human body, the sensitivity to human bodies and faces appears to be quite different. There is a known inversion effect for faces, in which face identity or other facial-information processing is impaired when an inverted face is viewed (Farah, Tanaka, & Drain, 1995). Neuroimaging studies have also demonstrated greater fMRI activation for upright than for inverted faces in fusiform gyrus (Kanwisher, Tong, & Nakayama, 1998). In contrast, N170 ERP activity is larger (but delayed) for inverted than for upright faces (Bentin, Allison, Puce, Perez, & McCarthy, 1996; Itier & Taylor, 2002; Rossion et al., 1999). Interestingly, an inversion effect is not observed when the head is removed from the body, which suggests that any inversion effect that might be observed when observing body motion is driven by the head and facial aspects of the stimulus (Brandman & Yovel, 2010). Yet, viewing upright and inverted human motion as depicted by an artist's wooden mannequin (with an oval head devoid of facial features) will activate the EBA (and the pSTS) to equal degrees (Thompson, Clarke, Stewart, & Puce, 2005). These data suggest that the features on the human head may activate this mechanism, underscoring the importance of the human head and face in interpreting others' behavior.

Over the years, a very large body of literature has stressed the importance of the face in human interactions, and different models for facial identity and emotion have been proposed (e.g., Adolphs, 2002; Bruce & Young, 1986; Farah, 1996; Hoffman &

Haxby, 2000). Traditionally, this literature has focused more on facial identity, in part because of the need to understand the basis for facial-recognition impairments, which can occur following a stroke or brain injury (Sorger, Goebel, Schiltz, & Rossion, 2007). Social interactions rely heavily on viewing changes in facial expression, and this focus begins early in life. Infants typically spend a lot of time gazing on the faces of others—any observed social interaction between an adult and an infant indicates this well enough. Human infants and toddlers go through a series of social developmental milestones during which the face and eyes are crucial to developing successful social interactions, the earliest being to learn to recognize that (1) eyes are an important part of the face, (2) eye gaze signals another's focus of attention, and (3) pointing with the finger can alter an observer's focus of attention (Farroni, Csibra, Simion, & Johnson, 2002; Farroni, Johnson, & Csibra, 2004; Henderson, Yoder, Yale, & McDuffie, 2002; Itier & Batty, 2009; Senju & Johnson, 2009; Wellman & Brandone, 2009).

The eyes and where they look, that is, an individual's social attention, are crucial for interpreting to whom a nonverbal cue is being directed. Strikingly, a preference for looking at eyes with direct gaze is already present in 2- to 5-day-old newborns (Farroni et al., 2002). Infants rely on their caregivers to nourish them and keep them warm and safe. Therefore, it is not surprising that direct gaze from another elicits longer preferential looking and more looks than an averted gaze, as well as ERPs that are larger to direct gaze in infants (Farroni et al., 2002). While direct gaze is clearly important in infants, infants ERPs are already preferentially modulated by averted gaze in the context of a fearful face (Hoehl & Striano, 2010). Adults typically are more sensitive to gaze aversion and can show larger ERPs to an averted than to a direct gaze (Puce, Smith, & Allison, 2000). This is in line with the idea that adults need to "keep an eye" not just on others in their sights but also on those in their surroundings. Having said that, there is a complex relationship between head and eye movements, as the head can face in one direction, but the eyes can look in another. In healthy adults, correlated fMRI activity between the fusiform gyrus and amygdala occurs in response to direct gaze, independent of head position (George, Driver, & Dolan, 2001). In contrast, averted gaze produces correlated activity between the fusiform gyrus and intraparietal sulcus, independent of head position (George et al., 2001). Data from ERP studies also indicate that the most important aspect of varied head or eye position is gaze direction, which elicits the strongest neurophysiological effects when gaze is direct and head position is averted (Conty, N'Diaye, Tijus, & George, 2007)

Thus far, visual cues have been discussed in terms of their importance in a social interaction. However, they are also powerful in that they can transcend distance, provided there is a line of sight between the sender and observer (e.g., de Gelder, 2006), which is crucial if the observer is out of earshot. In a similar vein, when there is no line of sight between individuals, auditory cues can link individuals. However, visual motion and sound rarely occur in isolation in everyday life—typically sounds accompany our actions, albeit in the form of vocalizations (including verbalizations) or sounds produced by hand or body actions. A number of neuroimaging studies have clearly identified preferential activation in the temporal cortex and amygdala elicited to human vocalizations (the so-called auditory face), particularly if the vocalization has emotional content (Belin, Zatorre, & Ahad, 2002; Belin, Zatorre, Lafaille, Ahad, & Pike, 2000; Fecteau, Belin, Joanette, & Armony, 2007). These regions of brain are also active in the presence of purely visual stimuli (Calvert et al., 1997) or audiovisual stimuli when the face (and mouth) is seen and the vocalization is heard. In this context, audiovisual speech has been studied (Campbell, 2008; Campbell et al., 2001). At a distance, however, the facial expression cannot always be clearly seen and may not always have an accompanying vocalization. In this case, emotions expressed by the body (e.g., fear, anger) can be readily identified and produce selective brain activation in a distinct brain network (de Gelder, 2006; Sinke, Sorger, Goebel, & de Gelder, 2010) that includes cortex that is sensitive to facial and hand movements (Kana & Travers, 2012; Wheaton et al., 2004).

When another individual is within one's reach, a tactile cue from another's arm movement into our personal space might serve as an intended social signal (Gallace & Spence, 2010). Typically, this type of cue is sent between individuals who are (nonsexually) comfortable with each other, who are sexually interested in one another, or who are already intimately familiar with one another (Moore, 2010). However, touch can also be a powerful nonverbal workplace cue when used by a dominant-status individual, such as a supervisor or boss. This type of action can have positive or negative consequences, depending on the context and the individuals concerned (Gallace & Spence, 2010). Given that touch is so important in social and dating situations, it is not surprising that it can create angst and discomfort in nonsexual situations such as the workplace.

Another potentially angst-creating cue can come in the olfactory modality. Strong smells such as lingering odors of cigarettes or cigars, garlic, or alcohol on the breath; sweat; and, to a lesser extent, strong perfume or cologne are rated as being unpleasant in a social interaction (Rosin, Tuorila, & Uutela, 1992). One would expect that this type of sensory bombardment might also produce a negative impression of the individual in question. However, the use of cologne or perfume to disguise body odors has been shown to impact positively and interact with visual cues in potential mate selection (Capparuccini, Berrie, & Mazzatenta, 2010).

Interestingly, one's surroundings can contribute to the judgments of others; for example, trustworthiness of other individuals may be increased in the presence of a "clean" smell in the room where the interaction is taking place (Liljenquist, Zhong, & Galinsky, 2010). To date, very little work has been done in this important area of research, perhaps in part because of the challenge of delivering a controlled stimulus in known quantities. Most of the literature on overtly detectable olfactory stimuli has dealt with plant or food odors (Levy et al., 1997; Rolls, Kringelbach, & de Araujo, 2003) rather than social stimuli such as fragrances and body odors. Preliminary work with human odorants does suggest that, in some human females, regions of the anterior inferior lateral prefrontal cortex (PFC) and pSTS respond more to odors of androstadienone (a component of male sweat) than to pleasant or unpleasant nonhuman odors (Gulyas, Keri, O'sullivan, Decety, & Roland, 2004). There is, however, a growing literature on the neural basis of unconscious odor perception and its importance to social interactions; this is discussed in the next section.

In summary, the human brain is equipped to preferentially deal with incoming sensory information from other humans, and some of these basic abilities are already available in rudimentary form to newborns and infants. Our brains have developed to integrate information from multiple sensory modalities, the integration of audiovisual speech being a prime example of how this ability has been distilled. Our ability to learn how to identify individuals, how to talk, and how to successfully interact with others, in terms of using socially acceptable rules, all hinge on our basic ability to learn from the nonverbal and verbal cues of our caregivers and others in our environment. These skills are continually called upon throughout life as we continue to learn new skills from others.

Unconscious vs. Conscious Nonverbal Cue Perception

Incoming cues that are not consciously perceived by the observer can influence subsequent decision-making. Such cues are investigated using experimental paradigms that implicitly test the attribute of interest (Ferguson & Bargh, 2004), and a number of attributes have been tested that are relevant to our discussion of unconsciously perceived nonverbal cues.

For human primates, one potentially underestimated and poorly studied nonverbal cue is that of chemosensory signaling—an important part of olfactory function for many animals (Touhara & Vosshall, 2009). Recent studies in humans are beginning to identify the functional neuroanatomy of our sensitivity to these subtle nonverbal cues, which typically are not accessible to conscious awareness. For instance, we are able to differentiate between emotional and physical stressors from chemosensory signals in the human sweat of others (Mujica-Parodi et al., 2009). This ability has been correlated with differential brain activation in the amygdala, despite participants being unable to explicitly discriminate between the two respective (generally odorless) stimuli when asked to. Orbitofrontal and fusiform cortices and hypothalamus are selectively active when women are exposed to sweat samples from sexually aroused men, but not when exposed to sweat samples obtained during other activities (Zhou & Chen, 2008). Similarly, men are responsive to chemosensory signals sent by ovulating women, which will trigger an increase in their testosterone levels (Miller & Maner, 2010). Studies such as these beg the question of how the receiver's behavior is altered when receiving these unconscious chemosensory signals from others. Prehn-Kristensen et al. (2009) reported the striking finding that unconscious perception of anxiety-related chemosensory signals in the sweat of others can trigger feelings of empathy in those being exposed to the chemosensory agent. This is an exciting new area of research that could potentially account for an important component of variance in social interaction studies. Findings thus far indicate clearly that these processes occur irrespective of whether we observe another individual sweating or not. A potentially important distinction to make in this line of work is the divide between chemosensory signaling itself (generated by the protagonist) and the neurochemical moderation of brain activity

in the observer. All of the studies discussed above fall into this latter category.

Another unconsciously evaluated nonverbal cue that can indicate an individual's stress or state of arousal is pupil size. Pupil size can increase as a function of anticipation (Bitsios, Szabadi, & Bradshaw, 2004), which can indicate a subject's state of arousal, but this tonic measure must be disentangled from phasic changes that occur as a result of individual visual-stimulus presentation (Granholm & Steinhauer, 2004). While pupil size is mediated by components of the autonomic nervous system, it is also altered as a function of local ambient light levels and the subject's depth of focus. An increase in sympathetic nervous system drive produces pupil dilation, whereas an increase in parasympathetic drive results in pupil constriction. As both components of the autonomic nervous system provide differential input to the pupillary control system, interpretation of pupil size changes is not a straightforward task (Steinhauer, Siegle, Condray, & Pless, 2004).

Recent neuroimaging investigations have made intriguing links between changes in pupil size to viewing potentially affective visual stimuli and amygdala activation. In a functional MRI study, male subjects passively viewed female faces whose pupils were presented at two different sizes (Demos, Kelley, Ryan, Davis, & Whalen, 2008). Amygdala activation was larger when viewing faces with larger pupils, even though the subjects did not report seeing any differences in pupil size in a post-scan debriefing session. The study's authors suggest that we may be sensitive to pupil size and the state of arousal of another individual without being aware that we are doing so. Harrison, Gray, and Critchley (2009) investigated this phenomenon in more detail and used an ingenious manipulation through which the pupil size of the stimulus face was made to vary with the subject's own pupil size while they viewed the visual stimulus display. In both of these studies, amygdala activation varied as a function of pupil size, despite subjects' not being aware that the pupils on the stimulus face had been manipulated. Earlier work by Harrison and colleagues demonstrated that "pupillary contagion" occurred when subjects viewed sad faces relative to neutral and other types of affective expressions: the observer's pupils shrank in size according to the stimuli being viewed (Harrison, Singer, Rotshtein, Dolan, & Critchley, 2006). This intriguing line of investigation has implications for potential differences in the processing of visually based affective stimuli and needs further study.

Another autonomically mediated nonverbal cue gleaned from others that might influence behavior is fear, an emotion closely linked with the flight-or-flight response and autonomic nervous system activity. The amygdala activates when healthy subjects observe this emotion in others (Fusar-Poli et al., 2009). Importantly, the amygdala activates when only a portion of a fearful face is presented in a manipulation but is not overtly perceived as such by the subject (e.g., Hardee, Thompson, & Puce, 2008). The amygdala is known for its response to fearful faces; however, consistent activation is also observed with faces depicting happiness and sadness (Fusar-Poli et al., 2009).

The amygdala, or amygdaloid complex, consists of at least nine nuclei. Probabilistic anatomical maps of the human amygdala, based on cytoarchitectonic criteria, have been constructed (Amunts et al., 2005). The human amygdala has been divided into broad relative anatomical subdivisions—the laterobasal, centromedial, and superficial subdivisions—based on fMRI studies examining resting-state connectivity (Roy et al., 2009), MRI investigations combining structural and functional information (Ball et al., 2007), and diffusion tensor imaging of white-matter terminating connections (Solano-Castiella et al., 2010). The lateral subdivision has been linked to changes in affect attention and vigilance, the medial subdivision to emotional novelty, and the central subdivision to the mediation of alimentary and gustatory behaviors (Knapska, Radwanska, Werka, & Kaczmarek, 2007). Different autonomic system inputs might also be expected across the subdivisions. If this is case in the human brain, then brain activation may occur in these regions when our own pupils change their size or when we observe these changes in others. Monitoring of pupil size and other autonomic variables, including heart-rate variability and electrodermal activity, is becoming more common in neuroimaging studies (Gray et al., 2009; Harrison et al., 2006; Iacovella & Hasson, 2011) and will no doubt provide valuable information on how the amygdala might influence our behavior in social situations that are highly pleasurable or very stressful.

Our ability to read nonverbal cues in others is somewhat at the mercy of the underlying state of our own autonomic nervous system and its neurochemistry. Some intriguing new research is beginning to highlight how specific changes in our neurochemistry, for example, via changes in oxytocin levels, can enhance or impair the ability to perceive nonverbal cues from others. Not surprisingly, we are unaware of these neurochemical changes and probably have no conscious control over them.

Oxytocin has been proposed to be a key factor in social behaviors involving a desire to seek affiliation and social approach and improved recognition of affective states in others (Heinrichs, von Dawans, & Domes, 2009; Ishak, Kahloon, & Fakhry, 2011). Oxytocin is a neuropeptide secreted in the hypothalamus (Buijs, De Vries, Van Leeuwen, & Swaab, 1983). In a study of 52 male subjects viewing neutral faces after receiving oxytocin or placebo, oxytocin increased the amount of time an individual spent looking at the eye region of a face (Guastella, Mitchell, & Dadds, 2008). Improved performance in "mind-reading" behavior has been reported following intranasal administration of oxytocin (Domes, Heinrichs, Michel, Berger, & Herpertz, 2007). In this double-blind placebo controlled study, 30 male participants were found to improve their performance on the Reading the Mind and the Eyes Test (Baron-Cohen, Wheelwright, Hill, Raste, & Plumb, 2001) following oxytocin administration.

Oxytocin is thought to modulate social cognition by altering activity levels in the amygdala (Kirsch et al., 2005). In a double blind study using oxytocin and placebo, male subjects had decreased amygdala activation to fear-inducing stimuli as a function of oxytocin administration. An fMRI study has shown that, following oxytocin administration, anterior portions of the amygdala have decreased activation to fearful faces and increased activation to happy faces (Gamer, Zurowski, & Buchel, 2010). In this same study, oxytocin administration linked with increased activation in the posterior subregions of the amygdala correlated with an increased tendency to gaze at the eye region of faces (Gamer et al., 2010); this latter finding was also demonstrated in an earlier study (Guastella et al., 2008). These studies support the idea that oxytocin can improve levels of trust, which is consistent with the idea that oxytocin as a social hormone (Heinrichs et al., 2009) has the potential to alter social responses to others.

Effects of oxytocin cannot be considered without some discussion of vasopressin, another neuropeptide that is also crucial to mediating reproductive behavior and various aspects of more "male-typical" behaviors, such as aggression and territoriality (Donaldson & Young, 2008; Heinrichs et al., 2009; Insel, 2010). Other hormones such as cortisol and testosterone, which can be elevated in socially stressful situations where dominance and power come into play, might also generate potent chemosensory signals and alter behaviors. Indeed, recent research suggests that adopted body postures (in terms of high-power or low-power poses) can actually alter the poser's neurochemistry: testosterone increases and cortisol decreases with high-power poses, and the converse occurs with low-power poses (Carney, Cuddy, & Yap, 2010).

Taken together, these data indicate that neurochemistry likely plays an important modulatory role in our responses to the nonverbal cues of others, irrespective of whether we are aware of them or not. In the future, neurochemical measures may have to be included as covariates or regressors in studies where behavior and brain activity is measured in the context of implicit and explicit experimental manipulations.

Unintentionally vs. Intentionally Sent Nonverbal Cues and Use of Nonverbal Cues for Deception

Nonverbal cues or signals can be intentional or unintentional on the part of the sender. In the latter case, the sender might not realize that he or she may be broadcasting a social message to others; for example, a yawn or a cough may simply reflect genuine tiredness or a throat irritation, whereas another individual might interpret this as signaling boredom or embarrassment, respectively. The interpretation can also be implicit on the part of the observer (Frith, 2009; Tamietto et al., 2009).

We habitually observe regular facial expressions depicting emotions such as happiness or surprise—basic emotions that are common across cultures (Ekman et al., 1987; Sauter, Eisner, Ekman, & Scott, 2010). However, sometimes it may not be socially appropriate to display our true feelings, so we "mask" those feelings by maintaining a face that shows a neutral expression. Yet, if the situation is emotionally powerful, it may not be possible to mask one's feelings completely. Facial expressions thought to be generated spontaneously and involuntarily can still manifest themselves, even though the individual may be making a conscious effort to not show them. These so-called involuntary facial microexpressions are so rapid that normal human observers can completely miss them in a social interaction (Porter & ten Brinke, 2008), and they are particularly difficult for those with Autistic Spectrum Disorders to identify (Clark, Winkielman, & McIntosh, 2008). Cosmetic procedures involving facial musculature require that facial motion and the ability to create expressions, including microexpressions, be preserved, but this is challenging in cases of Botox injection (Olson, 2007). Interestingly, recent work

on individuals who have undergone Botox injection into facial musculature suggests that any alteration in perceptual experiences of others' facial emotions may be subtle and complex (Davis, Senghas, Brandt, & Ochsner, 2010), thus the embodiment of emotion may not be as strong as previously suggested. The review by Neidenthal and colleagues (2010), as well as associated commentary on some of these issues, provides a multiperspective discussion on this topic (Niedenthal, Mermillod, Maringer, & Hess, 2010).

Another important transient nonverbal cue comes from human vocalizations. These cues are often sent involuntarily. Spontaneous nonverbal vocalizations such as sighs; expressions of pain, fear, or grief; or other rapid vocalizations such as coughs, yawns, sneezes, or grunts may also serve as informative social cues. These affective nonverbal vocalizations have been shown to selectively activate the amygdala (Fecteau et al., 2007). Another vocalization, laughter, can take a number of forms—that which occurs when someone is tickled is different from that occurring when an individual jokes with or taunts another person. Not surprisingly, the brain shows different activation patterns to different types of laughter: posterior temporal cortex is active when hearing laughter elicited by tickling, whereas so-called emotional laughter (associated with joy or taunt) elicits activation in anterior rostral medial frontal cortex (Szameitat et al., 2010).

Investigation of nonverbal cues from vocalizations is challenging, however, because social meaning can be altered as a function of not only different types of the same vocalization but also the acoustic complexity (Szameitat et al., 2010). An important nonverbal component of speech comes from vocal quality, such as modulation of the timbre and cadence of the speaker's voice, which can convey subtle nuances to very powerful social cues. Vocal prosody can be a particularly useful cue in the absence of visual cues, such as when one is speaking on the telephone. The superior temporal gyrus, particularly in the right hemisphere, is responsive to emotional prosody, and this is thought to occur due to a sensitivity to emotional arousal in the voice as well as to acoustic complexity (Wiethoff, Wildgruber, Grodd, & Ethofer, 2009). A right-hemisphere brain network consisting of the pSTS and areas of dorsolateral prefrontal and orbitofrontal cortices is thought to be critical for the comprehension of affective vocal prosody (Wildgruber et al., 2005).

The multisensory aspect of the evaluation of vocalizations should also be considered, as vocalizations typically co-occur with facial expressions, often in the case of expressing emotion. Given that facially generated emotional expressions are important for human face-to-face communication, it makes sense that the brain may have developed specialized mechanisms to handle the preferential sensory processing for these special types of multisensory cues in the cortex of the superior temporal gyrus (Adolphs & Tranel, 1999, 2004; Adolphs, Tranel, Damasio, & Damasio, 1994; Belin, Fecteau, & Bedard, 2004; Sauter et al., 2010). Indeed, this region is sensitive to the emotional content of the face *and* voice signal, and the strength of activation in this brain region is a function of the observer's trait emotional intelligence (Kreifelts, Ethofer, Huberle, Grodd, & Wildgruber, 2010). Findings such as these underscore the need to consider individual differences in the ability to process social signals, as well as the social or empathic skills of subjects who participate in these studies.

While the expressions of basic emotions such as happiness or anger—again, emotions regarded as being common across cultures (Ekman et al., 1987; Sauter et al., 2010)—are typically read from the human face (Frith, 2009), a growing body of work indicates that they can also be represented in body postures (de Gelder, 2006; Kret, Pichon, Grezes, & de Gelder, 2011). Indeed, recent work suggests that the human brain processes emotion from face, hand, and body movements in a modality-independent manner, and that this processing occurs in the medial prefrontal cortex and STS (Peelen, Atkinson, & Vuilleumier, 2010) as well as other brain regions, including the extrastriate body area, temporoparietal junction, and fusiform gyrus (Kret et al., 2011). Dynamic cues from body motion can be used to evaluate the collective emotional state of crowds of people (McHugh, McDonnell, O'sullivan, & Newell, 2010).

When we *consciously* send nonverbal cues, it is for the purpose of communicating something to another. Communication based on nonverbal cues and gestures has been used for millennia; it has been argued to predate language (Arbib, 2005; Corballis, 1992, 2003; Kelly et al., 2002; Steklis & Harnad, 1976). Even in modern times we can rely on this basic type of communication, best shown by travelers in countries where they cannot speak the local language. Sometimes this can create problems, as some nonverbal cues might send different messages in different cultures. The ability to navigate successfully among these different culturally idiosyncratic cues is known as cultural intelligence in the business world (Earley & Mosakowski, 2004) and should not be confused with the literature on cultural intelligence in nonhuman primates and animals (Reader, Hager, & Laland, 2011; van Schaik & Burkart, 2011).

Sometimes the intent of a sent nonverbal cue is to deceive another. The ability to do this convincingly varies among individuals and relies on one's ability to not only mask intended behavior but also sometimes to replace it with a completely different behavior entirely. The underlying intent on the part of the deceiver may be benign or malevolent. Unfortunately, the idea that someone's behavior can be a sign of malicious intent is being tested every day at airports around the world.

While work with microfacial expressions has offered some valuable clues into another's potentially deceptive behavior (Ekman & Friesen, 1969; Ekman & O'sullivan, 2006; Porter & ten Brinke, 2008), related work in other laboratories is offering a somewhat different perspective (Weinberger, 2010). Studies of deception detection, a growing area of cognitive neuroscience, investigate not only the ability to detect if another individual is lying or attempting to deceive but also what enables the execution of a lie and what underlies the intention to deceive (Ganis & Keenan, 2009). Increased rates of blinking and fidgeting have long been believed to accompany lying, as has the avoidance of eye contact. However, gaze avoidance and associated gaze shifts do not reliably indicate lying (DePaulo et al., 2003). Instead, they may signal that the person has a secret that he or she wishes not to divulge (Porter & ten Brinke, 2008). Direct eye contact accompanied by a raised chin and medially raised brows (the so called plus face) is a reliable indicator that someone may be attempting to deceive (Zivin, 1982, cited in DePaulo et al., 2003). Liars are also rated as being less pleasant, in studies where participants consider such facial behaviors as smiling (DePaulo et al., 2003). These important clues to an individual's potential lying all involve unintentionally generated nonverbal cues. Critically, then, being able to reliably detect if another's behavior is deceptive appears to rely on the evaluation and perhaps comparison of nonverbal *and* verbal cues, the current situational context, and knowledge of that individual's behavior patterns.

The other side of the coin with respect to deception detection is the extent to which we think we can trust someone. What types of behaviors or attributes make us think we can regard someone as being "trustworthy"? An individual's face is an important attribute in forming a trustworthiness judgment, in studies using neutral and static faces, without the presence of any nonverbal cues. Judgment of trustworthiness, however, is augmented by the presence of nonverbal cues, such as angry or happy facial expressions (Todorov, Said, Engell, & Oosterhof, 2008).

In an everyday social situation, one of the challenges for an observer is to determine which one of potentially multiple alternative meanings the perceived nonverbal cue is most likely to reflect, so that the observer can respond in a socially appropriate manner. Indeed, this can be particularly challenging when conflicting or incongruous messages are read from concurrently incoming nonverbal and verbal cues. Recent work indicates that different brain regions might be sensitive to various aspects of the conflict. Conflicting affective facial and body gestures selectively activated the cortex of the STS, inferior frontal gyrus and putamen (Zucker et al., 2011). When the observer had to overtly evaluate the conflicting social messages, the brain engaged not only social-cognition networks but also structures known to be involved in cognitive control and error monitoring, such as anterior cingulate cortex and lateral prefrontal cortex (Ruz & Tudela, 2011; Zaki, Hennigan, Weber, & Ochsner, 2010). This work addresses an important knowledge gap and may seed an interesting new line of research geared toward discovering how social-cognition systems in the brain interact with brain systems dealing with executive control.

Not only do we not have access to the workings of another's mind, but we also do not have conscious access to the ruminations occurring in our own social cognitive and executive control networks. So often people contemplate a past social situation and do not understand why they responded as they did. This reflective and introspective aspect of social cognition is also an understudied area.

Anomalies and Ambiguities in Nonverbal Cue Interpretation

It has been argued that one's own experience and sense of self is important in interpreting the actions of others. A "sense" of self relies on inputs from a number of different (nonverbal) sensory and vestibular cues available from one's own body. A large corpus of literature exists on the role of embodiment in the interpretation and prediction of others' actions and emotions and includes accounts of simulation, imitation, and mimicry, based heavily on elicited activation in sensorimotor systems to viewing the actions of others (see, e.g., Barsalou, 2008; Decety & Grezes, 2006; Gallese, 2007; Grafton, 2009; Hostetter & Alibali, 2008; Niedenthal, 2007; Wilson, 2002). Having said that, being born without one of the senses, such as hearing or vision, does not impoverish one's concept of self, nor does it preclude the ability to interpret the actions of others (Bigelow, 2003; Corina & Singleton, 2009).

In certain cases of neurological disease, however, the integration of cues from multiple senses can become disrupted, and the self may become fragmented. An excellent example of this disruption can be seen in the "out-of-body" experience for which the common neural substrate appears to be the cortex of the temporoparietal junction (Blanke, Landis, Spinelli, & Seeck, 2004; Blanke & Mohr, 2005), an area crucial for social cognition. Blanke and colleagues have studied a number of surgery patients with epilepsy who had complex characteristic visual and somatosensory experiential phenomena as essential parts of their focal seizures. A particular patient had the same stereotypical out-of-body experience during a seizure. The nature of an out-of-body experience varies from individual to individual. In its most extreme form it can include a visual and somatosensory experience of individuals observing themselves and feeling as if they were outside their own body.

The actual occurrence of out-of-body experience argues strongly for embodied cognition (see previous section). Our bodies influence and shape the nature of our inner mental life and our understanding of our external world (see, e.g., Niedenthal, 2007; Wilson, 2002). That incoming sensations from the body can color our interpretation of the affective or cognitive experiences of another individual and how we ourselves respond to that individual has been a position held in cognitive neuroscience for quite some time (Bechara, Damasio, & Damasio, 2003; Damasio, 1996) and can be an important component of empathy (Decety & Lamm, 2007; Hein & Singer, 2008). As discussed earlier, researchers are beginning to identify different profiles of autonomic nervous system activity in association with some basic emotions, for example disgust (Harrison, Gray, Gianaros, & Critchley, 2010). Such research will require the recording of physiological data from many different dimensions, including activity of the autonomic nervous system.

As stated earlier, the ability to read nonverbal cues and predict others' actions and intentions relies on an intact and fully developed neural system for recognizing these important social cues. When children do not exhibit these behaviors, this may signal a neuropsychiatric disorder such as autism. Much current research is devoted to finding out what is at the core of these difficulties (Bruinsma, Koegel, & Koegel, 2004; Hoehl et al., 2009). And much has been written about disorders such as autism and schizophrenia, in which the nonverbal and verbal messages of other individuals are either largely ignored or misinterpreted (reviewed by Caronna, Milunsky, & Tager-Flusberg, 2008; Fett et al., 2011; Ochsner, 2008; Uddin & Menon, 2009). In addition to these disorders, there are many other examples in neurology and psychiatry of individuals experiencing difficulty interacting with others in their social world, which may come from the person's inability to read cues and send them to others. Nowhere is this more dramatic than in the "locked-in" syndrome, where an individual is fully conscious but cannot move his or her body other than to open and close the eyes (Lule et al., 2009; Schnakers et al., 2008; Sorger et al., 2009). These individuals can be challenging to interact and communicate with, as they possess excellent cognitive ability and robust brain activation but cannot signal this to others (Schnakers et al., 2008; Sorger et al., 2009). In an extreme case of locked-in syndrome the individual was in this state for 16 years but was mistakenly thought to be in a vegetative state (Lukowicz, Matuszak, & Talar, 2010).

Patients with Parkinson's disease often generate a paucity of nonverbal cues, which can affect others' perception of that individual (Pitcairn, Clemie, Gray, & Pentland, 1990). In particular, the generation of facial expression can be impaired (known as "masking"), giving the impression of nonresponsiveness, emotional impoverishment, or depression (Mikos et al., 2009; Simons, Pasqualini, Reddy, & Wood, 2004). Facial-emotion recognition in others can also be impaired (Ariatti, Benuzzi, & Nichelli, 2008; Ibarretxe-Bilbao et al., 2009; Kan, Kawamura, Hasegawa, Mochizuki, & Nakamura, 2002). These two impairments underscore the embodied link between the generation and recognition of facial emotions (Heilman & Gilmore, 1998).

Difficulties with generating facial expressions can also occur in those with schizophrenia, depression, or right-hemisphere injury (Brozgold et al., 1998; Davison, Frith, Harrison-Read, & Johnstone, 1996; Pitman, Kolb, Orr, & Singh, 1987). Ironically, in the current age of obsession with physical attractiveness, we have the potential to induce impairments in social cognition in healthy individuals, through

Botox injection, as this may inactivate facial muscles (see previous section).

An aberration in signaling with the eyes can occur in Möbius syndrome, a rare form of bilateral facial paralysis in which facial expressions cannot be generated (Briegel, 2006). The inability to make lateral eye movements limits the sending of social attention signals, which instead need to be sent with the head or body. Eye movement difficulties extend to eye blinks, which when abnormal can be disconcerting in an interaction. We notice when someone blinks too often or too infrequently. In disorders such as schizophrenia, Tourette's syndrome, Parkinson's disease, and progressive supranuclear palsy, higher rates of blinking occur than in healthy individuals (Chan & Chen, 2004; Goldberg, Maltz, Bow, Karson, & Leleszi, 1987; Karson, Burns, LeWitt, Foster, & Newman, 1984; Swartzrauber & Fujikawa, 1998; Tulen et al., 1999). In Autism (Senju & Johnson, 2009) and schizophrenia (Morris, Weickert, & Loughland, 2009), the ability to read signals from the eyes and deal with the consequence of gaze changes appears to be particularly impaired. Individuals with autism and schizophrenia have also been known to shun direct eye contact with others (Richer & Coss, 1976; Senju & Johnson, 2009; Troisi, Pasini, Bersani, Di Mauro, & Ciani, 1991).

In sum, the inability to generate socially appropriate nonverbal behaviors and to read and interpret nonverbal behaviors in others puts sufferers of a number of neuropsychiatric disorders at a disadvantage for carrying out daily social activities. Others notice when behavior is "strange" or aberrant; this situation can be particularly challenging for children and adolescents in educational environments.

Interactions and Synchrony Between the Observer and Those Being Observed

A social action is an action directed at or involving another individual. In a regular social situation, protagonists typically participate in turn-taking interactions through which information from both verbal and nonverbal cues is sampled and integrated, to build up a model of the other's beliefs, desires, and intentions.

Emotional contagion is said to occur when an observer nonconsciously mimics or picks up on the emotions of another (Gump & Kulik, 1997; Shamay-Tsoory, 2011; Wild, Erb, & Bartels, 2001). The contagiousness of laughter (Gervais & Wilson, 2005) and of yawning (Schurmann et al., 2005) has been described. In an interesting experimental manipulation, activation in the right pSTS and bilateral anterior STS was shown on fMRI in response to viewing yawning, as opposed to other movements of the mouth and face. Activity in the region of the amygdala was negatively correlated with the STS activity (Schurmann et al., 2005). Activity in STS has been postulated to be crucial for social cognition (Redcay, 2008). The right posterior aspect of the STS has been linked with processing facial motion, particularly from the eyes (Allison, Puce, & McCarthy, 2000; Laube, Kamphuis, Dicke, & Thier, 2011; Puce & Perrett, 2003), whereas anterior bilateral STS may have a more evaluative role in processing the meaning of human (social) movements (Laube et al., 2011; but see also Deen & McCarthy, 2010).

The subtler aspects of emotional contagion (mimicry) have been studied by monitoring facial electromyographic (EMG) activity in observers looking at the facial expressions of others. Discernable EMG changes can be recorded in observers' facial musculature appropriate to the facial emotion being viewed. Importantly, these EMG changes occur in the presence of no discernable changes in the observer's facial expression. EMG changes have also been reported in response to viewing facial expressions of happiness, sadness, fear, and anger (Achaibou, Pourtois, Schwartz, & Vuilleumier, 2008; Schrammel, Pannasch, Graupner, Mojzisch, & Velichkovsky, 2009). Moreover, facial EMG changes specific to an emotion can occur when viewing body postures or listening to voices that convey the same emotion, indicating that facial EMG activity reflects a more generalizable evaluation and response to emotion (Magnee, Stekelenburg, Kemner, & de Gelder, 2007). Observers themselves are also unaware of any activity in their own facial musculature when viewing affective faces (Dimberg, Thunberg, & Elmehed, 2000).

Pupillometry is another technique that has been used to study unconscious social or emotional contagion, specifically through changes in pupil diameter. As discussed earlier, information relating to changes in pupil diameter is not typically available to conscious awareness. In an ingenious experimental manipulation, fMRI activation in amygdala, fusiform gyrus, and STS was observed when subjects viewed sad faces whose pupils were dynamically modulated to match the pupil diameter of observers while they were in the MRI scanner (Harrison et al., 2006). The subjects were unaware that these pupillary manipulations were occurring in the stimuli. That facial EMG activity can be detected when subjects view affective faces without conscious awareness (Dimberg et al., 2000) indicates that these nonverbal cues act at a level of nonconscious awareness. This factor should be considered when designing experiments to study neural responses to nonverbal cues.

Humans are not unique in decoding nonverbal signals from their conspecifics. Nonhuman primates and other animals use cues from different sensory modalities to recognize social hierarchies and to evade predators (Ouattara, Lemasson, & Zuberbuhler, 2009; Paxton et al., 2010). Animals also use signals from other species; for example, they may take evasive action upon hearing an alarm call signaling predators that is made by not only their own but also other cohabiting species (Seyfarth & Cheney, 2003). Humans use nonverbal cues from animals; that special relationship with "man's best friend," the dog, is an excellent example of how a reciprocal cross-species social relationship can exist based solely on nonverbal cues. Dogs can recognize human gaze cues (Miklosi et al., 2003) and gestures (Kaminski, Tempelmann, Call, & Tomasello, 2009; Tamietto et al., 2009). Dogs have also shown abilities similar to those of 2- to 3-year-old human children in decoding human index finger pointing gestures (Lakatos, Soproni, Doka, & Miklosi, 2009). There is a growing literature on these topics, which are beyond the scope of this chapter.

Conclusion

We have the ability to rapidly respond to and evaluate the multisensory nonverbal cues of others. Processing of nonverbal cues can also proceed with and without awareness, as shown by measures of autonomic and central nervous system activity that have been associated with behavior. State-of-the-art social cognitive neuroscience studies are beginning to collect multimodal data (e.g., brain blood flow or neurophysiological activity together with pupil dilation or galvanic skin response) in an attempt to more fully understand the embodied experience that can occur when we evaluate the behavior of another. This embodied experience involves many regions of the brain working in concert with one another, a process that is far from understood. Similarly, there is growing emphasis on the use of more naturalistic stimuli that might enable us to generate a better overall assessment of the brain–behavior continuum. Another important aspect of social-cognition studies that has been neglected is assessment of the basic social-cognitive and empathic abilities of subjects participating in these studies. Investigators are increasingly acknowledging these differences and are including these types of assessments (Dewall et al., 2012; Eisenberger, Gable, & Lieberman, 2007; Haruno & Frith, 2010; Krach et al., 2011; Prehn et al., 2008).

Future Directions

A large number of unsolved and interesting key questions remain regarding the perception of nonverbal cues. Listed below are some overarching questions that can be adequately tackled only through multimodal neuroimaging studies—for example, fMRI or EEG/MEG combined with behavioral monitoring and autonomic nervous system monitoring (e.g., pupil size, galvanic skin response or visceral activity) or monitoring of blood levels of various metabolites and hormones. These questions are multifaceted and form a line of investigation for a number of years to come.

1. How does information from incoming consciously and nonconsciously perceived cues become integrated in the human brain? How might incoming information from nonverbal cues acquired nonconsciously influence decisions we might ultimately make regarding the behavior of another? How do environmental sensory cues influence how we perceive and evaluate an individual?

2. How does our basic neurochemistry affect our responses to the nonverbal cues of others? Does our neurochemistry change only when experiencing powerful affective cues from others, or can it be modulated in a more muted social interaction? What are the time courses and durations for these neurochemical changes? What effect does gender have on these neurochemical changes, and in females, how does it vary as a function of the menstrual cycle?

3. The amygdala consists of multiple nuclei that have been potentially grouped along two main social and autonomic functional dimensions. How do these two dimensions interact to produce voluntary (and involuntary) reactions to the behavior of others? How do changes in pupil size of the individual being viewed affect our evaluation of them and perhaps also our own internal autonomic balance?

4. Generating an appropriate response to the nonverbal cues of others requires the coordinated activity of multiple brain systems that include specialized sensory and affective processors, as well as systems involved in response generation, error monitoring, conflict, and inhibition. How do these

systems interact with one another to produce a seamless and coordinated sequence of behavior?

5. What underlying neural processes are critical for the evaluation and self-reflection of one's own behaviors, especially those associated with past social situations that may have resulted in unfavorable or unpredictable outcomes on the part of the protagonist?

6. What underlies the inability to read, or generate, socially appropriate nonverbal cues in the various neuropsychiatric disorders? Can this inability be corrected with neurochemical or behavioral modifications?

References

Achaibou, A., Pourtois, G., Schwartz, S., & Vuilleumier, P. (2008). Simultaneous recording of EEG and facial muscle reactions during spontaneous emotional mimicry. *Neuropsychologia*, 46(4), 1104–1113.

Adolphs, R. (2002). Neural systems for recognizing emotion. *Current Opinion in Neurobiology*, 12(2), 169–177.

Adolphs, R., & Tranel, D. (1999). Intact recognition of emotional prosody following amygdala damage. *Neuropsychologia*, 37(11), 1285–1292.

Adolphs, R., & Tranel, D. (2004). Impaired judgments of sadness but not happiness following bilateral amygdala damage. *Journal of Cognitive Neuroscience*, 16(3), 453–462.

Adolphs, R., Tranel, D., Damasio, H., & Damasio, A. (1994). Impaired recognition of emotion in facial expressions following bilateral damage to the human amygdala. *Nature*, 372(6507), 669–672.

Allison, T., Puce, A., & McCarthy, G. (2000). Social perception from visual cues: Role of the STS region. *Trends in Cognitive Sciences*, 4(7), 267–278.

Amunts, K., Kedo, O., Kindler, M., Pieperhoff, P., Mohlberg, H., Shah, N. J., et al. (2005). Cytoarchitectonic mapping of the human amygdala, hippocampal region and entorhinal cortex: Intersubject variability and probability maps. *Anatomy and Embryology (Berlin)*, 210(5-6), 343–352.

Arbib, M. A. (2005). From monkey-like action recognition to human language: An evolutionary framework for neurolinguistics. *Behavioral and Brain Sciences*, 28(2), 105–124; discussion 125–167.

Ariatti, A., Benuzzi, F., & Nichelli, P. (2008). Recognition of emotions from visual and prosodic cues in Parkinson's disease. *Neurological Sciences*, 29(4), 219–227.

Astafiev, S. V., Stanley, C. M., Shulman, G. L., & Corbetta, M. (2004). Extrastriate body area in human occipital cortex responds to the performance of motor actions. *Nature Neuroscience*, 7(5), 542–548.

Ball, T., Rahm, B., Eickhoff, S. B., Schulze-Bonhage, A., Speck, O., & Mutschler, I. (2007). Response properties of human amygdala subregions: Evidence based on functional MRI combined with probabilistic anatomical maps. *PLoS One*, 2(3), e307.

Baron-Cohen, S., Wheelwright, S., Hill, J., Raste, Y., & Plumb, I. (2001). The "Reading the Mind in the Eyes" Test revised version: A study with normal adults, and adults with Asperger syndrome or high-functioning autism. *Journal of Child Psychology and Psychiatry*, 42(2), 241–251.

Barsalou, L. W. (2008). Grounded cognition. *Annual Review of Psychology, 59*, 617–645.

Beauchamp, M. S., Lee, K. E., Haxby, J. V., & Martin, A. (2003). FMRI responses to video and point-light displays of moving humans and manipulable objects. *Journal of Cognitive Neuroscience, 15*(7), 991–1001.

Bechara, A., Damasio, H., & Damasio, A. R. (2003). Role of the amygdala in decision-making. *Annals of the New York Academy of Sciences, 985*, 356–369.

Belin, P., Fecteau, S., & Bedard, C. (2004). Thinking the voice: Neural correlates of voice perception. *Trends in Cognitive Sciences, 8*(3), 129–135.

Belin, P., Zatorre, R. J., & Ahad, P. (2002). Human temporal-lobe response to vocal sounds. *Brain Research: Cognitive Brain Research, 13*(1), 17–26.

Belin, P., Zatorre, R. J., Lafaille, P., Ahad, P., & Pike, B. (2000). Voice-selective areas in human auditory cortex. *Nature, 403*(6767), 309–312.

Bentin, S., Allison, T., Puce, A., Perez, A., & McCarthy, G. (1996). Electrophysiological studies of face perception in humans. *Journal of Cognitive Neuroscience, 8*, 551–565.

Bigelow, A. E. (2003). The development of joint attention in blind infants. *Developmental Psychopathology, 15*(2), 259–275.

Bitsios, P., Szabadi, E., & Bradshaw, C. M. (2004). The fear-inhibited light reflex: Importance of the anticipation of an aversive event. *International Journal of Psychophysiology, 52*(1), 87–95.

Blanke, O., Landis, T., Spinelli, L., & Seeck, M. (2004). Out-of-body experience and autoscopy of neurological origin. *Brain, 127*(Pt 2), 243–258.

Blanke, O., & Mohr, C. (2005). Out-of-body experience, heautoscopy, and autoscopic hallucination of neurological origin: Implications for neurocognitive mechanisms of corporeal awareness and self-consciousness. *Brain Research: Brain Research Review, 50*(1), 184–199.

Bonda, E., Petrides, M., Ostry, D., & Evans, A. (1996). Specific involvement of human parietal systems and the amygdala in the perception of biological motion. *Journal of Neuroscience, 16*(11), 3737–3744.

Brandman, T., & Yovel, G. (2010). The body inversion effect is mediated by face-selective, not body-selective, mechanisms. *Journal of Neuroscience, 30*(31), 10534–10540.

Briegel, W. (2006). Neuropsychiatric findings of Mobius sequence—a review. *Clinical Genetics, 70*(2), 91–97.

Brozgold, A. Z., Borod, J. C., Martin, C. C., Pick, L. H., Alpert, M., & Welkowitz, J. (1998). Social functioning and facial emotional expression in neurological and psychiatric disorders. *Applied Neuropsychology, 5*(1), 15–23.

Bruce, V., & Young, A. (1986). Understanding face recognition. *British Journal of Psychology, 77*(Pt 3), 305–327.

Bruinsma, Y., Koegel, R. L., & Koegel, L. K. (2004). Joint attention and children with autism: A review of the literature. *Mental Retardation and Developmental Disabilities Research Reviews, 10*(3), 169–175.

Buccino, G., Binkofski, F., Fink, G. R., Fadiga, L., Fogassi, L., Gallese, V., et al. (2001). Action observation activates premotor and parietal areas in a somatotopic manner: an fMRI study. *European Journal of Neuroscience, 13*(2), 400–404.

Buijs, R. M., De Vries, G. J., Van Leeuwen, F. W., & Swaab, D. F. (1983). Vasopressin and oxytocin: distribution and putative functions in the brain. *Progress in Brain Research, 60*, 115–122.

Calvert, G. A., Bullmore, E. T., Brammer, M. J., Campbell, R., Williams, S. C., McGuire, P. K., et al. (1997). Activation of auditory cortex during silent lipreading. *Science, 276*(5312), 593–596.

Campbell, R. (2008). The processing of audio-visual speech: Empirical and neural bases. *Philosophical Transactions of the Royal Society of London, Series B: Biological Sciences, 363*(1493), 1001–1010.

Campbell, R., MacSweeney, M., Surguladze, S., Calvert, G., McGuire, P., Suckling, J., et al. (2001). Cortical substrates for the perception of face actions: An fMRI study of the specificity of activation for seen speech and for meaningless lower-face acts (gurning). *Brain Research: Cognitive Brain Research, 12*(2), 233–243.

Capparuccini, O., Berrie, C. P., & Mazzatenta, A. (2010). The potential hedonic role of olfaction in sexual selection and its dominance in visual cross-modal interactions. *Perception, 39*(10), 1322–1329.

Carney, D. R., Cuddy, A. J., & Yap, A. J. (2010). Power posing: Brief nonverbal displays affect neuroendocrine levels and risk tolerance. *Psychological Science, 21*(10), 1363–1368.

Caronna, E. B., Milunsky, J. M., & Tager-Flusberg, H. (2008). Autism spectrum disorders: Clinical and research frontiers. *Archives of Disease in Childhood, 93*(6), 518–523.

Cerveri, P., De Momi, E., Lopomo, N., Baud-Bovy, G., Barros, R. M., & Ferrigno, G. (2007). Finger kinematic modeling and real-time hand motion estimation. *Annals of Biomedical Engineering, 35*(11), 1989–2002.

Chan, R. C., & Chen, E. Y. (2004). Blink rate does matter: A study of blink rate, sustained attention, and neurological signs in schizophrenia. *Journal of Nervous and Mental Disease, 192*(11), 781–783.

Clark, T. F., Winkielman, P., & McIntosh, D. N. (2008). Autism and the extraction of emotion from briefly presented facial expressions: Stumbling at the first step of empathy. *Emotion, 8*(6), 803–809.

Conty, L., N'Diaye, K., Tijus, C., & George, N. (2007). When eye creates the contact! ERP evidence for early dissociation between direct and averted gaze motion processing. *Neuropsychologia, 45*(13), 3024–3037.

Corballis, M. C. (1992). On the evolution of language and generativity. *Cognition, 44*(3), 197–126.

Corballis, M. C. (2003). From mouth to hand: Gesture, speech, and the evolution of right-handedness. *Behavioral and Brain Sciences, 26*(2), 199–208; discussion 208–160.

Corina, D., & Singleton, J. (2009). Developmental social cognitive neuroscience: Insights from deafness. *Child Development, 80*(4), 952–967.

Damasio, A. R. (1996). The somatic marker hypothesis and the possible functions of the prefrontal cortex. *Philosophical Transactions of the Royal Society of London, Series B: Biological Sciences, 351*(1346), 1413–1420.

Davis, J. I., Senghas, A., Brandt, F., & Ochsner, K. N. (2010). The effects of BOTOX injections on emotional experience. *Emotion, 10*(3), 433–440.

Davison, P. S., Frith, C. D., Harrison-Read, P. E., & Johnstone, E. C. (1996). Facial and other non-verbal communicative behaviour in chronic schizophrenia. *Psychological Medicine, 26*(4), 707–713.

de Gelder, B. (2006). Towards the neurobiology of emotional body language. *Nature Reviews Neuroscience, 7*(3), 242–249.

Decety, J., & Grezes, J. (2006). The power of simulation: imagining one's own and other's behavior. *Brain Research, 1079*(1), 4–14.

Decety, J., & Lamm, C. (2007). The role of the right temporoparietal junction in social interaction: How low-level computational processes contribute to meta-cognition. *Neuroscientist*, *13*(6), 580–593.

Deen, B., & McCarthy, G. (2010). Reading about the actions of others: Biological motion imagery and action congruency influence brain activity. *Neuropsychologia*, *48*(6), 1607–1615.

Demos, K. E., Kelley, W. M., Ryan, S. L., Davis, F. C., & Whalen, P. J. (2008). Human amygdala sensitivity to the pupil size of others. *Cerebral Cortex*, *18*(12), 2729–2734.

DePaulo, B. M., Lindsay, J. J., Malone, B. E., Muhlenbruck, L., Charlton, K., & Cooper, H. (2003). Cues to deception. *Psychological Bulletin*, *129*(1), 74–118.

Dewall, C. N., Masten, C. L., Powell, C., Combs, D., Schurtz, D. R., & Eisenberger, N. I. (2012). Do neural responses to rejection depend on attachment style? An fMRI study. *Social, Cognitive & Affective Neuroscience*, *7*(2), 184–192.

Dimberg, U., Thunberg, M., & Elmehed, K. (2000). Unconscious facial reactions to emotional facial expressions. *Psychological Science*, *11*(1), 86–89.

Domes, G., Heinrichs, M., Michel, A., Berger, C., & Herpertz, S. C. (2007). Oxytocin improves "mind-reading" in humans. *Biological Psychiatry*, *61*(6), 731–733.

Donaldson, Z. R., & Young, L. J. (2008). Oxytocin, vasopressin, and the neurogenetics of sociality. *Science*, *322*(5903), 900–904.

Earley, P. C., & Mosakowski, E. (2004). Cultural intelligence. *Harvard Business Review*, *82*(10), 139–146, 158.

Eisenberger, N. I., Gable, S. L., & Lieberman, M. D. (2007) Functional magnetic resonance imaging responses relate to differences in real-world social experience. *Emotion*, *7*(4), 745–754.

Ekman, P., & Friesen, W. V. (1969). Nonverbal leakage and clues to deception. *Psychiatry*, *32*(1), 88–106.

Ekman, P., Friesen, W. V., O'sullivan, M., Chan, A., Diacoyanni-Tarlatzis, I., Heider, K., et al. (1987). Universals and cultural differences in the judgments of facial expressions of emotion. *Journal of Personality and Social Psychology*, *53*, 712–717.

Ekman, P., & O'sullivan, M. (2006). From flawed self-assessment to blatant whoppers: The utility of voluntary and involuntary behavior in detecting deception. *Behavioral Science Law*, *24*(5), 673–686.

Farah, M. J. (1996). Is face recognition "special"? Evidence from neuropsychology. *Behavioral and Brain Research*, *76*(1-2), 181–189.

Farah, M. J., Tanaka, J. W., & Drain, H. M. (1995). What causes the face inversion effect? *Journal of Experimental Psychology. Human Perception and Performance*, *21*(3), 628–634.

Farroni, T., Csibra, G., Simion, F., & Johnson, M. H. (2002). Eye contact detection in humans from birth. *Proceedings of the National Academy of Science U S A*, *99*(14), 9602–9605.

Farroni, T., Johnson, M. H., & Csibra, G. (2004). Mechanisms of eye gaze perception during infancy. *Journal of Cognitive Neuroscience*, *16*(8), 1320–1326.

Fecteau, S., Belin, P., Joanette, Y., & Armony, J. L. (2007). Amygdala responses to nonlinguistic emotional vocalizations. *Neuroimage*, *36*(2), 480–487.

Ferguson, M. J., & Bargh, J. A. (2004). How social perception can automatically influence behavior. *Trends in Cognitive Sciences*, *8*(1), 33–39.

Fett, A. K., Viechtbauer, W., Dominguez, M. D., Penn, D. L., van Os, J., & Krabbendam, L. (2011). The relationship between neurocognition and social cognition with functional outcomes in schizophrenia: A meta-analysis. *Neuroscience and Biobehavioral Reviews*, *35*(3), 573–588.

Fox, R., & McDaniel, C. (1982). The perception of biological motion by human infants. *Science*, *218*(4571), 486–487.

Frith, C. (2009). Role of facial expressions in social interactions. *Philosophical Transactions of the Royal Society of London, Series B: Biological Sciences*, *364*(1535), 3453–3458.

Fusar-Poli, P., Placentino, A., Carletti, F., Landi, P., Allen, P., Surguladze, S., et al. (2009). Functional atlas of emotional faces processing: A voxel-based meta-analysis of 105 functional magnetic resonance imaging studies. *Journal of Psychiatry Neuroscience*, *34*(6), 418–432.

Gallace, A., & Spence, C. (2010). The science of interpersonal touch: An overview. *Neuroscience and Biobehavioral Reviews*, *34*(2), 246–259.

Gallese, V. (2007). Before and below "theory of mind": Embodied simulation and the neural correlates of social cognition. *Philosophical Transactions of the Royal Society of London, Series B: Biological Sciences*, *362*(1480), 659–669.

Gamer, M., Zurowski, B., & Buchel, C. (2010). Different amygdala subregions mediate valence-related and attentional effects of oxytocin in humans. *Proceedings of the National Academy of Science U S A*, *107*(20), 9400–9405.

Ganis, G., & Keenan, J. P. (2009). The cognitive neuroscience of deception. *Social Neuroscience*, *4*(6), 465–472.

George, N., Driver, J., & Dolan, R. J. (2001). Seen gaze-direction modulates fusiform activity and its coupling with other brain areas during face processing. *Neuroimage*, *13*(6 Pt 1), 1102–1112.

Gervais, M., & Wilson, D. S. (2005). The evolution and functions of laughter and humor: A synthetic approach. *Quarterly Review of Biology*, *80*(4), 395–430.

Goldberg, T. E., Maltz, A., Bow, J. N., Karson, C. N., & Leleszi, J. P. (1987). Blink rate abnormalities in autistic and mentally retarded children: Relationship to dopaminergic activity. *Journal of the American Academy of Child and Adolescent Psychiatry*, *26*(3), 336–338.

Grafton, S. T. (2009). Embodied cognition and the simulation of action to understand others. *Annals of the New York Academy of Sciences*, *1156*, 97–117.

Granholm, E., & Steinhauer, S. R. (2004). Pupillometric measures of cognitive and emotional processes. *International Journal of Psychophysiology*, *52*(1), 1-6.

Gray, M. A., Minati, L., Harrison, N. A., Gianaros, P. J., Napadow, V., & Critchley, H. D. (2009). Physiological recordings: Basic concepts and implementation during functional magnetic resonance imaging. *Neuroimage*, *47*(3), 1105–1115.

Grossman, E. D., & Blake, R. (2002). Brain areas active during visual perception of biological motion. *Neuron*, *35*(6), 1167–1175.

Guastella, A. J., Mitchell, P. B., & Dadds, M. R. (2008). Oxytocin increases gaze to the eye region of human faces. *Biological Psychiatry*, *63*(1), 3–5.

Gulyas, B., Keri, S., O'sullivan, B. T., Decety, J., & Roland, P. E. (2004). The putative pheromone androstadienone activates cortical fields in the human brain related to social cognition. *Neurochemical International*, *44*(8), 595–600.

Gump, B. B., & Kulik, J. A. (1997). Stress, affiliation, and emotional contagion. *Journal of Personality and Social Psychology*, *72*(2), 305–319.

Hardee, J. E., Thompson, J. C., & Puce, A. (2008). The left amygdala knows fear: Laterality in the amygdala response to fearful eyes. *Social, Cognitive & Affective Neuroscience*, *3*(1), 47–54.

Harrison, N. A., Gray, M. A., & Critchley, H. D. (2009). Dynamic pupillary exchange engages brain regions encoding social salience. *Social Neuroscience*, *4*(3), 233–243.

Harrison, N. A., Gray, M. A., Gianaros, P. J., & Critchley, H. D. (2010). The embodiment of emotional feelings in the brain. *Journal of Neuroscience, 30*(38), 12878–12884.

Harrison, N. A., Singer, T., Rotshtein, P., Dolan, R. J., & Critchley, H. D. (2006). Pupillary contagion: central mechanisms engaged in sadness processing. *Social, Cognitive & Affective Neuroscience, 1*(1), 5–17.

Haruno, M., & Frith, C. D. (2010). Activity in the amygdala elicited by unfair divisions predicts social value orientation. *Nature Neuroscience, 13*(2), 160–161.

Heilman, K. M., & Gilmore, R. L. (1998). Cortical influences in emotion. *Journal of Clinical Neurophysiology, 15*(5), 409–423.

Hein, G., & Singer, T. (2008). I feel how you feel but not always: The empathic brain and its modulation. *Current Opinion in Neurobiology, 18*(2), 153–158.

Heinrichs, M., von Dawans, B., & Domes, G. (2009). Oxytocin, vasopressin, and human social behavior. *Frontiers in Neuroendocrinology, 30*(4), 548–557.

Henderson, L. M., Yoder, P. J., Yale, M. E., & McDuffie, A. (2002). Getting the point: Electrophysiological correlates of protodeclarative pointing. *International Journal of Developmental Neuroscience, 20*(3-5), 449–458.

Hoehl, S., Reid, V. M., Parise, E., Handl, A., Palumbo, L., & Striano, T. (2009). Looking at eye gaze processing and its neural correlates in infancy—implications for social development and autism spectrum disorder. *Child Development, 80*(4), 968–985.

Hoehl, S., & Striano, T. (2010). The development of emotional face and eye gaze processing. *Developmental Science, 13*(6), 813–825.

Hoffman, E. A., & Haxby, J. V. (2000). Distinct representations of eye gaze and identity in the distributed human neural system for face perception. *Nature Neuroscience, 3*(1), 80–84.

Hostetter, A. B., & Alibali, M. W. (2008). Visible embodiment: Gestures as simulated action. *Psychonomic Bulletin & Review, 15*(3), 495–514.

Iacovella, V., & Hasson, U. (2011). The relationship between BOLD signal and autonomic nervous system functions: Implications for processing of "physiological noise". *Magnetic Resonance Imaging, 29*(10), 1338–1345.

Ibarretxe-Bilbao, N., Junque, C., Tolosa, E., Marti, M. J., Valldeoriola, F., Bargallo, N., et al. (2009). Neuroanatomical correlates of impaired decision-making and facial emotion recognition in early Parkinson's disease. *European Journal of Neuroscience, 30*(6), 1162–1171.

Insel, T. R. (2010). The challenge of translation in social neuroscience: A review of oxytocin, vasopressin, and affiliative behavior. *Neuron, 65*(6), 768–779.

Ishak, W. W., Kahloon, M., & Fakhry, H. (2011). Oxytocin role in enhancing well-being: A literature review. *Journal of Affective Disorders, 130*(1-2), 1–9.

Itier, R. J., & Batty, M. (2009). Neural bases of eye and gaze processing: The core of social cognition. *Neuroscience and Biobehavioral Reviews, 33*(6), 843–863.

Itier, R. J., & Taylor, M. J. (2002). Inversion and contrast polarity reversal affect both encoding and recognition processes of unfamiliar faces: a repetition study using ERPs. *Neuroimage, 15*(2), 353–372.

Johansson, G. (1973). Visual perception of biological motion and a model of its analysis. *Perception and Psychophysiology, 14*, 202–211.

Kaminski, J., Tempelmann, S., Call, J., & Tomasello, M. (2009). Domestic dogs comprehend human communication with iconic signs. *Developmental Science, 12*(6), 831–837.

Kan, Y., Kawamura, M., Hasegawa, Y., Mochizuki, S., & Nakamura, K. (2002). Recognition of emotion from facial, prosodic and written verbal stimuli in Parkinson's disease. *Cortex, 38*(4), 623–630.

Kana, R. K., & Travers, B. G. (2012). Neural substrates of interpreting actions and emotions from body postures. *Social, Cognitive & Affective Neuroscience, 7*(4), 446–456.

Kanwisher, N., Tong, F., & Nakayama, K. (1998). The effect of face inversion on the human fusiform face area. *Cognition, 68*(1), B1–B11.

Karson, C. N., Burns, R. S., LeWitt, P. A., Foster, N. L., & Newman, R. P. (1984). Blink rates and disorders of movement. *Neurology, 34*(5), 677–678.

Kelly, S. D., Iverson, J. M., Terranova, J., Niego, J., Hopkins, M., & Goldsmith, L. (2002). Putting language back in the body: speech and gesture on three time frames. *Developmental Neuropsychology, 22*(1), 323–349.

Kirsch, P., Esslinger, C., Chen, Q., Mier, D., Lis, S., Siddhanti, S., et al. (2005). Oxytocin modulates neural circuitry for social cognition and fear in humans. *Journal of Neuroscience, 25*(49), 11489–11493.

Knapska, E., Radwanska, K., Werka, T., & Kaczmarek, L. (2007). Functional internal complexity of amygdala: Focus on gene activity mapping after behavioral training and drugs of abuse. *Physiological Reviews, 87*(4), 1113–1173.

Krach, S., Cohrs, J. C., de Echeverria Loebell, N. C., Kircher, T., Sommer, J., Jansen, A., et al. (2011). Your flaws are my pain: Linking empathy to vicarious embarrassment. *PLoS One, 6*(4), e18675.

Kreifelts, B., Ethofer, T., Huberle, E., Grodd, W., & Wildgruber, D. (2010). Association of trait emotional intelligence and individual fMRI-activation patterns during the perception of social signals from voice and face. *Human Brain Mapping, 31*(7), 979–991.

Kret, M. E., Pichon, S., Grezes, J., & de Gelder, B. (2011). Similarities and differences in perceiving threat from dynamic faces and bodies. An fMRI study. *Neuroimage, 54*(2), 1755–1762.

Lakatos, G., Soproni, K., Doka, A., & Miklosi, A. (2009). A comparative approach to dogs' (*Canis familiaris*) and human infants' comprehension of various forms of pointing gestures. *Animal Cognition, 12*(4), 621–631.

Laube, I., Kamphuis, S., Dicke, P. W., & Thier, P. (2011). Cortical processing of head- and eye-gaze cues guiding joint social attention. *Neuroimage, 54*(2), 1643–1653.

Levy, L. M., Henkin, R. I., Hutter, A., Lin, C. S., Martins, D., & Schellinger, D. (1997). Functional MRI of human olfaction. *Journal of Computed Assisted Tomography, 21*(6), 849–856.

Liljenquist, K., Zhong, C. B., & Galinsky, A. D. (2010). The smell of virtue: Clean scents promote reciprocity and charity. *Psychological Science, 21*(3), 381–383.

Lukowicz, M., Matuszak, K., & Talar, A. (2010). A misdiagnosed patient: 16 years of locked-in syndrome, the influence of rehabilitation. *Medical Science Monitor, 16*(2), CS18–CS23.

Lule, D., Zickler, C., Hacker, S., Bruno, M. A., Demertzi, A., Pellas, F., et al. (2009). Life can be worth living in locked-in syndrome. *Progress in Brain Research, 177*, 339–351.

Magnee, M. J., Stekelenburg, J. J., Kemner, C., & de Gelder, B. (2007). Similar facial electromyographic responses to faces, voices, and body expressions. *Neuroreport, 18*(4), 369–372.

McHugh, J. E., McDonnell, R., O'sullivan, C., & Newell, F. N. (2010). Perceiving emotion in crowds: The role of dynamic body postures on the perception of emotion in crowded scenes. *Experimental Brain Research, 204*(3), 361–372.

Michels, L., Lappe, M., & Vaina, L. M. (2005). Visual areas involved in the perception of human movement from dynamic form analysis. *Neuroreport, 16*(10), 1037–1041.

Miklosi, A., Kubinyi, E., Topal, J., Gacsi, M., Viranyi, Z., & Csanyi, V. (2003). A simple reason for a big difference: Wolves do not look back at humans, but dogs do. *Current Biology, 13*(9), 763–766.

Mikos, A. E., Springer, U. S., Nisenzon, A. N., Kellison, I. L., Fernandez, H. H., Okun, M. S., et al. (2009). Awareness of expressivity deficits in non-demented Parkinson disease. *Clinical Neuropsychology, 23*(5), 805–817.

Miller, S. L., & Maner, J. K. (2010). Scent of a woman: Men's testosterone responses to olfactory ovulation cues. *Psychological Science, 21*(2), 276–283.

Moore, M. M. (2010). Human nonverbal courtship behavior—a brief historical review. *Journal of Sex Research, 47*(2), 171–180.

Morris, R. W., Weickert, C. S., & Loughland, C. M. (2009). Emotional face processing in schizophrenia. *Current Opinion in Psychiatry, 22*(2), 140–146.

Mujica-Parodi, L. R., Strey, H. H., Frederick, B., Savoy, R., Cox, D., Botanov, Y., et al. (2009). Chemosensory cues to conspecific emotional stress activate amygdala in humans. *PLoS One, 4*(7), e6415.

Niedenthal, P. M. (2007). Embodying emotion. *Science, 316*(5827), 1002–1005.

Niedenthal, P. M., Mermillod, M., Maringer, M., & Hess, U. (2010). The Simulation of Smiles (SIMS) model: Embodied simulation and the meaning of facial expression. *Behavioral Brain Science, 33*(6), 417–433; discussion 433–480.

Ochsner, K. N. (2008). The social-emotional processing stream: Five core constructs and their translational potential for schizophrenia and beyond. *Biological Psychiatry, 64*(1), 48–61.

Olson, J. J. (2007). Balanced botox chemodenervation of the upper face: Symmetry in motion. *Seminars in Plastic Surgery, 21*(1), 47–53.

Ouattara, K., Lemasson, A., & Zuberbuhler, K. (2009). Campbell's monkeys concatenate vocalizations into context-specific call sequences. *Proceedings of the National Academy of Science U S A, 106*(51), 22026–22031.

Paxton, R., Basile, B. M., Adachi, I., Suzuki, W. A., Wilson, M. E., & Hampton, R. R. (2010). Rhesus monkeys (*Macaca mulatta*) rapidly learn to select dominant individuals in videos of artificial social interactions between unfamiliar conspecifics. *Journal of Comparative Psychology, 124*(4), 395–401.

Peelen, M. V., Atkinson, A. P., & Vuilleumier, P. (2010). Supramodal representations of perceived emotions in the human brain. *Journal of Neuroscience, 30*(30), 10127–10134.

Petrini, K., Pollick, F. E., Dahl, S., McAleer, P., McKay, L., Rocchesso, D., et al. (2011). Action expertise reduces brain activity for audiovisual matching actions: An fMRI study with expert drummers. *Neuroimage, 56*(3), 1480–1492.

Pilgramm, S., Lorey, B., Stark, R., Munzert, J., Vaitl, D., & Zentgraf, K. (2010). Differential activation of the lateral premotor cortex during action observation. *BMC Neuroscience, 11*, 89.

Pitcairn, T. K., Clemie, S., Gray, J. M., & Pentland, B. (1990). Non-verbal cues in the self-presentation of parkinsonian patients. *British Journal of Clinical Psychology, 29*(Pt 2), 177–184.

Pitman, R. K., Kolb, B., Orr, S. P., & Singh, M. M. (1987). Ethological study of facial behavior in nonparanoid and paranoid schizophrenic patients. *American Journal of Psychiatry, 144*(1), 99–102.

Porter, S., & ten Brinke, L. (2008). Reading between the lies: identifying concealed and falsified emotions in universal facial expressions. *Psychological Science, 19*(5), 508–514.

Prehn, K., Wartenburger, I., Meriau, K., Scheibe, C., Goodenough, O. R., Villringer, A., et al. (2008). Individual differences in moral judgment competence influence neural correlates of socio-normative judgments. *Social, Cognitive & Affective Neuroscience, 3*(1), 33–46.

Prehn-Kristensen, A., Wiesner, C., Bergmann, T. O., Wolff, S., Jansen, O., Mehdorn, H. M., et al. (2009). Induction of empathy by the smell of anxiety. *PLoS One, 4*(6), e5987.

Puce, A., Allison, T., Bentin, S., Gore, J. C., & McCarthy, G. (1998). Temporal cortex activation in humans viewing eye and mouth movements. *Journal of Neuroscience, 18*(6), 2188–2199.

Puce, A., & Perrett, D. (2003). Electrophysiology and brain imaging of biological motion. *Philosophical Transactions of the Royal Society of London, Series B: Biological Sciences, 358*(1431), 435–445.

Puce, A., Smith, A., & Allison, T. (2000). ERPs evoked by viewing facial movements. *Cognitive Neuropsychology, 17*, 221–239.

Puce, A., Syngeniotis, A., Thompson, J. C., Abbott, D. F., Wheaton, K. J., & Castiello, U. (2003). The human temporal lobe integrates facial form and motion: Evidence from fMRI and ERP studies. *Neuroimage, 19*(3), 861–869.

Reader, S. M., Hager, Y., & Laland, K. N. (2011). The evolution of primate general and cultural intelligence. *Philosophical Transactions of the Royal Society of London, Series B: Biological Sciences, 366*(1567), 1017–1027.

Redcay, E. (2008). The superior temporal sulcus performs a common function for social and speech perception: Implications for the emergence of autism. *Neuroscience and Biobehavioral Reviews, 32*(1), 123–142.

Reid, V. M., Hoehl, S., & Striano, T. (2006). The perception of biological motion by infants: an event-related potential study. *Neuroscience Letters, 395*(3), 211–214.

Richer, J. M., & Coss, R. G. (1976). Gaze aversion in autistic and normal children. *Acta Psychiatrica Scandinavica, 53*(3), 193–210.

Rolls, E. T., Kringelbach, M. L., & de Araujo, I. E. (2003). Different representations of pleasant and unpleasant odours in the human brain. *European Journal of Neuroscience, 18*(3), 695–703.

Rosin, S., Tuorila, H., & Uutela, A. (1992). Garlic: A sensory pleasure or a social nuisance? *Appetite, 19*(2), 133–143.

Rossion, B., Delvenne, J. F., Debatisse, D., Goffaux, V., Bruyer, R., Crommelinck, M., et al. (1999). Spatio-temporal localization of the face inversion effect: An event-related potentials study. *Biological Psychology, 50*(3), 173–189.

Roy, A. K., Shehzad, Z., Margulies, D. S., Kelly, A. M., Uddin, L. Q., Gotimer, K., et al. (2009). Functional connectivity of the human amygdala using resting state fMRI. *Neuroimage, 45*(2), 614–626.

Ruz, M., & Tudela, P. (2011). Emotional conflict in interpersonal interactions. *Neuroimage, 54*(2), 1685–1691.

Sauter, D. A., Eisner, F., Ekman, P., & Scott, S. K. (2010). Cross-cultural recognition of basic emotions through nonverbal emotional vocalizations. *Proceedings of the National Academy of Science U S A, 107*(6), 2408–2412.

Schnakers, C., Majerus, S., Goldman, S., Boly, M., Van Eeckhout, P., Gay, S., et al. (2008). Cognitive function in the locked-in syndrome. *Journal of Neurology*, *255*(3), 323–330.

Schrammel, F., Pannasch, S., Graupner, S. T., Mojzisch, A., & Velichkovsky, B. M. (2009). Virtual friend or threat? The effects of facial expression and gaze interaction on psychophysiological responses and emotional experience. *Psychophysiology*, *46*(5), 922–931.

Schurmann, M., Hesse, M. D., Stephan, K. E., Saarela, M., Zilles, K., Hari, R., et al. (2005). Yearning to yawn: The neural basis of contagious yawning. *Neuroimage*, *24*(4), 1260–1264.

Schwarzlose, R. F., Baker, C. I., & Kanwisher, N. (2005). Separate face and body selectivity on the fusiform gyrus. *Journal of Neuroscience*, *25*(47), 11055–11059.

Senju, A., & Johnson, M. H. (2009). Atypical eye contact in autism: models, mechanisms and development. *Neuroscience and Biobehavioral Reviews*, *33*(8), 1204–1214.

Seyfarth, R. M., & Cheney, D. L. (2003). Meaning and emotion in animal vocalizations. *Annals of the New York Academy of Sciences*, *1000*, 32–55.

Shamay-Tsoory, S. G. (2011). The neural bases for empathy. *Neuroscientist*, *17*(1), 18–24.

Simons, G., Pasqualini, M. C., Reddy, V., & Wood, J. (2004). Emotional and nonemotional facial expressions in people with Parkinson's disease. *Journal of the International Neuropsychology Society*, *10*(4), 521–535.

Sinke, C. B., Sorger, B., Goebel, R., & de Gelder, B. (2010). Tease or threat? Judging social interactions from bodily expressions. *Neuroimage*, *49*(2), 1717–1727.

Smeesters, C., Hayes, W. C., & McMahon, T. A. (2007). Determining fall direction and impact location for various disturbances and gait speeds using the articulated total body model. *Journal of Biomechanical Engineering*, *129*(3), 393–399.

Solano-Castiella, E., Anwander, A., Lohmann, G., Weiss, M., Docherty, C., Geyer, S., et al. (2010). Diffusion tensor imaging segments the human amygdala in vivo. *Neuroimage*, *49*(4), 2958–2965.

Sorger, B., Dahmen, B., Reithler, J., Gosseries, O., Maudoux, A., Laureys, S., et al. (2009). Another kind of "BOLD Response": Answering multiple-choice questions via online decoded single-trial brain signals. *Progress in Brain Research*, *177*, 275–292.

Sorger, B., Goebel, R., Schiltz, C., & Rossion, B. (2007). Understanding the functional neuroanatomy of acquired prosopagnosia. *Neuroimage*, *35*(2), 836–852.

Steinhauer, S. R., Siegle, G. J., Condray, R., & Pless, M. (2004). Sympathetic and parasympathetic innervation of pupillary dilation during sustained processing. *International Journal of Psychophysiology*, *52*(1), 77–86.

Steklis, H. D., & Harnad, S. R. (1976). From hand to mouth: Some critical stages in the evolution of language. *Annals of the New York Academy of Sciences*, *280*, 445–455.

Swartztrauber, K., & Fujikawa, D. G. (1998). An electroencephalographic study comparing maximum blink rates in schizophrenic and nonschizophrenic psychiatric patients and nonpsychiatric control subjects. *Biological Psychiatry*, *43*(4), 282–287.

Szameitat, D. P., Kreifelts, B., Alter, K., Szameitat, A. J., Sterr, A., Grodd, W., et al. (2010). It is not always tickling: Distinct cerebral responses during perception of different laughter types. *Neuroimage*, *53*(4), 1264–1271.

Tamietto, M., Castelli, L., Vighetti, S., Perozzo, P., Geminiani, G., Weiskrantz, L., et al. (2009). Unseen facial and bodily expressions trigger fast emotional reactions. *Proceedings of the National Academy of Science U S A*, *106*(42), 17661–17666.

Thompson, J. C., Clarke, M., Stewart, T., & Puce, A. (2005). Configural processing of biological motion in human superior temporal sulcus. *Journal of Neuroscience*, *25*(39), 9059–9066.

Todorov, A., Said, C. P., Engell, A. D., & Oosterhof, N. N. (2008). Understanding evaluation of faces on social dimensions. *Trends in Cognitive Sciences*, *12*(12), 455–460.

Touhara, K., & Vosshall, L. B. (2009). Sensing odorants and pheromones with chemosensory receptors. *Annual Review of Physiology*, *71*, 307–332.

Troisi, A., Pasini, A., Bersani, G., Di Mauro, M., & Ciani, N. (1991). Negative symptoms and visual behavior in DSM-III-R prognostic subtypes of schizophreniform disorder. *Acta Psychiatrica Scandinavica*, *83*(5), 391–394.

Tulen, J. H., Azzolini, M., de Vries, J. A., Groeneveld, W. H., Passchier, J., & van De Wetering, B. J. (1999). Quantitative study of spontaneous eye blinks and eye tics in Gilles de la Tourette's syndrome. *Journal of Neurology, Neurosurgery, and Psychiatry*, *67*(6), 800–802.

Uddin, L. Q., & Menon, V. (2009). The anterior insula in autism: Under-connected and under-examined. *Neuroscience and Biobehavioral Reviews*, *33*(8), 1198–1203.

Vaina, L. M., & Gross, C. G. (2004). Perceptual deficits in patients with impaired recognition of biological motion after temporal lobe lesions. *Proceedings of the National Academy of Science U S A*, *101*(48), 16947–16951.

van Schaik, C. P., & Burkart, J. M. (2011). Social learning and evolution: the cultural intelligence hypothesis. *Philosophical Transactions of the Royal Society of London, Series B: Biological Sciences*, *366*(1567), 1008–1016.

Weinberger, S. (2010). Airport security: Intent to deceive? *Nature*, *465*(7297), 412–415.

Wellman, H. M., & Brandone, A. C. (2009). Early intention understandings that are common to primates predict children's later theory of mind. *Current Opinion in Neurobiology*, *19*(1), 57–62.

Wheaton, K. J., Thompson, J. C., Syngeniotis, A., Abbott, D. F., & Puce, A. (2004). Viewing the motion of human body parts activates different regions of premotor, temporal, and parietal cortex. *Neuroimage*, *22*(1), 277–288.

Wiethoff, S., Wildgruber, D., Grodd, W., & Ethofer, T. (2009). Response and habituation of the amygdala during processing of emotional prosody. *Neuroreport*, *20*(15), 1356–1360.

Wild, B., Erb, M., & Bartels, M. (2001). Are emotions contagious? Evoked emotions while viewing emotionally expressive faces: Quality, quantity, time course and gender differences. *Psychiatry Research*, *102*(2), 109–124.

Wildgruber, D., Riecker, A., Hertrich, I., Erb, M., Grodd, W., Ethofer, T., et al. (2005). Identification of emotional intonation evaluated by fMRI. *Neuroimage*, *24*(4), 1233–1241.

Wilson, M. (2002). Six views of embodied cognition. *Psychonomic Bulletin and Review*, *9*(4), 625–636.

Zaki, J., Hennigan, K., Weber, J., & Ochsner, K. N. (2010). Social cognitive conflict resolution: Contributions of domain-general and domain-specific neural systems. *Journal of Neuroscience*, *30*(25), 8481–8488.

Zhou, W., & Chen, D. (2008). Encoding human sexual chemosensory cues in the orbitofrontal and fusiform cortices. *Journal of Neuroscience*, *28*(53), 14416–14421.

Zucker, N. L., Green, S., Morris, J. P., Kragel, P., Pelphrey, K. A., Bulik, C. M., et al. (2011). Hemodynamic signals of mixed messages during a social exchange. *Neuroreport*, *22*(9), 413–418.

chapter 11

Face Recognition

Rankin W. McGugin *and* Isabel Gauthier

Abstract

Facial recognition is generally regarded as being unique and distinct from object recognition; however, it may be possible to increase our understanding of it by framing it within the context of object recognition. Facial recognition can be viewed as a form of expert object recognition. Just as individuation can lead to holistic processing and specialization of the mechanisms for face recognition, the same behavioral and neural hallmarks of expertise are seen when individuation training is applied to novel objects. This chapter discusses how faces need to be compared to more than one object category at a time and how learning studies in non-face domains have advanced our understanding of the processes involved in face recognition. The chapter closes with a discussion of some challenges for ongoing research in this area, which have to do with brain behavior relationships, understanding the links between learning and development, and the need for computational models of expertise.

Key Words: perceptual expertise, object recognition, holistic processing, fusiform face area, prosopagnosia, autism

Face Recognition

Faces may be one of the most important categories of objects to which we are exposed. In recognizing others, we automatically identify them as individuals—Mom, Dad, Tom, stranger—from their faces. Even strangers' faces allow for rapid judgments of gender, age, and ethnicity, while also eliciting judgments of attractiveness and of many personality traits that underlie first impressions. In addition to these relatively stable attributes, we rely on dynamic information from faces to read the intentions, attentional status, and emotions of others. In cognitive neuroscience and related fields, this translates into a tremendous amount of research that concerns the processing of faces.

This chapter will not attempt to cover all such research. In fact, grouping disparate functions together simply because they operate on the same object—such as eye gaze processing, face identification and personality judgments—could lead to confusion in understanding any of them; for this reason, scientists often assume that these functions are inherently unique and largely subserved by independent brain systems. The extent of interactions is largely an empirical question of increasing interest in cognitive neuroscience (Martens, Leuthold, & Schweinberger, 2010; Perlman et al., 2009; Spangler, Schwarzer, Korell, & Maier-Karius, 2009). Therefore, while we may eventually find that other aspects of facial processing reciprocally affect how we identify faces, this chapter will address face identification independent of such influences. In addition, this chapter's discussion of face recognition is framed in the context of the identification and categorization of non-face stimuli. In contrast to the dominant tendency to dissociate face and object recognition research, this chapter explores face recognition as a special case of expert object recognition. While this framework is neither the only nor the dominant scheme for understanding face recognition, we argue that this approach may be most appropriate in the context of current knowledge.

We begin the chapter by introducing the debate over whether face recognition is special, then provide a review of related developmental, neuroimaging, and behavioral evidence. We end the chapter by briefly discussing computational models of face and object recognition and the challenges faced by modelers in trying to explain how the brain achieves expert face recognition.

Face Recognition as a Specialized Function: Behavioral Evidence
Behavioral Assessments of Face Processing Abound in the Literature

A broad range of phenomena suggest that upright faces are processed differently from other objects, with evidence often grounded in manipulations of up–down inversion in the stimulus plane. Turning faces upside down impairs recognition of them more than the equivalent change in most other objects (Hochberg & Galper, 1967; Yin, 1969; see Rossion, Gauthier, Goffaux, Tarr, & Crommelinck, 2002, for review). However, there is debate over whether these differences demonstrate the use of *qualitatively* different mechanisms for upright and inverted faces. At one extreme, Robbins and McKone (2003) suggest that it may be impossible to even train individuals to process inverted faces with the same holistic processing strategies that are automatically evoked with upright faces. At the opposite extreme, others argue that there are no qualitative differences in our processing of upright and inverted faces (Wenger & Townsend, 2001), or that observed differences exist only for familiar faces (Loftus, Oberg, & Dillon, 2004). Within the latter perspective, some research suggests that we generally seek to extract the same visual cues—namely, information near the eyes and eyebrows (Sekuler, Gaspar, Gold, & Bennett, 2004) within a 1.5 octave–wide band of spatial frequencies centered on seven cycles per face width (Gaspar, Sekuler, & Bennett, 2008)—to identify faces, regardless of orientation.

Thus, while inverted faces are sometimes considered a non-face object category that affords the best match in image properties with upright faces, they may not be comparable to other non-face objects. Relative to the processes recruited by upright faces, those recruited by non-face objects may differ qualitatively, whereas those recruited by inverted faces

may be only quantitatively different. Processing differences between upright and inverted faces may be simply due to our greater experience with front-facing upright faces, with limited generalization to the processing of inverted faces because the underlying features of identification are viewpoint specific (Grill-Spector et al., 1998; Logothetis, Pauls, & Poggio, 1995; Moses, Ullman, & Edelman, 1996; O'Toole, Edelman, & Bulthoff, 1998; O'Toole, Vetter, & Blanz, 1999; Troje & Kersten, 1999; Ullman, 1998).

There is more direct evidence that the magnitude of the inversion effect—namely, superior recognition for upright relative to inverted objects—correlates with the degree of experience with a category. For instance, a study of visual short-term memory (VSTM) capacity showed that typical observers could store more upright than inverted faces in VSTM (an inversion effect), whereas they showed no VSTM capacity difference in the number of upright and inverted cars (Curby & Gauthier, 2007). However, when individuals with expertise with cars were tested, an advantage for upright cars was also obtained (Curby, Glazek, & Gauthier, 2009). Furthermore, the number of upright cars maintained in VSTM correlated with an independent measure of perceptual expertise with cars. In sum, the differences between upright and inverted faces map well onto the differences that can be measured for the same category when novices and experts are compared (Curby & Gauthier, 2009a).

Some of the most interesting differences obtained between upright faces and non-face objects come from paradigms designed to measure configural and holistic processing.[1] The recognition of upright faces is particularly dependent on configural information, with observers easily detecting small changes in the distance between parts when a face is upright, whereas the same changes can be difficult to detect when the face is upside-down (Collishaw & Hole, 2002; Leder & Bruce, 2000; Leder, Candrian, Huber, & Bruce, 2001; Murray, Yong, & Rhodes, 2000; Rakover & Teucher, 1997; Rhodes, Brake, & Atkinson, 1993; Rotshtein, Malach, Hadar, Graif, & Hendler, 2001; Searcy & Bartlett, 1996; Tanaka & Sengco, 1997). In contrast, detecting a change in a feature (the shape or color of a face part) is much less affected by face inversion. A powerful demonstration of how upright face perception is particularly sensitive to configural changes is the "Thatcher effect" (first demonstrated on an image of Margaret Thatcher; Thompson, 1980). In this demonstration, face parts (e.g., the eyes and the mouth) are

Figure 11.1 Example of the "Thatcher effect" using the Mona Lisa, illustrating the sensitivity of upright face perception to configural changes. Turn the book upside down to see the dramatic change between upright and inverted perception.

turned upside-down, giving the face a grotesque expression that becomes almost undetectable when the entire image is inverted (see Figure 11.1). This example highlights the important role of configural information in face processing to encourage a holistic processing strategy whereby observers process all features of a face *together*, rather than independently.

Related research has shown that participants struggle to identify one face part accurately when other parts of the face are changed, even despite advance warning of the manipulation. For example, when asked to decide whether the nose in an image belongs to Elvis, observers make more mistakes or are slower if the eyes or mouth in the picture are replaced by those of Mick Jagger—a "whole-part" effect, discussed further in a later section. Phenomenologically, it seems that all parts of the composite face fuse together, taking the appearance of a new face that looks like neither of its "parents" (Young, Hellawell, & Hay, 1987). Holistic processing is influenced by the configuration of the parts: it becomes much easier to pay attention to one part and ignore the other parts if the parts of the composite face are misaligned in an abnormal configuration (e.g., Boutet, Gentes Hawn, & Chaudhuri, 2002; Carey & Diamond, 1994; Goffaux & Rossion,

2006; Hole, 1994; Le Grand, Mondloch, Maurer, & Brent, 2004).

Event-related potential (ERP) (Bentin, Allison, Puce, & Perez, 1996; Carmel & Bentin, 2002; Tanaka & Curran, 2001) and behavioral (de Heering, Rossion, Turati, & Simion, 2008; Le Grand, Mondloch, Maurer, & Brent, 2001, 2004) studies have shown that holistic processing can be obtained early during visual processing, and functional MRI (fMRI) studies have demonstrated that it can be correlated with activity in the fusiform gyrus (Gauthier & Tarr, 2002; Rotshtein, Geng, Driver, & Dolan, 2007). Originally, holistic effects were assumed to reflect the existence of a perceptual "holistic representation" in which parts of the face are not differentiated. This explanation has been challenged in the face of evidence suggesting a possible contribution from decisional mechanisms (Richler, Gauthier, Wenger, & Palmeri, 2008; Richler, Tanaka, Brown, & Gauthier, 2008; Wenger & Ingvalson, 2002, 2003). According to a decisional account of holistic effects face parts—like object parts—may be represented independently, but our experience with faces may have changed the way we make decisions about these parts. For instance, having learned that two faces with different eyes are likely to have different noses, we may be biased to expect (and amplify) such differences. The issue of the locus of holistic processing for faces is far from resolved. It is a relatively new question in face processing, one that is often completely ignored. The debate on this issue is only exacerbated by the limited number of tools available to probe such questions directly (Green & Swets, 1966; Kadlec, 1995, 1999; Kadlec & Townsend, 1992a, 1992b; Swets, 1996).

On the one hand, some studies agree that there is *no* evidence for a type of perceptual interaction that would arguably be the strongest form of perceptual dependence: a *violation of perceptual independence* between different features of a single face . Because perception is an inherently noisy process, a given face image perceived many times naturally will be perceived in different ways on several dimensions. For instance, with various viewing, the eyes of an image will be perceived as more or less distant, the mouth as more or less separated from the nose, the lips as more or less full, and so on. A violation of perceptual independence occurs if, over several presentations, the variations along one dimension prove to be correlated with those along another dimension (for instance, if the tendency to perceive the eyes as distant is correlated with the tendency to perceive the mouth as further away from the nose). Surprisingly, model simulations indicate that violations of perceptual independence cannot account for holistic processing as observed in the face composite effect (Richler, Gauthier, et al., 2008).

On the other hand, evidence suggests that the locus of holistic processing does not lie at the other extreme of the perceptual–decisional continuum, at the level of response interference. To test this, one study had observers learn the names of four different faces, two called "Fred" and two called "Bob" (Richler, Cheung, Wong & Gauthier, 2009). Participants were later asked to name parts of composites made by combining the top and bottom halves of these four faces. Response interference would be evidenced by finding more interference from a to-be-ignored (task-irrelevant) face part with a different name than from one that is equally unique *perceptually* but has the same name as the part to be identified. Unlike in Stroop-like paradigms (MacLeod, 1991), however, no such response interference was obtained. Instead, interference in this composite task was equivalent regardless of whether the to-be-ignored part had the same or a different name, or even if the to-be-ignored part was an unfamiliar face part with no attached name.

In sum, the nature of holistic processing appears to lie neither at the perceptual extreme nor at the level of response interference. There are other forms of perceptual and decisional types of interactions between face parts that may still prove to be the locus of these effects (e.g., Cheung, Richler, Palmeri, & Gauthier, 2008), but at the moment the methods that exist to tease them apart fail to produce unequivocal answers (Richler, Gauthier, et al., 2008; Wenger & Ingvalson, 2002).

As we evaluate the debate regarding whether holistic processing is uniquely dedicated to the processing of faces (Tanaka & Farah, 1993; Young et al., 1987), it is important to keep in mind how much remains unknown about the mechanism(s) behind holistic processing. Recent work suggests that individual differences in holistic processing do not predict face identification in younger adults, only in older adults (Crookes & McKone, 2009). Note also that holistic processing has been operationally defined in numerous ways, and it is unclear whether each definition gets at the same underlying phenomenon (see, e.g., Tanaka & Farah, 1993; Wenger & Townsend, 2001; Young et al., 1987). For instance, some work suggests that configural processing can break down relatively independently of holistic processing. Individuals with autism, like controls, experience interference from face parts that they are told to ignore. However, while such interference is released for controls if parts of face composites are misaligned, individuals with autism experience the same degree interference from irrelevant face parts regardless of alignment (Gauthier, Klaiman, & Schultz, 2009; Teunisse & de Gelder, 2003). In other work, face-like holistic effects can be obtained with novel objects because of contextual influences (e.g., if the encoding of a novel object is preceded by the encoding of a face). Like holistic effects in individuals with autism, however, such holistic effects are not sensitive to the configuration of the parts. These results suggest an attentional or strategic dimension to holistic processing that is not highly sensitive to the configuration of image parts but which may serve as a precursor for the more automatic level of holistic processing typically observed for faces.

A final note on holistic processing concerns one of the methods often used to measure this phenomenon, the composite face task, in which judgments regarding the top halves of two faces are influenced by irrelevant differences in the bottom haves of the faces (Carey & Diamond, 1994; Hole, 1994; Hole, George, & Dunsmore, 1999; Le Grand et al., 2004;

McKone, Kanwisher, & Duchaine, 2007; Young et al., 1987). There is evidence that the standard measure of holistic processing in the composite paradigm, the advantage for perceiving composite parts that are misaligned relative to those that are aligned, can be confounded by response biases—in other words, the observers' willingness to make a specific response as opposed to their ability to perceive the faces accurately. These response biases can be influenced by manipulations of the images (e.g., spatial frequencies; Cheung et al., 2008) or even by deceiving observers about the proportions of various kinds of trials in the experiment (Richler, Cheung, & Gauthier, 2011). A different version of the composite task, called the "complete composite paradigm," uses signal detection theory to separate holistic processing from response bias and is robust to various stimulus and strategic manipulations (Richler et al., 2011). While these issues may appear to be but methodological quibbles, the problems of measurement can contribute to conflicting results from studies using the composite task. For instance, while it has been argued that holistic processing can be acquired for non-face objects (Gauthier & Tarr, 2002; Wong, Palmeri, & Gauthier, 2009), other studies fail to replicate this result (Robbins & McKone, 2007). These opposite results are obtained with the two versions of the task, and they often produce incompatible answers (Cheung et al., 2008). The version of the composite task ultimately adopted as a standard will critically affect many conclusions about normal face processing, its development, face-processing deficits, and the expertise hypothesis. Here, as in other areas of studies, cognitive neuroscientists need to compare, evaluate, and standardize their measures.

Face Recognition as a Specialized Function: Neural Evidence

Face Cells and Face Areas in the Macaque

In addition to the behavioral evidence that face processing differs from that of other objects, converging evidence for a specialized response to faces comes from virtually every technique available to cognitive neuroscience. In the early 1970s, Gross and colleagues employed single-cell recording in monkeys to reveal the existence of a small proportion of temporal lobe neurons that respond selectively to biological stimuli such as hands, faces, and bodies (Desimone & Gross, 1979; Gross, Bender, & Rocha-Miranda, 1969; Gross, Rocha-Miranda, & Bender, 1972). Later work indicated two populations of face cells, one in inferior temporal (IT)

gyrus with cells differentially tuned to the identity of faces, and one in the superior temporal sulcus (STS) that was more sensitive to eye gaze and facial expression (Bruce, Desimone & Gross, 1981; Desimone, 1991; Desimone, Albright, Gross, & Bruce, 1984; Hasselmo, Rolls, & Bayliss, 1989; Perrett & Mistlin, 1990; Perrett, Rolls, & Cann, 1982; Perrett et al. 1984, 1985, 1990). Functional MRI studies (Tsao, Moeller, & Freiwald, 2008) have identified six areas of face selectivity in the temporal lobe of the macaque (compared to between four and five areas of selectivity in the human brain). We currently lack a clear understanding of the homologies between these areas in the two species, though the combination of neurophysiology with fMRI will facilitate this work. Whereas standard neurophysiological studies have found only a small fraction of recorded neurons selective for faces, use of fMRI to guide neurophysiological recordings has led to a much greater proportion of face-selective cells. Specifically, when face-selective patches are identified with fMRI, nearly all recorded neurons in these patches respond as face selective (Tsao et al., 2008).

An outstanding question concerns how these populations of neurons encode the information needed to support decisions about individual faces. One solution supports a very sparse neural code, whereby very few neurons encode the identity of each face (Quiroga, Kreiman, Koch, & Fried, 2008; Quiroga, Reddy, Kreiman, Koch, & Fried, 2005; Rolls & Tovee, 1995; Young & Yamane, 1992). An advantage of sparse coding is a limited overlap between the representations of different faces, minimizing interference on known faces when new faces are learned. In contrast to such sparse specialization is the demonstration of a distributed code, whereby the pattern of activity over a large population of cells represents the identity of a face (Riesenhuber & Poggio, 2002; Rolls, 2000; Rolls & Tovee, 1995; Young & Yamane, 1992). Relative to a sparse code, a coarse or distributed code has more capacity (the number of faces that can be stored grows exponentially, rather than linearly, with the number of neurons in the population), and the representation of any one face is more robust to damage. The current consensus specifies a relatively sparse neural code with a small number of cells that represent behaviorally relevant features diagnostic of identity, expression, and gaze direction, among other things (Bruce, Desimone, & Gross, 1981; Desimone, 1991; Desimone et al., 1984; Hasselmo et al., 1989; Perrett & Mistlin, 1990; Perrett et al., 1982, 1984, 1985, 1990). Analysis of the responses to cartoon

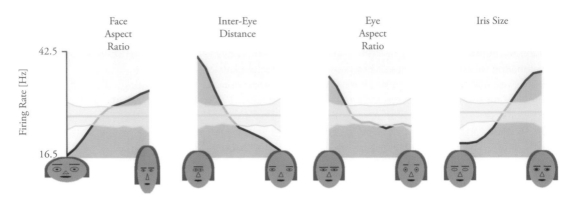

Figure 11.2 Four out of nineteen possible significant feature tuning curves of one middle face patch example neuron. The "cloud" in the center indicates the range of shuffle control–generated tuning curves, a baseline comparison for the tuning effect.

Figure courtesy of Weinrich Freiwald.

faces in one face-selective patch in monkey cortex, the "middle face patch," revealed a coarse coding of faces (Freiwald, Tsao, & Livingstone, 2009). Each neuron responded monotonically to variations of a few face parts (approximately three parts), and the results suggested that the cells lay somewhere halfway on the continuum of being part-based vs. holistic (Figure 11.2).

In addition to this sort of research, which describes the response of individual cells within the population of face selective cells, there is other research that is more concerned with how such responses are combined into perceptual decisions at later stages. For instance, work using linear classifier algorithms has shown that face and object categorization and even identification is robust when based on the accumulated responses of approximately 100 randomly selected IT neurons, using very few spikes in a short time window (little more than 10 ms; Hung, Kreiman, Poggio, & DiCArlo, 2005). However, a great deal of distributed information is found in randomly selected neurons, which also suggests that almost every neuron contributes. It is still unclear exactly how many neurons in each area actually participate in any given decision we make about a face.

Neuroimaging in Humans

Although a few intracranial recording studies have been conducted in surgical patients with intractable epilepsy (Allison, Ginter, et al., 1994; Allison, McCarthy, Nobre, Puce, & Belger, 1994), most human evidence for face selectivity comes from less invasive neuroimaging methods or neuropsychological studies. Positron emission tomography (PET) studies in the early 1990s highlighted a region in the temporal lobe that showed selective activation for faces (Haxby et al., 1991; Sergent, Ohta, & MacDonald, 1992). These early findings were confirmed and further investigated using fMRI (Kanwisher, McDermottk, & Chun, 1997; Tong, Nakayama, Moscovitch, Weinrib, & Kanwisher, 2000; Tong, Nakayama, Vaughan & Kanwisher, 1998), and the face-selective region of the temporal lobe was labeled the "fusiform face area" or FFA. The right FFA is the most studied face-selective region of the human brain, because its robust selectivity allows for easy identification in individual subjects. In addition, its stable location across subjects facilitates easy detection even with relatively crude methods of averaging brains of different individuals. An FFA is also observed in the left hemisphere, though typically smaller and more variable in this location than in its right counterpart. Furthermore, an occipital face area (OFA) is often observed in both hemispheres (Gauthier, Tarr, Anderson, Skudlarski, & Gore, 1999), as well as face-selective regions in the posterior STS (Haxby, Hoffman, & Gobbini, 2000; Puce, Allison, Gore, & McCarthy, 1995) and anterior temporal lobe (Bukach, Bub, Gauthier, & Tarr, 2006; Davies-Thompson, Gouws, & Andrews, 2009; Kriegeskorte, Formisano, Sorger, & Goebel, 2007; Tsao et al., 2008). Similar to work in the monkey, human studies suggest that the OFA and FFA are more important for the identification of faces (George et al., 1999; Haxby et al., 2001; Hoffman & Haxby, 2000; O'Toole, Jiang, Abdi, & Haxby, 2005; Sergent et al., 1992; Tong et al., 1998), whereas face-selective regions of the STS appear more important for processing eye gaze, expression, and dynamic facial movements (Beauchamp, Argall, Bodurka, Duyn, & Martin, 2004; Haxby et al., 2001; Hoffman & Haxby, 2000; Puce, Allison,

Bentin, Gore, & McCarthy, 1998). Recent mapping of tracts of white matter between face-selective areas in the human brain indicates that anomalies in the fibers that connect fusiform regions to the anterior temporal lobe and the frontal lobe are associated with congenital deficits in face processing (Thomas et al., 2006).

One controversy in the interpretation of hot spots of selectivity for object categories in the brain and, in particular the FFA, stems from experiments demonstrating distributed and overlapping responses to objects from various categories in the visual system and beyond. One view supported by classifier algorithms argues that faces—like other object categories—are represented in a distributed manner without a unique status for the FFA. Another view assumes that the recognition of most non-face objects is supported by distributed representations, while that of faces is unique and more dependent on a localized brain representation. For instance, two fMRI studies with a similar methodology found results that appear to contradict each other on these issues. Haxby et al. (2001) used multivariate pattern analysis (MVPA) to explore patterns of activity in response to faces and various object categories (e.g., cats, bottles, chairs). These authors found that information about the category membership of the object being viewed was distributed across visual cortex. In contrast, Spiridon and Kanwisher (2002) conducted different analyses on a similar dataset and found that the cluster of voxels most selective for faces was better at discriminating face from non-face categories than non-face from non-face categories. This was not the case for the voxels selective for other categories and was interpreted as evidence that faces, more so than other objects, are represented by highly category-selective neurons.

A recent computational study simulating a similar experiment with the stimuli from Haxby et al. (2001) has shed light on the discrepancy between the two findings (Cowell, Huber, & Cottrell, 2009). Within an unsupervised neural network, object representations were allowed to develop into a topographically organized map. Patterns of activity in the network were then analyzed using "virtual MVPA," and the results of both Haxby et al. (2001) and Spiridon and Kanwisher (2002) were successfully replicated. Most importantly, even in the context of this neural network, only clusters selective for faces were able to discriminate faces from other categories, which could solely occur owing to the similarity structure of the stimuli themselves. In other words, faces can appear to be "special" not because the brain represents them in a qualitatively different manner from that for other objects but merely because the face images used in a given experiment are less variable than those of other categories. These results by themselves do not argue against the special status of face-selective areas, but they do suggest that new standards are needed for determining the most appropriate stimuli required for answering this question.

In the temporal domain, ERP measured by electroencephalography (EEG) (or myeloencephalography [MEG]) also produces face-selective responses. In humans, electrophysiological studies have revealed a face-selective potential that peaks negatively at 170 ms post-stimulus onset and is thus conventionally called the N170 (Bentin et al., 1996; Carmel & Bentin, 2002; Tanaka & Curran, 2001). Typically, this potential is strongest over right hemisphere occipitotemporal electrodes and, specifically, appears to have a source near the face-selective areas in ventral cortex (Halgren, Raij, Marinkovic, Jousmaeki, & Hari, 2000; Liu, Harris, & Kanwisher, 2002). The N170 is slightly but faithfully delayed (~10 ms) and often larger in amplitude following the inversion of faces (Bentin et al., 1996; Rossion et al., 1999, 2000; Rossion, Gauthier, Goffaux, Tarr, & Crommelinck, 2002), and it shows a weakened response for repeated relative to novel upright but not inverted faces (Jacques, D'arripe, & Rossion, 2007; Jacques & Rossion, 2006a). Although the N170 is highly dependent on the presence of the eyes in the face (Bentin, Golland, Flevaris, Robertson, & Moscovitch, 2006), it is thought to reflect structural encoding more than emotional expression (Ashley, Vuilleumier, & Swick, 2003; Eimer & Holmes, 2002). In addition, the N170 waveform correlates with measures of holistic processing (Gauthier, Curran, Curby, & Collins, 2003; Jacques & Rossion, 2004, 2006a, 2006b; Rossion, Kung, & Tarr, 2004). Recently, a similar potential has been measured in scalp recordings in the monkey, which offers further promise of bridging animal and human work that traditionally depended on separate methods (de Haan, Pascalis, & Johnson, 2002).

Face-Selective Deficits

Regardless of deficits' origins, since there are anatomically localized areas in the brain that are functionally specialized for face processing, focal brain damage may sometimes result in lesions that selectively impair face recognition. Such deficits, collectively called "prosopagnosia" (Bodamer, 1947), are rare and generally follow damage to occipitotemporal cortex. Lesions resulting in prosopagnosia vary in their specific location, and perhaps expectedly, the patients also vary greatly in their pattern of impairments (Damasio, Damasio, & Van Hoesen, 1982). A meta-analysis surveyed case reports of patients with prosopagnosia and found that, in contrast to the locus of achromatopsia (a color recognition deficit that very often co-occurs with prosopagnosia), there was no single contiguous region damaged in the majority of patients (Bouvier & Engel, 2006). Most cases show lesions near the OFA, with surprisingly few cases showing damage in the STS or where the FFA proper is most routinely observed in fMRI studies, although there was a focus of overlap in a region medial to the typical FFA. The involvement of the OFA in many cases of prosopagnosia is consistent with transcranial magnetic stimulation (TMS) work in which transient lesions in the right OFA produced deficits in recognition of face parts (Pitcher, Walsh, Yovel, & Duchaine, 2007) or in the processing of facial expression (Pitcher, Garrido, Walsh, & Duchaine, 2008) but not the processing of relationships between face parts (Pitcher et al., 2007; Steeves et al., 2009). Thus, this area may be involved in many instances of face recognition deficits because its role is relatively basic.

In contrast to "acquired" prosopagnosia, which results from a brain damage, "congenital" or "developmental" prosopagnosia is a lifelong impairment in the absence of visible brain damage. Both forms of the disorder are associated with the inability to recognize familiar faces, yet they appear to reflect entirely different problems. Indeed, in many individuals with congenital prosopagnosia, faces induce normal levels of activity in visual areas (Avidan, Hasson, Malach, & Behrmann, 2005), and when faces are repeated, they produce normal patterns of decreasing activity or adaptation (Avidan & Berhmann, 2008). However, the integrity of the white matter tracts that connect face-selective areas in occipitoventral cortex to anterior temporal and frontal areas appears to be compromised in at least some individuals with prosopagnosia (Thomas et al., 2006). Research on congenital prosopagnosia adds to the evidence from acquired prosopagnosia to suggest that face recognition depends on a large network of interactive areas.

In addition to the structural and functional integrity of this network, experience must also be considered to account for our ability to recognize faces. Indeed, a lack of experience has been invoked

to explain problems with face recognition in another population: individuals with autism spectrum disorders (ASD). Individuals with ASD suffer from multifaceted impairments that include deficits in language and communication skills, repetitive behaviors, and restricted interests and difficulties with social interactions. Both fMRI and ERP studies suggest abnormal processing of faces in ASD; for example, a prolonged latency (McPartland, Dawson, Webb, Panagiotides, & Carver, 2004; O'Connor, Hamm, & Kirk, 2005; Webb, Dawson, Bernier, & Panagiotides, 2006) and reduced amplitude (Bailey, Braeutigam, Jousmaki, & Swithenby, 2005; O'Connor et al., 2005) of face-specific potentials (i.e., the N170) have been associated with ASD, and the right hemisphere face-processing bias routinely observed in healthy individuals is not present in individuals with ASD (Dawson, Webb, Carver, Panagiotides, & McPartland, 2004; McPartland et al., 2004; Senju, Tojo, Yaguchi, & Hasegawa, 2005; Webb et al., 2006). Behavioral evidence also suggests that people with ASD process faces using abnormal strategies (Klin, Jones, Schultz, Volkmar, & Cohen, 2002; Langdell, 1978; Rutherford, Clements, & Sekuler, 2007).

Interestingly, fewer and smaller neurons have been found in the fusiform gyrus of individuals with autism (van Kooten et al., 2008). According to one account, these abnormalities are the result, rather than the cause, of developing with the difficulty of the severe social impairments central to ASD (Schultz et al., 2000). This view is supported by the finding that when someone with an ASD develops expertise with a non-face category, they can show selective activation for this category in areas of the fusiform gyrus that are typically responsive to faces (Grelotti et al., 2005; Schultz et al., 2003). This finding suggests that hypoactivation for faces is due to a lack of general interest, experience, or both. In addition, a recent behavioral study characterizing holistic processing of faces in autism concluded that the abnormal processing strategy used for faces in ASD participants is similar to that observed in novice observers processing objects (Gauthier et al., 2009). This experience-based explanation of face deficits in ASD is not the only one available; for instance, people with ASD appear to have problems with configural perception that extend beyond the processing of faces (Behrmann, Thomas, & Humphreys, 2006), which could restrict normal development of face-processing skills while also acting as a more primary cause of the problem.

Whether or not a certain kind of practice with faces can alleviate this specific problem in ASD remains to be seen, but promise in the idea stems from a larger body of research on the role of expertise in producing behavioral and neural markers of face-like processing (discussed in the next section of this chapter).

Explaining the Origins of Face Specialization

As surveyed in the first part of this chapter, there are multiple sources of evidence suggesting that face recognition is "specialized" compared to the processing of other objects. There is at least one important caveat to this conclusion: most studies, neural or behavioral, that conclude that faces are special do so on the basis of a contrast between faces and a single non-face object category. Thus, while throughout the literature faces have been compared to many other categories, far less research has been collected regarding significant differences among non-face object categories on measures thought to capture an important aspect of face processing. The few exceptions (Haxby et al., 2001; Williams, Willenbockel, & Gauthier, 2009) often highlight surprising results that have the potential to change the way in which this literature is interpreted. For instance, one study compared the magnitude of the famous Thatcher effect (TE; Thompson, 1980) in faces to the same manipulation in other domains (see Figure 11.1). The ability to detect local inversion of parts when the whole stimulus is upright vs. inverted was tested with faces and with several other categories (Wong, Twedt, Sheinberg, & Gauthier, 2010). On the one hand, the effect was larger for faces than any other tested category (apart from letter strings), which would predict that a series of studies comparing faces to *one* other category at a time would nicely lead to the conclusion that the TE reflects a process unique to faces. But a different picture emerges when the relationship between the magnitude of the TE and upright performance for each category is considered. The magnitude of the TE was predicted by the averaged upright d' (upright: $r = .804$, $p = .029$; see Figure 11.1). In fact, the same trend was found when the human and animal face conditions were removed (upright: $r = .795$, $p = .11$). These results suggest that the TE can be predicted to a large extent by the ability of observers to detect local changes in upright images. This highlights a domain-general interpretation of the effect: our skill at detecting changes in an image varies across categories and may be influenced by experience, as we will discuss here.

To apply the modular account (see Fodor, 1983, 2000) to face specialization is to suggest that not only are faces processed differently but they are processed in a way that cannot be used with non-face objects even with extensive experience (Robbins & McKone, 2003). Before we review empirical evidence in favor of the main alternative account of this face specialization, the expertise hypothesis, it is important to highlight the fundamental importance of asking whether or not face perception is the product of a domain-specific brain module. As with any debate that goes on long enough, the controversy comes with drawbacks: complex issues become polarized and oversimplified, and the endless pendulum swinging between opposing views may suggest that there is no answer in sight. But we would argue that the question remains an important one. In this section, in reviewing the work on face-like behavioral and neural effects in perceptual experts with non-face objects, we hope to illustrate that much has been and will continue to be learned by asking this question.

First, by exploring beyond the visual system's general organization to study how it learns, we gain knowledge about the development of the system and associated plasticity of visual-processing mechanisms. Second, we learn about how practice—both controlled and non-controlled—in specific conditions and contexts can produce performance that rivals our exquisite face perception skills. Third, and perhaps most important, we can make progress on models that help understand category-specific responses across the brain.

Specifically, one potential limitation of modular accounts stems from the fact that they propose explanations that are domain-specific. This means that explaining the responses of a face cell or a face-selective area does not facilitate our understanding of the processing in any other cell or part of the visual system. To some extent it amounts to trying to understand the whole of the brain, one small area at a time. In contrast, expertise accounts, first inspired by attempts to explain the brain's selectivity for faces, have been adopted to explain specialized behaviors and neural responses in many domains (including in nonvisual modalities; Behrmann & Ewell, 2003; Chartrand, Peretz, & Belin, 2008; Kilgour & Lederman, 2006) and explain why some cases of expertise (e.g., car expertise, bird expertise) overlap with face processing while others do not (e.g., letter perception, reading of musical notation). In seeking a domain-general account of specialization for faces, general principles learned about the visual system can contribute to our understanding of face specialization. One example is work that reveals how visual areas beyond those classically considered retinotopic still have a topographic representation (Grill-Spector et al., 1998; Levy, Hasson, Avidan, Hendler, & Malach, 2001; Malach, Levy, & Hasson, 2002; Malach et al., 1995). This work suggests that one principle determining the part of the visual system specialized by experience with a given category of objects is the spatial-resolution requirements of the task generally performed with these objects during learning.

In sum, by asking whether faces are "special," scientists motivate studies that investigate the forces behind the specialization of faces while concurrently addressing more general learning mechanisms.

The Expertise Account of Face Specialization

When considering what makes face processing appear so distinct from the processing of other objects, the main hypothesis is that the differences are acquired through experience. By contrast, the main alternative is that experience plays no role and observed differences are innate (Crookes & McKone, 2009; McKone & Crookes, 2007). While we may be tempted to look to developmental studies to address this question, in reality one of the major challenges in this field remains to clarify the link between face processing as studied in newborns and infants and face processing in the adult (we discuss this challenge specifically toward the end of the chapter). To a great extent, conclusions regarding the origins of face specialization hinge on evidence that non-face objects can be processed similarly to faces by expert observers. In other words, while it is relatively difficult to obtain positive evidence for an innate basis of a specific ability, it is logically easier to challenge these claims by questioning the evidence for a domain-specific ability.

The idea that our expertise with faces can explain specialization for face perception is a specific case of a more general account that has been called the "process-map hypothesis" (Gauthier, 2000). The "map" in process-map refers to the layout of visual areas in the brain, with each area best suited for a certain kind of processing. The process-map hypothesis suggests that category selectivity observed in any given region (e.g., the selectivity of the FFA for faces) reflects task-driven differences even when the selectivity is measured in the absence of a task. Associations between a category and a task and, by extension, between a category and the processes best suited to perform this task (as well as the brain areas

that support these processes) arise from our prior history with a given category and tend to generalize to novel objects of the trained category.

Prior work on categorization suggests that psychological dimensions instructing object categorization can be given more weight than those deemed nondiagnostic; for instance, color is emphasized over shape if color is diagnostic for categorization (Kruschke, 1992; Nosofsky, 1986). In addition, perceptual discriminability can increase in a relatively stable and task-independent fashion for dimensions that are diagnostic during category learning (Goldstone, 1994; Goldstone & Styvers, 2001). The process-map hypothesis can be seen as a neural instantiation of these stable modulations of the psychological space. By virtue of intersecting gradients of different kinds (e.g., sensitivity to color, shape, motion, region of space, size of features, curvature, symmetry), extrastriate cortex may be thought of as a multidimensional map in which each location presents a unique combination of preferred attributes (Gauthier, 2000; Malach et al., 2002). Task-driven selective attention can enhance activity in some regions of the map; for example, attention to color or motion can enhance activity in color-selective area V4 or motion-selective area V5, respectively (Chawla, Ress, & Friston, 1999). Accompanying the repeated experience of performing a task with an object category may leave a lasting emphasis on certain diagnostic attributes, weighting part of the map accordingly. Consequently, the regions of the map best suited for the task may become associated with objects of a category and become automatically engaged by these objects, regardless of the current task.

In the case of expertise in face recognition, the task postulated to specialize regions of the occipitotemporal cortex and lead to holistic processing is individuation. In individuation, unique exemplars are represented according to distinguishing traits and characteristics. Individuation requires a shift in the level of abstraction with which observers identify objects. Naïve observers represent objects at the basic level (e.g., "house," "car," "chair"), whereas practice with individuation promotes subordinate-level recognition at a finer grain of detail (e.g., "Chalet bungalow," "Honda Accord," "Aeron office chair") (Rosch, Mervis, Gray, Johnson, & Boyes-Braem, 1976). Because it promotes automatic categorization at the subordinate level (detailed discriminations over individual exemplars sharing the same basic configuration), individuation has been found to promote a more "holistic" processing of exemplars of the trained category (Wong, Palmeri, & Gauthier, 2009).

THE EXPERTISE ACCOUNT: BEVAVIORAL EVIDENCE

The role individuation plays in the development of expertise has been explicitly manipulated in several training studies using diverse object domains. Some of the earliest evidence is from experimental studies in which participants were trained to individuate novel objects (Greebles) and in which they eventually demonstrated certain hallmarks of face-like expertise, such as the ability to learn new exemplars more rapidly and with increased sensitivity to small configural changes (Gauthier & Tarr, 1997; also see Gauthier & Tarr, 2002; Gauthier, Williams, Tarr, & Tanaka, 1998; Gauthier et al., 1999; Nishimura & Maurer, 2008; Rossion et al., 2004). Another study using yet another novel object set (Ziggerins) found similar results: participants that received individuation training acquired hallmarks of face-like processing, but participants that underwent categorization training did not (see Figure 11.3). Importantly, the development of these face-like effects through practice with the task of individuation is by no means limited to novel object categories. When trained to classify birds (wading birds or owls; Scott, Tanaka, Sheinberg, & Curran, 2008; Tanaka, Curran, & Sheinberg, 2005) and cars (sedans, SUVs, and antique cars; Scott et al., 2008) at either the subordinate level (species, or make or model, respectively) or the basic level (family or class, respectively), only participants with a subordinate-level individuation (as opposed to basic-level categorization) practice task showed characteristics of expertise.

These studies provide evidence that individuation can lead to the development of certain distinguishing hallmarks of expertise in novel objects, natural objects, and artificial manmade objects such as cars. Individuation training has even been shown to improve discrimination performance within a category of objects for which expertise is already very robust: human faces. It is commonly observed that most people are better able to recognize faces from their own race relative to faces of less familiar races (Allport, 1954; Anthony, Copper & Mullen, 1992; Bothwell, Brigham, & Malpass, 1989; Malpass & Kravitz, 1969; Meissner & Brigham, 2001), and this effect has been attributed to a tendency to individuate same-race faces at a more specific level of abstraction while categorizing other-race faces at a more general level (Lebrecht, Pierce, Tarr, & Tanaka, 2009; Levin, 1996; 2000; Tanaka & Pierce,

2009). When Caucasian participants were trained to individuate African-American faces (learn names) and make basic-level judgments on Hispanic faces (determine which of the two eyes is brighter), or vise versa, only the individuated race was associated with post-training, category-specific expert skills at the subordinate level (McGugin, Tanaka, Lebrecht, Tarr, & Gauthier, 2011).

Similar to this so-called other-race effect, an "other-age effect" has been documented. Individuals are better at recognizing same-age than other-age faces, and this ability can also be related to visual experience and, specifically, expert individuation (Anastasi & Rhodes, 2005; Kuefner, Macchi Cassia, Picozzi, & Bricolo, 2008; Lamont, Stewart-Williams, & Podd, 2005). For example, a group of preschool teachers (deemed "experts" at processing

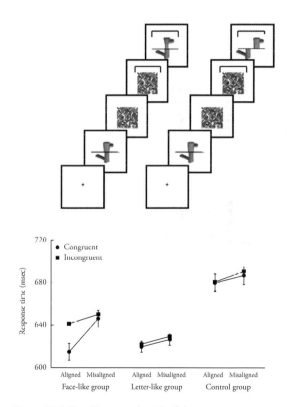

Figure 11.3 Top: Two example trials of the composite paradigm using Ziggerins. Images are presented in immediate succession at fixation, and the cue bracket indicates whether the top or bottom parts of the composite Ziggerin should be compared. *Left:* A "different aligned" trial, which is an incongruent trial because the response for cued and uncued parts is incongruent. *Right:* A "same misaligned" trial that is congruent. **Bottom:** Response time showing a congruency by configuration interaction indicating holistic processing, only in the group who practiced in the "face-like" training paradigm that requires individuation.

Adapted from Wong et al. (2009).

children faces) showed equal or even greater holistic processing for children's than for adult faces (de Heering & Rossion, 2008). An independent group of researchers found a larger composite effect (indicating more holistic processing) when child faces were viewed by children than when viewed by adults (Susilo, Crookes, McKone, & Turner, 2009). In addition to race and age, similar expertise-like effects have been observed at the species level: for instance, both human and monkeys demonstrate greater discrimination and recognition of faces from their own species (conspecific) than that of other species (nonconspecific) (Pascalis & Bachevalier, 1998). Certain hallmarks of expertise—such as the composite effect, inversion effect, and sensitivity to second-order relations—have been observed in chimpanzees for conspecific but not non-conspecific faces (Parr & Heintz, 2006; Parr, Heintz, & Akamagwuna, 2006; Parr, Winslow, & Hopkins, 1999; but see Martin-Malivel & Okada, 2007; Parr, Dove, & Hopkins, 1998). Discrepancies in processing capabilities across species—similar to those observed across races—can be attributed to differences in experience and practice.

These studies show the importance of individuation for the development of expertise. Critically, individuation with non-face objects leads to behavioral and neural markers of face-like expertise. Behavioral evidence for face-like processing of objects of expertise has been obtained for diverse paradigms and stimulus sets.

First, the whole-part paradigm was developed as the original operationalization of holistic recognition, according to which holistic processing is evidenced by superior identification of object features when presented within the context of the whole object ("whole" condition with configural information present) relative to when the components must be identified in isolation ("part" condition with no configural information) (Tanaka & Farah, 1993; Tanaka & Sengco, 1997). Superior recognition for parts presented in the context of the whole has been documented for novel objects in expert observers (Gauthier & Tarr, 1997). Importantly, however, while the whole-part paradigm assesses the interdependence among components in an object, the composite paradigm measures the ability to selectively attend to a face part–functionally speaking, the inverse of holistic processing (Carey & Diamond, 1994; Hole, 1994; Young et al., 1987). The paradigm requires selective attention to a "target" part (usually the top or bottom of an object) while measuring the influence of an irrelevant part, which can be in the correct configuration or not. This paradigm produces robust holistic processing for upright aligned face parts but also greater holistic processing associated with subordinate-level expertise more generally. For example, an increase in the influence of an irrelevant part on target-part matching of Greebles is observed following individuation Greeble training (Gauthier & Tarr, 2002) and for Ziggerins after individuation Ziggerin training (Wong, Palmeri & Gauthier, 2009).

Finally, because holistic processing (relative to processing by components) is highly vulnerable to shifts in orientation, stimulus inversion has been used as an effective, albeit indirect, measure (Farah, Wilson, Drain, & Tanaka; 1998; Tanaka & Farah, 1993; Young et al., 1987). Initially thought to be special for faces, inversion effects have subsequently been observed for objects of expertise: for example, inverted dogs processed by expert dog show hosts but not dog "novices" (Diamond & Carey, 1986; although see Robbins & McKone, 2007, for a failure to replicate this inversion effect), inverted cars with car experts (Curby et al., 2009), and same-race faces relative to other-race faces (Hancock & Rhodes, 2008; Rhodes, Tan, Brake, & Taylor, 1989).

Another behavioral effect originally assumed unique to faces but recently shown to extend to objects of expertise is sensitivity to the spatial-frequency content of an image (McGugin & Gauthier, 2009; Williams et al., 2009; see Figure 11.4). Relative to the perception of a common object, face perception is highly sensitive to manipulations of image format, including contrast reversal (Gaspar, Bennett, & Sekuler, 2008; Hayes, 1988; Subramaniam & Biederman, 1997), the use of line drawing (e.g., Bruce, Hanna, Dench, Healey, & Burton, 1992), and spatial-frequency filtering (Fiser, Subramaniam, & Biederman, 2001; Goffaux, Gauthier, & Rossion, 2003). If expertise leads to increased holistic processing as discussed above, and if holistic processing is sensitive to manipulations of spatial frequency, then we may suspect that sensitivity to spatial-frequency changes in the image content will increase with increasing expertise for the tested image category. Indeed, evidence shows that an observer's degree of perceptual expertise with modern cars can predict the magnitude of sensitivity to spatial-frequency manipulations in the image (Williams, Willenbockel, & Gauthier, 2009).

Both holistic processing and sensitivity to spatial frequency content suggest that information that experts have learned to use interferes with performance when the information is not relevant for

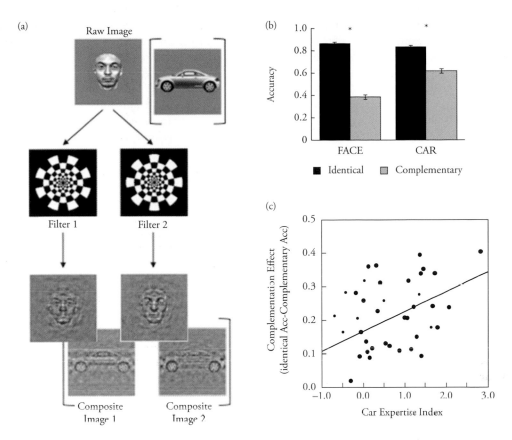

Figure 11.4 Illustration of sensitivity to the spatial-frequency content of visual objects. **a**. A raw image is filtered into two composite images such that each composite represents every other spatial frequency and orientation combination. Although two resulting composites represent the same physical identity, they share no mutual low-level visual information. **b**. Accuracy data from a same–different matching task. Individuals are better at matching identical composites than complementary composites, demonstrating viewer sensitivity to manipulations of spatial-frequency content. **c**. The magnitude of sensitivity to spatial-frequency manipulations of car images (Identical car accuracy–Complementary car accuracy) is associated with individual levels of car expertise (McGugin & Gauthier, 2009).

current goals. In the composite paradigm, the task-irrelevant half of a face or expert object interferes with processing of the target part (Cheung et al., 2008; Young et al., 1987). Similarly, vulnerability to manipulations of the spatial-frequency information in an image may occur because expert viewers find it especially difficult to ignore irrelevant information (i.e., low-level spatial frequency changes) while processing only the identity of an image. A different type of interference is observed between faces and objects of expertise that are simultaneously available for perceptual processing. If faces and objects of expertise rely on common perceptual mechanisms, their concurrent processing may lead to mutual interference, such that objects of expertise interfere with or limit the processing of other objects of expertise. Indeed, in one study participants were asked to identify which of two targets (either two faces, watches or cars) appeared in rapid

sequence of images alternating between items from the target category and items from a task-irrelevant category (McKeeff, McGugin, Tong, & Gauthier, 2010). With increasing car expertise (as measured in an independent task), participants required more time to identify a target car among distractor faces than that needed for watches, a finding indicating that faces interfered with car processing as a function of car expertise.

THE EXPERTISE ACCOUNT: NEURAL EVIDENCE

These behavioral markers of expert individuation—holistic processing, sensitivity to spatial frequency information, and competition for shared perceptual processes between objects of expertise—are not without their neural counterparts. Most neural evidence for the expert individuation explanation of face processing comes from fMRI and ERP recording studies. For example, in seven independent groups of subjects tested with a variety of stimulus sets and experimental tasks (six fMRI, one ERP) it was found that behavioral expertise correlated with FFA activity in response to non-face objects at a range of $r = 0.47–0.96$ (Gauthier & Bukach, 2007). The neural response recorded from the FFA, as well as the similarly face-selective OFA, has been correlated with many behavioral hallmarks, including holistic processing (Gauthier & Tarr, 2002; Rotshtein, Geng, Driver, & Dolan, 2007) and other measures of discriminability (Gauthier, Curby, Skudlarski, & Epstein, 2005; Gauthier, Skudlarski, Gore, & Anderson, 2000; Gauthier & Tarr, 2002; Xu, 2005). For example, novel objects trained to subordinate-level identification activated the FFA more than the same objects trained with basic-level categorization (Gauthier, Anderson, Tarr, Skularski, & Gore, 1997; Gauthier et al., 1999; Gauthier & Tarr, 2002; Rossion et al., 2004). Naturally acquired expertise also recruits this region, as seen when bird watchers process birds, car experts process cars (Gauthier et al ., 2000, 2005; Xu, 2005[2]), and practicing radiologists or fourth-year radiology residents process radiographs (Harley et al., 2009).

Expertise effects are also obtained as early as face-specific effects arise in ERP studies. For example, the early face-selective N170 component originating in occipitotemporal cortex is evoked when bird and dog experts process objects from their respective domains of expertise (Tanaka & Curran, 2001). Likewise, the N170 EEG component was delayed over the right parietal/temporal area when inverted fingerprints were processed by fingerprint experts (similar to the delay observed when all participants viewed inverted faces), and the effect was absent in novices (Busey & Vanderkolk, 2004). In addition, training with novel objects (Greebles) led to an electrophysiological face-like inversion effect for upright and inverted Greebles (Rossion et al., 2002) as well as competition (i.e., a reduced N170) during concurrent Greeble and face processing (Rossion et al., 2004) only in individuals trained in expert-level Greeble recognition. A weakened N170 for faces in the context of car processing is also obtained in car experts relative to car novices, including a positive correlation between car expertise and the magnitude of car–face interference (Gauthier & Curby, 2005; Gauthier et al., 2003; Rossion, Collins, Goffaux, & Curran, 2007).

Challenges in Contemporary Research on Face Recognition

We have painted a picture of some of what is currently known about face recognition, by placing it in the context of object recognition, arguably the most parsimonious approach given the existing evidence. Indeed, if expertise for words or musical notation can lead to category specialization in the brain (Wong & Gauthier, 2010; Wong, Jobard et al., 2009), and if individuation training can lead to face-like processing strategies and the recruitment of the fusiform gyrus and other parts of the face recognition network, then why could expertise not account for specialization for faces? There are many challenges remaining in the study of face recognition, and we summarize three of them here.

Understanding the Link Between Neural Markers and Behavior

This challenge is general to any domain in cognitive neuroscience, though is particularly salient for face perception when trying to account for individual differences in behavioral performance using brain-based measures. In the normal brain, there is a surprisingly strong correlation between activity in the FFA and behavioral measures of performance in various domains, including recognition of novel objects (Gauthier & Tarr, 2002; Wong, Palmeri, et al., 2009), cars (Gauthier et al., 2000, 2005; Xu, 2005), and chest radiographs (Harley et al., 2009). For instance, individuals' ability to match pictures of cars outside of the scanner can predict the level of activity to other cars relative to faces in the scanner ($r > .9$, Gauthier et al., 2005). Interestingly, the finding that 98% of the cells in the face-selective areas are highly face-selective (Tsao et al., 2008), if it applies to human fMRI as well, suggests that these expertise effects are produced to a large extent by face-selective cells. So far, no other local part of the brain or even distributed pattern of activity predicts performance better than this (this is not a so-called Voodoo correlation: Vul, Harris, Winkielman, & Pashler, 2009a, 2009b; but see Lazar, 2009; Lindquist & Gelman, 2009; Nichols & Poline, 2009). Despite this link between individuation performance and FFA activity, other work suggests that the anterior inferior temporal (aIT) cortex actually supports face identification while the FFA primarily supports face detection (Kriegeskorte et al, 2007; Nestor, Vettel, & Tarr, 2008).

Clearly, strong activity for faces in the FFA is not always indicative of good recognition performance. Patients with congenital prosopagnosia who have profound deficits in face perception can show a normal response to faces in the FFA (see, e.g., Avidan & Behrmann, 2008; Avidan et al., 2005). In contrast, although individuals with autism show abnormal processing strategies for face recognition that are nowhere near as impaired as those in individuals with prosopagnosia, they show little selectivity to faces in the FFA (Bailey et al., 2005; Dawson et al., 2004; Gauthier et al., 2009; McPartland et al., 2004; van Kooten et al., 2008). As reviewed earlier, lesions in acquired prosopagnosia (which is typically not a deficit of face detection but one of individuation) are generally posterior, typically falling on the OFA or near the FFA, but only rarely on aIT cortex.

There is no one general account that is consistent with all these findings. In attempts to link behavior and brain activity, recent studies have suggested that accounting for the integrity of fiber tracts between different parts of the face-selective network will be important (Thomas et al., 2006), as will a better understand of how various neuroimaging metrics, for instance, univariate and multivariate measures, relate to the information actually used by the brain during perception and decision-making (Nestor et al., 2008).

Linking Infant Findings to Adult Specialization

Faces have been postulated to be special for newborns and infants as well as for adults, but it is surprisingly difficult to relate findings obtained across these populations. There is little dispute over the existence of a preference for face-like stimuli in newborns; rather, the debate concerns what the preference is "about." This preference could reflect the action of an innate mechanism (termed "CONSPEC" by Morton & Johnson, 1991) whose function is to provide the newborn with a template of what a face looks like. Evidence suggests that CONSPEC depends on subcortical mechanisms (Tomalski, Johnson, & Csibra, 2009). CONSPEC is contrasted with another mechanism termed "CONLERN," which is cortical and responsible for learning to individuate faces, essentially the mechanism(s) responsible for the acquisition of expertise, as discussed earlier in this chapter.

It has been argued that a number of general biases having initially nothing to do with faces converge to give faces an advantage in newborn and infant preference studies. For instance, newborns prefer patterns with more elements in the upper part of a configuration: they prefer elements organized into a T or U rather than into an inverted T or U, respectively (Simion, Valenza, Macchi Cassia, Turati, & Umiltà, 2002). However, newborns do not prefer upright over inverted faces unless the faces are composed of darker areas around the eyes and mouth, a condition that would seem less consistent with a domain-general explanation and more with a preference tuned to detect faces (Farroni et al., 2005). On the other hand, computer models have consistently shown that an innate template is not necessary for a simple system to learn to detect faces (Butko, Fasel, & Movellan, 2006), and that while both an innate template and a combination of simple biases can locate faces, the latter may, in fact, be more efficient (Balas et al., 2010). In any case, even evidence for an inborn CONSPEC does not directly address whether CONSPEC is necessary to engage CONLERN. Findings of expertise in other domains acquired in adulthood without the benefit of a CONSPEC-like bias suggest that what is critical for the development of skilled individuation of faces and other objects is practice.

One phenomenon that links early experience to later performance is that of perceptual narrowing, which occurs when fairly general skills early in life narrow to result in a reduction of discrimination ability regarding those stimuli that were not experienced (Scott, Pascalis, & Nelson, 2007). The ability to discriminate two faces within an uncommonly experienced face category declines from 6 to 9 months of age (Kelly et al., 2007). As in the earlier discussion of acquisition of expertise, individuation appears to be critical to this development. For instance, in one study (Scott & Monesson, 2010), infants between 6 and 9 months of age who practiced individuating six monkey faces over a 3-month period maintained the ability to discriminate these monkey faces, whereas the ability was lost in infants who received the same exposure to the faces but for whom the faces were all labeled "monkey." Moreover, early exposure appears to have long-term implications. Three-year-old children with a younger sibling show an inversion effect for infant faces that is not observed in children of the same age who do not have a young sibling (Macchi, Picozzi, Kuefner, Bricolo, & Turati, 2009). Even more striking, in women who had a younger sibling when they were young, the same phenomenon can be observed once they become a mother (presumably due to experience with their infant's face). These women showed an inversion effect for infant faces, whereas mothers who did not have a younger sibling and women without children who had a younger sibling did not. These data suggest that considerable experience with just one face may have dormant effects that later experience can reactivate.

While some have suggested that perceptual narrowing represents evidence for innate mechanisms

(McKone & Crookes, 2007; Sugita, 2008), others have argued that they reflect domain-general tendencies (also observed for the perception of phonemes and musical rhythms) for the brain to tune to stimuli that are predominant in the environment (Pons, Lewkowicz, Soto-Faraco, & Sebastian-Galles, 2009; Scott, Pascalis, & Nelson, 2007). Understanding innate biasing mechanisms responsible for perceptual narrowing and underlying learning throughout life remains an important challenge.

Challenges in Modeling Face Recognition

Computational models build on verbal descriptive theories by specifying representations and processes using mathematical models and computer simulations. This forces the theorist to be explicit about all proposed aspects of information processing (Hintzman, 1990). Without precise models, theories cannot be rigorously evaluated and falsified. Yet, a considerable amount of research on face processing proceeds outside the context of such models, making it difficult to compare predictions from the many verbal theories that are in use for similar concepts. Perhaps the most salient example is the great difficulty in settling on a solid understanding of "holistic processing." Some investigators assume it reflects a certain kind of representation (Farah et al., 1998; Goffaux & Rossion, 2006; McKone et al., 2007; Robbins & McKone, 2007), with some arguing that it could have either a perceptual or decisional basis (Richler, Gauthier, et al., 2008; Wenger & Ingvalson, 2002, 2003); while others equate it with configural processing (Le Grand et al., 2004; Tanaka & Sengco, 1997), with some arguing that the two can be dissociated (Farah et al., 1998; Gauthier et al., 2003, 2009; Richler, Bukach, & Gauthier, 2009).

There are, of course, models that account for some of the phenomena that we observe with faces (for a review, see Palmeri & Cottrell, 2009). Some of these models are extremely specific to face processing and, in particular, the processing of familiar faces, with little coverage of unfamiliar face processing, addressing its different stages as independent modules and within a vacuum, without reference to nonface perception (e.g., Bruce & Young, 1986; Young, Hay, McWeeny, Flude, & Ellis, 1985; for review and discussion of this model, see Bruce, 1988; Young, 1998). Some models (Dailey & Cottrell, 1999; Joyce & Cottrell, 2004; Riesenhuber & Poggio, 1999, 2000, 2002; Serre, Oliva, & Poggio, 2007; Serre, Wolf, & Poggio, 2005) assume that the same, typically feed-forward, computational principles account for both object recognition and face recognition. The

multiple refinements of one of these models (Dailey & Cottrell, 1999) accounts for many of the hallmarks of face perception, such as holistic perception, patterns of generalization, inversion effects, and entry-level shift. This model stresses the significance of two distinct and independent systems for basic- and subordinate-level processing (Nguyen & Cottrell, 2005). But these approaches do not attempt to explain the transition from novice to expert perception, nor can they explain phenomena that involve interference or competition between faces and objects as a function of expertise (e.g., Gauthier & Curby, 2005; Gauthier et al., 2003, 2005; Rossion et al., 2007). They also do not provide a characterization of the temporal dynamics of the perceptual decisions (Curby & Gauthier, 2009b; Mack, Wong, Gauthier, Tanaka, & Palmeri, 2009).

Ultimately, a major challenge in this area is to decide precisely what to model, since a model can never replicate the entire complexity of the brain and its behavior. Because the field of face perception generally has been dominated by the view that faces are special, computational models have rarely striven to account for face perception in the context of the development of perceptual expertise.

This chapter advocates that the most promising framework for understanding face recognition is in the context of flexible but domain-general mechanisms. In this spirit, one approach that may be particularly successful is to build understanding from existing successful models of domain-general processing, such as models of categorization, attention, and general-object recognition (Jiang et al., 2006; Palmeri & Gauthier, 2004; Palmeri, Wong, & Gauthier, 2004).

Notes

1. Although configural and holistic processes are often discussed together, they represent separate phenomenon. The term *configural* or *relational* indicates the spatial relations between facial features. The term *holistic* refers to the integrative processing of all types of information contained in a face representation, including the unparsed gestalts or components and their spatial relations among each other (Farah et al., 1995; Tanaka & Farah, 1993).
2. One study (Grill-Spector, Knouf, & Kanwisher, 2004) that failed to obtain a car expertise effect in the FFA actually used images of antique cars when testing modern-car experts, such that the null effect could simply reflect testing outside the boundaries of participants' expertise.

References

Allison, T., Ginter, H., McCarthy, G., Nobre, A. C., Puce, A., Luby, M., & Spencer, D. D. (1994). Face recognition in human extrastriate cortex. *Journal of Neurophysiology, 71,* 821–825.

Allison, T., McCarthy, G., Nobre, A., Puce, A., & Belger, A. (1994). Human extrastriate visual cortex and the perception of faces, words, numbers, and colors. *Cerebral Cortex*, 4, 544–554.

Allport, G. W. (1954). *The nature of prejudice*. Cambridge, MA: Perseus Books.

Anastasi, J. S., & Rhodes, M. G. (2005). An own-age bias in face recognition for children and older adults. *Psychonomic Bulletin Review*, 12, 1043–1047.

Anthony, T., Copper, C., & Mullen, B. (1992). Cross-racial facial identification: A social cognitive integration. *Personality and Social Psychology Bulletin*, 18, 296–301.

Ashley, V., Vuilleumier, P., & Swick, D. (2003). Time course and specificity of event-related potentials to emotional expressions. *Neuroreport*, 15, 211–216

Avidan, G., & Behrmann, M. (2008). Implicit familiarity processing in congenital prosopagnosia. *Journal of Neuropsychology*, 2, 141–164.

Avidan, G., Hasson, U., Malach, R., & Behrmann, M. (2005). Detailed exploration of face-related processing in congenital prosopagnosia: 2. Functional neuroimaging findings. *Journal of Cognitive Neuroscience*, 17, 1150–1167.

Bailey, A. J., Braeutigam, S., Jousmaki, V., & Swithenby, S.J. (2005). Abnormal activation of face processing systems at early and intermediate latency in individuals with autism spectrum disorder: A magnetoencephalographic study. *European Journal Neuroscience*, 21, 2575–2585.

Balas, B., Nelson, C., Westerlund, A., Vogel-Farley, V., Riggins, T., & Kuefner, D. (2010). Personal familiarity influences the processing of upright and inverted faces in infants. *Frontiers in Human Neuroscience*, 4, 1.

Beauchamp, M. S., Argall, B. D., Bodurka, J., Duyn, J. H., & Martin, A. (2004). Unraveling multisensory integration: Patchy organization within human STS multisensory cortex. *Nature Neuroscience*, 7, 1190–1192.

Behrmann, M., & Ewell, C. (2003). Expertise in tactile pattern recognition. *Psychological Science*, 14, 480–486.

Behrmann, M., Thomas, C., & Humphreys, K. (2006). Autism: Seeing it differently. *Trends in Cognitive Sciences*, 10, 258–264.

Bentin, S., Allison, T., Puce, A., & Perez, E. (1996). Electrophysiological studies of face perception in humans. *Journal of Cognitive Neuroscience*, 8, 551–565.

Bentin, S., Golland, Y., Flevaris, A., Robertson, L. C., & Moscovitch, M. (2006). Processing the trees and the forest during initial stages of face perception: Electrophysiological evidence. *Journal of Cognitive Neuroscience*, 18, 1406–1421.

Bodamer, J. (1947). Die Prosopagnosie. *Archiv fuer Psychiatrie und Nervenkrankheiten*, 179, 6–54.

Bothwell, R. K., Brigham, J. C., & Malpass, R. S. (1989). Cross-racial identification. *Personality and Social Psychology Bulletin*, 15, 19–25.

Boutet, I., Gentes Hawn, A., & Chaudhuri, A. (2002). The influence of attention on holistic face encoding. *Cognition*, 84, 321–341.

Bouvier, S. E., & Engel, S. A. (2006). Behavioral deficits and cortical damage loci in cerebral achromatopsia. *Cerebral Cortex*, 16, 183–191.

Bruce, C., Desimone, R., & Gross, C. G. (1981). Visual properties of neurons in a polysensory area in superior temporal sulcus of the macaque. *Journal of Neurophysiology*, 46, 369–384.

Bruce, V. (1988). *Recognizing faces*. Hove: Lawrence Erlbaum Associates.

Bruce, V., Hanna, E., Dench, N., Healey, P., & Burton, M. (1992). The importance of "mass" in line drawings of faces. *Applied Cognitive Psychology*, 6, 619–628.

Bruce, V., & Young, A. W. (1986). Understanding face recognition. *British Journal of Psychology*, 77, 305–327.

Bukach, C. M., Bub, D., Gauthier, I., & Tarr, M. J. (2006). Perceptual expertise effects are not all or none: Spatially limited perceptual expertise for faces in a case of prosopagnosia. *Journal of Cognitive Neuroscience*, 18, 48–63.

Busey, T. A. & Vanderkolk, J. R. (2004). Behavioral and electrophysiological evidence for configural processing in fingerprint experts. *Vision Research*, 45, 431–448.

Butko, N. J., Fasel, I. & Movellan, J. R. (May 2006). Learning about humans during the first 6 minutes of life. Presented at the International Conference on Development and Learning, Bloomington, Indiana, May 31–June 3.

Carey, S., & Diamond, R. (1994). Are faces perceived as configurations more by adults than by children? *Visual Cognition*, 2, 253–274.

Carmel, D., & Bentin, S. (2002). Domain specificity versus expertise. Factors influencing distinct processing of faces. *Cognition*, 83, 1–29.

Chartrand, J. P., Peretz, I., & Belin, P. (2008). Auditory recognition expertise and domain specificity. *Brain Research*, 1220, 191–198.

Chawla, D., Rees, G., & Friston, K. J. (1999). The physiological basis of attentional modulation in extrastriate visual areas. *Nature Neuroscience*, 2, 671–676.

Cheung, O. S., Richler, J. J., Palmeri, T. J., & Gauthier, I. (2008). Revisiting the role of spatial frequencies in the holistic processing of faces. *Journal of Experimental Psychology: Human Perception and Performance*, 34, 1327–1336.

Collishaw, S. M., & Hole, G. J. (2002). Is there a linear or a nonlinear relationship between rotation and configural processing of faces? *Perception*, 31, 287–296.

Cowell, R., Huber, D., & Cottrell, G.W. (2009). Virtual brain reading: A connectionist approach to understanding fMRI. In *Proceedings of the 31st Annual Meeting of the Cognitive Science Society*.

Crookes, K., & McKone, E. (2009). Early maturity of face recognition: No childhood development of holistic processing, novel face-encoding, or face-space. *Cognition*, 111, 219–247.

Curby, K. M., & Gauthier, I. (2007). A visual short-term memory advantage for faces. *Psychonomic Bulletin & Review*, 14, 620–628.

Curby, K. M., Gauthier, I. (2009a). The temporal advantage for encoding objects of expertise. *Journal of Vision*, 9, 7.1–7.13.

Curby, K. M. & Gauthier, I. (2009b). To the trained eye: Perceptual expertise alters visual processing. *Topics in Cognitive Science*, 2, 189–201.

Curby, K., Glazek, K., & Gauthier, I. (2009). A visual short-term memory advantage for objects of expertise. *Journal of Experimental Psychology: Human Perception and Performance*, 35, 94–107.

Dailey, M. N., & Cottrell, G. W. (1999). Organization of face and object recognition in modular neural networks. *Neural Networks*, 12, 1053–1074.

Damasio, A. R., Damasio, H., & Van Hoesen, G. W. (1982). Prosopagnosia: Anatomic basis and behavioral mechanisms. *Neurology*, 32, 331–341.

Davies-Thompson, J., Gouws, A., & Andrews, T. J. (2009). An image-dependent representation of familiar and unfamiliar faces in the human ventral stream. *Neuropsychologia, 47*, 1627–1635.

Dawson, G., Webb, S. J., Carver, L., Panagiotides, H., & McPartland, J. (2004). Young children with autism show atypical brain responses to fearful versus neutral facial expressions of emotion. *Developmental Science, 7*, 340–359.

de Haan, M., Pascalis, O., & Johnson, M. (2002). Specialisation of neural mechanisms underlying face recognition in human infants. *Journal of Cognitive Neuroscience, 14*, 199–209.

de Heering, A., & Rossion, B. (2008). Prolonged visual experience in adulthood modulates holistic face perception. *PLOS One, 3*, e2317.

de Heering, A., Rossion, B., Turati, C., & Simion, F. (2008). Holistic face processing can be independent of gaze behavior: Evidence from the composite illusion. *Journal of Neuropsychologia, 2*, 183–195.

Desimone, R. (1991). Face-selective cells in the temporal cortex of monkeys. *Journal of Cognitive Neuroscience, 3*, 1–8.

Desimone, R., Albright, T. D., Gross, C. G., & Bruce, C. (1984). Stimulus selective properties of inferior temporal neurons in the macaque. *Journal of Neuroscience, 4*, 2051–2062.

Desimone, R., & Gross, C.G. (1979). Visual areas in the temporal cortex of the macaque. *Brain Research, 178*, 363–380.

Diamond, R., & Carey, S. (1986). Why faces, are an are not special: An effect of expertise. *Journal of Experimental Psychology: General, 115*, 107–117.

Eimer, M., & Holmes, A. (2002). An ERP study on the time course of emotional face processing. *Neuroreport, 13*, 427–431.

Farah, M. J., Wilson, K. D., Drain, M., & Tanaka, J. N. (1998). What is "special" about face perception? *Psychological Review, 105*, 482–498.

Farroni, T., Johnson, M. H., Menon, E., Zulian, L., Faraguna, D., & Csibra, G. (2005). Newborns' preference for face-relevant stimuli: Effects of contrast polarity. *Proceedings of the National Academy of Sciences of the United States of America, 102*(47), 17245–17250.

Fiser, J., Subramaniam, S., & Biederman, I. (2001). Size tuning in the absence of spatial frequency tuning in object recognition. *Vision Research, 41*, 1931–1950.

Fodor, J. (1983). *Modularity of mind*. Cambridge, MA: MIT Press.

Fodor, J. (2000). *The mind doesn't work that way*. Cambridge, MA: MIT Press.

Freiwald, W. A., Tsao, D. Y., & Livingstone, M. S. (2009). A face feature space in the macaque temporal lobe. *Nature Neuroscience, 12*, 1187–1196.

Gaspar, C. M., Bennett, P. J., & Sekuler, A. B. (2008). The effects of face inversion and contrast-reversal on efficiency and internal noise. *Vision Research, 48*, 1084–1095.

Gaspar, C. M., Sekuler, A. B., & Bennett, P. J. (2008). Spatial frequency tuning of upright and inverted face identification. *Vision Research, 48*, 2817–2826.

Gauthier, I. (2000). What constrains the organization of the ventral temporal cortex? *Trends in Cognitive Sciences, 4*, 1–2.

Gauthier, I., Anderson, A. W., Tarr, M. J., Skudlarski, P., & Gore, J. C. (1997). Levels of categorization in visual recognition studied using functional magnetic resonance imaging. *Current Biology, 7*, 645–651.

Gauthier, I., & Bukach, C. (2007). Should we reject the expertise hypothesis? *Cognition, 103*, 322–330.

Gauthier, I., & Curby, K. M. (2005). A perceptual traffic jam on highway N170: Interference between face and car expertise. *Current Directions in Psychological Science, 14*, 30–33.

Gauthier, I., Curby, K. M., Skudlarski, P., & Epstein, R. A. (2005). Individual differences in FFA activity suggest independent processing at different spatial scales. *Cognitive, Affective & Behavioral Neuroscience, 5*, 222–234.

Gauthier, I., Curran, T., Curby, K. M., & Collins, D. (2003). Perceptual interference supports a non-modular account of face processing. *Nature Neuroscience, 6*, 428–432.

Gauthier, I., Klaiman, C., & Schultz, R. T. (2009). Face composite effects reveal abnormal face processing in autism spectrum disorders. *Vision Research, 49*, 470–478.

Gauthier, I., Skudlarski, P., Gore, J. C., & Anderson, A. W. (2000). Expertise for cars and birds recruits brain areas involved in face recognition. *Nature Neuroscience, 3*, 191–197.

Gauthier, I., & Tarr, M. J. (1997). Becoming a "greeble" expert: Exploring mechanisms for face recognition. *Vision Research, 37*, 1673–1682.

Gauthier, I., & Tarr, M. J. (2002). Unraveling mechanisms for expert object recognition: Bridging brain activity and behavior. *Journal of Experimental Psychology: Human Perception and Performance, 28*, 431–446.

Gauthier, I., Tarr, M. J., Anderson, A. W., Skudlarski, P., & Gore, J. C. (1999). Activation of the middle fusiform "face area" increases with expertise in recognizing novel objects. *Nature Neuroscience, 2*, 568–573.

Gauthier, I., Williams, P., Tarr, M. J., & Tanaka, J. W. (1998). Training "greeble" experts: A framework for studying expert object recognition processes. *Vision Research, 38*, 2401–2428.

George, N., Dolan, R. J., Fink, G. R., Baylis, G. C., Russell, C., & Driver, J. (1999). Contrast polarity and face recognition in the human fusiform gyrus. *Nature Neuroscience, 2*, 574–580.

Goffaux, V., Gauthier, I., & Rossion, B. (2003). Spatial Scale contribution to early visual differences between face and object processing. *Cognitive Brain Research, 16*, 416–424.

Goffaux, V., & Rossion, B. (2006). Faces are "spatial"—holistic face perception is supported by low spatial frequencies. *Journal of Experimental Psychology: Human Perception and Performance, 32*, 1023–1039.

Goldstone, R. L. (1994). The role of similarity in categorization: Providing a groundwork. *Cognition, 52*, 125–157.

Goldstone, R. L. & Styvers, M. (2001). The sensitization and differentiation of dimensions during category learning. *Journal of Experimental Psychology: General, 130*, 116–139.

Green, D. M., & Swets, J. A. (1966). *Signal detection theory and psychophysics*. New York: John Wiley & Sons.

Grelotti, D. J., Klin, A. J., Gauthier, I., Skudlarski, P., Cohen, D. J., Gore, J. C., et al. (2005). fMRI activation of the fusiform gyrus and amygdala to cartoon characters but not to faces in a boy with autism. *Neuropsychologia, 43*, 373–385.

Grill-Spector, K., Knouf, .N, & Kanwisher, N. (2004). The FFA subserves face perception not generic within category identification. *Nature Neuroscience, 7*, 555-562.

Grill-Spector, K., Kushnir, T., Hendler, T., Edelman, S., Itzchak, Y., & Malach, R. (1998). A sequence of object-processing stages revealed by fMRI in the human occipital lobe. *Human Brain Mapping, 6*, 316–328.

Gross, C. G., Bender, D. B., & Rocha-Miranda, C. E. (1969). Visual receptive fields of neurons in inferotemporal cortex of the monkey. *Science, 166*, 1303–1306.

Gross, C. G., Rocha-Miranda, C. E., & Bender, D. B. (1972). Visual properties of neurons in inferotemporal cortex of the macaque. *Journal of Neurophysiology, 35*, 96–111.

Halgren, E., Raij, T., Marinkovic, K., Jousmaeki, V., & Hari, R. (2000). Cognitive response profile of the human fusiform face area as determined by MEG. *Cerebral Cortex, 10,* 69–81.

Hancock, K. J., & Rhodes, G. (2008). Contact, configural coding and the other-race effect in face recognition. *British Journal of Psychology, 99,* 45–56.

Harley, E. M., Pope, W. B., Villablanca, J. P., Mumford, J., Suh, R., Mazziotta, J. C., Enzmann, D., & Engel, S. A. (2009). Engagement of the fusiform cortex and disengagement of lateral occipital cortex in the acquisition of radiological expertise. *Cerebral Cortex, 19,* 2746–2754.

Hasselmo, M., Rolls, E. T., & Bayliss, G. C. (1989). The role of expression and identity in the face-selective responses of neurons in the temporal visual cortex of the monkey. *Behavioral Brain Research, 32,* 203–218.

Haxby, J. V., Gobbini, M. I., Furey, M. L., Ishai, A., Schouten, J. L., & Pietrini, P. (2001). Distributed and overlapping representations of faces and objects in ventral temporal cortex. *Science, 293,* 2425–2430.

Haxby, J. V., Grady, C. L., Horwitz, B., Ungerleider, L. G., Mishkin, M., Carson, R. E., Herscovitch, P., et al. (1991). Dissociation of object and spatial visual processing pathways in human extrastriate cortex. *Proceedings of the National Academy of Sciences U S A, 88,* 1621–1625.

Haxby, J. V., Hoffman, E. A., & Gobbini, M. I. (2000). The distributed human neural system for face perception. *Trends in Cognitive Neurosciences, 4,* 223–233.

Hayes, A. (1988). Identification of two-tone images: Some implications for high- and low-spatial-frequency processes in human vision. *Perception, 17,* 429–436.

Hintzman, D. L. (1990). Human learning and memory: connections and dissociations. *Annual Review Psychology, 41,* 109–139.

Hochberg, J., & Galper, R. E. (1967). Recognition of faces: I. An exploratory study. *Psychonomic Science, 9,* 619–620.

Hoffman, E., & Haxby, J. (2000). Distinct representations of eye gaze and identity in the distributed human neural system for face perception. *Nature Neuroscience, 3,* 80–84.

Hole, G. J. (1994). Configurational factors in the perception of unfamiliar faces. *Perception, 23,* 65–74.

Hole, G., George, P. A., & Dunsmore, V. (1999). Evidence for holistic processing of faces viewed as photographic negatives. *Perception, 28,* 341–359.

Hung, C. P., Kreiman, G., Poggio, T., & DiCarlo, J. J. (2005). Fast readout of object identity from macaque inferior temporal cortex. *Science, 310,* 863–866.

Jacques, C., d'Arripe, O., & Rossion, B. (2007). The time course of the inversion effect during individual face discrimination *Journal of Vision, 7,* 1–9.

Jacques, C., & Rossion, B. (2004). Concurrent processing reveals competition between visual representations of faces. *Neuroreport: For Rapid Communication of Neuroscience Research, 15,* 2417–2421.

Jacques, C., & Rossion, B. (2006a). The speed of individual face categorization. *Psychological Science, 17,* 485–492.

Jacques, C., & Rossion, B. (2006b). The time course of visual competition to the presentation of centrally fixated faces. *Journal of Vision, 6,* 154–162.

Jiang, X., Rosen, E., Zeffiro, T., Vanmeter, J., Blanz, V., & Riesenhuber, M. (2006). Evaluation of a shape-based model of human face discrimination using fMRI and behavioral techniques. *Neuron, 50,* 159–172.

Joyce, C., & Cottrell, G. W. (2004). Solving the visual expertise mystery. In H. Bowman & C. Labiouse (Eds.), *Connectionist models of cognition and perception II: Proceedings of the Eighth Neural Computation and Psychology Workshop* (pp. XX–XX). Hackensack, NJ: World Scientific.

Kadlec, H. (1995). Multidimensional signal detection analyses (MSDA) for testing separability and independence: A Pascal program. *Behavior Research Methods, Instruments and Computers, 27,* 442–458.

Kadlec, H. (1999). Statistical properties of *d'* and beta estimates of signal detection theory. *Psychological Methods, 4,* 22–43.

Kadlec, H., & Townsend, J. T. (1992a). Implications of marginal and conditional detection parameters for the separabilities and independence of perceptual dimensions. *Journal of Mathematical Psychology, 36,* 325–374.

Kadlec, H., & Townsend, J. T. (1992b). Signal detection analyses of dimensional interactions. In F. G. Ashby (Ed.), *Multidimensional models of perception and cognition* (pp. 188–227). Hillsdale, NJ: Lawrence Erlbaum Associates.

Kanwisher, N., McDermottk, J., & Chun, M. M. (1997). The fusiform face area: A module in human extrastriate cortex specialized for face perception. *Journal of Neuroscience, 17,* 4302–4311.

Kelly, D. J., Quinn, P. C., Slater, A., Lee, K., Ge, L., & Pascalis, O. (2007). The other-race effect develops during infancy: Evidence of perceptual narrowing. *Psychological Science, 18,* 1084–1089.

Kilgour, A. R., & Lederman, S. J. (2006). A haptic face-inversion effect. *Perception, 35,* 921–931.

Klin, A., Jones, W., Schulz, R., Volkmar, F., & Cohen, D. (2002). Visual fixation patterns during viewing of naturalistic social situations as predictors of social competence in individuals with autism. *Archives of General Psychiatry, 59,* 809–816.

Kriegeskorte, N., Formisano, E., Sorger, B., & Goebel, R. (2007). Individual faces elicit distinct response patterns in human anterior temporal cortex. *Proceedings of the National Academy of Sciences U S A, 104,* 20600–20605.

Kruschke, J. K. (1992) ALCOVE: An exemplar-based connectionist model of category learning. *Psychological Review, 99,* 22–44.

Kuefner, D., Macchi Cassia, V., Picozzi, M., & Bricolo, E. (2008). Do all kids look alike? Evidence for an other-age effect in adults. *Journal of Experimental Psychology: Human Perception and Performance, 34,* 811–817.

Lamont, A. C., Stewart-Williams, S., & Podd, J. (2005). Face recognition and aging: Effects of target age and memory load. *Memory and Cognition, 33,* 1017–1024.

Langdell, T. (1978). Recognition of faces: An approach to the study of autism. *Journal of Child Psychology and Psychiatry, 19,* 255–268.

Lazar, N. A. (2009). Discussion of "Puzzling high correlation in fMRI studies of emotion, personality and social cognition." *Perspectives on Psychological Science, 4,* 308–309.

Lebrecht, S., Pierce, L. J., Tarr, M. J., & Tanaka, J. W. (2009). Perceptual other-race training reduces implicit racial bias. *PLoS ONE, 4,* e4215.

Leder, H., & Bruce, V. (2000). When inverted faces are recognized: The role of configural information in face recognition. *Quarterly Journal of Experimental Psychology, 53,* 513–536.

Leder, H., Candrian, G., Huber, O., & Bruce, V. (2001). Configural features in the context of upright and inverted faces. *Perception, 30,* 73–83.

Le Grand, R., Mondloch, C. J., Maurer, D., & Brent, H. P. (2001). Early visual experience and face processing. *Nature, 410*, 890.

Le Grand, R., Mondloch, C. J., Maurer, D., & Brent, H. P. (2004). Impairment in holistic face processing following early visual deprivation. *Psychological Science, 15*, 762–768.

Levin, D. T. (1996). Classifying faces by race: The structure of face categories. *Journal of Experimental Psychology: Learning, Memory, and Cognition, 22*, 1364–1382.

Levin, D. T. (2000). Race as a visual feature: Using visual search and perceptual discrimination tasks to understand face categories and cross-race recognition deficit. *Journal of Experimental Psychology: General, 129*, 559–574.

Levy, I., Hasson, U., Avidan, G., Hendler, T., & Malach, R. (2001). Center-periphery organization of human object areas. *Nature Neuroscience, 4*, 533–539.

Lindquist, M. A., & Gelman, A. (2009). Correlations and multiple comparisons in functional imaging: A statistical perspective (Commentary on Vul et al., 2009). *Perspectives on Psychological Science, 4*, 310–313.

Liu, J., Harris, A., & Kanwisher, N. (2002) Stages of processing in face perception: An MEG study. *Nature Neuroscience, 5*, 910–916.

Loftus, G. R., Oberg, M. A., & Dillon, A. M. (2004). Linear theory, dimensional theory, and the face-inversion effect. *Psychological Review, 111*, 835–863.

Logothetis, N. K., Pauls, J., & Poggio, T. (1995). Shape representation in the inferior temporal cortex of monkeys. *Current Biology, 5*, 552–563.

Macchi, C. V., Picozzi, M., Kuefner, D., Bricolo, E., & Turati, C. (2009). Holistic processing for faces and cars in preschool-aged children and adults: Evidence from the composite effect. *Developmental Science, 12*, 236–248.

Mack, M. L., Wong, A.C.-N., Gauthier, I., Tanaka, J. W., & Palmeri, T. J. (2009). Time-course of visual object categorization: Fastest does not necessarily mean first. *Vision Research, 49*, 1961–1968.

MacLeod, C.M. (1991). Half a century of research on the Stroop effect: An integrative review. *Psychological Bulletin, 109*, 163–203.

Malach, R., Levy, I., & Hasson, U. (2002). The topography of high-order human object areas. *Trends in Cognitive Sciences, 6*, 176–184.

Malach, R. Reppas, J. B., Benson, R. R., Kwong, K. K., Jiang, H., Kennedy, W. A., Leden, P.J., et al . (1995). Object-related activity revealed by functional magnetic resonance imaging in human occipital cortex. *Proceedings of National Academy of Sciences U S A, 92*, 8135–8139.

Malpass, R. S., & Kravitz, J. (1969). Recognition for faces of own and other race. *Journal of Personality and Social Psychology, 13*, 330–334.

Martens, U., Leuthold, H., & Schweinberger, S. R. (2010). Parallel processing in face perception. *Journal of Experimental Psychology: Human Perception and Performance, 36*, 103–121.

Martin-Malivel, J., & Okada, K. (2007). Human and chimpanzee face recognition in chimpanzees (*Pan troglodytes*): Role of exposure and impact on categorical perception. *Behavioral Neuroscience, 121*, 1145–1125.

McGugin, R. W., & Gauthier, I. (2009). Perceptual expertise with objects predicts another hallmark of face perception. *Journal of Vision, 10*, 15.1–15.12.

McGugin, R. W., Tanaka, J. W., Lebrecht, S., Tarr, M. J., & Gauthier, I. (2011). Race-specific perceptual discrimination improvement following short individuation. *Cognitive Science, 35*, 330–347.

McKeeff, T., McGugin, R. W., Tong, F., & Gauthier, I. (2010). Expertise increases the functional overlap between face and object perception. *Cognition, 117*, 355–360.

McKone, E., & Crookes, K. (2007). Understanding the developmental origins of primate face recognition: Theoretical commentary on Martin-Malivel and Okada (2007). *Behavioural Neuroscience, 121*, 1437–1441.

McKone, E., Kanwisher, N. G., & Duchaine, B. C. (2007). Can generic expertise explain special processing for faces? *Trends in Cognitive Sciences, 11*, 8–15.

McPartland, J., Dawson, G., Webb, S. J., Panagiotides, H., & Carver, L. J. (2004). Event-related brain potentials reveal anomalies in temporal processing of faces in autism spectrum disorder. *Journal of Child Psychology: Psychiatry, 45*, 1235–1245.

Meissner, C. A., & Brigham, J. C. (2001). Thirty years of investigating the own-race bias in memory for faces: A meta-analytic review. *Psychology, Public Policy, and Law, 7*, 3–35.

Morton, J., & Johnson, M. H. (1991). CONSPEC and CONLERN: A two-process theory of infant face recognition. *Psychological Review, 98*, 164–181.

Moses, Y., Ullman, S., & Edelman, S. (1996). Generalization to novel images in upright and inverted faces. *Perception, 25*, 443–461.

Murray, J., Yong, E., & Rhodes, G. (2000). Revisiting the perception of upside-down faces. *Psychological Science, 11*, 492–496.

Nestor, A., Vettel, J. M., & Tarr, M. J. (2008). Task-specific codes for face recognition: How they shape the neural representation of features for detection and individuation. *PLoS One, 3*, e3978.

Nguyen, N., & Cottrell, G. W. (2005). Owls and wading birds: Generalization gradients in expertise. In *Proceedings of the 27th Annual Cognitive Science Conference, La Stresa, Italy*. Mahwah, NJ: Lawrence Erlbaum .

Nichols, T. E., & Poline, J-B. (2009). Commentary on Vul et al.'s (2009). "Puzzling high correlation in fMRI studies of emotion, personality and social cognition." *Perspectives on Psychological Science, 4*, 291–293.

Nishimura, M., & Maurer, D. (2008). The effect of categorization on sensitivity to second-order relations in novel objects. *Perception, 37*, 584–601.

Nosofsky, R. M. (1986). Attention, similarity and the identification-categorization relationship. *Journal of Experimental Psychology: General, 115*, 39–61.

O'Connor, K., Hamm, J. P., & Kirk, I. J. (2005). The neurophysiological correlates of face processing in adults and children with Asperger's syndrome. *Brain Cognition, 59*, 82–95.

O'Toole, A. J., Edelman, S., & Bulthoff, H. H. (1998). Stimulus-specific effects in face recognition over changes in viewpoint. *Vision Research, 38*, 2351–2363.

O'Toole, A. J., Jiang, F., Abdi, H., & Haxby, J. V. (2005). Partially distributed representations of objects and faces in ventral temporal cortex. *Journal of Cognitive Neuroscience, 17*, 580–590.

O'Toole, A. J., Vetter, T., & Blanz, V. (1999). Three-dimensional shape and two-dimensional surface reflectance contributions to face recognition: An application of three-dimensional morphing. *Vision Research, 39*, 3145–3155.

Palmeri, T. J., & Cottrell, G. (2009). Modeling perceptual expertise. In D. Bub, M. Tarr, & I. Gauthier (Eds.), *Perceptual expertise: Bridging brain and behavior* (pp. XX–XX). New York: Oxford University Press.

Palmeri, T. J., Gauthier, I. (2004). Visual object understanding. *Nature Reviews Neuroscience, 5*, 291–303.

Palmeri, T. J., Wong, A. C.-N., & Gauthier, I. (2004). Computational approaches to the development of perceptual expertise. *Trends in Cognitive Sciences, 8*, 378–386.

Parr, L. A., Dove, T., & Hopkins, W. D. (1998). Why faces may be special: Evidence of the inversion effect in chimpanzees. *Journal of Cognitive Neuroscience, 10*, 615–622.

Parr, L. A., & Heintz, M. (2006). The perception of unfamiliar faces and houses by chimpanzees: Influence of rotation angle. *Perception, 35*, 1473–1483.

Parr, L. A., Heintz, M., & Akamagwuna, U. (2006). Three studies on configural face processing by chimpanzees. *Brain Cognition, 62*, 30–42.

Parr, L. A., Winslow, J. T., & Hopkins, W. D. (1999). Is the inversion effect in rhesus monkeys face specific? *Animal Cognition, 2*, 123–129.

Pascalis, O., & Bachevalier, J. (1998). Face recognition in primates: A cross-species study. *Behavioral Processes, 43*, 87–96.

Perlman, S. B., Morris, J. P., Vander Wyk, B. C., Green, S. R., Doyle, J. L., & Pelphrey, K. A. (2009). Individual differences in personality predict how people look at faces. *PLoS One, 4*, e5952.

Perrett, D., Harries, M., Mistlin, A., et al. (1990). Social signals analyzed at the single cell level: Someone is looking at me, something touched me, something moved! *International Journal of Computational Psychology, 4*, 25–55

Perrett, D., & Mistlin, A. (1990). Perception of facial characteristics by monkeys. In W. Stebbins & M. Berkley (Eds.), *Comparative perception* (Vol. 2, pp. 187–215). Hoboken, NJ: Wiley.

Perrett, D. I., Rolls, E. T., & Cann, W. (1982). Visual neurones responsive to faces in the monkey temporal cortex. *Experimental Brain Research, 47*, 329–342

Perrett, D. I., Smith, P. A., Potter, D. D., Mistlin, A. J., Head, A. S., Milner, A. D., & Jeeves, M. A. (1984). Neurones responsive to faces in the temporal cortex: Studies of functional organization, sensitivity to identity and relation to perception. *Human Neurobiology, 3*, 197–208

Perrett, D. I., Smith, P. A., Potter, D. D., Mistlin, A. J., Head, A. S., Milner, A. D., & Jeeves, M. A. (1985) Visual cells in the temporal cortex sensitive to face view and gaze direction. *Proceedings of the Royal Society of London. Series B, Biological Sciences, 223*, 293–317

Pitcher, D., Garrido, L., Walsh, V., & Duchaine, B. C. (2008) Transcranial magnetic stimulation disrupts the perception and embodiment of facial expressions. *Journal of Neuroscience, 28*, 8929–8933.

Pitcher, D., Walsh, V., Yovel, G., & Duchaine, B. (2007). TMS evidence for the involvement of the right occipital face area in early face processing. *Current Biology, 17*, 1568–1573.

Pons, F., Lewkowicz, D. J., Soto-Faraco, S., & Sebastian-Galles, N. (2009). Narrowing of intersensory speech perception in infancy. *Proceedings of the National Academy of Sciences U S A, 106*, 10598–10602.

Puce, A., Allison, T., Bentin, S., Gore, J. C., & McCarthy, G. (1998). Temporal cortex activation of humans viewing eye and mouth movements. *Journal of Neuroscience, 18*, 2188–2199.

Puce, A., Allison, T., Gore, J. C., & McCarthy, G. (1995). Face-sensitive regions in human extrastriate cortex studied by functional MRI. *Journal of Neurophysiology, 74*, 1192–1199.

Quiroga, R. Q., Kreiman, G., Koch, C., & Fried, I. (2008). Sparse but not "grandmother-cell" coding in the medial temporal lobe. *Trends in Cognitive Sciences, 12*, 87–91.

Quiroga, R. Q., Reddy, R., Kreiman, G., Koch, C., & Fried, I. (2005). Invariant visual representation by single neurons in the human brain. *Nature, 435*, 1102–1107.

Rakover, S., & Teucher, B. (1997). Facial inversion effects: Parts and whole relationship. *Perception & Psychophysics, 59*, 752–761.

Rhodes, G., Brake, S., & Atkinson, A. P. (1993). What's lost in inverted faces? *Cognition, 47*, 25–57.

Rhodes, G., Tan, S., Brake, S., & Taylor, K. (1989). Expertise and configural coding in face recognition. *British Journal of Psychology, 80*, 313–331.

Richler, J. J., Bukach, C. M., & Gauthier, I. (2009). Context influences holistic processing of non-face objects in the composite task. *Perception and Psychophysics, 71*, 530–540.

Richler, J. J. Cheung, O. S., & Gauthier, I. (2011). Beliefs alter holistic face processing …If response bias is not taken into account. *Journal of Vision, 11*(13), 17.

Richler, J. J., Cheung, O. S., Wong, A. C.-N., & Gauthier, I. (2009). Does response interference contribute to face composite effects? *Psychonomic Bulletin & Review, 16*, 258–263.

Richler, J. J., Gauthier, I., Wenger, M. J., & Palmeri, T. J. (2008). Holistic processing of faces: Perceptual and decisional components. *Journal of Experimental Psychology: Learning, Memory and Cognition, 34*, 328–342.

Richler, J. J., Tanaka, J. W., Brown, D. D., & Gauthier, I. (2008). Why does selective attention fail in face processing? *Journal of Experimental Psychology: Learning, Memory, and Cognition, 34*, 1356–1368.

Riesenhuber, M., & Poggio, T. (1999). Hierarchical models of object recognition in cortex. *Nature Neuroscience, 2*, 1019–1025.

Riesenhuber, M., & Poggio, T. (2000). Models of object recognition. *Nature Neuroscience, 3*, 1199–1204.

Riesenhuber, M., & Poggio, T. (2002). Neural mechanisms of object recognition. *Current Opinions in Neurobiology, 12*, 162–168.

Robbins, R., & McKone, E. (2003). Can holistic processing be learned for inverted faces? *Cognition, 88*, 79–107.

Robbins, R., & McKone, E. (2007). No face-like processing for objects-of-expertise in three behavioural tasks. *Cognition, 103*, 34–79.

Rolls, E. T. (2000). Functions of the primate temporal lobe cortical visual areas in invariant visual object and face recognition. *Neuron, 27*, 205–218.

Rolls, E. T., & Tovee, M. J. (1995). Sparseness of the neuronal representation of stimuli in the primate temporal visual cortex. *Journal of Neurophysiology, 73*, 713–726.

Rosch, E., Mervis, C. B., Gray, W. D., Johnson, D. M., & Boyes-Braem, P. (1976). Basic objects in natural categories. *Cognitive Psychology, 8*, 382–439.

Rossion, B., Collins, D., Goffaux, V., & Curran, T. (2007). Long-term expertise with artificial objects increases visual competition with early face categorization processes. *Journal of Cognitive Neurosciences, 19*, 543–555.

Rossion, B., Delvenne, J. F., Debatisse, D., Goffaux, V., Bruyer, R., Crommelinck, M., et al. (1999). Spatio-temporal localization of the face inversion effect: An event-related potentials study. *Biological Psychology, 50,* 173–189.

Rossion, B., Gauthier, I., Goffaux, V., Tarr, M .J., & Crommelinck, M. (2002). Expertise training with novel objects leads to left-lateralized facelike electrophysiological responses. *Psychological Science, 13,* 250–257.

Rossion, B., Gauthier, I., Tarr, M. J., Despland, P., Bruyer, R., Linotte, S., et al. (2000). The N170 occipito-temporal component is delayed and enhanced to inverted faces but not to inverted objects: An electrophysiological account of face-specific processes in the human brain. *Neuroreport: For Rapid Communication of Neuroscience Research, 11,* 69–74.

Rossion, B., Kung, C. C., & Tarr, M. J. (2004). Visual expertise with nonface objects leads to competition with the early perceptual processing of faces in the human occipitotemporal cortex. *Proceedings of the National Academy of Sciences U S A, 101,* 14521–14526.

Rotshtein, P., Geng, J. J., Driver, J. & Dolan, R .J. (2007). Role of features and second-order spatial relations in face discrimination, face recognition, and individual face skills: Behavioral and functional magnetic resonance imaging data. *Journal of Cognitive Neurosciences, 19,* 1435–1452.

Rotshtein, P., Malach, R., Hadar, U., Graif, M., & Hendler, T. (2001). Feeling or features: Different sensitivity to emotion in high-order visual cortex and amygdala. *Neuron, 32,* 747–757.

Rutherford, M. D., Clements, K. A., & Sekuler, A. B. (2007). Differences in discrimination of eye and mouth displacement in autism spectrum disorders. *Vision Research, 47,* 2099–2110.

Schultz, R. T., Gauthier, I., Klin, A., Fulbright, R., Anderson, A., Volkmar, F., Skudlarski, P., et al. (2000). Abnormal ventral temporal cortical activity during face discrimination among individuals with autism and Asperger syndrome. *Archives of General Psychiatry, 57,* 331–340.

Schultz, R. T., Grelotti, D. J., Klin, A., Kleinman, J., Van der Gaag, C., Marois, R., & Skudlarski, P. (2003). The role of the fusiform face area in social cognition: Implications for the pathobiology of autism. *Proceedings of the Royal Society of London. Series B, Biological Sciences, 358,* 415–427.

Scott, L. S., & Monesson, A. (2010). Experience dependent neural specialization during infancy. *Neuropsychologia, 48,* 1857–1861.

Scott, L. S., Pascalis, O., & Nelson, C. A. (2007). A domain general theory of the development of perceptual discrimination. *Current Directions in Psychological Science, 16,* 197–201

Scott, L. S., Tanaka, J. T., Sheinberg, D. L ., & Curran, T. (2008). The role of category learning in the acquisition and retention of perceptual expertise: A behavioral and neurophysiological study. *Brain Research, 1210,* 204–215.

Searcy, J., & Bartlett, J. C. (1996). Inversion and processing of component and spatial–relational information in faces. *Journal of Experimental Psychology: Human Perception and Performance, 22,* 904–915.

Sekuler, A. B., Gaspar, C. M., Gold, J. M., & Bennett, P. J. 2004. Inversion leads to quantitative, not qualitative, changes in face processing. *Current Biology, 14,* 391–396.

Senju, A., Tojo, Y., Yaguchi, K., & Hasegawa, T. (2005). Deviant gaze processing in children with autism: An ERP study. *Neuropsychologia, 43,* 1297–1306.

Sergent, J., Ohta, S., & MacDonald, B. (1992). Functional neuroanatomy of face and object processing. A positron emission tomography study. *Brain, 115,* 15–36.

Serre, T., Oliva, A., & Poggio, T. (2007). A feedforward architecture accounts for rapid categorization. *Proceedings of National Academy of Sciences U S A, 104,* 6424–6429.

Serre, T., Wolf, L. & Poggio, T. (2005). Object recognition with features inspired by visual cortex. In Computer Vision and Pattern Recognition (CVPR 2005), San Diego, CA.

Simion, F., Valenza, E., Macchi Cassia, V., Turati, C., & Umiltà, C. (2002). Newborns preference for up–down asymmetrical configurations. *Developmental Science, 5,* 427–434.

Spangler, S. M., Schwarzer, G., Korell, M., & Maier-Karius, J. (2010). The relationships between processing facial identity, emotional expression, facial speech, and gaze direction during development. *Journal of Experimental Child Psychology, 105,* 1–19.

Spiridon, M., & Kanwisher, N. (2002). How distributed is visual category information in human occipito-temporal cortex? An fMRI study. *Neuron, 35,* 1157–1165, 2002.

Steeves, J., Dricot, J., Goltz, H. C., Sorger, B., Peters, J., Milner, A. D., et al. (2009). Abnormal face identity coding in the middle fusiform gyrus of two brain-damaged prosopagnosic patients. *Neuropsychologia, 47,* 2584–2592.

Subramaniam, S., & Biederman, I. (1997). Does contrast reversal affect object identification? *Investigative Ophthalmology and Visual Science, 38,* 998.

Sugita, Y. (2008). Face perception in monkeys reared with no exposure to faces. *Proceedings of the National Academy of Sciences U S A, 105,* 394–398.

Susilo, T., Crookes, K., McKone, E., & Turner, H. (2009). The composite task reveals stronger holistic processing in children than adults for child faces. *PLoS One, 4,* e6460.

Swets, J. A. (1996). *Signal detection theory and roc analysis in psychology and diagnostics: Collected papers.* Mahwah, NJ: Lawrence Erlbaum Associates.

Tanaka, J. W., & Curran, T. (2001). A neural basis for expert object recognition. *Psychological Science, 12*(1), 43–47.

Tanaka, J. W., Curran, T., & Sheinberg, D. (2005). The training and transfer of real-world, perceptual expertise. *Psychological Science, 16,* 141–151.

Tanaka, J. W., & Farah, M. J. (1993). Parts and wholes in face recognition. *Quarterly Journal of Experimental Psychology A: Human Experimental Psychology, 46,* 225–245.

Tanaka, J. W., & Pierce, L .J. (2009). The neural plasticity of other-race face recognition. *Cognitive, Affective & Behavioral Neuroscience, 9,* 122–131.

Tanaka, J. W., & Sengco, J.A. (1997). Features and their configuration in face recognition. *Memory & Cognition, 25,* 583–592.

Teunisse, J. P., & de Gelder, B. (2003). Face processing in adolescents with autistic disorder: The inversion and composite effects. *Brain Cognition, 52,* 285–294.

Thomas, C. P., Avidan, G., Humphreys, K., Jung, K. J., Gao, F., & Behrmann, M. (2006). Reduced structural connectivity in ventral visual cortex in congenital prosopagnosia. *Nature Neuroscience, 12,* 29–31.

Thompson, P. (1980). Margaret Thatcher: A new illusion. *Perception, 9,* 483–484.

Tomalski P., Johnson, M. H., & Csibra, G. (2009). Temporal-nasal asymmetry of rapid orienting to face-like stimuli. *Neuroreport, 20,* 1309–1312.

Tong, F., Nakayama, N., Moscovitch, M., Weinrib, O., & Kanwisher, N. (2000). Response properties of the human fusiform face area. *Cognitive Neuropsychology, 17,* 257–280.

Tong, F., Nakayama, K., Vaughan, J. T., & Kanwisher, N. G. (1998). Binocular rivalry and visual awareness in human extrastriate cortex. *Neuron, 21,* 753–759.

Troje, N. F., & Kersten, D. (1999). Viewpoint-dependent recognition of familiar faces. *Perception, 28,* 483–487.

Tsao, D. Y., Moeller, S., & Freiwald, W. A. (2008). Comparing face patch systems in macaques and humans. *Proceedings of the National Academy of Sciences U S A, 105,* 19514–19519.

Ullman, S. (1998). Three-dimensional object recognition based on the combination of views. In M. Tarr & H. Bulthoff (Eds.), *Object recognition in man, monkey, and machine.* Cambridge, MA: MIT Press.

van Kooten, I. A. J., Palmen, S. J. M. C., von Cappeln, P., Steinbusch, H. W. M., Korr, H., Heinsen, H., et al. (2008). Neurons in the fusiform gyrus are fewer and smaller in autism. *Brain, 131,* 987–999.

Vul, E., Harris, C., Winkielman, P., & Pashler, H. (2009a). Puzzling high correlation in fMRI studies of emotion, personality and social cognition. *Perspectives on Psychological Sciences, 4,* 279–290.

Vul, E., Harris, C., Winkielman, P., & Pashler, H. (2009b). Reply to comments on "Puzzlingly high correlations in fMRI studies of emotion, personality, and social cognition." *Perspectives in Psychological Sciences, 4,* 319–324.

Webb, S. J., Dawson, G., Bernier, R., & Panagiotides, H. (2006). ERP evidence of atypical face processing in young children with autism. *Journal of Autism Developmental Disorders, 36,* 881–890.

Wenger, M. J., & Ingvalson, E. M. (2002). A decisional component of holistic encoding. *Journal of Experimental Psychology: Learning, Memory & Cognition, 28,* 872–892.

Wenger, M. J., & Ingvalson, E. M. (2003). Preserving informational separability and violating decisional separability in facial perception and recognition. *Journal of Experimental Psychology: Learning, Memory, and Cognition, 29*(6), 1106–1118.

Wenger, M. J., & Townsend, J. T. (2001). Faces as gestalt stimuli: Process characteristics. In M. J. Wenger & J. T. Townsend (Eds.), *Computational, geometric, and process perspectives on facial cognition* (pp. 229–284). Mahwah, NJ: Lawrence Erlbaum.

Williams, N. R., Willenbockel, V., & Gauthier, I. (2009). Sensitivity to spatial frequency and orientation content is not specific to face perception, *Vision Research, 49,* 2353–2362.

Wong, C.-N., Jobard, G., James, K. H., James, T. W., & Gauthier, I. (2009). Expertise with characters in alphabetic and non-alphabetic writing systems engage overlapping occipito-temporal areas. *Cognitive Neuropsychology, 26,* 111–127.

Wong, A. C.-N., Palmeri, T. J., & Gauthier, I. (2009). Conditions for face-like expertise with objects: Becoming a Ziggerin expert—but which type? *Psychological Science, 20,* 1108–1117.

Wong, A. C.-N., Palmeri, T. J., Rogers, B. P., Gore, J. C., & Gauthier, I. (2009). Beyond shape: How you learn about objects affects how they are represented in visual cortex. *PLoS One, 2,* e8405.

Wong, Y. K. & Gauthier, I. (2010). A multimodal neural network recruited by expertise with musical notation. *Journal of Cognitive Neurosciences, 22,* 695–713.

Wong, Y., Twedt, E., Sheinberg, D., & Gauthier, I. (2010). Does Thompson's Thatcher effect reflect a face-specific mechanism? *Perception, 39,* 1125–1141.

Xu, Y. (2005). Revisiting the role of the fusiform face area in visual expertise. *Cerebral Cortex, 15,* 1234–1242.

Yin, R. K. (1969). Looking at upside-down faces. *Journal of Experimental Psychology, 81,* 141–145.

Young, A. W., Hay, D. C., McWeeny, K. H., Flude, B. M., & Ellis, A. W. (1985). Matching familiar and unfamiliar faces on internal and external features. *Perception, 14,* 737–746.

Young, A. W., Hellawell, D., & Hay, D. (1987). Configural information in face perception. *Perception, 10,* 747–759.

Young, A. W. (1998). *Face & mind.* Oxford: Oxford University Press.

Young, M. P. & Yamane, S. (1992). Sparse coding of faces in the inferotemporal cortex. *Science, 256,* 1227–1331.

The Cognitive and Neural Basis of Impression Formation

Alexander Todorov *and* Peter Mende-Siedlecki

Abstract

People rapidly form evaluative impressions of other people from minimal information. In the last decade, many cognitive neuroscience studies have explored the neural underpinnings of how impressions of other people, or person impressions, are made. This chapter reviews studies on the forming of impressions from facial appearance and from behavioral information. Across studies on impressions made from facial appearance, the most consistently activated brain regions include the amygdala, nucleus accumbens, medial orbitofrontal cortex, medial prefrontal cortex (PFC), and pregenual anterior cingulate cortex. Across studies on impressions made from behavioral information, the most consistently activated region is the dorsomedial PFC. Several studies have also identified the amygdala and ventromedial PFC as being critical in the updating of person impressions. The chapter concludes with a discussion of outstanding questions regarding the neural basis of forming impressions.

Key Words: impression formation, social cognition, face perception, face evaluation, person learning, amygdala, medial prefrontal cortex, trustworthiness, attractiveness

Introduction

In *Baboon Metaphysics*, a detailed investigation of the complexities of baboons' lives, Cheney and Seyfarth write, "Any way you look at it, most of the problems facing baboons can be expressed in two words: other baboons" (2007, p. 12). This statement applies to an even greater extent to humans. To successfully navigate the social world, human beings need to understand and predict other human beings' behavior (Ames, Fiske, & Todorov, 2011). We form impressions of other people in the service of this need. The processes underlying impression formation have been of central interest to social psychologists for many decades. In fact, more than 60 years ago, Asch insightfully characterized these processes:

> We look at a person and immediately a certain impression of his character forms itself in us. ... We

know that such impressions form with remarkable rapidity and with great ease. Subsequent observations may enrich or upset our view, but we can no more prevent its rapid growth than we can avoid perceiving a given visual object or hearing a melody." (Asch, 1946, p. 258)

Research unequivocally supports Asch's insights. First, as he argued, impressions of other people are formed from minimal information. People form such impressions from facial appearance (see, e.g., Bar, Neta, & Linz, 2006; Olson & Marshuetz, 2005; Willis & Todorov, 2006; Zebrowitz, 1999), "thin slices" of nonverbal behaviors (see, e.g., Albright, Kenny, & Malloy, 1988; Ambady, Hallahan, & Rosenthal, 1995; Ambady & Rosenthal, 1992), and behavioral information (see, e.g., Carlston & Skowronski, 1994; Todorov & Uleman, 2002, 2003, 2004; Uleman, Newman, & Moskowitz, 1996).

Second, people form impressions rapidly and efficiently (Bar et al., 2006; Olson & Marshuetz, 2005; Todorov, Pakrashi, & Oosterhof, 2009; Todorov & Uleman, 2003; Willis & Todorov, 2006). Finally, people spontaneously form these impressions even when their cognitive resources are severely limited (Todorov & Uleman, 2003; Uleman, Blader, & Todorov, 2005).

In the last decade, there has been a flurry of cognitive neuroscience research on the neural underpinnings of person impressions—the processes of forming evaluative judgments of other individuals. Although undoubtedly the evaluative processes underlying the formation of person impressions overlap with those underlying evaluations of nonsocial targets (Hare, Camerer, Knoeplfe, O'Doherty, & Rangel, 2010; Knutson, Fong, Bennett, Adams, & Hommer, 2003; Knutson, Taylor, Kaufman, Peterson, & Glover, 2005; Knutson & Wimmer, 2007; Rangel, Camerer, & Montague, 2008), research shows that both perception of faces and thinking about other people recruit distinctive functional networks of brain regions (Cunningham, Raye, & Johnson, 2004; Haxby, Hoffman, & Gobbini, 2000; Kanwisher & Yovel, 2006; Mitchell, 2008, 2009; Said, Haxby, & Todorov, 2011; Saxe, 2006; Todorov, 2012). Further, given that people are one of the more important classes of stimuli for human beings, we focus here on the forming of person impressions.

In this chapter, we aim to summarize the main findings from this research. In the first section, we review behavioral and event-related potential (ERP) studies on the efficiency of person impressions. In the second section, we review functional magnetic resonance imaging (fMRI) studies on person impressions. The first two sections focus primarily on impressions made from others' facial appearance. In the final section, we review lesion, fMRI, and ERP studies on the forming of impressions from multiple sources of information, including behavioral information and facial appearance.

The Efficiency of First Impressions

People make a variety of social inferences from appearances (Olivola & Todorov, 2010; Todorov, Said, Engell, & Oosterhof, 2008; Zebrowitz & Montepare, 2008). The most studied impressions include attractiveness (Langlois et al., 2000; Rhodes, 2006), facial maturity (Montepare & Zebrowiz, 1998), and trustworthiness (Todorov, 2008; Todorov, Said, et al., 2008). All of these impressions are formed rapidly from minimal information.

The efficiency of forming impressions is most frequently studied by presenting participants with unfamiliar faces for brief periods of time and testing whether participants can form impressions from these brief exposures. Locher, Unger, Sociedade, and Wahl (1993) showed that after a 100 ms exposure to faces, people were able to discriminate between different levels of facial attractiveness. Olson and Marshuetz (2005) replicated these findings using extremely short subliminal exposure (13 ms). Similar effects have been observed in the context of other social judgments, including competence, likeability, threat or aggressiveness, and trustworthiness (Ballew & Todorov, 2007; Bar et al., 2006; Todorov et al, 2009; Willis & Todorov, 2006). In all of these studies, judgments made after brief exposures to unfamiliar faces were highly correlated with judgments made in the absence of time constraints (criterion judgments).

Todorov and colleagues (2009, Experiment 2) systematically manipulated the time exposure to faces, ranging from 17 ms to unlimited time. After a 17 ms masked exposure to faces, judgments about trustworthiness were uncorrelated with criterion judgments, replicating a similar finding for judgments of threat (Bar et al., 2006). However, judgments made after 33 ms exposure were significantly correlated with the criterion judgments. This correlation increased dramatically with the increase in exposure from 33 to 100 ms and reached a plateau after 167 ms exposure.

The findings of Bar et al. (2006) and Todorov et al. (2009) suggest that social judgments made from faces are not made after subliminal exposure, unlike judgments of attractiveness (Olson & Marshuetz, 2005). However, using a subliminal priming paradigm, Todorov et al. (2009, Experiment 3) found that judgments of novel, neutral faces were more negative when the faces were preceded by their "untrustworthy" version—as manipulated by a computer model of face trustworthiness (Oosterhof & Todorov, 2008)—than when preceded by their "trustworthy" version. Specifically, the prime faces were presented for 20 ms and immediately masked by the neutral version of the face, which was presented for 50 ms. The effect of the prime faces was clearly detectable in the judgments of the neutral faces, although an objective test of awareness failed to find any evidence for the awareness of the prime faces.

To summarize the behavioral findings, people make a variety of social judgments after extremely brief exposures to emotionally neutral faces. These findings suggest that such judgments can be made automatically (Todorov, Loehr, & Oosterhof, 2010). Cues related to perceived attractiveness, trustworthiness, and dominance are rapidly extracted from facial appearance and, possibly, other appearance cues.

These findings are often misinterpreted as suggesting that people make up their mind within the exposure to the face. For example, findings that people can make a social judgment after 33 ms exposure are misinterpreted to mean that people make the judgment within 33 ms. This, of course, is highly unlikely, given that at least 100 ms is needed for visual information to travel from the retina to inferior temporal cortices (DiCarlo & Cox, 2007). Further, the first face-specific ERP responses emerge around 130 ms and peak at around 170 ms (Rossion & Jacques, 2008). Moreover, as we detail in the sections below, a wide, distributed network of brain regions, including subcortical and prefrontal regions, is engaged in face evaluation. Hence, effects specific to impression formation would be most likely detectable after 170 ms from stimulus onset.

ERP methods have an excellent temporal resolution and are an ideal tool to study the speed of forming person impressions. Surprisingly, there are very few studies using these methods to study impressions. One exception is a study by Rudoy and Paller (2009). In this study, they presented participants with faces that had been prerated as trustworthy- or untrustworthy-looking. Differences between these faces emerged between 200 and 400 ms after the stimulus onset of the faces in a cluster of frontal electrodes. These signals were similar to frontal signals observed in perception of emotional expressions (Eimer & Holmes, 2007), a finding consistent with theories positing that social judgments from emotionally neutral faces are based on similarity to emotional expressions (Montepare & Dobish, 2003; Oosterhof & Todorov, 2009; Said, Sebe, & Todorov, 2009; Zebrowitz, Kikuchi, & Fellous, 2010). The finding that differences between the two categories of faces started emerging at 200 ms after stimulus onset is quite remarkable, given that face-specific signals peak at around 170 ms (Rossion & Jacques, 2008). We will revisit these findings later, in the section on forming impressions from multiple sources of information.

The Neural Basis of Impressions Made from Facial Appearance

Most neuroimaging research on forming impressions from facial appearance has focused on either perceived attractiveness or perceived trustworthiness. The assumption in most attractiveness studies is that attractive faces should activate reward-related brain regions. Consistent with this assumption, many studies have observed increased activation to attractive faces in medial orbitofrontal cortex (mOFC; e.g., Cloutier, Heatherton, Whalen, & Kelley, 2008; Kranz & Ishai, 2006; O'Doherty et al., 2003; Winston, O'Doherty, Kilner, Perrett, & Dolan, 2007), and some studies have observed similar responses in the nucleus accumbens (NAcc; e.g., Aharon et al., 2001; Cloutier et al., 2008). However, many other studies have not observed activations in NAcc (e.g., Kampe, Frith, Dolan, & Frith, 2001; Kranz & Ishai, 2006; O'Doherty et al., 2003; Winston et al., 2007). Cloutier and colleagues (2008) have argued that NAcc would be activated only in a "mate-seeking" context in which participants are exposed to attractive faces of their preferred gender. Below, we consider an alternative interpretation based on a recent meta-analysis (Mende-Siedlecki, Said, & Todorov, 2013).

Following research on patients with bilateral amygdala lesions (Adolphs, Tranel, & Damasio, 1998), most neuroimaging studies on trustworthiness have focused on the role of the amygdala in evaluations of perceived trustworthiness. Adolphs and colleagues (1998) showed that patients with bilateral amygdala damage had a specific bias toward perceiving untrustworthy and unapproachable faces, as assessed by judgments of normal controls, as trustworthy and approachable (see also Todorov & Duchaine, 2008). Subsequent fMRI studies with normal participants have confirmed the amygdala's involvement in perceptions of trustworthiness (Engell, Haxby, &, Todorov, 2007; Winston, Strange, O'Doherty, & Dolan, 2002). In both of these studies, the amygdala's response increased with the decrease in trustworthiness of faces. However, after the initial reports of linear amygdala responses to face trustworthiness, several studies have found nonlinear responses (Said, Baron, & Todorov, 2009; Said, Dotsch, & Todorov, 2010; Todorov, Baron, & Oosterhof, 2008; Todorov, Said, Oosterhof, & Engell, 2011). In these studies, the amygdala responded more strongly to both trustworthy- and untrustworthy-looking faces than to faces in the middle of the continuum. Similar nonlinear amygdala responses have also been observed in studies on attractiveness (Liang, Zebrowitz, & Zhang, 2010; Winston et al., 2007): the amygdala responded more strongly to very attractive and very unattractive faces than to faces in the middle of the continuum.

Besides the inconsistencies within research on attractiveness and research on trustworthiness, it is also puzzling that these studies emphasize different sets of regions (Todorov, Said, & Verosky, 2011). Typically, judgments of attractiveness and trustworthiness are highly correlated with each other, with correlations ranging from .60 to .80 (Oosterhof & Todorov, 2008; Todorov, Said, et al., 2008). Such high correlations suggest that one should observe highly overlapping activations in neuroimaging studies on attractiveness and trustworthiness. The lack of such an overlap may be due to the researchers' a priori focus on specific regions. Alternatively, it may be that differences in brain activation across experiments studying different social evaluations are traceable to differences in experimental paradigms and face stimuli.

Meta-analytic methods, which combine data from multiple studies, are especially helpful in addressing these issues. These methods can be used to identify regions that are consistently activated across a large number of studies of the same psychological phenomenon. Two recent meta-analyses have analyzed studies on face evaluation (Bzdok et al., 2011; Mende-Siedlecki, Said, & Todorov, 2013). Both meta-analyses included data from whole-brain analyses in order to avoid biases due to researchers' a priori predictions about which regions might be involved in impressions of trustworthiness and attractiveness.

Bzdok and colleagues (2011) conducted an activation likelihood estimation (ALE) based meta-analysis of 16 studies on facial attractiveness and trustworthiness. Across both sets of studies, they observed consistent bilateral amygdala and right NAcc activations (see Table 12.1). They also observed amygdala and mOFC activations related to trustworthiness and attractiveness studies, respectively. However, they did not observe significant differences in activation between trustworthiness and attractiveness studies.

Mende-Siedlecki and colleagues (2013) conducted a multi-level kernel density analysis (MKDA)-based meta-analysis of 28 studies on face evaluation. In contrast to the ALE approach, the MKDA approach accounts for the fact that individual activation peaks are nested within contrast maps, making these maps the unit of analysis rather than the individual peaks (Wager et al., 2008). MKDA treats each contrast map within a study as a random effect, eliminating the possibility of one study with many peaks dominating the meta-analysis. It also weights contrasts so that studies with larger sample sizes and more statistically rigorous analyses contribute more to the results of the meta-analysis (Kober et al., 2008).

Mende-Siedlecki and colleagues (2013) performed separate analyses for negative and positive face evaluations. The negative MKDA comprised all contrasts across the collected 28 studies in which brain activity increased as facial stimuli *decreased* in either trustworthiness or attractiveness. Consequently, the positive MKDA comprised all contrasts in which brain activity increased as facial stimuli *increased* in either trustworthiness or attractiveness.

Across negative face evaluations, we observed the most consistent activations in bilateral amygdala, with less consistent activations observed in left amygdala, right anterior insula, right inferior frontal gyrus (IFG), right ventrolateral prefrontal cortex (vlPFC), and right globus pallidus (Figure 12.1). Across positive face evaluations, we observed the most consistent activations in medial prefrontal cortex (mPFC), pregenual anterior cingulate cortex (pgACC), mOFC, left caudate, and NAcc, as well as less consistent activations in right amygdala, bilateral insula, IFG, and vlPFC (Figure 12.2). These results are consistent with previous investigations of the neural responses to angry faces (Dannlowski et al., 2007; Monk et al., 2006; Morris et al., 1998; Whalen et al., 2001) and happy faces (Kesler-West et al., 2001; Morris et al., 1996; Phillips et al., 1998; Vrticka et al., 2008), respectively. These similarities are not surprising, given the perceptual similarities between these types of faces. For instance, in computer models of facial trustworthiness, extreme untrustworthiness resembles anger and extreme trustworthiness resembles happiness (Oosterhof & Todorov, 2008, 2009; Todorov, Said, Engell, & Oosterhof, 2008). As a result, evaluative social judgments of so-called affectively neutral faces may be based on underlying configurations of facial features that resemble emotional expressions (Said, Sebe, & Todorov, 2009; Todorov, Said et al., 2008).

After performing several smaller MKDAs to compare attractiveness and trustworthiness studies, we concluded that the negative and positive linear responses were driven by untrustworthiness and attractiveness studies, respectively. These two sets of studies were associated with different loci of activations: the right amygdala was more consistently active as facial trustworthiness decreased, while the NAcc/caudate and ventromedial prefrontal cortex (vmPFC)/pgACC were more consistently active as facial attractiveness increased.

Table 12.1. Peaks of Brain Areas Consistently Activated Across Studies on Impression Formation from Facial Appearance‡

Region	Lat	x	y	z		
Bzdok et al. (2011)						
Amygdala	R	26	0	−22		
Amygdala	R	18	−8	−14		
Amygdala	L	−18	−6	−18		
Nucleus accumbens	R	10	16	−2		

Region	Lat	x	y	z	#Vox	%Act
Mende-Siedlecki et al. (2013)						
Increased activity for negative evaluations, collapsed across untrustworthiness and unattractiveness						
Amygdala†**	R	20	−6	−18	1080	0.34
Amygdala**	L	−18	−6	−18	1328	0.29
Increased activity for positive evaluations, collapsed across trustworthiness and attractiveness						
Caudate/nucleus accumbens/ mOFC†**	L	−10	10	−4	1888	0.33
Ventromedial PFC†**	—	0	42	−6	344	0.30
Thalamus†**	R	14	−16	6	384	0.28
Pregenual cingulate cortex/dorsal anterior cingulate†**	—	−2	40	8	96	0.25
Cingulate†**						
Pregenual cingulate cortex†**	—	0	36	2	16	0.25
Caudate/right amygdala/anterior insula/inferior frontal gyrus**	R	4	22	0	76656	0.22
Ventral striatum/thalamus/anterior insula/inferior frontal gyrus/ventro-lateral prefrontal cortex*	R	14	−2	−2	34688	0.20

Stereotactic coordinates represent the areas most consistently activated across all studies in the two meta-analyses. Bzdok and colleagues (2011) analyzed 16 studies using an activation likelihood estimation approach. Mende-Siedlecki and colleagues (2013) analyzed 28 studies using a multilevel kernel density analysis approach. Abbreviations: Lat = laterality (right [R] or left [L]), PFC = prefrontal cortex; x, y, z coordinated represent peak activations within clusters. For the latter study, size of clusters in voxels (#Vox) and weighted percentage of CIMs that activated each cluster (%Act) are reported.
‡Data from two meta-analyses of fMRI studies. The peak coordinates are reported in MNI space.
†Areas withstanding height-based thresholding. **Areas withstanding extent-based thresholding ($p < .001$), *Areas withstanding extent-based thresholding ($p < .01$).

These differences between trustworthiness and attractiveness studies are puzzling because evaluations on these two dimensions are highly correlated. There were no obvious differences between these two sets of studies (e.g., implicit vs. explicit tasks) except for the nature of the face stimuli used in the studies. Whereas eight of the attractiveness studies used extremely attractive faces (e.g., faces of models), none of the trustworthiness studies used such faces. If the differences between attractiveness and trustworthiness studies are partly due to differences in stimuli, then the regions that differentiate these

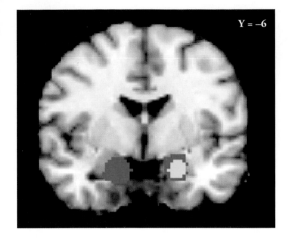

Figure 12.1 Consistently activated areas associated with negative evaluations based on facial appearance, across 28 studies. Negative evaluations were most associated with consistent bilateral amygdala activation. Yellow voxels withstood height-based thresholding, orange voxels withstood extent-based thresholding ($p < .001$), and pink voxels withstood extent-based thresholding ($p < .01$). The thresholding was based on Monte Carlo simulations (see Kober et al., 2008, and Mende-Siedlecki et al., 2013, for technical details).

studies should also appear in contrasts involving the extremeness of faces. In fact, comparisons of attractiveness studies that used extremely attractive faces and trustworthiness studies revealed more consistent activations in a region in the mOFC extending into NAcc, as well as activations centered in pgACC and extending broadly into both vmPFC and vlPFC, in the attractiveness studies as compared to the trustworthiness studies. As shown in Figure 12.3, these regions largely overlapped with the regions distinguishing between (all) attractiveness and trustworthiness studies. On the other hand, comparisons of attractiveness studies that did not use extremely attractive faces and trustworthiness studies did not produce areas of consistent activation for attractiveness studies. These findings suggest that some of the differences between attractiveness and trustworthiness studies can be attributed to differences in the face stimuli used in these studies.

Finally, we also compared contrasts identifying brain regions with linear responses to facial stimuli and contrasts identifying brain regions with nonlinear responses—that is, activity in

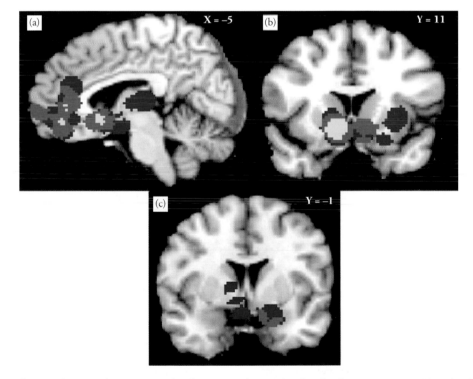

Figure 12.2 Consistently activated areas associated with positive evaluations based on facial appearance, across 28 studies. Positive evaluations were associated with consistent activation in (**a**) vmPFC, pgACC, mOFC; (**b**) NAcc and caudate; and (**c**), less consistently, in the right amygdala. Yellow voxels withstood height-based thresholding, orange voxels withstood extent-based thresholding ($p < .001$), and pink voxels withstood extent-based thresholding ($p < .01$). The thresholding was based on Monte Carlo simulations (see Kober et al., 2008, and Mende-Siedlecki et al., 2013, for technical details).

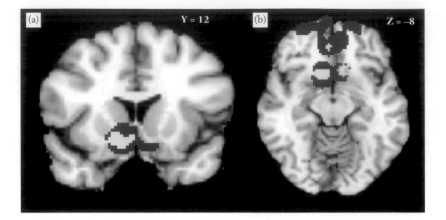

Figure 12.3 Atypical, or extremely attractive faces yielded consistent activations in (**a**) NAcc/caudate and (**b**) vmPFC/vlPFC. Studies that used more typical faces in the context of attractiveness evaluations were less likely to observe such activations. Yellow voxels withstood height-based thresholding, orange voxels withstood extent-based thresholding ($p < .001$), and pink voxels withstood extent-based thresholding ($p < .01$). The thresholding was based on Monte Carlo simulations (see Kober et al., 2008, and Mende-Siedlecki et al., 2013, for technical details).

these regions that increased with both increases *and* decreases in attractiveness or trustworthiness, relative to faces at the midpoint of these continua. This analysis yielded separate loci of activation within the amygdala for linear and nonlinear responses (Figure 12.4). Whereas a ventral portion responded more consistently to negative faces only, a dorsal portion of the amygdala responded more consistently to both negative and positive faces than to neutral faces. This dissociation of linear and nonlinear responses in the human amygdala parallels the findings of a high-resolution fMRI study on nonhuman primates (Hoffman, Gothard, Schmid, & Logothetis, 2007). Further, it is consistent with a hypothesis proposed by Whalen and colleagues (Kim et al., 2003; Whalen et al., 2001), who have argued that while the ventral portion of

the amygdala is involved in processing valence, the dorsal portion is involved in determining the value of particularly salient or ambiguous information in a given context (e.g., expressions of surprise, in Kim et al., 2003; or happiness, in Whalen et al., 1998).

These MKDAs revealed a host of brain regions consistently activated across studies on forming impressions from facial appearance: the right amygdala for negative evaluations and the NAcc/caudate, mOFC, mPFC, and pgACC for positive evaluations. These findings suggest that these regions comprise the core network for assessment of the affective value of faces, value that most likely determines the impressions formed about these faces. Most likely, the region that is central for the face evaluation network is the amygdala.

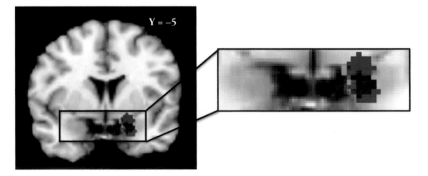

Figure 12.4 Linear and nonlinear response patterns in right amygdala. Blue indicates voxels consistently active across nonlinear contrasts, red indicates voxels consistently active across negative evaluations, and green indicates voxels consistently active across positive evaluations. Blue and red clusters withstood cluster- and extent-based thresholding, while the green cluster withstood extent-based thresholding ($p < .001$).

This is consistent with both anatomical studies of the macaque's brain (Amaral, Price, Pitkinen, & Carmichael, 1992) and neurophysiology findings of face-selective responses in the amygdala (Gothard, Battaglia, Erickson, Spitler, & Amaral, 2007; Nakamura, Mikami, & Kubota, 1992; Rolls, 2000). The amygdala receives input from the inferior temporal (IT) cortex and projects back not only to IT cortex but also to extrastriate and striate visual areas. The amygdala also has strong interconnections with rostral ACC, OFC, mPFC, basal ganglia, and anterior insula. This anatomical position of the amygdala allows it to serve as an affective hub of information. A recent meta-analysis of over 160 neuroimaging studies of emotions (which established the MKDA technique) found that the amygdala is consistently co-activated with rostral dorsal ACC, pgACC, dorsomedial (dm) PFC, and frontal operculum (Kober et al., 2008).

Highly processed face information in the fusiform gyrus (FG) can be further processed in the amygdala for determining the affective significance of the faces. Faces that are deemed significant by virtue of either their atypicality (Said et al., 2010) or emotional expressions (Vuilleumier et al., 2004) can be more deeply processed in FG regions via feedback projections from the amygdala. This accounts for findings that (a) FG activity is modulated when faces are associated with affective value (Petrovic, Kalisch, Pessiglione, Singer, & Dolan, 2008; Petrovic, Kalisch, Singer, & Dolan, 2008; Vuilleumier, Armony, Driver, & Dolan, 2001) and (b) when the amygdala is damaged, there is no enhanced response in the FG to fearful faces (Vuilleumier, Richardson, Armony, Driver, & Dolan, 2004).

The Neural Basis of Impressions Made from Multiple Sources of Information

As noted in the introduction, people form impressions from multiple sources of information. Impressions formed from the behaviors of others are among the most studied impressions in social psychology (e.g., Gilbert & Malone, 1995; Jones & Davis, 1965; Trope, 1986; for a review, see Gilbert, 1998). Behavioral studies have shown that people spontaneously infer evaluations and traits from behaviors and that such inferences are associated with the faces that accompanied the behaviors (Carlston & Skowronski, 1994; Goren & Todorov, 2009; Todorov & Uleman, 2002, 2003, 2004). Importantly, most of these studies randomly assign behaviors to faces to avoid effects of facial appearance on inferences and subsequent judgments. Hence, the observed effects of behavioral information on impressions cannot be attributed to facial appearance.

The first fMRI studies on impression formation used behavioral information to identify the brain regions involved in impression formation. In one of the earliest such studies (Mitchell, Macrae, & Banaji, 2004), participants read trait-related biographical information about a series of people (represented by faces) and were asked to either form impressions of those people or to remember the order in which this information appeared. Whereas the impression formation task was associated with activation in a large portion of dmPFC, the "sequencing" task was associated with activations in a separate set of brain regions (superior frontal and parietal gyri, precentral gyrus, and caudate). Furthermore, the authors found that dmPFC activity during the impression formation task predicted correct recall of the behavioral information during a subsequent memory test. In contrast, correct recall in the sequencing task was predicted by right hippocampal activity.

Subsequent studies have supported the link between the dmPFC and impression formation (Mitchel, Cloutier, Banaji, & Macrae, 2006; Mitchell, Macrae, & Banaji, 2005; Mitchell et al., 2004). In a follow-up study, Mitchell and colleagues (2006) observed that the dmPFC was involved in forming social impressions but not in forming nonsocial impressions. Specifically, participants either engaged in the impression formation or the sequencing task for both social (people) and nonsocial (objects such as cars and computers) targets. The social-impression formation condition elicited the greatest degree of dmPFC activation. The finding that only explicit impression formation activates the dmPFC is somewhat surprising in light of behavioral studies showing that impressions from behavioral information are formed even when people do not intend to form such impressions (Todorov & Uleman, 2002, 2003). Based on these studies, one would predict that the sequencing task should evoke responses in the dmPFC too. This apparent inconsistency seems to be related to the type of behavioral information that is used. In behavioral studies, such information is typically highly diagnostic with respect to both evaluative and trait inferences (e.g., "Henry kicked the puppy and laughed" leads to negative evaluations of Henry and that he is an aggressive person). In an additional study, Mitchell and colleagues (2006) varied the diagnosticity of the behavioral information. Once again, the dmPFC was found to be preferentially active in the impression formation task as opposed to the sequencing task. However, when the behavioral information was diagnostic, the dmPFC was as active in the sequencing as in the impression formation task.

These results are notably distinct from those described in the previous section. While appearance-based impression formation is associated primarily with amygdala (negative evaluations) and mOFC/NAcc (positive evaluations), behavior-based impression formation is most strongly associated with the dmPFC. This divergence most likely reflects the types of impressions being formed. Whereas appearance-based inferences are primarily about general evaluation of faces (Todorov, Said, et al., 2008), behavior-based inferences are about specific evaluations such as intelligence and honesty (Todorov & Uleman, 2002). Correspondingly, appearance-based inferences may depend more on brain areas coding for valence or motivational salience, whereas behavior-based inferences may depend more on regions coding for social content, potentially leading to inferences regarding mental states and intentions.

Since the initial studies on behavior-based impressions, further research has confirmed and clarified the nature of the dmPFC's involvement in forming evaluative impressions of others. For the most part, these studies continued to employ paradigms in which participants were presented with faces paired with behavioral information and were prompted to evaluate the targets (faces) in the context of this knowledge regarding their behavior or character. These studies have invariably observed dmPFC activity in association with this type of impression formation (Ames & Fiske, under invited revision; Baron, Gobbini, Engell, & Todorov, 2011; Chen, Welsh, Liberzon, & Taylor, 2010; Schiller, Freeman, Mitchell, Uleman, & Phelps, 2009). Moreover, this work has (a) identified other regions involved in person impressions (Schiller et al., 2009; Singer, Kiebel, Winston, Dolan, & Frith, 2004; Todorov, Gobbini, Evans, & Haxby, 2007); (b) studied how impressions from *multiple* sources of information are formed (Baron et al., 2011; Croft, Duffa, Kovacha, & Anderson,, 2010; Todorov & Olson, 2008); and (c) started exploring the possible interactions between regions involved in impression formation (Baron et al., 2011).

Schiller and colleagues (2009) showed that when biographical information varies in its relevance to the ultimate person evaluation, the posterior cingulate cortex (PCC) and amygdala show stronger responses to evaluation-relevant information than to evaluation-irrelevant information (Schiller et al., 2009). Notably, dmPFC activity did not vary as a function of evaluation relevance, which suggests a broader role of this region in supporting the formation of person impressions. Other studies have shown that once person impressions are formed, they seem to be automatically activated upon the presence of the person (Singer et al., 2004; Todorov et al., 2007). In one study, participants ostensibly played a sequential Prisoner's Dilemma Game with other people (Singer et al., 2004). Some of these people defected, some cooperated, and some were neutral. In a subsequent task, participants were asked to judge the gender of faces of the people they had played with. Although the task did not require person evaluation or retrieval of person knowledge, faces of cooperators and defectors that had attained affective value yielded stronger activation in a set of regions, including vmPFC, anterior insula, OFC, left amygdala, and left FG, than neutral-status faces.

In another study, participants learned associations between faces and four types of behaviors—aggressive, disgusting, nice, or neutral—that the pictured individual had carried out (Todorov et al., 2007). After the learning stage, participants were presented with the faces only during an implicit task (one back recognition). Consistent with the studies discussed above, although the participants' task did not demand retrieval of person knowledge, faces paired with behaviors elicited stronger dmPFC activation than novel faces (which had not previously been associated with behavioral information). Moreover, dmPFC activation was associated with better recall of the behaviors (cf., Mitchell et al., 2005). Critically, though, the authors observed that the type of behaviors associated with the faces affected the response to the faces. For example, faces associated with disgusting behaviors yielded stronger activation in the anterior insula, a region implicated in the processing of disgust-related stimuli (Calder, Keane, Manes, Antoun, & Young, 2000; Phillips et al., 1997), than faces associated with aggressive behaviors. These findings suggest that impression formation relies not only on regions such as the dmPFC, which supports general processes, but also on regions that represent the specific content of impressions.

So far, we have discussed impressions from one type of knowledge—faces in the previous sections, and behaviors in the present section—but people form impressions from *multiple* sources of information. Moreover, different sources of information are often conflicting with respect to impressions, and people need to integrate this conflicting information. From an adaptive point of view, people should be able to rapidly learn about other people and overwrite initial impressions in light of diagnostic information. For example, finding out that a trustworthy-looking person is a con artist should and does change one's impressions of trustworthiness (e.g., Todorov & Olson, 2008). In fact, person learning is highly robust. It occurs after minimal time exposure to faces and behaviors, is relatively independent of availability of cognitive resources, and is independent of explicit goals to form impressions. In addition, subsequent effects on perception and judgments are independent of explicit memory for the behaviors (Bliss-Moreau, Barrett, & Wright, 2008; Todorov & Uleman, 2003).

Several studies including patients with brain lesions provide evidence consistent with the idea of robust person-learning mechanisms (Croft et al., 2010; Johnson, Kim, & Risse, 1985; Tranel & Damasio, 1993; Todorov & Olson, 2008). In a particularly striking case, Tranel and Damasio (1993) described a patient (Boswell) with extensive damage in the medial temporal lobe and orbitofrontal cortex. Boswell had dense amnesia, did not recognize the faces of caregivers, and did not even show increased galvanic skin response to familiar faces, an index of implicit face processing. However, if consistently treated nicely by a caregiver, Boswell had a reliable preference for her face in forced-choice preference tasks.

Although Boswell's case is extreme, research with Korsakoff patients also shows that they can acquire and preserve affective responses to people's faces despite lacking explicit memory (Johnson et al., 1985). Johnson and colleagues presented such patients with two faces and described one of the people as bad (e.g., "… stole a car … robbed an old man who lived in the neighborhood") and the other as good (e.g., " … joined the Navy … saved a fellow sailor"). The patients reliably preferred the good person despite lacking memory for the origin of these impressions.

In a conceptual replication of Johnson and colleagues' study, Todorov and Olson (2008) studied how inferences from facial appearance and behavioral descriptions are integrated in person impressions. Normal participants and three patients with amnesia due to lesions in the hippocampus were presented with trustworthy- and untrustworthy-looking faces paired with trustworthy and untrustworthy behaviors. After the learning stage of the experiment, participants were asked to evaluate the faces. One of the patients with a localized lesion in the hippocampus showed excellent learning, as did young and older control participants. Faces associated with positive behaviors were evaluated more positively than faces associated with negative behaviors, and this learning effect was stronger than the effect of facial appearance on evaluation. The other two patients, whose lesions extended into the left amygdala and left temporal pole, showed little evidence of learning. At the same time, all patients showed effects of facial appearance on evaluation similar to the effects observed for developmental prosopagnosics (Todorov & Duchaine, 2008). These findings suggest that the hippocampus may not be necessary for forming affective associations with faces. Other structures in the medial temporal lobe such as the amygdala may be critical for this process (Somerville, Wig, Whalen, & Kelley, 2006).

Finally, Croft and colleagues (2010) studied patients with lesions in the hippocampus and in the vmPFC. In this study, participants were presented with pictures of people and then with visual depictions of positive or negative behaviors enacted by these people (e.g., drowning another person in a bathtub). As in the study by Todorov and Olson (2008), patients with hippocampal lesions were able to learn to associate the positive and negative information with the people, and their evaluations reflected this information. In contrast, patients with lesions in the vmPFC were unable to update their evaluations in light of the behavioral information. One possibility put forth by the authors is that the vmPFC is involved in associating emotional value with choices—individuals with damage to this region do not experience the emotionality of certain actions, and as a result, perform atypically on tasks such as updating person impressions.

In addition to the lesion studies described above, fMRI studies have also explored how different sources of information are integrated in person impressions. In one study, participants read biographical information about a series of individuals, who were described as morally good, morally dubious, or neutral (Delgado, Frank, & Phelps, 2005). Subsequently, when participants interacted with these individuals in a trust game (involving investing of money), they relied more heavily on prior knowledge of them than they did on actual behavior in the game. Participants were more likely to trust morally good partners than morally dubious ones, even when cooperation rates were held constant. In terms of the fMRI data, activity in the caudate nucleus differentiated between positive and negative outcomes in the Trust Game, consistent with prior work (Filoteo et al., 2005; Poldrack et al., 2001), but only for neutral partners. When participants had prior knowledge of their partner, caudate activity varied either very weakly between positive and negative outcomes (for "morally dubious" partners) or not at all (for "morally good" partners). In other words, choosing to rely on previously formed impressions of these targets dampened dependence on the neural mechanisms associated with trial-and-error reward learning.

In another fMRI study (Baron et al., 2011), participants were presented with faces previously rated as being either high or low on trustworthiness. Subsequently, some of these faces were paired with positive or negative behavioral information. Consistent with prior work (Todorov & Engell, 2008; Winston et al., 2002), the right amygdala responded more strongly to untrustworthy- than to trustworthy-looking faces before learning. During learning, dmPFC activity was stronger for faces paired with behaviors than for faces unpaired with behaviors. Moreover, similar to previous studies (Mitchell et al., 2004; Todorov et al., 2007), the authors found that dmPFC activity during learning predicted subsequent evaluation of the faces. Interestingly, this relationship between dmPFC activity and evaluation was moderated by the initial amygdala response to face trustworthiness, such that strong initial amygdala responses were associated with weaker relationships between dmPFC and behavioral learning. This lends support to the possibility of an interactive relationship between dmPFC and amygdala during impression formation (Baron et al., 2011).

There have been very few ERP studies on forming impressions from multiple sources of information, although ERP methods are invaluable for understanding how these sources are integrated over time. In the first section, we described a study by Rudoy and Paller (2009), which showed that differences between trustworthy- and untrustworthy-looking faces emerged between 200 and 400 ms after the stimulus onset of the faces. In the same study, the authors asked the participants to learn to associate positive and negative trait words with the faces. Differences between faces associated with positive and negative words emerged relatively late between 800 and 1000 ms in parietal electrodes.

These findings suggest that affective associations from learning do not change the initial, automatic impressions formed from facial appearance.

However, the type of learning may matter and possibly change the pattern of results. For example, witnessing a brutal behavior (cf., Croft et al., 2010) or learning an elaborate description of a person (cf., Delgado et al., 2005) may be more potent in changing face perception than learning to associate trait words with faces. In fact, intensive learning ("day in the life" stories) about unfamiliar people over a 5-day period modulated the N170 response to faces (Heisz & Shedden, 2009). Generally, N170 response is attenuated when unfamiliar faces are repeated. However, as in the case of perception of famous faces, the N170 response was not attenuated after repetition of the faces associated with rich behavioral information. Importantly, repetition of faces associated with nonsocial information (e.g., stories about volcanoes) did not attenuate the N170 response.

Further, the familiarity with the person or face may also be critical for the observed pattern of results. For example, Rahman (2011) showed that for highly familiar faces, effects of new affective knowledge (acquired before the ERP session) emerged between 200 and 300 ms. In contrast, for newly learned faces, as in Rudoy and Paller's experiment, these effects emerged later, between 500 and 600 ms.

While these ERP studies suggest that person learning has an observable impact on the temporal dynamics of impression formation, the range of these effects is considerable. Clearly, more studies are needed to understand how quickly affective knowledge influences face perception and evaluation.

Conclusions and Future Directions

In the first section, we reviewed evidence that people rapidly form impressions of other people based on minimal information. An ERP study showed that differences between faces with different evaluations emerged as early as 200 ms after stimulus onset (Rudoy & Paller, 2009). These findings suggest that person impressions are, indeed, rapidly formed, given that the first face-specific responses peaked at around 170 ms (Rossion & Jacques, 2008).

In the second section, we reviewed fMRI studies on forming impressions from facial appearance. A meta-analysis of 28 studies identified a number of regions that were consistently activated within specific evaluations (Mende-Siedlecki et al., 2013).

These included the right amygdala for negative evaluations and the NAcc/caudate, mOFC, mPFC, and pgACC for positive evaluations. In the next section we reviewed studies on forming impressions from behavioral information and from multiple sources of person information. There is strong behavioral evidence that people rapidly change their impressions in light of behavioral information. Although there are no quantitative summaries of these studies, it appears that dmPFC is consistently activated across studies that involve impression formation from behavioral or other biographical information. Several studies have also identified the amygdala (Baron et al., 2011; Schiller et al., 2009) and vmPFC (Croft et al., 2010) as being critical in the updating of person impressions.

It is interesting to note that there was relatively little overlap in the regions involved in forming impressions from facial appearance and from behavioral information. This may reflect different paradigms and stimulus materials in these studies (Ames et al., 2011) or different networks dedicated to different types of person learning. Meta-analyses that directly compare these types of studies would be helpful in clarifying this question. Similarly, ERP studies are needed to study the temporal dynamic of forming impressions from multiple sources of information. Although the behavioral findings show that learning can overwrite initial impressions, we lack models specifying how person representations are dynamically updated in the brain. One of the most important tasks for future research is to specify models of how different sources of person information are integrated in coherent person representations.

Another unresolved issue is the nature of the face properties that drive bottom-up neural responses. As we showed in the section on impressions made from facial appearance, some of the puzzling differences between attractiveness and trustworthiness studies (puzzling because these evaluations are highly correlated with each other) could be attributed to differences in face stimuli. This is worrisome given that face stimuli are rarely shared across different research groups and are often haphazardly sampled for individual studies. This could undermine the generalizability of findings. We need a general account of the face properties that drive neural responses. A recent study suggests that the critical property is face typicality, which is also highly correlated with a number of social attributions (Said et al., 2010). However, more work needs to be done.

Finally, very few studies have addressed the role of individual differences in impression formation (but see Bliss-Moreau et al., 2008), but such differences may be critical for the observed behavioral and neural responses. For example, although people agree in their impressions made from facial appearance, there are also individual differences (Engell et al., 2007; Hönekopp, 2006). Understanding these differences may be critical for understanding perceptual learning and top-down effects on social perception. Two likely sources of idiosyncratic contributions to evaluation of novel faces are self-resemblance (e.g., DeBruine, 2002, 2005; Verosky & Todorov, 2010a) and resemblance to faces of familiar people (Verosky & Todorov, 2010b). We know very little about the neural underpinnings of individual differences in face evaluation. Further, individual differences are also important for person learning (Bliss-Moreau et al., 2008). For example, Rudoy and Paller (2009) found a negative relationship between effects of facial appearance and effects of trait learning on person impressions. Specifically, participants who were likely to be influenced by facial appearance were less likely to be influenced by trait information. Similarly, Baron and colleagues (2011) found that individual differences in amygdala responses to unfamiliar faces modulated the relationship between dmPFC and person impressions.

To conclude, although considerable progress has been made in the study of the neural basis of impression formation, there are many exciting research questions awaiting answers.

Acknowledgments

The work presented here was supported by National Science Foundation grant 0823749 and the Russell Sage Foundation.

References

Adolphs, R., Tranel, D., & Damasio, A. R. (1998). The human amygdala in social judgment. *Nature, 393,* 470–474.

Aharon, I., Etcoff, N., Ariely, D., Chabris, C. F., O'Connor, E., & Breiter, H. C. (2001) Beautiful faces have variable reward value. fMRI and behavioral evidence. *Neuron, 32,* 537–551.

Albright, L., Kenny, D. A., & Malloy, T. E. (1988). Consensus in personality judgments at zero acquaintance. *Journal of Personality and Social Psychology, 55,* 387–395.

Amaral, D. G., Price, J. L., Pitkänen, A., & Carmichael, S. T. (1992). Anatomical organization of the primate amygdaloid complex. In J. P. Aggleton (Ed.), *The amygdala: Neurobiological aspects of emotion, memory, and mental dysfunction* (pp. 1–66). New York: Wiley-Liss.

Ambady, N., Hallahan, M., & Rosenthal, R. (1995). On judging and being judged accurately in zero-acquaintance situations. *Journal of Personality and Social Psychology, 69,* 518–529.

Ambady, N., & Rosenthal, R. (1992). Thin slices of expressive behavior as predictors of interpersonal consequences: A meta-analysis. *Psychological Bulletin, 111,* 256–274.

Ames, D. L., & Fiske, S. T. (under invited revision). Outcome dependency alters the neural substrates of impression formation. *NeuroImage*.

Ames, D. L., Fiske, S. T., & Todorov, A. (2011). Impression formation: A focus on others' intents. In J. Decety & J. Cacioppo (Eds.), *The handbook of social neuroscience*. New York: Oxford University Press.

Asch, S. E. (1946). Forming impressions of personality. *Journal of Abnormal and Social Psychology, 41*, 258–290.

Ballew, C. C., & Todorov, A. (2007). Predicting political elections from rapid and unreflective face judgments. *Proceedings of the National Academy of Sciences U S A, 104*, 17948–17953.

Bar, M., Neta, M., & Linz, H. (2006). Very first impressions. *Emotion, 6*, 269–278.

Baron, S. G., Gobbini, M. I., Engell, A. D., & Todorov, A. (2011). Amygdala and dorsomedial prefrontal cortex responses to appearance-based and behavior-based person impressions. *Social, Cognitive & Affective Neuroscience, 6*, 572–581.

Bliss-Moreau, E., Barrett, L. F., & Wright, C. I. (2008). Individual differences in learning the affective value of others under minimal conditions. *Emotion, 8*, 479–493.

Bzdok, D., Langner, R., Caspers, S., Furth, F., Habel, U., Zilles, K., Laird, A., & Eickhoff, S. B. (2011). ALE meta-analysis on facial judgments of trustworthiness and attractiveness. *Brain Structure and Function, 215*, 209–223.

Calder, A. J., Keane, J., Manes, F., Antoun, N., & Young, A. W. (2000). Impaired recognition and experience of disgust following brain injury. *Nature Neuroscience, 3*, 1077–1078.

Carlston, D. E., & Skowronski, J. J. (1994). Saving in the relearning of trait information as evidence for spontaneous inference generation. *Journal of Personality and Social Psychology, 66*, 840–856.

Chen, A. C., Welsh, R. C., Liberzon, I, & Taylor, S. F. (2010). "Do I like this person?" A network analysis of midline cortex during a social preference task. *Neuroimage, 51*, 930–939.

Cheyney, D. K., & Seyfarth, R. M. (2007). *Baboon metaphysics*. Chicago: University of Chicago Press.

Cloutier, J., Heatherton, T. F., Whalen, P. J., & Kelley, W. M. (2008). Are attractive people rewarding? Sex differences in the neural substrates of facial attractiveness. *Journal of Cognitive Neuroscience, 20*, 941–951.

Croft, K. E., Duffa, M. C., Kovacha, C. K., & Anderson, S. W. (2010). Detestable or marvelous? Neuroanatomical correlates of character judgments. *Neuropsychologia, 48*, 1789–1801.

Cunningham, W. A., Raye, C. L., & Johnson, M. K. (2004) Implicit and explicit evaluation: fMRI correlates of valence, emotional intensity, and control in the processing of attitudes. *Journal of Cognitive Neuroscience, 16*, 1717–1729.

Dannlowski, U., Ohrmann, P., Bauer, J., Kugel, H., Arolt, V., Heindel, W., Kersting, A., Baune, B.T., & Suslow, T. (2007). Amygdala reactivity to masked negative faces is associated with automatic judgmental bias in major depression: a 3-T fMRI study. *Journal of Psychiatry and Neuroscience, 32*, 423–429.

DeBruine, L. M. (2002). Facial resemblance enhances trust. *Proceedings of the Royal Society: Biological Sciences, 269*, 1307–1312.

DeBruine, L. M. (2005). Trustworthy but not lust-worthy: Context-specific effects of facial resemblance. *Proceedings of the Royal Society: Biological Sciences, 272*, 919–922.

Delgado, M. R., Frank, R. H., & Phelps, E. A. (2005). Perceptions of moral character modulate the neural systems of reward during the Trust Game. *Nature Neuroscience, 8*, 1611–1618.

DiCarlo, J. J., & Cox, D. D. (2007). Untangling invariant object recognition. *Trends in Cognitive Sciences, 11*, 333–340.

Eimer, M., & Holmes, A. (2007). Event-related brain potential correlates of emotional face processing. *Neuropsychologia, 45*, 15–31.

Engell, A. D., Haxby, J. V., & Todorov, A. (2007). Implicit trustworthiness decisions: Automatic coding of face properties in human amygdala. *Journal of Cognitive Neuroscience, 19*, 1508–1519.

Filoteo, J. V., Maddox, W. T., Simmons, A. N., Ing, A. D., Cagigas, X. E., Matthews, S., & Paulus, M. P. (2005). Cortical and subcortical brain regions involved in rule-based category learning. *Neuroreport, 16*, 111–115.

Gilbert, D. T. (1998). Ordinary personology. In D. T. Gilbert, S. T. Fiske, & G. Lindzey (Eds.), *The handbook of social psychology*, (Vol 2., pp. 89–150). New York: McGraw-Hill.

Gilbert, D. T., & Malone, P. S. (1995). The correspondence bias. *Psychological Bulletin, 117*, 21–38.

Goren, A., & Todorov, A. (2009). Two faces are better than one: Eliminating false trait associations with faces. *Social Cognition, 27*, 222–248.

Gothard, K. M., Battaglia, F. P., Erickson, C. A., Spitler, K. M., & Amaral, D. G. (2007). Neural responses to facial expression and face identity in the monkey amygdala. *Journal of Neurophysiology, 97*, 1671–1683.

Haxby, J. V., Hoffman, E. A., & Gobbini, M. I. (2000). The distributed human neural system for face perception. *Trends in Cognitive Sciences, 4*, 223–233.

Hare, T. A., Camerer, C. F., Knoepfle, D. T., O'Doherty, J. P., & Rangel, A. (2010). Value computations in ventral medial prefrontal cortex during charitable decision making incorporate input from regions involved in social cognition. *Journal of Neuroscience, 30*, 583–590.

Heisz, J. J., & Shedden, J. M. (2009). Semantic learning modifies perceptual face processing. *Journal of Cognitive Neuroscience, 21*, 1127–1134.

Hoffman, K. L., Gothard, K. M., Schmid, M. C., & Logothetis, N. K. (2007). Facial-expression and gaze-selective responses in the monkey amygdala. *Current Biology, 17*, 766–772.

Hönekopp, J. (2006). Once more: Is beauty in the eye of the beholder? Relative contributions of private and shared taste to judgments of facial attractiveness. *Journal of Experimental Psychology: Human Perception and Performance, 32*, 199–209.

Johnson, M. K., Kim, J. K., & Risse, G. (1985). Do alcoholic Korsakoff's syndrome patients acquire affective reactions? *Journal of Experimental Psychology: Learning, Memory, and Cognition, 11*, 22–36.

Jones, E. E., & Davis, K. E. (1965). From acts to dispositions: The attribution process in person perception. In L. Berkowitz (Ed.), *Advances in experimental social psychology* (Vol. 2, pp. 219–266). New York: Academic Press.

Kampe, K. K. W., Frith, C. D., Dolan, R. J., & Frith, U. (2001). Reward value of attractiveness and gaze. *Nature, 413*, 589–589.

Kanwisher, N., & Yovel, G. (2006). The fusiform face area: A cortical region specialized for the perception of faces. *Philosophical Transactions of the Royal Society of London B: Biological Sciences, 361*, 2109–2128.

Kesler-West, M. L., Andersen, A. H., Smith, C. D., Avison, M. J., Davis, C. E., Kryscio, R. J., & Blonder, L. X. (2001). Neural substrates of facial emotion processing using fMRI. *Cognitive Brain Research, 11*, 213–226.

Kim, H., Somerville, L. H., Johnstone, T., Alexander, A., & Whalen, P. J. (2003). Inverse amygdala and medial prefrontal cortex responses to surprised faces. *Neuroreport, 14,* 2317–2322.

Knutson, B., Fong, G. W., Bennett, S. M., Adams, C. S., & Hommer, D. (2003). A region of mesial prefrontal cortex tracks monetarily rewarding outcomes: Characterization with rapid event-related FMRI. *Neuroimage, 18,* 263–272.

Knutson, B., Taylor, J., Kaufman, M., Peterson, R., & Glover, G. (2005). Distributed neural representation of expected value. *Journal of Neuroscience, 25,* 4806–4812.

Knutson, B., Wimmer, G. E. (2007). Reward: Neural circuitry for social valuation. In Harmon-Jones, E., Winkielman, P. (Eds.) *Social neuroscience.* New York: Guilford Press, pp. 157–175.

Kober, H., Barrett, L. F., Joseph, J., Bliss-Moreau, E., Lindquist, K., & Wager, T. D. (2008). Functional grouping and cortical-subcortical interactions in emotion: A meta-analysis of neuroimaging studies, *Neuroimage, 42,* 998–1031.

Kranz, F., & Ishai, A. (2006). Face perception is modulated by sexual preference. *Current Biology, 16,* 63–68.

Langlois, J. H., Kalakanis, L., Rubenstein, A. J., Larson, A., Hallam, M., & Smoot, M. (2000). Maxims or myths of beauty? A meta-analytic and theoretical review. *Psychological Bulletin, 126,* 390–423.

Liang, X., Zebrowitz, L. A., & Zhang, Y. (2010). Neural activation in the "reward circuit" shows a nonlinear response to facial attractiveness. *Social Neuroscience, 5,* 320–334

Locher, P., Unger, R., Sociedade, P., & Wahl, J. (1993). At first glance: Accessibility of the physical attractiveness stereotype. *Sex Roles, 28,* 729–743.

Mende-Siedlecki, P., Said, C. P., & Todorov, A. (2013). The social evaluation of faces: A meta-analysis of functional neuroimaging studies. *Social, Cognitive & Affective Neuroscience, 8,* 285–299.

Mitchell, J. P. (2008). Contributions of functional neuroimaging to the study of social cognition. *Current Directions in Psychological Science, 17,* 142–146.

Mitchell, J. P. (2009). Inferences about other minds. *Philosophical Transactions of the Royal Society B, 364,* 1309–1316.

Mitchell, J. P., Cloutier, J., Banaji, M. R., & Macrae, C. N. (2006). Medial prefrontal dissociations during processing of trait diagnostic and nondiagnostic person information. *Social, Cognitive & Affective Neuroscience, 1,* 49–55.

Mitchell, J. P., Macrae, C. N., & Banaji, M. R. (2004). Encoding-specific effects of social cognition on the neural correlates of subsequent memory. *Journal of Neuroscience, 24,* 4912–4917.

Mitchell, J. P., Macrae, C. N., & Banaji, M. R. (2005). Forming impressions of people versus inanimate objects: Social-cognitive processing in the medial prefrontal cortex. *Neuroimage, 26,* 251–257.

Monk, C. S., Nelson, E. E., McClure, E. B., Mogg, K., Bradley, B. P., Leibenluft, E., Blair, R. J., Chen, G., Charney, D. S., Ernst, M., & Pine, D. S. (2006). Ventrolateral prefrontal cortex activation and attentional bias in response to angry faces in adolescents with generalized anxiety disorder. *American Journal of Psychiatry, 163,* 1091–1097.

Montepare, J. M., & Dobish, H. (2003). The contribution of emotion perceptions and their overgeneralizations to trait impressions. *Journal of Nonverbal Behavior, 27,* 237–254.

Montepare, J. M., & Zebrowitz, L. A. (1998). Person perception comes of age: The salience and significance of age in social judgments. *Advances in Experimental Social Psychology, 30,* 93–161.

Morris, J. S., Frith, C. D., Perrett, D. I., Rowland, D., Young, A. W., Calder, A. J., & Dolan, R. J. (1996). A differential neural response in the human amygdala to fearful and happy facial expressions. *Nature, 383,* 812–815.

Morris, J. S., Öhman, A., & Dolan, R. J. (1998). Conscious and unconscious emotional learning in the human amygdala. *Nature, 393,* 467–470.

Nakamura, K., Mikami, A., & Kubota, K. (1992). Activity of single neurons in the monkey amygdala during performance of a visual discrimination task. *Journal of Neurophysiology, 67,* 1447–1463.

O'Doherty, J., Winston, J., Critchley, H., Perrett, D., Burt, D. M., & Dolan, R. J. (2003). Beauty in a smile: The role of medial orbitofrontal cortex in facial attractiveness. *Neuropsychologia, 41,* 147–155.

Olivola, C. Y., & Todorov, A. (2010). Fooled by first impressions? Re-examining the diagnostic value of appearance-based inferences. *Journal of Experimental Social Psychology, 46,* 315–324.

Olson, I. R., & Marshuetz, C. (2005). Facial attractiveness is appraised in a glance. *Emotion, 5,* 498–502.

Oosterhof, N. N., & Todorov, A. (2008). The functional basis of face evaluation. *Proceedings of the National Academy of Sciences U S A, 105,* 11087–11092.

Oosterhof, N. N., & Todorov, A. (2009). Shared perceptual basis of emotional expressions and trustworthiness impressions from faces. *Emotion, 9,* 128–133.

Petrovic, P., Kalisch, R., Pessiglione, M., Singer, T., & Dolan, R. J. (2008). Learning affective values for faces is expressed in amygdala and fusiform gyrus. *Social, Cognitive & Affective Neuroscience, 3,* 109–118.

Petrovic, P., Kalisch, R., Singer, T., & Dolan, R. J. (2008). Oxytocin attenuates affective evaluations of conditioned faces and amygdala activity. *Journal of Neuroscience, 28,* 6607–6615.

Phillips, M. L., Young, A. W., Senior, C., Calder, A. J., Rowland, D., Brammer, M., Bullmore, E. T., Andrew, C., Willimas, S. C. R., Gray, J., & David, A. S. (1997). A specific neural substrate for perception of facial expressions of disgust. *Nature, 389,* 495–498.

Phillips, M. L., Bullmore, E. T., Howard, R., Woodruff, P. W. R., Wright, I. C., Williams, S. C. R., et al. (1998). Investigation of facial recognition memory and happy and sad facial expression perception: An fMRI study. *Psychiatry Research: Neuroimaging Section, 83,* 127–138.

Poldrack, R. A., Clark, J., Paré-Blagoev, E. J., Shohamy, D., Creso Moyano, J., Myers, C., & Gluck, M. A. (2001). Interactive memory systems in the human brain. *Nature, 414,* 546–550.

Rahman, R.A. (2011). Facing good and evil: Early brain signatures of affective biographical knowledge in face recognition. *Emotion, 11,* 1397–1405.

Rangel, A., Camerer, C., & Montague, P. R. (2008). A framework for studying the neurobiology of value-based decision making. *Nature Reviews Neuroscience, 9,* 545–556.

Rhodes, G. (2006). The evolutionary psychology of facial beauty. *Annual Review of Psychology, 57,* 199–226.

Rolls, E. T. (2000). Neurophysiology and function of the primate amygdala, and neural basis of emotion. In J. P. Aggleton (Ed.), *The amygdala: A functional analysis* (pp. 447–478). New York: Oxford University Press.

Rossion, B., & Jacques, C. (2008). Does physical interstimulus variance account for early electrophysiological face sensitive responses in the human brain? Ten lessons on the N170. *Neuroimage, 39*, 1959–1979.

Rudoy, J. D., & Paller, K. A. (2009). Who can you trust? Behavioral and neural differences between perceptual and memory-based influences. *Frontiers in Human Neuroscience, 3*, 1–6.

Said, C. P., Baron, S. G., & Todorov, A. (2009). Nonlinear amygdala response to face trustworthiness: Contributions of high and low spatial frequency information. *Journal of Cognitive Neuroscience, 21*, 519–528.

Said, C. P., Dotsch, R., & Todorov, A. (2010). The amygdala and FFA track both social and non-social face dimensions. *Neuropsychologia, 48*, 3596–3605.

Said, C. P., Haxby, J. V., & Todorov, A. (2011). Brain systems for assessing the affective value of faces. *Philosophical Transactions of the Royal Society, B, 336*, 1660–1670.

Said, C. P., Sebe, N., & Todorov, A. (2009). Structural resemblance to emotional expressions predicts evaluation of emotionally neutral faces. *Emotion, 9*, 260–264.

Saxe, R. (2006). Uniquely human social cognition. *Current Opinion in Neurobiology, 16*, 235–239.

Schiller, D., Freeman, J. B., Mitchell, J. P., Uleman, J. S., & Phelps, E. A. (2009). A neural mechanism of first impressions. *Nature Neuroscience, 12*, 508–514.

Singer, T., Kiebel, S. J., Winston, J. S., Dolan, R. J., & Frith, C.D. (2004). Brain responses to the acquired moral status of faces. *Neuron, 41*, 653–662.

Somerville, L. H., Wig, G. S., Whalen, P. J., & Kelley, W. M. (2006). Dissociable medial temporal lobe contributions to social memory. *Journal of Cognitive Neuroscience, 18*, 1253–1265.

Todorov, A. (2008). Evaluating faces on trustworthiness: An extension of systems for recognition of emotions signaling approach/avoidance behaviors. In A. Kingstone & M. Miller (Eds.), The Year in Cognitive Neuroscience 2008, *Annals of the New York Academy of Sciences, 1124*, 208–224.

Todorov, A. (2012). The role of the amygdala in face perception and evaluation. *Motivation & Emotion, 36*, 16–26.

Todorov, A., Baron, S., & Oosterhof, N. N. (2008). Evaluating face trustworthiness: A model based approach. *Social, Cognitive, & Affective Neuroscience, 3*, 119–127.

Todorov, A., & Duchaine, B. (2008). Reading trustworthiness in faces without recognizing faces. *Cognitive Neuropsychology, 25*, 395–410.

Todorov, A., & Engell, A. (2008). The role of the amygdala in implicit evaluation of emotionally neutral faces. *Social, Cognitive, & Affective Neuroscience, 3*, 303–312.

Todorov, A., Gobbini, M. I., Evans, K. K., & Haxby, J. V. (2007). Spontaneous retrieval of affective person knowledge in face perception. *Neuropsychologia, 45*, 163–173.

Todorov, A., Loehr, V., & Oosterhof, N. N. (2010). The obligatory nature of holistic processing of faces in social judgments. *Perception, 39*, 514–532.

Todorov, A., & Olson, I. (2008). Robust learning of affective trait associations with faces when the hippocampus is damaged, but not when the amygdala and temporal pole are damaged. *Social, Cognitive & Affective Neuroscience, 3*, 195–203.

Todorov, A., Pakrashi, M., & Oosterhof, N. N. (2009). Evaluating faces on trustworthiness after minimal time exposure. *Social Cognition, 27*, 813–833.

Todorov, A., Said, C. P., Engell, A.D., & Oosterhof, N. N. (2008) Understanding evaluation of faces on social dimensions. *Trends in Cognitive Sciences, 12*, 455–460.

Todorov, A., Said, C. P., Oosterhof, N. N., & Engell, A. D. (2011). Task-invariant brain responses to the social value of faces. *Journal of Cognitive Neuroscience, 23*, 2766–2781.

Todorov, A., Said, C. P., & Verosky, S. C. (2011). Personality impressions from facial appearance. In A. Calder, J. V. Haxby, M. Johnson, & G. Rhodes (Eds.), *Handbook of face perception* (pp. 631–652). Oxford, UK: Oxford University Press.

Todorov, A., & Uleman, J. S. (2002). Spontaneous trait inferences are bound to actor's faces: Evidence from a false recognition paradigm. *Journal of Personality and Social Psychology, 83*, 1051–1065.

Todorov, A., & Uleman, J. S. (2003). The efficiency of binding spontaneous trait inferences to actor's faces. *Journal of Experimental Social Psychology, 39*, 549–562.

Todorov, A., & Uleman, J. S. (2004). The person reference process in spontaneous trait inferences. *Journal of Personality and Social Psychology, 87*, 482–493.

Tranel, D., & Damasio, A. R. (1993). The covert learning of affective valence does not require structures in hippocampal system or amygdala. *Journal of Cognitive Neuroscience, 5*, 79–88.

Trope, Y. (1986). Identification and inferential processes in dispositional attribution. *Psychological Review, 93*, 239–257.

Uleman, J. S., Blader, S., & Todorov, A. (2005). Implicit impressions. In R. Hassin, J. S. Uleman, & J. A. Bargh (Eds.), *The new unconscious* (pp. 362–392). New York: Oxford University Press.

Uleman, J. S., Newman, L. S., & Moskowitz, G. B. (1996). People as flexible interpreters: Evidence and issues from spontaneous trait inference. In M. P. Zanna (Ed.), *Advances in experimental social psychology* (Vol. 28, pp. 211–279). San Diego, CA: Academic Press.

Verosky, S. C., & Todorov, A. (2010a). Differential neural responses to faces physically similar to the self as a function of their valence. *Neuroimage, 49*, 1690–1698.

Verosky, S. C., & Todorov, A. (2010b). Generalization of affective learning about faces to perceptually similar faces. *Psychological Science, 21*, 779–785.

Vrtička, P., Andersson, F., Grandjean, D., Sander, D., & Vuilleumier, P. (2008). Individual attachment style modulates human amygdala and striatum activation during social appraisal. *PLoS ONE 3*(8): e2868. doi:10.1371/journal.pone.0002868

Vuilleumier, P., Armony, J. L., Driver, J., & Dolan, R. J. (2001). Effects of attention and emotion on face processing in the human brain: an event-related fMRI study. *Neuron, 30*, 829–841.

Vuilleumier, P., Richardson, M., Armony, J. L., Driver, J., & Dolan, R. J. (2004). Distant influences of amygdala lesion on visual cortical activation during emotional face processing. *Nature Neuroscience, 7*, 1271–1278.

Wager, T. D., Barrett, L. F., Bliss-Moreau, E., Lindquist, K., Duncan, S., Kober, H., et al., (2008). The neuroimaging of emotion. In M. Lewis, J. M. Haviland-Jones, L. F. Barrett, (Eds.), *Handbook of emotion* (3rd ed., pp. 249–271). New York: Guilford.

Whalen, P. J., Bush, G., McNally, R. J., Wilhelm, S., McInerney, S. C., Jenike, M. A., & Rauch, S. L. (1998). The emotional counting stroop paradigm: A functional magnetic resonance imaging probe of the anterior cingulate affective division. *Biological Psychiatry, 44,* 1219–1228.

Whalen, P. J., Shin, L. M., McInerney, S. C., Fischer, H., Wright, C. I., & Rauch, S. L. (2001). A functional MRI study of human amygdala responses to facial expressions of fear vs. anger. *Emotion, 1,* 70–83.

Willis, J., & Todorov, A. (2006). First impressions: Making up your mind after 100 ms exposure to a face. *Psychological Science, 17,* 592–598.

Winston, J., O'Doherty, J., Kilner, J. M., Perrett, D. I., & Dolan, R. J. (2007). Brain systems for assessing facial attractiveness, *Neuropsychologia, 45,* 195–206.

Winston, J., Strange, B., O'Doherty, J., & Dolan, R. (2002). Automatic and intentional brain responses during evaluation of trustworthiness of face. *Nature Neuroscience, 5,* 277–283.

Zebrowitz, L. A. (1999). *Reading faces: Window to the soul?* Boulder, CO: Westview Press.

Zebrowitz, L. A, Kikuchi, M., & Fellous, J.M. (2010). Facial resemblance to emotions: Group differences, impression effects, and race stereotypes. *Journal of Personality and Social Psychology, 98,* 175–189.

Zebrowitz, L. A., & Montepare, J. M. (2008). Social psychological face perception: Why appearance matters. *Social and Personality Psychology Compass, 2,* 1497–1517.

Theory of Mind: How Brains Think about Thoughts

Rebecca Saxe *and* Liane Lee Young

Abstract

In the last decade, cognitive neuroscience research has begun to address key questions concerning Theory of Mind (ToM). Are there distinct brain regions for ToM? What are (and aren't) those regions doing? This chapter reviews evidence suggesting that key regions support social cognition, thinking about people (medial prefrontal cortex [MPFC]), and ToM, or thinking about thoughts (right temporoparietal junction [RTPJ]). Although we do appear to "simulate" others' actions (e.g., motor repertoires) and experiences (e.g., pain), the MPFC and RTPJ do not support social cognition and ToM via simulation. Evidence is presented showing that activity in these regions is not modulated by first-person experience or similarity between self and target. People can understand and evaluate others' actions, even when those actions depend on beliefs and desires they don't share or have never experienced. The chapter concludes with questions for the next decade of cognitive neuroscientific research regarding ToM.

Key Words: Theory of Mind (ToM), social cognition, medial prefrontal cortex, right temporoparietal junction, simulation

At the heart of comedy and tragedy, there is often a false belief. Titania doesn't know she's in love with a donkey. Romeo thinks Juliet is dead. Subsequently, human audiences are brought to laughter and tears. Imagine, though, an audience that doesn't have a concept of belief, that cannot think about other people's thoughts at all. Plots based on these aspects would make no sense. In fact, the whole notion of theatre, of watching actors depict a fictional story, could never get off the ground.

Our minds and brains have, among their most astonishing capacities, the ability to see behind people's physical actions to their internal causes, thoughts, and intentions. That is, we have a Theory of Mind (ToM) for understanding and interpreting the external actions of others. When the audience thinks, "Romeo doesn't know that Juliet wants her parents to think that she is dead," that thought consists of a pattern of firing across a group of neurons

somewhere in each person's brain. This fact is both obvious (what is the alternative?) and mind-boggling. How are those neurons doing this?

To get the answers to this question, we need to be able to study the human brain in action. Unlike the traditional neuroscience topics covered in this volume—perception, motor control, attention, memory, and emotion—uniquely human cognitive capacities, such as language and social cognition, cannot be studied in the brains of nonhuman animals. The invention of functional neuroimaging has therefore opened up many topics that historically belonged only to social sciences: how we think about people, how we think about thoughts, how we make moral judgments.

Although the neuroscience of ToM is only around a decade old, there is enough research that enables us to address some fundamental questions. What are the neural substrates of ToM? Are there distinct brain regions selectively recruited for ToM (just as there are for vision, audition, and motor control)? If so, what are (and aren't) these brain regions doing? Are there distinct cognitive components of ToM? Answers to these questions provide the foundation for a cognitive neuroscience of Theory of Mind.

Where in the Brain Do People Think about Thoughts?

Human adults can think about other people as having an infinite array of beliefs and desires, ranging from trivial to sublime, from familiar to exotic, from simple to remarkably complex.

For example, consider the following story: Sally and Anne go to the same high school. Sally doesn't suspect that Anne knows that Sally's boyfriend Tom believes that the tooth fairy stole the quarterback's lucky tooth before the big game, jinxing the team. Anne also knows that Tom will propose to Sally at graduation, so Anne realizes that only she can stop their engagement.

Even though this story is highly complex, the people are unfamiliar to you, and you likely have never considered the possibility of the tooth fairy's interference in a football game, you can nevertheless make sense of this story and predict and explain the characters' actions and emotions. How do you do this? What is happening in your brain while you read the story? Let's imagine following the story from the pattern on the page to the pattern in your brain.

First, the pattern of light and dark on the page reaches your eyes and then your visual cortex. Here the brain begins to recognize shapes and to test hypotheses about which letters and words are on the page. Soon, language brain regions are involved, helping to transform the representations from orthographic symbols to words and sentences that describe objects, events, and ideas—these representations are complex. As you build up a mental representation of all the elements in the story, your working memory helps to hold and manipulate the elements, while executive control supports shifts between the competing components of the event. In particular, executive control helps you keep track of what really happened, distinct from what Sally didn't suspect that Anne knew that Tom believed was happening. As you begin to understand and represent the events of the story, specific aspects of the story become clear. This is a story about people, social relationships, and human actions. This story requires you to think about different perspectives or representations of the same facts; that is, it requires

the capacity to form "meta-representations." And this story requires you to think about people's thoughts, beliefs, desires, motivations, and emotions.

Remarkably, human cognitive neuroscience can already help us pinpoint where in the brain each one of these different cognitive processes is occurring. Other chapters of this handbook describe the brain regions and processes involved in vision, word recognition, language comprehension, working memory, and executive function. Most interesting for our current purposes are three cognitive processes (and associated brain regions) that appear to be disproportionately necessary for reading and understanding a story about people and what they are thinking: (a) representing people and social relations (e.g., dorsal medial prefrontal cortex); (b) representing representations (including photographs, maps, as well as thoughts, e.g., left temporoparietal junction); and (c) representing *mental* representations (e.g., right temporoparietal junction), that is, thinking about thoughts.

All of these brain regions had a high metabolic response while you were reading the story about Sally, Anne, and Tom, but for different reasons—these brain regions perform different functions in helping you to perceive and reason about the story. To understand how we infer these different functions, it is helpful to imagine a hypothetical meta-experiment in which we present participants with five different kinds of stimuli and see which patterns of responses we would observe, and where. Each brain region or system would reveal different patterns of functional response across the categories (see Figure 13.1 for a schematic representation of the imaginary experiment, and Figure 13.2 for sample stimuli from actual experiments).

For example, there is a region near the calcarine sulcus that responds robustly when people read stories and look at pictures but not when people listen to stories or to music. Meanwhile, there is no difference in this region's response to the specific content of the stories, that is, whether the stories focus on physical objects, temporal changes, people, or their thoughts. However, the response in this brain region to the same story is very different depending on whether the story is presented visually (a high response) or aurally (a low response). Correspondingly, people with damage near the calcarine sulcus cannot perceive visually presented pictures or sentences but have no trouble understanding aural language or thinking about thoughts. Based on this pattern, we can diagnose that the cortex near the calcarine sulcus contains a brain region

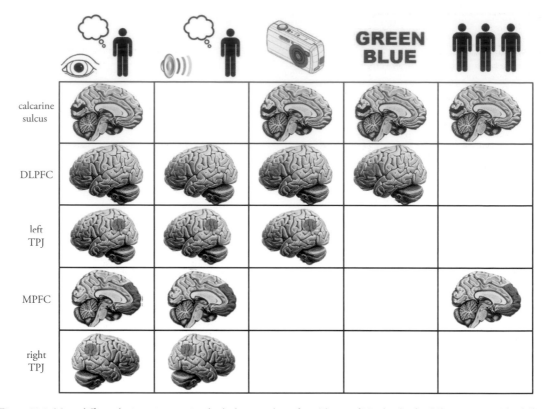

Figure 13.1 Many different brain regions are involved when people perform Theory of Mind tasks, for different reasons. The differences between brain regions could be revealed through an imaginary meta-experiment. For example, five different brain regions (rows) would show different patterns of functional response across five categories (columns, left to right): (1) visually presented stories depicting people's thoughts, (2) the same stories presented aurally, (3) nonmental meta-representations (e.g., stories about photographs, maps, signs), (4) a Stroop task manipulation of cognitive conflict, and (5) socially relevant (but nonmental) information about people. These distinct "functional profiles" of response could then be used to infer the function of each of these regions. DLPFC, dorsolateral prefrontal cortex; MPFC, medial prefrontal cortex; TPJ, temporoparietal junction.

involved in visual perception (see Chapters 11 and 12 in this Handbook). This, of course, would not be news. The visual system is one of the best-understood parts of the brain; none of the other brain regions we will consider here is affected by the modality of the stimulus.

Relying on a similar logic, we can look for patterns of functional responses and selective deficits to infer the cognitive functions of other less well-understood brain regions, and also to learn about how these cognitive functions are implemented in the brain. For example, there is a brain region in the left dorsolateral prefrontal cortex (DLPFC) that shows a high response for stimuli requiring difficult reasoning, especially for balancing competing ideas or responses. This brain region shows a high response when people read a story that describes two competing versions of reality: one past and one present, or one in a photograph and one in reality, or one that someone believes and one that actually happened.

This brain region also shows a high response when you try to name the red ink color of the word *green*, compared to the blue ink color of the word *blue*—the standard Stroop task manipulation of conflict (MacDonald, Cohen, Stenger, & Carter, 2000). Damage to this brain region thus makes it difficult to resolve such cognitive competition and, as a result, can make it difficult for people to reason accurately about another person's thoughts and beliefs in certain cases. For example, patients with left DLPFC damage wouldn't be able to balance their own ideas about Tom and the competing ideas about Tom held by Anne and Sally. Instead, these patients would just stick with their own perspective: if Tom is crazy, then Sally won't want to marry him. On the other hand, if there is no conflict in the story—for example, when we hear that Anne thinks only she can stop the engagement, which might be true or false and doesn't conflict with any other ideas—these patients have no problems

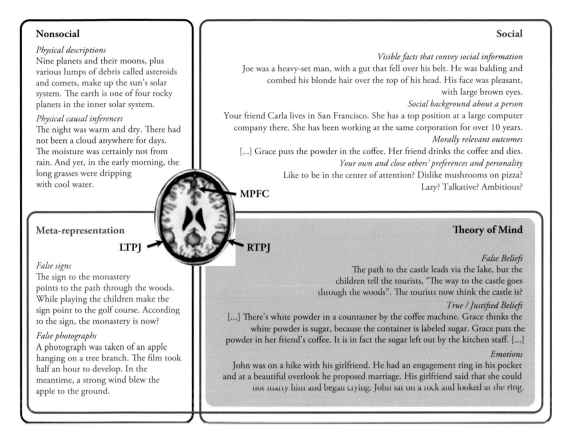

Nonsocial

Physical descriptions
Nine planets and their moons, plus various lumps of debris called asteroids and comets, make up the sun's solar system. The earth is one of four rocky planets in the inner solar system.

Physical causal inferences
The night was warm and dry. There had not been a cloud anywhere for days. The moisture was certainly not from rain. And yet, in the early morning, the long grasses were dripping with cool water.

MPFC

Social

Visible facts that convey social information
Joe was a heavy-set man, with a gut that fell over his belt. He was balding and combed his blonde hair over the top of his head. His face was pleasant, with large brown eyes.

Social background about a person
Your friend Carla lives in San Francisco. She has a top position at a large computer company there. She has been working at the same corporation for over 10 years.

Morally relevant outcomes
[...] Grace puts the powder in the coffee. Her friend drinks the coffee and dies.

Your own and close others' preferences and personality
Like to be in the center of attention? Dislike mushrooms on pizza? Lazy? Talkative? Ambitious?

Meta-representation

LTPJ   **RTPJ**

False signs
The sign to the monastery points to the path through the woods. While playing the children make the sign point to the golf course. According to the sign, the monastery is now?

False photographs
A photograph was taken of an apple hanging on a tree branch. The film took half an hour to develop. In the meantime, a strong wind blew the apple to the ground.

Theory of Mind

False Beliefs
The path to the castle leads via the lake, but the children tell the tourists, "The way to the castle goes through the woods". The tourists now think the castle is?

True / Justified Beliefs
[...] There's white powder in a container by the coffee machine. Grace thinks the white powder is sugar, because the container is labeled sugar. Grace puts the powder in her friend's coffee. It is in fact the sugar left out by the kitchen staff. [...]

Emotions
John was on a hike with his girlfriend. He had an engagement ring in his pocket and at a beautiful overlook he proposed marriage. His girlfriend said that she could not marry him and began crying. John sat on a rock and looked at the ring.

Figure 13.2 Sample stimuli from experiments that revealed the functional profile of three brain regions involved in Theory of Mind. The left temporoparietal junction (LTPJ) shows a higher response when reading stories that require thinking about representations, whether mental (such as thoughts) or physical (such as signs) than when reading stories with no such metarepresentational demands. Regions in the medial prefrontal cortex (MPFC) show a higher response when the stories contain socially relevant information about people. The right temporoparietal junction (RTPJ) is more selective than either of these, responding when the story contains descriptions of a range of different thoughts, beliefs, desires, or emotions, but not otherwise. Sample are stimuli from Saxe and Kanwisher (2003), Saxe and Powell (2006), Saxe and Wechsler (2005), Moran et al. (2006), Perner et al. (2009), Young et al. (2010), and Bruneau et al. (submitted) (Krienen et al., 2010; Mitchell et al., 2006).

thinking about beliefs per se, and predicting what Anne will do next (Apperly, Samson, Chiavarino, & Humphreys, 2004).

A brain region in the left temporoparietal junction (LTPJ) shows a second functional profile. The LTPJ response is high for any story, picture, or task that requires reasoning about perspectives, or representations of the world—whether those representations are mental representations (such as people's beliefs about the world) or physical representations (such as photographs of the world). Correspondingly, patients with damage to the LTPJ have difficulty with tasks that require reasoning about beliefs, photographs, and maps, but not with other "high-conflict" tasks, such as naming the ink color of the word *green*, printed in red ink. These patients have trouble thinking about any kind of belief or, indeed, any representation at all,

including a physical representation such as a photograph, regardless of whether these representations conflict with reality. So we can infer that the LTPJ is involved in metarepresentation, including but not limited to representing *mental* representations.

The functions of the DLPFC and the LTPJ may seem similar, but they have been elegantly dissociated by Samson, Apperly, and colleagues, in studies of patients with selective lesions. To get a sense for the dissociation, imagine that the story continues, to reveal who *actually* stole the lucky tooth: a crazy ex-girlfriend of the quarterback. Now, if you have to answer the question "what does Tom think happened to the quarterback's tooth?" you might consider three possible answers. First, the correct answer, which depends on keeping track of Tom's false belief, would be "he thinks the tooth fairy stole it." Second, if you couldn't hold on to Tom's belief in the face of the stronger competition from your knowledge of what really happened, then the "reality-error" answer would be "he thinks an ex-girlfriend stole it." This is the kind of error produced by DLPFC damage. Third, if you could resist competition from reality but couldn't hold on to a representation of Tom's belief, then you might just seek a likely explanation for a quarterback's missing tooth and make the "appearance-error": "he thinks it was knocked out during a game." LTPJ damage, but not DLFC damage, leads to "appearance" errors (Samson, Apperly, Chiavarino, & Humphreys, 2004).

In sum, thinking about thoughts depends on many cognitive functions that are not specific to ToM. ToM tasks are often hard logical problems, involving complex reasoning and perspective shifts, and thus rely on multiple brain regions—DLPFC and LTPJ are only examples. In addition, though, cognitive neuroscience research has revealed another group of brain regions, with a notably different pattern of response: these regions are involved specifically in thinking about other people.

Returning to our imaginary experiment, a third functional profile can be found in the medial prefrontal cortex (MPFC).[1] Here we would not see a high response to stories about photographs, physical interactions, or temporal changes; only stories with people and social relationships elicit a response in the MPFC. Thus, we can infer that the MPFC is involved specifically in social cognition.

Finally, a brain region near the right temporoparietal junction (RTPJ) shows a robust response during our original story (regardless of modality), but it does not respond to any of the other conditions in this imaginary experiment—not to difficult logical problems, or stories about photographs, or stories about people and social relationships (Saxe & Kanwisher, 2003; Saxe & Powell, 2006). Of the conditions in our imaginary experiment, the RTPJ region shows a high response only when the story describes someone's thoughts and beliefs.

Regions in the MPFC and RTPJ are most commonly recruited together, possibly because thinking about thoughts usually also involves thinking about people and social relationships (broadly construed; see Figure 13.2). However, careful experiments have revealed fascinating functional dissociations between these two regions. For example, activity in your RTPJ was high when you read about Sally, Anne, and Tom's true and false beliefs (Döhnel et al., 2012), but it would be low if you were reading instead about what Sally looks like (i.e., her physical traits) and whether she is stubborn or lazy

(i.e., her personality traits), where Anne comes from and how many siblings she has (i.e., her history and status), or what Tom prefers to eat for breakfast (i.e., his stable preferences) (Bedny, Pascual-Leone, Dodell-Feder, Fedorenko, & Saxe, 2011; Jenkins & Mitchell, 2009; Saxe & Powell, 2006; Saxe, Whitfield-Gabrieli, Scholz, & Pelphrey, 2009). Even reading about how Sally feels when she is hungry or tired or in physical pain would not elicit a robust response in the RTPJ (Saxe & Powell, 2006). Regions in the MPFC, by contrast, would show high activity for most of this information, especially descriptions of stable preferences and personality traits (Jenkins & Mitchell, 2009; Moran, Macrae, Heatherton, Wyland, & Kelley, 2006). One factor that matters to the response in MPFC, but not in RTPJ, is the person being described. The response in the MPFC region would be much higher if Sally, Anne, and Tom were friends of yours—either people you found similar to yourself or people who were emotionally close to you (Krienen, Tu, & Buckner, 2010; Mitchell, Macrae, & Banaji, 2006). By contrast, the RTPJ does not seem to care about the identity of the target.

What happens when the MPFC and the RTPJ are not functioning properly? Damage to MPFC often leads to problems, for example, in thinking about other people's emotions (Shamay-Tsoory, Tomer, Berger, & Aharon-Peretz, 2003), but not necessarily in thinking about people's thoughts (Bird, Castelli, Malik, Frith, & Husain, 2004). Selective damage to the RTPJ has not been as well studied, although similar evidence comes from an experiment in which we can produce a temporary or reversible "lesion," using a tool called transcranial magnetic stimulation (TMS). To understand the experiment, it will help to start with a new story about Sally and Anne.

Imagine that Sally is making dinner for Anne. Based on something Anne said, Sally believes that Anne is violently allergic to peanuts. Sally grinds up some peanuts and mixes them into the soup, which she then serves to Anne. In fact, Anne is allergic to coconuts but not peanuts, so she happily enjoys the soup. Now, did Sally do anything morally wrong? From the outside, nothing bad happened. Sally served Anne some delicious soup. Most people, however, would say that what Sally did was very wrong, because Sally *believed* she was doing something wrong. The opposite case presents an even starker contrast. Imagine that Sally adds coconut shavings to the soup, but she has absolutely no idea that Anne is allergic to coconuts or anything else.

Now, Anne eats the soup and becomes fatally ill. Did Sally do anything morally wrong? In spite of the tragic consequences of her actions, most people would say that what Sally did was not very wrong, because she reasonably believed her actions would not hurt anyone. These scenarios provide a sensitive measure of how much people are thinking about thoughts. The more you think about thoughts, the more you will blame Sally for attempting (but failing) to poison Anne, and the more you will forgive her for accidentally making Anne sick (and the more active your RTPJ will be; Young & Saxe, 2009).

To test the role of the RTPJ in thinking about thoughts, we briefly disrupted normal neural function specifically in the RTPJ, using fMRI-guided TMS. When the RTPJ is targeted with TMS, moral judgments shift. Innocent accidents appear more blameworthy, while failed attempts appear less blameworthy, as though it mattered less what Sally *believed* she was doing and mattered more what she actually did (Young, Camprodon, Hauser, Pascual-Leone, & Saxe, 2010). (People don't lose the ability to make moral judgments altogether; they still say it is completely morally wrong to intentionally kill, and it is not wrong at all to simply serve someone soup). These results fit very nicely with the fMRI study results. Activity in the RTPJ is correlated across time, across people, and across individual stories, specifically with the need to think about thoughts (Young & Saxe, 2008, 2009); when function in the RTPJ is disrupted, people think less about thoughts and more about other features of the stories.

Understanding the neural basis of ToM will thus probably begin with understanding the function(s) of these regions—that is, the MPFC, for thinking about people, and the RTPJ, for thinking about thoughts—along with the interactions between these regions with each other and with the rest of the brain. Provisionally, though, there seem to be patches of cortex in the human brain whose functions are specifically related to ToM (RTPJ) or social cognition (MPFC). This claim raises key questions that we address in the next section: What does it mean to say that a brain region's function is "specifically related to ToM"? What are and aren't these brain regions doing?

How Does the Brain Support Thinking about Thoughts?

From a certain perspective, ToM is a miracle. After all, we experience our own thoughts but not the thoughts of others—since we can't get into other people's heads, how do we know what's inside? How do our brains cross the gulf between our minds? One idea that may demystify the leap is that we understand other minds by "simulation" (Goldman, 2006). The central idea of simulation is that we understand other people because they are similar to us: they execute similar movements, experience similar sensations, and make similar decisions, using a body and mind similar to our own. As a result, we could use our own mind (and body) as an analogue for another person's mind. We could re-create in ourselves a copy of their actions and sensations and recapitulate our own experiences in order to understand theirs. Could *this* be the distinctive function of ToM brain regions—to construct appropriate and useful simulations of other people's minds?

People do seem to simulate the actions they observe, by activating matching motor representations in their own brain and body. When a person watches someone else act, the observer can't help but activate the same muscles and motor plans for that action (Fadiga, Craighero, & Olivier, 2005). As a result, action observation interferes with action execution, and action execution interferes with action observation (Kilner, Paulignan, & Blakemore, 2003; Zwickel, Grosjean, & Prinz, 2010a, 2010b). Even when the other person's actions are invisible, simply knowing about someone else's incompatible action can cause interference. In an elegant series of studies, Sebanz and colleagues showed that interference from thinking about *another* person's actions is comparable to competition from *one's own* actions (Atmaca, Sebanz, & Knoblich, 2011; Sebanz, Knoblich, & Prinz, 2003). That is, if you are trying to push the left button but you are thinking about pushing the right button, these two motor plans interfere with each other and slow you down. Amazingly, thinking about someone else's action has the same effect: when you know someone else is supposed to push the right button, you yourself are slower to push the left button. A similar pattern occurs when you observe what other people see. Seeing that another person sees more or less than you do can actually impair your ability to report what you yourself are seeing, as though you automatically computed the other person's view, which then competes with your own view for verbal report (Samson, Apperly, Braithwaite, Andrews, & Scott, 2010). These results show that watching and understanding another person's actions and experiences compete for the same cognitive and neural resources as those used for one's own actions and experiences.

Neural evidence converges on the same simulation story. Activity in the parietal cortex while watching someone else perform a simple hand action is suppressed if the participant had just previously made the same hand action. This response suggests that the representation of one's own action can be partially "recycled" during observation of someone else's (Chong, Cunnington, Williams, Kanwisher, & Mattingley, 2008). And, complementarily, watching someone else's hand movements leads to sub-threshold preparatory activity in one's own motor cortex and hand muscles; this activity can be seen if it is artificially pushed over the threshold by a pulse of TMS (Stürmer, Siggelkow, Dengler, & Leuthold, 2000). Furthermore, these activations seem to be modulated by experience: the more experience the observer has had actually performing a particular action, the more his or her motor cortex is activated while observing others performing the same action. In one example, the motor cortex of ballet dancers showed more activity when dancers observed gender-specific movements which they themselves had more experience executing (Calvo-Merino, Glaser, Grezes, Passingham, & Haggard, 2005; Casile & Giese, 2006; Cross, Hamilton, & Grafton, 2006). For example, male dancers showed more motor activity than female dancers when observing movements usually executed by male dancers, even though male and female dancers had equal experience observing these movements.

A similar pattern holds for observing physical sensations in another person, especially physical pain. A common group of brain regions is recruited when people feel their own pain and when they see someone else in pain. Experiencing pain leads to brain activity in the "pain matrix," including regions in cingulate cortex, secondary sensory cortex, and bilateral insula. When observers witness other people in physical pain, some of the same brain regions are activated (Botvinick et al., 2005; Jackson, Rainville, & Decety, 2006; Singer & Lamm, 2009; Singer et al., 2004). Activity in some of these regions is correlated with the intensity of pain, either experienced (Peyron, Laurent, & Garcia-Larrea, 2000) or attributed (Saarela et al., 2007).

In sum, we appear to "simulate" other people's actions and experience: as observers, we recruit (some of) the same representations as those of the target person. Simulations—the recycling of similar representations between first-person experience and third-person attributions—thus seem to reflect a general principle of how we bridge the gap between two separate human minds. Is activity in the RTPJ and MPFC also modulated by whether the mental states we attribute to other people are similar to

mental states we have experienced in the first person? Similar to the logic of "simulation" for actions and experiences, do we understand someone else's desire to become a neurosurgeon or belief that the Red Sox will win the World Series by activating the same representations in our own mind as those activated if we ourselves had that desire or held that belief?

As described above, regions in the MPFC are modulated by a related issue: whether the *target person* is, overall, similar or close to oneself. For example, MPFC is recruited when you are asked about the personality, preferences, and habits of people who are similar or emotionally important to you, like your mother, but not when asked about people who are dissimilar or less close, like President Obama (Mitchell et al., 2006). There even seems to be some "shared representation" of your own preferences and traits and those of similar others. If you have just been thinking about your own preferences, for example, and then transfer to thinking about the preferences of a similar other, the response in the MPFC is "adapted" (i.e., relatively low), which suggests that the two processes depend on shared neural substrates (Jenkins, Macrae, & Mitchell, 2008). When put to the test, however, the MPFC response does not depend on similarity (or first-person experience) but on emotional closeness. The MPFC response is higher for emotionally close friends who are not similar to oneself than for strangers who are very similar (Krienen et al., 2010). Specifically, when contrasting a close friend who is very different from oneself to a stranger who is very similar (in politics, food preferences, etc.), the MPFC response was higher during attributions to the close (but dissimilar) friend. Unlike the motor representations of ballet dancers, which really do depend on first-person experience, the response in MPFC during personality trait attribution reflects an assessment of social or personal significance.

The key region, though, for representing others' thoughts is the RTPJ. Here, too, the evidence against "simulation" of other minds is clear. The RTPJ does not recapitulate the observer's own analogous thoughts and experiences but is recruited for thinking about other people's thoughts, even when those thoughts are maximally different from one's own. Three lines of argument support the view that first-person experience does not determine the RTPJ response to other people's beliefs and desires.

First, we directly manipulated our participants' experience with specific beliefs and desires by generating examples of beliefs and desires unlikely to be frequently held by our participants (MIT under-graduates): a belief that conflicts are best resolved by physical violence, or a desire for one's partner to have an affair. Indeed, a postscan survey confirmed that our participants found these beliefs and desires unfamiliar. Nevertheless, the RTPJ did not show less (or more) activation when reading about cultur-ally distant beliefs and desires, compared to more familiar counterparts (Saxe & Wexler, 2005). First-person experience of the mental state (i.e., having similar beliefs and desires oneself) did not affect the response of the RTPJ when people attributed that state to somebody else. Instead, activation in RTPJ was modulated by a different factor: whether the specific belief or desire made sense, given the background and culture of the target person. Beliefs about violence are more expected in members of a gang; acceptance of an affair fits with a person who has joined a cult. Convergent evidence comes from a study in which people were described as having mental states that fit, or violated, expecta-tions based on the person's political views (e.g., a Democratic politician who wants a smaller govern-ment; Cloutier, Gabrieli, O'Young, & Ambady, 2011). Again, the RTPJ response depended not on the *participant's* beliefs, but on the fit between the target's background and their beliefs. That is, the RTPJ appeared to reflect a process of construct-ing a coherent model of the other person's mind (Hamilton & Sherman, 1996), without reference to the participant's own mental states.

We have also replicated this basic result with a different strategy. Instead of culturally unfamiliar beliefs, we asked participants to attribute common-sense beliefs ("John believes that swimming is a good way to cool off") or absurd beliefs ("John believes that swimming is a good way to grow fins" [Young, Dodell-Feder, & Saxe, 2010]). Activity in RTPJ was no higher for attributing common-sense beliefs (shared by the participant) than for absurd beliefs (not shared by the participant).

Second, we pushed the prediction even fur-ther: we asked people to attribute to other people a mental state that they themselves could never experience. To do this, we asked individuals who had been blind since birth to reason about experi-ences of hearing (which are very familiar) and seeing (which they could never experience themselves but frequently hear others describing). We found that first-person experience of seeing is not necessary for the development of normal neural representa-tions of another person's experiences of seeing. The RTPJ was recruited similarly for reasoning about beliefs formed on the basis of seeing and on that of hearing, in both sighted and blind adults (Bedny, Pascual-Leone, & Saxe, 2009). Apparently, reca-pitulating a similar first-person experience is not necessary for the normal representation of someone else's experience.

Finally, it is worth noting a key conceptual difference between the studies of action "simula-tion" and studies of Theory of Mind, beyond the empirical differences described above. Observation of actions elicits activity in the same brain regions used for executing actions, that is, actually making body movements. On a strict analogy then, simu-lation should predict that we understand beliefs and desires using the same brain regions we use for actually *having* beliefs and desires, or that we think about other people's personalities using the same brain regions that we use for *having* our own per-sonality. For example, we would recognize laziness in others using the brain regions we use for being lazy. But upon reflection, this prediction doesn't make sense. There can't be specific brain regions for having a personality or having a belief; personali-ties and beliefs are not specific cognitive processes or representations but summary descriptions of behavioral tendencies. By contrast, the RTPJ and MPFC are associated with attributing thoughts and personality traits, which do require specific cogni-tive processes and representations.

In sum, thinking about thoughts does not show the same functional profile as observing actions or experiences. Activity in the key brain regions, the MPFC and especially the RTPJ, is not affected by people's first-person experience or how similar the beliefs and desires are to their own beliefs and desires. This is part of what makes humans' Theory of Mind so powerful: we can understand, explain, predict, and judge other people's actions, even when they depend on beliefs and desires that we do not share and indeed have never experienced. We can imagine how Tom will act, given he believes in the tooth fairy, and what Anne will do to prevent Sally from marrying him, without knowing the people or without giving any actual credence to their beliefs. That's part of what makes watching tragedy and comedy so gripping, and the human actions that unfold in them so predictable.

Conclusions

This chapter summarizes the data that provide a foundation for a future neuroscience of Theory of Mind. Although there has been a furious burst of activity studying the neural basis of ToM in the last 10 years and hundreds of papers have been published, the most important questions remain unanswered. We have provided some evidence, for example, that the RTPJ and MPFC are not involved in "simulating" other people's minds, based on the observer's own first-person experience with similar beliefs and desires. So what computations *are* these brain regions doing? We have described evidence that the magnitude of average response in the RTPJ does not distinguish between true and false beliefs, or hard and easy inferences about beliefs. So which features of beliefs and desires *does* the RTPJ represent, and how? Ongoing research targeting the pattern of voxels in the RTPJ may shed light on the kinds of computations that this region performs and the cognitive dimensions to which the RTPJ is sensitive (Koster-Hale, Dungan, Saxe, Young, unpublished data; Young, Chakroff, Dungan, Koster-Hale, Saxe, unpublished data). Finally, we do not know how, or why, human adults come to have brain regions specifically involved in thinking about people and their thoughts. What are the homologues of RTPJ and MPFC in other animals, and what are their functions? When do these regions mature in the course of human childhood, and why? All of these questions are on the table for the next decade of the neuroscience of Theory of Mind.

Note

1. Here we describe the MPFC as a single region, although research has shown dissociable subregions within the MPFC, including the ventral MPFC and the dorsal MPFC. In some cases, these subregions have importantly different response profiles (Mitchell, Macrae, & Banaji, 2006). Here, for simplicity, we have focused on features of the response that are common across subdivisions of the MPFC, but we strongly urge readers specifically interested in the MPFC to consider these differences, as described in other reviews (e.g., Adolphs, 2009).

References

Adolphs, R. (2009). The social brain: Neural basis of social knowledge. *Annual Review of Psychology, 60,* 693–716.

Apperly, I. A., Samson, D., Chiavarino, C., & Humphreys, G. W. (2004). Frontal and temporo-parietal lobe contributions to theory of mind: Neuropsychological evidence from a false-belief task with reduced language and executive demands. *Journal of Cognitive Neurosciences, 16* (10), 1773–1784.

Atmaca, S., Sebanz, N., & Knoblich, G. (2011). The joint flanker effect: Sharing tasks with real and imagined co-actors. *Experimental Brain Research, 211* (3-4), 371–385.

Bedny, M., Pascual-Leone, A., Dodell-Feder, D., Fedorenko, E., & Saxe, R. Language processing in the occipital cortex of congenitally blind adults. *Proceedings of the National Academy of Sciences U S A, 108* (11), 4429–4434.

Bedny, M., Pascual-Leone, A., & Saxe, R. R. (2009). Growing up blind does not change the neural bases of Theory of Mind.

Proceedings of the National Academy of Sciences U S A, 106 (27), 11312–11317.

Bird, C. M., Castelli, F., Malik, O., Frith, U., & Husain, M. (2004). The impact of extensive medial frontal lobe damage on "Theory of Mind" and cognition. *Brain, 127* (Pt 4), 914–928.

Botvinick, M., Jha, A. P., Bylsma, L. M., Fabian, S. A., Solomon, P. E., & Prkachin, K. M. (2005). Viewing facial expressions of pain engages cortical areas involved in the direct experience of pain. *Neuroimage, 25* (1), 312–319.

Calvo-Merino, B., Glaser, D. E., Grezes, J., Passingham, R. E., & Haggard, P. (2005). Action observation and acquired motor skills: An FMRI study with expert dancers. *Cerebral Cortex, 15* (8), 1243–1249.

Casile, A., & Giese, M. A. (2006). Nonvisual motor training influences biological motion perception. *Current Biology, 16* (1), 69–74.

Chong, T. T., Cunnington, R., Williams, M. A., Kanwisher, N., & Mattingley, J. B. (2008). fMRI adaptation reveals mirror neurons in human inferior parietal cortex. *Current Biology, 18* (20), 1576–1580.

Cloutier, J., Gabrieli, J. D., O'Young, D., & Ambady, N. (2011). An fMRI study of violations of social expectations: When people are not who we expect them to be. *Neuroimage, 57* (2), 583–588.

Cross, E. S., Hamilton, A. F., & Grafton, S. T. (2006). Building a motor simulation de novo: Observation of dance by dancers. *Neuroimage, 31* (3), 1257–1267.

Döhnel, K., Schuwerk, T., Meinhardt, J., Sodian, B., Hajak, G., & Sommer, M. (2012). Functional activity of the right temporo-parietal junction and of the medial prefrontal cortex associated with true and false belief reasoning. *Neuroimage, 60*(3), 1652–1661.

Fadiga, L., Craighero, L., & Olivier, E. (2005). Human motor cortex excitability during the perception of others' action. *Current Opinion in Neurobiology, 15* (2), 213–218.

Goldman, A. (2006). *Simulating minds: The philosophy, psychology, and neuroscience of mindreading.* New York: Oxford University Press.

Hamilton, D., & Sherman, S. (1996). Perceiving persons and groups. *Psychological Review, 103* (2), 336–355.

Jackson, P. L., Rainville, P., & Decety, J. (2006). To what extent do we share the pain of others? Insight from the neural bases of pain empathy. *Pain, 125* (1-2), 5–9.

Jenkins, A. C., Macrae, C. N., & Mitchell, J. P. (2008). Repetition suppression of ventromedial prefrontal activity during judgments of self and others. *Proceedings of the National Academy of Sciences U S A, 105* (11), 4507–4512.

Jenkins, A. C., & Mitchell, J. P. Medial prefrontal cortex subserves diverse forms of self-reflection. *Social Neuroscience,* 1–8.

Jenkins, A. C., & Mitchell, J. P. (2009). Mentalizing under uncertainty: Dissociated neural responses to ambiguous and unambiguous mental state inferences. *Cerebral Cortex, 20* (2), 404–410.

Kilner, J. M., Paulignan, Y., & Blakemore, S. J. (2003). An interference effect of observed biological movement on action. *Current Biology, 13* (6), 522–525.

Krienen, F. M., Tu, P. C., & Buckner, R. L. (2010). Clan mentality: Evidence that the medial prefrontal cortex responds to close others. *Journal of Neuroscience, 30* (41), 13906–13915.

MacDonald, A. W., 3rd, Cohen, J. D., Stenger, V. A., & Carter, C. S. (2000). Dissociating the role of the dorsolateral prefrontal and anterior cingulate cortex in cognitive control. *Science, 288* (5472), 1835–1838.

Mitchell, J. P., Macrae, C. N., & Banaji, M. R. (2006). Dissociable medial prefrontal contributions to judgments of similar and dissimilar others. *Neuron, 50* (4), 655–663.

Moran, J. M., Macrae, C. N., Heatherton, T. F., Wyland, C. L., & Kelley, W. M. (2006). Neuroanatomical evidence for distinct cognitive and affective components of self. *Journal of Cognitive Neuroscience, 18* (9), 1586–1594.

Perner, (2009).

Peyron, R., Laurent, B., & Garcia-Larrea, L. (2000). Functional imaging of brain responses to pain. A review and meta-analysis (2000). *Neurophysiologie Clinique, 30* (5), 263–288.

Saarela, M. V., Hlushchuk, Y., Williams, A. C., Schurmann, M., Kalso, E., & Hari, R. (2007). The compassionate brain: Humans detect intensity of pain from another's face. *Cerebral Cortex, 17* (1), 230–237.

Samson, D., Apperly, I. A., Braithwaite, J., Andrews, B., & Scott, S. (2010). Seeing it their way: Evidence for rapid and involuntary computation of what other people see. *Journal of Experimental Psychology: Human Perception and Performance, 36* (5), 1255–1266.

Samson, D., Apperly, I. A., Chiavarino, C., & Humphreys, G. W. (2004). Left temporoparietal junction is necessary for representing someone else's belief. *Nature Neuroscience, 7* (5), 499–500.

Saxe, R., & Kanwisher, N. (2003). People thinking about thinking people. The role of the temporo-parietal junction in "theory of mind." *Neuroimage, 19* (4), 1835–1842.

Saxe, R., & Powell, L. (2006). It's the thought that counts: Specific brain regions for one component of theory of mind. *Psychological Science, 17* (8), 692–699.

Saxe, R., & Wexler, A. (2005). Making sense of another mind: The role of the right temporo-parietal junction. *Neuropsychologia, 43* (10), 1391–1399.

Saxe, R. R., Whitfield-Gabrieli, S., Scholz, J., & Pelphrey, K. A. (2009). Brain regions for perceiving and reasoning about other people in school-aged children. *Child Development, 80* (4), 1197–1209.

Sebanz, N., Knoblich, G., & Prinz, W. (2003). Representing others' actions: Just like one's own? *Cognition, 88* (3), B11–B21.

Shamay-Tsoory, S. G., Tomer, R., Berger, B. D., & Aharon-Peretz, J. (2003). Characterization of empathy deficits following prefrontal brain damage: The role of the right ventromedial prefrontal cortex. *Journal of Cognitive Neurosciences, 15* (3), 324–337.

Singer, T., & Lamm, C. (2009). The social neuroscience of empathy. *Annals of the New York Academy of Sciences, 1156,* 81–96.

Singer, T., Seymour, B., O'Doherty, J., Kaube, H., Dolan, R. J., & Frith, C. D. (2004). Empathy for pain involves the affective but not sensory components of pain. *Science, 303* (5661), 1157–1162.

Stürmer, B., Siggelkow, S., Dengler, R., & Leuthold, H. (2000). Response priming in the Simon paradigm. A transcranial magnetic stimulation study. *Experimental Brain Research, 135* (3), 353–359.

Young, L., Camprodon, J., Hauser, M., Pascual-Leone, A., & Saxe, R. (2010). Disruption of the right temporo-parietal junction with transcranial magnetic stimulation reduces the role of beliefs in moral judgment. *Proceedings of the National Academy of Sciences U S A, 107,* 6753–6758.

Young, L., Dodell-Feder, D., & Saxe, R. (2010). What gets the attention of the temporo-parietal junction? An fMRI investigation of attention and theory of mind. *Neuropsychologia, 48* (9), 2658–2664.

Young, L., & Saxe, R. (2008). The neural basis of belief encoding and integration in moral judgment. *Neuroimage, 40,* 1912–1920.

Young, L., & Saxe, R. (2009). Innocent intentions: a correlation between forgiveness for accidental harm and neural activity. *Neuropsychologia, 47* (10), 2065–2072.

Zwickel, J., Grosjean, M., & Prinz, W. (2010a). On interference effects in concurrent perception and action. *Psychological Research, 74* (2), 152–171.

Zwickel, J., Grosjean, M., & Prinz, W. (2010b). What part of an action interferes with ongoing perception? *Acta Psychologica, 134,* 403–409.

The Pleasures and Pains of Social Interactions: A Social Cognitive Neuroscience Perspective

Naomi I. Eisenberger *and* Keely A. Muscatell

Abstract

In the past decade, we have learned quite a bit about the "social brain" by examining the neural correlates of social interactions. This chapter reviews three key neural systems that seem to underpin many of these interactions: those involved in reward-related processing, those involved in processing painful experience, and those used to mentalize or understand the minds of others. Many studies examining social pleasures—such as receiving positive feedback, being treated fairly by others, and cooperating with others—indicate that such pleasures may rely in part on neural regions that process basic reward experience. Other work shows that social pains—such as being treated unfairly, being rejected, or losing a loved one—rely on neural regions involved in processing physical pain. Many of these socioemotional experiences rely critically on neural regions involved in mentalizing. The chapter concludes with a review of work exploring social attachment and love, experiences that seem to rely in part on neural regions involved in both pleasure and pain. Taken together, the studies discussed here provide a general sense of the landscape of the rich and developing literature on the cognitive neuroscience of social interactions.

Key Words: social interactions, functional magnetic resonance imaging, social cognitive neuroscience, pain, pleasure, mentalizing, ventral striatum, dorsal anterior cingulate cortex, anterior insula, medial prefrontal cortex

As humans, we are inherently social. We know this intuitively, as many of life's best and worst experiences involve the making and breaking of social bonds. Indeed, it is hard to imagine an event more pleasurable than one involving the formation of a loving relationship or an event more painful than one of losing or being rejected by those closest to us. We also know this empirically, as substantial evidence over the past half-century has documented the importance of social ties for humans and other mammalian species. This work has repeatedly demonstrated that not only do we have an inherent need for social connection, but those who lack social connection face severe psychological and physical health disturbances.

Harlow's seminal work—showing that infant monkeys preferred a cloth surrogate mother that

provided them with "contact comfort" to a wire surrogate mother that provided them with food— demonstrated the importance of a need for social connection, over and above the need for basic physical nourishment (Harlow, 1958). His infant monkeys reared in complete social isolation had psychological deficits so severe that they could never successfully form social attachments (Harlow, Dodsworth, & Harlow, 1965). Similar findings have been observed in humans; institutionalized children (orphans) experience a whole host of socioemotional disturbances, including atypical patterns of attachment and difficulties in establishing social bonds, as well as attentional and conduct problems that appear to last a lifetime (O'Connor & Rutter, 2000).

In addition to a lack of social connection setting the stage for later psychological and emotional disturbances, a lack of social ties can also take a toll on physical health. Thus, a lack of social relationships constitutes a major risk factor for mortality, comparable to other risk factors such as smoking, obesity, and high blood pressure (House, Landis, & Umberson, 1988). In a landmark study investigating the impact of social relationships on longevity, individuals with fewer social ties were two to three times more likely to die during a 9-year assessment period (Berkman and Syme, 1979).

In the past decade, researchers have started to explore the neural substrates of our inherently social nature in order to better understand *why* social relationships play such a large role in both mental and physical health. Interestingly, two salient findings continue to emerge from these studies. First, neural responses to complex social events—such as being accepted or rejected, being esteemed or devalued, and being treated fairly or unfairly—rely on basic neural circuitry that is typically associated with processing simple pleasures and pains (Lieberman & Eisenberger, 2009). Second, there appears to be a specialized neural network dedicated to understanding the minds of others, a phenomenon referred to as "mentalizing." These neural regions are dedicated exclusively to "social cognition" and are used whenever individuals process the intentions or minds of others (Frith & Frith, 2003; Lieberman, 2010; Mitchell, 2009).

In this chapter, we review a portion of the accumulating new research that has explored the neural substrates of social interactions—why these experiences have the capacity to affect us so deeply, and what makes them unique from nonsocial experiences. We will begin by reviewing the neural circuitry that underlies simple pleasures and pains as well as the set of neural regions that is specific to "social cognition," or understanding the minds of others (mentalizing). We will then use this general framework to review some of the studies that have investigated social interactions within the confines of the functional magnetic resonance imaging (fMRI) scanner. Along these lines, the chapter first reviews social processes typically experienced as pleasurable or rewarding, including cooperation, fairness, and altruism, and then reviews social processes that are typically experienced as painful, including rejection and grief. Although we often describe giving to charity as being a "rewarding" experience or being rejected as a "painful" one, we usually assume that these descriptions are largely metaphorical. However, accumulating evidence suggests that these

more complex social interactions do indeed rely on the same neural systems that process basic, physical pleasures and pains. Finally, we will touch on some of the studies that have examined the neural regions that underpin social attachment and love. We save these for last because these experiences appear to rely on regions involved in both pleasure and pain.

This chapter is meant to be inclusive, but not exhaustive. The focus here is on studies that have examined neural processes during real social interactions. However, given that real social interactions are difficult to re-create within the confines of the fMRI scanner (e.g., romantic exchanges, mother–infant interactions), we have also included some studies that have examined social experience without another individual (or a presumed other individual) present. Finally, certain topic areas that have not been examined extensively (e.g., gain or loss of social status) will not be included. Given these constraints, however, we hope to provide a general sense of the landscape of the literature on the cognitive neuroscience of social interactions.

Summary of Neural Regions Involved in Pleasure, Pain, and Social Cognition
The Neural Substrates of Pleasure (Reward)

Extensive research in animals and humans has delineated a network of neural regions involved in reward processing (reviewed more extensively by O'Doherty, 2004; Knutson & Cooper, 2005). These regions respond to basic rewarding stimuli such as food and sexual activity, as well as secondary reinforcers, such as monetary incentives (Knutson & Cooper, 2005). The reward circuitry consists of neural structures that receive dopaminergic projections from the ventral tegmental area (VTA) and includes the nucleus accumbens in the ventral striatum (VS), the caudate in the dorsal striatum, the ventromedial and medial prefrontal cortex (VMPFC, MPFC), and the amygdala[1] (see Figure 14.1). Delineating among these neural regions, some have suggested that certain regions, such as the VS, are activated preferentially to reward anticipation, whereas others, like the VMPFC and MPFC, are more responsive to rewarding outcomes or experience (Knutson & Cooper, 2005; Knutson, Fong, Adams, Varner, & Hommer, 2001; Knutson, Fong, Bennett, Adams, & Hommer, 2003; O'Doherty, Deichmann, Critchley, & Dolan, 2002).

The Neural Substrates of Pain
The network of neural regions involved in pain processing (i.e., the "pain matrix") has been well-

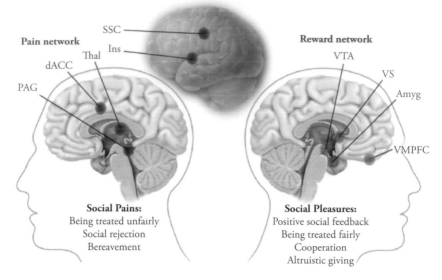

Figure 14.1 The pain network (on the left) consists of the dorsal anterior cingulate cortex (dACC), insula (Ins), somatosensory cortex (SSC), thalamus, (Thal), and periaqueductal gray (PAG). This network is also implicated in processing social pain. The reward network (on the right) consists on the ventral tegmental area (VTA), ventral striatum (VS), ventromedial prefrontal cortex (VMPFC), and the amygdala (Amyg). This network is also implicated in processing social rewards.

specified and includes regions such as the dorsal anterior cingulate cortex (dACC), anterior insula, somatosensory cortex, thalamus, and periaqueductal gray (Price, 2000; Rainville, 2002) (see Figure 14.1). Whereas the somatosensory cortex is associated with sensory aspects of cutaneous pain experience (e.g., pain localization), the dACC and anterior insula are associated with the affective or unpleasant aspects of pain experience (Apkarian, Bushnell, Treede, & Zubieta, 2005; Peyron, Laurent, & Garcia, 2000; Price, 2000; Rainville, 2002). As such, lesions to the dACC and anterior insula do not affect patients' ability to localize pain stimuli but result in patients reporting that they are no longer bothered by the pain (Foltz & White, 1962; Berthier, Starkstein, Leiguardia, & Carrea, 1988; Hebben, 1985). Conversely, lesions to somatosensory cortex compromise patients' ability to localize pain but leave the distress of painful experience intact (Ploner, Freund, & Schnitzler, 1999).

The Neural Substrates of Social Cognition

Researchers investigating mentalizing have uncovered a network of regions that appear to be specifically involved in social cognition, or understanding the minds of others. These areas of the "mentalizing network" include the medial and dorsomedial prefrontal cortex (MPFC, DMPFC), temporoparietal junction (TPJ), posterior superior temporal sulcus (pSTS), temporal poles, and precuneus/posterior cingulate cortex (PCC). These regions are reliably activated (especially the DMPFC and MPFC) when considering the mental states of others (Frith & Frith, 2003; Lieberman, 2010; Mitchell, 2009). For example, playing competitive games with a human partner in contrast to a computer algorithm activates these regions (Gallagher, Jack, Roepstorff, & Frith, 2002; Rilling, Dagenais, Goldsmith, Glenn, & Pagnoni, 2008; Rilling, Sanfey, Aronson, Nystrom, & Cohen, 2004a). Moreover, being given direct instructions to think about a specific person's mind by predicting their actions (Fletcher et al., 1995) or by forming an impression of them (Mitchell, Cloutier, Banaji, & Macrae, 2006; Mitchell, Macrae, & Banaji, 2004, 2005) activates these regions as well. Finally, some studies have demonstrated that lesions to these regions impair mentalizing abilities. Patients with damage to the MPFC show deficits in subtle mentalizing tasks, such as being able to detect a faux pas ("did that person say something they shouldn't have said?") (Stone, Baron-Cohen, & Knight, 1998). However, other work has shown the opposite, such that damage to the MPFC is not sufficient to impair mentalizing ability (Bird, Castelli, Malik, Frith, & Husain, 2004).

Summary

In sum, neuroimaging and neuropsychological research has successfully identified some of the neural regions involved in pleasure (reward), pain, and social cognition (mentalizing). Using each of these neural circuits as a framework, we now turn to work that has investigated the neural substrates of social interactions.

The Pleasures of Social Interaction

In the past decade, researchers from the fields of social cognitive neuroscience and neuroeconomics have been interested in exploring the neural underpinnings of basic types of human social interactions. Here we review several of the more positive forms of human social interactions, which for organizational purposes, are subdivided into social interactions that benefit the actor ("benefits for me": e.g., being esteemed by others, being treated fairly by others), social interactions that benefit the actor as well as the interaction partner ("benefits for us": e.g., cooperation), and social interactions that primarily benefit the interaction partner ("benefits for you": e.g., altruism, charity).

Benefits for "Me"
BEING ESTEEMD BY OTHERS

One of the most basic human motivations is to be esteemed and valued by others. This is likely based, in part, on a fundamental "need to belong," which can be satisfied by the feeling that one is liked, valued, or accepted by others (Baumeister & Leary, 1995). In line with this formulation, recent neuroimaging research has provided additional proof of the importance of being socially esteemed, by demonstrating that receiving social rewards (positive, self-relevant feedback from others) is processed neurally in a manner similar to receiving monetary rewards (Izuma, Saito, & Sadato, 2008).

To explore the neural correlates of social reward, participants were given positive social feedback (e.g., "trustworthy") or no social feedback ("XXX") that supposedly came from other individuals who had previously viewed information about the participant. In response to receiving positive vs. no social feedback, participants showed increased activity in the VS, in a region that overlapped with the VS activity observed during a monetary reward task (Izuma et al., 2008). A subsequent study demonstrated that gender moderates these effects. Thus, males showed widespread reward-related activity (dorsal and ventral striatum) to monetary reward but only limited activation for social reward (positive social feedback), whereas females showed widespread reward-related activity for both monetary and social rewards (Spreckelmeyer et al., 2009). In addition, other work has shown that simply receiving positive feedback—either from another person or a computer—is rewarding. Thus, both social and nonsocial positive feedback led to greater activity in the VS than did negative feedback (van den Bos, McClure, Harris, Fiske, & Cohen, 2007). In sum, being esteemed by others (and, in some cases, by a computer) appears to be processed neurally in a manner similar to that for more basic rewarding stimuli.

BEING TREATED FAIRLY BY OTHERS

Perhaps more fundamental than being esteemed by others is simply being treated fairly by others. Research using economic bargaining games has shown that being treated fairly by others activates reward-related neural circuitry (Tabibnia, Satpute, & Lieberman, 2008). In this study, participants played the Ultimatum Game, in which two players—a proposer and a responder—split a sum of money. During this game, the proposer decides how to divide a sum of money between the proposer and the responder, and the responder then has the opportunity to decide whether to accept or reject the offer. If the responder rejects the offer, neither party gets any money; if the responder accepts the offer, each player gets the amount of the proposed split. Participants in this study were scanned as they responded to fair and unfair offers, which were supposedly determined by other participants acting as the proposers. Results demonstrated that when participants were given fair, as opposed to unfair, offers, they reported greater happiness and showed increased activation in several reward-related regions, including the VS, VMPFC, and amygdala (Tabibnia et al., 2008). It should be noted that this study controlled for the pure monetary reward associated with the fair offers; thus the greater VS activity to fair ($3 out of $6) vs. unfair ($3 out of $10) trials was not simply due to greater monetary value in the fair trials.

In addition to being personally treated fairly by others, individuals also seem to be generally sensitive to fairness or equality in social interactions. In a recent study (Tricomi, Rangel, Camerer, & O'Doherty, 2010), each member of a pair of unacquainted participants received a monetary sum of $30, and then one member of the pair was randomly assigned to be "rich" (received a $50 bonus) while the other was assigned to be "poor" (received no bonus). Following this, participants were scanned as they received monetary transfers from the experimenter ($0 to $50, evenly distributed between the two players). In support of the notion that individuals prefer equality, the rich players showed greater reward-related activity (VS, VMPFC) when money was given to the poor player (vs. themselves), whereas poor players showed greater reward-related activity when money was given to themselves (vs. the rich player). This effect seemed to be due to an inherent desire for equality and not just different motives based on whether one is rich or poor. Thus, a subsequent behavioral study showed that this effect disappeared if the wealth of the two players was equalized. Here, pairs of participants who were both assigned to be rich or both assigned to be poor rated money transfers to themselves as significantly more rewarding than money transfers to the other individual. Hence, both fairness and equality appear to be processed by the brain as being pleasurable or rewarding.

BEING ACKNOWLEDGED BY OTHERS

Finally, some research has demonstrated that the mere act of being responded to by others in a contingent manner, or "being acknowledged" by others, may be rewarding as well. In one such study, participants completed two scans in which they (1) engaged in a face-to-face interaction with the experimenter via a live video feed and (2) viewed a videotaped recording of this interaction. During the scanning session, participants were instructed to complete the simple task of following the experimenter's (in the video) instructions to look at certain objects when prompted but were told that the experimenter would only be able to see and respond to them during the live interaction and not during the videotaped recording. When comparing neural activity during the live session vs. the prerecorded session, participants showed not only increased activity in mentalizing regions (pSTS, TPJ) but also increased activity in the VS (Redcay et al., 2010). Thus, there may be something inherently rewarding about knowing that one is being responded to in a contingent manner or that one's actions are being acknowledged (even in this most basic way) by someone else.

Benefits for "Us"
COOPERATION

For a social species, cooperation is critically important for smooth social interactions and, ultimately, survival. Cooperation between individuals has been hypothesized to require the ability to infer the mental state of another so that individuals can form shared expectations regarding mutual gains and make cooperative choices that realize these gains. To examine the neural underpinnings of cooperative interactions, researchers have used various economic games. One of these games is the Prisoner's Dilemma Game, which involves a participant deciding whether to (a) cooperate with another participant, which yields a greater joint outcome (each player gets $2), or (b) not cooperate, which yields a greater personal outcome (the participant gets $3 and the other player gets $0) (Rilling et al., 2002; Rilling, Sanfey, Aronson, Nystrom, & Cohen, 2004b). Another frequently used game is the Trust Game, in which one participant ("investor") decides how much money (if any) to transfer to another participant ("trustee"); this amount is then tripled and the trustee can decide how much money (if any) to return to the investor—a measure of cooperation (McCabe, Houser, Ryan, Smith, & Trouard, 2001).

Interestingly, studies on cooperation have shown that not only does cooperation activate neural regions involved in understanding the mental states of others (MPFC; DMPFC; McCabe et al., 2001; Decety, Jackson, Sommerville, Chaminade, & Meltzoff, 2004; Rilling et al., 2004a), but cooperation also activates reward-related regions, such as the VS and MPFC/VMPFC (McCabe et al., 2001; Rilling et al., 2002, 2004a, 2004b). Consistent with this, patients with damage to the MPFC and VMPFC are less likely to cooperate, as indexed by reduced sharing of monetary outcomes (Krajbich, Adolphs, Tranel, Denburg, & Camerer, 2009). Importantly, in studies in which cooperation results in monetary gain, it has been shown that the act of cooperating with another to receive a monetary reward leads to greater activity in reward-related regions than receiving the same amount of money in a nonsocial context (Rilling et al., 2002, 2004b).

Benefits for "You"
ALTRUISTIC GIVING

One of the most puzzling things about humans is their willingness to sacrifice their own material benefit for others. Indeed, humans will give altruistically not only to family and friends but also to individuals who they don't know, as well as to larger societal causes. Research on the neural correlates of charitable giving suggests that humans may behave altruistically because it is self-rewarding. Thus, across separate studies, it has been shown that giving to charity leads to reward-related activity in the VTA and VS (Harbaugh, Mayr, & Burghart, 2007; Moll et al., 2006) and that activity in the VS correlates directly with the number of decisions to donate to charity (Moll et al., 2006). Interestingly, it has also been shown that giving to charity leads to greater reward-related activity than receiving monetary reward for oneself (Moll et al., 2006); this was true for a region of the VS as well as for a region in the septal area, which is known to play a role in attachment and caregiving behavior (Young & Wang, 2004).

Building on this, another study demonstrated that individuals from cultures that value family assistance (helping other family members) showed greater reward-related activity when giving money to another family member (Telzer, Masten, Berkman, Lieberman, & Fuligni, 2010). Thus, Latino participants, who place a greater emphasis on family assistance, and White participants were scanned as they completed a task in which they made decisions about whether to contribute money to themselves or their families. Results revealed that, whereas Latino participants showed greater reward-related activity (dorsal striatum, VTA) while giving money to their families, White participants showed greater reward-related activity while giving money to themselves (VS, VTA). In addition, participants who felt more identified with their families showed greater activity in these regions (VS, dorsal striatum, VTA) when giving money to their families.

Finally, in a study examining the neural correlates of support-giving in long-term romantic relationships, participants who provided support to their partners (by holding their partner's arm as the partner went through painful stimulation) showed greater activity in the VS (Inagaki & Eisenberger, 2012). The VS was significantly more active during the support-giving condition than during a condition in which each participant simply held the partner's arm (without the partner receiving pain), which might be expected to be rewarding as well. Thus, this study suggests that not only can providing support to others be rewarding, but in some cases, supporting others may be more reinforcing than behaviors that are primarily self-rewarding, such as simple physical touch.

Although giving to others could be rewarding for any number of reasons (e.g., it may be evolutionarily adaptive to give altruistically), some have suggested that giving to others may be rewarding because of the social reward that is obtained when others know that one has behaved altruistically. Consistent with this, individuals who donated to charity in the presence of others showed greater activity in the VS than those who donated in the absence of others (Izuma, Saito, & Sadato, 2009). Nonetheless, the benefits of giving to others does not seem to be due exclusively to the rewarding aspects of others knowing, as donating to charity in the absence of others was still associated with significant VS activity in this study.

The Pains of Social Interaction

Like most things in life, experiences that create the most pleasure when they are present also tend to cause the most pain and distress when they are absent. Social relationships are no different. Simply put, although many aspects of social relationships are incredibly rewarding, our need for social connection can unfortunately lead to pain and suffering when this need is not met. Here we review the neural correlates underlying some of the more negative forms of social interactions: being treated unfairly, being rejected, and losing the ones we love.

Being Treated Unfairly

It is not too surprising that, in the same way that it is "rewarding" to be treated fairly, it is distressing to be treated unfairly. Using the Ultimatum Game to look at participants' neural responses to fair and unfair offers (supposedly proposed by another participant), it was found that unfair vs. fair offers led to greater activity in regions often associated with painful or distressing experience, such as the dACC and anterior insula (Boksem & De Cremer, 2010; Sanfey, Rilling, Aronson, Nystrom, & Cohen, 2003; Tabibnia et al., 2008). Similar results were found when the monetary values of the unfair offers ($3 out of $10) vs. fair offers ($3 out of $6) were controlled for, thus demonstrating that these activations were not due to receiving less money but rather to the perception that the offer was unfair (Tabibnia et al., 2008). In addition, anterior insula activity—often associated with negative affect and visceral pain sensation (Aziz, Schnitzler, & Enck, 2000; Cechetto & Saper, 1987; Lane, Reiman, Ahern, Schwartz, & Davidson, 1997; Phan, Wager, Taylor, & Liberzon, 2004)—correlated with the degree of the unfairness of the offer and the likelihood that an offer would be rejected (Sanfey et al., 2003).

Being Rejected

When individuals describe experiences in which they have been rejected or excluded, they will often use physical pain words to describe these events, complaining of "hurt feelings" and "broken hearts." Indeed, there may be a good reason for these physical pain-based descriptions. Research has demonstrated that the neural regions most often associated with pain unpleasantness (dACC, anterior insula) are also involved in the distressing experience of social exclusion. Thus, upon being socially excluded from a virtual ball-tossing game ("Cyberball"), supposedly being played with two other individuals, participants showed increased activity in both the dACC and anterior insula (Eisenberger, Lieberman, & Williams, 2003), a pattern very similar to what is observed in studies of physical pain (Apkarian et al., 2005). Furthermore, individuals who showed greater activity in the dACC reported greater levels of social distress (e.g., "I felt rejected," "I felt meaningless") in response to the exclusion episode.

Subsequent research, using various experimental designs, has provided analogous findings (Eisenberger, 2012). Replicating previous research, greater self-reports of social distress following an episode of social exclusion (Cyberball) were associated with greater activity in the dACC and anterior insula (DeWall, Masten, Powell, Combs, Schurtz & Eisenberger, 2012; Eisenberger, Taylor, Gable, Hilmert, & Lieberman, 2007; Masten et al., 2009; Onoda et al., 2009). Similarly, participants who felt socially devalued compared to others (although not outright rejected) showed greater activity in the dACC (Takahashi et al., 2009). Finally, participants who felt worse or "more hurt" in response to social-evaluative feedback showed greater activity in both the dACC and anterior insula (Eisenberger, Inagaki, Muscatell, Byrne Haltom, & Leary, 2011).

Consistent with these findings, it has also been shown that individual difference factors that typically increase or decrease responses to social rejection show the expected relationships with neural activity. Thus, individuals with lower levels of self-esteem (vs. higher levels of self-esteem), who should be more affected by social exclusion, reported feeling more hurt in response to social exclusion and also showed greater activity in the dACC (Onoda et al., 2010). Similarly, individuals who scored higher in anxious attachment, the tendency to worry about rejection from close others, showed increased activity in the dACC and anterior insula in response to social exclusion (DeWall et al., 2012). Conversely, individuals with more social support or who spend more time with friends—factors that should mitigate the negative effects of exclusion—showed reduced activity in the dACC and anterior insula in response to social exclusion (Eisenberger, Taylor et al., 2007; Masten, Telzer, Fuligni, Lieberman, & Eisenberger, 2012). Finally, individuals who reported feeling more socially rejected or disconnected in their real-world social interactions (assessed daily across a 10-day period) showed greater activity in the dACC and PAG (a pain-related region) in response to a Cyberball exclusion episode (Eisenberger, Gable, & Lieberman, 2007). This finding suggests a link between real-world experiences of social rejection and pain-related neural activation.

Building on these data, a recent study demonstrated that an experience of social rejection and an experience of physical pain activated overlapping pain-related neural regions within the same participants. In this study, participants who had recently experienced an unwanted romantic relationship breakup completed two tasks. In one task, they were asked to view a picture of the person who recently broke up with them and think back to that experience of rejection. In another task, they received painful heat stimulation. Results from this study showed increased activity in the dACC and anterior insula when thinking about this rejection experience and when feeling painful heat stimulation (Kross, Berman, Mischel, Smith, & Wager, 2011), providing additional evidence that experiences of social pain rely, in part, on pain-related neural regions.

In addition to studies examining the neural correlates underlying the *experience* of social rejection, studies using rejection-themed images or facial expressions, which signal rejection without necessarily triggering a full-blown experience of rejection, have shown similar effects. Kross and colleagues (Kross, Egner, Ochsner, Hirsch, & Downey, 2007) have shown both dACC and anterior insula activity in response to rejection-themed images (paintings by Edward Hopper) in contrast to acceptance-themed images. Moreover, for rejection-sensitive individuals, viewing videos of individuals making disapproving facial expressions, a potential cue of social rejection, is associated with greater activity in the dACC but not in other limbic regions (e.g., amygdala), a result suggesting that the dACC may be specifically responsive to these cues of rejection (Burklund, Eisenberger, & Lieberman, 2007).

Importantly, the hypothesis that experiences of social rejection ("social pain") rely on neural regions directly involved in the distress of physical pain has also been examined by looking at some of the expected consequences of such an overlap in neural circuitry. Hence, individual differences in sensitivity to one kind of pain relate to individual differences in sensitivity to the other. Those who are more sensitive to physical pain are also more sensitive to social pain (Eisenberger, Jarcho, Lieberman, & Naliboff, 2006; c.f. DeWall & Baumeister, 2006), and genetic polymorphisms that relate to increased physical pain sensitivity (mu-opioid receptor gene polymorphism, *OPRM1*) also relate to greater self-reported sensitivity to rejection as well as greater neural sensitivity (dACC, anterior insula) to an episode of exclusion (Way, Taylor, & Eisenberger, 2009). Additionally, factors that increase or decrease one type of pain experience seem to affect the other type of pain in a parallel manner. Thus, social support, which often reduces socially painful experience, also reduces the unpleasantness of physical pain stimuli (Eisenberger, et al., 2011; Master et al., 2009), and Tylenol, a common physical painkiller, reduces self-reported hurt feelings as well as neural sensitivity (dACC, anterior insula) to social rejection (DeWall et al., 2010).

Grief: Losing Those We Love

Other types of socially painful experiences, such as bereavement, have also been shown to activate pain-related neural regions. In one study (Gündel, O'Connor, Littrell, Fort, & Lane, 2003), bereaved participants were scanned while viewing pictures of their recently deceased first-degree relative and while viewing pictures of a stranger. In response to viewing pictures of the deceased, compared to pictures of a stranger, participants showed greater activity in regions of the dACC and anterior insula. A subsequent study, using a similar design, replicated these findings; bereaved individuals experiencing normal or complicated grief (grief that is prolonged and unabated) showed greater activity in both the dACC and anterior insula in response to viewing images of the deceased than when viewing images of a stranger (O'Connor et al., 2008). Interestingly, the only type of neural activation that differentiated those experiencing normal grief from those with complicated grief was greater activation in the VS for those with complicated grief. Moreover, greater activity in the VS correlated with greater self-reported yearning for the lost loved one. Finally, females who lost an unborn child after induced termination compared to females who delivered a healthy child showed greater activity in the dACC/midcingulate cortex in response to viewing pictures of smiling baby faces (Kersting et al., 2009). Thus, various types of "socially painful experience," not just experiences of social rejection or exclusion, may activate pain-related neural regions as well.

Love and Attachment

Attachment is an emotional and psychological bond with another individual. The earliest attachment relationship is between caregiver and child, with the express purpose of fostering the development of the infant, who cannot take care of him- or herself (Bowlby, 1969). Later on, attachment relationships form between romantic partners (Hazan & Shaver, 1987). Though difficult to recreate an attachment-related interaction in an fMRI scanner, researchers have started to use proxy measures to explore the neural underpinnings of one of the most significant types of human relationships— romantic and caregiver–infant attachments.

Typically, fMRI studies of attachment relationships have involved the viewing of pictures or videos of one's relationship partner or infant (compared to viewing a friend or familiar infant, respectively). As expected, many of these studies find that viewing one's romantic partner or infant activates regions involved in primitive reward-processing (VS, VTA). However, more puzzling is the fact that many of these studies also find significant activation in regions often associated with pain processing (dACC, anterior insula, PAG). One possible explanation for this is that viewing one's attachment figure may induce not only a sense of positive regard but also an increased sense of vigilance for potential separation from the attachment figure. Indeed, prior work has implicated certain pain-related neural regions, such as the dACC and the PAG, in distress-related as well as caregiving-related behaviors following maternal infant separation (Bandler & Shipley, 1994; Hadland, Rushworth, Gaffan, & Passingham, 2003; MacLean & Newman, 1988; Robinson, 1967; Smith, 1945). Another explanation for pain-related regions activating in response to viewing attachment figures may be common, underlying neurotransmitter activity. Many neural regions typically associated with pain processing have a high density of receptors for mu-opioids, which are released not only in response to pain (to reduce painful experience) but also in response to positive social interactions (Fields, 2007; Leknes & Tracey, 2008). Thus, it is possible that common neural activation in these regions during pain and pleasure reflects the action of similar neurotransmitter activity.

In this section, we first review the neural correlates underlying romantic love and then turn to those underlying maternal love.

Romantic Love

In the first study of the neural basis of romantic love (Bartels & Zeki, 2000), participants who reported being deeply in love with their romantic partners were scanned as they viewed pictures of their partner and as they viewed pictures of friends (known for the same amount of time as the partner). In response to viewing pictures of their partner, in contrast to viewing friends, participants showed increased activity in dopamine-rich areas associated with reward and approach motivation, including the caudate and putamen. Interestingly, participants also showed increased activation in the middle insula and dACC, which may reflect increased vigilance for separation from the romantic partner.[2] Finally, this study also showed that viewing partners, but not friends, led to reduced activity in mentalizing regions, including the DMPFC, PCC, pSTS, and temporal poles. This finding could either be interpreted as a deactivation in these neural regions when thinking about a loved one or as greater activity in these regions when thinking about a friend.

Subsequent studies have shown similar findings. Participants who reported being "intensely in love" with their partner showed increased activity in the VTA and caudate when viewing pictures of their partner relative to that when viewing a familiar individual, and greater scores on a passionate-love scale were associated with greater activity in the caudate (Aron et al., 2005). Even the subliminal priming of a loved one's name (without the participant's conscious awareness of seeing the name) elicited activity in some of these regions, including the caudate, VTA, and anterior and middle insula (Ortigue, Bianchi-Demicheli, Hamilton, & Grafton, 2007).

Maternal Love

Some would describe the attachment of a parent to his or her child as one of the most significant and affect-laden social bonds that an individual can ever experience. From an evolutionary perspective, the purpose of this bond is to foster the development of the infant, a process that is instantiated through attachment-related behaviors on the part of both the caregiver and infant. From the infant's vantage point, the attachment relationship allows for need fulfillment following distress and exploration when safety and satiety is achieved (Bowlby, 1969). From the caregiver's vantage point, which has been the focus of recent neuroimaging studies, the attachment relationship is fostered through rewarding caregiver–infant interactions, as well as caretaking behaviors when the infant experiences distress; both of these types of behaviors allow for the successful development of the offspring.

Studies of various mammalian species have demonstrated a tight coupling between maternal–infant attachment processes and the neural systems underlying reward (Insel & Young, 2001; Numan & Sheehan, 1997), which may relate to some of the intense, positive feelings associated with the attachment relationship. Moreover, theorists have also posited a role for thalamocingulate circuitry (the cingulate cortex and connected thalamic nuclei) in maternal behavior. This system is thought to be largely involved in responding to infants' distress and enacting appropriate caretaking behavior (MacLean, 1990). Consistent with this, studies have shown that anterior (as well as posterior) cingulate lesions impair maternal behavior in rats and hamsters (MacLean, 1990; Slotnick, 1967; Stamm, 1955). On the basis of these findings, one might expect both reward and distress-related neural regions to play a role in attachment experiences.

Like human studies of romantic love, human studies of maternal love have focused primarily on mothers viewing pictures or videos of their infants, in either a happy or distressed state. One of the first studies to do this found patterns of neural activity very similar to what is seen during romantic love (Bartels & Zeki, 2004). When mothers viewed pictures of their own child in contrast to those of another familiar child, they showed activation in reward-associated regions, including the VS and caudate. Mothers also showed increased activity in the dACC and middle insula. In addition, similar to what was found for romantic love, viewing one's own infant in contrast to another infant led to reduced activity in mentalizing regions (DMPFC, PCC/precuneus, pSTS, temporal pole). Interestingly, the PAG, a region involved in both pain processing and pain suppression through opioid-related mechanisms (Fields, 2007), was more active for maternal love than for romantic love.

To tease apart the reward and distress-related activations associated with maternal–infant attachment, subsequent studies have separately investigated the neural correlates associated with viewing a happy or a distressed infant. These efforts have yielded varying degrees of success, as many different neural processes seem to be recruited for processing positive in contrast to negative infant-related stimuli. In one study, viewing one's own infant in a separation situation (compared to a play situation) led to increased activity in regions involved in pain-related processing (dACC) and mentalizing (DMPFC, pSTS, precuneus), which might be expected, but it also led to increased activity in regions involved in reward-related processing (caudate) (Noriuchi, Kikuchi, & Senoo, 2008). Other studies have shown that seeing one's own infant (but not an unknown infant) led to greater activity in reward-related (VS, VTA), mentalizing (MPFC, pSTS, PCC), and distress-related neural regions (dACC), regardless of the type of facial expression displayed (happy, sad, neutral) (Strathearn, Li, & Montague, 2008).

Still other studies have shown that the attachment style of the mother, rather than the type of facial expression the infant displays, may be a better predictor of neural responses to infant pictures. Mothers identified as being securely attached showed greater VS activity when viewing their own baby than when viewing an unknown infant (Strathearn, Fonagy, Amico, & Montague, 2009). In addition, mothers who showed greater increases in oxytocin levels after interacting with their infants showed greater activity in the VS and the hypothalamus (both of which have a high density of oxytocin receptors) when viewing pictures of their infants (Strathearn et al., 2009).

Although all of the studies reviewed here used mother–infant dyads, a clever study manipulated baby-related features in pictures of infant faces to examine the neural correlates underlying sensitivity to baby features (Glocker et al., 2009). Females (who had not previously given birth) were scanned as they viewed images of babies that were manipulated to look more or less baby-like (high in baby-related features: round face, high forehead, big eyes, small nose and mouth). Pictures that were manipulated to look more baby-like were not only rated as cuter but led to greater activity in the VS. In addition, pictures high in baby-like features also led to increased activity in the dACC, which may relate to increased sensitivity to infant needs or distress and heightened caretaking motivation.

Summary and Conclusions

Although the study of the cognitive neuroscience of social interactions is relatively new, it has already revealed a great deal about our social nature. In this chapter we have reviewed a number of studies that investigated social interactions within the fMRI scanner. Two particularly important insights have emerged from these findings.

The first insight is that many complex social interactions that are typically described as being pleasurable (e.g., cooperation) or as being painful (e.g., rejection) actually rely on neural circuitry involved in responding to much more basic pleasures (e.g., food) and pains (e.g., physical injury) (Lieberman & Eisenberger, 2009). Thus, even though cooperating with others or being rejected seems like it would be rewarding or painful on a mental level, it is not always assumed that these experiences are interpreted as rewarding or painful on a more "physical" level. Nonetheless, growing evidence supports the notion that these social experiences are rooted in basic motivational and affective systems and that, at some level, social pleasures and pains are *basic* pleasures and pains. Whether one marvels at these findings or prefers to assert that "we knew it all along," neuroimaging research provides us with hard evidence to confirm our intuitions.

The second insight to emerge from the research on social interactions is that there is a dedicated set of neural regions that is uniquely involved in understanding the minds of others (Frith & Frith, 2003; Lieberman, 2010; Mitchell, 2009). These regions are specific to social cognition and are not activated when trying to understand objects without minds. Though perhaps overlooked because understanding the minds of others is a process that we engage in so easily and naturally, it is critical for our social nature and forms the basis for many of our most noble abilities as humans, including empathy, perspective-taking, self-reflection, and cooperation. Indeed, damage to these regions has been shown, in some cases, to severely impair fluid and appropriate social interaction (Beer, Heerey, Keltner, Scabini, & Knight, 2003).

Based on the studies reviewed here, it is important to note that many of the findings may not have been revealed without the use of real (or supposedly real) social interactions within the fMRI scanner. Because of the constraints associated with neuroimaging techniques (restriction of movement, small space), a lot of neuroimaging research has focused on understanding neural responses to pictures of social and affective stimuli. Although our understanding of the human brain has certainly benefited from evaluating neural responses to images (e.g., pictures of faces, threatening or pleasant scenes), looking at pictures is inherently different from being involved in a social interaction. Indeed, studies involving pictorial stimuli lack several features that are unique to studies involving social interactions.

First, when participants view pictures—even pictures of social stimuli—there is no expectation for social interaction. Although one *can*, one does not *need* to understand the mind of an individual in a picture (though this may happen automatically depending on the nature of the stimulus and the individual viewing it). As a result, neural regions involved in social cognition may be less likely to be engaged while viewing pictures of other individuals (unless specific instructions are given to try to understand the mind of the individual in the picture). Thus, with pictures alone, the mentalizing aspect of social cognition, which is so commonplace in real-world social interactions, may go uncaptured.

Second, viewing pictures is not a terribly meaningful or self-relevant experience. While pictures can be judged as positive or negative, emotionally arousing or nonarousing, most pictures are not processed as self-relevant and thus are not likely to elicit a large emotional response. In other words, without a stimulus that is self-relevant, it is unlikely that an experimental paradigm will trigger real emotional experience in participants. Without real emotional experience, it is impossible to truly understand the affective significance of social interactions. However, when studies begin to use real social interactions, it is possible that the self-relevance of these interactions increases for the participant and thus, as demonstrated in the studies reviewed here, pleasure and pain-related neural regions are activated in response to real (or supposedly real) social interactions.

One consequence of studying the brain's response to social interactions, rather than pictures of social stimuli, is that certain neural regions not typically activated by pictures of social stimuli may be activated in response to real social interactions. For example, whereas the amygdala is frequently engaged during tasks that involve the viewing of negative faces or threatening stimuli, other regions like the dACC and anterior insula are active more frequently in studies that involve negative social interactions. This may be due to the fact that social interactions are more engaging and more consequential and probably generate a fuller emotional experience. To the extent that our understanding of emotional and social experience comes from studies that examine neural responses to pictures of social stimuli, we will certainly be compromised in our understanding of real emotional experience. Perhaps the best way to truly capture these emotions is through measuring neural responses to social interactions.

In sum, although the studies reviewed here have revealed a great deal about the neural underpinnings of social experience, we are still at the earliest stages of understanding the social brain. For example, we have used here a very general scheme for classifying certain neural regions as being involved in pleasurable (rewarding) experience, others as being involved in painful experience, and still others as being involved in "social cognition." However, this conceptualization is undoubtedly too naïve. It is certainly the

case that the distinctions we made between these neural systems are not as clear or straightforward as we have portrayed them to be. For example, MPFC has been described as being involved in both reward processing as well as mentalizing; however, it is not yet clear how this same neural region instantiates both of these processes. Future work will be needed to sharpen our understanding and conceptualization of these neural regions and to illustrate how they contribute to social experience. It is our hope that researchers will continue to explore the neural substrates of social interactions to further specify the workings of the social brain.

Notes

1. Although most neuroimaging studies have focused on the amygdala's role in responding to aversive or threatening stimuli (e.g., fearful faces), this region has long been known to be involved in appetitive processing in animals (Holland & Gallagher, 1999). Recent neuroimaging evidence has confirmed the amygdala's role in responding to positive stimuli (Canli, Sivrs, Whitfield, Gotlib, & Gabrieli, 2002; O'Doherty, Rolls, Francis, Bowtell, & McClone, 2001; Tabibnia et al., 2008).

2. Although the dACC activation seen here is one that is commonly seen in studies of physical pain, correlating with the unpleasantness of the experience, the insular activation in this study—with its foci in the middle insula—was more caudal than that typically seen in studies of physical pain. Thus, this middle insula activation may be less related to pain processing and more related to positive emotional experience, which fits with other studies showing middle insula activation to pleasant physical touch (Olausson et al., 2002).

References

Apkarian, A. V., Bushnell, M. C., Treede, R.-D., & Zubieta, J.-K. (2005). Human brain mechanisms of pain perception and regulation in health and disease. *European Journal of Pain, 9*, 463–484.

Aron, A., Fisher, H., Mashek, D. J., Strong, G., Haifang, L., & Brown, L. (2005). Reward, motivation, and emotion systems associated with early-stage intense romantic love. *Journal of Neurophysiology, 94*, 327–337.

Aziz, Q., Schnitzler, A., & Enck, P. (2000). Functional neuroimaging of visceral sensation. *Journal of Clinical Neurophysiology, 17*, 604–612.

Bandler, R., & Shipley, M. T. (1994). Columnar organization in the midbrain periaqueductal gray: Modules for emotional expression? *Trends in Neurosciences, 17*, 379–389.

Bartels, A., & Zeki, S. (2000). The neural basis of romantic love. *Neuroreport, 11*, 3829–3834.

Bartels, A., & Zeki, S. (2004). The neural correlates of maternal and romantic love. *Neuroimage, 21*, 1155–1166.

Baumeister, R. F., & Leary, M. R. (1995). The need to belong: Desire for interpersonal attachments as a fundamental human motivation. *Psychological Bulletin, 117*, 497–529.

Beer, J. S., Heerey, E. A., Keltner, D., Scabini, D., & Knight, R. T. (2003). The regulatory function of self-conscious emotion: Insights from patients with orbitofrontal damage. *Journal of Personality and Social Psychology, 85*, 594–604.

Berkman, L. F., & Syme, S. L. (1979). Social networks, host resistance, and mortality: A nine-year follow-up study of Alameda County residents. *American Journal of Epidemiology*, *109*, 186–204.

Berthier, M., Starkstein, S., Leiguardia, R., & Carrea, R. (1988). Asymbolia for pain: A sensory-limbic disconnection system. *Annals of Neurology, 24*, 41–49.

Bird, C. M., Castelli, F., Malik, O., Frith, U., & Husain, M. (2004). The impact of extensive medial frontal lobe damage on "theory of mind" and cognition. *Brain, 127*, 914–928.

Boksem, M. A. S., & De Cremer, D. (2010). Fairness concerns predict medial frontal negativity amplitude in ultimatum bargaining. *Social Neuroscience, 5*, 118–128.

Bowlby, J. (1969). *Attachment and loss, Vol. I: Attachment.* New York: Basic Books.

Burklund, L. J., Eisenberger, N. I., & Lieberman, M. D. (2007). Rejection sensitivity moderates dorsal anterior cingulate activity to disapproving facial expressions. *Social Neuroscience, 2*, 238–253.

Canli, T., Sivrs, H., Whitfield, S. L., & Gotlib, I. H., & Gabrieli, J. D. E. (2002). Amygdala response to happy faces as a function of extraversion. *Science, 296*, 2191.

Cechetto, D. F., & Saper, C. B. (1987). Evidence for a viscerotopic sensory representation in the cortex and thalamus in the rat. *Journal of Comparative Neurology, 262*, 27–45.

Decety, J., Jackson, P. L., Sommerville, J. A., Chaminade, T., & Meltzoff, A. N. (2004). The neural bases of cooperation and competition: An fMRI investigation. *Neuroimage, 23*, 744–751.

DeWall, C. N., & Baumeister, R. F. (2006). Alone but feeling no pain. Effects of social exclusion on physical pain tolerance and pain threshold, affective forecasting, and interpersonal empathy. *Journal of Personality and Social Psychology, 91*, 1–15.

DeWall, C. N., MacDonald, G., Webster, G. D., Masten, C. L., Baumeister, R. F., Powell, C., et al. (2010). Tylenol reduces social pain: Behavioral and neural evidence. *Psychological Science, 21*, 931–937.

DeWall, C. N., Masten, C. L., Powell, C., Combs, D., Schurtz, D. R., & Eisenberger, N. I. (2012). Do neural responses to rejection depend on attachment style? An fMRI study. *Social, Cognitive & Affective Neuroscience, 7*, 184–192.

Eisenberger, N.I. (2012). The pain of social disconnection. Examining the shared neural underpinnings of physical and social pain. *Nature Reviews Neuroscience, 13*, 421–434.

Eisenberger, N. I., Gable, S. L., & Lieberman, M. D. (2007). fMRI responses relate to differences in real-world social experience. *Emotion, 7*, 745–754.

Eisenberger, N. I., Inagaki, T. K., Muscatell, K. A., & Leary, M. R. (2011). The neural sociometer: A mechanism for translating interpersonal appraisals into state self-esteem. *Journal of Cognitive Neuroscience, 23*, 3448–3455.

Eisenberger, N. I., Jarcho, J. M., Lieberman, M. D., & Naliboff, B. D. (2006). An experimental study of shared sensitivity to physical pain and social rejection. *Pain, 126*, 132–138.

Eisenberger, N. I., Lieberman, M. D., & Williams, K. D. (2003). Does rejection hurt? An fMRI study of social exclusion. *Science, 302*, 290–292.

Eisenberger, N.I., Master, S.L., Inagaki, T.I., Taylor, S.E., Shirinyan, D., Lieberman, M.D., & Naliboff, B. (2011). Attachment figures activate a safety signal-related neural region and reduce pain experience. *Proceedings of the National Academy of Sciences, 108*, 11721-11726.

Eisenberger, N. I., Taylor, S. E., Gable, S. L., Hilmert, C. J., & Lieberman, M. D. (2007). Neural pathways link social support to attenuated neuroendocrine stress responses. *Neuroimage, 35*, 1601–1612.

Fields, H. L. (2007). Understanding how opioids contribute to reward and analgesia. *Regional Anesthesia and Pain Medicine, 32*, 242–246.

Fletcher, P. C., Happé, S. C., Frith, U., Baker, S. C., Dolan, R. J., Frackowiak, R. S. J., & Frith, C. D. (1995). Other minds in the brain: A functional imaging study of "theory of mind" in story comprehension. *Cognition, 57*,109–128.

Foltz, E. L., & White, L. E. (1962). Pain "relief" by frontal cingulumotomy. *Journal of Neurosurgery, 89*, 89–100.

Frith, U., & Frith, C. D. (2003). Development and neurophysiology of mentalizing. *Philosophical Transactions: Biological Sciences, 358*, 459–473.

Gallagher, H. L., Jack, A. I., Roepstorff, A., & Frith, C. D. (2002). Imaging and the intentional stance in a competitive game. *Neuroimage, 16*, 814–821.

Glocker, M. L., Langleben, D. D., Ruparel, K., Loughead, J. W., Valdez, J. N., Griffin, M. D., et al. (2009). Baby schema modulates the brain reward system in nulliparous women. *Proceedings of the National Academy of Sciences U S A, 106*, 9115–9119.

Gündel, H., O'Connor, M.-F., Littrell, L., Fort, C., & Richard, L. (2003). Functional neuroanatomy of grief: An fMRI study. *American Journal of Psychiatry, 160*, 1946–1953.

Hadland, K. A, Rushworth, M. F. S., Gaffan, D., & Passingham, R. E. (2003). The effect of cingulate lesions on social behaviour and emotion. *Neuropsychologia, 41*, 919–931.

Harabaugh, W. T., Mayr, U., & Burghart, D. R. (2007). Neural responses to taxation and voluntary giving reveal motives for charitable donations. *Science, 316*, 1622–1625.

Harlow, H. F. (1958). The nature of love. *American Psychologist, 13*, 673–685.

Harlow, H. F., Dodsworth, R. O., & Harlow, M. K. (1965). Total social isolation in monkeys. *Proceedings of the National Academy of Sciences U S A, 54*, 90–97.

Hazan, C., & Shaver, P. (1987). Romantic love conceptualized as an attachment process. *Journal of Personality and Social Psychology, 52*, 511–524.

Hebben, N. (1985). Toward the assessment of clinical pain. In G. M. Aronoff (Ed.), *Evaluation and treatment of chronic pain* (pp. 451–462). Baltimore, MD: Urban & Schwarzenburg.

Holland, P. C., & Gallagher, M. (1999). Amygdala circuitry in attentional and representational processes. *Trends in Cognitive Sciences, 3*, 65–73.

House, J. S., Landis, K. R., & Umberson, D. (1988). Social relationships and health. *Science, 241*, 540–545.

Inagaki, T. K., & Eisenberger, N. I. (2012). Neural correlates of giving support to a loved one. *Psychosomatic Medicine, 74*, 3–7.

Insel, T. R., & Young, L. J. (2001). The neurobiology of attachment. *Nature Reviews Neuroscience, 2*, 129–136.

Izuma, K., Saito, D. N., & Sadato, N. (2008). Processing of social and monetary rewards in the human striatum. *Neuron, 58*, 284–294.

Izuma, K., Saito, D. N., & Sadato, N. (2009). Processing of the incentive for social approval in the ventral striatum during charitable donation. *Journal of Cognitive Neuroscience, 22*, 621–631.

Kersting, A., Ohrmann, P., Pedersen, A., Kroker, K., Samberg, D., Bauer, J., et al. (2009). Neural activation underlying acute grief in women after the loss of an unborn child. *American Journal of Psychiatry, 166,* 1402–1410.

Krajbich, I., Adolphs, R., Tranel, D., Denburg, N. L., & Camerer, C. F. (2009). Economic games quantify diminished sense of guilt in patients with damage to the prefrontal cortex. *Journal of Neuroscience, 29,* 2188–2192.

Kross, E., Berman, M. G., Mischel, W., Smith, E. E., & Wager, T. D. (2011). Social rejection shares somatosensory representations with physical pain. *Proceedings of the National Academy of Sciences U S A, 108,* 6270–6275.

Kross, E., Egner, T., Ochsner, K., Hirsch, J., & Downey, G. (2007). Neural dynamics of rejection sensitivity. *Journal of Cognitive Neuroscience, 19,* 945–956.

Knutson, B., & Cooper, J. C. (2005). Functional magnetic resonance imaging of reward prediction. *Current Opinion in Neurology, 18,* 411–417.

Knutson, B., Fong, G. W., Adams, C. M., Varner, J. L., & Hommer, D. (2001). Dissociation or reward anticipation and outcome with event-related fMRI. *Neuroreport, 12,* 3683–3687.

Knutson, B., Fong, G. W., Bennett, S. M., Adams, C. M., & Hommer, D. (2003). A region of mesial prefrontal cortex tracks monetarily rewarding outcomes: Characterization with rapid event-related fMRI. *Neuroimage, 18,* 263–272.

Lane, R. D., Reiman, E. M., Ahern, G. L., Schwartz, G. E., & Davidson, R. J. (1997). Neuroanatomical correlates of happiness, sadness, and disgust. *American Journal of Psychiatry, 154,* 926–933.

Leknes, S., & Tracey, I. (2008). A common neurobiology for pain and pleasure. *Nature Reviews Neuroscience, 9,* 314–320.

Lieberman, M. D. (2010). Social cognitive neuroscience. In S. T. Fiske, D. T. Gilbert, & G. Lindzey (Eds.) *Handbook of social psychology* (5th ed., pp. 143–193). New York: McGraw Hill.

Lieberman, M. D., & Eisenberger, N. I. (2009). Pains and pleasures of social life. *Science, 323,* 890–891.

MacLean, P. D. (1990). *The triune brain in evolution: Role in paleocerebral functions.* New York: Plenum.

MacLean, P. D., & Newman, J. D. (1988). Role of midline frontolimbic cortex in production of the isolation call of squirrel monkeys. *Brain Research, 45,* 111–123.

Masten, C. L., Eisenberger, N. I., Borofsky, L., Pfeifer, J. H., McNealy, K., & Dapretto, M. (2009). Neural correlates of social exclusion during adolescence: Understanding the distress of peer rejection. *Social, Cognitive & Affective Neuroscience, 4,* 143–157.

Masten, C. L., Telzer, E. H., Fuligni, A., Lieberman, M. D., & Eisenberger, N. I. (2012). Time spent with friends in adolescence relates to less neural sensitivity to later peer rejection. *Social, Cognitive & Affective Neuroscience, 7,* 106–114.

Master, S. L., Eisenberger, N. I., Taylor, S. E., Naliboff, B. D., Shirinyan, D., & Lieberman, M. D. (2009). A picture's worth: Partner photographs reduce experimentally induced pain. *Psychological Science, 20,* 1316–1318.

McCabe, K., Houser, D., Ryan, L., Smith, V., & Trouard, T. (2001). A functional imaging study of cooperation in two-person reciprocal exchange. *Proceedings of the National Academy of Sciences U S A, 98,* 11832–11835.

Mitchell, J. P. (2009). Inferences about mental states. *Philosophical Transactions of the Royal Society, Series B: Biological Sciences, 364,* 1309–1316.

Mitchell, J. P., Cloutier, J., Banaji, M. R., & Macrae, C. N. (2006). Medial prefrontal dissociations during processing of train diagnostic and nondiagnostic person information. *Social Cognitive and Affective Neuroscience, 1,* 49–55.

Mitchell, J. P., Macrae, C. N., & Banaji, M. R. (2004). Encoding-specific effects of social cognition on the neural correlates on subsequent memory. *Journal of Neuroscience, 24,* 4912–4917.

Mitchell, J. P., Macrae, C. N., & Banaji, M. R. (2005). Forming impressions of people versus inanimate objects: Social-cognitive processing in the medial prefrontal cortex. *Neuroimage, 26,* 251–257.

Moll, J., Krueger, F., Zahn, R., Padini, M., de Oliveira-Souza, R., & Grafman, J. (2006). Human fronto-mesolimbic networks guide decisions about charitable donation. *Proceedings of the National Academy of Sciences U S A, 103,* 15623–15628.

Noriuchi, M., Kikuchi, Y., & Senoo, A. (2008). The functional neuroanatomy of maternal love: Mother's response to infant's attachment behaviors. *Biological Psychiatry, 63,* 415–423.

Numan, M., & Sheehan, T. P. (1997). Neuroanatomical circuitry for mammalian behavior. In A. S. Carter, I. I. Lederhendler, & B. Kirkpatrick (Eds.), *The integrative neurobiology of affiliation* (pp. 275–299). Cambridge, MA: MIT Press.

O'Connor, T. G., & Rutter, M. (2000). Attachment disorder behavior following early severe deprivation: Extension and longitudinal follow-up. *Journal of the American Academy of Child and Adolescent Psychiatry, 39,* 703–712.

O'Connor, M. F., Wellisch, D. K., Stanton, A., Eisenberger, N. I., Irwin, M. R., & Lieberman, M.D. (2008). Craving love? Enduring grief activates brain's reward center. *Neuroimage, 42,* 969–972.

O'Doherty, J. P., Deichmann, R., Critchley, H. D., & Dolan, R. J. (2002). Neural responses during anticipation of a primary taste reward. *Neuron, 28,* 815–826.

O'Doherty, J. P. (2004). Reward representations and reward-related learning in the human brain: Insights from neuroimaging. *Current Opinion in Neurobiology, 14,* 769–776.

O'Doherty, J. P., Rolls, E. T., Francis, S., Bowtell, R., McGlone, F. (2001). Representation of pleasant and aversive taste in the human brain. *Journal of Neurophysiology, 85,* 1315–1321.

Olausson, H., Lamarre, Y., Backlund, H., Morin, C., Wallin, B. G., Starck, G., et al. (2002). Unmyelinated tactile afferents signal touch and project insular cortex. *Nature Neuroscience, 5,* 900–904.

Onoda, K., Okamoto, Y., Nakashima, K., Nittono, H., Ura, M., & Yamawaki, S. (2009). Decreased ventral anterior cingulated cortex activity is associated with reduced social pain during emotional support. *Social Neuroscience, 4,* 443–454.

Onoda, K., Okamoto, Y., Nakashima, K, Nittoni, H., Yoshimura, S., Yamawaki, S., Yamaguchi, S., & Ura, M. (2010). Does low self-esteem enhance social pain? The relationships between trait self-esteem and anterior cingulate cortex activation induced by ostracism. *Social, Cognitive & Affective Neuroscience, 5,* 383–391.

Ortigue, S., Bianchi-Demicheli, F., Hamilton, A. F., & Grafton, S. T. (2007). The neural basis of love as a subliminal prime: An event-related functional magnetic resonance imaging study. *Journal of Cognitive Neuroscience, 19,* 1218–1230.

Peyron, R., Laurent, B., & Garcia-Larrea, L. (2000). Functional imaging of brain responses to pain. A review and meta-analysis. *Neurophysiological Clinics, 30,* 263–288.

Phan, L., Wager, T. D., Taylor, S. F., & Liberzon, I. (2004). Functional neuroimaging studies of human emotions. *CNS Spectrums, 9,* 258–266.

Ploner, M., Freund, H. -J., & Schnitzler, A. (1999). Pain affect without pain sensation in a patient with postcentral lesion. *Pain, 81,* 211–214.

Price, D. D. (2000). Psychological and neural mechanisms of the affective dimensions of pain. *Science, 288,* 1769–1772.

Rainville, P. (2002). Brain mechanisms of pain affect and pain modulation. *Current Opinion in Neurobiology, 12,* 195–204.

Redcay, E., Dodell-Feder, D., Pearrow, M. J., Mavrose, P. L., Kleiner, M., Gabrieli, J. D. E., & Saxe, R. (2010). Live face-to-face interaction during fMRI: A new tool for social cognitive neuroscience. *Neuroimage, 50,* 1639–1647.

Rilling, J. K., Dagenais, J. E., Goldsmith, D. R., Glenn, A. L., & Pagnoni, G. (2008). Social cognitive neural networks during in-group and out-group interactions. *Neuroimage, 41,* 1447–1761.

Rilling, R. K., Gutman, D. A., Zeh, T. R., Pagnoni, G., Berns, G. S., & Kilts, C. D. (2002). A neural basis for social cooperation. *Neuron, 35,* 395–405.

Rilling, J. K., Sanfey, A. G., Aronson, J. A., Nystrom, L. E., & Cohen, J. D. (2004a). The neural correlates of theory of mind within interpersonal interactions. *Neuroimage, 22,* 1694–1703.

Rilling, J. K., Sanfey, A. G., Aronson, J. A., Nystrom, L. E., & Cohen, J. D. (2004b). Opposing BOLD responses to reciprocated and unreciprocated altruism in putative reward pathways. *Neuroreport, 15,* 2539–2543.

Robinson, B. W., (1967). Neurological aspects of evoked vocalizations. In S. A. Altmann (Ed.), *Social communication among primates* (pp. 135–147). Chicago: Chicago University Press.

Sanfey, A. G., Rilling, J. K., Aronson, J. A., Nystrom, L. E., & Cohen, J. D. (2003). The neural basis of economic decision-making in the Ultimatum Game. *Science, 300,* 1755–1758.

Slotnick, B. M. (1967). Disturbances in maternal behavior in the rat following lesions of the cingulate cortex. *Behaviour, 29,* 204–236.

Smith, W. (1945). The functional significance of the rostral cingular cortex as revealed by its responses to electrical excitation. *Journal of Neurophysiology, 8,* 241–255.

Spreckelmeyer, K. N., Krach, S., Rademacher, L., Irmak, A., Konrad, K., Kircher, T., et al. (2009). Dissocation of neural networks for anticipation and consumption of monetary and social rewards. *Social, Cognitive & Affective Neuroscience, 4,* 158–165.

Stamm, J. S. (1955). The function of the median cerebral cortex in maternal behavior in rats. *Journal of Comparative and Physiological Psychology, 48,* 347–356.

Stone, V. E., Baron-Cohen, S., & Knight, R. T. (1998). Frontal lobe contributions to theory of mind. *Journal of Cognitive Neuroscience, 10,* 640–656.

Strathearn, L., Fonagy, P., Amico, J., & Montague, P. R. (2009). Adult attachment predicts maternal brain and oxytocin responses to infant cues. *Neuropsychopharmacology, 34,* 2655–2666.

Strathearn, L., Li, J., & Montague, P. R. (2008). What's in a smile? Maternal brain responses to infant facial cues. *Pediatrics, 122,* 40–51.

Tabibnia, G., Satpute, A. B., & Lieberman, M. D. (2008). The sunny side of fairness: Preference for fairness activates reward circuitry (and disregarding unfairness activates self-control circuitry). *Psychological Science, 19,* 339–347.

Takahashi, H., Kato, M. Matsuura, M., Mobbs, D., Suhara, T., & Okubo, Y. (2009). When your gain in my pain and your pain is my gain: Neural correlates of envy and schadenfreude. *Science, 323,* 937–939.

Telzer, E. H., Masten, C. L, Berkman, E. T., Lieberman, M. D., & Fuligni, A. J. (2010). Gaining while giving: An fMRI study of the rewards of family assistance among White and Latino youth. *Social Neuroscience, 5,* 508–518.

Tricomi, E., Rangel, A., Camerer, C. F., & O'Doherty, J. P. (2010). Neural evidence for inequality-averse social preferences. *Nature, 463,* 1089–1091.

van den Bos, W. McClure, S. M., Harris, L. T., Fiske, S., T., & Cohen, J. (2007). Dissociating affective evaluation and social cognitive processes in the ventral medial prefrontal cortex. *Cognitive, Affective & Behavioral Neuroscience, 7,* 337–346.

Way, B. M., Taylor, S. E., & Eisenberger, N. I. (2009). Variation in the mu-opioid receptor gene (*OPRM1*) is associated with dispositional and neural sensitivity to social rejection. *Proceedings of the National Academy of Sciences U S A, 106,* 15079–15084

Young, L. J., & Wang, Z. (2004). The neurobiology of pair bonding. *Nature Neuroscience, 7,* 1048–1054.

The Neural Underpinnings of the Experience of Empathy: Lessons for Psychopathy

Jean Decety and Laurie R. Skelly

Abstract

Empathy is thought to play a key role in motivating prosocial behavior, guiding our preferences and behavioral responses, and providing the affective and motivational base for moral development. While this socioemotional ability has traditionally been examined using behavioral methods, recent work in affective neuroscience has begun to shed light on the neural circuitry within the amygdala, insula and orbitofrontal cortex that instantiates it. This chapter critically examines the current knowledge in affective neuroscience, including theory of mind, and provides an integrative and comprehensive view of the neurocomputational mechanisms that underlie interpersonal sensitivity. Also addressed is emotion-processing dysfunction in individuals with psychopathy and how this can account for their lack of empathy and callous disregard for the welfare of others.

Key Words: empathy, theory of mind, affective neuroscience, amygdala, insula, orbitofrontal cortex, neural circuitry

Introduction

A fundamental assumption of emotion theory is that emotion is an adaptive orienting system that evolved to guide behavior. Emotion is also, however, an interpersonal communication system that elicits response from others. Thus, emotions can be viewed as both intrapersonal and interpersonal states, and the construct of empathy is embedded in both of these dimensions. Empathy and sympathy (or concern for another's well-being), a related concept, play crucial roles in much of human social interaction and are necessary components for healthy coexistence. Sympathy is thought to be a conduit for prosocial behavior, guiding our preferences and behavioral responses and providing the affective and motivational base for moral development. Empathy is such a necessary component of healthy coexistence that its absence leads to serious social-cognitive dysfunctions. Empathy is known to inhibit aggressive behavior. Among the various psychopathologies marked by such deficits, the impact of the lack of empathy is most central to psychopathy (Hare, 1991; Mahmut, Homewood, & Stevenson, 2008). Thus better knowledge of the neural circuits that instantiate the experience of empathy will not only advance our understanding of interpersonal sensitivity in general but also shed light on the basic neural and cognitive mechanisms of emotion processing and their relation to cognition and motivation (i.e., empathic concern), individual differences in personality traits, and mental health.

The goal of this chapter is to critically examine our current knowledge about the neurophysiological underpinnings of empathy in humans. First we will clarify some definitional issues of empathy and associated phenomena. We argue that the construct of empathy needs to be decomposed in a model that includes the bottom-up processing of affective communication and top-down processing in which the perceiver's motivation, intentions, and self-regulation influence the sequelae of an empathic experience. Next, we critically review the empirical evidence that supports the notion of shared neural circuits for the generation of emotion and perception of emotion in others. We emphasize recent functional neuroimaging studies of empathy for pain that show a partial overlap in the neural circuits underlying the firsthand experience of pain and the observation of pain in others and how some interpersonal variables modulate empathic mimicry and sympathetic concern. We will briefly evaluate whether emotional disturbances observed in brain-damaged patients support the shared neural-circuit account of empathy. Finally, we address emotion-processing disorders in individuals with psychopathy and discuss how these can account for their lack of empathy and callous disregard for the welfare of others.

Empathy and Associated Phenomena

The term *empathy* is applied to various phenomena that cover a broad spectrum, ranging from feeling concern for other people that creates a motivation to help them, to experiencing emotions that match another individual's emotions, to knowing what another is thinking or feeling, to blurring the line between self and other (Decety, 2011; Hodges & Klein, 2001). These phenomena are related to one another, but they do not comprise one single thing that is "empathy," as one might say that an socioemotional ability consists of cognitive, affective, and behavioral components (Batson, 2009). Given this variety of phenomena, it is not surprising that philosophers and psychologists have long debated the nature of empathy. In developmental psychology and social psychology (the two academic disciplines that have produced most of the research on the subject), empathy is generally defined as an affective response stemming from the understanding of another's emotional state or condition, similar to what the other person is feeling or would be expected to feel in the given situation (Eisenberg, Shea, Carlo, & Knight, 1991). Other theorists more narrowly characterize empathy as one specific set of congruent emotions—those feelings that are more other-focused than self-focused (Batson, Fultz, & Schoenrade, 1987). Very often, empathy and sympathy are conflated. Here, we distinguish between *empathy* (the capacity to appreciate the emotions and feelings of others with a minimal distinction between self and other) and *sympathy* (feelings of

concern about the welfare of others). While empathy and sympathy are often confused, the two can be dissociated: although sympathy may stem from the apprehension of another's emotional state, it does not have to be congruent with the affective state of the other. The experience of empathy can lead to disparate outcomes: to empathic concern or sympathy, which includes an other-oriented motivation promoting helping or prosocial behavior, or to personal distress, an egoistic motivation to reduce stress by withdrawing from the stressor, thereby decreasing the likelihood of prosocial behavior.

Given the complexity of the phenomenological experience of empathy, investigation of its neurobiological underpinnings would be futile without first breaking down this construct into component processes. No psychological phenomena map in a one-to-one fashion onto some simple underlying neural substrate. Empathy, like other social cognitive processes, draws on a large array of brain structures and systems, including the cortex, the autonomic nervous system, hypothalamic–pituitary–adrenal axis (HPA), and endocrine systems—the entire gamut of systems that regulate bodily states, emotion, and reactivity. In the contemporary affective neuroscience literature, empathy is most often represented as a function of cortical processing. However, the underlying neurophysiological mechanisms necessary for the expression of empathy are shared with neurobiological systems instantiating emotionality in general, as well as sociality, attachment, and caring, which are dependent on lower brain structures, such as the brainstem, hypothalamus, and the autonomic nervous system (Decety, 2011).

Components of Empathy

Several scholars have argued that empathy includes both cognitive and affective components (Decety & Jackson, 2004; Eisenberg & Eggum, 2009; Hodges & Wegner, 1997; Roth-Hanania, Davidov, & Zahn-Waxler, 2011). Based on evidence from affective neuroscience and developmental psychology, Decety and collaborators (Decety, 2005, 2007; Decety & Meyer, 2008; Decety & Moriguchi, 2007) proposed a model that includes bottom-up processing of affective input and top-down processing in which the perceiver's motivation, intentions, and self-regulation influence the impact of an empathic experience and the likelihood of prosocial behavior. Under that working model, a number of distinct and interacting components contribute to the experience of empathy: (1) affective sharing or empathic arousal, a bottom-up process grounded in emotion perception; (2) the ability to keep apart self and other related representations, which relies on a sense of agency and self- and other-awareness and involves the medial prefrontal cortex (PFC) and temporoparietal junction; and (3) executive functions instantiated in the PFC, which operate as a top-down mediator, helping to understand and regulate emotions and yield mental flexibility. While this model is helpful and has exploratory and predictive value, it remains to be functionally connected with other biological systems implicated in interpersonal sensitivity, such as the autonomic nervous and endocrine systems, to create a comprehensive account of empathy at an organismal level. For instance, oxytocin is a putative mediator of empathy, facilitating social-approach related behaviors (Carter, Harris, & Porges, 2009).

Behavioral evidence indicates that the affective component of empathy develops earlier than the cognitive component. Affective responsiveness is present at an early age, is involuntary, and relies on somatovisceral resonance between other and self. Importantly, the brainstem (with reciprocal connections with the hypothalamus and amygdala), which handles primitive components of emotion and arousal, inborn reflexes such as crying and suckling, and regulation of basic homeostatic functions, is the most highly developed area of the brain at birth (Joseph, 2000). This explains why newborns and young infants become vigorously distressed when another infant begins to cry (Martin & Clark, 1987). Facial mimicry of basic emotional expressions also contributes to affective sharing, and this tendency starts very early in life, by approximately 10 weeks of age (Haviland & Lewica, 1987). The cognitive aspects of empathy are closely related to processes involved in theory of mind (ToM, the capacity to infer the explicit content of others' mental states such as emotions, intentions, and beliefs), executive function (attention, working memory, and inhibitory control), and self-regulation. The regulation of internal emotional states is particularly relevant to the modulation of vicarious emotion and the experience of empathy. Both ToM and emotion regulation tap into executive function resources of the PFC (Zelazo, Carlson, & Kesek, 2008), with different regions (medial and dorsolateral, respectively) subserving these distinct functions (Ochsner & Gross, 2005). The PFC develops more slowly than other brain areas, reaching maturation only late in adolescence (Bunge, Dudukovic, Thomasson, Vaidya, & Gabrieli, 2002). The maturation of the PFC allows children to use verbalizations to achieve

self-regulation of their feelings and to exercise inhibitory control over their thoughts, attention, and action (Diamond, 2002).

Overall, empathy draws on multiple components and neurological systems, which, as they mature, become progressively integrated. This underscores the complexity of the mechanisms underlying the experience of empathy and highlights how a multi-system approach is needed to understand individual differences that contribute to maladaptive socioemotional functioning.

Sharing the Emotions of Others

It has long been argued that empathy involves some form of unconscious resonance with the affective state of another. For instance, Ax proposed in 1964 that empathy can be thought of as a function of the autonomic nervous system in which the state of an observed person is simulated in the observer. Because facial emotional expressions are external manifestations of internal subjective states, empirical work of emotion sharing has largely focused on faces. Behavioral and electromyographic (EMG) studies indicate that viewing facial expressions triggers the viewer to produce similar expressions on their own face, even without conscious recognition of the stimulus (Hatfield, Rapson, & Le, 2009). Furthermore, a number of studies indicate that mimicry can result in the actual experience of the emotion. These findings trace a mechanism through which the observation of an emotion in another person may trigger the experience of the same emotion in the observer; this is described in a strong form as the perception–action model of empathy (Preston & de Waal, 2002). Further, this direct-matching hypothesis fits neatly with simulation models of emotion processing, which propose that our ability to understand the intentions and emotions expressed by others relies on internally simulating the same psychological state in ourselves (Goldman & Sripada, 2005).

Does mimicry actually facilitate emotional understanding? One study examined the relationship between facial mimicry (measured by facial EMG) and self-reported mood, upon exposure to static facial expressions of anger and happiness, in participants categorized as either high or low empathizers. The study found that the high-empathy participants produced greater facial mimicry than that of the low-empathy participants (Sonnby-Borgstrom, Jonsson, & Svensson, 2003). However, another study did not find any relation between emotion recognition performance and participants' tendency to mimic dynamic displays of emotions (Hess & Blairy, 2001). Selective facial EMG responses were detected in participants presented with computer-generated clips of morphed happy and angry facial expressions, but there was no correlation between the intensity of facial mimicry and dispositional empathy (Achaibou, Pourtois, Schwartz, & Vuilleumier, 2008). However, this finding may be due to task demands, since facial mimicry of video expressions of pain is detected only when subjects adopt an imagine-self perspective but not when they imagine that the pain occurred to another person (Lamm, Porges, Cacioppo, & Decety, 2008).

Importantly, there is little evidence to support the notion that individuals attribute the specific emotion they are feeling to the facial expression of their interaction partners. For example, one study investigated whether emotion recognition accuracy is associated with either facial mimicry, shared affect, or both (Blairy, Herrera, & Hess, 1999). The results confirmed that observers spontaneously mimic facial expressions and that the decoding of facial expressions is accompanied by shared affect. However, no evidence was found that emotion recognition accuracy or shared affects are mediated by mimicry, whether spontaneous or voluntary. What research suggests instead is that mimicry may lead to empathy and prosocial behavior via the associated increase in similarity—it fosters feelings of rapport between interaction partners and not via an increase in understanding of the other's emotional state (Hess, Philippot, & Blairy, 1999). Furthermore, affiliation between two interacting partners is moderated by the situational similarity of the affiliate, regardless of the emotional reaction of the affiliate (Gump & Kulik, 1997). These results are also consistent with other empirical research showing that facial movements alone carry simple affective information (whether the face should be approached or avoided), which is insufficient for perception of emotion, and context needs to be conjointly encoded to make more specific inference about an individual's emotion (Barrett & Kensinger, 2010).

For empathy to be fueled by a perceptual linking of self and other, the observation of an emotion in others must produce not only mimicry but also the experience of that emotion. In a well-known experiment, participants were instructed to produce facial configurations of basic emotions while heart rate, skin conductance, finger temperature, and somatic activity were monitored (Levenson, Ekman, & Friesen, 1990). Results showed that this voluntary facial activity produced significant levels of subjective experience of the associated emotions as well as specific and reliable autonomic measures. It is worth noting, however, that these results have not been reproduced, and a series of meta-analyses conducted by Cacioppo and colleagues (Cacioppo, Bernston, Larsen, Poehlmann, & Ito, 2000) indicated that even a limited set of discrete emotions such as happiness, sadness, anger, and disgust cannot be fully differentiated through visceral activity alone. The only consistent result is that negative emotions are associated with stronger autonomic nervous system responses than are the positive emotions.

Another physiological pathway that may account for the sharing of emotion is via the activation of facial feedback. The facial feedback hypothesis suggests that the control of facial expression produces parallel effects on subjective feelings. One study used functional imaging to compare brain activity during imitation of angry and sad expressions in groups who either did or did not receive BOTOX injections (Hennenlotter et al., 2009). The researchers found that during intentional imitation of anger, BOTOX decreased activity in the amygdala and its functional coupling with brainstem nuclei involved in autonomic control. Another study investigated the relationship between facial expression and emotional experience by comparing participants' self-reports of emotional experience before and after they had received one of two types of cosmetic facial injections used to treat facial wrinkles (Davis, Senghas, Brant, & Ochsner, 2010). One group received injections of BOTOX. The second group received injections of Restylane, a filler that has no effect on facial muscles. Results do not support strong versions of the facial feedback hypothesis that posit a necessary role for facial feedback in emotional experience, but only an influence in some circumstances. More neurophysiological work is clearly necessary to understand the neural pathways underpinning emotion contagion.

Shared Neural Circuits Between Self and Other

A number of functional neuroimaging studies have demonstrated that imagining emotional experiences from one's own and from someone else's perspective produce similar patterns of brain activation and psychophysiological reactions. For instance, Ruby and Decety (2004) presented participants with short written sentences depicting real-life situations that induce social emotions such as shame, guilt, or pride, (e.g., someone opens the bathroom door that you have forgotten to lock), as well as emotionally neutral situations, and asked them to imagine both how they would feel if they were in those situations and how their mother would feel in those situations. Cortical regions involved in emotional processing, the amygdala and the temporal poles, were similarly activated in the conditions that included emotionally laden situations for both self and other perspectives. Interestingly, interaction between the emotional content and perspective-taking factors led to a cluster in the right somatosensory cortex, which was stronger for the self-perspective.

Another study combined psychophysiology (heart rate and skin conductance) and neuroimaging measurements in participants who were required to imagine (1) a personal experience of fear or anger from their own past; (2) an equivalent experience from another person as if it were happening to them; and (3) a nonemotional experience from the participants' own past (Preston et al., 2007). When participants could relate to the scenario of the other person, they produced patterns of psychophysiological and neuroimaging activation equivalent to those of personal emotional imagery.

Single-pulse transcranial magnetic stimulation (TMS) applied to the right somatosensory cortex during emotion judgment tasks selectively disrupts the recognition of facial expression of fear, but not of happy expressions (Pourtois et al., 2004). Additional support for a role of the somatosensory cortex in emotion recognition comes from a study designed to test whether recognizing facial expressions requires visual processing followed by simulation of the somatovisceral responses associated with the perceived expression. Pitcher and colleagues (Pitcher, Garrigo, Walsh, & Duchaine, 2008) targeted the right occipital face area and the face region of right somatosensory cortex with repetitive transcranial magnetic stimulation (rTMS) while participants discriminated facial expressions. Results demonstrated that rTMS selectively impaired discrimination of facial expressions at both sites but had no effect on a face identity task.

It remains controversial whether the emotion-sharing mechanism requires involvement of the so-called mirror-neuron system in humans. Mirror neurons are a unique class of cells with sensorimotor properties that were first identified in monkey ventral premotor cortex (Gallese, Fadiga, Fogassi, & Rizzolatti, 1996). To date, evidence for mirror neurons in humans is indirect, given the technological difficulties of studying individual cells in behaving humans. Such evidence relies principally on functional neuroimaging studies that report overlapping activation between action observation and execution in regions where mirror neurons have been found in monkey homologues. These regions most frequently include the anterior part of the inferior frontal gyrus and the ventral premotor cortex, but also the anterior and posterior intraparietal sulcus and an area in the lateral occipital cortex (e.g., Dinstein, Hasson, Rubin, & Heeger, 2007). Further support for human mirror neuron activity comes from TMS studies, which have demonstrated changes in the excitability of the observer's motor and premotor cortices during action observation (e.g., Fadiga, Fogassi, Pavesi, & Rizzolatti, 1995) and impairment of motor facilitation effects after repetitive TMS to the premotor or somatosensory cortices (Catmur, Walsh, & Heyes, 2007). Similarly, magnetoencephalography (MEG) and electroencephalographic measurements have demonstrated suppression in the mu rhythm (8–13 Hz) over the sensorimotor cortex during observation of action that parallels the changes detected during action production (Cheng, Yang, Lin, Lee, & Decety, 2008). This mu rhythm could reflect downstream modulation of primary sensorimotor areas by mirror neuron activity, representing a critical information-processing function translating perception into action (Pineda, 2005). Recent meta-analyses, however, disagree on the location of putative mirror neurons in the human frontal cortex (Molenberghs, Cunnington, & Mattingley, 2009; Morin & Grèzes, 2008). A study using the asymmetric functional magnetic resonance imaging (fMRI) adaptation paradigm failed to reveal evidence for mirror neurons in humans at all (Lingnau, Gesierich, & Caramazza, 2009).

Although mirror neurons were first posited to be involved mainly in action understanding and imitation, many higher functions have been attributed to mirror neurons, including empathy and theory of mind. Studies have reported activation in the inferior frontal gyrus during the observation and imitation of facial expressions of emotions (e.g., Carr, Iacoboni, Dubeau, Mazziotta, & Lenzi, 2003). In one paradigm, subjects had to observe and imitate film clips of hand and face actions (Leslie, Johnson-Frey, & Grafton, 2004). The right ventral premotor cortex was commonly activated during observation and imitation of facial expressions. A more recent study demonstrated that even passive viewing of facial expressions activates a wide network of brain regions that are also involved in the execution of similar expressions, including the inferior frontal gyrus (IFG) and the posterior parietal cortex (van der Gaag, Minderaa, & Keysers, 2007). However, the majority of functional neuroimaging studies do not report activation of the IFG or other mirror neuron areas during the perception of facial expression of emotion (see Phan, Wager, Taylor, & Liberzon, 2002). For instance, Chakrabarti, Bullmore, and Baron-Cohen (2006) presented participants with video clips depicting happy, sad, angry and disgusted facial expressions. Activation of the left pars opercularis was seen during the viewing of happy faces, but no other activation was found in putative mirror neuron sites for other emotions.

More importantly, a fine conceptual analysis of empirical research on mirror neurons and their putative contribution to theory of mind concluded that motor resonance is neither necessary nor a sufficient mechanism for representing another individual's intentions, especially in a social context (Jacob, 2008). This argument relies on a hierarchical structure of intentionality, which distinguishes motor intention (or motor command) and prior intention. According to this view, motor resonance could at best generate a representation of an individual's motor intention, but not of his or her prior social and motivational intention. In addition, the recent discovery of mirror neurons in the primary motor cortex has prompted the argument that such cells may be best interpreted as motor system facilitators, acting via learned associations (Hickok, 2009). A similar view suggests that mirror neurons are formed in the course of individual development and via the same learning process that produces Pavlovian conditioning (Heyes, 2010).

To sum up, there is some solid evidence that shared neural substrates mediate both the experience and perception of emotion, in which the right somatosensory cortex seems to play a role (Heberlein & Atkinson, 2009). Importantly, though, shared neural circuits need not be synonymous with mirror neurons. Key questions remain largely unexplored in the simulation model of emotion recognition, such as whether specific emotions are processed by distinct neural mechanisms or a common circuit, and the extent to which emotion perception/sharing and emotion experience elicit similar or different brain responses. After all, such divergence is well known to exist in the behavioral sequelae following emotion perception and emotion experience; the perception of anger may elicit either approach or withdrawal tendencies in the observer, while the experience of anger is more likely to motivate approach toward the individual at which one is angry (Carver & Harmon-Jones, 2009).

Witnessing Others in Pain

Pain is a subjective experience triggered by the activation of a mental and neural representation of actual or potential tissue damage. This representation involves somatic sensory features, as well as affective-motivational reactions associated with the promotion of protective or recuperative visceromotor and behavioral responses. It is the affective experience of pain that signals an aversive state and motivates behavior to terminate, reduce, or escape exposure to the source of noxious stimulation (Price, 2000). The expression of pain also provides a crucial signal that can motivate soothing and caring behaviors in others. It is therefore a valuable and ecologically valid means to investigate the mechanisms underlying the experience of empathy.

The origin of empathy, evolutionarily, likely stems from the adaptive development of sensitivity to distress cues in mammalian young (Haidt, & Grahan, 2007), combined with motivation to care for offspring (Decety, 2011). This sensitivity came to extend beyond the mother–child relationship, such that normally developed individuals of many mammalian species are distressed by the suffering of others. For instance, rats that press a lever to obtain food stop doing so if their action is paired with the delivery of an electrical shock to a visible neighboring rat (Church, 1959). To investigate whether such pain related behavior can serve the function of soliciting social approach, Langford and colleagues (2010) tested test mice in various dyadic or triadic conditions, including "jailed" mice—some in pain via intraperitoneal injection of acetic acid—and test mice free to approach or avoid the jailed mice. Results showed a sex-specific effect whereby female, but not male, test mice approached a familiar same-sex conspecific in pain more frequently than an unaffected familiar conspecific or an unfamiliar but affected conspecific. Furthermore, the frequency of contact by the test mouse was negatively correlated with the pain behavior of the jailed mouse, which suggests that proximity of a familiar unaffected conspecific may have analgesic properties.

A growing body of research demonstrates shared neural mechanisms between the firsthand experience of pain and the perception of pain in others. In the first fMRI experiment on shared perception of pain, study participants were scanned during a condition of feeling a moderately painful pinprick stimulus to the fingertips and during another condition in which they watched another person's hand undergo similar stimulation (Morrison, Lloyd, di Pellegrino, & Roberts, 2004). Both conditions resulted in common hemodynamic activity in a pain-related area in the right dorsal anterior cingulate cortex (ACC). In contrast, the primary somatosensory cortex showed significant activations in response to noxious tactile (first person), but not visual (third person), stimuli. Another fMRI study demonstrated that the dorsal ACC, particularly the anterior midcingulate cortex (aMCC), the anterior insula (aINS), cerebellum, and brainstem, were activated when healthy participants experienced a painful stimulus, as well as when they observed a signal indicating that another person was receiving a similar stimulus. However, only the actual experience of pain resulted in activation in the somatosensory cortex and a more ventral region of the ACC (Singer et al., 2004). These findings were supported by two fMRI studies in which participants were shown still photographs depicting right hands and feet in painful or neutral everyday-life situations and then asked to imagine the level of pain that these situations would produce (Jackson, Brunet, Meltzoff & Decety, 2006; Jackson, Meltzoff, & Decety, 2005). Significant activation in regions involved in the affective aspects of pain processing, notably the aMCC, thalamus, and aINS, was detected. Unlike the first neuroimaging studies of pain empathy mentioned above, more recent functional MRI and MEG investigations have reported significant signal change in the somatosensory cortex/posterior insula, a region involved in the sensory discriminative dimension of pain (Akitsuki & Decety, 2009; Benuzzi, Lui, Duzzi, Nichelli, & Porro, 2008; Cheng et al., 2007, 2008; Decety & Michalska, 2010; Lamm, Meltzoff, & Decety, 2010; Moriguchi et al., 2007). Another recent study found that, compared to control stimuli (laughing and snoring), pain-related exclamations elicited increased activation in the superior and temporal gyri, insula, thalamus, and somatosensory cortices (Lang, Yu, Markl, Muller, & Kotchoubey, 2011). Overall, these results fit well with the perception–action coupling mechanism that underlies affective arousal and somatovisceral resonance between other and self.

Facial expressions of pain constitute an important category of facial expression that is readily understood by observers. One study investigated the neural response to pain expressions by performing functional MRI as subjects viewed short video sequences showing faces expressing either moderate pain or, for comparison, no pain (Botvinick et al.,

2005). In alternate blocks, the same subjects received both painful and nonpainful thermal stimulation. Facial expressions of pain were found to engage cortical areas also engaged by the firsthand experience of pain, including the anterior cingulate cortex and anterior insula. Similarly, Lamm, Baston, and Decety (2007) exposed study participants to videos of individuals expressing pain from listening to painful sounds, and also exposed the participants to the same painful sounds in the scanner. Overlapping activation between firsthand experience of pain and secondhand perception of pain in others was found in the aMCC, SMA, aINS, amygdala, and periaqueductal gray (PAG).

Most neuroimaging studies that have explored the overlap in brain response between the observation of behavior performed by others and the generation of the same behavior in self have used simple subtraction methods and generally have highlighted the commonalities between self and other processing and ignored the differences. This is particularly true for the series of fMRI studies reporting shared neural circuits for the firsthand experience of pain and the perception of pain in others (see Jackson, Rainville, & Decety, 2006). As argued by Zaki, Ochsner, Hanelin, Wager, and Mackey (2007), it is possible that common activity in the ACC and aINS reflects the operation of distinct but overlapping networks of regions that support perception of self or others' pain. To address this issue, the authors scanned participants while they received noxious thermal stimulation (self pain condition) or watched short videos of other people sustaining painful injuries (other pain condition). Analyses identified areas whose activity covaried with ACC and AI activity during self or other pain, either across time (intraindividual connectivity) or across participants (interindividual connectivity). Both connectivity analyses identified clusters in the midbrain and PAG with greater connectivity to the aINS during self-pain than during other pain. The opposite pattern was found in the dorsal medial PFC, which showed greater connectivity to the ACC and aINS during other pain than during self-pain, using both types of analysis. Intraindividual connectivity analyses also revealed regions in the superior temporal sulcus, posterior cingulate, and precuneus that became more connected to ACC during other pain than during self-pain. The results of this experiment document distinct neural networks associated with the ACC and aINS in response to firsthand experience of pain and to seeing other people in pain. These networks could not have been detected in prior work that examined overlap between self and other pain in terms of average activity but not connectivity.

Individual subject analyses in generic space similarly indicate that distinct neural networks in anterior and medial cingulate cortex (aMCC) are activated during firsthand but not secondhand experience of pain (Morrison & Downing, 2007). This is in line with a quantitative meta-analysis of studies on empathy for pain and pain in the self, using activation likelihood estimation (Decety & Lamm, 2009). This analysis revealed distinct subclusters in both ACC/aMCC and the insula. While activation in aMCC seems to be more left-lateralized, caudal, and dorsal during empathy for pain, a rostrocaudal activation gradient is evident in the insular cortex. These distinct activation patterns suggest the involvement of only partially overlapping neural subpopulations and indicate the involvement of distinct cognitive and affective processes.

Two nodes of this network play specific and distinctive roles in processing affective information. The aMCC is a functional and anatomical hub linking networks for negative affect, pain, and goal-directed behavior (Shackman et al., 2011), whereas the anterior insula is polysensory cortex involved in mapping internal states of bodily and subjective feeling and plays a crucial role in emotional awareness and sharing affective states of others (Craig, 2002). With extensive reciprocal connections with limbic forebrain areas, it is the most consistently and robustly activated region across all studies of empathy, even when there is no explicit cognitive demand to empathize with another individual (Gu et al., 2010).

Thus, current neurophysiological evidence indicates that perceiving, hearing, or imagining another individual in distress is associated with hemodynamic responses in the neural network processing the motivational-affective and the sensory dimensions of pain in oneself. This response is thought to reflect an aversive response in the observer, which may bring discomfort and act as a trigger to inhibit aggression or prompt motivation to help or care for the other.

Effect of Brain Lesions on Empathy

Supporting evidence for a role of the somatosensory cortex in emotion processing is provided by a lesion study in which damage of the right somatosensory cortex (including the anterior supramarginal gyrus) was associated with impaired recognition of facial expressions (Adolphs, Damasio, Tranel, Cooper, Damasio, 2000). This finding is consistent with a shared neural-circuits account of emotion recognition (i.e., we recognize the emotional expressions of others by relying on our own somatosensory representations).

Other neuropsychological observations speak against a shared-circuits interpretation (Heberlein & Atkinson, 2009). For instance, Keillor and colleagues (Keillor, Barrett, Crucian, Kortenkamp, & Heilman, 2002) reported the case of a patient with bilateral facial paralysis who was unable to convey emotions through facial expressions. Despite her complete facial paralysis, she did not show deficits in the experience of emotion or the recognition of facial expressions. Similarly, patients with Moebius syndrome, who suffer from bilateral, usually complete, facial paralysis, have difficulty communicating with facial expression but are not impaired at recognizing facial expressions of emotions of others (Bogart & Matsumoto, 2010; Calder, Keane, Cole, Campbell, & Young, 2000).

Another study of patients with congenital insensitivity to pain found pertinent results. In this rare syndrome, patients cannot rely on mirror-matching mechanisms to understand the pain of others because they have never experienced pain. Despite complete naiveté to the personal experience of pain, the patients showed similar hemodynamic responses to observed pain as those of control subjects in anterior mid cingulate cortex and anterior insula, two key regions of the "shared circuit" for pain in the self and others (Danziger, Faillenot, & Peyron, 2009).

Clinical reports have consistently indicated that acquired damage to the PFC may result in severe impairment in interpersonal behavior, including empathy and concern for others. For instance, a series of studies using the interpersonal reactivity index (IRI) in patients with neurological lesions showed reduced empathy following right hemisphere damage. Empathy was most severely impaired following lesions within the right frontal structures and, most notably, the ventromedial region, underscoring a role for right PFC structures in the mediation of empathy (Shamay-Tsoory, Tomer, Berger, & Aharon-Peretz, 2003; Shamay-Tsoory, Tomer, Berger, Goldsher, & Aharon-Peretz, 2005).

Another study by the same group found a behavioral and anatomical double dissociation between deficits in cognitive empathy (associated with ventromedial lesions) and emotional empathy (associated with lesions of the left inferior frontal gyrus (Shamay-Tsoory, Aharon-Peretz, & Perry, 2009). The pattern of empathy deficits among these patients represents the first direct evidence of a double disso-ciation between emotional and cognitive empathy. However, the fact that the lesion of inferior fron-tal gyrus was in the left hemisphere is at odds with neuroimaging studies of healthy volunteers that have consistently reported right-sided activation of the IFG in perception of emotion (Jabbi & Keysers, 2008; van der Gaag et al., 2007).

Impairment of the medial/cingulate PFC is com-monly associated with deficits in social interaction and self-conscious emotions (Sturm, Rosen, Allison, Miller, & Levenson, 2006). Such patients may become apathetic, disinterested in the environment, and unable to concentrate their attention on behav-ioral and cognitive tasks. It has also been suggested that frontal damage hinders perspective-taking abil-ity, a crucial component of empathic understanding (Price, Daffner, Stowe, & Mesulam, 1990).

Frontotemporal dementia (FTD), a family of conditions involving dramatic social impair-ment resulting from the progressive degeneration of the temporal and frontal lobes, constitutes an important source of knowledge in the relationship between empathy and cognition. Rankin and col-leagues (2006) measured empathy in several groups of patients with dementia. Both FTD and semantic dementia (SD) groups showed significantly lower levels of empathy than patients with Alzheimer's or healthy controls. However, SD patients showed dis-ruption of both emotional and cognitive empathy as measured with self-reports, whereas those with FTD showed only disruption of cognitive empathy (Rankin, Kramer, & Miller, 2005). In a second study by the same group (Rankin et al., 2006), the neuro-anatomical basis of empathy was investigated in 123 patients with FTD, Alzheimer's disease, corticobasal degeneration, and progressive supranuclear palsy, using the same measures of empathy. Subscales for empathic concern and perspective taking were cor-related with structural MRI brain volume using voxel-based morphometry. Across groups, voxels in the right temporal pole, right fusiform gyrus, right caudate, and right subcallosal gyrus correlated sig-nificantly with these scores. Further, empathy cor-related positively with the volume of right temporal structures in semantic dementia and with subcal-losal gyrus volume in frontotemporal dementia. These findings suggest that the right anterior tem-poral and medial frontal regions are essential for real-life empathic behavior.

The study of degenerative neurological diseases has also supplied evidence for relatively distinct routes to social cognition and empathy deficits.

For instance, Snowden et al. (2003) have shown that patients with FTD as well as patients with Huntington's disease (HD), a predominantly sub-cortical disorder characterized by involuntary movements, present with difficulties in social cogni-tion. Interestingly, patients with HD and those with FTD lack sympathy and empathy, but for different reasons: patients with FTD may suffer a breakdown in theory of mind, while patients with HD disease draw faulty inferences from social situations. In HD, therefore, the loss of empathy arises more at an emotional than a cognitive level, whereas FTD patients live in an egocentric world in which they do not ascribe independent mental states to others.

A compatible finding from a voxel-based mor-phometry analysis on FTD patients revealed that atrophy in bilateral temporal lobe and medial orb-itofrontal structures correlated with loss of cognitive empathy and that atrophy to the temporal pole cor-related significantly with loss of emotional empa-thy (Rankin et al., 2005). These findings support distinct neural underpinnings for the cognitive and affective aspects of empathy.

In sum, while neurological studies indicate a critical role of the medial and orbitofrontal cortex in social emotions, including empathy, there is little evidence that lesioning of the regions involved in the mirror neuron system (ventral premotor, motor cortex and anterior IPS) leads to any dysfunction in empathy.

Empathy and Psychopathy

Individuals classified as psychopaths are callous, shallow, and superficial. They often lack fear of pun-ishment and have difficulty regulating their emo-tions, and they do not experience insight into or empathy for the effect that their poor behavior has on others. The involvement of empathic deficits in the antisocial disorders is codified in the definitions of the major constructs used in research on adult antisocial behavior. Psychopathy itself is defined in part by a callous lack of regard for others (Hare, 1999). As such, psychopathy and related disorders serve as a functional lesion model for empathy; insights into the nature of neural deficits in these disorders are invaluable as a complement to other methods of empathy research usually conducted with typically developing individuals. Conversely, advances made in the description of the compo-nent processes and circuits underpinning healthy empathic responses may shed light on potential interventions or treatment options for individuals with these socioemotional disorders.

One theory of the origin of empathic deficits in psychopathy is the failure during development to form stimulus–reinforcement associations connecting harmful or aggressive actions with the pain and distress of others (Glenn & Raine, 2008). Negative reinforcement learning is known to involve the amygdala and the orbitofrontal cortex (OFC), and accordingly, these have become targets of study in the neuroscience of psychopathy. For instance, a study found individuals with psychopathy to have deficits in a gambling task and a reversal learning task used to probe OFC functioning, but no global deficit in attention shifting (Mitchell, Richell, Leonard, & Blair, 2006). Similar results were seen in a behavioral study of reversal learning in adolescents with psychopathic traits (Finger et al., 2008). Psychopathy has also been associated with difficulties in processing some face stimuli, particularly cues of fear and distress (Blair, Herrera, & Hess, 1997) as well as disgust (Kosson, Suchy, Mayer, & Libby, 2002), cues believed to be involved in aversive conditioning of behavior and thought to rely on activation in the amygdala. Adult psychopaths and children with psychopathic tendencies show reduced facilitation for processing emotional words during affective lexical decision tasks (Blair & Blair, 2009), and psychopaths do not show typical patterns of fear-potentiated startle during emotional picture processing (Levenston, Patrick, Bradley, & Lang, 2000). Taken together, these results support the notion of amygdala and OFC abnormality in psychopathy and the role of these structures in the development of abnormal empathic function.

Neuroanatomical models of neural circuits involved in psychopathy consistently hypothesize the involvement of an interconnected network of regions including the dorsolateral PFC and the amygdala (Blair & Blair, 2009). Consistent with this view, patients with focal brain lesions in the medial PFC and OFC, the insula, and the amygdala suffer dysfunctions of social sensitivity and morality, broadly defined (Moll, Zahn, de Oliveira-Souza, & Eslinger, 2003). A relation was found between ventromedial-frontal lesions and higher scores on measures of aggressiveness and violence in Vietnam War veterans (Grafman et al., 1996). Functional imaging studies have demonstrated that healthy inhibition of naturally occurring motivations (such as imagined aggressive or sexual impulses) recruits the activation of OFC and ACC, whereas a lack of inhibition is associated with a decrease in OFC activity (Blair, 2011).

Structural imaging studies support and extend these findings. Individuals diagnosed with antisocial personality disorder have lower prefrontal gray matter volume (but equal white matter) than that in psychiatric, substance abuse, and community-based control groups (Raine, Lenz, Bihrle, LaCasse, & Colletti, 2000). Bilateral areas of atrophy in the frontopolar cortex and OFC have been reported in violent offenders with antisocial personality disorder (Tiihonen et al., 2008). An interesting voxel-based morphometry study that combined the screening version of the Psychopathy Checklist investigated a matched sample of 15 community psychiatric patients with high scores on the Psychopathy Checklist–Screening Version (PCL-SV) and 15 healthy normal volunteers (de Oliveira-Souza et al., 2008). Gray matter reductions were observed in the frontopolar, orbitofrontal, and anterior temporal cortices; superior temporal sulcus; and insula of the patients. Further, the degree of structural abnormalities was significantly related to the severity of the interpersonal and affective dimension of psychopathy. The pattern of gray matter reductions in patients with high psychopathy scores comprised a distributed frontotemporal network, which plays a critical role in moral sensibility and behavior.

Another study was able to distinguish psychopaths from healthy controls on the basis of the integration between pattern recognition methods and gray matter quantification (Sato et al., 2011). In that study, the superior temporal sulcus was identified as a region containing the most relevant information to separate the two groups. This region is involved in different aspects of social cognition, including empathy, moral reasoning, and theory of mind (Decety & Lamm, 2007; Young & Dungan, 2012).

In adolescents with conduct disorder (CD), a voxel-based morphometry study found a significant reduction of gray matter in the aINS and left amygdala (Sterzer, Stadler, Poustka, & Kleinschmidt, 2007). Moreover, the aINS gray matter volume in CD correlated significantly with empathy scores on self-report questionnaires. These findings underscore the critical role of the insula in empathy, supporting research highlighting this area for empathic responses to others in pain and for general emotional functioning (Craig, 2002). A functional imaging study of youth with aggressive CD found increased activation in the striatum and amygdala when the adolescents watched people being intentionally hurt by others (Decety, Michalska, Akitsuki, & Lahey, 2009). The extent of amygdala activation to viewing pain in others was significantly correlated in a positive direction to their number of aggressive acts and their ratings of daring and sadism scores.

These findings would be consistent with at least two different hypotheses that should be tested in future studies. The first hypothesis is that highly aggressive antisocial youth may enjoy seeing their victims in pain and, because of their diminished PFC/amygdala connectivity, may not effectively regulate this positively reinforced aggressive behavior. Increased activity in the amygdala, particularly when coupled with activation in the striatum, may reflect a general arousing effect of reward (Murray, 2007).

The second hypothesis is that youth with CD have a lower threshold for responding to many situations with negative affect, including viewing pain in others, and are less able to regulate these negative emotions through cortical inhibition. Many studies indicate that individuals with CD tend to respond to aversive stimuli with greater negative affect than most other youth (Lahey & Waldman, 2003). This finding is potentially important, as their negative affect may increase the likelihood of aggression, especially in the absence of effective emotion regulation (Berkowitz, 1993). This interpretation fits well with the hypothesis of dysfunction in the neural circuitry of emotion regulation (Davidson, Putnam, & Larson, 2000) and is consistent with the analyses of effective PFC/amygdala connectivity. Two recent fMRI studies have reported that adolescents with disruptive psychopathic traits show reduced activity to increasing perceived pain intensity within structures typically implicated in affective responses to others' pain, including the rostral anterior cingulate cortex, insula and amygdala (Marsh et al. 2013). Another study also found reduced neural response to others' physical pain in children with conduct problems in the insula (Lockwood et al 2013).

As research proceeds toward the understanding of the neurophysiological contributions to psychopathy and related disorders, certain distinctions and considerations become crucial, as highlighted in a recent review by Koenigs and colleagues (Koenigs, Baskin-Sommers, Zeier, & Newman, 2011). For instance, while individuals with psychopathy and antisocial personality disorder and youth and adolescents with CD have many shared characteristics, these are overlapping but distinct constructs that may have identical or divergent neural origins. Within psychopathy itself, due care must be given to study design to ensure that proper groups are used as controls, with an eye to the fact that psychopaths

do not form a distinct taxon but are outliers along a continuum (Edens, Marcus, Lilienfeld, & Poythress, 2006). Factors and subtypes within psychopathy may also reflect distinct sources of aberrant neurological function.

One recent fMRI study (Decety, Skelly, & Kiehl, 2013) investigated brain responses in incarcerated males to dynamic visual stimuli depicting people injuring one another. The men were classified high and low in psychopathy using the Psychopathy Check List–Revised (PCLR). Inmates with high Psychopathy exhibited significantly less activation in the ventromedial prefrontal cortex, lateral orbitofrontal cortex, and periaqueductal gray relative to controls, but surprisingly showed greater activation in the insula. The major difference in brain response between psychopaths compared to incarcerated controls during the perception of others in pain was a reduced response in the brainstem and OFC/vmPFC, which was negatively associated with their severity on the PCL-R.

To sum up, individuals with psychopathic and/or antisocial tendencies have abnormal emotional processing, particularly in relation to distress and negative arousal cues, and these deficits are likely related to dysfunction within and among regions such as the OFC and amygdala, as commonly hypothesized, and also the anterior insula, which is uniquely situated to implement one's subjective awareness of one's own and others' affective states. The sharing of vicarious negative arousal provides a strong signal that can promote empathic concern. To be motivated to help another, one needs to be affectively, empathically aroused and needs to anticipate the cessation of mutually experienced personal distress. Such a signal may be lacking in psychopathic individuals, who exhibit weaker psychophysiological reactions to emotional stimuli and poor passive avoidance learning. Future studies should aim to elucidate whether these circuits are related primarily to behavior control and thus common to all antisocial disorders, or whether they are more aligned with the emotional processing deficits seen only in psychopathy and thus the impact of structural and functional differences seen in other brain areas.

Conclusion

Given the importance of empathy for human social interaction, it is not surprising that so many studies in affective neuroscience have explored facets of this construct. Much of this new work relies on functional neuroimaging studies that investigate the perception of a restricted number of primary facial expressions of emotions, such as disgust or fear, and pain (typically devoid of any social context). The combined results of these studies demonstrate a partial overlap between the neural regions involved in recognizing emotion and those involved in one's own emotional experience. In the case of pain, when individuals perceive or imagine others in painful or distressful situations, the pain matrix is activated to a great extent, and this activation can include the somatosensory cortex.

Such a shared neural mechanism offers an interesting foundation for intersubjectivity because it provides a functional bridge between first-person information and third-person information, is grounded in self–other equivalence (Decety & Sommerville, 2003), allows analogical reasoning, and offers a possible, yet incomplete, route to understanding the minds of others. However, while the capacity for two people to resonate with each other emotionally, prior to any cognitive understanding, is the basis for developing shared emotional meaning, it is not enough for mature empathic understanding. Such an understanding requires the forming of an explicit representation of the feelings of another person, an intentional agent, which necessitates additional computational mechanisms beyond the emotion-sharing level, as well as self-regulation to modulate negative arousal in the observer (Decety, Michalska, & Akitsuki, 2008; Decety & Moriguchi, 2007). In order to appreciate the emotions and feelings of others in relation to oneself, second-order representations of the other need to be available to awareness without confusion between self and other. This necessitates a decoupling computational mechanism between first-person and second-person information, for which the medial and ventromedial prefrontal cortices play crucial roles (Decety & Jackson, 2004). These representations become more abstract as we move forward, such that the most anterior region of the medial PFC is associated with metacognitive representations that enable us to reflect on the values linked to outcomes and actions (Amodio & Frith, 2006). This idea is strongly supported by lesion studies that consistently document the critical role of the OFC in empathy and emotion understanding. Direct evidence for the implication of the medial PFC in accurate identification of interpersonal emotional states was documented in a study in which adults participants were requested to rate how they believe target persons felt while talking about autobiographical emotional events (Zaki, Weber, Bolger, & Ochsner, 2009).

Whether the sharing of neural circuits really supports a simulationist model of emotion recognition remains an open question. There is little evidence for brain circuits that are selectively implicated in particular emotions, a key element for the theory of simulation. The current neurophysiological data are also compatible with the model of core affects (Barrett & Wager, 2006), which conceptualizes emotion states as the interaction of two orthogonal dimensions (valence and arousal). For instance, the neural circuit associated with the perception of pain in others (aMCC, aINS, PAG, and somatosensory cortex) may have more to do with the activation of the processing of threat-related (i.e., negative) information, which may trigger aversive or even defensive behavior. The aMCC works together with the SMA during pain observation to recognize the aversive nature of the event, to mount an appropriate motor response, and to modulate this response according to prevailing task constraints (Morrison, Peelen, & Downing, 2007). The SMA, as a result of feedback from the limbic system, represents one anatomical substrate for activating the motor response associated with danger and threats (Oliveri et al., 2003).

Breaking down empathy and related phenomena into component processes is also beneficial in the exploration of psychiatric conditions of disordered or abnormal emotional processing, such as psychopathy, antisocial personality disorder, or conduct disorder in children (Blair & Blair, 2009; Decety et al., 2009; Decety & Moriguchi, 2007). Trying to understand impairments of empathy and their related behaviors requires an examination of development, hormones and physiology, brain structure and function, behavior, personality, and social context. By focusing on fundamental mechanisms of the brain and behavior rather than on discrete psychiatric disorders, we can gain insights into therapeutic interventions that may be applied to a range of disorders. This fundamental approach may offer the biggest payoff in the final analysis.

Acknowledgement

The writing of this chapter was supported by a grant (#BCS-0718480) from the National Science Foundation and a grant from the John Templeton Foundation.

References

Achaibou, A., Pourtois, G., Schwartz, S., & Vuilleumier, P. (2008). Simultaneous recording of EEG and facial muscle reactions during spontaneous emotion mimicry. *Neuropsychologia, 46,* 1104–1113.

Adolphs, R., Damasio, H., Tranel, D., Cooper, G., & Damasio, A. R. (2000). A role for somatosensory cortices in the visual recognition of emotion as revealed by three-dimensional lesion mapping. *Journal of Neuroscience, 20,* 2683–2690.

Akitsuki, Y., & Decety, J. (2009). Social context and perceived agency modulate brain activity in the neural circuits underpinning empathy for pain: An event-related fMRI study. *Neuroimage, 47,* 722–734.

Amodio, D. M., & Frith, C. D. (2006). Meeting of minds: The medial frontal cortex and social cognition. *Nature Reviews in Neuroscience, 7,* 268–277.

Ax, A. F. (1964). Goals and methods of psychophysiology. *Psychophysiology, 62,* 8–25.

Barrett, L. F., & Kensinger, E. A. (2010). Context is routinely encoded during emotion perception. *Psychological Science, 21,* 595–599.

Barrett, L. F., & Wager, T. D. (2006). The structure of emotion. *Current Directions in Psychological Science, 15,* 79–83.

Batson, C. D. (2009). These things called empathy: Eight related but distinct phenomena. In J. Decety & W. Ickes (Eds.), *The Social Neuroscience of Empathy* (pp. 3–15). Cambridge, MA: MIT Press.

Batson, C. D., Fultz, J., & Schoenrade, P. (1987). Distress and empathy: Two qualitatively distinct vicarious emotions with different motivational consequences. *Journal of Personality, 55,* 19–39.

Benuzzi, F., Lui, F., Duzzi, D., Nichelli, P. F., & Porro, C. A. (2008). Does it look painful or disgusting? Ask your parietal and cingulate cortex. *Journal of Neuroscience, 28,* 923–931.

Berkowitz, L. (1993). Pain and aggression: Some findings and implications. *Motivation and Emotion, 17,* 277–293.

Blair, R. J. R. (2011). Psychopathy from the perspective of social and cognitive neuroscience. In J. Decety & J. T. Cacioppo (Eds.), *The Oxford Handbook of Social Neuroscience* (pp. 895–905). New York: Oxford University Press.

Blair, R. J. R., & Blair, K. S. (2009). Empathy, morality, and social convention: Evidence from the study of psychopathy and other psychiatric disorders. In J. Decety & W. Ickes (Eds.), *The Social Neuroscience of Empathy* (pp. 139–152). Cambridge, MA: MIT Press.

Blair, R. J. R., Jones, L., Clark, F., & Smith, M. (1997). The psychopathic individual: A lack of responsiveness to distress cues? *Psychophysiology, 342,* 192–198.

Blairy, S., Herrera, P., & Hess, U. (1999). Mimicry and the judgment of emotional facial expressions. *Journal of Nonverbal Behavior, 23,* 5–41.

Bogart, K. R., & Matsumoto, D. (2010). Facial mimicry is not necessary to recognize emotion: Facial expression recognition by people with Moebius syndrome. *Social Neuroscience, 5,* 241–251.

Botvinick, M., Jha, A. P., Bylsma, L. M., Fabian, S. A., Solomon, P. E., & Prkachin, K. M. (2005). Viewing facial expressions of pain engages cortical areas involved in the direct experience of pain. *Neuroimage, 25,* 312–319.

Bunge, S. A., Dudukovic, N. M., Thomasson, M. E., Vaidya, C. J., & Gabrieli, J. D. E. (2002). Immature frontal lobe contributions to cognitive control in children: Evidence from fMRI. *Neuron, 33,* 301–311.

Cacioppo, J. T., Berntson, G., Larsen, J., Poehlmann, K. M., & Ito, T. A. (2000). Psychophysiology of emotion. In M. Lewis & J. M. Haviland (Eds.), *Handbook of Emotions* (pp. 173–190). New York: Guilford Press.

Calder, A., J., Keane, J., Cole, J., Campbell, R., & Young, A. W. (2000). Facial expression recognition by people with Möbius syndrome. *Cognitive Neuropsychology, 17,* 73–87.

Carr, L., Iacoboni, M., Dubeau, M. C., Mazziotta, J. C., & Lenzi, G. L. (2003). Neural mechanisms of empathy in humans: A relay from neural systems for imitation to limbic areas. *Proceedings of the National Academy of Sciences U S A, 100,* 5497–5502.

Carter, S. S., Harris, J., & Porges, S. W. (2009). Neural and evolutionary perspectives on empathy. In J. Decety & W. Ickes (2009), *The Social Neuroscience of Empathy* (pp. 169–182). Cambridge, MA: MIT Press.

Carver, C., & Harmon-Jones, E. (2009). Anger is an approach-related affect: Evidence and implications. *Psychological Bulletin, 135,* 183–204.

Catmur, C., Walsh, V., & Heyes, C. (2007). Sensorimotor learning configures the human mirror system. *Current Biology, 17,* 1527–1531.

Chakrabarti, B., Bullmore, E., & Baron-Cohen, S. (2006). Empathizing with basic emotions: Common and discrete neural substrates. *Social Neuroscience, 1*(3-4), 364–384.

Cheng, Y., Lin, C., Liu, H. L., Hsu, Y., Lim, K., Hung, D., & Decety, J. (2007). Expertise modulates the perception of pain in others. *Current Biology, 17,* 1708–1713.

Cheng, Y., Yang, C. Y., Lin, C. P., Lee, P. R., & Decety, J. (2008). The perception of pain in others suppresses somatosensory oscillations: A magnetoencephalography study. *Neuroimage, 40,* 1833–1840.

Church, R. M. (1959) Emotional reactions of rats to the pain of others. *Journal of Comparative and Physiological Psychology, 52,* 132–134.

Craig, A. D. (2002). How do you feel? Interoception: the sense of the physiological condition of the body. *Nature Reviews Neuroscience, 3,* 655–666.

Danziger, N., Faillenot, I., & Peyron, R. (2009). Can we share a pain we never felt? Neural correlates of empathy in patients with congenital insensitivity to pain. *Neuron, 61,* 203–212.

Davidson, R. J., Putnam, K. M., & Larson, C. L. (2000). Dysfunction in the neural circuitry of emotion regulation—a possible prelude to violence. *Science, 289,* 591–594.

Davis, J. I., Senghas, A., Brandt, F., & Ochsner, K. N. (2010). The effects of BOTOX injections of emotional experience. *Emotion, 10,* 433–440.

Decety, J. (2005). Perspective taking as the royal avenue to empathy. In B. F. Malle & S. D. Hodges (Eds.), *Other Minds: How Humans Bridge the Divide Between Self and Others* (pp. 135–149). New York: Guilford Press.

Decety, J. (2007). A social cognitive neuroscience model of human empathy. In E. Harmon-Jones & P. Winkielman (Eds.), *Social Neuroscience: Integrating Biological and Psychological Explanations of Social Behavior* (pp. 246–270). New York: Guilford Press.

Decety, J. (2011). The neuroevolution of empathy. *Annals of the New York Academy of Sciences, 1231,* 35–45.

Decety, J., & Jackson, P. L. (2004). The functional architecture of human empathy. *Behavioral and Cognitive Neuroscience Reviews, 3,* 71–100.

Decety, J., & Lamm, C. (2007). The role of the right temporoparietal junction in social interaction: How low-level computational processes contribute to meta-cognition. *Neuroscientist, 13,* 580–593.

Decety, J., & Lamm, C. (2009). The biological basis of empathy and intersubjectivity. In J. T. Cacioppo & G. G. Berntson (Eds.), *Handbook of Neuroscience for the Behavioral Science* (pp. 940–957). New York: John Wiley & Sons.

Decety, J., & Meyer, M. (2008). From emotion resonance to empathic understanding: A social developmental neuroscience account. *Development and Psychopathology*, *20*, 1053–1080.

Decety, J., & Michalska, K. J. (2010). Neurodevelopmental changes in the circuits underlying empathy and sympathy from childhood to adulthood. *Developmental Science*, *13*, 886–899.

Decety, J., Michalska, K. J., & Akitsuki, Y. (2008). Who caused the pain? A functional MRI investigation of empathy and intentionality in children. *Neuropsychologia*, *46*, 2607–2614.

Decety, J., Michalska, K. J., Akitsuki, Y., & Lahey, B. (2009). Atypical empathic responses in adolescents with aggressive conduct disorder: A functional MRI investigation. *Biological Psychology*, *80*, 203–211.

Decety, J., & Moriguchi, Y. (2007). The empathic brain and its dysfunction in psychiatric populations: Implications for intervention across different clinical conditions. *Biopsychosocial Medicine*, *1*, 22–65.

Decety, J., Skelly, L., & Kiehl, K. A. (2013). Brain response to empathy-eliciting scenarios involving pain in incarcerated individuals with psychopathy. *JAMA Psychiatry*, epub ahead of print, doi:10.1001/jamapsychiatry.2013.27.

Decety, J., & Sommerville, J. A. (2003). Shared representations between self and others: A social cognitive neuroscience view. *Trends in Cognitive Sciences*, *7*, 527–533.

de Oliveira-Souza, R., Hare, R., Bramati, I. E., Garrido, G. J., Azevedo Ignácio, F., Tovar-Moll, F., & Moll, J. (2008). Psychopathy as a disorder of the moral brain: Fronto-temporo-limbic grey matter reductions demonstrated by voxel based morphometry. *Neuroimage*, *40*, 1202–1213.

Diamond, A. (2002). Normal development of prefrontal cortex from birth to young adulthood: cognitive functions, anatomy, and biochemistry. In D. T. Stuss & R. T. Knight (Eds.), *Principles of Frontal Lobe Function* (pp. 446–503). New York: Oxford University Press.

Dinstein, H., Hasson, U., Rubin, N., & Heeger, D. J. (2007). Brain areas selective for both observed and executed movements. *Journal of Neurophysiology*, *98*, 1415–1427.

Edens, J. F., Marcus, D. K., Lilienfeld, S. O., & Poythress Jr, N. G. (2006) Psychopathic, not psychopath: Taxometric evidence for the dimensional structure of psychopathy. *Journal of Abnormal Psychology*, *115*, 131–144.

Eisenberg, N., & Eggum, N. D. (2009). Empathic responding: Sympathy and personal distress. In J. Decety & W. Ickes (Eds.), *The Social Neuroscience of Empathy* (pp. 71–83). Cambridge, MA: MIT Press.

Eisenberg, N., Shea, C. L., Carlo, G., & Knight, G. P. (1991). Empathy-related responding and cognition: A chicken and the egg dilemma. In W. M. Kurtines (Ed.), *Handbook of Moral Behavior and Development*: Vol. 2. Research (pp. 63–88). Hillsdale, NJ: Lawrence Erlbaum.

Fadiga, L., Fogassi, L., Pavesi, G., & Rizzolatti, G. (1995). Motor facilitation during action observation: A magnetic stimulation study. *Journal of Neurophysiology*, *73*, 2608–2611.

Finger, E. C., Marsh, A. A., Mitchell, D. G. V., Reid, M. E., Sims, C., & Budhani, S. (2008). Abnormal ventromedial prefrontal cortex function in children with psychopathic traits during reversal learning. *Archives of General Psychiatry* *65*, 586–594.

Gallese, V., Fadiga, L., Fogassi, L., & Rizzolatti, G. (1996). Action recognition in the premotor cortex. *Brain*, *119*, 593–609.

Glenn, A. L., & Raine, A. (2008). The neurobiology of psychopathy. *Psychiatric Clinics of North America*, *31*, 463–475.

Goldman, A. I., & Sripada, C. S. (2005). Simulationist models of face-based emotion recognition. *Cognition*, *94*, 193–213.

Grafman, J., Schwab, K., Warden, D., Pridgen, A., Brown, H. R., & Salazar, A. M. (1996). Frontal lobe injuries, violence, and aggression: A report of the Vietnam Head Injury Study. *Neurology*, *46*, 1231–1238.

Gu, X., Liu, X., Guise, K. G., Naidich, T. P., Hof, P. R., & Fan, J. (2010). Functional dissociation of the frontoinsular and anterior cingulate cortices in empathy for pain. *Journal of Neuroscience*, *30*, 3739–3744.

Gump, B. B., & Kulik, J. A. (1997). Stress, affiliation, and emotional contagion. *Journal of Personality and Social Psychology*, *72*, 305–319.

Haidt, J., & Graham, J. (2007). When morality opposes justice: Conservatives have moral intuitions that liberals may not recognize. *Social Justice Research*, *20*, 98–116.

Hare, R. D. (1991). *The Hare Psychopathy Checklist—Revised*. North Tonawanda, NY: Multi-Health Systems.

Hare, R. D. (1999). *Without Conscience: The Disturbing World of the Psychopaths among Us*. New York: Guilford Press.

Hatfield, E., Rapson, R. L., & Le, Y. C. (2009). Emotional contagion and empathy. In J. Decety & W. Ickes (Eds.), *The Social Neuroscience of Empathy* (pp. 19–30). Cambridge, MA: MIT Press.

Haviland, J. M., & Lewica, M. (1987). The induced affect response: Ten-week old infants' responses to three emotion expressions. *Developmental Psychology*, *23*, 97–104.

Heberlein, A. S., & Atkinson, A. P. (2009). Neuroscientific evidence for simulation and shared substrates in emotion recognition: Beyond faces. *Emotion Review*, *1*, 162–177.

Hennenlotter, A., Dresel, C., Castrop, F., Ceballos Baumann, A. O., Wohlschager, A. M., & Haslinger, B. (2009). The link between facial feedback and neural activity within central circuites of emotion—New insights from botulinum toxin-induced denervation of frown muscles. *Cerebral Cortex*, *19*, 537–542.

Hess, U., & Blairy, S. (2001). Facial mimicry and emotional contagion to dynamic emotional facial expressions and their influence on decoding accuracy. *International Journal of Psychophysiology*, *40*, 129–141.

Hess, U., Philippot, P., & Blairy, S. (1999). Mimicry: Facts and fiction. In P. Philippot, R. Feldman, & E. J. Coats (Eds.). *The Social Context of Nonverbal Behavior, Studies in Emotion and Social Interaction* (pp. 213–241). New York: Cambridge University Press.

Heyes, C. (2010). Mesmerising mirror neurons. *Neuroimage*, *51*, 789–791.

Hickok, G. (2009). Eight problems for the mirror neuron theory of action understanding in monkeys and human. *Journal of Cognitive Neuroscience*, *21*, 1229–1243.

Hodges, S. D., & Klein, K. J. K. (2001). Regulating the costs of empathy: The price of being human. *Journal of Socio-Economics*, *30*, 437–452.

Hodges, S. D., & Wegner, D. M. (1997). The mental control of empathic accuracy. In W. Ickes (Ed.), *Empathic Accuracy* (pp. 311–339). New York: Guilford Press.

Jabbi, M., & Keysers, C. (2008). Frontal gyrus activity triggers anterior insula response to emotional facial expressions. *Emotion*, *8*, 775–780.

Jackson, P. L., Brunet, E., Meltzoff, A. N., & Decety, J. (2006). Empathy examined through the neural mechanisms involved in imagining how I feel versus how you feel pain. *Neuropsychologia, 44*, 752–761.

Jackson, P. L., Meltzoff, A. N., & Decety, J. (2005). How do we perceive the pain of others: A window into the neural processes involved in empathy. *Neuroimage, 24*, 771–779.

Jackson, P. L., Rainville, P., & Decety, J. (2006). From nociception to empathy: The neural mechanism for the representation of pain in self and in others. *Pain, 125*, 5–9.

Jacob, P. (2008). What do mirror neurons contribute to human social cognition? *Mind and Language, 23*, 190–223.

Joseph, R. (2000). Fetal brain and cognitive development. *Developmental Review, 20*, 81–98.

Keillor, J. M., Barrett, A. M., Crucian, G. P., Kortenkamp, S., & Heilman, K. M. (2002). Emotional experience and perception in the absence of facial feedback. *Journal of the International Neuropsychological Society, 8*, 130–135.

Koenigs, M., Baskin-Sommers, A., Zeier, J., & Newman, J. P. (2011). Investigating the neural correlates of psychopathy: A critical review. *Molecular Psychiatry, 16*, 792–799.

Kosson, D. S., Suchy, Y., Mayer, A. R., & Libby, J. (2002). Facial affect recognition in criminal psychopaths. *Emotion, 24*, 398–411.

Lahey, B.B., & Waldman, I.D. (2003). A developmental propensity model of the origins of conduct problems during childhood and adolescence. In B. B. Lahey, T. E. Moffitt, & A. Caspi (Eds.), *Causes of Conduct Disorder and Juvenile Delinquency* (pp. 76–117). New York: Guilford Press.

Lamm, C., Batson, C. D., & Decety, J. (2007). The neural basis of human empathy: Effects of perspective-taking and cognitive appraisal. *Journal of Cognitive Neuroscience, 19*, 42–58.

Lamm, C., Meltzoff, A. N., & Decety, J. (2010). How do we empathize with someone who is not like us? *Journal of Cognitive Neuroscience, 2*, 362–376.

Lamm, C., Porges, E. C., Cacioppo, J. T., & Decety, J. (2008). Perspective taking is associated with specific facial responses during empathy for pain. *Brain Research, 1227*, 153–161.

Lang, S., Yu, T., Markl, A., Muller, F., & Kotchoubey, B. (2011). Hearing others' pain: Neural activity related to empathy. *Cognitive, Affective & Behavioral Neuroscience, 11*, 386–395.

Langford, D. J., Tuttleb, A. H., Brown, K., Deschenes, S., Fischer, D. B., Mutso, A., et al. (2010). Social approach to pain in laboratory mice. *Social Neuroscience, 5*, 163–170.

Leslie, K. R., Johnson-Frey, S. H., & Grafton, S. (2004). Functional imaging of face and hand imitation: Towards a motor theory of empathy. *Neuroimage, 21*, 601–607.

Levenson, R. W., Ekman, P., & Friesen, W. V. (1990). Voluntary facial action generates emotion-specific autonomic nervous system activity. *Psychophysiology, 27*, 363–384.

Levenston, G. K., Patrick, C. J., Bradley, M. M., & Lang, P. J. (2000). The psychopath as observer: Emotion and attention in picture processing. *Journal of Abnormal Psychology, 109*, 373–385.

Lingnau, A., Gesierich, B., & Caramazza, A. (2009). Asymmetric fMRI adaptation reveals no evidence for mirror neurons in humans. *Proceedings of the National Academy of Sciences U S A, 106*(24), 9925–9930.

Lockwood, P. L., Sebastian, C. L., McCrory, E. J., Hyde, Z. H., Gu, X., De Brito, S. A., & Viding, E. (2013). Association of callous traits with reduced neural response to others' pain in children with conduct disorder. *Current Biology, 23*, 1-5.

Mahmut, M. K., Homewood, J., & Stevenson, R. J. (2008). The characteristics of non-criminals with high psychopathy traits: Are they similar to criminal psychopaths? *Journal of Research in Personality, 42*, 679–692.

Martin, G. B., & Clark, R. D. (1987). Distress crying in neonates: Species and peer specificity. *Developmental Psychology, 18*, 3–9.

Marsh, A. A, Finger, E. C., Fowler, K. A., Adalio, C. J., Jurkowitz, I. N., Schechter, J. C., Pine, D. S., Decety, J., & Blair, R. J. R. (2013). Empathic responsiveness in amygdala and anterior cingulate cortex in youths with psychopathic traits. *Journal of Child Psychology and Psychiatry*, epub ahead of print, doi:10.1111/jcpp.12063.

Mitchell, D. G. V., Richell, R. A., Leonard, A., & Blair, R. J. (2006). Emotion at the expense of cognition: Psychopathic individuals outperform controls on an operant response task. *Journal of Abnormal Psychology, 115*, 559–566.

Molenberghs, P., Cunnington, P., & Mattingley, J. B. (2009). Is the mirror neuron system involved in imitation? A short review and meta-analysis. *Neuroscience and Biobehavioral Reviews, 33*, 975–980.

Moll, J., Zahn, R., de Oliveira-Souza, R., & Eslinger, P. J. (2003). Morals and the human brain: A working model. *Neuroreport, 14*, 299–305.

Moriguchi, Y., Decety, J., Ohnishi, T., Maeda, M., Matsuda, H., & Komaki, G. (2007). Empathy and judging other's pain: An fMRI study of alexithymia. *Cerebral Cortex, 9*, 2223–2234.

Morin, O., & Grèzes, J. (2008). What is "mirror" in the premotor cortex? A review. *Neurophysiologie Clinique/Clinical Neurophysiology, 38*, 189–195.

Morrison, I., & Downing, P. E. (2007). Organization of felt and seen pain responses in anterior cingulate cortex. *Neuroimage, 37*, 642–651.

Morrison, I., Lloyd, D., di Pellegrino, G., & Roberts, N. (2004). Vicarious responses to pain in anterior cingulate cortex: Is empathy a multisensory issue? *Cognitive, Affective & Behavioral Neuroscience, 4*, 270–278.

Morrison, I., Peelen, M. V., & Downing, P. E. (2007). The sight of others' pain modulates motor processing in human cingulate cortex. *Cerebral Cortex, 17*, 2214–2222.

Murray, E. A. (2007). The amygdala, reward and emotion. *Trends in Cognitive Sciences, 11*, 489–497.

Ochsner, K. N., & Gross, J. J. (2005). The cognitive control of emotion. *Trends in Cognitive Sciences, 9*, 242–249.

Oliveri, M., Babiloni, C., Filippi, M. M., Caltagirone, C., Babiloni, F., Cicinelli, P., et al. (2003). Influence of the supplementary motor area on primary motor cortex excitability during movements triggered by neutral or emotionally unpleasant visual cues. *Experimental Brain Research, 149*, 214–221.

Phan, K. L., Wager, T., Taylor, S. F., & Liberzon, I. (2002). Functional neuroanatomy of emotion: A meta-analysis of emotion activation studies in PET and fMRI. *Neuroimage, 16*, 331–348.

Pineda, J. A. (2005). The functional significance of mu rhythms: Translating seeing and hearing into doing. *Brain Research Review, 50*, 57–68.

Pitcher, D., Garrigo, L., Walsh, V., & Duchaine, B. C. (2008). Transcranial magnetic stimulation disrupts the perception and embodiment of facial expressions. *Journal of Neuroscience, 28*, 8929–8933.

Pourtois, G., Sander, D., Andres, M., Grandjean, D., Reveret, L., Olivier, E., & Vuilleumier, P. (2004). Dissociable roles of the human somatosensory and superior temporal cortices for processing social face signals. *European Journal of Neuroscience, 20,* 3507–3515.

Preston, S. D., Bechara, A., Damasio, H., Grabowski, T. J., Stansfield, R. B., Mehta, S., & Damasio, A. R. (2007). The neural substrates of cognitive empathy. *Social Neuroscience, 2,* 254–275.

Preston, S. D., & de Waal, F. B. M. (2002). Empathy: Its ultimate and proximate bases. *Behavioral and Brain Sciences, 25,* 1–72.

Price, B. H., Daffner, K. R., Stowe, R. M., & Mesulam, M. M. (1990). The compartmental learning-disabilities of early frontal lobe damage. *Brain, 113,* 1383–1393.

Price, D. D. (2000). Psychological and neural mechanisms of the affective dimension of pain. *Science, 288,* 1769–1772.

Raine, A., Lenz, T., Bihrle, S., LaCasse, L., & Colletti, P. (2000). Reduced prefrontal gray matter volume and reduced autonomic activity in antisocial personality disorder. *Archives of General Psychiatry, 57,* 119–127.

Rankin, K. P., Gorno-Tempini, M. L., Allison, S. C., Stanley, C. M., Glenn, S., Weiner, M. W., & Miller, B. L. (2006). Structural anatomy of empathy in neurodegenerative disease. *Brain, 129,* 2945–2956.

Rankin, K. P., Kramer, J. H., & Miller, B. L. (2005). Patterns of cognitive and emotional empathy in frontotemporal lobar degeneration. *Cognitive and Behavioral Neurology, 18,* 28–36.

Ruby, P., & Decety, J. (2004). How would you feel versus how do you think she would feel? A neuroimaging study of perspective taking with social emotions. *Journal of Cognitive Neuroscience, 16,* 988–999.

Roth-Hanania, R., Davidov, M., & Zahn-Waxler, C. (2011). Empathy development from 8 to 16 months: Early signs of concern for others. *Infant Behavior and Development, 34,* 447–458.

Sato, J. R., de Oliviera-Souza, R., Thomaz, C. E, Basilio, R., Bramati, I. E., Amaro, E., et al. (2011). Identification of psychopathic individuals using pattern classification of MRI images. *Social Neuroscience, 6,* 627–639..

Shackman, A. J, Salomons, T. V., Slagter, H. A., Fox, A. S., Winter, J. J., & Davidson, R. J. (2011). The integration of negative affect, pain and cognitive control in the cingulate cortex. *Nature Review Neuroscience, 12,* 154–167.

Shamay-Tsoory, S. G., Aharon-Peretz, J., & Perry, D. (2009). Two systems for empathy: A double dissociation between emotional and cognitive empathy in inferior frontal gyrus versus ventromedial prefrontal lesions. *Brain, 132,* 617–627.

Shamay-Tsoory, S. G., Tomer, R., Berger, B. D., & Aharon-Peretz, J. (2003). Characterization of empathy deficits following prefrontal brain damage: The role of right ventromedial prefrontal cortex. *Cognitive and Behavioral Neurology, 18,* 55–67.

Shamay-Tsoory, S. G., Tomer, R., Berger, B. D., Goldsher, D., & Aharon-Peretz, J. (2005). Impaired affective theory of mind is associated with right ventromedial prefrontal damage. *Journal of Cognitive Neuroscience, 15,* 1–14.

Singer, T., Seymour, B., O'Doherty, J., Kaube, H., Dolan, R. J., & Frith, C. D. (2004). Empathy for pain involves the affective but not the sensory components of pain. *Science, 303,* 1157–1161.

Snowden, J. S., Gibbons, Z. C., Blackshaw, A., Doubleday, E., Thompson, J., Craufurd, D., et al. (2003). Social cognition in frontotemporal dementia and Huntington's disease. *Neuropsychologia, 41,* 688–701.

Sonnby-Borgstrom, M., Jonsson, P., & Svensson, O. (2003). Emotional empathy as related to mimicry reactions at different levels of information processing. *Journal of Nonverbal Behavior, 27,* 3–23.

Sterzer, P., Stadler, C., Poustka, F., & Kleinschmidt, A. (2007). A structural neural deficit in adolescents with conduct disorder and its association with lack of empathy. *Neuroimage, 37,* 335–342.

Sturm, V. E., Rosen, H. J., Allison, S., Miller, B. L., & Levenson, R. W. (2006). Self-conscious emotions deficits in frontotemporal lobar degeneration. *Brain, 129,* 2508–2516.

Tiihonen, J., Rossi, R., Laakso, M. P., Hodgins, S., Testa, C., Perez, J., et al. (2008). Brain anatomy of persistent violent offenders: More rather than less. *Psychiatry Research: Neuroimaging, 163,* 201–212.

Van der Gaag, C., Minderaa, R. B., & Keysers, C. (2007). Facial expressions: What the mirror neuron system can and cannot tell us. *Social Neuroscience, 2*(3), 179–222.

Wilson, E. O. (1988). *On Human Nature.* Cambridge, MA: Harvard University Press.

Young, L., & Dungan, J. (2012). Where in the brain is morality? Everywhere and maybe nowhere. *Social Neuroscience, 7*(1), 1–10..

Zaki, J., Ochsner, K. N., Hanelin, J., Wager, T. D., & Mackey, S. C. (2007). Different circuits for different pain: Patterns of functional connectivity reveal distinct networks for processing pain in self and others. *Social Neuroscience, 2,* 276–291.

Zaki, J., Weber, J., Bolger, N., & Ochsner, K. (2009). The neural bases of empathic accuracy. *Proceedings of the National Academy of Sciences U S A, 106,* 11382–11387.

Zelazo, P., Carlson, S., & Kesek, A. (2008). The development of executive function in childhood. In C. A. Nelson & M. Luciana (Eds.), *Handbook of Developmental Cognitive Neuroscience* (pp. 553–574). Cambridge, MA: MIT Press.

Mirror Neurons and the Perception–Action Link

Vittorio Gallese

Abstract

Social life depends in large part on the capacity to understand the intentional behavior of others. Which are the origins of this capacity? The classic cognitive view claims that intentional understanding can be explained only in terms of the ability to intellectually read the mind of others. Over the past few years, this view has been challenged by several neuroscientific findings regarding social cognition. In particular, the functional properties of mirror neurons and their direct matching mechanism indicate that intentional understanding is based primarily on the motor cognition that underpins one's own potentiality to act. The aim of this chapter is to present and discuss the role of such motor cognition, providing a biologically plausible and theoretically unitary account for the neural basis of basic forms of intentional understanding.

Key Words: motor cognition, intentional understanding, mirror neurons, social cognition

Introduction

Humans are social animals whose cognitive development capitalizes on the interaction with other conspecifics (e.g., adults, siblings). During social interactions we manifest our inner intentions, dispositions, and thoughts by means of overt behavior. At the same time we constantly try to understand the intentions, dispositions, and thoughts of others when witnessing their behavior. Detecting another agent's intentions, or other inner states, helps in anticipating this agent's future actions, which may be cooperative, noncooperative, or even threatening. Accurate understanding and anticipation enable the observer to adjust his or her responses appropriately.

For decades the prevalent opinion in cognitive science and in many quarters of philosophy of mind has been that in humans this capacity predominantly—or even exclusively—relies on the ability to "intellectually read" the mind of others. Mind reading, according to the mainstream view, consists of explaining others' actions, describable per se as

intentionally opaque instantiations of biological motion, by relating them to inner mental states that play a causal role in producing those very same behaviors. In this view, in order to understand others one would mind read others, that is, attribute mental states to others by mapping them as internal representations in propositional format.

Mind reading would also constitute a sort of "mental Rubicon" separating humans from all other living species of animals, including nonhuman primates, which are supposedly confined to a mere behaviorist account of others' behavior, relying on the extraction of procedural rules from observable regularities. According to this account, when interacting with other individuals nonhuman primates would be precluded from the capacity to infer mental states such as intentions, beliefs, and desires.

Many of these views can be challenged. As argued elsewhere (see Gallese, 2006, 2007, 2008; Gallese, Rochat, Cossu, & Sinigaglia, 2009; see also Iacoboni & Dapretto, 2006; Keysers & Gazzola, 2009), at the basis of the human capacity to understand others' intentional behavior, both from a phylogenetic and ontogenetic point of view, there is a more direct access to the world of the other. Such direct access is made possible by the fact that human beings, like nonhuman primates, are endowed with a functional mechanism, embodied simulation, that mediates the capacity to share the meaning of actions, basic motor intentions, feelings, and emotions with others, thus grounding the identification with and connectedness to others. According to this hypothesis, intersubjectivity should be viewed first and foremost as intercorporeity.

In this chapter I will first review the neuroscientific evidence for the neural underpinnings of action motor goals. I will then clarify how action goals can be understood and discuss the relation between action control and action understanding by introducing mirror neurons. An account of their functional relevance in social cognition, both in macaque monkeys and humans, will also be proposed.

The Neural Correlates of Motor Goals: Why Studying Macaque Monkey Brains Can Shed Light on Human Social Cognition

The empirical investigation of the neural basis of social cognition has been one of the most important targets of cognitive neuroscience during the last two decades. This research has repeatedly shown that a series of cortical regions (e.g., mesial frontal areas, the temporoparietal junction) are activated during explicit mentalizing tasks (for a review, see Frith & Frith, 2010). Unfortunately, most of these studies do not go beyond a mere correlational enterprise. The truth is that we do not know why these cortical areas are relevant to mind reading, unless we content ourselves with the tautological statement that mind reading is implemented in those brain areas.

Two further problems of this approach are the reification of mental notions like intention, desire, and belief into things found at specific brain locations and the questionable mind-reading specificity underlying the activation of the same brain regions. A possible way out of this impasse may stem from a comparative perspective on social cognition, enabling study of the neurophysiological mechanisms implicated in basic aspects of social cognition in nonhuman primates such as macaque monkeys (Gallese, 2007). As will be shown in this chapter, investigation of the functional properties of the cortical motor system of macaques has turned out to be quite fruitful.

For many years, the main focus of neurophysiological investigation of the cortical motor system of nonhuman primates was on the study of very elementary physical features of movement such as force, direction, and amplitude. However, a series of empirical results have suggested that the cortical motor system plays an important role in cognition. In particular, the neurophysiological study of the ventral premotor cortex and posterior parietal cortex of macaque monkeys has shown that the cortical motor system is functionally organized in terms of motor goals.

The most anterior region of the ventral premotor cortex of the macaque monkey controls hand and mouth movements (Hepp-Reymond, Hüsler, Maier, & Qi, 1994; Kurata & Tanji, 1986; Rizzolatti et al., 1988, Rizzolatti, Scandolara, Matelli, & Gentilucci, 1981). This sector, endowed with distinct histochemical and cytoarchitectonic features, has been termed "area F5" (Matelli, Luppino, & Rizzolatti, 1985). A fundamental functional property of area F5 is that most of its neurons, similar to neurons of other regions of the cortical motor system (Alexander & Crutcher, 1990; Crutcher & Alexander, 1990; Kakei, Hoffman, & Strick, 1999, 2001; Shen & Alexander, 1997), do not discharge in association with the activation of specific muscle groups or during the execution of elementary movements. Instead, they are active during motor acts—movements executed to accomplish a specific motor goal—such as grasping, tearing, holding, or manipulating objects (Rizzolatti et al., 1988; Rizzolatti, Fogassi, & Gallese, 2000; Rizzolatti & Gallese, 1997).

Premotor neurons of area F5 do not code merely physical parameters of movement such as force or movement direction but rather the relationship, in motor terms, between the agent and object of the motor act. F5 neurons become active only if a particular type of effector–object relation (e.g., hand–object) is executed, until the relation leads to a different state (e.g., taking possession of a piece of food, throwing it away, breaking it, bringing it to the mouth). Among F5 neurons, particularly interesting are those that discharge any time the monkey grasps an object, regardless of the effector employed, be it the right hand, the left hand, the mouth, or both hand and mouth (Rizzolatti et al., 1988; see also Rizolatti & Gallese, 1997; Rizzolatti et al., 2000).

The independence of the acting effector from the end-state attained suggests that the cortical motor system contains an abstract kind of means–end representation. A formal quantitative testing and validation of this hypothesis was carried out by Umiltà et al. (2008). In this study, hand-related neurons were recorded from premotor area F5 and the primary motor cortex (area F1) in monkeys trained to grasp objects using two different tools: "normal pliers" and "reverse pliers." These tools require opposite movements to grasp an object: With normal pliers the hand has to be first opened and then closed, as when grasping is executed with the bare hand, whereas with reverse pliers the hand has to be first closed and then opened. The use of the two tools enabled the dissociation of the neural activity related to hand movement from that related to the goal of the motor act, taking possession of the object.

All tested neurons in area F5 and half of the neurons recorded from the primary motor cortex discharged in relation to the accomplishment of the goal of grasping—when the tool closed on the object—regardless of whether the hand opened or closed during this phase, that is, regardless of the movements employed to accomplish the goal. The data of Umiltà et al. (2008) indicate that the coding of motor goals structures the way that action is mapped in area F5 and, to a minor extent, in the primary motor cortex.

The presence of a specific neural format for motor goal states in the motor system allows for a much simpler selection of a particular motor act within a given context (Rizzolatti et al., 1988). Wheher the motor act is self-generated or externally driven, only a few motor elements need to be selected.

Thus, the cortical motor system of primates is endowed with a neural format that generalizes across different instances in which a particular successful end-state of the organism (the goal state) can be achieved. Grasping-related neurons implement a goal-state "representation" whose content is both intentional and motor. It is intentional because it is a goal-centered motor representation that, although referring to a movement, cannot be reduced to a single sequence of movements. It is motor because the goal state is mapped in motor terms, as the endpoint of a motor act. This motor representation can be different in terms of single movements. However, it must have a coherent motor content enabling determination of a given behavior and control of its execution.

Beyond purely motor neurons, which constitute the overall majority of all F5 neurons, area F5 also contains two categories of "visuomotor" neurons. Neurons of both categories have motor properties that are indistinguishable from those of the purely motor neurons, and they have peculiar visual properties. The first category consists of neurons

that respond to the presentation of objects of particular size and shape in absence of any detectable action being aimed at them, either by the monkey or by the experimenter. These neurons have been called "canonical neurons" (Raos, Umiltà, Fogassi, & Gallese, 2006; Rizzolatti et al., 2000; Umiltà, Brochier, Spinks, & Lemon, 2007).

The second category consists of neurons that discharge when the monkey observes an action made by another individual and when it executes the same or a similar action. These neurons are called "mirror neurons" (Gallese, Fadiga, Fogassi, & Rizzolatti, 1996; Rizzolatti, Fadiga, Gallese, & Fogassi, 1996). Canonical and mirror neurons are the focus of the next two sections.

The World at Hand: Canonical Neurons

Most grasping actions are executed under visual guidance. This requires that a relationship be established among the most important relational features of three-dimensional (3D) visual objects, their affordances, and the motor programs controlling how to interact with them. The appearance of a graspable object in visual space will trigger the most appropriate "motor schema" enabling the intended type of hand–object relation. This process, in neurophysiological terms, implies that the same neuron must be able to not only code the motor act it is supposed to control but also respond to the situated visual features triggering it.

Consistent with these predictions, canonical neurons discharge at the visual presentation of objects of different size and shape in the absence of any detectable movement of the monkey (Jeannerod et al., 1995; Murata et al., 1997; Raos et al., 2006; Rizzolatti et al., 1988; Rizzolatti, Fogassi, & Gallese 2001; Umiltà et al., 2007). Very often, a strict congruence has been observed between the type of grip controlled by a given neuron and the size or shape of the object effective in triggering its "visual" response. The most interesting aspect, however, is the fact that in a considerable percentage of neurons, a congruence is observed between the response during the execution of a specific type of grip and the visual response to objects that, although differing in shape, nevertheless afford the same type of grip (see Murata et al., 1997; Raos et al., 2006). Thus, the very same neuron controlling a hand prehension suitable for grasping small objects will also fire equally well to the mere visual presentation of small objects such as a small sphere, small cone, or small cube. The objects' shapes are different, but they all specify a similar type of grasping.

The function of F5 canonical grasping neurons can hardly be defined in purely sensory or motor terms alone. Within the cortical motor system, objects are processed in motor relationally specified terms (Gallese, 2000). According to the logic of such a neural network, a series of physical entities, 3D objects, are identified, differentiated, and represented—not in relation to their mere visual appearance but in relation to the effect of the potential interaction with a situated acting agent. This property qualifies as an intentional type of representation, although still fully within the functional architecture of the cortical motor system. The first conclusion we can draw is that canonical neurons contribute to a multimodal representation of an organism–object relation. The visual world is always also the horizon of our potential pragmatic relation to it (Gallese & Sinigaglia, 2010). This evidence sheds light on how the brain maps intentional actions. The intentional character, the "aboutness," of the representational format of our mind could be deeply rooted in the intrinsic relational character of bodily action, which, in turn, suggests the intrinsic intertwined character of action, perception, and cognition (Gallese, 2000; see also Hurley, 1998).

Representational content cannot be fully explained without considering it as the result of the ongoing modeling process of an organism as currently integrated with the object to be represented, by intending it. This integration process between the representing organism and the represented object is articulated in a multiple fashion, for example, by intending to explore it by moving the eyes, intending to hold it in the focus of attention, intending to grasp it, and, ultimately, thinking about it (see Gallese, 2000; Gallese & Metzinger, 2003).

The same motor circuits that control the ongoing activity of the organism within its environment also map objects in that very same environment, thus defining and shaping in motor terms their representational content. The way the visual world is represented by the motor system incorporates agents' idiosyncratic way of interacting with it. In other words, the producer and repository of representational content are not the brain per se, but the brain-body system, by means of its interactions with the world in which it lives.

Mirror Neurons in Macaque Monkeys

Mirror neurons are premotor neurons that were first described in the most anterior sector of macaque monkey ventral premotor cortex, area F5 (di Pellegrino, Fadiga, Fogassi, & Gallese, 1992;

Gallese et al., 1996; Rizzolatti et al., 1996). They typically discharge both when a motor act is executed and when it is observed being performed by someone else. The same motor neuron that fires when the monkey grasps a peanut is also activated when the monkey observes another individual performing the same motor act. Neurons with similar properties were also discovered in a sector of the inferior parietal lobule reciprocally connected with premotor area F5 (Fogassi et al., 2005; Gallese, Fogassi, Fadiga, & Rizzolatti, 2002; Rozzi, Ferrari, Bonini, Rizzolatti, & Fogassi, et al., 2008).

Action observation causes in the observer the automatic activation of the same neural mechanism triggered by action execution. The novelty of this finding consists in the fact that, for the first time, a neural mechanism allowing a direct mapping between the visual description of a motor act and its execution has been identified. It has been proposed that this neural mapping mechanism provides a parsimonious solution to the problem of translating the results of visual analysis of an observed movement—in principle, devoid of meaning for the observer—into something that the observer is directly able to understand, because it can be directly mapped on the observer's motor representation (Gallese et al., 1996; Rizzolatti et al., 1996).

The proposal that mirror neurons' activity reflects an internal motor description of the meaning of the perceived motor act rather than a mere a visual description of its features has been demonstrated in two studies. In the first study, Umiltà et al. (2001) described a subset of F5 mirror neurons that discharged during the observation of partially hidden motor acts, coding the action outcome even in the absence of the complete visual information about it. Macaque monkeys' mirror neurons respond to observed acts not exclusively on the basis of their visual description but on the basis of the anticipation of their final goal-state, simulated through the activation of its neural motor "representation" in the observer's premotor cortex.

These data, of course, do not exclude the coexistence of a system that visually analyzes and describes the acts of others, most likely through the activation of extrastriate visual neurons sensitive to biological motion. However, such visual analysis per se is most likely insufficient to provide an understanding of the observed act (see below). Without reference to the observer's internal "motor knowledge," this description is devoid of factual meaning for the observing individual (Gallese et al., 2009).

A second study (Kohler et al., 2002) demonstrated that mirror neurons also code the meaning of the motor act performed by another individual on the basis of its related sound. A particular class of F5 mirror neurons ("audiovisual mirror neurons") responds not only when the monkey executes and observes a given hand action, such as breaking a peanut or tearing a sheet of paper, but also when it just hears the sound typically produced by the same motor acts. These neurons respond to the sound of specific motor acts and discriminate between the sounds of different motor acts, but they do not respond to other similarly interesting sounds, such as arousing noises or monkeys' and other animals' vocalizations.

Mirror neurons' activity reveals the existence of a mechanism through which perceived events as different as sounds or images are nevertheless equally responded to, hence coded as similar, to the extent that they represent the assorted sensory aspects of the motor act's goal. It has been proposed that mirror neurons, by mapping observed, implied, or heard goal-directed motor acts on their motor neural substrate in the observer's motor system, allow a direct form of action understanding (Gallese et al., 1996; Rizzolatti et al., 1996) through a mechanism of embodied simulation (Gallese, 2005, 2006; Gallese et al., 2009). Such a form of action understanding is considered *direct* to the extent that it does not require any inference by analogy or other more cognitively sophisticated and explicit forms of mentalization.

Rochat et al. (2010) showed that F5 mirror neurons respond to the execution and observation of motor acts—grasping objects—regardless of the effector (hand or reverse pliers) or the movements required to accomplish the goal. Tool-mediated grasp required opposite movements of the hand (fingers opening vs. fingers closing) with respect to natural grasping with the hand. In a third condition, mirror neurons were recorded during the observation of an experimenter spearing objects with a stick. Virtually all neurons responding to the observation of hand grasping also responded to the observation of grasping with pliers, and many of them responded to the observation of spearing with a stick. It appears, therefore, that what triggers mirror neurons is the identity of the goal—taking possession of an object—independent of the type of effector and of its movements.

Rochat et al. (2010) also demonstrated two important properties of F5 mirror neurons. First, the intensity of the discharge of the entire population of mirror neurons was significantly stronger during action execution than during action observation. This property indicates that the mirror mechanism is also sensitive to *who* the agent is. Second, the onset of mirror neuron response during observation of hand and tool grasping correlated with the monkey's motor expertise. The earliest discharge onset occurred during hand-grasping observation, whereas the latest one occurred during the observation of spearing. Grasping mirror neurons in area F5 map the goal of the observed motor act while simultaneously reflecting the reliability of this information with respect to the motor experience of the observing individual through the timing of their discharge.

However, it must be added that human social cognition is far more sophisticated than that. We not only understand what others are doing but also why—that is, we can attribute motor intentions to others. We do not limit ourselves to the knowledge that someone has grasped something, say an apple, but usually also determine to what particular purpose that grasping served (e.g., to eat the apple or to put it in a basket).

To what extent are mirror neurons also sensitive to the motor intention guiding an orderly sequence of motor acts? To address this question, two recent studies investigated the response of premotor and parietal mirror neurons while the monkey performed and observed a motor task consisting of two different actions: grasping to eat and grasping to place. The results showed that a conspicuous percentage of mirror neurons responded during the execution and observation of grasping according to the overarching goal of the action in which it was embedded: some neurons only responded when grasping led to bringing the object to the mouth but not when it led to putting the object into a container, and vice versa (Bonini et al., 2010; Fogassi et al., 2005).

Thus mirror neurons map integrated sequences of goal-related motor acts (grasping, holding, bringing, placing), clustering them into "syntactically" separate and parallel intentional actions. This "motor syntax" generates a hierarchically clustered, temporally chained sequence of motor acts properly assembled to accomplish a more distal goal-state. The core action intention (to eat, to place the food or object) is the goal-state of the ultimate goal-related motor act of the chain. Parietal and premotor mirror neurons, by virtue of this functional characteristic, might allow the observing monkey to anticipate the agent's next motor act, hence its core motor intention. This neural mechanism, present in a nonlinguistic species, could support more sophisticated social cognitive abilities, such as those characterizing our species (Gallese, 2006, 2007; Gallese et al., 2009).

Mirror Neurons and Nonhuman Primates' Social Cognition

The presence of a mirror mechanism within the cortical motor system of the macaque monkey brain in its premotor and posterior parietal components invites the question of what the relevance of such a mechanism is for macaque monkeys' social cognition. We have already seen that the mirror mechanism has the functional properties that could enable monkeys to understand what others are doing and for what basic purpose. These aspects, though, even if crucial, do not exhaust the realm of social cognition.

Empirical evidence shows that macaque monkeys are capable of shared attention behaviors (Ferrari, Kohler, Fogassi, & Gallese, 2000; Ferrari et al., 2008), are prone to social facilitation phenomena (Ferrari, Maiolini, Addessi, Fogassi, & Visaberghi, 2005), and are sensitive to the difference between cooperative and competitive relationships with other individuals by instantiating the capacity to establish a link between seeing and knowing in the latter case but not in the former (Flombaum & Santos 2005; Santos, Nissen, & Ferrugia, 2006). Shepherd et al. (Shepherd, Klein, Deaner, & Platt, 2009) discovered a class of neurons in the posterior parietal area LIP, known to be involved in oculomotor control, that fired both when the monkey looked in a given direction and when it observed another monkey looking in the same direction. Shepherd et al. suggested that LIP mirror neurons for gaze might contribute to the sharing of observed attention, thus playing a role in imitative behavior.

Furthermore, Rochat and colleagues (Rochat, Serra, Fadiga, & Gallese, 2008) investigated the phylogenetic origin of the ability to evaluate and predict the goal-directed action of others. Nonhuman primates' ability to discriminate between means and end and to use contextual cues to evaluate the ecological validity of a chosen means has been tested by adapting a looking-time paradigm previously used with human babies (Gergely, Nàdasdy, Csibra, & Bìro, et al., 1995). Results showed that macaque monkeys, similar to 9- to 12-month-old human infants, detected the goal of an observed motor act and, according to the physical characteristics of the context, construed expectancies about the most likely action that the agent would take in

a given context. This, however, is true only when observed motor acts are consonant with the observer's motor repertoire. Inadequate motor acts, non-goal-related movements, or unfamiliar goal-related motor acts do not allow any simulation and prediction. Although this study does not provide direct evidence about the neural mechanisms supporting the results, Rochat et al. (2008) hypothesized that monkeys evaluate the observed acts by mapping them on their own motor neural substrate, through activation of the mirror mechanism.

The relevance of mirror neurons for monkeys' social cognition is also evident from a study by Caggiano et al. (Caggiano, Fogassi, Rizzolatti, Their, & Casile, 2009), in which F5 mirror neurons were found to be modulated by the distance at which the observed action took place. About half of the recorded mirror neurons responded only when the observed agent acted either inside or outside the monkey's peripersonal space. Such modulation, however, didn't simply measure the physical distance between agent and observer. A consistent percentage of mirror neurons not responding to the experimenter's grasping actions carried out near the monkey resumed their discharge when a transparent barrier was placed between the object target of the action and the observing monkey. Blocking the monkey's potentiality for action on the target of action of someone else remaps the spatial location of the observed agent according to a system of coordinates dictated by and expressing the monkey's relational potentiality for interaction.

All of these studies are important, not only because they show that macaque monkeys are endowed with social cognitive abilities that only a few years ago were considered precluded from apes but also, and most importantly, because these cognitive abilities can be explained at the neurophysiological level by the motor resonance mechanism instantiated by mirror neurons. Given that this mechanism, as shown in the next section, is not unique to monkeys but has also been detected in the human brain, a new evolutionary scenario of the emergence of human social cognition is emerging (Gallese et al., 2009).

Mirroring Mechanisms in Humans

Nearly two decades of research have demonstrated the existence of a mechanism that directly maps action perception and execution in the human brain, called the mirror mechanism (for review, see Gallese 2003a, 2003b, 2006; Gallese, Keysers, & Rizzolatti, 2004; Rizzolatti et al., 2001; Rizzolatti

& Sinigaglia, 2008, 2010). During action observation, there is activation of premotor and posterior parietal areas, the likely human homologues of the monkey areas in which mirror neurons were originally described. The mirroring mechanism for actions in humans is coarsely somatotopically organized; the same regions within premotor and posterior parietal cortices that are normally active when we execute mouth, hand, and foot related acts are also activated when we observe the same motor acts done by others (Buccino et al., 2001; Gazzola, Aziz-Zadeh, & Keysers, 2006; see also Cattaneo & Rizzolatti, 2009). Watching someone grasping a cup of coffee, biting an apple, or kicking a football activates the same cortical regions of the brain that would be activated if we were doing these same activities.

The mirror mechanism in humans is directly involved in imitation of simple movements (Iacoboni et al., 1999, 2001) and in the imitation learning of complex skills (Buccino, Lui, et al., 2004). Furthermore, many interesting phenomena described by social psychologists, such as the "chameleon effect"—the unconscious mimicry by the observer of postures, expressions, and behaviors of one's social partners (Chartrand & Bargh, 1999)—with the mirror mechanism can find a neurophysiological explanation. It is worth noting that these instantiations of unconscious mimesis all share a prosocial character, because their occurrence tends to increase during social interactions with affiliative purposes.

Consistent with the goal-relatedness of mirror neurons in monkeys demonstrated by Rochat et al. (2010), a transcranial magnetic stimulation (TMS) study in humans showed that the amplitude of motor-evoked potentials (MEPs) recorded from participants' opponens pollicis during the observation of grasping performed with normal and reverse pliers was modulated by the goal of the observed motor act, regardless of the movements required to accomplish it (Cattaneo, Caruana, Jezzini, & Rizzolatti, 2009).

Functional magnetic resonance imaging (fMRI) evidence in humans shows that posterior parietal and ventral premotor areas, part of the network showing mirror mechanism-like functional properties, are activated by observation of hand goal-related motor acts when carried out by a nonanthropomorphic robotic arm (Gazzola, Rizzolatti, Wicker, & Keysers, 2007) or in observers born with no upper limbs, who thus could never have practiced hand grasping (Gazzola, van der Worp, et al.,

2007). In the latter case, the observed hand grasping activated the motor representations of mouth and foot grasping in the brains of the two patients. The results of another fMRI study showed that in humans the parietopremotor mirror mechanism can generalize motor goals when relying, as in the monkey, on action sounds through the auditory channel (Gazzola et al., 2006). A similar functional property was also found in congenitally blind patients (Ricciardi et al., 2009).

Finally, a recent TMS adaptation study confirmed the specific role of the motor system in generating a context-independent mapping of motor goal-relatedness. This property appears to be absent in extrastriate visual areas such as the STS, sensitive to the observation of biological motion, demonstrating that a visual description of motor behavior falls short of accounting for its goal-relatedness (Cattaneo, Sandrini, &Schwarzbach, 2010). The intentional character of behavior as it is mapped by the cortical motor system enables a direct appreciation of purpose without relying on explicit inference.

The mirror mechanism instantiated by parietopremotor areas can also map basic motor intentions, such as eating, drinking, and putting objects away (Cattaneo et al., 2007; Iacoboni et al., 2005). An fMRI study by Brass et al. (Brass, Schmitt, Spengler, & Gergely, 2007) showed that even when the observed goal-related motor act is unusual, like switching on the light with a knee, whether plausible (hands occupied) or not (hands free), it always leads to activation of the mirroring mechanism. This high level of motor abstraction generates the possibility of executing, hence also of recognizing in the perceptual domain, an orderly sequence of motor acts appropriately chained to accomplish a distal goal. When this level of motor mapping is present, motor behavior can be described at a higher level of abstraction, without implying an explicit language-mediated conceptualization. From the single motor goal (e.g., grasping) we move up to the level of goal hierarchy (e.g., grasping for eating), characterizing a whole motor action as such.

It should be added that the premotor cortex exhibiting the mirror mechanism is also involved in processing action-related words and sentences (Buccino et al., 2005; Hauk, Johnsrude, & Pulvermüller, 2004; Tettamanti et al., 2005; see also Pulvermüller, 2002). This suggests that mirror neurons, together with other parts of the sensory-motor system, could play a relevant role in language semantics (Gallese 2007, 2008; Gallese & Lakoff, 2005).

The neurofunctional architecture of the premotor system structures action execution and action perception, imitation, and imagination, with neural connections to motor effectors and/or other sensory cortical areas. When the action is executed or imitated, the corticospinal pathway is activated, leading to the excitation of muscles and ensuing movements. When the action is observed or imagined, its actual execution is inhibited. The cortical motor network is activated, but not in all of its components and likely not with the same intensity, but action is not produced, it is only simulated.

Other mirroring mechanisms seem to be involved with our capacity to share emotions and sensations with others (Bastiaansen, Thioux, & Keysers, 2009; de Vignemont & Singer 2006; Gallese, 2001, 2003a, 2003b, 2006). When we perceive others expressing a given basic emotion such as disgust, the same brain areas are activated as when we subjectively experience the same emotion (Wicker et al., 2003). This, of course, does not imply emotional contagion. In fact, in spite of a common shared focus of activation in the anterior insula, no matter whose disgust is at stake, different cortical areas are activated when disgust is subjectively experienced, when it is only observed in the facial expression of someone else (Jabbi, Bastiaansen, & Keysers, 2008). Similar direct matching mechanisms have been described for the perception of pain (Avenanti, Bueti, Galati, & Aglioti, 2005; Botvinick et al., 2005; Hutchison, Davis, Lozano, Tasker, & Dostrovsky, 1999; Jackson, Meltzoff, & Decety, 2005; Singer et al., 2004) and touch (Blakemore, Bristow, Bird, Frith, & Ward, 2005; Ebisch et al., 2008, 2011; Keysers et al., 2004; see also Keysers, Kaas, & Gazzola, 2010).

These results suggest that our capacity to empathize with others is mediated by embodied simulation mechanisms, that is, by the activation of the same neural circuits underpinning our own emotional and sensory experiences (see Gallese, 2005, 2006, 2009; Gallese et al., 2004). Following this perspective, empathy can be conceived of as the outcome of our natural tendency to experience our interpersonal relations first and foremost at the implicit level of intercorporeity, that is, the mutual resonance of intentionally meaningful sensory-motor behaviors.

Ontogenesis of Mirroring Mechanisms

The earliest indirect evidence available to date on the mirror mechanism in human infants is from a study by Shimada and Iraki (2006), who showed with near infrared spectroscopy (NIRS) the presence of an action execution/observation matching system in 6-month-old human infants. Southgate et al. (2008) showed with high-density electroencephalography (EEG) that 9-month-old infants exhibit alpha-band attenuation over central electrodes (a sign of motor resonance) during hand action execution and observation. The same authors (2010) showed a similar effect in 13-month-old infants during prediction of others' motor goals, with an experimental paradigm modeled based on that of Umiltà et al. (2001), in which monkeys' mirror neurons were tested during observation of a hidden hand grasping.

However, we do not know when and how the mirror mechanism appears. We do not know whether mirror neurons are innate and how they are shaped and modeled during development. Some authors have proposed that mirror neurons are the outcome of a mere associative mechanism binding the motor commands that enable action execution with visual perception of the same action (Heyes, 2010; Keysers & Perrett 2004). However, this hypothesis faces several problems. First, it does not account for mirroring mechanisms pertaining to motor acts performed with body parts that neither monkeys nor humans have direct visual access to, such as the mouth and face. Second, for the same reasons, one is forced to downplay or even deny the plausibility of neonatal imitation in both nonhuman primates (Ferrari et al., 2005; Myowa-Yamakoshi, Tomonaga, Tanaka, & Matsuzawa, 2004) and humans (Meltzoff & Moore, 1977). Third, the hypothesis falls short of explaining results such as those of Casile and Giese (2006) and of Glenberg et al. (2010), showing that motor experience without any visual feedback boosts perceptual ability when directed to human biological motion.

Del Giudice, Manera, and Keysers (2009) proposed that mirroring mechanisms might initially develop through experiential canalization of Hebbian learning, thus allowing for the possibility of some genetic preprogramming. According to this hypothesis, infants while acting would view themselves. Visual neurons in the temporal cortex would activate, responding selectively to the observed action as it unfolds, thus reinforcing the premotor neurons controlling its execution, inducing Hebbian potentiation. This hypothesis, however, bears the burden of explaining how visual selectivity for specific actions is achieved by temporal visual neurons. Furthermore, similar to the associative hypothesis, Del Giudice et al. (2009) cannot account for neonatal facial imitation and for the motor bias of perceptual recognition of biological motion.

An alternative account has been provided by Gallese (2009; Gallese et al., 2009). Recent data show that hand motor control is remarkably sophisticated well before birth (Myowa-Yamakoshi & Takeshita, 2006; Zoia et al., 2007). One study (Castiello et al., 2010) showed that already at the 14th week of gestation fetal twins display upper limb movements with different kinematic profiles according to whether they target their own body or the body of the other twin. Furthermore, between the 14th and the 18th week of gestation, the proportion of self-directed movements decreases, while that of movements targeting the sibling increases. These data show that well before birth the human motor system is already instantiating functional properties that enable social interactions, and that such social interactions are expressed obeying different motor potentialities. On the basis of this advanced prenatal development of the motor system, Gallese has hypothesized that before birth, specific connections may develop between the motor centers controlling mouth and hand movements and brain regions receiving visual inputs after birth. Such connectivity could provide functional templates (e.g., specific spatiotemporal patterns of neural firing) to areas of the brain that, once reached by visual information, would be ready to specifically respond to the observation of biological motion, such as hand or facial gestures, thus enabling, for example, neonatal imitation. Through specific neural connectivity developed during the late phase of gestation between motor and "to-become-visual" regions of the brain, neonates and infants would be ready to imitate the gestures performed by adult caregivers right in front of them and would be endowed with the neural resources enabling the reciprocal behaviors that characterize our postnatal life from its very beginning.

A similar motor conditioning of visual processing could also account for the advantages offered by motor experience with respect to visual familiarity observed in a variety of perceptual tasks performed by adults. Several brain-imaging studies conducted in humans have shown that the intensity of the mirror mechanism activation during action observation depends on the similarity between the observed actions and the participants' action repertoire (Buccino, Vogt, et al., 2004; Calvo-Merino, Glaser, Grèzes, Passingham, & Haggard, 2005). In particular, one fMRI study (Calvo-Merino, Grèzes, Glaser, Passingham, & Haggard, 2006) specifically investigated the distinction between the relative contribution of visual and motor experience in

processing an observed action. The results revealed greater activation of the mirror mechanism when the observed actions were frequently performed by the observers with respect to those that were only perceptually familiar but never practiced.

It can thus be hypothesized that an innate rudimentary mirror mechanism is already present at birth, to be subsequently and flexibly modulated by motor experience and gradually enriched by visuomotor associative learning. Lepage and Théoret (2007) proposed that the development of the mirror mechanism can be conceptualized as a process whereby the child learns to refrain from acting out the automatic mapping mechanism linking action perception and execution. This scenario has found support from data obtained from monkeys (Kraskov, Dancause, Quallo, Shepherd, & Lemon, 2010) and humans (Mukamel, Ekstrom, Kaplan, Iacoboni, & Fried, 2010). In fact, both studies presented neurophysiological evidence of mirror neurons activated during action execution but inhibited during observation of the same actions done by others. The development of cortical inhibitory mechanisms likely leads the gradual transition from mandatory re-enactment to mandatory embodied motor simulation.

Conclusions

The discovery of mirror neurons has shed new light on the relation between action, perception, and cognition. The mainstream view in cognitive science was, and to a certain extent today is, that action, perception, and cognition are separate domains. The discovery of the mirror neuron mechanism challenges this view, as it shows that such domains are intimately intertwined. It also provides a new empirically based notion of intersubjectivity, viewed first and foremost as intercorporeity—the mutual resonance of intentionally meaningful sensory-motor behaviors—as the basic source of knowledge we directly gather about others (Gallese, 2007, 2009). Intercorporeity describes a crucial aspect of intersubjectivity, not because the latter is grounded in the perceived similarity between our body and others' bodies, but because as human beings we all share the same intentional objects. Our situated sensory-motor systems are similarly wired to accomplish similar basic goals and experience similar emotions and sensations.

Anytime we meet other people, we are implicitly aware of their similarity to us, because we literally embody it. Some of the neural substrates activated when actions are executed or emotions and sensations are subjectively experienced are also activated when the same actions, emotions, and sensations are executed or experienced by others. It has been proposed that a common underlying functional mechanism, embodied simulation, mediates our capacity to share the meaning of actions, intentions, feelings, and emotions with others, thus grounding our identification with and connectedness to others (Gallese, 2005, 2006, 2007).

At odds with standard accounts of simulation theory of mind reading (see Goldman, 2006), embodied simulation is conceived as a mandatory, prerational, non-introspectionist process. Embodied simulation challenges the notion that the sole account of interpersonal understanding consists in explicitly attributing to others propositional attitudes such as beliefs and desires, mapped as symbolic representations. Parallel to the detached third-person sensory description of our social world, internal nonlinguistic "representations" of the body states associated with actions, emotions, and sensations are evoked in the observer, as if he or she were performing a similar action or experiencing a similar emotion or sensation. By means of an isomorphic format, we can map others' actions onto our own motor representations. We can also map others' emotions and sensations onto our own visceromotor and somatosensory representations.

Acknowledgments

This work was supported by MIUR (Ministero Italiano dell'Università e della Ricerca) and by the EU grant DISCOS and ROSSI.

References

Alexander, G. E., & Crutcher, M. D. (1990). Neural representations of the target (goal) of visually guided arm movements in three motor areas of the monkey. *Journal of Neurophysiology, 64*, 164–178.

Avenanti, A., Bueti, D., Galati G., & Aglioti S. M. (2005), Transcranial magnetic stimulation highlights the sensorimotor side of empathy for pain. *Nature Neuroscience, 8*, 955–960.

Bastiaansen, J. A., Thioux, M., & Keysers, C. (2009). Evidence for mirror systems in emotions. *Philosophical Transactions of the Royal Society of London, Series B: Biological Science, 364*(1528), 2391–2404.

Blakemore, S.-J., Bristow, D., Bird, G., Frith, C., & Ward, J. (2005). Somatosensory activations during the observation of touch and a case of vision–touch synaesthesia. *Brain 128*, 1571–1583.

Bonini, L., Rozzi, S., Serventi, F. U., Simone, L., Ferrari, P. F., & Fogassi, L. (2010). Ventral premotor and inferior parietal cortices make distinct contribution to action organization and intention understanding. *Cerebral Cortex, 2*, 1372–1385.

Botvinick, M., Jha, A. P., Bylsma, L. M., Fabian, S. A., Solomon, P. E., & Prkachin, K. M. (2005). Viewing facial expressions of pain engages cortical areas involved in the direct experience of pain. *Neuroimage, 25*, 315–319.

Brass, M., Schmitt, R. M., Spengler, S., & Gergely, G. (2007). Investigating action understanding: Inferential processes versus action simulation. *Current Biology, 17*, 2117–2121.

Buccino, G., Binkofski, F., Fink, G. R., Fadiga, L., Fogassi, L., Gallese, V., et al. (2001). Action observation activates premotor and parietal areas in a somatotopic manner: An fMRI study. *European Journal of Neuroscience, 13*, 400–404.

Buccino, G., Lui, F., Canessa, N., Patteri, I., Lagravinese, G., Benuzzi, F., et al. (2004). Neural circuits involved in the recognition of actions performed by nonconspecifics: An fMRI study. *Journal of Cognitive Neuroscience, 16*, 114–126.

Buccino, G., Riggio, L., Melli, G., Binkofski, F., Gallese, V., & Rizzolatti, G. (2005). Listening to action-related sentences modulates the activity of the motor system: A combined TMS and behavioral study. *Cognitive Brain Research, 24*, 355–363.

Buccino, G., Vogt, S., Ritzl, A., Fink, G. R., Zilles, K., Freund, H.-J., & Rizzolatti, G. (2004) Neural circuits underlying imitation learning of hand actions: An event-related fMRI study. *Neuron, 42*, 323–334.

Caggiano, V., Fogassi, L., Rizzolatti, G., Thier, P., & Casile, A. (2009) Mirror neurons differentially encode the peripersonal and extrapersonal space of monkeys. *Science, 324*, 403–406.

Calvo-Merino, B., Glaser, D. E, Grezes, J., Passingham, R. F., & Haggard, P. (2005). Action observation and acquired motor skills: An fMRI study with expert dancers. *Cerebral Cortex, 15*, 1243–1249.

Calvo-Merino, B., Grèzes, J., Glaser, D. E., Passingham, R. E., & Haggard, P. (2006). Seeing or doing? Influence of visual and motor familiarity in action observation. *Current Biology, 16*(19), 1905–1910.

Casile, A., & Giese, M. A. (2006) Nonvisual motor training influences biological motion perception. *Current Biology, 16*, 69–74.

Castiello, U., Becchio, C., Zoia, S., Nelini, C., Sartori, L., Blason, L., et al. (2010). Wired to be social: The ontogeny of human interaction. *PLoS ONE, 5*(10), e13199.

Cattaneo, L., Caruana, F., Jezzini, A., & Rizzolatti, G. (2009) Representation of goal and movements without overt motor behavior in the human motor cortex: A transcranial magnetic stimulation study. *Journal of Neuroscience, 29*, 11134–11138.

Cattaneo, L., Fabbri-Destro, M., Boria, S., Pieraccini, C., Monti, A., Cossu, G., & Rizzolatti, G. (2008). Impairment of action chains in autism and its possible role in intention understanding. *Proceedings of the National Academy of Sciences U S A, 104*, 17825–17830.

Cattaneo, L., & Rizzolatti, G. (2009). The mirror neuron system. Review. *Archives of Neurology, 66*(5), 557–560.

Cattaneo, L., Sandrini, M., & Schwarzbach, J. (2010). State-dependent TMS reveals a hierarchical representation of observed acts in the temporal, parietal, and premotor cortices. *Cerebral Cortex, 20*(9), 2252–2258.

Chartrand, T. L., & Bargh, J. A. (1999). The chameleon effect: The perception-behavior link and social interaction. *Journal of Personality & Social Psychology, 76*, 893–910.

Crutcher, M. D., & Alexander, G. E. (1990). Movement-related neuronal activity selectively coding either direction or muscle pattern in three motor areas of the monkey. *Journal of Neurophysiology, 64,* 151–163.

Cutting, J. E., & Kozlowski, L. T. (1977). Recognizing friends by their walk: Gait perception without familiarity cues. *Bulletin of the Psychonomic Society, 9,* 353–356.

Del Giudice, M., Manera, V., & Keysers, C. (2009). Programmed to learn? The ontogeny of mirror neurons. *Developmental Science, 12*(2), 350–363.

de Vignemont, F., & Singer, T. (2006). The emphatic brain: How, when, and why? *Trends in Cognitive Sciences, 10,* 435–441.

di Pellegrino, G., Fadiga, L., Fogassi, L., Gallese, V., & Rizzolatti, G. (1992). Understanding motor events: A neurophysiological study. *Experimental Brain Research, 91,* 176–180, 1992.

Ebisch, S. J. H., Ferri, F., Salone, A., d'Amico, L., Perrucci, M. G., Ferro, F. M., et al. (2011). Differential involvement of somatosensory and interoceptive cortices during the observation of affective touch. *Journal of Cognitive Neuroscience, 23*(7), 1808–1822..

Ebisch, S. J. H., Perrucci, M. G., Ferretti, A., Del Gratta, C., Romani, G. L., & Gallese, V. (2008). The sense of touch: Embodied simulation in a visuo-tactile mirroring mechanism for the sight of any touch. *Journal of Cognitive Neuroscience, 20,* 1611–1623.

Ferrari, P. F., Kohler, E., Fogassi, L., & Gallese, V. (2000). The ability to follow eye gaze and its emergence during development in macaque monkey. *Proceedings of the National Academy of Sciences, U S A, 97*(25), 13997–14002.

Ferrari, P. F., Maiolini, C., Addessi, E., Fogassi, L., & Visalberghi, E. (2005). The observation and hearing of eating actions activates motor programs related to eating in macaque monkeys. *Behavioural Brain Research, 161,* 95–101.

Ferrari, P. F[OUP-CE25]., Visalberghi, E., Paukner, A., Fogassi, L., Ruggiero, A., et al. (2006). Neonatal imitation in rhesus macaques. *PLoS Biology, 4*(9), e302.

Flombaum, J. L., & Santos, L. R. (2005). Rhesus monkeys attribute perceptions to others. *Current Biology, 15,* 447–452.

Fogassi, L., Ferrari, P. F., Gesierich, B., Rozzi, S., Chersi, F., & Rizzolatti, G. (2005). Parietal lobe: From action organization to intention understanding. *Science, 302,* 662–667.

Frith, U., & Frith, C. (2010). The social brain: Allowing humans to boldly go where no other species has been. *Philosophical Transactions of the Royal Society of London, Series B: Biological Science, 365*(1537), 165–176.

Gallese, V. (2000). The inner sense of action: Agency and motor representations. *Journal of Consciousness Studies, 7,* 23–40.

Gallese, V. (2001). The "shared manifold" hypothesis: From mirror neurons to empathy. *Journal of Consciousness Studies, 8*(5-7), 33–50.

Gallese, V. (2003a). The manifold nature of interpersonal relations: The quest for a common mechanism. *Philosophical Transactions of the Royal Society of London, Series B: Biological Science, 358,* 517–528.

Gallese, V. (2003b). The roots of empathy: The shared manifold hypothesis and the neural basis of intersubjectivity. *Psychopathology, 36*(4), 171–180.

Gallese, V. (2005). Embodied simulation: From neurons to phenomenal experience. *Phenomenology and the Cognitive Sciences, 4,* 23–48.

Gallese, V. (2006). Intentional attunement: A neurophysiological perspective on social cognition and its disruption in autism. *Brain Research, 1079,* 15–24.

Gallese V. (2007). Before and below theory of mind: Embodied simulation and the neural correlates of social cognition.

Proceedings of the Royal Society of London, Series B: Biological Science, 362, 659–669.

Gallese V. (2008). Mirror neurons and the social nature of language: The neural exploitation hypothesis. *Social Neuroscience, 3,* 317–333.

Gallese, V. (2009). Mirror neurons and the neural exploitation hypothesis: From embodied simulation to social cognition. In J. A. Pineda (Ed.), *Mirror Neuron Systems* (pp. 163–190). New York: Humana Press.

Gallese, V., Fadiga, L., Fogassi, L., & Rizzolatti, G. (1996). Action recognition in the premotor cortex. *Brain, 119,* 593–609.

Gallese, V., Fogassi, L., Fadiga, L., & Rizzolatti, G. (2002). Action representation and the inferior parietal lobule. In W. Prinz & B. Hommel (Eds.), *Attention & Performance XIX. Common Mechanisms in Perception and Action* (pp. 334–355). Oxford, UK: Oxford University Press.

Gallese, V., Keysers, C., & Rizzolatti, G. (2004). A unifying view of the basis of social cognition. *Trends Cognitive Sciences, 8,* 396–403.

Gallese, V., & Lakoff, G. (2005). The brain's concepts: The role of the sensory-motor system in reason and language. *Cognitive Neuropsychology, 22,* 455–479.

Gallese, V., & Metzinger, T. (2003). Motor ontology: The representational reality of goals, actions, and selves. *Philosophical Psychology, 16*(3), 365–388.

Gallese, V., Rochat, M., Cossu, G., & Sinigaglia, C. (2009). Motor cognition and its role in the phylogeny and ontogeny of intentional understanding. *Developmental Psychology, 45,* 103–113.

Gazzola, V., Aziz-Zadeh, L., & Keysers, C. (2006). Empathy and the somatotopic auditory mirror system in humans. *Current Biology, 16,* 1824–1829.

Gazzola, V., Rizzolatti, G., Wicker, B., & Keysers, C. (2007). The anthropomorphic brain: The mirror neuron system responds to human and robotic actions. *Neuroimage, 35,* 1674–1684.

Gazzola, V., van der Worp, H., Mulder, T., Wicker, B., Rizzolatti, G., & Keysers, C. (2007). Aplasics born without hands mirror the goal of hand actions with their feet. *Current Biology, 17,* 1235–1240.

Gergely, G., Nàdasdy, Z., Csibra, G., & Bìrò, S. (1995). Taking the intentional stance at 12 months of age. *Cognition, 56,* 165–193.

Glenberg, A. M., Lopez-Mobilia, G, McBeath, M., Toma, M., Sato, M., & Cattaneo, L. (2010). Knowing beans: Human mirror mechanisms revealed through motor adaptation. *Frontiers in Human Neuroscience, 4,* 206.

Goldman, A. (2006). *Simulating Minds: The Philosophy, Psychology and Neuroscience of Mindreading.* Oxford, UK: Oxford University Press.

Hauk, O., Johnsrude, I., & Pulvermuller, F. (2004). Somatotopic representation of action words in human motor and premotor cortex. *Neuron, 41*(2), 301–307.

Hepp-Reymond, M.-C., Hüsler, E. J., Maier, M. A., & Qi, H.-X. (1994). Force-related neuronal activity in two regions of the primate ventral premotor cortex. *Canadian Journal of Physiology and Pharmacology, 72,* 571–579.

Heyes, C. (2010). Where do mirror neurons come from? *Neuroscience and Biobehavioral Review, 34,* 575–583.

Hutchison, W. D., Davis, K. D., Lozano, A. M., Tasker, R. R., & Dostrovsky, J. O. (1999). Pain related neurons in the human cingulate cortex. *Nature Neuroscience, 2,* 403–405.

Iacoboni, M., & Dapretto, M. (2006). The mirror neuron system and the consequences of its dysfunction. *Nature Reviews Neuroscience*, *7*(12), 942–951.

Iacoboni, M., Molnar-Szakacs, I., Gallese, V., Buccino, G., Mazziotta, J., & Rizzolatti, G. (2005). Grasping the intentions of others with one's owns mirror neuron system. *PLOS Biology*, *3*, 529–535.

Iacoboni, M., Woods, R. P., Brass, M., Bekkering, H., Mazziotta, J. C., & Rizzolatti, G. (1999). Cortical mechanisms of human imitation. *Science*, *286*, 2526–2528.

Jabbi, M., Bastiaansen, J., & Keysers, C. (2008). A common anterior insula representation of disgust observation, experience and imagination shows divergent functional connectivity pathways. *PLoS ONE*, *3*(8), e2939.

Jackson, P. L., Meltzoff, A. N., & Decety, J. (2005). How do we perceive the pain of others: A window into the neural processes involved in empathy. *Neuroimage*, *24*, 771–779.

Kakei, S., Hoffman, D. S., & Strick, P. L. (1999). Muscle and movement representations in the primary motor cortex. *Science*, *285*, 2136–2139.

Kakei, S., Hoffman, D. S., & Strick, P. L. (2001). Direction of action is represented in the ventral premotor cortex. *Nature Neuroscience*, *4*, 1020–1025.

Keysers, C., & Perrett, D. I. (2004). Demystifying social cognition: A Hebbian perspective. *Trends in Cognitive Science*, *8*, 501–507.

Keysers, C., & Gazzola, V. (2009). Expanding the mirror: Vicarious activity for actions, emotions, and sensations. *Current Opinion in Neurobiology*, *19*(6), 666–671.

Keysers, C., Kaas, J. H., & Gazzola, V. (2010). Somatosensation in social perception. *Nature Reviews Neuroscience*, *11*(6), 417–428.

Keysers, C., Wickers, B., Gazzola, V., Anton, J. L., Fogassi, L., & Gallese, V. (2004). A Touching sight: SII/PV activation during the observation and experience of touch. *Neuron*, *42*, 1–20.

Kohler, E., Keysers, C., Umiltà, M. A., Fogassi, L., Gallese, V., & Rizzolatti, G. (2002). Hearing sounds, understanding actions: Action representation in mirror neurons. *Science*, *297*, 846–848.

Kraskov, A., Dancause, N., Quallo, M. M., Shepherd, S. & Lemon, R. N. (2010). Corticospinal neurons in macaque ventral premotor cortex with mirror properties: A potential mechanism for action suppression? *Neuron*, *64*, 922–930.

Lepage, J. F., & Théoret, H. (2007). The mirror neuron system: Grasping other's actions from birth? *Developmental Science*, *10*(5), 513–529.

Matelli, M., Luppino, G., & Rizzolatti, G. (1985). Patterns of cytochrome oxidase activity in the frontal agranular cortex of the macaque monkey. *Behavioral Brain Research*, *18*, 125–137.

Meltzoff, A. N., & Moore, M. K. (1977). Imitation of facial and manual gestures by human neonates. *Science*, *198*, 75–78.

Mukamel, R., Ekstrom, A. D., Kaplan, J., Iacoboni, M., & Fried, I. (2010). Single-neuron responses in humans during execution and observation of actions. *Current Biology*, *20*(8), 750–756.

Murata, A., Fadiga, L., Fogassi, L., Gallese, V., Raos, V., & Rizzolatti, G. (1997). Object representation in the ventral premotor cortex (area F5) of the monkey. *Journal of Neurophysiology*, *78*, 2226–2230.

Myowa-Yamakoshi, M., Tomonaga, M., Tanaka, M., & Matsuzawa, T. (2004). Imitation in neonatal chimpanzees (*Pan troglodytes*). *Developmental Science*, *7*, 437–442.

Oberman, L. M., & Ramachandran, V. S. (2007). The simulating social mind: Mirror neuron system and simulation in the social and communicative deficits of autism spectrum disorder. *Psychological Bulletin*, *133*, 310–327.

Pulvermüller, F. (2002). *The Neuroscience of Language*. Cambridge, UK: Cambridge University Press.

Raos, V., Umilta, M. A., Fogassi, L., & Gallese, V. (2006). Functional properties of grasping-related neurons in the ventral premotor area F5 of the macaque monkey. *Journal of Neurophysiology*, *95*, 709–729.

Ricciardi, E., Bonino, D., Sani, L., Vecchi, T., Guazzelli, M., Haxby, J. V., et al. (2009). Do we really need vision? How blind people "see" the actions of others. *Journal of Neuroscience*, *29*, 9719–9724.

Rizzolatti, G., Camarda, R., Fogassi, M., Gentilucci, M., Luppino, G., & Matelli, M. (1988). Functional organization of inferior area 6 in the macaque monkey: II. Area F5 and the control of distal movements. *Experimental Brain Research*, *71*, 491–507.

Rizzolatti, G, & Craighero, L. (2004). The mirror neuron system. *Annual Review of Neuroscience*, *27*, 169–192.

Rizzolatti, G., Fadiga, L., Gallese, V., & Fogassi, L. (1996). Premotor cortex and the recognition of motor actions. *Cognitive Brain Research*, *3*, 131–141.

Rizzolatti, G., Fogassi, L., & Gallese, V. (2000). Cortical mechanisms subserving object grasping and action recognition: A new view on the cortical motor functions. In M. S. Gazzaniga (Ed.), *The New Cognitive Neurosciences*, 2nd ed. (pp. 539–552). Cambridge, MA: MIT Press.

Rizzolatti G., Fogassi L., & Gallese V. (2001). Neurophysiological mechanisms underlying the understanding and imitation of action. *Nature Neuroscience Reviews*, *2*, 661–670.

Rizzolatti, G., & Gallese, V. (1997). From action to meaning. In J.-L. Petit (Ed.), *Les Neurosciences et la Philosophie de l'Action*. Paris: Librairie Philosophique J. Vrin.

Rizzolatti, G., Scandolara, C., Matelli, M., & Gentilucci, M. (1981). Afferent properties of periarcuate neurons in macaque monkey. II. Visual responses. *Behavioural Brain Research*, *2*, 147–163.

Rizzolatti, G., & Sinigaglia, C. (2008). *Mirrors in the Brain. How Our Minds Share Actions and Emotions*. New York: Oxford University Press.

Rizzolatti, G., & Sinigaglia, C. (2010). The functional role of the parieto-frontal mirror circuit: Interpretations and misinterpretations. *Nature Reviews Neuroscience*, *11*, 264–274.

Rochat, M. J., Caruana, F., Jezzini, A., Escola, L., Intskirveli, I., Grammont, F., et al. (2010). Responses of mirror neurons in area F5 to hand and tool grasping observation. *Experimental Brain Research*, *204*(4), 605–616.

Rochat, M. J., Serra, E., Fadiga, L., & Gallese, V. (2008). The evolution of social cognition: Goal familiarity shapes monkeys' action understanding. *Current Biology*, *18*, 227–232.

Rozzi, S., Ferrari, P. F., Bonini, L., Rizzolatti, G., & Fogassi, L. (2008). Functional organization of inferior parietal lobule convexity in the macaque monkey: Electrophysiological characterization of motor, sensory and mirror responses and their correlation with cytoarchitectonic areas. *European Journal of Neuroscience*, *28*, 1569–1588.

Santos, L. R., Nissen, A. G., & Ferrugia, J. A. (2006). Rhesus monkeys, *Macaca mulatta*, know what others can and cannot hear. *Animal Behavior*, *71*, 1175–1181.

Shen, L., & Alexander, G. E. (1997). Preferential representation of instructed target location versus limb trajectory in dorsal premotor area. *Journal of Neurophysiology*, *77*, 1195–1212.

Shepherd, S. V., Klein, J. T., Deaner, R. O., & Platt, M. L. (2009). Mirroring of attention by neurons in macaque parietal cortex. *Proceedings of the National Academy of Sciences U S A, 106*(23), 9489–9494.

Shimada, S., & Hiraki, K. (2006). Infant's brain responses to live and televised action. *Neuroimage, 32*(2), 930–939.

Singer, T., Seymour, B., O'Doherty, J., Kaube, H., Dolan, R. J., & Frith, C. F. (2004). Empathy for pain involves the affective but not the sensory components of pain. *Science, 303*, 1157–1162.

Tettamanti, M., Buccino, G., Saccuman, M. C., Gallese, V., Danna, M., Scifo, P., et al. (2005). Listening to action-related sentences activates fronto-parietal motor circuits. *Journal of Cognitive Neuroscience, 17*, 273–281.

Umiltà, M. A., Brochier, T., Spinks, R. L., & Lemon, R. N. (2007). Simultaneous recording of macaque premotor and primary motor cortex neuronal populations reveals different functional contributions to visuomotor grasp. *Journal of Neurophysiology, 98*, 488–501.

Umiltà, M. A., Escola, L., Intskirveli, I., Grammont, F., Rochat, M., Caruana, F., et al. (2008). How pliers become fingers in the monkey motor system. *Proceedings of the National Academy of Sciences U S A, 105*, 2209–2213.

Umiltà, M. A., Kohler, E., Gallese, V., et al. (2001). "I know what you are doing": A neurophysiological study. *Neuron, 32*, 91–101.

Wicker, B., Keysers, C., Plailly, J., Royet, J.-P., Gallese, V., & Rizzolatti, G. (2003). Both of us disgusted in my insula: The common neural basis of seeing and feeling disgust. *Neuron, 40*, 655–664.

Zoia, S., Blason, L., D'Ottavio, G., Bulgheroni, M., Pezzetta, E., Scabar, A., & Castiello, U. (2007). Evidence of early development of action planning in the human foetus: A kinematic study. *Experimental Brain Research. 176*, 217–226.

The Early Development of the Brain Bases for Social Cognition

Tobias Grossmann *and* Mark H. Johnson

Abstract

Much research has focused on how the adult human brain processes social information, yet until recently little was known about the early development of these abilities. This chapter reviews recent work examining the precursors of the human social brain network during infancy in several domains such as face and eye gaze processing, engaging in joint attention, decoding of biological motion, and understanding of human action. The findings from electroencephalography (EEG) and near-infrared spectroscopy (NIRS) studies in these domains suggest that some brain processes implicated in social cognition in adults become sensitive during infancy. While there seems to be emerging functional specialization for social cognition within individual brain regions during infancy, what still needs to be understood is how these regions become orchestrated into functional networks during development. Thus, in the final section on emerging networks, an account is put forward, based on prefrontal cortex functioning and computational modeling, of how such an integration might be achieved.

Key Words: social cognition, social brain, face, gaze, joint attention, biological motion, action

Introduction

Humans, like other primates, are intensely social creatures. One major function of our brains is to enable us to recognize and manipulate socially relevant information and behave accordingly. In the field of social cognition, researchers attempt to understand and explain how thoughts, feelings, and behavior of individuals are influenced by the presence of others and through interaction with others (Allport, 1985; Fiske, 1995).

There is evidence for the relative independence of social cognition from other aspects of cognition. For example, individuals with either frontal or prefrontal cortex damage show impaired social behavior and functioning, despite the retention of some intact cognitive skills, such as memory and language (Anderson, Bechara, Damasio, Tranel, & Damasio, 1999; Blair & Cipolotti, 2000; Fine, Lumsden, & Blair, 2001). The fact that social cognition can be

relatively impaired after such an injury while sparing aspects of nonsocial cognition raises the possibility that unique neural circuits may contribute to social cognition. A similar dissociation between social cognition and nonsocial cognitive skills is sometimes observed in persons with prosopagnosia, who can show selective impairments in the perception of faces despite preserved processing of nonsocial stimuli (Duchaine & Nakayama, 2006). Furthermore, it has been shown that while social and nonsocial behaviors are both heritable, they show a degree of partial independence, with some of the genetic variation dissociating social and nonsocial behaviors (Ronald, Happe, & Plomin, 2005). More evidence for the partial independence of social cognition has been gleaned from studies of persons with Williams' syndrome or autism. Individuals with Williams' syndrome appear to have relatively preserved basic social cognitive skills (i.e., facial processing and abilities in understanding mental states), despite having deficits in spatial cognition (Bellugi, Lichtenberger, Jones, Lai, & St George, 2000; Karmiloff-Smith, Klima, Bellugi, Grant, & Baron-Cohen, 1995). This partial preservation of social cognition is in direct contrast to persons with high-functioning autism and Asperger's syndrome, who show impairments in social cognition and social behavior that some suggest may not be related to general cognitive abilities (Heavey, Phillips, Baron-Cohen, & Rutter, 2000; Klin, 2000).

Together, these findings lend support to the hypothesis that there is a network of specific brain areas preferentially involved in the processing of social information. This network has been referred to as the "social brain" (Adolphs, 1999, 2001, 2003). This social brain hypothesis has also been maintained and influenced by thinking in the area of evolutionary anthropology (Brothers, 1990). To explain primates' and particularly humans' unusually large brains, it has even been claimed that the computational demands of living in complex social groups selected for increases in neocortex, a view put forward as the social brain hypothesis (Dunbar, 2003) or the Machiavellian intelligence hypothesis (Whiten & Byrne, 1997).

A new discipline called social cognitive neuroscience has emerged that investigates the neural underpinnings of human social behavior. Its agenda has been described as seeking "to understand phenomena in terms of interactions between three levels of analysis: the social level, which is concerned with the motivational and social factors that influence behavior and experience; the cognitive level, which is concerned with the information-processing mechanisms that give rise to social-level phenomena; and the neural level, which is concerned with the brain mechanisms that instantiate cognitive-level processes" (Ochsner & Lieberman, 2001, p. 717). The majority of the research activities in this area have focused on how adults' brains make sense of the social world (for reviews, see Adolphs, 1999, 2001, 2003; Beer & Ochsner, 2006; Blakemore & Frith, 2004; Frith & Frith, 1999, 2006; Lieberman, 2006). This provides us with important insights into the full-fledged, fully developed neural machinery that deals with complex social problems. However, from an ontogenetic perspective, the question arises: How do these capacities of the brain in reading others' social behavior develop? And what are the critical developmental precursors of these adult abilities? The answers to these questions are important for a variety of reasons since an understanding

of the early emergence of the social brain will not only inform theories of infant social development but will be of relevance for social, educational, and clinical policies (Blakemore & Frith, 2005).

The earliest stage of postnatal development, infancy (0–2 years), is the time of life during which enormous changes take place—the "helpless" newborn seems almost a different creature from the active, inquisitive 2-year-old. During this period, human infants develop in a world filled with other people. Relating socially to others not only has profound effects on what they feel, think, and do but is also essential for their healthy development and for optimal functioning throughout life. Indeed, the ability to learn from other humans is perhaps one of the most important adaptations of our species (Csibra & Gergely, 2009). Therefore, developing an understanding of other people is one of the most fundamental tasks infants face in learning about the world. The development of the brain circuitries involved in all kinds of cognitive processes depends on the interaction of two broad factors: nature (our inheritance or genetic factors) and nurture (environmental influences). If we aim to understand how these factors interact to "build" the mature brain network dealing with the social world, it seems of particular importance to look at how the human brain deals with social information during early development.

The ontogeny of the social brain network is one aspect of human postnatal functional brain development, and it is therefore useful to consider work in this field within the context of general perspectives on developing brain function (see Johnson, 2001, 2005a, for reviews). Specifically, in this chapter, we focus on advancing an interactive specialization (IS) view of functional brain specialization for social cognition in early development. The IS account assumes that postnatal functional brain development, at least within cerebral cortex, involves a process of organizing patterns of interregional interactions (Johnson, 2001, 2005a). According to this view, the response properties of a specific region are partly determined by its patterns of connectivity to other regions and, in turn, by their patterns of activity. During postnatal development changes in the response properties of cortical regions occur as they interact and compete with each other to acquire their role in new computational abilities. From this perspective, some cortical regions may begin with poorly defined functions and are consequently partially activated in a wide range of different contexts and tasks. During development, activity-dependent interactions between regions tunes up the functions of regions such that their activity becomes restricted to a narrower set of circumstances (e.g., a region originally activated by a wide variety of visual objects may come to confine its response to upright human faces). The onset of new behavioral competencies during infancy and childhood will therefore be associated with changes in activity (adjustments in tuning functions) over several regions and their patterns of connectivity, and not just by the onset of activity in one specific region.

In IS, the assumption is that cognitive functions are the emergent product of interactions between different brain regions and between the whole brain and its external environment. According to this view, brain regions do not develop in isolation but are heavily constrained by their connections and interactions with other regions, a phenomenon recently termed "embrainment" (Mareschal et al., 2007). In this respect, IS follows recent trends in adult functional neuroimaging in which the emphasis has shifted away from the attempt to localize particular functions to certain cortical regions and toward understanding the response properties of regions as determined by their patterns of functional connectivity to other regions (Fairhall & Ishai, 2007; Friston, 1994; Friston & Price, 2001; Summerfield et al., 2006). This is not to imply that there is not much to be gained from localizing cortical functions in infancy. It will become obvious throughout the chapter that much effort has been spent to map brain functions in infancy, and much more work needs to be done to achieve a fuller understanding of the functional specificity of certain brain regions. Nevertheless, the IS approach emphasizes the importance of interregional connectivity, as opposed to the maturation of intraregional connections.

The following sections will present and discuss empirical findings from several areas of processing social information in early development: (1) face and gaze processing, (2) joint attention, (3) biological motion, and (4) understanding human action. These findings are mainly based on electroencephalography (EEG) and event-related potential (ERP) methods, which are the most commonly used methods with this age group. These EEG/ERP methods, which provide precise information on the timing of brain and cognitive processes, were more recently complemented by near-infrared spectroscopy (NIRS) to localize cortical activation in infants (see Lloyd-Fox, Blasi, & Elwell, 2010, for a review). In recent years, this method has helped tremendously to map social cognitive processes in the infant brain.

Finally, after considering the empirical findings in these different areas of social cognition we will propose a model of how regionally specialized processes dedicated to social cognition become orchestrated into emerging networks.

Face

The face provides a wealth of socially relevant information. The ability to detect and recognize faces is thus commonly considered to be an important adaptation of social animals. From birth, human infants preferentially attend to some face-like patterns (Johnson, 2005b; Morton & Johnson, 1991), which suggests a powerful mechanism to bias the input that is processed by the newborn's brain. The face preference observed in newborns is thought to be guided largely by subcortical brain structures; it has been proposed that the maturation of visual cortical areas is necessary for the emergence of the more sophisticated competencies underlying identity recognition from faces (for a discussion, see Johnson, 2005b). Newborns first recognize their mother's face on the basis of information from the outer contour of the head, hairline, and the internal configuration of eyes, nose, and mouth (Bushnell, Sai, & Mullin, 1989). But it is not until 6 weeks of life that they become able to do this recognition solely on the basis of the face's internal configuration (de Schonen & Mathivet, 1990).

Investigations of brain areas involved in face processing in infants have been limited mainly by technical issues (de Haan & Thomas, 2002; Grossmann, 2008). One exception is a study by Tzourio-Mazoyer and colleagues (2002), who took advantage of the opportunity to perform positron emission tomography (PET) on infants in an intensive care unit as part of a clinical follow-up. In this small-scale study, a group of six 2-month-olds were imaged while they watched a face or an array of colored diodes used as a control stimulus. A subtraction analysis revealed that faces activated a network of areas in 2-month-old infants' brains similar to that described as the core system for face processing in adults (Haxby, Hofman, & Gobbini, 2000). More specifically, a significant activation was reported in an area in infants' right inferior temporal gyrus, which is thought to be the homologue of the adult fusiform face area (FFA) (Gauthier, Tarr, Anderson, Skudlarski, & Gore, 1999; Kanwisher, 2000). It is interesting to note that a cortical region that at the age of 2 months is neuroanatomically immature (Huttenlocher, 2002; Huttenlocher & Dabholkar, 1997) and has only a low level of metabolic activity (Chugani & Phelps,

1986; Chugani, Phelps, & Mazziotta, 1987) can exhibit functional activity. In addition, face perception activated bilateral inferior occipital and right inferior parietal areas in infants. The former has been implicated in early perceptual analysis of facial features, whereas the latter is thought to support spatially directed attention in adults (Haxby et al., 2000). Interestingly, and contrary to what is known from adults, face processing in 2-month-olds also recruited areas in the inferior frontal and superior temporal gyrus, which have been identified as part of the adult language network. One possible interpretation is that the coactivation of face and future language networks has a facilitatory effect on social interactions guiding language learning by attention toward the speaker's face and mouth (Tzourio-Mazoyer et al., 2002).

Bearing in mind the small sample size and nonoptimal control stimulus, the study by Tzourio-Mazoyer and colleagues nonetheless provided important information by identifying the neural substrates of the infant face-processing network. However, as mentioned earlier, because of ethical and technical concerns with the use of neuroimaging methods like PET and functional magnetic resonance imaging (fMRI) in infants, evidence coming from these kinds of studies is rare. Moreover, NIRS methods are not sensitive enough to image the ventral surface of the brain where the FFA is located (Grossmann, 2008). Therefore, most studies that have examined the brain basis of infant face perception rely on the more readily applicable recording of EEG measures, which provide an excellent temporal resolution but are relatively poor in their spatial resolution.

We now discuss briefly the empirical evidence available on infants' face processing using event-related brain potentials (ERPs; for a more detailed review, see de Haan, Johnson, & Halit, 2003). In adults, human faces elicit an N170 response, which is most prominent over posterior temporal sites and is larger in amplitude and longer in latency to inverted than to upright faces (Bentin, Allison, Puce, Perez, & McCarthy, 1996; de Haan, Pascalis, & Johnson, 2002). This component is not modulated by the inversion of monkey faces (de Haan et al., 2002) nor when upright objects are compared to inverted objects (Bentin et al., 1996). This selective inversion effect for human faces has been taken as evidence for a face-related processing mechanism generating the N170.

On the basis of waveform morphology and some of its response properties, it has been suggested that

the infant N290 is a precursor to the adult N170. In these studies, infants' and adults' ERPs were measured in response to upright and inverted human and monkey faces (de Haan et al., 2002; Halit, de Haan, & Johnson, 2003). The infant N290 is a negative-going deflection observed over posterior electrodes whose peak latency decreases from 350 ms at 3 months to 290 ms at 12 months of age (Halit et al., 2003). This is consistent with the latency of many prominent ERP components reducing with increasing age during childhood. The results of these studies indicate that at 12 months of age, the amplitude of the infant N290, like the adult N170, increases to inverted human but not inverted monkey faces when compared to the upright faces. However, the amplitude of the N290 was not affected by stimulus inversion at an earlier age (3 and 6 months).

It is important to point out that development of the brain processes reflected in the N170/N290 continues well beyond infancy (for a review, see Taylor, Batty, & Itier, 2004). While latency of the adult N170 is delayed by face inversion, no such effect is observed for the latency of the infant N290 at any age (de Haan et al., 2002; Halit et al., 2003). There is evidence that suggests that this latency effect is not apparent until 8 to 11 years (Taylor et al., 2004). Another important developmental finding is that while the amplitude of the adult N170 is larger to the monkey faces, infants' N290 shows the opposite pattern. A completely adult-like modulation of the amplitude of the N170 has not been reported to occur until age 13 to 14 years (Taylor et al., 2004).

To date, aside from speech perception (Dehaene-Lambertz, Dehaene, & Hertz-Pannier, 2002; Kuhl, 2004), face processing is the best studied aspect of infant brain development. The evidence available from PET and EEG/ERP studies suggests that most of the brain areas and mechanisms implicated in adult face processing can be activated within the first few months of postnatal life. However, there are differences, such as the activation of inferior frontal regions in 2-month-olds (Tzourio-Mazoyer et al., 2002), that do not directly map onto the face-processing system found in adults. In addition to the extra regions involved while infants perceive faces, another important observation in the infant ERP work is that the infant face-processing system possesses broader response properties that are not yet as finely tuned to upright human faces. This suggests that despite the gradual specialization seen throughout the first year of life, the system continues to specialize well beyond infancy. These changes in the degree of specialization of processing, and the spatial extent of cortical activation, are in accordance with the IS perspective alluded to earlier (Johnson, 2001, 2005a). A pattern of increasingly focal activation in response to faces in fusiform gyrus is supported by several recent fMRI studies comparing children and adults: faces resulted in a more distributed pattern of activation, and more broadly tuned neural responses, in 8- to 12-year-old children than in adults (see Johnson, Grossmann, & Cohen Kadosh, 2009, for a review).

Gaze

An important social signal encoded in faces is eye gaze. The detection and monitoring of eye gaze direction is essential for effective social learning and communication among humans (Bloom, 2000; Csibra & Gergely, 2009). Eye gaze provides information about the target of another person's attention and expression, and it also conveys information about communicative intentions and future behavior (Baron-Cohen, 1995). Eye contact is considered to be one of the most powerful modes of establishing a communicative link between humans (Kampe, Frith, & Frith, 2003). From birth, human infants are sensitive to another person's gaze, as reflected in their preference to look at faces that have their eyes open rather than closed (Batki, Baron-Cohen, Wheelwright, Connellan, & Ahluwalia, 2000). Furthermore, newborns look longer at faces with direct/mutual gaze than at faces with averted gaze (Farroni, Csibra, Simion, & Johnson, 2002). Eye gaze has also been shown to effectively cue newborn infants' attention to spatial locations, suggesting a rudimentary form of gaze following (Farroni, Pividori, Simion, Massaccesi, & Johnson, 2004). The question that arises is how the behaviorally expressed preference for direct gaze and the capacity to follow gaze are implemented in the infant brain.

By 4 months, the infant brain manifests enhanced processing of faces with direct gaze, as indexed by an increased amplitude of the N290 when compared to that of averted gaze (Farroni et al., 2002). This finding is obtained even when the head is averted but direct mutual gaze is maintained (Farroni, Johnson, & Csibra, 2004). However, enhanced neural processing of faces with direct gaze is only found when eyes are presented in the context of an upright face. Moreover, in a recent study, 4-month-old infants watched two kinds of dynamic scenarios in which a face either established mutual gaze or averted its gaze (Grossmann et al., 2008). Hemodynamic responses were measured by NIRS, permitting spatial localization of brain activation. The results

showed that processing of mutual gaze social interactions activates areas in the infant right superior temporal and prefrontal cortex that correspond to the brain regions implicated in these processes in adults (Kampe et al., 2003; Pelphrey, Viola, & McCarthy, 2004). This pattern of ERP and NIRS results suggests the early specialization of brain processes involved in mutual gaze detection.

Another communicative function of eye gaze is to direct attention to certain locations, events, and objects. Understanding the relations between eye gaze and target objects is particularly important for aspects of development such as word learning. Comprehending that another's gaze direction refers to a specific object allows the child to associate the object with a name or an emotional expression (Baldwin & Moses, 1996).

In an ERP study, 9-month-old infants and adults watched a face whose gaze shifted either toward (object-congruent) or away from (object-incongruent) the location of a previously presented object (Senju, Johnson, & Csibra, 2006). This paradigm was based on that used in an earlier fMRI study (Pelphrey, Singerman, Allison, & McCarthy, 2003) and was designed to reveal the neural basis of "referential" gaze perception. When the ERPs elicited by object-incongruent gaze shifts were compared to the object-congruent gaze shifts, an enhanced negativity around 300 ms over occipitotemporal electrodes was observed in both infants and adults. This suggests that infants encode referential information of gaze using similar neural mechanisms to those engaged in adults. However, only infants showed a frontocentral negative component that was larger in amplitude for object-congruent gaze shifts. It is thus possible that in the infant brain the referential information about gaze is encoded in more widespread cortical circuits than in the more specialized adult brain. We will return to this interesting finding on referential gaze in the next section, in which the neural basis of a very closely related social-cognitive phenomenon called joint attention is discussed.

Joint Attention

One of the major developmental changes in infants' engagement with others is thought to be the transition from participating in dyadic (face-to-face) interactions to developing a capacity to engage in triadic (infant–other person–object) joint-attention exchanges (Scaife & Bruner, 1975). Besides attending to an external object or event herself, the ability to jointly attend with another person requires the infant to monitor (a) the other person's attention in relation to the self and (b) the other person's attention toward the same object or event. Behavioral studies suggest that triadic representations between two minds and a shared object of attention emerge at around 9 months of age. They are thought to be uniquely human representations (Baron-Cohen, 1995; Tomasello, Carpenter, Call, Behne, & Moll, 2005) supporting shared attention and collaborative goals. The dorsal part of the medial prefrontal cortex (PFC) has been identified as a critical region to support these kinds of representations in the adult human brain (Frith & Frith, 2006; Saxe, 2006; Williams, Waiter, Perro, Perrett, & Whiten, 2005).

Striano, Reid, and Hoehl (2006) used a novel interactive paradigm to examine the ERP correlates of joint attention in 9-month-old infants in which an adult interacted live with each infant in two contexts. In the joint-attention context, the adult looked at the infant and then at the computer screen displaying a novel object. In the non-joint-attention context, the adult only looked at the chest of the infant and then at the novel object presented on the screen. Objects presented in the joint-attention context, compared to objects in the non-joint-attention context, were found to elicit a greater negative component (Nc), peaking at around 500 ms with a maximum amplitude over frontal and central channels. The Nc is thought to be generated within the PFC and may indicate the allocation of attention to a visual stimulus (with a greater amplitude indexing more allocation of attentional resources; Reynolds & Richards, 2005). Therefore, Striano et al. (2006) suggested that infants benefit from the joint-attention interaction and thus devote more attentional resources to those objects presented in this context. This ERP paradigm has also been used to examine joint attention in younger infants (see Parise, Reid, Stets, & Striano, 2008). This study found that even by the age of 5 months, infants show an increased allocation of attention to the object in a joint-attention condition, as indexed by an increased Nc.

It is worth noting that in Senju et al.'s (2006) study on referential gaze perception, discussed earlier, a very similar frontocentral negativity to that in Striano et al.'s (2006) and Parise et al.'s (2008) live joint-attention studies was observed. This is not surprising, given the similarities between the two studies and the joint-attentional nature of the situations presented to the infant in the two studies. In Senju et al.'s (2006) study, the frontocentral negativity was observed in 9-month-olds who watched a person on the screen make eye contact and then look at an object. In Striano et al.'s (2006) and Parise et al.'s

(2008) studies, this brain response was obtained when a live experimenter established eye contact with the infant and then looked at an object on the screen. It is thus possible that the infant frontocentral negativity found in these two studies reflects brain processes related to joint attention.

Despite these insights from using ERP methods, it still remains unclear which brain regions are involved in engaging in triadic interactions. However, in a recent study NIRS was used to localize infant brain responses during triadic interactions (Grossmann & Johnson, 2010). In this study, 5-month-old infants showed increased left prefrontal cortical responses when engaged in joint triadic interactions compared to that in two (nontriadic) control conditions, in which either no eye contact was established or the person looked away from the object. These findings are in line with previous fMRI work with adults implicating left prefrontal regions in joint attention (Williams et al., 2005). Thus, during triadic social interactions 5-month-olds infants seem to engage the same prefrontal regions as those engaged in adults.

Further support for the notion that left PFC plays a critical role in joint attention comes from a clinical study in which cortical metabolism in infants was measured using PET prior to hemispherectomy for intractable seizure disorder (Caplan et al., 1993). In this study, higher rates of preoperative glucose metabolism in frontal cortical regions, especially left frontal region, was a positive predictor of the postoperatively assessed tendency to initiate joint-attention bids. To further assess the role of the frontal cortex, resting EEG coherence and its relation to joint-attention skills in typically developing infants was examined (Mundy, Card, & Fox, 2000). EEG coherence is a measure of phase synchrony between spatially separated EEG generators, which provides an index of aspects of neural network integration (Thatcher, Krause, & Hrybyk, 1986). EEG coherence measures of left frontal cortical activity were found to be associated with the infants' tendency to initiate joint attention at 14 and 18 months. Furthermore, in a follow-up study, it was shown that behavioral measures of joint attention and EEG coherence at 14 months were both related to language development at 24 months (Mundy, Fox, & Card, 2003).

In summary, ERP and NIRS data suggest that, as earlier as 5 months, infants are sensitive to triadic social interactions. This early sensitivity to joint attention appears to depend on left prefrontal brain areas. At the outset of this section, based on behavioral findings, it was stated that one of the major developmental changes in infants' engagement with others is the transition from participating in dyadic (face-to-face) to triadic (infant–other–object) joint-attention exchanges at around 9 months of age. This proposed transition does not seem to be present in the neuroimaging data reviewed in this section. This suggests that changes might take place much earlier, that is, before 5 months of age, or they may simply emerge more gradually than previously thought. Supporting the gradual emergence of developing joint-attention skills, it has been shown that by the age of 3 months, infants are able to behaviorally discriminate between dyadic and triadic joint-attention interactions (Striano & Stahl, 2005). In this study, infants gazed and smiled more when, in the joint-attention condition, an experimenter alternated visual attention between the infant and the object than when she simply looked at the object without engaging or addressing the infant.

Another speculation is that the behavioral transition observed at around 9 months might be reflected in the emerging sensitivity of other brain systems involved in a deeper understanding of social interactions. This notion of a more elaborate understanding of other's gazing behavior has received some support from behavioral work showing that, when infants watched an adult turning his or her head toward a target with either open or closed eyes, 10- and 11-month-old infants followed adult turns significantly more often in the open-eyes than the closed-eyes condition, whereas 9-month-olds did not behave differently across conditions. This finding suggests that older infants begin to understand "seeing" in others (see Brooks & Meltzoff, 2005) and are thus able to adjust their behavior accordingly. The emergence of this kind of understanding of others' gazing behavior might have important implications for the early development of joint-attentional capacities. However, to our knowledge, its brain basis has not yet been examined.

Biological Motion

Another important function of the social brain is the detection of biological agents. The detection and interpretation of biological motion is thought to be a critical process for this identification. Behavioral research using point-light displays (PLDs; Johansson, 1973) suggests that, from birth, human infants detect biological motion (e.g., walking hen) by preferring it to other forms of nonbiological motion (e.g., randomly drifting dots), and

they also show a specific preference for upright biological movement (Simion, Regolin, & Bulf, 2008; see also Bertenthal, 1993, for similar findings with 3-month-old infants, using human point-light walkers). The basis for this orientation preference may be the characteristic motion patterns of the feet (see Troje & Westhoff, 2006). These findings suggest that human infants possess an inborn species-unspecific system that allows for the detection of and preferential attention to biological motion involving limbs.

In an ERP study, 8-month-old infants' processing of upright and inverted PLDs depicting human movement was examined (Reid, Hoehl, & Striano, 2006). Inverted compared to upright human motion elicited a greater right posterior N290 in infants' ERPs. These results suggest that 8-month-olds process upright and inverted human motion differently, providing corroborating evidence to what is already known from the behavioral work. Both inverted compared to upright human motion (Reid et al., 2006) and inverted human faces compared to upright human faces (Halit et al., 2003) have been found to elicit a greater N290. This similarity observed in infants' human face and human motion processing suggests that in infants the cortical processes underlying the N290 might be more generally tuned to "humanness" of a visual stimulus independent of whether the stimulus is a face or a PLD. In another ERP study, 8-month-olds were found to show a greater N290 over right posterior sites in response to human motion than to scrambled motion (Hirai & Hiraki, 2005). This finding has been extended to 5-month-old infants using walking, kicking, throwing, and running actions (Marshall & Shipley, 2009). However, in 5-month-olds the ERP effect was observed over both hemispheres and not lateralized to the right hemisphere as in 8-month-olds. This suggests that the right-hemisphere dominance in dealing with biological motion may only emerge after 5 months of age (see also Reid, Csibra, Belsky, & Johnson, 2007, for a discussion).

The posterior superior temporal sulcus (STS) has been implicated in the processing of biological motion in human adults (Allison, Puce, & McCarthy, 2000). Lloyd-Fox and colleagues (2009) used NIRS to measure hemodynamic responses in the temporal lobes in response to biological motion in 5-month-olds infants. Human infants showed increased bilateral activation in response to biological motion (human eye, mouth, and hand movements) around the posterior superior temporal cortex compared to that in response to static control images and, importantly, to nonbiological motion (clips of machine cogs and pistons and moving mechanical toys). These findings suggest not only that infants as young as 5 months of age recruit fairly specialized brain regions in temporal cortices when processing biological human motion, but also that the brain regions employed by these young infants are very similar to those engaged in adults (see Beauchamp, Lee, Haxby, & Martin, 2002). Despite this early cortical specialization for biological motion in young infants, similar to what we have seen for the face-processing system, fMRI work with 7- to 10-year-old children has demonstrated an increasing specificity for biological motion with age in the STS (Carter & Pelphrey, 2006). This suggests that, in accord with the IS account and with what we have learned about the FFA in the context of face processing, the STS continues to develop functional specificity in processing biological motion well into mid-childhood.

Action

Human actions are an exceedingly complex set of visual stimuli providing dynamic and continuous information about the behavior of other humans. The capacity to parse ongoing actions into meaningful segments is critical for the interpretation of others' behavior. There is evidence to suggest that in adults and infants, this parsing of action sequences is partly based on understanding the goal of an action (Baldwin, Baird, Saylor, & Clark, 2001; Blakemore & Decety, 2001). For example, when 8-month-old infants were presented with video clips showing complete and incomplete goal-directed actions (pouring liquid from a bottle into a glass). they looked longer at the incomplete than at the complete action (Reid, Csibra, Belsky, & Johnson, 2007). It is possible that the infants detected a mismatch between anticipated and perceived actions, which resulted in increased looking time when an action is terminated before a goal is achieved. This detection might be based on a process called forward-mapping, which involves the continuous prediction of possible motion trajectories and future actions based on their own motor representations (see, e.g., Falck-Ytter, Gredebäck, & von Hofsten, 2006).

Researchers have also asked the question of whether infants come to understand other people's actions through a mirror neuron system (Rizzolatti & Craighero, 2004) that maps an observed action onto infants' own motor representation of that action. According to the mirror neuron system view, infants are not expected to predict others' action goals before they can perform the action themselves. In a behavioral study (Falck-Ytter et al., 2006), 12-month-olds but not 6-month-olds were found to show proactive (anticipatory) goal-directed eye movements during observation of an action (putting objects into a box). Because it is known that infants do not master this kind of motor task until 7 to 9 months of age (Bruner, 1973), this finding was taken as evidence for the mirror neuron system view of action understanding. Furthermore, based on the finding that proactive eye movements were only found when a human agent produced the action but not when the objects were self-propelled (Falck-Ytter et al., 2006), it was argued that a human agent is required to activate the mirror neuron system. These findings are also interesting in light of evidence showing that good motor skills in 8-month-old infants correlate with their sensitivity to discriminate biologically possible from impossible arm movements (Reid, Belsky, & Johnson, 2005). Despite the value of these interesting behavioral findings, a shortcoming is that they provide only indirect evidence for a neural mechanistic explanation.

A candidate neural signature that has been shown to be useful for the study of action perception in adults is the mu wave (oscillatory bursts at 9–11 Hz), which can be measured with EEG. This wave activity appears to be associated with the motor cortex and is diminished with movement or an intent to move or when others are observed performing actions (Oberman et al., 2005). Therefore, EEG oscillations in the mu-wave range recorded over sensorimotor cortex are thought to reflect mirror neuron activity and have been associated with enabling an adult observer to understand an action through motor simulation.

Southgate, Johnson, Osborne, and Csibra (2009) investigated 9-month-olds' mu-wave activity over sensorimotor cortex during elicited reaching for objects. Critically, they also examined whether mu activity was modulated when observing a grasping action performed by someone else. The results obtained in this study revealed that, like adults, 9-month-old infants display a reduction in mu activity while performing and observing a grasping action. Another interesting finding in this study was that motor activation (mu suppression) was measured before the actual onset of the observed action. Infants must have learned to anticipate the occurrence of the action because they were presented with repeated trials and no mu suppression was evident during the first three trials. This finding of predictive motor activation during action observation supports accounts claiming that the mirror neuron system plays an important role in action prediction (Csibra, 2007).

In a follow-up study, 9-month-old infants watched an action (a hand grasping behind an occluder) that could only be interpreted as goal-directed if they are able to predict a hidden outcome (Southgate, Johnson, El Karoui, & Csibra, 2010). As in the previous study, motor activity was measured as indexed by mu activity over sensorimotor cortex. Motor activity during this goal prediction condition was compared to three control conditions that consisted of (1) a turned hand, unable to reach, going behind an occluder; (2) an open grasping hand being placed on the table in front of an occluder; and (3) a turned hand, unable to reach, being placed on the table in front of an occluder. Only when infants watched the grasping hand going behind the occluder was mu activity suppressed, whereas no such suppression was observed during any of the control conditions. This finding provides further evidence for 9-month-old infants' ability to predict the goal of an action and strengthens the notion that the motor system plays a critical role in action understanding. In addition, it shows that already by the age of 9 months motor activity is influenced by top-down processes such goal prediction rather than simply being driven by observing any kind of action.

However, in both studies (Southgate et al. 2009, 2010) the grasping actions presented to the infants in the action observation conditions were in their action repertoire. In another study (van Elk, van Schie, Hunnius, Vesper, & Bekkering, 2008), the role of motor experience with an action was investigated with 14- to 16-month-old infants. As predicted on the basis of infants' limited motor experience with walking at this age, infants exhibited stronger mu suppression during the observation of crawling than during the observation of walking. Furthermore, the size of this suppression effect was strongly correlated with the infants' own crawling experience such that infants who had longer crawling experience showed a stronger mu suppression. These findings provide some first evidence that motor activity during action observation in infants depends on motor experience with an action.

All the studies concerning action understanding presented up to this point relied on EEG scalp recordings placed over sensorimotor cortex. However, these scalp recordings cannot be localized to motor cortex activation with certainty during these tasks. Therefore, Shimada and Hiraki (2006) used NIRS to examine whether motor cortex is activated during action execution and action observation. They found that 6- to 7-month-old infants and adults activated motor cortex during the execution and observation of an action. Interestingly, at both ages, the activation of the motor system during action observation was only evoked when the action was presented live, but not when it was presented on video (see Shimada & Hiraki, 2006, for a discussion). However, the mu-suppression effects reported using EEG were obtained under live (Southgate et al., 2009, 2010) and videos conditions (van Elk et al., 2008) alike. It therefore seems critical to coregister EEG and NIRS in infants in order to clarify this issue. In any case, Shimada and Hiraki's (2006) findings further support the notion that there is an intricate link between observing and executing an action in the motor system.

Finally, a different line of research has investigated the assumption that action understanding, like language comprehension, relies on the use of semantic rules. That is, in order to anticipate the conclusion of an observed action, infants of a certain age may use semantic processes. Semantic processing in adults has been linked to the N400 component measured with ERPs (Kutas & Federmeier, 2000). Reid and colleagues (2009) presented 7- and 12-month old infants and adults with action sequences that ended with either an anticipated action (e.g., spoon to mouth) or an unanticipated action (e.g., spoon to forehead) while measuring ERPs. In this study, adults and 9-month-olds showed enhanced N400 responses while watching anticipated action conclusions, whereas no such effect was found for 7-month-old infants. This indicates that 9-month-olds and adults use similar, perhaps semantic, brain processes when processing action sequences in terms of outcomes. It is interesting to note that infants show an N400 response in the language domain only much later in development, at around 19 months of age (Friederici, 2006), lending some credence to the hypothesis that language understanding may originate from, or at least partly be linked to, action understanding.

In summary, the studies presented here suggest that action understanding and goal prediction may rely on both motor and semantic processes. Whether these processes are dissociable or interdependent during early development remains an open question that should be addressed in future research. Nevertheless, what can be said on the basis of the reviewed findings is that at least by the age of 9 months the brain processes that underlie motor and semantic action cognition seem to emerge. There is also some initial evidence that experience with a motor skill influences motor cortex activation during action observation, suggesting that with development, as new motor skills and action patterns are integrated into the developing child's repertoire, a better understanding of these actions may be acquired.

Emerging Networks

This systematic review of the emerging work on the early development of social cognition has shown that newborns enter the world with biases that help them to dedicate increased processing resources to their social world. Newborns show strong preferences for faces, eye contact and biological motion. These biases, which might be hard-wired and based on subcortical processes, could pave the way for the development and specialization of cortical processes that help infants to interact with, and learn about and from, social agents (see Johnson, 2005b, for a similar argument).

The most intriguing insight from this review is that some of the brain regions that have been implicated in the adult social brain network appear to become sensitive to social interaction and cognition in the first year of life. Faces specifically activate the right fusiform gyrus of 2-month-olds, eye contact cues activate the posterior STS and PFC in 4-month-olds, watching biological motion results in functional activation in posterior STS in 5-month-olds, joint triadic interaction appears to be processed in specialized regions in the left PFC in 5-month-olds, and observing and executing actions result in specific brain activation in the motor system in 6- to 7-month-olds. These findings suggest that some of the brain processes implicated in social cognition become specialized during infancy, raising the question of what develops beyond infancy.

One answer already alluded to throughout the individual sections based on fMRI work with children and adolescents is that there seems to be a substantial amount of region-specific fine-tuning occurring throughout childhood and adolescence (see Blakemore, 2008; Johnson et al., 2009, for review). Another important aspect to consider is that while we have observed activation of individual regions during infancy, we do not know whether the activity of these regions is coordinated into functional networks, as seen in adults. In other words, we are still in the dark about how the larger scale

of cortical function develops in terms of networks of regions (Johnson & Munakata, 2005). Here, we present some fragments of the answer to this important issue for the emerging social brain network.

The first piece of the puzzle comes from a study by Fair et al. (2007), who used functional connectivity analyses in fMRI to study resting-state "control" networks in children and adults. They found that development entailed both segregation (i.e., decreased short-range connectivity) and integration (i.e., increased long-range connectivity) of brain regions that contribute to a network. The decrease in short-range interregional functional connectivity is readily explicable in terms of the IS view. As neighboring regions of cortical tissue become increasingly specialized for different functions (e.g., objects versus faces), they will less commonly be coactivated. This process may also involve synaptic pruning and has been simulated in neural network models of cortex in which nodes with similar response properties cluster together spatially distinct from nodes with other response properties (Oliver, Johnson, & Schrager, 1996). Thus, decreasing functional connectivity between neighboring areas of cortex is readily predicted by neural network models implementing the IS account. More challenging from the current perspective is accounting for the increase in long-range functional connections.

A maturational explanation of the increase in long-range functional connectivity would suggest that this increase is due to the establishment or strengthening of the relevant fiber bundles. However, the increase in functional connectivity during development may occur after the relevant long-range fiber bundles are in place (see Fair et al., 2007, for discussion). While increased myelination is likely to be a contributing factor, (1) myelination itself can be a product of the activity/usage of a connection (Markham & Greenough, 2004), and (2) a general increase in myelin does not in itself account for the specificity of interregional activity into functional networks that support particular computations (but see Nagy, Westerberg, & Klingberg, 2004).

Most of the long-range functional connections studied by Fair et al. (2007) involve links to parts of the PFC. This part of the cortex is generally considered to have a special role during development in childhood and in skill acquisition in adults (Gilbert & Sigman, 2007; Thatcher, 1992). Johnson (2005) reviewed a number of studies consistent with the idea that the PFC may play a role in orchestrating the collective functional organization of other cortical regions during development. While there are several neural network models of PFC functioning in adults (e.g., O'Reilly, 2006), few if any of these have addressed development. However, another class of model intended to simulate aspects of development may be relevant both to PFC and to the issue of how networks of specialized regions come to coordinate their activity to support cognition. Knowledge-based cascade correlation (KBCC; Shultz, Rivest, Egri, Thivierge, & Dandurand, 2007) involves an algorithm and architecture that recruit previously learned functional networks when required during learning. Computationally, this dynamic neural network architecture has a number of advantages over other learning systems. Put simply, it can learn many tasks faster, or learn tasks that other networks cannot, because it can recruit the "knowledge" and computational ability of other self-contained networks as and when required. In a sense, it selects from a library of available computational systems to orchestrate the best combination for the learning problem at hand. While this class of model is not intended to be a detailed model of brain circuits (Shultz & Rivest, 2001; Shultz et al., 2007), it has been used to characterize frontal systems (Thivierge, Titone, & Schultz, 2005) and may capture important elements of the emerging interactions between the PFC and other cortical regions at an abstract level. In addition, it offers initially attractive accounts of (1) why PFC is required for the acquisition of new skills, (2) why the PFC is active from early in development, but also shows prolonged developmental change, and (3) why early damage to the PFC can have widespread effects over many domains (see also Johnson et al. , 2009).

Under this scenario of the emerging social brain network, the PFC may be activated from early on (Grossmann et al., 2008; Grossmann & Johnson, 2010) but at that point may play little role in selectively activating other regions because of their own lack of functional specialization and a lack of myelination of the relevant long-range connections. Once more posterior regions such as the STS and the FFA become more finely tuned to their different functions, the role of the PFC, or other frontal areas, becomes more important in orchestrating the combinations of regions activated for a given social cognition task. These prefrontal areas will be required more when learning a task or acquiring a new skill than once it is acquired (with the appropriate combination of other posterior regions already selected). This may explain the observation from a number of fMRI studies that there is a general migration of activity during childhood from greater activity in medial PFC than in the STS and FFA to the reverse pattern in adulthood (see Johnson et al., 2009). It is possible that once the PFC has learned the appropriate pattern of posterior regional activation to succeed in a task, cortical activity will tend to migrate to these posterior regions and decrease in the PFC itself.

Top-down feedback from the PFC may also have a direct role in shaping the functional response properties of posterior cortical areas. In cellular recording studies from both humans and animals, evidence has accrued that the selectivity of response of neurons in areas such as the fusiform cortex may increase in real time following the presentation of a stimulus. For example, Puce, Allison, Bentin, Gore, and McCarthy (1998) measured local field potentials in regions of lateral fusiform cortex in human adults and found that responses of these neurons go from being face-selective at around 200 ms after stimulus presentation to being modulated by top-down information such as face identity at later temporal windows. This suggests that top-down cortical feedback pathways, in addition to their importance in attention and object processing (Spratling & Johnson, 2004, 2006), may increase the degree of specialization and localization in real time, as well as in developmental time. Thus, some of the changes in functional specialization and localization seen in face-, gaze-, or biological motion-sensitive regions may reflect the increasing influence of interregional coordination with other regions, including the PFC.

Conclusion

We have reviewed here the currently available studies on the early development of brain processes dedicated to social cognition. There is now emerging evidence demonstrating early cortical specialization of the brain processes for social cognition during infancy. Despite this early specialization, for most of these brain processes dynamic developmental changes are observed beyond infancy. Development after the period of infancy seems to be characterized by a dynamic interplay between prefrontal and posterior regions, indicating that the influence of the PFC might be one of the sources of constraint on the specialization and functional development of some posterior structures. We discussed a class of learning system that may explain the role of prefrontal areas in orchestrating the differential activation of regions into functional networks, including those that underlie social cognition. Clearly, much work is required to test these speculative proposals about the emergence of certain networks involved in social cognition during development. This research will specifically require studies that simultaneously combine the study of structural and functional changes in the brain during development. Ideally, these empirical data will be compared to results from theoretical computational models of functional brain development.

References

Adolphs, R. (1999). Social cognition and the human brain. *Trends in Cognitive Sciences*, *3*, 469–479.

Adolphs, R. (2001). The neurobiology of social cognition. *Current Opinion in Neurobiology*, *11*, 231–239.

Adolphs, R. (2003). Cognitive neuroscience of human social behaviour. *Nature Reviews Neuroscience*, *4*, 165–178.

Allison, T., Puce, A., & McCarthy, G. (2000). Social perception: Role of the STS region. *Trends in Cognitive Sciences*, *4*, 267–278.

Allport, A. (1985). The historical background of social psychology. In G. Lindzey & E. Aronson (Eds.), *Handbook of Social Psychology* (pp. 1–46). New York: Random House.

Anderson, S. W., Bechara, A., Damasio, H., Tranel, D., & Damasio, A. R. (1999). Impairment of social and moral behavior related to early damage in human prefrontal cortex. *Nature Neuroscience*, *2*, 469–479.

Baldwin, D. A., Baird, J. A., Saylor, M. M., & Clark, M. A. (2001). Infants parse dynamic action. *Child Development*, *72*, 708–717.

Baldwin, D. A., & Moses, L. J. (1996). The ontogeny of social information gathering. *Child Development*, *67*, 1915–1939.

Baron-Cohen, S. (1995). *Mindblindness: An Essay on Autism and Theory of Mind*. Cambridge, MA: MIT Press.

Batki, A., Baron-Cohen, S., Wheelwright, S., Connellan, J., & Ahluwalia, J. (2000). Is there an innate gaze module? Evidence from human neonates. *Infant Behaviour & Development*, *23*, 223–229.

Beauchamp, M. S., Lee, K. E., Haxby, J. V., & Martin, A. (2002). Parallel visual motion processing streams for manipulable objects and human movements. *Neuron*, *34*, 149–159.

Beer, J., & Ochsner, K. (2006). Social cognition: A multi-level analysis. *Brain Research*, *1079*, 98–105.

Bellugi, U., Lichtenberger, L., Jones, W., Lai, Z., & St George, M. (2000). The neurocognitive profile of Williams syndrome. *Journal of Cognitive Neuroscience*, *12*, 7–29.

Bentin, S., Allison, T., Puce, A., Perez, A., & McCarthy, A. (1996). Electrophysiological studies of face perception in humans. *Journal of Cognitive Neuroscience*, *8*, 551–565.

Bertenthal, B. I. (1993). Perception of biomechanical motions by infants: Intrinsic image and knowledge-based constraints. In C. Granrud (Ed.), *Carnegie Symposium on Cognition: Visual Perception and Cognition in Infancy* (pp. 175–214). Hillsdale, NJ: Lawrence Erlbaum.

Blair, R. J. R., & Cipolotti, L. (2000). Impaired social response reversal: A case of acquired "sociopathy." *Brain*, *123*, 1122–1141.

Blakemore, S. J. (2008). The social brain in adolescence. *Nature Reviews Neuroscience*, *9*, 267–277.

Blakemore, S. J., & Decety, J. (2001). From the perception of action to the understanding of intention. *Nature Reviews Neuroscience*, *2*, 561–567.

Blakemore, S. J., & Frith, U. (2004). How does the brain deal with the social world? *Neuroreport*, *15*, 119–128.

Blakemore, S. J., & Frith, U. (2005). *The Learning Brain: Lessons for Education*. Oxford: Blackwell.

Bloom, P. (2000). *How Children Learn the Meanings of Words*. Cambridge, MA: MIT Press.

Brooks, R., & Meltzoff, A. N. (2005). The development of gaze following and its relation to language. *Developmental Science*, *8*, 535–543.

Brothers, L. (1990). The social brain: A project for integrating primate behavior and neurophysiology in a new domain. *Concepts Neuroscience*, *1*, 27–51.

Bruner, J. S. (1973). Organization of early skilled action. *Child Development*, *44*, 1–11.

Bushnell, I. W. R., Sai, F., & Mullin, J. T. (1989). Neonatal recognition of the mother's face. *British Journal of Development Psychology*, *7*, 3–15.

Caplan, R., Chugani, H. T., Messa, C., Guthrie, D., Sigman, M., de Traversay, J., & Mundy, P. (1993). Hemispherectomy for intractable seizures: Presurgical cerebral glucose metabolism and post-surgical non-verbal communication. *Developmental Medicine & Child Neurology*, *35*, 582–592.

Carter, E. J., & Pelphrey, K. A. (2006). School-aged children exhibit domain-specific responses to biological motion. *Social Neuroscience*, *1*, 396–411.

Chugani, H. T., & Phelps, M. E. (1986). Maturational changes in cerebral function in infants determined by 18FDG positron emission tomography. *Science*, *231*, 840–843.

Chugani, H. T., Phelps, M. E., & Mazziotta, J. C. (1987). Positron emission tomography study of human brain functional development. *Annals of Neurology*, *22*, 487–497.

Csibra, G. (2007). Action mirroring and action interpretation: An alternative account. In P. Haggard, Y. Rosetti, & M. Kawato (Eds.), *Sensorimotor Foundations of Higher Cognition. Attention and Performance XXII* (pp. 435–459). Oxford, UK: Oxford University Press.

Csibra, G. & Gergely, G. (2009). Natural pedagogy. *Trends in Cognitive Sciences*, *13*, 148–153.

de Haan, M., Johnson, M. H., & Halit, H. (2003). Development of face-sensitive event-related potentials during infancy: A review. *International Journal of Psychophysiology*, *51*, 45–58.

de Haan, M., Pascalis, O., & Johnson, M. H. (2002). Specialization of neural mechanisms underlying face recognition in human infants. *Journal of Cognitive Neuroscience*, *14*, 199–209.

de Haan, M. & Thomas, K.M. (2002). Applications of ERP and fMRI techniques to developmental science. *Developmental Science*, *5*, 335–343.

Dehaene-Lambertz, G., Dehaene, S., & Hertz-Pannier, L. (2002). Functional neuroimaging of speech perception in infants. *Science*, *298*, 2013–2015.

de Schonen, S., & Mathivet, E. (1990). Hemispheric asymmetry in a face discrimination task in infants. *Child Development*, *61*, 1192–1205.

Duchaine, B., & Nakayama, K. (2006). Developmental prosopagnosia: A window to content-specific face processing. *Current Opinion in Neurobiology*, *16*, 166–173.

Dunbar, R. (2003). The social brain: Mind, language and society in evolutionary perspective. *Annual Review of Anthropology*, *32*, 163–181.

Fair, D. A., Dosenbach, N. U. F., Church, J. A., Cohen, A. L., Brahmbhatt, S., Miezin, F., et al. (2007). Development of distinct control networks through segregation and integration.

Proceedings of the National Academy of Sciences U S A, 104, 13507–13512.

Fairhall, S. L., & Ishai, A. (2007). Effective connectivity within distributed cortical network for face perception. *Cerebral Cortex, 17,* 2400–2406.

Falck-Ytter, T., Gredebäck, G., & von Hofsten, C. (2006). Infants predict other people's action goals. *Nature Neuroscience, 9,* 878–879.

Farroni, T., Csibra, G., Simion, F., & Johnson, M. H. (2002). Eye contact detection in humans from birth. *Proceedings of the National Academy of Sciences U S A, 99,* 9602–9605.

Farroni, T., Johnson, M. H., & Csibra, G. (2004). Mechanisms of eye gaze perception during infancy. *Journal of Cognitive Neuroscience, 16,* 1320–1326.

Farroni, T., Pividori D., Simion F., Massaccesi, S., & Johnson M. H. (2004). Eye gaze cueing of attention in newborns. *Infancy, 5,* 39–60.

Fine, C., Lumsden, J., & Blair, R. J. R. (2001). Dissociation between "theory of mind" and executive functions in a patient with early left amygdala damage. *Brain, 124,* 287–298.

Fiske, S. T. (1995). Social cognition. In A. Tesser (Ed.), *Advanced Social Psychology* (pp. 149–193). New York: McGraw Hill.

Friederici, A. D. (2006). The neural basis of language development and its impairment. *Neuron, 52,* 941–952.

Friston, K. (1994). Functional and effective connectivity in neuroimaging: A synthesis. *Human Brain Mapping, 2,* 56–78.

Friston, K. J., & Price, C. J. (2001). Dynamic representations and generative models of brain function. *Brain Research Bulletin, 54,* 275–285.

Frith, C. D., & Frith, U. (1999). Interacting minds. A biological basis. *Science, 286,* 1692–1695.

Frith, C. D., & Frith, U. (2006). The neural basis of mentalizing. *Neuron, 50,* 531–534.

Gauthier, I., Tarr, M.J., Anderson A.W., Skudlarski, P., & Gore, J C. (1999) Activation of the middle fusiform "face area" increases with expertise in recognizing novel objects. *Nature Neuroscience, 2,* 568–573.

Gilbert, C. D., & Sigman, M. (2007). Brain states: Top-down influences in sensory processing. *Neuron, 54,* 677–696.

Grossmann, T. (2008). Shedding light on infant brain function: The use of near-infrared spectroscopy (NIRS) in the study of face perception. *Acta Paediatrica, 97,* 1156–1158.

Grossmann, T., & Johnson, M. H. (2010). Selective prefrontal cortex responses to joint attention. *Biology Letters, 6,* 540–543.

Grossmann, T., Johnson, M. H., Lloyd-Fox, S., Blasi, A., Deligianni, F., Elwell, C., & Csibra, G. (2008). Early cortical specialization for face-to-face communication in human infants. *Proceedings of the Royal Society, Series B: Biological Sciences, 275,* 2803–2811.

Halit, H., de Haan, M., & Johnson, M. H. (2003). Cortical specialisation for face processing: Face-sensitive event-related potential components in 3- and 12- month-old infants. *Neuroimage, 19,* 1180–1193.

Haxby, J. V., Hoffman, E. A., & Gobbini, M. I. (2000). The distributed human neural system for face perception. *Trends in Cognitive Sciences, 4,* 223–233.

Heavey, L., Phillips, W., Baron-Cohen, S., & Rutter, M. (2000). The awkward moments test: A naturalistic measure of social understanding in autism. *Journal of Autism & Developmental Disorders, 30,* 225–236.

Hirai, M., & Hiraki, K. (2005) An event-related potentials study of biological motion perception in human infants. *Cognitive Brain Research, 22,* 301–304.

Huttenlocher, P. R. (2002). *Neural Plasticity.* Cambridge, MA: Harvard University Press.

Huttenlocher, P. R., & Dabholkar, A. S. (1997). Regional differences in synaptogenesis in human cerebral cortex. *Journal of Comparative Neurology, 387,* 167–178.

Johansson, G. (1973). Visual perception of biological motion and a model for its analysis. *Perception & Psychophysics, 14,* 201–211.

Johnson, M. H. (2001). Functional brain development in humans. *Nature Reviews Neuroscience, 2,* 475–483.

Johnson, M. H. (2005a). *Developmental Cognitive Neuroscience,* 2nd ed. Oxford: Blackwell.

Johnson, M. H. (2005b). Subcortical face processing. *Nature Reviews Neuroscience, 6,* 766–774.

Johnson, M. H., Grossmann, T., & Cohen Kadosh, K. (2009). Mapping functional brain development: Building a social brain through interactive specialization. *Developmental Psychology, 45,* 151–159.

Johnson, M. H., & Munakata, Y. (2005). Processes of change in brain and cognitive development. *Trends in Cognitive Sciences, 9,* 152–158.

Kampe, K., Frith, C. D., & Frith, U. (2003). "Hey John": Signals conveying communicative intention toward self activate brain regions associated with "mentalizing," regardless of modality. *Journal of Neuroscience, 12,* 5258–5263.

Kanwisher, N. (2000). Domain specificity in face processing. *Nature Neuroscience, 3,* 759–763.

Karmiloff-Smith, A., Klima, E., Bellugi, U., Grant, J., & Baron-Cohen, S. (1995). Is there a social module? Language, face processing, and theory of mind in individuals with Williams syndrome. *Journal of Cognitive Neuroscience, 7,* 196–208.

Klin, A. (2000). Attributing social meaning to ambiguous visual stimuli in higher-functioning autism and Asperger syndrome: The social attribution task. *Journal of Child Psychology & Psychiatry, 41,* 831–846.

Kuhl, P. (2004). Early language acquisition: Cracking the speech code. *Nature Reviews Neuroscience, 5,* 831–841.

Kutas, M., & Federmeier, K. D. (2000). Electrophysiology reveals semantic memory use in language comprehension. *Trends in Cognitive Sciences, 4,* 463–470.

Lieberman, M. D. (2006). Social cognitive neuroscience: A review of core processes. *Annual Review of Psychology, 58,* 18.1–18.31.

Lloyd-Fox, S., Blasi, A., & Elwell, C. E. (2010). Illuminating the developing brain: The past, present and future of functional near infrared spectroscopy. *Neuroscience and Biobehavioural Reviews, 34,* 269–284.

Lloyd-Fox, S., Blasi, A., Volein, A., Everdell, N., Elwell, C. E., & Johnson, M. H. (2009). Social perception in infancy: A near infrared spectroscopy study. *Child Development, 80,* 986–999.

Mareschal, D., Johnson, M. H., Sirios, S., Spratling, M., Thomas, M., & Westermann, G. (2007). *Neuroconstructivism, Vol. I: How the Brain Constructs Cognition.* Oxford, UK: Oxford University Press.

Markham, J. A., & Greenough, W. T. (2004). Experience-driven brain plasticity: Beyond the synapse. *Neuron Glia Biology, 1,* 351–363.

Marshall, P. J., & Shipley, T. F. (2009). Event-related potentials to point-light displays of human actions in 5-month-old infants. *Developmental Neuropsychology, 34,* 368–377.

Morton, J., & Johnson, M. H. (1991). CONSPEC and CONLERN: A two-process theory of infant face recognition. *Psychological Review, 98,* 164–181.

Mundy, P., Card, J., & Fox, N. (2000). Fourteen-month cortical activity and different infant joint attention skills. *Developmental Psychobiology, 36*, 325–338.

Mundy, P., Fox, N., & Card, J. (2003). EEG coherence, joint attention and language development in the second year. *Developmental Science, 6*, 48–54.

Nagy, Z., Westerberg, H., & Klingberg, T. (2004). Maturation of white matter is associated with the development of cognitive functions during childhood. *Journal of Cognitive Neuroscience, 16*, 1227–1233.

Oberman, L. M., Hubbard, E. M., McCleery, J. P., Altschuler, E. L., Ramachandran, V. S., & Pineda, J. A. (2005). EEG evidence for mirror neuron dysfunction in autism spectrum disorders. *Brain Research, 24*, 190–198.

Ochsner, K. N., & Lieberman, M. D. (2001). The emergence of social cognitive neuroscience. *American Psychologist, 56*, 717–734.

Oliver, A., Johnson, M. H., & Shrager, J. (1996). The emergence of hierarchical clustered representations in a Hebbian neural network model that simulates development in the neocortex. *Network: Computation in Neural Systems, 7*, 291–299.

O'Reilly, R. C. (2006). Biologically based computational models of high-level cognition. *Science, 314*, 91–94.

Parise, E., Reid, V. M., Stets, M., & Striano, T. (2008). Direct eye contact influences the neural processing of objects in 5-month-old infants. *Social Neuroscience, 3*, 141–150.

Pelphrey, K. A., Singerman, J. D., Allison, T., & McCarthy, G. (2003). Brain activation evoked by perception of gaze shifts: The influence of context. *Neuropsychologia, 41*, 156–170.

Pelphrey, K. A., Viola R. J., & McCarthy, G. (2004). When strangers pass: Processing of mutual and averted gaze in the superior temporal sulcus. *Psychological Science, 15*, 598–603.

Puce, A., Allison, T., Bentin, S., Gore, J. C., & McCarthy, G. (1998). Temporal cortex activation in humans viewing eye and mouth movements. *Journal of Neuroscience, 18*, 2188–2199.

Reid, V. M., Belsky, J. & Johnson, M. H. (2005). Infant perception of human action: Toward a developmental cognitive neuroscience of individual differences. *Cognition, Brain & Behaviour, 9*, 35–52.

Reid, V. M., Csibra, G., Belsky, J., & Johnson, M. H. (2007). Neural correlates of the perception of goal-directed action in infants. *Acta Psychologica, 124*, 129–138.

Reid, V. M., Hoehl, S., & Striano, T. (2006). The perception of biological motion by infants: An event-related potential study. *Neuroscience Letters, 395*, 211–214.

Reid, V. M., Hoehl, S., Grigutsch, M., Groendahl, A., Parise, E., & Striano, T. (2009). The Neural Correlates of Infant and Adult Goal Prediction: Evidence for Semantic Processing Systems. *Developmental Psychology, 45*(3), 620–629.

Reynolds, G. D., & Richards, J. E. (2005). Familiarization, attention, and recognition memory in infancy: An ERP and cortical source analysis study. *Developmental Psychology, 41*, 598–615.

Rizzolatti, G., & Craighero, L. (2004). The mirror-neuron system. *Annual Review of Neuroscience, 27*, 169–192.

Ronald, A., Happe, F., & Plomin, R. (2005). The genetic relationship between individual differences in social and nonsocial behaviours characteristic of autism. *Developmental Science, 8*, 444–458.

Saxe, R. (2006). Uniquely human social cognition. *Current Opinion in Neurobiology, 16*, 235–239.

Scaife, M., & Bruner, J. S. (1975). The capacity for joint visual attention in the infant. *Nature, 253*, 265–266.

Senju, A., Johnson, M. H., & Csibra, G. (2006). The development and neural basis of referential gaze perception. *Social Neuroscience, 1*, 220–234.

Shimada, S., & Hiraki, K. (2006). Infant's brain responses to live and televised action. *Neuroimage, 32*, 930–939.

Shultz, T. R., & Rivest, F. (2001). Knowledge-based cascade-correlation: Using knowledge to speed learning. *Connection Science, 13*, 43–72.

Shultz, T. R., Rivest, F., Egri, L., Thivierge, J. P., & Dandurand, F. (2007). Could knowledge-based neural learning be useful in developmental robotics? The case of KBCC. *International Journal of Humanoid Robotics, 4*, 245–279.

Simion, F., Regolin, L., & Bulf, H. (2008). A predisposition for biological motion in the newborn baby. *Proceedings of the National Academy of Sciences U S A, 15*, 809–813.

Southgate, V., Johnson, M. H., El Karoui, I., & Csibra, G. (2010). Motor system activation reveals infants' online prediction of others' goals. *Psychological Science, 21*, 355–359.

Southgate, V., Johnson, M. H., Osborne, T., & Csibra, G. (2009). Predictive motor activation during action observation in human infants. *Biology Letters, 5*, 769–772.

Spratling, M., & Johnson, M. H. (2004). A feedback model of visual attention. *Journal of Cognitive Neuroscience, 16*, 219–237.

Spratling, M., & Johnson, M. H. (2006). A feedback model of perceptual learning and categorization. *Visual Cognition, 13*, 129–165.

Striano, T., Reid, V. M. & Hoehl, S. (2006). Neural mechanisms of joint attention in infancy. *European Journal of Neuroscience, 23*, 2819–2823.

Striano, T., & Stahl, D. (2005). Sensitivity to triadic attention in early infancy. *Developmental Science, 4*, 333–343.

Summerfield, C., Egner, T., Greene, M., Koechlin, E., Mangels, J., & Hirsch, J. (2006). Predictive codes for forthcoming perception in the frontal cortex. *Science, 314*, 1311–1314.

Taylor, M. J., Batty, M., & Itier, R. J. (2004). The faces of development: A review of early face processing over childhood. *Journal of Cognitive Neuroscience, 16*, 1426–1442.

Thatcher, R. W. (1992). Cyclic cortical reorganization during early childhood. Special issue: The role of frontal lobe maturation in cognitive and social development. *Brain & Cognition, 20*, 24–50.

Thatcher, R. W., Krause, P. J., & Hrybyk, M. (1986). Cortico-cortical associations and EEG coherence: A two-compartmental model. *Electroencephalography & Clinical Neurophysiology, 64*, 123–143.

Thivierge, J. P., Titone, D., & Schultz, T. R. (2005). Simulating fronto-temporal pathways involved in lexical ambiguity resolution. *Proceedings of the Twenty-seventh Annual Conference of the Cognitive Science Society*, 2178–2183.

Tomasello, M., Carpenter, M., Call, J., Behne, T., & Moll, H. (2005). Understanding and sharing intentions: The origins of cultural cognition. *Behavioural & Brain Sciences, 28*, 675–691.

Troje, N. F., & Westhoff, C. (2006). The inversion effect in biological motion perception: Evidence for a "life detector"? *Current Biology, 16*, 821–824.

Tzourio-Mazoyer, N., De Schonen, S., Crivello, F., Reutter, B., Aujard, Y., & Mazoyer, B. (2002). Neural correlates of woman face processing by 2-month-old infants. *Neuroimage, 15*, 454–461.

van Elk, M., van Schie, H. T., Hunnius, S., Vesper, C., & Bekkering, H. (2008). You'll never crawl alone: Neurophysiological evidence for experience-dependent motor resonance in infancy. *Neuroimage, 43*, 808–814.

Whiten, A. & Byrne, R. W. (1997). *Machiavellian Intelligence II: Evaluations and Extensions*. Cambridge, UK: Cambridge University Press.

Williams, J. H. G., Waiter, G. D., Perro, O., Perrett, D. I., & Whiten, A. (2005). An fMRI study of joint attention experience. *Neuroimage, 25*, 133–140.

PART 3

Higher Cognitive Functions

Conflict Monitoring and Cognitive Control

Nick Yeung

Abstract

Neural mechanisms of cognitive control are hypothesized to support flexible, goal-directed behavior by representing task-relevant information in order to guide thought and action. The conflict monitoring theory proposes that anterior cingulate cortex (ACC) contributes to cognitive control by detecting conflicts in information processing and signaling when increased top-down control is required. This theory provides a computationally specified framework for understanding how cognitive control is recruited and explains a large literature of human neuroimaging studies reporting ACC activity in conditions of increased cognitive demand. Predictions from the theory have been tested and consistently confirmed in behavioral and neuroimaging experiments with human subjects. However, challenging findings from patients with ACC lesions and from studies of ACC function in nonhuman primates suggest that conflict monitoring may be just one facet of the broader role of ACC in performance monitoring and the optimization of behavior.

Key words: cognitive control, conflict monitoring, anterior cingulate cortex, neuroimaging, computational models, neuropsychology, reinforcement learning, performance monitoring

Introduction

A central challenge in cognitive neuroscience research is to account for intelligent, purposive human behavior without relying on an unspecified intelligent agent—a controlling homunculus—for explanatory power (Monsell & Driver, 2000). Framed differently, the challenge is to explain how the richness and flexibility of human cognition emerges from interactions among component processes that are themselves fixed and algorithmically specifiable. As a first step toward meeting this challenge, it is often proposed that dedicated mechanisms of cognitive control support flexible cognition by representing task-relevant information and using this information to guide thought and action in accordance with current goals and intentions (Miller & Cohen, 2001). Regions in lateral prefrontal cortex (PFC) are thought to play a particularly important role in exerting this control (Sakai, 2008).

However, the notion that lateral PFC exerts control raises the question of how this region itself knows which information is task-relevant: There is a clear danger here of theoretical regress. Recent years have thus seen considerable effort devoted to understanding how the inputs to this region might support its functioning. Various functional connections of lateral PFC are relevant in this regard: Interactions with the medial temporal lobe might support the recall of goals set during earlier prospective planning (Cohen & O'Reilly, 1996; Schacter, Addis, & Buckner, 2007), input from orbitofrontal cortex could provide information about the likely payoffs of those plans (Koechlin & Hyafil, 2007; Wallis, 2007), and anterior prefrontal regions might facilitate the coordination of multiple task goals (Badre & D'Esposito, 2009; Koechlin, Ody, & Kouneiher, 2003; Shallice & Burgess, 1991). Complementing these ideas, a major focus of recent research has been the hypothesis that recruitment of control by lateral PFC might depend on input from medial PFC regions that monitor ongoing performance for indications of success or failure in the chosen task.

The conflict monitoring theory is the most influential articulation of the hypothesis that medial and lateral PFC regions form a regulatory feedback loop (Figure 18.1). According to this theory, control is recruited following the detection in medial PFC of competition—or *conflict*—in information processing (Botvinick, Braver, Carter, Barch, & Cohen, 2001; Botvinick, Cohen, & Carter, 2004; Carter et al., 1998). This chapter surveys recent empirical and theoretical developments in research on this hypothesis. The first section reviews the conceptual and empirical foundations of the theory. The second section reviews empirical debates stimulated by the theory, for example, regarding the neural basis of conflict monitoring and the varying forms of conflict that might be monitored in the human brain. The final section places the theory in a broader theoretical context, discussing challenging findings from studies of medial PFC function in other species that suggest a wider conception of the role of this region in the control of behavior.

Theoretical Foundations
Conflict and Competitive Interactions

The idea that processing conflicts impose a fundamental constraint on human cognition has been articulated in several influential theories of visual attention (Desimone & Duncan, 1995; Treisman & Gelade, 1980), action selection (Allport, 1987; Norman & Shallice, 1986), working memory (Baddeley, 1996), and executive function (Logan, 2003; Miller & Cohen, 2001). In each domain, top-down cognitive control is thought to be needed to impose coherence on thought and action. In

particular, the central role of processing conflict, and the need for top-down modulation, is inferred to follow from three basic and interrelated features of human cognition: that behavior is flexible, that it is goal directed, and that it is an emergent property of coordinated activity across distributed neural circuits.

The flexibility of human cognition is apparent even in the artificial simplicity of the laboratory. Presented with words on a screen, for example, subjects can read them aloud, memorize them, classify each as a living or manmade thing, search for a certain word, etc., and can switch fluently between these tasks according to whim or instruction (Logan, 1985; Monsell, 1996). Given that behavior is only loosely constrained by the environment, some form of control must be exerted to select among the available tasks and actions (Duncan, 1986; Miller & Cohen, 2001; Monsell, 1996). However, purposeful behavior need not always rely on effortful control: We often follow established routines that we execute with little thought or effort. The essence of flexible, goal-directed behavior lies in our ability to act effectively when we lack these routines and, perhaps even more critically, when achieving our behavioral goals requires us to override our habits (Norman & Shallice, 1986; Shiffrin & Schneider, 1977). Control is required in the Stroop task, for example, to suppress an established habit of reading words to allow naming of the ink color of those words (Cohen, Dunbar, & McClelland, 1990; Stroop, 1935). Cognitive control is thus needed because our behavioral goals are often in conflict with established response tendencies.

The importance of conflict in constraining our ability to behave coherently arises critically from the distributed nature of neural processing: Even the simplest cognitive task requires the coordination of activity across multiple brain regions. The distributed architecture of cognition is exemplified by the structure of the cortical visual system in which a proliferation of functionally specialized regions feeds into memory and action systems in a massively parallel manner. Within this parallel processing system, coordination is vital to ensure the coherent activation—or binding—of object features represented in distant regions (Treisman & Gelade, 1980), and to ensure that features of selected objects are transmitted to appropriate action systems (Allport, 1980). This coordination is thought to depend on mechanisms of top-down cognitive control implemented in lateral PFC (Desimone & Duncan, 1995).

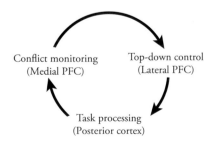

Figure 18.1 Schematic illustration of the conflict-control regulatory feedback loop involving medial and lateral prefrontal cortex (PFC) regions.

These considerations converge to suggest that regulating conflict is a core function of cognitive control. It follows that identifying these conflicts as they arise could provide a crucial signal of when increased control is required. This idea is at the heart of the conflict monitoring theory (Botvinick et al., 2001; Carter et al., 1998), which proposes specifically that anterior cingulate cortex (ACC), a region in medial PFC, monitors for the occurrence of conflict between incompatible actions. A canonical example of response conflict comes from the Stroop task, in which the presence of competing responses associated with incongruent color and word attributes (e.g., *BLUE* in red ink) results in impaired performance relative to the case in which color and word are congruent (e.g., *RED* in red ink). Response conflict similarly occurs in the flanker task when the central target is flanked by distracting peripheral stimuli associated with a different response (e.g., > > < > >) relative to the case when target and flankers are congruent (e.g., > > > > >). The conflict theory proposes that ACC detects these conflicts as they emerge during the action selection process and uses this information to signal the need for increased

control. Increased control by lateral PFC regions, which serve to enhance task-relevant stimulus and response representations, in turn leads to reduced conflict during subsequent task performance, thus closing the conflict-control loop (Figure 18.1).

Anterior Cingulate Cortex

The ACC lies bilaterally around the rostrum of the corpus callosum (Figure 18.2). The conflict monitoring theory focuses in particular on dorsal-caudal ACC, Brodmann's areas 24c′ and 32′ (Devinsky, Morrell, & Vogt, 1995; Vogt, Nimchinsky, Vogt, & Hof, 1995). As well as being densely interconnected with neighboring premotor regions (Dum & Strick, 1993), this part of ACC shares strong anatomical connections with lateral PFC and parietal cortex (Beckmann, Johansen-Berg, & Rushworth, 2009; van Hoesen, Morecraft, & Vogt, 1993) and co-activates with these regions in human neuroimaging studies during task performance (Duncan & Owen, 2000; Koski & Paus, 2000; Nee, Wager, & Jonides, 2007; Paus, Koski, Caramanos, & Westbury, 1998) and in a slowly evolving manner at rest (Margulies et al., 2007; Raichle, 2010; but see Dosenbach et al., 2007). The

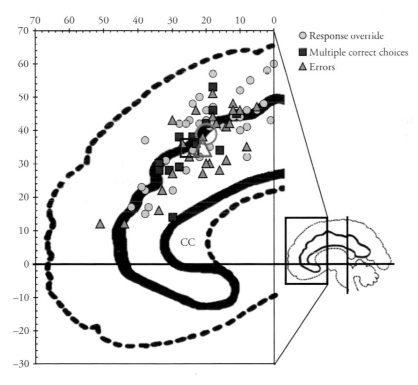

Figure 18.2 Meta-analysis of conflict-related activations on the medial surface of the frontal lobes. Activation peaks are plotted from published PET and fMRI studies of tasks involving response override, choice between multiple correct responses, and error commission. The plot combines data from a previous meta-analysis (Ridderinkhof et al., 2004) with results from more recent studies. The large open data points correspond to the average coordinates across studies, and cluster together around the cingulate sulcus. CC, corpus callosum.

region thus forms part of a well-characterized control (or "executive") network with precisely the connectivity required by a conflict monitoring system: Interconnections with motor structures would provide access to information about co-activation of competing actions—at the level of both abstract motor plans and specific planned movements—while connections with lateral PFC would enable the region to signal the need for increased top-down control when such conflicts are detected.

Evidence that the ACC plays this role in response conflict monitoring has come primarily from human neuroimaging studies. Using a variety of methods, including positron emission tomography (PET), functional magnetic resonance imaging (fMRI), and electroencephalography (EEG), increased ACC activity has been found in conditions characterized by conflict between different actions: when subjects override habitual responses, when they select one of a number of potentially correct responses, and when they make errors (Figure 18.2; Botvinick et al., 2001, 2004). Perhaps the most replicated neuroimaging finding regarding ACC is its increased activity when the required response conflicts with a prepotent or habitual alternative. Thus, ACC activity is observed in the Stroop task when the written word is incongruent with the required color-naming response (Bench et al., 1993; Liotti, Woldorff, Perez, & Mayberg, 2000; Pardo, Pardo, Janer, & Raichle, 1990), in the flanker task when peripheral distractors cue a different response than the attended target (Botvinick, Nystrom, Fissell, Carter, & Cohen, 1999; Kopp, Rist, & Mattler, 1996), and in corresponding conditions of many other tasks (e.g., Braver, Barch, Gray, Molfese, & Snyder, 2001; Nieuwenhuis, Yeung, van den Wildenberg, & Ridderinkhof, 2003; Paus, Petrides, Evans, & Meyer, 1993; Peterson et al., 2002; Rubia et al., 2001; Taylor, Kornblum, Minoshima, Oliver, & Koeppe, 1994).

ACC activation is similarly observed in underdetermined response tasks that induce conflict between multiple potentially correct responses, such as generating verbs associated with particular nouns (Crosson et al., 1999; Petersen, Fox, Posner, Mintun, & Raichle, 1989), or producing random sequences of finger movements (Frith, Friston, Liddle, & Frackowiak, 1991). Importantly, ACC activity in these tasks increases when the response is less constrained by the stimulus, for example, when verbs are generated for nouns with many possible actions (e.g., a *ball* can be thrown, kicked, bounced, etc.) compared with nouns with one main associate (e.g., a *bell* tends to be rung) (Barch, Braver,

Sabb, & Noll, 2000; Thompson-Schill, D'Esposito, Aguirre, & Farah, 1997). Thus, ACC activity varies in relation to the level of conflict between responses even when there is no defined correct response.

However, ACC also strongly activates when subjects make errors. Error-related ACC activity was first found using electrophysiological recordings in nonhuman primates (Gemba, Sasaki, & Brooks, 1986) and scalp EEG studies in humans (Falkenstein, Hohnsbein, Hoorman, & Blanke, 1990; Gehring, Goss, Coles, Meyer, & Donchin, 1993). In human EEG, a component labeled the error-related negativity (ERN) is robustly observed within 100 ms of incorrect responses in choice decision tasks such as the Stroop and flanker tasks. Dipole modeling of the ERN suggests ACC as its likely neural source (Dehaene, Posner, & Tucker, 1994), a supposition confirmed using methods with more precise spatial localization (Carter et al., 1998; Debener et al., 2005; Wang, Ulbert, Schomer, Marinkovic, & Halgren, 2005). These converging findings suggest that ACC is active following errors, when conflict would be expected to occur between correct and incorrect responses.

Evidence that conflict-related ACC activity reflects its role in the recruitment of control has come from studies of sequential adaptation effects. In the Stroop task, for example, interference from an incongruent word is reduced when the immediately preceding stimulus was also incongruent, relative to trials following a congruent stimulus (Kerns et al., 2004). The conflict theory explains this finding in terms of conflict detection on one trial leading to increased top-down control, and hence reduced conflict, on the subsequent trial. Consistent with this hypothesis, neuroimaging evidence indicates that lateral PFC activity increases after high-conflict trials (indicating increased top-down control, Egner, Delano, & Hirsch, 2007; Egner & Hirsch, 2005), whereas ACC activity is reduced (reflecting the reduction in conflict, Botvinick et al., 1999). Indeed, conflict-related ACC activity on one trial is predictive of lateral PFC activity and concomitant performance improvements on the next (Kerns et al., 2004). Collectively, these findings support the hypothesis that ACC and lateral PFC have dissociable but complementary functional roles, with the former involved in recruiting control and the latter involved in the execution of control.

Computational Models of Conflict Monitoring

The two central claims of the conflict monitoring theory—that ACC monitors for the occurrence of response conflict, and that it uses this information to signal the need for increased top-down control—have been formalized in computational models (Botvinick et al., 2001). One such model (Figure 18.3a) simulates behavior in the flanker task, in which subjects indicate the direction of a central arrow while ignoring task-irrelevant flankers. The model comprises a task network (black) and conflict-control feedback loop (blue). In the task network, units representing possible stimuli activate corresponding left- and right-hand responses under the influence of top-down attention. Incongruent

flankers (e.g., in the stimulus < > <) activate the incorrect response, producing conflict with the correct response and, hence, slower and less accurate responding than congruent flankers (e.g., in the stimulus > > >) (Cohen, Servan-Schreiber, & McClelland, 1992; Spencer & Coles, 1999).

Importantly, the level of conflict in the response layer of the network accurately predicts empirically observed patterns of ACC activity in neuroimaging studies of the flanker task (Botvinick et al., 1999) and provides a computational basis for recruiting appropriate levels of top-down attentional control (Botvinick et al., 2001). Hopfield energy (Hopfield, 1982) provides a simple formulation of the conflict signal:

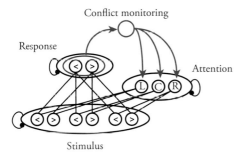

(a) **Model architecture:**

Conflict monitoring

Response

Attention

Stimulus

$$(1) \qquad Conflict = -\sum_{i=1}^{N}\sum_{j-1}^{N} a_i * a_j * w_{ij}$$

where a denotes unit activity, w the connection weight between pairs of units, and i and j are indexed over competing network units. Thus defined, conflict increases when there is co-activation of units that share a mutually inhibitory connection. This product measure of conflict is not the only possible formulation (Botvinick et al., 2001; Yu, Dayan, & Cohen, 2009), but it formalizes conflict in an intuitive and straightforward way: On incongruent trials, the target and flankers activate different responses such that the product of response activation levels is large and conflict is high. On congruent trials, incorrect response activity is low or zero, the product is correspondingly low, and there is little or no conflict.

Closing the conflict-control loop, detected conflict can be used to adjust the level of attentional control according to the following equation (Botvinick et al., 2001):

$$(2) \qquad C(t+1) = \lambda C(t) + (1-\lambda)(\alpha E(t)+\beta)$$

where C indicates the strength of top-down control, adjusted on a trial-by-trial basis (t) as a function of previously experienced conflict (energy, E), scaled by a learning rate parameter λ within limits imposed by parameters α and β. According to this equation, control increases when high levels of conflict are experienced, leading to enhancement of task-relevant stimulus and response representations on subsequent trials, thus enabling the model to account for sequential adaptation effects observed in experimental studies (Botvinick et al., 2001): Strengthening of

(b) **Conflict simulation:**

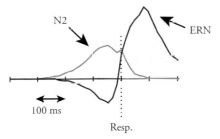

N2

ERN

100 ms

Resp.

(c) **EEG data:**

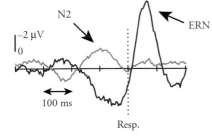

N2

ERN

$-2\ \mu V$
0

100 ms

Resp.

—— Incongruent minus congruent
—— Error minus correct

Figure 18.3 Conflict model architecture, predictions, and empirical test. **a.** Schematic diagram of a computational model of conflict monitoring in the flanker task. **b.** Model predictions for the timing of conflict-related ACC activity time-locked to correct and error responses. **c.** Empirical results from an EEG study of the error-related negativity (ERN) and N2, two components generated in the ACC (Yeung et al., 2004).

control after a high-conflict incongruent trial leads to reduced conflict on the next trial (cf. Gratton, Coles, & Donchin, 1992). Equations 1 and 2 together, therefore, provide a computationally straightforward framework for dynamic and flexible recruitment of control.

As well as the flanker task model described above, this computational approach has been applied to Stroop and underdetermined word generation tasks (Botvinick et al., 2001) and used to simulate both conflict- and error-related adjustments in control (Rabbitt, 1966). In each case, the proposed model implements flexible control without a controlling homunculus: Conflict monitoring uses readily available information about activation levels of competing responses, and the conflict signal is converted algorithmically to set the level of top-down control. Crucially, these models have generated novel predictions that have spurred subsequent empirical work. For example, a core prediction is that increased conflict-related ACC activity on one trial should lead to increased cognitive control and improved performance on the subsequent trial. This prediction has been borne out in fMRI studies (Kerns et al., 2004; Liston, Matalon, Hare, Davidson, & Casey, 2006). Meanwhile, EEG methods have confirmed key model predictions regarding the timing of ACC activity: Whereas ACC activity is predicted to occur after incorrect responses are produced, as reflected in the ERN component of the EEG, conflict on trials with correct responses is predicted to occur primarily before the response (Figure 18.3b), a prediction confirmed in EEG studies of a second component, the N2 (Figure 18.3c; Nieuwenhuis et al., 2003; van Veen & Carter, 2002; Yeung, Botvinick, & Cohen, 2004). Predictions derived from computational models of conflict monitoring have thus been borne out in studies of both the level (using fMRI) and timing (using EEG) of activity in ACC during task performance.

Current Directions in Conflict Monitoring Research

The preceding section summarizes the core claims of the conflict monitoring theory: Conflict and competitive interactions place a fundamental constraint on human cognition; activity in ACC varies with conflict in a manner predictive of changes in the level of top-down cognitive control; and conflict monitoring provides a computationally tractable mechanism for the flexible recruitment and allocation of control. Along the way, we have seen a number of claims—for example, about the neural basis

of conflict monitoring, its relation to error detection, and its role in sequential adaptation—that have each become the focus of considerable research interest in recent years. This section reviews emerging evidence on these topics and others, emphasizing the fertility of the conflict monitoring theory in stimulating new research, while also considering important challenges to the theory.

Neural Basis of Conflict Monitoring

The foregoing discussion identifies dorsal-caudal parts of ACC (areas 24c′ and 32′) as the likely neural basis of conflict monitoring. This region is variously referred to as dorsal ACC (Botvinick et al., 2004), posterior medial frontal cortex (Ridderinkhof, Ullsperger, Crone, & Nieuwenhuis, 2004), anterior mid-cingulate cortex (Vogt, Berger, & Derbyshire, 2003), and the rostral cingulate zone or rostral cingulate motor area (Debener et al., 2005; Fink, Frackowiak, Pietrzyk, & Passingham, 1997; Picard & Strick, 1996, 2001). The variability in nomenclature at least in part reflects disagreement about the precision with which conflict-related activity has been localized and about the functional anatomy of the region of interest. There is nevertheless broad consensus that if conflict monitoring occurs within ACC, then the relevant region lies in the caudal-dorsal "cognitive" division rather than the rostral-ventral "affective" division (Bush, Luu, & Posner, 2000; Devinsky et al., 1995).

However, it has been argued that conflict-related activity may localize outside ACC within the neighboring pre-supplementary motor area (pre-SMA, Rushworth, Walton, Kennerley, & Bannerman, 2004; Ullsperger & von Cramon, 2004). Evidence for this view has come from studies of the flanker, go/no-go, and Simon tasks, in which contrasts between high- and low-conflict trials identify regions extending dorsally into the pre-SMA, whereas contrasts between correct and error trials identify regions only in ACC (Garavan, Ross, Kaufman, & Stein, 2003; Ullsperger & von Cramon, 2001, 2004; Wittfoth, Kustermann, Fahle, & Herrmann, 2008). Pre-SMA activity has also been observed in some tasks that would be expected to produce conflict, for example, when subjects are required to override a preplanned movement (Nachev, Rees, Parton, Kennard, & Husain, 2005). Correspondingly, single-unit activity in nonhuman primates has been found to vary with response conflict in pre-SMA and the supplementary eye field (Isoda & Hikosaka, 2007; Stuphorn, Taylor, & Schall, 2000), but not in ACC (Emeric et al., 2008; Nakamura, Roesch, & Olson, 2005).

Attempts to precisely localize conflict-related activity in the medial wall are hindered by inherent limitations of neuroimaging methods that involve spatial smoothing and group averaging of data, such that the location of peak activity varies considerably even across studies with comparable methodologies (Barch et al., 2000; Ridderinkhof et al., 2004). There is also considerable individual variability in sulcal anatomy in this region, where the dorsal cingulate areas of interest may lie buried in the cingulate sulcus or may appear in an adjacent paracingulate region (Paus, Otaky et al., 1996; Paus, Tomaiuolo et al., 1996; Vogt et al., 1995; Yucel et al., 2001). Adding yet further complication, many functions ascribed to pre-SMA, such as willed action selection (Lau, Rogers, & Passingham, 2006; Passingham, 1993; Passingham, Bengtsson, & Lau, 2010) and behavioral switching (Hikosaka & Isoda, 2010; Rushworth, Hadland, Paus, & Sipila, 2002), would lead to co-activation with putative conflict monitoring signals in ACC.

Converging evidence nevertheless points to the ACC as the consistent source of conflict-related activity in medial PFC. First, despite variability across individual studies, meta-analyses consistently localize the center of mass of conflict-related activity around the cingulate sulcus (Figure 18.2; Barch et al., 2000; Beckmann et al., 2009; Bush et al., 2000; Paus et al., 1998; Peyron, Laurent, & Garcia-Larrea, 2000; Ridderinkhof et al., 2004; Roberts & Hall, 2008). Second, studies that explicitly consider anatomical variability across subjects—using high-resolution single-subject analyses (Lutcke & Frahm, 2008) or contrasting activation patterns according to sulcal anatomy (Crosson et al., 1999)—localize conflict-related activity to the paracingulate sulcus and gyrus when present, and to the cingulate sulcus otherwise, tracking the known location of ACC areas 24c′ and 32′. Finally, error-related activity is rarely observed in pre-SMA, yet errors should produce high levels of conflict (Botvinick et al., 2001; Yeung et al., 2004), suggesting that observed pre-SMA activity reflects its role in action selection rather than conflict monitoring. In contrast, dorsal ACC is very consistently activated by both conflict and errors (Braver et al., 2001; Carter et al., 1998; Garavan et al., 2003; Holroyd et al., 2004; Kiehl, Liddle, & Hopfinger, 2000; Lutcke & Frahm, 2008; Mathalon, Whitfield, & Ford, 2003; Taylor et al., 2006). Collectively, these considerations indicate that regions around the cingulate sulcus are the neural basis of conflict signals in the medial wall.

Conflict and Error Processing

According to the conflict monitoring theory, error-related ACC activity can be explained in terms of response conflict that develops following errors, when continued stimulus processing leads to activation of the correct response that conflicts with the initial error (Botvinick et al., 2001). In computational simulations, this post-error conflict signal replicates key properties of the ERN component of the scalp-recorded EEG, such as its timing and sensitivity to factors including stimulus frequency and speed-accuracy emphasis (Yeung et al., 2004). Consistent with the hypothesis that the ERN reflects continuous conflict monitoring rather than explicit error detection as originally proposed (Falkenstein et al., 1990; Gehring et al., 1993; Scheffers & Coles, 2000), ERN amplitude is insensitive to whether or not errors are consciously detected (Klein et al., 2007; Nieuwenhuis, Ridderinkhof, Blom, Band, & Kok, 2001). Subsequent empirical studies have shown, as predicted, that ERN amplitude varies with levels of response conflict (Frank, Woroch, & Curran, 2005), for example, being greater when correct and incorrect responses are similar and therefore in more direct competition (Gehring & Fencsik, 2001).

As described above, a key prediction arising from conflict model simulations—that on correct trials ACC should primarily be active before the response—has been borne out in studies of a second EEG component, the N2 (Folstein & Van Petten, 2008; Kopp et al., 1996; Nieuwenhuis et al., 2003; van Veen & Carter, 2002; Yeung et al., 2004; Yeung & Nieuwenhuis, 2009). However, the hypothesis that the ERN and N2 both index conflict monitoring has been challenged by findings that the two components may be affected in opposite ways by cingulate lesions (Swick & Turken, 2002) and some psychoactive drugs (Riba, Rodriguez-Fornells, Morte, Munte, & Barbanoj, 2005; Ridderinkhof et al., 2002). In response, subsequent simulation studies have shown how such dissociations might arise in a conflict monitoring system—for example, if cingulate lesions cause attentional deficits by disconnecting ACC from lateral PFC (Yeung & Cohen, 2006). Predictions arising from these simulations—for example, mimicking the attentional effects of ACC lesions by increasing the salience of irrelevant stimuli in the flanker task—have since been confirmed in empirical work (Danielmeier, Wessel, Steinhauser, & Ullsperger, 2009; Yeung, Ralph, & Nieuwenhuis, 2007).

Also important to address are findings of anatomical dissociations between conflict and errors. Whereas conflict primarily activates dorsal ACC, error-related activity typically extends into the affective rostral-ventral subdivision of ACC (Kiehl et al., 2000; Mathalon et al., 2003; Menon, Adleman, White, Glover, & Reiss, 2001; Taylor et al., 2006; Wittfoth et al., 2008). This anatomical dissociation is not directly predicted by the conflict monitoring theory, but nor is it unexpected given that conflicts and errors may require different compensatory reactions. Thus, whereas conflict detection should primarily drive adjustments in attentional control (Fan, Hof, Guise, Fossella, & Posner, 2008; Kerns et al., 2004), errors may elicit affective responses (Pourtois et al., 2010; Taylor et al., 2006) and strategic speed-accuracy trade-offs (Botvinick et al., 2001; Rabbitt, 1966) that could impose additional cognitive demands (Jentzsch & Dudschig, 2009; Notebaert et al., 2009).

Nevertheless, there remain substantial challenges to the conflict account of error-related ACC activity. First, the theory cannot explain evidence of ACC activity following the presentation of feedback indicating that an error has occurred (Gehring & Willoughby, 2002; Holroyd & Coles, 2002; Miltner, Braun, & Coles, 1997), as discussed below in relation to reinforcement learning theories of ACC function. Second, the theory predicts that ACC activity on correct trials should primarily occur before the response, yet a correct-response negativity (CRN) is sometimes observed with timing comparable to the ERN (Gehring & Knight, 2000; Pailing & Segalowitz, 2004; Vidal, Hasbroucq, Grapperon, & Bonnet, 2000), although arguably reflecting different neural mechanisms (Coles, Scheffers, & Holroyd, 2001; Roger, Benar, Vidal, Hasbroucq, & Burle, 2010; Vidal, Burle, Bonnet, Grapperon, & Hasbroucq, 2003; Yordanova, Falkenstein, Hohnsbein, & Kolev, 2004). Finally, some predictions from conflict model simulations have been disconfirmed (Burle, Roger, Allain, Vidal, & Hasbroucq, 2008; Carbonnell & Falkenstein, 2006; Steinhauser, Maier, & Hubner, 2008). For example, the theory predicts greater conflict when errors are quickly corrected, a prediction confirmed in some studies (Rodriguez-Fornells, Kurzbuch, & Muente, 2002) but not others (Burle et al., 2008). Thus, although the conflict theory successfully explains and predicts a range of findings regarding conflict and errors, debate continues as to whether it provides a comprehensive account of error-related ACC activity.

Conflict Adaptation

The conflict monitoring theory claims that detection of conflict should lead to increased recruitment of cognitive control (Botvinick et al., 2001), reflected in increased activation of high-level task representations in lateral PFC (Kerns et al., 2004) and, subsequently, enhancement of task-relevant information in sensory and motor cortices (Egner & Hirsch, 2005). Experimental tests of this claim have focused on trial-to-trial sequential adaptation effects observed in the Stroop (Kerns et al., 2004), flanker (Gratton et al., 1992), and Simon (Sturmer, Leuthold, Soetens, Schroter, & Sommer, 2002) tasks, among others, in which the effects of task-irrelevant information—interference on incongruent trials and facilitation on congruent trials—are reduced following high-conflict incongruent trials (Figure 18.4). The theory explains these findings in terms of conflict detected on trial N-1 leading to increased control on trial N that attenuates the effects of task-irrelevant information on behavior.

It has been argued, however, that sequential adaptation effects are problematically confounded with low-level repetition and priming effects (e.g., Hommel, 2004; Mayr, Awh, & Laurey, 2003). For example, performance may improve on successive incongruent trials simply because this trial sequence includes many exact repetitions of the stimulus and required response (Mayr et al., 2003). Excluding exact repetitions has been found to abolish sequential adaptation effects in some studies (Fernandez-Duque & Knight, 2008; Mayr et al., 2003; Nieuwenhuis et al., 2006). Moreover, sequential adaptation effects have sometimes been found only during the early stages of testing (Mayr & Awh, 2009) and to be somewhat independent of conflict experienced on trial N-1 as measured through electromyographic (EMG) activity corresponding to the competing responses (Burle, Allain, Vidal, & Hasbroucq, 2005).

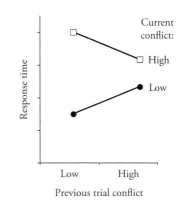

Figure 18.4 Schematic illustration of conflict adaptation in response time data.

Nevertheless, it seems unlikely that repetition and priming fully account for observed sequential adaptation effects, which may be evident even when repetition effects are factored out via multiple regression (Notebaert & Verguts, 2007) or excluded from analysis (Kunde & Wuhr, 2006; Notebaert, Gevers, Verbruggen, & Liefooghe, 2006; Ullsperger, Bylsma, & Botvinick, 2005). Critically, repetition trials were excluded in neuroimaging studies reporting that increased ACC activity on high-conflict trials is predictive of increased PFC activity and reduced conflict on subsequent trials (Egner & Hirsch, 2005; Kerns, 2006; Kerns et al., 2004; Larson, Kaufman, & Perlstein, 2009). Feature repetition provides no ready account of these findings, nor of why sequential adaptation should be lost following ACC lesions (di Pellegrino, Ciaramelli, & Ladavas, 2007), transcranial magnetic stimulation of lateral PFC (Sturmer, Redlich, Irlbacher, & Brandt, 2007), the presentation of positive feedback to counteract aversive effects of conflict (van Steenbergen, Band, & Hommel, 2009), or reduction in the time between trials (Notebaert et al., 2006). Moreover, experiments favoring the feature repetition account may have overlooked other sequential factors, such as negative priming (Tipper, 1985), that could mask conflict adaptation (Bugg, 2008; Davelaar & Stevens, 2009). Taken together, these combined findings provide strong support for the existence of conflict adaptation independent of feature repetition.

Recent studies have extended this conclusion to evaluate the specificity of conflict adaptation, asking whether conflict detection in one task can lead to subsequent control adjustments in another. Although cross-task adaptation is sometimes observed, for example, when flanker task conflict on trial N-1 leads to reduced Stroop interference on trial N (Freitas, Bahar, Yang, & Banai, 2007; Kunde & Wuhr, 2006), many studies report that conflict adaptation is task-specific (Brown, Reynolds, & Braver, 2007; Egner et al., 2007; Fernandez-Duque & Knight, 2008; Funes, Lupianez, & Humphreys, 2010a; Kiesel, Kunde, & Hoffmann, 2006). Similarity between two tasks appears to be the critical factor: Cross-task adaptation is observed when tasks share similar stimuli, responses, or stimulus-response mappings (Akcay & Hazeltine, 2008; Cho, Orr, Cohen, & Carter, 2009; Notebaert & Verguts, 2008), but not otherwise. These findings suggest that conflict adaptation is process-specific: Adaptation generalizes when tasks share processes such as attending to particular stimulus features

or selecting specific responses. Neuroimaging dissociations between conflict-control mechanisms in the Stroop and Simon tasks are consistent with this hypothesis (Egner et al., 2007). A question for future research is whether such dissociations reflect the existence of dissociable process-specific conflict monitoring systems in ACC, or if instead a common conflict monitoring system interacts with dissociable control systems depending on task structure (Akcay & Hazeltine, 2008).

Uses of Conflict Signals

Most research to date has focused on trial-to-trial conflict adaptation, but conflict-control feedback may operate over both shorter and longer time scales, recruiting control online within a trial and setting levels of control over extended periods. Relevant to the latter, conflict is reduced when incongruent trials occur frequently across blocks of the Stroop and flanker tasks (Gratton et al., 1992; Tzelgov, Henik, & Berger, 1992), and ACC activity covaries with this effect (Carter et al., 2000). Computational simulations show how accumulated trial-to-trial sequential adjustments in control might account for these block-level adjustments (Blais, Robidoux, Risko, & Besner, 2007; Botvinick et al., 2001; Verguts & Notebaert, 2008). However, block-level and sequential adjustments seem to differ in their generalization across tasks (Funes, Lupianez, & Humphreys, 2010b), persistence over training (Mayr & Awh, 2009), and influence on specific processing stages (Purmann, Badde, & Wendt, 2009). One intriguing hypothesis is that these dissociations reflect the operation of a unitary conflict monitoring system as it interacts with cognitive control systems operating over different time scales (cf. Braver, Reynolds, & Donaldson, 2003). This issue is ripe for investigation, for example, using neuroimaging designs sensitive to both transient and sustained neural activity (Donaldson, 2004).

Still less is known about within-trial conflict adaptation. fMRI and EEG studies indicate that functional connectivity between ACC and frontoparietal regions dynamically increases on high-conflict trials (Cavanagh, Cohen, & Allen, 2009; Fan et al., 2008; Hanslmayr et al., 2008; Wang et al., 2010), but these interactions might serve primarily to influence future conflict adaptation. Perhaps more conclusive is recent evidence that trials with increased ACC activity are associated with reduced activation of incorrect responses (Pastotter, Hanslmayr, & Bauml, 2010), suggestive of ACC-mediated control adjustments within trials. Future research might usefully study such within-trial effects in other paradigms in which online recruitment of control has been inferred, such as suppression of direct response activation in the Simon and Stroop tasks (Davelaar, 2008; Ridderinkhof, 2002; Yu et al., 2009), reduction of conflict when the presented stimulus has previously been associated with high levels of conflict (Crump, Gong, & Wmiken, 2006; Jacoby, Lindsay, & Hessels, 2003; Wendt, Kluwe, & Vietze, 2008), and reduced sensitivity to task-irrelevant information on trials in which a high level of conflict is experienced (Goschke & Dreisbach, 2008). The question currently remains open whether ACC conflict monitoring might contribute to these effects.

Recent computational modeling studies have meanwhile suggested uses of conflict signals beyond simple recruitment of control. First, conflict may act as an online "braking signal" that prompts selective or cautious responding. This idea has been incorporated in models of cognitive control in task switching (Brown et al., 2007), as well as in models of optimal decision-making by the basal ganglia (Bogacz & Gurney, 2007) in which conflict signals from the ACC prompt response inhibition by the subthalamic nucleus (Bogacz, Wagenmakers, Forstmann, & Nieuwenhuis, 2010; Frank, 2006). Second, conflict has been proposed as a useful signal driving learning (Blais et al., 2007; Botvinick, 2007; Verguts & Notebaert, 2009). For example, conflict adaptation effects have been simulated using models in which conflict modulates Hebbian learning between top-down control and bottom-up stimulus representations (Blais et al., 2007; Verguts & Notebaert, 2008). Conflict might also serve as an aversive signal to drive reinforcement learning of behavioral strategies to minimize cognitive effort (Botvinick, 2007). Specifically, whereas transient conflict indicates the need for increased control, conflict over an extended period might indicate that alternative strategies should be sought (Aston-Jones & Cohen, 2005). Thus, conflict monitoring may provide a valuable source of information that can be used in various ways to optimize behavioral performance, although a coherent and comprehensive account of these varied uses remains to be developed.

Dissociable Forms of Conflict

Comparisons between conflict tasks have typically identified overlapping activation patterns in ACC (Fan, Flombaum, McCandliss, Thomas, & Posner, 2003; Rubia et al., 2001; Wager et al., 2005), regardless of the stimuli inducing the conflict (Roberts & Hall, 2008) and the response modality in which the conflict occurs (Barch et al., 2001). Collectively, these findings suggest that a common ACC system monitors for conflicts among representations of very different kinds. However, one dissociation now well established is between stimulus and response conflict (Davelaar, 2008; Liston et al., 2006; Milham et al., 2001; Schulte et al., 2009; van Veen & Carter, 2002; van Veen, Cohen, Botvinick, Stenger, & Carter, 2001; Wendelken, Ditterich, Bunge, & Carter, 2009). Stimulus and response conflict can be dissociated using flanker tasks in which two stimuli require left-hand responses (e.g., *H* and *P*) and two require right-hand responses (e.g., *S* and *M*), so that response conflict trials (e.g., *HHSHH*) can be compared with trials in which the stimuli conflict but their associated responses do not (e.g., *HHPHH*). Stimulus conflict has been found to activate lateral frontal and parietal cortex (Liston et al., 2006; Wendelken et al., 2009) but produces little activity in ACC (van Veen et al., 2001), as one might expect, given that ACC receives little direct sensory input (Beckmann et al., 2009; Margulies et al., 2007; van Hoesen et al., 1993).

A proposed dissociation between cognitive and emotional conflict has a similarly strong basis in the differential connectivity of the dorsal-caudal and rostral-ventral subdivisions of ACC (Bush et al., 2000; Devinsky et al., 1995). Rostral ACC activity is observed in conflict tasks in which task-irrelevant information is affectively valenced (Bishop, Duncan, & Lawrence, 2004; Vuilleumier, Armony, Driver, & Dolan, 2001; Whalen et al., 1998), for example, when subjects judge whether faces are happy or fearful while ignoring an irrelevant superimposed word (*HAPPY* or *FEAR*) (Etkin, Egner, Peraza, Kandel, & Hirsch, 2006). This activity is functionally and anatomically dissociable from response conflict-related activity in dorsal ACC (Mohanty et al., 2007). However, dorsal and rostral ACC do not appear to independently monitor response and emotional conflicts, but rather interact during emotional conflict in a way that mirrors the interaction between dorsal ACC and lateral PFC in resolving response conflict (Egner, Etkin, Gale, & Hirsch, 2008). Thus, dorsal ACC activity is also observed in emotional conflict tasks (Davis et al., 2005; Egner et al., 2008; Mohanty et al., 2007; Wittfoth et al., 2010), and, in emotional conflict adaptation, rostral ACC activity increases rather than reduces following high-conflict trials (Etkin et al., 2006).

Within dorsal ACC, dissociable activity patterns have been reported as a function of the nature of conflicting representations. Most research and theorizing to date has focused on conflict between simple actions, typically key-presses made with different fingers, but efforts have been made to study conflict between more abstract response representations. Thus, decision conflict, which occurs when subjects choose between options that are not (or not yet) associated with particular actions, has been found to activate more anterior portions of ACC than conflict between defined actions (Pochon, Riis, Sanfey, Nystrom, & Cohen, 2008; Venkatraman, Rosati, Taren, & Huettel, 2009). The opposite organization is suggested by studies of conflict between high-level task and semantic representations (Aarts, Roelofs, & van Turennout, 2009; Melcher & Gruber, 2009; Milham & Banich, 2005; Ruff, Woodward, Laurens, & Liddle, 2001; van Veen & Carter, 2005). Task-level Stroop conflict can be identified, for example, by contrasting congruent (e.g., *RED* in red ink) and neutral stimuli (e.g., *XXX* in red ink). Response conflict should be low in both cases, but the irrelevant word in congruent stimuli should lead to conflict between the word-reading and color-naming tasks. Task conflict has been found to activate posterior regions of ACC and pre-SMA, contrasting with anterior activation seen to decision conflict (Melcher & Gruber, 2009; Milham & Banich, 2005; but see Roelofs, van Turennout, & Coles, 2006). Thus, although findings from decision, semantic, and task-level conflict suggest subdivisions within dorsal ACC, the precise functional architecture of the region remains unknown.

Finally, recent studies have investigated whether the ACC activates solely during the experience of conflict—our focus thus far—or also during anticipation of conflict, using pre-cues that indicate the expected level of conflict prior to stimulus presentation. Despite some evidence to the contrary (Luks, Simpson, Dale, & Hough, 2007; MacDonald, Cohen, Stenger, & Carter, 2000; Nieuwenhuis, Schweizer, Mars, Botvinick, & Hajcak, 2007), it now seems clear that anticipatory activity occurs in ACC (Aarts, Roelofs, & Van Turennout, 2008; Dosenbach et al., 2006; Fan et al., 2007; Luks, Simpson, Feiwell, & Miller, 2002), and more so for cues indicating high conflict to come (Barber & Carter, 2005; Sohn, Albert, Jung, Carter, & Anderson, 2007; Weissman, Gopalakrishnan, Hazlett, & Woldorff, 2005). One recent study found that anticipatory activity dissociates from conflict-related activity in ACC (Orr & Weissman, 2009), with the former lying more posterior and extending into pre-SMA. There is notable overlap between this anticipatory activity and task-level conflict effect discussed above. In both cases, it has yet to be determined whether the focus of activity lies within ACC or pre-SMA, and whether the activity is conflict-related or rather reflects processes related to attention and task preparation (Brass & von Cramon, 2002; Orr & Weissman, 2009).

Neuropsychology of Conflict Monitoring

The vast majority of conflict monitoring studies have used correlational neuroimaging methods, but there is obvious value in establishing more causal evidence. Although ACC lesions are consistently associated with deficits in executive function (Devinsky et al., 1995), evidence specific to conflict monitoring has proven controversial. Several studies have found that Stroop interference is not markedly increased in patients with cingulate lesions (Baird et al., 2006; Fellows & Farah, 2005; Stuss, Floden, Alexander, Levine, & Katz, 2001), and these patients—including some with extensive bilateral damage—may show intact conflict adaptation (Fellows & Farah, 2005), even if their subjective experience of conflict is markedly reduced (Naccache et al., 2005). However, there are also several reports of impaired performance in a variety of conflict tasks in patients with ACC lesions (Modirrousta & Fellows, 2008; Picton et al., 2007), including some with very focal damage (Cohen, Kaplan, Moser, Jenkins, & Wilkinson, 1999; Cohen, Kaplan, Zuffante et al., 1999; Ochsner et al., 2001; Swick & Turken, 2002; Turken & Swick, 1999; Yen et al., 2009), and with crucial lesion sites mapping on well to the localization of conflict-related activity in neuroimaging studies (Swick & Jovanovic, 2002). Impaired conflict adaptation and error monitoring have also been observed following damage to dorsal ACC (Modirrousta & Fellows, 2008; Swick & Jovanovic, 2002) and in patients with damage affecting more rostral ACC regions (di Pellegrino et al., 2007).

These discrepancies may at least partly reflect methodological issues: Many patient studies use blocked designs in which conflict is predictable, yet ACC is primarily important when adapting to varying levels of conflict (Floden, Vallesi, & Stuss, 2011). Nevertheless, whereas cingulate patients only inconsistently show increased sensitivity to response conflict, the same patients very consistently exhibit general slowing of responding across tasks irrespective of conflict (Alexander, Stuss, Shallice, Picton, & Gillingham, 2005; Picton et al., 2007; Stuss et al.,

2005). Such findings have suggested a role for ACC in "energizing" responding (Stuss et al., 2005), but this hypothesis is challenged by evidence that ACC is sensitive to tasks requiring response inhibition (Nieuwenhuis et al., 2003; Rubia et al., 2001; Tsuchida & Fellows, 2009). Instead, the combined findings are intriguing when taken with the recent proposal that conflict signals from ACC may be used to set an appropriate response threshold to optimize decision making (Bogacz et al., 2010; Frank, 2006). If correct, this interpretation would support the view that the role of ACC extends beyond conflict-control regulation to include more general functions relevant to setting appropriate response strategies.

Conflict monitoring has also been investigated in psychiatric patient populations. Abnormalities in conflict-related activity are inconsistent in mood disorder and attention-deficit hyperactivity disorder but are well established in patients with schizophrenia and obsessive-compulsive disorder (Melcher, Falkai, & Gruber, 2008; Ullsperger, 2006). As part of a broader pattern of hypofrontality (Benes, 2000; Cohen & Servan-Schreiber, 1992) and performance-monitoring deficits (Malenka, Angel, Hampton, & Berger, 1982), patients with schizophrenia exhibit reduced conflict-related ACC activity (Carter, Mintun, Nichols, & Cohen, 1997; McNeely, West, Christensen, & Alain, 2003) and reduced conflict adaptation (Kerns et al., 2005). These findings are suggestive of conflict-monitoring deficits that might contribute to both the positive (psychotic) symptoms and the cognitive deficits evident in these patients. In contrast, ACC tends to be hyperactive in patients with obsessive-compulsive disorder, both in association with errors (Gehring, Himle, & Nisenson, 2000; but see Nieuwenhuis, Nielen, Mol, Hajcak, & Veltman, 2005) and response conflict (Maltby, Tolin, Worhunsky, O'Keefe, & Kiehl, 2005; Ursu, Stenger, Shear, Jones, & Carter, 2003; Yucel et al., 2007), with the degree of ACC hyperactivity predictive of symptom severity. There is obvious intuitive appeal to the notion that patients with obsessive-compulsive disorder have an overactive action-monitoring system.

Such findings suggest that performance-monitoring deficits may contribute to the symptoms apparent in patient groups and may provide useful diagnostic measures in clinical settings (Melcher et al., 2008; Ullsperger, 2006). Such inferences must be drawn with caution, however, because disruptions in ACC performance monitoring might be secondary symptoms rather than a primary cause of observed deficits (Yeung & Cohen, 2006). ACC

function is known to be sensitive to damage to a widespread network of regions, including lateral PFC and the basal ganglia (Gehring & Knight, 2000; Ullsperger & von Cramon, 2006). Existing findings nevertheless provide grounds for optimism that conflict monitoring might provide a useful framework for investigating cognitive deficits associated with ACC dysfunction. A crucial open question is whether therapeutic interventions targeted at conflict monitoring can ameliorate the cognitive deficits in these patient populations (cf. Edwards, Barch, & Braver, 2010).

Conflict Monitoring in Context

The research reviewed above has been conducted within the framework of the conflict monitoring theory, providing extensions and challenges to parts of that framework. This final section considers the theory in the context of wider research on ACC function. As will become apparent, consideration of evidence gathered via other methodologies, in other species, and involving wider conceptions of the functional role of ACC brings into question the degree to which conflict monitoring provides a comprehensive account of the role of this region in control and in cognition more widely.

Conflict Monitoring in Nonhuman Primates

Nonhuman primate studies have to date provided little support for the conflict monitoring theory. Whereas recordings of spiking activity and local field potentials in human ACC reveal evidence of conflict-related activity (Davis, Hutchison, Lozano, Tasker, & Dostrovsky, 2000; Davis et al., 2005; Wang et al., 2005), no such effects have been observed in monkey ACC (Emeric et al., 2008; Ito, Stuphorn, Brown, & Schall, 2003; Nakamura et al., 2005). Moreover, ACC lesions in primates have been found to have no effect on conflict adaptation, which is instead primarily sensitive to lateral PFC damage (Mansouri, Buckley, & Tanaka, 2007). More promising evidence of conflict-related activity in primates has been observed in the pre-SMA and supplementary eye field (Isoda & Hikosaka, 2007; Nakamura et al., 2005; Stuphorn et al., 2000). However, conflict effects in these regions typically reflect modulations of movement-selective task-related activity, rather than pure signals of conflict independent of the responses selected (Isoda & Hikosaka, 2007; Nakamura et al., 2005). Indeed, these findings have led to the suggestion that conflict-related activity in human neuroimaging studies may be an artifact of coarse-grained neuroimaging methods averaging activity across populations of neurons that selectively code for conflicting responses (Nakamura et al., 2005).

Given the serious implications this conclusion would have for all of the research considered in this chapter, it is unsurprising that alternative accounts of the between-species discrepancy have been proposed (Botvinick et al., 2004; Cole, Yeung, Freiwald, & Botvinick, 2009). However, several potential explanations can be immediately ruled out. First, the discrepancy is unlikely to reflect the fact that human studies typically use manual responses whereas primate work mostly uses saccadic tasks, because conflict-related activity is observed in human ACC when saccadic tasks are used (Curtis, Cole, Rao, & D'Esposito, 2005; Paus et al., 1993). Nor is it likely that primate studies have simply failed to find conflict-signaling neurons that are nonetheless present, given that these studies sampled widely in ACC and had little trouble identifying error-related activity, suggesting that the regions under scrutiny are homologous (Nakamura et al., 2005). Moreover, although human ACC contains cell types not found in monkeys (Nimchinsky et al., 1999), these large spindle neurons are restricted to the cingulate gyrus rather than the sulcal regions that are the focus of conflict-related activity.

Several possible accounts of the between-species discrepancy remain after excluding these alternatives. First, and perhaps most strikingly, human conflict-related activity localizes to area 32′— an area of cingulofrontal transition cortex interposed between the cingulate motor areas and the pre-SMA and SMA—which has no direct homolog in dorsal ACC in monkeys (Vogt et al., 1995). As such, conflict monitoring functions may be substantially more developed in humans than in nonhuman primates (Cole et al., 2009). Second, conflict-related activity may be less evident in single-unit spiking activity than in neuroimaging recordings that are sensitive to synchronization and synaptic activity within local neural circuits (Botvinick et al., 2004). Consistent with this interpretation, a recent fMRI study of awake behaving monkeys found strong ACC activity in a conflict-inducing antisaccade task (Ford, Gati, Menon, & Everling, 2009). Third, it may be misguided to expect conflict-related activity in single-unit recordings to occur independent of the particular responses selected. Recent computational modeling suggests that conflict may be detected in a response-specific manner (Brown et al., 2007) and may lead to modulation of control that is similarly stimulus- and response-specific (Blais et al., 2007; Verguts & Notebaert, 2008).

Each of these possibilities identifies important avenues for future research. Thus, if conflict monitoring is uniquely developed in humans, it becomes important to explain why primate behavior is nonetheless sensitive to conflict (Mansouri et al., 2007; Nakamura et al., 2005) and to identify cognitive abilities that might depend critically on this supposedly unique function. Conversely, if conflict signals are apparent in both humans and monkeys but only in regional activity, it becomes vital to identify the functional role of these signals, given that spiking activity is required if conflict signals are to be conveyed to other cortical regions (Nakamura et al., 2005). One hypothesis could be that local activity in ACC varies with conflict, as envisioned by the theory, but its spiking output may convey much more than a simple scalar signal of conflict, for example, indicating specific changes in control strategy. According to this hypothesis, activation patterns in ACC should correlate with specific behavioral strategies, a prediction ripe for evaluation using multivariate fMRI analysis approaches. Finally, if conflict is detected in a response-specific manner, as envisioned in recent computational models, the behavior of units in these models should be meaningfully related to single unit activity recorded in monkey ACC. Thus, although studies in nonhuman primates have so far provided little support for the conflict monitoring theory, they suggest a number of intriguing avenues for its development in future research.

Reinforcement and Reward-Guided Decision-Making

Conflict monitoring research typically focuses on ACC activity in tasks in which the required response is clearly defined: The challenge for subjects is to produce this response in the face of conflict from a prepotent or habitual alternative (Miller & Cohen, 2001). However, ACC activity has also been widely studied using tasks in which the correct response is not instructed but must be learned by trial-and-error using feedback. In such tasks, robust ACC activity is not only observed as subjects choose their response (Blair et al., 2006; Holroyd et al., 2004; Marsh, Blair, Vythilingam, Busis, & Blair, 2007; Walton, Devlin, & Rushworth, 2004)—a finding that might reflect conflict between the different options—but also as subjects anticipate or receive feedback about their choices (Bush et al., 2002; Gehring & Willoughby, 2002; Holroyd et al., 2004; Knutson, Taylor, Kaufman, Peterson, & Glover, 2005; Miltner et al., 1997; Yeung & Sanfey, 2004).

This evidence supports the view that the ACC plays a critical role in reward-guided decision-making and learning, serving to guide behavior by associating actions with their outcomes (Alexander & Brown, 2011; Holroyd & Coles, 2002; Rushworth, Behrens, Rudebeck, & Walton, 2007). Consistent with this hypothesis, feedback-related ACC activity increases with the unpredictability (Holroyd, Nieuwenhuis, Yeung, & Cohen, 2003) and volatility (Behrens, Woolrich, Walton, & Rushworth, 2007) of experienced outcomes and is predictive of whether subjects will avoid repeating incorrect responses in the future (Hester, Barre, Murphy, Silk, & Mattingley, 2008).

This view of ACC function is supported by single-unit recordings in nonhuman primates where, in contrast to the apparent absence of conflict-sensitive neurons, coding of reward and reinforcement is well established (Amiez, Joseph, & Procyk, 2006; Shidara & Richmond, 2002). Indeed, when comparable tasks are used in humans and nonhuman primates, close correspondences are observed between ACC activity across species (Bush et al., 2002; Shima & Tanji, 1998; Williams, Bush, Rauch, Cosgrove, & Eskandar, 2004). ACC neuron activity specifically appears to code the value of experienced outcomes in relation to selected actions (Hayden & Platt, 2010; Luk & Wallis, 2009), for example, increasing when unexpected reductions in reward lead to changes in behavior (Shima & Tanji, 1998; Williams et al., 2004). This activity appears to play a causal role in learning: Focal lesions in ACC impair animals' ability to use reinforcement to learn to select appropriate actions (Amiez et al., 2006; Hadland, Rushworth, Gaffan, & Passingham, 2003; Kennerley, Walton, Behrens, Buckley, & Rushworth, 2006; Shima & Tanji, 1998).

Given these successes, an important question concerns the relation between reward-guided decision-making and conflict monitoring. It could be that they are dissociable functions of separate ACC subregions (Marsh et al., 2007; Rogers et al., 2004). However, meta-analyses indicate substantial overlap in conflict- and feedback-related activity within the ACC (Beckmann et al., 2009; Ridderinkhof et al., 2004). Moreover, reinforcement learning and conflict monitoring in certain cases provide contrasting accounts of the same phenomenon (Alexander & Brown, 2011; Holroyd & Coles, 2002; Yeung et al., 2004), suggesting the importance of reconciling the theories. One suggestion has been that conflict-related activity in ACC is artifactual: a by-product of coding the likelihood of errors or anticipation

of negative outcomes that correlate with conflict (Brown & Braver, 2005). However, this hypothesis struggles to explain ACC activity seen in tasks in which errors are rare (e.g., in the Stroop task; Carter et al., 2000) or absent (e.g., in word generation tasks in which the conflict occurs between multiple correct responses; Barch et al., 2000; Thompson-Schill et al., 1997). Moreover, when conflict and error likelihood are dissociated on the basis of response speed—because slow responses produce high conflict but low error likelihood—ACC activity varies with the level of conflict (Yeung & Nieuwenhuis, 2009). Recent computational modeling work has attempted to address these criticisms of reinforcement learning approaches, using more complex algorithms that are capable of learning vector representations of expected response outcomes rather than simple scalar predictions of expected reward (Alexander & Brown, 2011). However, this model fails to account for benchmark features of ACC activity seen during reinforcement learning, such as its specific sensitivity to negative outcomes even when those outcomes are as likely as positive outcomes (Holroyd et al., 2003; Yeung & Sanfey, 2004). As such, a reductive model of conflict- and learning-related activity in ACC remains elusive.

Instead, conflict monitoring and reinforcement learning seem to provide complementary rather than competing accounts of ACC function (Botvinick, 2007). In particular, ACC might contribute broadly to the optimization of behavior through its sensitivity to signals indicating the efficiency and effectiveness of actions, both internal (in the case of conflict) and environmental (in the case of reinforcement learning). One specific proposal is that conflict registers as a cost to drive avoidance learning against effortful or error-prone options (Botvinick, 2007). This interpretation is consistent with evidence from animal studies that the ACC plays a crucial role in evaluating the effort associated with actions (Rudebeck, Walton, Smyth, Bannerman, & Rushworth, 2006; Walton, Bannerman, Alterescu, & Rushworth, 2003) and extends this notion to encompass mental as well as physical effort. More generally, these ideas begin to situate the conflict monitoring theory within the broader context of ACC function as it is understood in a range of task contexts and in a variety of species.

Contrasting Theories of ACC Function

A broader conception of ACC function might also help relate the conflict monitoring theory to other perspectives on the role of ACC. One influential hypothesis is that the ACC supports action selection (Dum & Strick, 1991; Picard & Strick, 1996), particularly when responding is voluntary rather than cued by stimuli in the environment (Paus, 2001). Thus, patients with cingulate lesions produce fewer spontaneous verbalizations and movements than controls and demonstrate corresponding deficits in unstructured tasks (e.g., when asked simply to draw as many pictures or designs as possible over a fixed period; Cohen, Kaplan, Zuffante et al., 1999). Deficits in voluntary action are seen in extreme form in akinetic mutism, in which patients become immobile and unresponsive to external stimuli following bilateral damage to the ACC and nearby cortex (Nemeth, Hegedus, & Molnar, 1988). Neuroimaging studies report greater ACC activity during self-initiated movement—for example, when movements are produced in an irregular rhythm—than when the same movements are made in response to external stimuli (Deiber, Honda, Ibanez, Sadato, & Hallett, 1999; Krieghoff, Brass, Prinz, & Waszak, 2009). Corresponding single-unit recordings in nonhuman primates demonstrate that this activity may precede movement initiation by more than a second (Shima et al., 1991).

Conflict monitoring provides no ready account of these findings. Although the neuroimaging findings might reflect increased conflict when actions are self-initiated (Barch et al., 2000; Botvinick et al., 2001), it is unclear why a lesion-induced conflict monitoring deficit should reduce spontaneous speech and action. Instead, a more productive reconciliation might be in relation to the view that conflict monitoring represents one facet of the role of ACC in evaluating the costs and benefits of actions (Botvinick, 2007). Such evaluation would be vital in voluntary action selection, which must normally depend on a cost-benefit analysis of action choices (Holroyd & Yeung, 2012). Within this framework, an important open question is whether ACC itself directly selects or initiates actions (Paus, 2001), or rather supports action selection indirectly via its connections with premotor and prefrontal cortex (Kouneiher, Charron, & Koechlin, 2009). Recent neuroimaging evidence has been taken to favor the former view (Banich, 2009; Dosenbach, Fair, Cohen, Schlaggar, & Petersen, 2008).

The notion that ACC plays a regulative role, directly exerting control rather than simply evaluating performance, has been a longstanding alternative view of ACC function (Posner & Petersen, 1990). Although this hypothesis is challenged by conflict adaptation effects—after high-conflict trials, ACC activity reduces with the level of conflict rather than increasing with the level of control (Botvinick et al., 1999)—recent findings have reignited interest in regulative accounts of ACC function (Banich, 2009; Dosenbach et al., 2008). Evidence that the ACC activates transiently not only during conflict but also during preparation and in a sustained manner throughout task performance (Dosenbach et al., 2006) has led to the view that the ACC is part of a core system for maintaining a stable cognitive state over time (Dosenbach et al., 2008). Meanwhile, evidence that conflict-related changes in ACC activity may disappear when between-condition differences in reaction time are controlled for (Grinband et al., 2011) has led to the suggestion that the ACC plays a more general role in decision-making. Finally, EEG evidence that ACC activity follows lateral PFC activity in the Stroop task, and modulates its influence on behavioral performance (Silton et al., 2010), has been taken to show that ACC operates at a relatively late stage of a control "cascade," making transient contributions to the selection of specific actions (Banich, 2009).

These theories present a different view of ACC function than that proposed by the conflict monitoring theory. However, given disagreement about the supposed nature of control exerted by ACC—sustained task-level control vs. transient response selection—it remains unclear whether a coherent integration is possible. Moreover, current evidence is far from definitive in challenging the conflict monitoring theory. Preparatory ACC activity could reflect task-level conflict (Aarts et al., 2008; Melcher & Gruber, 2009; Milham & Banich, 2005; Ruff et al., 2001; van Veen & Carter, 2005), sustained activity might reflect the integration of conflict over an extended period (Aston-Jones & Cohen, 2005; Botvinick et al., 2001), activity related to variation in reaction time is well explained by existing models of conflict monitoring (Yeung, Cohen & Botvinick, 2011), and ACC-related modulation of control by lateral PFC might reflect within-trial conflict adaptation (Cavanagh et al., 2009; Fan et al., 2008; Hanslmayr et al., 2008; Wang et al., 2010). Thus, ACC involvement in regulative rather than evaluative aspects of control remains to be determined. It is nevertheless increasingly clear, particularly given evidence of ACC involvement in voluntary action selection and reinforcement learning, that conflict monitoring is just one aspect of the role of ACC in the evaluation and control of thought and action.

Conclusion

The conflict monitoring theory has been a significant success story of cognitive neuroscience research. Countering claims that neuroimaging is of limited relevance to theories of cognition (Coltheart, 2006), the initial impetus for the theory came primarily from imaging work—specifically, emerging evidence of ACC activity associated with a diverse range of cognitive demands—but the theory itself is truly cognitive. It proposes a computationally specified process that explains not only the original neuroimaging evidence but also established findings in the behavioral literature. In three critical respects, therefore, the theory has proven highly successful. First, it has given substantial impetus to a research field—on performance monitoring and the recruitment of control—that had been largely neglected in prior work. Second, it has provided a powerful set of behavioral, neuroimaging, and computational tools with which to probe these functions. And third, it has proven immensely productive in generating testable predictions about behavior and brain activity that have, by and large, been borne out experimentally. The original empirical (Carter et al., 1998) and conceptual (Botvinick et al., 2001) expositions of the theory have now been cited over 1,000 times each, attesting to the influence of the theory in cognitive neuroscience. Ongoing efforts to enrich understanding of the ways conflict might be detected and used (Aston-Jones & Cohen, 2005; Blais et al., 2007; Botvinick, 2007; Brown et al., 2007; Frank, 2006; Verguts & Notebaert, 2009) bode well for the continuing vitality of the theory as a source of new research.

These successes notwithstanding, scientific theories are ultimately judged according to whether or not they are right, and in this respect the legacy of the conflict monitoring theory is far less assured. Several substantive challenges have been discussed, but two issues in particular seem fundamental. The first arises from human neuropsychological studies: Conflict monitoring is proposed as a fundamental mechanism underpinning the recruitment of control, yet patients with ACC lesions only inconsistently exhibit deficits in conflict monitoring, adaptation, and control and are notably spared in overall intellect and executive function. The second challenge arises from the failure to find evidence of conflict monitoring in nonhuman primates (and other animals). Again, if conflict monitoring is a fundamental cognitive function, one would expect it to be present in our near-relatives, or for there to be obvious between-species differences in the experience or expression of conflict, yet evidence for either possibility is currently lacking.

The continuing success and influence of the conflict monitoring theory suggest that it would be premature to abandon it in the face of these challenges. Instead, these issues are perhaps most productively viewed as identifying key questions for future research. As discussed above, one such question is the relation between conflict monitoring, action selection, and reinforcement learning. Recent work has begun to reconcile these views (Botvinick, 2007; Holroyd & Yeung, 2012), but it remains unclear whether these integrative accounts can explain the wealth of evidence supporting the conflict monitoring theory as originally presented. Meanwhile, the relative insensitivity of current lab paradigms to lesions in ACC suggests a need to identify tasks that more effectively index this functioning. On the assumption that cognitive control crucially supports the structuring of behavior through time (Duncan, 2010) and rapid, flexible adaptation to new requirements (Monsell, 2003), the immediate theoretical challenge is to articulate clearly the role that conflict monitoring might play in these abilities. The corresponding empirical challenge is to design tasks that precisely probe this contribution and to evaluate their sensitivity to hypothesized deficits following ACC lesions and between-species differences in ACC function. Efforts towards these goals would represent an important step in the continuing evolution of the conflict monitoring theory: from an account primarily inspired by findings from constrained laboratory paradigms, toward a mature and detailed theory that makes direct contact with established principles of cognitive control.

Future Directions

1. Why do recordings of regional activity (e.g., using EEG and fMRI) show evidence of conflict-related activity in ACC while single-unit recordings generally fail to do so? Is the regional conflict signal merely an artifact of averaging across populations of neurons whose spiking activity is affected by, but does not code for, conflict? Or:

a. Is conflict detected in a stimulus/response-specific manner, such that it would be misguided to search for conflict signals that are independent of the response selected?

b. Does the spiking output of ACC contain more information than a simple scalar signal of experienced conflict, such as instructions about specific changes in behavioral strategy?

2. Can the conflict monitoring theory explain why performance on conflict tasks is only inconsistently affected by ACC lesions in humans? Is conflict-related activity seen in neuroimaging studies epiphenomenal? Or:

a. Do the deficits suffered by these patients provide important clues regarding additional uses of the ACC conflict signal, for example, in setting an appropriate response threshold?

b. Are typical laboratory tasks too simple to capture the contribution of conflict monitoring to flexible, structured human behavior? If so, how does conflict monitoring by the ACC support rapid behavioral shifting or the structured sequencing of thought and action?

3. How can the conflict monitoring theory be reconciled with the presumed role of ACC in reinforcement learning and voluntary action selection? Can a reconciled view account for the large corpus of existing data collected in support of the theory?

References

Aarts, E., Roelofs, A., & van Turennout, M. (2008). Anticipatory activity in anterior cingulate cortex can be independent of conflict and error likelihood. *Journal of Neuroscience, 28,* 4671–4678.

Aarts, E., Roelofs, A., & van Turennout, M. (2009). Attentional control of task and response in lateral and medial frontal cortex: Brain activity and reaction time distributions. *Neuropsychologia, 47,* 2089–2099.

Akcay, C., & Hazeltine, E. (2008). Conflict adaptation depends on task structure. *Journal of Experimental Psychology: Human Perception and Performance, 34,* 958–973.

Alexander, M. P., Stuss, D. T., Shallice, T., Picton, T. W., & Gillingham, S. (2005). Impaired concentration due to frontal lobe damage from two distinct lesion sites. *Neurology, 65,* 572–579.

Alexander, W. H., & Brown, J. W. (2011). Medial prefrontal cortex as an action-outcome predictor. *Nature Neuroscience, 14,* 1338–1344.

Allport, D. A. (1980). Attention and performance. In G. L. Claxton (Ed.), *Cognitive psychology: New directions* (pp. 112–153). London: Routledge and Kegan Paul.

Allport, D. A. (1987). Selection for action: Some behavioural and neurophysiological considerations of attention and action. In H. Heuer & A. F. Sanders (Eds.), *Perspectives on perception and action* (pp. 395–419). Hillsdale, NJ: Lawrence Erlbaum.

Amiez, C., Joseph, J. P., & Procyk, E. (2006). Reward encoding in the monkey anterior cingulate cortex. *Cerebral Cortex, 16,* 1040–1055.

Aston-Jones, G., & Cohen, J. D. (2005). An integrative theory of locus coeruleus-norepinephrine function: Adaptive gain and optimal performance. *Annual Review of Neuroscience, 28,* 403–450.

Baddeley, A. (1996). The fractionation of working memory. *Proceedings of the National Academy of Sciences of the USA, 93,* 13468–13472.

Badre, D., & D'Esposito, M. (2009). Is the rostro-caudal axis of the frontal lobe hierarchical? *Nature Reviews Neuroscience, 10,* 659–669.

Baird, A., Dewar, B. K., Critchley, H., Gilbert, S. J., Dolan, R. J., & Cipolotti, L. (2006). Cognitive functioning after medial frontal lobe damage including the anterior cingulate cortex: A preliminary investigation. *Brain and Cognition, 60,* 166–175.

Banich, M. T. (2009). Executive function: The search for an integrated account. *Current Directions in Psychological Science, 18,* 89–94.

Barber, A. D., & Carter, C. S. (2005). Cognitive control involved in overcoming prepotent response tendencies and switching between tasks. *Cerebral Cortex, 15,* 899–912.

Barch, D. M., Braver, T. S., Akbudak, E., Conturo, T., Ollinger, J., & Snyder, A. (2001). Anterior cingulate cortex and response conflict: Effects of response modality and processing domain. *Cerebral Cortex, 11,* 837–848.

Barch, D. M., Braver, T. S., Sabb, F. W., & Noll, D. C. (2000). Anterior cingulate and the monitoring of response conflict: Evidence from an fMRI study of overt verb generation. *Journal of Cognitive Neuroscience, 12,* 298–309.

Beckmann, M., Johansen-Berg, H., & Rushworth, M. F. S. (2009). Connectivity-based parcellation of human cingulate cortex and its relation to functional specialization. *Journal of Neuroscience, 29,* 1175–1190.

Behrens, T. E., Woolrich, M. W., Walton, M. E., & Rushworth, M. F. (2007). Learning the value of information in an uncertain world. *Nature Neuroscience, 10,* 1214–1221.

Bench, C. J., Frith, C. D., Grasby, P. M., Friston, K. J., Paulesu, E., Frackowiak, R. S. J., et al. (1993). Investigations of the functional anatomy of attention using the Stroop test. *Neuropsychologia, 9,* 907–922.

Benes, F. M. (2000). Emerging principles of altered neural circuitry in schizophrenia. *Brain Research Reviews, 31,* 251–269.

Bishop, S., Duncan, J., & Lawrence, A. D. (2004). Prefrontal cortical function and anxiety: Controlling attention to threat-related stimuli. *Nature Neuroscience, 7,* 184–188.

Blair, K., Marsh, A. A., Morton, J., Vythilingam, M., Jones, M., Mondillo, K., et al. (2006). Choosing the lesser of two evils, the better of two goods: Specifying the roles of ventromedial prefrontal cortex and dorsal anterior cingulate in object choice. *Journal of Neuroscience, 26,* 11379–11386.

Blais, C., Robidoux, S., Risko, E. F., & Besner, D. (2007). Item-specific adaptation and the conflict-monitoring hypothesis: A computational model. *Psychological Review, 114,* 1076–1086.

Bogacz, R., & Gurney, K. (2007). The basal ganglia and cortex implement optimal decision making between alternative actions. *Neural Computation, 19,* 442–477.

Bogacz, R., Wagenmakers, E. J., Forstmann, B. U., & Nieuwenhuis, S. (2010). The neural basis of the speed-accuracy tradeoff. *Trends in Neurosciences, 33,* 10–16.

Botvinick, M. M. (2007). Conflict monitoring and decision making: reconciling two perspectives on anterior cingulate function. *Cognitive, Affective & Behavioral Neuroscience, 7,* 356–366.

Botvinick, M. M., Braver, T. S., Carter, C. S., Barch, D. M., & Cohen, J. D. (2001). Conflict monitoring and cognitive control. *Psychological Review, 108,* 624–652.

Botvinick, M. M., Cohen, J. D., & Carter, C. S. (2004). Conflict monitoring and anterior cingulate cortex: An update. *Trends in Cognitive Sciences, 8,* 539–546.

Botvinick, M. M., Nystrom, L. E., Fissell, K., Carter, C. S., & Cohen, J. D. (1999). Conflict monitoring versus selection-for-action in anterior cingulate cortex. *Nature, 402,* 179–181.

Brass, M., & von Cramon, D. Y. (2002). The role of the frontal cortex in task preparation. *Cerebral Cortex, 12,* 908–914.

Braver, T. S., Barch, D. M., Gray, J. R., Molfese, D. L., & Snyder, A. (2001). Anterior cingulate cortex and response conflict: Effects of frequency, inhibition and errors. *Cerebral Cortex, 11,* 825–836.

Braver, T. S., Reynolds, J. R., & Donaldson, D. I. (2003). Neural mechanisms of transient and sustained cognitive control during task switching. *Neuron, 39,* 713–726.

Brown, J. W., & Braver, T. S. (2005). Learned predictions of error likelihood in the anterior cingulate cortex. *Science, 307,* 1118–1121.

Brown, J. W., Reynolds, J. R., & Braver, T. S. (2007). A computational model of fractionated conflict-control mechanisms in task-switching. *Cognitive Psychology, 55,* 37–85.

Bugg, J. M. (2008). Opposing influences on conflict-driven adaptation in the Eriksen flanker task. *Memory & Cognition, 36,* 1217–1227.

Burle, B., Allain, S., Vidal, F., & Hasbroucq, T. (2005). Sequential compatibility effects and cognitive control: Does conflict really matter? *Journal of Experimental Psychology: Human Perception and Performance, 31,* 831–837.

Burle, B., Roger, C., Allain, S., Vidal, F., & Hasbroucq, T. (2008). Error negativity does not reflect conflict: A reappraisal of conflict monitoring and anterior cingulate cortex activity. *Journal of Cognitive Neuroscience, 20,* 1637–1655.

Bush, G., Luu, P., & Posner, M. I. (2000). Cognitive and emotional influences in anterior cingulate cortex. *Trends in Cognitive Sciences, 4,* 215–222.

Bush, G., Vogt, B. A., Holmes, J., Dale, A. M., Greve, D., Jenike, M. A., et al. (2002). Dorsal anterior cingulate cortex: A role in reward-based decision making. *Proceedings of the National Academy of Sciences of the USA, 99,* 523–528.

Carbonnell, L., & Falkenstein, M. (2006). Does the error negativity reflect the degree of response conflict? *Brain Research, 1095,* 124–130.

Carter, C. S., Braver, T. S., Barch, D. M., Botvinick, M. M., Noll, D., & Cohen, J. D. (1998). Anterior cingulate cortex, error detection, and the online monitoring of performance. *Science, 280,* 747–749.

Carter, C. S., Macdonald, A. M., Botvinick, M. M., Ross, L. L., Stenger, V. A., Noll, D., et al. (2000). Parsing executive processes: Strategic vs. evaluative functions of the anterior cingulate cortex. *Proceedings of the National Academy of Sciences of the USA, 97,* 1944–1948.

Carter, C. S., Mintun, M., Nichols, T., & Cohen, J. D. (1997). Anterior cingulate gyrus dysfunction and selective attention deficits in schizophrenia: [150]H20 PET study during single-trial Stroop task performance. *American Journal of Psychiatry, 154,* 1670–1675.

Cavanagh, J. F., Cohen, M. X., & Allen, J. J. B. (2009). Prelude to and resolution of an error: EEG phase synchrony reveals cognitive control dynamics during action monitoring. *Journal of Neuroscience, 29,* 98–105.

Cho, R. Y., Orr, J. M., Cohen, J. D., & Carter, C. S. (2009). Generalized signaling for control: Evidence from postconflict and posterror performance adjustments. *Journal of Experimental Psychology: Human Perception and Performance, 35,* 1161–1177.

Cohen, J. D., Dunbar, K., & McClelland, J. L. (1990). On the control of automatic processes: A parallel distributed processing account of the Stroop effect. *Psychological Review, 97,* 332–361.

Cohen, J. D., & O'Reilly, R. C. (1996). A preliminary theory of the interactions between prefrontal cortex and hippocampus that contribute to planning and prospective memory. In M. Brandimonte, G. O. Einstein, & M. McDaniel (Eds.), *Prospective memory: Theory and applications* (pp. 267–295). Hillsdale, NJ: Lawrence Erlbaum.

Cohen, J. D., & Servan-Schreiber, D. (1992). Context, cortex and dopamine: A connectionist approach to behaviour and biology in schizophrenia. *Psychological Review, 99,* 45–77.

Cohen, J. D., Servan-Schreiber, D., & McClelland, J. L. (1992). A parallel distributed processing approach to automaticity. *American Journal of Psychology, 105,* 239–269.

Cohen, R. A., Kaplan, R. F., Moser, D. J., Jenkins, M. A., & Wilkinson, H. (1999). Impairments of attention after cingulotomy. *Neurology, 53,* 819–824.

Cohen, R. A., Kaplan, R. F., Zuffante, P., Moser, D. J., Jenkins, M. A., Salloway, S., et al. (1999). Alteration of intention and self-initiated action associated with bilateral anterior cingulotomy. *Journal of Neuropsychiatry and Clinical Neuroscience, 11,* 444–453.

Cole, M. W., Yeung, N., Freiwald, W. A., & Botvinick, M. (2009). Cingulate cortex: Diverging data from humans and monkeys. *Trends in Neurosciences, 32,* 566–574.

Coles, M. G. H., Scheffers, M. K., & Holroyd, C. B. (2001). Why is there an ERN/Ne on correct trials? Response representations, stimulus-related components, and the theory of error-processing. *Biological Psychology, 56,* 173–189.

Coltheart, M. (2006). What has functional neuroimaging told us about the mind (so far)? *Cortex, 42,* 323–331.

Crosson, B., Sadek, J. R., Bobholz, J. A., Gokcay, D., Mohr, C. M., Leonard, C. M., et al. (1999). Activity in the paracingulate and cingulate sulci during word generation: An fMRI study of functional anatomy. *Cerebral Cortex, 9,* 307–316.

Crump, M. J. C., Gong, Z. Y., & Wmiken, B. (2006). The context-specific proportion congruent Stroop effect: Location as a contextual cue. *Psychonomic Bulletin & Review, 13,* 316–321.

Curtis, C. E., Cole, M. W., Rao, V. Y., & D'Esposito, M. (2005). Canceling planned action: An FMRI study of countermanding saccades. *Cerebral Cortex, 15,* 1281–1289.

Danielmeier, C., Wessel, J. R., Steinhauser, M., & Ullsperger, M. (2009). Modulation of the error-related negativity by response conflict. *Psychophysiology, 46,* 1288–1298.

Davelaar, E. J. (2008). A computational study of conflict-monitoring at two levels of processing: Reaction time distributional analyses and hemodynamic responses. *Brain Research, 1202,* 109–119.

Davelaar, E. J., & Stevens, J. (2009). Sequential dependencies in the Eriksen flanker task: A direct comparison of two competing accounts. *Psychonomic Bulletin & Review, 16,* 121–126.

Davis, K. D., Hutchison, W. D., Lozano, A. M., Tasker, R. R., & Dostrovsky, J. O. (2000). Human anterior cingulate cortex neurons modulated by attention-demanding tasks. *Journal of Neurophysiology, 83,* 3575–3577.

Davis, K. D., Taylor, K. S., Hutchison, W. D., Dostrovsky, J. O., McAndrews, M. P., Richter, E. O., et al. (2005). Human anterior cingulate cortex neurons encode cognitive and emotional demands. *Journal of Neuroscience, 25,* 8402–8406.

Debener, S., Ullsperger, M., Siegel, M., Fiehler, K., von Cramon, D. Y., & Engel, A. K. (2005). Trial-by-trial coupling of concurrent electroencephalogram and functional magnetic resonance imaging identifies the dynamics of performance monitoring. *Journal of Neuroscience, 25*, 11730–11737.

Dehaene, S., Posner, M. I., & Tucker, D. M. (1994). Localization of a neural system for error detection and compensation. *Psychological Science, 5,* 303–305.

Deiber, M.-P., Honda, M., Ibanez, V., Sadato, N., & Hallett, M. (1999). Mesial motor areas in self-initiated versus externally triggered movements examined with fMRI: Effect of movement type and rate. *Journal of Neurophysiology, 81*, 3065–3077.

Desimone, R., & Duncan, J. (1995). Neural mechanisms of selective attention. *Annual Review of Neuroscience, 18*, 193–222.

Devinsky, O., Morrell, M. J., & Vogt, B. A. (1995). Contributions of anterior cingulate cortex to behaviour. *Brain, 118*, 279–306.

di Pellegrino, G., Ciaramelli, E., & Ladavas, E. (2007). The regulation of cognitive control following rostral anterior cingulate cortex lesion in humans. *Journal of Cognitive Neuroscience, 19*, 275–286.

Donaldson, D. I. (2004). Parsing brain activity with fMRI and mixed designs: What kind of a state is neuroimaging in? *Trends in Neurosciences, 27*, 442–444.

Dosenbach, N. U. F., Fair, D. A., Cohen, A. L., Schlaggar, B. L., & Petersen, S. E. (2008). A dual-networks architecture of top-down control. *Trends in Cognitive Sciences, 12*, 99–105.

Dosenbach, N. U. F., Fair, D. A., Miezin, F. M., Cohen, A. L., Wenger, K. K., Dosenbach, R. A. T., et al. (2007). Distinct brain networks for adaptive and stable task control in humans. *Proceedings of the National Academy of Sciences of the USA, 104*, 11073–11078.

Dosenbach, N. U. F., Visscher, K. M., Palmer, E. D., Miezin, F. M., Wenger, K. K., Kang, H. S. C., et al. (2006). A core system for the implementation of task sets. *Neuron, 50*, 799–812.

Dum, R. P., & Strick, P. L. (1991). The origin of corticospinal projections from the premotor areas in the frontal lobe. *Journal of Neuroscience, 11*, 667–689.

Dum, R. P., & Strick, P. L. (1993). Cingulate motor areas. In B. A. Vogt & M. Gabriel (Eds.), *Neurobiology of cingulate cortex and limbic thalamus: A comprehensive handbook* (pp. 415–441). Boston: Birkhauser.

Duncan, J. (1986). Disorganisation of behaviour after frontal lobe damage. *Cognitive Neuropsychology, 3*, 271–290.

Duncan, J. (2010). The multiple-demand (MD) system of the primate brain: Mental programs for intelligent behaviour. *Trends in Cognitive Sciences, 14*, 172–179.

Duncan, J., & Owen, A. M. (2000). Common regions of the human frontal lobe recruited by diverse cognitive demands. *Trends in Neurosciences, 23*, 475–483.

Edwards, B. G., Barch, D. M., & Braver, T. S. (2010). Improving prefrontal cortex function in schizophrenia through focused training of cognitive control. *Frontiers in Human Neuroscience, 4*.

Egner, T., Delano, M., & Hirsch, J. (2007). Separate conflict-specific cognitive control mechanisms in the human brain. *Neuroimage, 35*, 940–948.

Egner, T., Etkin, A., Gale, S., & Hirsch, J. (2008). Dissociable neural systems resolve conflict from emotional versus non-emotional distracters. *Cerebral Cortex, 18*, 1475–1484.

Egner, T., & Hirsch, J. (2005). Cognitive control mechanisms resolve conflict through cortical amplification of task-relevant information. *Nature Neuroscience, 8*, 1784–1790.

Emeric, E. E., Brown, J. W., Leslie, M., Pouget, P., Stuphorn, V., & Schall, J. D. (2008). Performance monitoring local field potentials in the medial frontal cortex of primates: Anterior cingulate cortex. *Journal of Neurophysiology, 99*, 759–772.

Etkin, A., Egner, T., Peraza, D. M., Kandel, E. R., & Hirsch, J. (2006). Resolving emotional conflict: A role for the rostral anterior cingulate cortex in modulating activity in the amygdala. *Neuron, 51*, 871–882.

Falkenstein, M., Hohnsbein, J., Hoorman, J., & Blanke, L. (1990). Effects of errors in choice reaction tasks on the ERP under focused and divided attention. In C. H. M. Brunia, A. W. K. Gaillard, & A. Kok (Eds.), *Psychophysiological brain research* (Vol. 1, pp. 192–195). Tilburg, The Netherlands: Tilburg University Press.

Fan, J., Flombaum, J. I., McCandliss, B. D., Thomas, K. M., & Posner, M. I. (2003). Cognitive and brain consequences of conflict. *Neuroimage, 18*, 42–57.

Fan, J., Hof, P. R., Guise, K. G., Fossella, J. A., & Posner, M. I. (2008). The functional integration of the anterior cingulate cortex during conflict processing. *Cerebral Cortex, 18*, 796–805.

Fan, J., Kolster, R., Ghajar, J., Suh, M., Knight, R. T., Sarkar, R., et al. (2007). Response anticipation and response conflict: An event-related potential and functional magnetic resonance imaging study. *Journal of Neuroscience, 27*, 2272–2282.

Fellows, L. K., & Farah, M. J. (2005). Is anterior cingulate cortex necessary for cognitive control? *Brain, 128*, 788–796.

Fernandez-Duque, D., & Knight, M. (2008). Cognitive control: Dynamic, sustained, and voluntary influences. *Journal of Experimental Psychology: Human Perception and Performance, 34*, 340–355.

Fink, G. R., Frackowiak, R. S. J., Pietrzyk, U., & Passingham, R. (1997). Multiple nonprimary motor areas in the human cortex. *Journal of Neurophysiology, 77*, 2164–2174.

Floden, D., Vallesi, A., & Stuss, D. T. (2011). Task context and frontal lobe activation in the Stroop task. *Journal of Cognitive Neuroscience, 23*, 867–879.

Folstein, J. R., & Van Petten, C. (2008). Influence of cognitive control and mismatch on the N2 component of the ERP: A review. *Psychophysiology, 45*, 152–170.

Ford, K. A., Gati, J. S., Menon, R. S., & Everling, S. (2009). BOLD fMRI activation for anti-saccades in nonhuman primates. *Neuroimage, 45*, 470–476.

Frank, M. J. (2006). Hold your horses: A dynamic computational role for the subthalamic nucleus in decision making. *Neural Networks, 19*, 1120–1136.

Frank, M. J., Woroch, B. S., & Curran, T. (2005). Error-related negativity predicts reinforcement learning and conflict biases. *Neuron, 47*, 495–501.

Freitas, A. L., Bahar, M., Yang, S., & Banai, R. (2007). Contextual adjustments in cognitive control across tasks. *Psychological Science, 18*, 1040–1043.

Frith, C. D., Friston, K. J., Liddle, P. F., & Frackowiak, R. S. J. (1991). Willed action and the prefrontal cortex in man: a study with PET. *Proceedings of the Royal Society of London: Series B, 244*, 241–246.

Funes, M. J., Lupianez, J., & Humphreys, G. (2010a). Analyzing the generality of conflict adaptation effects. *Journal of Experimental Psychology: Human Perception and Performance, 36*, 147–161.

Funes, M. J., Lupianez, J., & Humphreys, G. (2010b). Sustained vs. transient cognitive control: Evidence of a behavioral dissociation. *Cognition, 114*, 338–347.

Garavan, H., Ross, H., Kaufman, T. J., & Stein, E. A. (2003). A midline dissociation between error processing and response conflict monitoring. *Neuroimage, 20*, 1132–1139.

Gehring, W. J., & Fencsik, D. (2001). Functions of the medial frontal cortex in the processing of conflict and errors. *Journal of Neuroscience, 21*, 9430–9437.

Gehring, W. J., Goss, B., Coles, M. G. H., Meyer, D. E., & Donchin, E. (1993). A neural system for error detection and compensation. *Psychological Science, 4*, 385–390.

Gehring, W. J., Himle, J., & Nisenson, L. G. (2000). Action-monitoring dysfunction in obsessive-compulsive disorder. *Psychological Science, 11*, 1–6.

Gehring, W. J., & Knight, R. T. (2000). Prefrontal-cingulate interactions in action monitoring. *Nature Neuroscience, 3*, 516–520.

Gehring, W. J., & Willoughby, A. R. (2002). The medial frontal cortex and the rapid processing of monetary gains and losses. *Science, 295*, 2279–2282.

Gemba, H., Sasaki, K., & Brooks, V. B. (1986). "Error" potentials in limbic cortex (anterior cingulate area 24) of monkeys during motor learning. *Neuroscience Letters, 70*, 223–227.

Goschke, T., & Dreisbach, G. (2008). Conflict-triggered goal shielding: Response conflicts attenuate background monitoring for prospective memory cues. *Psychological Science, 19*, 25–32.

Gratton, G., Coles, M. G. H., & Donchin, E. (1992). Optimizing the use of information: Strategic control of activation of responses. *Journal of Experimental Psychology: General, 121*, 480–506.

Grinband, J., Savitsky, J., Wager, T. D., Teichert, T., Ferrera, V. P., & Hirsch, J. (2011). The dorsal medial frontal cortex is sensitive to time on task, not response conflict or error likelihood. *Neuroimage, 57*, 303–311.

Hadland, K. A., Rushworth, M. F. S., Gaffan, D., & Passingham, R. E. (2003). The anterior cingulate and reward-guided selection of actions. *Journal of Neurophysiology, 89*, 1161–1164.

Hanslmayr, S., Pastotter, B., Bauml, K. H., Gruber, S., Wimber, M., & Klimesch, W. (2008). The electrophysiological dynamics of interference during the Stroop task. *Journal of Cognitive Neuroscience, 20*, 215–225.

Hayden, B. Y., & Platt, M. L. (2010). Neurons in anterior cingulate cortex multiplex information about reward and action. *Journal of Neuroscience, 30*, 3339–3346.

Hester, R., Barre, N., Murphy, K., Silk, T. J., & Mattingley, J. B. (2008). Human medial frontal cortex activity predicts learning from errors. *Cerebral Cortex, 18*, 1933–1940.

Hikosaka, O., & Isoda, M. (2010). Switching from automatic to controlled behavior: Cortico-basal ganglia mechanisms. *Trends in Cognitive Sciences, 14*, 154–161.

Holroyd, C. B., & Coles, M. G. H. (2002). The neural basis of human error processing: Reinforcement learning, dopamine, and the error-related negativity. *Psychological Review, 109*, 679–709.

Holroyd, C. B., Nieuwenhuis, S., Yeung, N., & Cohen, J. D. (2003). Errors in reward prediction are reflected in the event-related brain potential. *Neuroreport, 14*, 2481–2484.

Holroyd, C. B., Nieuwenhuis, S., Yeung, N., Nystrom, L. E., Mars, R. B., Coles, M. G. H., et al. (2004). Dorsal anterior cingulate cortex shows fMRI response to internal and external error signals. *Nature Neuroscience, 7*, 497–498.

Holroyd C. B., & Yeung, N. (2012). Motivation of extended behaviors by anterior cingulate cortex. *Trends in Cognitive Sciences, 16*, 122–128.

Hommel, B. (2004). Event files: Feature binding in and across perception and action. *Trends in Cognitive Sciences, 8*, 494–500.

Hopfield, J. J. (1982). Neural networks and physical systems with emergent collective computational abilities. *Proceedings of the National Academy of Sciences of the USA, 79*, 2554–2558.

Isoda, M., & Hikosaka, O. (2007). Switching from automatic to controlled action by monkey medial frontal cortex. *Nature Neuroscience, 10*, 240–248.

Ito, S., Stuphorn, V., Brown, J. W., & Schall, J. D. (2003). Performance monitoring by anterior cingulate cortex: Comparison not conflict during countermanding. *Science, 302*, 120–122.

Jacoby, L. L., Lindsay, D. S., & Hessels, S. (2003). Item-specific control of automatic processes: Stroop process dissociations. *Psychonomic Bulletin & Review, 10*, 638–644.

Jentzsch, I., & Dudschig, C. (2009). Why do we slow down after an error? Mechanisms underlying the effects of posterror slowing. *Quarterly Journal of Experimental Psychology, 62*, 209–218.

Kennerley, S. W., Walton, M. E., Behrens, T. E., Buckley, M. J., & Rushworth, M. F. (2006). Optimal decision making and the anterior cingulate cortex. *Nature Neuroscience, 9*, 940–947.

Kerns, J. G. (2006). Anterior cingulate and prefrontal cortex activity in an FMR1 study of trial-to-trial adjustments on the Simon task. *Neuroimage, 33*, 399–405.

Kerns, J. G., Cohen, J. D., MacDonald, A. W., 3rd, Cho, R. Y., Stenger, V. A., & Carter, C. S. (2004). Anterior cingulate conflict monitoring and adjustments in control. *Science, 303*, 1023–1026.

Kerns, J. G., Cohen, J. D., MacDonald, A. W., Johnson, M. K., Stenger, V. A., Aizenstein, H., et al. (2005). Decreased conflict- and error-related activity in the anterior cingulate cortex in subjects with schizophrenia. *American Journal of Psychiatry, 162*, 1833–1839.

Kiehl, K. A., Liddle, P. F., & Hopfinger, J. B. (2000). Error processing and the rostral anterior cingulate: An event-related fMRI study. *Psychophysiology, 37*, 216–223.

Kiesel, A., Kunde, W., & Hoffmann, J. (2006). Evidence for task-specific resolution of response conflict. *Psychonomic Bulletin & Review, 13*, 800–806.

Klein, T. A., Endrass, T., Kathmann, N., Neumann, J., von Cramon, D. Y., & Ullsperger, M. (2007). Neural correlates of error awareness. *Neuroimage, 34*, 1774–1781.

Knutson, B., Taylor, J., Kaufman, M., Peterson, R., & Glover, G. (2005). Distributed neural representation of expected value. *Journal of Neuroscience, 25*, 4806–4812.

Koechlin, E., & Hyafil, A. (2007). Anterior prefrontal function and the limits of human decision-making. *Science, 318*, 594–598.

Koechlin, E., Ody, C., & Kouneiher, F. (2003). The architecture of cognitive control in the human prefrontal cortex. *Science, 302*, 1181–1185.

Kopp, B., Rist, F., & Mattler, U. (1996). N200 in the flanker task as a neurobehavioral tool for investigating executive control. *Psychophysiology, 33*, 282–294.

Koski, L., & Paus, T. (2000). Functional connectivity of the anterior cingulate cortex within the human frontal lobe: A brain-mapping meta-analysis. *Experimental Brain Research, 133*, 55–65.

Kouneiher, F., Charron, S., & Koechlin, E. (2009). Motivation and cognitive control in the human prefrontal cortex. *Nature Neuroscience, 12,* 939–945.

Krieghoff, V., Brass, M., Prinz, W., & Waszak, F. (2009). Dissociating what and when of intentional actions. *Frontiers in Human Neuroscience, 3,* 3 (1–10).

Kunde, W., & Wuhr, P. (2006). Sequential modulations of correspondence effects across spatial dimensions and tasks. *Memory & Cognition, 34,* 356–367.

Larson, M. J., Kaufman, D. A. S., & Perlstein, W. M. (2009). Neural time course of conflict adaptation effects on the Stroop task. *Neuropsychologia, 47,* 663–670.

Lau, H., Rogers, R. D., & Passingham, R. E. (2006). Dissociating response selection and conflict in the medial frontal surface. *Neuroimage, 29,* 446–451.

Liotti, M., Woldorff, M. G., Perez, R., & Mayberg, H. S. (2000). An ERP study of the temporal course of the Stroop color-word interference effect. *Neuropsychologia, 38,* 701–711.

Liston, C., Matalon, S., Hare, T. A., Davidson, M. C., & Casey, B. J. (2006). Anterior cingulate and posterior parietal cortices are sensitive to dissociable forms of conflict in a task-switching paradigm. *Neuron, 50,* 643–653.

Logan, G. D. (1985). Executive control of thought and action. *Acta Psychologica, 60,* 193–210.

Logan, G. D. (2003). Executive control of thought and action: In search of the wild homunculus. *Current Directions in Psychological Science, 12,* 45–48.

Luk, C. H., & Wallis, J. D. (2009). Dynamic encoding of responses and outcomes by neurons in medial prefrontal cortex. *Journal of Neuroscience, 29,* 7526–7539.

Luks, T. L., Simpson, G. V., Dale, C. L., & Hough, M. G. (2007). Preparatory allocation of attention and adjustments in conflict processing. *Neuroimage, 35,* 949–958.

Luks, T. L., Simpson, G. V., Feiwell, R. J., & Miller, W. J. (2002). Evidence for anterior cingulate cortex involvement in monitoring preparatory attentional set. *Neuroimage, 17,* 792–802.

Lutcke, H., & Frahm, J. (2008). Lateralized anterior cingulate function during error processing and conflict monitoring as revealed by high-resolution fMRI. *Cerebral Cortex, 18,* 508–515.

MacDonald, A. W., Cohen, J. D., Stenger, V. A., & Carter, C. S. (2000). Dissociating the role of dorsolateral prefrontal and anterior cingulate cortex in cognitive control. *Science, 288,* 1835–1838.

Malenka, R. C., Angel, R. W., Hampton, B., & Berger, P. A. (1982). Impaired central error-correcting behavior in schizophrenia. *Archives of General Psychiatry, 39,* 101–107.

Maltby, N., Tolin, D. F., Worhunsky, P., O'Keefe, T. M., & Kiehl, K. A. (2005). Dysfunctional action monitoring hyperactivates frontal-striatal circuits in obsessive-compulsive disorder: an event-related fMRI study. *Neuroimage, 24,* 495–503.

Mansouri, F. A., Buckley, M. J., & Tanaka, K. (2007). Mnemonic function of the dorsolateral prefrontal cortex in conflict-induced behavioral adjustment. *Science, 318,* 987–990.

Margulies, D. S., Kelly, A. M., Uddin, L. Q., Biswal, B. B., Castellanos, F. X., & Milham, M. P. (2007). Mapping the functional connectivity of anterior cingulate cortex. *Neuroimage, 37,* 579–588.

Marsh, A. A., Blair, K. S., Vythilingam, M., Busis, S., & Blair, R. J. (2007). Response options and expectations of reward in decision-making: the differential roles of dorsal and rostral anterior cingulate cortex. *Neuroimage, 35,* 979–988.

Mathalon, D. H., Whitfield, S. L., & Ford, J. M. (2003). Anatomy of an error: ERP and fMRI. *Biological Psychology, 64,* 119–141.

Mayr, U., & Awh, E. (2009). The elusive link between conflict and conflict adaptation. *Psychological Research, 73,* 794–802.

Mayr, U., Awh, E., & Laurey, P. (2003). Conflict adaptation effects in the absence of executive control. *Nature Neuroscience, 6,* 450–452.

McNeely, H. E., West, R., Christensen, B. K., & Alain, C. (2003). Neurophysiological evidence for disturbances of conflict processing in patients with schizophrenia. *Journal of Abnormal Psychology, 112,* 679–688.

Melcher, T., Falkai, P., & Gruber, O. (2008). Functional brain abnormalities in psychiatric disorders: Neural mechanisms to detect and resolve cognitive conflict and interference. *Brain Research Reviews, 59,* 96–124.

Melcher, T., & Gruber, O. (2009). Decomposing interference during Stroop performance into different conflict factors: An event-related fMRI study. *Cortex, 45,* 189–200.

Menon, V., Adleman, N. E., White, C. D., Glover, G. H., & Reiss, A. L. (2001). Error-related brain activation during a go/no-go response inhibition task. *Human Brain Mapping, 12,* 131–143.

Milham, M. P., & Banich, M. T. (2005). Anterior cingulate cortex: An fMRI analysis of conflict specificity and functional differentiation. *Human Brain Mapping, 25,* 328–335.

Milham, M. P., Banich, M. T., Webb, A., Barad, V., Cohen, N. J., Wszalek, T., et al. (2001). The relative involvement of anterior cingulate and prefrontal cortex in attentional control depends on nature of conflict. *Cognitive Brain Research, 12,* 467–473.

Miller, E. K., & Cohen, J. D. (2001). An integrative theory of prefrontal cortex function. *Annual Review of Neuroscience, 24,* 167–202.

Miltner, W. H. R., Braun, C. H., & Coles, M. G. H. (1997). Event related potentials following incorrect feedback in a time-estimation task: Evidence for a "generic" neural system for error detection. *Journal of Cognitive Neuroscience, 9,* 788–798.

Modirrousta, M., & Fellows, L. K. (2008). Dorsal medial prefrontal cortex plays a necessary role in rapid error prediction in humans. *Journal of Neuroscience, 28,* 14000–14005.

Mohanty, A., Engels, A. S., Herrington, J. D., Heller, W., Ho, M.-H. R., Banich, M. T., Webb, A. G., Warren S. L., & Miller G. A. (2007). Differential engagement of anterior cingulate cortex subdivisions for cognitive and emotional function. *Psychophysiology, 44,* 343–351.

Monsell, S. (1996). Control of mental processes. In V. Bruce (Ed.), *Unsolved mysteries of the mind* (pp. 93–148). Hove, E. Sussex: Lawrence Erlbaum.

Monsell, S. (2003). Task switching. *Trends in Cognitive Sciences, 7,* 134–140.

Monsell, S., & Driver, J. S. (2000). *Attention and Performance XVIII: Control of cognitive processes.* Cambridge, MA: MIT Press.

Naccache, L., Dehaene, S., Cohen, L., Habert, M. O., Guichart-Gomez, E., Galanaud, D., et al. (2005). Effortless control: executive attention and conscious feeling of mental effort are dissociable. *Neuropsychologia, 43,* 1318–1328.

Nachev, P., Rees, G., Parton, A., Kennard, C., & Husain, M. (2005). Volition and conflict in human medial frontal cortex. *Current Biology, 15,* 122–128.

Nakamura, K., Roesch, M. R., & Olson, C. R. (2005). Neuronal activity in macaque SEF and ACC during performance of tasks involving conflict. *Journal of Neurophysiology*, *93*, 884–908.

Nee, D. E., Wager, T. D., & Jonides, J. (2007). Interference resolution: Insights from a meta-analysis of neuroimaging tasks. *Cognitive Affective & Behavioral Neuroscience*, *7*, 1–17.

Nemeth, G., Hegedus, K., & Molnar, L. (1988). Akinetic mutism associated with bicingular lesions: Clinicopathological and functional anatomical correlates. *European Archives of Psychiatry and Neurological Sciences*, *237*, 218–222.

Nieuwenhuis, S., Nielen, M. M., Mol, N., Hajcak, G., & Veltman, D. J. (2005). Performance monitoring in obsessive-compulsive disorder. *Psychiatry Research*, *134*, 111–122.

Nieuwenhuis, S., Ridderinkhof, K. R., Blom, J., Band, G. P. H., & Kok, A. (2001). Error-related brain potentials are differentially related to awareness of response errors: Evidence from an antisaccade task. *Psychophysiology*, *38*, 752–760.

Nieuwenhuis, S., Schweizer, T. S., Mars, R. B., Botvinick, M. M., & Hajcak, G. (2007). Error-likelihood prediction in the medial frontal cortex: A critical evaluation. *Cerebral Cortex*, *17*, 1570–1581.

Nieuwenhuis, S., Stins, J. F., Posthuma, D., Polderman, T. J. C., Boomsma, D. I., & de Geus, E. J. (2006). Accounting for sequential trial effects in the flanker task: Conflict adaptation or associative priming? *Memory & Cognition*, *34*, 1260–1272.

Nieuwenhuis, S., Yeung, N., van den Wildenberg, W., & Ridderinkhof, K. R. (2003). Electrophysiological correlates of anterior cingulate function in a go/no-go task: Effects of response conflict and trial-type frequency. *Cognitive, Affective & Behavioral Neuroscience*, *3*, 17–26.

Nimchinsky, E. A., Gilissen, E., Allman, J. M., Perl, D. P., Erwin, J. M., & Hof, P. R. (1999). A neuronal morphological type unique to humans and great apes. *Proceedings of the National Academy of Sciences of the USA*, *96*, 5268–5273.

Norman, D. A., & Shallice, T. (1986). Attention to action: Willed and automatic control of behaviour. In R. J. Davidson, G. E. Schwartz, & D. Shapiro (Eds.), *Consciousness and self-regulation* (Vol. 4, pp. 1–18). New York: Plenum.

Notebaert, W., Gevers, W., Verbruggen, F., & Liefooghe, B. (2006). Top-down and bottom-up sequential modulations of congruency effects. *Psychonomic Bulletin & Review*, *13*, 112–117.

Notebaert, W., Houtman, F., Van Opstal, F., Gevers, W., Fias, W., & Verguts, T. (2009). Post-error slowing: An orienting account. *Cognition*, *111*, 275–279.

Notebaert, W., & Verguts, T. (2007). Dissociating conflict adaptation from feature integration: A multiple regression approach. *Journal of Experimental Psychology: Human Perception and Performance*, *33*, 1256–1260.

Notebaert, W., & Verguts, T. (2008). Cognitive control acts locally. *Cognition*, *106*, 1071–1080.

Ochsner, K. N., Kosslyn, S. M., Cosgrove, G. R., Cassem, E. H., Price, B. H., Nierenberg, A. A., et al. (2001). Deficits in visual cognition and attention following bilateral anterior cingulotomy. *Neuropsychologia*, *39*, 219–230.

Orr, J. M., & Weissman, D. H. (2009). Anterior cingulate cortex makes 2 contributions to minimizing distraction. *Cerebral Cortex*, *19*, 703–711.

Pailing, P. E., & Segalowitz, S. J. (2004). The effects of uncertainty in error monitoring on associated ERPs. *Brain and Cognition*, *56*, 215–233.

Pardo, J. V., Pardo, P. J., Janer, K. W., & Raichle, M. E. (1990). The anterior cingulate cortex mediates processing selection in the Stroop attentional conflict paradigm. *Proceedings of the National Academy of Sciences of the USA*, *87*, 256–259.

Passingham, R. (1993). *The frontal lobes and voluntary action*. Oxford, UK: Oxford University Press.

Passingham, R. E., Bengtsson, S. L., & Lau, H. C. (2010). Medial frontal cortex: From self-generated action to reflection on one's own performance. *Trends in Cognitive Sciences*, *14*, 16–21.

Pastotter, B., Hanslmayr, S., & Bauml, K. H. T. (2010). Conflict processing in the anterior cingulate cortex constrains response priming. *Neuroimage*, *50*, 1599–1605.

Paus, T. (2001). Primate anterior cingulate cortex: Where motor control, drive and cognition interface. *Nature Reviews Neuroscience*, *2*, 417–424.

Paus, T., Koski, L., Caramanos, Z., & Westbury, C. (1998). Regional differences in the effects of task difficulty and motor output on blood flow response in the human anterior cingulate cortex: A review of 107 PET activation studies. *Neuroreport*, *9*, R37–R47.

Paus, T., Otaky, N., Caramanos, Z., MacDonald, D., Zijdenbos, A., D'Avirro, D., et al. (1996). In vivo morphometry of the intrasulcal gray matter in the human cingulate, paracingulate, and superior-rostral sulci: Hemispheric asymmetries, gender differences and probability maps. *Journal of Comparative Neurology*, *376*, 664–673.

Paus, T., Petrides, M., Evans, A. C., & Meyer, E. (1993). Role of human anterior cingulate cortex in the control of oculomotor, manual, and speech responses: A positron emission tomography study. *Journal of Neurophysiology*, *20*, 453–469.

Paus, T., Tomaiuolo, F., Otaky, N., MacDonald, D., Petrides, M., Atlas, J., et al. (1996). Human cingulate and paracingulate sulci: Pattern, variability, asymmetry, and probabilistic map. *Cerebral Cortex*, *6*, 207–214.

Petersen, S. E., Fox, P. T., Posner, M. I., Mintun, M., & Raichle, M. E. (1989). Positron emission tomographic studies of the processing of single words. *Journal of Cognitive Neuroscience*, *1*, 153–170.

Peterson, B. S., Kane, M. J., Alexander, G. M., Lacadie, C., Skudlarski, P., Leung, H. C., et al. (2002). An event-related functional MRI study comparing interference effects in the Simon and Stroop tasks. *Brain Research Cognitive Brain Research*, *13*, 427–440.

Peyron, R., Laurent, B., & Garcia-Larrea, L. (2000). Functional imaging of brain responses to pain. A review and meta-analysis. *Neurophysiology Clinique—Clinical Neurophysiology*, *30*, 263–288.

Picard, N., & Strick, P. L. (1996). Motor areas of the medial wall: A review of their location and functional activation. *Cerebral Cortex*, *6*, 342–353.

Picard, N., & Strick, P. L. (2001). Imaging the premotor areas. *Current Opinion in Neurobiology*, *11*, 663–672.

Picton, T. W., Stuss, D. T., Alexander, M. P., Shallice, T., Binns, M. A., & Gillingham, S. (2007). Effects of focal frontal lesions on response inhibition. *Cerebral Cortex*, *17*, 826–838.

Pochon, J. B., Riis, J., Sanfey, A. G., Nystrom, L. E., & Cohen, J. D. (2008). Functional imaging of decision conflict. *Journal of Neuroscience*, *28*, 3468–3473.

Posner, M. I., & Petersen, S. E. (1990). The attention system of the human brain. *Annual Review of Neuroscience*, *13*, 25–42.

Pourtois, G., Vocat, R., N'Diaye, K., Spinelli, L., Seeck, M., & Vuilleumier, P. (2010). Errors recruit both cognitive and emotional monitoring systems: Simultaneous intracranial recordings in the dorsal anterior cingulate gyrus and amygdala combined with fMRI. *Neuropsychologia, 48*, 1144–1159.

Purmann, S., Badde, S., & Wendt, M. (2009). Adjustments to recent and frequent conflict reflect two distinguishable mechanisms. *Psychonomic Bulletin & Review, 16*, 350–355.

Rabbitt, P. M. A. (1966). Errors and error correction in choice-response tasks. *Journal of Experimental Psychology, 71*, 264–272.

Raichle, M. E. (2010). Two views of brain function. *Trends in Cognitive Sciences, 14*, 180–190.

Riba, J., Rodriguez-Fornells, A., Morte, A., Munte, T. F., & Barbanoj, M. J. (2005). Noradrenergic stimulation enhances human action monitoring. *Journal of Neuroscience, 25*, 4370–4374.

Ridderinkhof, K. R. (2002). Micro- and macro-adjustments of task set: Activation and suppression in conflict tasks. *Psychological Research, 66*, 312–323.

Ridderinkhof, K. R., de Vlugt, Y., Bramlage, A., Spaan, M., Elton, M., Snel, J., et al. (2002). Alcohol consumption impairs detection of performance errors in mediofrontal cortex. *Science, 298*, 2209–2211.

Ridderinkhof, K. R., Ullsperger, M., Crone, E. A., & Nieuwenhuis, S. (2004). The role of the medial frontal cortex in cognitive control. *Science, 306*, 443–447.

Roberts, K. L., & Hall, D. A. (2008). Examining a supra-modal network for conflict processing: A systematic review and novel functional magnetic resonance Imaging data for related visual and auditory Stroop tasks. *Journal of Cognitive Neuroscience, 20*, 1063–1078.

Rodriguez-Fornells, A., Kurzbuch, A. R., & Muente, T. F. (2002). Time course of error detection and correction in humans: neurophysiological evidence. *Journal of Neuroscience, 22*, 9990–9996.

Roelofs, A., van Turennout, M., & Coles, M. G. H. (2006). Anterior cingulate cortex activity can be independent of response conflict in Stroop-like tasks. *Proceedings of the National Academy of Sciences of the USA, 103*, 13884–13889.

Roger, C., Benar, C. G., Vidal, F., Hasbroucq, T., & Burle, B. (2010). Rostral cingulate zone and correct response monitoring: ICA and source localization evidences for the unicity of correct- and error-negativities. *Neuroimage, 51*, 391–403.

Rogers, R. D., Ramnani, N., Mackay, C., Wilson, J. L., Jezzard, P., Carter, C. S., et al. (2004). Distinct portions of anterior cingulate cortex and medial prefrontal cortex are activated by reward processing in separable phases of decision-making cognition. *Biological Psychiatry, 55*, 594–602.

Rubia, K., Russell, T., Overmeyer, S., Brammer, M. J., Bullmore, E. T., Sharma, T., et al. (2001). Mapping motor inhibition: Conjunctive brain activations across different versions of go/no-go and stop tasks. *Neuroimage, 13*, 250–261.

Rudebeck, P. H., Walton, M. E., Smyth, A. N., Bannerman, D. M., & Rushworth, M. F. (2006). Separate neural pathways process different decision costs. *Nature Neuroscience, 9*, 1161–1168.

Ruff, C. C., Woodward, T. S., Laurens, K. R., & Liddle, P. F. (2001). The role of anterior cingulate cortex in conflict processing: Evidence from reverse Stroop interference. *Neuroimage, 14*, 1150–1158.

Rushworth, M. F., Behrens, T. E., Rudebeck, P. H., & Walton, M. E. (2007). Contrasting roles for cingulate and orbitofrontal cortex in decisions and social behaviour. *Trends in Cognitive Sciences, 11*, 168–176.

Rushworth, M. F., Hadland, K. A., Paus, T., & Sipila, P. K. (2002). The role of the human medial frontal cortex in task switching: A combined fMRI and TMS study. *Journal of Neurophysiology, 87*, 2577–2592.

Rushworth, M. F., Walton, M. E., Kennerley, S. W., & Bannerman, D. M. (2004). Action sets and decisions in the medial frontal cortex. *Trends in Cognitive Sciences, 8*, 410–417.

Sakai, K. (2008). Task set and prefrontal cortex. *Annual Review of Neuroscience, 31*, 219–245.

Schacter, D. L., Addis, D. R., & Buckner, R. L. (2007). Remembering the past to imagine the future: The prospective brain. *Nature Reviews Neuroscience, 8*, 657–661.

Scheffers, M. K., & Coles, M. G. H. (2000). Performance monitoring in a confusing world: Error-related brain activity, judgements of response accuracy, and types of errors. *Journal of Experimental Psychology: Human Perception and Performance, 26*, 141–151.

Schulte, T., Muller-Oehring, E. M., Vinco, S., Hoeft, F., Pfefferbaum, A., & Sullivan, E. V. (2009). Double dissociation between action-driven and perception-driven conflict resolution invoking anterior versus posterior brain systems. *Neuroimage, 48*, 381–390.

Shallice, T., & Burgess, P. W. (1991). Deficits in strategy application following frontal lobe damage in man. *Brain, 114* (Pt 2), 727–741.

Shidara, M., & Richmond, B. J. (2002). Anterior cingulate: Single neuronal signals related to degree of reward expectancy. *Science, 296*, 1709–1711.

Shiffrin, R. M., & Schneider, W. (1977). Controlled and automatic human information processing: II. Perceptual learning, automatic attending, and a general theory. *Psychological Review, 84*, 127–190.

Shima, K., Aya, K., Mushiake, H., Inase, M., Aizawa, H., & Tanji, J. (1991). Two movement-related foci in primate cingulate cortex observed in signal-triggered and self-paced forelimb movements. *Journal of Neurophysiology, 65*, 188–202.

Shima, K., & Tanji, J. (1998). Role for cingulate motor area cells in voluntary movement selection based on reward. *Science, 282*, 1335–1338.

Silton, R. L., Heller, W., Towers, D. N., Engels, A. S., Spielberg, J. M., Edgar, J. C., et al. (2010). The time course of activity in dorsolateral prefrontal cortex and anterior cingulate cortex during top-down attentional control. *Neuroimage, 50*, 1292–1302.

Sohn, M. H., Albert, M. V., Jung, K. J., Carter, C. S., & Anderson, J. R. (2007). Anticipation of conflict monitoring in the anterior cingulate cortex and the prefrontal cortex. *Proceedings of the National Academy of Sciences of the USA, 104*, 10330–10334.

Spencer, K. M., & Coles, M. G. H. (1999). The lateralized readiness potential: Relationship between human data and response activation in a connectionist model. *Psychophysiology, 36*, 364–370.

Steinhauser, M., Maier, M., & Hubner, R. (2008). Modeling behavioral measures of error detection in choice tasks: Response monitoring versus conflict monitoring. *Journal of Experimental Psychology: Human Perception and Performance, 34*, 158–176.

Stroop, J. R. (1935). Studies in interference in serial verbal reactions. *Journal of Experimental Psychology, 18*, 643–662.

Stuphorn, V., Taylor, T. L., & Schall, J. D. (2000). Performance monitoring by the supplementary eye field. *Nature, 408*, 857–860.

Sturmer, B., Leuthold, H., Soetens, E., Schroter, H., & Sommer, W. (2002). Control over location-based response activation in the Simon task: Behavioral and electrophysiological evidence. *Journal of Experimental Psychology: Human Perception and Performance, 28*, 1345–1363.

Sturmer, B., Redlich, M., Irlbacher, K., & Brandt, S. (2007). Executive control over response priming and conflict: A transcranial magnetic stimulation study. *Experimental Brain Research, 183*, 329–339.

Stuss, D. T., Alexander, M. P., Shallice, T., Picton, T. W., Binns, M. A., Macdonald, R., et al. (2005). Multiple frontal systems controlling response speed. *Neuropsychologia, 43*, 396–417.

Stuss, D. T., Floden, D., Alexander, M. P., Levine, B., & Katz, D. (2001). Stroop performance in focal lesion patients: Dissociation of processes and frontal lobe lesion location. *Neuropsychologia, 39*, 771–786.

Swick, D., & Jovanovic, J. (2002). Anterior cingulate cortex and the Stroop task: Neuropsychological evidence for topographic specificity. *Neuropsychologia, 40*, 1240–1253.

Swick, D., & Turken, A. U. (2002). Dissociation between conflict detection and error monitoring in the human anterior cingulate cortex. *Proceedings of the National Academy of Sciences of the USA, 99*, 16354–16359.

Taylor, S. F., Kornblum, S., Minoshima, S., Oliver, L. M., & Koeppe, R. A. (1994). Changes in medial cortical blood flow with a stimulus-response compatibility task. *Neuropsychologia, 32*, 249–255.

Taylor, S. F., Martis, B., Fitzgerald, K. D., Welsh, R. C., Abelson, J. L., Liberzon, I., et al. (2006). Medial frontal cortex activity and loss-related responses to errors. *Journal of Neuroscience, 26*, 4063–4070.

Thompson-Schill, S. L., D'Esposito, M., Aguirre, G. K., & Farah, M. J. (1997). Role of left inferior prefrontal cortex in retrieval of semantic knowledge: A reevaluation. *Proceedings of the National Academy of Sciences of the USA, 94*, 14792–14797.

Tipper, S. P. (1985). The negative priming effect: Inhibitory priming by ignored objects. *Quarterly Journal of Experimental Psychology, 37A*, 571–590.

Treisman, A. M., & Gelade, G. (1980). A feature-integration theory of attention. *Cognitive Psychology, 12*, 97–136.

Tsuchida, A., & Fellows, L. K. (2009). Lesion evidence that two distinct regions within prefrontal cortex are critical for N-back performance in humans. *Journal of Cognitive Neuroscience, 21*, 2263–2275.

Turken, A. U., & Swick, D. (1999). Response selection in the human anterior cingulate cortex. *Nature Neuroscience, 2*, 920–924.

Tzelgov, J., Henik, A., & Berger, J. (1992). Controlling Stroop effects by manipulating expectations for color words. *Memory and Cognition, 20*, 727–735.

Ullsperger, M. (2006). Performance monitoring in neurological and psychiatric patients. *International Journal of Psychophysiology, 59*, 59–69.

Ullsperger, M., Bylsma, L. M., & Botvinick, M. M. (2005). The conflict adaptation effect: It's not just priming. *Cognitive, Affective, & Behavioral Neuroscience, 5*, 467–472.

Ullsperger, M., & von Cramon, D. Y. (2001). Subprocesses of performance monitoring: A dissociation of error processing and response competition revealed by event-related fMRI and ERPs. *Neuroimage, 14*, 1387–1401.

Ullsperger, M., & von Cramon, D. Y. (2004). Neuroimaging of performance monitoring: error detection and beyond. *Cortex, 40*, 593–604.

Ullsperger, M., & von Cramon, D. Y. (2006). The role of intact frontostriatal circuits in error processing. *Journal of Cognitive Neuroscience, 18*, 651–664.

Ursu, S., Stenger, V. A., Shear, M. K., Jones, M. R., & Carter, C. S. (2003). Overactive action monitoring in obsessive-compulsive disorder: Evidence from functional magnetic resonance imaging. *Psychological Science, 14*, 347–353.

van Hoesen, G. W., Morecraft, R. J., & Vogt, B. A. (1993). Connections of the monkey cingulate cortex. In B. A. Vogt & M. Gabriel (Eds.), *Neurobiology of cingulate cortex and limbic thalamus: A comprehensive handbook* (pp. 249–284). Boston: Birkhauser.

van Steenbergen, H., Band, G. P. H., & Hommel, B. (2009). Reward counteracts conflict adaptation: Evidence for a role of affect in executive control. *Psychological Science, 20*, 1473–1477.

van Veen, V., & Carter, C. S. (2002). The timing of action monitoring in rostral and caudal anterior cingulate cortex. *Journal of Cognitive Neuroscience, 14*, 593–602.

van Veen, V., & Carter, C. S. (2005). Separating semantic conflict and response conflict in the Stroop task: A functional MRI study. *Neuroimage, 27*, 497–504.

van Veen, V., Cohen, J. D., Botvinick, M. M., Stenger, V. A., & Carter, C. S. (2001). Anterior cingulate cortex, conflict monitoring, and levels of processing. *Neuroimage, 14*, 1302–1308.

Venkatraman, V., Rosati, A. G., Taren, A. A., & Huettel, S. A. (2009). Resolving response, decision, and strategic control: Evidence for a functional topography in dorsomedial prefrontal cortex. *Journal of Neuroscience, 29*, 13158–13164.

Verguts, T., & Notebaert, W. (2008). Hebbian learning of cognitive control: Dealing with specific and nonspecific adaptation. *Psychological Review, 115*, 518–525.

Verguts, T., & Notebaert, W. (2009). Adaptation by binding: A learning account of cognitive control. *Trends in Cognitive Sciences, 13*, 252–257.

Vidal, F., Burle, B., Bonnet, M., Grapperon, J., & Hasbroucq, T. (2003). Error negativity on correct trials: A reexamination of available data. *Biological Psychology, 64*, 265–282.

Vidal, F., Hasbroucq, T., Grapperon, J., & Bonnet, M. (2000). Is the "error negativity" specific to errors? *Biological Psychology, 51*, 109–128.

Vogt, B. A., Berger, G. R., & Derbyshire, S. W. (2003). Structural and functional dichotomy of human midcingulate cortex. *European Journal of Neuroscience, 18*, 3134–3144.

Vogt, B. A., Nimchinsky, E. A., Vogt, L. J., & Hof, P. R. (1995). Human cingulate cortex: Surface features, flat maps, and cytoarchitecture. *Journal of Comparative Neurology, 359*, 490–506.

Vuilleumier, P., Armony, J. L., Driver, J., & Dolan, R. J. (2001). Effects of attention and emotion on face processing in the human brain: An event-related fMRI study. *Neuron, 30*, 829–841.

Wager, T. D., Sylvester, C. Y. C., Lacey, S. C., Nee, D. E., Franklin, M., & Jonides, J. (2005). Common and unique components of response inhibition revealed by fMRI. *Neuroimage, 27*, 323–340.

Wallis, J. D. (2007). Orbitofrontal cortex and its contribution to decision-making. *Annual Review of Neuroscience, 30*, 31–56.

Walton, M. E., Bannerman, D. M., Alterescu, K., & Rushworth, M. F. (2003). Functional specialization within medial frontal cortex of the anterior cingulate for evaluating effort-related decisions. *Journal of Neuroscience, 23*, 6475–6479.

Walton, M. E., Devlin, J. T., & Rushworth, M. F. (2004). Interactions between decision making and performance monitoring within prefrontal cortex. *Nature Neuroscience, 7*, 1259–1265.

Wang, C., Ulbert, I., Schomer, D. L., Marinkovic, K., & Halgren, E. (2005). Responses of human anterior cingulate cortex microdomains to error detection, conflict monitoring, stimulus-response mapping, familiarity, and orienting. *Journal of Neuroscience, 25*, 604–613.

Wang, L., Liu, X., Guise, K. G., Knight, R. T., Ghajar, J., & Fan, J. (2010). Effective connectivity of the fronto-parietal network during attentional control. *Journal of Cognitive Neuroscience, 22*, 543–553.

Weissman, D. H., Gopalakrishnan, A., Hazlett, C. J., & Woldorff, M. G. (2005). Dorsal anterior cingulate cortex resolves conflict from distracting stimuli by boosting attention toward relevant events. *Cerebral Cortex, 15*, 229–237.

Wendelken, C., Ditterich, J., Bunge, S. A., & Carter, C. S. (2009). Stimulus and response conflict processing during perceptual decision making. *Cognitive, Affective & Behavioral Neuroscience, 9*, 434–447.

Wendt, M., Kluwe, R. H., & Vietze, I. (2008). Location-specific versus hemisphere-specific adaptation of processing selectivity. *Psychonomic Bulletin & Review, 15*, 135–140.

Whalen, P. J., Bush, G., McNally, R. J., Wilhelm, S., McInerny, S. C., Jenike, M. A., et al. (1998). The emotional counting Stroop paradigm: A functional magnetic resonance imaging probe of the anterior cingulate affective division. *Biological Psychiatry, 44*, 1219–1228.

Williams, Z. M., Bush, G., Rauch, S. L., Cosgrove, G. R., & Eskandar, E. N. (2004). Human anterior cingulate neurons and the integration of monetary reward with motor responses. *Nature Neuroscience, 7*, 1370–1375.

Wittfoth, M., Kustermann, E., Fahle, M., & Herrmann, M. (2008). The influence of response conflict on error processing: Evidence from event-related fMRI. *Brain Research, 1194*, 118–129.

Wittfoth, M., Schroder, C., Schardt, D. M., Dengler, R., Heinze, H. J., & Kotz, S. A. (2010). On emotional conflict: Interference resolution of happy and angry prosody reveals valence-specific effects. *Cerebral Cortex, 20*, 383–392.

Yen, C. P., Kuan, C. Y., Sheehan, J., Kung, S. S., Wang, C. C., Liu, C. K., et al. (2009). Impact of bilateral anterior cingulotomy on neurocognitive function in patients with intractable pain. *Journal of Clinical Neuroscience, 16*, 214–219.

Yeung, N., Botvinick, M. M., & Cohen, J. D. (2004). The neural basis of error detection: Conflict monitoring and the error-related negativity. *Psychological Review, 111*, 931–959.

Yeung, N., & Cohen, J. D. (2006). The impact of cognitive deficits on conflict monitoring: Predictable dissociations between the error-related negativity and N2. *Psychological Science, 17*, 164–171.

Yeung, N., Cohen, J. D., & Botvinick, M. M. (2011). Errors of interpretation and modeling: A reply to Grinband et al. *Neuroimage, 57*, 316–319.

Yeung, N., & Nieuwenhuis, S. (2009). Dissociating response conflict and error likelihood in anterior cingulate cortex. *Journal of Neuroscience, 29*, 14506–14510.

Yeung, N., Ralph, J., & Nieuwenhuis, S. (2007). Drink alcohol and dim the lights: The impact of cognitive deficits on medial frontal cortex function. *Cognitive, Affective & Behavioral Neuroscience, 7*, 347–355.

Yeung, N., & Sanfey, A. G. (2004). Independent coding of reward magnitude and valence in the human brain. *Journal of Neuroscience, 24*, 6258–6264.

Yordanova, J., Falkenstein, M., Hohnsbein, J., & Kolev, V. (2004). Parallel systems of error processing in the brain. *Neuroimage, 22*, 590–602.

Yu, A. J., Dayan, P., & Cohen, J. D. (2009). Dynamics of attentional selection under conflict: Toward a rational Bayesian account. *Journal of Experimental Psychology: Human Perception and Performance, 35*, 700–717.

Yucel, M., Harrison, B. J., Wood, S. J., Fornito, A., Wellard, R. M., Pujol, J., et al. (2007). Functional and biochemical alterations of the medial frontal cortex in obsessive-compulsive disorder. *Archives of General Psychiatry, 64*, 946–955.

Yucel, M., Stuart, G. W., Maruff, P., Velakoulis, D., Crowe, S. F., Savage, G., et al. (2001). Hemispheric and gender-related differences in the gross morphology of the anterior cingulate/paracingulate cortex in normal volunteers: An MRI morphometric study. *Cerebral Cortex, 11*, 17–25.

Hierarchical Cognitive Control and the Functional Organization of the Frontal Cortex

David Badre

Abstract

Cognitive control refers to the ability of humans and other primates to internally guide behavior in concert with goals, plans, and broader contextual knowledge. However, in everyday life, we often must manage multiple goals at once over different time scales and at different levels of abstraction with respect to an overt response. Recent cognitive neuroscience research has suggested that cognitive control processing in the frontal lobes of the brain may be hierarchically organized along their rostrocaudal axis in order to deal with this problem. This chapter provides a brief overview of current research on hierarchical cognitive control and how this function may emerge from the functional organization of the frontal lobes.

Key Words: cognitive control, executive function, prefrontal cortex, learning and generalization, planning

Introduction

Human behavior is marked by its flexibility. We choose the courses of action that are likely to achieve our goals from a vast space of candidate actions. Moreover, as circumstances change and previous plans become obsolete, we can rapidly change our behavior to accommodate the new situation and still reach our goals. However, having such a large behavioral repertoire comes with a cost, namely, the problem of choice. With so many ways to act, how do we navigate this broad space and maintain coherent, goal-directed behavior?

Part of the answer to this question lies in our capacity for cognitive control, or the mechanisms by which we use plans, goals, or features of our environment to constrain action selection (Badre & Wagner, 2004; Bunge, 2004; Miller & Cohen, 2001; O'Reilly & Frank, 2006). However, another important consideration is the way that we structure action representations and the cognitive control system itself in order to reduce the number of alternatives from which a choice must be made (Badre,

2008; Botvinick, Niv, & Barto, 2009; Cooper & Shallice, 2006; Lashley, 1951; Schank & Abelson, 1977). Consider, for example, the task of making a sandwich. Even if one eliminates the problem of deciding which type of sandwich to make, there are many different ways of constructing a particular sandwich, such as spreading mayonnaise before or after the mustard. Moreover, consider how difficult this problem becomes if we could plan only in terms of sequences of motor-effector movements. It is clear that the spread of potential options would be vast, and comparison among them in order to choose one plan over another by a cognitive control system would be intractable.

Hierarchies are useful in dealing with large spaces of options, such as in the problem of action, because they permit a divide-and-conquer approach (Newell, 1990; Rosenbaum, 1987). Returning to our sandwich example, one can represent this task as a very abstract goal: "make a sandwich." This abstract goal can be broken down into a more specific series of subgoals like slicing bread, spreading mayonnaise, etc. These subgoals can be broken down further into more specific sub-subgoals and so forth until the task is decomposed into a highly specific sequence of neuromuscular outputs. Thus, choices about which actions to take can be made at multiple levels of abstraction. This has the benefit of separating updating, monitoring, and maintenance of contextual information relevant to each level independently. And, importantly, choices at the higher levels will constrain the space of possible actions at lower levels, reducing complexity and the demands on choice.

Recent evidence has suggested that the cognitive control of action is hierarchical in nature and emerges from the functional organization of the frontal cortex (Badre, 2008; Badre & D'Esposito, 2009; Botvinick, 2008; Koechlin & Summerfield, 2007; O'Reilly, 2010). In this chapter, we will consider evidence for hierarchical control as it relates to frontal lobe function, how this type of architecture may support flexibility and abstraction in action, and, finally, a model for how hierarchical control mechanisms may operate in the brain.

Policy Abstraction: Rules that Govern Rules

Cognitive control refers to our ability to guide our behavior on the basis of internal representations of goals, plans, and context (Cohen, Dunbar, & McClelland, 1990; Miller & Cohen, 2001). Consider the everyday example of entering a colleague's office and finding a place to sit down. On a daily basis, in one's own office, the chair behind one's desk is the appropriate seat. However, in another's office, even one with which we have no prior experience, we easily alter our behavior and look for the chair in front of the desk. Our ability to flexibly shift our behavior without multiple trials of reinforcement and based on an abstract social rule depends on cognitive control. In the brain, the frontal lobes are known to be necessary for cognitive control function (Stuss & Benson, 1987).

Cognitive control mechanisms are generally thought to operate through a process of biased competition, whereby maintenance of a distributed neural representation of the task context ("colleague's office") by frontal neurons biases processing throughout the action system in favor of an appropriate course of action ("sit in the chair in front of desk") over competing ones ("sit in the chair behind the desk") (Cohen et al., 1990; Cohen & Servan-Schreiber, 1992; Desimone & Duncan, 1995; Miller & Cohen, 2001). Thus, cognitive control permits a state of the system (i.e., "context") to influence

selection of an operator, such as a particular action, that is likely to achieve a desired outcome state (the "goal"). A rule that relates a state, an action, and a desired outcome has been termed *policy* in the reinforcement learning literature (Botvinick, 2008; Botvinick et al., 2009). Thus, from this perspective, the investigation of cognitive control is centrally concerned with how the brain acquires, selects, and implements action policy.

Policy provides a useful way of conceptualizing hierarchical abstraction in a cognitive control system. In particular, a policy can be considered abstract to the extent that it determines a class of simpler policy based on a state. For example, consider two simple rules: a circle cues a left-hand response and a rectangle a right-hand response (Figure 19.1a). This first-order policy is concrete because the state (the identity of the shape) fully specifies what action to take (which hand to move). However, consider an independent set of first-order policy, based on size, in which a large stimulus cues a left-hand response and a small stimulus a right-hand response (Figure 19.1b). Because the shape and size rule sets are independent, both cannot simultaneously govern responding. For instance, if the relevant set of first-order policy is unknown, a stimulus that is both circular and small cues opposing responses. Consequently, a more abstract rule (second-order policy) is required in order to specify which set of first-order rules (shape or size) should govern responding in the current context. For example, coloring the stimulus red might indicate that the

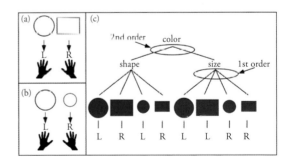

Figure 19.1 Schematic example of a second-order policy structure. **a.** First-order policy mappings based on shape. Circles cue a left (L)-hand response and rectangles cue a right (R)-hand response. **b.** First-order policy mappings based on size. Large shapes cue a left-hand response and small shapes cue a right-hand response. **c.** In this example, the color of the stimulus determines whether to use the shape or size rules. The rule relating color to first-order policy sets is second-order policy. Expressed as a tree structure, the order of policy abstraction can be determined by the number of branch points that must be traversed in order to determine a response.

shape set is the appropriate first-order policy, while blue might indicate size (Figure 19.1c). Because this second-order policy based on color specifies a class of simpler rule sets (shape or size) but not a specific response, it is more abstract.

Considerable research in both humans and animals has implicated the frontal cortex in the acquisition and implementation of simple behavioral rules (Asaad, Rainer, & Miller, 1998, 2000; Bunge, 2004; Bunge, Kahn, Wallis, Miller, & Wagner, 2003; Wallis, Anderson, & Miller, 2001; Wallis & Miller, 2003; White & Wise, 1999), particularly those involving first-order policy. Recently, our lab and others have become interested in how the brain's cognitive control system is organized to processes more complex policy structures that are likely critical in accounting for the massive flexibility and vast behavioral repertoire evident in human and nonhuman primates.

Policy Abstraction and the Rostrocaudal Axis of Frontal Cortex

Fuster's perception–action cycle theory was the first to associate a concept of abstraction in action control with the functional organization of frontal cortex (Fuster, 1997, 2001, 2004). Fuster proposed a series of loops between perceptual hierarchy in posterior neocortex and an action hierarchy along the rostrocaudal axis of the frontal lobes. According to the theory, as abstract plans are translated into concrete responses, progressively posterior regions of lateral frontal cortex are responsible for integrating more concrete inputs from sensory systems over more proximate time intervals. Thus, in the perception–action cycle, the hierarchical structure of action may be represented in the organization of cortical areas from rostral to caudal frontal cortex.

The first empirical evidence regarding a rostrocaudal organization of the frontal cortex came from an fMRI study in which participants were tested while performing response and task-set selection tasks (Koechlin, Ody, & Kouneiher, 2003). In the response selection task, participants selected a finger response based on a colored cue. In the task-set selection task, participants chose a letter classification task based on a colored cue. Selection of a finger response in the response selection task was associated with dorsal premotor cortex (PMd), whereas selection of the task set for letter classification was associated with the more rostral anterior premotor cortex (prePMd). In addition, across both experiments, prior to a block of trials, an instruction indicated what the mappings between color,

and task and response were going to be in the upcoming block. Importantly, on blocks when the mappings were infrequent, this instruction had to be maintained or refreshed in some way in order to interpret the color and select the right rule on each trial. The low-frequency conditions elicited activation inclusive of a further anterior region, mid-dorsolateral PFC (area 9/46). Thus, because the contextual information required to make a choice became more abstract and temporally remote, more rostral regions of the frontal cortex were required to engage in control.

To what extent did this rostrocaudal gradient in frontal cortex reflect differences in policy abstraction, as defined above? In order to test this, we developed a paradigm that permitted manipulation of cognitive control demands over four levels of policy abstraction (Badre & D'Esposito, 2007). Importantly, we parametrically taxed policy at one level at a time while keeping demands on higher-level policy minimal and lower-level policy constant. Thus, we were able to distinguish which regions of the brain were selectively sensitive to each level of policy independently from correlated changes in control demands at lower levels and from overall changes in difficulty.

In order to understand the logic of the experiment, it is helpful to return to our example of second-order policy from the preceding section. Mapping out the decisions (Figure 19.1c) results in a two-tiered decision tree with each branch point representing a decision, or a point at which some contextual information will bias selection of one action path over another. The depth of the decision tree remaining to be traversed from any branch point in order to reach a response determines the order of policy abstraction. Thus, in our example, deciding which rule set, color or shape, is appropriate requires traversing two branch points and so represents a decision at a second order of policy abstraction. Deciding what response to make based on shape, by contrast, requires traversing only one branch point and so is at a first order of policy abstraction. In an experiment, one can continue to add layers of contingency and thus additional branch points to the tree, thereby requiring decisions to be made at higher orders of policy abstraction. The order of policy abstraction, then, may be determined by the depth of the tree (number of branch points) to be traversed to determine a response.

Of course, making a choice more abstract will arguably increase complexity of the rule and, in some cases, its difficulty. Thus, one wants to be sure that differences in fMRI activation can be attributed to changes in abstraction and not to "task difficulty" in general. Importantly, the decisions at any branch point can also be made more difficult without increasing abstractness by increasing the number of alternatives at that level (or reducing the frequency of any one alternative). For example, at a second order of policy abstraction, choosing among four orthogonal rule sets (e.g., defined by shape, size, texture, and orientation) will be more difficult than choosing among two rule sets. Increasing the number of alternatives increases competition and thus will demand greater control at a second level

of policy abstraction. Increasing competition puts greater demands on cognitive control mechanisms to make a choice, but adding alternatives does not produce a deeper tree. Although difficulty increases, the order of policy abstraction does not. Thus, policy abstraction and competition may be unconfounded by separately varying the depth and width of the tree.

Using this logic, Badre and D'Esposito (2007) independently tested the response of frontal cortex to increasing cognitive control demands at four levels of policy abstraction during fMRI scanning (Figures 19.2 and 19.3).

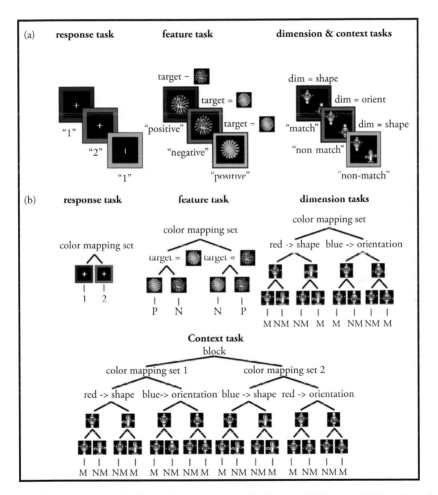

Figure 19.2 Task used for testing four levels of policy abstraction in study by Badre and D'Esposito (2007). **a.** Task schematics showing trial events for the response, feature, dimension, and context tasks. In the response task, the color of the box on every trial determined what response to make. In the feature task, the color determined the target feature (indicated as a particular texture above each trial). When the target texture appeared, this resulted in a positive response; other textures received a negative response. In the dimension and context tasks, the color determined the relevant dimension (shape, size, orientation, or texture) along which to compare two presented objects. Participants decided if the objects matched or not along the relevant dimension. In the context task, the frequency of mapping between the color and the relevant dimension was also varied to add an additional level of selection. **b.** Policy structures associated with each of the four tasks. The mid- and high-competition conditions of each experiment require selection at first (response), second (feature), third (dimension), and fourth (context) orders of policy abstraction, respectively. P, positive; N, negative; M, match; NM, non-match.

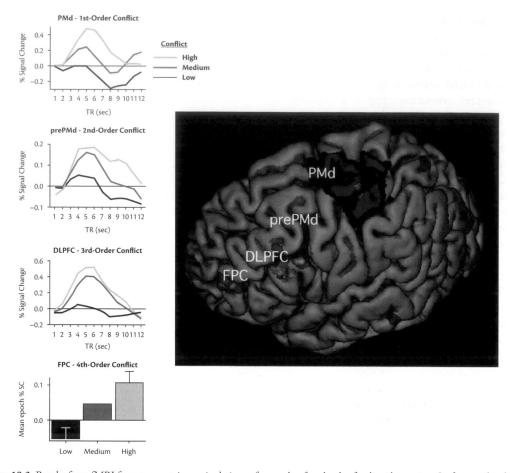

Figure 19.3 Results from fMRI from parametric manipulations of control at four levels of policy abstraction. Surface-rendered activation (right) and selectively averaged time courses from regions of interest (left) show that increasing the competition from low to mid to high in the response, feature, dimension, and context experiments resulted in selective, parametric increases in fMRI activation in dorsal premotor cortex (PMd; ~BA 6), anterior PMd (prePMd; ~BA 8), inferior frontal sulcus (IFS; ~BA 9/46), and frontal polar cortex (FPC; ~BA 46 or 10).

Response Task

During the response task (first-order control), participants were required to select a response on each trial based on the color of a presented square (Figure 19.2a). Competition at a first order of policy abstraction was manipulating by requiring a choice from among one, two, or four alternative responses. Increasing competition at a first order of policy abstraction (Figure 19.2b) resulted in a parametric increase in activation in PMd (Figure 19.3).

Feature Task

On each trial of the feature task (second-order control), participants were presented with a single object inside a colored box (Figure 19.2a). From trial to trial, the object varied along one dimension, such as texture. The participant looked for a particular target texture and made a positive response if the

target texture was present and a negative response to any other texture. On any trial, only one texture entailed a positive response and other textures entailed a negative response. However, on the next trial, the target could change (as cued by a different color), and so a different texture could require a positive response. Knowledge of the texture alone was insufficient to determine which response mapping (positive or negative) was required on that trial. Rather, the participant knew the set of mappings between textures and responses based on the colored box. Thus, control at a second level was required in that one set of texture-to-response mappings had to be selected over competing sets (Figure 19.2b). As the number of sets of feature-defined mapping sets increased from one to two to four, activation increased in caudal PFC/anterior PMd (prePMd) (Figure 19.3).

Dimension Task

On each trial of the dimension task (third-order control), participants were presented with two objects appearing inside a colored box (Figure 19.2a). From trial to trial, objects varied along four dimensions: texture, orientation, shape, and size. The participant decided whether the objects matched or mismatched along one of the dimensions. The color of the surrounding box was required in order to decide which dimension was relevant to the decision. Control at a third order of abstraction was necessary to the extent that the relevant dimension had to be selected from two or more competitors (Figure 19.2b). As the number of candidate dimensions increased from one to two to four, activation increased in dorsolateral PFC (DLPFC), specifically along the upper bank of the inferior frontal sulcus (IFS) (Figure 19.3).

Context Task

Finally, during the context task (fourth-order control), participants were again required to make a match decision between two objects (Figure 19.2a). They also had to choose which of two dimensions was relevant based on the color of the surrounding square. However, in the context task, a given color could map to different dimensions on different blocks. To the extent that a given color-to-dimension mapping is infrequent across blocks, fourth-order control is required to select the relevant mapping (Figure 19.2b). Thus, as the frequency of a given color to dimension mapping decreased from 100% to 50% to 25%, activation increased in frontal polar cortex (FPC) (Figure 19.3).

To summarize, across these four separate tasks, competition and policy abstraction were independently varied. Policy abstraction affected the locus of activation, with progressively anterior regions being associated with added orders of abstraction. By contrast, competition at any level of policy abstraction was associated with greater BOLD activation but not increases in more rostral regions. This finding is important because it indicates that difficulty alone does not account for the caudal-to-rostral organization. Rather, increases in policy abstraction elicit activation of progressively rostral frontal cortex.

Alternatives to Policy Abstraction

These data provide motivation for characterizing the rostrocaudal axis in terms of policy abstraction, but this experiment does leave open important alternatives regarding how to rank the levels of hierarchy in frontal cortex. Indeed, abstraction has been defined in different ways across separate bodies of evidence concerning rostrocaudal functional organization (Badre, 2008). Most notable among the alternatives to policy abstraction are temporal abstraction and relational complexity.

Temporal Abstraction

Temporal abstraction is a concept highly related to policy abstraction and refers to a time scale over which a contextual representation must influence action. It has also been hypothesized that regions along the rostrocaudal axis are differentiated on the basis of temporal abstraction (Botvinick, 2007, 2008; Botvinick et al., 2009; Fuster, 2001; Koechlin & Summerfield, 2007). Simply put, separable pools of neurons along the rostrocaudal axis of the frontal cortex may differ in their ability to maintain information and resolve contingencies over longer time intervals. As action representations become more concrete, going from abstract goals down to a specific sequence of neuromuscular outputs, goal and subgoal information must be updated more frequently and sustained over shorter intervals and so temporal abstraction decreases.

The relationship between temporal abstraction and the rostrocaudal axis of the frontal lobe has received support from a number of convergent sources. In particular, electrophysiological evidence has distinguished PFC from premotor regions on the basis of neurons in PFC mediating longer cross-temporal contingencies (Fuster, Bodner, & Kroger, 2000). FPC, at the most anterior extent of the rostrocaudal axis, has been associated across a range of experiments with a sustained response relative to higher-frequency event-related responses in posterior PFC (Braver, Reynolds, & Donaldson, 2003; Donaldson, Petersen, Ollinger, & Buckner, 2001; Visscher et al., 2003).

Most directly, however, the data from the response and task-set selection experiments by Koechlin et al. (Koechlin & Summerfield, 2007) described above have been argued to demonstrate a rostrocaudal organization in the integration of control signals arising from increasingly temporally remote contexts. In their model, from premotor to posterior DLPFC, control relies on information available in the immediate environment. Within this posterior zone, regions are distinguished from one another on the basis of demand to select longer sequences or sets of responses (Koechlin & Jubault, 2006). Anterior DLPFC and FPC engage in control relying on information that is not present in the current environment but occurred either in the current temporal frame, such as an ongoing task condition (anterior DLPFC) (Koechlin et al., 2003), or during a previous context (FPC) (Koechlin, Basso, Pietrini, Panzer, & Grafman, 1999; Koechlin, Corrado, Pietrini, & Grafman, 2000), such as is required during subgoaling (Braver & Bongiolatti, 2002).

Relational Integration

Abstraction through relational integration suggests that regions along the rostrocaudal axis are differentially required given the number of variable dimensions that must be integrated in order to determine a response (Bunge, 2004; Bunge, Wendelken, Badre, & Wagner, 2005; Christoff & Gabrieli, 2000; Christoff & Keramatian, 2007; Christoff, Ream, Geddes, & Gabrieli, 2003; Halford, 1993; Ramnani & Owen, 2004; Robin & Holyoak, 1995). A first order of relational complexity requires only a single dimension be considered, as in assigning a simple property to a specific item ("What is the color?"), and has been associated with ventrolateral PFC (VLPFC) (Bunge et al., 2003, 2005; Christoff & Keramatian, 2007; Kostopoulos & Petrides, 2003; Wagner, Paré-Blagoev, Clark, & Poldrack, 2001). By contrast, a second order of complexity requires drawing simple relations between concrete properties ("Do the colors match?") and is associated with DLPFC according to neuroimaging and neurophysiological evidence (Bunge et al., 2003; Christoff & Keramatian, 2007; Wallis et al., 2001; Wallis & Miller, 2003). A second-order relation is more abstract because it does not depend on a specific property of an item and may be generalized to novel items. A higher, third order of relational complexity, with a hypothesized association with FPC, entails evaluation of relations among relations. For example, deciding whether the mismatching dimension (texture or shape) of a target pair matches the mismatching dimension of a subsequently presented target pair is associated with activation in FPC (Christoff et al., 2003). Thus, from the perspective of relational complexity, abstraction can be varied experimentally to the extent that a task requires generation of relationships that become increasingly removed from the specific properties of a stimulus. Increasing the number of relations that must be integrated should result in processing progressing from VLPFC (first order) to DLPFC (second order) to FPC (third order).

Of course, these types of abstraction are not necessarily mutually exclusive with respect to each other or policy abstraction and may share a number of common properties. For example, temporal and policy abstraction are highly correlated.

Representations that are more abstract in policy terms are also likely to be relevant over longer time scales. Similarly, policy abstraction and relational integration both require monitoring and updating of increasing numbers of independent contextual dimensions as abstraction increases. Thus, although precisely defining abstraction with respect to rostrocaudal frontal organization is a key theoretical point to be clarified in future research, there is a common theme that more rostral regions of the frontal cortex are involved in more abstract, higher-order control operations. Consequently, in the interest of conceptual clarity, the remainder of the chapter will use policy abstraction as its working framework for discussing frontal hierarchy.

Evidence for a Processing Hierarchy in the Frontal Cortex

In light of the previous discussion, there is now fairly strong convergent evidence for a gradient of abstraction along the rostrocaudal axis of frontal cortex that could support hierarchical cognitive control. However, a key feature of a hierarchy is that influence and inheritance are asymmetrical from superordinate to subordinate levels relative to the reverse order. Thus, a key question is whether this gradient of abstraction in cognitive control actually reflects a processing hierarchy in lateral frontal cortex, whereby rostral neurons influence activity in caudal neurons more than the reverse situation.

In a review of the corticocortical anatomy of frontal cortex, Badre and D'Esposito (2009) suggested that rostrocaudal frontal connectivity displays two features that are prerequisites for a processing hierarchy such as that described above (Figure 19.4a). In particular, adjacent regions along the rostrocaudal axis are directly connected to one another. Notably, it is not the case that every frontal region shares connections with all regions adjacent to it. For example, the dorsal or ventral adjacent regions may not share direct connections (such as ventral vs. dorsal 9/46). Thus, this contiguity principle is a specific property of the rostrocaudal connectivity of the frontal lobe. More importantly, frontal subregions do not project to more rostral regions beyond those regions immediately adjacent, whereas rostral regions do project to caudal regions beyond those immediately adjacent. This asymmetry of input from rostral to caudal is consistent with a processing hierarchy.

In line with the anatomy, evidence from functional connectivity analysis at rest has provided evidence that the regions along the rostrocaudal axis of frontal cortex (46/10, 9/46, 8, and 6) couple

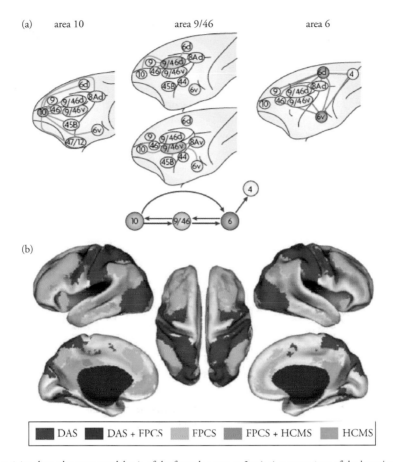

(a)　area 10　　　　　area 9/46　　　　　area 6

(b)

| ■ DAS | ■ DAS + FPCS | FPCS | ■ FPCS + HCMS | ■ HCMS |

Figure 19.4 Connectivity along the rostrocaudal axis of the frontal cortex. **a.** Intrinsic connections of the lateral prefrontal cortex (PFC; top) and a schematic summary of the connections of the principal frontal regions (area 10, shown in orange; area 9/46, shown in green; and area 6, shown in blue) that are proposed to be part of a rostrocaudal functional gradient based on functional studies (bottom). Area 4 depicts the primary motor cortex. **b.** Results from Vincent et al. (2008) showing that spontaneous activity in regions along the rostrocaudal axis of the PFC and in parietal and medial frontal cortex is correlated with activity in the frontopolar cortex (shown in light green). Also depicted in the figure is the spatial relationship of these regions to two other networks: the dorsal attention system (DAS) and the hippocampal-cortical memory system (HCMS), which were identified using visual motion area MT+ and the hippocampus as seeds, respectively. FPCS, frontoparietal control system.

Reproduced with permission from Badre and D'Esposito (2009).

as a coherent functional network (Vincent, Kahn, Snyder, Raichle, & Buckner, 2008), along with regions of parietal cortex and the posterior temporal lobe (Figure 19.4b). Owing to its general association with cognitive control, this network has been termed the *frontoparietal control system*, and is distinguishable from at least two other coherent networks: a more dorsal attentional network and a ventral hippocampal network. Importantly, effective connectivity values, which provide a direction of influence as estimated with structural equation modeling of fMRI data, have been shown to differentially flow from front to back in the frontal cortex within this network (Koechlin et al., 2003; Kouneiher, Charron, & Koechlin, 2009).

However, the neuroimaging data cannot be conclusive on this point. Indeed, some perspectives can account for a rostrocaudal functional gradient without a requirement that the processing architecture be hierarchical (Christoff & Gabrieli, 2000; Christoff & Keramatian, 2007; Christoff et al., 2003; Petrides, 2005). Thus, a fundamental issue to resolve is whether the observed rostrocaudal gradient reflects a hierarchical or nonhierarchical organization of function (Badre, 2008). To test the asymmetry hypothesis, we asked 12 individuals with focal frontal lobe lesions and 24 age-matched controls to perform the four response selection tasks (response, feature, dimension, and context) performed previously and for which we had fMRI data (see Figure 19.2) (Badre, Hoffman, Cooney, & D'Esposito, 2009).

An anterior-to-posterior flow of control processing in the frontal lobes predicts that performance on tasks involving higher-order control should be impaired by disruptions to lower-order processors, even when the higher-order processors are intact. However, the reverse prediction should not hold. Performance should be unaffected for tasks involving only intact lower-order processors when higher-order processors are impaired. Put more concretely, a deficit in third-order control would affect performance on the dimension task but not the feature or response tasks. Conversely, a deficit in second-order control would impact the feature and dimension tasks.

The results from this experiment provided evidence for this type of asymmetrical deficit pattern. On this task, patients showed a greater deficit compared to controls as the task rules became more abstract.

There can be two explanations for this finding: (1) higher-order control demands could increasingly challenge all patients, regardless of the site of their lesion, thus their performance would become differentially impaired as the task complexity increases, or (2) because of the asymmetrical dependencies predicted by a hierarchy, deficits in higher-level tasks would be more likely across patients, regardless of the site of their lesion, resulting in a greater aggregate likelihood of a deficit. If the aggregation account is the case, then the presence of an impairment at any level should increase the likelihood of an impairment at all higher levels but should not increase the odds of an impairment at a lower level.

The probability of a deficit on any task, p(D), was 62% across the patients. Critically, however, the probability of a deficit at any level given a deficit at a lower level, p(D|L), was 91% across patients, a significant change over p(D) on any task. By contrast, the probability of a deficit at any level given a deficit at a higher level, p(D|H), was only 76%, a weak change over the prior probability of a deficit on any task. This asymmetry provides initial support for the hierarchical dependencies among deficits at the different levels and the aggregation account of the group data.

We then used an observer-independent method to assign patients to lesion-overlap groups based on their behavioral performance across the four tasks. Vectors were created that corresponded to the idealized behavior of a patient with a selective deficit at a

particular hierarchical level. These vectors served as regressors in a multiple regression on each patient's performance differences from age-matched controls across all conditions of all experiments. Based on this regression, a patient was assigned to a particular lesion-overlap group. Two groups of patients were found (Figure 19.5).

Figure 19.5a shows the lesion-overlap map of patients that had a behavioral pattern consistent with a deficit at the feature level. In other words, they were impaired on the second-, third-, and fourth-level tasks but not at the first-level task. The site of their maximal lesion shown in dark red was within area 8, pre-PMD, in an almost identical location to that identified in our prior fMRI study, which is shown directly above the lesion overlap.

Figure 19.5b shows the lesion overlap of patients that had a behavioral pattern consistent with a deficit at the dimension level. In other words, they were impaired on the third- and fourth-level tasks but not at the lower first and second levels. The site of maximal lesion was within IFS, area 9/46, in an almost identical location to that identified in our prior fMRI study.

Taken together, these results provide evidence of a rostral-to-caudal asymmetry in the flow of cognitive control, which is consistent with a hierarchical processing architecture in the frontal cortex.

Hierarchical Learning and Abstraction

Flexible behavior requires the ability to rapidly adapt to novel circumstances and apply abstract rules to concrete actions. In this regard, hierarchies are convenient structures. Because a hierarchy represents a task at multiple levels of abstraction (Estes, 1982; Lashley, 1951; Miller, Galanter, & Pribram, 1960; Newell, 1990), analogy and the application of existing knowledge is easier at higher levels when encountering a novel task. Thus, hierarchical structures can support chunking, whereby a known higher-order relationship eases the learning of specific examples (Chase & Simon, 1973). Hierarchies can support transfer of a strategy or rule set to a novel task because analogies can be drawn at abstract levels of task structure (Gick & Holyoak, 1980, 1983; Speed, 2010). And, failures to perceive these higher-order relationships may underlie deficits in abstract reasoning seen in various patient groups (Butterfield, Wambold, & Belmont, 1973; Solomon, Ozonoff, Cummings, & Carter, 2008).

It remains an open question whether these putative advantages conveyed by hierarchies are supported by a hierarchical control system along the rostrocaudal

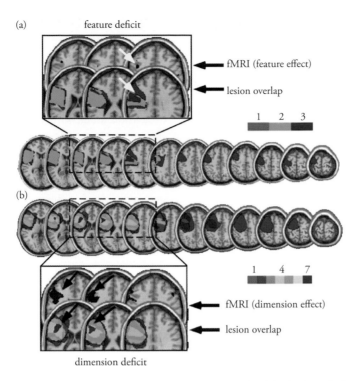

(a) feature deficit

fMRI (feature effect)

lesion overlap

1　2　3

(b)

1　4　7

fMRI (dimension effect)

lesion overlap

dimension deficit

Figure 19.5 Patient overlap maps showing selective, asymmetrical deficits at second and third orders of policy abstraction. Patients were assigned using an observer-independent method to "feature" or "dimension" deficit groups depending on whether their behavior showed an asymmetrical deficit at second or third levels of policy abstraction. Sites of highest overlap are shown in red and correspond to prePMd and IFS for the feature and dimension groups, respectively. Results associated with second- and third-order control from fMRI (Badre & D'Esposito, 2007) are shown for comparison.

Reproduced with permission from Badre et al. (2009).

axis of the frontal lobe. However, some evidence supports the role of the frontal lobe in this type of higher-order cognition. For example, more anterior regions of the PFC have been associated with the ability to draw analogies and higher-order relations. Explicit tests of analogy, such as verifying the statement "sailor is to boat as pilot is to plane," are associated with FPC (Bunge et al., 2005). By contrast, activation is observed in VLPFC during simple retrieval of semantic information, as in "who operates a boat?" (Badre, Poldrack, Pare-Blagoev, Insler, & Wagner, 2005; Badre & Wagner, 2007; Bunge et al., 2005; Wagner et al., 2001). Recently, increasing numbers of studies have tied the rostrocaudal organization of frontal cortex to relational and fluid reasoning and analogy (Badre, 2010; Christoff, Keramatian, Gordon, Smith, & Madler, 2009; Golde, von Cramon, & Schubotz, 2010; Krawczyk, McClelland, Donovan, Tillman, & Maguire, 2010; Krawczyk, Michelle McClelland, & Donovan, 2011; Speed, 2010; Volle, Gilbert, Benoit, & Burgess, 2010).

So, in order to more directly connect policy abstraction to learning and generalization, we conducted an fMRI experiment to assess whether the rostrocaudal axis of frontal cortex helps in the discovery of abstract rules when they are available in a novel learning context (Badre, Kayser, & D'Esposito, 2010). Specifically, using the policy abstraction definition, we designed a novel reinforcement learning task that contrasted a learning context when participants had an opportunity to acquire an abstract rule (second-order policy) against one in which only concrete (first-order policy) rules were available.

During fMRI scanning, participants were required to learn two sets of rules, in separate epochs, that linked each of 18 different stimuli uniquely and deterministically to one of three button-press responses. For each rule set, an individual stimulus consisted of one of three shapes, at one of three orientations, inside a box that was one of two colors, for a total of 18 unique stimuli (3 shapes × 3 orientations x 2 colors). Participants were instructed to learn the correct response for each stimulus based on auditory feedback (Figure 19.6a).

For one of the two rule sets, termed the *flat set*, each of the 18 rules had to be learned individually

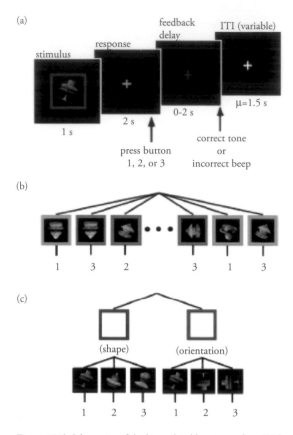

(a)

stimulus

response

feedback delay

ITI (variable)

1 s

2 s

0-2 s

μ=1.5 s

press button
1, 2, or 3

correct tone
or
incorrect beep

(b)

1   3   2   · · ·   3   1   3

(c)

(shape)   (orientation)

1   2   3   1   2   3

Figure 19.6 Schematics of the hierarchical learning task. **a.** Trial events during all epochs of the hierarchical learning task. On each trial, participants received a shape, at a particular orientation, surrounded by a colored box. Based on these features they selected one of three responses on the keypad. This was followed by feedback indicating whether the response was correct or not. ITI, Inter-trial-interval. **b.** Policy structure for the flat condition. The arrangement of mappings was such that 18 unique mappings had to be learned between each conjunction of shape, orientation, and color and a response, yielding a very wide flat first-order structure. **c.** Policy structure for the hierarchical condition. The arrangement of mappings was such that participants could select either a limited set of shape or orientation rules based on color. This results in a second-order policy structure.

as one-to-one mappings (first-order policy) between a conjunction of color, shape, and orientation and a response (Figure 19.6b). In the other set, termed the *hierarchical set*, stimulus display parameters and instructions were identical to those for the flat set. Indeed, the hierarchical set could also be learned as 18 individual first-order rules. However, the arrangement of response mappings was such that a second-order relationship could be learned instead, thereby reducing the number of first-order rules to be learned (Figure 19.6c). Specifically, in the context of one colored box, only the shape dimension was relevant to the response, with each of the three

unique shapes mapping to one of the three button responses regardless of orientation. Conversely, in the context of the other colored box, only the orientation dimension was relevant to the response. Thus, the hierarchical rule set permitted learning of abstract, second-order rules mapping color to dimension along with two sets of first-order rules (i.e., specific shape-to-response and orientation-to-response mappings).

Critically, all instructions, stimulus presentation parameters, and between-subject stimulus orderings were identical between the two rule sets. The flat and hierarchical rule sets only differed in that the organization of mappings in the hierarchical set permitted learning of a second-order rule. Hence, these two sets contrast a learning context in which abstract rules can be discovered with an analogous context in which no such rules can be learned.

Results from this experiment provide fundamental insights into the way that humans approach novel learning problems. First, participants were clearly capable of rapidly acquiring abstract rules when they were available. Relative to flat-set learning, which showed a slow, monotonic increase over the course of learning, learning curves during the hierarchical set were associated with rapid, step-function increases (Figure 19.7a). Behavioral analysis indicated that this rapid increase was due to generalization of an abstract rule to multiple specific instances.

Second, consistent with prior evidence, activation was greater in prePMd for hierarchical- than for flat-set learning epochs. Importantly, however, this pattern emerged because of a decline in prePMd over learning (Figure 19.7b). In other words, activation was evident in both PMd and prePMd early in learning but declined in the more rostral prePMd by the end of learning of the flat set, which contained no second-order rules. This pattern suggests that participants were searching, early on, for any higher-order rules—a search process that depended on prePMd. However, during flat set learning, when such rules were not rewarded, this activation declined progressively.

Consistent with the search hypothesis, behavioral differences between the hierarchical- and flat-set learning curves correlated with individual differences in early activation in prePMd. In other words, to the extent that an individual activated prePMd (though not PMd) early in learning, this individual was more likely to discover the abstract rule when it was available.

Overall, these results provide potential insight into the advantage that a hierarchical architecture conveys over other schemes, particularly where the

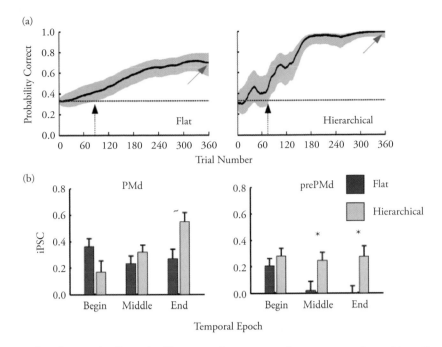

Figure 19.7 Results from fMRI study of hierarchical learning. **a.** Learning curves from a representative participant from the task. For the flat condition, learning increased gradually over the course of the trial. For the hierarchical condition, learning demonstrated a step function rapidly reaching ceiling. The learning trial, or point when learning is better than chance (light arrow), was reliably earlier, and the terminal accuracy (dark arrow) was reliably greater in the group between the hierarchical and flat conditions. **b.** Integrated percent signal change (iPSC) (y-axis) across early, middle, and late phases of learning (x-axis) for flat (dark bar) and hierarchical (light bar) conditions for PMd (left) and prePMd (right) regions of interest. PrePMd showed activation early for both hierarchical and flat conditions. In contrast to PMd, activation in prePMd declined by the middle phase of learning.

ability to make abstractions with regard to action selection is of central benefit. It has been demonstrated that though complex action may be represented hierarchically (i.e., in terms of goals, subgoals, etc.), the existence of hierarchical representations does not require that the action system itself segregate these representations among spatially separate pools of neurons (Botvinick, 2007; Botvinick & Plaut, 2004). However, one advantage of having such an organization is that structural hierarchies can facilitate learning of tasks that require acquisition of abstract policy relationships (Paine & Tani, 2005). One reason for this efficiency could be the capability of hierarchical structures to search independently for rules at multiple levels of abstraction in parallel. The results from the learning experiment are consistent with this perspective in that frontal cortex appears to leverage its hierarchical organization in order to engage in search at multiple levels of abstraction from the outset of learning.

Mechanisms of Hierarchical Control

A fundamental open question concerns the mechanisms by which the brain carries out hierarchical control. Moreover, what mechanisms support higher-order rule discovery, such as that described above? To begin to address these questions, we sought to model the Badre et al. (2010) learning task by adapting an established neural model of cognitive control (Frank & O'Reilly, 2006; O'Reilly & Frank, 2006) for hierarchical control (Badre & Frank, 2012; Frank & Badre, 2012). However, before describing the hierarchical model, we need to first introduce the concept of adaptive gating.

As described at the outset of the chapter, cognitive control is hypothesized to operate through a system of biased competition whereby relevant contextual information is maintained in the PFC to bias selection of relevant over irrelevant action pathways. However, we often encounter many aspects of our world that are simply irrelevant to our present purposes. Thus, for biased competition to work, it is important to selectively input relevant contextual information into working memory while keeping irrelevant information out. This function is termed *input gating*. Moreover, even when relevant information is gleaned from the environment and maintained in working memory, one may want to hang onto it for a period of time without its mere maintenance in the PFC actually influencing our behavior. Consider, for example, in a task with many subgoal steps, some information may need to be maintained but not influence the task until a specific time in the sequence of steps. Thus, one also needs a mechanism of *output gating* that determines which items currently maintained in working memory can currently influence behavior.

O'Reilly and Frank (2006) proposed a neural network architecture in which both input and output gating are achieved through interactions between the PFC and the striatum. From this perspective, the striatum disinhibits thalamic units to permit certain components of the sensory input to pass into the PFC (i.e., input gating). The striatum also determines which representations maintained in PFC influence selection of a motor response (i.e., output gating) via similar mechanism. However, in this case, the striatum disinhibits thalamic units that interact with the "output" cortical layers of PFC (corresponding to lamina 5/6). Importantly, the selection of which representations to input and output gate is learned via a common dopaminergic reward prediction error (RPE) signal that modulates activity in go and no-go striatal neuronal populations expressing D1 and D2 dopamine receptors, respectively (Frank, 2005; O'Reilly & Frank, 2006; Shen, Flajolet, Greengard, & Surmeier, 2008).

To adapt this model for hierarchical control and learning, we proposed that information maintained in rostral regions of PFC influences the striatal units that output-gate more caudal regions of PFC (Figure 19.8). To be concrete, consider our example second-order policy (see Figure 19.1) in which color determines which dimensions, shape or size, of the stimulus determine a response. The model would learn to input-gate color for maintenance by prePMd, and shape and orientation by PMd. Importantly, the maintenance of color by prePMd would influence the striatal output-gating units for the PMd. So, depending on the color maintained by prePMd, these units would gate the appropriate maintained stimulus feature (shape or orientation) into the output layer of PMd. And maintenance of this feature by PMd would influence selection of the motor response by the motor basal ganglia circuit.

Thus, in this model, hierarchical control, and the observed rostrocaudal organization of the frontal cortex, emerges from a series of nested corticostriatal loops. This proposed architecture is consistent with evidence from monkey tracing studies and probabilistic connectivity in humans showing a rostrocaudal organization of inputs from premotor/prefrontal cortex to corresponding regions of striatum (Draganski et al., 2008; Inase, Tokuno, Nambu, Akazawa, & Takada, 1999; Lehericy, Ducros, Krainik, et al., 2004; Lehericy, Ducros, Van de Moortele, et al., 2004; Postuma & Dagher, 2006). It also follows from the general anatomical property that inputs to striatum are strongest from cortical areas of closest proximity (Kemp & Powell, 1970).

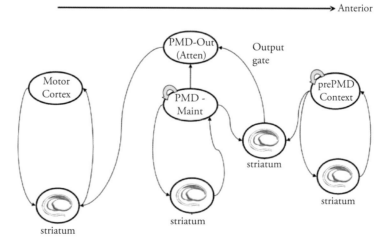

Figure. 19.8 Schematic of the neural net model of hierarchical control in frontal corticostriatal loops, from Frank and Badre (2012). Circles represent labeled regions of frontal cortex or striatum. Arrows indicate direction of influence, with a recursive arrow indicating a recurrent maintenance loop. From the model, rostral frontal regions influence output-gating dynamics between striatum and caudal regions of frontal cortex. So, in the schematic, maintenance of context by prePMd, influences the output gating loop between striatum and deep output layers of PMd, which in turn affects motor response gating by the motor loop.

A central feature of this nested architecture is that it permits rapid learning of hierarchical structure, as was observed in Badre et al. (2010). By contrast, in other versions of the model, which do not include a hierarchical architecture, learning is not as efficient or successful. Moreover, it suggests a mechanistic account for the decline in prePMd activation observed by Badre et al. (2010). Specifically, in the model, the representation of contextual information in prePMd, which constrains attention to one of the dimensions in PMd, is not adaptive during flat blocks in which no hierarchical structure is present. As such, prePMd layer activity comes to be associated with negative value and generates a negative RPE, which in turn, allows the striatum to learn not to gate contextual representations into this layer.

In order to test predictions of the neural net model with fMRI, we developed a second probabilistic "mixture of experts" model that abstracts the key computations of the neural net circuitry. However, this model can be fitted to the behavioral data of each participant in Badre et al. (2010) and so can provide estimates of the "latent states" of the participant at each point during the task. In other words, for a given trial, are they attending to the hierarchical rule? And, which rule are they using to determine their response? Based on these estimates, we were able to analyze two key components of the model in our fMRI data. First, we could assess which regions of the brain changed depending on the extent to which a participant attended to hierarchical rules vs. other rules. Second, because we would have an estimate of which rule and thus what outcome a participant anticipated for each, we could compute RPE.

The results from this analysis confirmed key predictions of the model and provided novel evidence for the nested corticostriatal structure it proposes. Specifically, we found greater prePMd activation in participants who searched for hierarchical rules more during learning than in those who did not. RPE estimates were generally associated with activation in striatum and frontal cortex (Figure 19.9a). However, when RPE was weighted by attention to hierarchical rules, only prePMD and a focal subregion of the striatum at the same rostrocaudal extent were activated (Figure 19.9b–d). Moreover, the hierarchical RPE signal in this striatal subregion (but not RPE in others) correlated with the decline in prePMd activity when no hierarchical structure existed (i.e., in the flat condition). This provided empirical support for the mechanistic explanation of this decline that emerged from the neural net model.

Thus, our results suggest that a specific corticostriatal circuit is involved in learning second-order hierarchical structure. This is in line with the broader hypothesis that each level of the hierarchy is associated with a specific corticostriatal loop and that hierarchical control emerges from this nested structure. Put another way, the observed rostrocaudal functional organization of the frontal cortex may emerge as a consequence of the way that frontal cortex interacts with the striatum, as a series of nested gating loops.

Conclusions

Our cognitive control system is hierarchical in nature. We can update and maintain information relevant to decisions at multiple levels of abstraction. This capacity for abstraction in control is likely a source of our remarkable cognitive flexibility.

Hierarchical control emerges from the functional organization of the frontal cortex. Progressively rostral regions of the frontal cortex appear to support cognitive control representations at increasing levels of abstraction. Moreover, the relationship of these subregions to each other is hierarchical, in the sense that neural activity in rostral regions appears to influence neural activity in caudal regions more than the reverse. Finally, at least in the context of hierarchical learning, it appears that this hierarchical architecture may emerge from a series of nested corticostriatal loops that permit rostral regions of PFC to differentially affect gating in caudal regions of the PFC. Given the ability of only a few such loops to support control over large policy structures, this simple nested gating architecture may be one key to the remarkable flexibility in our thought and action.

Future Directions

Following are questions to pursue further in future research:

• What is the relationship between the rostrocaudal organization of frontal cortex as observed in cognitive control of action and analogical and relational reasoning and intelligence?

• How does this organization develop, and how does its development affect learning and cognitive control in children?

• How does hierarchical cognitive control in goal-directed behavior relate to habitual behavior, which can also be expressed hierarchically?

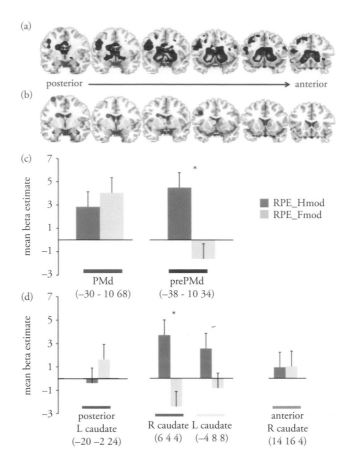

Figure 19.9 Results from tests of model predictions with fMRI (Badre & Frank, 2012). **a.** BOLD response to brain areas that track reward prediction error (RPE). Significant activations were observed across the entire striatum and prePMd. **b.** Functionally defined regions of interest (ROIs) for PMd, prePMd, and areas within caudate that are posterior to, at the same level as, and anterior to prePMd. **c.** Within cortical ROIs, prePMd tracked RPE specifically when the model-derived attentional weight to hierarchical rule (RPE_Hmod) was high, but not the flat rule (RPE_Fmod). PMd did not distinguish between hierarchical and flat rules in its sensitivity to RPE. **d.** Within caudate, areas at the same anterior-to-posterior level as prePMd tracked RPE modulated by attention to hierarchical relative to flat rule. Caudate areas more posterior and more anterior to prePMd were not sensitive to this distinction.

• How does this frontal organization fit within a broader network for cognitive control in the brain beyond local interactions in frontal cortex?

• Some evidence exists for a similar rostrocaudal organization along ventrolateral prefrontal cortex. What distinguishes this pathway from the dorsal gradient that has been the focus of research to date?

Acknowledgments

This work was supported by the National Institutes of Health (NS065046). I also wish to acknowledge my collaborators, including M. J. Frank, A. Kayser, and M. D'Esposito, on the work described in this chapter.

References

Asaad, W. F., Rainer, G., & Miller, E. K. (1998). Neural activity in the primate prefrontal cortex during associative learning. *Neuron, 21*(6), 1399–1407.

Asaad, W. F., Rainer, G., & Miller, E. K. (2000). Task-specific neural activity in the primate prefrontal cortex. *Journal of Neurophysiology, 84*(1), 451–459.

Badre, D. (2008). Cognitive control, hierarchy, and the rostrocaudal organization of the frontal lobes. *Trends in Cognitive Sciences, 12*(5), 193–200.

Badre, D. (2010). Is prefrontal cortex necessary for the storage and acquisition of relational concepts? *Cognitive Neuroscience, 1*(2), 140–141.

Badre, D., & D'Esposito, M. (2007). Functional magnetic resonance imaging evidence for a hierarchical organization of the prefrontal cortex. *Journal of Cognitive Neuroscience, 19*(12), 2082–2099.

Badre, D., & D'Esposito, M. (2009). Is the rostro-caudal axis of the frontal lobe hierarchical? *Nature Reviews Neuroscience, 10*(9), 659–669.

Badre, D., & Frank, M. J. (2012). Mechanisms of hierarchical reinforcement learning in corticostriatal circuits, Part II: Evidence from fMRI. *Cerebral Cortex*, *22*(3), 527–536.

Badre, D., Hoffman, J., Cooney, J. W., & D'Esposito, M. (2009). Hierarchical cognitive control deficits following damage to the human frontal lobe. *Nature Neuroscience*, *12*(4), 515–522.

Badre, D., Kayser, A. S., & D'Esposito, M. (2010). Frontal cortex and the discovery of abstract action rules. *Neuron*, *66*(2), 315–326.

Badre, D., Poldrack, R. A., Pare-Blagoev, E. J., Insler, R. Z., & Wagner, A. D. (2005). Dissociable controlled retrieval and generalized selection mechanisms in ventrolateral prefrontal cortex. *Neuron*, *47*(6), 907–918.

Badre, D., & Wagner, A. D. (2004). Selection, integration, and conflict monitoring; Assessing the nature and generality of prefrontal cognitive control mechanisms. *Neuron*, *41*(3), 473–487.

Badre, D., & Wagner, A. D. (2007). Left ventrolateral prefrontal cortex and the cognitive control of memory. *Neuropsychologia*, *45*(13), 2883–2901.

Botvinick, M., & Plaut, D. C. (2004). Doing without schema hierarchies: A recurrent connectionist approach to normal and impaired routine sequential action. *Psychological Review*, *111*(2), 395–429.

Botvinick, M. M. (2007). Multilevel structure in behaviour and in the brain: A model of Fuster's hierarchy. *Philosophical Transactions of the Royal Society of London Series B: Biological Science*, *362*(1485), 1615–1626.

Botvinick, M. M. (2008). Hierarchical models of behavior and prefrontal function. *Trends in Cognitive Sciences*, *12*(5), 201–208.

Botvinick, M. M., Niv, Y., & Barto, A. C. (2009). Hierarchically organized behavior and its neural foundations: A reinforcement learning perspective. *Cognition*, *113*(3), 262–280.

Braver, T. S., & Bongiolatti, S. R. (2002). The role of frontopolar cortex in subgoal processing during working memory. *Neuroimage*, *15*(3), 523–536.

Braver, T. S., Reynolds, J. R., & Donaldson, D. I. (2003). Neural mechanisms of transient and sustained cognitive control during task switching. *Neuron*, *39*(4), 713–726.

Bunge, S. A. (2004). How we use rules to select actions: A review of evidence from cognitive neuroscience. *Cognitive, Affective & Behavioral Neuroscience*, *4*(4), 564–579.

Bunge, S. A., Kahn, I., Wallis, J. D., Miller, E. K., & Wagner, A. D. (2003). Neural circuits subserving the retrieval and maintenance of abstract rules. *Journal of Neurophysiology*, *90*(5), 3419–3428.

Bunge, S. A., Wendelken, C., Badre, D., & Wagner, A. D. (2005). Analogical reasoning and prefrontal cortex: Evidence for separable retrieval and integration mechanisms. *Cerebral Cortex*, *15*(3), 239–249.

Butterfield, E. C., Wambold, C., & Belmont, J. M. (1973). On the theory and practice of improving short-term memory. *American Journal of Mental Deficiency*, *77*, 654–669.

Chase, W. G., & Simon, H. A. (1973). The mind's eye in chess. In W. G. Chase (Ed.), *Visual information processing* (pp. 215–281). New York: Academic Press.

Christoff, K., & Gabrieli, J. D. E. (2000). The frontopolar cortex and human cognition: Evidence for a rostrocaudal hierarchal organization within the human prefrontal cortex. *Psychobiology*, *28*, 168–186.

Christoff, K., & Keramatian, K. (2007). Abstraction of mental representations: Theoretical considerations and neuroscientific evidence. In S. A. Bunge & J. D. Wallis (Eds.), *Perspectives on rule-guided behavior* (pp. 107–126). New York: Oxford University Press.

Christoff, K., Keramatian, K., Gordon, A. M., Smith, R., & Madler, B. (2009). Prefrontal organization of cognitive control according to levels of abstraction. *Brain Research*, *1286*, 94–105.

Christoff, K., Ream, J. M., Geddes, L. P. T., & Gabrieli, J. D. E. (2003). Evaluating self-generated information: Anterior prefrontal contributions to human cognition. *Behavioral Neuroscience*, *117*(6), 1161–1168.

Cohen, J. D., Dunbar, K., & McClelland, J. L. (1990). On the control of automatic processes: A parallel distributed processing account of the Stroop effect. *Psychological Review*, *97*, 332–361.

Cohen, J. D., & Servan-Schreiber, D. (1992). Context, cortex, and dopamine: A connectionist approach to behavior and biology in schizophrenia. *Psychological Review*, *99*, 45–77.

Cooper, R. P., & Shallice, T. (2006). Hierarchical schemas and goals in the control of sequential behavior. *Psychological Review*, *113*, 887–916.

Desimone, R., & Duncan, J. (1995). Neural mechanisms of selective visual attention. *Annual Review of Neuroscience*, *18*, 193–222.

Donaldson, D. I., Petersen, S. E., Ollinger, J. M., & Buckner, R. L. (2001). Dissociating state and item components of recognition memory using fMRI. *Neuroimage*, *13*(1), 129–142.

Draganski, B., Kherif, F., Kloppel, S., Cook, P. A., Alexander, D. C., Parker, G. J., et al. (2008). Evidence for segregated and integrative connectivity patterns in the human basal ganglia. *Journal of Neuroscience*, *28*(28), 7143–7152.

Estes, W. K. (1982). Learning, memory, and intelligence. In R. J. Sternberg (Ed.), *Handbook of intelligence* (pp. 170–224). New York: Cambridge University Press.

Frank, M. J. (2005). Dynamic dopamine modulation in the basal ganglia: a neurocomputational account of cognitive deficits in medicated and nonmedicated Parkinsonism. *Journal of Cognitive Neuroscience*, *17*(1), 51–72.

Frank, M. J., & Badre, D. (2012). Mechanisms of hierarchical reinforcement learning in corticostriatal circuits, Part I: Theory. *Cerebral Cortex*, *22*(3), 509–526.

Frank, M. J., & O'Reilly R. C. (2006). A mechanistic account of striatal dopamine function in human cognition: Psychopharmacological studies with cabergoline and haloperidol. *Behavioral Neuroscience*, *120*(3), 497–517.

Fuster, J. M. (1997). *The prefrontal cortex: Anatomy, physiology, and neuropsychology of the frontal lobe* (3rd ed.). Philadelphia: Lippincott-Raven.

Fuster, J. M. (2001). The prefrontal cortex—an update: Time is of the essence. *Neuron*, *30*(2), 319–333.

Fuster, J. M. (2004). Upper processing stages of the perception-action cycle. *Trends in Cognitive Sciences*, *8*(4), 143–145.

Fuster, J. M., Bodner, M., & Kroger, J. (2000). Cross-modal and cross-temporal association in neurons of frontal cortex. *Nature*, *405*, 347–351.

Gick, M. L., & Holyoak, K. J. (1980). Analogical problem solving. *Cognitive Psychology*, *12*, 306–355.

Gick, M. L., & Holyoak, K. J. (1983). Schema induction and analogical transfer. *Cognitive Psychology*, *15*, 1–38.

Golde, M., von Cramon, D. Y., & Schubotz, R. I. (2010). Differential role of anterior prefrontal and premotor cortex in the processing of relational information. *Neuroimage*, *49*(3), 2890–2900.

Halford, G. S. (1993). *Children's understanding: The development of mental models*. Hillsdale, NJ: Lawrence Erlbaum.

Inase, M., Tokuno, H., Nambu, A., Akazawa, T., & Takada, M. (1999). Corticostriatal and corticosubthalamic input zones from the presupplementary motor area in the macaque monkey: Comparison with the input zones from the supplementary motor area. *Brain Research*, *833*(2), 191–201.

Kemp, J. M., & Powell, T. P. (1970). The cortico-striate projection in the monkey. *Brain*, *93*(3), 525–546.

Koechlin, E., Basso, G., Pietrini, P., Panzer, S., & Grafman, J. (1999). The role of the anterior prefrontal cortex in human cognition. *Nature*, *399*(6732), 148–151.

Koechlin, E., Corrado, G., Pietrini, P., & Grafman, J. (2000). Dissociating the role of the medial and lateral anterior prefrontal cortex in human planning. *Proceedings of the National Academy of Sciences U S A*, *97*(13), 7651–7656.

Koechlin, E., & Jubault, T. (2006). Broca's area and the hierarchical organization of human behavior. *Neuron*, *50*(6), 963–974.

Koechlin, E., Ody, C., & Kouneiher, F. (2003). The architecture of cognitive control in the human prefrontal cortex. *Science*, *302*(5648), 1181–1185.

Koechlin, E., & Summerfield, C. (2007). An information theoretical approach to prefrontal executive function. *Trends in Cognitive Sciences*, *11*(6), 229–235.

Kostopoulos, P., & Petrides, M. (2003). The mid-ventrolateral prefrontal cortex: Insights into its role in memory retrieval. *European Journal of Neuroscience*, *17*(7), 1489–1497.

Kouneiher, F., Charron, S., & Koechlin, E. (2009). Motivation and cognitive control in the human prefrontal cortex. *Nature Neuroscience*, *12*(7), 939–945.

Krawczyk, D. C., McClelland, M. M., Donovan, C. M., Tillman, G. D., & Maguire, M. J. (2010). An fMRI investigation of cognitive stages in reasoning by analogy. *Brain Research*, *1342*, 63–73.

Krawczyk, D. C., Michelle McClelland, M., & Donovan, C. M. (2011). A hierarchy for relational reasoning in the prefrontal cortex. *Cortex*, *47*(5), 588–597.

Lashley, K. S. (1951). The problem of serial order in behavior. In L. A. Jeffress (Ed.), *Cerebral mechanisms in behavior* (pp. 112–136). New York: Wiley.

Lehericy, S., Ducros, M., Krainik, A., Francois, C., Van de Moortele, P. F., Ugurbil, K., et al. (2004). 3-D diffusion tensor axonal tracking shows distinct SMA and pre-SMA projections to the human striatum. *Cerebral Cortex*, *14*(12), 1302–1309.

Lehericy, S., Ducros, M., Van de Moortele, P. F., Francois, C., Thivard, L., Poupon, C., et al. (2004). Diffusion tensor fiber tracking shows distinct corticostriatal circuits in humans. *Annals of Neurology*, *55*(4), 522–529.

Miller, E. K., & Cohen, J. D. (2001). An integrative theory of prefrontal cortex function. *Annual Review of Neuroscience*, *24*, 167–202.

Miller, G. A., Galanter, E., & Pribram, K. H. (1960). *Plans and the structure of behavior*. New York: Holt, Rinehart and Winston.

Newell, A. (1990). *Unified theories of cognition*. Cambridge, MA: Harvard University Press.

O'Reilly, R. C. (2010). The what and how of prefrontal cortical organization. *Trends in Neuroscience*, *33*(8), 355–361.

O'Reilly, R. C., & Frank, M. J. (2006). Making working memory work: A computational model of learning in the prefrontal cortex and basal ganglia. *Neural Computation*, *18*(2), 283–328.

Paine, R. W., & Tani, J. (2005). How hierarchical control self-organizes in artificial adaptive systems. *Adaptive Behavior*, *13*, 211–225.

Passingham, R. E., & Rowe, J. B. (2002). Dorsal prefrontal cortex: Maintenance in memory or attentional selection? In D. T. Stuss & R. T. Knight (Eds.), *Principles of frontal lobe function* (pp. 221–232). Oxford: Oxford University Press.

Petrides, M. (2005). Lateral prefrontal cortex: Architectonic and functional organization. *Philosophical Transactions of the Royal Society of London, Series B: Biological Science*, *360*(1456), 781–795.

Postuma, R. B., & Dagher, A. (2006). Basal ganglia functional connectivity based on a meta-analysis of 126 positron emission tomography and functional magnetic resonance imaging publications. *Cerebral Cortex*, *16*(10), 1508–1521.

Ramnani, N., & Owen, A. M. (2004). Anterior prefrontal cortex: Insights into function from anatomy and neuroimaging. *Nature Reviews Neuroscience*, *5*(3), 184–194.

Robin, N., & Holyoak, K. J. (1995). Relational complexity and the functions of the prefrontal cortex. In M. S. Gazzaniga (Ed.), *The cognitive neurosciences* (pp. 987–997). Cambridge, MA: MIT Press.

Rosenbaum, D. A. (1987). Hierarchical organization of motor programs. In S. Wise (Ed.), *Neural and behavioral approaches to higher brain functions* (pp. 45–66). New York: Wiley.

Schank, R. C., & Abelson, R. (1977). *Scripts, plans, goals, and understanding*. Hove, UK: Lawrence Erlbaum Associates.

Shen, W., Flajolet, M., Greengard, P., & Surmeier, D. J. (2008). Dichotomous dopaminergic control of striatal synaptic plasticity. *Science*, *321*(5890), 848–851.

Solomon, M., Ozonoff, S. J., Cummings, N., & Carter, C. S. (2008). Cognitive control in autism spectrum disorders. *International Journal of Developmental Neuroscience*, *26*(2), 239–247.

Speed, A. (2010). Abstract relational categories, graded persistence, and prefrontal cortical representation. *Cognitive Neuroscience*, *1*(2), 126–152.

Stuss, D. T., & Benson, D. F. (1987). The frontal lobes and control of cognition and memory. In E. Perecman (Ed.), *The frontal lobes revisited* (pp. 141–158). New York: IRBN Press.

Vincent, J. L., Kahn, I., Snyder, A. Z., Raichle, M. E., & Buckner, R. L. (2008). Evidence for a frontoparietal control system revealed by intrinsic functional connectivity. *Journal of Neurophysiology*, *100*(6), 3328–3342.

Visscher, K. M., Miezin, F. M., Kelly, J. E., Buckner, R. L., Donaldson, D. I., McAvoy, M. P., et al. (2003). Mixed blocked/event-related designs separate transient and sustained activity in fMRI. *Neuroimage*, *19*(4), 1694–1708.

Volle, E., Gilbert, S. J., Benoit, R. G., & Burgess, P. W. (2010). Specialization of the rostral prefrontal cortex for distinct analogy processes. *Cerebral Cortex*, *20*(11), 2647–2659.

Wagner, A. D., Paré-Blagoev, E. J., Clark, J., & Poldrack, R. A. (2001). Recovering meaning: Left prefrontal cortex guides controlled semantic retrieval. *Neuron, 31,* 329–338.

Wallis, J. D., Anderson, K. C., & Miller, E. K. (2001). Single neurons in prefrontal cortex encode abstract rules. *Nature, 411,* 953–956.

Wallis, J. D., & Miller, E. K. (2003). From rule to response: Neuronal processes in the premotor and prefrontal cortex. *Journal of Neurophysiology, 90*(3), 1790–1806.

White, I. M., & Wise, S. P. (1999). Rule-dependent neuronal activity in the prefrontal cortex. *Experimental Brain Research, 126*(3), 315–335.

Thinking

Kalina Christoff

Abstract

Most neuroscientific investigations of human thought have examined it through the prism of task-based paradigms. Thinking is often seen in terms of reasoning and problems solving, or the goal-directed mental processes that occur in the course of solving a particular task. Such goal-directed thought has been closely linked to the functions of the lateral prefrontal cortex and its associated mechanism of cognitive control. Goal-directed thought is often organized in a hierarchical fashion and can rely on relational reasoning and different levels of abstraction in processing—all functions that have been linked to lateral prefrontal function and organization. The last decade of research, however, has seen an upsurge of interest in undirected thought phenomena such as mind wandering and spontaneous thought. Undirected thought processes have been linked to recruitment of the default network of brain regions, the executive system, and the temporal lobe memory network. The terminology and paradigms for investigating undirected thought are still being developed, and research is moving beyond strictly task-based paradigms and toward incorporating introspective first-person reports in order to better understand undirected thought. While goal-directed and undirected thought appear to be in some ways opposites, another form of thought, creative thinking, can bring them together to form a unique approach in tapping the fullness of human mental resources. Finally, recursive thought phenomena such as meta-awareness and introspection appear to be closely linked to the functions of the anterior prefrontal cortex. However, a distinction between meta-awareness of content and process may need to be made in order to better explain the role of this region in recursive thought.

Key Words: goal-directed thought, relational processing, levels of abstraction, undirected thought, mind wandering, spontaneous thought, creative thought, default network, executive network, memory network

Introduction

In the vast majority of textbooks on psychology, the term *thinking* appears in chapters on problem solving, reasoning, creativity, and decision-making (e.g., Sternberg, 2006). This reflects the predominant view of thinking as a goal-directed phenomenon, a mental process deliberately employed toward solving a problem or making progress on a task. In contrast, another much less dominant view of thinking has emphasized its undirected, spontaneous nature—from William James' discussion of

the thought's tendency to "drift" (James, 1980), to research on daydreaming, during the 1960s (Antrobus, Singer, & Greenberg, 1966; Singer & Schonbar, 1961), to more recent research on spontaneous thought and mind wandering (Christoff, Gordon, Smallwood, Smith, & Schooler, 2009; Christoff, Ream, & Gabrieli, 2004; Klinger & Cox, 1987; Smallwood & Schooler, 2006; Teasdale et al., 1995).

Within cognitive neuroscience, goal-directed aspects of thinking have received the most scientific attention, until recently. The last decade has seen an upsurge of interest in undirected thought phenomena such as mind wandering and spontaneous cognition. This chapter reviews the different forms of thought that have been subject to neuroscientific investigation and the state of knowledge about each one of them.

Different Forms of Thought from a Neuroscientific Perspective

Based on theoretical understanding of the functions of the brain's executive, default, and memory networks, three general types of thought can be outlined: goal-directed, spontaneous, and creative (Christoff, Gordon, & Smith, 2011). The most studied is *goal-directed* thought, which occurs frequently during reasoning, problem-solving, and decision-making paradigms. Goal-directed thought is achieved by consciously representing current and desired states and linking these representations through a series of actions that attempt to transform the current to the desired state. The other two forms of thought are studied to a much lesser extent. *Undirected* thought, including mind wandering, appears to be in many ways the opposite of goal-directed thought. Between these two extreme ends of a thought continuum lies yet another form of thinking, *creative* thought, which appears to share commonalities with both goal-directed and undirected thought.

Goal-Directed Thinking

The region of the brain most closely linked to goal-directed thought is the prefrontal cortex (PFC). Patient studies throughout the last century have repeatedly demonstrated that lesions to the PFC lead to profound deficits in goal-directed thought (e.g., Duncan, Burgess, & Emslie, 1995; Luria, 1966; Milner, 1964; Shallice, 1982). Neuroimaging findings have yielded further support for this link, arguing for a specific role of the two most anterior lateral prefrontal subregions, the dorsolateral PFC (DLPFC) and the rostrolateral PFC (RLPFC), in planning, reasoning, and problem solving (for reviews, see Christoff & Gabrieli, 2000; Unterrainer & Owen, 2006).

The crucial role that PFC plays in goal-directed thought is closely linked to its ability to influence other cortical regions—a function known as cognitive control (Miller & Cohen, 2001). Cognitive control is the process by which PFC selectively biases currently relevant representations in other parts of the brain, thereby helping focus attention on currently relevant stimuli while diminishing attention toward other competing stimuli (Desimone &

Duncan, 1995). The PFC may play an analogous role during goal-directed thinking, by biasing those thoughts that are relevant to the current goal and allowing them to be selected among other competing thoughts, thus keeping mental content "on track" and producing a logically connected train of thought (Christoff, Gordon, et al., 2011). Cognitive control and its implementation through the recruitment of lateral PFC appear to be some of the characteristic features of goal-directed thinking.

HIERARCHICAL ORGANIZATION

Goal-directed thought is often hierarchically organized in the sense that it aims at the achievement of a number of goals and subgoals. It also tends to proceed in sequential steps, each step working with the products and outcomes of previous mental steps. During the last decade, a number of models of goal-directed thought organization within the lateral PFC have been proposed (Badre & D'Esposito, 2007; Christoff & Gabriel, 2000; Christoff & Keramatian, 2007; Koechlin, Ody, & Kouneiher, 2003; Koechlin & Summerfield, 2007). Although the specific mapping of regions to functions differs across models, all share some common properties: more posterior PFC regions control relatively simple mappings of stimuli to actions, while increasingly anterior PFC regions control increasingly complex and abstract relationships among rules. It is generally agreed that cognitive control within the PFC can be organized in a hierarchical fashion, with more anterior PFC regions exerting control over more posterior PFC regions (Christoff & Gabriel, 2000; Koechlin et al., 2003).

The hierarchy of goal-directed thought in the PFC is often described in processing terms, with more anterior regions assumed to work by re-representing the products of processes performed by more posterior regions (Badre & D'Esposito, 2007; Christoff & Gabriel, 2000; Fletcher & Henson, 2001; Koechlin et al., 2003). This hierarchical processing arrangement, however, is not a permanent characteristic of prefrontal function, but appears to be only one of the ways in which lateral PFC regions can organize themselves to meet current task demands (Christoff, Keramatian, Gordon, Smith, & Madler, 2009). A different way in which the PFC can organize goal-directed thinking is according to the level of abstraction in thought.

LEVELS OF ABSTRACTION

Discussions of abstraction are ubiquitous in the cognitive neuroscience of goal-directed thought, with terms such as *abstract cognitive abilities*, *abstract thought*, and *abstract rules* almost invariably employed when lateral PFC functions are discussed (e.g., Baker et al., 1996; Bunge, Kahn, Wallis, Miller, & Wagner, 2003; Christoff & Gabriel, 2000; Luria, 1966; Miller, Nieder, Freedman, & Wallis, 2003; Milner, 1963; O'Reilly, Noelle, Braver, & Cohen, 2002; Sakai & Passingham, 2003). Indeed, the PFC has been implicated in maintaining information at varying degrees of abstraction: from concrete information such as specific objects and perceptual features (e.g., Fuster, 1980; Goldman-Rakic, 1987), to abstract rules about the relationship between objects (e.g., "same" vs. "different"; Wallis, Anderson, & Miller, 2001), to highly abstract task contexts that are themselves comprised of multiple abstract rules (Cohen, Dunbar, & McClelland, 1990; Koechlin et al., 2003; O'Reilly et al., 2002; Sakai & Passingham, 2003).

Research in nonhuman primates (Dias, Robbins, & Roberts, 1996, 1997) has suggested that different prefrontal regions may support information at varying levels of abstraction (O'Reilly et al., 2002; Rougier, Noelle, Braver, Cohen, & O'Reilly, 2005), with dorsal PFC supporting abstract dimensional representations and orbitofrontal PFC supporting concrete featural representations. Adding to these results, human neuroimaging studies have implicated the most anterior part of the lateral PFC, the RLPFC, in supporting representations at some of the highest levels of abstraction, while associating less abstract representations with more posterior PFC regions such as the dorsolateral (DLPFC) and ventrolateral (VLPFC) PFC (Bunge, Wallis, et al., 2005; Christoff, Keramatian, et al., 2009; Christoff, Ream, Geddes, & Gabrieli, 2003; Koechlin et al., 2003; Sakai & Passingham, 2003; Smith, Keramatian, & Christoff, 2007; Wendelken, Nakhabenko, Donohue, Carter, & Bunge, 2008).

A recently emerging view is that the lateral PFC can organize itself according to cognitive control at minimally three levels of abstraction (Bunge & Zelazo, 2006; Christoff, 2003; Christoff & Keramatian, 2007; Christoff, Keramatian, et al., 2009), with the most anterior part corresponding to the highest level of abstraction. One of the biggest challenges in providing evidence for this view has been the confound of task difficulty. In general, tasks that are associated with relatively low task difficulty typically recruit posterior PFC regions. As task difficulty increases, however, PFC recruitment spreads in an increasingly anterior direction to include first DLPFC and then RLPFC (e.g., Baker

et al., 1996; Braver et al., 1997; Christoff et al., 2001; D'Esposito, Postle, Ballard, & Lease, 1999; Kroger et al., 2002; Rypma, Prabhakaran, Desmond, Glover, & Gabrieli, 1999; Smith & Jonides, 1997; van den Heuvel et al., 2003). While difficulty frequently increases in experimental paradigms that have been used to demonstrate lateral PFC organization according to level of abstraction (e.g., Badre & D'Espositio, 2007; Koechlin & Summerfield, 2007), a recent study shows that that such organization can also be demonstrated in the absence of increasing difficulty (Christoff, Keramatian et al., 2009). Thus, above and beyond complexity of mental processing, the level of abstraction in human thought appears to map onto an organization of lateral PFC.

RELATIONAL REASONING

A unique quality of human thought is our highly developed ability to reason about relations among items. This includes reasoning by analogy and comprehending metaphors (Gentner, Holyoak, & Kokinov, 2001). Such relational reasoning, and, in particular, our ability to process multiple relations simultaneously, has been linked to the functions of the lateral PFC (Robin & Holyoak, 1995; Waltz et al., 1999). A dominant trend of the research in goal-directed thought has examined the specific linkages between relational reasoning processes and lateral PFC functions.

Many goal-directed forms of thought involve relational processing (Halford, Wilson, & Phillips, 2010). For example, complex planning requires working with the relationships between multiple subgoals and organizing them in a subgoal hierarchy (Carpenter, Just, & Shell, 1990; Shallice & Burgess, 1991). Building an optimal subgoal hierarchy would require considering multiple subgoal relations simultaneously (Halford, Wilson, & Phillips, 1998). Similarly, dual tasks require executing two action sequences in parallel. The management of dual tasks, therefore, would demand the integration of the temporal relations between these action sequences (Christoff et al., 2001). The integration of relations may be one of the common factors linking diverse goal-directed thought processes.

The neuroimaging literature on relational reasoning has demonstrated the presence of an overall hierarchy of relational reasoning in the lateral PFC (Bunge, Wendelken, Badre, & Wagner, 2005; Christoff et al., 2001; Green, Fugelsang, Kraemer, Shamosh, & Dunbar, 2006; Krawczyk, Michelle McClelland, & Donovan, 2011; Kroger et al., 2002;

Wendelken et al., 2008). Problem-solving tasks that involve reasoning about only one relation at a time tend to recruit mostly posterior lateral PFC cortices (Christoff et al., 2001; Krawczyk et al., 2011; Kroger et al., 2002). When multiple relations need to integrated, however, neural recruitment extends more and more anteriorly; one of the more consistent findings from the relational reasoning literature is that the process of relational integration recruits specifically the most anterior lateral PFC subregion, the RLPFC (Bunge, Wendelken, et al., 2005; Christoff et al., 2001, 2003; Green et al., 2006; Krawczyk et al., 2011; Kroger et al., 2002; Wendelken et al., 2008). This hierarchical pattern of recruitment has been linked to the hierarchical organization of lateral PFC functions according to levels of abstraction: Reasoning about single relations tends to involve more concrete representations, and as the complexity of relational reasoning and integration increases, the level of abstraction in thought increases as well (Christoff & Keramatian, 2007; Krawczyk et al., 2011).

In summary, goal-directed thought seems closely linked to the functions of the lateral PFC and its associated mechanism of cognitive control. It is often organized in a hierarchical fashion and can rely on relational reasoning and different levels of abstraction in processing—all functions that have been linked to lateral prefrontal function and organization. Although the role of regions outside of the PFC has also been discussed, such discussion has been relatively sparse. However, the processes related to goal-directed thought are most likely subserved by an interconnected and widely distributed system of cortical and subcortical regions. A more complete understanding of goal-directed thought will ultimately require a fuller appreciation of how the PFC, with its subregional distinction and functional organization, influences, and is in turn influenced by, other brain regions.

Undirected Thinking

While goal-directed thinking has received the lion's share of neuroscientific attention, its counterpart, the undirected thought flow that comes to mind unbidden and without effort, has remained largely on the sidelines of scientific research. The last decade, however, marked a resurgence of interest in the neural basis of undirected thought. There is no clear agreement about the most appropriate terminology to use. For example, is all daydreaming undirected? Is mind wandering the same as daydreaming? These questions remain unanswered. It is clear, however, that undirected thought forms a large part of our mental experience. Ninety-six percent of American adults report some kind of daydreaming each day (Singer & McCraven, 1961), and approximately 30% of thoughts that people experience in their daily lives can be classified as mind wandering, as defined by their lack of relation to the current task (Kane et al., 2007; Klinger & Cox, 1987). Furthermore, as many as 50% of thoughts can be classified as daydreaming, defined as a nonworking thought that was either spontaneous or fanciful (Klinger, 2009). Given this striking prevalence of undirected thought in our mental experience, it is clear that understanding its neuroscientific underpinnings is a necessary step toward improving our overall understanding of human thought.

The terms *spontaneous thought* (Christoff, Gordon et al., 2011; Christoff et al., 2004), *stimulus-independent thought* (Gilbert, Dumontheil, Simons, Frith, & Burgess, 2007; Mason et al., 2007a, b; McGuire, Paulesu, Frackowiak, & Frith, 1996), and *mind wandering* (Christoff, Gordon et al., 2009; Schooler et al., 2011; Smallwood & Schooler, 2006) have been used most frequently during the last decade of neuroscientific investigations. These terms are sometimes used interchangeably, although they are by no means the same thing. Furthermore, the definition of each of these terms is often different across different researchers and sometimes even across different publications by the same researchers.

This terminological fluidity is understandable; the neuroscience of undirected thought is still in its infancy. To some extent, such fluidity is useful in that it allows researchers to continue to improve their definitions as they learn more about the relevant phenomena. Partly because of this terminological uncertainty and partly because the experimental paradigms for its study are still developing, it is impossible to say at this point that undirected thinking is preferentially linked to any one brain system in the same way that goal-directed thought is preferentially linked to the lateral PFC functions. A connection between undirected thought and the default network has been empirically demonstrated on a number of occasions (e.g., Christoff, Gordon, et al., 2009; Mason et al., 2007a, b). However, other brain networks such as the executive system and the temporal lobe memory network appear to be equally involved (Christoff, Gordon et al., 2009; Christoff et al., 2004; Stark & Squire, 2001).

This section reviews the three most frequently investigated forms of thought that are considered to be largely undirected. Almost all of neuroscientific investigations thus far have used rest as an experimental paradigm to study undirected thought. During rest, subjects are simply instructed to do nothing. No experimental task is given to them, and they are typically presented with a blank screen in front of them while they are lying in the scanner. This minimizes the external perceptual and cognitive demands on subjects, and as behavioral research has consistently shown (Filler & Giambra, 1973; Giambra & Grodsky, 1989), conditions of low external demands result in high rates of undirected thoughts, such as daydreaming, mind wandering, or stimulus-independent thought. However, the existence of such undirected thoughts during rest is only indirectly inferred. By contrast, using experience sampling—a procedure during which subjects are asked to report on the quality of their thought experience in an online fashion, as these thoughts occur in the scanner—offers a more direct way of investigating undirected thought processes but has only begun to be used (Christoff, Gordon et al., 2009). As the field progresses, both the experimental paradigms and the terminology will undoubtedly become more sophisticated.

SPONTANEOUS THOUGHT

Spontaneous thought can be defined as the unintended, nonworking, noninstrumental mental content that comes to mind unbidden and effortlessly (Klinger, 2009). What distinguishes spontaneous thoughts from deliberate thoughts is the way in which they occur and the extent to which the thinker deliberately directs them (Klinger, 2009). Conceptually, spontaneous thought differs from mind wandering and stimulus-independent thought. For example, if *mind wandering* is defined as thinking that's unrelated to the ongoing task or activity, then mind wandering can occur either spontaneously (as in when we catch our mind having wandered off during the last paragraph of whatever we were reading) or deliberately (as in when we "tune out" during a boring lecture and instead direct our thoughts toward some future event of greater interest). Similarly, stimulus-independent thought—thinking about something that is unrelated to what we are currently perceiving—can also occur either spontaneously or deliberately.

In neuroscientific practice so far, spontaneous thought has only been examined in terms of the mental processes that occur during rest. During conditions of low external demands such as rest or a highly practiced task, individuals often report experiencing spontaneously arising thoughts (Klinger

& Cox, 1987; Singer, 1966). The contents of such spontaneous thoughts often have to do with personally significant or concerning events (Singer, 1966). Assuming that the neural activations observed during rest conditions reflect to a large extent the occurrence of spontaneous cognition, investigators have identified a number of brain region that appear to be preferentially linked to spontaneous thought, including midline default network regions (posterior cingulate cortex/precuneus and anterior medial PFC), temporopolar cortex and medial temporal lobe structures (hippocampus and parahippocampus), and the RLPFC.

What role does each of these brain areas play in spontaneous thought? Researchers have hypothesized that activation of the posterior cingulate cortex (PCC) and the anterior medial PFC may reflect the affective, self-relevant nature of spontaneous thoughts (Andrews-Hanna, Reidler, Sepulcre, Poulin, & Buckner, 2010). Medial PFC recruitment may also reflect acts of spontaneous mentalizing, that is, imagining the thoughts and intentions of other individuals (Spiers & Maguire, 2006). The temporopolar cortex may also contribute to spontaneous mentalizing (Spiers & Maguire, 2006). By virtue of its anatomical connectivity with medial temporal lobe structures and its role in autobiographical memory (Graham, Lee, Brett, & Patterson, 2003), the temporopolar cortex may also participate in experiencing spontaneously arising memories (Christoff et al., 2004).

The functional role of the precuneus is currently a subject for intense investigation; findings are starting to converge to show that it plays an important role in episodic memory retrieval and self-related mental imagery during rest (Cavanna & Trimble, 2006). Similarly, the medial temporal lobe structures may contribute to spontaneously retrieved memories (Christoff et al., 2004; Gelbard-Sagiv, Mukamel, Harel, Malach, & Fried, 2008; Stark & Squire, 2001) and the simulation of future events (Buckner, 2010).

Finally, the link between RLPFC and spontaneous thought may seem at first surprising, given extensive evidence from task-based paradigms that this brain region is specifically involved in deliberate, metacognitive processes such as monitoring one's own internal cognitive states and higher-order reasoning (Christoff & Gabrieli, 2000; Christoff et al., 2001, 2003). The consistent RLPFC recruitment during rest (Christoff et al., 2004; Shulman et al., 1997) has been suggested to reflect the metacognitive evaluation and manipulation of self-generated thoughts (Christoff et al., 2004; Dumontheil, Gilbert, Frith, & Burgess, 2010). However, such evaluation and manipulation are generally considered to be deliberate, goal-oriented mental processes and do not generally occur spontaneously. Instead, RLPFC's role in spontaneous thought may be more closely linked to the maintenance of an abstract mindset (Christoff & Keramatian, 2007; Christoff, Keramatian, et al., 2009), which may enable the spontaneous thought flow to occur uninterrupted by attention to our ongoing concrete (i.e., sensory and specific) perceptions.

It should be emphasized, however, that all these hypotheses regarding the role of different brain regions in spontaneous thought are based on indirect inferences and our knowledge of these regions' functions from task-based research. To further our knowledge of the neuroscience of spontaneous thought, it will be necessary to conduct direct empirical investigations in which subject's introspective reports about their spontaneously occurring thoughts, obtained in a trial-by-trial basis, can be linked to neural recruitment (Christoff, Cosmelli, Legrand, & Thompson, 2011). This method, known as thought sampling (Christoff et al., 2004; Teasdale, Proctor, Lloyd, & Baddeley, 1993) or experience sampling (Christoff, Gordon et al., 2009; Kahneman, Krueger, Schkade, Schwarz, & Stone, 2004), has not yet been used in the neuroscientific study of spontaneous thought.

STIMULUS-INDEPENDENT THOUGHT

Within the context of cognitive neuroscience, the term *stimulus independent thought* is sometimes used interchangeably with the term *mind wandering* (e.g., Mason et al., 2007a, b). However, the two are conceptually different. In general, stimulus-independent thought is easier to define than mind wandering. By definition, stimulus-independent thought is decoupled from current sensory information (Antrobus, 1968; Teasdale et al., 1993). This could occur in the form of mind wandering away from a task (Mason et al., 2007a, b), but it can also occur in the form of complex task-related thought that goes beyond the current sensory information (Gilbert, Simons, Frith, & Burgess, 2006). Stimulus-independent thought is typically contrasted to stimulus-oriented thought, which reflects attention toward the current external sensory environment (Gilbert, Simons, et al., 2006; Ritter & Weber, 1973). Stimulus-oriented thought can involve watchfulness toward upcoming task-related stimuli, but it can also occur in the form of mind wandering away from a task (e.g., paying attention

to scanner noise or incidental light) (Gilbert et al., 2007). Thus, theoretically, stimulus-independent thought and mind wandering are independent dimensions of thought (Klinger, 2009), but in practice they do tend to be correlated in the sense that most mind wandering tends to be decoupled from current sensory information.

As with spontaneous thought, the neuroscientific study of stimulus-independent thought has come exclusively from brain recruitment during rest. The medial PFC has received the most attention within this literature, with a number of studies suggesting its involvement in stimulus-independent thought (Mason et al., 2007a, b; McGuire et al., 1996). Other researchers, however, have argued against this by using task-based paradigms to suggest that the medial PFC is involved in stimulus-oriented thought (Gilbert et al., 2007; Gilbert, Simons, et al., 2006). This controversy (Gilbert et al., 2007; Mason et al., 2007a, b) remains unresolved. Once again, the evidence so far relies on indirect inferences about the presence of stimulus-independent or stimulus-oriented thought based on the level of task requirements (e.g., stimulus-independent thought is more likely to occur during easier task-blocks than during difficult task-blocks). Here, too, the field would benefit from a neurophenomenological approach (Christoff, Cosmelli, et al., 2011)—combining moment-to-moment introspective reports collected through experience sampling with concurrent fMRI measures of brain recruitment.

MIND WANDERING

Although there have been relatively few studies of mind wandering (Christoff, Gordon, et al., 2009; Mason et al., 2007a, b; McKiernan, D'Angelo, Kaufman, & Binder, 2006), our neuroscientific knowledge of this phenomenon is greater than that for either spontaneous thought or stimulus-independent thought because of these studies' use of individual differences analysis and experience sampling approach combined with fMRI measures.

So far, *mind wandering* has most often been defined as thinking that is unrelated to the currently ongoing task or activity (Christoff, Gordon, et al., 2009; Smallwood & Schooler, 2006). One brain network that has been linked to mind wandering is the default network of brain regions (Raichle et al., 2001), which includes, most prominently, the medial PFC, posterior cingulate/precuneus region, and the temporoparietal junction (TPJ). Studies have demonstrated correlations between reported frequency of task-unrelated thoughts and default network activation during conditions of low cognitive demand (Mason et al., 2007a, b; McKiernan et al., 2006), as well as stronger default network activation during highly practiced tasks than during novel tasks in people with a higher propensity for mind wandering (Mason et al., 2007a, b). Furthermore, evidence collected using trial-by-trial experience sampling during fMRI has shown the three main default network regions to be significantly more activated immediately before reports of mind wandering than immediately before reports of being "on-task" (Christoff, Gordon, et al., 2009). Therefore, there is strong evidence to suggest that recruitment of default network regions co-occurs with mind-wandering episodes.

However, in addition to default network recruitment, Christoff, Gordon, et al. (2009) also observed significantly greater executive network recruitment during episodes of mind wandering than in episodes of on-task attention. These executive network regions include the DLPFC and the anterior cingulate cortex (ACC). This joint activation of the default and executive networks during mind wandering may seem highly surprising at first. In general, the executive and default networks are thought to act in opposition to each other so that when the executive network becomes activated, the default network becomes deactivated or actively suppressed (Fox et al., 2005; Greicius, Krasnow, Reiss, & Menon, 2003; Weissman, Roberts, Visscher, & Woldorff, 2006). This mutually exclusive relationship between the two networks may characterize their behavior during experimental conditions such as standard tasks and conditions of rest, but mental phenomena such as mind wandering fall outside the range of such standard experimental conditions. As well, the parallel recruitment of default and executive brain regions during mind wandering is reminiscent of the neural recruitment observed during creative thinking (Kounios et al., 2006, 2008; Subramaniam, Kounios, Parrish, & Jung-Beeman, 2009), during which executive regions such as the dorsal ACC and default network regions such as the PCC are activated prior to solving problems with insight. Furthermore, a similar parallel recruitment of executive and default regions has been observed during naturalistic film viewing (Golland et al., 2007), which is related to immersive simulative mental experience (Mar & Oatley, 2008). Thus, mind wandering may be part of a larger class of mental phenomena that enable executive processes to occur without diminishing the potential contribution of the default network for creative

thought (Christoff, Gordon et al., 2011; Ellamil, Dobson, Beeman, & Kalina, 2012; Kounios et al., 2006, 2008; Subramaniam et al., 2009) and mental simulation (Buckner, Andrews-Hanna, & Schacter, 2008; Schacter, Addis, & Buckner, 2008; Spreng, Mar, & Kim, 2009).

Creative Thinking

Creative thought is a unique mental ability that relies on the skilled engagement of both goal-directed and undirected thought (Christoff, Gordon, et al., 2011). Often defined in terms of its product, *creativity* is the ability to produce ideas that are both novel (original and unique) and useful (appropriate and meaningful) (Amabile & Tighe, 1993; Besemer & Treffinger, 1981; Bruner, 1962; Gardner, 1989; Sternberg, 1985). The neuroscientific study of creative thinking has a relatively long tradition, beginning with an earlier emphasis on large-scale brain distinctions (e.g., hemispheric differences) and leading to a more recent emphasis on specific brain region and networks.

HEMISPHERIC CONTRIBUTIONS AND INTERACTIONS

One of the earliest and best-known brain theories of creativity emphasized the importance of the right hemisphere and was supported by findings that patients often demonstrate enhanced artistic creativity following damage to the left prefrontal area, an area thought to inhibit creative right hemisphere processes (Finkelstein, Vardi, & Hod, 1991; Mendez, 2004; Miller, Boone, Cummings, Read, & Mishkin, 2000; Miller et al., 1998). Furthermore, Sperry's (1964) research into split-brain patients suggested that the right hemisphere carries out associative, intuitive, and holistic processing that may facilitate creative generation (Barrett, Beversdorf, Crucian, & Heilman, 1998; Beeman et al., 1994; Faust & Lavidor, 2003; Robertson, Lamb, & Knight, 1988). Consistent with this, EEG studies have found evidence of right hemisphere dominance in artists (Bhattacharya & Petsche, 2002, 2005), as well as during insight (Jung-Beeman et al., 2004; Kounios et al., 2008) and divergent thinking tasks (Martindale, Hines, Mitchell, & Covello, 1984).

Follow-up studies of Sperry's split-brain patients, however, found that these patients lacked integrated thought and had an impoverished fantasy life (Hoppe & Kyle, 1990; TenHouten, 1994). Furthermore, EEG and PET studies have also found increased activation in the left parietal cortex during hypothesis generation (Jin, Kwon, Jeong, Kwon,

& Shin, 2006) and word association (Starchenko, Bekhtereva, Pakhomov, & Medvedev, 2003), as well as activation in both hemispheres during creative story generation (Bekhtereva, Dan'ko, Starchenko, Pakhomov, & Medvedev, 2001; Bekhtereva et al., 2000; Carlsson, Wendt, & Risberg, 2000). These findings suggest that left hemisphere functions, such as logical and detail-oriented processing (Sperry, 1964), may be as important as right-hemisphere processes for creative thinking. Thus, despite the original emphasis on right hemisphere processes, the body of neuroscientific research indicates that hemispheric interactions may be more important for creativity than isolated right hemisphere recruitment.

DIFFERENT NETWORK CONTRIBUTIONS

Recent findings point to the possible involvement of specific networks and brain regions in different components of creative thought. The default, executive, and memory networks all seem to play a key role.

The DLPFC and dorsal ACC, two main executive network regions, are known to be activated during a variety of creative tasks, including piano improvisation (Bengtsson, Csíkszentmihályi, & Ullén, 2007; Berkowitz & Ansari, 2008), creative story generation (Bekhtereva et al., 2000, 2001; Howard-Jones, Blakemore, Samuel, Summers, & Claxton, 2005), word association (Bekhtereva et al., 2004), divergent thinking (Carlsson et al., 2000; Seger, Desmond, Glover, & Gabrieli, 2000), fluid analogy formation (Geake & Hansen, 2005), insight problem solving (Geake & Hansen, 2005; Kounios et al., 2008; Subramaniam et al., 2009), and visual art design (Kowatari et al., 2009). The executive brain network's contribution during creative thinking may be to enable a goal-directed, analytic mode of processing through which the evaluation of the usefulness of novel ideas can be achieved (Howard-Jones & Murray, 2003). Goal-directed thinking would also enable individuals to focus on the pertinent task details and to select the relevant ideas among the many they may have spontaneously generated (Dorfman, Martindale, Gassimova, & Vartanian, 2008; Gabora, 2010; Heilman, Nadeau, & Beversdorf, 2003; Lepine, Bernardin, & Barrouillet, 2005; Vartanian, Martindale, & Kwiatkowski, 2007).

The three main regions of the default network have all been found to contribute to creative thought. Enhanced TPJ activity has been observed during divergent thinking tasks (Fink & Neubauer,

2006; Grabner, Fink, & Neubauer, 2007), creative story generation (Bekhtereva et al., 2004), hypothesis generation (Jin et al., 2006), fluid analogy formation (Geake et al., 2005), and remote associate insight problems (Jung-Beeman et al., 2004; Subramaniam et al., 2009). As well, medial PFC is recruited during creative story generation (Howard-Jones et al., 2005). Insight problems activate both the MPFC and PCC/precuneus (Geake & Hansen, 2005; Jung-Beeman et al., 2004; Kounios et al., 2008; Subramaniam et al., 2009). The recruitment of default network regions during creative thought may reflect undirected thought processes that support the generation of novel ideas (Dorfman et al., 2008; Howard-Jones & Murray, 2003; Vartanian et al., 2007). However, it may also contribute to creative evaluative processes, through its role in affective and visceroceptive evaluation demonstrated during emotional paradigms (Damasio, 2000; Fossati et al., 2003; Gusnard, Akbudak, Shulman, & Raichle, 2001; Lane, Fink, Chau, & Dolan, 1997; Mitchell, Banaji, & Macrae, 2005; Ochsner, Knierim et al., 2004; Ruby & Decety, 2004; Zysset, Huber, Ferstl, & von Cramon, 2002).

Recruitment of medial temporal lobe (MTL) memory regions such as the hippocampus and the parahippocampus occurs frequently during creative thinking, although it has received relatively little attention to date. For example, the hippocampus exhibits greater recruitment during visual art design (Kowatari et al., 2009), divergent thinking (Fink et al., 2009), and creative generation (Ellamil et al., 2012). In general, studies have linked the MTL to memory retrieval (Squire, Stark, & Clark, 2004) and associative processing (Eichenbaum, 2000). The associative function of the MTL may play an important role in creative thought by facilitating the generation of novel ideas and associations and the recombination of old ones (Ellamil et al., 2012).

CREATIVE GENERATION AND EVALUATION

In following with the twofold definition of the creative product as both novel and useful, psychological findings have suggested a twofold creative process that includes generative and evaluative components (Basadur, Graen, & Green, 1982; Campbell, 1960; Finke, Ward, & Smith, 1992; Israeli, 1962; Wallas, 1926). Creative generation and evaluation can occur in parallel, but creating a temporal separation between the two is known to increase the creativity of outputs (Basadur et al., 1982; Parnes & Meadow, 1959)—a principle which is used in the practice of brainstorming.

Recent findings (Ellamil et al., 2012) show that creative generation is preferentially associated with recruitment of MTL regions. Creative evaluation, by contrast, is preferentially associated with joint recruitment of executive and default network regions and activation of the RLPFC, insula, and temporopolar cortex (Ellamil et al., 2012). Thus, the MTL regions may be central to creative-thought generation. This is consistent with previous studies that have linked MTL to the spontaneous generation of thoughts and memories (Christoff et al., 2004; Gelbard-Sagiv et al., 2008; Stark & Squire, 2001). It is likely that it is particularly the associative and constructive functions of the MTL (Aminoff, Gronau, & Bar, 2007; Bar, Aminoff, & Schacter, 2008; Henke, Buck, Weber, & Wieser, 1997; Henke, Weber, Kneifel, Wieser, & Buck, 1999; Rombouts et al., 1997) that allow it to generate novel ideas and thought content. The preferential recruitment of MTL regions during creative generation is also consistent with psychological accounts that describe creative generation as enhanced associative processing (Gabora, 2010) and the restructuring of preexisting ideas (Hospers, 1985; Weisberg, 1995).

The joint recruitment of executive, default network, and limbic brain regions during creative evaluation (Ellamil et al., 2012) suggests that this process extends beyond the analytical goal-directed thought supported by executive network regions to include more spontaneous, affective, and possibly visceroceptive evaluative processes supported by default and limbic regions. The default network of brain regions is known to engage in a range of affective evaluative processes, including evaluation of self and of others' emotional reactions (Fossati et al., 2003; Ochsner, Knierim et al., 2004; Ruby & Decety, 2004), and, more generally, the evaluation of internally generated affective information (Damasio, 2000; Gusnard et al., 2001; Lane et al., 1997; Zysset et al., 2002). Related to this, the anterior insula and temporopolar cortex, which are also recruited during creative evaluation, are thought to integrate highly processed sensory data with interoceptive-autonomic information (Craig, 2002; Critchley, Wiens, Rotshtein, Ohman, & Dolan, 2004; Olson, Plotzker, & Ezzyat, 2007; Seeley et al., 2007). The enhanced activation of default and salience network regions during creative evaluation may therefore convey the importance of affective and visceroceptive forms of evaluative processing during creative thought. Indeed, while evaluating the products of one's own creative activity, creative individuals frequently pay attention to their "gut

reactions" (de Bono, 2000). Finally, the joint activation and positive functional connectivity between default and executive network regions during creative evaluation suggests that this component of creative thought may involve a rare combination of goal-directed and undirected thought processes, as well as cognitive and affective components (Ellamil et al., 2012).

Recursiveness of Thought

Although people often assume that they are aware of every thought they have, it is empirically possible to demonstrate that our thoughts can occur even when we are not aware of them. For example, while reading a novel, we may suddenly realize that during the last page or two our thoughts had drifted off to something else; during that interval of mind wandering we must not have been aware of our thoughts or else we would have stopped reading.

The act of becoming aware of our own thoughts is an act of recursive thinking. The terms *introspection* and *meta-awareness* are most often used to describe the recursiveness of thought. In general, *meta-awareness* implies a more passive observation of our thoughts, without an attempt to evaluate them or modify them. By contrast, *introspection* is often used to indicate a more active observation of one's own thoughts, often accompanied by an evaluation of their appropriateness or usefulness.

The brain region that is beginning to be recognized as most closely linked to meta-awareness and introspection is the anterior PFC (Broadmann area 10), including the RLPFC but also the anterior medial PFC (Christoff & Gabrieli, 2000; Christoff et al., 2003; Fleming, Weil, Nagy, Dolan, & Rees, 2010; McCaig, Dixon, Keramatian, Liu, & Christoff, 2011; Stuss, 2007). Thus, lesion studies have suggested that a defining function of the anterior PFC may be the process of reflecting on one's own mental contents (Stuss, 2007; Stuss & Levine, 2002; Wheeler, Stuss, & Tulving, 1997). More recently, neuroimaging studies have focused on possible subregional differences in anterior PFC (Gilbert, Spengler, Simons, Frith, & Burgess, 2006; Gilbert, Spengler, Simons, Steele et al., 2006). The lateral sector, the RLPFC, seems to play a reflective or monitoring function that coordinates, integrates, and evaluates the outputs of prior stages of cognitive processing (Christoff & Gabrieli, 2000; Fleming et al., 2010; Fletcher et al., 2001; Petrides, 2005; Ramnani & Owen, 2004; Tsujimoto, Genovesio, & Wise, 2010). The outputs that RLPFC appears to operate on—a self-generated rule in the context of reasoning, a subgoal in the context of multitasking, or a memory episode in the context of retrieval—seem more related to conceptual thought than to other possible mental contents such as visceral, emotional, or external body sensations. This suggests that RLPFC may specifically subserve meta-cognitive awareness of one's own thoughts (McCaig et al., 2011). In contrast, evidence suggests that medial BA10 may be preferentially linked to meta-awareness of one's own emotional states (Lane et al., 1997; Ochsner & Gross, 2005; Ochsner, Ray, et al., 2004). It appears, therefore, that both medial and lateral anterior PFC sectors contribute to recursive thought but may be differentially recruited, based on whether or not the mental content being reflected on is affectively charged.

The fact that anatomically, the anterior PFC is predominately connected to multimodal association areas in the superior temporal and posterior frontal cortices (Petrides & Pandya, 2007) supports its proposed role in recursive thought. Moreover, based on evidence that the DLPFC plays a role in monitoring the contents of working memory and the hierarchical anatomical relationship between the DLPFC and the RLPFC, it has been suggested that RLPFC may monitor the monitoring process in DLPFC (Christoff & Gabrieli, 2000; Fletcher et al., 2001; Petrides, 2005). Additional kinds of metamonitoring have been suggested through interactions between RLPFC and other brain regions, such as the inferior frontal, pre-motor, and insular cortices (Farb et al., 2007; Koechlin et al., 2003; Sakai & Passingham, 2006). Thus, the RLPFC may allow us to become aware that we are aware of something—a self-reflective knowledge of our mental contents. The considerable expansion of this region during the course of primate evolution (Semendeferi, Armstrong, Schleicher, Zilles, & Van Hoesen, 2001) may, therefore, be at least in part linked to the remarkable levels and varieties of self-awareness possessed by humans (Wheeler et al., 1997).

In the context of this remarkable consistency of evidence for increased anterior PFC recruitment during goal-directed meta-awareness, there comes the seemingly contradictory finding that meta-awareness of undirected thought such as mind wandering is associated with *decreased* recruitment of anterior PFC (Christoff, Gordon et al., 2009). When mind wandering with meta-awareness is directly compared to mind wandering in the absence of meta-awareness, decreased recruitment of both medial and lateral anterior PFC is observed (Christoff, Gordon et al., 2009). Although the meta-awareness of undirected thought has just begun to be investigated, one possible explanations for this seemingly contradictory finding is that during mind wandering subjects may be aware of the contents of their consciousness without being aware of the fact that they are mind wandering, or the process of mind wandering itself. Although this possible distinction between meta-awareness of process and content is not part of current theoretical models of anterior PFC function (Burgess, Simons, Dumontheil, & Gilbert, 2005; Christoff & Gabrieli, 2000; Christoff et al., 2004; Koechlin, Basso, Pietrini, Panzer, & Grafman, 1999; Lane et al., 1997; Ochsner, Knierim et al., 2004; Ramnani & Owen, 2004) and meta-consciousness (Lambie & Marcel, 2002; Schooler, 2002), it may prove instrumental for their future development.

Conclusion

It is clear that cognitive neuroscience has contributed important new concepts and theoretical distinctions to the overall scientific investigation of thought. For example, the importance of different levels of abstraction in thought and thought's hierarchical aspects have been mainly emphasized from a neuroscientific perspective. As well, the way that creative thought combines goal-directed and undirected aspects of thought has been highlighted mainly through neuroscientific research. But perhaps the biggest contribution of the cognitive neuroscience of thought is the newly emerged emphasis on undirected thought processes—emphasis that originally came from the ubiquitously observed neural recruitment during rest and that has been expanded in the more recent empirical investigation of mind wandering. These investigations have revealed that, contrary to most people's intuitive beliefs, the mind may be most active when it is freely wandering outside the confines of particular tasks or goals.

Much remains to be done toward improving the definitions, terminology, and experimental paradigms used to study undirected thought. Some of the biggest challenges may be moving beyond exclusively task-based paradigms while successfully incorporating first-person introspective reports in scientific investigations. Overcoming these challenges, however, bears the promise of improving our understanding of our own thought processes, including how our brains enable this understanding.

Questions for Future Research
• How are relational reasoning, hierarchical processing, and level of abstraction in thought

related to each other at the cognitive level? Are they supported by the same neural processes, or is there a fundamental difference in the way lateral PFC implements each of these thought phenomena?

• How can we investigate spontaneous thought processes without exclusively relying on tasks or their absence?

• What is the role of the temporopolar cortex in spontaneous thought? This is one of the least discussed and yet frequently activated brain regions when it comes to spontaneous thought and mind wandering.

• Why does temporally separating evaluation and generation during creative thought increase the creativity of outputs?

• Why do memories sometimes evade us during deliberate attempt at recall but "come to us" later, spontaneously, when we're not deliberately trying to retrieve them? Does recruitment of executive network regions in the service of goal-directed thought lead to suppression of spontaneous retrieval and generation of thought in MTL structures?

• How does anterior PFC support meta-awareness of mental *processes*, and does this differ from the way it supports meta-awareness of mental *contents*?

• What are the circumstances that lead to joint recruitment of the brain's executive and default networks, and how do they differ from circumstances that lead to an opposition (either-or recruitment) between the two networks?

References

Amabile, T. M., & Tighe, E. (1993). Questions of creativity. In J. Brockman (Ed.), *Creativity* (pp. 7–27). New York: Simon & Schuster.

Aminoff, E., Gronau, N., & Bar, M. (2007). The parahippocampal cortex mediates spatial and nonspatial associations. *Cerebral Cortex, 17*(7), 1493–1503.

Andrews-Hanna, J. R., Reidler, J. S., Sepulcre, J., Poulin, R., & Buckner, R. L. (2010). Functional-anatomic fractionation of the brain's default network. *Neuron, 65*(4), 550–562.

Antrobus, J. S. (1968). Information theory and stimulus-independent thought. *British Journal of Psychology, 59*, 423–430.

Antrobus, J. S., Singer, J. L., & Greenberg, S. (1966). Studies in the stream of consciousness: Experimental enhancement and suppression of spontaneous cognitive processes. *Perceptual & Motor Skills, 23*(2), 399–417.

Badre, D., & D'Esposito, M. (2007). Functional magnetic resonance imaging evidence for a hierarchical organization of the prefrontal cortex. *Journal of Cognitive Neuroscience, 19*(12), 2082–2099.

Baker, S. C., Rogers, R. D., Owen, A. M., Frith, C. D., Dolan, R. J., Frackowiak, R. S. J., & Robbins, T. W. (1996). Neural systems engaged by planning: A PET study of the Tower of London task. *Neuropsychologia, 34*(6), 515–526.

Bar, M., Aminoff, E., & Schacter, D. L. (2008). Scenes unseen: The parahippocampal cortex intrinsically subserves contextual associations, not scenes or places per se. *Journal of Neuroscience, 28*(34), 8539–8544.

Barrett, A. M., Beversdorf, D. Q., Crucian, G. P., & Heilman, K. M. (1998). Neglect after right hemisphere stroke: A smaller floodlight for distributed attention. *Neurology, 51*(4), 972–978.

Basadur, M., Graen, G. B., & Green, S. G. (1982). Training in creative problem solving: Effects on ideation and problem finding and solving in an industrial research organization. *Organizational Behavior and Human Performance, 30*(1), 41–70.

Beeman, M., Friedman, R. B., Grafman, J., Perez, E., Diamond, S., & Lindsay, M. B. (1994). Summation priming and coarse semantic coding in the right hemisphere. *Journal of Cognitive Neuroscience, 6*(1), 26–45.

Bekhtereva, N. P., Dan'ko, S. G., Starchenko, M. G., Pakhomov, S. V., & Medvedev, S. V. (2001). Study of the brain organization of creativity: 3. Brain activation assessed by the local cerebral blood flow and EEG. *Human Physiology, 27*(4), 390–397.

Bekhtereva, N. P., Korotkov, A. D., Pakhomov, S. V., Roudas, M. S., Starchenko, M. G., & Medvedev, S. V. (2004). PET study of brain maintenance of verbal creative activity. *International Journal of Psychophysiology, 53*(1), 11–20.

Bekhtereva, N. P., Starchenko, M., Klyucharev, V., Vorob'ev, V., Pakhomov, S., & Medvedev, S. (2000). Study of the brain organization of creativity: 2. Positron-emission tomography data. *Human Physiology, 26*(5), 516–522.

Bengtsson, S. L., Csíkszentmihályi, M., & Ullén, F. (2007). Cortical regions involved in the generation of musical structures during improvisation in pianists. *Journal of Cognitive Neuroscience, 19*(5), 830–842.

Berkowitz, A. L., & Ansari, D. (2008). Generation of novel motor sequences: The neural correlates of musical improvisation. *Neuroimage, 41*(2), 535–543.

Besemer, S. P., & Treffinger, D. J. (1981). Analysis of creative products: Review and synthesis. *Journal of Creative Behavior, 15*(3), 158–178.

Bhattacharya, J., & Petsche, H. (2002). Shadows of artistry: Cortical synchrony during perception and imagery of visual art. *Cognitive Brain Research, 13*(2), 179–186.

Bhattacharya, J., & Petsche, H. (2005). Drawing on mind's canvas: Differences in cortical integration patterns between artists and non-artists. *Human Brain Mapping, 26*(1), 1–14.

Braver, T. S., Cohen, J. D., Nystrom, L. E., Jonides, J., Smith, E. E., & Noll, D. C. (1997). A parametric study of prefrontal cortex involvement in human working memory. *Neuroimage, 5*(1), 49–62.

Bruner, J. S. (1962). The conditions of creativity. In H. Gruber, G. Terrell, & M. Wertheimer (Eds.), *Contemporary approaches to creative thinking* (pp. 1–30). New York: Atherton.

Buckner, R. L. (2010). The role of the hippocampus in prediction and imagination. *Annual Review of Psychology, 61*, 27–48, C21–C28.

Buckner, R. L., Andrews-Hanna, J. R., & Schacter, D. L. (2008). The brain's default network: Anatomy, function, and relevance to disease. *Annals of the New York Academy of Sciences, 1124*, 1–38.

Bunge, S. A., Kahn, I., Wallis, J. D., Miller, E. K., & Wagner, A. D. (2003). Neural circuits subserving the retrieval and maintenance of abstract rules. *Journal of Neurophysiology*, *90*(5), 3419–3428.

Bunge, S. A., Wallis, J. D., Parker, A., Brass, M., Crone, E. A., Hoshi, E., & Sakai, K. (2005). Neural circuitry underlying rule use in humans and nonhuman primates. *Journal of Neuroscience*, *25*(45), 10347–10350.

Bunge, S. A., Wendelken, C., Badre, D., & Wagner, A. D. (2005). Analogical reasoning and prefrontal cortex: Evidence for separable retrieval and integration mechanisms. *Cerebral Cortex*, *15*(3), 239–249.

Bunge, S. A., & Zelazo, P. D. (2006). A brain-based account of the development of rule use in childhood. *Current Directions in Psychological Science*, *15*(3), 118–121.

Burgess, P. W., Simons, J. S., Dumontheil, I., & Gilbert, S. J. (2005). The gateway hypothesis of rostral prefrontal cortex (area 10) function. In J. Duncan, L. Phillips, & P. McLeod (Eds.), *Measuring the mind: Speed, control, and age* (pp. 217–248). Oxford: Oxford University Press.

Campbell, D. (1960). Blind variation and selective retention in creative thought as in other knowledge processes. *Psychological Review*, *67*, 380–400.

Carlsson, I., Wendt, P. E., & Risberg, J. (2000). On the neurobiology of creativity. Differences in frontal activity between high and low creative subjects. *Neuropsychologia*, *38*(6), 873–885.

Carpenter, P. A., Just, M. A., & Shell, P. (1990). What one intelligence test measures: A theoretical account of the processing in the Raven Progressive Matrices Test. *Psychological Review*, *97*(3), 404–431.

Cavanna, A. E., & Trimble, M. R. (2006). The precuneus: A review of its functional anatomy and behavioural correlates. *Brain*, *129*(Pt 3), 564–583.

Christoff, K. (2003). Using and musing of abstract behavioural rules: Peculiarities of prefrontal function in humans. *Neuroimage*, *19*(2, AbsTrak ID: 18325).

Christoff, K., Cosmelli, D., Legrand, D., & Thompson, E. (2011). Specifying the self for cognitive neuroscience. *Trends in Cognitive Sciences*, *15*(3), 104–112.

Christoff, K., & Gabrieli, J. D. E. (2000). The frontopolar cortex and human cognition: Evidence for a rostrocaudal hierarchical organization within the human prefrontal cortex. *Psychobiology*, *28*(2), 168–186.

Christoff, K., Gordon, A. M., Smallwood, J., Smith, R., & Schooler, J. W. (2009). Experience sampling during fMRI reveals default network and executive system contributions to mind wandering. *Proceedings of the National Academy of Sciences U S A*, *106*(21), 8719–8724.

Christoff, K., Gordon, A. M., & Smith, R. (2011). The role of spontaneous thought in human cognition. In O. Vartanian & D. R. Mandel (Eds.), *Neuroscience of decision making* (pp. 259–284). New York: Psychology Press.

Christoff, K., & Keramatian, K. (2007). Abstraction of mental representations: Theoretical considerations and neuroscientific evidence. In S. A. Bunge & J. D. Wallis (Eds.), *The neuroscience of rule-guided behavior* (pp. 107–126). New York: Oxford University Press.

Christoff, K., Keramatian, K., Gordon, A. M., Smith, R., & Madler, B. (2009). Prefrontal organization of cognitive control according to levels of abstraction. *Brain Research*, *1286*, 94–105.

Christoff, K., Prabhakaran, V., Dorfman, J., Zhao, Z., Kroger, J. K., Holyoak, K. J., & Gabrieli, J. D. E. (2001). Rostrolateral prefrontal cortex involvement in relational integration during reasoning. *Neuroimage*, *14*(5), 1136–1149.

Christoff, K., Ream, J. M., & Gabrieli, J. D. (2004). Neural basis of spontaneous thought processes. *Cortex*, *40*(4-5), 623–630.

Christoff, K., Ream, J. M., Geddes, L. P. T., & Gabrieli, J. D. E. (2003). Evaluating self-generated information: Anterior prefrontal contributions to human cognition. *Behavioral Neuroscience*, *117*(6), 1161–1168.

Cohen, J. D., Dunbar, K., & McClelland, J. L. (1990). On the control of automatic processes: A parallel distributed processing account of the Stroop effect. *Psychological Review*, *97*(3), 332–361.

Craig, A. D. (2002). How do you feel? Interoception: the sense of the physiological condition of the body. *Nature Reviews Neuroscience*, *3*(8), 655–666.

Critchley, H. D., Wiens, S., Rotshtein, P., Ohman, A., & Dolan, R. J. (2004). Neural systems supporting interoceptive awareness. *Nature Neuroscience*, *7*(2), 189–195.

Damasio, A. R. (2000). Subcortical and cortical brain activity during the feeling of self-generated emotions. *Nature Neuroscience*, *3*(10), 1049–1056.

de Bono, E. (2000). *Six thinking hats*. New York: Penguin Books.

Desimone, R., & Duncan, J. (1995). Neural mechanisms of selective visual attention. *Annual Review of Neuroscience*, *18*, 193–222.

D'Esposito, M., Postle, B. R., Ballard, D., & Lease, J. (1999). Maintenance versus manipulation of information held in working memory: An event-related fMRI study. *Brain and Cognition*, *41*(1), 66–86.

Dias, R., Robbins, T. W., & Roberts, A. C. (1996). Dissociation in prefrontal cortex of affective and attentional shifts. *Nature*, *380*(6569), 69–72.

Dias, R., Robbins, T. W., & Roberts, A. C. (1997). Dissociable forms of inhibitory control within prefrontal cortex with an analog of the Wisconsin Card Sort Test: Restriction to novel situations and independence from "on-line" processing. *Journal of Neuroscience*, *17*(23), 9285–9297.

Dorfman, L., Martindale, C., Gassimova, V., & Vartanian, O. (2008). Creativity and speed of information processing: A double dissociation involving elementary versus inhibitory cognitive tasks. *Personality and Individual Differences*, *44*(6), 1382–1390.

Dumontheil, I., Gilbert, S. J., Frith, C. D., & Burgess, C. W. (2010). Recruitment of lateral rostral prefrontal cortex in spontaneous and task-related thoughts. *Quarterly Journal of Experimental Psychology*, *63*(9), 1740–1756.

Duncan, J., Burgess, P., & Emslie, H. (1995). Fluid intelligence after frontal lobe lesions. *Neuropsychologia*, *33*(3), 261–268.

Eichenbaum, H. (2000). A cortical-hippocampal system for declarative memory. *Nature Reviews Neuroscience*, *1*(1), 41–50.

Ellamil, M., Dobson, C., Beeman, Mark, & Kalina, C. (2012). Evaluative and generative modes of thought during the creative process. *Neuroimage*, *59*(2), 1783–1794.

Farb, N. A. S., Segal, Z. V., Mayberg, H., Bean, J., McKeon, D., Fatima, Z., & Anderson, A. K. (2007). Attending to the present: mindfulness meditation reveals distinct neural modes of self-reference. *Social, Cognitive & Affective Neuroscience*, *2*, 313–322.

Faust, M., & Lavidor, M. (2003). Semantically convergent and semantically divergent priming in the cerebral hemispheres: lexical decision and semantic judgment. *Cognitive Brain Research*, *17*(3), 585–597.

Filler, M. S., & Giambra, L. M. (1973). Daydreaming as a function of cueing and task difficulty. *Perceptual and Motor Skills, 37,* 503–509.

Fink, A., Grabner, R. H., Benedek, M., Reishofer, G., Hauswirth, V., Fally, M., Neuper, C., Ebner, F., & Neubauer, A. C. (2009). The creative brain: Investigation of brain activity during creative problem solving by means of EEG and fMRI. *Human Brain Mapping, 30*(3), 734–748.

Fink, A., & Neubauer, A. C. (2006). EEG alpha oscillations during the performance of verbal creativity tasks: Differential effects of sex and verbal intelligence. *International Journal of Psychophysiology, 62*(1), 46–53.

Finke, R., Ward, T., & Smith, S. (1992). *Creative cognition: Theory, research and applications.* Cambridge, MA: MIT Press.

Finkelstein, Y., Vardi, J., & Hod, I. (1991). Impulsive artistic creativity as a presentation of transient cognitive alterations. *Behavioral Medicine, 17*(2), 91–94.

Fleming, S. M., Weil, R. S., Nagy, Z., Dolan, R. J., & Rees, G. (2010). Relating introspective accuracy to individual differences in brain structure. *Science, 329*(5998), 1541–1543.

Fletcher, P. C., & Henson, R. N. A. (2001). Frontal lobes and human memory: Insights from functional neuroimaging. *Brain, 124*(5), 849–881.

Fossati, P., Hevenor, S. J., Graham, S. J., Grady, C., Keightley, M. L., Craik, F., & Mayberg, H. (2003). In search of the emotional self: An FMRI study using positive and negative emotional words. *American Journal of Psychiatry, 160*(11), 1938–1945.

Fox, M. D., Snyder, A. Z., Vincent, J. L., Corbetta, M., Van Essen, D. C., & Raichle, M. E. (2005). The human brain is intrinsically organized into dynamic, anticorrelated functional networks, *Proceedings of the National Academy of Sciences U S A, 102,* 9673–9678.

Fuster, J. M. (1980). *The prefrontal cortex. Anatomy, physiology and neuropsychology of the frontal lobe.* New York: Raven Press.

Gabora, L. (2010). Revenge of the "neurds": Characterizing creative thought in terms of the structure and dynamics of memory. *Creativity Research Journal, 22*(1), 1–13.

Gardner, H. (1989). *To open minds.* New York: Basic.

Geake, J. G., & Hansen, P. C. (2005). Neural correlates of intelligence as revealed by fMRI of fluid analogies. *Neuroimage, 26*(2), 555–564.

Gelbard-Sagiv, H., Mukamel, R., Harel, M., Malach, R., & Fried, I. (2008). Internally generated reactivation of single neurons in human hippocampus during free recall. *Science, 322*(5898), 96–101.

Gentner, D., Holyoak, K. J., & Kokinov, B. N. (Eds.). (2001). *The analogical mind: Perspectives from cognitive science.* Cambridge, MA: MIT Press.

Giambra, L. M., & Grodsky, A. (1989). Task-unrelated images and thoughts while reading. In J. E. Shorr, P. Robin & J. A. Connella, & Wolpin, M. (Eds.), *Imagery: Current perspectives* (pp. 27–31). New York: Plenum.

Gilbert, S. J., Dumontheil, I., Simons, J. S., Frith, C. D., & Burgess, P. W. (2007). Comment on "Wandering minds: the default network and stimulus-independent thought." *Science, 317*(5834), 43.

Gilbert, S. J., Simons, J. S., Frith, C. D., & Burgess, P. W. (2006). Performance-related activity in medial rostral prefrontal cortex (area 10) during low-demand tasks. *Journal of Experimental Psychology. Human Perception and Performance, 32*(1), 45–58.

Gilbert, S. J., Spengler, S., Simons, J. S., Frith, C. D., & Burgess, P. W. (2006). Differential functions of lateral and medial rostral prefrontal cortex (area 10) revealed by brain-behavior associations. *Cerebral Cortex, 16*(12), 1783–1789.

Gilbert, S. J., Spengler, S., Simons, J. S., Steele, J. D., Lawrie, S. M., Frith, C. D., & Burgess, P. W. (2006). Functional specialization within rostral prefrontal cortex (area 10): A meta-analysis. *Journal of Cognitive Neuroscience, 18*(6), 932–948.

Goldman-Rakic, P. S. (1987). Circuitry of primate prefrontal cortex and regulation of behavior by representational memory. In F. Plum & V. B. Mountcastle (Eds.), *Handbook of physiology* (Vol. 5, pp. 373–417). Bethesda, MD: American Physiological Society.

Golland, Y., Bentin, S., Gelbard, H., Benjamini, Y., Heller, R., Nir, Y., Hasson, U., & Malach, R. (2007). Extrinsic and intrinsic systems in the posterior cortex of the human brain revealed during natural sensory stimulation. *Cerebral Cortex, 17*(4), 766–777.

Grabner, R. H., Fink, A., & Neubauer, A. C. (2007). Brain correlates of self-rated originality of ideas: Evidence from event-related power and phase-locking changes in the EEG. *Behavioral Neuroscience, 121*(1), 224–230.

Graham, K. S., Lee, A. C., Brett, M., & Patterson, K. (2003). The neural basis of autobiographical and semantic memory: New evidence from three PET studies. *Cognitive, Affective, & Behavioral Neuroscience, 3*(3), 234–254.

Green, A. E., Fugelsang, J. A., Kraemer, D. J., Shamosh, N. A., & Dunbar, K. N. (2006). Frontopolar cortex mediates abstract integration in analogy. *Brain Research, 1096*(1), 125–137.

Greicius, M. D., Krasnow, B., Reiss, A. L., & Menon, V. (2003). Functional connectivity in the resting brain: A network analysis of the default mode hypothesis. *Proceedings of the National Academy of Sciences U S A, 100*(1), 253–258.

Gusnard, D. A., Akbudak, E., Shulman, G. L., & Raichle, M. E. (2001). Medial prefrontal cortex and self-referential mental activity: Relation to a default mode of brain function. *Proceedings of the National Academy of Sciences U S A, 98*(7), 4259–4264.

Halford, G. S., Wilson, W. H., & Phillips, S. (1998). Processing capacity defined by relational complexity: Implications for comparative, developmental, and cognitive psychology. *Behavioral and Brain Sciences, 21*(6), 803–831; discussion 831–864.

Halford, G. S., Wilson, W. H., & Phillips, S. (2010). Relational knowledge: The foundation of higher cognition. *Trends in cognitive sciences, 14*(11), 497–505.

Heilman, K. M., Nadeau, S. E., & Beversdorf, D. O. (2003). Creative innovation: Possible brain mechanisms. *Neurocase, 9*(5), 369–379.

Henke, K., Buck, A., Weber, B., & Wieser, H. G. (1997). Human hippocampus establishes associations in memory. *Hippocampus, 7*(3), 249–256.

Henke, K., Weber, B., Kneifel, S., Wieser, H. G., & Buck, A. (1999). Human hippocampus associates information in memory. *Proceedings of the National Academy of Sciences U S A, 96*(10), 5884–5889.

Hoppe, K. D., & Kyle, N. L. (1990). Dual brain, creativity, and health. *Creativity Research Journal, 3*(2), 150–157.

Hospers, J. (1985). Artistic creativity. *Journal of Aesthetics and Art Criticism, 43*(3), 243–255.

Howard-Jones, P. A., Blakemore, S.-J., Samuel, E. A., Summers, I. R., & Claxton, G. (2005). Semantic divergence and creative story generation: An fMRI investigation. *Cognitive Brain Research, 25*(1), 240–250.

Howard-Jones, P. A., & Murray, S. (2003). Ideational productivity, focus of attention, and context. *Creativity Research Journal, 15*(2-3), 153–166.

Israeli, N. (1962). Creative processes in painting. *Journal of General Psychology, 67*(2), 251–263.

James, W. (1980). *The principles of psychology* (Vol. 1). New York: Dover.

Jin, S. H., Kwon, Y. J., Jeong, J. S., Kwon, S. W., & Shin, D. H. (2006). Differences in brain information transmission between gifted and normal children during scientific hypothesis generation. *Brain and Cognition, 62*(3), 191–197.

Jung-Beeman, M., Bowden, E. M., Haberman, J., Frymiare, J. L., Arambel-Liu, S., Greenblatt, R., Reber, P. J., & Kounios, J. (2004). Neural activity when people solve verbal problems with insight. *PLoS Biology, 2*(4), E97.

Kahneman, D., Krueger, A. B., Schkade, D. A., Schwarz, N., & Stone, A. A. (2004). A survey method for characterizing daily life experience: the day reconstruction method. *Science, 306*(5702), 1776–1780.

Kane, M. J., Brown, L. H., McVay, J. C., Silvia, P. J., Myin-Germeys, I., & Kwapil, T. R. (2007). For whom the mind wanders, and when: An experience-sampling study of working memory and executive control in daily life. *Psychological Science, 18*(7), 614–621.

Klinger, E. (2009). Daydreaming and fantasizing: Thought flow and motivation. In K. D. Markman, W. M. P. Klein, & J. A. Suhr (Eds.), *Handbook of imagination and mental simulation* (pp. 225–240). New York: Psychology Press.

Klinger, E., & Cox, W. M. (1987). Dimensions of thought flow in everyday life. *Imagination, Cognition and Personality, 7*(2), 105–128.

Koechlin, E., Basso, G., Pietrini, P., Panzer, S., & Grafman, J. (1999). The role of the anterior prefrontal cortex in human cognition. *Nature, 399*(6732), 148–151.

Koechlin, E., Ody, C., & Kouneiher, F. (2003). The architecture of cognitive control in the human prefrontal cortex. *Science, 302*(5648), 1181–1185.

Koechlin, E., & Summerfield, C. (2007). An information theoretical approach to prefrontal executive function. *Trends in Cognitive Sciences, 11*(6), 229.

Kounios, J., Fleck, J. I., Green, D. L., Payne, L., Stevenson, J. L., Bowden, E. M., & Jung-Beeman, M. (2008). The origins of insight in resting-state brain activity. *Neuropsychologia, 46*(1), 281–291.

Kounios, J., Frymiare, J. L., Bowden, E. M., Fleck, J. I., Subramaniam, K., Parrish, T. B., & Jung-Beeman, M. (2006). The prepared mind: Neural activity prior to problem presentation predicts subsequent solution by sudden insight. *Psychological Science, 17*(10), 882–890.

Kowatari, Y., Lee, S. H., Yamamura, H., Nagamori, Y., Levy, P., Yamane, S., & Yamamoto, M. (2009). Neural networks involved in artistic creativity. *Human Brain Mapping, 30*(5), 1678–1690.

Krawczyk, D. C., Michelle McClelland, M., & Donovan, C. M. (2011). A hierarchy for relational reasoning in the prefrontal cortex. *Cortex, 47*(5), 588–597.

Kroger, J. K., Sabb, F. W., Fales, C. L., Bookheimer, S. Y., Cohen, M. S., & Holyoak, K. J. (2002). Recruitment of anterior dorsolateral prefrontal cortex in human reasoning: A parametric study of relational complexity. *Cerebral Cortex, 12*(5), 477–485.

Lambie, J. A., & Marcel, A. J. (2002). Consciousness and the varieties of emotion experience: A theoretical framework. *Psychological Review, 109*(2), 219–259.

Lane, R. D., Fink, G. R., Chau, P. M., & Dolan, R. J. (1997). Neural activation during selective attention to subjective emotional responses. *Neuroreport, 8*(18), 3969–3972.

Lepine, R., Bernardin, S., & Barrouillet, P. (2005). Attention switching and working memory spans. *European Journal of Cognitive Psychology, 17*(3), 329–345.

Luria, A. R. (1966). *Higher cortical functions in man*. London: Tavistock Publications.

Mar, R. A., & Oatley, K. (2008). The function of fiction is the abstraction and simulation of social experience. *Perspectives on Psychological Science, 3*(3), 173–192.

Martindale, C., Hines, D., Mitchell, L., & Covello, E. (1984). EEG alpha-asymmetry and creativity. *Personality and Individual Differences, 5*(1), 77–86.

Mason, M. F., Norton, M. I., Van Horn, J. D., Wegner, D. M., Grafton, S. T., & Macrae, C. N. (2007a). Response to comment on "Wandering minds: The default network and stimulus-independent thought." *Science, 317*(5834), 43.

Mason, M. F., Norton, M. I., Van Horn, J. D., Wegner, D. M., Grafton, S. T., & Macrae, C. N. (2007b). Wandering minds: The default network and stimulus-independent thought. *Science, 315*(5810), 393–395.

McCaig, R. G., Dixon, M., Keramatian, K., Liu, I., & Christoff, K. (2011). Improved modulation of rostrolateral prefrontal cortex using real-time fMRI training and meta-cognitive awareness. *Neuroimage, 55*(3), 1298–1305.

McGuire, P. K., Paulesu, E., Frackowiak, R. S., & Frith, C. D. (1996). Brain activity during stimulus independent thought. *Neuroreport, 7*(13), 2095–2099.

McKiernan, K. A., D'Angelo, B. R., Kaufman, J. N., & Binder, J. R. (2006). Interrupting the "stream of consciousness": An fMRI investigation. *Neuroimage, 29*(4), 1185–1191.

Mendez, M. F. (2004). Dementia as a window to the neurology of art. *Medical Hypotheses, 63*(1), 1–7.

Miller, B. L., Boone, K., Cummings, J. L., Read, S. L., & Mishkin, F. (2000). Functional correlates of musical and visual ability in frontotemporal dementia. *British Journal of Psychiatry, 176*, 458–463.

Miller, B. L., Cummings, J., Mishkin, F., Boone, K., Prince, F., Ponton, M., & Cotman, C. (1998). Emergence of artistic talent in frontotemporal dementia. *Neurology, 51*(4), 978–982.

Miller, E. K., & Cohen, J. D. (2001). An integrative theory of prefrontal cortex function. *Annual Review of Neuroscience, 24*, 167–202.

Miller, E. K., Nieder, A., Freedman, D. J., & Wallis, J. D. (2003). Neural correlates of categories and concepts. *Current Opinion in Neurobiology, 13*(2), 198–203.

Milner, B. (1963). Effects of different brain lesions on card sorting. *Archives of Neurology, 9*, 90–100.

Milner, B. (1964). Some effects of frontal lobectomy in man. In J. M. Warren & K. Akert (Eds.), *The frontal granular cortex and behavior* (pp. 313–334). New York: McGraw-Hill.

Mitchell, J. P., Banaji, M. R., & Macrae, C. N. (2005). The link between social cognition and self-referential thought in the medial prefrontal cortex. *Journal of Cognitive Neuroscience, 17*(8), 1306–1315.

Ochsner, K. N., & Gross, J. J. (2005). The cognitive control of emotion. *Trends in Cognitive Sciences, 9*(5), 242–249.

Ochsner, K. N., Knierim, K., Ludlow, D. H., Hanelin, J., Ramachandran, T., Glover, G., & Mackey, S. C. (2004). Reflecting upon feelings: An fMRI study of neural systems supporting the attribution of emotion to self and other. *Journal of Cognitive Neuroscience, 16*(10), 1746–1772.

Ochsner, K. N., Ray, R. D., Cooper, J. C., Robertson, E. R., Chopra, S., Gabrieli, J. D., & Gross, J. J. (2004). For better or for worse: Neural systems supporting the cognitive down- and up-regulation of negative emotion. *Neuroimage, 23*(2), 483–499.

Olson, I. R., Plotzker, A., & Ezzyat, Y. (2007). The enigmatic temporal pole: A review of findings on social and emotional processing. *Brain, 130*(Pt 7), 1718–1731.

O'Reilly, R. C., Noelle, D. C., Braver, T. S., & Cohen, J. D. (2002). Prefrontal cortex and dynamic categorization tasks: Representational organization and neuromodulatory control. *Cerebral Cortex, 12*(3), 246–257.

Parnes, S. J., & Meadow, A. (1959). Effects of brainstorming instructions on creative problem-solving by trained and untrained subjects. *Journal of Educational Psychology, 50*(4), 171–176.

Petrides, M. (2005). Lateral prefrontal cortex: architectonic and functional organization. *Philosophical Transactions of the Royal Society of London, Series B, 360*(1456), 781–795.

Petrides, M., & Pandya, D. N. (2007). Efferent association pathways from the rostral prefrontal cortex in the macaque monkey. *Journal of Neuroscience, 27*(43), 11573–11586.

Raichle, M. E., MacLeod, A. M., Snyder, A. Z., Powers, W. J., Gusnard, D. A., & Shulman, G. L. (2001). A default mode of brain function. *Proceedings of the National Academy of Sciences U S A, 98*(2), 676–682.

Ramnani, N., & Owen, A. M. (2004). Anterior prefrontal cortex: insights into function from anatomy and neuroimaging. *Nature Reviews Neuroscience, 5*(3), 184–194.

Ritter, G. W., & Weber, R. J. (1973). Production of stimulus-independent and stimulus-dependent thoughts as a function of word imagery and meaningfulness. *Perceptual & Motor Skills, 37*(1), 123–127.

Robertson, L. C., Lamb, M. R., & Knight, R. T. (1988). Effects of lesions of temporal-parietal junction on perceptual and attentional processing in humans. *Journal of Neuroscience, 8*(10), 3757–3769.

Robin, N., & Holyoak, K. J. (1995). Relational complexity and the functions of prefrontal cortex. In M. S. Gazzaniga (Ed.), *The cognitive neurosciences* (pp. 987–997). Cambridge, MA: MIT Press.

Rombouts, S. A., Machielsen, W. C., Witter, M. P., Barkhof, F., Lindeboom, J., & Scheltens, P. (1997). Visual association encoding activates the medial temporal lobe: A functional magnetic resonance imaging study. *Hippocampus, 7*(6), 594–601.

Rougier, N. P., Noelle, D. C., Braver, T. S., Cohen, J. D., & O'Reilly, R. C. (2005). Prefrontal cortex and flexible cognitive control: Rules without symbols. *Proceedings of the National Academy of Sciences U S A, 102*(20), 7338–7343.

Ruby, P., & Decety, J. (2004). How would you feel versus how do you think she would feel? A neuroimaging study of perspective-taking with social emotions. *Journal of Cognitive Neuroscience, 16*(6), 988–999.

Rypma, B., Prabhakaran, V., Desmond, J. E., Glover, G. H., & Gabrieli, J. D. (1999). Load-dependent roles of frontal brain regions in the maintenance of working memory. *Neuroimage, 9*(2), 216–226.

Sakai, K., & Passingham, R. E. (2003). Prefrontal interactions reflect future task operations. *Nature Neuroscience, 6*(1), 75–81.

Sakai, K., & Passingham, R. E. (2006). Prefrontal set activity predicts rule-specific neural processing during subsequent cognitive performance. *Journal of Neuroscience, 26*(4), 1211–1218.

Schacter, D. L., Addis, D. R., & Buckner, R. L. (2008). Episodic simulation of future events: Concepts, data, and applications. *Annals of the New York Academy of Sciences, 1124*, 39–60.

Schooler, J. W. (2002). Re-representing consciousness: Dissociations between experience and meta-consciousness. *Trends in Cognitive Sciences, 6*(8), 339–344.

Schooler, J. W., Smallwood, J., Christoff, K., Handy, T. C., Reichle, E. D., & Sayette, M. A. (2011). Meta-awareness, perceptual decoupling and the wandering mind. *Trends in Cognitive Sciences, 15*(7), 319–326.

Seeley, W. W., Menon, V., Schatzberg, A. F., Keller, J., Glover, G. H., Kenna, H., Reiss, A. L., & Greicius, M. D. (2007). Dissociable intrinsic connectivity networks for salience processing and executive control. *Journal of Neuroscience, 27*(9), 2349–2356.

Seger, C. A., Desmond, J. E., Glover, G. H., & Gabrieli, J. D. E. (2000). Functional magnetic resonance imaging evidence for right-hemisphere involvement in processing unusual semantic relationships. *Neuropsychology, 14*(3), 361–369.

Semendeferi, K., Armstrong, E., Schleicher, A., Zilles, K., & Van Hoesen, G. W. (2001). Prefrontal cortex in humans and apes: A comparative study of area 10. *American Journal of Physical Anthropology, 114*(3), 224–241.

Shallice, T. (1982). Specific impairments of planning. *Philosophical Transactions of the Royal Society of London. Series B, Biological Sciences, 298*(1089), 199–209.

Shallice, T., & Burgess, P. W. (1991). Higher-order cognitive impairments and frontal lobe lesions in man. In H. S. Levin, H. M. Eisenberg & A. L. Benton (Eds.), *Frontal lobe function and dysfunction* (pp. 125–138). New York: Oxford University Press.

Shulman, G. L., Fiez, J. A., Corbetta, M., Buckner, R. L., Miezin, F. M., Raichle, M. E., & Petersen, S. E. (1997). Common blood flow changes across visual tasks: II. Decreases in cerebral cortex. *Journal of Cognitive Neuroscience, 9*(5), 648–663.

Singer, J. L. (1966). *Daydreaming: An introduction to the experimental study of inner experience.* New York: Random House.

Singer, J. L., & McCraven, V. G. (1961). Some characteristics of adult daydreaming. *Journal of Psychology 51*, 151–164.

Singer, J. L., & Schonbar, R. A. (1961). Correlates of daydreaming: A dimension of self-awareness. *Journal of Consulting Psychology, 25*(1), 1.

Smallwood, J., & Schooler, J. W. (2006). The restless mind. *Psychological Bulletin, 132*(6), 946–958.

Smith, F. F., & Jonides, J. (1997). Working memory: A view from neuroimaging. *Cognitive Psychology, 33*(1), 5–42.

Smith, R., Keramatian, K., & Christoff, K. (2007). Localizing the rostrolateral prefrontal cortex at the individual level. *Neuroimage, 36*, 1387–1396.

Sperry, R. W. (1964). The great cerebral commissure. *Scientific American, 210*(1), 42–52.

Spiers, H. J., & Maguire, E. A. (2006). Spontaneous mentalizing during an interactive real world task: An fMRI study. *Neuropsychologia, 44*(10), 1674–1682.

Spreng, R. N., Mar, R. A., & Kim, A. S. N. (2009). The common neural basis of autobiographical memory, prospection, navigation, theory of mind and the default mode: A quantitative meta-analysis. *Journal of Cognitive Neuroscience, 21*(3), 489–510.

Squire, L. R., Stark, C. E. L., & Clark, R. E. (2004). The medial temporal lobe. *Annual Review of Neuroscience, 27*, 279–306.

Starchenko, M. G., Bekhtereva, N. P., Pakhomov, S. V., & Medvedev, S. V. (2003). Study of the brain organization of creative thinking. *Human Physiology, 29*, 652–653.

Stark, C. E., & Squire, L. R. (2001). When zero is not zero: The problem of ambiguous baseline conditions in fMRI. *Proceedings of the National Academy of Sciences of the United States of America U S A, 98*(22), 12760–12766.

Sternberg, R. J. (1985). Implicit theories of intelligence, creativity, and wisdom. *Journal of Personality and Social Psychology, 49*(3), 607–627.

Sternberg, R. J. (2006). *Cognitive psychology* (5th ed.). Belmont, CA: Wadsworth.

Stuss, D. T. (2007). New approaches to prefrontal lobe testing. In B. L. Miller & J. L. Cummings (Eds.), *The human frontal lobes: Functions and disorders* (2nd ed., pp. 292–305). New York: Guilford Publications.

Stuss, D. T., & Levine, B. (2002). Adult clinical neuropsychology: Lessons from studies of the frontal lobes. *Annual Review of Psychology, 53*, 401–433.

Subramaniam, K., Kounios, J., Parrish, T. B., & Jung-Beeman, M. (2009). A brain mechanism for facilitation of insight by positive affect. *Journal of Cognitive Neuroscience, 21*, 415–432.

Teasdale, J. D., Dritschel, B. H., Taylor, M. J., Proctor, L., Lloyd, C. A., Nimmo-Smith, I., & Baddeley, A. D. (1995). Stimulus-independent thought depends on central executive resources. *Memory and Cognition, 23*(5), 551–559.

Teasdale, J. D., Proctor, L., Lloyd, C. A., & Baddeley, A. D. (1993). Working memory and stimulus-independent thought: Effects of memory load and presentation rate. *European Journal of Cognitive Psychology, 5*(4), 417–433.

TenHouten, W. D. (1994). Creativity, intentionality, and alexithymia: A graphological analysis of split-brained patients and normal controls. In M. P. Shaw & M. A. Runco (Eds.), *Creativity and affect*. Westport, CT: Ablex Publishing.

Tsujimoto, S., Genovesio, A., & Wise, S. P. (2010). Evaluating self-generated decisions in frontal pole cortex of monkeys. *Nature Neuroscience, 13*(1), 120–126.

Unterrainer, J. M., & Owen, A. M. (2006). Planning and problem solving: From neuropsychology to functional neuroimaging. *Journal of Physiology* (*Paris*), *99*(4-6), 308–317.

van den Heuvel, O. A., Groenewegen, H. J., Barkhof, F., Lazeron, R. H., van Dyck, R., & Veltman, D. J. (2003). Frontostriatal system in planning complexity: A parametric functional magnetic resonance version of Tower of London task. *Neuroimage, 18*(2), 367–374.

Vartanian, O., Martindale, C., & Kwiatkowski, J. (2007). Creative potential, attention, and speed of information processing. *Personality and Individual Differences, 43*(6), 1470–1480.

Wallas, G. (1926). *The art of thought*. New York: Harcourt: Brace and Company.

Wallis, J. D., Anderson, K. C., & Miller, E. K. (2001). Single neurons in prefrontal cortex encode abstract rules. *Nature, 411*(6840), 953–956.

Waltz, J. A., Knowlton, B. J., Holyoak, K. J., Boone, K. B., Mishkin, F. S., de Menezes Santos, M., Thomas, C. R., & Miller, B. L. (1999). A system for relational reasoning in human prefrontal cortex. *Psychological Science, 10*(2), 119–125.

Weisberg, R. W. (1995). Case studies of creative thinking: Reproduction versus restructuring in the real world. In S. M. Smith, T. B. Ward & R. A. Finke (Eds.), *The creative cognition approach* (pp. 53–72). Cambridge, MA: MIT Press.

Weissman, D. H., Roberts, K. C., Visscher, K. M., & Woldorff, M. G. (2006). The neural bases of momentary lapses in attention. *Nature neuroscience, 9*(7), 971–978.

Wendelken, C., Nakhabenko, D., Donohue, S. E., Carter, C. S., & Bunge, S. A. (2008). "Brain is to thought as stomach is to ??": Investigating the role of rostrolateral prefrontal cortex in relational reasoning. *Journal of Cognitive Neuroscience, 20*(4), 682–693.

Wheeler, M. A., Stuss, D. T., & Tulving, E. (1997). Toward a theory of episodic memory: The frontal lobes and autonoetic consciousness. *Psychological Bulletin, 121*(3), 331–354.

Zysset, S., Huber, O., Ferstl, E., & von Cramon, D. Y. (2002). The anterior frontomedian cortex and evaluative judgment: An fMRI study. *Neuroimage, 15*(4), 983–991.

CHAPTER 21

Decision Neuroscience

Maya U. Shankar *and* Samuel M. McClure

Abstract

For the most part, human decision-making is well captured by the assumption that we act in order to maximize benefits. However, the assumption that humans are rational agents fails to account for many interesting nuances of human behavior. This chapter examines three instances in which our behavior violates basic tenets of rationality. In order to shed light on the underlying mechanisms that may govern these behaviors, the chapter discusses the role that neuroscience has played in understanding the cognitive processes that underlie these behaviors. One theme from this work is that decisions arise from the combined activity of multiple functionally distinct neural systems. Broadly, these findings support the many "dual system" theories from decision science in that the processes that underlie decision-making fall into two qualitatively distinct categories: one is automatic and rapid, while the other is associated with cognitive control and deliberative thought. Overall, and in a relatively short time, cognitive neuroscience has contributed to our theoretical understanding of choice behavior by lending support for such dual system models of decision-making and opening the door to understanding how these systems interact during choice. This input from cognitive neuroscience will certainly increase in its scope as the details of these choice dynamics become better understood with future research.

Key Words: decision-making, rational agent theory, expected utility theory, multiple-systems approach, ultimatum game, intertemporal choice, framing

Introduction: A Rational Approach to Decision Making

Decision-making pervades nearly every aspect of our lives. From the time we wake up in the morning until the moment we go to sleep, we are inundated by a wealth of choices, the consequences of which range from trivial to life altering. Our decisions of whether to hit the snooze button on our alarm clock, to eat whole-grain cereal or its sugary counterpart, or to take the bus or a car to work represent just a few of the hundreds of decisions we face on a daily basis.

In part because of the ubiquity and diversity of our choices, understanding how we make decisions is a daunting problem. Certainly the biggest

advance in overcoming the challenge derives from the assumption that humans and other animals seek to maximize the (subjective) utility of returns. Following from this assumption, social scientists have developed myriad models that describe behavior as it ought to be. Together, these models comprise *rational agent theory*, the fundamental tenet being that acting rationally involves choosing that option which results in the optimal outcome.

Under this umbrella theory fall a number of precise models that capture ideal behavior in specific decision-making contexts. For example, *expected utility* integrates probability into outcomes of arbitrary magnitudes, describing optimal behavior for decisions involving risk. According to this model, value (based on personal preference) is assigned to all possible choice alternatives. These values are weighted by their probability of occurrence. Rational behavior entails selecting that outcome which yields the highest total expected utility (Von Neumann & Morgenstern, 1947). This is summarized by the following equation:

$$\text{Utility} = \sum_i (\text{probability}_i \times \text{value}_i)$$

where i indexes the (possibly numerous) outcomes that result from a considered choice alternative.

To make this concrete, imagine that you are asked to choose between the following two outcomes:

A. A 20% chance of winning $45, or else nothing.
B. A 25% chance of winning $30, or else nothing.

In this simple example, expected utility theory asserts that the optimal choice is option A, since its calculated utility (i.e., .20 × $45 = $9.00) is greater than that of option B (i.e., .20 × $45 = $7.50).

Likewise, *discounted utility* describes how to make optimal decisions when the consequences of the decision are spread out over time (e.g., a choice between receiving a dollar today and two dollars in a week from now). Rational choice in these contexts commonly requires trading off the magnitude of the reward with time; that is to say, is the extra payoff worth the wait? To decide between temporally distinct outcomes requires discounting their absolute value based on the delay until receipt and then choosing the greater of these two discounted values. This delay discounting process places a premium on time, so that we always prefer to receive an identical reward sooner rather than later. Rationality in these choices generally focuses on the requirement that preferences be stable over time. For example, if you do in fact prefer one dollar today to two dollars in a week, you should similarly prefer one dollar in a year to two dollars in a year and a week.

Rational models of decision-making have tremendous appeal. They are quantitatively precise and generally make very good predictions about human behavior. More importantly, people are sensitive to incentives in the ways assumed by rational models. Increasing the value of an outcome, shortening its delay to receipt, and increasing the likelihood of occurrence all increase subjective appeal. However, despite the explanatory power of these rational models, a wealth of research has revealed their numerous limits in accounting for the full extent of human decision-making behavior. As should become clear, our choices routinely violate basic tenets of rationality, yielding suboptimal choices and inconsistent preferences over time.

To see this, consider the case of deciding in which of two different cities to buy a home (cf. Gigerenzer, 2007). There are likely a large number of attributes along which we are inclined to make this choice: weather, cost, job opportunities, safety, cultural richness, quality of the school systems. The rational approach to solving this conflict is to first assign a value to each dimension for each city, then take the sum and select the city with the highest value from this calculation. While we may occasionally strive to take this approach, most of us find that our final choices in these difficult contexts are driven not by this kind of deliberative choice procedure but instead by a "gut feeling." Indeed, neuroscience suggests that without such gut feelings we become hopelessly incapable of behaving in such scenarios (Damasio, 1995). As a result, while our decisions may sometimes align with the optimal outcome, it is certainly not guaranteed.

Our reliance on gut feelings is perhaps to be expected. Many of these behavioral patterns stem from the fact that our cognitive resources are limited in both capacity and speed. The computational challenges required to estimate the expected value of all possible outcomes can be overwhelming. If we were to deliberately reason through every choice we face, we would hardly be able to make it out of our homes in the morning. This is especially true given the rapidly changing demands of our environment. In cases such as this that overwhelm our ability to maintain relevant information in working memory, automatic judgments may in fact be more adaptive than more reasoned preferences (Dijksterhuis, Bos, Nordgren, & von Baaren, 2006; Wilson & Schooler, 1991).

The distinction between seemingly automatic, feeling-based decision-making and exhaustive deliberative consideration has long been recognized in behavioral psychology. Many *dual systems* models have been proposed to capture the presumed cognitive processes that underlie decision-making. These models all assert that behavior stems not simply from one unitary rational system, as normative models presuppose, but instead choices follow from the interactions of distinguishable cognitive systems. Of particular interest is the fact that research from cognitive neuroscience supports this view as well, by revealing that these distinctions are similarly instantiated on a neural level.

Many terms have been used for the two cognitive systems involved in decision-making. While acknowledging that no set of terms seems completely satisfactory, we use *automatic* and *controlled* in this chapter. Automatic processes are defined as fast, effortless, associative in nature, and stereotyped in function such that they are generally insensitive to behavioral contexts or overarching goals. In some sense, automatic processing serves as a "cognitive shortcut," allowing us to evaluate choice alternatives with an emphasis on efficiency and speed. This is especially valuable when the computational challenges inherent to a decision are large, such as when there are multiple relevant attributes to consider, as illustrated in the example above. By contrast, controlled processing is slower, serial, effortful, deliberative, goal directed, and flexible, since it depends on general rules (i.e. reasoning) that are adaptable to the specific circumstances at hand (cf. Kahneman, 2003). The vast majority of the time, these systems work in concert, directing behavior toward the same goal and allowing us to rapidly respond to the myriad daily choices we face. However, sometimes automatic and controlled evaluations stand in direct opposition, producing different dispositions toward the same stimulus. These latter circumstances are clearly of greatest interest to experimentalists. They allow investigation of how these different processes interact to determine behavior.

In this chapter, we investigate decision-making in three contexts in which human behavior deviates from the maxims of economic rationality. Each of the instances we explore involves an interaction between these competing value systems. Building from this behavioral data, we examine how insights from cognitive neuroscience have increased our understanding of the mechanisms that underlie both automatic and controlled processing. We begin our discussion with a brief overview of the distinction between automatic and controlled processes and the brain regions associated with each. In the subsequent section, we describe the results of a number of classic behavioral psychology experiments which serve as descriptive evidence that we do not always adhere to rational models of behavior. We supplement our discussion of each of these behavioral findings with new neuroscience research that provides compelling evidence for a dual systems approach to understanding choice behavior. We conclude that cognitive neuroscience provides an ideal explanatory system for human decision-making behavior by uncovering the primary mechanisms that are at play when we make choices. In

this way, it serves as an important complement to existing economic and psychological research if the ultimate goal is to construct a comprehensive and predictive model of decision-making.

The Controlled-Automatic Distinction

Before delving into the brain, it is first important that we clarify our use of the terms *automatic* and *controlled* processing. A number of different terms have been used to describe these distinct modes of processing: emotional vs. cognitive, System 1 vs. System 2, bottom-up vs. top-down, habitual vs. cognitive, fast vs. slow, hot vs. cold, and implicit vs. explicit reasoning (Stanovich & West, 2000; Evans, 2003; Sloman, 1996; see Frank, Cohen, & Sanfey, 2009, for a comprehensive review). While there is contention surrounding which terms most accurately reflect the distinctions between these two systems, there is consensus surrounding their defining features.

Automatic processing refers to low-level psychological processes that are engaged by events that elicit strongly valenced or stereotyped behavioral responses. This processing is rapid and yields instinctive responses to specific stimuli or events. The downside of this kind of processing is that it is not particularly flexible and thus is suited to certain situations and not others (Kahneman, 2003). In the brain, numerous structures have been associated with automatic processing. For sensory processing, such as rapidly and effortlessly identifying a friend, posterior cortical structures are directly implicated. Processes that involve emotional or valenced responses implicate numerous other regions, including (among other regions) the mid-brain dopamine system and its primary targets in the striatum, as well as the amygdala and ventral parts of the anterior insular cortex. Several areas in so-called perilimbic regions of the prefrontal cortex have also been associated with automatic processes. These regions receive direct input from dopamine neurons and amygdala projection neurons. For the purposes of decision-making, the ventromedial prefrontal cortex (including the orbitofrontal cortex) will be most important of these prefrontal areas in the discussion that follows.

Controlled processing is defined by the ability to flexibly respond to different contexts and circumstances, to rationally consider the long-term consequences of behavior, and to plan behavior for the sake of accomplishing arbitrary goals. This mode of reasoning is associated with problem solving and planning. For goal-directed behavior, controlled processing considers the desired outcome during processing and is thus malleable to the requirements of the task at hand. Controlled processes depend principally on lateral regions of the prefrontal cortex, which influence behavior through dense efferent projections to posterior parietal cortex (Miller and Cohen, 2001). (Important distinctions are made between ventro- and dorsolateral prefrontal cortex, but these are beyond the scope of this chapter.) The anterior cingulate cortex (ACC) is also important for controlled processing but is believed to serve a regulatory role, triggering the lateral prefrontal cortex when things are going awry (Botvinick, Braver, Barch, Carter, & Cohen, 2001).

While empirical evidence supports categorizing brain regions as we have done, some important moderating comments are warranted before we proceed. Specifically, the implicated brain regions are not involved in automatic or controlled processing exclusively. One fact about anatomy illustrates the importance of this point: all of the brain areas listed above are interconnected. It therefore follows that they interact in ways that are critical for understanding decision-making and that the distinction between their functions is fluid. This point is easily illustrated with respect to mid-brain dopamine function. Dopamine is acknowledged to be associated with automatic, rationality-defying valuation processes, such as the compulsion that drives addiction. However, dopaminergic dysfunction also underlies the disordered deliberative thought that defines schizophrenia. In decision research, these functions are generally dissociated. Similarly, LeDoux (1996) discusses "low road" and "high road" neural pathways and functions for the amygdala that roughly align with our automatic and controlled distinction. Despite this forewarning, and as evidenced by the case studies that follow in the remainder of this chapter, the automatic vs. controlled distinction certainly captures important fundamental functional differences in the brain areas we discuss. It is just that, as always seems to be the case in science, important subtleties defy a strict categorical division.

Undermining Rationality: Three Examples from Psychological Research

In the past several decades, descriptive data, emerging principally from the field of psychology, have illuminated numerous features of human decision-making that can produce clearly irrational behavior. Together, these studies pose a major challenge to normative theories of decision-making.

Rational agent models can certainly be adapted to account for these behaviors. However, this requires making new assumptions to sculpt normative predictions by changing how utility is calculated. We feel that the more fruitful approach is to first understand the general styles of decision-making and to then use this understanding to derive principles for understanding behavior. To this end, cognitive neuroscience research has played an important role. These findings make the importance of automatic and controlled modes of reasoning even clearer.

We have selected three particularly illustrative experimental paradigms in which people's behavior deviates from rational doctrine: situations involving temporal delay (intertemporal choice), risk taking under different cognitive framing, and social interactions in the Ultimatum Game. For each of these cases, we provide empirical evidence from neuroscience that support a multiple-systems (brain areas) approach.

Hyperbolic Discounting: A Challenge to Discounted Utility Theory

A paradigmatic example of decision-making behavior that deviates from rationality can be found in our responses to intertemporal decisions. Intertemporal choices capture a ubiquitous and broad class of decisions between outcomes that are realized at different points in time. As discussed above, choosing in these circumstances often requires determining whether postponing the consumption of a reward (e.g., spending money now) is worth its respective increase in value (e.g., through savings and investment). To decide between temporally distinct outcomes requires one to discount their absolute value based on the delay until receipt and then choose the greater of these two discounted values. The criterion used for rationality asserts that preferences should not vary across time. If we prefer to save a percentage of our upcoming paycheck now, then this preference should hold even when the money is "burning a hole in our pocket."

The discount function required by this model of rationality decays exponentially with delay (Frederick, Loewenstein, & O'Donoghue, 2003; Koopmans, 1960; Samuelson, 1937). Any other discount function necessarily produces inconsistent preferences. To be clear, consider a simple choice between receiving $10 next week and $12 in 2 weeks and assume a preference for the larger $12 outcome. Holding consistent preferences implies that if asked again at any point during the initial 1-week delay, the preference for $12 should remain. So, if asked again in 1 week, one should still prefer $12 (now to be received in only 1 week) to $10 immediately.

It is not hard to come up with examples in which our behavior fails to show such consistency. Thaler and Shefrin (1981) argued that when people are asked to choose between one apple today and two apples tomorrow, they consistently choose the former. However, when this offer is delayed by a year, they select the latter option instead. More problematically, people commonly profess to want to save more but fail to do so, presumably because of the temptation posed by having money available to spend now. These preference reversals have been associated with a number of human failings, spanning everything from the difficulty in maintaining a healthy diet to procrastination.

Generally, we tend to act more impulsively for rewards that are available immediately but hold more far-sighted preferences when outcomes are remote. Impulsivity also depends on emotional arousal (Loewenstein, 1996; Wilson & Daly, 2004); we are far more capable of being patient when we are not aroused. (Loewenstein illustrates this point by reporting our extreme patience for mundane goods like gasoline and writing paper.) However, when an outcome is known to satisfy a visceral desire, like the consumption of food when hungry, we become far more susceptible to impulsive behavior. In this way, time-dependent preference reversals indicate a relative overvaluation of rewards available in the immediate future and thus violate rationality. This is commonly taken to reflect a conflict between the emotions that underlie immediate temptation and our cognitive appraisal of what actions coincide with long-term interest.

INIGHTS FROM NEUROSCIENCE

Cognitive neuroscience has provided evidence supporting the conflict assumed to exist for intertemporal choice. The making of intertemporal choices recruits separate neural systems. One system preferentially responds when considered rewards are immediately available, whereas the other system does not have such time dependence and is associated with more far-sighted choices (Figner et al., 2010; Hare, O'Doherty, Camerer, Schultz, & Rangel, 2008; McClure, Ericson, Laibson, Loewenstein, & Cohen, 2007; McClure, Laibson, Loewenstein, & Cohen, 2004). Furthermore, these brain systems include areas associated with automatic and deliberative processing.

Consider the experiment performed by McClure et al. (2004). Participants were asked to select from among a series of rewards that carried different monetary values available at different points in the future. Some choices included an immediate reward, while others were composed of only delayed payments. In this experiment, automatic processing should be preferentially engaged when participants consider an immediately available reward, and should be significantly less responsive when both outcomes in a choice are delayed. Controlled processing, by contrast, should be engaged in all decisions equally. Regions associated with the mesolimbic dopamine system, including the ventral striatum and ventromedial prefrontal cortex, showed greater activity during choices that involved the opportunity for monetary rewards on the day of the experiment than that during choices involving only delayed rewards. By contrast, regions of the dorsolateral prefrontal cortex (DLPFC) and the posterior parietal cortex were much less sensitive to delay. Interestingly, the relative strength of activity in both systems predicted the resulting behavior. More recently, it has been shown that disrupting DLPFC function increases impulsivity (Figner et al., 2010), demonstrating the necessity of assaying the function of both brain systems in order to predict choice.

Framing Effects: A Challenge to Expected Utility Theory

A second example in which people clearly violate rationality concerns decisions under risk. One reasonable requirement of rationality is that preferences should be constant as long as the attributes of the choice are held the same. In other words, the way in which options are presented should be irrelevant as long as nothing fundamental is altered. However, investigators have routinely demonstrated violations of this tenet, referred to as extensionality, in carefully crafted experiments. In general, humans do not make decisions in ways that are description-invariant. An example derived from Kahneman and Teversky (1979) illustrates this nicely:

1. Imagine that you are given $1,000 and now must choose between earning an additional
   (A) $1,000 with a 50% probability or (B) $500 with certainty.

2. Imagine that you are given $2,000 and now must choose between losing
   (A') -$1,000 with a 50% probability or (B') -$500 with certainty.

In this example, the majority of people prefer option B in the first problem but option A' in the second problem—despite the fact that these preferences are clearly contradictory. It seems that people consider the gambles as gains or losses without appropriately integrating the initial bonuses they were given. The final preferences reflect a general tendency to be risk-averse when considering gains, but risk-seeking for outcomes involving losses. One hypothesis for explaining why this may occur is that people rely too much on automatic heuristics for such problems without adequately, and deliberatively, considering the full implications of the choice.

INSIGHTS FROM NEUROSCIENCE

Research from neuroscience has demonstrated that more intuitive, automatic processes do in fact govern the irrational decision-making tendencies that we see in the loss–gain risk aversion paradigms. According to de Martino et al. (de Martino, Kumaran, Seymour, & Dolan, 2006), when decisions involve incomplete information, or overly complex information, participants end up relying on simplifying heuristics or rules of thumb. The authors investigated the underlying mechanisms that drive this effect using fMRI and a decision-making task that manipulated framing. In their study, participants were alerted to the total amount of money that would be involved in the trial at its start (e.g., £50). They were then asked to make a choice between two options: the certain option (which was framed as either gaining some fraction of the total sum—e.g., keep £20 of the £50—or as losing the difference between that fraction and the initial sum—e.g., lose £30 of the £50) or the risky option (which consisted of a pie chart that conveyed the probabilities of either winning or losing that amount). As expected, participants' responses were significantly affected by the framing manipulation. More specifically, they were risk-averse in the gain frame (indicated by preferences for the sure outcomes over the gambles) and were risk-seeking in the loss frame (preferring the gambles).

The results showed differential activation in brain regions depending on whether people's behaviors fell in line with the framing effect or whether they ran counter to this general tendency. There was a substantial increase in amygdala activation when participants were risk-averse when the outcome was framed in terms of gains and risk-seeking than when the scenario was framed in terms of losses, highlighting the involvement of automatic processing in these cases. On the contrary, there was greater activity in the ACC when subjects' choices ran counter to this general behavioral tendency. This suggests that there is competition between these two competing neural systems, with controlled processes associated with increased ACC activation, and more automatic behavior associated with amygdala activity.

The Ultimatum Game: Irrationality in Social Norms

A final example of clearly irrational behavior is found in a number of related bargaining games, captured most famously in the simple Ultimatum Game (Thaler, 1988). In the classic paradigm, two participants, a proposer and a responder, must agree on how to divide a sum of money. The game begins with the proposer who offers a split, which the responder must then either accept or reject. If the responder accepts the offer, the endowment is divided as proposed. However, if the offer is rejected, neither individual receives any money.

Rationality suggests that there is only one sensible way for both participants to proceed. First, consider the responder. This person will receive an offer and has the option to accept some money or condemn both participants to no earnings. Since some earnings ought to always be preferred to nothing, the responder should accept any non-zero offer. Knowing this, the proposer is set to take advantage of the responder by offering as tiny an amount as possible of the total sum. The responder may begrudge this gesture, but nonetheless should accept.

Interestingly, this outcome is seldom realized (Güth, Schmittberger, & Schwarz, 1982; Thaler, 1988). Instead, proposers' offers generally fall between 30 and 40% of the total endowment. Responders also reject at a high rate if the offer is 20% or less of the total endowment (Hoffman, McCabe, & Smith, 1995). It has been hypothesized that perhaps we reject these offers because we have a negative emotional (automatic) response to the unfairness of the offer. This behavioral tendency may certainly be adaptive. In small social groups, reputations can have profound influences on how we are treated by others. Developing a reputation for accepting unequal shares could have tremendously negative consequences in the long run. Many experiments that use the Ultimatum Game account for this by making the offers anonymous and "one-shot" so that reputation building is not a factor. Still, it is reasonable to speculate that we have an automatic preference for fairness that manifests as an acute negative response to unfair treatment.

INSIGHTS FROM NEUROSCIENCE RESEARCH

In an fMRI experiment conducted by Sanfey et al. (Sanfey, Rilling, Aaronson, Nystrom, & Cohen, 2003), participants' brain activity was measured as they responded to a series of ultimatum offers. Participants were informed that offers were generated by one of two sources: either by a person whose picture they saw alongside the proposed split, or by a computer program. In both cases, half of the offers were (approximately) fair (50:50 and 70:30 splits) and the other half unfair (80:20 and 90:10). As expected, nearly all of the fair offers were accepted and a significant number of unfair offers were rejected. Interestingly, people were much more likely to reject unfair offers from a person than from a computer program. Furthermore, unfair offers from people elicited activity in the insula, a region of the brain associated with negative emotions (Britton et al., 2006; Calder, Lawrence, & Young, 2001; Knutson & Greer, 2008; Phillips et al., 1997; Shapira et al., 2003). The DLPFC was also activated during the decision-making process, perhaps reflecting an overall goal to earn money. Critically, level of activity in the insula predicted eventual choice, with greater insula responses co-occurring with rejected offers. These findings suggest two things. First, violations of fairness elicit negative emotions (insula activity). Second, in order to overcome the desire to turn down money, deliberative reasoning (as reflected by DLPFC activity) is essential.

Concluding Remarks

In this chapter, we have investigated those contexts in which our decisions stray from the basic tenets of rationality. From these examples it follows that while rational models are precise and, for the most part, good predictors of human behavior, on their own they are insufficient in describing the entirety of decision-making behavior. In order to shed light on the underlying mechanisms that govern these irrational tendencies, we appealed to emerging research from the field of cognitive neuroscience. More specifically, we discussed three classic behavioral psychology paradigms—temporal discounting, risk preferences under varying cognitive frames, and the Ultimatum Game—each of which involves the interaction of competing neural systems. The brain regions identified in these experiments are associated with automatic and controlled processing through a wealth of prior neuroscience research. Overall, research in cognitive neuroscience has successfully revealed some of the physical mechanisms that govern our behaviors. In doing so, this research has enabled further investigation of how precisely these regions should be characterized and the variables that likely influence their recruitment.

It is important to note that while both automatic and controlled processing are associated with distinguishable brain regions, they are, in fact, highly *interactive*. Understanding the dynamic interplay between these systems is especially useful when trying to predict behavior in situations that involve conflict—that is, when lower-level, automatic processes favor one behavior and controlled, flexible processes favor something different. Future research will undoubtedly examine the interactions between these competing systems and reveal details concerning the means by which behavior changes dynamically, with and between individual choices. So far there has been limited work done on this in decision science, largely because of the difficulty of assessing underlying mechanisms from overt behavior (although see Chapter XX for a neural analysis of how these systems interact).

We believe that, since the goal of decision science is to construct a truly comprehensive model of human decision-making, foundational decision-making research from both economics and behavioral psychology must be considered together with findings from the field of cognitive neuroscience. Neuroscience techniques can be used to directly identify and measure underlying processes. The initial results from this fusion are apparent in this chapter: neuroimaging has supported the dual systems model proposed to account for behavior in numerous classic experiments. We anticipate that decision neuroscience will eventually transform the way in which we conceptualize decision-making and lend insights into the underlying nature of our choice processes.

References

Botvinick, M. M., Braver, T. S., Barch, D. M., Carter, C. S., & Cohen, J. D. (2001). Conflict monitoring and cognitive control. *Psychological Review, 108*, 624–652.

Britton, J. C., Phan, K. L., Taylor, S. F., Welsh, R. C., Berridge, K. C., & Liberzon, I. (2006). Neural correlates of social and nonsocial emotions: An fMRI study. *Neuroimage, 31*, 397–409.

Calder, A. J., Lawrence, A. D., & Young, A. W. (2001). Neuropsychology of fear and loathing. *Nature Reviews Neuroscience, 2*(5), 352–363.

Damasio, A. (1995). *Descartes' error: Emotion, reason, and the human brain*. New York: Macmillan.

de Martino, B., Kumaran, D., Seymour, B., & Dolan, R. J. (2006). Frames, biases, and rational decision-making in the human brain. *Science, 313*, 684–687.

Dijksterhuis, A., Bos, M. W., Nordgren, L. F., & von Baaren, R. B. 2006. On making the right choice: The deliberation-without-attention effect. *Science, 311*, 1005–1007

Evans, J. S. (2003). In two minds: Dual-process accounts of reasoning. *Trends in Cognitive Sciences, 7*, 454–459.

Figner, B., Knoch, D., Johnson, E. J., Krosch, A. R., Lisanby, S. H., Fehr, E., & Weber E. U. (2010). Lateral prefrontal cortex and self-control in intertemporal choice. *Nature Neuroscience*, *13*, 538–539.

Frank, M. J., Cohen, M. X., & Sanfey, A. G. (2009). Multiple systems in decision making: A neurocomputational perspective. *Current Directions in Psychological Science*, *18*, 73–77.

Frederick, S., Loewenstein, G., & O'Donoghue, T. (2003). Time discounting and time preference: A critical review. In G. Loewenstein, D. Read, & R. Baumeister (Eds.), *Decision and time* (pp. 13–86). New York: Russell Sage.

Gigerenzer G. (2007). *Gut feelings: The intelligence of the unconscious*. New York: Viking.

Güth, W., Schmittberger, R., & Schwarze, B. (1982). An experimental analysis of ultimatum bargaining. *Journal of Economic Behavior and Organization*,

Hare, T. A., O'Doherty J., Camerer, C. F., Schultz, W., & Rangel, A. (2008). Dissociating the role of the orbitofrontal cortex and the striatum in the computation of goal values and prediction errors. *Journal of Neuroscience*, *28*, 5623–5630.

Hoffman, E., McCabe K., & Smith, V. (1995) On expectations and the monetary stakes in ultimatum games. *International Journal of Game Theory*, *86*, 653.

Kahneman, D. (2003). A perspective on judgment and choice: Mapping bounded rationality. *American Psychologist*, *58*, 697–720.

Kahneman, D., & Tversky, A. (1979) Prospect theory: An analysis of decisions under risk. *Econometrica*, *47*, 262–291.

Knutson, B., & Greer, S. M. (2008). Anticipatory affect: Neural correlates and consequences for choice. *Philosophical Transactions of the Royal Society, Series B: Biological Science*, *363*, 3771–3786.

Koopmans, T. C. (1960). Stationary ordinal utility and impatience. *Econometrica*, *28*, 287–309.

LeDoux, J. (1996). *The emotional brain: The Mysterious underpinnings of emotional life*. New York: Simon & Schuster.

Loewenstein, G. (1996). Out of control: Visceral influences on behavior. *Organizational Behavior and Human Decision Processes*, *65*, 272–292.

McClure, S. M., Ericson, K. M., Laibson, D. I., Loewenstein, G., & Cohen, J. D. (2007). Time discounting for primary rewards. *Journal of Neuroscience*, *27*, 5796–5804.

McClure, S. M., Laibson, D. I., Loewenstein, G., & Cohen, J. D. (2004) Separate neural systems value immediate and delayed monetary rewards. *Science*, *306*, 503–507.

Miller, E. K., & Cohen, J. D. (2001). An integrative theory of prefrontal cortex function. *Annual Review of Neuroscience*, *24*, 167–202.

Phillips, M. L., Young, A. W., Senior, C., Brammer, M., Andrew, C., Calder, A. J., et al. (1997). A specific neural substrate for perceiving facial expressions of disgust. *Nature*, *389*(6650), 495–449

Samuelson, P. (1937). A note on measurement of utility. *Review of Economic Studies*, *4*, 155–161.

Sanfey, A., Rilling, J., Aaronson, J., & Nystrom, L., Cohen, J. (2003). The neural basis of economic decision-making in the Ultimatum Game. *Science*, *300*(5626), 1755–1758.

Shapira, N. A., Liu, Y., He, A. G., Bradley, M. M., Lessig, M. C., James, G. A., et al. (2003). Brain activation by disgust-inducing pictures in obsessive-compulsive disorder. *Biological Psychiatry*, *54*, 751–756.

Sloman, S. A. (1996). The empirical case for two systems of reasoning. *Psychological Bulletin*, *119*(1), 3–22.

Stanovich, K. E., & West, R. F. (2000). Advancing the rationality debate. *Behavioral and Brain Sciences*, *23*, 701–726.

Thaler, R. H. (1988). Anomalies: The Ultimatum Game. *Journal of Economic Perspectives*, *2*, 195–206.

Thaler, R. H., & Shefrin, H. M. (1981). An economic-theory of self-control. *Journal of Political Economy*, *89*, 392–406.

Von Neumann, J., & Morgenstern, O. (1947). *Theory of games and economic behavior* (2nd ed.). Princeton, NJ: Princeton University Press.

Wilson, M., & Daly, M. (2004). Do pretty women inspire men to discount the future? *Proceedings of Biological Sciences*, *271*(Suppl 4), S177–S179.

Wilson, T., & Schooler, J. (1991). Thinking too much: Introspection can reduce the quality of preferences and decisions. *Journal of Personality and Social Psychology*, *60*(2), 181–192.

CHAPTER 22

Categorization

Bradley C. Love

Abstract

Judging a person as a friend or foe, a mushroom as edible or poisonous, or a sound as an *l* or *r* are examples of categorization problems. This chapter considers the relative merits of four basic types of category learning models: rule-, prototype-, exemplar-, and cluster-based models. The history of model progression is marked by descendant models displaying increasingly sophisticated processing mechanisms that can manifest the behaviors of ancestral models. These four basic model types are related to the computations performed by four candidate learning systems in the human brain, which rely on prefrontal cortex, posterior occipital cortex, the striatum, and the medial temporal lobes. One issue raised is whether the prefrontal cortex and posterior occipital cortex support true learning systems or are better viewed as supporting general cognitive and perceptual abilities. Use of well-specified cognitive models can help answer related theoretical questions, such as how multiple learning systems contribute to categorization behavior.

Key Words: categorization, category learning, classification, memory systems, learning systems

Introduction

The act of categorization is ubiquitous in human behavior. Judging a person as a friend or a foe, a mushroom as edible or poisonous, or a sound as an *l* or *r* are examples of categorization problems. Because people never encounter the same exact stimulus twice, they must develop categorization schemes that capture the useful regularities in their environment. One key research challenge is to determine how humans acquire and represent categories. The focus of this chapter will be on proposed category learning mechanisms and their brain basis. While there are a number of other valuable topics in categorization research, such as how semantic information is organized (Cree & McRae, 2003), the nature of category-specific deficits (Caramazza & Shelton, 1998), and how prior knowledge guides category acquisition (Rehder & Murphy, 2003), this chapter will focus on models and studies that

address how people acquire novel categories from observed examples. For a review of how well-learning categories are represented in the brain, see work by Martin (2007).

Category learning is a theory- and model-rich area within cognitive psychology. Models have played a prominent role in shaping our understanding of human category learning. Accordingly, proposed mechanisms are diverse, including rule-, prototype-, and exemplar-based models, as well as clustering models and models that contain multiple systems. One general trend is toward models with increasingly sophisticated processing mechanisms that can mimic the behaviors of existing models, as well as address behaviors outside the scope of previous models.

Cognitive models are beginning to play an important role in cognitive neuroscience research as well, particularly in the area of category learning.

Cognitive models are distinguished from other useful analysis tools, such as multivoxel pattern recognition (see Pereira, Mitchell, & Botvinick, 2009), in that cognitive models are theories of the mental operations that support behavior, rather than simply analysis tools. Operations and components in cognitive models can be linked to brain measures (such as the BOLD signal in fMRI studies; see Daw, O'Doherty, Dayan, Seymour, & Dolan, 2006) to understand the brain basis of interesting behaviors, such as the operations that support categorization (Davis, Love, & Preston, 2012). Model-based analysis can help us understand how human behavior arises from the interaction of numerous brain regions. In addition to aiding data analysis, formal cognitive models make clear predictions that can be evaluated analytically or through simulation. Successful models are formal characterizations of the field's best theories, and unlike verbal theories, formal models can be evaluated quantitatively.

Cognitive models may help overcome common century-old criticisms of cognitive neuroscience research. Franz remarked in his 1912 essay "New Phrenology" that "the individual parts of the brain do not work independently; they work interdependently, and it is because of the possible functional and anatomical connections that certain types or kinds of mental states are more in evidence than others." To Franz, the allure of localizing mental activities in the brain begot overly simplistic and crude theories of mental processes and brain function. Cognitive models may offer a solution to these difficulties (see Love & Gureckis, 2007). Localizing mental function need not be problematic. The issue is what to localize. The value of a theory that localizes mental function lies in both the characterization of the mental process and the bridge theory that links this characterization to the brain. Starting with an ill-specified or folk psychological theory of mental function ultimately limits the value of the overall enterprise and invites comparison to Franz's new phrenology.

For these reasons, this chapter places an emphasis on model mechanisms and their linkage to the brain. One claim is that well-specified, process models of cognitive functions are the appropriate targets for localization. Successful cognitive models, which are quantitatively validated on a broad range of data sets, offer a number of advantages over folk psychological, ad hoc, or traditional psychological theories. In addition to being predictive, behavioral models have mechanisms and dynamics that can be related to brain measures. For example, models of decision processes (a component process in categorization) have been useful for understanding how choice is implemented in the brain (Purcell et al., 2010). Although not naive accounts of mental function, cognitive models are typically idealized and relatively simple. This clarity provides a good starting point for localizing function. Given that debates persist over the basic function of areas as well studied as the hippocampus (Eichenbaum, 1999; Stark, Bayley, & Squire, 2002), starting simple makes sense.

In the course of reviewing a variety of category learning models, I will emphasize what the relative merits of each model reveal about the nature of human learning. After reviewing the basic model types, the relationship between models of category learning and candidate learning systems in the brain will be considered. Finally, a number of challenges for understanding the brain basis of categorization will be discussed.

Models of Category Learning

In this section, I will briefly review several models of human category learning. Presentation order is organized chronologically, from oldest to most recent accounts of category learning. Although more recent models offer some advantages over their ancestors, it would be a mistake to view ancestral models as being supplanted by their descendants. Each model class addresses some key aspects of human category learning and serves an important theoretical role. In fact, many older models have taken on new life as components in recently proposed multiple systems models. One common component in these multiple systems models is a rule-based system, which is the first model class considered here.

Rule-Based Models

The classical view of categories holds that categories are defined by logical rules. This view has a long history, dating back to Aristotle. In Figure 22.1, any item that is a square is a member of category A. This simple rule determines category membership. According to the rule view, our category of category A can be represented by this simple rule. Discovering this rule would involve a rational hypothesis-testing procedure. Through this procedure one attempts to discover a rule that is satisfied by all of the positive examples of a category, but none of the negative examples of the category (i.e., items that are members of other categories). In trying to come up with such a rule for category A, one might first try the rule *if dark, then in category A*. After rejecting this rule (because there are counterexamples), other rules would be tested (starting with simple rules and progressing toward more complex rules) until the correct rule is eventually discovered. For example, in learning about birds, one might first try the rule *if it flies, then it is a bird*. This rule works pretty well, but not perfectly (penguins do not fly and bats do). Another simple rule like *if it has feathers, then it is a bird* would not work either because a pillow filled with feathers is not a bird. Eventually, a more complex rule might be discovered, such as *if it has feathers and wings, then it is a bird*.

For decades psychologists have conducted experiments to characterize the relative difficulty people have in learning various types of rules (Bruner, Goodnow, & Austin, 1956; Shepard, Hovland, & Jenkins, 1961). These studies have provided the primary data used to develop and validate models of hypothesis testing. Some models, such as RULEX (Nosofsky, Palmeri, & McKinley, 1994), embody the hypothesis testing procedure described above. RULEX starts with simple hypotheses and progresses toward more complex hypotheses until a set of rules and exceptions is discovered that properly discriminates between the categories.

The term *rule* has various, somewhat conflicting, interpretations. Here, I focus on rule-based models, like RULEX, that engage in explicit, hypothesis testing. RULEX's mechanistic approach (i.e., algorithmic in the sense of Marr, 1982) contrasts with other approaches that aim to predict how difficult learning should be, based on calculations of how complex the correct hypothesis is (Feldman, 2000). The latter approaches, which are not concerned with the actual process of learning, have more in common with measures of complexity and compression (Pothos & Chater, 2002). Yet other approaches, such as General Recognition Theory (Maddox & Ashby, 1993), aim to assess and compactly describe people's performance rather than characterize the learning process. Unlike these more abstract approaches, mechanistic models of hypothesis testing, such as RULEX, largely implement the strategic and conscious thought processes that we feel (by introspection) that we are carrying out when solving classification problems. These explicit processes are thought to rely on limited working memory capacity (Zeithamova & Maddox, 2006).

Although rules can in principle provide a concise representation of a category, often more elaborate representations would serve us better. Category representation needs to be richer than a simple rule, because we use categories for much more than simply classifying objects we encounter. For instance, we often use categories to support inference (e.g., a child infers that members of the category stove can be dangerously hot). Using categories to make inferences is a very important use of categories (Markman & Ross, 2003). Knowing something is an example of a category tells us a great deal about the item. For example, after classifying a politician from the United States as a Republican, one can readily infer the politician's position on a number of issues. The point is that our representations of categories must include information beyond what is needed to classify items as examples of the category. For example, the rule *if square, then in category A* correctly classifies all members of category A in Figure 22.1, but it doesn't capture the knowledge that all category A members are *dark*. One problem with rule representations of categories is that potentially useful information is discarded. In fact, even when people explicitly use rules to classify item, performance is heavily influenced by rule-irrelevant information (Allen & Brooks, 1991; Lacroix, Giguere, & Larochelle, 2005; Sakamoto & Love, 2004), which is inconsistent with rules serving as the sole basis for category representations.

Perhaps the biggest problem with the rule approach to categories is that most of our everyday categories do not seem to be describable by a tractable rule. To demonstrate this point, Wittgenstein (1953) noted that the category game lacks a defining property. Most games are fun, but Russian roulette is not fun. Most games are competitive, but ring around the roses is not competitive. While most games have characteristics in common, there is not a rule that unifies them all. Rather, we can think of

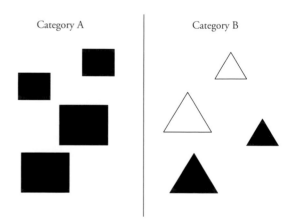

Figure 22.1 Examples of category A and category B. A simple rule on shape discriminates between the two categories.

the members of the category game as being organized around a family resemblance structure (analogous to how members of your family resemble one another). Rosch and colleagues' (Rosch & Mervis, 1975) seminal work demonstrated the psychological reality of many of Wittgenstein's intuitions. Even some paradigmatic examples of rule-based classification reveal a non-rule-based underbelly (see Love, Tomlinson, & Gureckis, 2008, for a review). Hahn and Ramscar (2001) offer one such example. Tigers are defined as having tiger DNA, which is a seemingly rule-based category definition. However, determining whether an animal has tiger DNA amounts to assessing the similarity of the animal's DNA to known examples of tiger DNA.

A related weakness of the rule account of categories is that examples of a category differ in their typicality (Barsalou, 1985; Posner & Keele, 1968; Reed, 1972; Rosch & Mervis, 1975). If all a category consisted of was a rule that determined membership, then all examples should have equal status. According to the rule account, all that should matter is whether an item satisfies the rule. Our categories do not seem to have this definitive flavor. For example, some games are better examples of the category game than others. Basketball is a very typical example of the category of games. Children play basketball in a playground, it is competitive, there are two teams, each team consists of multiple players, you score points, etc. Basketball is a typical example of the category of games because it has many characteristics in common with other games. Russian roulette, by contrast, is not a very typical game—it requires a gun and one of the two players dies. Russian roulette does not have many properties in common with other games. In terms of family resemblance structure, we can think of basketball as having a central position and Russian roulette being a distant cousin to the other family members. These findings extend to categories in which a simple classification rule exists. For example, people judge the number 3 to be a more typical odd number than the number 47, even though membership in the category odd number can be defined by a simple rule (Gleitman, Gleitman, Miller, & Ostrin, 1996).

The fact that category membership follows a gradient as opposed to being all or none affords us flexibility in how we apply our categories. Of course, this flexibility can lead to ambiguity. Consider the category mother (see Lakoff, 1987, for a thorough analysis). It is a category that we are all familiar with that seems straightforward—a mother is a woman who becomes pregnant and gives birth to a child. But what about a woman who adopts a neglected infant and raises it in a nurturing environment? Is the birth mother who neglected the infant a mother? What if a woman is implanted with an embryo from another woman? Court cases over maternity arise because the category of motherhood is ambiguous. The category exhibits greater flexibility and productivity than is even indicated above. For example, is it proper to refer to an architect as the mother of a building? All the above examples of the category mother share a family resemblance structure (i.e., they are organized around some commonalities), but the category is not rule based. Some examples of the category mother are better than others.

I do not want to imply that rule-based approaches do not have their place. For example, rule-based approaches might be viable for some socially defined categories. For example, determining whether currency is legal tender might largely involve applying a series of rules (Hampton, 2001). Also, as we will see later in this chapter, rule-based approaches figure prominently in multiple systems accounts. While rule-based approaches might not provide a sufficient explanation of human learning in isolation, such approaches might prove viable in certain domains or as components of multiple systems models.

Prototype-Based Models

The prototype approach to category learning and representation was developed by Rosch and colleagues to address some of the shortcomings of the rule approach. Prototype models represent information about all the possible properties (i.e., stimulus dimensions), instead of focusing on only a few properties like rule models do. The prototype of a category is a summary of all of its members (Posner & Keele, 1968; Reed, 1972; Smith & Minda, 2001). Mathematically, the prototype is the average or central tendency of all category members. Figure 22.2 displays the prototypes for two categories, simply named categories A and B. Notice that all the items differ in size and luminance (i.e., there are two stimulus dimensions) and that the prototype is located amidst all of its category members. The prototype for each category has the average value on both the stimulus dimensions of size and luminance for the members of its category.

The prototype of a category is used to represent the category. According to the prototype model, a novel item is classified as a member of the category whose prototype it is most similar to. For example, a large bright item would be classified as a member

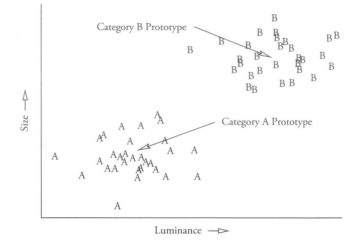

Figure 22.2 Two categories and their prototypes.

of category B because category B's prototype is large and bright (see Figure 22.2). The position of the prototype is updated when new examples of the category are encountered. For example, if one encountered a very small and dark item that is a member of category A, then category A's prototype would move slightly toward the bottom left corner in Figure 22.2. As an outcome of learning, the position of the prototype shifts toward the newest category member in order to take it into account. A prototype can be very useful for determining category membership in domains where there are many stimulus dimensions that each provide information useful for determining category membership, but no dimension is definitive. For example, members of a family may tend to be tall and have large noses, a medium complexion, brown eyes, and good muscle tone, but no family member possesses all of these traits. Matching on some subset of these traits would provide evidence for being a family member.

Notice the economy of the prototype approach. Each cloud of examples in Figure 22.2 can be represented by just the prototype. The prototype is intended to capture the critical structure in the environment without having to encode every detail or example. It is also fairly simple to determine which category a novel item belongs to by determining which category prototype is most similar to the item.

Unlike the rule approach, the prototype model can account for typicality effects. According to the prototype model, the more typical category members should be those members that are most similar to the prototype. In Figure 22.2, similarity can

be viewed in geometric terms—the closer together items are in the plot, the more similar they are. Thus, the most typical items for categories A and B are those that are closest to the appropriate prototype. Accordingly, the prototype approach can explain why robins are more typical birds than penguins. The bird prototype represents the average bird: has wings, has feathers, can fly, can sing, lives in trees, lays eggs, etc. Robins share all of these properties with the prototype, whereas penguins differ in a number of ways (e.g., penguins can't fly, but they do swim). Extending this line of reasoning, the best example of a category should be the prototype, even if the actual prototype has never been viewed (or doesn't even exist). Indeed, numerous learning studies support this conjecture. After viewing a series of examples of a category, human participants are more likely to categorize the prototype as a category member (even though they never actually viewed the prototype) than they are to categorize an item they have seen before as a category member (Posner & Keele, 1968).

Because the prototype approach does not represent categories in terms of a logical rule that is either satisfied or not, it can explain how category membership has a graded structure that is not all or none. Some examples of a category are simply better examples than other examples. Also, categories do not need to be defined in terms of logical rules but are rather defined in terms of family resemblance to the prototype. In other words, members of a category need not share a common defining thread, but can have many characteristic threads in common with one another.

The prototype approach, while preferable to the rule approach for the reasons just discussed, does fail to account for important aspects of human category learning. The main problem with the prototype model is that it does not retain enough information about examples encountered in learning. For instance, prototypes do not store any information about the frequency of each category, yet people are sensitive to frequency information. If an item was about equally similar to the prototype of two different categories and one category had 100 times more members than the other, people would be more likely to assign the item to the more common category (under most circumstances, see Kruschke, 1996). Of course, some of these concerns could be addressed by expanding the information that a prototype encodes.

However, other concerns seem fundamental to the prototype approach. Prototypes are not sensitive to the correlations and substructure within a category. For example, a prototype model would not be able to represent that spoons tend to be large and made of wood or small and made of steel. These two subgroups would simply be averaged together into one prototype. This averaging makes some categories unlearnable with a prototype model. One example of such a category structure is shown in Figure 22.3. Each category consists of two subgroups. Members of category A are either *small* and *dark* or they are *large* and *light*, whereas members of category B are either *large* and *dark* or they are *small* and *light*. The prototypes for the two categories are both in the center of the stimulus space (i.e., medium size and medium luminance). Items cannot be classified correctly by which prototype they are most similar to because the prototypes provide little guidance.

In general, prototype models can only be used to learn category structures that are linearly separable. A learning problem involving two categories is linearly separable when a line or plane can be drawn that separates all the members of the two categories. The category structure shown in Figure 22.2 is linearly separable because a diagonal line can be drawn that separates the category A and B members (i.e., the category A members fall on one side of the line and the category B members fall on the other side of the line). Thus, this category structure can be learned with a prototype model. The category structure illustrated in Figure 22.3 is nonlinear—no single line can be drawn to segregate the category A and B members. Mathematically, a category structure is linearly separable when there exists a weighting of the feature dimensions that yields an additive

rule that correctly indicates one category when the sum is below a chosen threshold and the other category when the sum is above the threshold.

The inability of the prototype model to learn nonlinear category structures detracts from its worth as a model of human category learning because people are not biased against learning nonlinear category structures. While the extent to which natural categories deviate from linear structures is contested (Murphy, 2002), the general consensus is that people in the laboratory do not show a preference for linear structures in supervised learning (Medin & Schwanenflugel, 1981), though they might in unsupervised learning (Love, 2002). Some nonlinear category structures may actually be easier to acquire than linear category structures. For example, it seems quite natural that small birds sing, whereas large birds do not sing. Many categories have subtypes within them that we naturally pick out. One way for the prototype model to address this learnability problem is to include complex features that represent the presence of multiple simple features (e.g., large and blue). Unfortunately, this approach quickly becomes unwieldy as the number of stimulus dimensions increases (e.g., Gluck & Bower, 1988).

Related to the prototype model's inability to account for substructure within categories is its inadequacy as a model of item recognition. Unlike exemplar models considered in the following section (Medin & Schaffer, 1978; Nosofsky, 1986), prototypes models do not readily account for how people recognize specific items because the category prototype averages away item-distinguishing information that people retain in some situations.

Exemplar-Based Models

Exemplar models store every training example in memory instead of just the prototype (i.e., the summary) of each category. Perhaps surprising upon first consideration, exemplar models can account for findings marshaled in support of prototype models, such as sensitivity to family resemblance structure. At the same time, by retaining all of the information from training, exemplar models address many of the shortcomings of prototype model. Exemplar models are sensitive to the frequency, the variability, and the correlations among items. In this section, I will discuss how exemplar-based models can display these behaviors.

Unlike prototype models, exemplar models can master category structures that contain substructure. For the learning problem illustrated in Figure 22.3,

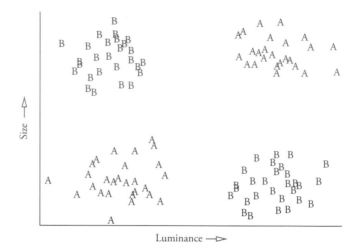

Figure 22.3 Two categories and their prototypes.

an exemplar model would store every training example. New items are classified by how similar they are to all items in memory (not just the prototype). For the category structure illustrated in Figure 22.3, the pairwise similarity of a novel item and every stored item would be calculated. If the novel item tended to be more similar to the category A members (i.e., the item was small and dark) than to the category B members, then the novel item would be classified as a member of category A.

One aspect of exemplar models that seems counterintuitive is their lack of any abstraction in category representation. It seems that humans do learn something more abstract about categories than a list of examples. Surprisingly, exemplar models are capable of displaying abstraction. For instance, exemplar models can correctly predict that humans more strongly endorse the underlying prototype (even if it has not been seen) than an actual item that has been studied (a piece of evidence previously cited in favor of the prototype model). How could this be possible without the prototype actually being stored? It would be impossible if exemplar models simply functioned by retrieving the exemplar in memory that was most similar to the current item and classified the current item in the same category as the retrieved exemplar (this is essentially how processing works in a prototype model, except that a prototype is stored in memory instead of a bunch of exemplars).

Instead, exemplar models engage in more sophisticated processing and calculate the similarity between the current item (the item that is to be classified) and every item in memory. Some exemplars

in memory will be very similar to the current item, whereas others will not be very similar. The current item is classified in the category in which the sum of its similarities to all the exemplars is greatest. When a previously unseen prototype is presented to an exemplar model, it can be endorsed as a category member more strongly than a previously seen item. The prototype (which is the central tendency of the category) will tend to be somewhat similar to every item in the category, whereas any given non-prototype item will tend to be very similar to some items (especially itself!) in memory, but not so similar to other items. Overall, the prototypical item can display an advantage over an item that has actually been studied. Abstraction in an exemplar model is indirect and results from processing (i.e., calculating and summing pairwise similarities), whereas abstraction in a prototype model is rather direct (i.e., prototypes are stored).

By and large, exemplar models can mimic all the behaviors of prototype models, but the opposite is not true. There are some subtle behaviors that the prototype model can display that versions of exemplar models cannot. For example, prototype and exemplar models predict slightly different category endorsement gradients (i.e., probability of membership) as one moves toward the center of a category (see Nosofsky & Zaki, 2002; and Smith, 2002, for a recent debate).

Although exemplar models are decent models of recognition, they do have some fundamental shortcomings. Exemplar models calculate recognition strength as the sum of similarity to all items stored in memory. Thus, the pairwise similarity relations among items govern recognition. However, humans often appear to build schema-like structures in memory and store items preferentially that deviate from these structures (see Sakamoto & Love, 2004, for a review). Thus, exemplar models do not correctly predict enhanced recognition for items that violate salient rules or patterns (Palmeri & Nosofsky, 1995). Exemplar models do not capture these results because exception items that violate these patterns are not exceptional in terms of their pairwise similarity relations to other items. Exception items are exceptional in terms of violating a knowledge structure stored in memory (Sakamoto & Love, 2004, 2006).

At a more philosophical level, exemplar models seem to make some questionable assumptions. For example, exemplar models store every training example, which seems excessive. Also, every exemplar is retrieved from memory every time an item is classified (though see Nosofsky & Palmeri, 1997, for an exception). In addition to these assumptions, one worries that the exemplar model does not make strong enough theoretical commitments because it retains all information about training and contains a great deal of flexibility in how it processes information. In support of this conjecture, Sakamoto, Matsuka, and Love (2004) built an exemplar model that effectively built distributed knowledge structures and could account for exception recognition findings (also see Rodrigues & Murre, 2007). While their model did not explicitly build schema or exception representations, the model did learn to selectively tune exemplars (broad tunings for rule-following items and tight tunings for exception items) and properly weight these exemplars to give rise to an exemplar model that functionally contained exception and schema-like knowledge structures. If there are no constraints on how items are processed, then in principle an exemplar model can account for any pattern of results, thereby reducing the exemplar model's theoretical utility. However, in practice, exemplar models often follow previously published formalisms and serve as valuable theoretical tools.

Clustering Models

Prototype and exemplar models can be seen as opposite ends of a continuum of category representation. On one extreme, prototype models store every category member together in memory. At the other extreme, exemplar models store every category member separately in memory. Between these two extremes lie a wealth of possibilities. Categories in the real world contain multiple subtypes and exceptions. For example, the category mammals contains subcategories like cats, dogs, horses, and bats. Ideally, our mental representations would reflect this structure. Both prototype and exemplar models are inflexible in that they treat the structure of each category as predetermined. These models do not let the distribution of category members influence the form category representations take. For example, prototype models assume that categories are always represented by one node (i.e., the prototype) in memory, whereas exemplar models assume that categories are always represented by one node in memory for every category example encountered.

One reasonable intuition is that similar items should cluster together in memory (Anderson, 1991; Love, Medin, & Gureckis, 2004; Vampaemel & Storms, 2008). For example, a person walking down Congress Avenue in Austin in the fall will encounter thousands of seemingly identical grackles. The rationale for storing each of these birds separately in memory is unclear. At the same time, someone walking down the street probably would mentally note unusual or otherwise surprising birds.

Clustering models embody these intuitions about memory. For example, Anderson's (1991) rational model (also see Sanborn, Griffiths, & Navarro, 2006) computes the probability that an item belongs to an existing cluster (a prototype can be thought of as a cluster that encodes all category members). If this probability is sufficiently high, the cluster is updated to reflect its new member. However, if the item is more likely from a new cluster, then a new cluster is created. The overarching goal of Anderson's model is to create clusters that are maximally predictive.

Love et al.'s SUSTAIN model operates along similar lines in that it incrementally adds clusters as it learns, but its recruitment process is somewhat different from the rational model's. In the SUSTAIN model, new clusters are recruited in response to surprising events. What counts as a surprising event depends on the learner's current goals. When the learner's goals are somewhat diffuse, as in unsupervised learning, SUSTAIN's operation is very similar to that of the rational model. In such cases, items that are dissimilar from existing clusters result in a new cluster being recruited to encode the item. However, in supervised learning situations, such as in classification learning (the learner's goal is to properly name the stimulus's category), items are recruited when a surprising error results. For example, upon encountering a bat for the first time and being asked to name it, a child surprised to learn that a bat is not a bird would recruit a new cluster to capture this example. If the child activates this cluster in the future to successfully classify other bats, then the cluster would come to resemble a bat prototype.

Both the rational model and SUSTAIN can be viewed as multiple prototype models in which the number of prototypes is determined by the complexity of the category structure. When categories are very regular, these models will function like prototype models. When categories are very irregular (i.e., there is no discernable pattern linking members to one another), these models will tend to function like exemplar models. SUSTAIN's sensitivity to a learner's goal allows it to capture performance differences across different induction tasks. For example, people learning through inference (e.g., *This is a mammal. Does it have fur?*) tend to focus on the internal structure of categories, whereas people learning through classification (e.g., *This has fur. Is it a mammal?*) tend to focus on information that discriminates between categories (see Markman & Ross, 2003, for a review). These two ways of interacting with stimuli during learning have very different acquisition and retention profiles (Sakamoto & Love, 2010).

Clustering models, like exemplar and prototype models, can be coupled with selective attention mechanisms that can learn to emphasize critical stimulus properties. For example, in learning to classify car makes, SUSTAIN would learn to weight shape more than color because shape reliably indicates model type whereas color varies idiosyncratically. The motivation for selective attention comes from the observation that people can only process a limited number of stimulus properties simultaneously. Selective attention mechanisms have been developed through consideration of human and animal learning data (see Kruschke, 2003, for a review). In tasks that require people to actively sample stimulus dimensions, selective attention mechanisms predict which dimensions are fixated (Rehder & Hoffman, 2005).

Importantly, selective attention mechanisms allow non-rule models to display rule-like behaviors. When a prototype, exemplar, or clustering model places all of its attention on one stimulus dimension, a model's operation is indistinguishable from the application of a simple rule. In terms of accounting for human data, SUSTAIN outperforms RULEX in some respects on learning problems that require acquiring a simple rule and storing

exceptions to these rules (Sakamoto & Love, 2004). SUSTAIN creates a small set of clusters to encode items that follow the rules and encodes exceptions in their own clusters. Attention is heavily biased to the rule-relevant dimensions. This allows SUSTAIN to show enhanced recognition for exceptions and rule-like behavior for rule-following items, while maintaining some sensitivity to non-rule-relevant dimensions like human subjects do.

The incorporation of selective attention mechanisms into non-rule models invites a number of theoretical questions. It is not entirely clear whether these selective attention mechanisms should be viewed as an integral part of non-rule models or as rule mechanisms grafted onto non-rule models. One possibility is that people are relying on rule and non-rule systems, thus necessitating the need for selective attention mechanisms in non-rule models.

Multiple Systems Models

Determining the best psychological model can be difficult, as one model may perform well in one situation but be bested by a competing model in a different situation. One possibility is that there is not a single "true" model. In category learning, this line of reasoning has led to the development of models containing multiple learning systems. These more complex models hold that category learning behavior reflects the contributions of different systems organized around discrepant principles that use qualitatively distinct representations. The idea that multiple learning systems support category learning behavior enjoys widespread support among researchers in the cognitive neuroscience of category learning (see Ashby & O'Brien, 2005, for a review and Nosofsky & Zaki, 1998, for a dissenting opinion).

Multiple systems models of category learning detail the relative contributions of the component learning systems. For each categorization decision, some multiple systems models select which individual system governs the response (Ashby, Alfonso-Reese, Turken, & Waldron, 1998). Over time, one system might prove more useful and dominate responding. Alternatively, the modeler can predetermine the timing of the shift from one system to another. This is sensible in cases where there is good evidence for predictable shifts, such as the shift from rule-based to exemplar-based responding in classification learning (Johansen & Palmeri, 2002).

Both of these multiple systems approaches are somewhat inadequate in that they do not allow the current situation to dictate which system is operable. For example, when trying to learn how to operate a new piece of machinery, a person might use a hypothesis (i.e., rule) system, but when riding a bicycle, a more procedural system might govern responding and be updated. In some models, like ATRIUM (Erickson & Kruschke, 1998), the relative contributions of divergent systems can depend on the circumstances (cf., Yang & Lewandowsky, 2004). ATRIUM contains a rule-and-exemplar learning system. The system that is operable is determined by a gating system, allowing different classification procedures to be applied to different parts of the stimulus space. For example, familiar items could be classified by the exemplar system, whereas rules could be applied to unfamiliar items.

Somewhat muddying the waters, ostensibly single-system models have been developed that also manifest this ability. In CLUSTER (Love & Jones, 2006), clusters can tune themselves (i.e., attend) to different stimulus properties and encode categories at various levels of granularity. This allows CLUSTER to apply different procedures to different parts of the stimulus space, like ATRIUM does. For example, clusters would heavily weight color in the domain of clothing and processor type in the domain of laptops. This tuning is accomplished by minimizing an error term that reflects the model's predictive accuracy, a technique commonly used in connectionist modeling. Tunable parameters that encode each cluster's specificity and attentional weighting of different properties are shaped by experience.

Models like CLUSTER are very rich. Consideration of such models leads to the question of what constitutes or defines a system. As previously discussed, one could even construe the selective attention mechanism of various models as being a separate system (see Poldrack & Foerde, 2008, for a related discussion on model parameters). Fortunately, models are mathematically well specified and allow researchers to make predictions and state their theories clearly without having to be overly concerned with the semantics of what constitutes a system. The mathematical specification of models can free researchers from some potentially thorny debates.

The notion of a system perhaps takes on greater significance when considered in the context of the brain (Ashby & Crossley, 2010). Within cognitive neuroscience, it is generally accepted that there is a hypothesis-testing system that relies on frontal circuitry (Ashby et al., 1998), a dopamine-mediated procedural learning system that involves the striatum (Ashby et al., 1998), a repetition priming system that involves early visual areas (Reber, Gitelman, Parrish, & Mesulam, 2003), and a medial temporal lobe (MTL) learning system that maps onto exemplar- or cluster-based learning (Love & Gureckis, 2007). For each system, there are behavioral manipulations that tend to emphasize the one system over the other systems. Lesion, patient, and imaging studies provide compelling evidence for the multiple systems view. The relationship between the models discussed above and proposed learning systems in the brain is discussed in greater detail in the next section.

Brain Basis of Category Learning

In this section, the relationship between the models described above and candidate learning systems in the brain is considered. Successful models that have been developed in light of these learning systems' detailed circuitry (e.g., Becker & Wojtowicz, 2007; Frank, Seeberger, & O'Reilly, 2004; Norman & O'Reilly, 2003) will not be discussed. Instead, the focus will be on linking the basic computational properties of category learning models to learning systems in the brain.

Posterior Occipital Cortex

Forms of implicit learning (i.e., learning without awareness) with visual stimuli are thought to rely on the posterior occipital cortex (see Smith & Grossman, 2008, for a review). The best support for this hypothesis comes from prototype abstraction studies in which subjects view numerous stimuli that are similar to an underlying prototype (e.g., dot pattern tasks). In these tasks, patients with impaired declarative memory, such those with lesions in the MTL (Knowlton & Squire, 1993; Kolodny, 1994; Reed, Squire, Patalano, Smith, & Jonides, 1999) and Alzheimer's disease (Bozoki, Grossman, & Smith, 2006; Eldridge, Masterman, & Knowlton, 2002), retain the ability to extract a single prototype through implicit means.

After exposure to items that coalesce around a prototype, imaging studies find deactivations of posterior occipital cortex (roughly V2) for items that are similar to the prototype (Aizenstein et al., 2000; Koenig et al., 2008; Reber, Stark, & Squire, 1998; Reber et al., 2003). High accuracy in prototype extraction tasks does not appear to require involvement of declarative memory areas, though such areas can be engaged by these learning tasks (Koenig et al., 2008).

Interestingly, this form of implicit learning seems to be very limited in terms of the types of categories that can be learned. Alzheimer's patients and amnesiacs can extract a single prototype but are unable to discriminate two prototypes (Sinha, 1999; Zaki, Nosofsky, Jessup, & Unversagt, 2003). These results suggest that the learning supported by posterior occipital cortex is better viewed as a perceptual priming system than as a general mechanism for acquiring category knowledge. One possibility is that people experience a feeling of fluency (based on deactivations in visual areas) for items similar to the average of recent items and that this feeling of fluency supports categorization performance for tasks in which there is a single prototype. Such a learning system would not be useful for discriminating categories. In terms of the models discussed, a prototype model restricted to a single prototype provides the best characterization of the reviewed findings. The other models all master a greater variety of discriminations than the posterior occipital cortex appears to support. An open issue is whether perceptual priming for prototypical stimuli leads to lasting representations or is short-lived.

Prefrontal Cortex

The prefrontal cortex (PFC) and head of the caudate nucleus are theorized to engage a rule-based category learning system that depends on working memory (WM) to support maintenance of rules and new hypothesis testing (Ashby et al., 1998; Monchi, Petrides, Petre, Worsley, & Dagher, 2001; Seger et al., 2000; Smith, Patalano, & Jonides, 1998). This learning system appears to correspond with explicit hypothesis testing in which learners are aware of applying a rule and can accurately verbally report the hypothesis they are entertaining. Manipulations that disrupt WM or executive attention are particularly detrimental to this form of rule-based learning (DeCaro, Thomas, & Beilock, 2008; Waldron & Ashby, 2001; Zeithamova & Maddox, 2006).

Patient studies indicate that explicit learning of rules does not rely on intact MTL (Janowsky, Shimamura, Kritchevsky, & Squire, 1989; Leng & Parkin, 1988). One possibility is that people solve simple rule-based tasks by entertaining rules in WM. Indeed, executive attention is mediated by structures in the PFC (Posner & Petersen, 1990). Imaging results of rule-based learning corroborate this interpretation (Konishi et al., 1999; Monchi et al., 2001; Smith et al., 1998). Here, the PFC may be better viewed as supporting rule-based reasoning during category learning tasks than as a dedicated category learning system. Like the posterior occipital cortex, it is not clear to what extent learned PFC representations persist over time (though see Asaad, Rainer, & Miller, 1998).

In terms of the models reviewed, the PFC best corresponds to a rule-based model in which there is no permanent store of inferred rules (i.e., inferred rules reside in a WM and are subject to disruption). Like the perceptual priming system, the explicit rule system is extremely limited in the types of categories that it can learn. All the aforementioned studies involve acquiring rules with one or two antecedents (e.g., "If the item is big and bright, then it is a member of Category A"). Multiple prototype, exemplar, and clustering models all provide more general and powerful learning mechanisms. That said, common laboratory and neuropsychology tasks, such as the Wisconsin Card Sorting Task, likely rely on the PFC (Joel, Weiner, & Feldon, 1997). Additionally, subtle category discriminations can involve a rule component supported by the PFC (especially during initial acquisition).

Striatum and Midbrain Dopaminergic Areas

The tail and body of the caudate nucleus are theorized to support a category learning system that involves the strengthening of associations between individual stimuli and category responses, often described as procedural learning (Ashby et al., 1998; Foerde, Knowlton, & Poldrack, 2006; Knowlton, Mangels, & Squire, 1996; Knowlton, Squire, & Gluck, 1994; Poldrack et al., 2001). Unlike the previously discussed learning systems, the procedural learning system appears able to learn arbitrary category discriminations under appropriate conditions.

Necessary conditions for learning include corrective feedback arriving shortly after responding (Shohamy, Myers, Kalanithi, & Gluck, 2008). Following Schultz, Dayan, and Montague (1997), one hypothesis is that delaying feedback disrupts dopamine-mediated learning (Maddox, Ashby, & Bohil, 2003). Likewise, manipulations that disrupt procedural learning in serial reaction time tasks (e.g., Willingham, 1998) also disrupt category learning tasks based on subtle (non-rule-based) discriminations (Ashby, Noble, Filoteo, Waldron, & Ell, 2003). Further supporting the linkage of procedural learning to dopamine-mediated striatal learning, patients with Parkinson's disease have deficits in processing feedback in procedural learning tasks (Shohamy et al., 2004). Neuroimaging studies further support this linkage (Nomura et al., 2007; Poldrack & Foerde, 2008; Shohamy et al., 2008).

In terms of the previously reviewed models, variants of exemplar models are the best computational analog to the procedural learning system. Like human procedural learning, exemplar models can master arbitrary category discriminations and are sensitive to the details of their inputs. The best matching variant is the covering map version of Kruschke's (1992) connectionist exemplar model. This model seeds the space of possible stimuli uniformly with a number of exemplar nodes and uses error-driven learning to associate stimuli with category responses. Such a model corresponds to a standard exemplar model when training examples are uniformed sampled over the space of possible items. The Striatal Pattern Classifier (SPC; Ashby & Waldron, 1999) has a similar operation, though the high-level motivation for this model is quite different. In the SPC, the mechanisms in the model are described as associating regions of stimulus space with motor responses, not as storing experienced exemplars in memory. Nevertheless, at an abstract computational level, these approaches are highly similar.

Medial Temporal Lobe

One neurobiological system that has proven difficult to characterize in terms of its role in category learning is the MTL. The essential role of the MTL for encoding and retrieval of declarative memories, long-term memory for facts and events, is well established (Scoville & Milner, 1957; Squire, 1992). However, the role of the MTL in category learning remains controversial; each of the major fixed representational forms (e.g., rules, prototypes, exemplars) has been ascribed to the function of the MTL by different groups of researchers. For example, many theories suggest that the MTL uses exemplar-based representations (Ashby & Maddox, 2005; Ashby & O'Brien, 2005; Pickering, 1997). However, empirical work has suggested that the MTL may be essential for the storage of category rules (Nomura et al., 2007; Seger & Cincotta, 2006) or representations of category prototypes (Aizenstein et al., 2000; Reber et al., 2003; Zaki et al., 2003; Zeithamova, Maddox, & Schnyer, 2008). In contrast, other theorists question whether the MTL is involved in category learning at all (Ashby et al., 1998; Maddox & Ashby, 2004). Given these difficulties in ascribing a single, fixed representational type to the function of the MTL, one plausible alternative that may integrate these disparate theories is that the MTL builds representations that are appropriate for a specific learning context, like those proposed by clustering models (e.g., Anderson, 1991; Love et al., 2004).

One hypothesis is that the SUSTAIN clustering model corresponds to the operation of MTL and its subregions (Davis et al., 2012; Love & Gureckis, 2007). In terms of declarative memory, the hippocampus is thought to play a critical role in rapidly forming conjunctive representations that bind together different sources of information into a single flexible memory (Brown & Aggleton, 2001; Eichenbaum, Yonelinas, & Ranganath, 2007; Norman & O'Reilly, 2003). Conjunctive representations are thought to be encoded by the hippocampus in response to novelty (Stark & Squire, 2001; Tulving, Markowitsch, Craik, Habib, & Houle, 1996; Yamaguchi, Hale, Desposito, & Knight, 2004) in as little as a single trial (Morris, Garrud, Rawlins, & O'Keefe, 1982; Rutishauser, Mamelak, & Schuman, 2006), as well as code information about the spatiotemporal context in which an item occurred (Staresina & Davachi, 2009; Wallenstein, Eichenbaum, & Hasselmo, 1998). SUSTAIN's clusters resemble hippocampal conjunctive representations in that they can be dynamically recruited in response to novelty on a single trial. They also bind together multiple-item features and category information into a single flexible representation that can promote generalization to novel contexts (Love et al., 2004).

Many real-world categories often appear to be describable by simple representations, such as logical rules, but upon closer inspection are found to be more complex (Wittgenstein, 1953). For example, natural categories such as birds and mammals are often associated with verbalizable rules such as, if it has wings, it is a bird, but also contain violations of these rules, such as bats. People can verbally report descriptions of bats and explicitly relate bats to other mammals, but these descriptions are not rules per se. In order for people to learn that examples as diverse as bats and ponies are all members of the category mammals, people need to build representations of the category mammals that are appropriate for this goal. The SUSTAIN model would predict that people achieve this goal by forming a separate cluster for birds and mammals, and then creating additional specialized clusters for exceptions, like bats, as they are encountered. One possibility is that the MTL acquires declarative knowledge that eclipses the limitations of rule-based models through mechanisms similar to that of the SUSTAIN model.

Conclusion

In this chapter, I have reviewed the relative merits of a variety of category learning models, including rule-, prototype-, and exemplar-based models, as well as clustering models and multiple systems models that combine two or more of these model types. Also considered was how inclusion of selective attention mechanisms can increase the capabilities of these models by endowing them with the ability to manifest rule-following behavior.

To review briefly each model family's merits, rule-based models conform to our intuition that we effortfully search for patterns that we can verbally communicate to others. In contrast to rule models, prototype models successfully reflect the graded nature of category membership. Exemplar models address deficiencies in the prototype model and can capture correlations within categories. Exemplar models also capture aspects of recognition memory performance. Clustering models successfully transition between prototype- and exemplar-like representations, depending on the complexity of the category structure.

All of these models have played a critical role in advancing the theory and design of key experiments. The development of new models is informed by the failings of preceding models. The history of model development is marked by the arrival of models with increasingly sophisticated processing mechanisms that can manifest the behaviors of previous models as well as additional human behaviors beyond the reach of previous models. Of course, the value in models lie more in predicting unanticipated behaviors than in simply accounting for known behaviors. Thus, it is important for models to be somewhat constrained to have theoretical value.

Later in the chapter, these four basic model types were related to four candidate learning systems in the brain: a PFC-supported rule-based system, a perceptual priming system that operates like a restricted prototype model, a procedural learning system that has some characteristic of exemplar models and related variants, and an MTL-supported flexible clustering model. One important question for future research is how these multiple mechanisms interact.

Some researchers may question whether it is even useful to think in terms of multiple learning systems. After all, many behavioral findings thought to indicate the need for multiple systems of representation have subsequently been shown to be consistent with a single-system interpretation (Johansen & Palmeri, 2002; Nosofsky & Johansen, 2000; Nosofsky & Zaki, 1998). At first blush, this position might seem recalcitrant, but given the mounting evidence that many brain areas perform cooperatively in learning tasks (Koenig et al., 2008; Sadeh, Shohamy, Levy, Reggev, & Maril, 2011), one could reasonably argue there is a single system at a functional level as long as it is acknowledged that certain brain areas are best suited to certain learning conditions. For example, secondary task load impairs PFC- and MTL-mediated learning but not procedural learning (Foerde et al., 2006), whereas delayed feedback impairs procedural learning but not rule-based learning (Maddox & Ing, 2005). Our recommendation is to specify model-based mechanisms and relate these mechanisms to brain function, not to argue for or against a particular number of learning systems. We believe that, in practice, the criteria for delineating separate systems is often underspecified and can lead to needless controversy. Indeed, SUSTAIN, which is a single-system model, can act as an exemplar-, prototype-, or rule-based model depending on the nature of the category learning task.

Future Directions

1. Now that many in the field are confident that several learning systems have been identified, basic questions surround how these learning systems interact during learning. Under what conditions do systems cooperate or compete? For a given situation, what determines which learning system guides behavior? Answering these questions will likely require the specifying of model gating mechanisms that determine how the outputs of systems influence behavior.

2. I suggested that two learning systems, the rule-based and perceptual priming systems, may be better viewed as general cognitive and perceptual abilities than as proper learning systems. One question for future research is how processes outside of category learning systems, such as those engaged in analogy and language use, impact categorization behavior.

3. For decades, cognitive psychologists have made theoretical progress by comparing the predictions and fits of models to behavioral data. One fruitful area for future research may be to extend this endeavor to incorporate brain imaging and neuropsychological data.

Acknowledgments

This work was supported by AFOSR grant FA9550-10-1-0268 and NIH grant MH09152.

Further Reading

Ashby, F. G., & Crossley, M. (2010). The neurobiology of categorization. In D. Mareschal, P. Quinn, & S. Lea (Eds.), *The making of human concepts* (p. 75–98). New York: Oxford University Press.

Poldrack, R. A., & Foerde, K. (2008). Category learning and memory systems debate. *Neuroscience and Biobehavioral Reviews, 32,* 197–205.

Seger, C. A., & Miller, E. (2010). Category learning in the brain. *Annual Review of Neuroscience, 33,* 203–219.

Smith, E. E., & Grossman, M. (2008). Multiple systems of category learning. *Neuroscience and Biobehavioral Reviews, 32,* 249–264.

References

Aizenstein, H. J., MacDonald, A. W., Stenger, V. A., Nebes, R.D., Larson, J. K., Ursu, S., & Carter, C. S. (2000). Complementary category learning systems identified using event-related functional MRI. *Journal of Cognitive Neuroscience, 12,* 977–987.

Allen, S. W., & Brooks, L. R. (1991). Specializing the operation of an explicit rule. *Journal of Experimental Psychology: General, 120,* 3–19.

Anderson, J. R. (1991). The adaptive nature of human categorization. *Psychological Review, 98,* 409–429.

Asaad, W., Rainer, G., & Miller, E. (1998). Neural activity in the primate prefrontal cortex during associative learning. *Neuron, 21,* 1399–1407.

Ashby, F. G., Alfonso-Reese, L., Turken, A., & Waldron, E. (1998). A neuropsychological theory of multiple-systems in category learning. *Psychological Review, 105,* 442–481.

Ashby, F. G., & Crossley, M. (2010). The neurobiology of categorization. In D. Mareschal, P. Quinn, & S. Lea (Eds.), *The making of human concepts* (pp. 75–98). New York: Oxford University Press.

Ashby, F. G., & Maddox, W. T. (2005). Human category learning. *Annual Review of Psychology, 56,* 149–178.

Ashby, F. G., Noble, S., Filoteo, J. V., Waldron, E. M., & Ell, S. W. (2003). Category learning deficits in Parkinson's disease. *Neuropsychology, 17,* 115–124.

Ashby, F. G., & O'Brien, J. B. (2005). Category learning and multiple memory systems. *Trends in Cognitive Sciences, 9,* 83–89.

Ashby, F. G., & Waldron, E. M. (1999). On the nature of implicit categorization. *Psychonomic Bulletin & Review, 6,* 363–378.

Barsalou, L. W. (1985). Ideals, central tendency, and frequency of instantiation as determinants of graded structure of categories. *Journal of Experimental Psychology: Learning, Memory, & Cognition, 11,* 629–654.

Becker, S., & Wojtowicz, J. (2007). A model of hippocampal neurogenesis in memory and mood disorders. *Trends in Cognitive Science, 11,* 70–76.

Bozoki, A., Grossman, M., & Smith, E. E. (2006). Can patients with Alzheimer's disease learn a category implicitly? *Neuropsycholgia, 44,* 816–827.

Brown, M. W., & Aggleton, J. P. (2001). Recognition memory: What are the roles of the perirhinal cortex and hippocampus? *Nature Reviews Neuroscience, 2,* 51–61.

Bruner, J. S., Goodnow, J. J., & Austin, G. A. (1956). *A study of thinking.* New York: Wiley.

Caramazza, A., & Shelton, J. R. (1998). Domain-specific knowledge systems in the brain: The animate-inanimate distinction. *Journal of Cognitive Neuroscience, 10,* 1–34.

Cree, G. S., & McRae, K. (2003). Analyzing the factors underlying the structure and computation of the meaning of chipmunk, cherry, chisel, cheese, and cello (and many other such concrete nouns). *Journal of Experimental Psychology: General, 132,* 63201.

Davis, T., Love, B. C. & Preston, A. R. (2012). Learning the exception to the rule: Model-based fmri reveals specialized representations for surprising category members. *Cerebral Cortex, 22* (2), 260–273.

Daw, N. D., O'Doherty, J. P., Dayan, P., Seymour, B., & Dolan, R. J. (2006). Cortical substrates for exploratory decisions in humans. *Nature, 441*(7095), 876–879.

DeCaro, M. S., Thomas, R. D., & Beilock, S. L. (2008). Individual differences in category learning: Sometimes less working memory capacity is better than more. *Cognition, 107,* 284–294.

Eichenbaum, H. (1999). Conscious awareness, memory, and the hippocampus. *Nature Neuroscience, 2,* 775–776.

Eichenbaum, H., Yonelinas, A., & Ranganath, C. (2007). The medial temporal lobe and recognition memory. *Annual Review of Neuroscience, 30,* 123–152.

Eldridge, L., Masterman, D., & Knowlton, B. (2002). Intact implicit habit learning in Alzheimer's disease. *Behavioral Neuroscience, 116,* 722–726.

Erickson, M. A., & Kruschke, J. K. (1998). Rules and exemplars in category learning. *Journal of Experimental Psychology: General, 127,* 107–140.

Feldman, J. (2000). Minimization of Boolean complexity in human concept learning. *Nature, 407,* 630–633.

Foerde, K., Knowlton, B. J., & Poldrack, R. A. (2006). Modulation of competing memory systems by distraction. *Proceedings of the National Academy of Sciences U S A, 103,* 11778–11783.

Frank, M., Seeberger, L., & O'Reilly R. C. (2004). By carrot or by stick: Cognitive reinforcement learning in parkinsonism. *Science, 306,* 1940–1943.

Franz, S. I. (1912). New phrenology. *Science, 35,* 321–328.

Gleitman, L. R., Gleitman, H., Miller, C., & Ostrin, R. (1996). Similar, and similar concepts. *Cognition, 58,* 321–376.

Gluck, M. A., & Bower, G. H. (1988). From conditioning to category learning. An adaptive network model. *Journal of Experimental Psychology: General, 117,* 225–244.

Hahn, U., & Ramscar, M. (2001). Conclusion: Mere similarity? In U. Hahn & M. Ramscar (Eds.), *Similarity and categorization* (p. 257–272). New York: Oxford University Press.

Hampton, J. A. (2001). The role of similarity in natural categorization. In U. Hahn & M. Ramscar (Eds.), *Similarity and categorization* (p. 13–28). New York: Oxford University Press.

Janowsky, J. S., Shimamura, A. P., Kritchevsky, M., & Squire, L. R. (1989). The effects of concurrent task interference on category learning: Evidence for multiple category learning systems. *Behavioral Neuroscience, 103,* 548–560.

Joel, D., Weiner, I., & Feldon, J. (1997). Electrolytic lesions of the medial prefrontal cortex in rats disrupt performance on an analog of the Wisconsin Card Sorting Test, but do not disrupt latent inhibition: Implications for animal models of schizophrenia. *Behavioral Brain Research, 85,* 187–201.

Johansen, M. K., & Palmeri, T. J. (2002). Are there representational shifts during category learning? *Cognitive Psychology, 45,* 482–553.

Knowlton, B., Mangels, J., & Squire, L. (1996). Neostriatal habit learning system in humans. *Science, 273,* 1399–1402.

Knowlton, B., & Squire, L. R. (1993). The learning of categories: Parallel brain systems for item memory and category knowledge. *Science, 262,* 1747–1749.

Knowlton, B., Squire, L., & Gluck, M. (1994). Probabilistic classification in amnesia. *Learning and Memory, 1,* 106–120.

Koenig, P., Smith, E. E., Troiani, V., Antani, S., McCawely, G., Moore, P., et al. (2008). Medial temporal lobe involvement in an implicit memory task: Evidence of collaborating implicit and explicit memory systems from fmri and Alzheimer's disease. *Cerebral Cortex, 18*, 2831–2843.

Kolodny, J. (1994). Memory processes in classification learning: an investigation of amnesic performance in categorization of dot patterns and artistic styles. *Psychological Science, 5*, 164–169.

Konishi, S., Karwazu, M., Uchida, I., Kikyo, H., Asakura, I., & Miyashita, Y. (1999). Contribution of working memory to transient activation in human inferior prefrontal cortex during performance of the Wisconsin Card Sorting Test. *Cerebral Cortex, 9*, 745–753.

Kruschke, J. K. (1992). ALCOVE: An exemplar-based connectionist model of category learning. *Psychological Review, 99*, 22–44.

Kruschke, J. K. (1996). Base rates in category learning. *Journal of Experimental Psychology: Learning, Memory, & Cognition, 22*, 3–26.

Kruschke, J. K. (2003). Attention in learning. *Current Directions in Psychological Science, 12*, 171–175.

Lacroix, G. L., Giguere, G., & Larochelle, S. (2005). The origin of exemplar effects in rule-driven categorization. *Journal of Experimental Psychology: Learning, Memory, & Cognition, 31*, 272–288.

Lakoff, G. (1987). *Women, fire, and dangerous things: What categories reveal about the mind.* Chicago: University of Chicago Press.

Leng, N. R., & Parkin, A. J. (1988). Double dissociation of frontal dysfunction in organic amnesia. *British Journal of Clinical Psychology, 27*, 359–362.

Love, B. C. (2002). Comparing supervised and unsupervised category learning. *Psychonomic Bulletin & Review, 9*, 829–835.

Love, B. C., & Gureckis, T. M. (2007). Models in search of a brain. *Cognitive, Affective, & Behavioral Neuroscience, 7*, 90–108.

Love, B. C., & Jones, M. (2006). The emergence of multiple learning systems. *Proceedings of the Cognitive Science Society.*

Love, B. C., Medin, D. L., & Gureckis, T. (2004). SUSTAIN: A network model of human category learning. *Psychological Review, 111*, 309–332.

Love, B. C., Tomlinson, M., & Gureckis, T. (2008). The concrete substrates of abstract rule use. In B. H. Ross (Ed.), *The psychology of learning and motivation: Advances in research and theory.* 49, 167–207.

Maddox, W. T., & Ashby, F. G. (1993). Comparing decision bound and exemplar models of categorization. *Perception & Psychophysics, 53*, 49–70.

Maddox, W. T., & Ashby, F. G. (2004). Dissociating explicit and procedural-learning based systems of perceptual category learning. *Behavioral Processes, 66*, 309–332.

Maddox, W. T., Ashby, F. G., & Bohil, C. J. (2003). Delayed feedback effects on rule-based and information-integration category learning. *Journal of Experimental Psychology: Learning, Memory, & Cognition, 29*, 650–662.

Maddox, W. T., & Ing, A. D. (2005). Delayed feedback disrupts the procedural-learning system but not the hypothesis testing system in perceptual category learning. *Journal of Experimental Psychology: Learning, Memory, & Cognition, 31*, 100–107.

Markman, A. B., & Ross, B. H. (2003). Category use and category learning. *Psychological Bulletin, 129*, 592–613.

Marr, D. (1982). *Vision.* San Francisco: W. H. Freeman.

Martin, A. (2007). The representation of object concepts in the brain. *Annual Review of Psychology, 58*, 25–45.

Medin, D. L., & Schaffer, M. M. (1978). Context theory of classification learning. *Psychological Review, 85*, 207–238.

Medin, D. L., & Schwanenflugel, P. J. (1981). Linear separability in classification learning. *Journal of Experimental Psychology: Human Learning & Memory, 7*, 355–368.

Monchi, O., Petrides, M., Petre, V., Worsley, K., & Dagher, A. (2001). Wisconsin Card Sorting revisited: Distinct neural circuits participating in different stages of the task identified by event-related functional magnetic resonance imaging. *Journal of Neuroscience, 21*, 7733–7741.

Morris, R., Garrud, P., Rawlins, J., & O'Keefe, J. (1982). Place navigation impaired in rats with hippocampal lesions. *Nature, 297*, 681–683.

Murphy, G. L. (2002). *The big book of concepts.* Cambridge, MA: MIT Press.

Nomura, E. M., Maddox, W. T., Filoteo, J. V., Ing, A. D., Gitelman, D. R., Parrish, T. B., et al. (2007). Neural correlates of rule-based and information-integration visual category learning. *Cerebral Cortex, 17*(1), 37–43.

Norman, K., & O'Reilly, R. (2003). Modeling hippocampal and neocortical contributions to recognition memory: A complementary learning systems approach. *Psychological Review, 110.*

Nosofsky, R. M. (1986). Attention, similarity, and the identification-categorization relationship. *Journal of Experimental Psychology: General, 115*, 39–57.

Nosofsky, R. M., & Johansen, M. (2000). Exemplar-based accounts of multiple-system phenomena in perceptual categorization. *Psychonomic Bulletin & Review, 7*, 375–402.

Nosofsky, R. M., & Palmeri, T. J. (1997). An exemplar-based random walk model of speeded classification. *Psychological Review, 104*, 266–300.

Nosofsky, R. M., Palmeri, T. J., & McKinley, S. C. (1994, January). Rule-plus-exception model of classification learning. *Psychological Review, 101*(1), 53–79.

Nosofsky, R. M., & Zaki, S. F. (1998). Dissociations between categorization and recognition in amnesic and normal individuals. *Psychological Science, 9*, 247–255.

Nosofsky, R. M., & Zaki, S. F. (2002). Exemplar and prototype models revisited: Response strategies, selective attention, and stimulus *generalization. Journal of Experimental Psychology: Learning, Memory, & Cognition, 28*, 924–940.

Palmeri, T. J., & Nosofsky, R. M. (1995). Recognition memory for exceptions to the category rule. *Journal of Experimental Psychology: Learning, Memory, & Cognition, 21*, 548–568.

Pereira, F., Mitchell, T., & Botvinick, M. (2009). Machine learning classifiers and fMRI: A tutorial overview. *Neuroimage, 45*, S199–S209.

Pickering, A. (1997). New approaches to the study of amnesic patients: What can a neurofunctional philosophy and neural network methods offer? *Memory, 5*, 255–300.

Poldrack, R. A., Clark, J., Pare-Blagoev, E., Shohamy, D., Creso Moyano, J., Myers, C., et al. (2001). Interactive memory systems in the human brain. *Nature, 414*, 546–550.

Poldrack, R. A., & Foerde, K. (2008). Category learning and memory systems debate. *Neuroscience and Biobehavioral Reviews, 32*, 197–205.

Posner, M. I., & Keele, S. W. (1968). On the genesis of abstract ideas. *Journal of Experimental Psychology, 77*, 241–248.

Posner, M. I., & Petersen, S. E. (1990). Attention systems in the human brain. *Annual Review of Neuroscience, 13*, 25–42.

Pothos, E. M., & Chater, N. (2002). A simplicity principle in unsupervised human categorization. *Cognitive Science, 26*, 303–343.

Purcell, B., Heitz, R., Cohen, J., Schall, J., Logan, G., & Palmeri, T. (2010). Neurally constrained modeling of perceptual decision making. *Psychological Review, 117*, 1113–1143.

Reber, P., Gitelman, D., Parrish, T., & Mesulam, M. (2003). Dissociating explicit and implicit category knowledge with fmri. *Journal of Cognitive Neuroscience, 15*, 574–583.

Reber, P., Stark, C., & Squire, L. (1998). Contrasting cortical activity associated with category memory and recognition memory. *Learning and Memory, 5*, 420–428.

Reed, J., Squire, L., Patalano, A., Smith, E., & Jonides, J. (1999). Learning about categories that are defined by object-like stimuli despite impaired declarative memory. *Behavioral Neuroscience, 113*, 411–419.

Reed, S. (1972). Pattern recognition and categorization. *Cognitive Psychology, 3*, 382–407.

Rehder, B., & Hoffman, A. B. (2005). Eyetracking and selective attention in category learning. *Cognitive Psychology, 51*, 1–41.

Rehder, B., & Murphy, G. L. (2003). A knowledge-resonance (KRES) model of category learning. *Psychonomic Bulletin & Review, 10*, 759–784.

Rodrigues, P. M., & Murre, J. M. J. (2007). Rules-plus-exception tasks: A problem for exemplar models? *Psychonomic Bulletin & Review, 14*, 640–646.

Rosch, E., & Mervis, C. B. (1975). Family resemblences: Studies in the internal structure of categories. *Cognitive Psychology, 7*, 573–605.

Rutishauser, U., Mamelak, A., & Schuman, E. (2006). Single-trial learning of novel stimuli by individual neurons of the human hippocampus-amygdala complex. *Neuron, 49*, 805–813.

Sadeh, T., Shohamy, D., Levy, D., Reggev, N., & Maril, A. (2011). Cooperation between the hippocampus and the striatum during episodic encoding. *Journal of Cognitive Neuroscience, 23*, 1597–1608.

Sakamoto, Y., & Love, B. C. (2004). Schematic influences on category learning and recognition memory. *Journal of Experimental Psychology: General, 33*, 534–553.

Sakamoto, Y., & Love, B. C. (2006). Vancouver, toronto, montreal, austin: Enhanced oddball memory through differentiation, not isolation. *Psychonomic Bulletin & Review, 13*, 474–479.

Sakamoto, Y., & Love, B. C. (2010). Learning and retention through predictive inference and classification. *Journal of Experimental Psychology: Applied, 16*, 361–377.

Sakamoto, Y., Matuska, T., & Love, B. C. (2004). Dimension-wide vs. exemplar-specific attention in category learning and recognition. In M. Lovett, C. Schunn, C. Lebiere, & P. Munro (Eds.), *Proceedings of the international conference of cognitive modeling* (Vol. 27, p. 261–266). Mahwah, NJ: Lawrence Erlbaum.

Sanborn, A. N., Griffiths, T. L., & Navarro, D. J. (2010). Rational approximations to rational models: Alternative algorithms for category learning. *Psychological Review, 117*, 1144–1167.

Schultz, W., Dayan, P., & Montague, P. R. (1997). A neural substrate of prediction and reward. *Science, 275*(5306), 1593–1599.

Scoville, W., & Milner, B. (1957). Loss of recent memory after bilateral hippocampal lesions. *Journal of Neurology, Neurosurgery, & Psychiatry, 20*, 11–21.

Seger, C. A., & Cincotta, C. (2006). Dynamics of frontal, striatal, and hippocampal systems during rule learning. *Cerebral Cortex, 16*, 1546–1555.

Seger, C. A., Poldrack, R. A., Prabhakaran, V., Zhao, M., Glover, G., & Gabrieli, J. (2000). Hemispheric asymmetries and individual differences in visual concept learning as measured by functional mri. *Neuropsychologia, 38*, 1316–1324.

Shepard, R. N., Hovland, C. L., & Jenkins, H. M. (1961). Learning and memorization of classifications. *Psychological Monographs, 75*(13, Whole No. 517).

Shohamy, D. S., Myers, C. E., Grossman, S., Sage, J., Gluck, M. A., & Poldrack, R. A. (2004). Cortico-striatal contributions to feedback-based learning: converging data from neuroimaging and neuropsychology. *Brain, 127*, 851–859.

Shohamy, D. S., Myers, C., Kalanithi, J., & Gluck, M. (2008). Basal ganglia and dopamine contributions to probabilistic category learning. *Biobehavioral Reviews., 32*, 219–236.

Sinha, R. R. (1999). Neuropsychological substrates of category learning. *Dissertation Abstracts International: Section B: The Sciences and Engineering, 60* (5-B), *2381*, UMI No. AEH9932480.

Smith, E. E., & Grossman, M. (2008). Multiple systems of category learning. *Neuroscience and Biobehavioral Reviews, 32*, 249–264.

Smith, E. E., Patalano, A. L., & Jonides, J. (1998). Alternative strategies of categorization. *Cognition, 65*, 167–196.

Smith, J. (2002). Exemplar theory's predicted typicality gradient can be tested and disconfirmed. *Psychological Science, 13*, 437–442.

Smith, J. D., & Minda, J. P. (2001). Journey to the center of the category: The dissociation in amnesia between categorization and recognition. *Journal of Experimental Psychology: Learning, Memory, & Cognition, 27*, 984–1002.

Squire, L. R. (1992). Memory and the hippocampus: A synthesis from findings with rats, monkeys, and humans. *Psychological Review, 99*, 195–231.

Staresina, B.P., & Davachi, L. (2009). Mind the gap: Binding experience across space and time in the human hippocampus. *Neuron, 63*, 267–276.

Stark, C. E. L., Bayley, P. J., & Squire, L. R. (2002). Recognition memory for single items and for associations is similarity impaired following damage to the hippocampal region. *Learning & Cognition, 9*, 238–242.

Stark, C. E. L., & Squire, L. R. (2001). When zero is not zero: The problem of ambiguous baseline conditions in fMRI. *Proceedings of the National Academy of Sciences U S A, 98*(22), 12760–12766.

Tulving, E., Markowitsch, H., Craik, F., Habib, R., & Houle, S. (1996). Novelty and familiarity activations in PET studies of memory encoding and retrieval. *Cerebral Cortex, 6*, 71–79.

Vampaemel, W., & Storms, G. (2008). In search of abstraction: The varying abstraction model of categorization. *Psychonomic Bulletin & Review, 15*, 732–749.

Waldron, E. M., & Ashby, F. G. (2001). The effects of concurrent task interference on category learning: Evidence for multiple category learning systems. *Psychonomic Bulletin & Review, 8*, 168–176.

Wallenstein, G. V., Eichenbaum, H., & Hasselmo, M. E. (1998). The hippocampus as an associator of discontiguous events. *Trends in Neuroscience, 21*(8), 317–323.

Willingham, D. (1998). A neuropsychological theory of motor skill learning. *Psychological Review, 105,* 558–584.

Wittgenstein, L. (1953). *Philosophical investigations* (G. E. M. Anscombe, trans.). Oxford, England: Blackwell.

Yamaguchi, S., Hale, L., Desposito, M., & Knight, R. (2004). Rapid prefrontal-hippocampal habituation to novel events. *Journal of Neuroscience, 24,* 5356–5363.

Yang, L. X., & Lewandowsky, S. (2004). Context-gated knowledge partitioning in categorization. *Journal of Experimental Psychology: Learning, Memory, & Cognition, 30,* 1045–1064.

Zaki, S. R., Nosofsky, R. M., Jessup, N. M., & Unversagt, F. W. (2003). Categorization and recognition performance of a memory-impaired group: Evidence for single-system models. *Journal of the International Neuropsychological Society, 9,* 394–406.

Zeithamova, D., & Maddox, W. T. (2006). Dual-task interference in perceptual category learning. *Memory & Cognition, 34,* 387–398.

Zeithamova, D., Maddox, W. T., & Schnyer, D. M. (2008). Dissociable prototype learning systems: Evidence from brain imaging and behavior. *Journal of Neuroscience, 28*(49), 13194–13201.

CHAPTER 23

Expectancies and Beliefs: Insights from Cognitive Neuroscience

Lauren Y. Atlas *and* Tor D. Wager

Abstract

Expectations influence clinical outcomes and ongoing experience across nearly all psychological domains. They color our perceptions, drive learning and memory, and shape the generation of emotional responses. Despite their profound influence, researchers have only recently begun to focus on the mechanisms by which expectancies actually modulate subjective experience. This chapter describes a cognitive neuroscience approach to the study of expectations, focusing on expectancy effects on affective experience. First a brief history is provided of the development of expectation as a construct with explanatory power in psychology, and several distinct types of expectancy are discussed. Next, the chapter describes the role of expectations in affective processes, both during anticipation and during the experience of hedonic outcomes. The chapter ends with a discussion on the brain mechanisms currently thought to underlie expectations and their effects, first focusing on expectancies across domains, and then specifically on pain, an area that has proven to be a particularly tractable and informative model system.

Key Words: expectancy, beliefs, placebo, anticipation, emotion, cognitive neuroscience, conditioning, pain, learning

High expectations are the key to everything.
—Sam Walton, founder of Wal-Mart

I find my life is a lot easier the lower I keep my expectations.
—Calvin, from "Calvin and Hobbes," by Bill Watterson

Expect nothing, live frugally on surprise.
—Alice Walker

Expectations shape the world we perceive, for better and for worse. Students tend to score lower on IQ tests when teachers expect them to perform poorly (Raudenbush, 1984; Rosenthal, 1994). Experimenters' expectations influence experimental outcomes (Rosenthal & Rubin, 1978), even in simple observational studies of animal behavior: Rats are slower when they are tested by experimenters who believe the rats were specifically bred to perform poorly in mazes, in contrast to experimenters who believe the rats come from a brighter breed (Rosenthal & Fode, 1963). Expectations can also be profoundly beneficial. Expectations that a medical treatment will be beneficial can elicit placebo effects that influence pain (Price, Craggs, Verne, Perlstein, & Robinson, 2007), depression (Kirsch & Sapirstein,

1998), symptoms of Parkinson's disease (de la Fuente-Fernandez et al., 2001), and other physiological outcomes (Meissner, Distel, & Mitzdorf, 2007). Although outcomes are shaped toward expectations in all of these examples, expectations can also bias perception in the opposite direction. Individuals often complain when peers rave about a popular new film, for fear of experiencing disappointment if the film fails to live up to expectations. In sum, expectancies color all areas of affective experience. They fill us with dread or excitement. They affect how we experience events themselves. They bias our memories of significant occasions, sometimes outweighing the influence of our feelings during the event. Thus, it is not surprising to see disagreement over whether it is better to expect the best, expect the worst, or attempt to live life without expectations.

The study of expectations is a very broad one indeed, as expectations play a critical role in virtually every area of psychology and neuroscience. Their effects operate across multiple levels of analysis, from social behavior to low-level neurobiological responses. They are critical in perception, learning (from simple conditioning to complex problem solving), memory, attention, judgment and decision-making, social behavior, and disorders of the mind and brain. Their study is embedded within each field of psychology and is encapsulated by none. Despite the pervasive influence of expectancy, researchers have only recently begun to examine the precise brain mechanisms by which expectancies modulate perception, emotion, and judgment.

Here, we describe a cognitive neuroscience approach to the study of expectations, focusing on the effects of expectations on brain processes and behavior, and on the cognitive and brain mechanisms that underlie them. Rather than comprehensively reviewing expectancy effects across all areas of psychology, we will focus on expectancy effects in affective processes, including the experience of pain and other responses to events with high relevance for physical and social well-being. Among all the domains of affective and clinical outcomes influenced by expectations, pain is the most well studied, with strong evidence for causal effects of expectations on the experience of both clinical and experimental pain (Benedetti, Carlino, & Pollo, 2011; Vase, Petersen, Riley, & Price, 2009; Vase, Riley, & Price, 2002).

A Brief History: Conditioning vs. Expectancy

Expectancies have been defined in many ways, but a basic commonality across definitions is that expectations involve a belief that something will happen in the future (Kirsch, Lynn, Vigorito, & Miller, 2004). Expectancy theory dates back to the middle of the twentieth century, when behaviorism dominated the field. Woodworth (1947) and Tolman (1949) argued that when an animal learns that a tone predicts a shock, the animal is essentially developing an expectation about the timing of the shock and the relationship between the tone and the stimulus. These ideas were further developed by Bolles (1972), who argued that conditioned stimuli do not directly elicit responses; instead, contingent reinforcements cause animals to develop expectancies about outcomes, which in turn elicit responses insofar as the animal is motivated to achieve or avoid that outcome. More formally, animals learn either stimulus-outcome contingencies (S-S^*) or response-outcome contingencies (R-S^*), and behaviors are exhibited as a function of the value of the expected outcome (S^*); thus a hungry animal will be more likely to exhibit responses than a satiated one because of a difference in S^*. Finally, Rescorla and Wagner (1972) formalized a model of classical conditioning to explain phenomena such as blocking and conditioned inhibition, which suggest that learning does not depend on simple contiguity between conditioned and unconditioned stimuli. Instead, conditioned responses are elicited on the basis of the information value of conditioned cues, not simply as reflexive responses to the cues themselves (Rescorla, 1988). Thus, according to this perspective, expectancies underlie most forms of learning (Reiss, 1980). Notably, these accounts also suggest that expectancies can be studied in basic animal models.

The definition of expectancy evolved with the cognitive revolution. Researchers focused on a more cognitive interpretation of the notion of expectancy, requiring that expectancies involve explicit, verbalizable awareness of contingencies. This gave rise to important distinctions between conditioning and expectancy. Conditioning in humans can produce explicit awareness of stimulus contingencies and thus lead to conscious expectancies (Brewer, 1974; Kirsch, 1985). Expectancies of this type can be distinguished from other types of conditioned learning that are unconscious, in several ways (Benedetti et al., 2003; Kirsch et al., 2004). First, insofar as conditioning can occur without conscious awareness (Clark, Manns, & Squire, 2002; Lovibond & Shanks, 2002), it is distinct from expectancy. Second, conscious expectations can be elicited by verbal information or social observation, without any previous experience with a given stimulus or situation. Third, if conditioned effects are impervious to changes in expectations, they are likely distinct from expectancy.

Interest in the relationship between conditioning and expectancy grew when the medical community began to acknowledge the power of expectancy. At the same time that Tolman and others were arguing for a new interpretation of classical conditioning, Henry Beecher published an influential article entitled "The Powerful Placebo" (Beecher, 1955), which included an early meta-analysis of 15 studies that administered placebos for conditions as diverse as wound pain, seasickness, anxiety, and the common cold. Beecher reported that placebos were clinically effective for ~35% of the patients in these studies and reported placebo effects on objective outcomes (both clinically relevant and side effects), such as rashes and pupil diameter. In the half-century following his article, researchers focused on identifying the mechanisms underlying the placebo response, motivated at least in part by an effort to harness the body's endogenous healing capabilities to assist modern medicine in providing better patient care (Benson & Friedman, 1996; Brown, 1998; Chaput de Saintonge & Herxheimer, 1994; Stefano, Fricchione, Slingsby, & Benson, 2001). As part of this effort, a heated debate focused on whether placebo effects depend on expectancy or conditioning.

Conditioning accounts explained placebo effects as arising from a lifetime of associations between pills, white coats, and hospital settings and treatment induced positive outcomes. Those who held this perspective argued that when these contextual factors are presented in the absence of drug treatment, they elicit healing as a conditioned response (Voudouris, Peck, & Coleman, 1985, 1989, 1990; Wickramasekera, 1980). Indeed, conditioned drug effects are prevalent in rats as well as humans (Herrnstein, 1962), though rats may develop some forms of expectations as well (Schoenbaum, Takahashi, Liu, & Mcdannald, 2011). Others argued that placebo effects depend on explicit beliefs, rather than conditioning (De Jong, van Baast, Arntz, & Merckelbach, 1996; Kirsch, 1985; Montgomery & Kirsch, 1997). From this perspective, placebos should only affect clinical outcomes insofar as patients believe in the treatment and expect relief.

A number of studies attempted to directly isolate the effects of conscious expectancies from other conditioned learning (Amanzio & Benedetti, 1999; Benedetti et al., 2003; De Jong et al., 1996;

Montgomery & Kirsch, 1997; Voudouris et al., 1985, 1989, 1990; for a thorough review, see Stewart-Williams & Podd, 2004). One influential experiment (Benedetti et al., 2003) tested the basis of placebo effects on consciously accessible outcomes (pain in healthy controls and motor performance in patients with Parkinson's disease) and physiological outcomes that are not accessible to direct conscious experience (cortisol and growth hormone secretion). The critical groups went through conditioning phases (pretreatment with the analgesic ketorolac for pain conditioning, subthalamic nucleus stimulation for Parkinson's patients, and treatment with sumatriptan for cortisol and growth hormone secretion) and then received verbal information that induced expectations that were either consistent or inconsistent with the conditioned response. For instance, one group that was exposed to ketorolac was told that a treatment (really a placebo) would induce hyperalgesia (increased pain, opposing the analgesic effects of ketorolac). If pain increased with placebo during the test phase, that would indicate that placebo effects were due to conscious belief, whereas if they decreased, that would show that placebo effects depend on conditioning. Using this logic, Benedetti et al. showed that placebo effects on biophysical and hormonal responses depend on conditioning (i.e., they did not reverse with instructions), whereas effects on physical responses (pain and motor performance) depend on conscious belief.

Understanding the contributions of conscious and nonconscious processes continues to be a critical issue for the field of expectancy research. However, the vast majority of studies of expectancy effects combine both verbal information and conditioning in order to maximize expectancy effects on outcome measures, as illustrated in the typical paradigms described below. Thus, unless otherwise noted, we include both conscious beliefs and nonconscious anticipatory processes in our consideration of expectancy effects.

Types of Expectancies

There are two broad classes of expectancy: *stimulus expectancies* and *response expectancies*. The former focuses on beliefs about stimuli in the external world, while the latter focuses on beliefs about one's own responses to the external world.

Stimulus expectancies can be divided into beliefs about the *timing* of an event, and beliefs about *stimulus characteristics*; in the stress literature, these have been referred to as "contingency predictability" and "what-kind-of-event predictability," respectively

(Miller, 1981). To study stimulus expectancies, researchers often pair arbitrary cues with verbal information and/or conditioning, so that cues acquire predictive value and induce expectations. Very large bodies of literature on "fear conditioning" in the aversive domain (Delgado, Olsson, & Phelps, 2006; Rogan, Stäubli, & LeDoux, 1997) and conditioned reinforcement in the appetitive domain (Balleine & Killcross, 2006; Dayan & Balleine, 2002) focus on the effects of the cues themselves on brain and behavior, but there are also effects of cues with learned information value on perceptions of and responses to subsequent outcomes. To study these effects, researchers test whether behavioral and brain responses to a single subsequent stimulus are affected by cue-based expectancies, as illustrated in Figure 23.1. For example, to examine the effects of expectations about stimulus characteristics, colored shapes might be paired with two intensities of aversive electric shocks: a mild stimulus and a highly aversive stimulus. During a later test phase, each shape might be paired with a moderately aversive stimulus, and researchers can assess whether cue-based expectancies influence how the stimulus is perceived. Using this approach, researchers have examined whether perception is affected by expectations about stimulus intensity (Arntz, van den Hout, van den Berg, & Meijboom, 1991; Brown, Seymour, Boyle, Elderedy, & Jones, 2008; Keltner et al., 2006; Lorenz et al., 2005; Ploghaus et al., 2000; Wallace, 1985), location (Coull &

Nobre, 1998; Downing, 1988; Kastner, Pinsk, De Weerd, Desimone, & Ungerleider, 1999), and category (Bollinger, Rubens, Zanto, & Gazzaley, 2010; Zellner, Strickhouser, & Tornow, 2004). Results from these paradigms are summarized in Figure 23.1A. As described later in this review, the dominant finding is that perceived outcomes are assimilated toward expected values.

A similar approach can be used to study expectations about timing, as illustrated in Figure 23.1B. One cue (e.g., an arbitrary shape) might be consistently followed 5 seconds later by an aversive shock stimulus, whereas another might be unrelated to the time of shock onset, inducing uncertainty. If researchers are interested in studying anticipation or dread, researchers can examine responses to the cue itself. To study the effects of predictability or uncertainty, analyses can focus on responses to the shock as a function of the antecedent cue. Using this approach, researchers have studied behavioral and neural effects of predictability (Alink, Schwiedrzik, Kohler, Singer, & Muckli, 2010; Berns, McClure, Pagnoni, & Montague, 2001; Carlsson et al., 2006; Crombez, Baeyens, & Eelen, 1994), anticipation (Carlsson, Petrovic, Skare, Petersson, & Ingvar, 2000; Hsieh, Stone-Elander, & Ingvar, 1999; Jensen et al., 2003; Kahnt, Heinzle, Park, & Haynes, 2010; Knutson, Adams, Fong, & Hommer, 2001; Koyama, Tanaka, & Mikami, 1998; Ploghaus et al., 1999; Porro et al., 2002; van Boxtel & Böcker, 2004), and dread or anticipatory anxiety (Berns et al., 2006; Mobbs et al.,

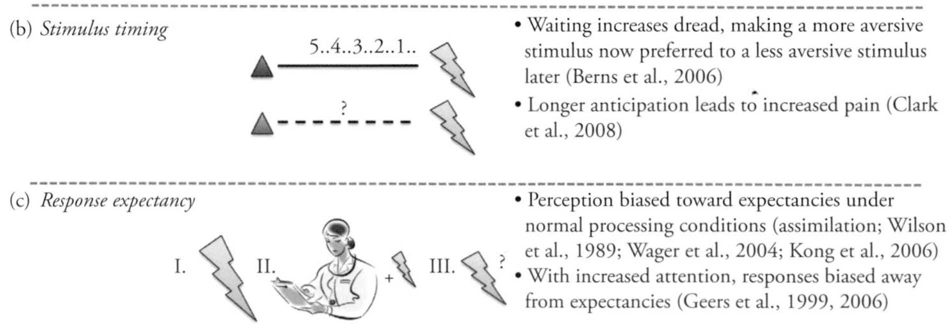

Expectancy type	Standard paradigm	Effect on perception
(a) *Stimulus characteristics*		• Perception biased toward expectancies • Potential asymmetry: more evidence for modulatory effects of positive expectations than negative expectations (e.g. Arntz et al., 1991, Koyama et al., 2005, Keltner et al., 2006; cf. Colloca et al., 2010) • Uncertainty about intensity intensifies emotion (Bar-Anan, Wilson, and Gilbert, 2009; Grupe & Nitschke, 2011; Sawamoto et al., 2000; cf. Brown et al., 2008)
(b) *Stimulus timing*	5..4..3..2..1..	• Waiting increases dread, making a more aversive stimulus now preferred to a less aversive stimulus later (Berns et al., 2006) • Longer anticipation leads to increased pain (Clark et al., 2008)
(c) *Response expectancy*		• Perception biased toward expectancies under normal processing conditions (assimilation; Wilson et al., 1989; Wager et al., 2004; Kong et al., 2006) • With increased attention, responses biased away from expectancies (Geers et al., 1999, 2006)

Figure 23.1 Types of expectancies. **A.** Stimulus characteristics. **B.** Stimulus timing. **C.** Response expectancy.

2007, 2009; Nitschke, Sarinopoulos, Mackiewicz, Schaefer, & Davidson, 2006; Simmons, Matthews, Stein, & Paulus, 2004; Somerville, Whalen, & Kelley, 2010). As summarized in Figure 23.1, and as discussed in more detail below, expectations about stimulus timing also influence perception, affecting both brain and behavioral responses. For example, shock after a long delay is perceived as more unpleasant than shock after a short delay, and individuals who report the highest sensation of dread show greater activation in pain-related regions during this delay period (Berns et al., 2006).

A second class of expectancies is concerned primarily with one's internal response to the outside world, rather than the state of the outside world per se. When beliefs concern one's own *nonvolitional responses* (e.g., emotional reactions, physiological responses, pain), they are referred to as *response expectancies* (Kirsch, 1985). Examples of response expectancies include the placebo response (expectations for healing that accompany otherwise inert treatments; Kirsch, 1985, 1999, 2004) and affective forecasting (beliefs about one's future state; Wilson & Gilbert, 2003). To study response expectancies, researchers generally manipulate the context surrounding an experience. This is most often accomplished through placebo manipulations, which combine conditioning and verbal information to induce expectations about a treatment that, unbeknownst to subjects, is actually pharmacologically inert (see Figure 23.1C). During a later test phase, the placebo treatment is administered, and researchers test whether participants' experience is affected.

These different types of expectations often occur in tandem in natural situations. For example, a host might inform a dinner party guest that his or her ex-partner was also invited and will arrive any second. Chances are that this guest will feel a sense of dread (expectation about timing), anticipating an unpleasant conversation (expectation about stimulus characteristics) and expecting to feel uncomfortable (response expectancy). As these expectancies are therefore often linked, they are regularly discussed interchangeably in the expectancy literature, particularly in the case of pain-related stimulus expectancies and response expectancies. However, each can be effectively isolated and brought under experimental control, using the experimental approaches described above. One important outstanding question is whether these expectancies are supported by distinct or overlapping mechanisms.

The Role of Expectancy in Affective Processing

Expectancies are particularly powerful in affective domains. Expectations influence responses to pleasant and unpleasant tastes (Berns et al., 2001; Nitschke, Dixon, et al., 2006; O'Doherty, Dayan, Friston, Critchley, & Dolan, 2003; Sarinopoulos, Dixon, Short, Davidson, & Nitschke, 2006), monetary reward and punishment (Breiter, Aharon, Kahneman, Dale, & Shizgal, 2001; Christakou, Brammer, Giampietro, & Rubia, 2009; Elliott, Friston, & Dolan, 2000; Rolls, McCabe, & Redoute, 2007; Spicer et al., 2007), positive and negative emotional images (Bermpohl et al., 2006; Petrovic et al., 2005), and other affect-eliciting material such as humorous cartoons and films (Geers & Lassiter, 1999, 2002; Wilson, Lisle, Kraft, & Wetzel, 1989). A great number of studies have demonstrated that expectancies modify pain perception; we review this work in detail in the final section of this review. In each of these domains, expectations influence each stage of affective processing: before, during, and after emotional experience (see Figure 23.2). We review expectancy effects on each of these stages in detail in the following sections.

Anticipatory Expectancy Effects

The period immediately preceding the appearance of an expected stimulus or event has garnered a great deal of attention in emotion and learning research. While anticipatory emotions and learning mechanisms are highly related, they are also dissociable, as described below. Anticipation is characterized by approach and avoidance behaviors and emotions, illustrated in the top panel of Figure 23.2. When a positive stimulus is expected, this results in approach behavior and a subjective sense of excitement or reward anticipation. This anticipatory state can be characterized as a kind of "wanting" (Berridge & Robinson, 1998), depending on the motivational state of the organism, and is likely to be mediated by phasic dopamine release in the nucleus accumbens and other forebrain areas from the ventral tegmental area (Schott et al., 2008; Tsai et al., 2009). An expected aversive stimulus elicits avoidance behavior and may cause subjective sensations of fear, dread, or anxiety, depending on the level of certainty (*anxiety* is the state of aversive anticipation without a specific object, whereas *fear* involves expectations about specific events).

While a detailed discussion of the literature on these emotions is outside the scope of this review, a substantial number of neuroimaging studies have focused on identifying neural mechanisms

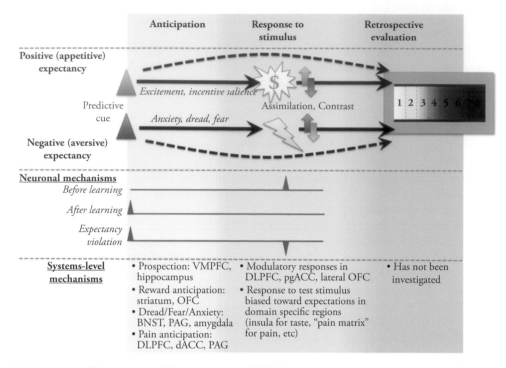

Figure 23.2 Expectancy effects on stages of affective processing. BNST, bed nucleus of the stria terminalis; dACC, dorsal anterior cingulate cortex; DLPFC, dorsolateral prefrontal cortex; OFC, orbitofrontal cortex; PAG, periacqueductal gray; pgACC, pregenual anterior cingulate cortex; VMPFC, ventromedial prefrontal cortex.

underlying the generation of each of these affective responses (Berns et al., 2006; Knutson, Adams, et al., 2001; Knutson, Fong, Adams, Varner, & Hommer, 2001; LaBar, Gatenby, Gore, LeDoux, & Phelps, 1998; Mobbs et al., 2007, 2009; Phelps et al., 2001). Some current claims about the brain substrates underlying different types of affective responses related to expectancy are summarized at the bottom of Figure 23.2. A number of individual studies imply that varieties of anticipatory affect are associated with distinct neural signatures, but the sensitivity and specificity of brain activity in these areas for particular types of affective states has not been established in humans. Meta-analyses indicate that claims of one-to-one mappings between affective states and gross anatomical brain regions are not likely to be warranted (Barrett & Wager, 2006; Lindquist, Wager, Kober, Bliss-Moreau, & Barrett, 2012; Wager, Phan, Liberzon, & Taylor, 2003; cf. Phan, Wager, Taylor, & Liberzon, 2002).

In addition, the rather straightforward view that "positive" and "negative" affective responses are natural categories respected by the brain, and that positive and negative affect are de facto triggered by appetitive and aversive cues, is likely to require substantial revision. A major contribution

of appraisal and psychological construction-based theories of emotion (Barrett & Wager, 2006; Ellsworth & Scherer, 2003; Scherer, 1999) is to illustrate the powerful influences of complex social and situational information on the types of affective responses that might be elicited by predictive cues. Cues that predict desired rewards, for example, could trigger arousal, eagerness, and approach behavior if rewards are accessible, but frustration and aggression if they are not. Cues that predict aversive outcomes can elicit avoidance behavior if escape strategies are available, anxiety if the cues are ambiguous with respect to the timing and nature of outcomes, fear if outcomes are aversive and impeding, or aggression if the perceived cause of threat is another individual.

As illustrated in cartoon form in the middle panel of Figure 23.2 (adapted from Schultz, 2007), the anticipation period is also critical in the context of computational and neural models of reinforcement learning. These models, discussed in detail later in this review (see section below, "How Do Expectancies Emerge?"), suggest that when an organism has learned that a cue predicts a subsequent reward, dopaminergic midbrain neurons fire in response to the cue (Schultz, 2007; Schultz,

Dayan, & Montague, 1997; Schultz & Dickenson, 2000). Similar patterns have been observed in primate amygdala for both appetitive and aversive outcomes (Belova, Paton, Morrison, & Salzman, 2007). The neuronal and neurochemical levels of analysis are not incompatible with the specific anticipatory emotions discussed above, and current perspectives generally attempt to integrate across these levels, but this is a challenging endeavor. For example, whereas the amygdala was once thought of as one of the main "seats of emotion" and many have posited a specific role for it in signaling fear, current theories focus on amygdala involvement in processes that are related, but not specific, to fear, such as cue value (Salzman, Paton, Belova, & Morrison, 2007) and vigilance or stimulus salience (Whalen et al., 2009).

Expectancy Effects on Affective Experience

Expectations affect not only anticipatory responses but also responses to emotional stimuli themselves. For example, cue-based expectancies influence whether tastes are perceived as pleasant or unpleasant (Nitschke et al., 2006; Sarinopoulos et al., 2006). Information about the price of a wine influences how much it is enjoyed (Plassmann, O'Doherty, Shiv, & Rangel, 2008). Beliefs about anxiolytic treatments reduce the unpleasantness of aversive images (Petrovic et al., 2005). Expectancy effects on subjective experience also extend to social influences. Knowing that other people enjoyed a cartoon causes people to find it more humorous (Wilson et al., 1989). Appraisal theories of emotion suggest that emotion generation depends critically on an individual's evaluation of his or her context, which is influenced by current, remembered, and imagined future circumstances (Ellsworth & Scherer, 2003; Scherer, 1999). Thus, as with expectancy effects on anticipatory processes, affective responses to outcomes can potentially be influenced by complex appraisals.

In 1989, Timothy Wilson and co-authors formalized the Affective Expectancy Model (AEM; Wilson et al., 1989), which posits that subjective emotional responses depend as much on expectations as they do on emotional stimuli themselves. According to the AEM, affective experiences stem from an interaction between affective expectations (expectations about what one will feel) and stimulus characteristics. When emotional responses are biased in the direction of expectancies, this is referred to as *assimilation*. The AEM suggests that assimilation conserves processing resources by allowing faster, shallower processing of stimuli when a priori

expectations about emotional meaning are strong. Thus, emotional responses will assimilate to expectancies when (1) affective expectations are congruent with a stimulus (e.g., when individuals expect to like a *New Yorker* cartoon that is indeed funny), or (2) when affective expectancies are incongruent with a stimulus but processing is minimal (e.g., when individuals expect to like a boring *New Yorker* cartoon and therefore turn the page quickly after a chuckle). In both of these cases, attentional resources are conserved during stimulus processing and introspection, as demonstrated by speeded response times during stimulus viewing and during reaction probes (Wilson et al., 1989); thus, the discrepancy between the stimulus and expectancies is not noticed in the incongruent case because of superficial attention. Laboratory investigations find evidence of assimilation across a host of domains, including pain (Atlas, Bolger, Lindquist, & Wager, 2010; Keltner et al., 2006; Kong et al., 2006, 2008; Koyama, McHaffie, Laurienti, & Coghill, 2005; Wager et al., 2004; Wager, Scott, & Zubieta, 2007), taste (Nitschke, Dixon, et al., 2006; Plassmann et al., 2008; Sarinopoulos et al., 2006), emotion (Klaaren, Hodges, & Wilson, 1994; Wilson et al., 1989), and person perception (Hamilton & Sherman, 1996; Rosenthal, 1987, 1994; Rosenthal & Rubin, 1978).

While experimentally manipulated expectancies generally lead to assimilation, common belief suggests that having positive expectations can actually lead to negative outcomes. The statement "I didn't want to get my hopes up" belies the notion that expecting something positive will only lead to disappointment. Individuals often avoid seeing a film that has received rave reviews from friends and critics, for fear that the experience will not "live up to expectations" and will instead be less enjoyable than if the film had been seen without prior information. *Contrast* describes the phenomenon whereby subjective experience is biased away from expectancies. Echoing earlier theories from work in priming and categorization (Herr, 1986; Herr, Sherman, & Fazio, 1983; Lombardi, Higgins, & Bargh, 1987), Wilson hypothesized that contrast occurs when affective expectations are incongruent with stimulus valence and individuals notice this discrepancy. In this case, stimulus processing and the formation of affective responses will take longer.

While Wilson failed to find evidence of contrast effects on perception in his original studies, subsequent work did find evidence of contrast effects. One experiment (Geers & Lassiter, 1999) tested

Wilson's predictions about level of encoding using a unitization paradigm, in which subjects segment films on the basis of meaningful actions. One group was instructed to segment a film that was not funny into the *largest* meaningful actions (gross-level attention), while a second group was instructed to segment behavior based on the *smallest* meaningful actions (fine-grained attention). This attention manipulation was crossed with an expectancy manipulation (positive expectation vs. no expectation about the film). Results confirmed the predictions of the AEM: within the gross-level attention group, participants with positive expectations enjoyed the film more than those with no expectations (assimilation), but within the fine-grained attention group, participants with positive expectations enjoyed the film *less* than those without expectations (contrast).

Contrast also occurs when individuals have prior exposure to an expectation-inconsistent stimulus (Geers, Helfer, Kosbab, Weiland, & Landry, 2005). Geers and colleagues crossed an expectancy manipulation (positive expectation vs. no expectation) with prior exposure to a relatively humorless film. Half the group saw the film and returned several weeks later to participate in a supposedly unrelated experiment that happened to show the same film. Those in the positive expectation group who had seen the film rated it as less funny than those who had seen the film but had no expectations in the subsequent session, and those who had positive expectations without prior exposure to the film.

Contrast is also observed when expectations are accompanied by uncertainty (Zellner et al., 2004): When unfamiliar food products are paired with congruent or incongruent expectations, incongruent expectations lead to contrast, rather than assimilation.

Finally, individual differences can influence whether contrast or assimilation will occur. Assimilation is more likely for optimists (Geers & Lassiter, 2002) and for individuals low in need for cognition (Geers & Lassiter, 2003), whereas pessimists and those high in need for cognition take longer to process stimuli and hence notice discrepancies and show contrast effects.

Thus, in each of these examples, attention seems to moderate the relationship between expectations and affective experience. Prior exposure, uncertainty, pessimism, and need for cognition all increase fine-grained attention and lead to contrast, whereas assimilation is dominant with broad attention. Notably, neuroimaging studies of expectancy have focused on identifying the mechanisms underlying effects that assimilate with expectations. Understanding the mechanisms underlying contrast effects, the conditions under which they arise, and the relationship between contrast and feelings of disappointment or surprise are important directions for future work.

Retrospective Expectancy Effects

Affective expectations can directly influence retrospective evaluations of affective experiences, independent of responses to the event. For example, in one study that took place at the end of a fall semester (Klaaren et al., 1994), students predicted how much they expected to enjoy their upcoming winter vacation. Several weeks after students returned from break, Klaaren and colleagues collected ratings of overall vacation enjoyment, as well as ratings of specific experiences during the vacation. Retrospective ratings of overall enjoyment were predicted by not only experiences while on the vacation but also pre-vacation expectancies. (In this case, expectancies did *not* influence the enjoyableness of vacation experiences themselves.) In a follow-up study, the authors experimentally manipulated expectations and found similar results. Participants who were invited to take part in an "enjoyable" study enjoyed watching a film at the lab more than a separate group that was given no information about the study, but also reported greater willingness to return and more overall enjoyment several weeks later, independent of their experience during the film. Similar results have been found in studies of placebo analgesia, which have sometimes been found to be larger in retrospective reports than immediate ratings of pain (De Pascalis, Chiaradia, & Carotenuto, 2002; Price, Milling, Kirsch, & Duff, 1999).

Taken together, these findings suggest that pre-experience expectancies may directly influence retrospective evaluations, represented by the dashed line in Figure 23.2. Expectancy effects on retrospective reports may result from biased memories of pretreatment (baseline) experiences (Feine, Lavigne, Dao, Morin, & Lund, 1998) or biased memories of affective experiences relative to concurrent ratings of those experiences (De Pascalis et al., 2002; Price et al., 1999). In addition, different factors may influence online vs. retrospective ratings: Retrospective ratings of colonoscopies depend on peak pain and pain at the end of the procedure, rather than integrating across the entire duration of real-time ratings (Redelmeier & Kahneman, 1996; Redelmeier, Katz, & Kahneman, 2003). Finally, expectancy effects on retrospective reports may reflect self-consistency biases (Wells & Sweeney, 1986), whereby individuals report experiences consistent with expectations simply to maintain self-esteem and avoid psychological uncertainty. As discussed in more detail later, the question of whether expectations affect retrospective evaluations without affecting stimulus processing has caused a heated debate in the field of placebo research, and is one of the critical reasons to test whether expectations affect more objective outcome measures, such as pain-related brain responses.

Mechanisms of Expectancy

It is clear that expectancies strongly modify affective experience. We now turn to the psychological processes and neural mechanisms hypothesized to support these effects. We focus here on the processes that give rise to expectancies, those likely to be involved in maintaining expectancies, and those thought to play a modulatory role in affecting perception.

How do Expectancies Emerge?

There are two main routes to expectancy formation: experience-dependent expectancies (e.g., those elicited by conditioning), and expectancies formed without direct exposure (e.g., those elicited by verbal instructions). While both routes might lead to similar mechanisms of expectancy maintenance and downstream modulation, the pathways involved in the development of these two types of expectancies are likely to be quite distinct.

First, expectations can be based on one's own experiences or previous reactions to a stimulus. This can occur for both simple classical conditioning-based expectancies and more complex response expectancies. One important line of work in the field of reinforcement learning provides a mechanistic account of how experience-based expectations are developed in the simple case of stimulus expectancies that arise through classical conditioning. A cartoon depicting this chain of events (adapted from Schultz, 2007) is presented in the middle panel of Figure 23.2. In brief, in response to an unpredicted rewarding event, dopaminergic midbrain neurons increase their firing rates, signaling a prediction error (Schultz et al., 1997; Schultz & Dickinson, 2000). Over time, as an animal learns that rewards are predicted by an antecedent cue, the same neuron will respond to the cue, now signaling predictive value. Hence, this value signal represents an expectation about the reward that will be delivered. After learning, if the cue is presented but a reward is not delivered, the firing rate in the same neurons will decrease relative to baseline at the time when the reward was expected. This decrease in firing rate signals a negative prediction error (reward expected, but not delivered), which will update expected value on the following trial. These patterns of neural responses can be described by computational models (Rescorla & Wagner, 1972; Sutton & Barto, 1981), and neuroimaging studies have shown that the same models predict brain responses in humans during reward learning (O'Doherty, 2004; O'Doherty et al., 2003) as well as during aversive learning (Delgado, Li, Schiller, & Phelps, 2008; Ploghaus et al., 2000; Seymour et al., 2004, 2005) and even in purely cognitive domains (Aron et al., 2004; Rodriguez, Aron, & Poldrack, 2006). Medial and lateral orbitofrontal cortex, which contains neurons that flexibly encode both aversive and rewarding outcomes (Morrison & Salzman, 2009), appears to represent the expected values of specific cues and outcomes (Mcdannald, Lucantonio, Burke, Niv, & Schoenbaum, 2011; Murray, O'Doherty, & Schoenbaum, 2007; Schoenbaum & Roesch, 2005; Schoenbaum, Roesch, Stalnaker, & Takahashi, 2009; Schoenbaum, Saddoris, & Stalnaker, 2007). Prediction errors are encoded primarily by the ventral striatum (Hare, O'Doherty, Camerer, Schultz, & Rangel, 2008; Mcdannald et al., 2011; O'Doherty et al., 2004; Rutledge, Dean, Caplin, & Glimcher, 2010; Schoenbaum & Setlow, 2003) and basolateral amygdala (Belova, Paton, & Salzman, 2008; Roesch, Calu, Esber, & Schoenbaum, 2010; Schoenbaum, Chiba, & Gallagher, 1998; Schoenbaum, Setlow, Saddoris, & Gallagher, 2003). The dynamic effects of expected value and prediction errors on responses in these systems illustrate how expectancies emerge, how expectancy violations affect neural responses, and how experiences update expectations over time in the case of simple conditioning-based learning.

Response expectancies that involve predictions about more complex scenarios are unlikely to be fully explained by these simple computational models. Research on affective forecasting focuses on understanding how individuals predict future emotional responses to hypothetical situations, and why these predictions are generally incorrect (Gilbert & Wilson, 2009). A dominant hypothesis is that previous experiences influence future expectations through mental simulation, or *prospection*. Individuals may use memories of prior experiences to imagine themselves in a future situation, and use their feelings about the imaginary situation to generate predictions about future emotions and affective events (Gilbert & Wilson, 2007, 2009; Schacter, Addis, & Buckner, 2007).

Explicit prospection is thought to depend on interactions between self-related processing and episodic memory, both of which converge in the ventromedial prefrontal cortex (VMPFC). Self-related processing is a placeholder term for the representation of information relevant for the status and well-being of the social and physical self. Such representations appear to involve the VMFPC in connection with (a) dorsomedial prefrontal and lateral temporal systems important in social cognition and (b) subcortical regions involved in valuation and affect. Episodic memory involves VMPFC in connection with a circuit that includes the hippocampus and surrounding medial temporal regions and the posterior cingulate (Addis, Pan, Vu, Laiser, & Schacter, 2009; Buckner & Carroll, 2007; Fellows & Farah, 2005; Schacter et al., 2007; Wheeler, Stuss, & Tulving, 1997). In addition, mental simulation might elicit hedonic reactions that would in turn affect domain-specific mechanisms associated with the imagined experience (Gilbert & Wilson, 2007). Consistent with this hypothesis, humans and primates show increased activation of brain regions involved in nociception when anticipating pain (Koyama et al., 1998; Porro et al., 2002), and similarly, when anticipating reward, individuals activate brain regions that are also activated in response to rewarding events (Bray, Rangel, Shimojo, Balleine, & O'Doherty, 2008; Knutson, Adams, et al., 2001; Knutson, Fond, et al., 2001). It is important to note that it may be impossible to dissociate anticipatory affect associated with prospection from computations of expected value. Value and anticipatory affect go hand in hand and might very well involve the same underlying processes.

People also form affective expectancies in the absence of direct experience with a stimulus or situation. An individual might expect to like a film on the basis of friends' impressions and critics' reviews. Expectations might also stem from knowledge of how one is supposed to behave in a certain situation; for example, one might never have spoken in public, but might know that giving a talk is generally anxiety provoking. A number of studies have investigated the neural systems underlying learning in these contexts. Observational learning has been studied with vicarious conditioning paradigms (Colloca & Benedetti, 2009; Hygge & Ohman, 1978; Mineka & Cook, 1993; Olsson & Phelps, 2004). Rule-based learning can be tested by

delivering verbal information about contingencies and testing responses without actual reinforcement (Amanzio & Benedetti, 1999; Colloca & Benedetti, 2006; Colloca, Sigaudo, & Benedetti, 2008; Colloca, Tinazzi, et al., 2008; Funayama, Grillon, Davis, & Phelps, 2001; Grillon, Ameli, Woods, Merikangas, & Davis, 1991; Phelps et al., 2001). These studies suggest that these different routes to learning elicit similar effects as experience-dependent learning, including physiological responses (e.g., differential skin conductance responses; Hygge & Ohman, 1978; Mineka & Cook, 1993) and placebo and nocebo effects (Colloca & Benedetti, 2009), though placebo effects based on verbal information without conditioning are smaller than those based on experience or social observation (Amanzio & Benedetti, 1999; Colloca & Benedetti, 2009). Both routes are associated with amygdala activation during fear learning, similar to standard fear conditioning (Phelps, 2006). Vicarious learning or its autonomic expression, however, might depend critically on the left amygdala, as patients with left temporal lobe lesions fail to show potentiated startle responses as a function of verbal information (Funayama et al., 2001).

How Are Expectancies Maintained?

Expectancy involves maintenance of a belief, particularly in the case of conscious, verbalizable expectancies. Two regions have been consistently observed in studies of expectancy effects in various domains that are likely to support expectancy maintenance: the dorsolateral prefrontal cortex (DLPFC), and the ventrolateral prefrontal cortex (VLPFC)/lateral orbitofrontal cortex (OFC) (Atlas, Wager, Dahl, & Smith, 2009; Wager, 2005b; see Figure 23.3). Studies of executive working memory consistently activate the DLPFC (Wager & Smith, 2003), and it is activated during anticipation and experience in a number of experimental investigations of expectancy effects on pain (Atlas et al., 2010; Craggs, Price, Perlstein, Verne, & Robinson, 2008; Wager, Atlas, Leotti, & Rilling, 2011; Wager et al., 2004; Watson et al., 2009), taste (Sarinopoulos et al., 2006), and emotion (Petrovic et al., 2005). Direct stimulation of the DLPFC also appears to block placebo-based expectancy effects on pain (Krummenacher, Candia, Folkers, Schedlowski, & Schönbächler, 2009). Interestingly, the DLPFC is not only critical for working memory, but it also plays a key role in cognitive control (Kim, Johnson, Cilles, & Gold, 2011; Miller, 2000; Miller & Cohen, 2001; Taren, Venkatraman, & Huettel, 2011). Thus, this region

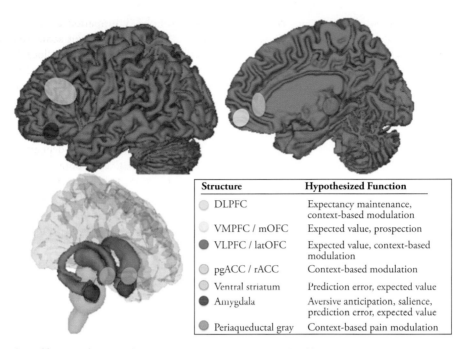

Structure	Hypothesized Function
DLPFC	Expectancy maintenance, context-based modulation
VMPFC / mOFC	Expected value, prospection
VLPFC / latOFC	Expected value, context-based modulation
pgACC / rACC	Context-based modulation
Ventral striatum	Prediction error, expected value
Amygdala	Aversive anticipation, salience, prediction error, expected value
Periaqueductal gray	Context-based pain modulation

Figure 23.3 General brain mechanisms of expectancy. See Figure 23.2 and text for abbreviations.

has been thought to be key in maintaining expectancies and in modulating perception in accordance with expectancies, as described in more detail below (Lorenz, Minoshima, & Casey, 2003). The VLPFC/lateral OFC has also been activated in a number of placebo studies (Lieberman et al., 2004; Petrovic et al., 2005; Wager et al., 2004, 2011) and is generally thought to support affective value, expectancy maintenance, and regulation of emotion (Kringelbach, 2005; Lieberman et al., 2004; Petrovic et al., 2010; Wager, 2005b).

When expectancies concern affective stimuli or outcomes, they involve predictions about affective value. As mentioned above, learning studies suggest that the OFC tracks—and is necessary for representing—the expected value of anticipated outcomes (Hare et al., 2008; Mcdannald et al., 2011; Murray et al., 2007; Schoenbaum & Roesch, 2005; Schoenbaum et al., 2007, 2009). Recent evidence suggests that it is less important for tracking the overall expected value of cues, and rather is necessary for representing specific outcomes associated with specific cues (Schoenbaum, Takahashi, Liu, & Mcdannald, 2011). It also may be most important for "model-based" expectancies (Daw, Niv, & Dayan, 2005; Daw, O'Doherty, Dayan, Seymour, & Dolan, 2006), in which expected value is determined by forward-looking conceptualization and prediction of future outcomes. Thus, in studies of stimulus expectancies like those depicted in Figure 23.1, lateral OFC may become activated in anticipation of pain—that is, in response to pain-predictive cues—in order to represent the value of the upcoming pain associated with that cue. Similarly, it may be active in placebo conditions, because the expected value is heavily determined by conceptual processes, placing metabolic demands on expectancy formation in lateral OFC. Lateral OFC is one of the most consistently activated areas in placebo studies (Wager & Fields, 2013) and by this view, lateral OFC may also be essential for placebo effects.

How Do Expectancies Modulate Affective Responses?

Whether they lead to assimilation or contrast, expectancies are likely to affect perception through specific mediating psychological mechanisms (Wager, 2005a). Here, we consider both the psychological processes likely to give rise to these effects and the neural mechanisms that may support expectancy-based changes in downstream processes that in turn affect perception.

Three specific regions have emerged as central in expectancy-based modulation across domains. These are the DLPFC, particularly in the left hemisphere, the lateral OFC, and the pregenual/rostral anterior cingulate cortex (rACC). Each of these regions is associated with expectancy-based *increases* that are correlated with the magnitude of expectancy effects on subjective experience, and the magnitude of expectancy effects on downstream domain-specific responses (e.g., amygdala activation during emotion processing, insula responses during taste perception, insula and thalamus responses during pain) (Atlas et al., 2010; Bingel, Lorenz, Schoell, Weiller, & Buchel, 2006; Craggs, Price, Verne, & Perlstein, 2007; Kong et al., 2006; Sarinopoulos et al., 2006; Wager et al., 2004, 2011). While these patterns of interactions among brain regions suggest that these regions are involved in expectancy-based modulation, it is unknown whether this modulation comes about through expectancy-related changes in intervening psychological processes.

First, as hypothesized in the AEM (Wilson et al., 1989), expectancies may induce changes in attention. As a result of expectations, individuals may engage in more superficial encoding or might attend selectively to congruent information. This hypothesis is supported by research suggesting that expectancies that are congruent with stimulus properties lead to faster processing and decision-making than incongruent expectancies (Wilson et al., 1989). Individuals adjust somatic attention in response to expectations for high pain (Johnston, Atlas, & Wager, 2012) and during placebo treatment (Geers, Helfer, Weiland, & Kosbab, 2006). Interestingly, in one recent study (Johnston, Atlas, & Wager, 2012), cue-based expectations for high pain increased focus on the body, and focus on the body actually *reduced* expectancy effects on pain reports. Thus expectancy-based changes in attention produced effects opposite in sign from those of expectancies, suggesting that robust expectancy effects on pain experience must be supported at least in part by mechanisms other than changes in attention. Similarly, other recent work suggests that at least some types of expectancy effects, particularly those elicited by placebo treatments, are not reducible to changes in attention. Buhle and Wager (Buhle, Stevens, Friedman, & Wager, 2012) found that both placebo and a difficult, attention-demanding working memory task reduced pain, but that these effects were essentially completely additive. The fact that the placebo treatment and the difficult cognitive task neither interfered with nor potentiated one another suggests that their mechanisms and processing resources may be independent.

Second, in the case of response expectancies or expectations about negative or positive stimuli, affective expectancies might increase or decrease stress and anxiety (Aslaksen & Flaten, 2008; Wager, 2005a).

This hypothesis is supported by research demonstrating that individuals with low state anxiety show larger placebo responses (McGlashan, Evans, & Orne, 1969; Vase, Robinson, Verne, & Price, 2005), that individual differences in placebo analgesia are correlated with changes in subjective stress (Aslaksen & Flaten, 2008), and that nocebo effects, or effects of expectations that a treatment will *increase* pain, are abolished by benzodiazepines, a class of anxiolytics (Benedetti, Amanzio, Vighetti, & Asteggiano, 2006). Expectancy-induced changes in anxiety, stress, and general affective state are likely to cause nonspecific effects that would be additive with stimulus effects.

A third possibility, mentioned above, is that expectancies might modulate evaluations and decision-making without changing stimulus processing (Wager, 2005a). This hypothesis is supported by sensory decision theory (SDT) studies that suggest that placebo treatments change response criteria, but not discriminability of pain processing (Clark, 1969; Feather, Chapman, & Fisher, 1972), and that expectancies influence retrospective pain ratings by biasing memories of pretreatment pain (Price et al., 1999). In addition, in many cases placebo effects on reported pain are substantially larger than corresponding effects on brain markers of pain-processing (Wager, Matre, & Casey, 2006).

Finally, expectancy-based modulation might involve unique mechanisms unexplained by these proposed mediating psychological factors. One specific line of research has focused on the endogenous opioid system and its role in placebo analgesia. Placebo effects are abolished by the opioid antagonist naloxone (Eippert, Bingel et al., 2009; Levine, Gordon, & Fields, 1978), and PET imaging studies indicate that placebo responses are accompanied by increased μ-opioid receptor (MOR) binding in limbic regions (Scott et al., 2007, 2008; Wager, Scott, & Zubieta, 2007; Zubieta et al., 2005). Consistent with the idea that opioids are critical for expectancy-based modulation, placebo analgesia is also associated with increases in activation in the MOR-rich rACC and the periaqueductal gray (PAG) (Bingel et al., 2006; Petrovic, Kalso, Petersson, & Ingvar, 2002; Wager et al., 2004), as well as increased connectivity between these regions (Bingel et al., 2006; Wager et al., 2007) that is abolished with naloxone (Eippert, Bingel et al., 2009). The PAG produces analgesia when stimulated in humans (Baskin et al., 1986; Boivie & Meyerson, 1982) and has inhibitory connections with primary afferent nociceptors in the spinal cord's dorsal horn (Basbaum & Fields, 1984; Fields, 2004). Several studies have demonstrated that placebo analgesia can reduce responses to noxious events in the spinal cord, consistent with descending modulation (Eippert, Finsterbusch, Bingel, & Buchel, 2009; Goffaux, de Souza, Potvin, & Marchand, 2009; Goffaux, Redmond, Rainville, & Marchand, 2007). While this literature supports the idea that placebo treatments can engage "gate control" mechanisms that can block nociceptive afferents at the spinal level (Melzack & Wall, 1965), the scope and importance of these potential spinal effects for overall analgesia are unknown. In addition, it is unknown whether opioids underlie stimulus expectancy effects, or whether opioid-based modulation or other specific mechanisms could mediate expectancy effects in non-nociceptive affective domains.

Expectancy Effects on Affective Experience

While research on conditioning and learning models has provided a strong picture of the neural mechanisms that give rise to expectations about reward and punishments, we know far less about how expectations affect *perception* of affective events. As mentioned in the previous sections, a critical question has been whether expectancies modulate affective processing, or whether they modulate decision-making and subjective reports independent of actual experience. Early studies used sensory decision theory to separate changes in stimulus discriminability from changes in report criterion and found that placebo analgesia was associated with changes in decision criteria but not sensitivity (Clark, 1969; Feather et al., 1972), suggesting that expectancies affect decision-making but not sensory processing. However, later studies have used neuroimaging and electrophysiological approaches to demonstrate that expectancies modulate responses within brain regions relevant for processing pain (Atlas et al., 2010; Brown, Seymour, Boyle et al., 2008; Brown, Seymour, El-Deredy, & Jones, 2008; Koyama et al., 2005; Price et al., 2007; Wager et al., 2004, 2006; Watson et al., 2009), taste (Nitschke, Dixon, et al., 2006; Sarinopoulos et al., 2006), and emotion (Petrovic et al., 2005; Sharot, De Martino, & Dolan, 2009). This suggests that affective expectancies do indeed modulate brain responses.

However, expectancies can affect brain responses in a domain-relevant region without that region driving subjective experience. There are many examples of stimulus effects on domain-relevant brain responses that do not contribute to conscious perception, such as amygdala activation to unperceived laser stimulation (Bornhovd et al., 2002) and masked emotional faces (Whalen et al., 1998, 2004). Further,

many of the regions involved in affective processing have multiple roles. For example, expectancy effects have been observed on insula responses to noxious stimulation (Koyama et al., 2005; Price et al., 2007; Wager et al., 2004) as well as to pleasant and aversive tastes (Nitschke, Dixon, et al., 2006; Sarinopoulos et al., 2006). While the insula is reliably activated by noxious and gustatory stimuli, it is also affected by interoception (Craig, 2002, 2009), general task set (Dosenbach et al., 2006), negative affect (Shackman et al., 2011), and a variety of emotions (Lindquist et al., 2012). Each of these processes might be affected by changes in expectancy. Thus, expectancy-induced changes in the insula or other affective regions might reflect changes in attention, anxiety, or other processes that are affected by expectancy, rather than changes in basic stimulus processing. This account would be consistent with Wilson's idea that an experience that fails to meet expectations is processed the same, but also involves disappointment (Wilson et al., 1989). It might be this disappointment (or relief, in the case of positive experiences like analgesia) that contributes to subjective experience. Thus, while expectations might modulate activation in domain-relevant regions, subjective reports may still be driven by regions involved in decision-making and evaluation independent of activation within primary regions. In order to isolate the mechanisms whereby expectations affect subjective experience, expectancy effects on the brain need to be related to expectancy effects on behavioral outcomes.

This has been accomplished through individual differences analyses, which suggest that the magnitude of expectancy effects on perception is correlated with the magnitude of expectancy effects on the brain. For example, individuals who report larger placebo effects on pain also show larger placebo effects on rACC and DLPFC responses (Wager et al., 2004, 2011), and those who report larger nocebo effects show larger increases in dACC (Kong et al., 2008). While this suggests that there is indeed a relationship between subjective experience and the magnitude of expectancy effects on brain activation, individual differences analyses cannot show that these factors are causally related. A number of personality variables are related to placebo-based expectancy effects on pain responses, including optimism (Geers et al., 2005; Morton, Watson, El-Deredy, & Jones, 2009), suggestibility (De Pascalis et al., 2002), and reward responsiveness (Scott et al., 2007). Thus, these factors may independently influence expectancy effects on behavior as well as expectancy effects on the brain.

To identify the pathways whereby expectancies modulate *ongoing* affective experience, expectancy effects on brain and behavior must be measured and related within subjects and over time. One can thus isolate whether manipulated expectations affect activation within domain-specific regions and whether those changes in turn affect responses, or whether responses reflect decision-making biases independent of activation within sensory regions. In a recent fMRI study (Atlas et al., 2010), we used an approach called multilevel mediation analysis to identify the brain regions that support the dynamic relationships between cue-based stimulus expectancies and expectancy effects on affective experience. We focused on expectancy effects on pain, as pain provides an ideal model system of affective processing. We found that expectancy effects on dynamic pain were mediated by three classes of brain regions: those thought to support changes in value (e.g., OFC, striatum), those implicated in cognitive control and downstream modulation (e.g., DLPFC, pgACC), and those that were also specifically activated by painful stimulation, which are described in more detail below. In the following section, we review the brain mechanisms that underlie pain processing and review findings from our lab and others

isolating the paths by which expectations modulate pain perception.

Expectancy Effects on Pain

The hedonic domain of pain processing provides an ideal platform by which to study the transfer from external stimulus to subjective perception and to test where along this pathway expectancies affect perception. First, noxious stimuli are objectively quantifiable. In thermal pain models, temperature is a characteristic of the external stimulus, and it is possible to measure the effects of small changes in the noxious stimulus; the direct effects of objective changes in noxious input are referred to as *nociception*.

Second, nociception is well studied in both human and animal models, and the brain regions that are affected by changes in noxious stimuli, often referred to as the "pain matrix," are highly conserved across species. This has led to a well-characterized understanding of the ascending pathways that transfer a noxious input (e.g., a small pinprick, or a hot flame) from peripheral nociceptors to the spinal cord to the central nervous system, depicted in Figure 23.4 (lower right). In brief, noxious input is registered by Aδ, Aβ, and C-fiber primary afferent nociceptors (PANs) in the periphery, which synapse

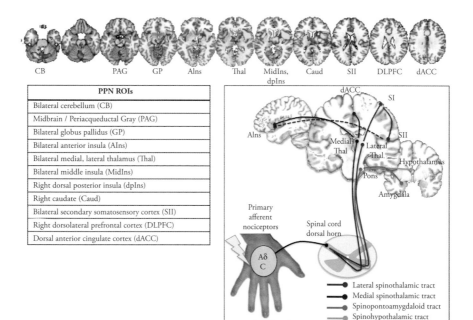

Figure 23.4 The pain processing network (PPN). Top row: Results of a mega-analysis of five studies comparing High vs Low intensity thermal stimulation (n=114; Atlas et al., 2010; Atlas et al., 2012) reveal pain processing network regions of interest (PPN ROIs). We note that primary somatosensory cortex (SI) is generally included in the "pain matrix" and is activated by noxious stimuli in animal and human models. However it was not identified within the boundaries of our PPN mega-analysis. This may be because thermode position varied slightly across stidies. Because of the wide literature on S1 involvement in somatosensory and pain processing, we consider this region part of the PPN as well. Bottom right: Schematic illustrating cortical targets of main ascending nociceptive pathways.

at in the spinal cord's dorsal horn. Many PANs project via the *lateral spinothalamic tract* to contralateral thalamus (ventral posterior lateral and ventral posterior inferior nuclei), which in turn project to primary and secondary somatosensory cortex (SI and SII). Other PANs project via the *medial spinothalamic tract* to medial thalamus (ventral medial posterior and central lateral nuclei) followed by dorsal anterior cingulate and anterior insula. In addition to these spinothalamic pathways, there are also direct projections to the hypothalamus (spinohypothalamic tract; Giesler, Katter, & Dado, 1994); to the amygdala by way of pontine nuclei (spinopontoamygdaloid tract); to midbrain structures including the periaqueductal gray (spinomesencephalic tract); and to the caudal medulla and reticular formation (spinoreticular tract). (For more detailed reviews, see Almeida, Roizenblatt, & Tufik, 2004; Price, 2000; Treede, Kenshalo, Gracely, & Jones, 1999; Willis & Westlund, 1997.) The central nervous system regions that receive input from these various pathways are reliably activated by noxious input, as shown in the top row of Figure 23.4. In an analysis that tested the effects of noxious stimulus intensity across five different studies of thermal heat pain (*n* = 114) (Atlas et al., 2010, 2012), we observed heat-related activation (high- vs. low-intensity stimulation) of all of the targets of these afferent pathways, with the exception of S1 (see Figure 23.4). For the remainder of this review, these regions are defined as the pain-processing network, or PPN.

Third, the concept of pain actually refers to a subjective percept that is distinct from nociception. Pain involves both sensory and affective components (Loeser & Treede, 2008); in other words, the subjective percept has location and intensity information, but also involves unpleasantness and a motivation to escape the noxious stimulus. This dissociation makes pain unique from other perceptual domains and allows it to serve as a model of affective processing. Interestingly, the precise central nervous system mechanisms that give rise to subjective pain have not been fully distinguished from those that are associated with nociception. Researchers have focused more directly on dissociating sensory and affective components of subjective pain; a general consensus is that lateral spinothalamic targets are associated with pain's sensory components, while targets of the medial spinothalamic tract are relevant for the motivational and affective components of pain (Price, 2000; Rainville, 2002). It is important to note that this distinction is primarily supported by a series of studies that used hypnosis to modify

pain unpleasantness. When participants focused on decreasing pain unpleasantness, dACC activation decreased, but noxious stimulus-evoked responses in S1 and insula were unaffected (Rainville, Carrier, Hofbauer, Bushnell, & Duncan, 1999; Rainville, Duncan, Price, Carrie, & Bushnell, 1997). Another study showed that ratings of pain unpleasantness were correlated with pain-related regional cerebral blood flow (rCBF) responses in dACC, while intensity ratings were correlated with posterior cingulate responses Tolle et al., 1999. However, findings from studies that have attempted to dissociate "bottom-up," stimulus-driven brain responses from those that predict pain reports have not been consistent (Apkarian, Darbar, Krauss, Gelnar, & Szeverenyi, 1999; Craig, Chen, Bandy, & Reiman, 2000), and thus the roles of specific individual brain structures in creating the subjective experience of pain are still not entirely clear. It is likely that pain emerges from integrated activity across regions (Coghill, Sang, Maisog, & Iadarola, 1999) and that one cannot point to some regions as evidence for "sensory" modulation and others as evidence for "affective" modulation.

Finally, pain is highly modifiable by expectations. Unpredictable noxious stimuli and those preceded by longer anticipation are perceived as more painful than predictable stimuli (Carlsson et al., 2006; Hauck et al., 2007; Miller, 1981; cf. Crombez et al., 1994). Cue-based expectations about the intensity of a noxious stimulus bias perception of the stimulus in the direction of expectations (Atlas et al., 2010; Keltner et al., 2006; Lorenz et al., 2005; Ploghaus et al., 2001), although several studies have found an asymmetry whereby cue-based expectations for low pain decrease pain ratings (similar to the placebo effect), but cue-based expectations for high pain do not increase pain (Arntz, 1996; Koyama et al., 2005). Interestingly, when expectations about stimulus timing *and* intensity are combined there is an interaction whereby certain expectations for high-intensity stimuli lead to increased dread (Berns et al., 2006) and higher pain reports than uncertain expectations (Brown, Seymour, Boyle, et al., 2008; Lorenz et al., 2005).

Pain perception is also highly affected by response expectancies, or expectations about one's internal affective experiences and responses. This is most obvious in the case of placebo analgesia, whereby individuals experience less pain in response to an inert treatment when conditioning and/or instructions lead them to believe the treatment will reduce pain (for reviews, see Atlas et al., 2009; Benedetti, 2007; Benedetti et al., 2011; Benedetti, Mayberg, Wager, Stohler, & Zubieta, 2005; Bingel, Schoell, &

Buchel, 2007; Cavanna, Strigaro, & Monaco, 2007; Colloca, Benedetti, & Porro, 2008; Faria, Fredrikson, & Furmark, 2008; Hoffman, Harrington, & Fields, 2005; Kaptchuk, 2002; Price, Finniss, & Benedetti, 2007; Wager, 2005c). Placebo responses are highest in pain (Hróbjartsson & Gøtzsche, 2001, 2004; Vase et al., 2009). Chronic pain, a debilitating condition that costs the United States an estimated $635 billion annually in medical treatment and lost productivity (Committee on Advancing Pain Research, 2011), is effectively treated with cognitive interventions that involve changes in beliefs about pain (Keefe, Dunsmore, & Burnett, 1992; Morley, Eccleston, & Williams, 1999; Nicholas, Wilson, & Goyen, 1992; Vlaeyen & Morley, 2005). Thus, experienced pain is strongly affected by expectations about the self, expectations about the intensity of a stimulus, and expectations about stimulus timing. The question remains whether these effects reflect changes in nociception, changes in processes like anxiety or positive affect that are additive with nociception, or changes in decision-making and pain evaluation mechanisms.

To address this question, we manipulated stimulus expectancies and examined the brain mechanisms that link cue-based expectancies with trial-by-trial changes in subjective pain experience (Atlas et al., 2010). In a task similar to the one depicted in the top row of Figure 23.1, auditory cues elicited expectations for barely painful or highly painful thermal stimulation, and we assessed how cues influenced pain reports and brain responses to a single level of medium heat. As mentioned above, we used multilevel mediation analysis to identify brain regions that (1) are modulated by predictive cues, (2) predict trial-to-trial variations in pain reports, and (3) formally mediate the relationship between cues and reported pain. Cues influenced heat-evoked responses in all PPN regions, including both medial and lateral pain pathways. A subset of PPN regions, including anterior cingulate cortex, anterior insula, and thalamus, formally mediated cue effects on pain. Effects on these regions were in turn mediated by cue-evoked anticipatory activity in the medial OFC and ventral striatum, areas not previously directly implicated in nociception but discussed earlier in supporting more general processes such as expected value and prediction. Thus, these findings illustrate that domain-general anticipatory processes in OFC and striatum link to domain-specific expectancy effects (i.e., effects on PPN), which in turn directly predict trial-by-trial expectancy effects on subjective pain. Future research should test whether parallel mechanisms support expectancy effects on other hedonic domains.

Conclusions

Expectations and beliefs play a pervasive role in the workings of the brain. Expectations are central to learning, affect and emotion, and the coordination of adaptive behavior. Even in the heyday of behaviorism, some theorists argued that expectations—explicit mental representations of specific future outcomes—played a fundamental role in shaping animal behavior, and research since then has reinforced the notion that mental representations operate alongside simpler forms of neural plasticity to drive learning. We do not simply react to events; we anticipate them, and we respond—often in advance—to pursue opportunities and ward off threats. In a world where second chances were hard to come by, our ancestors could not afford not to anticipate the future and respond proactively, and we have inherited this legacy. Because of the fundamental importance of expectations in physical and social well-being, they are also of fundamental importance in driving emotion, and they color our experiences in many ways. They can elicit basic affective responses and full-blown emotions in their own right, and they can influence how we perceive expected events, including those that are clinically and medically relevant. Thus, the emerging study of the brain mechanisms that underlie expectancy belongs to many fields—the study of affect and emotion, learning, and the clinical sciences—and has something to contribute to all of them.

References.

Addis, D. R., Pan, L., Vu, M.-A., Laiser, N., & Schacter, D. L. (2009). Constructive episodic simulation of the future and the past: Distinct subsystems of a core brain network mediate imagining and remembering. *Neuropsychologia, 47* (11), 2222–2238.

Alink, A., Schwiedrzik, C. M., Kohler, A., Singer, W., & Muckli, L. (2010). Stimulus predictability reduces responses in primary visual cortex. *Journal of Neuroscience, 30*(8), 2960–2966.

Almeida, T. F., Roizenblatt, S., & Tufik, S. (2004). Afferent pain pathways: A neuroanatomical review. *Brain Research, 1000*(1-2), 40–56.

Amanzio, M., & Benedetti, F. (1999). Neuropharmacological dissection of placebo analgesia: Expectation-activated opioid systems versus conditioning-activated specific subsystems. *Journal of Neuroscience, 19*(1), 484–494.

Apkarian, A. V., Darbar, A., Krauss, B. R., Gelnar, P. A., & Szeverenyi, N. M. (1999). Differentiating cortical areas related to pain perception from stimulus identification: Temporal analysis of fMRI activity. *Journal of Neurophysiology, 81*(6), 2956–2963.

Arntz, A. (1996). Why do people tend to overpredict pain? On the asymmetries between underpredictions and overpredictions of pain. *Behaviour Research and Therapy, 34*(7), 545–554.

Arntz, A., van den Hout, M. A., van den Berg, G., & Meijboom, A. (1991). The effects of incorrect pain expectations on acquired fear and pain responses. *Behaviour Research and Therapy, 29*(6), 547–560.

Aron, A. R., Shohamy, D., Clark, J., Myers, C., Gluck, M. A., & Poldrack, R. A. (2004). Human midbrain sensitivity to cognitive feedback and uncertainty during classification learning. *Journal of Neurophysiology, 92*(2), 1144–1152.

Aslaksen, P., & Flaten, M. A. (2008). The roles of physiological and subjective stress in the effectiveness of a placebo on experimentally induced pain. *Psychosomatic Medicine, 70*(7), 811–818.

Atlas, L. Y., Bolger, N., Lindquist, M. A., & Wager, T. D. (2010). Brain mediators of predictive cue effects on perceived pain. *Journal of Neuroscience, 30*(39), 12964–12977.

Atlas, L. Y., Wager, T. D., Dahl, K., & Smith, E. (2009). Placebo effects. In J. T. Cacioppo & G. G. Berntson (Eds.), *Handbook of neuroscience for the behavioral sciences* (pp. 1236–1259). Hoboken, NJ: John Wiley & Sons,.

Atlas, L. Y., Whittington, R. A., Lindquist, M. A., Wielgosz, J., Sonty, N., & Wager, T.D. (2012). Dissociable influences of opiates and expectations on pain. *Journal of Neuroscience, 32*(23), 8053–8064.

Balleine, B. W., & Killcross, S. (2006). Parallel incentive processing: An integrated view of amygdala function. *Trends in Neuroscience, 29*(5), 272–279.

Barrett, L. F., & Wager, T. (2006). The structure of emotion: Evidence from neuroimaging studies. *Current Directions in Psychological Science, 15*(2), 79–83.

Basbaum, A. I., & Fields, H. L. (1984). Endogenous pain control systems: Brainstem spinal pathways and endorphin circuitry. *Annual Review of Neuroscience, 7*, 309–338.

Baskin, D. S., Mehler, W. R., Hosobuchi, Y., Richardson, D. E., Adams, J. E., & Flitter, M. A. (1986). Autopsy analysis of the safety, efficacy and cartography of electrical stimulation of the central gray in humans. *Brain Research, 371*(2), 231–236.

Beecher, H. K. (1955). The powerful placebo. *Journal of the American Medical Association, 159*(17), 1602–1606.

Belova, M. A., Paton, J. J., Morrison, S. E., & Salzman, C. D. (2007). Expectation modulates neural responses to pleasant and aversive stimuli in primate amygdala. *Neuron, 55*(6), 970–984.

Belova, M. A., Paton, J. J., & Salzman, C. D. (2008). Moment-to-moment tracking of state value in the amygdala. *Journal of Neuroscience, 28*(40), 10023–10030.

Benedetti, F. (2007). Mechanisms of placebo and placebo related effects across diseases and treatments. *Annual Review of Pharmacology and Toxicology, 48*, 2.1–2.27.

Benedetti, F., Amanzio, M., Vighetti, S., & Asteggiano, G.(2006). The biochemical and neuroendocrine bases of the hyperalgesic nocebo effect. *Journal of Neuroscience, 26*(46), 12014–12022.

Benedetti, F., Carlino, E., & Pollo, A. (2011). How placebos change the patient's brain. *Neuropsychopharmacology, 36*(1), 339–354.

Benedetti, F., Mayberg, H. S., Wager, T. D., Stohler, C. S., & Zubieta, J.-K. (2005). Neurobiological mechanisms of the placebo effect. *Journal of Neuroscience, 25*(45), 10390–10402.

Benedetti, F., Pollo, A., Lopiano, L., Lanotte, M., Vighetti, S., & Rainero, I. (2003). Conscious expectation and unconscious conditioning in analgesic, motor, and hormonal placebo/nocebo responses. *Journal of Neuroscience, 23*(10), 4315–4323.

Benson, H., & Friedman, R. (1996). Harnessing the power of the placebo effect and renaming it "remembered wellness." *Annual Review of Medicine, 47*, 193–199.

Bermpohl, F., Pascual-Leone, A., Amedi, A., Merabet, L. B., Fregni, F., Gaab, N., et al. (2006). Dissociable networks for the expectancy and perception of emotional stimuli in the human brain. *Neuroimage, 30*(2006), 588–600.

Berns, G. S., Chappelow, J., Cekic, M., Zink, C. F., Pagnoni G., & Martin-Skurski, M. E. (2006). Neurobiological substrates of dread. *Science, 312* (5774), 754–758.

Berns, G. S., McClure, S. M., Pagnoni G., & Montague, P. R. (2001). Predictability modulates human brain response to reward. *Journal of Neuroscience, 21*(8), 2793–2798.

Berridge, K. C., & Robinson, T. E. (1998). What is the role of dopamine in reward: Hedonic impact, reward learning, or incentive salience? *Brain Research. Brain Research Reviews, 28*(3), 309–369.

Bingel, U., Lorenz, J., Schoell, E., Weiller, C., & Buchel, C. (2006). Mechanisms of placebo analgesia: rACC recruitment of a subcortical antinociceptive network. *Pain, 120*, 8–15.

Bingel, U., Schoell, E., & Buchel, C. (2007). Imaging pain modulation in health and disease. *Current Opinion in Neurology, 20*(4), 424–431.

Boivie, J., & Meyerson, B. A. (1982). A correlative anatomical and clinical study of pain suppression by deep brain stimulation. *Pain, 13*(2), 113–126.

Bolles, R. (1972). Reinforcement, expectancy, and learning. *Psychological Review, 79*(5), 394–409.

Bollinger, J., Rubens, M. T., Zanto, T. P., & Gazzaley, A. (2010). Expectation-driven changes in cortical functional connectivity influence working memory and long-term memory performance. *Journal of Neuroscience, 30*(43), 14399–14410.

Bornhovd, K., Quante, M., Glauche, V., Bromm, B., Weiller, C., & Buchel, C. (2002). Painful stimuli evoke different stimulus-response functions in the amygdala, prefrontal, insula and somatosensory cortex: A single-trial fMRI study. *Brain, 125*(Pt 6), 1326–1336.

Bray, S., Rangel, A., Shimojo, S., Balleine, B. W., & O'Doherty, J. P. (2008). The neural mechanisms underlying the influence of Pavlovian cues on human decision making. *Journal of Neuroscience, 28*(22), 5861–5866.

Breiter, H. C., Aharon, I., Kahneman, D., Dale, A. M., & Shizgal, P. (2001). Functional imaging of neural responses to expectancy and experience of monetary gains and losses. *Neuron, 30*(2), 619–639.

Brewer, W. F. (1974). There is no convincing evidence for operant or classical conditioning in adult humans. In W. B. Weimer & D. S. Palermo (Eds.), *Cognition and the symbolic processes* (pp. 1–42). Hillsdale, NJ: Lawrence Erlbaum.

Brown, C., Seymour, B., Boyle, Y., Elderedy, W., & Jones, A. (2008). Modulation of pain ratings by expectation and uncertainty: Behavioral characteristics and anticipatory neural correlates. *Pain, 135*(3), 240–250.

Brown, C., Seymour, B., El-Deredy, W., & Jones, A. K. (2008). Confidence in beliefs about pain predicts expectancy effects on pain perception and anticipatory processing in right anterior insula. *Pain, 139*(2), 324–332.

Brown, W. A. (1998). The placebo effect. *Scientific American, 278*(1), 90–95.

Buckner, R. L., & Carroll, D. C. (2007). Self-projection and the brain. *Trends in Cognitive Sciences, 11*(2), 49–57.

Buhle, J., Stevens, B., Friedman, J., & Wager, T. (2012). Distraction and placebo: Two separate routes to pain control. *Psychological Science*, *23*(3), 246–253.

Carlsson, K., Andersson, J., Petrovic, P., Petersson, K. M., Ohman, A., & Ingvar, M. (2006). Predictability modulates the affective and sensory-discriminative neural processing of pain. *Neuroimage*, *32*(4), 1804–1814.

Carlsson, K., Petrovic, P., Skare, S., Petersson, K. M., & Ingvar, M. (2000). Tickling expectations: Neural processing in anticipation of a sensory stimulus. *Journal of Cognitive Neuroscience*, *12*(4), 691–703.

Cavanna, A. E., Strigaro, G., & Monaco, F. (2007). Brain mechanisms underlying the placebo effect in neurological disorders. *Functional Neurology*, *22*(2), 89–94.

Chaput de Saintonge, D. M., & Herxheimer, A. (1994). Harnessing placebo effects in health care. *Lancet*, *344*(8928), 995–998.

Christakou, A., Brammer, M., Giampietro, V., & Rubia, K. (2009). Right ventromedial and dorsolateral prefrontal cortices mediate adaptive decisions under ambiguity by integrating choice utility and outcome evaluation. *Journal of Neuroscience*, *29*(35), 11020–11028.

Clark, R. E., Manns, J. R., & Squire, L. R. (2002). Classical conditioning, awareness, and brain systems. *Trends in Cognitive Sciences*, *6*(12), 524–531.

Clark, W. C. (1969). Sensory-decision theory analysis of the placebo effect on the criterion for pain and thermal sensitivity. *Journal of Abnormal Psychology*, *74*(3), 363–371.

Coghill, R. C., Sang, C. N., Maisog, J. M., & Iadarola, M. J. (1999). Pain intensity processing within the human brain: A bilateral, distributed mechanism. *J Neurophysiology*, *82*(4), 1934–1943.

Colloca, L., & Benedetti, F. (2006). How prior experience shapes placebo analgesia. *Pain*, *124*(1-2), 126–133.

Colloca, L., & Benedetti, F. (2009). Placebo analgesia induced by social observational learning. *Pain*, *144*(1-2), 28–34.

Colloca, L., Benedetti, F., & Porro, C. A. (2007). Experimental designs and brain mapping approaches for studying the placebo analgesic effect. *European Journal of Applied Physiology*, *102*(4), 371–380.

Colloca, L., Sigaudo, M., & Benedetti, F. (2008). The role of learning in nocebo and placebo effects. *Pain*, *136*(1-2), 211–218.

Colloca, L., Tinazzi, M., Recchia, S., Le Pera, D., Fiaschi, A., Benedetti, F., et al. (2008). Learning potentiates neurophysiological and behavioral placebo analgesic responses. *Pain*, *139*(2), 306–314.

Committee on Advancing Pain Research and Education. (2011). *Relieving Pain in America: A Blueprint for Transforming Prevention, Care, Education, and Research.*

Coull, J. T., & Nobre, A. C. (1998). Where and when to pay attention: The neural systems for directing attention to spatial locations and to time intervals as revealed by both PET and fMRI. *Journal of Neuroscience*, *18*(18), 7426–7435.

Craggs, J., Price, D., Perlstein, W., Verne, G. N., & Robinson, M. (2008). The dynamic mechanisms of placebo induced analgesia: Evidence of sustained and transient regional involvement. *Pain*, *139*(660–669).

Craggs, J., Price, D. D., Verne, G. N., & Perlstein, W. (2007). Functional brain interactions that serve cognitive–affective processing during pain and placebo analgesia. *Neuroimage*, *38*(720–729).

Craig, A. D. (2002). How do you feel? Interoception: The sense of the physiological condition of the body. *Nature Reviews Neuroscience*, *3*(8), 655–666.

Craig, A. D. (2009). How do you feel—now? The anterior insula and human awareness. *Nature Reviews Neuroscience*, *10*, 12.

Craig, A. D., Chen, K., Bandy, D., & Reiman, E. M. (2000). Thermosensory activation of insular cortex. *Nature Neuroscience*, *3*(2), 184–190.

Crombez, G., Baeyens, F., & Eelen, P. (1994). Sensory and temporal information about impending pain: The influence of predictability on pain. *Behaviour Research and Therapy*, *32*(6), 611–622.

Daw, N. D., Niv, Y., & Dayan, P. (2005). Uncertainty-based competition between prefrontal and dorsolateral striatal systems for behavioral control. *Nature Neuroscience*, *8*(12), 1704–1711.

Daw, N. D., O'Doherty, J. P., Dayan, P., Seymour, B., & Dolan, R. J. (2006). Cortical substrates for exploratory decisions in humans. *Nature*, *441*(7095), 876–879.

Dayan, P., & Balleine, B. W. (2002). Reward, motivation, and reinforcement learning. *Neuron*, *36*(2), 285–298.

De Jong, P. J., van Baast, R., Arntz, A., & Merckelbach, H. (1996). The placebo effect in pain reduction: The influence of conditioning experiences and response expectancies. *International Journal of Behavioral Medicine*, *3*(1), 14–29.

de la Fuente-Fernandez, R., Ruth, T., Sossi, V., Schulzer, M., Calne, D., & Stoessl, A. (2001). Expectation and dopamine release: Mechanism of the placebo effect in Parkinson's disease. *Science*, *293*, 1164–1166.

Delgado, M. R., Li, J., Schiller, D., & Phelps, E. A. (2008). The role of the striatum in aversive learning and aversive prediction errors. *Philosophical Transactions of the Royal Society of London, Series B, Biological Sciences*, *363*(1511), 3787–3800.

Delgado, M. R., Olsson, A., & Phelps, E. A. (2006). Extending animal models of fear conditioning to humans. *Biological Psychology*, *73*(1), 39–48.

De Pascalis, V., Chiaradia, C., & Carotenuto, E. (2002). The contribution of suggestibility and expectation to placebo analgesia phenomenon in an experimental setting. *Pain*, *96*, 393–402.

Dosenbach, N. U. F., Visscher, K. M., Palmer, E. D., Miezin, F. M., Wenger, K. K., Kang, H. C., et al. (2006). A core system for the implementation of task sets. *Neuron*, *50*(5), 799–812.

Downing, C. J. (1988). Expectancy and visual-spatial attention: Effects on perceptual quality. *Journal of Experimental Psychology. Human Perception and Performance*, *14*(2), 188–202.

Eippert, F., Bingel, U., Schoell, E. D., Yacubian, J., Klinger, R., Lorenz, J., et al. (2009). Activation of the opioidergic descending pain control system underlies placebo analgesia. *Neuron*, *63*(4), 533–543.

Eippert, F., Finsterbusch, J., Bingel, U., & Buchel, C. (2009). Direct evidence for spinal cord involvement in placebo analgesia. *Science*, *326*(5951), 404.

Elliott, R., Friston, K. J., & Dolan, R. J. (2000). Dissociable neural responses in human reward systems. *Journal of Neuroscience*, *20*(16), 6159–6165.

Ellsworth, P. C., & Scherer, K. R. (2003). Appraisal processes in emotion. In R. J. Davidson, K. R. Scherer & H. H. Goldsmith (Eds.), *Handbook of affective sciences* (pp. 572–595). New York: Oxford University Press.

Faria, V., Fredrikson, M., & Furmark, T. (2008). Imaging the placebo response: A neurofunctional review. *European Neuropsychopharmacology, 18*(7), 473–485.

Feather, B., Chapman, C. R., & Fisher, S. (1972). The effect of a placebo on the perception of painful radiant heat stimuli. *Psychosomatic Medicine, 34*(4), 290–294.

Feine, J. S., Lavigne, G. J., Dao, T. T., Morin, C., & Lund, J. P. (1998). Memories of chronic pain and perceptions of relief. *Pain, 77*(2), 137–141.

Fellows, L. K., & Farah, M. J. (2005). Dissociable elements of human foresight: A role for the ventromedial frontal lobes in framing the future, but not in discounting future rewards. *Neuropsychologia, 43*(8), 1214–1221.

Fields, H. L. (2004). State-dependent opioid control of pain. *Nature Reviews Neuroscience, 5*(7), 565–575.

Funayama, E. S., Grillon, C., Davis, M., & Phelps, E. A. (2001). A double dissociation in the affective modulation of startle in humans: Effects of unilateral temporal lobectomy. *Journal of Cognitive Neuroscience, 13*(6), 721–729.

Geers, A. L., Helfer, S. G., Kosbab, K., Weiland, P. E., & Landry, S. J. (2005). Reconsidering the role of personality in placebo effects: dispositional optimism, situational expectations, and the placebo response. *Journal of Psychosomatic Research, 58*(2), 121–127.

Geers, A. L., Helfer, S. G., Weiland, P. E., & Kosbab, K. (2006). Expectations and placebo response: A laboratory investigation into the role of somatic focus. *Journal of Behavioral Medicine, 29*(2), 171–178.

Geers, A. L., & Lassiter, G. D. (1999). Affective expectations and information gain: Evidence for assimilation and contrast effects in affective experience* 1. *Journal of Experimental Social Psychology, 35*(4), 394–413.

Geers, A. L., & Lassiter, G. (2002). Effects of affective expectations on affective experience: The moderating role of optimism-pessimism. *Personality and Social Psychology Bulletin, 28*(8), 1026–1039.

Geers, A. L., & Lassiter, G. D. (2003). Need for cognition and expectations as determinants of affective experience. *Basic and Applied Social Psychology, 25*(4), 313–325.

Giesler, G. J., Katter, J. T., & Dado, R. J. (1994). Direct spinal pathways to the limbic system for nociceptive information. *Trends in Neuroscience, 17*(6), 244–250.

Gilbert, D. T., & Wilson, T. D. (2007). Prospection: Experiencing the future. *Science, 317*(5843), 1351–1354.

Gilbert, D. T., & Wilson, T. D. (2009). Why the brain talks to itself: Sources of error in emotional prediction. *Philosophical Transactions of the Royal Society of London, Series B, Biological Sciences, 364*(1521), 1335–1341.

Goffaux, P., de Souza, J., Potvin, S., & Marchand, S. (2009). Pain relief through expectation supersedes descending inhibitory deficits in fibromyalgia patients. *Pain, 145*(1-2), 18–23.

Goffaux, P., Redmond, W. J., Rainville, P., & Marchand, S. (2007). Descending analgesia—when the spine echoes what the brain expects. *Pain, 130*(1-2), 137–143.

Grillon, C., Ameli, R., Woods, S. W., Merikangas, K., & Davis, M. (1991). Fear-potentiated startle in humans: Effects of anticipatory anxiety on the acoustic blink reflex. *Psychophysiology, 28*(5), 588–595.

Hamilton, D. L., & Sherman, S. J. (1996). Perceiving persons and groups. *Psychological Review, 103*(2), 336.

Hare, T., O'Doherty, J. P., Camerer, C., Schultz, W., & Rangel, A. (2008). Dissociating the role of the orbitofrontal cortex and the striatum in the computation of goal values and prediction errors. *Journal of Neuroscience, 28*(22), 5623–5630.

Hauck, M., Lorenz, J., Zimmermann, R., Debener, S., Scharein, E., & Engel, A. K. (2007). Duration of the cue-to-pain delay increases pain intensity: A combined EEG and MEG study. *Experimental Brain Research, 180*(2), 205–215.

Herr, P. M. (1986). Consequences of priming: Judgment and behavior. *Journal of Personality and Social Psychology, 51*(6), 1106.

Herr, P. M., Sherman, S. J., & Fazio, R. H. (1983). On the consequences of priming: Assimilation and contrast effects. *Journal of Experimental Social Psychology, 19*(4), 323–340.

Herrnstein, R. J. (1962). Placebo effect in the rat. *Science, 138*, 677–678.

Hoffman, G. A., Harrington, A., & Fields, H. L. (2005). Pain and the placebo: What we have learned. *Perspectives in Biological Medicine, 48*(2), 248–265.

Hróbjartsson, A., & Gøtzsche, P. C. (2001). Is the placebo powerless? An analysis of clinical trials comparing placebo with no treatment. *New England Journal of Medicine, 344*(21), 1594–1602.

Hróbjartsson, A., & Gøtzsche, P. C. (2004). Is the placebo powerless? Update of a systematic review with 52 new randomized trials comparing placebo with no treatment. *Journal of Internal Medicine, 256*(2), 91–100.

Hsieh, J.-C., Stone-Elander, S., & Ingvar, M. (1999). Anticipatory coping of pain expressed in the human anterior cingulate cortex: A positron emission tomography study. *Neuroscience Letters, 262*(1), 61–64.

Hygge, S., & Ohman, A. (1978). Modeling processes in the acquisition of fears: Vicarious electrodermal conditioning to fear-relevant stimuli. *Journal of Personality and Social Psychology, 36*(3), 271–279.

Jensen, J., McIntosh, A. R., Crawley, A., Mikulis, D., Remington, G., & Kapur, S. (2003). Direct activation of the ventral striatum in anticipation of aversive stimuli. *Neuron, 40*(6), 1251–1257.

Johnston, N. E., Atlas, L. Y., & Wager, T. D. (2012). Opposing effects of expectancy and somatic focus on pain. *PLoS One, 7*(6), e38854.

Kahnt, T., Heinzle, J., Park, S. Q., & Haynes, J.-D. (2010). The neural code of reward anticipation in human orbitofrontal cortex. *Proceedings of the National Academy of Sciences U S A, 107*(13), 6010–6015.

Kaptchuk, T. J. (2002). The placebo effect in alternative medicine: Can the performance of a healing ritual have clinical significance? *Annals of Internal Medicine, 136*(11), 817–825.

Kastner, S., Pinsk, M. A., De Weerd, P., Desimone, R., & Ungerleider, L. G. (1999). Increased activity in human visual cortex during directed attention in the absence of visual stimulation. *Neuron, 22*(4), 751–761.

Keefe, F. J., Dunsmore, J., & Burnett, R. (1992). Behavioral and cognitive-behavioral approaches to chronic pain: Recent advances and future directions. *Journal of Consulting and Clinical Psychology, 60*(4), 528.

Keltner, J., Furst, A., Fan, C., Redfern, R., Inglis, B., & Fields, H. L. (2006). Isolating the modulatory effect of expectation on pain transmission: A functional magnetic resonance imaging study. *Journal of Neuroscience, 26*(16), 4437–4443.

Kim, C., Johnson, N. F., Cilles, S. E., & Gold, B. T. (2011). Common and distinct mechanisms of cognitive flexibility in prefrontal cortex. *Journal of Neuroscience, 31*(13), 4771–4779.

Kirsch, I. (1985). Response expectancy as a determinant of experience and behavior. *American Psychologist*, *40*(11), 1189–1202.

Kirsch, I. (1999). Hypnosis and placebos: Response expectancy as a mediator of suggestion effects. *Anales de Psicología, 15*(1), 99–110.

Kirsch, I. (2004). Conditioning, expectancy, and the placebo effect: Comment on Stewart-Williams and Podd (2004). *Psychological Bulletin*, *130*(2), 341–343; discussion 344–345.

Kirsch, I., Lynn, S. J., Vigorito, M., & Miller, R. R. (2004). The role of cognition in classical and operant conditioning. *Journal of Clinical Psychology*, *60*(4), 369–392.

Kirsch, I., & Sapirstein, G. (1998). Listening to Prozac but hearing placebo: A meta-analysis of antidepressant medication. *Prevention & Treatment, 1* .

Klaaren, K. J., Hodges, S. D., & Wilson, T. D. (1994). The role of affective expectations in subjective experience and decision-making. *Social Cognition*, *12*(2), 77–101.

Knutson, B., Adams, C. M., Fong, G. W., & Hommer, D. (2001). Anticipation of increasing monetary reward selectively recruits nucleus accumbens. *Journal of Neuroscience*, *21*(16), RC159.

Knutson, B., Fong, G. W., Adams, C. M., Varner, J. L., & Hommer, D. (2001). Dissociation of reward anticipation and outcome with event-related fMRI. *Neuroreport*, *12*(17), 3683–3687.

Kong, J., Gollub, R. L., Polich, G., Kirsch, I., Laviolette, P., Vangel, M., et al. (2008). A functional magnetic resonance imaging study on the neural mechanisms of hyperalgesic nocebo effect. *Journal of Neuroscience*, *28*(49), 13354–13362.

Kong, J., Gollub, R. L., Rosman, I. S., Webb, J. M., Vangel, M. G., Kirsch, I., et al. (2006). Brain activity associated with expectancy-enhanced placebo analgesia as measured by functional magnetic resonance imaging. *Journal of Neuroscience*, *26*(2), 381–388.

Koyama, T., McHaffie, J. G., Laurienti, P., & Coghill, R. C. (2005). The subjective experience of pain: Where expectations become reality. *Proceedings of the National Academy of Science U S A*, *102*(36), 12950–12955.

Koyama, T., Tanaka, Y. Z., & Mikami, A. (1998). Nociceptive neurons in the macaque anterior cingulate activate during anticipation of pain. *Neuroreport*, *9*(11), 2663–2667.

Kringelbach, M. L. (2005). The human orbitofrontal cortex: Linking reward to hedonic experience. *Nature Reviews Neuroscience*, *6*(9), 691–702.

Krummenacher, P., Candia, V., Folkers, G., Schedlowski, M., & Schönbächler, G. (2009). Prefrontal cortex modulates placebo analgesia. *Pain*, *148*(3), 368–374.

LaBar, K. S., Gatenby, J. C., Gore, J. C., LeDoux, J. E., & Phelps, E. A. (1998). Human amygdala activation during conditioned fear acquisition and extinction: a mixed-trial fMRI study. *Neuron*, *20*(5), 937–945.

Levine, J. D., Gordon, N. C., & Fields, H. L. (1978). The mechanism of placebo analgesia. *Lancet*, *2*(8091), 654–657.

Lieberman, M. D., Jarcho, J. M., Berman, S., Naliboff, B. D., Suyenobu, B., Mandelkern, M., et al. (2004). The neural correlates of placebo effects: A disruption account. *Neuroimage*, *22* , 447–455.

Lindquist, K., Wager, T., Kober, H., Bliss-Moreau, E., & Barrett, L. F. (2012). The brain basis of emotion: A meta-analytic review. *Behavioral and Brain Sciences*, *35*(3), 172–202.

Loeser, J. D., & Treede, R.-D. (2008). The Kyoto Protocol of IASP Basic Pain Terminology. *Pain*, *137*(3), 473–477.

Lombardi, W., Higgins, E. T., & Bargh, J. A. (1987). The role of consciousness in priming effects on categorization: Assimilation versus contrast as a function of awareness of the priming task. *Personality and Social Psychology Bulletin*, *13*(3), 411–429.

Lorenz, J., Hauck, M., Paur, R. C., Nakamura, Y., Zimmermann, R., Bromm, B., et al. (2005). Cortical correlates of false expectations during pain intensity judgments—a possible manifestation of placebo/nocebo cognitions. *Brain, Behavior, and Immunity*, *19*(4), 283–295.

Lorenz, J., Minoshima, S., & Casey, K. L. (2003). Keeping pain out of mind: The role of the dorsolateral prefrontal cortex in pain modulation. *Brain*, *126*(Pt 5), 1079–1091.

Lovibond, P. F., & Shanks, D. R. (2002). The role of awareness in Pavlovian conditioning: Empirical evidence and theoretical implications. *Journal of Experimental Psychology: Animal Behavior Processes*, *28*(1), 3–26.

Mcdannald, M. A., Lucantonio, F., Burke, K. A., Niv, Y., & Schoenbaum, G. (2011). Ventral striatum and orbitofrontal cortex are both required for model-based, but not model-free, reinforcement learning. *Journal of Neuroscience*, *31*(7), 2700–2705.

McGlashan, T. H., Evans, F. J., & Orne, M. T. (1969). The nature of hypnotic analgesia and placebo response to experimental pain. *Psychosomatic Medicine*, *31*(3), 227–246.

Meissner, K., Distel, H., & Mitzdorf, U. (2007). Evidence for placebo effects on physical but not on biochemical outcome parameters: A review of clinical trials. *BMC Medicine*, *5* , 3.

Melzack, R., & Wall, P. D. (1965). Pain mechanisms: A new theory. *Science*, *150*(699), 971–979.

Miller, E. K. (2000). The prefrontal cortex and cognitive control. *Nature Reviews Neuroscience*, *1*(1), 59–65.

Miller, E. K., & Cohen, J. D. (2001). An integrative theory of prefrontal cortex function. *Annual Review of Neuroscience*, *24* , 167–202.

Miller, S. M. (1981). Predictability and human stress: Toward a clarification of evidence and theory. *Advances in Experimental Social Psychology*, *14* , 203–255.

Mineka, S., & Cook, M. (1993). Mechanisms involved in the observational conditioning of fear. *Journal of Experimental Psychology. General*, *122*(1), 23–38.

Mobbs, D., Marchant, J. L., Hassabis, D., Seymour, B., Tan, G., Gray, M., et al. (2009). From threat to fear: The neural organization of defensive fear systems in humans. *Journal of Neuroscience*, *29*(39), 12236–12243.

Mobbs, D., Petrovic, P., Marchant, J. L., Hassabis, D., Weiskopf, N., Seymour, B., et al. (2007). When fear is near: Threat imminence elicits prefrontal-periaqueductal gray shifts in humans. *Science*, *317*(5841), 1079–1083.

Montgomery, G. H., & Kirsch, I. (1997). Classical conditioning and the placebo effect. *Pain*, *72*(1-2), 107–113.

Morley, S., Eccleston, C., & Williams, A. (1999). Systematic review and meta-analysis of randomized controlled trials of cognitive behaviour therapy and behaviour therapy for chronic pain in adults, excluding headache. *Pain*, *80*(1-2), 1–13.

Morrison, S. E., & Salzman, C. (2009). The convergence of information about rewarding and aversive stimuli in single neurons. *Journal of Neuroscience*, *29*(37), 11471–11483.

Morton, D. L., Watson, A., El-Deredy, W., & Jones, A. K. P. (2009). Reproducibility of placebo analgesia: Effect of dispositional optimism. *Pain*, *146*(1-2), 194–198.

Murray, E. A., O'Doherty, J. P., & Schoenbaum, G. (2007). What we know and do not know about the functions of the orbitofrontal cortex after 20 years of cross-species studies. *Journal of Neuroscience, 27*(31), 8166–8169.

Nicholas, M. K., Wilson, P. H., & Goyen, J. (1992). Comparison of cognitive-behavioral group treatment and an alternative non-psychological treatment for chronic low back pain. *Pain, 48*(3), 339–347.

Nitschke, J. B., Dixon, G. E., Sarinopoulos, I., Short, S. J., Cohen, J. D., Smith, E. E., et al. (2006). Altering expectancy dampens neural response to aversive taste in primary taste cortex. *Nature Neuroscience, 9*(3), 435–442.

Nitschke, J.B., Sarinopoulos, I., Mackiewicz, K., Schaefer, H., & Davidson, R. (2006). Functional neuroanatomy of aversion and its anticipation. *Neuroimage, 29*(1), 106–116.

O'Doherty, J. P. (2004). Reward representations and reward-related learning in the human brain: Insights from neuroimaging. *Current Opinion in Neurobiology, 14*(6), 769–776.

O'Doherty, J. P., Dayan, P., Friston, K., Critchley, H., & Dolan, R. J. (2003). Temporal difference models and reward-related learning in the human brain. *Neuron, 38*(2), 329–337.

O'Doherty, J. P., Dayan, P., Schultz, J., Deichmann, R., Friston, K., & Dolan, R. J. (2004). Dissociable roles of ventral and dorsal striatum in instrumental conditioning. *Science, 304*(5669), 452–454.

Olsson, A., & Phelps, E. A. (2004). Learned fear of "unseen" faces after Pavlovian, observational, and instructed fear. *Psychological Science, 15*(12), 822–828.

Petrovic, P., Dietrich, T., Fransson, P., Andersson, J., Carlsson, K., & Ingvar, M. (2005). Placebo in emotional processing— induced expectations of anxiety relief activate a generalized modulatory network. *Neuron, 46*(6), 957–969.

Petrovic, P., Kalso, E., Petersson, K. M., Andersson, J., Fransson, P., & Ingvar, M. (2010). A prefrontal non-opioid mechanism in placebo analgesia. *Pain, 150* , 59–65.

Petrovic, P., Kalso, E., Petersson, K. M., & Ingvar, M. (2002). Placebo and opioid analgesia— imaging a shared neuronal network. *Science, 295*(5560), 1737–1740.

Phan, K. L., Wager, T., Taylor, S. F., & Liberzon, I. (2002). Functional neuroanatomy of emotion: A meta-analysis of emotion activation studies in PET and fMRI. *Neuroimage, 16*(2), 331–348..

Phelps, E. A. (2006). Emotion and cognition: insights from studies of the human amygdala. *Annual Review of Psychology, 57* , 27–53.

Phelps, E. A., O'Connor, K. J., Gatenby, J. C., Gore, J. C., Grillon, C., & Davis, M. (2001). Activation of the left amygdala to a cognitive representation of fear. *Nature Neuroscience, 4*(4), 437–441.

Plassmann, H., O'Doherty, J., Shiv, B., & Rangel, A. (2008). Marketing actions can modulate neural representations of experienced pleasantness. *Proceedings of the National Academy of Sciences U S A, 105*(3), 1050–1054.

Ploghaus, A., Narain, C., Beckmann, C. F., Clare, S., Bantick, S. J., Wise, R. G., et al. (2001). Exacerbation of pain by anxiety is associated with activity in a hippocampal network. *Journal of Neuroscience, 21*(24), 9896–9903.

Ploghaus, A., Tracey, I., Clare, S., Gati, J. S., Rawlins, J. N., &.Matthews, P. M. (2000). Learning about pain: The neural substrate of the prediction error for aversive events. *Proceedings of the National Academy of Sciences U S A, 97*(16), 9281–9286.

Ploghaus, A., Tracey, I., Gati, J. S., Clare, S., Menon, R. S., Matthews, P. M., et al. (1999). Dissociating pain from

its anticipation in the human brain. *Science, 284*(5422), 1979–1981.

Porro, C. A., Baraldi, P., Pagnoni, G., Serafini, M., Facchin, P., Maieron, M., et al. (2002). Does anticipation of pain affect cortical nociceptive systems? *Journal of Neuroscience, 22*(8), 3206–3214.

Price, D. D. (2000). Psychological and neural mechanisms of the affective dimension of pain. *Science, 288*(5472), 1769–1772.

Price, D. D., Craggs, J., Verne, G., Perlstein, W., & Robinson, M. E. (2007). Placebo analgesia is accompanied by large reductions in pain-related brain activity in irritable bowel syndrome patients. *Pain, 127* , 63–72.

Price, D. D., Finniss, D. G., & Benedetti, F. (2007). A comprehensive review of the placebo effect: Recent advances and current thought. *Annual Review of Psychology, 59* , 565–590.

Price, D. D., Milling, L., Kirsch, I., & Duff, A. (1999). An analysis of factors that contribute to the magnitude of placebo analgesia in an experimental paradigm. *Pain, 83*, 147–156.

Rainville, P. (2002). Brain mechanisms of pain affect and pain modulation. *Current Opinion in Neurobiology, 12*(2), 195–204.

Rainville, P., Carrier, B., Hofbauer, R. K., Bushnell, M. C., & Duncan, G. H. (1999). Dissociation of sensory and affective dimensions of pain using hypnotic modulation. *Pain, 82*(2), 159–171.

Rainville, P., Duncan, G. H., Price, D. D., Carrier, B., & Bushnell, M. C.. (1997). Pain affect encoded in human anterior cingulate but not somatosensory cortex. *Science, 277*(5328), 968–971.

Raudenbush, S. (1984). Magnitude of teacher expectancy effects on pupil IQ as a function of the credibility of expectancy induction: A synthesis of findings from 18 experiments. *Journal of Educational Psychology, 76*(1), 85–97.

Redelmeier, D. A., & Kahneman, D. (1996). Patients' memories of painful medical treatments: Real-time and retrospective evaluations of two minimally invasive procedures. *Pain, 66*(1), 3–8.

Redelmeier, D. A., Katz, J., & Kahneman, D. (2003). Memories of colonoscopy: A randomized trial. *Pain, 104*(1-2), 187–194.

Reiss, S. (1980). Pavlovian conditioning and human fear: An expectancy model. *Behavior Therapy, 11* , 380–396.

Rescorla, R. A. (1988). Pavlovian conditioning. It's not what you think it is. *American Psychologist, 43*(3), 151–160.

Rescorla, R. A., & Wagner, A. (1972). A theory of Pavlovian conditioning: Variations in the effectiveness of reinforcement and nonreinforcement. In A. H. Black & W. F. Prokasy (Eds.), *Classical conditioning II* (pp. 64–99). Appleton-Century-Crofts.

Rodriguez, P., Aron, A. R., & Poldrack, R. A. (2006). Ventral-striatal/nucleus-accumbens sensitivity to prediction errors during classification learning. *Human Brain Mapping, 27* , 306–313.

Roesch, M. R., Calu, D. J., Esber, G. R., & Schoenbaum, G. (2010). Neural correlates of variations in event processing during learning in basolateral amygdala. *Journal of Neuroscience, 30*(7), 2464–2471.

Rogan, M. T., Stäubli, U. V., & LeDoux, J. E. (1997). Fear conditioning induces associative long-term potentiation in the amygdala. *Nature, 390*(6660), 604–607.

Rolls, E., McCabe, C., & Redoute, J. (2007). Expected value, reward outcome, and temporal difference error representations in a probabilistic decision task. *Cerebral Cortex, 18*(3), 652–663.

Rosenthal, R. (1987). Pygmalion effects: Existence, magnitude, and social importance. *Educational Researcher, 16*(9), 37.

Rosenthal, R. (1994). Interpersonal expectancy effects: A 30-year perspective. *Current Directions in Psychological Science,* 176–179.

Rosenthal, R., & Fode, K. (1963). The effect of experimenter bias on the performance of the albino rat. *Behavioral Science, 8*(3), 183–189.

Rosenthal, R., & Rubin, D. (1978). Interpersonal expectancy effects: The first 345 studies. *Behavioral and Brain Sciences, 1*(3), 377–415.

Rutledge, R. B., Dean, M., Caplin, A., & Glimcher, P. W. (2010). Testing the reward prediction error hypothesis with an axiomatic model. *Journal of Neuroscience, 30*(40), 13525–13536.

Salzman, C. D., Paton, J. J., Belova, M. A., & Morrison, S. E. (2007). Flexible neural representations of value in the primate brain. *Annals of the New York Academy of Sciences, 1121*, 336–354.

Sarinopoulos, I., Dixon, G. E., Short, S. J., Davidson, R. J., & Nitschke, J. B. (2006). Brain mechanisms of expectation associated with insula and amygdala response to aversive taste: Implications for placebo. *Brain, Behavior, and Immunity, 20*(2), 120–132.

Schacter, D. L., Addis, D. R., & Buckner, R. L. (2007). Remembering the past to imagine the future: The prospective brain. *Nature Reviews Neuroscience, 8*(9), 657–661.

Scherer, K. R. (1999). Appraisal theory. In T. Dalgleish & M. Power (Eds.), *Handbook of cognition and emotion* (pp. 637–663). New York: John Wiley & Sons.

Schoenbaum, G., Chiba, A. A., & Gallagher, M. (1998). Orbitofrontal cortex and basolateral amygdala encode expected outcomes during learning. *Nature Neuroscience, 1*(2), 155–159.

Schoenbaum, G., & Roesch, M. (2005). Orbitofrontal cortex, associative learning, and expectancies. *Neuron, 47*(5), 633–636.

Schoenbaum, G., Roesch, M. R., Stalnaker, T. A., & Takahashi, Y. K. (2009). A new perspective on the role of the orbitofrontal cortex in adaptive behaviour. *Nature Reviews Neuroscience, 10*(12), 885–892.

Schoenbaum, G., Saddoris, M. P., & Stalnaker, T. A. (2007). Reconciling the roles of orbitofrontal cortex in reversal learning and the encoding of outcome expectancies. *Annals of the New York Academy of Sciences, 1121*, 320–335.

Schoenbaum, G., & Setlow, B. (2003). Lesions of nucleus accumbens disrupt learning about aversive outcomes. *Journal of Neuroscience, 23*(30), 9833–9841.

Schoenbaum, G., Setlow, B., Saddoris, M. P., & Gallagher, M. (2003). Encoding predicted outcome and acquired value in orbitofrontal cortex during cue sampling depends upon input from basolateral amygdala. *Neuron, 39*(5), 855–867.

Schoenbaum, G., Takahashi, Y. K., Liu, T.-L., & Mcdannald, M. A. (2011). Does the orbitofrontal cortex signal value? *Annals of the New York Academy of Sciences, 1239*, 87–99.

Schott, B. H., Minuzzi, L., Krebs, R. M., Elmenhorst, D., Lang, M., Winz, O. H., et al. (2008). Mesolimbic functional magnetic resonance imaging activations during reward anticipation correlate with reward-related ventral striatal dopamine release. *Journal of Neuroscience, 28*(52), 14311–14319.

Schultz, W. (2007). Behavioral dopamine signals. *Trends in Neuroscience, 30*(5), 203–210.

Schultz, W., Dayan, P., & Montague, P. R. (1997). A neural substrate of prediction and reward. *Science, 275*(5306), 1593–1599.

Schultz, W., & Dickinson, A. (2000). Neuronal coding of prediction errors. *Annual Review of Neuroscience, 23*, 473–500.

Scott, D. J., Stohler, C. S., Egnatuk, C. M., Wang, H., Koeppe, R., & Zubieta, J. K. (2007). Individual differences in reward responding explain placebo-induced expectations and effects. *Neuron, 55*, 325–336.

Scott, D. J., Stohler, C. S., Egnatuk, C. M., Wang, H., Koeppe, R., & Zubieta, J. K. (2008). Placebo and nocebo effects are defined by opposite opioid and dopaminergic responses. *Archives of General Psychiatry, 65*(2), 1–12.

Seymour, B., O'Doherty, J. P., Dayan, P., Koltzenburg, M., Jones, A. K., Dolan, R. J., et al. (2004). Temporal difference models describe higher-order learning in humans. *Nature, 429*(6992), 664–667.

Seymour, B., O'Doherty, J. P., Koltzenburg, M., Wiech, K., Wiech, K., Frackowiak, R., & Dolan, R. J. (2005). Opponent appetitive-aversive neural processes underlie predictive learning of pain relief. *Nature Neuroscience, 8*(9), 1234–1240.

Shackman, A. J., Salomons, T. V., Slagter, H. A., Fox, A. S., Winter, J. J., & Davidson, R. J. (2011). The integration of negative affect, pain and cognitive control in the cingulate cortex. *Nature Reviews Neuroscience, 12*(3), 154–167.

Sharot, T., De Martino, B., & Dolan, R. J. (2009). How choice reveals and shapes expected hedonic outcome. *Journal of Neuroscience, 29*(12), 3760–3765.

Simmons, A., Matthews, S. C., Stein, M. B., & Paulus, M. P. (2004). Anticipation of emotionally aversive visual stimuli activates right insula. *Neuroreport, 15*(14), 2261–2265.

Somerville, L. H., Whalen, P. J., & Kelley, W. M. (2010) Human bed nucleus of the stria terminalis indexes hypervigilant threat monitoring. *Biological Psychiatry, 68*(5), 416–424.

Spicer, J. A., Galvan, A., Hare, T. A., Voss, H., Glover, G. C., & Casey, B. J. (2007). Sensitivity of the nucleus accumbens to violations in expectation of reward. *Neuroimage, 34*(1), 455–461.

Stefano, G. B., Fricchione, G., Slingsby, B. T., & Benson, H. (2001). The placebo effect and relaxation response: Neural processes and their coupling to constitutive nitric oxide. *Brain Research. Brain Research Reviews, 35*(1), 1–19.

Stewart-Williams, S., & Podd, J. (2004). The placebo effect: Dissolving the expectancy versus conditioning debate. *Psychological Bulletin, 130*(2), 324–340.

Sutton, R. S., & Barto, A. G. (1981). Toward a modern theory of adaptive networks: Expectation and prediction. *Psychological Review, 88*(2), 135–170.

Taren, A. A., Venkatraman, V., & Huettel, S. A. (2011). A parallel functional topography between medial and lateral prefrontal cortex: Evidence and implications for cognitive control. *Journal of Neuroscience, 31*(13), 5026–5031.

Tölle, T. R., Kaufmann, T., Siessmeier, T., Lautenbacher, S., Berthele, A., Munz, F., ... & Bartenstein, P. (1999). Region-specific encoding of sensory and affective components of pain in the human brain: a positron emission tomography correlation analysis. *Annals of neurology, 45*(1), 40–47.

Tolman, E. (1949). There is more than one kind of learning. *Psychological Review, 56*(3), 144–155.

Treede, R.-D., Kenshalo, D. R., Gracely, R. H., & Jones, A. K. P. (1999). The cortical representation of pain. *Pain, 79*(2-3), 105–111.

Tsai, H.-C., Zhang, F., Adamantidis, A., Stuber, G. D., Bonci, A., de Lecea, L., et al. (2009). Phasic firing in dopaminergic neurons is sufficient for behavioral conditioning. *Science*, *324*(5930), 1080–1084.

van Boxtel, G., & Böcker, K. (2004). Cortical measures of anticipation. *Journal of Psychophysiology*, *18*, 61–76.

Vase, L., Petersen, G., Riley, J., & Price, D. (2009). Factors contributing to large analgesic effects in placebo mechanism studies conducted between 2002 and 2007. *Pain*, *145*, 36–44.

Vase, L., Riley 3rd, J., & Price, D. D. (2002). A comparison of placebo effects in clinical analgesic trials versus studies of placebo analgesia. *Pain*, *99*, 443–452.

Vase, L., Robinson, M., Verne, G., & Price, D. D. (2005). Increased placebo analgesia over time in irritable bowel syndrome (IBS) patients is associated with desire and expectation but not endogenous opioid mechanisms. *Pain*, *115*, 338–347.

Vlaeyen, J. W. S., & Morley, S. (2005). Cognitive-behavioral treatments for chronic pain: What works for whom? *Clinical Journal of Pain*, *21*(1), 1–8.

Voudouris, N. J., Peck, C. L., & Coleman, G. (1985). Conditioned placebo responses. *Journal of Personality and Social Psychology*, *48*(1), 47–53.

Voudouris, N. J., Peck, C. L., & Coleman, G. (1989). Conditioned response models of placebo phenomena: Further support. *Pain*, *38*(1), 109–116.

Voudouris, N. J., Peck, C. L., & Coleman, G. (1990). The role of conditioning and verbal expectancy in the placebo response. *Pain*, *43*(1), 121–128.

Wager, T. D. (2005a). Expectations and anxiety as mediators of placebo effects in pain. *Pain*, *115*, 225–226.

Wager, T. D. (2005b). The neural bases of placebo effects in anticipation and pain. *Seminars in Pain Medicine*, *3*(1), 22–30.

Wager, T. D. (2005c). The neural bases of placebo effects in pain. *Current Directions in Psychological Science*, *14*(4), 175–179.

Wager, T. D., Atlas, L. Y., Leotti, L. A., & Rilling, J. K. (2011). Predicting individual differences in placebo analgesia: Contributions of brain activity during anticipation and pain experience. *Journal of Neuroscience*, *31*(2), 439–452.

Wager, T. D., & Fields, H. (2013). Placebo analgesia. In McMahon, Koltzenburg, Tracey, and Turk (Eds), *Textbook of pain* (pp. 362–373). Philadelphia: Saunders, an imprint of Elsevier Ltd.

Wager, T. D., Matre, D., & Casey, K. L. (2006). Placebo effects in laser-evoked pain potentials. *Brain, Behavior, and Immunity*, *20*, 219–230.

Wager, T. D., Phan, K. L., Liberzon, I., & Taylor, S. F. (2003). Valence, gender, and lateralization of functional brain anatomy in emotion: A meta-analysis of findings from neuroimaging. *Neuroimage*, *19*(3), 513–531.

Wager, T. D., Rilling, J. K., Smith, E. E., Sokolik, A., Casey, K. L., Davidson, R. J., et al. (2004). Placebo-induced changes in FMRI in the anticipation and experience of pain. *Science*, *303*(5661), 1162–1167.

Wager, T. D., Scott, D. J., & Zubieta, J. K. (2007). Placebo effects on human μ-opioid activity during pain. *Proceedings of the National Academy of Sciences U S A*, *104*(26), 11056–11061.

Wager, T. D., & Smith, E. E. (2003). Neuroimaging studies of working memory: A meta-analysis. *Cognitive, Affective & Behavioral Neuroscience*, *3*(4), 255–274.

Wallace, L. M. (1985). Surgical patients' expectations of pain and discomfort: Does accuracy of expectations minimise post-surgical pain and distress? *Pain*, *22*(4), 363–373.

Watson, A., El-Deredy, W., Iannetti, G., Lloyd, D., Tracey, I., Vogt, B., et al. (2009). Placebo conditioning and placebo analgesia modulate a common brain network during pain anticipation and perception. *Pain*, *145*, 24–30.

Wells, L., & Sweeney, P. (1986). A test of three models of bias in self-assessment. *Social Psychology Quarterly*, *49*, 1–10.

Whalen, P. J., Davis, F. C., Oler, J. A., Kim, H., Kim, M. J., & Neta, M. (2009). Human amygdala responses to facial expressions of emotion. In P. J. P. Whalen, E.A (Ed.), *The human amygdala* (pp. 265–288). New York: Guilford Press.

Whalen, P. J., Kagan, J., Cook, R. G., Davis, F. C., Kim, H., Polis, S., et al. (2004). Human amygdala responsivity to masked fearful eye whites. *Science*, *306*(5704), 2061.

Whalen, P. J., Rauch, S. L., Etcoff, N. L., McInerney, S. C., Lee, M. B., & Jenike, M. A. (1998). Masked presentations of emotional facial expressions modulate amygdala activity without explicit knowledge. *Journal of Neuroscience*, *18*(1), 411–418.

Wheeler, M. A., Stuss, D. T., & Tulving, E. (1997). Toward a theory of episodic memory: The frontal lobes and autonoetic consciousness. *Psychological Bulletin*, *121*(3), 331–354.

Wickramasekera, I. (1980). A conditioned response model of the placebo effect predictions from the model. *Biofeedback and Self Regulation*, *5*(1), 5–18.

Willis, W. D., & Westlund, K. N. (1997). Neuroanatomy of the pain system and of the pathways that modulate pain. *Journal of Clinical Neurophysiology*, *14*(1), 2–31.

Wilson, T. D., & Gilbert, D. T. (2003). Affective forecasting. *Advances in Experimental Social Psychology*, *35*, 345–411.

Wilson, T. D., Lisle, D. J., Kraft, D., & Wetzel, C. G. (1989). Preferences as expectation-driven inferences: Effects of affective expectations on affective experience. *Journal of Personality and Social Psychology*, *56*(4), 519–530.

Woodworth, R. (1947). Reinforcement of perception. *American Journal of Psychology*, *60*(1), 119–124.

Zellner, D. A., Strickhouser, D., & Tornow, C. E. (2004). Disconfirmed hedonic expectations produce perceptual contrast, not assimilation. *American Journal of Psychology*, *117*(3), 363–387.

Zubieta, J.-K., Bueller, J. A., Jackson, L., Scott, D. J., Xu, J., Koeppe, R., et al. (2005). Placebo effects mediated by endogenous opioid activity on μ-opioid receptors. *Journal of Neuroscience*, *25*(34), 7754–7762.

Cognitive Neuroscience of Numerical Cognition

Daniel Ansari *and* Stephan E. Vogel

Abstract

Over the past two decades, cognitive neuroscientists have begun to investigate the neural mechanisms underlying number processing using cutting-edge neuroimaging methods. These investigations have allowed researchers to map out brain regions that appear to be fundamental to our ability to represent and process numerical magnitude. They have addressed questions concerning the overlap between the processing of numerical and non-numerical magnitude, and the relationship between processing numerical magnitude and numerical order. Moreover, questions regarding the shared and dissociated neuronal correlates of symbolic (e.g., Arabic numerals) and nonsymbolic (e.g. arrays of dots) number processing have received much attention. Beyond these investigations, studies have also been conducted to map out the correlates of the typical and atypical development of number processing. This chapter provides an overview of these developments and critically discusses some of the key questions that are the focus of current research in the cognitive neuroscience of numerical cognition. The chapter concludes with a discussion of some of the open questions in this relatively new subdiscipline of cognitive neuroscience.

Key Words: cognitive neuroscience, numerical cognition, numerical magnitude, numerical order, number processing, brain regions, neuroimaging

Introduction

Numbers are a frequent feature of our everyday lives. Most of the time we process numbers so effortlessly that we are not consciously aware of using numerical information to guide our decisions and behaviors. For example, when you get up in the morning and glance at your alarm clock, you are processing numbers, when you check the weather to decide what to wear, you use numbers to guide your decisions, and when you read the latest news, you need to process numerical information in order to make sense of most news stories. The list of examples from everyday life that involve number processing is countless.

How does our brain enable us to process numerical information? Is there a specialized brain circuit for the representation and processing of numbers?

Questions such as these have driven the development of a subfield within cognitive neuroscience that is concerned with the characterization of neuronal mechanisms underlying the representation and processing of numerical information. This field of study is the cognitive neuroscience of numerical cognition.

Investigation into the brain regions that support the processing of numerical information began at the beginning of the twentieth century. Neurologists such as Henschen (1919) studied brain-damaged patients and observed that damage to parietal regions of the brain (in particular to the left parietal lobe) was associated with calculation deficits. In other words, patients with parietal lobe damage had great difficulties solving basic arithmetic problems. Numerous reports of the association between parietal lobe damage and calculation in the neuropsychological literature followed. More recently, functional neuroimaging studies have provided evidence convergent with that from study of neuropsychological patients to suggest that the parietal cortex is activated when healthy individuals engage in calculation. Much progress has been made in better characterizing the neuronal architecture underlying arithmetic problem solving. Many of these findings have been reviewed elsewhere (for a useful review, see Zamarian, Ischebeck, & Delazer, 2009).

The focus of this chapter, however, is on the recently uncovered brain mechanisms underlying more foundational aspects of numerical cognition upon which more complex number-processing operations, such as mental arithmetic, are thought to be built. In particular, we will review how and where numerical magnitudes (i.e., the total number of items in a set) are represented and processed in the human brain. Following a review of the classic findings in the study of numerical-magnitude representation in the brain that has provided the basis of the cognitive neuroscience of numerical cognition, a series of topics and questions addressed in current research will be discussed.

Numerical Magnitudes in the Brain

A growing body of evidence suggests qualitatively similar representations of numerical magnitude in non-human animals (Boysen, Bernston, Hannan, & Cacioppo, 1996; Brannon & Terrace, 1998; Cantlon & Brannon, 2006), infants (Feigenson, Carey, & Spelke, 2002; Xu & Spelke, 2000; Xu, Spelke, & Goddard, 2005), and children (Halberda & Feigenson, 2008, Halberda, Mazzocco, & Feigenson, 2008). In view of this, it has been suggested that aspects of the representation of numerical magnitude have a long evolutionary history and

that humans are born with a "sense of magnitude," or "number sense" (Dehaene, 1997).

How does one go about measuring numerical-magnitude representations? A significant number of studies have employed number comparison tasks, similar to the one used in a pioneering study by Moyer and Landauer (1967), to tap into basic representation and processing of numerical magnitude. In their study, adult participants were presented with pairs of single digits and were asked to decide which of the simultaneously presented digits was the numerically larger one. Examination of the reaction time data revealed an inverse relationship between how long it took participants to compare the relative numerical magnitude of the digits and the numerical difference or distance between them (see Figure 24.1a). In other words, participants were significantly slower when the numerical distance between the digits they were comparing was relatively small (e.g., 1 vs. 2, numerical distance = 1) than when the distance was comparatively large (e.g. 1 vs. 8, numerical distance = 7). These findings have been interpreted to reflect an internal, analogue representation of numerical magnitude, in which numbers that are close together (i.e., have a relatively small numerical distance) share more representational overlap than those that are far apart.

Another effect that can be measured using numerical-magnitude comparison tasks is the numerical size or ratio effect. Instead of using the distance between two numbers as the independent variable, researchers use their ratio. In this way, consistent with Weber's law, the relative size of the magnitudes is taken into account (see Figure 24.1b).

As already stated by Moyer and Landauer (1967) in their seminal paper, the numerical ratio explains more variability in numerical-magnitude comparison data than does the numerical distance. Take, for example, the comparisons of (a) 8 vs. 9 and (b) 1

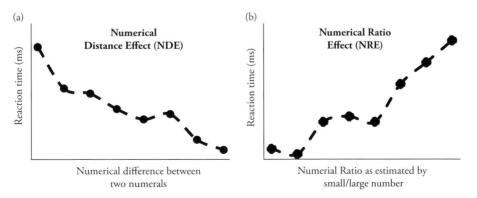

Figure 24.1 Typical reaction time data observed for a) the numerical distance effect (NDE) and b) the numerical ratio effect (NRE).

vs. 2. Both of these number pairs have a numerical distance of 1, but their ratio is different. Thus, a numerical distance effect would predict similar response times for both pairs, while the ratio effect predicts larger reaction times for 8 vs. 9 compared to 1 vs. 2. Despite the better prediction of reaction time data during comparison when ratio and not distance is used as the independent variable, distance and ratio are highly correlated and thus make very similar predictions, resulting in slight differences in the variance explained, instead of representing radically different models of numerical-magnitude comparison data.

Both distance and ratio have been used as independent variables in behavioral studies to characterize the representation and processing of numerical magnitude in adults (Moyer & Landauer, 1967; Verguts & Van Opstal, 2005), infants (Xu & Spelke, 2000; Xu et al., 2005), children (Holloway & Ansari, 2008, 2009; Sekuler & Mierkiewicz, 1977), and non-human primates (Brannon & Terrace, 1998; Cantlon & Brannon, 2006). Thus, number comparison has become somewhat of a litmus test for the representation and processing of numerical magnitude.

In view of this, it is not surprising that most of the first neuroimaging studies investigating the neural basis of numerical-magnitude processing used number comparison paradigms (for example stimuli of a number comparison task; see Figure 24.2).

The early neuroimaging studies of number comparison used event-related brain potentials (ERPs) to measure how the neuronal time course of number processing is affected by numerical distance. In one of the earliest investigations of this kind, Grune, Mecklinger, and Ullsperger (1993) asked participants to compare two simultaneously presented digits while ERPs were recorded from their scalp. The findings from this study revealed that numerical distance affects ERPs 300 milliseconds (ms) following the presentation of digits pairs. In other words, a positive ERP (the P300) differs between pairs of digits separated by a relatively small numerical distance and pairs that have a large numerical distance

separating them, with a larger P300 for large than for small distances. This finding is important, as it suggests that numerical distance affects brain activation before participants make a response and, hence, seems to affect processes related to stimulus encoding and activation of representations that will enable discrimination to occur.

These findings were subsequently extended in an ERP study by Dehaene (1996). Participants were presented with both Arabic digits and number words and asked to judge whether the presented digit or number word was smaller or larger than 5 while ERPs were acquired. Using an additive-factors method, Dehaene (1996) identified several temporally separate stages that occurred during numerical-magnitude comparison. He found an initial difference between words and digits in early components that could be localized (using source localization) to visual areas of the brain. These components were not sensitive to the numerical distance and hence were likely to be reflective of visual identification and not semantic processing. This was followed by a distance effect on components occurring at electrodes over bilateral parietal sites, between 170 and 200 ms following stimulus onset. The effect of numerical distance on this component did not differ between number words and digits. A later effect was also reported that related to differences in the electrophysiology as a function of the response side for a given trial.

These findings are interesting for a number of reasons. First, they reveal a temporal independence in the brain of semantic processing of numerical magnitude (as indexed by the numerical distance effect) from the visual identification of the numerical stimuli and the response execution. Second, these findings extend those by Grune and colleagues (1993), by demonstrating that numerical distance affects brain activation at very early processing stages (within the first 200 ms). Finally, the source localization data presented by Dehaene (1996) suggest that areas of the parietal cortex may play a critical role in numerical-magnitude processing.

While providing exquisite information about when certain processes happen in the brain (even when source localization algorithms are used), cannot be used to precisely pinpoint the regions of the brain involved in numerical-magnitude processing. Using functional magnetic resonance imaging (fMRI) of the brain, Pinel et al. (1999) were the first to study the neural basis of the numerical distance effect. Their findings indicated that brain activations of bilateral regions of the intraparietal sulcus (IPS,

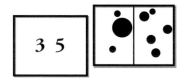

Figure 24.2 Examples of stimuli used in a symbolic and non-symbolic comparison task.

see Figure 24.3) within the parietal lobe are parametrically modulated by numerical distance during numerical-magnitude comparison tasks.

In other words, the amount of brain activation in these brain regions is inversely related to the numerical distance of the numerical magnitudes being compared. These seminal findings have since been replicated by other authors and laboratories (for examples see Ansari, Garcia, Lucas, Hamon, & Dhital, 2005; Kaufmann et al., 2006; Pinel, Dehaene, Rivière, & LeBihan, 2001). It is important to note, however, that investigations of the neural basis of the numerical distance effect do not merely reveal distance effects on activation of parietal regions. Many of these published studies reported distance effects across a distributed network of regions, including areas of the frontal cortex, whose activity is also modulated by numerical distance.

Response Selection Rather than Number Representation in the Parietal Cortex?

While neuroimaging studies of number comparison provided novel insights into the neural basis of numerical-magnitude processing, questions were soon raised concerning the extent to which distance effects on the activity of parietal brain regions, measured through the use of comparison tasks, were indeed reflective of the semantic processing of numerical magnitude or whether they might be indicative of more domain-general processes related to comparison and response-selection mechanisms. In other words, might activation of the parietal cortex during number comparison be nothing more than a reflection of the well-known role played by this region in response selection (resolving and implementing the choice between two response options)? In order to evaluate this alternative explanation, Göbel, Johansen-Berg, Behrens, and Rushworth (2004) conducted an fMRI study in which they compared parietal brain activation during numerical (digit comparison) and non-numerical (judgments of line orientation) tasks. Their findings revealed no significant differences in the activation of the parietal cortex during numerical and non-numerical comparison, supporting the hypothesis that parietal activation during number comparison may not be reflective (or at least not exclusively so) of the semantic processing of numbers, but instead may be driven by processes of response selection that are not number-specific. In a similar vein, in behavioral research, it has been proposed that the numerical distance effect is not reflective of overlapping, analogue representations of numerical magnitude, but instead indexes a reflection of the comparison process, which is common to both numerical and non-numerical comparison tasks (Van Opstal, Gevers, De Moor, & Verguts, 2008).

While this explanation of IPS activation during number comparison is compelling, there is a growing body of evidence implicating activation of the IPS in numerical-magnitude processing in the absence of response selection. For example, Eger, Sterzer, Russ, Giraud, and Kleinschmidt (2003) presented participants with letters, colors, or numbers in both visual (single letters, patches of color, and Arabic digits) and auditory (letter, color, and number names) formats. Participants were required to attend to one of

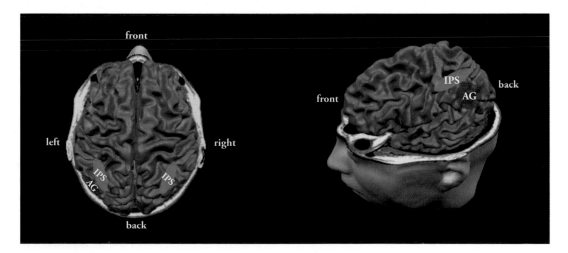

Figure 24.3 Reconstruction of the human brain, showing important areas involved in number processing. In green bilateral regions of the intraparietal sulcus (IPS) are displayed and in red the left angular gyrus (AG) is shown.

the three categories (different categories in different runs) and to press a button whenever an example of this category was presented. Thus, in this task, the response-selection criteria were minimal and were equal across the three categories. The results of this study showed greater activation of bilateral regions of the IPS during the visual and auditory perception of numbers than that for letter and colors. Even in a paradigm where only minimal response selection is required and this response selection is equivalent across conditions, it is the numerical stimuli that elicit the greatest amount of activation in the IPS. Thus, these findings run counter to an account positing that IPS activation during number-processing tasks is merely a reflection of domain-general response-selection mechanisms implemented by this brain region.

Another way of studying brain function that does not require paradigms involving response selection is to use fMRI adaptation (fMRA). The principle behind fMRA is that the repeated presentation of a particular stimulus leads to decreasing responsiveness of neurons that encode that particular stimulus (Grillspector, Henson, & Martin, 2006). This adaptation (sometimes also referred to as habituation) can be measured in a number of ways. For example, pairs of stimuli can be presented that either are repetitions of the same stimulus (e.g., 1 1) or represent pairs of different stimuli (e.g., 1 2). The prediction is that repeated stimuli will lead to greater adaptation (reduction of activity) in stimulus-specific brain regions than the presentation of different stimuli from within the same category. Another approach is to present trains of repeated stimuli (e.g., arrays of 8 dots) that are occasionally interspersed by stimuli that deviate in numerical magnitude (e.g., arrays of 16 dots). The latter approach was used by Piazza, Izard, Pinel, Le Bihan, and Dehaene (2004). Participants were presented with streams of dot arrays that each contained 16 dots in different spatial locations, controlling for different overall and individual surface area as well as density. Occasionally, this stream of repetition of 16 dots was interrupted by the presentation of a deviant numerical magnitude of 8, 10, 13, 20, 24, or 32 dots. When the brain activation to these deviant events was modeled, bilateral activation in the IPS was observed, suggesting that the change in numerical magnitude led to a recovery of neurons adapted to 16 dots in the IPS. More importantly, the amount of recovery in the response of the IPS following adaptation to 16 dots varied as a function of the numerical distance between the habituation

numerical magnitude and the deviant numerical magnitude. More specifically, Piazza et al. (2004) observed that the greater the distance between the habituation and deviant numerosities, the larger the deviant-related activation of the IPS. The same pattern of data was observed when the habituation numerical magnitude was 32 instead of 16. Thus, in a completely passive design, the IPS exhibits a numerical distance effect. It appears that number-sensitive neurons in the IPS adapt to the repeated presentation of a particular numerical magnitude and that when this numerical magnitude is changed, the response of these neurons recovers or dishabituates. Furthermore, the observed distance effects support the notion of overlapping representations of numerical magnitude in the IPS. Put differently, the closer the deviant numerical magnitude to the adapted numerical magnitude, the greater their overlap and, thus, the greater the similarity (and the lower the amount of dishabituation) in IPS responses.

These findings strongly argue against a response-selection account of activation in the IPS during number processing. Instead, they suggest that the IPS is engaged in numerical-magnitude processing in the way predicted by the numerical-distance and ratio effects, even in the absence of a task that requires response selection. Piazza et al.'s (2004) results are further strengthened by the finding that when a change in stimulus shape (from dots to triangles), while holding numerical magnitude constant, was introduced, brain regions other than the IPS exhibited dishabituation responses. Thus, the responses to the sparse-number deviants (among trains of stimuli that contained the same number of items) were number-specific rather than reflecting some kind of shift in attention that might feasibly be induced by the presentation of any stimulus. Using a different design, Ansari, Dhital, and Siong (2006) uncovered an effect of nonsymbolic numerical distance on activation of bilateral regions of the IPS in a completely passive design that had no response-selection component. These findings have since been replicated, not only for nonsymbolic stimuli (Cantlon, Brannon, Carter, & Pelphrey, 2006; Piazza, Pinel, Le Bihan, & Dehaene, 2007) but also for symbolic stimuli (Cohen Kadosh, Cohen Kadosh, Kaas, Henik, & Goebel, 2007; Notebaert, Nelis, & Reynvoet, 2011).

Taken together, these findings constitute a body of evidence that, through the use of passive imaging paradigms, reveals numerical magnitude–related responses in the IPS that are consistent with the classic distance and size effects in the absence of response selection. Given these findings, it is implausible that activation of the IPS during number discrimination paradigms is exclusively accounted for by response selection. However, it is important to note that different levels of numerical-magnitude representation may be tapped by passive and active paradigms. In other words, it is possible that the activations observed in passive paradigms are not strong enough to inform decision-making about number. Acting on number requires additional response-selection mechanisms represented by populations of IPS neurons that are intermingled with those involved in response selection. There is also much cross-talk between these when participants have to act on number (such as in the context of number discrimination tasks). As Göbel and Rushworth (2004) point out, it is important to distinguish between representations of number and processes of acting on numbers. Related to this point, it is important to challenge the notion of "purely" passive designs. Since the brain is known to be constantly involved in the process of prediction (Bar, 2009), it is plausible that during adaptation to a particular numerical magnitude, the brain uses numerical-magnitude information to form predictions about upcoming stimuli which are then evaluated against the information accumulated during adaptation. This can be argued to be some kind of action, if not response selection, in the way of making an explicit decision.

Number-Specific or Magnitude-General Coding in the Parietal Cortex?

Another related question that is the subject of ongoing research concerns the degree to which number representation in the IPS is domain-specific, or whether similar patterns of activation can be detected for the comparison and processing of continuous non-numerical magnitudes (such as size, height, luminance, or length). In other words, does the parietal cortex, as hypothesized by Walsh (2003) and Cantlon and Brannon (2007), support a general representation of magnitude?

This question has been addressed in a number of functional neuroimaging studies. In one of the first studies, Fias, Lammertyn, Caessens, and Orban (2007) asked participants to compare pairs of angles, line lengths, and two-digit numbers. A conjunction analysis revealed that, after subtracting out a low-level control task, the three magnitude comparison tasks were associated with common activation in the left IPS. In a similar study, using

different analyses, Pinel, Piazza, Le Bihan, and Dehaene (2004) used fMRI to investigate brain activation while participants engaged in the comparison of size, luminance, and numerical magnitude. Participants had to decide which of the two presented numerals was brighter, physically larger or numerically larger. The authors found that number and size judgments were associated with overlapping responses in the IPS, while luminance and size comparisons were found to share responses in the occipitotemporal cortex. Using a similar design, Cohen Kadosh et al. (2005) found overlapping representations for size, luminance, and numerical magnitude in the bilateral regions of the parietal cortex. In addition, the authors also reported evidence to indicate that a region within the left IPS was specifically modulated by the numerical-magnitude comparison condition and exhibited a numerical distance effect. In a more recent investigation, Dormal and Pesenti (2009) studied the common and distinct brain representations of length and numerical-magnitude (dot arrays) processing. Their results suggested that while the right IPS exhibits overlapping neuronal representations for length and numerical magnitude, the left IPS was found to be involved in numerical-magnitude processing only.

Taken together, the available data, while not providing a particularly coherent picture of the precise anatomical localization of common and segregated neuronal correlates of numerical and non-numerical magnitude processing, suggest that the parietal cortex contains regions that code for numerical magnitude alone as well as areas that appear to respond in similar ways to both numerical and non-numerical quantities.

Perhaps one of the reasons for the results from the available fMRI data not yielding a straightforward picture is that there is both segregation and integration of numerical and non-numerical quantity at a microlevel, which cannot be detected by the comparatively coarse spatial resolution of fMRI. One explanation for the seemingly conflicting fMRI data comes from a single-cell recording study with primates, by Tudusciuc and Nieder (2007). In their study, primates were trained to discriminate between dot arrays and line lengths. Recordings from areas of the primate IPS revealed neurons that were either tuned to numerical or non-numerical magnitude or exhibited tuning to both types of magnitude. These three different types of responses from single neurons were found to be in very close spatial proximity to one another, supporting the hypothesis that both overlapping and discrete neuronal processing of continuous and discrete magnitude occurs in the IPS. Thus, these data suggest close spatial proximity of single neurons tuned to either continuous or discrete magnitude, or both. In view of the fact that fMRI blurs over millions of neurons within a single region, it is quite plausible that the differences in the spatial localization of discrete and continuous-magnitude representations in the fMRI studies reflect slight biases in the patterns of overlapping or segregated neuronal responses being sampled that may well vary as a function of the paradigm being used. In this vein, modern imaging fMRI analysis techniques, such as multivoxel pattern analysis (MVPA), that are sensitive to differences in the spatial patterns of activations between conditions may yield more consistent results.

Taken together, the results from functional neuroimaging and single-unit recording studies converge to suggest that the IPS contains number-specific representations as well as regions in which numerical and non-numerical magnitudes are coded in similar ways.

Symbolic and Non-symbolic Brain Representations of Number?

Most neuroimaging research on numerical cognition has focused on commonalities between symbolic (e.g., Hindu-Arabic digits) and non-symbolic (e.g., patterns of dot arrays) number processing rather than on differences between these formats. As discussed above, most of the empirical research in the cognitive neuroscience of numerical cognition has largely emphasized that areas in and around the IPS, located within the parietal cortex of the human brain, are thought to encode an abstract and, therefore, notation-independent representation of numerical magnitude (Dehaene, Dehaene-Lambertz, & Cohen, 1998). For example, Piazza et al. (2007) used a passive fMRI adaptation study, with single digits and dot arrays, to investigate whether the IPS encodes for a common representation of symbolic and non-symbolic numerical magnitudes. The study revealed a numerical distance-related cross-notation adaptation between symbolic and non-symbolic stimuli. In other words, when participants were repeatedly shown 16 dots, the IPS would exhibit distance-related activation recovery to deviants that were Arabic numerals rather than dots. Conversely, following adaptation to a particular quantity represented by an Arabic numeral, the parietal cortex exhibited distance-related deviant responses to dot arrays. This finding of an adaptation effect regardless of the presentation format (i.e., numerical symbols

or dot arrays) has been interpreted as evidence for a common and notation-independent underlying neuronal substrate for the processing of symbolic and non-symbolic magnitudes within the IPS.

However, recent empirical evidence has challenged this assumption, fostering an increased interest in the segregation and integration of brain functions involved in the processing of symbolic and non-symbolic numerical magnitudes. The similarities and differences between symbolic and non-symbolic numerical-magnitude representations in the brain are important, as many theoretical accounts (Dehaene & Changeux, 1993; Verguts & Fias, 2004) posit that cultural, symbolic representations of numerical magnitude, such as Arabic numerals, are mapped onto basic (perhaps innate) non-symbolic representations.

The results from the study by Piazza et al. (2007), while supporting the notion of abstract representations of number (that are common across symbolic and non-symbolic formats), also point to subtle differences in the neural mechanisms underlying symbolic and non-symbolic representations of numerical magnitude. Specifically, the neural tuning curves obtained by plotting the responses to deviants of various distances differed significantly between the two presentation formats. The data reported by Piazza et al. (2007) suggest that there is a more precise representation of symbolic numerical magnitude in the left IPS (with no format differences in the right hemisphere). This sharper, or more precise, representation is characterized by narrower tuning curves, reflecting greater sensitivity to differences between the adaptation and deviant numerosities. Thus, it can be argued that not only commonalities between formats but also differences between symbolic and non-symbolic processing exist. The left hemisphere may play a critical role in the process of mapping numerical symbols onto non-symbolic numerical-magnitude representation, a process which may, in part, rely on linguistic functions subserved by left hemisphere regions.

In a computational model of symbolic and non-symbolic numerical-magnitude processing, Verguts and Fias (2004) formulated a mechanistic account of the relationship between symbolic and non-symbolic numerical-magnitude processing. In particular, their model proposed the existence of initially separated, neuronally distinct, format-specific pathways for the processing of symbolic and non-symbolic numerical magnitudes. However, at the level of representations, both formats converge onto a common representation of numerical magnitude.

Using this model as a starting point, Holloway, Price, and Ansari (2010) investigated through fMRI analysis whether segregated and common areas in the human brain, which mediate the processing of symbolic and non-symbolic numerical magnitude, can be identified. Subjects were asked to perform a number comparison task with Hindu-Arabic symbols and dot patterns. Results of this study showed that neural activation of both presentation formats significantly overlapped in the right IPS, supporting the notion of a common, abstract representation of symbolic and non-symbolic numerical magnitude. However, in addition to this activation overlap, format-specific effects for non-symbolic stimuli were reported in other areas of the brain, such as the left angular gyrus, superior temporal gyri, and the posterior superior parietal cortex (Holloway et al., 2010). This study provides experimental evidence for the existence of both distinct and common neuronal processing pathways for symbolic and non-symbolic numerical magnitudes.

In another fMRI study (Santens, Roggeman, Fias, & Verguts, 2010), differences in the neuronal processing pathways underlying symbolic and non-symbolic numerical-magnitude processing were investigated using functional connectivity analysis (in which the degree of connectivity between brain regions as a function of experimental conditions is probed). This specific analysis revealed different encoding systems for the processing of symbolic and non-symbolic numerical magnitude that converge onto a common area within the IPS. The first pathway is involved in the processing of non-symbolic numerical information and includes areas of the visual cortex, the posterior parietal lobe, and the IPS. In contrast, connectivity analysis of the symbolic numerical condition suggested a functional pathway that connects areas of the visual cortex directly to the IPS, bypassing areas of the posterior parietal lobe. These data provide evidence for two different pathways involved in the processing of symbolic and non-symbol numerical information. Consistent with Holloway et al.'s (2010) data, the authors found a zone of convergence between symbolic and non-symbolic processing within the IPS, suggesting that both format-specific pathways feed into a common, abstract representation of numerical magnitude (Santens et al., 2010).

Taken together, the investigation of differences and similarities in the neural correlates of symbolic and non-symbolic numerical magnitudes has provided evidence to suggest that symbolic and non-symbolic numerical-magnitude processing is correlated with overlapping activation of the IPS, perhaps reflecting abstract-magnitude representation in the IPS. Furthermore, it has been shown that distinct and format-specific pathways in the human brain mediate the processing of symbolic and non-symbolic magnitudes.

While these neuroimaging studies investigating symbolic and non-symbolic numerical magnitude converge to suggest the existence of an abstract, format-independent representation of numerical magnitude, there has been a significant amount of discussion concerning the extent to which numerical representations in the IPS are format independent or dependent. For example, using fMRI adaptation, Cohen Kadosh et al. (2007) reported evidence pointing to both format-dependent and independent representation of numerical magnitude in the IPS, by comparing within and cross-format adaptation to number words and digits. In view of these data and others (Cohen Kadosh, Cohen Kadosh, & Henik, 2008; Cohen Kadosh & Walsh, 2009), it has been proposed that numerical-magnitude representations in the IPS are nonabstract and format dependent.

Different Brain Representations of Numerical Order and Numerical Magnitude?

Numerical magnitude is not the only semantic information that is represented by numerical symbols. In addition, ordinal information is also represented by digits. For example, the digit 5 stands not only for five objects (i.e., the five-ness) but also for the fifth position within the number sequence. The focus of research in cognitive neuroscience of numerical cognition has concentrated predominantly on the processing of numerical magnitude, and relatively little is known about how the human brain may encode numerical order and how the processing of numerical order both relates to and differs from numerical-magnitude representation and the processing of non-numerical, but ordered, stimuli (such as letters).

Initial evidence for differences in the brain basis of numerical magnitude and order was provided by neuropsychological studies that reported a double dissociation for the processing of numerical magnitude and numerical order (Delazer & Butterworth, 1997; Turconi & Seron, 2002). In other words, brain damage can selectively impair either numerical-magnitude or numerical-order processing while leaving the other function intact.

Moreover, functional neuroimaging studies have revealed that regions of the IPS are involved in the processing of numerical order and that differences exist in the parietal responses during numerical-magnitude and numerical-order processing. For example, in one ERP study, subjects had to judge whether a visually presented Arabic digit was smaller or larger than 15 (i.e., numerical-magnitude task), or whether a presented numeral came before or after 15 (i.e., numerical-order task). The results of this study demonstrated a significant difference in the time course of neural processing underlying numerical-magnitude and numerical-order processing. Specifically, numerical-magnitude processing was associated with a P2 component over the left parietal lobe. In contrast, the numerical-order task evoked a delayed and bilateral parietal response. Furthermore, a significant distance effect for both conditions was found at the P3 component over parietal areas (Turconi, Jemel, Rossion, & Seron, 2004). However, an fMRI study suggested spatial overlap between the processing of numerical order and numerical magnitude within the IPS (Franklin & Jonides, 2009).

In addition to investigations focusing on differences between numerical-order and numerical-magnitude processing, imaging studies have reported functional overlap for the processing of numerical- and non-numerical-ordered sequences such as letters of the alphabet or months of the year. For example, in one fMRI study, a standard number comparison task (i.e., which number is larger or smaller) and a letter comparison task, in which subjects were asked to decide which letter appeared later or earlier in the alphabet, were used. A conjunction analysis demonstrated that anterior regions of the IPS were significantly activated in response to both tasks, suggesting that similar brain mechanisms might underlie the processing of different ordinal sequences (Fias et al., 2007). In another, similar fMRI study investigating the processing of order, participants were asked to silently recite months of the year and single-digit sequences. Consistent with the results obtained by Fias et al. (2007), the authors showed that anterior regions of the IPS were specifically sensitive to sequential information independent of the presentation format (Ischebeck et al., 2008).

Using MVPA, a more recent fMRI analysis method that identifies differences in activation patterns (i.e., the spatial pattern of activation) rather than differences in the activation extent of one region, Zorzi, Di Bono, and Fias (2011) reanalyzed the data from the Fias et al. (2007) study. While results from the earlier study reported a spatial overlap in brain activation in response to the processing

of numbers and letters, the new statistical analysis showed that a trained classifier (support vector machine) is able to discriminate different patterns of activation underlying the processing of order in letters and numbers. This result strongly suggests that, although overlapping regions within the IPS might be involved in the processing of ordered information, different patterns of activity encode numerical- and non-numerical-ordered formats. It might well be the case, therefore, that distinct neural representations underlie the processing of numerical and non-numerical order.

Although little is known about numerical- and non-numerical-order processing, the above reported studies suggest that the IPS might be involved in the processing of abstract—that is, format-independent—ordinal knowledge. However, the relationship between the brain mechanisms underlying the processing of numerical order and numerical magnitude are less clear and are yet to be further investigated. It could be the case that distinct neural representations within the same region of the IPS are involved in the processing of numerical and non-numerical order.

Development of Numerical-Magnitude Representations in the Brain

Until recently, much of the research on the cognitive neuroscience of numerical cognition was focused on work with adult participants and little attention had been paid to the ways in which learning and development might modulate the brain circuits underlying number processing. In recent years a small but growing body of research has accumulated, investigating the differences and similarities in the neural mechanisms underlying numerical-magnitude processing in infants, children, and adults. These studies have provided evidence for both dynamic changes in the neural correlates of numerical-magnitude processing as well as similarities in the brain areas engaged during number processing between children and adults.

In one of the first studies to investigate the neural basis of the symbolic distance effect in children and adults, Ansari et al. (2005) found differences in the brain areas modulated by numerical distance between a group of 9- to 12-year-old children and a group of adults. Children were found to exhibit a symbolic distance effect on right frontal brain regions (right inferior and middle frontal gryri), whereas adults exhibited a distance effect on parietal brain regions such as the right IPS and bilateral regions of the precuneus. These findings suggested a shift from the initial reliance on frontal brain regions to an increasing age-related specialization of the parietal cortex for the processing of symbolic, numerical magnitude. These results were supported by a similar observation by Kaufmann et al. (2006) using a number Stroop paradigm. In addition, the hypothesis that the parietal cortex undergoes a process of age-related specialization for the processing of numerical magnitude was supported by an fMRI study that compared the non-symbolic distance effect in children and in adults (Ansari & Dhital, 2006). This study revealed that the non-symbolic (comparison of arrays of squares) numerical distance effect on activation in a region of the left IPS increases over developmental time. Adults exhibited a significantly greater distance effect (larger activation for relatively small compared to large numerical distance) on the left IPS than did the group of children. Furthermore, in an analysis of the neuronal correlates of the distance effect in the two groups separately, children exhibited distance-related modulation of the right frontal brain areas, whereas in adults the strongest distance effect was found in the bilateral parietal regions. These data have been interpreted as evidence for a gradual specialization of parietal brain regions for the representation and processing of numerical magnitude. The engagement of frontal brain regions in children (distance-related modulations of frontal brain areas) has been posited to reflect the engagement of frontal brain resources such as cognitive control and conflict resolution. More specifically, it has been argued that the parietal brain representations of numerical magnitude in children may be, consistent with behavioral evidence (Holloway & Ansari, 2008; Sekuler & Mierkiewicz, 1977), more overlapping than they are in adults. In order to resolve this representational overlap in the context of number comparison, children require frontal brain resources that are tuned to resolving response competition and conflict.

It should be noted that the strongest evidence to date points towards an age-related specialization of the parietal cortex for the processing of numerical magnitude. The finding of greater frontal engagement during both symbolic and non-symbolic numerical-magnitude processing in children is less clearly understood. While studies indicate that children, analyzed as a group by themselves, exhibit distance related responses in frontal brain regions, there exists, to the best of our knowledge, no data that shows that these frontal distance effects are statistically greater in children compared to adults. Clearly, more evidence is needed in this area. There is a great need for studies that move beyond the relatively coarse comparison of children and adults towards a characterization of the full developmental trajectory underlying the neural correlates of both symbolic and non-symbolic numerical-magnitude processing.

In addition to findings suggesting that the neuronal mechanisms underlying both symbolic and non-symbolic number processing undergo age-related changes, there is also a body of data suggesting similarities between children and adults. For example, Cantlon et al. (2006) using fMRI adaptation (similar to the procedures used by Piazza et al., 2004, reviewed above) revealed that the right IPS responds to non-symbolic numerical deviants (presented among trains of non-symbolic stimuli of equivalent numerical magnitude) in a comparable way in both adults and 4-year-old children. These findings suggest that, in children as young as 4 years of age, the parietal cortex responds similarly to numerical magnitudes when a passive (fMRI adaptation) design is used. Furthermore, evidence using ERPs with human infants combined with source localization has indicated that parietal brain regions are modulated by numerical magnitude in very young infants and children (Izard, Dehaene-Lambertz, & Dehaene, 2008; Libertus & Brannon, 2009), suggesting that parietal brain regions are responsive to manipulations of numerical magnitude early in development.

In this context, it should be noted that the first study to ever investigate symbolic and non-symbolic numerical magnitude processing (using a comparison task) showed similar modulations of the time course of neuronal processing in 5-year-old children and adults for both symbolic and non-symbolic numerical distance effects (Temple & Posner, 1998). However, this particular study did not provide a quantitative comparison of the ERP responses recorded from children and adults, making it difficult to evaluate the extent to which age-related differences in the symbolic and non-symbolic distance effect on ERPs recorded over parietal brain regions existed in these data.

The findings of developmental similarities in the brain representations of numerical magnitude are intriguing, as they may suggest that different levels of numerical magnitude representation are associated with diverging developmental trajectories. More specifically, it can be hypothesized that young children and adults exhibit similar representations of non-symbolic numerical magnitude in the parietal cortex when no action on these representations is required. However, when participants are required to make a decision on these representations (such as judging which of two numerical magnitudes is numerically larger), additional brain resources need to be engaged. It is thus important for future studies to conduct developmental neuroimaging studies of numerical cognition using both passive and active paradigms. Such investigations could reveal important differences in the levels of processing of numerical magnitude information in the brain and how these are differentially modulated by ontogenesis.

The Neuronal Basis of Developmental Dyscalculia

The discussion of the cognitive neuroscience of numerical cognition in this chapter thus far has described the brain circuits involved in the processing and representation of numerical magnitude in typically developing individuals and how these brain processes change over developmental time. An important question within this field concerns the degree to which such brain circuits develop and respond atypically in individuals with mathematical difficulties.

It is a little known fact that approximately 5% of the general population (Butterworth, Varma, & Laurillard, 2011; Shalev & Gross-Tsur, 2001) suffers from specific difficulties in calculation, while performing within the normal range on tests of intelligence and reading competence. These individuals are thought to have a specific learning difficulty in the domain of mathematics (specifically, arithmetic) called "developmental dyscalculia" (DD). Until recently, it was not known whether the function and structure of the brains of individuals with DD differ from those unaffected by this disorder.

In one of the first brain imaging studies to investigate differences between individuals with and those without mathematical difficulties, Isaacs, Edmonds, Lucas, and Gadian (2001) compared the brain structures of two groups of adolescents who had been born with very low birth weight. Interestingly, one of the groups had a specific difficulty in calculation but functioned at the same level of intelligence as their peers in the control group, who also had the same birth weight but exhibited no calculation deficits. Using voxel-based morphometry (a method to quantify white and gray matter volumes in the brain and compare them between groups of participants), Isaacs et al. (2001) found that the group of individuals with very low birth weight and calculation deficits had significantly less volume of gray matter in an area of the left IPS than did their peers with

very low birth weight, who were matched on birth weight and intelligence but did not have a calculation deficit. This clinical study provided the first evidence to suggest neuroanatomical differences between individuals with and those without calculation deficits.

Using both functional and structural neuroimaging, Molko et al. (2003) investigated differences between women with and those without Turner syndrome (TS). One of the hallmarks of TS is that affected individuals struggle with doing math. In seeking a neural correlate for their math difficulties, Molko et al. (2003) found that individuals with TS exhibited abnormalities in the IPS. Furthermore, in a calculation task, individuals with TS exhibited atypical parietal responses during calculation.

In the first functional neuroimaging study of DD, Kucian et al. (2006) imaged the brains of children with and without DD while they performed both exact and approximate calculation tasks (the approximate task required participants to choose which of two inaccurate answers was closest to the correct answer) and a magnitude comparison task (choosing which of two collections of objects was numerically larger). The authors found similar activation profiles between children with and those without DD in the tasks used to measure brain activation. However, additional region of interest (ROI) analyses suggested weaker activation in the IPS in the group of children with DD, pointing toward atypical recruitment of this brain region in DD during numerical and calculation tasks.

In another fMRI study comparing children with and without DD, Price, Holloway, Räsänen, Vesterinen, and Ansari (2007) found that children with DD exhibit an atypical activation of the right IPS during comparison of non-symbolic sets of items (arrays of squares). Children in both groups were to determine which of two simultaneously presented sets of squares was numerically larger. The numerical distance between the sets was varied, and a brain imaging analysis was conducted to compare the effect of non-symbolic distance on the brains of children with and without DD. The authors showed that while children without DD exhibited a normal distance effect on activation in the right IPS (more activation for pairs separated by a relatively small non-symbolic numerical distance than for those with a large one), children with DD had considerably lower activation in this brain region and did not exhibit a distance effect. These findings point to an impairment of parietal brain circuits during basic, non-symbolic numerical magnitude processing in children with DD. In view of the developmental evidence from typically developing children, in children with DD, parietal brain circuits may fail to specialize for the processing of numerical magnitude in a typical way.

Further evidence of a parietal impairment in the processing of numerical magnitude in children with DD comes from a study by Mussolin et al. (2010), who used a symbolic (Arabic numerals) comparison task to compare the neural correlates of the numerical distance effect between children with and those without DD. Their findings, consistent with those of Price et al. (2007), demonstrated a smaller symbolic distance effect in children with DD than that in their typically developing peers.

In another fMRI study, Kaufmann et al. (2009) investigated functional brain activation differences between a group of nine children diagnosed with DD and a group of nine children without DD. Both groups were asked to solve a new version of a non-symbolic numerical magnitude comparison task, in which children were presented with two real photographs of hands that differed in the number of fingers raised. The activation patterns acquired while the children were judging whether the hand on the right or that on the left displayed more fingers suggested that children with DD exhibited significant activation differences in the left and right inferior parietal areas, including the IPS. Children with DD showed relatively stronger activations than their peers, which the authors interpreted as compensatory activation of areas involved in numerical processing in children with DD. Both groups had a comparable behavioral performance level. Thus, this study provides evidence that, compared to their peers, children with DD need to activate number-processing areas more strongly in order to perform low-level number-processing tasks at an equal (at the same behavioral level as their peers) performance level.

In addition to fMRI, electrophysiological measures, particularly ERPs, have been used to understand potential differences in the time course of brain activation during numerical-magnitude comparison between children with and those without DD. Soltesz, Szucs, Dekany, Markus, and Csepe (2007) found that, during a symbolic comparison task, children with and without DD exhibited a numerical distance effect on an early time window of brain processing, in electrodes over right parietal brain regions, typically associated with this effect. However, at a later time window, individuals with DD did not exhibit a distance effect, whereas children without DD had a trend toward a significant distance effect. These findings may indicate subtle differences in the neural time course underlying numerical-magnitude processing between children with and those without DD.

What about structural abnormalities in children with DD? The evidence presented above suggests that children with very low birth weight who suffer from calculation difficulties, as well as women with TS, exhibit structural abnormalities in parietal brain regions that have been associated with number processing. Is the same true for children with DD? To answer this question, Rotzer et al. (2008) used voxel-based morphometry to compare the gray and white matter volumes of groups of children with and without DD. Their findings indicated that children with DD have reduced gray matter volume in the right IPS as well as in several frontal brain regions (the anterior cingulate, left inferior frontal gyrus, and bilateral regions of the middle frontal gyri). Furthermore, these authors also detected reduced white matter volumes in left frontal regions and the parahippocampal gyrus in children with DD compared to their typically developing controls.

Taken together, this growing body of research suggests that children with mathematical difficulties, be they associated with low birth weight, genetic abnormalities, or DD, exhibit neuronal abnormalities at both the structural and functional levels of analyses. Some, but certainly not all, of the data point to atypical function and structure of the IPS, which, as the evidence from typically developing individuals demonstrates, plays a critical role in the representation and processing of numerical magnitude. However, the few pieces of evidence that are currently available imply that the picture is far more complicated than atypical structure and function of the IPS alone causing individuals' difficulties in the processing of numerical and mathematical information. Some findings provide little evidence for a specific deficit in parietal brain function (Kucian et al., 2006; Soltesz et al., 2007). Moreover, some data point to compensatory brain activation among children with DD (Kaufmann et al., 2009). In addition, the structural data reviewed above indicate abnormalities in brain structure in individuals with DD that extend beyond the parietal cortex and involve areas of the frontal cortex and medial temporal lobe. Thus, currently there is no clear picture of the neural correlates of DD. Finally, a recent fMRI study (Rotzer et al., 2009) showed that children with DD, relative to a group of nonimpaired controls, exhibited atypical activation of the right IPS. These findings suggest that the neuronal deficits of children with DD may generalize beyond numerical-magnitude processing to deficits in domain-general functions, such as working memory.

More studies are needed that take into account different diagnostic criteria and their impact on functional and structural data. Also needed is a concerted effort to study the neuronal correlates of the heterogeneity of cognitive profiles associated with DD, and comorbidity between DD and other difficulties, such as developmental dyslexia (Rubinsten & Henik, 2009).

How Is Numerical Magnitude Represented in the Brain?

Besides mapping out the brain regions involved in numerical magnitude processing and determining whether they are domain-specific and how they relate to other processes and development, the field of cognitive neuroscience of numerical cognition also needs to provide mechanistic accounts of how numerical magnitude is represented in the brain.

Summation vs. Place Coding

In a seminal paper, Dehaene and Changeux (1993) presented a computational neural model of how numerical magnitude is processed in the human mind. The model itself consists of four distinct processing stages. First, there is the input system (representing the retina) on which objects of varying physical sizes can be projected at different locations. The computational task of the next stage is to normalize various object sizes, by representing each object with a fixed setting of units. For example, a small object will activate three units in the input layer, whereas a large object will activate six units. In the second layer both objects are normalized such

that each object is represented by four units. The activity of the normalized objects is projected onto the next layer, which reflects a numerical summation (adding up) of all items presented. Activity in this module increases monotonically and is highly correlated with the numerical magnitude of the initial visual display (see Figure 24.4). Because of its summation characteristic, this process is often termed "summation-coding."

In the final stage, input is received from the summation code module and the summed activity is projected onto a topographically organized "number line." In other words, the summed activity is mapped onto a selective numerical magnitude unit that only responds to a selective range of values, but not if the value is larger or smaller. For example, the summed activity of seven objects is projected onto a unit, which prefers the numerical magnitude 7. However, this unit will also respond to the numerical magnitude 6 and 8, although to a lesser degree. Therefore, each projected numerical magnitude creates a bell-curved Gaussian activity distribution where the peak activation is centered on the preferred numerical magnitude. This type of representation is termed "place-coding" because the resulting bell-curved activation relates to a specific position on the number line. In addition, Dehaene and Changeux (1993) assumed that the number line is logarithmically compressed and thus obeys Weber's law. This compression leads to a relative overrepresentation of small numbers compared to larger numbers.

Convincing evidence for the existence of place and summation-coding comes from electrophysiological investigations probing the responses of single neurons in awake, behaving primates. Nieder and Miller (2003) trained monkeys to perform a delayed

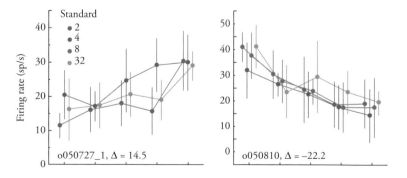

Figure 24.4 Neurons in the lateral intraparietal area (LIP) of monkeys displaying 'summation coding'. The neural activity increases or decreases monotonically with an increase of numerical magnitude (reprinted from Roitman, Brannon & Platt, 2007, with permission from PLoS Biology.)

match-to-sample task. In this experiment, a series of visual displays containing different numbers of items are consecutively presented on a screen. The task of the monkey is to decide whether the target contains the same number of items as the sample. Importantly, the authors were able to identify neurons in the ventral intraparietal area (VIP)[1] that were selectively tuned to different numerical magnitudes. More specifically, the identified number of selective neurons showed maximum activity in response to a preferred numerical magnitude and a systematic decrease in activity as the numerical magnitude departed from the preferred number. In other words, the characteristics of these neurons resembled the proposed properties of place-coding units described in the model of Dehaene and Changeux (1993). The existence of number-selective neurons provides compelling evidence that a place-coding system is involved in representing non-symbolic numerical magnitude.

A different electrophysiological study provided evidence for summation-coding at the level of single neurons. Roitman, Brannon, and Platt (2007) showed that neuronal activity in the LIP[2] in monkeys increases or decreases monotonically with an increase of numerical magnitude. Monotonic activity is a critical feature for summation-coding; therefore, the data provide direct evidence for summation coding in the monkey brain. Evidence for the existence of both systems in the primate brain, in different parts of the parietal cortex, lends support for the computational models that contain both summation and place-coding mechanisms (Dehaene & Changeux, 1993; Verguts & Fias, 2004).

In addition to these electrophysiological studies, there is increasing evidence that both systems also exist in the human brain. For example, in an fMRI adaptation study, Piazza et al. (2007) found numerical magnitude selective activation (i.e., place coding), while Santens et al. (2010) reported direct evidence for summation-coding in the human parietal lobe. They showed that numerical processes within the posterior parietal lobe of the non-symbolic processing pathway exhibit certain computational characteristics that reflect summation-coding— that is, the neurofunctional activation in this area increases monotonically with an increase in numerical magnitude. In other words, the more items present of a given non-symbolic stimuli, the higher the neurofunctional activation within the posterior parietal lobe. It seems likely that the identified summation code neurons resemble an intermediate step and directly project onto place-coding neurons

(Santens et al., 2010). Nieder and Dehaene (2009) have argued in favor of this possibility since the neurons, reported by Roitman et al. (2007), encode numerical magnitude only within their restricted receptive fields. The extraction of abstract numerical magnitude, however, requires integration across visual space. It is unclear if and how both identified systems interact.

There is some evidence from computational modeling that summation-coding could be the only coding scheme underlying numerical magnitude representation. Pearson, Roitman, Brannon, Platt, and Raghavachari (2010) tested the hypothesis that a neural summation-coding model (created by using experimental data from the Roitman et al. [2007] study) would be able to perform a decision process within a number bisection task. Results of this study clearly showed that summation-coding can inform numerical decision processes and suggested that such numerical decision processes do not necessarily require place-coding representation of numerical magnitude to be implemented.

Converging evidence from electrophysiological studies, using single-cell recording in monkeys, and from neurofunctional studies in humans have provided compelling evidence that numerical magnitudes can be neuronally encoded through both summation and place-coding. Establishing a mechanistic account of magnitude representation within the neural framework is an important step toward understanding how representations of numerical magnitudes might be implemented in the human brain.

Logarithmic vs. Linear Representation

As discussed in the previous sections, recent empirical evidence has suggested that numerical magnitudes are represented in ways that resemble other non-numerical, analogue magnitudes, such as size or line length. A distinct feature of this internal analogue number system is that discrimination between numerical magnitudes varies as a function of the relative size of the ratio of compared numerical magnitudes (i.e., Weber's law). In other words, it is more difficult (as displayed by reaction times and accuracy) to discriminate between two numerals that are relatively large, such as 8 and 9, than numerals that are relatively small, such as 1 and 2. This effect has been described as the numerical ratio effect, described in more detail earlier in this chapter. How can we model this effect mathematically? Currently, there are at least two theoretical models: the linear and the logarithmic that have been drawn upon to explain how magnitudes are represented in the brain and give rise to ratio effects. What both accounts have in common is that they both hypothesize that numbers are organized along a hypothetical number line, on which each numeral is represented by a Gaussian distribution (see Figure 24.5). In other words, each numeral is not represented exactly (i.e., discrete) but approximately. The two models differ substantially, however, in how the hypothetical number line is organized and in how the Gaussian distribution that represents each numerical magnitude on the "mental number line" is characterized.

Gallistel and Gelman (2000) argue in favor of a linear representation, in which the variability of the Gaussian distribution increases in proportion to a linear increase of the numerical magnitude (i.e., scalar variability of Gaussian distribution—the hypothetical number line is linear). In contrast, in the logarithmic compressed model (see Figure 24.5, panel b), proposed by Dehaene and Changeux (1993), the width of the Gaussian distribution for each numeral remains constant, but the relative distance between numerals decreases with a logarithmic function (i.e., variability of numerals is constant but the hypothetical number line is logarithmically compressed). In other words, the distance between numerals on a hypothetical number line remains the same in the linear model, whereas in the logarithmic model, the representational distance between two numerals is logarithmically compressed. Furthermore, the variability of the Gaussian distribution in the logarithmic model is the same for each numeral, whereas the linear model assumes scalar variability (the width of the distribution is proportional to the numerical magnitude). Although both models differ in their explanation of how the ratio

effect arises, a dissociation between the two theoretical models on a behavioral level has been proven to be impossible, since both models predict identical behavioral outputs (i.e., the ratio effect; although see Siegler and Opfer's [2003] work on number line estimation for one approach to dissociating the two models using behavioral data).

Recent investigations have tried to tease the two models apart on a neurofunctional level. For instance, strong evidence in favor of a logarithmically compressed numerical magnitude organization comes from single-cell recordings in monkeys. As discussed above, Nieder and Miller (2003) trained monkeys to discriminate dot arrays in a delayed match-to-sample task while recording firing rates of single neurons. The authors found number-selective neurons within the monkeys' IPS that were specifically tuned to certain numerosities. In addition, the identified number-selective neurons displayed a Gaussian distribution in such a way that the firing rates of neurons systematically decreased as the numerical distance to the preferred numerical magnitude increased. Of note, the authors showed that the variability in the firing rate of number-selective neurons was best explained by assuming a logarithmic compressed number line compared to a linear number line. A similar result was reported in the fMRI adaptation study by Piazza and colleagues (2004). The tuning curves in the IPS mapped out from the fMRI responses to sparse numerical deviants among trains of repeated numerical magnitude were found to be best described by a logarithmic rather than a linear function.

Numerosity Code

Both the linear and logarithmic models of numerical-magnitude representations posit that the

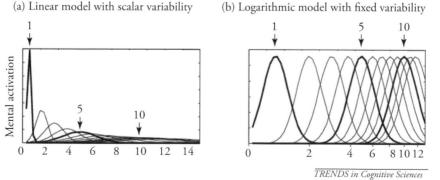

(a) Linear model with scalar variability   (b) Logarithmic model with fixed variability

Figure 24.5 Models for representing numbers on a linear or logarithmic scale (reprinted from Feigenson, Dehaene, & Spelke, 2004, with permission from Elsevier).

representation of numerical magnitude is analogue and, therefore, inherently noisy and approximate. In contrast to this account, Zorzi et al. (2011) proposed a different computational model for number representation and discrimination. In their model, each number is represented by a set of activated units in which every single unit corresponds to a number step of one. For example, a numerical magnitude of 3 would activate three units, whereas a numerical magnitude of 5 would activate five units of the system. Thus, this system of representation is exact, rather than approximate. Using a neuronal network, the authors tested whether this simple computational model for number representation would be sufficient to explain simple behavioral effects such as the distance effect. Indeed, results suggested that this model is able to model the commonly observed distance effect in number comparison tasks. Furthermore, it showed that effects usually thought to indicate an underlying analogue magnitude representation can be modeled by assuming a simple one-to-one correspondence of numerical magnitude and activation units, without necessarily assuming an underlying analogue representation. In this model, the numerical distance effect does not arise from the noise in the underlying magnitude representations but occurs at the level of implementing the decision. In other words, the greater the similarity in the exact numerical-magnitude codes, the greater the competition between left- and right-hand responses and, thus, the longer the reaction times.

Taken together, different neural computational models have been used to predict how numerical information is processed and represented in the human brain. Neurophysiological and functional imaging studies have successfully used these conceptual models to guide their investigations of how neuronal structures might implement the processing of numerical information in the brain. For example, it has been shown with single-cell recordings that both summation-coding and place-coding is a possible solution to code for numerical magnitude within a neuronal framework. In addition to these advances, functional neuroimaging studies can aid in the clarification of certain properties of conceptual models that are hard to differentiate on the behavioral level (see the logarithmic vs. linear discussion).

Conclusions and Future Directions

The aim of this chapter was to provide an overview of the tremendous scientific progress made in uncovering and describing the neuronal mechanisms underlying the representation and processing of numerical magnitude. These advances have led to the establishment of an important and steadily growing subdiscipline within the field of cognitive neuroscience, which we have referred to here as the cognitive neuroscience of numerical cognition. As reviewed above, in its relatively short history, this field of inquiry has moved beyond simply documenting which brain regions are correlated with the processing and representation of numerical magnitude toward a deeper characterization of the mechanisms carried out by the brain regions activated in tasks designed to tap into numerical cognition. In this vein, questions have been tackled concerning the specificity of numerical magnitude representation in the parietal cortex, their overlap with domain-general functions such as response selection, and the possibility of brain mechanisms that subserve both numerical and non-numerical magnitudes. Furthermore, growing progress has been made toward a better understanding of both the atypical and typical development of brain mechanisms underlying numerical cognition. At the level of understanding the computational architecture underlying numerical magnitude processing in the brain, mechanistic computational models have been put forward, and invasive and noninvasive brain imaging methods have been used to test predictions.

While much progress has been made, there are many outstanding questions that require further research. Many of these have been reviewed in this chapter. Here, we highlight just a few that are particularly pressing in order to make progress in this field. For example, while it has been shown that there are both segregated and common mechanisms for symbolic and non-symbolic numerical magnitude processing in the brain, it is yet unclear how the representational formats interact over the course of developmental time. Specifically, it has been frequently hypothesized that cultural representations of numerical magnitude (such as Arabic numerals and number words) get mapped onto early developing (perhaps even innate) non-symbolic representations. However, exactly how this mapping process is achieved at the neuronal level is largely unknown. In order to understand how basic systems of numerical magnitude representations interact with those that are the outcome of enculturation processes, a better understanding of the hypothesized mapping process is required. The insights gained through investigating this process will also inform our understanding of the development of mathematical learning difficulties.

A related outstanding question in the cognitive neuroscience of numerical cognition concerns the neuronal mechanisms underlying non-symbolic numerical magnitude processing. One of the challenges that researchers face when attempting to delineate neurocognitive mechanisms underlying the processing of the numerical magnitude represented by sets of items is to control for variables that covary with numerical magnitude, such as area, density, and contour length. This raises the question of how the brain abstracts numerical magnitude from all these continuous variables and how variations—the degree to which the numerical magnitude of a non-symbolic array of objects is either correlated or anticorrelated with a non-numerical continuous variable—influence the neuronal correlates of numerical magnitude processing. The processes related to the extraction of numerical magnitude from non-symbolic sets has largely largely ignored. The investigation of these processes will further constrain our understanding of the nature and mechanisms underlying numerical magnitude representations in the brain.

A final question we would like to raise concerns the relationship between numerical magnitude processing in the parietal lobe and other functions carried out by this large brain region. It is well known that the parietal cortex is involved in multiple functions, ranging from top-down attentional control (Corbetta & Shulman, 2002) to visuomotor integration (Culham & Valyear, 2006). There are too many functions that have been associated with the parietal cortex to be listed here. Despite the large heterogeneity of function of this brain region, with the exception of a few studies (Simon et al., 2004; Simon, Mangin, Cohen, Le Bihan, & Dehaene, 2002), research into the neural correlates of numerical cognition has largely ignored the relationships between parietal representations of numerical magnitude and other parietally mediated sensory, motor, and cognitive processes. We contend that a major challenge for future studies in the cognitive neuroscience of numerical cognition will be to relate parietal correlates of numerical cognition to other parietal functions. Such investigations will help to address the relationship among domains of brain functions. They also have the potential to further hone our understanding of the precise role of parietal cortex in numerical cognition and determine why this brain region is so prominently associated with the representation and processing of numerical magnitude.

Notes

1. An area within the fundus of the intraparietal sulcus (IPS) of the parietal lobe.
2. Located at the lateral wall of the IPS in monkeys.

References

Ansari, D., & Dhital, B. (2006). Age-related changes in the activation of the intraparietal sulcus during nonsymbolic magnitude processing: An event-related functional magnetic resonance imaging study. *Journal of Cognitive Neuroscience, 18*(11), 1820–1828.

Ansari, D., Dhital, B., & Siong, S. C. (2006). Parametric effects of numerical distance on the intraparietal sulcus during passive viewing of rapid numerosity changes. *Brain Research, 1067*(1), 181–188.

Ansari, D., Garcia, N., Lucas, E., Hamon, K., & Dhital, B. (2005). Neural correlates of symbolic number processing in children and adults. *Neuroreport, 16*(16), 1769–1773.

Bar, M. (2009). The proactive brain: Memory for predictions. *Philosophical Transactions of the Royal Society of London. Series B, Biological Sciences, 364*(1521), 1235–1243.

Boysen, S. T., Bernston, G. G., Hannan, M. B., & Cacioppo, J. T. (1996). Quantity-based interference and symbolic representations in chimpanzees (*Pan troglodytes*). *Journal of Experimental Psychology. Animal Behavior Processes, 22*(1), 76–86.

Brannon, E. M., & Terrace, H. S. (1998). Ordering of the numerosities 1 to 9 by monkeys. *Science, 282*(5389), 746.

Butterworth, B., Varma, S., & Laurillard, D. (2011). Dyscalculia: From brain to education. *Science, 332*(6033), 1049–1053.

Cantlon, J. F., & Brannon, E. M. (2006). Shared system for ordering small and large numbers in monkeys and humans. *Psychological Science, 17*(5), 401–406.

Cantlon, J. F., & Brannon, E. M. (2007). Adding up the effects of cultural experience on the brain. *Trends in Cognitive Sciences, 11*(1), 1–4.

Cantlon, J. F., Brannon, E. M, Carter, E. J., & Pelphrey, K. (2006). Functional imaging of numerical processing in adults and 4-year-old children. *PLoS Biology, 4*(5), e125.

Cohen Kadosh, R., Cohen Kadosh, K., & Henik, A. (2008). When brightness counts: The neuronal correlate of numerical-luminance interference. *Cerebral Cortex, 18*(2), 337–343.

Cohen Kadosh, R., Cohen Kadosh, K., Kaas, A., Henik, A., & Goebel, R. (2007). Notation-dependent and -independent representations of numbers in the parietal lobes. *Neuron, 53*(2), 307–314.

Cohen Kadosh, R., Henik, A., Rubinsten, O., Mohr, H., Dori, H., van de Ven, V., et al. (2005). Are numbers special? The comparison systems of the human brain investigated by fMRI. *Neuropsychologia, 43*(9), 1238–1248.

Cohen Kadosh, R., & Walsh, V. (2009). Numerical representation in the parietal lobes: Abstract or not abstract? *Behavioral and Brain Sciences, 32*(3-4), 313–328; discussion 328–373.

Corbetta, M., & Shulman, G. L. (2002). Control of goal-directed and stimulus-driven attention in the brain. *Nature Reviews Neuroscience, 3*(3), 201–215.

Culham, J. C., & Valyear, K. F. (2006). Human parietal cortex in action. *Current Opinion in Neurobiology, 16*(2), 205–212.

Dehaene, S. (1996). The organization of brain activations in number comparison: Event-related potentials and the additive-factors method. *Journal of Cognitive Neuroscience, 8*(1), 47–68.

Dehaene, S. (1997). *The number sense* (p. 274). New York: Oxford University Press.

Dehaene, S., & Changeux, J. P. (1993). Development of elementary numerical abilities—a neuronal model. *Journal of Cognitive Neuroscience, 5*(4), 390–407.

Dehaene, S, Dehaene-Lambertz, G, & Cohen, L. (1998). Abstract representations of numbers in the animal and human brain. *Trends in Neurosciences, 21*(8), 355–361.

Delazer, M., & Butterworth, B. (1997). A dissociation of number meanings. *Cognitive Neuropsychology, 14*(4), 613–636.

Dormal, V., & Pesenti, M. (2009). Common and specific contributions of the intraparietal sulci to numerosity and length processing. *Human Brain Mapping, 30*(8), 2466–2476.

Eger, E., Sterzer, P., Russ, M. O., Giraud, A.-L., & Kleinschmidt, A. (2003). A supramodal number representation in human intraparietal cortex. *Neuron, 37*(4), 719–725.

Feigenson, L., Dehaene, S., & Spelke, E. (2004). Core systems of number. *Trends in Cognitive Sciences, 8*(7), 307–314.

Feigenson, L., Carey, S., & Spelke, E. (2002). Infants' discrimination of number vs. continuous extent. *Cognitive Psychology, 44*(1), 33–66.

Fias, W., Lammertyn, J., Caessens, B., & Orban, G. (2007). Processing of abstract ordinal knowledge in the horizontal segment of the intraparietal sulcus. *Journal of Neuroscience, 27*(33), 8952–8956.

Franklin, M. S., & Jonides, J. (2009). Order and magnitude share a common representation in parietal cortex. *Journal of Cognitive Neuroscience, 21*(11), 2114–2120.

Gallistel, C. R., & Gelman, I. I. (2000). Non-verbal numerical cognition: From reals to integers. *Trends in Cognitive Sciences, 4* (2), 59–65.

Göbel, S. M., Johansen-Berg, H., Behrens, T., & Rushworth, M. F. S. (2004). Response-selection-related parietal activation during number comparison. *Journal of Cognitive Neuroscience, 16*(9), 1536–1551.

Göbel, S. M., & Rushworth, M. F. S. (2004). Cognitive neuroscience: Acting on numbers. *Current Biology, 14*(13), R517–R519.

Grillspector, K., Henson, R., & Martin, A. (2006). Repetition and the brain: Neural models of stimulus-specific effects. *Trends in Cognitive Sciences, 10*(1), 14–23.

Grune, K., Mecklinger, A., & Ullsperger, P. (1993). Mental comparison: P300 component of the ERP reflects the symbolic distance effect. *Neuroreport, 4*(11), 1272.

Halberda, J., & Feigenson, L. (2008). Developmental change in the acuity of the "number sense": The approximate number system in 3-, 4-, 5-, and 6-year-olds and adults. *Developmental Psychology, 44*(5), 1457–1465.

Halberda, J., Mazzocco, M. M. M., & Feigenson, L. (2008). Individual differences in non-verbal number acuity correlate with maths achievement. *Nature, 455*(7213), 665–668.

Henschen, S. E. (1919). Über Sprach-, Musik- und Rechenmechanismen und ihre Lokalisationen im Großhirn. *Zeitschrift für die gesamte Neurologie und Psychiatrie, 52*(1), 273–298.

Holloway, I. D., & Ansari, D. (2008). Domain-specific and domain-general changes in children's development of number comparison. *Developmental Science, 11*(5), 644–649.

Holloway, I. D., & Ansari, D. (2009). Mapping numerical magnitudes onto symbols: The numerical distance effect and individual differences in children's mathematics achievement. *Journal of Experimental Child Psychology, 103*(1), 17–29.

Holloway, I. D., Price, G. R., & Ansari, D. (2010). Common and segregated neural pathways for the processing of symbolic and nonsymbolic numerical magnitude: An fMRI study. *Neuroimage, 49*(1), 1006–1017.

Isaacs, E. B., Edmonds, C. J., Lucas, A., & Gadian, D. G. (2001). Calculation difficulties in children of very low birth weight: A neural correlate. *Brain, 124* (Pt 9), 1701–1707.

Ischebeck, A., Heim, S., Siedentopf, C., Zamarian, L, Schocke, M., Kremser, C., et al. (2008). Are numbers special? Comparing the generation of verbal materials from ordered categories (months) to numbers and other categories (animals) in an fMRI study. *Human Brain Mapping, 29*(8), 894–909.

Izard, V., Dehaene-Lambertz, G., & Dehaene, S. (2008). Distinct cerebral pathways for object identity and number in human infants. *PLoS Biology, 6*(2), e11.

Kaufmann, L., Koppelstaetter, F., Siedentopf, C., Haala, I., Haberlandt, E., Zimmerhackl, L. B., et al. (2006). Neural correlates of the number-size interference task in children. *Neuroreport, 17*(6), 587–591.

Kaufmann, L., Vogel, S. E., Starke, M., Kremser, C., Schocke, M., & Wood, G. (2009). Developmental dyscalculia: Compensatory mechanisms in left intraparietal regions in response to nonsymbolic magnitudes. *Behavioral and Brain Functions, 5*, 35.

Kucian, K., Loenneker, T., Dietrich, T., Dosch, M., Martin, E., & von Aster, M. (2006). Impaired neural networks for approximate calculation in dyscalculic children: A functional MRI study. *Behavioral and Brain Functions, 2*, 31.

Libertus, M. E., & Brannon, E. M. (2009). Behavioral and neural basis of number sense in infancy. *Current Directions in Psychological Science, 18*(6), 346–351.

Molko, N., Cachia, A., Bruandet, M., Bihan, D. L., Cohen, L., Dehaene, S., et al. (2003). Functional and structural alterations of the intraparietal sulcus in a developmental dyscalculia of genetic origin. *Neuron, 40*, 847–858.

Moyer, R. S., & Landauer, T. K. (1967). Time required for judgements of numerical inequality. *Nature, 215*(2), 1519–1520.

Mussolin, C., De Volder, A., Grandin, C., Schlögel, X., Nassogne, M. C., & Noël, M.-P. (2010). Neural correlates of symbolic number comparison in developmental dyscalculia. *Journal of Cognitive Neuroscience, 22*(5), 860–874.

Nieder, A., & Dehaene, S. (2009). Representation of number in the brain. *Annual Review of Neuroscience, 32*, 185–208.

Nieder, A., & Miller, E. K. (2003). Coding of cognitive magnitude: Compressed scaling of numerical information in the primate prefrontal cortex. *Neuron, 37*(1), 149–157.

Notebaert, K., Nelis, S., & Reynvoet, B. (2011). The magnitude representation of small and large symbolic numbers in the left and right hemisphere: An event-related fMRI study. *Journal of Cognitive Neuroscience, 23*(3), 622–630.

Pearson, J., Roitman, J. D., Brannon, E. M., Platt, M. L., & Raghavachari, S. (2010). A physiologically-inspired model of numerical classification based on graded stimulus coding. *Frontiers in Behavioral Neuroscience, 4*(January), 1.

Piazza, M., Izard, V., Pinel, P., Le Bihan, D., & Dehaene, S. (2004). Tuning curves for approximate numerosity in the human intraparietal sulcus. *Neuron, 44*(3), 547–555.

Piazza, M., Pinel, P., Le Bihan, D., & Dehaene, S. (2007). A magnitude code common to numerosities and number symbols in human intraparietal cortex. *Neuron, 53*(2), 293–305.

Pinel, P., Dehaene, S., Rivière, D., & LeBihan, D. (2001). Modulation of parietal activation by semantic distance in a number comparison task. *Neuroimage, 14*(5), 1013–1026.

Pinel, P., Le Clec, H. G., Moortele, P. F. van de, Naccache, L., Le Bihan, D, & Dehaene, S. (1999). Event-related fMRI analysis of the cerebral circuit for number comparison. *Neuroreport, 10*(7), 1473–1479.

Pinel, P., Piazza, M., Le Bihan, D., & Dehaene, S. (2004). Distributed and overlapping cerebral representations of number, size, and luminance during comparative judgments. *Neuron, 41*(6), 983–993.

Price, G. R., Holloway, I., Räsänen, P., Vesterinen, M., & Ansari, D. (2007). Impaired parietal magnitude processing in developmental dyscalculia. *Current Biology, 17*(24), R1042–R1043.

Roitman, J. D., Brannon, E. M., & Platt, M. L. (2007). Monotonic coding of numerosity in macaque lateral intraparietal area. *PLoS Biology, 5*(8), e208.

Rotzer, S., Kucian, K., Martin, E., von Aster, M., Klaver, P., & Loenneker, T. (2008). Optimized voxel-based morphometry in children with developmental dyscalculia. *Neuroimage, 39*(1), 417–422.

Rotzer, S., Loenneker, T., Kucian, K., Martin, E., Klaver, P., & von Aster, M. (2009). Dysfunctional neural network of spatial working memory contributes to developmental dyscalculia. *Neuropsychologia, 47*(13), 2859–2865.

Rubinsten, O., & Henik, A. (2009). Developmental dyscalculia: Heterogeneity might not mean different mechanisms. *Trends in Cognitive Sciences, 13*(2), 92–99.

Santens, S., Roggeman, C., Fias, W., & Verguts, T. (2010). Number processing pathways in human parietal cortex. *Cerebral Cortex, 20* (1), 77–88.

Sekuler, R., & Mierkiewicz, D. (1977). Children's judgments of numerical inequality. *Child Development, 48*(2), 630–633.

Shalev, R. S., & Gross-Tsur, V. (2001). Developmental dyscalculia. *Pediatric Neurology, 24*(00), 337–342.

Siegler, R. S., & Opfer, J. E. (2003). The development of numerical estimation: Evidence for multiple representations of numerical quantity. *Psychological Science, 14* , 237–243.

Simon, O., Kherif, F., Flandin, G., Poline, J. B., Rivière, D., Mangin, J. F., et al. (2004). Automatized clustering and functional geometry of human parietofrontal networks for language, space, and number. *Neuroimage, 23*(3), 1192–1202.

Simon, O., Mangin, J. F., M., Cohen, L., LeBihan, D., & Dehaene, S. (2002). Topographical layout of hand, eye, calculation and language related areas in the human parietal lobe. *Neuron, 33*, 475–487, 2002.

Soltesz, F., Szucs, D., Dekany, J., Markus, A., & Csepe, V. (2007). A combined event-related potential and neuropsychological investigation of developmental dyscalculia. *Neuroscience Letters, 417*, 181–186.

Temple, E., & Posner, M. I. (1998). Brain mechanisms of quantity are similar in 5-year-old children and adults. *Proceedings of the National Academy of Sciences U S A, 95*(13), 7836–7841.

Tudusciuc, O., & Nieder, A. (2007). Neuronal population coding of continuous and discrete quantity in the primate posterior parietal cortex. *Proceedings of the National Academy of Sciences U S A, 104*(36), 14513–14518.

Turconi, E., Jemel, B., Rossion, B., & Seron, X. (2004). Electrophysiological evidence for differential processing of numerical quantity and order in humans. *Brain Research. Cognitive Brain Research, 21*(1), 22–38.

Turconi, E. & Seron, X. (2002). Dissociation between order and quantity meaning in a patient with Gerstmann syndrome. *Cortex, 38*(5), 911–914.

Van Opstal, F., Gevers, W., De Moor, W., & Verguts, T. (2008). Dissecting the symbolic distance effect: Comparison and priming effects in numerical and nonnumerical orders. *Psychonomic Bulletin & Review, 15*(2), 419–425.

Verguts, T., & Fias, W. (2004). Representation of number in animals and humans: A neural model. *Journal of Cognitive Neuroscience, 16*(9), 1493–1504.

Verguts, T., & Van Opstal, F. (2005). Dissociation of the distance effect and size effect in one-digit numbers. *Psychonomic Bulletin & Review, 12*(5), 925–930.

Walsh, V. (2003). A theory of magnitude: common cortical metrics of time, space and quantity. *Trends in Cognitive Sciences, 7*(11), 483–488.

Xu, F, & Spelke, E. S. (2000). Large number discrimination in 6-month-old infants. *Cognition, 74*(1), B1–B11.

Xu, F., Spelke, E. S., & Goddard, S. (2005). Number sense in human infants. *Developmental Science, 8*(1), 88–101.

Zamarian, L, Ischebeck, A., & Delazer, M. (2009). Neuroscience of learning arithmetic—evidence from brain imaging studies. *Neuroscience and Biobehavioral Reviews, 33*(6), 909–925.

Zorzi, M., Di Bono, M. G., & Fias, W. (2011). Distinct representations of numerical and non-numerical order in the human intraparietal sulcus revealed by multivariate pattern recognition. *Neuroimage, 56*(2), 674–680.

Psychopharmacology of Cognition

T. W. Robbins

Abstract

In this chapter the neuroscientific basis and clinical rationale of cognitive psychopharmacology are reviewed. Effects of drugs in humans and animals are surveyed on different forms of memory and a number of aspects of executive function, including attention, working memory, cognitive flexibility, and response inhibition. The main drug classes covered include the benzodiazepines and the stimulants, but their cognitive effects are mainly analyzed in terms of their neurochemical modes of action, for example, at GABAergic, glutamatergic, monoaminergic, or cholinergic receptors, and in relation to their neuroanatomical sites. Particular attention is paid to cognitive-enhancing drugs and their prospects. The main factors determining the benefits and costs of drugs on cognitive performance are identified. The utility of psychopharmacology in dissecting cognitive processes is also considered.

Key Words: memory, executive function, attention, neurotransmitter, cognitive enhancement

Introduction

Cognitive psychopharmacology is an increasingly important discipline in view of the large number of neuropsychiatric and neurological disorders requiring treatment and the plethora of both old and new candidate mechanisms of cognitive-enhancing drugs. Moreover, the subtlety of such mechanisms promises to tell us much about the functional organization of the brain through pharmacological manipulation. The ethical, legal, and scientific controversies surrounding the use of cognitive enhancers by healthy human subjects also requires careful evaluation of possible costs and benefits of such compounds in terms of neuropsychological test batteries ultimately deriving from the application of cognitive theory.

Evidence relevant to this discipline has traditionally come from three main sources: correlation of chemical neurotransmitter deficits postmortem with cognitive status in life, the study of systemically administered agents on human cognition, and extrapolation from animal studies. Each of these approaches suffers from considerable limitations. The study of chemical neuropathology, as in the case of relating central cholinergic loss from the cerebral cortex to mental performance during life, runs into the usual problems of interpreting correlative evidence. Studies in human psychopharmacology usually cannot easily construct dose–response curves for practical and ethical reasons, and the receptors for the drug effects may be distributed in widely divergent neural systems with different functions, often resulting in irrelevant, adverse, and confounding side effects. Moreover, access to the brain itself is limited by pharmacokinetic factors, and identification of the precise neural locus of any given effect is not possible using the usual systemic route of administration, unless combined with functional brain imaging in pharmacological fMRI studies. A further frustration with human studies is that they often are unable to use drugs with selective modes of action, either for reasons of safety and toxicity or simply because the drugs are unavailable for investigation from the parent companies. Although data for such compounds are often available from published animal studies, it is often unclear to what extent the findings of such studies can be extrapolated to humans; this "translational gap" is a central issue not only for pharmaceutical companies but also for the development of the discipline itself. Fortunately, there have been impressive attempts to bridge this divide, which have also had the effect of strengthening the range and power of the underlying neuropsychological constructs.

Cognitive Psychopharmacology in the Context of Neuroscience

Research in cognitive psychopharmacology is most effectively carried out in the context of advances in neuroscience. Drugs affect chemical neurotransmitter function by interacting generally with receptors that mediate various components of synaptic processes, including the synthesis, storage, release, reuptake, and catabolism of neurotransmitters, as well as the simulation or antagonism of their effects at pre- or postsynaptic receptors. Neurotransmitter actions have to be understood in the context of

their functions in order to optimize transmission in neuronal networks. Thus, the connectivity of neuronal networks in major forebrain structures such as the cerebral cortex, hippocampus, and striatum is mediated by fast-signaling excitatory (glutamate) or inhibitory (GABAergic) transmission. Neuronal networks are also modulated by slower-acting neurotransmitters, such as the monoamines (dopamine, noradrenaline, and serotonin), and by acetylcholine, as well as by neuropeptide-type transmitters that may coexist as transmitters in the same neurons as, for example, dopamine (cholecystokinin), noradrenaline (neuropeptide Y), or acetylcholine (vasoactive intestinal polypeptide [VIP]), and have a dual role in the periphery (Table 25.1). These neuropeptides are often equivalent to hormones in the nature and slow time-course of their effects and are particularly important in producing state changes.

Added to this complexity is the frequent existence of multiple neurotransmitter receptors for a given neurotransmitter, mediating different aspects of their functions, in ways we are still striving to understand completely. In a few cases the precise neuroanatomical distribution of these different receptors offers opportunities for producing selective

Table 25.1. Major Chemical Neurotransmitters

Classical Neurotransmitters	Receptors
Fast Signaling	
Glutamate (excitatory) (GLU)	NMDA, AMPA, Kainate
Gamma-aminobutyric acid (inhibitory) (GABA)	GABA-a, GABA-b
Slow Modulatory	
Acetylcholine (ACh)	nicotinic, muscarinic
Dopamine (DA)	D1-D5
Noradrenaline (NA)	alpha1,2; beta 1,2
(norepinephrine)	
Serotonin (5-hydroxytryptamine, 5-HT)	At least 15, including 5-HT1a, 5-HT1b, 5HT2a, 5-HT2c, 5-HT3, 5-HT6, etc.
Neuropeptides	
Very slow modulators/co-transmitters	
Cholecystokinin (CCK)—co-transmitter for DA	CCK-A, CCK-B
Neuropeptide Y—co-transmitter for NA	NPY1R, NPY2R
Vasoactive intestinal polypeptide (VIP)—co-transmitter for ACh	$VPAC_1$, $VPAC_2$
Oxytocin, vasopressin, etc.	OXTR, V1-V3.

drug effects on particular aspects of cognition. For the purposes of the discussion in this chapter it is worth mentioning that acetylcholine has at least two main forms of receptor (muscarinic and nicotinic), dopamine (DA) has five main receptors (D1–D5), serotonin (or 5-hydroxytryptamine [5-HT]) has at least 15, and glutamate at least three main types (AMPA, NMDA, and kainate). AMPA is primarily responsible for the fast-signaling functions of this transmitter, and NMDA is linked to mechanisms of neural plasticity, including learning (see Cooper, Bloom, & Roth, 2002, for further details).

The Translational Imperative: A Case Study of the Cholinergic Hypothesis of Dementia

Perhaps the earliest example of the translational approach comes from the demonstration that the intellectual status of patients with Alzheimer's disease is related to cortical cholinergic loss (Perry et al., 1978). This observation helped spark the notion that remediation of the cognitive deficits might occur after treatment with cholinergic agents, parallel to the well-known treatment of Parkinson's disease with levodopa (L-dopa) to restore lost dopaminergic function. This resulting research program depended to a large extent on the widespread use of the cholinergic muscarinic receptor antagonist scopolamine in healthy volunteers to simulate (reversibly) the effects of aging or dementia in young adult subjects (see Bartus & Dean, 2009). Such studies, combined with parallel observations in nonhuman primates and rodents, have been successful in demonstrating significant detrimental effects of scopolamine on both working memory and long-term memory, including recognition and recall, probably working at sites in the medial temporal lobe and prefrontal cortex, respectively (e.g., Tang, Mishkin, & Aigner, 1997). Antagonizing these deleterious effects with cholinergic agents, such as the acetylcholine esterase inhibitors (examples being physostigmine, tacrine, donepezil, and rivastigmine), or the cholinergic agonist nicotine seemed to provide a strong case for expecting a positive therapeutic effect of such drugs in humans with dementia (e.g., Aigner & Mishkin, 1986). Moreover, psychopharmacological (Davis et al., 1978) and neuroimaging (Furey, Pietrini, & Haxby, 2000) evidence in healthy volunteers showed that drugs such as physostigmine could enhance aspects of memory while changing the balance of cerebral blood flow in circuits of the medial temporal lobe and prefrontal cortex. However, the therapeutic benefits of cholinergic drug therapy in Alzheimer's disease, while producing small, measurable improvements and clinical benefit in some patients, have not in general been fulfilled. This is probably because the cholinergic deficit in Alzheimer's disease co-occurs with severe pathology and nerve cell loss to parts of the cerebral cortex innervated by the forebrain cholinergic projections, and so any boosting of cholinergic function that may occur with treatment is likely to be compromised. Further promising examples of translation will be considered below; however, their prospects of therapeutic success should all be tempered by this seminal example.

Drug Effects on Cognition via Arousal-like Processes

Many drugs affecting cognition probably do so by affecting modulatory or state-dependent motivational or arousal-type mechanisms, although it is frequently difficult to dissociate these from the core cognitive processes. Thus, for example, d-amphetamine and related stimulant drugs such as methylphenidate, cocaine, and possibly also caffeine and modafinil may influence cognitive functions via their arousing, alerting, or motivational actions. Traditional evidence points to benefits of such drugs on standard vigilance tasks such as continuous performance, especially when fatigue develops (Koelega, 1993; Weiss & Laties, 1962), which can be offset by their positive effects on arousal. Whether positive effects on tasks involving working memory or inhibitory self-control, for example, Logan's stop-signal reaction time task (Logan, Cowan, & Davis, 1984), can similarly be attributed to effects on arousal seems less likely. The existence of well-defined projections of the catecholamine (dopamine and noradrenaline) systems to the cerebral cortex in humans, including the prefrontal cortex, appear likely to have specific functional roles based on their neuromodulatory effects, for example, the "stabilization of neuronal ensembles" (Durstewicz, Seamans, & Sejnowski, 2000; Robbins & Roberts, 2007) or the boosting of working memory by strengthening the memory trace and protecting it from disruption (Goldman-Rakic, 1998), rather than simply modulating arousal per se. Indeed, it is now more productive to consider how drug effects on cognition might be mediated by specific receptors that mediate specific forms of processing.

However, the Yerkes-Dodson principle (1908), which has its origins in theories of arousal (e.g., Berlyne, 1960; Hebb, 1955) has been useful in describing how typical inverted-U-shaped dose–response effects, that is, improvements in performance at low doses and deficits at higher ones, may arise (see Figure 25.1). Instead of the traditional plot of arousal level on the abscissa and performance efficiency on the ordinate, the usual trend is to refer more specifically to a neurochemical variable such as "level of D1 receptor stimulation" vs. a more precisely defined task-related dependent parameter. Such functions generally define an optimal level of performance produced by an optimal dose, and this serves to highlight the fact that cognitive performance may peak between particular levels of chemical neuromodulation.

A corollary to the Yerkes-Dodson principle is that performance may also vary as a function of the task. Early formulations suggested that difficult tasks were performed optimally at lower levels of arousal than easy ones (Figure 25.1). While the notions of "easy" and "difficult" have not always been straightforward to apply, there is no doubt that drugs may sometimes affect cognitive performance in the opposite direction in the same individual, producing both benefit and detriment. A contemporary example of this is the effect of L-dopa on cognition in Parkinson's disease. The medication is primarily for the movement disorder, but it may have beneficial effects on some aspects of cognition, such as working memory and planning function (Lange et al., 1992; Swainson et al., 1999). However, the same dose can lead to impairments in other aspects of cognition (reversal learning and risky decision-making), probably as a consequence of its actions on a different neural substrate (Cools, Barker, Sahakian, & Robbins, 2001, 2003; Cools, Lewis, Clark, Barker, & Robbins, 2007; Swainson et al., 1999).

The Yerkes-Dodson principle has not, in general, been very popular in psychology when applied to more obviously psychological processes such as motivation or levels of stress (Broadbent, 1971; Eysenck, 1982). This is partly because of the difficulty of testing the predictions of the inverted U–shaped function; it often appears that almost any data can be fitted to it, and probably as many as seven levels of arousal level (or, in this case, dose) are necessary to produce an unambiguous test. Drugs with apparently opposite effects on arousal, as defined, for example, by effects to desynchronize or synchronize the EEG, such as amphetamine and scopolamine, do not merely cancel out their deleterious effects, as might be explained by a single inverted U–shaped function; in fact, much evidence exists to suggest that their deleterious effects on performance may even be potentiated. Such findings first stimulated Broadbent (1971) to speculate that drugs may exert effects on more than one type of arousal mechanism ("upper" and "lower," see also Robbins, 1984). Indeed, it now appears that there may well be separate inverted U–shaped functions for different neurotransmitters, and indeed, their receptors, in common brain regions. This is fully compatible with the neuroscientific evidence that the anatomical details of these chemically identified ascending neurotransmitter systems serve to fractionate the old, diffuse reticular formation that was held to maintain cortical arousal (e.g., Hebb, 1955).

Despite these problems, there have been important applications of the inverted U–shaped function to explain how a given dose of drug may produce both beneficial and deleterious effects on performance in the same individual, and how genetic influences may drive individual responses to drug actions (see below). The introduction of computational modeling approaches into cognitive psychopharmacology, as exemplified by the use of logistic sigmoid functions, and associated concepts such as "inverse temperature" to define effects of drugs or manipulations on signal-to-noise processing (Servan-Schreiber, Printz, & Cohen, 1990) may be consistent with a more sophisticated understanding in terms of the Yerkes-Dodson principle.

Complementary to accounts of stimulant drug effects on cognition in terms of elevated arousal are accounts of amnesic effects of benzodiazepine-like drugs such as diazepam and chlordiazepoxide in terms of their sedative actions. The anterograde amnesia generated by these drugs resembles the effects of medial temporal lobe lesions. Thus, the

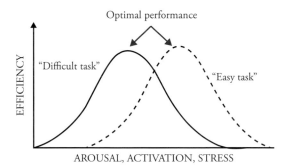

Figure 25.1 The Yerkes-Dodson principle, which defines a curvilinear relationship between level of arousal (or activation, or stress) and cognitive performance. The inverted U–shaped function may also differ as a function of task difficulty. The relevance of this principle to psychopharmacology comes from the very frequent finding of inverted U–shaped dose–response curves, relating dose of drug to cognitive performance.

consolidation of new information or new learning is compromised, rather than implicit priming effects or short-term memory capacity (Curran, 1991). Despite this apparent specificity of action, these anterograde amnesic effects nonetheless have been ascribed to the sedative effects of the benzodiazepines. Simply speaking, efficient encoding or retrieval is impaired by their sleep-inducing or hypnotic properties. However, it is significant for arousal-type hypotheses that this common-sense explanation has been refuted by three distinct lines of evidence: first, the sedative and amnestic effects do not correlate well; second, the sedative effects show tolerance (i.e., get smaller) upon repeated administration whereas the amnestic effects do not; and third, the sedative effects can be antagonized by a benzodiazepine receptor antagonist at doses that are not effective against the amnestic actions. Thus, the simple arousal hypothesis is clearly shown to be inadequate.

A more illuminating explanation of the effects of benzodiazepines on memory derives from an understanding of how these drugs act as positive allostearic modulators to boost neurotransmission at the GABA receptor. The GABA receptor comprises a number of protein subunits which are expressed in different combinations in a distributed fashion at different neuroanatomical locations and which are also associated with different aspects of benzodiazepine action, notably the alpha-1 and alpha-2 subunits, associated with sedative and hypnotic properties of the drugs, and an alpha-5 subunit, which is mainly restricted to the hippocampus and has been associated with their amnestic effects (Mohler, 2007).

In theory, it should be feasible to produce drugs acting as inverse agonists that have opposite effects to those of the benzodiazepines. Given that their actions to act as anticonvulsants, anxiolytics, and amnestic agents can clearly be dissociated as a function of which receptor subunits are implicated, it should be theoretically possible to produce a drug with a promnestic (i.e., memory-enhancing) action. Indeed, a drug that acts as an inverse agonist at GABA-A receptors containing the alpha-5 subunits has been produced. The drug attenuates the effects of GABA at GABA-A receptors with the alpha-5 subunit. While not apparently conferring any memory-enhancing effects, this drug has been shown specifically to antagonize the detrimental effects on memory (delayed verbal recall) of alcohol in intact human volunteers (Nutt, Besson, Wilson, Dawson, & Lingford-Hughes, 2007). However,

this antagonism is not extended to the other effects of alcohol, including its sedative effects. Whether such a drug could be used in a productive manner in society and not simply to enhance the tendency to drink alcohol but avoid some its detrimental effects is an issue that will require careful regulatory attention.

Effects of Drugs on Learning: Long-Term Potentiation and Prediction Errors

Neuronal networks mediate associative learning functions, and one appealing description of the underlying neurophysiological processes, originating with Hebb, is that "neurons that fire together, wire together." It is thus a natural assumption that the weights that accrue to the nodes within neuronal assemblies might well be subject to modulation and drug effects. Despite the apparent existence of several forms of memory, for example, declarative and procedural memory, and within the declarative category, semantic and episodic memory, with probably distinct underlying anatomical systems (Squire, 1992), it remains plausible that the underlying neuronal processes share common elements. Candidate processes depend on so-called long-term potentiation (LTP) or long-term depression (LTD), which vary subtly in their exact mechanisms but are now known to depend crucially on glutamatergic transmission, with the NMDA receptor especially implicated in neuronal plasticity and in hippocampal memory function (Morris, Anderson, Lynch, & Baudry, 1986).

Despite this solid neuroscience backdrop, little has emerged so far in terms of drugs that demonstrably modify human learning processes as a direct consequence of their actions on LTP or LTD, although a wealth of evidence has been amassed in the form of studies of learning in experimental animals. In general, treatment with NMDA receptor antagonists, such as APV (or AP-5), impair learning without necessarily affecting performance when administered post-training. For example, Young, Bohenek, and Fanselow (1994) found that NMDA receptor blockade in the hippocampus impaired the normal learning of associations between an environmental setting or context and an electric shock ("contextual fear"). While there was initially thought to be some special relationship between NMDA receptors and spatial or contextual learning dependent on the hippocampus, other studies showed the generality of the effects of NMDA receptor blockade for other neural structures and other behavioral paradigms. Thus, deficits in the acquisition of both fear conditioning and appetitive conditioning to discrete stimuli in rats (i.e., approach behavior to food-predictive cues) were shown to depend on NMDA receptors within the amygdala (Burns, Everitt, & Robbins, 1994; Miserendino, Sananes, Melia, & Davis, 1990). A form of stimulus–response learning dependent on the dorsal striatum (approaching cues predictive of reward) has also been shown to depend on NMDA receptors (Packard & Teather, 1997). Moreover, Dalley et al. (2005) showed that the consolidation of memory of a conditioned stimulus predictive of food delivery which elicits appetitive approach behavior was similarly dependent on NMDA (as well as dopamine D1) receptors in the ventral striatum. This growing list of learning and memory deficits following NMDA receptor blockade has led to several questions. Which aspects of learning and memory are impaired? What is the precise role of other glutamate receptors (such as the AMPA subtype, which mediates fast signaling by the glutamate-containing neurons)? What significance for human studies, especially in the therapeutic sense, do these findings have?

One way of addressing these questions is by comparing effects of dissociative anesthetic drugs on human cognition, such as ketamine, an NMDA receptor antagonist, whose effects have often been used to simulate psychotic symptoms in human volunteers (Krystal et al., 1994). Ketamine produces a rich range of subjective and objectively measured cognitive effects in a dose-dependent fashion. These include specific deficits at low doses on discrimination learning and on human causal-learning paradigms specifically in the formation of prediction errors, which are computed as the difference between obtained and expected outcomes and have been correlated with changes in the BOLD signal in a number of brain regions, including the midbrain, nucleus accumbens, and prefrontal cortex (Corlett et al., 2006). Moreover, low-dose ketamine in humans produces impairments not in basic short-term memory capacity (e.g., digit or spatial span) but in the manipulation of material in verbal (though not visuospatial) working memory, such as the reordering of digits or letters, abilities that are probably relevant to the ability to encode new information (Honey et al., 2003). These selective effects of ketamine on higher-order cognitive processes suggest that the drug first affects so-called executive functions, considered in more detail below.

These findings for animal and human models lead to the conjecture that it might be feasible to *enhance* rather than impair learning or memory by manipulating glutamatergic transmission, based on new discoveries in glutamate receptor pharmacology. Of course, such findings are especially relevant to those clinical disorders in which there is likely impairment in glutamate receptor function, such as schizophrenia and Alzheimer's disease (see below).

However, there is much more to learning than glutamate-dependent neuronal activity. A putative role of dopamine in reinforcement learning process has been bolstered by the discovery that the midbrain dopamine neurons behave in a manner consistent with their encoding of a prediction error for associative learning in the Rescorla-Wagner equation (Schultz, 2002). The prediction error in animal studies is evident when expectancies are violated, for example, when expected food rewards are omitted. The finding that dopamine neurons appear to track the prediction of reward by conditioned stimuli by exhibiting changes in fast phasic burst activity complements the previous understanding that this system generally operates in a rather slow, tonic-like manner (which may reflect different functions such as incentive motivation). It has proven difficult to provide definitive evidence that the dopamine system is causally related to certain forms of learning, despite clear indications in the animal literature (such as the experiment by Dalley et al., 2005, discussed above). Nevertheless, a recent study by Pessiglione and colleagues (Pessiglione, Seymour, Flandin, Dolan, & Frith, 2006) showed that L-dopa produced facilitatory effects on a discrimination learning task reinforced by money in human volunteers, when contrasted with the dopamine-blocking drug haloperidol. The experiment was carried out in a functional imaging paradigm through which the authors were able to parcellate error-prediction-like responses from the accompanying BOLD responses that occurred during learning in the striatum.

The discoveries concerning dopamine raise several interesting questions. How precisely are the dopamine neurons "informed" about these complex contingencies? How do these findings relate to those regarding NMDA receptor antagonists, described above? One way of integrating these results is to suggest that prefrontal cortical networks governed in part by glutamatergic transmission mediate at least some of the computations contributing to the prediction error and influence the midbrain dopamine neurons top-down via their anatomical projections to them. It should be noted, however, that this hypothesis remains to be tested, and other structures, including the amygdala and the habenula (Matsumoto & Hikosaka, 2007), may also help to influence or "educate" the dopamine neurons.

A further issue is the representation of punishment rather than reward prediction errors. The studies by Schultz (2002) showed that dopamine neurons respond to the omission of a reward by inhibiting their activity, which might constitute a negative prediction error. However, punishment may also implicate the presentation of aversive stimuli as well as the omission of rewarding stimuli. Other neurochemical systems, notably serotonin, have been considered as possibly contributing to the prediction of punishing stimuli (Cools, Roberts, & Robbins, 2008).

Pharmacological Dissection of Encoding, Consolidation, and Retrieval Memory Processes

Animal studies can also be used to dissect the effects of drugs on different memory subprocesses, such as initial encoding, subsequent consolidation and storage, and the ultimate retrieval of the memory trace. These factors can be unraveled in rodent studies using so-called one-trial memory tasks in which the agent of interest can be administered either prior to or just after initial learning and its effects on memory retrieval assessed at some subsequent retention test, possibly several days or more later. Such a paradigm has rarely been used in human studies, thus it is difficult to be sure about its clinical utility. However, possible new applications of drug treatments in such conditions as post-traumatic stress disorder and even drug addiction, where it may be desirable to manipulate prior memory traces, may change this state of affairs.

A drug that is only effective for a limited time-interval *after* training can be said to affect consolidation rather than the initial encoding of the trace. The drug is often also administered just before retention, to test possible effects on memory retrieval (as well as state-dependent effects, in which the state change associated with the drug potentially acts as a memory retrieval cue). In this way, the effects of NMDA receptor blockade, as well as other receptors, on different stages of memory can be determined. In one-trial place memory tests, NMDA receptor blockade disrupted encoding and consolidation of the memory but not retrieval (Bast, da Silva, & Morris, 2005). A similar pattern has been found for learned fear of contexts (Kim, Fanselow, DeCola, & Landeira-Fernandez, 1992). These findings imply that NMDA receptors have a selective role in the processes by which initially encoded events are made more permanent in long-term memory.

By contrast, blockade of AMPA/kainate receptors with a selective AMPA receptor antagonist such as LY326325 disrupts not only encoding but also consolidation and retrieval of spatial memories, showing that fast synaptic transmission via AMPA receptors is required more generally for all of these processes (Packard & Teather, 1997). This distinction between the roles of NMDA and AMPA receptors has also been demonstrated for other forms of memory mediated by the hippocampus, such as event–place associations in the rat, which can perhaps be more readily linked to the forms of episodic memory deficits shown by patients with Alzheimer's disease. Rats were trained to associate flavors with particular places where they had found those flavors in single episodes. Blockade of NMDA receptors within the hippocampus impaired encoding but not retrieval of the flavor–place associations, whereas blockade of AMPA receptors using LY326325 disrupted retrieval (Day, Langston, & Morris, 2003).

Recognition Memory

Involvement of NMDA and AMPA receptors has been demonstrated in another aspect of memory—the ability to recognize objects, which is markedly impaired in Alzheimer's disease. There is now strong evidence that object recognition is more dependent on a specific region of the medial temporal lobe, the perirhinal cortex, rather than the hippocampus (Murray & Bussey, 1999). Winters and Bussey (2005) capitalized on this functional localization by infusing selective NMDA and AMPA receptor antagonists into the perirhinal cortex in rats at varying stages of performance of a visual object recognition task. In this test, rats are allowed to interact with and explore a novel object before experiencing that now-familiar object again at a later time in the presence of another object. Recognition memory (or at least the sense of familiarity) can be inferred by the relative proportion of time the rats spend exploring the familiar and novel objects at a retention test carried out either a short or longer time following the original presentation of the first object. They found that NMDA receptor blockade (with AP-5) impaired long- but not short-term object recognition memory when infusion occurred prior to encoding the initial object. This result suggests that NMDA receptors within the perirhinal cortex are not necessary for the initial perceptual encoding of the object but are required for the induction of synaptic plasticity needed for the long-term storage of its trace. Moreover, NMDA receptor blockade soon *after* experience of the initial object also blocked its subsequent recognition, showing that NMDA receptors are directly implicated in memory consolidation. By contrast, NMDA receptor blockade immediately prior to the retention test had no effects on recognition memory, whereas AMPA receptor blockade (via the drug CNQX) did disrupt retrieval, paralleling the findings for spatial memory in the hippocampus. AMPA receptor blockade also detrimentally affected all three stages of memory: encoding, consolidation, and retrieval. Thus, it appears that there is considerable generality in the glutamate mechanisms mediating memory across not only domains (i.e., the nature of the memories) but also common memory processes, such as consolidation.

It should be noted that although glutamatergic mechanisms in the cortex appear to be crucial for recognition memory, there are modulatory roles of other neurotransmitters on these cortical networks, as in the case of cholinergic influences (Tang et al., 1997; see above). One of the most intriguing of these is via the neuropeptide oxytocin, which has been suggested to have selective effects on social recognition memory in animals (Bielsky & Young, 2004) and in human subjects, where there is evidence of selective improvement of memory for faces but not nonfacial stimuli (Rimmele, Hediger, Heinrichs, & Klaver, 2009). Indeed, other studies using conventional (i.e., nonsocial) paired associates or recall tests of human memory find only deficits following similar doses of oxytocin (Heinrichs, Meinlschmidt, Wippich, Ehlert, & Hellhammer, 2004). Presumably, these contrasting results represent the actions of this neuropeptide to bias processing toward the social rather than the nonsocial modalities and indicate an important role in memory for neuroendocrine factors. How such modulation would affect neural networks under the control of glutamatergic or GABAergic influences remains an important question.

Working Memory

Evidence from mice lacking the AMPA receptor subunit A (GluRA/GluR1) supports the role of fast synaptic transmission in working memory functions, as measured in a delayed alternation paradigm in which the mice simply have to remember which arm they last visited in a T maze (Schmitt, Deacon, Seeburg, Rawlins, & Bannerman, 2003). These mice were relatively unimpaired in a spatial task requiring longer-term memory and NMDA receptor involvement in the hippocampus, which suggests that different neuronal mechanisms within

the hippocampus contribute to different (though probably interactive) types of information processing. NMDA receptors had already been implicated in spatial working memory functions in rodents, based on behavioral pharmacological evidence (e.g., Riedel et al., 1999; Steele & Morris, 1999).

Cognitive Enhancement via Glutamate Receptors

Increasing knowledge about the nature of the glutamate receptors and the regulation of glutamatergic transmission prompts the question of how such information might be used to develop new agents for improving memory and cognitive function (see Kew & Kemp, 2005). The rather specific effects of NMDA receptor agents on the processes linking encoding to consolidation might encourage the further testing of this hypothesis by postulating selective enhancements with appropriate agonist drugs. However, this strategy is weakened by the likelihood of serious side effects (e.g., epilepsy and neurotoxicity) of surplus activity of glutamate receptors. Some ground for optimism is provided, however, by a report of effects on long-term memory recall in healthy elderly human volunteers by ampakine drugs that enhance excitatory glutamate transmission via their actions as positive allosteric modulators of the AMPA receptor (Lynch, 2002; see Figure 25.2). Robust and substantial improvements in recognition memory, as measured in a delayed-non-match-to-sample task, were also produced by a prominent ampakine compound (CX717) in rhesus monkeys (Figure 25.3; Porrino, Daunais, Rogers, Hampson, & Deadwyler, 2005). Dose-dependent effects were obtained in this study that also depend on both the delay between sample and retention test and the difficulty of the task (in terms of the length of list of the objects to be remembered). Moreover, improvements were observed in monkeys that were not only sleep-deprived but also in a sleep-non-deprived state; thus although sleep deprivation clearly impaired performance, the drug improved it independently of the baseline. These striking findings were correlated with predictable changes in regional cerebral metabolism, as measured by positron emission tomography (PET). However, robust as they are, these positive results have not yet been translated into a medication for humans.

Interest has also focused on partial agonists that facilitate NMDA receptor activity more indirectly. For example, D-cycloserine acts at the strychnine-insensitive glycine recognition site of the NMDA receptor complex to enhance NMDA

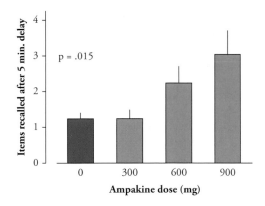

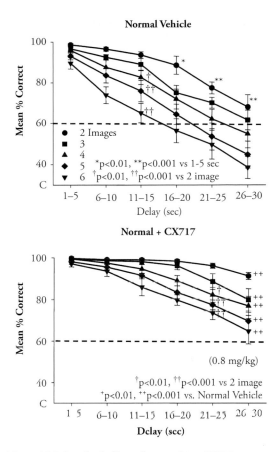

Figure 25.2 Beneficial, dose-related effects of an ampakine on delayed verbal recall in a subset of poor-performing, elderly volunteers.

Redrawn from Lynch (2002) with the permission of the author and publishers.

Figure 25.3 Beneficial effects of an ampakine, CX717, on recognition memory in rhesus monkeys. Significant dose- and delay-dependent improvements were found at several levels of difficulty compared to the normal vehicle (placebo control).

From Porrino et al (2005), reproduced with permission of the authors and publishers.

receptor functioning and has been reported to improve learning and memory in several animal tests, including visual recognition memory in non-human primates (Matsuoka & Aigner, 1996) and maze learning and associative learning in rodents (Monahan, Handelmann, Hood, & Cordi, 1989; Pitkanen et al., 1995). There have also been reports of small beneficial effects in clinical studies on schizophrenia (Goff et al., 1999) and Alzheimer's disease (Tsai, Falk, Gunther, & Coyle, 1999). These promising results have sometimes proven difficult to replicate (see Goff et al., 2005). However, recent work has shown reproducible effects of D-cycloserine in experimental animals on a special sort of learning process—extinction learning, which is also dependent on NMDA receptors—and has considerable implications for the treatment of other neuropsychiatric disorders (Walker, Ressler, Lu, & Davis, 2002). One possible application has been in the area of phobic anxiety. Concomitant treatment of patients with vertigo with cognitive behavior therapy based on extinction and with D-cycloserine had lasting benefits over and above those produced by either treatment alone (Ressler et al., 2004).

These effects on extinction may be related to those produced with another experimental paradigm termed "reconsolidation." This paradigm requires memory trace reactivation through the presentation of a memory retrieval cue, that is, a subset of the original memory associations. The reactivation of the memory apparently renders it labile and susceptible to further modulation. Thus, for example, a fear memory can be summoned and

then abolished by treatment with a protein synthesis inhibitor, indicating that the memory requires further protein synthesis for its reconsolidation (Nader, 2003). The reactivation may also lead to selective amnesia if the memory is treated with an NMDA receptor inhibitor or propranolol. This has possible implications for the treatment of post-traumatic stress disorder (Pitman, Brunet, Orr, Tremblay, & Nader, 2006). Reconsolidation then appears to represent another avenue for memory modification in a therapeutic context, although whether the process can be demonstrated unequivocally in humans is still uncertain.

Despite these major advances in basic knowledge concerning the role of glutamate receptors in cognition, there has been little application to human clinical disorders, though much is promised. The NMDA receptor antagonist memantine has found an application in the treatment of moderately impaired patients with Alzheimer's disease; its precise mechanism of action is not well understood.

Executive Cognition: Working Memory, Attention, Cognitive Flexibility, and Response Inhibition

There is still considerable controversy over the definition and nature of "executive" processes, which include processes contributing to future planning, and complex decision-making such as working memory, response inhibition, and responding to novel situations. Previously, executive functions had been defined as those cognitive control processes that serve to optimize performance in complex tasks involving the coordination of systems in control of perception, representations in short-term memory, and other modular cognitive functions. The term is meant to embrace those functions that appear to depend on intact functions of the prefrontal cortex, although it is accepted that executive deficits may arise from damage or impairment to structures other than the prefrontal cortex itself, which is presumed to be implicated within a neural network of interconnected structures.

One view is that these executive functions are "unitary" and may even be equivalent to Spearman's *g* in tests of fluid intelligence (Duncan et al., 2000). Others take the view that the executive system comprises several, fractionable processes (Robbins, 1996; Shallice & Burgess, 1996). A recent informative psychometric analysis of test performance in a large number of healthy volunteers used a range of tests to validate the definition of three major components of executive function: response inhibition (e.g., when a prepotent response has to be suppressed to allow adaptive behavior); updating working memory (e.g., incorporating novel information into planning); and cognitive flexibility (i.e., responding adaptively when environmental contingencies change or in novel circumstances). Factor analysis showed these constructs to receive significant validation by intercorrelation of performance on distinct clusters of tasks putatively sharing some common functions (Friedman et al., 2006). However, structural equation modeling showed that although these constructs were related to one another (justifying their clustering as components of executive cognition), only that of updating working memory was correlated with measures of fluid intelligence. In neural terms, these psychometric data are probably compatible with the view that executive functions recruit distinct but interrelated networks in different prefrontal cortical regions.

The fact that the monoaminergic and cholinergic neurotransmitter systems all innervate the prefrontal cortex to varying extents, depending on the details of their innervation of different cytoarchitectonic regions, suggests that they may exert differential forms of modulation on executive cognition. Animal studies have highlighted the roles of these chemically defined systems in such functions as arousal, motivation, and stress, and these factors are known to exert significant effects on cognitive function—for example, to reduce debilitating effects of fatigue, to enhance mood and thereby performance, or to produce disruptive side effects that may impair performance according to the Yerkes-Dodson principle (see above). Given that drugs such as amphetamine and methylphenidate are known to enhance the functioning of catecholamine (i.e., noradrenaline and dopamine) systems within the prefrontal cortex, it is likely that such drugs may affect cognition, perhaps by affecting such modulatory factors. One of the drivers for this research has been the need to understand how drugs such as methylphenidate (Ritalin) and d-amphetamine actually work in both juvenile and adult attention deficit/hyperactivity disorder (ADHD). The balance of evidence indicates that these stimulants sometimes have remarkable effects on behavior and cognitive performance in these patients (Greenhill, 2001). Indeed, their efficacy provides probably the best examples of cognitive-enhancing drugs currently available. However, the analysis of the roles of the cortical monoamine systems has largely derived from studies of rodents and especially nonhuman primates.

Working Memory

The seminal demonstration of a role for dopamine (specifically D1 receptors) in spatial working memory in rhesus monkeys (Goldman-Rakic, 1998) has not been possible to confirm in humans because of the lack of suitable D1 agents for human studies. However, impairments in a test of self-ordered spatial working memory analogous to tests used in animals (e.g., of delayed alternation) for humans in patients with Parkinson's disease have been shown to be remediated by treatment with L-dopa (which probably restores dopaminergic function in the prefrontal cortex or striatum) (Lange et al., 1992). Moreover, the catecholaminergic agent methylphenidate improves spatial working memory in healthy young adult volunteers (Elliott et al., 1997). Intriguingly, a subsidiary analysis showed that the beneficial effects of methylphenidate could be predicted from the baseline working memory capacity of the volunteers, as measured by verbal digit span task; those subjects with lower span scores tended to benefit more from the drug (Mehta et al., 2000). In another study of the working memory–enhancing capacities of methylphenidate, the drug was concomitantly shown on PET to *reduce* cerebral blood flow in frontoparietal regions (Mehta et al., 2000). This might be interpreted as reflecting enhanced efficiency of prefrontal function produced by the drug. A similar principle had already been suggested by similar studies of effects of d-amphetamine on working memory using the n-back procedure (Mattay et al., 1996).

Even more remarkably, such effects of stimulants such as d-amphetamine in humans have been linked to putative measures of prefrontal cortical dopamine function, as determined by individuals bearing polymorphisms of the catecholamine-*O*-methyl transferease (*COMT*) gene, which regulates prefrontal dopamine function (Mattay et al., 2003). Those individuals with the val/val alleles associated with reduced prefrontal dopamine function tend to show greater degrees of improvement in performance and cognitive efficiency after amphetamine use than those with met/met alleles associated with enhanced prefrontal dopamine. These data are consistent with the inverted U–shaped Yerkes-Dodson function (see above).

There are several other examples of baseline-dependent effects of dopaminergic drugs on working memory, notably of the dopamine D2 receptor agonist bromocriptine (Cools, Sheridan, Jacobs, & D'Esposito, 2007; Kimberg, D'Esposito, & Farah, 1997), which lead us to conclude that the facilitatory effects of drugs such as amphetamine and methylphenidate do indeed depend on dopamine for at least some of their effects. However, there is a considerable amount of evidence from studies in rhesus monkeys that prefrontal noradrenaline also contributes to working memory function, again according to an inverted U–shaped function (Arnsten, 2009). Facilitatory and decremental effects have been observed depending crucially on dosage and which adrenoceptors or dopamine receptors are involved. Complementary modulations are produced by D1 and alpha-1 and alpha-2 receptors on signal-to-noise processing. Arnsten (2009) has developed a sophisticated account of how these effects might be related to postsynaptic intracellular processes. This work raises questions about the role of these systems in modulating input

to the prefrontal cortex and about the possible roles of attention-like functions contributing to working memory, for example, by preventing rehearsal of the memory trace over delays. This issue has generally been addressed by studies in rodents, for example, in tests of sustained attention.

Attention

A classic test of sustained attention in humans, related to the continuous performance task, is the five choice serial reaction time task. Essentially the same task has been configured for rats in an apparatus in which the animals have to detect brief visual targets presented randomly in one of five locations in order to earn food. The task can be used to measure attentional accuracy, impulsive responding, and vigilance across long test sessions, and its difficulty can be manipulated by varying the temporal predictability and discriminability of the targets, as well as the influence of distractibility and working memory load (Robbins, 2002). Optimal performance of the task depends on the integrity of the prefrontal cortex; different subregions contribute to different aspects of performance. Additionally, manipulations of the different ascending chemical systems produce sometimes overlapping and sometimes contrasting effects: accuracy is particularly susceptible to manipulations of the basal forebrain cholinergic system, a finding consistent with more recent elegant studies by measuring prefrontal cholinergic function with in vitro voltammetry (Parikh & Sarter, 2008). The disruptive effects of cholinergic depletion on accuracy can be remediated by treatment with cholinergic agents, including acetylcholine esterase inhibitors and nicotine (Muir, Everitt, & Robbins, 1995). Moreover, it has been shown for human patients with Alzheimer's disease that boosting cholinergic function with an acetylcholine esterase inhibitor also improves the accuracy of performance on this task (Sahakian et al., 1993) and in other attentional paradigms (Bentley, Driver, & Dolan, 2008).

Infusion of D1 receptor agents directly into the dorsomedial prefrontal cortex of rats also improves attentional accuracy, although this cannot be shown with systemic treatment (Granon et al., 2000). Manipulations of the coeruleocortical noradrenergic system also impair accuracy, but only other conditions of temporal unpredictability or distractibility (Carli, Robbins, Evenden, & Everitt, 1983; Cole & Robbins, 1992). Finally, while there is some evidence that depletion of cortical 5-HT may improve attentional discriminability, the major effect of

5-HT manipulations is on impulsive responding (Harrison, Everitt, & Robbins, 1997). Thus, 5-HT2A receptor antagonists, whether infused directly into the infralimbic cortex (ventromedial frontal cortex) or systemically, reduce premature responding (Winstanley et al., 2003).

Cognitive Flexibility

An analogous analysis has been made of a test of cognitive flexibility based on the Wisconsin Card Sort Test (WCST)—the intradimensional/extradimensional set-shifting paradigm from the CANTAB test battery (Dias, Robbins, & Roberts, 1996). Briefly, animals (or humans) are trained to discriminate elements from a compound stimulus comprising two perceptual dimensions (in the Wisconsin test, colors or shapes; in the CANTAB test, shapes and superimposed lines). They have to learn which dimension is relevant by trial and error, and then (with novel exemplars of the stimuli) the relevant dimension may be switched (extradimensional shift). Alternatively, the relevant dimension may remain the same with different exemplars (intradimensional shift). Reversal learning (when the compound stimuli remain the same but the one that is rewarded is switched and vice versa) is a third form of cognitive flexibility.

Accumulating data using this suite of tasks or analogous tests in humans, rodents, and monkeys are beginning to support the idea that ascending chemical modulatory systems subserve different effects on these functions (see Robbins & Roberts, 2007). In summary, reversal learning appears to be affected by 5-HT manipulations, especially in the orbitofrontal cortex of marmoset monkeys, whereas comparable manipulation of prefrontal dopamine has no effect on reversal learning per se but does impair the formation of attentional sets (i.e., serial intradimensional shifting) and, possibly, as a consequence, incidentally enhances extradimensional set-shifting. The finding of impaired intradimensional set-shifting is consistent with a recent psychopharmacological study in humans of talcapone, a drug that inhibits COMT (Apud et al., 2007). However, there may be some discrepancy among the primate and rodent studies; inconsistent effects of prefrontal cortical dopamine manipulations have been reported for extradimensional shifting, but the evidence for facilitation after treatment with selective dopamine agonists is limited to certain receptor types (Robbins & Roberts, 2007). There is a clearer pattern of evidence for cortical noradrenergic modulation of extradimensional set-shifting in rodents, whether disruption by cortical

noradrenaline loss (Tait et al., 2007) or facilitation by noradrenergic agents (Lapiz & Morilak, 2006). Nevertheless, a dissociation between reversal learning and the flexibility of attentional sets following 5-HT and catecholamine treatments appears valid. Perhaps it is due to anatomically distinct modulation in the prefrontal cortex, with reversal learning sensitive to 5-HT-dependent orbitofrontal manipulations, and attentional functions sensitive to catecholamine-dependent lateral prefrontal cortical manipulations.

The psychopharmacology of set-shifting tasks is receiving great emphasis from their extensive use in animal models of cognitive deficits in schizophrenia when screening putative cognitive-enhancing drugs with diverse novel mechanisms of action. This popularity stems in part from well-known deficits of schizophrenic patients on WCST performance and the deleterious effects of the NMDA receptor antagonist ketamine on this task (Krystal et al., 1994). The effects of novel compounds targeting glutamatergic transmission remain to be characterized in full.

Response Inhibition

This construct is generally invoked in explanations of performance on tasks in which inhibition has to be exerted, for example, of a prepotent response, which is often motor in nature (e.g., the stop signal reaction time [SSRT] task or other go/no-go tasks, of which SSRT is a special case). However, inhibition or cognitive control can also be exerted in relation to emotions (including their autonomic and behavioral expression) or memories or, indeed, thoughts. Typically, serotoninergic mechanisms have been linked to behavioral inhibition, mainly from experiments in animals. However, this action may relate more to a role for 5-HT in motivational processes, for example, aversive contingencies that lead to behavioral suppression. Perhaps surprisingly, manipulations of 5-HT through dietary (tryptophan depletion) or pharmaceutical means (e.g., treatment with selective serotonin reuptake inhibitors [SSRIs]) have been shown not to affect SSRT, even when individual genetic differences in the 5-HT transporter-promoter polymorphism are taken into account (Clark et al., 2005).

SSRT performance, however, is remediated by drugs affecting catecholaminergic neurotransmission, such as methylphenidate and atomoxetine. The beneficial effects of atomoxetine in speeding SSRT have been shown in adults with ADHD, healthy adult volunteers, and rats (Chamberlain et al., 2006, see Figure 25.4; Robinson et al.,

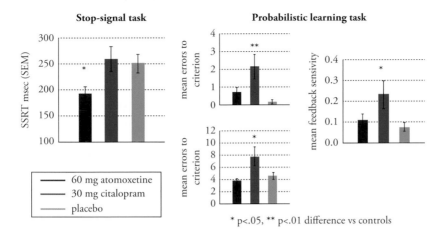

Figure 25.4 Double dissociation of effects of atomoxetine (SNRI) and citalopram (SSRI) on stop-signal reaction time performance and probabilistic discrimination learning in healthy adult volunteers.

Redrawn from Chamberlain et al. (2006) with permission of the author and publishers of *Science*.

2008). There is strong evidence that this effect can be attributed to increased synaptic concentrations of NA via blockade of the NA transporter, but this remains to be confirmed. A pharmacological fMRI study of atomoxetine's effect on SSRT task performance showed that the drug appears to enhance activation of the right inferior prefrontal cortex region often associated with performance on this task. It did so in a manner dependent on plasma levels of the drug, for successful rather than failed stop responses (Figure 25.5; Chamberlain et al., 2009). The positive effects of atomoxetine on SSRT in the rat are paralleled by analogous effects on other measures of impulsivity (which commonly tend not to intercorrelate very highly). Thus, atomoxetine also reduces impulsivity in the five-choice serial reaction time test of sustained attention in the rat and promotes choice of large, delayed rewards in a temporal discounting situation that measures "impulsive choice." These effects all occur optimally at the same dosage of the drug; however, the drug's action to promote cognitive flexibility (i.e., extradimensional shifting) may occur at a much lower dosage (Newman, Darling, & McGaughy, 2008). The precise relevance of these findings to human psychiatric disorders such as ADHD remains unclear.

Analysis of the traditional go/no-go paradigm produces a rather different pharmacological finding which suggests that there may be different neurochemical mechanisms implicated in this and the SSRT paradigm, despite their superficial similarities. A key difference appears to be in the effects of 5-HT agents or manipulations, which are much more consistent with 5-HT's purported role in behavioral inhibition. One possible explanation is that the go/no-go task reflects response selection, whereas the SSRT measure indicates a response-stopping process. Another possibility is that SSRT tasks for humans commonly provide little in the way of reinforcing feedback, in

The SNRI atomoxetine enhances task-dependent SSRT activity in right inferior frontal gyrus

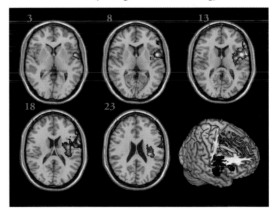

Figure 25.5 Atomoxetine significantly enhanced the BOLD response in the inferior prefrontal cortex during stop-signal reaction time performance (Reprinted from Biological Psychiatry, Vol. 65 Issue 7, Samuel R. Chamberlain et al., "Atomoxetine modulates right inferior frontal activation during inhibitory control: a pharmacological functional magnetic resonance imaging study," 550–555, Copyright 2009, with permission from Elsevier).

contrast to the go/no-go paradigm (see Eagle, Bari, & Robbins, 2008). That the motivational state may be important in determining effects of serotoninergic manipulations has been demonstrated by an investigation of the effects of low tryptophan on go/no-go performance; Crockett, Clark, and Robbins (2009) found that there was a selective effect of this treatment to produce disinhibition only when responding was punished.

Cognitive Enhancers

Clearly, much work needs to be done to evaluate the specific effects of monoaminergic agents on the main forms of executive control: attention and working memory, cognitive flexibility, and inhibition. Does a positive effect on one imply a similar effect on the other, or are dissociations evident? It is intriguing that in healthy volunteers there appear to be some differences in the profile of improvements produced by different stimulant drugs. Thus, for example, the atypical drug modafinil produced a highly significant effect on healthy volunteers' performance of the Tower of London planning test (Figure 25.6), but, unlike methylphenidate, it did not significantly eliminate errors on a self-ordered spatial working memory task (Turner et al., 2003). While modafinil improved measures of verbal working memory capacity such as digit span, it was ineffective at enhancing long-term memory and learning.

Results such as these for modafinil are interesting for a number of reasons. First, the effects were produced in non-sleep-deprived individuals, although the main therapeutic use of modafinil is for treatment of narcolepsy (with some off-label use in the treatment of jet-lag and shift-workers). Second, the mechanism by which modafinil exerts its effects are essentially unknown, although recent work has stressed its (weak) catecholaminergic action. Lastly, modafinil has attracted media interest as a cognitive-enhancing drug that can potentially improve cognitive performance in healthy normal subjects. In turn, this has catalyzed ethical debate about whether and under which circumstances it might be appropriate to boost cognition by these artificial means (e.g., Sahakian & Morein-Zamir, 2007).

This debate has been useful because, from the findings reviewed here, it seems likely that several other drugs with vastly different modes of action from those of modafinil and "typical" stimulants such as methylphenidate will be available with putative cognitive-enhancing effects. Such drugs may display quite different profiles from that of modafinil, affecting, for example, long-term memory and learning in the case of some GABAergic and glutamatergic agents. Neuropeptides such as oxytocin may also have selective effects on social cognition, if recent reports are confirmed.

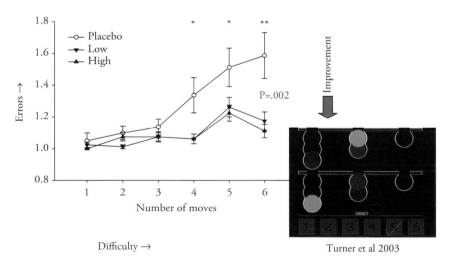

Figure 25.6 Modafinil significantly improved cognitive planning performance relative to placebo, as a function of task difficulty on the computerized Tower of London task (or Stockings of Cambridge [SoC] task; Turner et al., 2003).

Reproduced by permission of the authors and publishers. (Insert, screen-shot of the SoC task, reproduced with permission from Cambridge Cognition plc).

Conclusions

Psychoactive drugs can affect cognitive function in a bewilderingly large number of ways, often influencing diverse aspects of cognitive processing that use different neural networks. These effects will sometimes offset possible benefits of the drug, thus producing obvious costs (or side effects). Further issues will have to be resolved concerning chronic use. For example, would benefits be sustained? Might the agent have some cumulative toxic effect on the brain (or produce dependence)? It will thus be important to not only examine the validity of any claims of sustained cognitive enhancement but also screen putative cognitive enhancers for possible costs to performance or harms in the long term. In evaluating possible benefits, the nature and neural substrate of the cognitive task at hand will have to be taken into account, as will individual differences, possibly relating to genotype but also in terms of state (e.g., pathology, age, sleep deprivation, fatigue, mood). All of these factors can influence baseline level of performance, which is often a potent determinant of drug efficacy. The next period will see an accumulation of crucial information on effects of drugs on cognitive performance, whether for specific patient groups or for nonmedical purposes.

Overall, we can expect refined methodological advances as well as new theoretical approaches to contribute to this field. In experimental animals, the provision of genetic manipulations, including optogenetics and transgenic preparations that can be controlled conditionally to enhance the precision of neurochemical manipulations in restricted regions, will undoubtedly complement a burgeoning armamentarium of new compounds for further dissection of mnemonic and executive processes. This work will have to be matched in human experimental studies by enhanced and multimodal neuroimaging methodologies, including PET with a wider range of ligands than is currently available. A proper understanding of the genomic factors that affect performance in cognitive tasks and influence drug effects will also be needed, as will development of well-understood cognitive paradigms that predict real-life scenarios and can be translated readily into the building blocks of cognition shared with other species.

Acknowledgments

The author's research is supported by the Wellcome Trust and the Medical Research Council. Thanks are due to Ms. Nicola Richmond for manuscript preparation.

References

Aigner, T. G., & Mishkin, M. (1986). The effects of physostigmine and scopolamine on recognition memory in monkeys. *Behavioral Neural Biology, 45* (1), 81–87.

Apud, J. A., Mattay, V., Chen, J., Kolachana, B. S., Callicott, J. H., Rasetti, R., et al. (2007). Tolcapone improves cognition and cortical information processing in normal human subjects. *Neuropsychopharmacology, 32* (5), 1011–1020.

Arnsten, A. F. (2009). Stress signalling pathways that impair prefrontal cortex structure and function. *Nature Reviews Neuroscience, 10* (6), 410–422.

Bartus, R. T., & Dean, R. L., 3rd. (2009). Pharmaceutical treatment for cognitive deficits in Alzheimer's disease and other neurodegenerative conditions: Exploring new territory using traditional tools and established maps. *Psychopharmacology (Berlin), 202* (1-3), 15–36.

Bast, T., da Silva, B. M., & Morris, R. G. (2005). Distinct contributions of hippocampal NMDA and AMPA receptors to encoding and retrieval of one-trial place memory. *Journal of Neuroscience, 25* (25), 5845–5856.

Bentley, P., Driver, J., & Dolan, R. J. (2008). Cholinesterase inhibition modulates visual and attentional brain responses in Alzheimer's disease and health. *Brain, 131* (Pt 2), 409–424.

Berlyne, D. (1960). *Conflict, arousal and curiosity*. New York: McGraw-Hill.

Bielsky, I. F., & Young, L. J. (2004). Oxytocin, vasopressin, and social recognition in mammals. *Peptides, 25* (9), 1565–1574.

Broadbent, D. (1971). *Decision and stress*. San Diego: Academic Press.

Burns, L. H., Everitt, B. J., & Robbins, T. W. (1994). Intraamygdala infusion of the N-methyl-D-aspartate receptor antagonist AP5 impairs acquisition but not performance of discriminated approach to an appetitive CS. *Behavioral and Neural Biology, 61*, 242–250.

Carli, M., Robbins, T. W., Evenden, J. L., & Everitt, B. J. (1983). Effects of lesions to ascending noradrenergic neurones on performance of a 5-choice serial reaction task in rats; implications for theories of dorsal noradrenergic bundle function based on selective attention and arousal. *Behavioral Brain Research, 9* (3), 361–380.

Chamberlain, S. R., Hampshire, A., Muller, U., Rubia, K., Del Campo, N., Craig, K., et al. (2009). Atomoxetine modulates right inferior frontal activation during inhibitory control: A pharmacological functional magnetic resonance imaging study. *Biological Psychiatry, 65* (7), 550–555.

Chamberlain, S. R., Muller, U., Blackwell, A. D., Clark, L., Robbins, T. W., & Sahakian, B. J. (2006). Neurochemical modulation of response inhibition and probabilistic learning in humans. *Science, 311* (5762), 861–863.

Clark, L., Roiser, J. P., Cools, R., Rubinsztein, D. C., Sahakian, B. J., & Robbins, T. W. (2005). Stop signal response inhibition is not modulated by tryptophan depletion or the serotonin transporter polymorphism in healthy volunteers: Implications for the 5-HT theory of impulsivity. *Psychopharmacology (Berlin), 182* (4), 570–578.

Cole, B. J., & Robbins, T. W. (1992). Forebrain norepinephrine: Role in controlled information processing in the rat. *Neuropsychopharmacology, 7* (2), 129–142.

Cools, R., Barker, R. A., Sahakian, B. J., & Robbins, T. W. (2001). Enhanced or impaired cognitive function in Parkinson's disease as a function of dopaminergic medication and task demands. *Cerebral Cortex, 11* (12), 1136–1143.

Cools, R., Barker, R. A., Sahakian, B. J., & Robbins, T. W. (2003). L-dopa medication remediates cognitive inflexibility, but increases impulsivity in patients with Parkinson's disease. *Neuropsychologia, 41* (11), 1431–1441.

Cools, R., Lewis, S. J., Clark, L., Barker, R. A., & Robbins, T. W. (2007). L-DOPA disrupts activity in the nucleus accumbens during reversal learning in Parkinson's disease. *Neuropsychopharmacology, 32* (1), 180–189.

Cools R., Roberts A. C., & Robbins, T. W. (2008) Serotoninergic regulation of emotional and behavioural control processes. *Trends in Cognitive Sciences, 12,* 31–40.

Cools, R., Sheridan, M., Jacobs, E., & D'Esposito, M. (2007). Impulsive personality predicts dopamine-dependent changes in frontostriatal activity during component processes of working memory. *Journal of Neuroscience, 27* (20), 5506–5514.

Cooper, B., Bloom, F., & Roth, R. H. (2002). *The biochemical basis of neuropharmacology* (8th ed. p. 405). New York: Oxford University Press.

Corlett, P. R., Honey, G. D., Aitken, M. R., Dickinson, A., Shanks, D. R., Absalom, A. R., et al. (2006). Frontal responses during learning predict vulnerability to the psychotogenic effects of ketamine: Linking cognition, brain activity, and psychosis. *Archives of General Psychiatry, 63* (6), 611–621.

Crockett, M. J., Clark, L., & Robbins, T. W. (2009). Reconciling the role of serotonin in behavioral inhibition and aversion: Acute tryptophan depletion abolishes punishment-induced inhibition in humans. *Journal of Neuroscience, 29* (38), 11993–11999.

Curran, H. V. (1991). Benzodiazepines, memory and mood: A review. *Psychopharmacology (Berlin), 105* (1), 1–8.

Dalley, J. W., Laane, K., Theobald, D. E., Armstrong, H. C., Corlett, P. R., Chudasama, Y., et al. (2005). Time-limited modulation of appetitive Pavlovian memory by D1 and NMDA receptors in the nucleus accumbens. *Proceedings of the National Academy of Sciences U S A, 102* (17), 6189–6194.

Davis, K. L., Mohs, R. C., Tinklenberg, J. R., Pfefferbaum, A., Hollister, L. E., & Kopell, B. S. (1978). Physostigmine: Improvement of long-term memory processes in normal humans. *Science, 201* (4352), 272–274.

Day, M., Langston, R., & Morris, R. G. (2003). Glutamate-receptor-mediated encoding and retrieval of paired-associate learning. *Nature, 424* (6945), 205–209.

Dias, R., Robbins, T. W., & Roberts, A. C. (1996). Primate analogue of the Wisconsin Card Sorting Test: Effects of excitotoxic lesions of the prefrontal cortex in the marmoset. *Behavioral Neuroscience, 110* (5), 872–886.

Duncan, J., Seitz, R. J., Kolodny, J., Bor, D., Herzog, H., Ahmed, A., et al. (2000). A neural basis for general intelligence. *Science, 289* (5478), 457–460.

Durstewicz, D., Seamans, J. K., & Sejnowski, T. (2000). Dopamine-mediated stabilization of delay-period activity in a network model of prefrontal cortex. *Journal of Neurophysiology, 19* , 2807–2822.

Eagle, D. M., Bari, A., & Robbins, T. W. (2008). The neuropsychopharmacology of action inhibition: Cross-species translation of the stop-signal and go/no-go tasks. *Psychopharmacology (Berlin), 199* (3), 439–456.

Elliott, R., Sahakian, B. J., Matthews, K., Bannerjea, A., Rimmer, J., & Robbins, T. W. (1997). Effects of methylphenidate on spatial working memory and planning in healthy young adults. *Psychopharmacology (Berlin), 131* (2), 196–206.

Eysenck, M. (1982). *Attention and arousal.* Heidelberg: Springer-Verlang.

Friedman, N. P., Miyake, A., Corley, R. P., Young, S. E., Defries, J. C., & Hewitt, J. K. (2006). Not all executive functions are related to intelligence. *Psychological Science, 17* (2), 172–179.

Furey, M. L., Pietrini, P., & Haxby, J. V. (2000). Cholinergic enhancement and increased selectivity of perceptual processing during working memory. *Science, 290* (5500), 2315–2319.

Goff, D. C., Herz, L., Posever, T., Shih, V., Tsai, G., Henderson, D. C., et al. (2005). A six-month, placebo-controlled trial of D-cycloserine co-administered with conventional antipsychotics in schizophrenia patients. *Psychopharmacology (Berlin), 179* (1), 144–150.

Goff, D. C., Tsai, G., Levitt, J., Amico, E., Manoach, D., Schoenfeld, D. A., et al. (1999). A placebo-controlled trial of D-cycloserine added to conventional neuroleptics in patients with schizophrenia. *Archives of General Psychiatry, 56* (1), 21–27.

Goldman-Rakic, P. S. (1998). The prefrontal landscape: Implications of functional architecture for understanding human mentation and the central executive. In A. C. Roberts, T. W. Robbins, & L. Weiskrantz (Eds.), *The prefrontal cortex: Executive and cognitive functions* (pp. 97–102). Oxford: Oxford University Press.

Granon, S., Passetti, F., Thomas, K. L., Dalley, J. W., Everitt, B. J., & Robbins, T. W. (2000). Enhanced and impaired attentional performance after infusion of D1 dopaminergic receptor agents into rat prefrontal cortex. *Journal of Neuroscience, 20* (3), 1208–1215.

Greenhill, L. (2001). Clinical effects of stimulant medication in ADHD. In M. Solanto, A. F. Arnsten, & F. Castellanos (Eds.), *Stimulant drugs and ADHD* (pp. 31–71). New York: Oxford University Press.

Harrison, A. A., Everitt, B. J., & Robbins, T. W. (1997). Central 5-HT depletion enhances impulsive responding without affecting the accuracy of attentional performance: Interactions with dopaminergic mechanisms. *Psychopharmacology (Berlin), 133* (4), 329–342.

Hebb, D. O. (1955). Drives and the C.N.S. (conceptual nervous system). *Psychological Review, 62* (4), 243–254.

Heinrichs, M., Meinlschmidt, G., Wippich, W., Ehlert, U., & Hellhammer, D. H. (2004). Selective amnesic effects of oxytocin on human memory. *Physiological Behavior, 83* (1), 31–38.

Honey, R. A., Turner, D. C., Honey, G. D., Sharar, S. R., Kumaran, D., Pomarol-Clotet, E., et al. (2003). Subdissociative dose ketamine produces a deficit in manipulation but not maintenance of the contents of working memory. *Neuropsychopharmacology, 28* (11), 2037–2044.

Kew, J. N., & Kemp, J. A. (2005). Ionotropic and metabotropic glutamate receptor structure and pharmacology. *Psychopharmacology (Berlin), 179* (1), 4–29.

Kim, J. J., Fanselow, M. S., DeCola, J. P., & Landeira-Fernandez, J. (1992). Selective impairment of long-term but not short-term conditional fear by the N-methyl-D-aspartate antagonist APV. *Behavioral Neuroscience, 106* (4), 591–596.

Kimberg, D. Y., D'Esposito, M., & Farah, M. J. (1997). Effects of bromocriptine on human subjects depend on working memory capacity. *Neuroreport, 8* (16), 3581–3585.

Koelega, H. S. (1993). Stimulant drugs and vigilance performance: A review. *Psychopharmacology (Berlin), 111* (1), 1–16.

Krystal, J. H., Karper, L. P., Seibyl, J. P., Freeman, G. K., Delaney, R., Bremner, J. D., et al. (1994). Subanesthetic effects of the noncompetitive NMDA antagonist, ketamine, in humans. Psychotomimetic, perceptual, cognitive, and neuroendocrine responses. *Archives of General Psychiatry, 51* (3), 199–214.

Lange, K. W., Robbins, T. W., Marsden, C. D., James, M., Owen, A. M., & Paul, G. M. (1992). L-dopa withdrawal in Parkinson's disease selectively impairs cognitive performance in tests sensitive to frontal lobe dysfunction. *Psychopharmacology (Berlin), 107* (2-3), 394–404.

Lapiz, M. D., & Morilak, D. A. (2006). Noradrenergic modulation of cognitive function in rat medial prefrontal cortex as measured by attentional set shifting capability. *Neuroscience, 137* (3), 1039–1049.

Logan, G. D., Cowan, W. B., & Davis, K. A. (1984). On the ability to inhibit simple and choice reaction time responses: a model and a method. *Journal of Experimental Psychology. Human Perception and Performance, 10* (2), 276–291.

Lynch, G. (2002). Memory enhancement: The search for mechanism-based drugs. *Nature Neuroscience, 5*(Suppl), 1035–1038.

Matsumoto, M, &, Hikosaka, O. (2007) Lateral habenula as a source of negative reward signals in dopamine neurons. *Nature Neuroscience, 447,* 1111–1115.

Matsuoka, N., & Aigner, T. G. (1996). D-cycloserine, a partial agonist at the glycine site coupled to N-methyl-D-aspartate receptors, improves visual recognition memory in rhesus monkeys. *Journal of Pharmacology and Experimental Therapeutics, 278* (2), 891–897.

Mattay, V. S., Berman, K. F., Ostrem, J. L., Esposito, G., Van Horn, J. D., Bigelow, L. B., et al. (1996). Dextroamphetamine enhances "neural network-specific" physiological signals: A positron emission tomography rCBF study. *Journal of Neuroscience, 16* (15), 4816–4822.

Mattay, V. S., Goldberg, T. E., Fera, F., Hariri, A. R., Tessitore, A., Egan, M. F., et al. (2003). Catechol O-methyltransferase val158-met genotype and individual variation in the brain response to amphetamine. *Proceedings of the National Academy of Sciences U S A, 100* (10), 6186–6191.

Mehta, M. A., Owen, A. M., Sahakian, B. J., Mavaddat, N., Pickard, J. D., & Robbins, T. W. (2000). Methylphenidate enhances working memory by modulating discrete frontal and parietal lobe regions in the human brain. *Journal of Neuroscience, 20* (6), RC65.

Miserendino, M. J. D., Sananes, C. B., Melia, K. R., & Davis, M. (1990). Blocking of acquisition but not expression of conditioned fear- potentiated startle by NMDA antagonists in the amygdala. *Nature, 345,* 716–718.

Mohler, H. (2007). Functional relevance of GABA-A receptor subtypes. In S. Enna & H. Mohler (Eds.), *The Receptors: The GABA receptors* (3rd ed., pp. 23–40). Totowa NJ: Humana Press.

Monahan, J. B., Handelmann, G. E., Hood, W. F., & Cordi, A. A. (1989). D-cycloserine, a positive modulator of the N-methyl-D-aspartate receptor, enhances performance of learning tasks in rats. *Pharmacology, Biochemistry, and Behavior, 34* (3), 649–653.

Morris, R. G., Anderson, E., Lynch, G. S., & Baudry, M. (1986). Selective impairment of learning and blockade of long-term potentiation by an N-methyl-D-aspartate receptor antagonist, AP5. *Nature, 319* (6056), 774–776.

Muir, J. L., Everitt, B. J., & Robbins, T. W. (1995). Reversal of visual attentional dysfunction following lesions of the cholinergic basal forebrain by physostigmine and nicotine but not by the 5-HT3 receptor antagonist, ondansetron. *Psychopharmacology (Berlin), 118* (1), 82–92.

Murray, E. A., & Bussey, T. J. (1999). Perceptual-mnemonic functions of the perirhinal cortex. *Trends in Cognitive Sciences, 3* (4), 142–151.

Nader, K. (2003). Memory traces unbound. *Trends in Neuroscience, 26* (2), 65–72.

Newman, L. A., Darling, J., & McGaughy, J. (2008). Atomoxetine reverses attentional deficits produced by noradrenergic deafferentation of medial prefrontal cortex. *Psychopharmacology (Berlin), 200* (1), 39–50.

Nutt, D. J., Besson, M., Wilson, S. J., Dawson, G. R., & Lingford-Hughes, A. R. (2007). Blockade of alcohol's amnestic activity in humans by an alpha5 subtype benzodiazepine receptor inverse agonist. *Neuropharmacology, 53* (7), 810–820.

Packard, M. G., & Teather, L. A. (1997). Double dissociation of hippocampal and dorsal-striatal memory systems by post-training intracerebral injections of 2-amino-5-phosphonopentanoic acid. *Behavioral Neuroscience, 111* (3), 543–551.

Parikh, V., & Sarter, M. (2008). Cholinergic mediation of attention: contributions of phasic and tonic increases in prefrontal cholinergic activity. *Annals of the New York Academy of Sciences, 1129,* 225–235.

Perry, E. K., Tomlinson, B. E., Blessed, G., Bergmann, K., Gibson, P. H., & Perry, R. H. (1978). Correlation of cholinergic abnormalities with senile plaques and mental test scores in senile dementia. *British Medical Journal, 2* (6150), 1457–1459.

Pessiglione, M., Seymour, B., Flandin, G., Dolan, R. J., & Frith, C. D. (2006). Dopamine-dependent prediction errors underpin reward-seeking behaviour in humans. *Nature, 442* (7106), 1042–1045.

Pitkanen, M., Sirvio, J., MacDonald, E., Niemi, S., Ekonsalo, T., & Riekkinen, P., Sr. (1995). The effects of D-cycloserine and MK-801 on the performance of rats in two spatial learning and memory tasks. *European Neuropsychopharmacology, 5* (4), 457–463.

Pitman, R., Brunet, A., Orr, S., Tremblay, J., & Nader, K. (2006). A novel treatment for post-traumatic stress disorder by reconsolidation blockade with propanolol. *Neuropsychopharmacology, 31,* S8–S9.

Porrino, L. J., Daunais, J. B., Rogers, G. A., Hampson, R. E., & Deadwyler, S. A. (2005). Facilitation of task performance and removal of the effects of sleep deprivation by an ampakine (CX717) in nonhuman primates. *PLoS Biology, 3* (9), e299.

Ressler, K. J., Rothbaum, B. O., Tannenbaum, L., Anderson, P., Graap, K., Zimand, E., et al. (2004). Cognitive enhancers as adjuncts to psychotherapy: Use of D-cycloserine in phobic individuals to facilitate extinction of fear. *Archives of General Psychiatry, 61* (11), 1136–1144.

Riedel, G., Micheau, J., Lam, A. G., Roloff, E. L., Martin, S. J., Bridge, H., et al. (1999). Reversible neural inactivation reveals hippocampal participation in several memory processes. *Nature Neuroscience, 2* (10), 898–905.

Rimmele, U., Hediger, K., Heinrichs, M., & Klaver, P. (2009). Oxytocin makes a face in memory familiar. *Journal of Neuroscience, 29* (1), 38–42.

Robbins, T. W. (1984). Cortical noradrenaline, attention and arousal. *Psychological Medicine, 14* (1), 13–21.

Robbins, T. W. (1996). Dissociating executive functions of the prefrontal cortex. *Philosophical Transactions of the Royal Society of London, Series B: Biological Sciences, 351* (1346), 1463–1470; discussion 1470–1461.

Robbins, T. W. (2002). The 5-choice serial reaction time task: Behavioural pharmacology and functional neurochemistry. *Psychopharmacology (Berlin), 163* (3-4), 362–380.

Robbins, T. W., & Roberts, A. C. (2007). Differential regulation of fronto-executive function by the monoamines and acetylcholine. *Cerebral Cortex, 17*(Suppl 1), i151–i160.

Robinson, E. S., Eagle, D. M., Mar, A. C., Bari, A., Banerjee, G., Jiang, X., et al. (2008). Similar effects of the selective noradrenaline reuptake inhibitor atomoxetine on three distinct forms of impulsivity in the rat. *Neuropsychopharmacology, 33* (5), 1028–1037.

Sahakian, B., & Morein-Zamir, S. (2007). Professor's little helper. *Nature, 450* (7173), 1157–1159.

Sahakian, B. J., Owen, A. M., Morant, N. J., Eagger, S. A., Boddington, S., Crayton, L., et al. (1993). Further analysis of the cognitive effects of tetrahydroaminoacridine (THA) in Alzheimer's disease: Assessment of attentional and mnemonic function using CANTAB. *Psychopharmacology (Berlin), 110* (4), 395–401.

Schmitt, W. B., Deacon, R. M., Seeburg, P. H., Rawlins, J. N., & Bannerman, D. M. (2003). A within-subjects, within-task demonstration of intact spatial reference memory and impaired spatial working memory in glutamate receptor-A-deficient mice. *Journal of Neuroscience, 23* (9), 3953–3959.

Schultz, W. (2002). Getting formal with dopamine and reward. *Neuron, 36* (2), 241–263.

Servan-Schreiber, D., Printz, H., & Cohen, J. D. (1990). A network model of catecholamine effects: Gain, signal-to-noise ratio, and behavior. *Science, 249* (4971), 892–895.

Shallice, T., & Burgess, P. (1996). The domain of supervisory processes and temporal organization of behaviour. *Philosophical Transactions of the Royal Society London, Series B: Biological Sciences, 351* (1346), 1405–1411; discussion 1411–1402.

Squire, L. R. (1992). Memory and the hippocampus: A synthesis from findings with rats, monkeys, and humans. *Psychological Review, 99* (2), 195–231.

Steele, R. J., & Morris, R. G. (1999). Delay-dependent impairment of a matching-to-place task with chronic and intrahippocampal infusion of the NMDA-antagonist D-AP5. *Hippocampus, 9* (2), 118–136.

Swainson, R., Rogers, R. D., Sahakian, B. J., Summers, B. A., Polkey, C. E., & Robbins, T. W. (1999). Probabilistic learning and reversal deficits in patients with Parkinson's disease

or frontal or temporal lobe lesions: Possible adverse effects of dA-ergic medication. *Neuropsychologia, 38* , 596–612.

Tait, D. S., Brown, V. J., Farovik, A., Theobald, D. E., Dalley, J. W., & Robbins, T. W. (2007). Lesions of the dorsal noradrenergic bundle impair attentional set-shifting in the rat. *European Journal of Neuroscience, 25* (12), 3719–3724.

Tang, Y., Mishkin, M., & Aigner, T. G. (1997). Effects of muscarinic blockade in perirhinal cortex during visual recognition. *Proceedings of the National Academy of Sciences U S A, 94* (23), 12667–12669.

Tsai, G. E., Falk, W. E., Gunther, J., & Coyle, J. T. (1999). Improved cognition in Alzheimer's disease with short-term D-cycloserine treatment. *American Journal of Psychiatry, 156* (3), 467–469.

Turner, D. C., Robbins, T. W., Clark, L., Aron, A. R., Dowson, J., & Sahakian, B. J. (2003). Cognitive enhancing effects of modafinil in healthy volunteers. *Psychopharmacology (Berlin), 165* (3), 260–269.

Walker, D. L., Ressler, K. J., Lu, K. T., & Davis, M. (2002). Facilitation of conditioned fear extinction by systemic administration or intra-amygdala infusions of D-cycloserine as assessed with fear-potentiated startle in rats. *Journal of Neuroscience, 22* (6), 2343–2351.

Weiss, B., & Laties, V. G. (1962). Enhancement of human performance by caffeine and the amphetamines. *Pharmacology Review, 14* , 1–36.

Winstanley, C. A., Chudasama, Y., Dalley, J. W., Theobald, D. E., Glennon, J. C., & Robbins, T. W. (2003). Intra-prefrontal 8-OH-DPAT and M100907 improve visuospatial attention and decrease impulsivity on the five-choice serial reaction time task in rats. *Psychopharmacology (Berlin), 167* (3), 304–314.

Winters, B. D., & Bussey, T. J. (2005). Glutamate receptors in perirhinal cortex mediate encoding, retrieval, and consolidation of object recognition memory. *Journal of Neuroscience, 25* (17), 4243–4251.

Yerkes, R. M., & Dodson, J. D. (1908). The relation of strength of stimulus to rapidity of habit-formation. *Journal of Comparative Neurology and Psychiatry, 18* , 459–482.

Young, S. L., Bohenek, D. L., & Fanselow, M. S. (1994). NMDA processes mediate anterograde amnesia of contextual fear conditioning induced by hippocampal damage: immunization against amnesia by context preexposure. *Behavioral Neuroscience, 108* (1), 19–29.

Clinical Applications

Attention Deficit/Hyperactivity Disorder (ADHD)

Chandan J. Vaidya

Abstract

Convergent evidence from brain imaging, behavioral, and molecular genetic studies indicates that neuropathophysiology of attention deficit/hyperactivity disorder (ADHD) is rooted in dopamine-mediated circuits encompassing prefrontal cortex and basal ganglia, which are important for executive control and motivational behavior. However, cognitive deficits in ADHD extend beyond executive and motivational domains to include spatial attention, temporal processing, and motor execution. Atypical structural and functional anatomy also includes parietal and temporal cortices. A primary challenge for future work is identifying genetic and neurobiological underpinnings of the observed neurocognitive heterogeneity in ADHD that is also paralleled in its phenotypic expression.

Key Words: prefrontal, striatal, dopamine, catecholamine, stimulants

Introduction

Attention deficit hyperactivity disorder (ADHD) is estimated to occur in 8.6% of 8- to 15-year-old children, with higher rates in males than in females (2.1:1) (Merikangas et al., 2010). Its symptoms include age-inappropriate and maladaptive levels of inattention, hyperactivity, and impulsivity. Symptoms persist, fully or partially, in 78% of American children into young adulthood (Biederman, Petty, Clarke, Lomedico, & Faraone, 2011). The disorder characterizes 4% of adults worldwide (Faraone, Sergeant, Gillberg, & Biederman, 2003). The primary form of treatment includes stimulant medications such as methylphenidate and amphetamines that enhance catecholaminergic transmission. ADHD is an inherited condition, with a polygenic mode of transmission suspected to include catecholaminergic genes (Faraone et al., 2005). Research conducted over the past 20 years has confirmed that ADHD is a brain-based disorder, dispelling notions of it being the outcome of poor parenting or cultural changes. This chapter describes current knowledge about

the neuropathophysiology of ADHD gleaned from behavioral, brain imaging, and molecular genetic studies of children and adults.

Neuropsychological Profile of ADHD

The diagnosis of ADHD involves parent and teacher reports of behaviors indicating age-inappropriate levels of inattention (e.g., making careless mistakes, difficulty concentrating), hyperactivity (e.g., fidgeting, excessive running or climbing), and/or impulsivity (e.g., difficulty waiting one's turn, talking excessively). These behaviors must be present before 7 years of age and persist for 6 months in at least two settings (e.g., home and school) (American Psychiatric Association, 2000). Although three subtypes are recognized (combined-type, predominantly inattentive, predominantly impulsive) in the *Diagnostic and Statistical Manual for Mental Disorders, 4th Edition* (DSM-IV), they do not account for the high degree of symptom heterogeneity observed in ADHD. Further heterogeneity is induced by comorbidity with other psychiatric conditions such as mood disorders (e.g., depression, anxiety), conduct disorder, oppositional defiant disorder, obsessive-compulsive disorder, Tourette's, developmental dyslexia, or autism spectrum disorders, as well as nonpsychiatric conditions such as sleep disorders. Assessment of symptoms varies across settings; primary care settings rely primarily on parent-teacher reports, whereas specialty care settings supplement them with observational reports, assessment of academic achievement, and/or performance measures of sustained attention (e.g., Test of Variables of Attention [TOVA]; Chan, Hopkins, Perrin, Herrerias, & Homer, 2005).

The primary cognitive domain affected in ADHD is executive function. Executive function involves the control of attention and action in the service of goals and is accomplished by component processes of working memory, inhibitory control, flexible switching of task-set, and self-monitoring. Impaired performance in children with ADHD is readily apparent on problem-solving tasks that evoke multiple component processes (e.g., Tower of Hanoi). However, this deficit results from reduced performance in all component processes as observed in a meta-analysis of 83 studies involving 6,700 subjects with effect sizes ranging from 0.4 to 0.7 (Willcutt, Doyle, Nigg, Faraone, & Pennington, 2005). Among component processes of executive function, behavioral studies have focused most on working memory, the temporary maintenance, manipulation or both of information and response inhibition, the ability to inhibit prepotent responses. Spatial working memory appears to be more sensitive to ADHD than verbal working memory, with effect sizes ranging from .85 to 1.14 (Martinussen, Hayden, Hogg-Johnson, & Tannock, 2005). Response inhibition as measured by go/no-go and stop signal tasks is also highly sensitive to ADHD (effect size .58 in meta-analysis of 17 studies including 1,200 children; Lijffijt, Kenemans, Verbaten, & van Engeland, 2005). Thus, executive dysfunction is thought to be a cardinal feature of ADHD.

It is important to note, however, that executive function is neither necessary nor sufficient to account for all cases of ADHD. When performance distributions are compared between ADHD and control children, there is a high degree of overlap, yielding the fairly modest effect sizes mentioned above (Nigg, Willcutt, Doyle, & Sonuga-Barke, 2005). Nigg et al. (2005) compared the co-occurrence of deficits on five component processes of executive function and found that only 10% of ADHD children were impaired on all five; further, 21% of ADHD children and 53% of control children were unimpaired

on all five processes. Thus, there is significant heterogeneity in the degree of executive dysfunction among children with ADHD. Many such children exhibit deficits on reward-related decision-making tasks in the form of delay aversion, preference for immediate albeit small rewards relative to delayed larger rewards, and more risky decision-making on gambling tasks (reviewed in Luman, Oosterlaan, & Sergeant, 2005). Most importantly, such motivational deficits and those on executive tasks are dissociable; within the same group of ADHD children, response inhibition and delay aversion were uncorrelated but together accounted for 90% of the ADHD cases (Solanto et al., 2001).

Several nonexecutive deficits have also been observed in ADHD. Specifically, reaction times are slower on early trials, suggesting arousal deficiencies (Oosterlaan & Sergeant, 1998), and vary to a greater degree from trial to trial within individuals, suggesting cognitive inefficiency (Castellanos et al., 2005). In addition, numerous studies, using time estimation and reproduction tasks, have documented deficits in temporal processing in children and adults with ADHD (reviewed in Toplak, Dockstader, & Tannock, 2006). Further, studies of spatial attention have found a rightward attentional bias (i.e., left-sided inattention) in children with ADHD (Bellgrove et al., 2008; Chan et al., 2009). Studies of skill learning showed that automatic acquisition of cognitive skills, both with higher and lower working memory demands, was slower in children with ADHD (Huang-Pollock & Karalunas, 2010). Implicit learning was also selectively impaired for perceptual-motor sequences but not for visual context (Barnes, Howard, Howard, Kenealy, & Vaidya, 2010). Therefore, cognitive impairment in ADHD is not limited to executive and motivational function but extends to lower-level motoric, temporal, and selective attention processes.

Summary

Diagnosis of ADHD symptoms is confounded by a high degree of phenotypic heterogeneity that is not fully accounted for by current diagnostic taxonomy. Although deficits in the domain of executive function have been consistently identified across studies, recent studies suggest more widespread impairment, including motivational function and lower-level nonexecutive processes.

Neuroanatomical Basis of ADHD
Structural Imaging of ADHD

A large body of studies using structural magnetic resonance imaging (MRI) has documented altered brain morphology in ADHD. Most significant among these are studies of growth trajectories using mixed cross-sectional and longitudinal designs in large samples (e.g., >150) of 5- to 18-year-old children. The main findings from this work are presented below.

Developmental trajectories show that ADHD is characterized by reduced brain volume and delayed global cortical maturation. Children with ADHD had approximately 4% smaller volume, relative to controls, of the total cerebrum, cerebellum, and the four lobes, and total and lobular gray and white matter, despite adjusting for differences in vocabulary scores, medication status, and height (Castellanos et al., 2002). Furthermore, these differences were not moderated by age, gender, or medication status. Examination of the thickness of the cortical mantle, thought to reflect maturational changes in synaptic density, showed that children with ADHD had thinner cortices globally with a delayed maturational course, in studies employing mixed (Shaw, Eckstrand, et al., 2007) and cross-sectional (Narr et al., 2009) designs. While the sequence of changes in cortical thickness proceeded from sensory to association cortices in both groups, children with ADHD attained peak cortical thickness later, between 10 and 11 years of age rather than 7 and 8 years. Further evidence for the association of slower cortical thinning with symptoms of ADHD also comes from examining typically developing children who vary in severity of behaviors exhibiting hyperactivity and impulsivity (Shaw et al., 2011): those with higher rates of these behaviors had a slower rate of cortical thinning, particularly in frontal cortex. Thus, ADHD is characterized by delayed maturation rather than an aberrant course of brain development.

In addition to the global differences noted above, regionally selective differences have also been observed. Volumetric developmental trajectories converged between groups in adolescence for the caudate nucleus, in that it was smaller in ADHD in childhood but normalized by adolescence (Castellanos et al., 2002). Development of the cortical mantle in children with ADHD did not show the same hemispheric asymmetries as controls, particularly for frontal cortex (Shaw, Lalonde, et al., 2009). Specifically, as right-handed control children entered adolescence, cortical thickness increased in the right orbital and inferior frontal cortex and in the left occipital cortex. Children with ADHD, however, showed the occipital increase but not that in frontal cortex. Further, precentral gyrus and superior and medial prefrontal cortex showed more pronounced cortical thinning in ADHD children

than in controls (Shaw et al., 2006). Taken together, these findings suggest that regions within frontal cortex and striatum have altered maturational courses in ADHD.

Brain maturation in selected regions is moderated by stimulant use (Shaw, Sharp, et al., 2009) and clinical outcome (Shaw et al., 2006) in children with ADHD. Children whose symptoms persisted into adolescence had thinner medial prefrontal cortex at initial scanning (mean age, 8.7 [1.9] years) relative to those whose symptoms resolved and to controls. Further, developmental trajectories of cortical thickness were parallel except in right parietal cortex, where they converged in adolescence with controls for the group with symptom remittance. During the period between ages 12.5 and 16.4 years, which is dominated by cortical thinning, more rapid cortical thinning was observed in the subset of ADHD children who went off medication during that span of 4 years than in those who stayed on medication and in controls, selectively in right motor cortex, left ventrolateral prefrontal cortex, and right parieto-occipital cortex. Thus, stimulant use appears to exert a protective effect on cortical maturation in those regions. These findings suggest that stimulant use and clinical outcome alter the maturation of selective anterior and posterior cortical regions.

Nondevelopmental studies comparing small samples of ADHD subjects with age-matched controls have reported localized differences in regions other than those revealed by the developmental studies discussed above (see reviews by Seidman, Valera, & Makris, 2005; Shaw & Rabin, 2009). Across studies, there were smaller volumes of frontal cortex as a whole and of its subregions—premotor cortex, posterior cingulate, as well as anterior and medial temporal lobes, amygdala, cerebellar lobules, and basal ganglia structures (caudate, globus pallidus, putamen, ventral striatum). Further, a meta-analysis of studies reporting voxel-based gray matter differences found that reductions in right-hemispheric putamen/globus pallidus in ADHD subjects were consistently observed across multiple studies (Ellison-Wright, Ellison-Wright, & Bullmore, 2008). However, many findings are not equivocal, as there is at least one study for each region reporting no differences between groups. Also, while most studies have found smaller regions in those with ADHD than in controls, one study found larger inferior parietal and posterior temporal regions in ADHD adolescents than in controls (Sowell et al., 2003). In addition to these differences in gray matter, several studies have observed thinner corpus collosum in children with ADHD, particularly in posterior aspects (see Konrad & Eickhoff, 2010, for a review). Two studies comparing white matter microstructure rather than volume found reduced integrity of white matter in right premotor and striatal areas, cerebellum, and left parieto-occipital areas in children with ADHD (Ashtari et al., 2005) and in the cingulum bundle and the superior fasciculus, which are medial and lateral tracts, respectively, connecting frontal to parietal lobes, in adults with ADHD (Makris et al., 2008). Thus, both gray and white matter characteristics of multiple regions in frontal, parietal, and temporal lobes are affected in ADHD.

Functional Imaging of ADHD—with Cognitive Challenge

Findings from functional magnetic resonance imaging (fMRI) of ADHD support abnormal engagement of the regions implicated by the structural findings reviewed above. It is useful to view the functional anatomical findings in the context of functional circuits, as they elucidate cognitive domains that are most sensitive to ADHD. From that viewpoint, atypical functional anatomy in ADHD includes frontostriato-cerebellar circuitry subserving executive function, mesolimbic circuits important for reward-related decision-making, motor-execution circuitry, and parieto-temporal circuitry important for visual-spatial attentional function and its contribution to executive processes (see reviews by Makris, Biederman, Monuteaux, & Seidman, 2009; Vaidya & Stollstorff, 2008). Figure 26.1 shows the

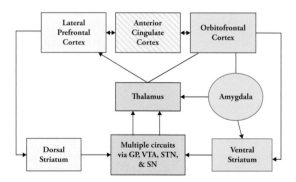

Figure 26.1 Primary circuitry affected in ADHD. Red outline denotes components executive control circuits; green outline denotes structures of the limbic system important for motivational functions. Regions in yellow form the mesocortical dopaminergic pathway and those in blue form the mesolimbic dopaminergic pathway; yellow-blue stripes show regions important for both pathways. Regions in grey are subcortical structures (thalamus, GP – Globus Pallidus) and midbrain nuclei (VTA – Ventral Tegmentum Area; STN – Subthalamic Nuclei; SN – Substantia Nigra) that are part of multiple circuits.

affected circuitry in ADHD as reflected by the most consistent findings across studies.

Studies of executive function that draws on frontal cortex and dorsal striatum, regions comprising mesocortical circuitry, and its thalamic connections to the cerebellum for the most part reveal *reduced* engagement in ADHD (see meta-analysis by Dickstein, Bannon, Castellanos, & Milham, 2006). It has been evoked on tasks requiring relatively process-pure component processes of executive function, such as response inhibition (e.g., stop-signal, go/no-go, Stroop), working memory (e.g., n-back task, PASAT, mental rotation), interference control (e.g., flanker, multi-source interference task), and response switching (e.g., Meiran switch task). Indeed, these functions rely on subregions within frontal cortex to different extents, such as dorsal anterior cingulate for monitoring response conflict, ventrolateral prefrontal cortex for inhibition and selection of responses, and dorsolateral prefrontal cortex for maintaining information in working memory. All of these regions, in addition to the striatum, were underactivated in ADHD subjects relative to controls. However, level of performance appears to influence prefrontal engagement; lower-performing adolescents with ADHD (also with persisting symptoms) activated inferior ventrolateral and frontopolar cortices to a greater extent than controls in some studies (Schulz et al., 2004; Schulz, Newcorn, Fan, Tang, & Halperin, 2005). Further, response inhibition and selection tasks drawing on use of temporal information were associated with reduced cerebellar involvement in children and adolescents with ADHD (Durston et al., 2007). In sum, atypical frontostriato-cerebellar involvement during processes contributing to executive function is ubiquitous in ADHD.

Studies of motivational function in ADHD have revealed a pattern of increases and decreases in activation of orbitofrontal cortex, ventral striatum, medial temporal regions, and anterior cingulate structures comprising mesolimbic circuitry. Adolescents and adults with ADHD showed underactivation of the ventral striatum during anticipation of rewards (Scheres, Milham, Knutson, & Castellanos, 2007; Strohle et al., 2008). However, this region was activated in ADHD adolescents upon delivery of reward, as was the orbitofrontal cortex in ADHD adults. During a gambling task, adults with ADHD had reduced activation in medial temporal regions but greater activation in dorsal anterior cingulate (Ernst et al., 2003). This pattern suggests that altered functional connectivity among prefrontal and limbic regions may mediate abnormal reward processing in ADHD.

Parietal-temporal regions have shown atypical activation in ADHD subjects during a variety of tasks, including executive function. During mental rotation, children with ADHD had reduced activation in right inferior parietal cortex (Vance et al., 2007) and in right superior parietal and temporal cortices (Silk et al., 2005). Right parietal reduction in activation in children with ADHD was also observed during visual search tasks involving voluntary attention (Booth et al., 2005). Further, lateral and medial parietal-temporal reductions in activation were observed in ADHD subjects during attentional tasks evoking involuntary attention (e.g., oddball; Rubia, Smith, Brammer, & Taylor, 2007; Stevens, Pearlson, & Kiehl, 2007; Tamm, Menon, & Reiss, 2006). Interestingly, these regions were often more activated in ADHD subjects than in controls on a variety of executive tasks, including mental rotation (Silk et al., 2005), response inhibition (Durston et al., 2003; Rubia et al., 1999; Vaidya et al., 2005), flanker interference (Vaidya et al., 2005), and working memory (Schweitzer et al., 2000). The mixed pattern of increases and decreases of the same regions depending on functional domain indicates age-inappropriate involvement of posterior cortices, perhaps owing to use of different strategies or to reduced prefrontal control of posterior association areas.

In addition to atypical activation subserving executive and attentional functions, motor circuitry involved in execution of responses has also shown atypicalities in ADHD. During self-paced finger-to-thumb sequencing, contralateral primary motor and right superior parietal regions were less activated in ADHD than in control children (Mostofsky et al., 2006). Further, transcranial magnetic stimulation revealed reduced neural inhibition in the corticospinal tract (Moll, Heinrich, Trott, Wirth, & Rothenberger, 2000). These findings suggest immature motor-execution circuitry, supporting findings of greater motor overflow (i.e., contralateral motor movements), a sign of motor immaturity, in children with ADHD (Mostofsky, Newschaffer, & Denckla, 2003). This immaturity may contribute to reduced executive function, as Mostofsky et al. reported that motor overflow movements predicted response inhibition performance in children with ADHD.

Functional Imaging of ADHD—without Cognitive Challenge

Studies of intrinsic functional connectivity that examine low-frequency synchrony between regions while subjects rest with their eyes open or closed have shown two abnormalities in ADHD subjects (see Konrad & Eickhoff, 2010, for a review). First, a network comprising dorsal and ventral medial prefrontal cortex and posterior cingulate, termed "default mode," showed atypical connectivity in adults with ADHD. In healthy subjects, during task states requiring attention to external stimuli, the default-mode network is deactivated and anticorrelated with regions engaged by the task (e.g., dorsal anterior cingulate). This pattern was altered in ADHD adults, who showed weak connectivity within nodes of the default-mode network (e.g., posterior cingulate cortex) (Uddin et al., 2008) and stronger connectivity with task-evoked regions (e.g., dorsal anterior cingulate) (Castellanos et al., 2008). Weak default-mode connectivity and more acrossnetwork connectivity have been associated with greater behavioral variability, an index of distractibility, in adults with ADHD.

The second abnormality found is that resting-state functional connectivity among regions involved in executive function, frontal cortex, striatum, and cerebellum was weaker in ADHD children (Cao et al., 2006) and altered in amplitude, with reductions in some regions (e.g., right inferior frontal, left sensorimotor, cerebellum) but increases in others (e.g., right anterior cingulate, brainstem) (Zang et al., 2007). These studies indicate that functional properties of networks associated with executive function are atypical in ADHD at baseline, without task engagement.

Summary

Neuroimaging of ADHD has revealed structural and functional brain differences between individuals with ADHD and their typically developing peers, most prominently in frontal-striatal-cerebellar circuitry but also in motor, limbic, and parietal-temporal regions. Longitudinal structural imaging studies provide robust evidence for a model supporting delayed brain maturation in ADHD, rather than aberrant development. This view concurs with the diagnostic criteria of ADHD that require age-inappropriate levels of certain behaviors.

Assessment of developmental delay from functional imaging findings is not straightforward, as no studies have used longitudinal designs or cross-sectional ones including multiple ages. However, across studies and tasks, children with ADHD engage the same circuitry as controls, but to a lesser or greater degree. This pattern is more supporting of a developmental-delay model, the notion that *typical* circuitry is recruited *atypically*, rather than an aberrant developmental model that would require different regions to be recruited relative to controls. Posterior regions were often recruited by ADHD individuals but not by controls during tasks drawing on inhibitory and working memory processes. This recruitment has been interpreted as being compensatory to weak frontostriatal functioning. It is possible that factors such as persistence or remittance of symptoms and stimulant medication use that moderate structural maturation determine their engagement.

Atypical properties of connectivity between networks showing atypical engagement in functional imaging studies with cognitive challenge (e.g., frontostriato-cerebellar) were apparent in the "task-free" resting state, suggesting that task engagement is not necessary for revealing dysfunctional circuitry in ADHD. Altered properties of resting-state connectivity are relevant to cognitive dysfunction observed in ADHD because they have been associated with mind wandering, distractibility, and disorders of executive function (e.g., schizophrenia, autism spectrum disorder; see review Broyd et al., 2009).

Lastly, it is important to note that although the conclusions drawn here are gleaned from the most consistent findings across studies, there are many contradictory findings among structural studies (e.g., nonsignificant differences in all described regions) and functional imaging studies with cognitive challenge (e.g., different subregions of described circuits activated across studies for the same function or task) and those without (e.g., contradictory pattern of increases and decreases in connectivity). While some of these differences could be attributed to differences across studies in sample sizes, age, and intellectual functioning of subjects, they are also likely to reflect the phenotypic heterogeneity that is inherent to the disorder (see Nigg et al., 2005; Toplak et al., 2009).

Neurochemical Basis of ADHD

ADHD is considered a dopaminergic disorder, primarily based on the action of medications that produce temporary relief of ADHD symptoms. Methylphenidate hydrochloride (MPH), which is effective in 60 to 70% of children with ADHD, increases striatal synaptic dopamine by blocking the dopamine transporter (DAT) that regulates reuptake following release. Amphetamines, which are effective in a third of the cases, increase synaptic dopamine by blocking DAT and stimulating release. DAT is most abundantly expressed in the striatum where it is the primary means of dopamine clearance relative to any other region of the brain (Madras, Miller, & Fischman, 2005). Indeed, increased extracellular

dopamine in the striatum following administration of MPH correlated with severity of impulsivity and inattention in adolescents with ADHD (Rosa-Neto et al., 2005). The striatum is a key node in thalamocortical circuits that connect prefrontal cortex to posterior cortical regions. Thus, striatal modulation by MPH has widespread influence, extending to multiple cortical regions.

Most functional imaging studies of MPH response in ADHD subjects reveal that MPH normalized involvement of regions that were atypically activated without MPH in comparison with controls (but see Kobel et al., 2009, for null effects). MPH increased activation in striatal structures during response inhibition (Vaidya et al., 1998) and divided attention (Shafritz, Marchione, Gore, Shaywitz, & Shaywitz, 2004) in ADHD children, and in prefrontal cortex laterally during response inhibition in children (Vaidya et al., 1998) and medially during interference control in adults (Bush et al., 2008) with ADHD. Further, MPH increased suppression of ventromedial prefrontal cortex during response inhibition in ADHD children (Peterson et al., 2009). In contrast to these selective increases in ADHD subjects, MPH increased involvement of fronto-striato-thalamo-cerebellar and parietotemporal networks during sustained attention and reduced involvement of orbitofrontal and superior temporal cortices during monetarily-rewarded sustained attention (Rubia et al., 2009). Normalizing effects of MPH have also been observed after prolonged MPH treatment, without acute administration during imaging. After 1 year of MPH treatment in ADHD children relative to before start of treatment, activation associated with spatial attention was reduced in the insula and putamen, regions that were more activated in ADHD children before treatment relative to controls. Thus it appears that MPH enables *typical* regional engagement during executive function in ADHD children and adults.

Findings of studies directly examining dopaminergic function suggest that it is reduced in ADHD. First, several studies measuring availability of DAT found increased expression in the striatum of ADHD subjects relative to controls (see review Krause, Dresel, Krause, la Fougere, & Ackenheil, 2003). Higher DAT expression in ADHD subjects suggests increased reuptake resulting in reduced synaptic dopamine. Second, D2/D3 receptor activity associated with dopamine release in the striatum was reduced in adults with ADHD relative to controls (Volkow et al., 2009), and further, correlated with inattention symptoms (Volkow, Wang, Newcorn,

Telang, et al., 2007). Third, dopamine synthesis was higher in midbrain regions (e.g., substantia nigra, ventral tegmentum) in adolescents with ADHD relative to controls (Ernst et al., 1999); higher dopamine synthesis may result from reduced extracellular dopamine or increased transporter activity. Taken together, these findings provide evidence for ADHD as a hypo- dopaminergic condition.

Characterizing ADHD as a hypo- or hyperdopaminergic condition, however, is not straightforward for several reasons. In contrast to the above findings, studies have also reported reductions (Volkow, Wang, Newcorn, Fowler, et al., 2007) and no difference in DAT availability in the striatum (van Dyck et al., 2002) in adults with ADHD relative to controls. Further, DAT availability was reduced in the midbrain of adolescents with ADHD in the absence of striatal differences (Jucaite, Fernell, Halldin, Forssberg, & Farde, 2005). Greater dopamine signaling in ADHD has also been suggested by a report of increased homovanillic acid levels, a metabolite of dopamine in cerebrospinal fluid, in children with ADHD; further homovanillic acid levels correlated with symptoms and their attenuation following MPH administration (Castellanos et al., 1996). While these mixed findings could reflect differences in subject (e.g., nicotine use, history of stimulant exposure, age) or ligand (e.g., measuring internalized vs. externalized DAT) characteristics, they could also reflect differences in adaptive processes compensating for greater dopamine release or reduced storage. Further, functional properties of the dopaminergic system are sensitive to contextual factors such as experience of task difficulty or interest. Indeed, dopamine release following MPH administration varied with subjects' reports of interest during a mathematical task (Volkow et al., 2004). In addition to contextual factors, trait-related factors such as hypertrophy of dopaminergic neurons due to insufficient pruning during development or genetic factors are likely to also induce individual variability in dopaminergic signaling.

Summary

Based on the effects of MPH and findings from ligand-based studies, there is strong support for dopaminergic dysfunction in ADHD. Behavioral and functional imaging studies of the effects of MPH reveal normalizing effects for reducing symptoms and changing functional anatomy mediating executive control to resemble healthy subjects. Further, imaging of dopaminergic signaling revealed that enhanced dopamine by MPH was context-selective, suggesting that increased dopamine serves to enhance the saliency of the cognitively demanding task. Thus, MPH is posited to bring about its beneficial effects by enhancing dopaminergic signaling in the striatum as well as enhancing the saliency of the task at hand (Volkow, Wang, Fowler, & Ding, 2005). A more nuanced view has distinguished between phasic release of dopamine that is stimulus-driven and tonic activity from chronic accumulation of extracellular dopamine. Seeman and Madras posit that tonic activity is lower and phasic activity is higher than optimal levels in ADHD and both are modulated by MPH to bring them to optimal levels (Seeman & Madras, 2002). Specifically, they posit that MPH increases tonic activity by DAT blockade, which leads to stimulation of autoreceptors that serve to attenuate phasic release. This model reconciles findings of both reduced and greater dopamine signaling in ADHD.

Less is known about the role of other catecholamines in ADHD. They are suspected to play a role because pure dopamine agonists such as L-dopa do not relieve ADHD symptoms (Overtoom et al., 2003). Indeed, norepinephrine agonists (e.g., atomoxetine by inhibiting norepinephrine transporter and guanfacine by stimulating alpha-2-adrenorecptors) are effective for some cases (Spencer & Biederman, 2002). Further, MPH increases both dopamine and norepinephrine in prefrontal cortex (Berridge et al., 2006). Thus, pathophysiology of ADHD likely involves interaction between dopaminergic and noradrenergic systems, although the nature of the interaction remains to be fully specified (see review Vaidya & Lee, 2009).

Neurogenetics of ADHD

ADHD is an inherited condition with a mode of transmission that is unknown but suspected to be polygenic. The heritability of ADHD has been estimated to be .76 based on twin studies. Meta-analysis of molecular genetic studies indicates that seven catecholaminergic genes have risk alleles that are over-transmitted in ADHD (Faraone et al., 2005). These candidate genes include four for dopaminergic transmission (dopamine receptor 4 [DRD4] and 5 [DRD5], dopamine transporter [DAT1], dopamine-beta-hydroxylase [DBH]), two for serotoninergic transmission (serotonin transporter [5HTT], serotonin-1B-receptor [HTR1B]), and SNAP25. While these genes are variably expressed in different brain regions, when considered together they are represented in circuitry known to be dysfunctional in ADHD (see review by Durston, de Zeeuw, & Staal,

2009). More recent work has also identified association with ADHD of rare chromosomal deletions and duplications known as copy number variations (CNVs) of multiple genes previously implicated in other psychiatric conditions that are important for multiple psychological and neural functions (Elia et al., 2009; Williams et al., 2010).

Studies of siblings and parents of children with ADHD have elucidated the heritability of prefrontal-striatal-cerebellar properties in ADHD. Like their affected siblings, siblings without ADHD have smaller right prefrontal and left occipital lobular volumes than those of controls; however, smaller cerebellar volumes have been observed only in the affected siblings (Durston et al., 2004). A preliminary monozygotic twin study found no cortical regions that differed between affected and unaffected twins; however, smaller caudate volumes were observed in affected but not unaffected twins (Castellanos et al., 2003). Thus, smaller cerebellar and caudate volumes were associated with the ADHD phenotype, but cortical volume, especially of right prefrontal lobe, may mediate familial risk for ADHD. Further, integrity of prefrontal-striatal white matter was lower in children with ADHD and in their affected parents than in children without ADHD and their unaffected parents (Casey et al., 2007). Ventrolateral prefrontal activation during inhibitory control was reduced in ADHD children and their unaffected siblings (Durston, Mulder, Casey, Ziermans, & van Engeland, 2006). Taken together, these results suggest that inheritance of prefrontal-striatal structural and functional properties plays a role in mediating genetic risk for ADHD.

Studies of structural and functional brain characteristics associated with risk alleles of candidate genes suggest neuropathological pathways mediating risk for ADHD. In children with ADHD, their unaffected siblings, and control children, homozygosity of the 10-repeat *DAT1* allele was associated with smaller caudate volumes, whereas the 7-repeat *DRD4* allele was associated with smaller prefrontal volumes (Durston et al., 2005). Right orbitofrontal/inferior prefrontal and posterior parietal cortex was thinner in carriers of the 7-repeat *DRD4* alleles; cortical thickness did not differ by *DAT1* alleles (Shaw, Gornick, et al., 2007). The anatomical dissociation of these gene effects is consistent with their expression in that DAT regulates dopamine levels primarily in the striatum, and *DRD4* is selectively expressed cortically. Further, functional activation during inhibitory control was reduced in

the caudate in ADHD children and their unaffected siblings who were 10-repeat homozygous carriers relative to heterozygotes; the genotype difference was not observed in the controls (Durston et al., 2008) but has been observed in another study with larger samples (Stollstorff et al., 2010). These results suggest that prefrontal-striatal dopaminergic function associated with *DAT1* and *DRD4* alleles is one neurobiological pathway for developing ADHD.

Summary

Studies of children with ADHD and their family members suggest that shared properties of prefrontal-striatal regions mediate risk for ADHD. Further, this circuitry is modulated by two dopamine-regulating genes, *DAT1* and *DRD4*, that have been associated with ADHD. Less is understood about the role that CNVs may play in selective susceptibility to ADHD. Thus, while inherited suboptimal dopaminergic function of prefrontal-striatal circuitry appears to be part of ADHD etiology, risk for the disorder appears to be mediated by more complex genetic alterations including chromosomal factors.

Conclusion

Convergent evidence from brain imaging, behavioral, and genetic studies indicates that the neuropathophysiology of ADHD is rooted in dopamine-mediated circuits encompassing the prefrontal cortex and basal ganglia, which are important for executive control and motivational behavior (see Figure 26.1). However, structural and functional imaging studies also provide evidence for atypicalities in other regions, such as parietal and temporal lobes. Further, while most physiological evidence has focused on dopaminergic dysfunction in ADHD, dysfunction of the noradrenergic system is also suspected. Currently, these observations are not accounted for in a single model of ADHD. Rather, different models emphasize different aspects of ADHD or anatomy. One model designed to account for heterogeneity in executive and motivational function in ADHD posits that alterations in mesocortical and mesolimbic dopaminergic circuits lead to executive and motivational dysfunction, respectively (Sonuga-Barke, 2002). A computational account posits that dopaminergic deficiency leads to executive and motivational deficits, whereas noradrenergic deficiency leads to response speed deficits (e.g., greater behavioral variability in ADHD) (Frank, Santamaria, O'Reilly, & Willcutt, 2007). Finally, a model based on animal studies of ADHD posits altered reinforcement and extinction-mediated learning resulting from dopamine deficiency in mesolimbic circuitry as the basis of ADHD symptoms and behavioral deficits (Sagvolden, Johansen, Aase, & Russell, 2005).

Future Directions

The following gaps remain in our current knowledge of the cognitive neuroscience of ADHD.

First, structural imaging studies suggest that ADHD represents a developmental delay rather than an aberrant developmental trajectory. Whether this is borne out in functional brain organization in ADHD is unknown. Functional imaging studies employing a longitudinal design to build growth curves of regional brain involvement during cognitive functions affected in ADHD will be useful.

Second, while many brain regions are identified as being functionally atypical in ADHD, there is no clear understanding of whether connectivity among these is disrupted and how it is relevant to ADHD symptomatology. While resting-state studies suggest altered connectivity, the way in which it impacts cognitive function in ADHD remains to be fully elaborated. Weak cognitive control in ADHD is thought to stem from weak prefrontal signals to sensory and motor modalities. Whether weak cognitive control is coupled with stronger "bottom-up" signals for salient or rewarding stimuli in ADHD is worth investigating. Thus, individual differences in inattention and impulsivity and hyperactivity symptoms may be represented in the relationship of "top-down" prefrontal regions to "bottom-up" limbic structures, rather than in the engagement of individual regions.

Third, researchers agree that there is a high degree of phenotypic heterogeneity in ADHD. Subtyping and identification of comorbid conditions are useful for broad classifications but are inadequate for probing neurobiological individual differences. Studies examining how genetic and environmental variation influences phenotype expression and modulates structural and functional anatomy are needed. Further, studies both of single genes and in combination are needed to identify neurobiological sources of phenotypic variation.

Fourth, pharmacological treatment of ADHD involves a cumbersome trial-and-error process in making prescription decisions. Pharmacogenetic studies hold promise for informing clinicians about predictive relationships between genotype and effective medication response that would make decisions regarding prescriptions for children less cumbersome (Froehlich, McGough, & Stein, 2010). These studies need to be coupled with brain imaging to enable us to understand the neurobiological basis of individual variability in treatment efficacy. Further, the extent to which pharmacological treatment can be supplemented by or substituted with cognitive training regimens (e.g., working memory training; Klingberg et al., 2005) will be important to investigate.

Acknowledgments

Preparation of this manuscript was supported by NIMH grant MH65395.

References

American Psychiatric Association (2000). *Diagnostic and statistical manual for mental disorders, 4th Edition—Text Revision.* Washington, DC: American Psychiatric Association.

Ashtari, M., Kumra, S., Bhaskar, S. L., Clarke, T., Thaden, E., Cervellione, K. L., et al. (2005). Attention-deficit/hyperactivity disorder: A preliminary diffusion tensor imaging study. *Biological Psychiatry, 57*(5), 448–455.

Barnes, K. A., Howard, J. H., Jr., Howard, D. V., Kenealy, L., & Vaidya, C. J. (2010). Two forms of implicit learning in childhood ADHD. *Developmental Neuropsychology, 35*(5), 494–505.

Bellgrove, M. A., Barry, E., Johnson, K. A., Cox, M., Daibhis, A., Daly, M., et al. (2008). Spatial attentional bias as a marker of genetic risk, symptom severity, and stimulant response in ADHD. *Neuropsychopharmacology, 33*(10), 2536–2545.

Berridge, C. W., Devilbiss, D. M., Andrzejewski, M. E., Arnsten, A. F., Kelley, A. E., Schmeichel, B., et al. (2006). Methylphenidate preferentially increases catecholamine neurotransmission within the prefrontal cortex at low doses that enhance cognitive function. *Biological Psychiatry, 60*(10), 1111–1120.

Biederman, J., Petty, C. R., Clarke, A., Lomedico, A., & Faraone, S. V. (2011). Predictors of persistent ADHD: An 11-year follow-up study. *Journal of Psychiatric Research, 45*(2), 150–155.

Booth, J. R., Burman, D. D., Meyer, J. R., Lei, Z., Trommer, B. L., Davenport, N. D., et al. (2005). Larger deficits in brain networks for response inhibition than for visual selective attention in attention deficit hyperactivity disorder (ADHD). *Journal of Child Psychology and Psychiatry, 46*(1), 94–111.

Broyd, S. J., Demanuele, C., Debener, S., Helps, S. K., James, C. J., & Sonuga-Barke, E. J. (2009). Default-mode brain dysfunction in mental disorders: A systematic review. *Neuroscience and Biobehavioral Reviews, 33*(3), 279–296.

Bush, G., Spencer, T. J., Holmes, J., Shin, L. M., Valera, E. M., Seidman, L. J., et al. (2008). Functional magnetic resonance imaging of methylphenidate and placebo in attention-deficit/hyperactivity disorder during the multi-source interference task. *Archives of General Psychiatry, 65*(1), 102–114.

Cao, Q., Zang, Y., Sun, L., Sui, M., Long, X., Zou, Q., et al. (2006). Abnormal neural activity in children with attention deficit hyperactivity disorder: A resting-state functional magnetic resonance imaging study. *Neuroreport, 17*(10), 1033–1036.

Casey, B. J., Epstein, J. N., Buhle, J., Liston, C., Davidson, M. C., Tonev, S. T., et al. (2007). Frontostriatal connectivity and its role in cognitive control in parent-child dyads with ADHD. *American Journal of Psychiatry*, *164*(11), 1729–1736.

Castellanos, F. X., Elia, J., Kruesi, M. J., Marsh, W. L., Gulotta, C. S., Potter, W. Z., et al. (1996). Cerebrospinal fluid homovanillic acid predicts behavioral response to stimulants in 45 boys with attention deficit/hyperactivity disorder. *Neuropsychopharmacology*, *14*(2), 125–137.

Castellanos, F. X., Lee, P. P., Sharp, W., Jeffries, N. O., Greenstein, D. K., Clasen, L. S., et al. (2002). Developmental trajectories of brain volume abnormalities in children and adolescents with attention-deficit/hyperactivity disorder. *Journal of the American Medical Association*, *288*(14), 1740–1748.

Castellanos, F. X., Margulies, D. S., Kelly, C., Uddin, L. Q., Ghaffari, M., Kirsch, A., et al. (2008). Cingulate-precuneus interactions: A new locus of dysfunction in adult attention-deficit/hyperactivity disorder. *Biological Psychiatry*, *63*(3), 332–337.

Castellanos, F. X., Sharp, W. S., Gottesman, R. F., Greenstein, D. K., Giedd, J. N., & Rapoport, J. L. (2003). Anatomic brain abnormalities in monozygotic twins discordant for attention deficit hyperactivity disorder. *American Journal of Psychiatry*, *160*(9), 1693–1696.

Castellanos, F. X., Sonuga-Barke, E. J., Scheres, A., Di Martino, A., Hyde, C., & Walters, J. R. (2005). Varieties of attention-deficit/hyperactivity disorder-related intra-individual variability. *Biological Psychiatry*, *57*(11), 1416–1423.

Chan, E., Hopkins, M. R., Perrin, J. M., Herrerias, C., & Homer, C. J. (2005). Diagnostic practices for attention deficit hyperactivity disorder: A national survey of primary care physicians. *Ambulatory Pediatrics*, *5*(4), 201–208.

Chan, E., Mattingley, J. B., Huang-Pollock, C., English, T., Hester, R., Vance, A., et al. (2009). Abnormal spatial asymmetry of selective attention in ADHD. *Journal of Child Psychology and Psychiatry*, *50*(9), 1064–1072.

Dickstein, S. G., Bannon, K., Castellanos, F. X., & Milham, M. P. (2006). The neural correlates of attention deficit hyperactivity disorder: An ALE meta-analysis. *Journal of Child Psychology and Psychiatry*, *47*(10), 1051–1062.

Durston, S., Davidson, M. C., Mulder, M. J., Spicer, J. A., Galvan, A., Tottenham, N., et al. (2007). Neural and behavioral correlates of expectancy violations in attention-deficit hyperactivity disorder. *Journal of Child Psychology and Psychiatry*, *48*(9), 881–889.

Durston, S., de Zeeuw, P., & Staal, W. G. (2009). Imaging genetics in ADHD: A focus on cognitive control. *Neuroscience and Biobehavioral Reviews*, *33*(5), 674–689.

Durston, S., Fossella, J. A., Casey, B. J., Hulshoff Pol, H. E., Galvan, A., Schnack, H. G., et al. (2005). Differential effects of DRD4 and DAT1 genotype on fronto-striatal gray matter volumes in a sample of subjects with attention deficit hyperactivity disorder, their unaffected siblings, and controls. *Molecular Psychiatry*, *10*(7), 678–685.

Durston, S., Fossella, J. A., Mulder, M. J., Casey, B. J., Ziermans, T. B., Vessaz, M. N., et al. (2008). Dopamine transporter genotype conveys familial risk of attention-deficit/hyperactivity disorder through striatal activation. *Journal of the American Academy of Child and Adolescent Psychiatry*, *47*(1), 61–67.

Durston, S., Hulshoff Pol, H. E., Schnack, H. G., Buitelaar, J. K., Steenhuis, M. P., Minderaa, R. B., et al. (2004). Magnetic resonance imaging of boys with attention-deficit/hyperactivity disorder and their unaffected siblings. *Journal of the American Academy of Child and Adolescent Psychiatry*, *43*(3), 332–340.

Durston, S., Mulder, M., Casey, B. J., Ziermans, T., & van Engeland, H. (2006). Activation in ventral prefrontal cortex is sensitive to genetic vulnerability for attention-deficit hyperactivity disorder. *Biological Psychiatry*, *60*(10), 1062–1070.

Durston, S., Tottenham, N. T., Thomas, K. M., Davidson, M. C., Eigsti, I. M., Yang, Y., et al. (2003). Differential patterns of striatal activation in young children with and without ADHD. *Biological Psychiatry*, *53*(10), 871–878.

Elia, J., Gai, X., Xie, H. M., Perin, J. C., Geiger, E., Glessner, J. T., et al. (2009). Rare structural variants found in attention-deficit hyperactivity disorder are preferentially associated with neurodevelopmental genes. *Molecular Psychiatry*, *15*(6), 637–646.

Ellison-Wright, I., Ellison-Wright, Z., & Bullmore, E. (2008). Structural brain change in attention deficit hyperactivity disorder identified by meta-analysis. *BMC Psychiatry*, *8* , 51.

Ernst, M., Kimes, A. S., London, E. D., Matochik, J. A., Eldreth, D., Tata, S., et al. (2003). Neural substrates of decision making in adults with attention deficit hyperactivity disorder. *American Journal of Psychiatry*, *160*(6), 1061–1070.

Ernst, M., Zametkin, A. J., Matochik, J. A., Pascualvaca, D., Jons, P. H., & Cohen, R. M. (1999). High midbrain [18F] DOPA accumulation in children with attention deficit hyperactivity disorder. *American Journal of Psychiatry*, *156*(8), 1209–1215.

Faraone, S. V., Perlis, R. H., Doyle, A. E., Smoller, J. W., Goralnick, J. J., Holmgren, M. A., et al. (2005). Molecular genetics of attention-deficit/hyperactivity disorder. *Biological Psychiatry*, *57*(11), 1313–1323.

Faraone, S. V., Sergeant, J., Gillberg, C., & Biederman, J. (2003). The worldwide prevalence of ADHD: Is it an American condition? *World Psychiatry*, *2*(2), 104–113.

Frank, M. J., Santamaria, A., O'Reilly, R. C., & Willcutt, E. (2007). Testing computational models of dopamine and noradrenaline dysfunction in attention deficit/hyperactivity disorder. *Neuropsychopharmacology*, *32*(7), 1583–1599.

Froehlich, T. E., McGough, J. J., & Stein, M. A. (2010). Progress and promise of attention-deficit hyperactivity disorder pharmacogenetics. *CNS Drugs*, *24*(2), 99–117.

Huang-Pollock, C. L., & Karalunas, S. L. (2010). Working memory demands impair skill acquisition in children with ADHD. *Journal of Abnormal Psychology*, *119*(1), 174–185.

Jucaite, A., Fernell, E., Halldin, C., Forssberg, H., & Farde, L. (2005). Reduced midbrain dopamine transporter binding in male adolescents with attention-deficit/hyperactivity disorder: Association between striatal dopamine markers and motor hyperactivity. *Biological Psychiatry*, *57*(3), 229–238.

Klingberg, T., Fernell, E., Olesen, P. J., Johnson, M., Gustafsson, P., Dahlstrom, K., et al. (2005). Computerized training of working memory in children with ADHD—a randomized, controlled trial. *Journal of the American Academy of Child and Adolescent Psychiatry*, *44*(2), 177–186.

Kobel, M., Bechtel, N., Weber, P., Specht, K., Klarhofer, M., Scheffler, K., et al. (2009). Effects of methylphenidate on working memory functioning in children with attention deficit/hyperactivity disorder. *European Journal of Paediatric Neurology*, *13*(6), 516–523.

Konrad, K., & Eickhoff, S. B. (2010). Is the ADHD brain wired differently? A review on structural and functional connectivity in attention deficit hyperactivity disorder. *Human Brain Mapping*, *31*(6), 904–916.

Krause, K. H., Dresel, S. H., Krause, J., la Fougere, C., & Ackenheil, M. (2003). The dopamine transporter and neuroimaging in attention deficit hyperactivity disorder. *Neuroscience and Biobehavioral Reviews, 27*(7), 605–613.

Lijffijt, M., Kenemans, J. L., Verbaten, M. N., & van Engeland, H. (2005). A meta-analytic review of stopping performance in attention-deficit/hyperactivity disorder: Deficient inhibitory motor control? *Journal of Abnormal Psychology, 114*(2), 216–222.

Luman, M., Oosterlaan, J., & Sergeant, J. A. (2005). The impact of reinforcement contingencies on AD/HD: A review and theoretical appraisal. *Clinical Psychology Review, 25*(2), 183–213.

Madras, B. K., Miller, G. M., & Fischman, A. J. (2005). The dopamine transporter and attention-deficit/hyperactivity disorder. *Biological Psychiatry, 57*(11), 1397–1409.

Makris, N., Biederman, J., Monuteaux, M. C., & Seidman, L. J. (2009). Towards conceptualizing a neural-systems based anatomy of attention deficit/hyperactivity disorder. *Developmental Neuroscience, 31* , 36–49.

Makris, N., Buka, S. L., Biederman, J., Papadimitriou, G. M., Hodge, S. M., Valera, E. M., et al. (2008). Attention and executive systems abnormalities in adults with childhood ADHD: A DT-MRI study of connections. *Cerebral Cortex, 18*(5), 1210–1220.

Martinussen, R., Hayden, J., Hogg-Johnson, S., & Tannock, R. (2005). A meta-analysis of working memory impairments in children with attention-deficit/hyperactivity disorder. *Journal of the American Academy of Child and Adolescent Psychiatry, 44*(4), 377–384.

Merikangas, K. R., He, J. P., Brody, D., Fisher, P. W., Bourdon, K., & Koretz, D. S. (2010). Prevalence and treatment of mental disorders among US children in the 2001–2004 NHANES. *Pediatrics, 125*(1), 75–81.

Moll, G. H., Heinrich, H., Trott, G., Wirth, S., & Rothenberger, A. (2000). Deficient intracortical inhibition in drug naive children with attention-deficit hyperactivity disorder is enhanced by methylphenidate. *Neuroscience Letters, 284*(1-2), 121–125.

Mostofsky, S. H., Newschaffer, C. J., & Denckla, M. B. (2003). Overflow movements predict impaired response inhibition in children with ADHD. *Perceptual and Motor Skills, 97*(3 Pt 2), 1315–1331.

Mostofsky, S. H., Rimrodt, S. L., Schafer, J. G., Boyce, A., Goldberg, M. C., Pekar, J. J., et al. (2006). Atypical motor and sensory cortex activation in attention-deficit/hyperactivity disorder: A functional magnetic resonance imaging study of simple sequential finger tapping. *Biological Psychiatry, 59*(1), 48–56.

Narr, K. L., Woods, R. P., Lin, J., Kim, J., Phillips, O. R., Del'Homme, M., et al. (2009). Widespread cortical thinning is a robust anatomical marker for attention-deficit/hyperactivity disorder. *Journal of the American Academy of Child and Adolescent Psychiatry, 48*(10), 1014–1022.

Nigg, J. T., Willcutt, E. G., Doyle, A. E., & Sonuga-Barke, E. J. (2005). Causal heterogeneity in attention-deficit/hyperactivity disorder: Do we need neuropsychologically impaired subtypes? *Biological Psychiatry, 57*(11), 1224–1230.

Oosterlaan, J., & Sergeant, J. A. (1998). Effects of reward and response cost on response inhibition in AD/HD, disruptive, anxious, and normal children. *Journal of Abnormal Child Psychology, 26*(3), 161–174.

Overtoom, C. C., Verbaten, M. N., Kemner, C., Kenemans, J. L., van Engeland, H., Buitelaar, J. K., et al. (2003). Effects of methylphenidate, desipramine, and L-dopa on attention

and inhibition in children with attention deficit hyperactivity disorder. *Behavioural Brain Research, 145*(1-2), 7–15.

Peterson, B. S., Potenza, M. N., Wang, Z., Zhu, H., Martin, A., Marsh, R., et al. (2009). An FMRI study of the effects of psychostimulants on default-mode processing during Stroop task performance in youths with ADHD. *American Journal of Psychiatry, 166*(11), 1286–1294.

Rosa-Neto, P., Lou, H. C., Cumming, P., Pryds, O., Karrebaek, H., Lunding, J., et al. (2005). Methylphenidate-evoked changes in striatal dopamine correlate with inattention and impulsivity in adolescents with attention deficit hyperactivity disorder. *Neuroimage, 25*(3), 868–876.

Rubia, K., Halari, R., Cubillo, A., Mohammad, A. M., Brammer, M., & Taylor, E. (2009). Methylphenidate normalises activation and functional connectivity deficits in attention and motivation networks in medication-naive children with ADHD during a rewarded continuous performance task. *Neuropharmacology, 57*(7-8), 640–652.

Rubia, K., Overmeyer, S., Taylor, E., Brammer, M., Williams, S. C., Simmons, A., et al. (1999). Hypofrontality in attention deficit hyperactivity disorder during higher-order motor control: A study with functional MRI. *American Journal of Psychiatry, 156*(6), 891–896.

Rubia, K., Smith, A. B., Brammer, M. J., & Taylor, E. (2007). Temporal lobe dysfunction in medication-naive boys with attention-deficit/hyperactivity disorder during attention allocation and its relation to response variability. *Biological Psychiatry, 62*(9), 999–1006.

Sagvolden, T., Johansen, E. B., Aase, H., & Russell, V. A. (2005). A dynamic developmental theory of attention-deficit/hyperactivity disorder (ADHD) predominantly hyperactive/impulsive and combined subtypes. *Behavioural Brain Science, 28*(3), 397–419; discussion 419–368.

Scheres, A., Milham, M. P., Knutson, B., & Castellanos, F. X. (2007). Ventral striatal hyporesponsiveness during reward anticipation in attention-deficit/hyperactivity disorder. *Biological Psychiatry, 61*(5), 720–724.

Schulz, K. P., Fan, J., Tang, C. Y., Newcorn, J. H., Buchsbaum, M. S., Cheung, A. M., et al. (2004). Response inhibition in adolescents diagnosed with attention deficit hyperactivity disorder during childhood: An event-related FMRI study. *American Journal of Psychiatry, 161*(9), 1650–1657.

Schulz, K. P., Newcorn, J. H., Fan, J., Tang, C. Y., & Halperin, J. M. (2005). Brain activation gradients in ventrolateral prefrontal cortex related to persistence of ADHD in adolescent boys. *Journal of the American Academy of Child and Adolescent Psychiatry, 44*(1), 47–54.

Schweitzer, J. B., Faber, T. L., Grafton, S. T., Tune, L. E., Hoffman, J. M., & Kilts, C. D. (2000). Alterations in the functional anatomy of working memory in adult attention deficit hyperactivity disorder. *American Journal of Psychiatry, 157*(2), 278–280.

Seeman, P., & Madras, B. (2002). Methylphenidate elevates resting dopamine which lowers the impulse-triggered release of dopamine: A hypothesis. *Behavioural Brain Research, 130*(1-2), 79–83.

Seidman, L. J., Valera, E. M., & Makris, N. (2005). Structural brain imaging of attention-deficit/hyperactivity disorder. *Biological Psychiatry, 57*(11), 1263–1272.

Shafritz, K. M., Marchione, K. E., Gore, J. C., Shaywitz, S. E., & Shaywitz, B. A. (2004). The effects of methylphenidate on neural systems of attention in attention deficit hyperactivity disorder. *American Journal of Psychiatry*, *161*(11), 1990–1997.

Shaw, P., Eckstrand, K., Sharp, W., Blumenthal, J., Lerch, J. P., Greenstein, D., et al. (2007). Attention-deficit/hyperactivity disorder is characterized by a delay in cortical maturation. *Proceedings of the National Academy of Sciences U S A*, *104*(49), 19649–19654.

Shaw, P., Gilliam, M., Liverpool, M., Weddle, C., Malek, M., Sharp, W., et al. (2011). Cortical development in typically developing children with symptoms of hyperactivity and impulsivity: Support for a dimensional view of attention deficit hyperactivity disorder. *American Journal of Psychiatry*, *168*(2), 143–151.

Shaw, P., Gornick, M., Lerch, J., Addington, A., Seal, J., Greenstein, D., et al. (2007). Polymorphisms of the dopamine D4 receptor, clinical outcome, and cortical structure in attention-deficit/hyperactivity disorder. *Archives of General Psychiatry*, *64*(8), 921–931.

Shaw, P., Lalonde, F., Lepage, C., Rabin, C., Eckstrand, K., Sharp, W., et al. (2009). Development of cortical asymmetry in typically developing children and its disruption in attention-deficit/hyperactivity disorder. *Archives of General Psychiatry*, *66*(8), 888–896.

Shaw, P., Lerch, J., Greenstein, D., Sharp, W., Clasen, L., Evans, A., et al. (2006). Longitudinal mapping of cortical thickness and clinical outcome in children and adolescents with attention-deficit/hyperactivity disorder. *Archives of General Psychiatry*, *63*(5), 540–549.

Shaw, P., & Rabin, C. (2009). New insights into attention-deficit/hyperactivity disorder using structural neuroimaging. *Current Psychiatry Report*, *11*(5), 393–398.

Shaw, P., Sharp, W. S., Morrison, M., Eckstrand, K., Greenstein, D. K., Clasen, L. S., et al. (2009). Psychostimulant treatment and the developing cortex in attention deficit hyperactivity disorder. *American Journal of Psychiatry*, *166*(1), 58–63.

Silk, T., Vance, A., Rinehart, N., Egan, G., O'Boyle, M., Bradshaw, J. L., et al. (2005). Fronto-parietal activation in attention-deficit hyperactivity disorder, combined type: Functional magnetic resonance imaging study. *British Journal of Psychiatry*, *187*, 282–283.

Solanto, M. V., Abikoff, H., Sonuga-Barke, E., Schachar, R., Logan, G. D., Wigal, T., et al. (2001). The ecological validity of delay aversion and response inhibition as measures of impulsivity in AD/HD: A supplement to the NIMH multimodal treatment study of AD/HD. *Journal of Abnormal Child Psychology*, *29*(3), 215–228.

Sonuga-Barke, E. J. (2002). Psychological heterogeneity in AD/HD—a dual pathway model of behaviour and cognition. *Behavioural Brain Research*, *130*(1-2), 29–36.

Sowell, E. R., Thompson, P. M., Welcome, S. E., Henkenius, A. L., Toga, A. W., & Peterson, B. S. (2003). Cortical abnormalities in children and adolescents with attention-deficit hyperactivity disorder. *Lancet*, *362*(9397), 1699–1707.

Spencer, T., & Biederman, J. (2002). Non-stimulant treatment for attention-deficit/hyperactivity disorder. *Journal of Attention Disorders*, *6* Suppl 1, S109–S119.

Stevens, M. C., Pearlson, G. D., & Kiehl, K. A. (2007). An FMRI auditory oddball study of combined-subtype attention deficit hyperactivity disorder. *American Journal of Psychiatry*, *164*(11), 1737–1749.

Stollstorff, M., Foss-Feig, J., Cook, E. H., Jr., Stein, M. A., Gaillard, W. D., & Vaidya, C. J. (2010). Neural response

to working memory load varies by dopamine transporter genotype in children. *Neuroimage*, *53*(3), 970–977.

Strohle, A., Stoy, M., Wrase, J., Schwarzer, S., Schlagenhauf, F., Huss, M., et al. (2008). Reward anticipation and outcomes in adult males with attention-deficit/hyperactivity disorder. *Neuroimage*, *39*(3), 966–972.

Tamm, L., Menon, V., & Reiss, A. L. (2006). Parietal attentional system aberrations during target detection in adolescents with attention deficit hyperactivity disorder: Event-related fMRI evidence. *American Journal of Psychiatry*, *163*(6), 1033–1043.

Toplak, M. E., Dockstader, C., & Tannock, R. (2006). Temporal information processing in ADHD: Findings to date and new methods. *Journal of Neuroscience Methods*, *151*(1), 15–29.

Toplak, M. E., Pitch, A., Flora, D. B., Iwenofu, L., Ghelani, K., Jain, U., et al. (2009). The unity and diversity of inattention and hyperactivity/impulsivity in ADHD: Evidence for a general factor with separable dimensions. *Journal of Abnormal Child Psychology*, *37*(8), 1137–1150.

Uddin, L. Q., Kelly, A. M., Biswal, B. B., Margulies, D. S., Shehzad, Z., Shaw, D., et al. (2008). Network homogeneity reveals decreased integrity of default-mode network in ADHD. *Journal of Neuroscience Methods*, *169*(1), 249–254.

Vaidya, C. J., Austin, G., Kirkorian, G., Ridlehuber, H. W., Desmond, J. E., Glover, G. H., et al. (1998). Selective effects of methylphenidate in attention deficit hyperactivity disorder: A functional magnetic resonance study. *Proceedings of the National Academy of Sciences U S A*, *95*(24), 14494–14499.

Vaidya, C. J., Bunge, S. A., Dudukovic, N. M., Zalecki, C. A., Elliott, G. R., & Gabrieli, J. D. (2005). Altered neural substrates of cognitive control in childhood ADHD: Evidence from functional magnetic resonance imaging. *American Journal of Psychiatry*, *162*(9), 1605–1613.

Vaidya, C. J., & Lee, P. S. (2009). Attention deficit hyperactivity disorder: Methylphenidate (Ritaline) and dopamine. In L. R. Squire (Ed.), *Encyclopedia of neuroscience* (Vol. 1, pp. 625–631). Oxford: Academic Press.

Vaidya, C. J., & Stollstorff, M. (2008). Cognitive neuroscience of attention deficit hyperactivity disorder: Current status and working hypotheses. *Developmental Disabilities Research Reviews*, *14*(4), 261–267.

van Dyck, C. H., Quinlan, D. M., Cretella, L. M., Staley, J. K., Malison, R. T., Baldwin, R. M., et al. (2002). Unaltered dopamine transporter availability in adult attention deficit hyperactivity disorder. *American Journal of Psychiatry*, *159*(2), 309–312.

Vance, A., Silk, T. J., Casey, M., Rinehart, N. J., Bradshaw, J. L., Bellgrove, M. A., et al. (2007). Right parietal dysfunction in children with attention deficit hyperactivity disorder, combined type: A functional MRI study. *Molecular Psychiatry*, *12*(9), 826–832, 793.

Volkow, N. D., Wang, G. J., Fowler, J. S., & Ding, Y. S. (2005). Imaging the effects of methylphenidate on brain dopamine: New model on its therapeutic actions for attention-deficit/hyperactivity disorder. *Biological Psychiatry*, *57*(11), 1410–1415.

Volkow, N. D., Wang, G. J., Fowler, J. S., Telang, F., Maynard, L., Logan, J., et al. (2004). Evidence that methylphenidate enhances the saliency of a mathematical task by increasing dopamine in the human brain. *American Journal of Psychiatry*, *161*(7), 1173–1180.

Volkow, N. D., Wang, G. J., Kollins, S. H., Wigal, T. L., Newcorn, J. H., Telang, F., et al. (2009). Evaluating dopamine reward pathway in ADHD: clinical implications. *Journal of the American Medical Association, 302*(10), 1084–1091.

Volkow, N. D., Wang, G. J., Newcorn, J., Fowler, J. S., Telang, F., Solanto, M. V., et al. (2007). Brain dopamine transporter levels in treatment and drug naive adults with ADHD. *Neuroimage, 34*(3), 1182–1190.

Volkow, N. D., Wang, G. J., Newcorn, J., Telang, F., Solanto, M. V., Fowler, J. S., et al. (2007). Depressed dopamine activity in caudate and preliminary evidence of limbic involvement in adults with attention-deficit/hyperactivity disorder. *Archives of General Psychiatry, 64*(8), 932–940.

Willcutt, E. G., Doyle, A. E., Nigg, J. T., Faraone, S. V., & Pennington, B. F. (2005). Validity of the executive function theory of attention-deficit/hyperactivity disorder: A meta-analytic review. *Biological Psychiatry, 57*(11), 1336–1346.

Williams, N. M., Zaharieva, I., Martin, A., Langley, K., Mantripragada, K., Fossdal, R., et al. (2010). Rare chromosomal deletions and duplications in attention-deficit hyperactivity disorder: A genome-wide analysis. *Lancet, 376*(9750), 1401–1408.

Zang, Y. F., He, Y., Zhu, C. Z., Cao, Q. J., Sui, M. Q., Liang, M., et al. (2007). Altered baseline brain activity in children with ADHD revealed by resting-state functional MRI. *Brain Development, 29*(2), 83–91.

CHAPTER

27

Post-Traumatic Stress Disorder (PTSD)

J. Douglas Bremner

Abstract

Post-traumatic stress disorder (PTSD) is a mental disorder specifically linked to traumatic stress that is associated with considerable disability. PTSD has been shown to be associated with changes in brain structure and function. Brain regions affected by PTSD include the amygdala, hippocampus, and prefrontal cortex, all brain areas involved in memory as well as the stress response. Neuroimaging studies in patients with PTSD have replicated findings in animal studies by finding alterations in these brain areas. Abnormalities in these brain areas are hypothesized to underlie symptoms of PTSD.

Key Words: positron emission tomography (PET), depression, stress, post-traumatic stress disorder (PTSD)

Introduction

Post-traumatic stress disorder (PTSD) was defined for the first time in 1980 by the American Psychiatric Association's (APA) manual for psychiatric disorders, the *Diagnostic and Statistical Manual*, 3rd edition (Saigh & Bremner, 1999). This was the first time when it was recognized that psychological trauma could cause lasting mental disturbances, even when there was no physical injury. Subsequent research showed that PTSD is associated with lasting changes in the brain, cognition, and physiological responding. The diagnosis of PTSD represented a departure from the approach to war trauma in the first DSM of 1952. In DSM-I, "gross stress reaction" was a diagnosis that could be applied to veterans of World War II who suffered from mental disturbances as a result of exposure to the trauma of war. The conception of gross stress reaction was of a transient disorder. If symptoms persisted, it was assumed that there was pathology that had preceded the war.

In a delayed response to dealing with the ongoing mental health issues of veterans of the Vietnam War, there was a call for research into PTSD in the 1980s. Up until 1988, however, the diagnosis of PTSD was rarely made, possibly a result of a delay in education or changes in diagnostic practice of clinicians (Bremner, Southwick, Darnell, & Charney, 1996). Since that time there has been an acceleration of research into PTSD, which has led to an increased acceptance of the fact that trauma can have lasting consequences for the individual.

PTSD affects 8% of people at some time during their lives (Kessler, Sonnega, Bromet, Hughes, & Nelson, 1995). Risk factors for the development of PTSD include lower education, young age, history of prior trauma, reaction at the time of the trauma, and absence of social support (Brewin, Andrews, & Valentine, 2000).

The diagnosis of PTSD requires exposure to an event that involves a threat to one's life or self-integrity, and is associated with intense fear, horror, or helplessness. In addition, the diagnosis requires the presence of symptoms in three clusters: intrusions, avoidance and hyperarousal, and the presence of clinically significant distress or impairment. The diagnosis requires at least one symptom in the intrusion category, three in the avoidance category, and two in the hyperarousal category.

Intrusive symptoms include recurrent intrusive memories and nightmares, feeling as if the event were recurring, feeling a lot worse with reminders of the event, and having increased physiological reactivity with the event. Avoidant symptoms include avoidance of reminders of the event, avoidance of thoughts and feelings related to the event, trouble remembering an important aspect of the trauma, decreased interest, feeling detached or cut off from others, emotional numbing, and a sense of foreshortened future. Hyperarousal symptoms include difficulty falling or staying asleep, irritability or outbursts of anger, difficulty concentrating, hypervigilance, and exaggerated startle response.

Symptoms of PTSD are a behavioral manifestation of stress-induced changes in brain structure and function. Stress results in acute and chronic changes in neurochemical systems and specific brain regions that result in long-term changes in brain circuits involved in the stress response. Brain regions thought to play an important role in PTSD include the hippocampus, amygdala, and medial prefrontal cortex. The hypothalamic–pituitary–adrenal (HPA) axis (which produces cortisol) and norepinephrine (or noradrenergic) systems are two neurochemical systems that are critical in the stress response.

One brain area sensitive to stress in animals is the hippocampus, which plays a critical role in learning and memory. Studies in animals exposed to stress showed deficits in memory function (Luine, Villegas, Martinez, & McEwen, 1994) and damage to the hippocampus (Sapolsky, Uno, Rebert, & Finch, 1990; Uno, Tarara, Else, Suleman, & Sapolsky, 1989). Stress interfered with hippocampal-based mechanisms of memory function, including long-term potentiation (LTP) (Diamond, Fleshner, Ingersoll, & Rose, 1996; Luine et al., 1994). A variety of mechanisms have been proposed for these findings, including elevated levels of glucocorticoids released during stress (Lawrence & Sapolsky, 1994; Sapolsky, 1996), stress-related inhibition of brain-derived neurotrophic factor (BDNF) (Nibuya, Morinobu, & Duman, 1995; Smith, Makino, Kvetnansky, & Post, 1995), changes in serotonergic function (McEwen et al., 1992), or inhibition of neurogenesis (or the growth of new neurons) (Fowler, Liu, Oimet, & Wang, 2001; Gould, McEwen, Tanapat, Galea, & Fuchs, 1997) in the hippocampus.

Animal studies have demonstrated several agents with potentially beneficial effects on stress-induced hippocampal damage. Antidepressant treatments block the effects of stress, promote neurogenesis in the hippocampus, or both (Czeh et al., 2001; D'Sa & Duman, 2002; Duman, Heninger, & Nestler, 1997; Duman, Malberg, & Nakagawa, 2001; Duman, 2004; Garcia, 2002; Lucassen, Fuchs, & Czeh, 2004; Malberg, Eisch, Nestler, & Duman, 2000; McEwen & Chattarji 2004; Nibuya et al., 1995; Santarelli et al., 2003; Watanabe, Gould, Cameron, Daniels, & McEwen, 1992).

Brain Structure and Cognitive Functioning in PTSD

Patients with PTSD show a wide range of memory alterations that are mediated in part by the hippocampus (Bremner, 2003b; Bremner et al., 1993; Bremner, Krystal, Southwick, & Charney, 1995; Bremner, Randall, Scott, Capelli, et al., 1995). Neuroimaging studies have shown smaller volume of hippocampus in patients with PTSD, using magnetic resonance imaging (MRI) to measure the volume of the hippocampus (Bremner, Randall, Scott, Bronen, et al., 1995). Decreases in right hippocampal volume in PTSD patients were associated with deficits in short-term memory (Bremner, Randall, Scott, Bronen, et al., 1995). Smaller hippocampal volume or a reduction in N-acetyl aspartate (NAA) in the hippocampus (a marker of neuronal integrity) in adults with chronic PTSD has been found in multiple studies (Bonne et al., 2008; Bossini et al., 2008; Bremner, Randall, et al., 1997; Bremner, Vythilingam, Vermetten, Southwick, McGlashen, & Nazeere, et al., 2003; Bremner et al., 2002; Emdad et al., 2006; Felmingham, Williams, Whitford, et al., 2009; Freeman, Cardwell, Karson, & Komoroski, 1998; Freeman et al., 2006; Gilbertson et al., 2002; Gurvits et al., 1996; Hedges et al., 2003; Irle, Lange, & Sachsse, 2005; Kimbrell, Leulf, Cardwell, Komoroski, & Freeman, 2005; Kitayama, Vaccarino, Kutner, Weiss, & Bremner, 2005; Li et al., 2006; Lindauer et al., 2005; Lindauer, Olff, van Meijel, Carlier, & Gersons, 2006; Lindauer, Vlieger, et al., 2004; Mahmutyazicioglu et al., 2005; Mohanakrishnan Menon et al., 2003; Pavic et al., 2007; Schuff et al., 1997, 2001, 2008; Shin, Shin, et al., 2004; Stein, Koverola, Hanna, Torchia, & McClarty, 1997; Thomaes et al., 2010; Villarreal et al., 2002; Wang, Neylan, et al., 2010b; Woon, Sood, & Hedges, 2010). Not all studies in adults, however, have shown smaller hippocampal volume with PTSD (Hedges et al., 2007; Jatzko et al.,

2006; Landré et al., 2010; Pederson et al., 2004): some individuals with new-onset PTSD (Bonne et al., 2001; Fennema-Notestine, Stein, Kennedy, Archibald, & Jernigan, 2002) and Holocaust survivors with PTSD did not have smaller hippocampal volume (Golier et al., 2005). One study showed a correlation between PTSD symptoms and hippocampal volume in unaffected twin brothers, suggesting a genetic contribution to smaller hippocampal volume (Gilbertson et al., 2002). Other studies of cancer survivors found a correlation between intrusive memories and smaller hippocampal volume (Hara et al., 2008; Nakano et al., 2002). Studies of children with PTSD have consistently not shown smaller hippocampal volume (Carrion et al., 2001; De Bellis et al., 1999; De Bellis, Hall, Boring, Frustaci, & Moritz, 2001), whereas studies of abused adult women showed that stress at specific periods of development are associated with risk for smaller hippocampal volume (Andersen et al., 2008).

Patients with PTSD exhibit alterations in learning and memory that are thought to be mediated by the hippocampus (Brewin, 2001; Buckley, Blanchard, & Neill, 2000; Elzinga & Bremner, 2002; Golier & Yehuda, 1998). Several studies, using a variety of measures (including the Wechsler Memory Scale, the visual and verbal components of the Selective Reminding Test, the Auditory Verbal Learning Test, the California Verbal New Learning Test, and the Rivermead Behavioral Memory Test), have found specific deficits in verbal declarative memory function, with a relative sparing of visual memory and IQ (Barrett, Green, Morris, Giles, & Croft, 1996; Bremner et al., 1993; Bremner, Randall, Scott, Capelli, et al. 1995; Gil, Calev, Greenberg, Kugelmass, & Lerer, 1990; Gilbertson, Gurvits, Lasko, Orr, & Pitman, 2001; J. Golier et al., 1997; Jenkins, Langlais, Delis, & Cohen. 1998; Moradi, Doost, Taghavi, Yule, & Dagleish, 1999; Roca & Freeman, 2001; Sachinvala et al., 2000; Uddo, Vasterling, Brailey, & Sutker, 1993; Vasterling, Brailey, Constans, & Sutker, 1998; Vasterling et al., 2002; Yehuda et al., 1995). These studies were conducted in patients with PTSD that was related to Vietnam combat (Barrett et al., 1996; Bremner et al., 1993; Gilbertson et al., 2001; Golier et al., 1997; Roca & Freeman, 2001; Sachinvala et al., 2000; Uddo et al., 1993; Vasterling et al., 1998, 2002; Yehuda et al., 1995), patients with PTSD related to rape (Jenkins et al., 1998), adults with early childhood abuse (Bremner, Randall, Scott, Capelli, et al. 1995), and traumatized

children (Moradi et al., 1999). Studies suggest that cognitive deficits are specifically associated with PTSD and are not due to the nonspecific effects of trauma exposure (Bremner, Vermetten, Afzal, & Vythillingham, 2004; Jenkins et al., 1998). Some investigators have not been able to find specific deficits in verbal memory function (Stein, Hanna, Vaerum, & Koverola, 1999; Zalewski, Thompson, & Gottesman, 1994). These studies indicate that PTSD is associated with deficits in verbal declarative memory. Also, one study found that cognitive deficits in early-abuse survivors are specific to PTSD and not a nonspecific effect of exposure to trauma (Bremner, Vermeten, Afzal, et al., 2004).

Studies have shown changes in brain volume, as measured with MRI, in other brain structures in patients with PTSD. Thinner cortical volumes have been found in the frontal and temporal cortex (Geuze, Westenberg, et al., 2008). Several studies have found smaller anterior cingulate volume, based on MRI measurements, in individuals with PTSD (Kasai et al., 2008; Kitayama et al., 2005; Rauch et al., 2003; Rogers et al., 2009; Thomaes et al., 2010; Woodward et al., 2006; Yamasue et al., 2003). Some investigators have found reduced anterior cingulate NAA (De Bellis, Keshavan, Spencer, & Hall, 2000; Mahmutyazicioglu et al., 2005), while others did not (Seedat, Videen, Kennedy, & Stein, 2005). Studies have also found a decrease in gray matter density in association with PTSD (Corbo, Clément, Armony, Pruessner, & Brunet, 2005) and a smaller volume of corpus callosum in children who suffered neglect (De Bellis et al., 2002; Teicher et al., 2004). In adults with PTSD (Kitayama et al., 2007; Villarreal et al., 2004), reduced gray matter density was found in left posterior cingulate and the left posterior parahippocampal gyrus (Nardo et al., 2009), as well as smaller volume of the insula (Chen et al., 2006), cavum septum pellucidum (May et al., 2004) and orbitofrontal cortex (Hakamata et al., 2007; Thomaes et al., 2010). Other studies have found no difference in volume of cerebellar vermis (Levitt et al., 2006) and increased volume of the right caudate (Looi et al., 2009). Another study (Lim et al., 2003) showed decreased NAA in the basal ganglia in PTSD. Although some studies have reported smaller amygdala volume in PTSD (Rogers et al., 2009; Thomaes et al., 2010) or in cancer patients with intrusive recollections (Matsuoka, Yamawaki, Inagaki, Akechi, & Uchitomi, 2003), a recent meta-analysis did not find smaller amygdala volumes in PTSD when results from multiple studies were combined (Woon & Hedges, 2008, 2009).

Damage to the amygdala, medial prefrontal cortex, or both was associated with a decreased risk of development of PTSD, suggesting that these structures play a role in the genesis of the disorder after traumatic stress (Koenigs et al., 2007).

Studies have used measures of fractional anisotropy (FA) to assess white matter integrity, with a decrease in FA indicating decreased white matter integrity in PTSD. Decreased FA was found in the medial and posterior portions of the corpus callosum in children with PTSD (Jackowski et al., 2008) and in in the hippocampus, cingulum bundle (Wang, Zhang, et al. 2010), left side of rostral, subgenual and dorsal cingulum bundle (Kim et al., 2006), and left anterior cingulate (Kim et al., 2005, 2006) in adults with PTSD. Children with PTSD had increased gray matter volume in the right and left inferior and superior quadrants of the prefrontal cortex and decreased pons and posterior vermis as measured by volumetric MRI (Carrion et al., 2009).

The noradrenergic system plays a critical role in stress (Bremner, Krystal, Southwick, & Charney, 1996a, 1996b). The majority of noradrenergic cell bodies are located in the locus coeruleus, a nucleus in the dorsal pons region of the brainstem, with a dense network of axons extending throughout the cerebral cortex and to multiple cortical and subcortical areas. These areas include the hippocampus, amygdala, thalamus and hypothalamus, bed nucleus of stria terminalis, nucleus accumbens, and descending projections that synapse at the level of the thoracic spinal cord (Foote, Bloom, & Aston-Jones, 1983). Exposure to stressors results in activation of the locus coeruleus, with release of norepinephrine throughout the brain (Abercrombie & Jacobs, 1987; Levine, Litto, & Jacobs, 1990), including the hippocampus and medial prefrontal cortex (Finlay, Zigmond, & Abercrombie, 1995). Chronic stress is associated with potentiated release of norepinephrine in the hippocampus with exposure to subsequent stressors (Bremner, Southwick, et al., 1996; Nisenbaum, Zigmond, Sved, & Abercrombie, 1991).

Norepinephrine sharpens the senses, focuses attention, raises the level of fear, quickens the heart rate and blood pressure and, in general, helps prepares us for "fight or flight." The norepinephrine system is like a fire alarm that alerts all areas of the brain simultaneously.

A variety of studies have found long-term dysregulation of the noradrenergic system in PTSD (Bremner, Krystal, et al., 1996b). Psychophysiology

studies have demonstrated an increase in sympathetic responses (heart rate, blood pressure, and galvanic skin response) to traumatic reminders, such as slides and sounds of trauma or traumatic scripts, in PTSD (Pitman, Orr, Forgue, de Jong, & Claiborn, 1987). There are increased concentrations of norepinephrine in plasma and urine at baseline, and traumatic reminders result in a potentiated release of norepinephrine (McFall, Murburg, Ko, & Veith, 1990). Administration of the α_2 antagonist yohimbine, which causes an increased release of norepinephrine in the brain, to PTSD patients resulted in an increase in PTSD-specific symptomatology, as well as greater release of norepinephrine metabolites in plasma (Southwick et al., 1993). Alterations in central metabolic responses to yohimbine were also found in PTSD patients, as measured with positron emission tomography (PET) (Bremner, Innis, et al., 1997).

The HPA-cortisol system also plays an important role in the stress response. Like norepinephrine, cortisol is released during times of threat and is critical to survival. Cortisol redistributes energy, suppressing functions not needed for immediate survival, including reproduction, the body's immune response, digestion, and the feeling of pain. Cortisol shunts energy to the brain and muscles to promote quick thinking and fast escapes. Stress is associated with activation of the HPA axis. Corticotropin-releasing factor (CRF) is released from the hypothalamus, with stimulation of adrenocorticotropic hormone (ACTH) release from the pituitary. This results in glucocorticoid (cortisol) release from the adrenal, which in turn has a negative feedback effect on the axis at the level of the pituitary and central brain sites, including the hypothalamus and hippocampus (Arborelius, Owens, Plotsky, & Nemeroff, 1999) Exposure to stressful situations is associated with a marked increase in cortisol release from the adrenal gland, and following chronic stress there is an increased glucocorticoid response to subsequent stressors (Levine, Weiner, & Coe, 1993; Stanton, Gutierrez, & Levine, 1988).

PTSD is associated with long-term dysregulation of the HPA axis (Yehuda, 2006). Baseline levels of urinary cortisol have been found to be either decreased or unchanged in chronic PTSD, while decreased levels were found in 24-hour samples of plasma cortisol levels (Bremner, Vythillingham, Anderson, et al. 2003; Yehuda, 2006; Yehuda, Teicher, Levengood, Trestman, & Siever, 1994). In individuals with PTSD, exposure to a stressor (Bremner, Vythillingham, Vermetten, et al., 2003) or a traumatic reminder (Elzinga, Schmal, Vermetten, van Dyck, & Bremner, 2003) was associated with a potentiated release of cortisol. A replicated finding has been a supersuppression of the cortisol response to lower doses of dexamethasone (0.5 mg), the opposite response of patients with major depression, who are nonsuppressers with the standard 1 mg dexamethasone suppression test (DST) (Yehuda et al., 1993). Patients with PTSD had elevated levels of CRF in the cerebrospinal fluid (Baker et al., 1999; Bremner, Licinio, et al., 1997). One possible explanation for these findings is that patients with PTSD have an increase in neuronal CRF release, increased central glucocorticoid receptor responsiveness, and resultant low levels of peripheral cortisol due to enhanced negative feedback.

Results from the few studies of the effects of early stress on neurobiology that have been conducted in clinical populations of traumatized children have generally been consistent with findings from animal studies. They suggest that early abuse is associated with long-term changes in the HPA axis, although the direction of those changes is not always consistent (De Bellis & Keshavan, 2003; Gunnar, Morison, Chisholm, & Schuder, 2001).

Functional Neuroimaging Studies in PTSD

Functional neuroimaging studies have been performed to map the neural circuitry of PTSD (Bremner, 2003a, 2007; Bremner & Vermetten 2001). These studies are consistent with dysfunction in a network of related brain areas, including the amygdala, medial prefrontal cortex, and hippocampus, that mediate memory and the stress response and may mediate symptoms of PTSD (Bremner, 2002b, 2003b; Pitman, 2001). The amygdala plays a central role in conditioned fear responses (Davis, 1992; LeDoux, 1993). The medial prefrontal cortex consists of several related areas, including the orbitofrontal cortex, anterior cingulate (Brodmann's area 25—the subcallosal gyrus—and area 32), and anterior prefrontal cortex (area 9) (Devinsky, Morrell, & Vogt, 1995; Vogt, Ficnh, & Olson, 1992). Lesions in this area result in a failure to mount the peripheral cortisol and sympathetic response to stress (Devinsky et al., 1995; Vogt et al., 1992). Early stress is associated with a reduction in dendritic branching in this area (Radley et al., 2004). The medial prefrontal cortex also has inhibitory inputs to the amygdala that mediate extinction to fear responding (Morgan & LeDoux, 1995; Quirk, 2002). These findings suggest that dysfunction of the medial prefrontal cortex plays a role in mediating symptoms of PTSD.

Imaging studies of brain function in PTSD are consistent with dysfunction of the medial prefrontal cortex, amygdala, and hippocampus (Bremner, 1998, 2002a, 2007; Cannistraro & Rauch, 2003; Liberzon, Britton, & Phan, 2003; Liberzon & Martis, 2006; Liberzon & Phan, 2003; Pitman, 2001; Rauch, Shin, & Phelps, 2006). PET and SPECT studies of resting blood flow or metabolism have shown alterations at rest in medial prefrontal, temporal, and dorsolateral prefrontal cortex; cerebellum; amygdala (Bonne et al., 2003; Bremner, Innis, et al. 1997; Chung et al., 2006); thalamus (Kim et al., 2007); and mid-cingulate (Shin et al., 2009).

In one study, activation of the noradrenergic system with yohimbine resulted in a failure of activation in dorsolateral prefrontal, temporal, parietal, and orbitofrontal cortex, and decreased function in the hippocampus (Bremner, Innis, et al. 1997). Exposure to traumatic reminders on slides or through sounds or traumatic scripts was associated with an increase in PTSD symptoms, decreased blood flow, and/or failure of activation in the medial prefrontal cortex/anterior cingulate, including Brodmann's area 25, or subcallosal gyrus, and areas 32 and 24, as measured with PET, SPECT, or fMRI (Bremner, Narayan, et al., 1999; Bremner, Staib, et al., 1999; Britton, Phan, Taylor, Fig, & Liberzon, 2005; Britton et al., 2007; Etkin & Wager, 2007; Fonzo et al., 2010; Hopper, Frewen, van der Kolk, & Lanius, 2007; Hou et al., 2007; Lanius et al. 2001, 2003; Liberzon et al., 1999; Lindauer, Booji, et al., 2004; Phan, Britton, Taylor, Fig, & Liberzon, 2006; Semple et al., 2000; Shin et al., 1997, 1999, 2001, 2005; Shin, Orr, et al., 2004; Yang, Wu, Hsu, & Ker, 2004). Other findings from studies of traumatic reminder exposure include decreased function in the hippocampus (Bremner, Narayan, et al., 1999), thalamus (Lanius et al., 2001, 2003), visual association cortex (Bremner, Narayan, et al., 1999; Lanius et al., 2003; Shin et al., 1997; Shin, Orr, et al., 2004a), parietal cortex (Bremner, Narayan, et al., 1999; Rauch et al., 1996; Sakamoto et al., 2005; Shin et al., 1997, 1999), and inferior frontal gyrus (Bremner, Narayan, et al., 1999; Lanius et al., 2003; Rauch et al., 1996; Sakamoto et al., 2005; Shin et al., 1997, 1999, 2001), and increased function in the amygdala (Liberzon et al. 1999; Rauch et al., 1996; Shin, Orr, et al., 2004), insula (Fonzo et al., 2010; Hopper et al., 2007; Simmons et al., 2008), posterior cingulate (Bremner, Narayan, et al., 1999; Bremner, Staib, et al., 1999; Lanius et al., 2001; Shin et al., 1997), ventromedial prefrontal cortex (Morey, Petty, Cooper, Labar, & McCarthy, 2008), and parahippocampal gyrus (Bremner, Narayan, et al. 1999; Bremner, Staib, et al., 1999; Liberzon et al., 1999). Shin and colleagues found a correlation between increased amygdala function and decreased medial prefrontal function with traumatic reminders (Shin, Orr, et al., 2004). A failure of inhibition of the amygdala by the medial prefrontal cortex could account for increased PTSD symptoms with traumatic reminders. Another study showed that increased amygdala reactivity predicted increased stress symptom response to combat, while increased hippocampal activity paralleled the increase in stress symptoms (Admon et al., 2009). Other studies have found increased amygdala and parahippocampal function and decreased medial prefrontal function during performance of an attention task (Felmingham, Williams, Kemp, et al., 2009; Semple et al., 2000). Increased amygdala function was found at rest (Chung et al., 2006) during a working memory task (Bryant et al., 2005), during recall of traumatic words (Protopopescu et al., 2005), and with exposure to masked fearful faces (Armony, Corbo, Clément, & Brunel, 2005; Bryant, Kemp, et al., 2008; Felmingham et al., 2010; Kemp et al., 2007, 2009; Rauch et al., 2000), overt fearful faces (Fonzo et al., 2010; Shin et al., 2005), negative pictures (Brohawn et al., 2010), neutral pictures (Brunetti et al., 2010), traumatic sounds (Liberzon et al., 1999; Pissiota et al., 2002), traumatic scripts (Rauch et al., 1996), extinction learning (Milad et al., 2009), and classical fear conditioning (Bremner, Vermetten, et al., 2005).

Children with post-traumatic stress symptoms showed increased medial prefrontal and decreased middle frontal gyrus activation with a go/no-go working memory task (Carrion, Garrett, Menon, Weems, & Reiss, 2008).

Studies have also looked at neural correlates of acute traumatization. Patients with acute PTSD from surgical trauma had increased blood flow in the hippocampus, anterior cingulate, and amygdala upon exposure to traumatic memories (Piefke et al., 2007). One study of survivors of an acute motor vehicle accident indicated decreased amygdala blood flow during exposure to traumatic scripts, and a negative correlation was found between symptom improvement at 3 months and hippocampal blood flow during exposure to traumatic scripts (Osuch et al., 2008).

Several studies have examined neural correlates of cognitive tasks in PTSD. Studies using specific declarative memory tasks have found decreased activation of the hippocampus (Astur et al., 2006; Bremner, Vythillingham, Vermetten, Southwick, McGlashan, Nazeere, et al., 2003; Shin, Shin, et al., 2004) and insula (Chen, Li, Xu, & Liu, 2009; Whalley, Rugg, Smith, Dolan, & Brewin, 2009) in PTSD. During performance of working memory tasks, patients with PTSD had decreased inferior frontal (Clark et al., 2003), parietal (Bryant et al., 2005; Clark et al., 2003), hippocampal, and anterior cingulate function (Moores et al., 2008). Also in PTSD patients performing a working memory task, presentation of combat-related distractors was associated with increased activation in the amygdala, ventrolateral prefrontal cortex, and fusiform gyrus, and decreased activation in the dorsolateral prefrontal cortex (Morey et al., 2008). An emotional oddball task was associated with activation in peri-amygdala areas, ventrolateral prefrontal cortex, and orbitofrontal cortex (Pannu Hayes, Labar, Petty, McCarthy, & Morey, 2009). Patients with PTSD showed reduced anterior cingulate activation during a same-different emotional conflict task (Kim et al., 2008). One study of individuals with PTSD found a relative failure of connectivity in the right inferior frontal gyrus and right inferior parietal lobule during performance of working memory tasks, as well as stronger connectivity between the posterior cingulate cortex and right superior frontal gyrus and between the medial prefrontal cortex and left parahippocampal gyrus (Daniels et al., 2010) during the same tasks.

Retrieval of emotionally valenced words (Bremner et al., 2001) (e.g., *rape-mutilate*) in women with PTSD from early abuse resulted in decreases in blood flow in an extensive area that included the orbitofrontal cortex, anterior cingulate, and medial prefrontal cortex (Brodmann's areas 25, 32, 9); left hippocampus; and fusiform gyrus/inferior temporal gyrus (Bremner, Vythillingham, Vermetten, Southwick, McGlashan, Staib, et al., 2003). Encoding of neutral words was associated with a failure of frontal, temporal (Geuze, Vermetten, Ruf, de Kloet, & Westenberg, 2008), and precuneus activation in PTSD (Geuze, Vermetten, de Kloet, & Westenberg, et al., 2008). Neutral-word retrieval was associated with impaired activation of the hippocampus, middle temporal gyrus, and frontal cortex (Geuze, Vermetten, Ruf, et al., 2008) and parahippocampal gyrus (Hou et al. 2007). Performance of the emotional Stroop task in PTSD (e.g., naming the color of a word, such as *rape*) was associated with failure of activation or decreased function in medial prefrontal cortical/anterior cingulate (Bremner, Vermetten, Vythillingham, et al. 2004; Shin et al., 2001), visual association, parietal cortex (Bremner, Vermetten, Vythillingham, et al., 2004), and dorsolateral prefrontal cortex (Bremner, Vermetten, Vythillingham, et al., 2004; Shin et al., 2001), and with increased function in posterior cingulate and parahippocampal gyrus (Shin et al., 2001). During a facial-profession encoding task, patients with PTSD had increased hippocampal and weaker prefrontal activation, and during retrieval a decrease in left parahippocampal gyrus and other memory-related brain regions (Werner et al., 2009).

Functional imaging studies have also shown evidence for deficits in neural circuits involved in motivation and reward systems in PTSD. During the processing of gains in the late phase of learning in a decision-making task, patients with PTSD showed lower activation in the nucleus accumbens and the mesial prefrontal cortex than that in controls (Sailer et al., 2008). In PTSD patients there was a failure of prefrontal cortex activation during attempts to diminish emotional responses to emotional pictures (New et al., 2009). Other studies have shown decreased insula activation during an affective set-shifting task (Simmons, Strigo, Matthews, Paulus, & Stein, 2009). One study showed a failure of right dorsolateral frontal and increased striatal activity in PTSD during a task involving inhibitory control (Falconer et al., 2009). Levels of emotional awareness were negatively correlated with activation of the anterior cingulate in patients with PTSD (Frewen et al., 2008).

Studies have also examined neural correlates of pain processing in PTSD, with affected individuals having decreased sensitivity to pain. During the processing of pain, PTSD subjects had increased insula (Geuze et al., 2007; Strigo et al., 2010) and dorsolateral prefrontal cortex activation (Strigo et al., 2010). Other studies have shown increased hippocampal and amygdala activation and decreased ventrolateral prefrontal function (Geuze et al., 2007).

More recently, investigators have looked at connectivity between different brain areas in PTSD. Increased connectivity between amygdala and anterior cingulate in acutely traumatized patients was associated with current PTSD symptom severity as well as risk for chronicity of future PTSD symptoms (Lanius et al., 2010). Patients with PTSD showed increased connectivity between the amygdala, anterior cingulate, visual cortex, and subcallosal gyrus (Gilboa et al., 2004). Other studies have reported a decrease in posterior cingulate–precuneus

connectivity during a resting state in patients with PTSD (Bluhm et al., 2009).

Studies have also looked at neural correlates of treatment response in PTSD. Treatment with paroxetine for up to a year in PTSD patients resulted in significant improvements in verbal declarative memory and a 4.6% increase in mean hippocampal volume (Vermetten, Vythillingham, Southwick, Charney, & Bremner, 2003). Another study showed an increase in hippocampal volume with sertraline treatment in patients with PTSD (Bossini et al., 2007). An increase in right hippocampal and cerebral cortical brain volume with phenytoin treatment for PTSD has also been reported (Bremner, Mletzko, et al., 2005).

PTSD patients who did not respond to eye movement desensitization and reprocessing (EMDR) therapy showed lower gray matter density than that of responders in bilateral posterior cingulate, anterior insula, anterior parahippocampal gyrus, and amygdala in the right hemisphere (Nardo et al., 2009). Patients with subthreshold PTSD had significant increases in perfusion following psychotherapy, as measured with SPECT HMPAO in the parietal lobes, left hippocampus, thalamus, and left prefrontal cortex during a memory retrieval task (Peres et al., 2007). Patients with PTSD showed decreased frontal and hippocampal perfusion with SPECT HMPAO, compared to controls, that normalized with successful EMDR treatment (Pagani et al., 2007). Treatment of PTSD with EMDR resulted in decreases in perfusion in the left and right occipital lobe, left parietal lobe, and right precentral frontal lobe, as well as significant increased perfusion in the left inferior frontal gyrus, as measured with SPECT HMPAO (Lansing, Amen, Hanks, & Rudy, 2005).

Cognitive behavioral therapy (CBT) resulted in a decreased amygdala and increased anterior cingulate response to fearful faces in those with PTSD (Felmingham et al., 2007). PTSD patients who responded to CBT had larger rostral anterior cingulate volumes (rACC) than those who did not (Bryant, Felmington, Whitford, et al., 2008), while those who were poor responders to CBT had increased amygdala and ventral ACC response to masked fearful faces, compared to positive responders (Bryant, Felmington, Kemp, et al., 2008).

In summary, successful treatment of PTSD is associated with changes in brain areas that have been implicated in PTSD, including the hippocampus and prefrontal cortex. Increased function in the amygdala may be a predictor of poor response to CBT.

Neuroreceptor Studies in PTSD

Studies have begun to use PET and SPECT to measure neuroreceptors in PTSD. Reduced binding of benzodiazepine receptors has been found in the frontal cortex in combat veterans in some studies (Bremner et al., 2000; Geuze, van Berckel, et al., 2008) but not in others (Fujita et al., 2004). One study found no changes in binding of the 5HT1A serotonin receptor (Bonne et al., 2005). Other studies have found a reduction in anterior cingulate opiate receptor binding (Liberzon et al., 2007) and an increase in hippocampal beta2 nicotinic acetylcholine receptor binding in PTSD (Czermak et al., 2008).

Conclusions

PTSD is a common condition that can be associated with considerable morbidity and mortality. This disorder is associated with long-term changes in the brain and stress-responsive systems. Brain areas affected include the amygdala, hippocampus, and frontal cortex. These changes may lead to both memory problems and maintenance of abnormal fear responses and other symptoms of PTSD. Some studies have shown that treatment can affect the hippocampus and prefrontal cortex, possibly facilitating the ability of the brain to extinguish troubling intrusive memories and thereby facilitate recovery. Future studies are required to examine the neurochemical substrates of PTSD and response to treatment.

References

Abercrombie, E. D., & Jacobs, B. L. (1987). Single-unit response of noradrenergic neurons in the locus coeruleus of freely moving cats. II. Adaptation to chronically presented stressful stimuli. *Journal of Neuroscience, 7,* 2844–2848.

Admon, R., Lubin, G., Stern, O., Rosenberg, K., Sela, L., Ben-Ami H., & Hendler, T. (2009). Human vulnerability to stress depends on amygdala's predisposition and hippocampal plasticity. *Proceedings of the National Academy of Sciences U S A, 106*(33), 14120–14125.

Andersen, S. L., Tomada, A., Vincow, E. S., Valente, E., Polcari, A., & Teicher, M. H. (2008). Preliminary evidence for sensitive periods in the effect of childhood sexual abuse on regional brain development. *Journal of Neuropsychiatry & Clinical Neuroscience, 20*(3), 292–301.

Arborelius, L., Owens, M. J., Plotsky, P. M., & Nemeroff, C. B. (1999). The role of corticotropin-releasing factor in depression and anxiety disorders. *Journal of Endocrinology, 160,* 1–12.

Armony, J. L., Corbo, V., Clément, M. H., & Brunet, A. (2005). Amygdala response in patients with acute PTSD to masked and unmasked emotional facial expressions. *American Journal of Psychiatry, 162*(10), 1961–1963.

Astur, R. S., St Germain, S. A., Tolin, D., Ford, J., Russell, D., & Stevens, M. (2006). Hippocampus function predicts severity of post-traumatic stress disorder. *Cyberpsychology & Behavior, 9*(2), 234–240.

Baker, D. G., West, S. A., Nicholson, W. E., Ekhator, N. N., Kasckow, J. W., Hill, K. K., et al. (1999). Serial CSF corticotropin-releasing hormone levels and adrenocortical activity in combat veterans with posttraumatic stress disorder. *American Journal of Psychiatry, 156,* 585–588.

Barrett, D. H., Green, M. L., Morris, R., Giles, W. H., & Croft, J. B. (1996). Cognitive functioning and posttraumatic stress disorder. *American Journal of Psychiatry, 153*(11), 1492–1494.

Bluhm, R. L., Williamson, P. C., Osuch, E. A., Frewen, P. A., Stevens, T. K., Boksman, K., et al. (2009). Alterations in default network connectivity in posttraumatic stress disorder related to early-life trauma. *Journal of Psychiatry and Neuroscience, 34*(3), 187–194.

Bonne, O., Bain, E., Neumeister, A., Nugent, A. C., Vythilingham, M., Carson, R. E., et al. (2005). No change in serotonin type 1A receptor binding in patients with posttraumatic stress disorder. *American Journal of Psychiatry, 162*(2), 383–385.

Bonne, O., Brandes, D., Gilboa, A., Gomori, J. M., Shenton, M. E., Pitman, R. K., & Shalev, A. Y. (2001). Longitudinal MRI study of hippocampal volume in trauma survivors with PTSD. *American Journal of Psychiatry, 158,* 1248–1251.

Bonne, O., Gilboa, A., Louzoun, Y., Brandes, D., Yona, I., Lester, H., et al. (2003). Resting regional cerebral perfusion in recent posttraumatic stress disorder. *Biological Psychiatry, 54*(10), 1077–1086.

Bonne, O., Vythilingham, M., Inagaki, M., Wood, S., Neumeister, A., Nugent, A. C., et al. (2008). Reduced posterior hippocampal volume in posttraumatic stress disorder. *Journal of Clinical Psychiatry, 69*(7), 1087–1091.

Bossini, L., Tavanti, M., Lombardelli, A., Calossi, S., Polizzotto, N. R., Galli, R., et al. (2007). Changes in hippocampal volume in patients with post-traumatic stress disorder after sertraline treatment. *Journal of Clinical Psychopharmacology, 27*(2), 233–235.

Bossini, L., Tavanti, M., Calossi, S., Lombardelli, A., Polizzotto, N. R., Galli, R., et al. (2008). Magnetic resonance imaging volumes of the hippocampus in drug-naïve patients with post-traumatic stress disorder without comorbidity conditions. *Journal of Psychiatric Research, 42*(9), 752–762.

Bremner, J. D. (1998). Neuroimaging of posttraumatic stress disorder. *Psychiatric Annals, 28,* 445–450.

Bremner, J. D. (2002a). Neuroimaging of childhood trauma. *Seminars in Clinical Neuropsychiatry, 7,* 104–112.

Bremner, J. D. (2002b). *Does stress damage the brain? Understanding trauma-related disorders from a mind-body perspective.* New York: W.W. Norton.

Bremner, J. D. (2003a). Long-term effects of childhood abuse on brain and neurobiology. *Child and Adolescent Psychiatric Clinics of North America, 12*(2), 271–292.

Bremner, J. D. (2003b). Functional neuroanatomical correlates of traumatic stress revisited 7 years later, this time with data. *Psychopharmacology Bulletin, 37*(2), 6–25.

Bremner, J. D. (2007). Functional neuroimaging in posttraumatic stress disorder. *Expert Reviews in Neurotherapeutics, 7*(4), 393–405.

Bremner, J. D., Innis, R. B., Ng, C. K., Staib, L. H., Salomon, R. M., Bronen, R. A., et al. (1997). Positron emission tomography measurement of cerebral metabolic correlates of yohimbine administration in posttraumatic stress disorder. *Archives of General Psychiatry, 54,* 246–256.

Bremner, J. D., Innis, R. B., White, T., Fujita, M., Silbersweig, D., Goddard, A. W., et al. (2000). SPECT [I-123]iomazenil measurement of the benzodiazepine receptor in panic disorder. *Biological Psychiatry, 47*, 96–106.

Bremner, J. D., Krystal, J. H., Southwick, S. M., & Charney, D. S. (1995). Functional neuroanatomical correlates of the effects of stress on memory. *Journal of Traumatic Stress, 8*, 527–554.

Bremner, J. D., Krystal, J. H., Southwick, S. M., & Charney, D. S. (1996a). Noradrenergic mechanisms in stress and anxiety: I. Preclinical studies. *Synapse, 23*, 28–38.

Bremner, J. D., Krystal, J. H., Southwick, S. M., & Charney, D. S. (1996b). Noradrenergic mechanisms in stress and anxiety: II. Clinical studies. *Synapse, 23*, 39–51.

Bremner, J. D., Licinio, J., Darnell, A., Krystal, J. H., Owens, M. J., Southwick, S. M., et al. (1997). Elevated CSF corticotropin-releasing factor concentrations in posttraumatic stress disorder. *American Journal of Psychiatry, 154*, 624–629.

Bremner, J. D., Mletzko, T., Welter, S., Quinn, S., Williams, C., Brummer, M., et al. (2005). Effects of phenytoin on memory, cognition and brain structure in posttraumatic stress disorder: A pilot study. *Journal of Psychopharmacology, 19*(2), 159–165.

Bremner, J. D., Narayan, M., Staib, L. H., Southwick, S. M., McGlashan, T., & Charney, D. S. (1999). Neural correlates of memories of childhood sexual abuse in women with and without posttraumatic stress disorder. *American Journal of Psychiatry, 156*, 1787–1795.

Bremner, J. D., Randall, P., Scott, T. M., Bronen, R. A., Seibyl, J. P., Southwick, S. M., et al. (1995). MRI-based measurement of hippocampal volume in patients with combat-related posttraumatic stress disorder. *American Journal of Psychiatry, 152*, 973–981.

Bremner, J. D., Randall, P., Scott, T. M., Capelli, S., Delaney, R., McCarthy, G., & Charney, D. S. (1995). Deficits in short-term memory in adult survivors of childhood abuse. *Psychiatry Research, 59*, 97–107.

Bremner, J. D., Randall, P., Vermetten, E., Staib, L., Bronen, R. A., Mazure, C., et al. (1997). Magnetic resonance imaging-based measurement of hippocampal volume in posttraumatic stress disorder related to childhood physical and sexual abuse: A preliminary report. *Biological Psychiatry, 41*, 23–32.

Bremner, J. D., Scott, T. M., Delaney, R., Southwick, S. M., Mason, J. W., Johnson, D. R., et al. (1993). Deficits in short-term memory in post-traumatic stress disorder. *American Journal of Psychiatry, 150*, 1015–1019.

Bremner, J. D., Soufer, R., McCarthy, G., Delaney, R., Staib, L. H., Duncan, J. S., & Charney, D. S. (2001). Gender differences in cognitive and neural correlates of remembrance of emotional words. *Psychopharmacology Bulletin, 35*, 55–87.

Bremner, J. D., Southwick, S. M., Darnell, A., & Charney, D. S. (1996). Chronic PTSD in Vietnam combat veterans: Course of illness and substance abuse. *American Journal of Psychiatry, 153*, 369–375.

Bremner, J. D., Staib, L. H., Kaloupek, D., Southwick, S. M., Soufer, R., & Charney, D. S. (1999). Neural correlates of exposure to traumatic pictures and sound in Vietnam combat veterans with and without posttraumatic stress disorder: A positron emission tomography study. *Biological Psychiatry, 45*, 806–816.

Bremner, J. D., & Vermetten, E. (2001). Stress and development: Behavioral and biological consequences. *Development & Psychopathology, 13*, 473–489.

Bremner, J. D., Vermetten, E., Afzal, N., & Vythillingham, M. (2004). Deficits in verbal declarative memory function

in women with childhood sexual abuse-related posttraumatic stress disorder. *Journal of Nervous and Mental Disease, 192*(10), 643–649.

Bremner, J. D., Vermetten, E., Schmal, C., Vaccarino, V., Vythillingham, M., Afzal, N., et al. (2005). Positron emission tomographic imaging of neural correlates of a fear acquisition and extinction paradigm in women with childhood sexual abuse-related posttraumatic stress disorder. *Psychological Medicine, 35*(6), 791–806.

Bremner, J. D., Vermetten, E., Vythillingham, M., Afzal, N., Schmal, C., Elzinga, B., & Charney, D. S. (2004). Neural correlates of the classic color and emotional Stroop in women with abuse-related posttraumatic stress disorder. *Biological Psychiatry, 55*(6), 612–620.

Bremner, J. D., Vythillingham, M., Anderson, G., Vermetten, E., McGlashan, T., Heninger, G., et al. (2003). Assessment of the hypothalamic-pituitary-adrenal axis over a 24-hour diurnal period and in response to neuroendocrine challenges in women with and without early childhood sexual abuse and posttraumatic stress disorder. *Biological Psychiatry, 54*(7), 710–718.

Bremner, J. D., Vythillingham, M., Vermetten, E., Adil, J., Khan, S., Nazeere, A., et al. (2003). Cortisol response to a cognitive stress challenge in posttraumatic stress disorder (PTSD) related to childhood abuse. *Psychoneuroendocrinology, 28*, 733–750.

Bremner, J. D., Vythillingham, M., Vermetten, E., Southwick, S. M., McGlashan, T., Nazeere, A., et al. (2003). MRI and PET study of deficits in hippocampal structure and function in women with childhood sexual abuse and posttraumatic stress disorder. *American Journal of Psychiatry, 160* (5), 924–932.

Bremner, J. D., Vythillingham, M., Vermetten, E., Southwick, S. M., McGlashan, T., Staib, L. H., et al. (2003). Neural correlates of declarative memory for emotionally valenced words in women with posttraumatic stress disorder related to early childhood sexual abuse. *Biological Psychiatry, 53*, 289–299.

Brewin, C. R. (2001). A cognitive neuroscience account of posttraumatic stress disorder and its treatment. *Behavior Research and Therapy, 39*, 373–393.

Brewin C. R. (2003). MRI and PET study of deficits in hippocampal structure and function in women with childhood sexual abuse and posttraumatic stress disorder (PTSD). *American Journal of Psychiatry, 160*, 924–932.

Brewin, C. R., Andrews, B., & Valentine, J. D. (2000). Meta-analysis of risk factors for posttraumatic stress disorder in trauma-exposed adults. *Journal of Consulting & Clinical Psychology, 68*(5), 748–766.

Britton, J. C., Phan, K. L., Taylor, S. F., Fig, L. M., & Liberzon, I. (2005). Corticolimbic blood flow in posttraumatic stress disorder during script-driven imagery *Biological Psychiatry, 57*(8), 832–840.

Brohawn, K. H., Offringa, R., Pfadd, D. L., Hughes, K. C., & Shin, L. M. (2010). The neural correlates of emotional memory in posttraumatic stress disorder. *Biological Psychiatry, 68*(11), 1023–1030.

Brunetti, M., Sepede, G., Mingoia, G., Catani, C., Ferretti, A., Merla, A., et al. (2010). Elevated response of human amygdala to neutral stimuli in mild post traumatic stress disorder: Neural correlates of generalized emotional response. *Neuroscience, 168*(3), 670–679.

Bryant, R. A., Felmington, K., Kemp, A., Barton, M., Peduto, A., Rennie, C., et al. (2005). Neural networks of information processing in posttraumatic stress disorder: A functional magnetic resonance imaging study. *Biological Psychiatry*, 58(2), 111–118.

Bryant, R. A., Felmington, K., Kemp, A., Das, P., Hughes, G., Peduto, A., & Williams, L. M. (2008). Amygdala and ventral anterior cingulate activation predicts treatment response to cognitive behaviour therapy for post-traumatic stress disorder. *Psychological Medicine*, 38(4), 555–561.

Bryant, R. A., Felmington, K., Whitford, T. J., Kemp, A., Hughes, G., Peduto, A., & Williams, L. M. (2008). Rostral anterior cingulate volume predicts treatment response to cognitive-behavioural therapy for posttraumatic stress disorder. *Journal of Psychiatry and Neuroscience*, 33(2), 142–146.

Bryant, R. A., Kemp, A., Felmington, K., Liddell, B., Olivieri, G., Peduto, A., et al. (2008). Enhanced amygdala and medial prefrontal activation during nonconscious processing of fear in posttraumatic stress disorder: an fMRI study. *Human Brain Mapping*, 29(5), 517–523.

Buckley, T. C., Blanchard, E. B., & Neill, W. T. (2000). Information processing and PTSD: A review of the empirical literature. *Clinical Psychology Reviews*, 28(8), 1041–1065.

Cannistraro, P. A., & Rauch, S. L. (2003). Neural circuitry of anxiety: Evidence from structural and functional neuroimaging studies. *Psychopharmacology Bulletin*, 37(4), 8–25.

Carrion, V. G., Garrett, A., Menon, V., Weems, C. F., & Reiss, A. L. (2008). Posttraumatic stress symptoms and brain function during a response-inhibition task: An fMRI study in youth. *Depression and Anxiety*, 25(6), 514–526.

Carrion, V. G., Weems, C. F., Eliez, S., Patwardhan, A., Brown, W., Ray, R. D., & Reiss, A. L. (2001). Attenuation of frontal asymmetry in pediatric posttraumatic stress disorder. *Biological Psychiatry*, 50, 943–951.

Carrion, V. G., Weems, C. F., Watson, C., Eliez, S., Menon, V., & Reiss, A. L. (2009). Converging evidence for abnormalities of the prefrontal cortex and evaluation of midsagittal structures in pediatric posttraumatic stress disorder: An MRI study. *Psychiatry Research*, 172(3), 226–234.

Chen, S., Li, L., Xu, B., & Liu, J. (2009). Insular cortex involvement in declarative memory deficits in patients with posttraumatic stress disorder. *BMC Psychiatry*, 9, 39.

Chen, S., Xia, W., Li, L., Liu, J., He, Z., Zhang, Z., et al. (2006). Gray matter density reduction in the insula in fire survivors with posttraumatic stress disorder: A voxel-based morphometric study. *Psychiatry Research*, 146(1), 65–72.

Chung, Y. A., Kim, S. H., Chung, S. K., Chae, J. H., Yang, D. W., Sohn, H. S., & Jeong, J. (2006). Alterations in cerebral perfusion in posttraumatic stress disorder patients without re-exposure to accident-related stimuli. *Clinical Neurophysiology*, 117(3), 637–642.

Clark, C. R., McFarlane, A. C., Morris, P., Weber, D. L., Sonkkilla, C., Shaw, M., et al. (2003). Cerebral function in posttraumatic stress disorder during verbal working memory updating: A positron emission tomography study. *Biological Psychiatry*, 53, 474–481.

Corbo, V., Clément, M. H., Armony, J. L., Pruessner, J. C., & Brunet, A. (2005). Size versus shape differences: Contrasting voxel-based and volumetric analyses of the anterior cingulate cortex in individuals with acute posttraumatic stress disorder. *Biological Psychiatry*, 58(2), 119–124.

Czeh, B., Michaelis, T., Watanabe, T., Frahm, J., de Biurrun, G., van Kampen, M., et al. (2001). Stress-induced changes in cerebral metabolites, hippocampal volume, and cell proliferation are prevented by antidepressant treatment with tianeptine. *Proceedings of the National Academy of Sciences U S A*, 98, 12796–12801.

Czermak, C., Staley, J. K., Kasserman, S., Bois, F., Young, T., Henry, S., et al. (2008). Beta-2 nicotinic acetylcholine receptor availability in post-traumatic stress disorder. *International Journal of Neuropsychopharmacology*, 11(3), 419–424.

Daniels, J. K., McFarlane, A. C., Blume, R. L., Moores, K. A., Clark, C. R., Shaw, M. E., et al. (2010). Switching between executive and default mode networks in posttraumatic stress disorder: Alterations in functional connectivity. *Journal of Psychiatry & Neuroscience*, 35(4), 258–266.

Davis, M. (1992). The role of the amygdala in fear and anxiety. *Annual Review of Neuroscience*, 15, 353–375.

De Bellis, M. D., Hall, J., Boring, A. M., Frustaci, K., & Moritz, G. (2001). A pilot longitudinal study of hippocampal volumes in pediatric maltreatment-related posttraumatic stress disorder. *Biological Psychiatry*, 50, 305–309.

De Bellis, M. D., & Keshavan, M. S. (2003). Sex differences in brain maturation in maltreatment-related pediatric posttraumatic stress disorder. *Neuroscience & Biobehavioral Reviews*, 27(1-2), 103–117.

De Bellis, M. D., Keshavan, M. S., Shifflett, H., Iyengar, S., Beers, S. R., Hall, J., & Moritz, G. (2002). Brain structures in pediatric maltreatment-related posttraumatic stress disorder: A sociodemographically matched study. *Biological Psychiatry*, 52(11), 1066–1078.

De Bellis, M. D., Keshavan, M. S., Spencer, S., & Hall, J. (2000). N-Acetylaspartate concentration in the anterior cingulate of maltreated children and adolescents with PTSD. *American Journal of Psychiatry*, 157, 1175–1177.

De Bellis, M. D., Keshavan, M. S., Clark, D. B., Casey, B. J., Giedd, J. N., Boring, A. M., et al. (1999). A.E. Bennett Research Award: Developmental traumatology: Part II. Brain development. *Biological Psychiatry*, 45, 1271–1284.

Devinsky, O., Morrell, M. J., & Vogt, B. A. (1995). Contributions of anterior cingulate to behavior. *Brain*, 118, 279–306.

Diamond, D. M., Fleshner, M., Ingersoll, N., & Rose, G. M. (1996). Psychological stress impairs spatial working memory: Relevance to electrophysiological studies of hippocampal function. *Behavioral Neuroscience*, 110, 661–672.

D'Sa, C., & Duman, R. S. (2002). Antidepressants and neuroplasticity. *Bipolar Disorder*, 4, 183–194.

Duman, R. S. (2004). Depression: A case of neuronal life and death? *Biological Psychiatry*, 56, 140–145.

Duman, R. S., Heninger, G. R., & Nestler, E. J. (1997). A molecular and cellular theory of depression. *Archives of General Psychiatry*, 54, 597–606.

Duman, R. S., Malberg, J. E., & Nakagawa, S. (2001). Regulation of adult neurogenesis by psychotropic drugs and stress. *Journal of Pharmacology & Experimental Therapeutics*, 299, 401–407.

Elzinga, B. M., & Bremner, J. D. (2002). Are the neural substrates of memory the final common pathway in PTSD? *Journal of Affective Disorders*, 70, 1–17.

Elzinga, B. M., Schmal, C. G., Vermetten, E., van Dyck, R., & Bremner, J. D. (2003). Higher cortisol levels following exposure to traumatic reminders in abuse-related PTSD. *Neuropsychopharmacology*, 28(9), 1656–1665.

Emdad, R., Bonekamp, D., Sondergaard, H. P., Bjorklund, T., Agartz, I., Ingvar, M., & Theorell, T. (2006). Morphometric and psychometric comparisons between non-substance-abusing patients with posttraumatic stress disorder and normal controls. *Psychotherapy and Psychosomatics*, 75(2), 122–132.

Etkin, A., & Wager, T. D. (2007). Functional neuroimaging of anxiety: A meta-analysis of emotional processing in PTSD, social anxiety disorder, and specific phobia. *American Journal of Psychiatry, 164*(10), 1476–1488.

Falconer, E., Bryant, R., Felmingham, K. L., Kemp, A. H., Gordon, E., Peduto, A., et al. (2009). The neural networks of inhibitory control in posttraumatic stress disorder. *Journal of Psychiatry and Neuroscience, 33*(3), 413–422.

Felmingham, K., Kemp, A., Williams, L., Das, P., Hughes, G., Peduto, A., & Bryant, R. (2007). Changes in anterior cingulate and amygdala after cognitive behavior therapy of posttraumatic stress disorder. *Psychological Sciences, 18*(2), 127–129.

Felmingham, K., Williams, L., Kemp, A. H., Lidell, B., Falconer, E., Peduto, A., & Bryant, R. (2010). Neural responses to masked fear faces: Sex differences and trauma exposure in posttraumatic stress disorder. *Journal of Abnormal Psychology, 119*(1), 241–247.

Felmingham, K. L., Williams, L., Kemp, A. H., Renni, C., Gordon, E., & Bryant, R. A. (2009). Anterior cingulate activity to salient stimuli is modulated by autonomic arousal in posttraumatic stress disorder. *Psychiatry Research, 173*(1), 59–62.

Felmingham, K., Williams, L., Whitford, T. J., Falconer, E., Kemp, A. H., Peduto, A., & Bryant, R. (2009). Duration of posttraumatic stress disorder predicts hippocampal grey matter loss. *Neuroreport, 20*(16), 1402–1406.

Fennema-Notestine, C., Stein, M. B., Kennedy, C. M., Archibald, S. L., & Jernigan, T. L. (2002). Brain morphometry in female victims of intimate partner violence with and without posttraumatic stress disorder. *Biological Psychiatry, 51*, 1089–1101.

Finlay, J. M., Zigmond, M. J., & Abercrombie, E. D. (1995). Increased dopamine and norepinephrine release in medial prefrontal cortex induced by acute and chronic stress: Effects of diazepam. *Neuroscience, 64*, 619–628.

Fonzo, G. A., Simmons, A. N., Thorp, S. R., Norman, S. B., Paulus, M. P., & Stein, M. B. (2010). Blood oxygenation level-dependent response to threat-related emotional faces in women with intimate-partner violence posttraumatic stress disorder. *Biological Psychiatry, 68*, 433–441.

Foote, S. L., Bloom, F. E., & Aston-Jones, G. (1983). Nucleus locus coeruleus: new evidence of anatomical and physiological specificity. *Physiology & Behavior, 63*, 844–914.

Fowler, C. D., Liu, Y., Ouimet, C., & Wang, Z. (2001). The effects of social environment on adult neurogenesis in the female prairie vole. *Journal of Neurobiology, 51*, 115–128.

Freeman, T. W., Cardwell, D., Karson, C. N., & Komoroski, R. A. (1998). In vivo proton magnetic resonance spectroscopy of the medial temporal lobes of subjects with combat-related posttraumatic stress disorder. *Magnetic Resonance in Medicine, 40*, 66–71.

Freeman, T. W., Kimbrell, T., Booe, L., Myers, M., Cardwell, D., Lindquist, D. M., et al. (2006). Evidence of resilience: Neuroimaging in former prisoners of war. *Psychiatry Research, 146*(1), 59–64.

Frewen, P., Lane, R. D., Neufeld, R. W., Densmore, M., Stevens, T., & Lanius, R. (2008). Neural correlates of levels of emotional awareness during trauma script-imagery in posttraumatic stress disorder. *Psychosomatic Medicine, 70*(1), 27–31.

Fujita, M., Southwick, S. M., Denucci, C. C., Zoghbi, S. S., Dillon, M. S., Baldwin, R. M., et al. (2004). Central type benzodiazepine receptors in Gulf War veterans with posttraumatic stress disorder. *Biological Psychiatry, 56*(2), 95–100.

Garcia, R. (2002). Stress, metaplasticity, and antidepressants. *Current Molecular Medicine, 2*, 629–638.

Geuze, E., van Berckel, B. N., Lammerstma, A. A., Boellaard, R., de Kloet, C. S., Vermetten, E., & Westenberg, H. G. (2008). Reduced GABAA benzodiazepine receptor binding in veterans with post-traumatic stress disorder. *Molecular Psychiatry, 13*(1), 74–83, 3.

Geuze, E., Vermetten, E., de Kloet, C. S., & Westenberg, H. G. (2008). Precuneal activity during encoding in veterans with posttraumatic stress disorder. *Progress in Brain Research, 167*, 293–297.

Geuze, E., Vermetten, E., Ruf, M., de Kloet, C. S., & Westenberg, H. G. (2008). Neural correlates of associative learning and memory in veterans with posttraumatic stress disorder. *Journal of Psychiatric Research, 42*(8), 659–669.

Geuze, E., Westenberg, H. G., Heinecke, A., de Kloet, C. S., Goebel, R., & Vermetten, E. (2008). Thinner prefrontal cortex in veterans with posttraumatic stress disorder. *Neuroimage, 41*(3), 675–681.

Geuze, E., Westenberg, H. G., Jochims, A., de Kloet, C. S., Bohus, M., & Vermetten, E. (2007). Altered pain processing in veterans with posttraumatic stress disorder. *Archives of General Psychiatry, 64*(1), 76–85.

Gil, T., Calev, A., Greenberg, D., Kugelmass, S., & Lerer, B. (1990). Cognitive functioning in posttraumatic stress disorder. *Journal of Traumatic Stress, 3*, 29–45.

Gilbertson, M. W., Gurvits, T. V., Lasko, N. B., Orr, S. P., & Pitman, R. K. (2001). Multivariate assessment of explicit memory function in combat veterans with posttraumatic stress disorder. *Journal of Traumatic Stress, 14*, 413–420.

Gilbertson, M. W., Shenton, M. E., Ciszewski, A., Kasai, K., Lasko, N. B., Orr, S. P., & Pitman, R. K. (2002). Smaller hippocampal volume predicts pathologic vulnerability to psychological trauma. *Nature Neuroscience, 5*(11), 1242–1247.

Gilboa, A., Shalev, A. Y., Laor, L., Lester, H., Louzon, Y., Chisin, R., & Bonne, O. (2004). Functional connectivity of the prefrontal cortex and the amygdala in posttraumatic stress disorder. *Biological Psychiatry, 55*(3), 263–272.

Golier, J., & Yehuda, R. (1998). Neuroendocrine activity and memory-related impairments in posttraumatic stress disorder. *Development & Psychopathology, 10*(4), 857–869.

Golier, J., Yehuda, R., Cornblatt, B., Harvey, P., Gerber, D., & Levengood, R. (1997). Sustained attention in combat-related posttraumatic stress disorder. *Integrative Physiological & Behavioral Science, 32*(1), 52–61.

Golier, J. A., Yehuda, R., De Santi, S., Segal, S., Dolan, S., & de Leon, M. J. (2005). Absence of hippocampal volume differences in survivors of the Nazi Holocaust with and without posttraumatic stress disorder. *Psychiatry Research, 139*(1), 53–64.

Gould, E., McEwen, B. S., Tanapat, P., Galea, L. A., & Fuchs, E.. (1997). Neurogenesis in the dentate gyrus of the adult tree shrew is regulated by psychosocial stress and NMDA receptor activation. *Journal of Neuroscience, 17*, 2492–2498.

Gunnar, M. R., Morison, S. J., Chisholm, K., & Schuder, M. (2001). Salivary cortisol levels in children adopted from Romanian orphanages. *Development & Psychopathology, 13*, 611–628.

Gurvits, T. V., Shenton, M. E., Hokama, H., Ohta, H., Lasko, N. B., Gilbertson, M. W., et al. (1996). Magnetic resonance imaging study of hippocampal volume in chronic combat-related posttraumatic stress disorder. *Biological Psychiatry*, *40*, 192–199.

Hakamata, Y., Matsuoka, Y., Inagaki, M., Nagamine, M., Hara, E., Imoto, S., et al. (2007). Structure of orbitofrontal cortex and its longitudinal course in cancer-related post-traumatic stress disorder. *Neuroscience Research*, *59*(4), 383–389.

Hara, E., Matsuoka, Y., Hakamata, Y., Nagamine, M., Inagaki, M., Imoto, S., et al. (2008). Hippocampal and amygdalar volumes in breast cancer survivors with posttraumatic stress disorder. *Journal of Neuropsychiatry & Clinical Neuroscience*, *20*(3), 302–308.

Hedges, D. W., Allen, S., Tate, D. F., Thatcher G. W., Miller, M. J., Rice, S. A., et al. (2003). Reduced hippocampal volume in alcohol and substance naive Vietnam combat veterans with posttraumatic stress disorder. *Cognitive and Behavioral Neurology*, *16*(4), 219–224.

Hedges, D. W., Thatcher G. W., Bennett P. J., Sood, S., Paulson, D., Creem-Regehr, S., et al. (2007). Brain integrity and cerebral atrophy in Vietnam combat veterans with and without posttraumatic stress disorder. *Neurocase*, *13*(5), 402–410.

Hopper, J. W., Frewen, P. A., van der Kolk, B. A., & Lanius, R. A. (2007). Neural correlates of reexperiencing, avoidance, and dissociation in PTSD: Symptom dimensions and emotion dysregulation in responses to script-driven trauma imagery. *Journal of Traumatic Stress*, *20*(5), 713–725.

Hou, C., Liu, J., Wang, K., Li, L., Liang, M., He, Z., et al. (2007). Brain responses to symptom provocation and trauma-related short-term memory recall in coal mining accident survivors with acute severe PTSD. *Brain Research*, *1144*, 165–174.

Irle, E., Lange, C., & Sachsse, U. (2005). Reduced size and abnormal asymmetry of parietal cortex in women with borderline personality disorder. *Biological Psychiatry*, *57*(2), 173–182.

Jackowski, A. P., Douglas-Palumberi, H., Jackowski, M., Win, L., Schultz, R. T., Staib, L. W., et al. (2008). Corpus callosum in maltreated children with posttraumatic stress disorder: A diffusion tensor imaging study. *Psychiatry Research*, *162*(3), 256–261.

Jatzko, A., Rothenhöfer, S., Schmitt, A., Gaser, C., Demirakca, T., Weber-Fahr, W., et al. (2006). Hippocampal volume in chronic posttraumatic stress disorder (PTSD): MRI study using two different evaluation methods. *Journal of Affective Disorders*, *94*(1-3), 121–126.

Jenkins, M. A., Langlais, P. J., Delis, D., & Cohen, R. (1998). Learning and memory in rape victims with posttraumatic stress disorder. *American Journal of Psychiatry*, *155*, 278–279.

Kasai, K., Yamasue, H., Gilbertson, M. W., Shenton, M. E., Rauch, S. L., & Pitman, R. K. (2008). Evidence for acquired pregenual anterior cingulate gray matter loss from a twin study of combat-related posttraumatic stress disorder. *Biological Psychiatry*, *63*(6), 550–556.

Kemp, A. H., Felmingham, K. L., Das, P., Hughes, G., Peduto, A. S., Bryant, R. A., & Williams, L. M. (2007). Influence of comorbid depression on fear in posttraumatic stress disorder: An fMRI study. *Psychiatry Research*, *155*(3), 265–269.

Kemp, A. H., Felmingham, K. L., Falconer, E., Liddell, B. J., Bryant, R. A., & Williams, L. M. (2009). Heterogeneity of non-conscious fear perception in posttraumatic stress disorder as a function of physiological arousal: An fMRI study. *Psychiatry Research*, *174*(2), 158–161.

Kessler, R. C., Sonnega, A., Bromet, E., Hughes, M., & Nelson, C. B. (1995). Posttraumatic stress disorder in the National Comorbidity Survey. *Archives of General Psychiatry*, *52*, 1048–1060.

Kim, M. J., Chey, J., Chung, A., Bae, S., Khang, H., Ham, B., et al. (2008). Diminished rostral anterior cingulate activity in response to threat-related events in posttraumatic stress disorder. *Journal of Psychiatric Research*, *42*(4), 268–277.

Kim, M. J., Lyoo, I. K., Kim, S. J., Sim, M., Kim, N., Choi, N., et al. (2005). Disrupted white matter tract integrity of anterior cingulate in trauma survivors. *Neuroreport*, *16*(10), 1049–1053.

Kim, S. J., Jeong, D. U., Sim, M. E., Bae, S. C., Chung, A., Kim, M. J., et al. (2006). Asymmetrically altered integrity of cingulum bundle in posttraumatic stress disorder. *Neuropsychobiology*, *54*(2), 120–125.

Kim, S. J., Lyoo, I. K., Lee, Y. S., Kim, J., Sim, M. E., Bae, S. C., et al. (2007). Decreased cerebral blood flow of thalamus in PTSD patients as a strategy to reduce re-experience symptoms. *Acta Psychiatrica Scandinavica*, *116*(2), 145–153.

Kimbrell, T., Leulf, C., Cardwell, D., Komoroski, R. A., & Freeman, T. W. (2005). Relationship of in vivo medial temporal lobe magnetic resonance spectroscopy to documented combat exposure in veterans with chronic posttraumatic stress disorder. *Psychiatry Research*, *140*(1), 91–94.

Kitayama, N., Brummer, M., Hertz, L., Quinn, S., Kim, Y., & Bremner, J. D. (2007). Morphologic alterations in the corpus callosum in abuse-related posttraumatic stress disorder: A preliminary study. *Journal of Nervous and Mental Disease*, *195*(12), 1027–1029.

Kitayama, N., Vaccarino, V., Kutner, M., Weiss, P., & Bremner, J. D. (2005). Magnetic resonance imaging (MRI) measurement of hippocampal volume in posttraumatic stress disorder: A meta-analysis. *Journal of Affective Disorders*, *88*(1), 79–86.

Koenigs, M., Huey, E. D., Raymont, V., Cheon, B., Solomon, J., Wasserman, E. M., & Grafman, J. (2007). Focal brain damage protects against post-traumatic stress disorder in combat veterans. *Nature Neuroscience*, *11*, 232–237.

Landré, L., Destrieux, C., Baudry, M., Barantin, L., Cottier, J. P., Martineau, J., et al. (2010). Preserved subcortical volumes and cortical thickness in women with sexual abuse-related PTSD. *Psychiatry Research*, *183*(3), 181–186.

Lanius, R. A., Bluhm, R. L., Coupland, N. J., Hegadoren, K. M., Roew, B., Théberge, J., et al. (2010). Default mode network connectivity as a predictor of post-traumatic stress disorder. *Acta Psychiatrica Scandinavica*, *121*, 33–40.

Lanius, R. A., Williamson, P. C., Densmore, M., Boksman, K., Gupta, M. A., Neufeld, R. W., et al. (2001). Neural correlates of traumatic memories in posttraumatic stress disorder: A functional MRI investigation. *American Journal of Psychiatry*, *158*, 1920–1922.

Lanius, R. A., Williamson, P. C., Hopper, J., Densmore, M., Boksman, K., Gupta, M. A., et al. (2003). Recall of emotional states in posttraumatic stress disorder: An fMRI investigation. *Biological Psychiatry*, *53*(3), 204–210.

Lansing, K., Amen, D. G., Hanks, C., & Rudy, L. (2005). High-resolution brain SPECT imaging and eye movement desensitization and reprocessing in police officers with PTSD. *Journal of Neuropsychiatry & Clinical Neuroscience*, *17*(4), 526–532.

Lawrence, M. S., & Sapolsky, R. M. (1994). Glucocorticoids accelerate ATP loss following metabolic insults in cultured hippocampal neurons. *Brain Research*, *646*, 303–306.

LeDoux, J. L. (1993). In search of systems and synapses. *Annals of the New York Academy of Sciences, 702,* 149–157.

Levine, E. S., Litto, W. J., & Jacobs, B. L. (1990). Activity of cat locus coeruleus noradrenergic neurons during the defense reaction. *Brain Research, 531,* 189–195.

Levine, S., Weiner, S. G., & Coe, C. L. (1993). Temporal and social factors influencing behavioral and hormonal responses to separation in mother and infant squirrel monkeys. *Psychoneuroendocrinology, 4,* 297–306.

Levitt, J. J., Chen, Q. C., May, F. S., Gilbertson, M. W., Shenton, M. E., & Pitman, R. K. (2006). Volume of cerebellar vermis in monozygotic twins discordant for combat exposure: Lack of relationship to post-traumatic stress disorder. *Psychiatry Research, 148*(2-3), 143–149.

Li, L., Chen, S., Liu, J., Zhang, J., He, Z., & Lin, X. (2006). Magnetic resonance imaging and magnetic resonance spectroscopy study of deficits in hippocampal structure in fire victims with recent-onset posttraumatic stress disorder. *Canadian Journal of Psychiatry, 51*(7), 431–437.

Liberzon, I., Britton, J. C., & Phan, K. L. (2003). Neural correlates of traumatic recall in posttraumatic stress disorder. *Stress, 6*(3), 151–156.

Liberzon, I., & Martis, B. (2006). Neuroimaging studies of emotional responses in PTSD. *Annals of the New York Academy of Science, 1071,* 87–109.

Liberzon, I., & Phan, K. L. (2003). Brain-imaging studies of posttraumatic stress disorder. *CNS Spectrum, 8*(9), 641–650.

Liberzon, I., Taylor, S. F., Amdur, R., Jung, T. D., Chamberlain, K. R., Minoshima, S., et al. (1999). Brain activation in PTSD in response to trauma-related stimuli. *Biological Psychiatry, 45,* 817–826.

Liberzon, I., Taylor, S. F., Phan, K. L., Britton, J. C., Fig, L. M., Bueller, J. A., et al. (2007). Altered central micro-opioid receptor binding after psychological trauma. *Biological Psychiatry, 61*(9), 1030–1038.

Lim, M. K., Suh, C. H., Kim, H. J., Kim, S. T., Lee, J. S., Kang, M. H., et al. (2003). Fire-related post-traumatic stress disorder: brain 1H-MR spectroscopic findings. *Korean Journal of Radiology, 4*(2), 79–84.

Lindauer, R. J., Vlieger, E. J., Jalink, M., Olff, M., Carlier, I. V., Majoie, C. B., et al. (2005). Effects of psychotherapy on hippocampal volume in out-patients with post-traumatic stress disorder: A MRI investigation. *Psychological Medicine, 35*(10), 1421–1431.

Lindauer, R. J., Booij, J., Habraken, J. B., Uylings, H. B., Olff, M., Carlier, I. V., et al. (2004). Cerebral blood flow changes during script-driven imagery in police officers with posttraumatic stress disorder. *Biological Psychiatry, 56*(11), 853–861.

Lindauer, R. J., Olff, M., van Meijel, E. P., Carlier, I. V., & Gersons, B. P. (2006). Cortisol, learning, memory, and attention in relation to smaller hippocampal volume in police officers with posttraumatic stress disorder. *Biological Psychiatry, 59*(2), 171–177.

Lindauer, R. J., Vlieger, E. J., Jalink, M., Olff, M., Carlier, I. V., Majoie, C. B., et al. (2004). Smaller hippocampal volume in Dutch police officers with posttraumatic stress disorder. *Biological Psychiatry, 56*(5), 356–363.

Looi, J. C., Maller, J. J., Pagani, M., Högberg, G., Lindberg, O., Liberg, B., et al. (2009). Caudate volumes in public transportation workers exposed to trauma in the Stockholm train system. *Psychiatry Research: Neuroimaging, 171,* 138–143.

Lucassen, P. J., Fuchs, E., & Czeh, B. (2004). Antidepressant treatment with tianeptine reduces apoptosis in the hippocampal dentate gyrus and temporal cortex. *European Journal of Neuroscience, 14,* 161–166.

Luine, V., Villegas, M., Martinez, C., & McEwen, B. S. (1994). Repeated stress causes reversible impairments of spatial memory performance. *Brain Research, 639,* 167–170.

Mahmutyazicioglu, K., Konuk, N., Ozdemir, H., Atasoy, N., Atik, L., & Gündogdu, S. (2005). Evaluation of the hippocampus and the anterior cingulate gyrus by proton MR spectroscopy in patients with post-traumatic stress disorder. *Diagnostic and Interventional Radiology, 11*(3), 125–129.

Malberg, J. E., Eisch, A. J., Nestler, E. J., & Duman, R. S. (2000). Chronic antidepressant treatment increases neurogenesis in adult rat hippocampus. *Journal of Neuroscience, 20,* 9104–9110.

Matsuoka, Y., Yamawaki, S., Inagaki, M., Akechi, T., & Uchitomi, Y. (2003). A volumetric study of amygdala in cancer survivors with intrusive recollections. *Biological Psychiatry, 54*(7), 736–743.

May, F. S., Chen, Q. C., Gilbertson, M. W., Shenton, M. E., & Pitman, R. K. (2004). Cavum septum pellucidum in monozygotic twins discordant for combat exposure: Relationship to posttraumatic stress disorder. *Biological Psychiatry, 55*(6), 656–658.

McEwen, B. S., Angulo, J., Cameron, H., Chao, H. M., Daniels, D., Gannon, M. N., et al. (1992). Paradoxical effects of adrenal steroids on the brain: Protection versus degeneration. *Biological Psychiatry, 31,* 177–199.

McEwen, B. S., & Chattarji, S. (2004). Molecular mechanisms of neuroplasticity and pharmacological implications: The example of tianeptine. *European Neuropsychopharmacology, 14*(Suppl 5), S497–S502.

McFall, M. E., Murburg, M. M., Ko, G. N., & Veith, R. C. (1990). Autonomic responses to stress in Vietnam combat veterans with posttraumatic stress disorder. *Biological Psychiatry, 27,* 1165–1175.

Milad, M. R., Pitman, R. K., Ellis, C. B., Gold, A. L., Shin, L. M., Lasko, N. B., et al. (2009). Neurobiological basis of failure to recall extinction memory in posttraumatic stress disorder. *Biological Psychiatry, 66*(12), 1075–1082.

Mohanakrishnan Menon, P., Nasrallah, H. A., Lyons, J. A., Scott, M. F., & Liberto, V. (2003). Single-voxel proton MR spectroscopy of right versus left hippocampi in PTSD. *Psychiatry Research, 123*(2), 101–108.

Moores, K. A., Clark, C. R., McFarlane, A. C., Brown, G. C., Puce, A., Taylor, D. J. (2008). Abnormal recruitment of working memory updating networks during maintenance of trauma-neutral information in post-traumatic stress disorder. *Psychiatry Research, 163*(2), 156–170.

Moradi, A. R., Doost, H. T., Taghavi, M. R., Yule, W., & Dagleish, T. (1999). Everyday memory deficits in children and adolescents with PTSD: performance on the Rivermead Behavioural Memory Test. *Journal of Child Psychology and Psychiatry, 40,* 357–361.

Morey, R. A., Petty, C. M., Cooper, D. A., Labar, K. S., & McCarthy, G. (2008). Neural systems for executive and emotional processing are modulated by symptoms of posttraumatic stress disorder in Iraq War veterans. *Psychiatry Research, 162*(1), 59–72.

Morgan, C. A., & LeDoux, J. E. (1995). Differential contribution of dorsal and ventral medial prefrontal cortex to the acquisition and extinction of conditioned fear in rats. *Behavioral Neuroscience, 109,* 681–688.

Nakano, T., Wenner, M., Inagaki, M., Kugaya, A., Akechi, T., Matsuoka, Y., et al. (2002). Relationship between distressing cancer-related recollections and hippocampal volume in cancer survivors. *American Journal of Psychiatry, 159,* 2087–2093.

Nardo, D., Högberg, G., Looi, J. C., Larsson, S., Hällström, T., & Pagani, M. (2009). Gray matter density in limbic and paralimbic cortices is associated with trauma load and EMDR outcome in PTSD patients. *Journal of Psychiatric Research, 44,* 477–485.

New, A. S., Fan, J., Murrough, J. W., Liu, X., Lieberman, R. E., Guise, K. G., et al. (2009). A functional magnetic resonance imaging study of deliberate emotion regulation in resilience and posttraumatic stress disorder. *Biological Psychiatry, 66*(7), 656–664.

Nibuya, M., Morinobu, S., & Duman, R. S. (1995). Regulation of BDNF and trkB mRNA in rat brain by chronic electroconvulsive seizure and antidepressant drug treatments. *Journal of Neuroscience, 15,* 7539–7547.

Nisenbaum, L. K., Zigmond, M. J., Sved, A. F., & Abercrombie, E. D. (1991). Prior exposure to chronic stress results in enhanced synthesis and release of hippocampal norepinephrine in response to a novel stressor. *Journal of Neuroscience, 11,* 1478–1484.

Osuch, E. A., Willis, M. W., Bluhm, R., CSTS Neuroimaging Study Group, Ursano, R. J., Drevets, W. C. (2008). Neurophysiological responses to traumatic reminders in the acute aftermath of serious motor vehicle collisions using [15O]-H2O positron emission tomography. *Biological Psychiatry, 64*(4), 327–335.

Pagani, M., Högberg, G., Salmaso, D., Nardo, D., Sundin, O., Jonsson, C., et al. (2007). Effects of EMDR psychotherapy on 99mTc-HMPAO distribution in occupation-related posttraumatic stress disorder. *Nuclear Medicine Communications, 28*(10), 757–765.

Pannu Hayes, J., Labar K. S., Petty, C. M., McCarthy, G., & Morey, R. A. (2009). Alterations in the neural circuitry for emotion and attention associated with posttraumatic stress symptomatology. *Psychiatry Research, 172*(1), 7–15.

Pavic, L., Gregurek, R., Rados, M., Brkljacic, B. Brajkovic, L., Simetin-Pavic, I., et al. (2007). Smaller right hippocampus in war veterans with posttraumatic stress disorder. *Psychiatry Research, 154*(2), 191–198.

Pederson, C. L., Maurer, S. H., Kaminski, P. L., Zander, K. A., Peters, C. M., et al. (2004). Hippocampal volume and memory performance in a community-based sample of women with posttraumatic stress disorder secondary to child abuse. *Journal of Traumatic Stress, 17*(1), 37–40.

Peres, J. F., Newberg, A. B., Mercante, J. P., Simão, M., Albuquerque, V. E., Peres, M. J., & Nasello, A. G., et al. (2007). Cerebral blood flow changes during retrieval of traumatic memories before and after psychotherapy: A SPECT study. *Psychological Medicine 37*(10), 1481–1491.

Phan, K. L., Britton, J. C., Taylor, S. F., Fig, L. M., & Liberzon, I. (2006). Corticolimbic blood flow during nontraumatic emotional processing in posttraumatic stress disorder. *Archives of General Psychiatry, 63*(2), 184–192.

Piefke, M., Pestinger, M., Arin, T., Kohl, B., Kastrau, F., Schnitker, R., et al. (2007). The neurofunctional mechanisms of traumatic and non-traumatic memory in patients with acute PTSD following accident trauma. *Neurocase, 13*(5), 342–357.

Pissiota, A., Frans, O., Fernandez, M., von Knorring, L., Fischer, H., & Fredrikson, M. (2002). Neurofunctional correlates of posttraumatic stress disorder: A PET symptom provocation study. *European Archives of Psychiatry & Clinical Neuroscience, 252,* 68–75.

Pitman, R. K. (2001). Investigating the pathogenesis of posttraumatic stress disorder with neuroimaging. *Journal of Clinical Psychiatry, 62,* 47–54.

Pitman, R. K., Orr, S. P., Forgue, D. F., de Jong, J. B., & Claiborn, J. M. (1987). Psychophysiologic assessment of posttraumatic stress disorder imagery in Vietnam combat veterans. *Archives of General Psychiatry, 44,* 970–975.

Protopopescu, X., Pan, H., Tuescher, O., Cloitre, M., Goldstein, M., Engelien, W., et al. (2005). Differential time courses and specificity of amygdala activity in posttraumatic stress disorder subjects and normal control subjects. *Biological Psychiatry, 57*(5), 464–473.

Quirk, G. J. (2002). Memory for extinction of conditioned fear is long-lasting and persists following spontaneous recovery. *Learning & Memory, 9,* 402–407.

Radley, J. J., Sisti, H. M., Hao, J., Rocher, A. B., McCall, T., Hof, P. R., et al. (2004). Chronic behavioral stress induces apical dendritic reorganization in pyramidal neurons of the medial prefrontal cortex. *Neuroscience, 125*(1), 1–6.

Rauch, S. L., Shin, L. M., & Phelps, E. A. (2006). Neurocircuitry models of posttraumatic stress disorder and extinction: Human neuroimaging research past, present, and future. *Biological Psychiatry, 60*(4), 376–382.

Rauch, S. L., Shin, L. M., Segal, E., Pitman, R. K., Carson, M. A., McMullin, K., et al. (2003). Selectively reduced regional cortical volumes in post-traumatic stress disorder. *Neuroreport, 14*(7), 913–916.

Rauch, S. L., van der Kolk, B. A., Fisler, R. E., Alpert, N. M., Orr, S. P., Savage, C. R., et al. (1996). A symptom provocation study of posttraumatic stress disorder using positron emission tomography and script driven imagery. *Archives of General Psychiatry, 53,* 380–387.

Rauch, S. L., Whalen, P. J., Shin, L. M., McInerney, S. C., Macklin, M. L., Lasko, N. B., et al. (2000). Exaggerated amygdala response to masked facial stimuli in posttraumatic stress disorder: A functional MRI study. *Biological Psychiatry, 47*(9), 769–776.

Roca, V., & Freeman, T. W. (2001). Complaints of impaired memory in veterans with PTSD. *American Journal of Psychiatry, 158,* 1738.

Rogers, M. A., Yamasue, H., Abe, O., Yamada, H., Ohtani, T., Iwanami, A., et al. (2009). Smaller amygdala volume and reduced anterior cingulate gray matter density associated with history of post-traumatic stress disorder. *Psychiatry Research, 174*(3), 210–216.

Sachinvala, N., von Scotti, H., McGuire, M., Fairbanks, L., Bakst, K., McGuire, M., & Brown, N. (2000). Memory, attention, function, and mood among patients with chronic posttraumatic stress disorder. *Journal of Nervous and Mental Disease, 188,* 818–823.

Saigh, P. A., & Bremner, J. D. (1999). The history of posttraumatic stress disorder. in P.A. Saigh and J.D. Bremner (eds.), *Posttraumatic stress disorder: A comprehensive text* (pp. 1–17). Needham Heights, MA: Allyn & Bacon.

Sailer, U., Robinson, S., Fischmeister, F. P., König, D., Oppenauer, C., Lueger-Schuster, B., et al. (2008). Altered reward processing in the nucleus accumbens and mesial prefrontal cortex of patients with posttraumatic stress disorder. *Neuropsychologia, 46*(11), 2836–2844.

Sakamoto, H., Fukuda, R., Okuaki, T., Rogers, M., Kasai, K., Machida, T., et al. (2005). Parahippocampal activation evoked by masked traumatic images in posttraumatic stress disorder: A functional MRI study. *Neuroimage, 26*(3), 813–821.

Santarelli, L., Saxe, M., Gross, C., Surget, A., Battaglia, F., Dulawa, S., et al. (2003). Requirement of hippocampal neurogenesis for the behavioral effects of antidepressants. *Science, 301*(5634), 805–809.

Sapolsky, R. M. (1996). Why stress is bad for your brain. *Science, 273*, 749–750.

Sapolsky, R. M., Uno, H., Rebert, C. S., & Finch, C. E. (1990). Hippocampal damage associated with prolonged glucocorticoid exposure in primates. *Journal of Neuroscience, 10*, 2897–2902.

Schuff, N., Marmar, C. R., Weiss, D. S., Neylan, T. C., Schoenfeld, F., Fein, G., & Weiner, M. W. . (1997). Reduced hippocampal volume and n-acetyl aspartate in posttraumatic stress disorder. *Annals of the New York Academy of Sciences, 821*, 516–520.

Schuff, N., Neylan, T. C., Fox-Bosetti, S., Lenoci, M. A., Samuelson, K. W., Studholme, C., et al. (2008). Abnormal N-acetylaspartate in hippocampus and anterior cingulate in posttraumatic stress disorder. *Psychiatry Research, 162*(2), 147–157.

Schuff, N., Neylan, T. C., Lenoci, M. A., Du, A. T., Weiss, D. S., Marmar, C. R., & Weiner, M. W. (2001). Decreased hippocampal N-acetylaspartate in the absence of atrophy in posttraumatic stress disorder. *Biological Psychiatry, 50*, 952–959.

Seedat, S., Videen, J. S., Kennedy, C. M., & Stein, M. B. (2005). Single voxel proton magnetic resonance spectroscopy in women with and without intimate partner violence-related posttraumatic stress disorder. *Psychiatry Research, 139*(3), 249–258.

Semple, W. E., Goyer, P. F., McCormick, R., Donovan, B., Muzic, R. F., Jr., Rugle, L., et al. (2000). Higher brain blood flow at amygdala and lower frontal cortex blood flow in PTSD patients with comorbid cocaine and alcohol abuse compared to controls. *Psychiatry, 63*, 65–74.

Shin, L. M., Kosslyn, S. M., McNally, R. J., Alpert, N. M., Thompson, W. L., Rauch, S. L., et al. (1997). Visual imagery and perception in posttraumatic stress disorder: A positron emission tomographic investigation. *Archives of General Psychiatry, 54*, 233–237.

Shin, L. M., Lasko, N. B., Macklin, M. L., Karpf, R. D., Milad, M. R., Orr, S. P., et al. (2009). Resting metabolic activity in the cingulate cortex and vulnerability to posttraumatic stress disorder. *Archives of General Psychiatry, 66*(10), 1099–1107.

Shin, L. M., McNally, R. J., Kosslyn, S. M., Thompson, W. L., Rauch, S. L., Alpert, N. M., et al. (1999). Regional cerebral blood flow during script-driven imagery in childhood sexual abuse-related PTSD: A PET investigation. *American Journal of Psychiatry, 156*, 575–584.

Shin, L. M., Orr, S. P., Carson, M. A., Rauch, S. L., Macklin, M. L., Lasko, N. B., et al. (2004). Regional cerebral blood flow in the amygdala and medial prefrontal cortex during traumatic imagery in male and female Vietnam veterans with PTSD. *Archives of General Psychiatry, 61*(2), 168–176.

Shin, L. M., Shin, P. S., Heckers, S., Krangel, T. S., Macklin, M. L., Orr, S. P., et al. (2004). Hippocampal function in posttraumatic stress disorder. *Hippocampus, 14*(3), 292–300.

Shin, L. M., Whalen, P. J., Pitman, R. K., Bush, G., Macklin, M. L., Lasko, N. B., et al. (2001). An fMRI study of anterior cingulate function in posttraumatic stress disorder. *Biological Psychiatry, 50*, 932–942.

Shin, L. M., Wright, C. I., Cannistraro, P. A., Wedig, M. M., McMullin, K., Martis, B., et al. (2005). A functional magnetic resonance imaging study of amygdala and medial prefrontal cortex responses to overtly presented fearful faces in posttraumatic stress disorder. *Archives of General Psychiatry, 62*(3), 273–281.

Simmons, A. N., Paulus, M. P., Thorp, S. R., Matthews, S. C., Norman, S. B., & Stein, M. B. (2008). Functional activation and neural networks in women with posttraumatic stress disorder related to intimate partner violence. *Biological Psychiatry, 64*(8), 681–690.

Simmons, A., Strigo, I. A., Matthews, S. C., Paulus, M. P., & Stein, M. B. (2009). Initial evidence of a failure to activate right anterior insula during affective set shifting in posttraumatic stress disorder. *Psychosomatic Medicine, 71*, 373–377.

Smith, M. A., Makino, S., Kvetnansky, R., & Post, R. M. (1995). Stress and glucocorticoids affect the expression of brain-derived neurotrophic factor and neurotrophin-3 mRNA in the hippocampus. *Journal of Neuroscience, 15*, 1768–1777.

Southwick, S. M., Krystal, J. H., Morgan, C. A., Johnson, D., Nagy, L. M., Nicolaou, A., et al. (1993). Abnormal noradrenergic function in posttraumatic stress disorder. *Archives of General Psychiatry, 50*(4), 295–305.

Stanton, M. E., Gutierrez, Y. R., & Levine, S. (1988). Maternal deprivation potentiates pituitary-adrenal stress responses in infant rats. *Behavioral Neuroscience, 102*, 692–700.

Stein, M. B., Hanna, C., Vaerum, V., & Koverola, C. (1999). Memory functioning in adult women traumatized by childhood sexual abuse. *Journal of Traumatic Stress, 12*(3), 527–534.

Stein, M. B., Koverola, C., Hanna, C., Torchia, M., & McClarty, B. (1997). Hippocampal volume in women victimized by childhood sexual abuse. *Psychological Medicine, 27*, 951–959.

Strigo, I. A., Simmons, A. N., Matthews, S. C., Grimes, E. M., Allard, C. B., Reinhardt, L. E., et al. (2010). Neural correlates of altered pain response in women with posttraumatic stress disorder from intimate partner violence. *Biological Psychiatry, 68*(5), 442–450.

Teicher, M. H., Dumont, N. L., Ito, Y., Vaituzis, C., Giedd, J. N., & Andersen, S. L. (2004). Childhood neglect is associated with reduced corpus callosum area. *Biological Psychiatry, 56*, 80–85.

Thomaes, K., Dooepaal, E., Draijer, N., de Ruiter, M. B., van Balkom, A. J., Smit, J. H., & Veltman, D. J. (2010). Reduced anterior cingulate and orbitofrontal volumes in child abuse-related complex PTSD. *Journal of Clinical Psychiatry, 71*(12), 1636–1644.

Uddo, M., Vasterling, J. J., Brailey, K., & Sutker, P. B. (1993). Memory and attention in posttraumatic stress disorder. *Journal of Psychopathology and Behavioral Assessment, 15*, 43–52.

Uno, H., Tarara, R., Else, J. G., Suleman, M. A., & Sapolsky, R. M. (1989). Hippocampal damage associated with prolonged and fatal stress in primates. *Journal of Neuroscience, 9*, 1705–1711.

Vasterling, J. J., Brailey, K., Constans, J. I., & Sutker, P. B. (1998). Attention and memory dysfunction in posttraumatic stress disorder. *Neuropsychology, 12*, 125–133.

Vasterling, J. J., Duke, L. M., Brailey, K., Constans, J. I., Allain, A. N., & Sutker, P. B. (2002). Attention, learning, and memory performance and intellectual resources in Vietnam veterans: PTSD and no disorder comparisons. *Neuropsychology, 16,* 5–14.

Vermetten, E., Vythillingham, M., Southwick, S. M., Charney, D. S., & Bremner, J. D. (2003). Long-term treatment with paroxetine increases verbal declarative memory and hippocampal volume in posttraumatic stress disorder. *Biological Psychiatry, 54*(7), 693–702.

Villarreal, G., Hamilton, D. A., Graham, D. P., Driscoll, I., Qualls, C., Petropoulos, H., et al. (2004). Reduced area of the corpus callosum in posttraumatic stress disorder. *Psychiatry Research: Neuroimaging, 131,* 227–235.

Villarreal, G., Hamilton, D. A., Petropoulos, H., Driscoll, I., Rowland, L. M., Griego, J. A., et al. (2002). Reduced hippocampal volume and total white matter in posttraumatic stress disorder. *Biological Psychiatry, 52,* 119–125.

Vogt, B. A., Finch, D. M., & Olson, C. R.(1992). Functional heterogeneity in cingulate cortex: The anterior executive and posterior evaluative regions. *Cerebral Cortex, 2,* 435–443.

Wang, H.-H., Zhang, Z. J., Tan, Q. R., Yin, H., Chen, Y. C., et al. (2010). Psychopathological, biological, and neuroimaging characterization of posttraumatic stress disorder in survivors of a sever coalmining disaster in China. *Journal of Psychiatric Research, 44,* 385–392.

Wang, Z., Neylan, T. C., Mueller, S. G., Lenoci, M., Truran, D., Marmar, C. R., et al. (2010). Magnetic resonance imaging of hippocampal subfields in posttraumatic stress disorder. *Archives of General Psychiatry, 67*(3), 296–303.

Watanabe, Y. E., Gould, H., Cameron, D., Daniels, D., & McEwen, B. S. (1992). Phenytoin prevents stress and corticosterone induced atrophy of CA3 pyramidal neurons. *Hippocampus, 2,* 431–436.

Werner, N. S., Meindl, T., Engel, R. R., Rosner, R., Riedel, M., Reiser, M., et al. (2009). Hippocampal function during associative learning in patients with posttraumatic stress disorder. *Journal of Psychiatric Research, 43*(3), 309–318.

Whalley, M. G., Rugg, M. D., Smith, A. P., Dolan, R. J., & Brewin, C. R. (2009). Incidental retrieval of emotional contexts in post-traumatic stress disorder and depression: An fMRI study. *Brain and Cognition, 69,* 98–107.

Woodward, S. H., Kaloupek, D. G., Street, C. C., Martinez, C., Schaer, M., & Eliez, S. (2006). Decreased anterior cingulate volume in combat-related PTSD. *Biological Psychiatry, 59*(7), 582–587.

Woon, F. L., & Hedges, D. W. (2008). Hippocampal and amygdala volumes in children and adults with childhood maltreatment-related posttraumatic stress disorder: A meta-analysis. *Hippocampus, 18*(8), 729–736.

Woon, F. L., & Hedges, D. W. (2009). Amygdala volume in adults with posttraumatic stress disorder: A meta-analysis. *Journal of Neuropsychiatry & Clinical Neuroscience, 21*(1), 5–12.

Woon, F. L., Sood, S., & Hedges, D. W. (2010). Hippocampal volume deficits associated with exposure to psychological trauma and posttraumatic stress disorder in adults: A meta-analysis. *Progress in Neuropsychopharmacology and Biological Psychiatry, 34*(7), 1181–1188.

Yamasue, H., Kasai, A., Iwanami, T., Ohtani, H., Yamada, O., Abe, N., et al. (2003). Voxel-based analysis of MRI reveals anterior cingulate gray-matter volume reduction in posttraumatic stress disorder due to terrorism. *Proceedings of the National Academy of Sciences U S A, 100*(15), 9039–9043.

Yang, P., Wu, M-T., Hsu, C-C., & Ker, J-H. (2004). Evidence of early neurobiological alternations in adolescents with posttraumatic stress disorder: A functional MRI study. *Neuroscience Letters, 370*(1), 13–18.

Yehuda, R. (2006). Advances in understanding neuroendocrine alterations in PTSD and their therapeutic implications. *Annals of the New York Academy of Sciences, 1071,* 137–166.

Yehuda, R., Teicher, M. H., Levengood, R. A., Trestman, R. L., & Siever, L. J. (1994). Circadian regulation of basal cortisol levels in posttraumatic stress disorder. *Annals of the New York Academy of Sciences,* 378–380.

Yehuda, R., Southwick, S. M., Krystal, J. H., Bremner, D., Charney, D. S., & Mason, J. W. (1993). Enhanced suppression of cortisol with low dose dexamethasone in posttraumatic stress disorder. *American Journal of Psychiatry, 150,* 83–86.

Yehuda, R., Keefe, R. S., Harvey, P. D., Levengood, R. A., Gerber, D. K., Geni, J., & Siever, L. J. (1995). Learning and memory in combat veterans with posttraumatic stress disorder. *American Journal of Psychiatry, 152,* 137–139.

Zalewski, C., Thompson, W., & Gottesman, I. (1994). Comparison of neuropsychological test performance in PTSD, generalized anxiety disorder, and control Vietnam veterans. *Assessment, 1,* 133–142.

Generalized Anxiety Disorder and Social Phobia Considered from a Cognitive Neuroscience Perspective

Karina S. Blair *and* R. J. R. Blair

Abstract

Generalized anxiety disorder (GAD) and social phobia (SP) are two of the major anxiety disorders identified by DSM-IV. They are highly comorbid and overlap in symptoms yet present with distinct features (e.g., worry in GAD and fear of embarrassment in SP). Given the overlap in symptoms and suggestions that conditioning-based accounts may explain all anxiety disorders, this chapter first evaluates whether hyperconditioning or hypersensitivity to threat is found in both or either disorder. On the basis of the current literature, this cannot currently be concluded in the case of GAD but may be the case for SP, as least for social-threat stimuli. The chapter then examines potential neurocognitive functions that might be aberrant in specific ways in the two disorders. Much remains to be discovered before any adequate cognitive neuroscience account of GAD can be considered. However, one form of neurocognitive function that appears markedly aberrant in SP relates to self-referential processing.

Key Words: generalized anxiety disorder, social phobia, threat processing, emotion regulation, self-referential processing

Introduction

This chapter reviews work on two of the major forms of anxiety disorder described by the *Diagnostic and Statistical Manual of Mental Disorders* (4th ed., Revised) (DSM-IV-R): generalized anxiety disorder (GAD) and social phobia (SP). Other recent reviews have considered the neurobiology of these two disorders (e.g., Martin, Ressler, Binder, & Nemeroff, 2010; Shin & Liberzon, 2010; Stein, 2009). However, these reviews have not considered GAD and SP from a more cognitive neuroscience perspective. Cognitive neuroscience models of a disorder take into account the computational processes *and* their neural substrates that, when dysfunctional, lead to the emergence of the disorder. To say, for example, that amygdala dysfunction leads to the emergence of the disorder is not a cognitive

neuroscience account—the model is purely anatomical. To say, however, that the amygdala's response to face stimuli is maladaptively strong would be the beginning of a cognitive neuroscience model. Moreover, such an account implies that the amygdala's role in other functions, such as appetitive processing, need not be compromised in the disorder. In contrast, the purely anatomical model should predict that they are. Cognitive neuroscience accounts typically pay particular attention to functional neuroimaging and psychophysiological and behavioral data.

The goal of this chapter is to consider GAD and SP from a cognitive neuroscience perspective. As such, work on the genetics of GAD and SP will not be directly considered (but see Hettema, Neale, & Kendler, 2001; Norrholm & Ressler, 2009, for excellent reviews of this literature), and purely cognitive work will receive less attention than it deserves (but see Alden & Taylor, 2004; Behar, DiMarco, Hekler, Mohlman, & Staples, 2009; Hirsch & Clark, 2004).

The chapter begins with short clinical descriptions of GAD and SP. This is followed by a consideration of general threat processing across the two disorders. The chapter concludes with a discussion of neurocognitive dysfunctions that might be specific to GAD but not to SP.

Clinical Features of GAD and SP

Patients with anxiety disorders show some indications of symptom overlap at least when it comes to self-report (Craske et al., 2009). Thus, patients with anxiety disorders report increased escape behaviors, physiological arousal (though this is lessened in patients with GAD), tension, and thoughts of imminent and future threat. A reduction in positive affect is more notable in patients with SP than in those with other anxiety disorders (Craske et al., 2009).

Generalized anxiety disorder (GAD) is characterized by persistent (more days than not for at least 6 months) and excessive worry about aspects of life or the welfare of loved ones that is difficult to control. While patients might not report the worry as excessive, they do complain of significant distress or impairment as a result. Patients with GAD must also have three associated symptoms, such as restlessness, fatigue, sleep difficulties, impaired concentration, irritability, muscle tension, or insomnia.

Social phobia (SP) is marked by an acute anxiety response to social or performance situations, related to the concern of scrutiny or humiliation by others. Patients with SP may seek to reduce the fear of embarrassment and distress by avoiding social situations.

Threat Processing in GAD and SP

Much of the work involving patients with anxiety disorders has its roots in our understanding of the neural systems mediating fear in animals (cf. Shin & Liberzon, 2010). This is unsurprising. Excessive fear is a key component of most anxiety disorders. Phobias have been thought to potentially reflect hypersensitivity in the pathways that mediate innate fear (Ohman & Mineka, 2001). This argument has also been made for SP (cf. Milad & Rauch, 2007), though it rests on the assumption that social stimuli are innately fear inducing. On a related note, conditioning-based accounts have been proposed for the pathogenesis of anxiety disorders for most of the last century (Watson & Rayner, 1920). In their classical

form, the suggestion is that pathological anxiety develops through classical conditioning (Watson & Rayner, 1920); the individual experiences an aversive unconditioned stimulus (US) that is associated with an event or experience that becomes the focus of the individual's anxiety. A variant of this position, with the addition of dysfunctional extinction of the fear memory (see below), is currently probably the dominant model of post-traumatic stress disorder (PTSD; Milad & Rauch, 2007) and is a prevalent position with respect to anxiety disorders generally (e.g., Eysenck, 1979; Lissek et al., 2005).

Heightened fear- and conditioning-based accounts of GAD and SP might assume that these disorders reflect (a) heightened sensitivity to innate threats generally (GAD) or social threats specifically (SP), and/or (b) heightened propensity to learn to avoid threats generally (GAD) or social threats specifically (SP), and/or (c) that the individual has previously experienced particularly aversive experiences associated with threats generally (GAD) or social threats specifically (SP). The third (c) possibility is included here primarily for completion. While it is considered relevant to other phobias (Watson & Rayner, 1920), it receives less attention with respect to SP and no attention in GAD. The following section will consider threat sensitivity in patients with GAD and SP as indexed through fear conditioning, extinction, and emotional attention paradigms.

Fear Conditioning

Fear conditioning involves the pairing of a neutral stimulus with an aversive US. The neutral stimulus initially elicits no emotional reaction, but after repeated pairings with the US, the neutral stimulus becomes a conditioned stimulus (CS) initiating a conditioned response comparable to the unconditioned response initiated by the US. Fear conditioning can be indexed through both simple and differential conditioning paradigms. Simple conditioning simply involves the CS being paired with a US. Differential conditioning involves the CS+ being paired with a US, but a CS- that is never paired with the US. As such, the CS- can be viewed as a "safety stimulus" in comparison to the CS+ in that the CS- signals the absence of the US (Barlow, 2002). The amygdala is critical for fear conditioning (e.g., Davis, 2000; LeDoux, 2000), associating reinforcement values with stimuli such that these will come to be regarded as aversive or appetitive. This has been shown in both animal (e.g., Davis, 2000; LeDoux, 2000) and human studies (e.g., Shin & Liberzon, 2010).

On the basis of a meta-analysis of the literature, Lissek and colleagues (2005) concluded that anxiety-disordered adults show enhanced simple conditioning (elevated responses to CS+) and reduced differential conditioning (because of elevated responses to the CS+ *and* the CS-). While this appears relatively clear for patients with PTSD (Craske et al., 2009; Lissek et al., 2005), the situation is complicated with respect to GAD and SP.

Only two studies have examined differential conditioning in patients with GAD (Pitman & Orr, 1986; Thayer, Friedman, Borkovec, Johnsen, & Molina, 2000). The first study, by Pitman and Orr, indicated increased responsiveness to the CS+; however, there was significant comorbidity, with almost 50% of the patients with GAD also presenting with panic disorder. The second study, by Thayer et al., involved dot cues for anticipating either threat or neutral words, and conditioned heart rate deceleration as the indexed conditioned response. Unfortunately, this conditioned response was not shown by the healthy comparison individuals, making the validity of the paradigm unclear. In this context, it is worth noting the results of a third study that examined the impact on startle reflex of cues that were either (1) predictive of aversive stimuli, (2) associated with aversive stimuli that were administered *unpredictably*, or (3) predictive of the absence of social stimuli (Grillon et al., 2009). Across conditions, the patients with GAD showed no differences from control participants in the impact of these cues on startle reflex. In short, the existing literature does not unequivocally support the suggestion of heightened fear conditioning in patients with GAD.

The literature on SP is far less ambiguous. Three studies have examined fear conditioning in patients with SP (Hermann, Ziegler, Birbaumer, & Flor, 2002; Schneider et al., 1999; Veit et al., 2002), and all reported heightened conditioning in SP. However, all three studies used face stimuli as the CS. Thus, the literature cannot disentangle whether the effects represent a general propensity for increased conditionability or a specific propensity to condition toward social stimuli.

Extinction

During extinction, the CS+ is repeatedly presented in the absence of the US, leading to a reduction in the conditioned response (e.g., reduced freezing and skin conductance responses to the CS). Extinction appears to rely on the appropriate activation of a CS+–non-threat association (Bouton, 2002, 2004). Extinction has been thought to implicate the amygdala and ventromedial prefrontal cortex (VMPFC) (Milad et al., 2007).

A deficiency in the ability to engage in extinction has been related to the emergence of the anxiety disorders, particularly PTSD (Milad & Rauch, 2007). On the basis of their meta-analysis of the literature, Lissek and colleagues (2005) also concluded that anxiety-disordered adults show reduced extinction. Again, this effect is relatively clear for patients with PTSD (see also Craske et al., 2009). However, only one study has examined the issue in patients with GAD, and that study involved a population with a variety of comorbid conditions (Pitman & Orr, 1986). Of the two studies examining extinction in patients with SP, one indicated reduced extinction (Hermann et al., 2002) while the other did not (Schneider et al., 1999).

In short, the literature does not support or refute the suggestion of impaired extinction in GAD or SP.

Emotional Attention

Specific aspects of attention are core to models of conditioning in animals (Holland & Gallagher, 1999; Maddux, Kerfoot, Chatterjee, & Holland, 2007). In particular, studies in animals have shown that the rate of learning about a CS is enhanced by the surprise or prediction error generated when that CS is an inconsistent predictor of its emotional consequences. The underlying circuit that underlies the changes in CS associability implicates both the amygdala and parietal cortex (Holland & Gallagher, 1999; Maddux et al., 2007). The impact of emotion on attention is important for models of anxiety. It has been suggested that anxious individuals initially show rapid orienting of attention toward (Ohman, Flykt, & Esteves, 2001) and engagement in and difficulty disengaging from (Yiend & Mathews, 2001) threat stimuli. This is then followed by the eventual direction of attention away from the threat in an effort to reduce subjective distress (Mogg & Bradley, 2002). It is hypothesized that this "vigilance-avoidance" pattern of cognitive bias is maladaptive, because it may enhance sensitization and interfere with habituation, thereby maintaining anxiety in the long term (e.g., Mogg, Millar, & Bradley, 2000; Ohman et al., 2001).

Emotional attention can be understood as a function of the interaction between the amygdala and cortical regions (Blair et al., 2007; Blair & Mitchell, 2009; Pessoa & Ungerleider, 2004). Aversive and appetitive conditioning involves the interaction of temporal cortex and the amygdala

(LeDoux, 1998); stimuli represented within temporal cortex that become associated with valence information represented within the amygdala come to activate the amygdala. As the connections between temporal cortex and the amygdala are reciprocal (Amaral, Price, Pitkanen, & Carmichael, 1992), the activity of neurons representing emotional stimuli in temporal cortex is further augmented by reciprocal feedback from the amygdala. This means that if the emotional stimulus is a distracter to the stimulus determining task performance, then representational interference will be greater than if this distracter stimulus were neutral (Blair & Mitchell, 2009). Indeed, a variety of studies have shown that emotional stimuli cause greater interference than neutral stimuli (Blair et al., 2007; Erthal et al., 2005; Vuilleumier, Armony, Driver, & Dolan, 2001). Conversely, if the emotional stimulus is relevant to task performance, then there will be facilitation of performance, induced by the emotional nature of the stimulus (due to reciprocal activation from the amygdala), relative to neutral stimuli (Blair & Mitchell, 2009). This can be seen in emotional lexical decision paradigms in which healthy volunteers are usually significantly faster and more accurate to judge that emotional (e.g., "murder") rather than neutral letter strings (e.g., "table") are letter strings (Graves, Landis, & Goodglass, 1981; Nakic, Smith, Busis, Vythilingam, & Blair, 2006).

There is a general consensus that patients with anxiety disorders, including GAD and SP, show a heightened attention bias toward threat-related stimuli across a variety of emotional attention paradigms (Craske et al., 2009); that is, reactions to stimuli presented in the spatial vicinity of previously presented emotional stimuli will be faster, whereas performance will decline if the emotional information serves as a distracter to task performance. There is also a strong assumption in the literature that the threat-related stimuli that produce attention biases are disorder specific.

This threat disorder specificity is not obviously the case for patients with GAD, however. Both pediatric and adult patients with GAD have been found to show attention bias toward threat words and angry faces (Bradley, Mogg, White, Groom, & de Bono, 1999; Taghavi, Dalgleish, Moradi, Neshat-Doost, & Yule, 2003; Waters, Mogg, Bradley, & Pine, 2008), though attention biases *away* from angry faces have also been reported in pediatric patients with GAD (Monk et al., 2006; Waters et al., 2008, in less anxious patients with GAD). Moreover, the attention bias need not be specific for threat stimuli in GAD.

Both pediatric and adult patients with GAD have been found to show attention bias toward happy expressions in some studies (Martin, Williams, & Clark, 1991; Waters et al., 2008) but not in others (Mogg, Bradley, Williams, & Mathews, 1993; Monk et al., 2006; Taghavi et al., 2003). In short, there does appear to be evidence of attention bias to emotional stimuli in patients with GAD. However, this may not be specific for threat but may also be shown for positive stimuli.

In SP, the issue regarding disorder specificity is uncertain. Patients with SP show heightened, particularly early, orientation toward social threat (e.g., angry faces) (e.g., Gamble & Rapee, 2010; Mogg, Philippot, & Bradley, 2004; Roy et al., 2008). Unfortunately, though, few studies have examined the presence or absence of attention bias for general threat in patients with SP, although it should be noted that patients with SP do appear to exhibit selective heightened responsiveness in non-attention paradigms. Thus, patients with SP exhibit enhanced startle reflex and autonomic responding during social but not survival threat (McTeague et al., 2009). In short, patients with SP show attention biases to social threats. What remains unclear is whether they also have attention biases to nonsocial threats.

GAD from a Cognitive Neuroscience Perspective

While an animal learning–based theory has not been clearly proposed as a model of GAD, there have certainly been proposals that a similar neural, and presumably computational, architecture mediate all anxiety disorders, including GAD (see Martin et al., 2010). However, as noted above, there is currently relatively little reason to believe that patients with GAD show heightened conditionability or reduced extinction. There are indications, though, that patients with GAD experience generally increased attention to emotional stimuli. This increased attention occurs with both social and word threats in patients with GAD (Bradley et al., 1999; Taghavi et al., 2003; Waters et al., 2008) and may also be seen with positive stimuli (see above). The emotional-attention data are slightly surprising in the context of no clearly increased conditionability in patients with GAD because it might be logically assumed that heightened amygdala-cortical interactions mediating enhanced emotional attention would also heighten conditionability. Of course, the absence of definitive data regarding increased conditionability in patients with GAD may reflect the lack of studies rather than the absence of the phenomenon. But it would seem plausible that increased attention to threatening stimuli should be associated with increased physiological responsiveness to these stimuli. Yet studies have found that GAD is characterized by either reduced, or at least not significantly increased, physiological arousal to stressors (Grillon et al., 2009; Hoehn-Saric, McLeod, & Zimmerli, 1989). In these studies, there were no group differences in startle magnitude and autonomic responsiveness under baseline conditions.

But is GAD marked by increased amygdala responsiveness to threatening stimuli? Studies with pediatric patients have indicated hyperactivity to negative emotional expression faces in GAD (McClure et al., 2007; Monk et al., 2008). However, three studies with adult patients, consistent with the physiological literature (Grillon et al., 2009; Hoehn-Saric et al., 1989), have not (Blair, Shaywitz, et al., 2008; Palm, Elliott, McKie, Deakin, & Anderson, 2010; Whalen et al., 2008). A further study also found no significant increased amygdala response to the anticipation or receipt of threatening images (Nitschke et al., 2009), although this study did find that patients with GAD showed a heightened amygdala response to the anticipation or receipt of *neutral* images. Only one study has indicated an increased amygdala response to threatening images in patients with GAD (Etkin, Prater, Hoeft, Menon, & Schatzberg, 2010). This study reported increased amygdala responses to the receipt of fearful facial expressions in patients with GAD (Etkin et al., 2010). However, this study also found that their population of patients with GAD had increased responsiveness to facial expressions of happiness, a finding suggestive of a generally increased emotional responsiveness rather than a threat-specific hyper-responsiveness.

While these data consistently indicate no increased amygdala responsiveness to specifically threatening stimuli in GAD (except perhaps in pediatric GAD), they also (particularly the studies of Blair, Shaywitz, et al., 2008; Etkin et al., 2010; Nitschke et al., 2009) do not suggest the absence of amygdala abnormalities in GAD. In this respect, it is interesting to note the resting-state findings of Etkin et al. (Etkin, Prater, Schatzberg, Menon, & Greicius, 2009). This study indicated group differences in amygdala structure as well as group differences in the connectivity between the basolateral (BLA) and centromedial (CMA) subregions of the amygdala and regions of cortex. Patients with GAD showed a general reduction in correlated activity between the amygdala and insula/ventrolateral prefrontal cortex, dorsal/midcingulate cortex, and striatal regions. In contrast, patients with GAD exhibited a general increase in correlated activity between the amygdala and dorsolateral and posterior parietal cortices. This increase in correlated amygdala-dorsolateral/posterior parietal cortex activity was inversely related to anxiety measures (i.e., most marked for the least anxious patients), which suggests that it reflected some form of compensatory neural adaptation rather than a direct component of the pathophysiology of GAD.

The inconsistency between the pediatric and adult findings regarding responsiveness to threatening stimuli in patients with GAD could mean that GAD in adulthood reflects an accommodation to the increased responsiveness that was present when the patients were children. As such, GAD should not be considered an increased responsiveness to threat stimuli (this is particularly the case, since increased responsiveness to threatening facial stimuli is seen in pediatric patients with SP who do not present with GAD; see below). Rather, GAD might reflect an adaptation to this increased responsiveness to threatening stimuli that, while pathological, is at least successful in negating the original phenomena. In short, increased responsiveness to threat might be a nonspecific risk factor that can, but need not, lead to the development of GAD.

It has been suggested that worry reflects an overlearned compensatory strategy for dulling emotional experience (Borkovec, Alcaine, & Behar, 2004). Indeed, there are considerable data indicating that worrying appears to dampen somatic arousal at rest and in response to threatening stimuli (for a review, see Behar et al., 2009). The hallmark feature of GAD is, of course, an increased propensity to worry (American Psychiatric Association, 1994). However, excessive worry does not solve objective and subjective difficulties; worrying people do not plan complex responses to overwhelming events but rather repeat to themselves that things will get worse (Paulesu et al., 2010). It has been argued that patients with GAD resort to worry because of an underlying abnormality in regulating emotional processing (McLaughlin, Mennin, & Farach, 2007; Mennin, Heimberg, Turk, & Fresco, 2005; Mennin, Holaway, Fresco, Moore, & Heimberg, 2007). In line with this, Etkin et al. (2010) found reduced automatic emotional regulation and reduced regulatory activity within pregenual anterior cingulate in patients with GAD. However, recent fMRI work found similar disruption in the recruitment of attention-related regions during emotion regulation in patients with GAD and patients with SP, suggesting that emotion dysregulation is not specific to GAD but rather could be a general risk factor for many of the anxiety disorders (Blair et al., 2012). The unique feature of GAD is the increased propensity to worry. Thus to understand GAD we need to understand worry. However, only two, small N-studies have investigated worry in patients with GAD (Hoehn-Saric, Schlund, & Wong, 2004; Paulesu et al., 2010). Hoehn-Saric et al. (2004) found that treatment with citalopram reduced differential BOLD responses to worry relative to neutral statements, within several regions of the prefrontal cortex and the insula, in 7 patients with GAD. However, this study involved no comparison group. Paulesu et al. (2010) compared the differential response of 8 patients with GAD and 12 comparison individuals to worry relative to neutral statements. They observed no group differences in responsiveness to these statements at time of presentation; however, the patients with GAD maintained a differential response within rostral anterior cingulate cortex and a region of medial frontal cortex in the rest period following stimuli presentation (neither region was implicated in the Hoehn-Saric et al., 2004, study). In short, these studies on worry in patients with GAD are interesting but must be considered preliminary. The prefrontal regions implicated by Hoehn-Saric and Paulesu were not consistent. Moreover, no computational details of worry have been provided. Thus we are left with the suggestion of frontal pathology in GAD, with little understanding of what that might mean.

SP from a Cognitive Neuroscience Perspective

Animal learning–based theories have been offered for SP. It has been argued that SP might reflect hypersensitivity in the pathways mediating a potential innate fear of social threat, difficulty in extinguishing the aversive emotional memory, or both (cf. Milad & Rauch, 2007). However, interpretation of the existent literature is complicated. It does appear that patients with SP show a heightened ability to associate aversive unconditioned stimuli with neutral facial stimuli (Hermann et al., 2002; Schneider et al., 1999; Veit et al., 2002). Moreover, patients with SP show greater amygdala responses while associating neutral facial expressions with aversive stimuli (Schneider et al., 1999). However, there is less reason to believe that patients with SP have difficulty extinguishing these associations (Hermann

et al., 2002; Schneider et al., 1999). Indeed, no difference in activation during extinction between this patient population and comparison individuals has been reported (Schneider et al., 1999) for.

Importantly, though, these data indicate that SP is associated with a greater preparedness to associate aversive outcomes with social stimuli rather than an increased *innate fear* of social threat. The studies discussed above demonstrate that patients with SP show a heightened ability to associate aversive unconditioned stimuli with neutral facial stimuli (Hermann et al., 2002; Schneider et al., 1999; Veit et al., 2002). To conclude that patients with SP show an increased innate fear of social threat we have to assume that neutral facial expressions *are* innate social threats. Perhaps they are. But it is also possible that patients with SP have heightened conditioning to threat more generally. Moreover, it is uncertain whether this heightened ability to associate aversive unconditioned stimuli with neutral facial stimuli is a risk factor for the development of SP or a developmental consequence of *having* SP. Finally, some work that has been interpreted in terms of conditioning models should perhaps be reinterpreted. For example, Lissek and colleagues (2008) reported heightened fear conditioning to neutral faces with an "unconditioned stimulus" that was negative insults. Importantly, the conditionability of negative insults likely reflects an individual's propensity to process such insults as an aversive stimulus. Notably, the healthy comparison individuals in this study showed no conditioning. In other words, this study appeared to have more to do with differential responsiveness to negative insults than an increased propensity to condition to social stimuli (see below for more details).

With respect to emotional attention, it appears that SP is associated with increased attention to social threat stimuli. While it has not been shown that attention biases are *selective* for social stimuli (i.e., not also shown to general threat stimuli), this appears likely given that inappropriately increased responsiveness is only seen regarding social but not survival threat (McTeague et al., 2009). If we understand emotional attention to reflect increased reciprocal priming, by the amygdala, of representations within temporal cortex that activated the amygdala (Blair & Mitchell, 2009), we should expect patients with SP to show heightened amygdala and temporal cortical activity in response to social threat stimuli. Partially in line with this expectation, relatively consistent work with adult patients with SP has revealed heightened amygdala and temporal cortical activity in response to angry facial expressions (Evans et al., 2008; Phan, Fitzgerald, Nathan, & Tancer, 2006; Stein, Goldin, Sareen, Zorrilla, & Brown, 2002; Straube, Kolassa, Glauer, Mentzel, & Miltner, 2004; Straube, Mentzel, & Miltner, 2005). Angry expressions are those most likely to elicit the attention biases in patients with SP (e.g., Gamble & Rapee, 2010; Mogg et al., 2004). Interestingly, an increased amygdala response to physical-threat stimuli has not been reported in patients with SP (Goldin, Manber-Ball, Werner, Heimberg, & Gross, 2009), consistent with the lack of increased physiological response to physical threat (McTeague et al., 2009) and suggesting that the attention biases might be unique to social stimuli.

Interestingly, the amygdala response to fearful faces, the stimulus class most consistently shown to engage the amygdala of healthy adolescents and adults (Blair, Morris, Frith, Perrett, & Dolan, 1999; Murphy, Nimmo-Smith, & Lawrence, 2003; Whalen et al., 2001), has only been examined twice in patients with SP, and the results have been inconsistent (Blair, Shaywitz, et al., 2008; Stein et al., 2002). One study reported increased amygdala responses to fearful expressions in SP (Blair, Shaywitz, et al., 2008), the other did not (Stein et al., 2002). The response to neutral expressions is also of interest. Neutral expressions activate the amygdala, albeit to a significantly less extent than fearful expressions (Murphy et al., 2003). However, patients with SP do not typically show enhanced amygdala responses to neutral expressions (Blair, Shaywitz, et al., 2008; Phan et al., 2006; Stein et al., 2002; Straube et al., 2005; but see Birbaumer et al., 1998; Cooney, Atlas, Joormann, Eugene, & Gotlib, 2006). If neutral expressions were innate social threats and patients with SP showed an increased innate fear of social threat, one might expect that patients with SP would show enhanced amygdala responses to neutral expressions. Yet, it appears that they do not.

There is, however, a significant disadvantage to using facial-expression stimuli to understand SP. While facial-expression stimuli serve as reinforcers (happy expressions increase the probability of the repetition of actions that elicited the response, while fearful or sad expressions decrease this probability; see Blair, 2003), they may be either primary innately specified unconditioned stimuli, learned secondary reinforcers and conditioned stimuli, or both. In other words, the heightened amygdala responses to angry expressions in SP may reflect (1) an innately specified hypersensitivity to this expression; (2) heightened learning of an association between aversive experiences and this expression; or (3) both. It is thus important to determine whether patients with SP show heighted amygdala responses to socially aversive experiences that are unlikely to be innately specified aversive social unconditioned stimuli. In this regard, several studies have investigated the response of patients with SP to anticipated public speaking. Of these, two have reported increased amygdala-hippocampal and temporal cortical activity in patients SP (Lorberbaum et al., 2004; Tillfors, Furmark, Marteinsdottir, & Fredrikson, 2002). Two others did not (Nakao et al., 2011; Van Ameringen et al., 2004), although it should be noted that the Nakao et al. study did not investigate anticipated public speaking as such, rather participants were shown pictures of social stimuli (e.g., going to a reception) and asked to imagine themselves in that situation. Also, both the Van Ameringen et al. and Nakao et al. studies involved very small sample sizes (N = 5/6 patients with SP). Importantly, a recent study examining the response of patients with SP revealed significantly increased amygdala (and orbital frontal cortex) responses during indirect processing (when asked to judge a grammatical category) of SP-related relative to SP-unrelated words (Schmidt, Mohr, Miltner, & Straube, 2010). In short, the larger N public speaking studies (Lorberbaum et al., 2004; Tillfors et al., 2002) and the phobia word study (Schmidt et al., 2010) all suggest heightened responding to aversive, social-conditioned stimuli in patients with SP.

So what atypical computational processes might be unique to SP and lead to the diagnostic symptoms? A core concern in SP is the fear of being negatively evaluated. Indeed, social anxiety has been related to elevated levels of self-criticism (Blair, Geraci, et al., 2008; Blair et al., 2011). These data have led to the suggestion that disordered self-referential processing, relating to dysfunctional medial prefrontal cortex (MPFC) activity, is a core component of this disorder. This was first suggested by Blair et al. (2008) in a study that examined self-referential processing in SP using fMRI. Patients were assessed when processing self vs. other-referential criticism (e.g., "You're ugly" vs. "He's ugly") and praise (e.g., "You're beautiful" vs. "He's beautiful"). This study revealed selectively increased BOLD responses to self-referential criticism, within both the amygdala and a dorsal-lateral region of MPFC in patients with SP. In short, these data indicated that the heightened sensitivity to self-referential criticism in patients with SP implicates dorsal-lateral MPFC as well as the amygdala. Since then a series of studies have examined issues related to self-referential processing in patients with SP (Blair et al., 2010, 2011; Goldin & Gross, 2010; Goldin, Manber, Hakimi, Canli, & Gross, 2009; Guyer et al., 2008; Sripada et al., 2009).

With respect to the finding of increased amygdala responses in patients with SP to self-referential criticism, subsequent studies have largely replicated this result. Blair and colleagues (2011) again found increased amygdala responses in patients with SP for self-referential statements. Moreover, Goldin et al. (2009) and Goldin and Gross (2010) reported increased amygdala activity in association with negative self-beliefs in patients with SP (though only Goldin et al. [2009] showed that this was elevated relative to comparison subjects; there were no comparison subjects in the Goldin and Gross [2010] study). In addition, Guyer et al. (2008) found heightened amygdala responses in anticipation of self-referential comments.

With respect to MPFC, regions proximal to the dorsal-lateral region of MPFC noted by Blair et al. (2008) were identified in the context of the group main effects in the Blair, Geraci, et al. (2010) and Blair et al. (2011) studies. Patients with SP showed increased activity within these regions for self-referential statements irrespective of valence and when processing intentional, unintentional (embarrassing inducing), and normative social interaction vignettes. However, notable activity has also been reported within VMPFC in patients with SP in these contexts. Guyer et al. (2008) found heightened VMPFC responses in anticipation of effectively self-referential comments. Goldin and Gross (2010) reported an increase in VMPFC activity in response to negative self-beliefs in patients with SP. Moreover, a study by Blair and colleagues (2011) went beyond documenting increased activity in this region in patients with SP. VMPFC is a relatively large region, typically encompassing BA10, BA11, and rostral regions of BA32. It has been implicated in a series of functions, including the representation of valence (Blair et al., 2006; Knutson, Fong, Adams, Varner, & Hommer, 2001; O'Doherty, 2004), emotional regulation (Beauregard, Levesque, & Bourgouin, 2001; Urry et al., 2006), and self-referential processing (for review see Gillihan & Farah, 2005; Legrand & Ruby, 2009; Northoff et al., 2006; Schmitz & Johnson, 2007; van der Meer, Costafreda, Aleman, & David, 2010). It is this latter function that is of particular relevance to the Blair et al. (2010, 2011) studies.

The 2010 study by Blair and colleagues involved subjects processing intentional and unintentional (embarrassing) conventional (social disorder–based) transgressions. The study used an adaptation of a previously published paradigm (Berthoz, Armony, Blair, & Dolan, 2002). Berthoz et al. (2002) had demonstrated that healthy individuals exhibit significantly greater activity for intentional conventional social transgressions than for unintentional ones. This response is thought to reflect heightened representation of the protagonist's intent to challenge the social order (Berthoz et al., 2002; Finger, Marsh, Kamel, Mitchell, & Blair, 2006). Blair et al. (2010) replicated this finding in the healthy comparison adults. However, the adults with SP had a notably different pattern: increased activity in response to the unintentional, relative to intentional, social transgressions. Blair et al. (2011) examined the response of patients with SP and comparison individuals to the participants' own (first person; e.g., "I'm ugly") or other individuals' (second person; e.g., "you're ugly") negative, positive, and neutral opinions about the self. They found that healthy comparison adults showed increased activation in response to first-person ("I") relative to second-person ("you") viewpoints within this region. This was in line with an EEG study by Eisslen et al. that also reported increased activity in the VMPFC of healthy individuals in response to presentations of "I" relative to "he/she" trait adjectives (Esslen, Metzler, Pascual-Marqui, & Jancke, 2008). However, in contrast to the healthy adults, the patients with SP did not show increased activation to first- ("I") relative to second-person ("you") viewpoints within this region. Instead, they showed significantly greater activation to the "you" than to the "I" comments. Moreover, their activation to "I" comments correlated negatively with their level of social symptomatology.

Taken together, the data from these two studies suggest a profound reorganization of self-referential reasoning in SP. While a detailed computational account of self-referential reasoning remains to be provided, it appears to involve the matching of information to the individual's self-concept (Northoff et al., 2006). For healthy individuals, this appears to be particularly related to the potential status challenges indicated by intentional social transgressions and self-generated viewpoints ("am I really like this?"). In contrast, evaluations of the self in SP primarily focus on potentially embarrassing events and are particularly related to others' viewpoints ("am I really like what this other person considers me to be?"). Moreover, the finding of an inverse relationship between symptom levels and activity to first-person viewpoints within ventral MPFC suggests that not only do patients with SP reflect more on the self through the eyes of others as perceived by the person with SP but also that they reflect *less* on the self through self-evaluation. Indeed, it is notable that work has shown a relationship between self-clarity and social anxiety (Stopa, 2009); individuals experiencing high social anxiety not only have reduced confidence in their judgments of self-descriptive words but also take longer making those judgments (Stopa, 2009; Wilson & Rapee, 2006). Of course, these suggestions are speculative. However, they prediction future work that needs to be done. Notably, these data indicate that the pathophysiology of SP extends, perhaps developmentally, beyond a heightened amygdala response to social threat.

Future Directions

As should now be clear, considerable work remains for gaining an adequate understanding of GAD and SP. In this section, we present three outstanding empirical and conceptual questions that ought to be addressed in order to clarify or eliminate current theoretical positions.

1. Is fear conditioning and extinction impaired in GAD and SP? Specifically, do patients with GAD have heightened fear conditioning and reduced extinction? Studies need to be conducted in which the GAD study population does not show marked comorbidity with other anxiety disorders and in which the paradigm reliably elicits fear conditioning in healthy individuals. This has not yet been done. With respect to SP, we need to know whether patients show enhanced fear conditioning when the conditioned stimuli are not social (or whether the impairment is specific to social conditioned stimuli). We also need to know whether the enhanced fear conditioning with social (and maybe also nonsocial) conditioned stimuli is coupled with impaired extinction. Currently, the results are inconsistent.

2. How should worry be quantified? What computational processes might mediate worry, and how can they be indexed? It is possible that no substantial progress will be made in understanding the unique features of GAD without these conceptual and empirical issues being addressed.

3. What is the precise nature of the self-referential processing abnormality in SP? While the fMRI work has indicated that self-referential processing may be dysfunctional in SP, the specifics of the atypical processing will remain difficult to understand without adequate behavioral work delineating the specifics of the atypical processing. Importantly, determining these specifics may have clear clinical impact, enabling the augmentation of cognitive behavioral interventions to specifically target the atypical processing.

Conclusion

GAD and SP are two highly comorbid anxiety disorders, and similar computational architectures have been proposed for the two disorders. In this chapter, we considered GAD and SP within a cognitive neuroscience framework by considering first general threat processing in terms of fear conditioning, extinction, and emotional attention. In GAD, there appears to be little evidence to suggest increased fear conditioning and reduced extinction, although there is some data to suggest increased attention to threat stimuli. In addition, fMRI work involving children and adolescents with the disorder suggests an increased neural response to these threat stimuli. This finding is, however, not typically observed in adults with GAD. In line with other authors, we suggest that this is due to a disorder-specific adaption (worry) to deal with the initial increased response to threat stimuli.

Regarding SP, there are data to suggest an increased propensity for fear conditioning, at least if the conditioned stimuli are social. There are also data suggesting heightened attention to social threats in patients with SP. Indeed, this heightened attention to social threats, particularly expressions of anger, is mirrored by increased amygdala and temporal cortical responsiveness to these expressions in patients with SP. But SP may be more than just an increased responsiveness to social threats. Recent data suggest that patients with SP show atypical self-referential processing. This may suggest that the pathophysiology of social phobia extends, perhaps developmentally, beyond a heightened amygdala response to social threat.

References

Alden, L. E., & Taylor, C. T. (2004). Interpersonal processes in social phobia. *Clinical Psychology Review, 24*(7), 857–882.

Amaral, D. G., Price, J. L., Pitkanen, A., & Carmichael, S. T. (1992). Anatomical organization of the primate amygdaloid complex. In J. P. Aggleton (Ed.), *The amygdala: Neurobiological aspects of emotion, memory, and mental dysfunction* (pp. 1–66). New York: Wiley.

American Psychiatric Association. (1994). *Diagnostic and statistical manual of mental disorders*, 4th ed. text revision.. Washington, DC: American Psychiatric Association.

Barlow, D. H. (2002). *Anxiety and its disorders: The nature and treatment of anxiety and panic*. New York: Guilford Press.

Beauregard, M., Levesque, J., & Bourgouin, P. (2001). Neural correlates of conscious self-regulation of emotion. *Journal of Neuroscience*, 21(18), RC165.

Behar, E., DiMarco, I. D., Hekler, E. B., Mohlman, J., & Staples, A. M. (2009). Current theoretical models of generalized anxiety disorder (GAD): Conceptual review and treatment implications. *Journal of Anxiety Disorders*, 23(8), 1011–1023.

Berthoz, S., Armony, J., Blair, R. J. R., & Dolan, R. (2002). Neural correlates of violation of social norms and embarrassment. *Brain*, 125(8), 1696–1708.

Birbaumer, N., Grodd, W., Diedrich, O., Klose, U., Erb, M., Lotze, M., et al. (1998). fMRI reveals amygdala activation to human faces in social phobics. *Neuroreport*, 9(6), 1223–1226.

Blair, R. J. R. (2003). Facial expressions, their communicatory functions and neuro-cognitive substrates. *Philosophical Transactions of the Royal Society London B: Biological Science*, 358(1431), 561–572.

Blair, K. S., Geraci, M., Devido, J., McCaffrey, D., Chen, G., Vythilingam, M., et al. (2008). Neural response to self- and other referential praise and criticism in generalized social phobia. *Archives of General Psychiatry*, 65(10), 1176–1184.

Blair, K. S., Geraci, M., Hollon, N., Otero, M., DeVido, J., Majestic, C., et al. (2010). Social norm processing in adult social phobia: Atypically increased ventromedial frontal cortex responsiveness to unintentional (embarrassing) transgressions. *American Journal of Psychiatry*, 167(12), 1526–1532.

Blair, K. S., Geraci, M., Otero, M., Majestic, K., Odenheimer, S., Jacobs, M., et al. (2011). Atypically reduced modulation of medial prefrontal cortex to self-referential comments in generalized social phobia. *Psychiatry Research: Neuroimaging*, 193(1), 38–45.

Blair, K. S., Marsh, A. A., Morton, J., Vythilingam, M., Jones, M., Mondillo, K., et al. (2006). Choosing the lesser of two evils, the better of two goods: Specifying the roles of ventromedial prefrontal cortex and dorsal anterior cingulate cortex in object choice. *Journal of Neuroscience*, 26(44), 11379–11386.

Blair, K. S., Shaywitz, J., Smith, B. W., Rhodes, R., Geraci, M., Jones, M., et al. (2008). Response to emotional expressions in generalized social phobia (GSP) and generalized anxiety disorder (GAD): Evidence for separate disorders. *American Journal of Psychiatry*, 165(9), 1193–1202.

Blair, K. S., Smith, B. W., Hollon, N., Geraci, M., DeVido, J., Otero, M., Jones, M., Blair, R. J. R., & Pine, D. S. (2012). Reduced dorsal anterior cingulate cortical activity during emotional regulation and top-down attentional control in Generalized Social Phobia (GSP), Generalized Anxiety Disorder (GAD) and comorbid GSP/GAD. *Biological Psychiatry*, 72(6), 476–482.

Blair, K. S., Smith, B. W., Mitchell, D. G., Morton, J., Vythilingam, M., Pessoa, L., et al. (2007). Modulation of emotion by cognition and cognition by emotion. *Neuroimage*, 35(1), 430–440.

Blair, R. J., & Mitchell, D. G. (2009). Psychopathy, attention and emotion. *Psychological Medicine*, 39(4), 543–555.

Blair, R. J. R., Morris, J. S., Frith, C. D., Perrett, D. I., & Dolan, R. (1999). Dissociable neural responses to facial expressions of sadness and anger. *Brain*, 122, 883–893.

Borkovec, T. D., Alcaine, O., & Behar, E. (2004). Avoidance theory of worry and generalized anxiety disorder. In R. G. Heimberg, C. L. Turk, & D. S. Mennin (Eds.), *Generalized anxiety disorder: Advances in theory and practice* (pp. 77–108). New York: Guilford Press.

Bouton, M. E. (2002). Context, ambiguity, and unlearning: sources of relapse after behavioral extinction. *Biological Psychiatry*, 52(10), 976–986.

Bouton, M. E. (2004). Context and behavioral processes in extinction. *Learning & Memory*, 11(5), 485–494.

Bradley, B. P., Mogg, K., White, J., Groom, C., & de Bono, J. (1999). Attentional bias for emotional faces in generalized anxiety disorder. *British Journal of Clinical Psychology*, 38(Pt 3), 267–278.

Cooney, R. E., Atlas, L. Y., Joormann, J., Eugene, F., & Gotlib, I. H. (2006). Amygdala activation in the processing of neutral faces in social anxiety disorder: Is neutral really neutral? *Psychiatry Research*, 148(1), 55–59.

Craske, M. G., Rauch, S. L., Ursano, R., Prenoveau, J., Pine, D. S., & Zinbarg, R. E. (2009). What is an anxiety disorder? *Depression and Anxiety*, 26(12), 1066–1085.

Davis, M. (2000). The role of the amygdala in conditioned and unconditioned fear and anxiety. In J. P. Aggleton (Ed.), *The amygdala: A functional analysis* (pp. 289–310). Oxford: Oxford University Press.

Erthal, F. S., de Oliveira, L., Mocaiber, I., Pereira, M. G., Machado-Pinheiro, W., Volchan, E., et al. (2005). Load-dependent modulation of affective picture processing. *Cognitive, Affective & Behavioral Neuroscience*, 5(4), 388–395.

Esslen, M., Metzler, S., Pascual-Marqui, R., & Jancke, L. (2008). Pre-reflective and reflective self-reference: A spatiotemporal EEG analysis. *Neuroimage*, 42(1), 437–449.

Etkin, A., Prater, K. E., Hoeft, F., Menon, V., & Schatzberg, A. F. (2010). Failure of anterior cingulate activation and connectivity with the amygdala during implicit regulation of emotional processing in generalized anxiety disorder. *American Journal of Psychiatry*, 167(5), 545–554.

Etkin, A., Prater, K. E., Schatzberg, A. F., Menon, V., & Greicius, M. D. (2009). Disrupted amygdalar subregion functional connectivity and evidence of a compensatory network in generalized anxiety disorder. *Archives of General Psychiatry*, 66(12), 1361–1372.

Evans, K. C., Wright, C. I., Wedig, M. M., Gold, A. L., Pollack, M. H., & Rauch, S. L. (2008). A functional MRI study of amygdala responses to angry schematic faces in social anxiety disorder. *Depression & Anxiety*, 25(6), 496–505.

Eysenck, H. J. (1979). The conditioning model of neurosis. *Behavioral and Brain Sciences*, 2, 155–199.

Finger, E. C., Marsh, A. A., Kamel, N., Mitchell, D. G., & Blair, J. R. (2006). Caught in the act: The impact of audience on the neural response to morally and socially inappropriate behavior. *Neuroimage*, 33(1), 414–421.

Gamble, A. L., & Rapee, R. M. (2010). The time-course of attention to emotional faces in social phobia. *Journal of Behavior Therapy and Experimental Psychiatry*, 41(1), 39–44.

Gillihan, S. J., & Farah, M. J. (2005). Is self special? A critical review of evidence from experimental psychology and cognitive neuroscience. *Psychological Bulletin*, 131(1), 76–97.

Goldin, P. R., & Gross, J. J. (2010). Effects of mindfulness-based stress reduction (MBSR) on emotion regulation in social anxiety disorder. *Emotion*, 10(1), 83–91.

Goldin, P. R., Manber, T., Hakimi, S., Canli, T., & Gross, J. J. (2009). Neural bases of social anxiety disorder: Emotional reactivity and cognitive regulation during social and physical threat. *Archives of General Psychiatry, 66*(2), 170–180.

Goldin, P. R., Manber-Ball, T., Werner, K., Heimberg, R., & Gross, J. J. (2009). Neural mechanisms of cognitive reappraisal of negative self-beliefs in social anxiety disorder. *Biological Psychiatry, 66*(12), 1091–1099.

Graves, R., Landis, T., & Goodglass, H. (1981). Laterality and sex differences for visual recognition of emotional and non-emotional words. *Neuropsychologia, 19* , 95–102.

Grillon, C., Pine, D. S., Lissek, S., Rabin, S., Bonne, O., & Vythilingam, M. (2009). Increased anxiety during anticipation of unpredictable aversive stimuli in posttraumatic stress disorder but not in generalized anxiety disorder. *Biological Psychiatry, 66*(1), 47–53.

Guyer, A. E., Lau, J. Y., McClure-Tone, E. B., Parrish, J., Shiffrin, N. D., Reynolds, R. C., et al. (2008). Amygdala and ventrolateral prefrontal cortex function during anticipated peer evaluation in pediatric social anxiety. *Archives of General Psychiatry, 65*(11), 1303–1312.

Hermann, C., Ziegler, S., Birbaumer, N., & Flor, H. (2002). Psychophysiological and subjective indicators of aversive Pavlovian conditioning in generalized social phobia. *Biological Psychiatry, 52*(4), 328–337.

Hettema, J. M., Neale, M. C., & Kendler, K. S. (2001). A review and meta-analysis of the genetic epidemiology of anxiety disorders. *American Journal of Psychiatry, 158*(10), 1568–1578.

Hirsch, C. R., & Clark, D. M. (2004). Information-processing bias in social phobia. *Clinical Psychology Review, 24*(7), 799–825.

Hoehn-Saric, R., McLeod, D. R., & Zimmerli, W. D. (1989). Somatic manifestations in women with generalized anxiety disorder. Psychophysiological responses to psychological stress. *Archives of General Psychiatry, 46*(12), 1113–1119.

Hoehn-Saric, R., Schlund, M. W., & Wong, S. H. (2004). Effects of citalopram on worry and brain activation in patients with generalized anxiety disorder. *Psychiatry Research, 131*(1), 11–21.

Holland, P. C., & Gallagher, M. (1999). Amygdala circuitry in attentional and representational processes. *Trends in Cognitive Sciences, 3*(2), 65–73.

Knutson, B., Fong, G. W., Adams, C. M., Varner, J. L., & Hommer, D. (2001). Dissociation of reward anticipation and outcome with event-related fMRI. *Neuroreport, 12*(17), 3683–3687.

LeDoux, J. (1998). *The emotional brain*. New York: Weidenfeld & Nicolson.

LeDoux, J. E. (2000). Emotion circuits in the brain. *Annual Review of Neuroscience, 23* , 155–184.

Legrand, D., & Ruby, P. (2009). What is self-specific? Theoretical investigation and critical review of neuroimaging results. *Psychological Review, 116*(1), 252–282.

Lissek, S., Levenson, J., Biggs, A. L., Johnson, L. L., Ameli, R., Pine, D. S., et al. (2008). Elevated fear conditioning to socially relevant unconditioned stimuli in social anxiety disorder. *American Journal of Psychiatry, 165*(1), 124–132.

Lissek, S., Powers, A. S., McClure, E. B., Phelps, E. A., Woldehawariat, G., Grillon, C., et al. (2005). Classical fear conditioning in the anxiety disorders: A meta-analysis. *Behaviour Research and Therapy, 43*(11), 1391–1424.

Lorberbaum, J. P., Kose, S., Johnson, M. R., Arana, G. W., Sullivan, L. K., Hamner, M. B., et al. (2004). Neural correlates of speech anticipatory anxiety in generalized social phobia. *Neuroreport, 15*(18), 2701–2705.

Maddux, J. M., Kerfoot, E. C., Chatterjee, S., & Holland, P. C. (2007). Dissociation of attention in learning and action: Effects of lesions of the amygdala central nucleus, medial prefrontal cortex, and posterior parietal cortex. *Behavioral Neuroscience, 121*(1), 63–79.

Martin, E. I., Ressler, K. J., Binder, E., & Nemeroff, C. B. (2010). The neurobiology of anxiety disorders: Brain imaging, genetics, and psychoneuroendocrinology. *Clinics in Laboratory Medicine, 30*(4), 865–891.

Martin, M., Williams, R. M., & Clark, D. M. (1991). Does anxiety lead to selective processing of threat-related information? *Behavioral Research and Therapy, 29* , 147–160.

McClure, E. B., Monk, C. S., Nelson, E. E., Parrish, J. M., Adler, A., Blair, R. J., et al. (2007). Abnormal attention modulation of fear circuit function in pediatric generalized anxiety disorder. *Archives of General Psychiatry, 64*(1), 97–106.

McLaughlin, K. A., Mennin, D. S., & Farach, F. J. (2007). The contributory role of worry in emotion generation and dysregulation in generalized anxiety disorder. *Behaviour Research and Therapy, 45*(8), 1735–1752.

McTeague, L. M., Lang, P. J., Laplante, M. C., Cuthbert, B. N., Strauss, C. C., & Bradley, M. M. (2009). Fearful imagery in social phobia: Generalization, comorbidity, and physiological reactivity. *Biological Psychiatry, 65*(5), 374–382.

Mennin, D. S., Heimberg, R. G., Turk, C. L., & Fresco, D. M. (2005). Preliminary evidence for an emotion dysregulation model of generalized anxiety disorder. *Behaviour Research and Therapy, 43*(10), 1281–1310.

Mennin, D. S., Holaway, R. M., Fresco, D. M., Moore, M. T., & Heimberg, R. G. (2007). Delineating components of emotion and its dysregulation in anxiety and mood psychopathology. *Behavioral Therapy, 38*(3), 284–302.

Milad, M. R., & Rauch, S. L. (2007). The role of the orbitofrontal cortex in anxiety disorders. *Annals of the New York Academy of Sciences, 1121* , 546–561.

Milad, M. R., Wright, C. I., Orr, S. P., Pitman, R. K., Quirk, G. J., & Rauch, S. L. (2007). Recall of fear extinction in humans activates the ventromedial prefrontal cortex and hippocampus in concert. *Biological Psychiatry, 62*(5), 446–454.

Mogg, K., & Bradley, B. P. (2002). Selective orienting of attention to masked threat faces in social anxiety. *Behaviour Research and Therapy, 40*(12), 1403–1414.

Mogg, K., Bradley, B. P., Williams, R., & Mathews, A. (1993). Subliminal processing of emotional information in anxiety and depression. *Journal of Abnormal Psychology, 102*(2), 304–311.

Mogg, K., Millar, N., & Bradley, B. P. (2000). Biases in eye movements to threatening facial expressions in generalized anxiety disorder and depressive disorder. *Journal of Abnormal Psychology, 109*(4), 695–704.

Mogg, K., Philippot, P., & Bradley, B. P. (2004). Selective attention to angry faces in clinical social phobia. *Journal of Abnormal Psychology, 113*(1), 160–165.

Monk, C. S., Nelson, E. E., McClure, E. B., Mogg, K., Bradley, B. P., Leibenluft, E., et al. (2006). Ventrolateral prefrontal cortex activation and attentional bias in response to angry faces in adolescents with generalized anxiety disorder. *American Journal of Psychiatry, 163*(6), 1091–1097.

Monk, C. S., Telzer, E. H., Mogg, K., Bradley, B. P., Mai, X., Louro H. M. C,., et al. (2008). Amygdala and ventromedial prefrontal cortex activation to masked angry faces in children and adolescents with generalized anxiety disorder. *Archives of General Psychiatry, 65*(5), 568–576.

Murphy, F. C., Nimmo-Smith, I., & Lawrence, A. D. (2003). Functional neuroanatomy of emotions: A meta-analysis. *Cognitive, Affective & Behavioral Neuroscience, 3*(3), 207–233.

Nakao, T., Sanematsu, H., Yoshiura, T., Togao, O., Murayama, K., Tomita, M., et al. (2011). fMRI of patients with social anxiety disorder during a social situation task. *Neuroscience Research, 69*(1), 67–72.

Nakic, M., Smith, B. W., Busis, S., Vythilingam, M., & Blair, R. J. (2006). The impact of affect and frequency on lexical decision: The role of the amygdala and inferior frontal cortex. *Neuroimage, 31*(4), 1752–1761.

Nitschke, J. B., Sarinopoulos, I., Oathes, D. J., Johnstone, T., Whalen, P. J., Davidson, R. J., et al. (2009). Anticipatory activation in the amygdala and anterior cingulate in generalized anxiety disorder and prediction of treatment response. *American Journal of Psychiatry, 166*(3), 302–310.

Norrholm, S. D., & Ressler, K. J. (2009). Genetics of anxiety and trauma-related disorders. *Neuroscience, 164*(1), 272–287.

Northoff, G., Heinzel, A., de Greck, M., Bermpohl, F., Dobrowolny, H., & Panksepp, J. (2006). Self-referential processing in our brain—a meta-analysis of imaging studies on the self. *Neuroimage, 31*(1), 440–457.

O'Doherty, J. P. (2004). Reward representations and reward-related learning in the human brain: Insights from neuroimaging. *Current Opinion in Neurobiology, 14*(6), 769–776.

Ohman, A., Flykt, A., & Esteves, F. (2001). Emotion drives attention: Detecting the snake in the grass. *Journal of Experimental Psychology. General, 130*(3), 466–478.

Ohman, A., & Mineka, S. (2001). Fears, phobias, and preparedness: Toward an evolved module of fear and fear learning. *Psychological Review, 108*(3), 483–522.

Palm, M. E., Elliott, R., McKie, S., Deakin, J. F., & Anderson, I. M. (2010). Attenuated responses to emotional expressions in women with generalized anxiety disorder. *Psychological Medicine,* 1–11.

Paulesu, E., Sambugaro, E., Torti, T., Danelli, L., Ferri, F., Scialfa, G., et al. (2010). Neural correlates of worry in generalized anxiety disorder and in normal controls: A functional MRI study. *Psychological Medicine, 40*(1), 117–124.

Pessoa, L., & Ungerleider, L. G. (2004). Neuroimaging studies of attention and the processing of emotion-laden stimuli. *Progress in Brain Research, 144*, 171–182.

Phan, K. L., Fitzgerald, D. A., Nathan, P. J., & Tancer M. E. (2006). Association between amygdala hyperactivity to harsh faces and severity of social anxiety in generalized social phobia. *Biological Psychiatry, 59*(5), 424–429.

Pitman, R. K., & Orr, S. P. (1986). Test of the conditioning model of neurosis: Differential aversive conditioning of angry and neutral facial expressions in anxiety disorder patients. *Journal of Abnormal Psychology, 95*(3), 208–213.

Roy, A. K., Vasa, R. A., Bruck, M., Mogg, K., Bradley, B. P., Sweeney, M., et al. (2008). Attention bias toward threat in pediatric anxiety disorders. *Journal of the American Academy of Child and Adolescent Psychiatry, 47*(10), 1189–1196.

Schmidt, S., Mohr, A., Miltner, W. H., & Straube, T. (2010). Task-dependent neural correlates of the processing of verbal threat-related stimuli in social phobia. *Biological Psychology, 84*(2), 304–312.

Schmitz, T. W., & Johnson, S. C. (2007). Relevance to self: A brief review and framework of neural systems underlying appraisal. *Neuroscience and Biobehavioral Reviews, 31*(4), 585–596.

Schneider, F., Weiss, U., Kessler, C., Muller-Gartner, H. W., Posse, S., Salloum, J. B., et al. (1999). Subcortical correlates of differential classical conditioning of aversive emotional reactions in social phobia. *Biological Psychiatry, 45*(7), 863–871.

Shin, L. M., & Liberzon, I. (2010). The neurocircuitry of fear, stress, and anxiety disorders. *Neuropsychopharmacology, 35*(1), 169–191.

Sripada, C. S., Angstadt, M., Banks, S., Nathan, P. J., Liberzon, I., & Phan, K. L. (2009). Functional neuroimaging of mentalizing during the trust game in social anxiety disorder. *Neuroreport, 20*(11), 984–989.

Stein, M. B. (2009). Neurobiology of generalized anxiety disorder. *Journal of Clinical Psychiatry, 70*(Suppl 2), 15–19.

Stein, M. B., Goldin, P. R., Sareen, J., Zorrilla, L. T., & Brown, G. G. (2002). Increased amygdala activation to angry and contemptuous faces in generalized social phobia. *Archives of General Psychiatry, 59*(11), 1027–1034.

Stopa, L. (2009). Why is the self important in understanding and treating social phobia? *Cognitive Behaviour Therapy, 38*(Suppl 1), 48–54.

Straube, T., Kolassa, I. T., Glauer, M., Mentzel, H. J., & Miltner, W. H. (2004). Effect of task conditions on brain responses to threatening faces in social phobics: An event-related functional magnetic resonance imaging study. *Biological Psychiatry, 56*(12), 921–930.

Straube, T., Mentzel, H. J., & Miltner, W. H. (2005). Common and distinct brain activation to threat and safety signals in social phobia. *Neuropsychobiology, 52*(3), 163–168.

Taghavi, M. R., Dalgleish, T., Moradi, A. R., Neshat-Doost, H. T., & Yule, W. (2003). Selective processing of negative emotional information in children and adolescents with generalized anxiety disorder. *British Journal of Clinical Psychology, 42* (Pt 3), 221–230.

Thayer, J. F., Friedman, B. H., Borkovec, T. D., Johnsen, B. H., & Molina, S. (2000). Phasic heart period reactions to cued threat and nonthreat stimuli in generalized anxiety disorder. *Psychophysiology, 37*(3), 361–368.

Tillfors, M., Furmark, T., Marteinsdottir, I., & Fredrikson, M. (2002). Cerebral blood flow during anticipation of public speaking in social phobia: A PET study. *Biological Psychiatry, 52*(11), 1113–1119.

Urry, H. L., van Reekum, C. M., Johnstone, T., Kalin, N. H., Thurow, M. E., Schaefer, H. S., et al. (2006). Amygdala and ventromedial prefrontal cortex are inversely coupled during regulation of negative affect and predict the diurnal pattern of cortisol secretion among older adults. *Journal of Neuroscience, 26*(16), 4415–4425.

Van Ameringen, M., Mancini, C., Szechtman, H., Nahmias, C., Oakman, J. M., Hall, G. B., et al. (2004). A PET provocation study of generalized social phobia. *Psychiatry Research, 132*(1), 13–18.

van der Meer, L., Costafreda, S., Aleman, A., & David, A. S. (2010). Self-reflection and the brain: A theoretical review and meta-analysis of neuroimaging studies with implications for schizophrenia. *Neuroscience and Biobehavioral Reviews, 34*(6), 935–946.

Veit, R., Flor, H., Erb, M., Hermann, C., Lotze, M., Grodd, W., et al. (2002). Brain circuits involved in emotional learning in antisocial behavior and social phobia in humans. *Neuroscience Letters, 328*(3), 233–236.

Vuilleumier, P., Armony, J. L., Driver, J., & Dolan, R. J. (2001). Effects of attention and emotion on face processing in the human brain: an event-related fMRI study. *Neuron, 30*(3), 829–841.

Waters, A. M., Mogg, K., Bradley, B. P., & Pine, D. S. (2008). Attentional bias for emotional faces in children with generalized anxiety disorder. *Journal of the American Academy of Child and Adolescent Psychiatry, 47*(4), 435–442.

Watson, J. B., & Rayner, R. (1920). Conditioned emotional reactions. *Journal of Experimental Psychology, 3*(1), 1–14.

Whalen, P. J., Johnstone, T., Somerville, L. H., Nitschke, J. B., Polis, S., Alexander, A. L., et al. (2008). A functional magnetic resonance imaging predictor of treatment response to venlafaxine in generalized anxiety disorder. *Biological Psychiatry, 63*(9), 858–863.

Whalen, P. J., Shin, L. M., McInerney, S. C., Fischer, H., Wright, C. I., & Rauch, S. L. (2001). A functional MRI study of human amygdala responses to facial expressions of fear versus anger. *Emotion, 1*(1), 70–83.

Wilson, J. K., & Rapee, R. M. (2006). Self-concept certainty in social phobia. *Behaviour Research and Therapy, 44*(1), 113–136.

Yiend, J., & Mathews, A. (2001). Anxiety and attention to threatening pictures. *Quarterly Journal of Experimental Psychology A, 54*(3), 665–681.

The Neurobiology of Obsessive-Compulsive Disorder

Samuel R. Chamberlain *and* Naomi A. Fineberg

Abstract

Obsessive-compulsive disorder (OCD) is a debilitating and prevalent neuropsychiatric disorder characterized by obsessions and/or compulsions. This chapter selectively reviews OCD from several perspectives. It begins by considering clinical features of the disorder and its relationship with putative OC spectrum conditions such as trichotillomania and Tourette's syndrome. Existing first-line pharmacological and psychological interventions are outlined. The chapter then considers what is known of the neurobiology of OCD, focusing on relatively functionally segregated frontostriatal circuitry and underlying neurochemical mediators. It is proposed that OCD symptoms, and associated cognitive deficits, can be conceptualized in terms of aberrant function of orbitofrontocortical and dorsolateral prefrontocortical circuitry. This model is supported by translational studies relating to three specific cognitive functions: reversal learning, set-shifting, and response inhibition. Problems in these domains, along with associated neural abnormalities, have been found in patients with OCD and in their clinically unaffected first-degree relatives. Shortcomings in the literature are then discussed and future research directions provided, including the search for validated endophenotypes and novel treatment approaches for OCD and related disorders.

Key Words: obsessive-compulsive disorder (OCD), impulsivity, compulsivity, translational, inhibition, flexibility, serotonin, dopamine

Introduction

Obsessive-compulsive disorder (OCD) is a prevalent and disabling neuropsychiatric disorder with a lifetime prevalence of 2–3% worldwide (Weissman et al., 1994; Zohar, 1999). The condition is characterized by recurrent intrusive thoughts that enter into the stream of consciousness, which tend to be unpleasant and distressing (obsessions), and/or repetitive mental acts or physical rituals designed to neutralize obsessions or undertaken according to rigid rules (American Psychiatric Association, 2000). Individuals with OCD typically report symptoms cutting across a number of behavioral domains, which can change over time (Katerberg et al., 2010; Mataix-Cols, Rosario-Campos, & Leckman, 2005). These behavioral domains have been explored using

factor analysis, which supports the existence of several distinct symptom dimensions or clusters: washing, checking, ordering/symmetry, and hoarding (Mataix-Cols et al., 2004, 2005). Hoarding in particular represents a relatively distinct subtype that is more common in males and is often treatment refractory. OCD typically emerges in childhood or early adulthood (earlier in males) and follows a lifelong course with fluctuating severity (Skoog & Skoog, 1999). Unfortunately, existing treatment algorithms, while helpful for many sufferers, do not lead to adequate clinical response in up to a third of patients (Fineberg, Sivakumaran, Roberts, & Gale, 2005).

Studies have often identified cognitive deficits and structural–functional abnormalities of frontostriatal circuitry in patients with the OCD, in comparison to matched healthy controls with no known family history of the condition (Chamberlain, Blackwell, Fineberg, Robbins, & Sahakian, 2005). In some case reports, OCD has been linked with specific structural brain abnormalities (Berthier, 2000; Irle, Exner, Thielen, Weniger, & Ruther, 1998; Stengler-Wenzke, Muller, & Matthes-von-Cramon, 2003); however, in most cases of the disorder, findings are subtle and there are no gross macroscopic brain abnormalities that can be identified "by eye," highlighting the importance of sensitive methods of imaging analysis. Brain-based approaches to the study of OCD can help elucidate brain correlates of symptoms and cognitive deficits. Such approaches represent an important means of accounting for the mechanisms by which treatments exert their clinically beneficial effects. Convergent tiers of evidence implicate impairments of top-down control processes governing habitual responses, and overzealous activity of basal ganglia nodes mediating such habits, in the manifestation of OCD and related disorders (Chamberlain et al., 2005; Chamberlain, Fineberg, Blackwell, Robbins, & Sahakian, 2006; Chamberlain & Menzies, 2009; Fineberg et al., 2011).

Many of the symptoms observable in OCD bear similarities with rituals of childhood that usually disappear during brain development (Evans, Lewis, & Iobst, 2004). Children will often walk across the pavement avoiding cracks, dress in a certain order, and have certain mannerisms; if disrupted, children may become very distressed. The tendency toward habits makes evolutionary sense in that repetitive behaviors can be automated, thereby freeing up higher cortical regions for cognitive functions necessary for adapting rapidly to the changing world around us. Such functions include working memory, adaptive responding, and executive planning (Leckman et al., 2010). In normal development, the maturation of the frontal cortex and its subcortical connections that occurs in the adolescent years results in the natural suppression of these habitual tendencies, in favor of more adaptive, goal-directed behaviors (Gillan et al., 2011). Disruption of this sensitive balance between habit-mediating basal ganglia circuitry and top-down regulatory cortical circuitry is posited to at least in part underlie the repetitive hard-to-suppress habitual behaviors seen in OCD and related conditions (Fineberg et al., 2010; Graybiel & Rauch, 2000).

Clinical Aspects

The hallmark symptoms of OCD are unwanted and distressing (1) repetitive intrusive thoughts (obsessions) and/or (2) repetitive mental or behavioral rituals (compulsions). To warrant a diagnosis, such symptoms must be functionally impairing and not due to another psychiatric or medical disorder. For example, patients with schizophrenia may experience troubling thoughts or undertake stereotypies, which may form part of schizophrenia itself; less commonly, they may be part of a "schizo-OCD" presentation where both disorders co-occur (Patel et al., 2010). Careful clinical assessment is vital in order to provide correct diagnosis and appropriate treatment. OCD symptoms have been split into putatively distinct categories, with clinical relevance—hoarding is harder to treat.

Comorbid axis I disorders are common in OCD, especially depression, other anxiety disorders, and impulse control disorders. There is also considerable overlap between OCD and the so-called cluster C personality traits, as manifested in anankastic/obsessive-compulsive personality disorder (Fineberg, Fourie, Gale, & Sivakumaran, 2005; Peris et al., 2010). There is evidence that depression in patients with OCD differs somewhat from "stand-alone" clinical depression: the former tends to be associated with relatively increased worry and rumination and less vegetative disturbance compared with the latter (Fineberg, Fourie, et al., 2005). Moreover, depressive symptoms respond in tandem with the OCD during pharmacotherapy (Hoehn-Saric et al., 2000).

That many clinicians regard OCD as an anxiety disorder, and indeed it is conceptualized as such in the *Diagnostic and Statistical Manual of Mental Disorders* (4th ed., text revision; DSM-IV), is perhaps not surprising given that compulsions can be viewed as anxiety reducing: they are undertaken in response to obsessions, often to avoid some dreaded catastrophe. Likewise, if a patient with OCD is prevented from undertaking rituals, anxiety increases in the short term. This "neutralizing" influence of compulsions can lead to a vicious cycle (Drummond & Fineberg, 2007), and the main psychological treatment for OCD—exposure and response prevention (ERP)—uses this notion to therapeutic ends. The role of anxiety in OCD nonetheless remains controversial, and OCD's nosological position is under active review (Hollander, 2008; Hollander, Braun, & Simeon, 2008; Phillips et al., 2010).

In this regard, it is noteworthy that a number of nosologically separate conditions bear phenomenological similarity with OCD and may constitute a new category broadly conceptualized as obsessive-compulsive (OC) spectrum disorders (Hollander, 2008; Hollander, Stein, Fineberg, Marteau, & Legault,

2010; Phillips et al., 2010). Tics and Tourette's syndrome commonly occur together with an obsessive-compulsive syndrome that looks identical to OCD (Hranov & Fineberg, 2010). Patients with OCD are likely to be at increased risk of pathological grooming disorders, including trichotillomania, pathological skin-picking, and pathological nail-biting. There is also overlap between OCD, body dysmorphic disorder (BDD), and eating disorders in terms of an "obsessional" quality that is hard to suppress and often leads to ritualistic or "habitual" behavior (Cavallini, Bertelli, Chiapparino, Riboldi, & Bellodi, 2000; Hollander et al., 2008). These conditions may share overlapping etiologies, as they co-occur in related family members more frequently than would be expected by chance alone (Bienvenu et al., 2000; Hollander et al., 1996; Jaisoorya, Reddy, & Srinath, 2003; Matsunaga et al., 2005; Phillips, 2002; Phillips et al., 2010; Richter, Summerfeldt, Antony, & Swinson, 2003; Swedo & Leonard, 1992). In view of these findings, it is likely that DSM-V will include a new category of "OC and related disorders" (http://www.dsm5.org) that includes OCD, BDD, trichotillomania, pathological skin-picking and hoarding as separate diagnoses. The presence of comorbid tics in children and adolescents with OCD is predictive of a positive outcome in adulthood, whereas primary hoarding symptoms are associated with refractory OCD (Bloch et al., 2009).

Pharmacological Intervention in OCD

There is considerable high-quality evidence from double-blind, randomized, placebo-controlled studies showing that serotonin reuptake inhibitors are effective in the treatment of OCD (Fineberg & Gale, 2004). Effective treatments range from the nonselective tricyclic clomipramine to the more highly selective serotonin reuptake inhibitors (SSRIs, e.g., citalopram/escitalopram), which are reasonably effective in approximately two-thirds of cases. Treatment benefits are gradual over weeks to months and can require higher doses to come about (Fineberg & Gale, 2004). It is important to note that treatments found to be effective in some other anxiety and affective disorders, such as noradrenergic reuptake inhibitors, benzodiazepines, and mood stabilizers, are not regarded as clinically effective in the treatment of OCD. In treatment-refractory OCD, treatment options include increasing SSRI dosing beyond formulary limits, SSRI switching, or augmenting with a low-dose antipsychotic (Fineberg, Nigam, & Silvakumaran, 2006; Pampaloni et al., 2010). Tic-related OCD may respond better to an adjunctive antipsychotic than OCD without tic behavior (Fineberg, Stein, et al., 2006).

The serotonin and dopamine systems in particular have been implicated in the pathophysiology of OCD and in its treatment. Administration of the nonselective serotonin receptor agonist meta-chlorophenylpiperazine (mCPP) was found to induce OCD symptoms, and these effects were found to be blocked by pretreatment with clomipramine/SSRI (Hollander et al., 1991; Zohar, Insel, Zohar-Kadouch, Hill, & Murphy, 1988). Ligand-based PET studies have identified striatal and cortical alterations in 5-HT2A receptors and in striatal D2 receptors in patients with OCD (Denys, Van Der Wee, Janssen, De Geus, & Westenberg, 2004; Westenberg, Fineberg, & Denys, 2007). In rats, co-administration of SSRI and antipsychotic medication increased dopamine release in the prefrontal cortex (Denys, Klompmakers, & Westenberg, 2004). Other neurotransmitter systems have also been implicated in OCD, albeit to a lesser degree, for example, cholinergic (Lucey, Butcher, Clare, & Dinan, 1993), glutamatergic (McGrath, Campbell, Parks, & Burton, 2000), NMDA, and peptide systems (Lochner et al., 2004a, b).

The mechanisms by which existing pharmacological treatments for OCD exert their beneficial effects on symptoms are far from fully explained. It is likely that there are complex and gradual effects that may involve serotonin receptor changes in the orbitofrontal cortices and caudate nucleus (Blier & de Montigny, 1998; El Mansari & Blier, 2005, 2006; El Mansari, Bouchard, & Blier, 1995). Clinical benefits of serotoninergic agents are unlikely to be accounted for by a simple "reuptake inhibition increases free serotonin neurotransmitter levels" account. Tryptophan depletion, which involves putative depletion of brain serotonin via consumption of an amino acid cocktail lacking the necessary precursors (Bell, Abrams, & Nutt, 2001; Young, 1993), does not appear to exacerbate or induce OCD symptoms in patients with OCD (Berney, Sookman, Leyton, Young, & Benkelfat, 2006; Kulz, Meinzer, Kopasz, & Voderholzer, 2007). Nonetheless, tryptophan supplementation was reported to be clinically beneficial when used in conjunction with an SRI plus administration of the 5-HT1A partial agonist pindolol in one study of OCD patients (Blier & Bergeron, 1996).

Quantifying Neurobiological Dysfunction in OCD

Cognitive functions and consequent overt behaviors are thought to be dependent upon relatively

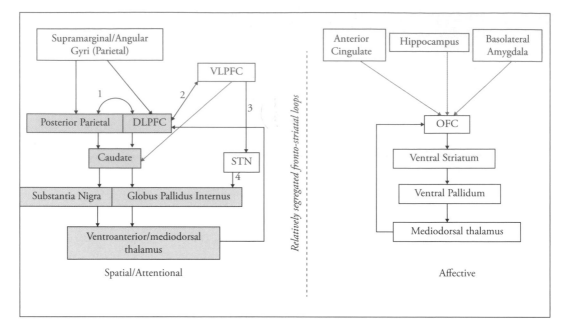

Figure 29.1 Affected brain circuitry in OCD. OCD can be conceptualized in terms of dysfunction of the dorsolateral network (principally involved in higher-order cognitive functioning) and orbitofrontal network (principally involved in emotional processing and lower-order cognitive functioning). These networks are under the neuromodulatory influences of monoamine systems, including dopamine and serotonin. DLPFC, dorsolateral prefrontal cortex; OFC, orbitofrontal cortex; STN, subthalamic nucleus; VLPFC, ventrolateral prefrontal cortex.

Reprinted with permission from Menzies, Chamberlain, et al. (2008).

segregated circuits within the brain, based on work in animals and in humans (Alexander, DeLong, & Strick, 1986; Robbins & Arnsten, 2009). Aberrant structure and function of nodes within corticosubcortical networks have frequently been reported in patients with OCD (as compared to healthy volunteers), as have abnormalities in the white matter tracts interconnecting such regions (Atmaca et al., 2006; Menzies, Chamberlain, et al., 2008; Nordahl et al., 1989; Radua & Mataix-Cols, 2009; Rotge et al., 2009; Saxena & Rauch, 2000). Based on comprehensive review of imaging and cognitive studies (Menzies, Chamberlain, et al., 2008), it has been proposed that the neurobiology of OCD might best be accounted for by a model that includes dysfunction of the orbitofrontostriatal loop and dorsolateral frontostriatal loop (Figure 29.1).

Neuropsychological studies in OCD patients, and in patients' clinically unaffected first-degree relatives, have highlighted performance deficits across several cognitive domains: (1) reversal learning, (2) extradimensional set-shifting, and (3) response inhibition (Chamberlain et al., 2005, 2006, 2008; Chamberlain, Fineberg et al., 2007). Reversal learning is a low-level cognitive function that involves adapting one's behavior in light of emotionally salient feedback (e.g., being told one is wrong), such as switching from choosing one simple stimulus to another in an ongoing reinforcement task (Roberts, Robbins, Everitt, & Muir, 1992). Extradimensional set-shifting is a higher-order cognitive function whereby individuals inhibit and shift attention from one aspect of the environment to another previously irrelevant aspect, as investigated in early work using the Wisconsin Card Sorting Test of frontal integrity. Response inhibition involves the ability to suppress simple prepotent motor responses that have already been triggered (Aron, Fletcher, Bullmore, Sahakian, & Robbins, 2003; Logan, Cowan, & Davis, 1984). Collectively, these three cognitive domains have proven valuable in OCD research—they are thought to be relatively dissociable from neural and neurochemical points of view. Reversal, set-shifting, and response inhibition are under the neuromodulatory influences (in humans and in other animals) of serotonin, noradrenaline/dopamine, and noradrenaline, respectively (for further discussion, see Robbins, 2000, 2005).

More recent work has expanded on findings of problems with these cognitive abilities in people with OCD, by using structural and functional imaging in conjunction with recently developed

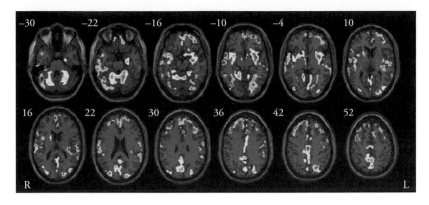

Figure 29.2 Patients with OCD and their unaffected first-degree relatives showed underactivation of the bilateral lateral orbitofrontal cortex/prefrontal cortex (top graphs) and bilateral parietal cortices (bottom graphs) during a functional brain imaging test requiring flexible reversal of behavioral responses. $^*p < .05$, $^{**}p < .01$, $^{***}p < .001$. These neural regions constitute part of the circuitry shown in Figure 29.1.

Reprinted with permission from Chamberlain et al. (2008).

methods of imaging analysis. During reversal learning, patients with OCD and their clinically unaffected first-degree relatives showed underactivation of the bilateral orbitofrontal and bilateral posterior parietal cortices as compared to healthy volunteers (Chamberlain et al., 2008; Figure 29.2). There was also a trend toward underactivation of the dorsolateral prefrontal cortices during set-shifting (it should be noted that set-shifting is more difficult to assess in repeated event study designs than reversal learning). Gray matter abnormalities in distributed corticosubcortical circuitry were significantly associated with response inhibition deficits in patients and in their relatives, and a brain-based marker was found to be significantly heritable (Menzies et al., 2007; Figure 29.3). Follow-up work indicated the presence of structural abnormalities in white matter tracts interconnecting these regions, in patients and in relatives (Menzies, Williams et al., 2008). Collectively, these cognitive deficits and their associated structural–functional correlates are thought to reflect disposition toward "cognitive inflexibility" and "motor impulsivity" and thus OC spectrum disorders within OCD families (Chamberlain & Menzies, 2009).

Translational Modeling of Select Cognitive Problems in OCD

The features of OCD and related disorders that are most readily captured by animal models are the rigid cognitive styles and repetitive motor outputs of various forms relating to compulsivity (Boulougouris, Chamberlain, & Robbins, 2009); obsessive thoughts are not studied in animals since they are not accessible in nonhumans. Validation criteria for animal models are determined by the objective of the model and its intended use, rather than its capturing of a given disorder per se (Geyer & Markou, 1995, 2002; Matthysse, 1986; Mckinney, 2000; McKinney & Bunney, 1969; Willner, 1991). Criteria for assessing animal models are described in detail elsewhere (Boulougouris, Chamberlain, & Robbins, 2009; Geyer & Markou, 1995; Willner, 1984) but in brief comprise face validity (phenomenological similarity), predictive validity (the extent to which an animal model allows accurate predictions about the human disorder, e.g., in terms of pharmacological treatment), construct validity (overlapping underlying neurobiology), and reliability (consistency across studies and research units). Geyer and Markou (1995) have suggested that the evaluation of animal models in this context should principally rely on reliability and predictive validity. We consider here, selectively, animal models relating to the three cognitive domains highlighted as being abnormal (in behavior and/or neural substrates) in OCD patients and in their relatives: (1) reversal learning, (2) extradimensional set-shifting, and (3) response inhibition.

As noted earlier, patients with OCD and their unaffected relatives have been shown to exhibit underactivation (vs. controls) in the orbitofrontal and parietal cortices during visual reversal learning, suggesting a possible neuroendophenotype for OCD (Chamberlain et al., 2008). In marmosets, impaired reversal learning occurs following orbitofrontal lesions (Dias, Robbins, & Roberts, 1996) and also following 5-HT depletion within the orbitofrontal

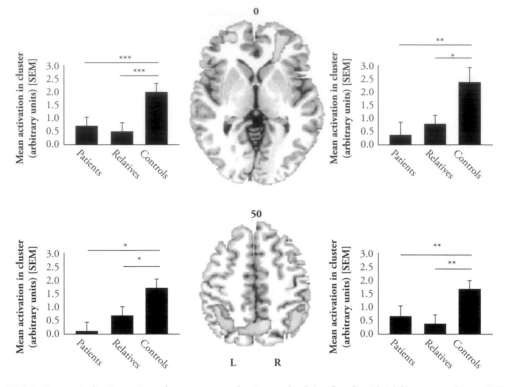

Figure 29.3 Brain maps indicating regions where gray matter density correlated significantly with inhibitory control in an OCD study. Response inhibition impairments in people with OCD and their unaffected first-degree relatives were associated with increased gray matter in cingulate, parietal, and striatal regions, and with reduced gray matter in the right orbitofrontal and inferior frontal regions. These findings support the model outlined in Figure 29.1.

Reprinted with permission from Menzies et al. (2007).

cortices (Clarke et al., 2005; Clarke, Walker, Dalley, Robbins, & Roberts, 2007). The orbitofrontal cortices project to the medial striatum and nucleus accumbens in marmosets (Roberts et al., 2007). Moreover, excitotoxic lesions of the medial striatum lead to impaired reversal learning (Clarke, Robbins, & Roberts, 2008). There has been little attempt so far to remediate reversal learning deficits in studies of nonhuman primates, although reversal learning has been used to assess 5-HT agents in rats (Boulougouris, Glennon, & Robbins, 2008). Predictive validation of the reversal learning model therefore remains to be undertaken. Nonetheless, in a recent study, a relationship between reversal, 5-HT, and effects of stress in rats was demonstrated (Lapiz-Bluhm, Soto-Pina, Hensler, & Morilak, 2009). This may demonstrate an important relationship between rigidity induced by a cortical lesion and stress-induced anxiety, mediated by the ascending 5-HT system.

Set-shifting deficits have been commonly reported in OCD on a variety of tasks (Chamberlain

et al., 2006; Chamberlain, Fineberg et al., 2007). OCD patients with concurrent obsessive-compulsive personality disorder (OCPD) were significantly more affected (Fineberg, Sharma, Sivakumaran, Sahakian, & Chamberlain, 2007). Groups of patients with body dysmorphic disorder (Jefferies, Laws, & Fineberg, 2010) and schizophrenia with OCD (Patel et al., 2010), as well as schizophrenia without OCD (Pantelis et al., 1999), have also shown extradimensional impairment compared to a matched controls. Impaired extradimensional shifting may represent a hallmark of compulsive responding associated with cognitive inflexibility. In healthy volunteers, set-shifting is dependent on distributed circuitry including the lateral prefrontal cortices (Hampshire & Owen, 2006). There is remarkable consistency across species in this regard. This form of attentional set-shifting modeled in the marmoset is impaired by lateral frontal, but not orbitofrontal, cortex lesions and by catecholamine, but not 5-HT, depletion (see Robbins, 2005, for review). Also, whereas the impaired extradimensional shifting in OCD patients is also seen in their unaffected first-degree relatives (Chamberlain, Fineberg, et al. 2007), this is not the case for schizophrenia (Ceaser et al., 2008), which suggests that this may be a specific endophenotype for OCD itself.

Individuals with OCD also exhibit impaired inhibition on a variety of tasks (Bannon, Gonsalvez, Croft, & Boyce, 2002; Enright & Beech, 1993; Rosenberg, Dick, O'Hearn, & Sweeney, 1997; Tien, Pearlson, Machlin, Bylsma, & Hoehn-Saric, 1992; see Chamberlain et al., 2005, for a review). The stop-signal test of response inhibition, used in the previously described work in OCD, identified behavioral motor inhibition deficits in OCD and in symptom-unaffected patient relatives, linked with structural abnormalities of frontostriatal circuitry. The ability to inhibit responses in humans is dependent on distributed circuitry including the right inferior frontal gyrus (Aron et al., 2003; Hampshire, Chamberlain, Monti, Duncan, & Owen, 2010). A method of measuring response inhibition in rats has been developed, which appears to be dependent on homologous brain structures (Eagle & Robbins, 2003; Eagle, Tufft, Goodchild, & Robbins, 2007). The task is insensitive to serotoninergic manipulations in both rats and humans (Chamberlain & Sahakian, 2007), but inhibitory performance is improved by noradrenergic manipulations (Chamberlain, Del Campo, et al., 2007; DeVito et al., 2009).

Conclusions and Implications

The translational findings considered in this chapter implicate cognitive rigidity and response disinhibition not only as problems that manifest in patients with OCD but also as candidate vulnerability factors—such problems were also found in unaffected "at-risk" relatives of patients. While reversal learning problems would fit with dysregulation of the serotonin system in OCD, the manifestation of set shift and response inhibition deficits implicates super-added dysregulation of the dopamine and noradrenaline systems. These data also highlight that OCD is likely to be associated not with specific orbitofrontal dysfunction, as previously supposed in the literature, but with more general dysregulation of other corticosubcortical circuitry, including dorsolateral.

Considerable advances are being made in exploring these cognitive problems in families with OCD and in modeling them translationally. The development of useful theoretically motivated models of OCD, particularly with regard to repetitive motoric

habits and inhibitory failure, are promising but require further validation with stringent criteria. For example, it will be important to probe these models using a variety of pharmacological agents chronically to assess whether they are differentially responsive to SSRI monotherapy. If validated, novel pharmacological agents could be tested in these cognitive models before potential use in human studies.

These findings raise as many questions as answers. If cognitive problems precede OCD, can they be targeted with psychotherapy, pharmacotherapy, or both to stem the progress of the condition, which, once ingrained, is hard to treat? How selective are these cognitive problems for OCD itself as opposed to unrelated conditions? Do they occur at increased rates in relatives of people with related conditions such as trichotillomania? Given the heterogeneity and etiological complexity of OCD, the findings emerging from the combined use of different models may provide insight to the various aspects and etiology of the disorder and lead to new treatment targets.

Acknowledgments and Disclosures

Dr. S. R. Chamberlain has consulted for Cambridge Cognition, Shire, Lilly, and P1Vital. Dr. Fineberg has consulted for Lundbeck, GlaxoSmith Kline, Servier, and Bristol Myers Squibb; has received research support from Lundbeck, GlaxoSmithKline, Astra Zeneca, Wellcome, Cephalon, ECNP, and Servier; has received honoraria for lectures at scientific meetings from Janssen, Jazz, Lundbeck, Servier, Astra Zeneca, and Wyeth; and has received financial support to attend scientific meetings from Janssen, Bristol Myers Squibb, Jazz, Lundbeck, Servier, Astra Zeneca, Wyeth, Cephalon, and the International College of OC Spectrum Disorders. This chapter was derived in part from an adaptation of a previously published manuscript (Fineberg et al., 2011).

References

Alexander, G. E., DeLong, M. R., & Strick, P. L. (1986). Parallel organization of functionally segregated circuits linking basal ganglia and cortex. *AnnualReview of Neuroscience, 9,* 357–381.

American Psychiatric Association. (2000). *Diagnostic and statistical manual of mental disorders* (4th ed., text revision). Washington, DC: American Psychiatric Association.

Aron, A. R., Fletcher, P. C., Bullmore, E. T., Sahakian, B. J., & Robbins, T. W. (2003). Stop-signal inhibition disrupted by damage to right inferior frontal gyrus in humans. *Nature Neuroscience, 6*(2), 115–116.

Atmaca, M., Yildirim, B. H., Ozdemir, B. H., Aydin, B. A., Tezcan, A. E., & Ozler, A. S. (2006). Volumetric MRI assessment of brain regions in patients with refractory obsessive-compulsive disorder. *Progress in Neuropsychopharmacology and Biological Psychiatry, 30*(6), 1051–1057.

Bannon, S., Gonsalvez, C. J., Croft, R. J., & Boyce, P. M. (2002). Response inhibition deficits in obsessive-compulsive disorder. *Psychiatry Research, 110*(2), 165–174.

Bell, C., Abrams, J., & Nutt, D. (2001). Tryptophan depletion and its implications for psychiatry. *British Journal of Psychiatry, 178*, 399–405.

Berney, A., Sookman, D., Leyton, M., Young, S. N., & Benkelfat, C. (2006). Lack of effects on core obsessive-compulsive symptoms of tryptophan depletion during symptom provocation in remitted obsessive-compulsive disorder patients. *Biological Psychiatry, 59*(9), 853–857.

Berthier, M. L. (2000). [Cognitive function in the obsessive-compulsive disorder associated with cerebral lesions]. *Revue Neurologe, 30*(8), 769–772.

Bienvenu, O. J., Samuels, J. F., Riddle, M. A., Hoehn-Saric, R., Liang, K. Y., Cullen, B. A., et al. (2000). The relationship of obsessive-compulsive disorder to possible spectrum disorders: Results from a family study. *Biological Psychiatry, 48*(4), 287–293.

Blier, P., & Bergeron, R. (1996). Sequential administration of augmentation strategies in treatment-resistant obsessive-compulsive disorder: Preliminary findings. *International Clinical Psychopharmacology, 11*(1), 37–44.

Blier, P., & de Montigny, C. (1998). Possible serotonergic mechanisms underlying the antidepressant and anti-obsessive-compulsive disorder responses. *Biological Psychiatry, 44*(5), 313–323.

Bloch, M. H., Craiglow, B. G., Landeros-Weisenberger, A., Dombrowski, P. A., Panza, K. E., Peterson, B. S., et al. (2009). Predictors of early adult outcomes in pediatric-onset obsessive-compulsive disorder. *Pediatrics, 124*(4), 1085–1093.

Boulougouris, V., Chamberlain, S. R., & Robbins, T. W. (2009). Cross-species models of OCD spectrum disorders. *Psychiatry Research, 170*(1), 15–21.

Boulougouris, V., Glennon, J. C., & Robbins, T. W. (2008). Dissociable effects of selective 5-HT2A and 5-HT2C receptor antagonists on serial spatial reversal learning in rats. *Neuropsychopharmacology, 33*(8), 2007–2019.

Cavallini, M. C., Bertelli, S., Chiapparino, D., Riboldi, S., & Bellodi, L. (2000). Complex segregation analysis of obsessive-compulsive disorder in 141 families of eating disorder probands, with and without obsessive-compulsive disorder. *American Journal of Medical Genetics, 96*(3), 384–391.

Ceaser, A. E., Goldberg, T. E., Egan, M. F., McMahon, R. P., Weinberger, D. R., & Gold, J. M. (2008). Set-shifting ability and schizophrenia: A marker of clinical illness or an intermediate phenotype? *Biological Psychiatry, 64*(9), 782–788.

Chamberlain, S. R., Blackwell, A. D., Fineberg, N., Robbins, T. W., & Sahakian, B. J. (2005). The neuropsychology of obsessive compulsive disorder: The importance of failures in cognitive and behavioural inhibition as candidate endophenotypic markers. *Neuroscience and Biobehavioral Review, 29*(3), 399–419.

Chamberlain, S. R., Del Campo, N., Dowson, J., Müller, U., Clark, L., Robbins, T. W., et al. (2007). Atomoxetine improved response inhibition in adults with attention deficit/hyperactivity disorder. *Biological Psychiatry, 62*, 977–984.

Chamberlain, S. R., Fineberg, N. A., Blackwell, A. D., Robbins, T. W., & Sahakian, B. J. (2006). Motor inhibition and cognitive flexibility in obsessive-compulsive disorder and trichotillomania. *American Journal of Psychiatry, 163*(7), 1282–1284.

Chamberlain, S. R., Fineberg, N. A., Menzies, L. A., Blackwell, A. D., Bullmore, E. T., Robbins, T. W., et al. (2007). Impaired cognitive flexibility and motor inhibition in unaffected first-degree relatives of patients with obsessive-compulsive disorder. *American Journal of Psychiatry, 164*(2), 335–338.

Chamberlain, S. R., & Menzies, L. (2009). Endophenotypes of obsessive-compulsive disorder: Rationale, evidence and future potential. *Expert Review of Neurotherapeutics, 9*(8), 1133–1146.

Chamberlain, S. R., Menzies, L., Hampshire, A., Suckling, J., Fineberg, N. A., del Campo, N., et al. (2008). Orbitofrontal dysfunction in patients with obsessive-compulsive disorder and their unaffected relatives. *Science, 321*(5887), 421–422.

Chamberlain, S. R., & Sahakian, B. J. (2007). The neuropsychiatry of impulsivity. *Current Opinion in Psychiatry, 20*(3), 255–261.

Clarke, H. F., Robbins, T. W., & Roberts, A. C. (2008). Lesions of the medial striatum in monkeys produce perseverative impairments during reversal learning similar to those produced by lesions of the orbitofrontal cortex. *Journal of Neuroscience, 28*(43), 10972–10982.

Clarke, H. F., Walker, S. C., Crofts, H. S., Dalley, J. W., Robbins, T. W., & Roberts, A. C. (2005). Prefrontal serotonin depletion affects reversal learning but not attentional set shifting. *Journal of Neuroscience, 25*(2), 532–538.

Clarke, H. F., Walker, S. C., Dalley, J. W., Robbins, T. W., & Roberts, A. C. (2007). Cognitive inflexibility after prefrontal serotonin depletion is behaviorally and neurochemically specific. *Cerebral Cortex, 17*(1), 18–27.

Denys, D., Klompmakers, A. A., & Westenberg, H. G. (2004). Synergistic dopamine increase in the rat prefrontal cortex with the combination of quetiapine and fluvoxamine. *Psychopharmacology* (Berlin), *176*(2), 195–203.

Denys, D., Van Der Wee, N., Janssen, J., De Geus, F., & Westenberg, H. G. (2004). Low level of dopaminergic D(2) receptor binding in obsessive-compulsive disorder. *Biological Psychiatry, 55*(10), 1041–1045.

DeVito, E. E., Blackwell, A. D., Clark, L., Kent, L., Dezsery, A. M., Turner, D. C., et al. (2009). Methylphenidate improves response inhibition but not reflection-impulsivity in children with attention deficit hyperactivity disorder (ADHD). *Psychopharmacology* (Berlin), *202*(1-3), 531–539.

Dias, R., Robbins, T. W., & Roberts, A. C. (1996). Dissociation in prefrontal cortex of affective and attentional shifts. *Nature, 380*(6569), 69–72.

Drummond, L. M., & Fineberg, N. A. (2007). Obsessive-compulsive disorders. In G. Stein (Ed.), *College seminars in adult psychiatry* (pp. 270–286). London: Gaskell.

Eagle, D. M., & Robbins, T. W. (2003). Inhibitory control in rats performing a stop-signal reaction-time task: Effects of lesions of the medial striatum and d-amphetamine. *Behavioral Neuroscience, 117*(6), 1302–1317.

Eagle, D. M., Tufft, M. R., Goodchild, H. L., & Robbins, T. W. (2007). Differential effects of modafinil and methylphenidate on stop-signal reaction time task performance in the rat, and interactions with the dopamine receptor antagonist cis-flupenthixol. *Psychopharmacology* (Berlin), *192*(2), 193–206.

El Mansari, M., & Blier, P. (2005). Responsiveness of 5-HT(1A) and 5-HT2 receptors in the rat orbitofrontal cortex after long-term serotonin reuptake inhibition. *Journal of Psychiatry & Neuroscience, 30*(4), 268–274.

El Mansari, M., & Blier, P. (2006). Mechanisms of action of current and potential pharmacotherapies of obsessive-compulsive disorder. *Progress in Neuropsychopharmacology & Biological Psychiatry, 30*(3), 362–373.

El Mansari, M., Bouchard, C., & Blier, P. (1995). Alteration of serotonin release in the guinea pig orbito-frontal cortex by selective serotonin reuptake inhibitors. Relevance to treatment of obsessive-compulsive disorder. *Neuropsychopharmacology, 13*(2), 117–127.

Enright, S. J., & Beech, A. R. (1993). Reduced cognitive inhibition in obsessive-compulsive disorder. *British Journal of Clinical Psychology, 32*(Pt 1), 67–74.

Evans, D. W., Lewis, M. D., & Iobst, E. (2004). The role of the orbitofrontal cortex in normally developing compulsive-like behaviors and obsessive-compulsive disorder. *Brain Cognition, 55*(1), 220–234.

Fineberg, N. A., Fourie, H., Gale, T. M., & Sivakumaran, T. (2005). Comorbid depression in obsessive compulsive disorder (OCD): Symptomatic differences to major depressive disorder. *Journal of Affective Disorders, 87*(2-3), 327–330.

Fineberg, N. A., & Gale, T. M. (2004). Evidence-based pharmacotherapy of obsessive-compulsive disorder. *International Journal of Neuropsychopharmacology*, 1–23.

Fineberg, N. A., Nigam, A., & Silvakumaran, T. (2006). Pharmacological strategies for treatment-resistant obsessive compulsive disorder. *Psychiatric Annals, 36*(7), 464–474.

Fineberg, N. A., Potenza, M. N., Chamberlain, S. R., Berlin, H. A., Menzies, L., Bechara, A., et al. (2010). Probing compulsive and impulsive behaviors, from animal models to endophenotypes: a narrative review. *Neuropsychopharmacology, 35*(3), 591–604.

Fineberg, N. A., Potenza, M. N., Chamberlain, S. R., Berlin, H. A., Menzies, L., Bechara, A., et al. (2011). Probing compulsive and impulsive behaviors, from animal models to endophenotypes: A narrative review. *Neuropsychopharmacology, 35*(3), 591–604.

Fineberg, N. A., Sharma, P., Sivakumaran, T., Sahakian, B., & Chamberlain, S. R. (2007). Does obsessive-compulsive personality disorder belong within the obsessive-compulsive spectrum? *CNS Spectrum, 12*(6), 467–482.

Fineberg, N. A., Sivakumaran, T., Roberts, A., & Gale, T. (2005). Adding quetiapine to SRI in treatment-resistant obsessive-compulsive disorder: A randomized controlled treatment study. *International Clinical Psychopharmacology, 20*(4), 223–226.

Fineberg, N. A., Stein, D. J., Premkumar, P., Carey, P., Sivakumaran, T., Vythilingum, B., et al. (2006). Adjunctive quetiapine for serotonin reuptake inhibitor-resistant obsessive-compulsive disorder: A meta-analysis of randomized controlled treatment trials. *International Clinical Psychopharmacology, 21*(6), 337–343.

Geyer, M. A., & Markou, A. (1995). Animal models of psychiatric disorders. In F. E. Bloom & D. J. Kupfer (Eds.), *Psychopharmacology: The fourth generation of progress* (pp. 787–798). New York: Raven Press.

Geyer, M. A., & Markou, A. (2002). The role of preclinical models in the development of psychotropic drugs. In K. L. Davis, J. T. Coyle, & C. Nemeroff (Eds.), *Psychopharmacology: The fifth generation of progress* (pp. 445–455). Philadelphia: Lippincott Williams & Wilkins.

Gillan, C. M., Papmeyer, M., Morein-Zamir, S., Sahakian, B. J., Fineberg, N. A., Robbins, T. W., & de Wit, S. (2011). Disruption in the balance between goal-directed behavior and habit learning in obsessive-compulsive disorder. *American Journal of Psychiatry, 168*(7), 718–726.

Graybiel, A. M., & Rauch, S. L. (2000). Toward a neurobiology of obsessive-compulsive disorder. *Neuron, 28*(2), 343–347.

Hampshire, A., Chamberlain, S. R., Monti, M. M., Duncan, J., & Owen, A. M. (2010). The role of the right inferior frontal gyrus: Inhibition and attentional control. *Neuroimage, 50*(3), 1313–1319.

Hampshire, A., & Owen, A. M. (2006). Fractioning attentional control using event-related fMRI. *Cerebral Cortex, 16*(12), 1679–1689.

Hoehn-Saric, R., Ninan, P., Black, D. W., Stahl, S., Greist, J. H., Lydiard, B., et al. (2000). Multicenter double-blind comparison of sertraline and desipramine for concurrent obsessive-compulsive and major depressive disorders. *Archives of General Psychiatry, 57*(1), 76–82.

Hollander, E. (2008). Obsessive-compulsive spectrum phenomena and the DSM-V developmental process. *CNS Spectrum, 13*(2), 107–108.

Hollander, E., Braun, A., & Simeon, D. (2008). Should OCD leave the anxiety disorders in DSM-V? The case for obsessive compulsive-related disorders. *Depression & Anxiety, 25*(4), 317–329.

Hollander, E., DeCaria, C., Gully, R., Nitescu, A., Suckow, R. F., Gorman, J. M., et al. (1991). Effects of chronic fluoxetine treatment on behavioral and neuroendocrine responses to meta-chlorophenylpiperazine in obsessive-compulsive disorder. *Psychiatry Research, 36*(1), 1–17.

Hollander, E., Kwon, J. H., Stein, D. J., Broatch, J., Rowland, C. T., & Himelein, C. A. (1996). Obsessive-compulsive and spectrum disorders: Overview and quality of life issues. *Journal of Clinical Psychiatry, 57* Suppl 8, 3–6.

Hollander, E., Stein, D. J., Fineberg, N. A., Marteau, F., & Legault, M. (2010). Quality of life outcomes in patients with obsessive-compulsive disorder: Relationship to treatment response and symptom relapse. *Journal of Clinical Psychiatry, 71*(6), 784–792.

Hranov, G., & Fineberg, N. A. (2010). Are tics an essential symptom of the obsessive compulsive syndrome? *European Neuropsychopharmacology, 20*(2), s521.

Irle, E., Exner, C., Thielen, K., Weniger, G., & Ruther, E. (1998). Obsessive-compulsive disorder and ventromedial frontal lesions: Clinical and neuropsychological findings. *American Journal of Psychiatry, 155*(2), 255–263.

Jaisoorya, T. S., Reddy, Y. C., & Srinath, S. (2003). The relationship of obsessive-compulsive disorder to putative spectrum disorders: Results from an Indian study. *Comprehensive Psychiatry, 44*(4), 317–323.

Jefferies, K., Laws, K., & Fineberg, N. A. (2010). Cognitive and perceptual processing in body dysmorphic disorder. *European Neuropsychopharmacology, 20*(3), s309.

Katerberg, H., Delucchi, K. L., Stewart, S. E., Lochner, C., Denys, D. A., Stack, D. E., et al. (2010). Symptom dimensions in OCD: Item-level factor analysis and heritability estimates. *Behavioral Genetics, 40*(4), 505–517.

Kulz, A. K., Meinzer, S., Kopasz, M., & Voderholzer, U. (2007). Effects of tryptophan depletion on cognitive functioning, obsessive-compulsive symptoms and mood in obsessive-compulsive disorder: Preliminary results. *Neuropsychobiology, 56*(2-3), 127–131.

Lapiz-Bluhm, M. D., Soto-Pina, A. E., Hensler, J. G., & Morilak, D. A. (2009). Chronic intermittent cold stress and serotonin depletion induce deficits of reversal learning in an attentional set-shifting test in rats. *Psychopharmacology* (Berlin), *202*(1-3), 329–341.

Leckman, J. F., Denys, D., Simpson, H. B., Mataix-Cols, D., Hollander, E., Saxena, S., et al. (2010). Obsessive-compulsive disorder: A review of the diagnostic criteria and possible subtypes and dimensional specifiers for DSM-V. *Depression & Anxiety, 27*(6), 507–527.

Lochner, C., Hemmings, S. M., Kinnear, C. J., Moolman-Smook, J. C., Corfield, V. A., Knowles, J. A., et al. (2004a). Corrigendum to "gender in obsessive-compulsive disorder: Clinical and genetic findings". *European Neuropsychopharmacology, 14*(5), 437–445.

Lochner, C., Hemmings, S. M., Kinnear, C. J., Moolman-Smook, J. C., Corfield, V. A., Knowles, J. A., et al. (2004b). Gender in obsessive-compulsive disorder: Clinical and genetic findings. *European Neuropsychopharmacology, 14*(2), 105–113.

Logan, G. D., Cowan, W. B., & Davis, K. A. (1984). On the ability to inhibit simple and choice reaction time responses: A model and a method. *Journal of Experimental Psychology. Human Perception and Perform*ance, *10*(2), 276–291.

Lucey, J. V., Butcher, G., Clare, A. W., & Dinan, T. G. (1993). Elevated growth hormone responses to pyridostigmine in obsessive-compulsive disorder: Evidence of cholinergic supersensitivity. *American Journal of Psychiatry, 150*(6), 961–962.

Mataix-Cols, D., Rosario-Campos, M. C., & Leckman, J. F. (2005). A multidimensional model of obsessive-compulsive disorder. *American Journal of Psychiatry, 162*(2), 228–238.

Mataix-Cols, D., Wooderson, S., Lawrence, N., Brammer, M. J., Speckens, A., & Phillips, M. L. (2004). Distinct neural correlates of washing, checking, and hoarding symptom dimensions in obsessive-compulsive disorder. *Archives of General Psychiatry, 61*(6), 564–576.

Matsunaga, H., Kiriike, N., Matsui, T., Oya, K., Okino, K., & Stein, D. J. (2005). Impulsive disorders in Japanese adult patients with obsessive-compulsive disorder. *Comprehensive Psychiatry, 46*(1), 43–49.

Matthysse, S. (1986). Animal models in psychiatric research. *Progress in Brain Research, 65*, 259–270.

McGrath, M. J., Campbell, K. M., Parks, C. R., & Burton, F. H. (2000). Glutamatergic drugs exacerbate symptomatic behavior in a transgenic model of comorbid Tourette's syndrome and obsessive-compulsive disorder. *Brain Research, 877*(1), 23–30.

Mckinney, W. T. (2000). Animal research and its relevance to psychiatry. In B. J. Sadock & V. A. Sadock (Eds.), *Kaplan & Sadock's comprehensive textbook of psychiatry* (7th ed., pp. 545–562). Philadelphia: Lippincott, Williams, & Wilkins.

McKinney, W. T., Jr., & Bunney, W. E., Jr. (1969). Animal model of depression. I. Review of evidence: implications for research. *Archives of General Psychiatry, 21*(2), 240–248.

Menzies, L., Achard, S., Chamberlain, S. R., Fineberg, N., Chen, C. H., del Campo, N., et al. (2007). Neurocognitive endophenotypes of obsessive-compulsive disorder. *Brain, 130*(Pt 12), 3223–3236.

Menzies, L., Williams, G. B., Chamberlain, S. R., Ooi, C., Fineberg, N., Suckling, J., et al. (2008). White matter abnormalities in patients with obsessive-compulsive disorder and their first-degree relatives. *American Journal of Psychiatry, 165*(10), 1308–1315.

Menzies, L. A., Chamberlain, S. R., Laird, A. R., Thelen, S. M., Sahakian, B. J., & Bullmore, E. T. (2007). Integrating evidence from neuroimaging and neuropsychological studies of obsessive compulsive disorder: The orbitofronto-striatal

model revisited. *Neuroscience and Biobehavioral Review, 32*(3), 525–549.

Nordahl, T. E., Benkelfat, C., Semple, W. E., Gross, M., King, A. C., & Cohen, R. M. (1989). Cerebral glucose metabolic rates in obsessive compulsive disorder. *Neuropsychopharmacology, 2*(1), 23–28.

Pampaloni, I., Sivakumaran, T., Hawley, C. J., Al Allaq, A., Farrow, J., Nelson, S., et al. (2010). High-dose selective serotonin reuptake inhibitors in OCD: A systematic retrospective case notes survey. *Journal of Psychopharmacology, 24*(10), 1439–1445.

Pantelis, C., Barber, F. Z., Barnes, T. R., Nelson, H. E., Owen, A. M., & Robbins, T. W. (1999). Comparison of set-shifting ability in patients with chronic schizophrenia and frontal lobe damage. *Schizophrenia Research, 37*(3), 251–270.

Patel, D. D., Laws, K. R., Padhi, A., Farrow, J. M., Mukhopadhaya, K., Krishnaiah, R., et al. (2010). The neuropsychology of the schizo-obsessive subtype of schizophrenia: A new analysis. *Psychological Medicine, 40*(6), 921–933.

Peris, T. S., Bergman, R. L., Asarnow, J. R., Langley, A., McCracken, J. T., & Piacentini, J. (2010). Clinical and cognitive correlates of depressive symptoms among youth with obsessive compulsive disorder. *Journal of Clinical Child and Adolescent Psychology, 39*(5), 616–626.

Phillips, K. A. (2002). The obsessive-compulsive spectrums. *Psychiatric Clinics of North America, 25*(4), 791–809.

Phillips, K. A., Stein, D. J., Rauch, S. L., Hollander, E., Fallon, B. A., Barsky, A., et al. (2010). Should an obsessive-compulsive spectrum grouping of disorders be included in DSM-V? *Depression & Anxiety, 27*(6), 528–555.

Radua, J., & Mataix-Cols, D. (2009). Voxel-wise meta-analysis of grey matter changes in obsessive-compulsive disorder. *British Journal of Psychiatry, 195*(5), 393–402.

Richter, M. A., Summerfeldt, L. J., Antony, M. M., & Swinson, R. P. (2003). Obsessive-compulsive spectrum conditions in obsessive-compulsive disorder and other anxiety disorders. *Depression & Anxiety, 18*(3), 118–127.

Robbins, T. W. (2000). Chemical neuromodulation of frontal-executive functions in humans and other animals. *Experimental Brain Research, 133*(1), 130–138.

Robbins, T. W. (2005). Chemistry of the mind: Neurochemical modulation of prefrontal cortical function. *Journal of Comparative Neurology, 493*(1), 140–146.

Robbins, T. W., & Arnsten, A. F. (2009). The neuropsychopharmacology of fronto-executive function: Monoaminergic modulation. *Annual Review of Neuroscience, 32*, 267–287.

Roberts, A. C., Robbins, T. W., Everitt, B. J., & Muir, J. L. (1992). A specific form of cognitive rigidity following excitotoxic lesions of the basal forebrain in marmosets. *Neuroscience, 47*(2), 251–264.

Roberts, A. C., Tomic, D. L., Parkinson, C. H., Roeling, T. A., Cutter, D. J., Robbins, T. W., et al. (2007). Forebrain connectivity of the prefrontal cortex in the marmoset monkey (*Callithrix jacchus*): An anterograde and retrograde tract-tracing study. *Journal of Comprehensive Neurology, 502*(1), 86–112.

Rosenberg, D. R., Dick, E. L., O'Hearn, K. M., & Sweeney, J. A. (1997). Response-inhibition deficits in obsessive-compulsive disorder: An indicator of dysfunction in frontostriatal circuits. *Journal of Psychiatry Neuroscience, 22*(1), 29–38.

Rotge, J. Y., Guehl, D., Dilharreguy, B., Tignol, J., Bioulac, B., Allard, M., et al. (2009). Meta-analysis of brain volume changes in obsessive-compulsive disorder. *Biological Psychiatry, 65*(1), 75–83.

Saxena, S., & Rauch, S. L. (2000). Functional neuroimaging and the neuroanatomy of obsessive-compulsive disorder. *Psychiatric Clinics of North America, 23*(3), 563–586.

Skoog, G., & Skoog, I. (1999). A 40-year follow-up of patients with obsessive-compulsive disorder [see comments]. *Archives of General Psychiatry, 56*(2), 121–127.

Stengler-Wenzke, K., Muller, U., & Matthes-von-Cramon, G. (2003). [Compulsive-obsessive disorder after severe head trauma: Diagnosis and treatment]. *Psychiatric Praxis, 30*(1), 37–39.

Swedo, S. E., & Leonard, H. L. (1992). Trichotillomania. An obsessive compulsive spectrum disorder? *Psychiatric Clinics of North America, 15*(4), 777–790.

Tien, A. Y., Pearlson, G. D., Machlin, S. R., Bylsma, F. W., & Hoehn-Saric, R. (1992). Oculomotor performance in obsessive-compulsive disorder. *American Journal of Psychiatry, 149*(5), 641–646.

Weissman, M. M., Bland, R. C., Canino, G. J., Greenwald, S., Hwu, H. G., Lee, C. K., et al. (1994). The cross national epidemiology of obsessive compulsive disorder. The Cross National Collaborative Group. *Journal of Clinical Psychiatry, 55*(Suppl). 5–10.

Westenberg, H. G., Fineberg, N. A., & Denys, D. (2007). Neurobiology of obsessive-compulsive disorder: Serotonin and beyond. *CNS Spectrum, 12*(2 Suppl 3), 14–27.

Willner, P. (1984). The validity of animal models of depression. *Psychopharmacology* (Berl), *83*(1), 1–16.

Willner, P. (1991). Behavioural models in psychopharmacology. In P. Willner (Ed.), *Behavioural models in psychopharmacology: Theoretical, industrial and clinical perspectives*. Cambridge, UK: Cambridge University Press.

Young, S. N. (1993). The use of diet and dietary components in the study of factors controlling affect in humans: A review. *Journal of Psychiatry & Neuroscience, 18*(5), 235–244.

Zohar, A. H. (1999). The epidemiology of obsessive-compulsive disorder in children and adolescents. *Child & Adolescent Psychiatric Clinics of North America, 8*(3), 445–460.

Zohar, J., Insel, T. R., Zohar-Kadouch, R. C., Hill, J. L., & Murphy, D. L. (1988). Serotonergic responsivity in obsessive-compulsive disorder. Effects of chronic clomipramine treatment. *Archives of General Psychiatry, 45*(2), 167–172.

PART 5

Conclusion

Epilogue to *The Oxford Handbook of Cognitive Neuroscience* Cognitive Neuroscience: Where Are We Going?

Kevin N. Ochsner *and* Stephen M. Kosslyn

Abstract

This epilogue looks at themes and trends that hint at future developments in cognitive neuroscience. It first considers how affective neuroscience merged the study of neuroscience and emotion, how social neuroscience merged the study of neuroscience and social behavior, and how social cognitive neuroscience merged the study of cognitive neuroscience with social cognition. It also considers how the level of analysis of behavior/experience can be linked to psychological process and neural instantiation. It also addresses two topics that have not yet been approached from a cognitive neuroscience perspective, but seem ripe for near-term future progress, namely the study of the development across the lifespan of the various abilities described in the book, and the study of the functional organization of the frontal lobes and their contributions to behaviors (e.g., the ability to exert self-control). This epilogue also explores the multiple methods, both behavioral and neuroscientific, used in cognitive neuroscience, new ways of modeling relationships between levels of analysis, and the question of how to make cognitive neuroscience relevant to everyday life.

Key Words: cognitive neuroscience, emotion, social behavior, social cognition, functional organization, frontal lobes, behaviors, methods, analysis, neural instantiation

Whether you have read the two-volume *Oxford Handbook of Cognitive Neuroscience* from cover to cover or have just skimmed a chapter or two, we hope that you take away a sense of the breadth and depth of work currently being conducted in the field. Since the naming of the field in the backseat of a New York City taxicab some 35 years ago, the field and the approach it embodies have become a dominant—if not the dominant—mode of scientific inquiry in the study of human cognitive, emotional, and social functions.

But where will it go from here? Where will the next 5, 10, or even 20 years take the field and its approach? Obviously, nobody can say for sure—but there are broad intellectual themes and trends that run throughout this two-volume set, and a discussion of them can be used as a springboard to thinking about possible directions future work might take.

Themes and Trends

Here we discuss themes and trends that hint at possible future developments, focusing on those that may be more likely to occur in the relatively near term.

What's in a Name?

It is said that imitation is the sincerest form of flattery. Given the proliferation of new areas of research with names that seemingly mimic *cognitive neuroscience*, the original has reason to feel flattered.

Consider, for example, the development of three comparatively newer fields and the dates of their naming: social neuroscience (Cacioppo, 1994), affective neuroscience (Panksepp 1991), and social cognitive neuroscience (Ochsner & Lieberman, 2001). Although all three fields are undoubtedly the products of unique combinations of influences (see, e.g., Cacioppo, 2002; Ochsner, 2007; Panksepp, 1998), they each followed in the footsteps of cognitive neuroscience. In cognitive neuroscience the study of cognitive abilities and neuroscience were merged, and in the process of doing so, the field has made considerable progress. In like fashion, affective neuroscience combined the study of emotion with neuroscience; social neuroscience, the study of social behavior with neuroscience; and social cognitive neuroscience, the study of social cognition with cognitive neuroscience.

All three of these fields have adopted the same kind of multilevel, multimethod constraints and convergence approach embodied by cognitive neuroscience (as we discussed in the Introduction to this *Handbook*). In addition, each of these fields draws from and builds on, to differing degrees, the methods and models developed within what we can now call "classic" cognitive neuroscience (see Vol. 1 of the *Handbook*). These new fields are siblings in a family of fields that have the similar, if not identical, research "DNA."

It is for these reasons that Volume 2 of this *Handbook* has sections devoted to affect and emotion and to self and social cognition. The topics of the constituent chapters in these sections could easily appear in handbooks of affective or social or social cognitive neuroscience (and in some cases, they already have, see, e.g., Cacioppo & Berntson, 2004; Todorov et al., 2011). We included this material here because it represents the same core approach that guides research on the classic cognitive topics in Volume 1 and in the latter half of Volume 2.

One might wonder whether these related disciplines are on trajectories for scientific and popular impact similar to that of classic cognitive neuroscience. In the age of the Internet, one way of quantifying impact is simply to count the number of Google hits returned by a search for specific terms, in this case, "cognitive neuroscience," "affective neuroscience," and so on. The results of an April 2012 Google search for field names is shown in the tables at right. The top table compares cognitive neuroscience with two of its antecedent fields: cognitive psychology (Neisser, 1967) and neuroscience. The bottom table compares the descendants of classic cognitive neuroscience that were noted above. As can be seen, cognitive psychology and neuroscienceare the oldest fields and the ones with the most online mentions. By comparison, their descendant, cognitive neuroscience, which describes a narrower field than either of its ancestors, is doing quite well. And the three newest fields of social, affective, and social cognitive

	Year term was coined	Approx Age	Google hits
Cognitive Psychology	~1967	~45 yrs	5,910,000
Neuroscience	~1960?	50+	38,600,000
Cognitive Neuroscience	late 70's	~34 yrs	2,750,000
Affective Neuroscience	1991	21 yrs	280,000
Social Neuroscience	1994	18 yrs	290,000
Social Cognitive Neuroscience	2001	11 yrs	370,000

Google hit counts for the names of fields as of April 2012

neuroscience, each of which describes fields even narrower than that of cognitive neuroscience, also are doing well, with combined hit counts totaling about one-third that of cognitive neuroscience, in spite of the fact that the youngest field is only about one-third of cognitive neuroscience's age.

How Do We Link Levels of Analysis?

A theme running throughout the chapters concerns the different ways in which we can link the levels of analysis of behavior/experience, psychological process, and neural instantiation. Here, we focus on two broad issues that were addressed, explicitly or implicitly, by many of the authors of chapters in these volumes.

The first issue is the complexity of the behaviors that one is attempting to map onto underlying processes and neural systems. For example, one might ask whether we should try to map what might be called "molar" abilities, such as memory or attention, onto sets of processes and neural systems, or instead whether we should try to map "molecular" *subtypes* of memory and subtypes of attention onto their constituent processes and neural systems. As alluded to in the Introduction, for most of the abilities described in Volume 1, it was clear as early as 20 years ago that a more molecular, subtype, method of mapping makes the most sense in the context of neuroscience data. The current state-of-the-art in the study of perception, attention, memory, and language (reviewed in Volume 1 of this *Handbook*) clearly bears this out. All the chapters in these sections describe careful ways in which researchers have used combinations of behavioral and brain data to fractionate the processes that give rise to specific subtypes of abilities.

This leads us to the second issue, which concerns the fact that for at least some of the topics discussed in Volume 2, only recently has it become clear that more molecular mappings are possible. This is because for at least some of the Volume 2 topics, behavioral research before the rise of the cognitive neuroscience approach had not developed clearly articulated process models that specied explicitly how information is represented and processed to accomplish a particular task. This limitation was perhaps most evident for topics such as the self, some aspects of higher level social cognition such as mental state inference, and some aspects of emotion, including how emotions are generated and regulated. Twenty years ago, when functional neuroimaging burst on the scene, researchers had proposed few if any process models of these molar phenomena. Hence, initial functional imaging and other types of neuroscience studies on these topics had more of a "let's induce an emotional state or evoke a behavior and see what happens" flavor, and often they did not attempt to test specific theories. This is not to fault these researchers; at the time, they did not have the advantage of decades of process-oriented behavioral research from cognitive psychology and vision research to help guide them (see, e.g., Ochsner & Barrett, 2001; Ochsner & Gross, 2004). Instead, researchers had to develop process models on the fly.

However, times have changed. As attested by the chapters in the first two sections of Volume 2, the incorporation of brain data into research on the self, social perception, and emotion has been very useful in developing increasingly complex, "molecular" theories of the relationships between the behavior/experience, psychological process, and neural instantiation.

Just as the study of memory moved beyond single-system models and toward multiple-system models (Schacter & Tulving, 1994), the study of the self, social cognition, and emotion has begun to move beyond simplistic notions that single brain regions (such as the medial prefrontal cortex or amygdala) are the seat of these abilities.

Looking Toward the Future

Without question, progress has been made. What might the current state of cognitive neuroscience research auger for the future of cognitive neuroscience research? Here we address this question in four ways.

New Topics

One of the ideas that recurs in the chapters of this *Handbook* is that the cognitive neuroscience approach is a general-purpose scientific tool. This approach can be used to ask and answer questions about any number of topics. Indeed, even within the broad scope of this two-volume set, we have not covered every topic already being fruitfully addressed using the cognitive neuroscience approach.

That said, of the many topics that have not yet been approached from a cognitive neuroscience perspective, do any appear particularly promising? Four such topics seem ripe for near-term future progress. These topics run the gamut from the study of specific brain systems to the study of lifespan development and differences in group or social network status, to forging links with the study of mental and physical health.

The first topic is the study of the functional organization of the frontal lobes and the contributions they make to behaviors such as the ability to exert self-control. At first blush, this might seem like a topic that already has received a great deal of attention. From one perspective, it has. Over the past few decades numerous labs have studied the relationship of the frontal lobes to behavior. From another perspective, however, not much progress has been made. What is missing are coherent process models that link specific behaviors to specific subregions of prefrontal cortex. Notably, some chapters in this *Handbook* (e.g., those by Badre, Christoff, and Silvers et al.) attempt to do this within specific domains. But no general theory of prefrontal cortex has yet emerged that can link the myriad behaviors in which it is involved to specific and well-described processes that in turn are instantiated in specific portions of this evolutionarily newest portion of our brain.

The second topic is the study of the development across the lifespan of the various abilities described in the *Handbook*. Although some *Handbook* sections include chapters on development and aging, many do not—precisely because the cognitive neuroscientific study of lifespan changes in many abilities has only just begun. Clearly, the development from childhood into adolescence of various cognitive, social, and affective abilities is crucially important, as is the ways in which these abilities change as we move from middle adulthood into older age (Casey et al, 2010; Charles & Carstensen, 2010; Mather, 2012). The multilevel approach that characterizes the cognitive neuroscience approach holds promise of deepening our understanding of such phenomena. Toward this end, it is important to note that new journals devoted to some of these topics have appeared (e.g., *Developmental Cognitive Neuroscience*, which was first published in 2010), and various institutes within the National Institutes of Health (NIH) have called for research on these topics.

The third topic is the study of the way in which group-level variables impact the development and operation of the various processing systems described in both Volumes of this *Handbook*. Notably, this is an area of research that is not yet represented in the *Handbook*, although interest in connecting the study of group-level variables to the study of the brain has been growing over the past few years. Consider, for example, emerging research suggesting that having grown up as a member of different cultural groups can dictate whether and how one engages perceptual, memory, and affective systems both when reflecting on the self and in social settings (Chiao, 2009). There is also evidence that the size of one's social networks can impact the structure of brain systems involved in affect and affiliation, and that one's status within these networks (Bickart et al., 2011) can determine whether and when one recruits brain systems implicated in emotion and social cognition (Bickart et al., 2011; Chiao, 2010; Muscatell et al., 2012). Forging links between group-level variables and the behavior/experience, process, and brain levels that are the focus in the current *Handbook* will prove challenging and may require new kinds of collaborative relationships with other disciplines, such as sociology and anthropology. As these collaborations grow to maturity, we predict this work will make its way into future editions of the *Handbook*.

The fourth topic is the way in which specific brain systems play important roles in physical, as well as mental, health. The *Handbook* already includes chapters that illustrate how cognitive neuroscience approaches are being fruitfully translated to understand the nature of dysfunction, and potential treatments for it, in various kinds of psychiatric and substance use disorders (see e.g., Barch et al., 2009; Johnstone et al., 2007; Kober et al., 2010; Ochsner, 2008 and the section below on *Translation*). This type of translational work is sure to grow in the future. What the current *Handbook* is missing, however, is discussion of how brain systems are critically involved in physical health via their interactions with the immune system. This burgeoning area of interest seeks to connect fields such as health psychology with cognitive neuroscience and allied disciplines to understand how variables like chronic stress or disease, or social connection vs. isolation, can boost or diminish physical health. Such an effect would arise via interactions between the immune systems

and brain systems involved in emotion, social cognition, and control (Muscatell & Eisenberger, 2012; Eisenberger & Cole, 2012). This is another key area of future growth that we expect to be represented in this *Handbook* in the future.

New Methods

How are we going to make progress on these questions and the countless others posed in the chapters of the *Handbook*? On the one hand, the field will undoubtedly continue to make good use of the multiple methods—both behavioral and neuroscientific—that have been its bread and butter for the past decades. As noted in the Introduction, certain empirical and conceptual advances were only made possible by technological advances, which enabled us to measure activity with dramatically new levels of spatial and temporal resolution. The advent of positron emission tomography, and later functional magnetic resonance imaging (20–30 years ago), were game-changing advances.

On the other hand, these functional imaging techniques are still limited in terms of their spatial and temporal resolution, and the areas of the brain they allow researchers to focus on reflect the contributions of many thousands of neurons. Other techniques, such as magnetoencephalography and scalp electroencephalography, offer relatively good temporal resolution, but their spatial localization is relatively poor. Moreover, they are best suited to studying cortical rather than subcortical regions.

We could continue to beat the drum for the use of converging methods: What one technique can't do, another can, and by triangulating across methods, better theories can be built and evaluated. But for the next stage of game-changing methodological advances to be realized, either current technologies will need to undergo a transformation that enables them to combine spatial and temporal resolution in new ways or new techniques that have better characteristics will need to be invented.

New Ways of Modeling Relationships Between Levels of Analysis

All this said, even the greatest of technological advances will not immediately be useful unless our ability to conceptualize the cognitive and emotional processes that lie between brain and behavior becomes more sophisticated.

At present, most theorizing in cognitive neuroscience makes use of commonsense terminology for describing human abilities. We talk about memory, perception, emotion, and so on. We break these molar abilities into more molecular parts and characterize them in terms of their automatic or controlled operation, whether the mental representations are relational, and so on. Surely, however, the computations performed by specific brain regions did not evolve to instantiate our folk-psychological ideas about how best to describe the processes underlying behavior.

One possible response to this concern is that the description of phenomena at multiple levels of analysis allows us to sidestep this problem. One could argue that at the highest level of description, it's just fine to use folk-psychological terms to describe behavior and experience. After all, our goal is to map these terms—which prove extremely useful for everyday discourse about human behavior—onto precise descriptions of underlying neural circuitry by reference to a set of information processing mechanisms.

Unfortunately, however, many researchers do not restrict intuitively understandable folk-psychological terms to describe behavior and experience, but also use such terms to describe information processing itself. In this case, process-level descriptions are not likely to map in a direct way onto neural mechanisms.

Marr (1982) suggested a solution to this problem: Rely on the language of computation to characterize information processing. The language of computation characterizes what computers do, and this language often can be applied to describe what brains do. But brains are demonstrably not digital computers, and thus it is not clear whether the technical vocabulary that evolved to characterize information processing in computers can in fact always be appropriately applied to brains. Back in the 1980s, many researchers hoped that connectionist models might provide an appropriate kind of computational specificity. More recently, computational models from the reinforcement learning and neuroeconomic literatures have been advanced as offering a new level of computational specificity.

Although no existing approach has yet offered a computational language that is powerful enough to describe more than thin slices of human information processing, we believe that such a medium will become a key ingredient of the cognitive neuroscience approach in the future.

Translation

In an era in which increasing numbers of researchers are applying for a static or shrinking pool of grant funding, some have come to focus on the question of how to use cognitive neuroscience to solve problems that arise in everyday life (and therefore address the concerns of funding agencies, which often are pragmatic and applied).

Research is often divided into two categories (somewhat artificially): "Foundational" research focuses on understanding phenomena for its own sake, whereas "translational" research focuses on using such understanding to solve a real-world problem. Taking cognitive neuroscience models of abilities based on studies of healthy populations and applying them to understand and treat the bases of dysfunction in specific groups is one form of translational research. This will surely be an area of great future growth.

Already, a number of areas of psychiatric and substance use research have adopted a two-step translational research sequence (e.g., Barch et al., 2004, 2009; Carter et al., 2009; Ochsner, 2008; Paxton et al., 2008). The first step involves building a model of normal behavior, typically in healthy adults, using the cognitive neuroscience approach. The second step involves translating that model to a population of interest, and using the model to explain the underlying bases of the disorder or other deviation from the normal baseline-and this would be a crucial step in eventually developing effective treatments.. This population could suffer from some type of clinically dysfunctional behavior, such as the four psychiatric groups described in Part 4 of Volume 2 of the *Handbook*. It could be an adolescent or older adult population, as described in a handful of chapters scattered across sections of the *Handbook*. Or—as was not covered in the *Handbook*, but might be in the future—it could be a vulnerable group for whom training in a specific type of cognitive, affective, or social skill would improve the quality of life.

The possibilities abound—and it would behoove researchers in cognitive neuroscience to capitalize on as many of them as possible. Not just for the pragmatic reason that they may be more likely to be funded but, more importantly, for the principled reason that *it matters*. It matters that we understand real-world, consequential behavior. Yes, we need to start by studying the ability to learn a list of words in the lab, and we need to understand the brain systems responsible for such relatively simple tasks. But then we need to move toward understanding, for example, how these brain systems do or do not function normally in a child growing up in an impoverished household compared with a child afforded every advantage (Noble et al., 2007).

Happily, there is evidence that federal funding agencies are beginning to understand the importance of this two-step, foundational-to-translational research sequence. In 2011, the National Institute of Mental Health (NIMH) announced the Research Domain Criteria (RDoC) framework as part of NIMH's Strategic Plan to "Develop, for research purposes, new ways of classifying mental disorders based upon dimensions of observable behavior and neurobiological functioning" (http://www.nimh.nih.gov/about/strategic-planning-reports/index.shtml). In essence, the RDoC's framework aims to replace the traditional symptom-based means of describing abnormal behavior (and that characterizes traditional psychiatric diagnosis) with a means of describing the full range of normal to abnormal behavior in terms of fundamental underlying processes. The idea is that, over time, researchers will seek to target and understand the nature of these processes, the ways in which they can go awry, and the behavioral variability to which they can give rise—as opposed to targeting traditionally defined clinical groups. For example, a researcher could target processes for generating positive or negative affect, or their control, or the ways in which interactions between affect and control processes break down to produce anhedonia or a preponderance of negative affect—as opposed to focusing on a discretely defined disorder such as major depression.

The two-step approach allows initial research to focus on understanding core processes—considered in the context of different levels of analysis—but with an eye toward then understanding how variability in these processes gives rise to the full range of normal to abnormal behavior. Elucidating the fundamental nature of these cognitive and emotional processes, and their relation to the behavioral/experiential level above and to the neural level below, is the fundamental goal of cognitive neuroscience.

Concluding Comment

How do we measure the success of a field? By the number of important findings and insights? By the number of scientists and practitioners working within it?

If we take that late 1970s taxicab ride, when the term *cognitive neuroscience* was first used as the inception point for the field, then by any and all of these metrics, cognitive neuroscience has been enormously successful. Compared with physics, chemistry, medicine, and biology, however—or even compared with psychology and neuroscience—cognitive neuroscience is just beginning to hit its stride. This is to be expected, given that it has existed only for a very short period of time. Indeed, the day for cognitive neuroscience is still young.

This is good news. Even though cognitive neuroscience is entering its mid-30s, compared with these other broad disciplines that were established hundreds of years ago, this isn't even middle age. The hope, then, is that the field can continue to blossom and grow from its adolescence to full maturity—and make good on the promising returns it has produced so far.

References

Barch, D. M., Braver, T. S., Carter, C. S., Poldrack, R. A., & Robbins, T. W. (2009). CNTRICS Final task selection: Executive control. *Schizophrenia Bulletin, 35*, 115–135.

Barch, D. M., Mitropoulou, V., Harvey, P. D., New, A. S., Silverman, J. M., & Siever, L. J. (2004). Context-processing deficits in schizotypal personality disorder. *Journal of Abnormal Psychology, 113*, 556–568.

Bickart, K. C., Wright, C. I., Dautoff, R. J., Dickerson, B. C., & Barrett, L. F. (2011). Amygdala volume and social network size in humans. *Nature Neuroscience, 14*, 163–164.

Cacioppo, J. T. (1994). Social neuroscience: Autonomic, neuroendocrine, and immune responses to stress. *Psychophysiology, 31*, 113–128.

Cacioppo, J. T. (2002). Social neuroscience: Understanding the pieces fosters understanding the whole and vice versa. *American Psychologist, 57*, 819–381.

Cacioppo, J. T., & Berntson, G. G. (2004). (Eds.) *Social neuroscience: Key readings* (Vol. 14). New York: Ohio State University Psychology Press.

Carter, C. S., Barch, D. M., Gur, R., Pinkham, A., & Ochsner, K. (2009). CNTRICS Final task selection: Social cognitive and affective neuroscience-based measures. *Schizophrenia Bulletin, 35*, 153–162.

Casey, B. J., Jones, R. M., Levita, L., Libby, V., Pattwell, S. S., et al. (2010). The storm and stress of adolescence: Insights from human imaging and mouse genetics. *Developmental Psychobiology, 52*, 225–235.

Charles, S. T., & Carstensen, L. L. (2010). Social and emotional aging. *Annual Review Psychology, 61*, 383–409.

Chiao, J. Y. (2009). Cultural neuroscience: a once and future discipline. *Progress in brain research, 178*, 287–304.

Chiao, J. Y. (2010). Neural basis of social status hierarchy across species. *Current opinion in neurobiology, 20*, 803–809.

Eisenberger, N. I., & Cole, S. W. (2012). Social neuroscience and health: neurophysiological mechanisms linking social ties with physical health. *Nature neuroscience, 15*, 669–674.

Johnstone, T., van Reekum, C. M., Urry, H. L., Kalin, N. H., & Davidson, R. J. (2007). Failure to regulate: counterproductive recruitment of top-down prefrontal-subcortical circuitry in major depression. *The Journal of neuroscience : the official journal of the Society for Neuroscience, 27*, 8877–8884.

Kober, H., Mende-Siedlecki, P., Kross, E. F., Weber, J., Mischel, W., et al. (2010). Prefrontal-striatal pathway underlies cognitive regulation of craving. *Proceedings of the National Academy of Sciences of the United States of America, 107*, 14811–14816.

Mather, M. (2012). The emotion paradox in the aging brain. *Annals of the New York Academy of Sciences, 1251*, 33–49.

Marr, D. (1982). *Vision: A computational investigation into the human representation and processing of visual information* (397pp). San Francisco: W.H. Freeman.

Muscatell, K. A., & Eisenberger, N. I. (2012). A Social Neuroscience Perspective on Stress and Health. *Social and personality psychology compass, 6,* 890–904.

Muscatell, K. A., Morelli, S. A., Falk, E. B., Way, B. M., Pfeifer, J. H., et al. 2012. Social status modulates neural activity in the mentalizing network. *NeuroImage, 60,* 1771–7.

Neisser, U. (1967). *Cognitive psychology* (Vol. 16). New York: Appleton-Century-Crofts.

Noble, K. G., McCandliss, B. D., & Farah, M. J. (2007). Socioeconomic gradients predict individual differences in neurocognitive abilities. *Developmental Science, 10,* 464–480.

Ochsner, K. (2007). Social cognitive neuroscience: Historical development, core principles, and future promise. In A. Kruglanksi & E. T. Higgins (Eds.), *Social psychology: a handbook of basic principles* (pp. 39–66). New York: Guilford Press.

Ochsner, K. N. (2008). The social-emotional processing stream: Five core constructs and their translational potential for schizophrenia and beyond. *Biological Psychiatry, 64,* 48–61.

Ochsner, K. N., & Barrett, L. F. (2001). A multiprocess perspective on the neuroscience of emotion. In T. J. Mayne & G. A. Bonanno (Eds.), *Emotions: Current issues and future directions* (pp. 38–81). New York: Guilford Press.

Ochsner, K. N., & Gross, J. J. (2004). Thinking makes it so: A social cognitive neuroscience approach to emotion regulation. In R. F. Baumeister & K. D. Vohs (Eds.), *Handbook of self-regulation: Research, theory, and applications* (pp. 229–255). New York: Guilford Press.

Ochsner, K. N., & Lieberman, M. D. (2001). The emergence of social cognitive neuroscience. *American Psychologist, 56,* 717–734.

Panksepp, J. (1991). Affective neuroscience: A conceptual framework for the neurobiological study of emotions. *International Review of Studies on Emotion, 1,* 59–99.

Panksepp, J. (1998). *Affective neuroscience: The foundations of human and animal emotions.* New York: Oxford University Press.

Paxton, J. L., Barch, D. M., Racine, C. A., & Braver, T. S. (2008). Cognitive control, goal maintenance, and prefrontal function in healthy aging. *Cerebral Cortex, 18,* 1010–1028.

Pizzagalli, D. A., Holmes, A. J., Dillon, D. G., Goetz, E. L., Birk, J. L., Bogdan, R., et al. (2009). Reduced caudate and nucleus accumbens response to rewards in unmedicated individuals with major depressive disorder. *Am J Psychiatry, 166*(6), 702–710.

Schacter, D. L., & Tulving, E. (1994). *Memory systems 1994* (Vol. 8). Cambridge, MA: MIT Press.

Todorov, A. B., Fiske, S. T., & Prentice, D. A. (2011). *Social neuroscience: Toward understanding the underpinnings of the social mind* (Vol. 8). New York: Oxford University Press.

INDEX